AFRIKAANS-ENGLISH
ENGLISH-AFRIKAANS
DICTIONARY

Hippocrene Practical Dictionary

AFRIKAANS-ENGLISH ENGLISH-AFRIKAANS DICTIONARY

Revised and Expanded Edition

JAN KROMHOUT
B.Com., FCIS, M.A., D. Litt.

Hippocrene Books
New York

Originally published by Pharos Dictionaries, Cape Town, South Africa.
Copyright© 1997 by Pharos Dictionaries. Published under license.

Hippocrene edition 2001.
Third printing, 2004.

For information, address:
HIPPOCRENE BOOKS, INC.
171 Madison Avenue
New York, NY 10016

ISBN 0-7818-0846-4

Printed in the United States of America.

Inhoud / Contents

Foreword

This thirteenth edition of *Little Dictionary* has been thoroughly updated to reflect, within the constraints of a "little" dictionary, the language patterns of a new South Africa.

Special attention has been given to vocabulary growth through transitional and technological developments, especially in the field of computer science.

The list of abbreviations and acronyms has been expanded considerably. Useful new features are the names of the nine provinces and eleven official languages of our country.

Furthermore, thousands of word options and near-synonyms have been included. This increases without doubt the dictionary's functional flexibility.

As an aid to correct pronunciation, stress marks have been added to the countless derivations and composites as well.

Jan Kromhout
Johannesburg, June 1997

Vooraf

Hierdie dertiende uitgawe van *Klein Woordeboek* is ingrypend bygewerk sodat dit binne die beperkinge van 'n "klein" woordeboek die taalgebruik van 'n nuwe Suid-Afrika bydertyds weerspieël.

Besondere aandag is gegee aan nuwe woorde wat vanweë die veranderende situasie in die land en tegnologiese ontwikkelinge, veral op die gebied van die rekenaarwese, in omloop gekom het.

Die lys afkortings en akronieme is aansienlik uitgebrei.

'n Nuttige nuwigheid is die bylaes met die name van die nege provinsies en die elf ampstale.

Voorts is duisende keusewoorde en amper-sinonieme bygevoeg om die boek as *woorde*boek nóg bruikbaarder te maak.

As riglyn by die regte uitspraak van woorde het nou nie meer slegs die trefwoorde nie maar ook die tallose afleidings en samevoegings *binne* die lemmas klemtekens gekry.

Jan Kromhout
Johannesburg, Junie 1997

AFRIKAANS – ENGELS

Afkortings en tekens

Die volgende verkorte afkortings dui, waar nodig, die woordsoort van die trefwoord aan:

(b)	= byvoeglike naamwoord	(tw)	= tussenwerpsel
(bw)	= bywoord	(vgw)	= voegwoord
(lw)	= lidwoord	(vnw)	= voornaamwoord
(s)	= selfstandige naamwoord	(vs)	= voorsetsel
(telw)	= telwoord	(w)	= werkwoord

Ander afkortings wat in hierdie woordeboek gebruik word, is onder meer: (advert.) advertensie(wese); (Afro-Am.) Afro-Amerikaans; (Am.) Amerika/-aans; (betr.) betreklike (met "vnw"); (besit.) besitlike (met "vnw"); (biol.) biologie; (bot.) botanie/-s; (bv.) byvoorbeeld; (ekon.) ekonomie/-s; (elektr.) elektrisiteit/elektries/elektronies; (Eng.) Engeland; (Eur.) Europa/ -ees; (fig.) figuurlik; (fot.) fotografie; (geol.) geologie/-s; (gimn.) gimnastiek/gimnasium; (gram.) grammatika/grammaties; (hist.) histories; (idiom.) idiomaties; (imp.) imperatief; (lett.) letter= kunde/-ig; (med.) medies/medisyne; (mil.) militêr; (mus.) musiek; (mv) meervoud; (neerh.) neerhalend; (onbep.) onbepaalde (met "vnw"); (pers.) persoonlike (met "vnw"); (Prot.) Protestants; (rek.) rekenaar(wese); (R.K.) Rooms-Katoliek; (SA) Suid-Afrika/-aans; (S.Am.) Suid-Amerika/-aans; (sl) sleng; (stat.) statistiek/statistiese wetenskap; (tegn.) tegnologie; (telef.) telefoon; (verklw) verkleinwoord; (veroud.) verouderd/verouderend; (vr.) vraende (met "vnw"); (wisk.) wiskunde/-ig.

1. Die **tilde** of **slangetjie** (~) vervang die trefwoord soos hy staan:
   a) **nippertjie:** op die ~ beteken: *op die nippertjie.*
   b) **aand:** ~ete, ~kerk beteken: **aandete, aandkerk.**
2. **Koppelteken** (-):
   a) Ná selfstandige naamwoorde beteken dit: voeg die letter(s) by die woord vir die meervoud: **eend -e = eend, eende; kind -ers = kind, kinders.**
   b) Twee letters of lettergrepe voorafgegaan deur koppeltekens beteken die selfstandige naamwoord (s) het twee meervoude: **aanbeveling -s, -e = aanbeveling, aanbevelings, aanbevelinge.**
   c) Na byvoeglike naamwoorde en bywoorde gee dit te kenne: voeg die letters by vir die trappe van vergelyking: **lelik -e; -er, -ste = lelik, lelike, leliker, lelikste.**
   d) Na werkwoorde beteken dit: voeg, vir die verlede deelwoord, **ge-** voor die woord: **speel ge- = speel, gespeel.** So ook: voeg **-ge-** tussen die dele van die woord: **wegkruip -ge- = wegkruip, weggekruip.**
   e) Aan die end van 'n reël dui die koppelteken aan dat die betrokke samevoeging met 'n koppelteken geskryf word.
3. **Afbreekteken** (=): Die afbreekteken aan die end van 'n reël dui aan dat die betrokke woord aanmekaar geskryf word.
4. **Kolletjies** (..): Oral waar die spelling van verboë vorme verander, word sulke verandering voorafgegaan deur twee kolletjies: **musikaal ..kale = musikaal, musikale.**
5. **Ronde hakies** ( ) om 'n letter of letters in 'n woord beteken dat die woord met of sonder daardie letter(s) gespel kan word: **agte(r)losig; verjaar(s)dag.**
6. Die **klemteken** (′) verskyn net na die letter of lettergreep wat die hoofklem het in 'n woord: **kie′wiet; mu′sikus; musikant′.**
7. Die **balk** (/) beteken die gebruiker het 'n keuse tussen die twee vorme: **keuse/keur.**

A

aak'lig -e; -er, -ste horrible, nasty, awful; *'n ~e gesig* a horrible sight
aal'moes -e alms, charity, dole
aal'wyn -e/**aal'wee** -s aloe
aam'beeld -e anvil; *altyd op dieselfde ~ slaan* keep on harping on the same string
aam'bei -e piles, haemorrhoids
aambors'tig e-; -er, -ste asthmatic
aan¹ (b, bw) on, in, upon; *ek wil weet waar ek ~ of af is* I want to know where I stand
aan² (vs) at, near, next to, upon; *~ boord* on board; *~ die gang* on the go; *~ tafel* at table; *~ tering sterf* die of consumption; *wat is ~ die gang?* what is going on?
aan'beveel *~* recommend; **aan'bevole prys** recommended price *ook* **rig'prys**
aan'beveling -s, -e recommendation; *op ~ van* on the recommendation of
aanbid' *~* adore, worship, idolise
aan'bied -ge- offer; present; volunteer; tender; *~ing* presentation
aan'bly -ge- continue, remain; hold on; *bly asseblief aan* please hold the line
aan'bod ..biedinge, ..biedings offer, propo-sal; supply; *vraag en ~* demand and supply
aan'bou (w) -ge- build on; *~ing* addition (to building)
aan'breek -ge- dawn; come; *die dag sal ~* the day will come
aand -e evening, eve *ook* **voor'nag**
aan'dag attention, devotion; *die ~ vestig op* draw attention to
aandag'tig -e; -er, -ste attentive
aan'deel ..dele share; portion, part; *~ hê in* have a share in; *~hou'er* shareholder
aan'dele: *~beurs* stock exchange; *~bewys'* share certificate; (pl) scrip; *~kapitaal'* share capital
aan'denking -s, -e remembrance, keepsake, souvenir, memento
aand: *~e'te* supper; dinner; *~kerk* evening service; *~klas* evening/night class(es); *~klokreël* curfew *ook* **klok'reël**
aan'doen -ge- call at (port); cause, affect, move; *smart/leed ~* cause grief/sorrow; *~'lik* touching, pathetic
aand'pak -ke dress suit
aan'dra -ge- bring to, carry to; tell, inform
aan'draai -ge- screw tighter, turn on

aan'dring -ge- urge, press on, insist on; *op 'n saak ~* insist on a matter
aand'rok -ke evening dress (lady)
aand: *~sit'ting* evening/night session; *~ske'-mering* twilight, dusk
aan'dui -ge- indicate, point out
aan'duiding -s, -e indication, designation
aan'durf -ge- dare; *'n taak ~* tackle a job
aan'gaan -ge- concern; begin; proceed, con-tinue; *koste ~* incur expenses; *'n ooreen'-koms ~* conclude/enter into an agreement; *wat my ~* as far as I am concerned.
aangaan'de as for, concerning, regarding
aan'gaap -ge- stare/gape at
aan'gee (s) ..geë pass (rugby); (w) -ge- hand on, pass; *die pas ~* set the pace *kyk* **pas'aangeër**
aan'gehoudene (s) detainee (person)
aan'geklaagde -s accused, defendant
aan'geklam -de tipsy, groggy *ook* **geko'ring**
aan'geleentheid ..hede affair, concern, matter *ook* **saak**, **on'derwerp**
aan'genaam ..name; ..namer, -ste pleasant, agreeable, enjoyable *ook* **genot'vol**; *~!/ ..name kennismaking* how do you do?, pleased to meet you
aan'genome (b) accepted; adopted; *~ kind* adopted child
aan gesien because, as, considering, since
aan'gesig -te face, countenance
aan'geteken -de noted; registered; *~de pos* registered post
aan'gewese obvious, right, proper; *die ~ per-soon* the right person
aangren'send -e adjacent, bordering on, ad-joining; *~e bin'neland* adjacent interior; *~e pla'se* adjoining farms
aan'gryp -ge- seize, catch hold of; attack; *'n geleentheid ~* grasp/seize an opportunity
aangry'pend -e; -er, -ste touching, moving, gripping *ook* **ontroe'rend**
aan'haak -ge- hook on, fasten; hitch on
aan'haal -ge- quote, cite; *~ ..afhaal* quote ..unquote; *bewyse ~* produce proof/evidence; *~te'kens* quotation marks
aan'haling -s, -e quoted passage
aan'hang (s) following; adherents, party; *~er* follower, disciple; fan (person)
aan'hangsel -s supplement, appendix/annex-ure *ook* **by'lae**

aan'hef (s) beginning, preamble; *die ~ van 'n brief* the beginning/salutation of a letter

aan'heg -ge- affix, annex, attach; aan'gehegte kwitan'sie attached receipt

aan'help -ge- help on with

aan'hits -ge- instigate, incite *ook* op'stook

aan'hoor -ge- listen to; ~der listener

aan'hou -ge- continue; insist; persevere; keep (servant); keep on (clothes); detain, arrest; *in ~ding* detained, in custody; aan'gehoudene detainee (person)

aanhou'dend -e continual, incessant; ~ droogte prolonged drought

aan'houer -s perseverer; ~ *wen* perseverance will be rewarded

aan'kla -ge- accuse, charge with

aan'klaer -s prosecutor; plaintiff

aan'klag -te accusation, charge *ook* aan'klagte; ~kantoor' charge office (police)

aan'kleef/aan'klewe -ge- stick/adhere to

aan'klop -ge- knock, beat (at the door); *om hulp ~* ask for help

aan'knoop -ge- fasten; enter into (conversation); tie on to

aan'kom -ge- arrive, get at; acquire, obtain; drop in; *betyds/op tyd ~* arrive in time

aan'komeling -e newcomer, beginner

aan'koms arrival

aan'kondig -ge- announce, publish, inform, advertise; ~er announcer; ~ing announcement, notification

aan'koop (s, w) purchase; *verkry deur ~* acquired through purchase; aan'koper buyer (for firm)

aan'kweek -ge- cultivate, grow, rear; *'n goeie gewoonte ~* cultivate a good habit

aan'kyk -ge- look at; *iem. skeef ~* look askance/doubtingly at someone

aan'las -ge- join, attach

aan'lê -ge- aim at; apply; plan, build, lay out; court; *~ met 'n geweer* take aim; *by 'n nooi ~* court a girl

aan'leer -ge- learn, acquire (a skill)

aan'leg -te plan; arrangement; talent, disposition; installation; ~ **en masjinerie'** plant and machinery; ~toets aptitude test

aan'leiding -s, -e cause, reason, motive; *na ~ van* with reference to, concerning

aanlok'lik attractive, charming, inviting

aan'loop (s) patronage; takeoff; (w) -ge- go on walking; walk faster; call in passing; *agter meisies ~* run after girls; ~baan runway

ook styg'baan

aan'maak -ge- prepare, mix

aan'maan -ge- warn, admonish; remind

aan'maning -s, -e warning, reminder; relapse (disease)

aan'matigend -e; -er, -ste presumptuous, arrogant; ~e houding arrogant bearing/attitude

aan'mekaar together, connected; consecutively, continuously; *die twee is ~* the two of them are fighting

aan'meld -ge- announce, report; *jy moet jou môre ~* you must report tomorrow; ~bare siekte notifiable disease

aan'merking -s, -e remark; criticism; observation; *in ~ kom vir* qualify for; *in ~ neem* take into consideration; bele'digende ~ insulting remark

aanmerk'lik -e; -er, -ste considerable, notable, appreciable; ~e verbe'tering a remarkable improvement

aan'moedig -ge- encourage *ook* aan'spoor; ~ing encouragement

aan'neem -ge- accept, adopt; assume, admit; *'n vriendelike houding ~* adopt a friendly attitude; *'n uitnodiging ~* accept an invitation

aanneem'lik -e; -er, -ste acceptable, credible, reasonable

aan'nemer -s contractor *ook* kontrakteur'; (funeral) undertaker

aan'pak -ge- seize, take hold of; tackle

aan'pas -ge- try on, fit; adapt, adjust; *by omstandighede ~* adapt to circumstances; ~ser adapter (elect.) *ook* pas'stuk; ~sing adjustment; ~(sings)vermo'ë adaptability

aan'plak -ge- post up (bills), stick; ~bord notice board *ook* aan'speldbord

aan'por -ge- prod, rouse, urge, instigate

aan'prys -ge- commend, extol

aan'raai -ge- advise, suggest, recommend *kyk* af'raai

aan'raak -ge- touch

aan'raking -s, -e touch, contact; *in ~ kom met* get in touch with

aan'rand -ge- assault, attack; ~ing assault, attack; onse'delike ~ing indecent assault

aan'rig -ge- cause, commit, do; *skade ~* cause damage

aan'roer -ge- touch upon, broach, mention; stir up; hasten; *'n saak ~* broach a subject/matter

aan'ryg -ge- string (beads); lace up (boots); baste

aan'sê -ge- announce, inform; instruct
aan'sien (s) appearance; respect, esteem; *hoog in ~ wees* be highly respected
aansien'lik -e; -er, -ste respectable; consider= able, notable; handsome
aan'sit -ge- sit down at table; put on; instigate; start (motor); ~**ka'bel** booster cable, jumper lead; ~**ter** starter (motor)
aan'skaf -ge- procure, buy, secure
aanskou' ~ view, behold; *die lewenslig ~* be born; ~**ingson'derwys** visual education; ~**lik** (b) attractive, striking
aan'skryf/aan'skrywe -ge- notify; send a letter of demand, sue
aan'skrywing -s, -e letter of demand; summons
aan'slaan -ge- touch, strike, assume (a tone); assess; salute; knock on (rugby); *die regte toon ~* strike the right note
aan'slag ..slae stroke; attempt; touch (mus.); assessment (income tax); *'n ~ op sy lewe* an attempt on his life
aan'sluit -ge- join, follow; enlist, enrol; con= nect; *by die leër ~* join the army; ~**ing** connection; junction (road)
aan'soek -e application, request, proposal; ~ *doen om 'n betrekking* apply for a post/job; *'n ~ rig* apply; ~**er** applicant *ook* **appli= kant'**
aan'spoor -ge- spur on, urge on, encourage; ~**bo'nus** incentive bonus
aan'sporing encouragement; incentive
aan'spraak ..sprake address; claim, title; ~ *maak op iets* lay claim to something; ~**ma= ker** contender (for a sporting title)
aan'spreek -ge- address, speak to; accost
aanspreek'lik -e; -er, -ste responsible, liable; ~ *hou vir die koste* hold responsible for the cost; ~**heid** liability
aan'staan -ge- please, like, suit; *hy staan my glad nie aan nie* I don't like him at all
aanstaan'de (s) -s intended; fiancé (man), fiancée (lady) *ook* **verloof'de (s)**; (b) next; prospective; forthcoming
aan'staar -ge- stare at, gaze at
aan'stalte -s preparation; ~ *maak* getting ready
aan'stap -ge- walk on; walk briskly
aan'steek -ge- infect; light, kindle; pin on
aansteek'lik -e; -er, -ste infectious, contagious
aan'steker -s (cigarette) lighter
aan'stel -ge- appoint; pretend; sham, put on; *moenie jou so ~ nie* do not put on such airs
aan'stellerig -e; -er, -ste affected, conceited

ook **verwaand'/geveins'**
aan'stelling -s, -e appointment
aan'sterk -ge- recuperate, convalesce; ~**ver= lof'** convalescent leave
aan'stip -ge- jot down, touch on, hint at
aan'stons presently, directly *ook* **nou-nou**
aan'stoot (s) ..stote offence; ~ *gee of neem* give or take offence/umbrage
aanstoot'lik -e; -er, -ste objectionable, offen= sive, indecent *ook* **kwet'send/walg'lik**
aan'stryk -ge- walk on; brush over
aan'stuur -ge- send on, despatch
aan'suiwer -ge- settle; adjust; *'n tekort ~* make up a deficit; ~**ings** adjustments (book= keeping)
aan'sukkel -ge- struggle/trudge along
aan'tal -le number; *'n hele ~ foute* quite a few mistakes
aan'tas -ge- touch; attack, affect; *sy gesond= heid was aangetas* his health was impaired
aan'teken -ge- note down, record; register; score; *'n brief ~* register a letter; *'n drie ~* score a try (rugby); *protes ~* lodge a protest; ~**ing** (s) note; record; registration; ~**ing= boek** notebook, scribbler
aan'toon -ge- show, demonstrate, indicate *ook* **aan'dui, toon (w)**
aan'tref -ge- meet, find; *iem. tuis ~* find somebody at home
aan'trek -ge- dress; draw tighter; attract
aan'trekking attraction; ~**s'krag** gravitation (of earth), appeal, attractiveness
aantrek'lik -e; -er, -ste attractive, handsome (man); pleasing *ook* **bekoor'lik**; sensitive
aan'tyging -s, -e allegation, accusation *ook* **beskul'diging**
aanvaar' ~ accept, assume
aan'val (s) -le attack, charge; fit; *'n ~ afslaan* repel an attack; (w) attack, assail, charge
aan'valler -s assailant, attacker
aanval'lig (b) attractive; lovely, charming *ook* **aantrek'lik/bekoor'lik**
aan'vang (s) beginning, start; (w) begin, commence; *wat het jy aangevang?* what have you been up to?; ~**s'kol'wer** opening batsman; ~**sta'dium** initial stage
aanvoel'bare: ~ temperatuur' wind-chill (am= bient) factor
aan'voer (w) -ge- supply; allege; advance; lead; ~**der** commander, leader
aan'voor -ge- begin, commence; *'n saak ~* take the first steps

aan'vra -ge- apply for, request

aan'vraag ..vrae application, demand, request, requisition; *hierdie artikel is in* ~ this article is in demand

aan'vul -ge- fill up, replenish, supplement; ~(lings)eksa'men supplementary examination

aan'wakker -ge- encourage; fan (hatred); *be*langstelling ~ rouse interest

aan'was (s) growth; increase (in population); (w) grow, increase

aan'wend -ge- use, employ, apply; appropriate; ~*ing van fondse* application of funds (bookkeeping); *'n poging* ~ make an attempt

aanwe'sig -e present; *veertien leerlinge is* ~ fourteen pupils are present

aan'wins gain, profit, acquisition, asset

aan'wys -ge- show, point out, indicate; allocate; ~stok pointer

aan'wyser -s pointer, indicator; ekono'miese ~ economic indicator

aap ape; monkey; fool; *die* ~ *kom uit die mou* the cat is out of the bag; ~stre'ke monkey tricks

aap'stuipe: *hy kry die* ~ he is beside himself/ very upset

aar[1] are ear (of corn)

aar[2] are vein; underground watercourse; core (electr.); ~voe'ding intravenous feeding

aar'bei -e strawberry; ~konfyt' strawberry jam

aard[1] (s) nature, kind, temper; *niks van die* ~ *nie,* nothing of the kind; *'n* ~*jie na sy vaartjie* like father, like son; (w) ge- take after; thrive

aard[2] (w) ge- earth (electr.)

aard: ~be'wing earthquake; ~bol globe

aar'de earth; *hemel en* ~ *beweeg* leave no stone unturned; *moeder* ~ mother earth

aar'dig (b) nice, agreeable; unpleasant, queer; *'n* ~*e sommetjie geld* a considerable sum of money

aard: ~kun'de geology; ~rykskun'de geography

aardrykskun'dig -e geographical; ~e -s geographer (person)

aards -e worldly, mundane; down to earth

aard: ~skok/~skud'ding earth tremor

aar'sel ge- hesitate, waver *ook* wei'fel

aart'appel -s potato *ook* ert'appel; ~moer seed potato; ~sky'fie (potato) chip

aarts: ~bis'kop archbishop; ~en'gel archangel; ~va'der patriarch; ~vy'and archenemy

aas[1] (s) carrion; bait; (w) ge- feed on, prey on; scrounge

aas[2] (s) ase ace

aas'voël -s vulture; glutton

ab -te abbot (*person*)

ab'attoir -s abattoir; public slaughterhouse *ook* slag'plaas

ab'ba (w) ge- carry on one's back (baby); ~hart piggy-back heart

abdis' -se abbess

abdy' -e abbey, monastery

abnormaal' ..male; ..maler, -ste abnormal

abor'sie -s abortion *ook* vrug'afdrywing

ab'seil (w) abseil; ~er abseiler (person)

absent' absent; ~isme absenteeism

abses' -se abscess, ulcer *ook* et'tersweer

absoluut' (b) ..lute absolute; (bw) absolutely *ook* volstrek', volko'me

absorbeer' ~, ge- absorb

abstrak' -te abstract

absurd' -e absurd, preposterous; ~e tea'ter theatre of the absurd

abuis' mistake, error; *per* ~ by mistake *ook* per on'geluk

a'dams: ~ap'pel Adam's apple; ~kostuum' in nature's garb, nude

ad'der -s adder, viper; ~gebroed'sel breed of vipers; vermin

addisioneel' ..nele additional; extra *ook* by-ko'mend

a'del nobility

a'delaar -s eagle *ook* a'rend

a'delbors (s) marine cadet; midshipman

a' del: ~lik noble, high-born; *hy is van* ~*like afkoms* he is of noble birth; ~stand nobility, peerage

a'dem (s) -s breath; (w) breathe (fig.); ~*lose stilte* breathless silence

adjektief' ..tiewe adjective

adjudant' -e adjutant, aide-de-camp

adjunk' -te deputy, assistant; ~president' deputy president

administra'sie administration

administrateur' -s administrator

admiraal' -s admiral

administratief' (b) ..iewe administrative

admis'sie admission; ~-eksa'men entrance examination (mostly theology)

adolessen'sie adolescence *ook* tie'nerjare

adrenalien'/adrenali'ne adrenalin(e)
adres' -se address *ook* **woon'plek**
adresseer' ~, **ge-** address, direct
adverteer' ~, **ge-** advertise
adverten'sie -s advertisement *kyk* **rekla'me**
advies' advice; *op* ~ *van* on the advice of; *van* ~ *(be)dien* advise; ~**raad** advisory council
adviseer' (w) ~, **ge-** advise
adviseur' -s adviser *ook* **raad'gewer** (mens)
advokaat[1] **..kate** advocate, barrister-at-law, lawyer; *hy praat/pleit soos 'n* ~ he has the gift of the gab
advokaat[2] eggflip
af off, down, from; *van sy jeug* ~ since his (early) youth; *~ en toe* now and then
af'baken **-ge-** divide; beacon off, mark out; ~**ing** delimitation, demarcation
af'beeld **-ge-** picture, portray, depict; ~**ing** picture, portrait, illustration
af'been cripple(d)
af'betaal ~ (w) pay off, discharge; settle
af'betaling -s, -e payment, settlement; *op* ~ *koop* buy on terms
af'brand **-ge-** burn down (house)
af'breek **-ge-** demolish; destroy; break off
af'breuk damage; ~ *doen aan* injure, prejudice
af'bring **-ge-** bring down, reduce; come off
af'byt **-ge-** bite off; *die spit* ~ bear the brunt
af'dak **-ke** shed, lean-to; penthouse; **mo'tor**~ carport *ook* **mo'torskuiling**
af'dank **-go** dismiss, discharge, fire, retrench *ook* **af'betaal, ontslaan'**
af'deling **-s, -e** division, section, department; detachment; *'n* ~ *soldate* a squad of soldiers; ~**-swin'kel** department(al) store
af'doen **-ge-**, **afgedaan** finish, complete; take off, expedite; ~**de bewys'** clear/conclusive proof
af'draai **-ge-** turn off, twist off, branch off
af'draand(e) slope, descent; *hy is op die* ~ he is going down-hill
af'dreig **-ge-** blackmail; extort; ~**ing** (s) blackmail; extortion *ook* **af'persing**
af'druk (s) **-ke** imprint; copy, impression, reproduction
af'dwaal **-ge-** stray, deviate, wander
affère -s affair, thing, matter *ook* **petal'je**
affilia'sie affiliation *ook* **aan'sluiting**
affodil' **-le** daffodil *ook* **mô'rester** (blom)
af'gaan **-ge-** go down, descend; wear off
afgedank'ste confounded; ~ **loe'sing/pak slae** severe thrashing

af'gee **-ge-** deliver, hand over; come off; *on= enigheid* ~ cause dissension
af'gelas ~ call off; *die polisie gelas die soek= tog af* the police are calling off the search
af'geleë meer ~, **mees** ~ remote, distant
af'geleef **-de** worn with age, decrepit
af'gemat tired, weary, exhausted *ook* **uit'geput**
af'gesaag hackneyed, stale; ~**de grap** stale joke
af'gesant **-e** messenger; envoy, emissary
af'gesien: ~ *van* apart from; notwithstanding
af'gesonder **-de** isolated; retired, lonely
af'gestorwene **-s** (the) deceased, (the) dear departed
af'getrokke meer ~, **mees** ~ absent-minded; abstract; ~ **profes'sor** absent-minded pro= fessor
af'gevaardigde **-s** deputy, delegate (person)
af'god **-e** idol; *geld tot 'n* ~ *maak* idolise/ worship money
af'gooi **-ge-** throw down; cast off
af'grond **-e** precipice, abyss
afgrys'lik **-e; -er, -ste** horrible, hideous, dread= ful, ghastly *ook* **afsku'welik/aak'lig**
af'guns (s) envy, jealousy, spite
afguns'tig **-e; -er, -ste** envious, jealous *ook* **jaloers'**
af'haak **-ge-** unhook, detach; let go, let loose; deliver a blow; *wanneer gaan julle* ~? when are you getting married?
af'haal **-ge-** take down; call for; unquote
af'handel **-ge-** settle, terminate, conclude
af'hang **-ge-** hang down; depend (up)on; *alles hang van jou af* everything depends on you
afhank'lik (b) dependent; (s) ~**e** dependant (person)
af'jak (s) **-ke** rating, rebuff; snub; (w) scold, chide, snub
af'kam **-ge-** comb off; run down (by criti= cism), denigrate
af'kap **-ge-** cut off, chop off; apostrophise; ~**te'ken/~pingsteken** apostrophe
af'keer[1] (s) aversion, dislike; *'n* ~ *hê van* have a dislike of
af'keer[2] (w) **-ge-** avert, ward off
afkeur' **-ge-** disapprove, condemn; reject
af'keuring (s) disapproval, censure; *sy* ~ *uitspreek* express his disapproval
af'klim **-ge-** climb down, descend; *van sy perdjie* ~ come down a notch or two
af'knou **-ge-** hurt, bully; ~**er** (s) bully *ook* **baas'speler/boe'lie** (mens)
af'koel **-ge-** cool down

af'kom -ge- come down, descend; *met 'n boete daarvan* ~ get off with a fine; *die rivier sal* ~ the river will be in flood; ~**eling** descendant; ~**s** descent, extraction, origin; *van hoë* ~*s* of noble birth

afkoms'tig derived from, descended from; ~ *van die Karoo* hailing from the Karoo

af'kondig -ge- proclaim, promulgate, publish; *gebooie* ~ publish the banns

af'konkel -ge- coax away; alienate

af'koop (w) -ge- surrender (insurance policy); redeem; ~**boe'te** spotfine; ~**waar'de** surrender value (insurance)

af'kort -ge- shorten, abbreviate, abridge; ~**ing** abbreviation, abridgment

af'kyk -ge- copy, crib; look down; spy

af'laai[1] -ge- unload/offload; discharge

af'laai[2] (w) download; (s) downloading (comp.)

af'lê -ge- lay down, part with; lay out; take (oath); pass (examination); give (evidence); pay (visit); *'n besoek* ~ pay a visit; *'n eed* ~ take an oath; *eksamen* ~ take/pass an examination; *getuienis* ~ give evidence

af'leer -ge- unlearn, forget

af'leggingspakket' (s) severance package *ook* **skei'dingspakket'**, **uit'treepakket'**

af'lei -ge- deduce, infer, derive; divert; ~**ding** derivation, deduction; diversion, distraction, recreation; ~**er** (lightning) conductor; distractor (in multiple-choice questions)

af'lewer -ge- deliver; ~**ing** delivery

af'loer -ge- spy, watch

af'loop (s) end, result, issue; expiration; run-off; *na* ~ *van die vergadering* after the meeting

af'los -ge- relieve, redeem; *mekaar* ~ take turns; ~**baar** redeemable; ~**wed'loop** relay race

af'luister (w) -ge- eavesdrop; bug, tap (tel.) *ook* **mee'luister** *kyk* **luis'tervlooi**

af'maak -ge- kill, finish

af'mat: (b) ~**tend** tiresome; ~**ting** weariness, exhaustion *kyk* **af'gemat**

af'merk -ge- tick off, mark; mark down

af'meting -s, -e measurement, dimension

af'neem -ge- take away, deprive; decrease, shrink; take a photo, photograph (v) *ook* **fotografeer'**; *'n eksamen* ~ conduct an examination; *sy kragte neem vinnig af* his strength is rapidly declining

af'pen -ge- peg out (claim)

af'pers -ge- extort, exact from *ook* **af'dreig**; blackmail; ~**er** blackmailer, racketeer; ~**ing** extortion; blackmail

af'plat level off, slow down (economy)

af'pluk -ge- pick (off); gather

af'praat -ge- arrange, agree upon, settle

af'raai -ge- dissuade from; discourage

af'rammel -ge- rattle off; prattle; *die voordrag* ~ rattle off the recitation

af'ransel -ge- thrash, flog *ook* **foe'ter/ta'kel**

af'reken -ge- settle, get even with

af'rig -ge- train, coach (sport); ~**ter** trainer, coach *ook* **brei'er**; ~**ting** training, coaching

A'frika Africa; ~**ta'le** African languages

Afrikaan' ..**kane** African

Afrikaans' (s) Afrikaans; (b) -e Afrikaans

Afrika'ner[1] -s Afrikaner (person) *ook* **Afrikaan'** (van Afrika)

afrika'ner[2] -s marigold (flower)

af'rit -te offramp, exit (traffic) *ook* **uit'rit**

Af'ro-Asia'ties -e Afro-Asian

af'rokkel -ge- coax away, wheedle away

af'rond -ge- round off, finish off; ~**ing** rounding off; finish; ~**(ing)skool** finishing school

af'saag/af'sae -ge- saw off; **af'gesaagde grap** stale joke

af'sê -ge- sack; countermand; *die nooi het hom afgesê* the girl gave him the sack (broke the engagement)

af'send -ge- send off, forward, consign *ook* **versend'** (w); ~**er** sender, consignor

af'set turnover, sales; ~**gebied'** market, sales area; ~**punt** outlet

af'setter -s swindler, conman, cheat (person)

afsien -ge- give up, abandon; see off; *van 'n plan* ~ give up a plan

afsig'telik (b) ugly, hideous *ook* **afsku'welik**

af'sit -ge- put down; dismiss; dethrone (a king); ~**ter** starter (person; sport)

af'skaal (w) -ge- scale down

af'skaf -ge- abolish, abrogate, repeal; ~**fer** abstainer, teetotaller (person)

af'skeep -ge- do work in a slip-shod manner, treat shabbily; *jou werk* ~ neglect your work

af'skeer -ge- shear; shave

af'skei -ge- separate; sever from; secrete

af'skeid parting, departure, farewell; ~ *toe'wuif* wave farewell

af'skeids: ~**geskenk'** farewell gift/present; ~**maal** farewell dinner; ~**preek** farewell/valedictory sermon

af'skil -ge- peel, rind

af'skilfer -ge- scale, peel off

af'skop (w) -ge- kick off

af'skort -ge- partition off; ~**ing** partition;

cubicle *ook* **kleed'hokkie**
af'skrif -te copy, duplicate; **gewaar'merkte**
~ certified copy
af'skrik (w) -ge- frighten, scare away, dis=
courage; ~**mid'del** deterrent
afskrikwek'kend -e; -er, -ste terrifying
af'skryf/af'skrywe -ge- copy, crib; cancel,
write off; *R5 van 'n rekening* ~ write off
R5 from an account
af'sku (s) abomination, horror, abhorrence
af'skud -ge- shake off
afsku'welik -e; -er, -ste abominable, horrible
ook **aak'lig, afgrys'lik**
af'slaan -ge- decline, refuse (an invitation);
repulse, beat off (the enemy); serve, service
(tennis); *'n aanbod* ~ refuse an offer
af'slaer -s auctioneer (person)
af'slag[1] (s) rebate, discount *ook* **kor'ting**
af'slag[2] (w) -ge- flay, skin
af'slagwinkel -s discount store
af'sloof (w) -ge- drudge, toil; flog oneself
af'sluit -ge- close, shut off; fence in; seclude;
jou ~ seclude oneself; *rekenings* ~ *aan die
einde van die boekjaar* close off accounts at
the end of the financial year
af'slyt -ge- wear out, waste
af'smeer -ge- palm off on; *hy het daardie ou
fiets aan my afgesmeer* he palmed off that
old bicycle on me
af'snou -ge- speak harshly to, snub; bully
af'sny -ge- cut off, curtail, lop off
af'sonder -ge- isolate, separate; ~**ing** seclusion,
retirement; ~**ingshospitaal** isolation hospital
afson'derlik (b) -e separate, isolated; ~**e
geval'le** isolated cases; ~**e ontwik'keling**
separate development; (bw) separately
af'sper (w) cordon off (street)
af'spraak ..**sprake** appointment; agreement;
~ *met tandarts* appointment with dentist;
~**verkrag'ting** date rape
af'spreek -ge- agree upon, arrange
af'spring -ge- jump off, alight; ~**plek** spring=
board (for attacks)
af'staan -ge- give up, yield, surrender
af'stam -ge- descend, spring from; ~**meling'**
descendant
af'stand (s) ~**e** distance; ~**(s)beheer** remote
control; ~**on'derrig** distance education/
teaching, teletuition
af'steek -ge- contrast with; deliver (speech);
cut off; mark out; *iem. die loef* ~ outdo
someone

af'stof -ge- dust
af'stoot -ge- push off; repel; *jy stoot al jou vrien=
de van jou af* you alienate all your friends
afstoot'lik (b) -e repulsive *ook* **walg'lik**
af'studeer (v) -ge- complete studies
af'sweer -ge- abjure, swear off, renounce; *hy
het alle aardse genietinge afgesweer* he re=
nounced all worldly pleasures
af'takel -ge- unrig (ship); dismantle; thrash; *hy
takel vinnig af* he is getting weak and decrepit
af'tas (w) scan *ook* **skandeer'** *kyk* **brein=
tas'ting**; **(af)tas'ter** scanner
af'teken -ge- mark; draw; sign off; *die berge
staan afgeteken teen die lug* the mountains
are silhouetted against the sky
af'tel[1] -ge- lift off
af'tel[2] -ge- count out; count down; ~**ling**
count off; countdown (space launch)
af'tog retreat; *die* ~ *blaas* sound the retreat
af'trap -ge- wear out (heels); break by treading;
'n lelike stel ~ have a nasty experience
af'trede/af'treding resignation, retirement
af'tree[1] (w) -ge- pace, measure
af'tree[2] (w) -ge- resign; retire; ~**-annuïteit'**
retirement annuity; ~**oord** retirement village
af'trek (s) sale, demand; subtraction; *die boek
kry baie* ~ the book is much in demand;
~**som** subtraction sum
af'vaardig -ge- delegate, return, depute; ~**ing**
deputation, delegation
af'val (s) head and trotters of a sheep; offal;
refuse, trash, waste; (w) -ge- fall off
afval'lig -e; -er, -ste faithless; disagreeing,
dissident; ~**e** dissident (person)
af'val: ~**produk'** (s) -te byproduct; ~**waar'de**
scrap value
af'vee(g) -ge- wipe off, dry; polish
af'voer (w) -ge- lead away, carry off; ~**pyp**
waste/overflow pipe; downpipe (gutter)
af'vra -ge- ask, request; *die boer die kuns* ~
fish for information
af'vry -ge- oust (in courting), cut out
af'vryf/af'vrywe -ge- rub off
af'wag -ge- await, abide; *sy beurt* ~ take his
turn; ~**re'kening** suspense account
af'water (w) -ge- drain, pour off; **af'gewaterde
teks** watered-down text/version; (s) effluent
af'weer -ge- ward off, prevent, avert
af'wend -ge- turn aside, divert; *die gevaar* ~
avert the danger
af'werk -ge- complete, finish; put finishing
touches to; ~**ing** finish; workmanship

af'werp -ge- throw off, shake off

afwe'sig -e absent; ~heid absence

af'wissel -ge- change, alternate; take turns; vary; ~end (b) alternative, diversified; ~ende kleu're varying colours

af'wyk -ge- deviate, depart from, differ from; deflect; van die waarheid ~ swerve from the truth

af'wys -ge- reject, refuse, decline

ag¹ (s) attention, care; in ~ neem take into consideration; ~ slaan op pay attention to; (w) ge- esteem, value; iets nodig ~ consider something necessary

ag/agt² (telw) eight

ag³ (tw) alas! oh!

ag'baar ..bare respectable, venerable, hon= ourable; ag'bare voor'sitter (voor'sitster) Mr Chairman (Madam Chair), Chairperson

ageer' ~, ge- act (for someone), deputise

agen'da -s agenda ook sa'kelys; verskuil'de ~ hidden agenda

agent' -e agent; ~skap agency

aggressief' (b) aggressive ook aanval'lend

a'gie -s quidnunc, Paul Pry; nuuskierige ~s hoort in die wolwehok curiosity killed the cat

agita'tor -s agitator ook op'stoker; demagogue

agiteer' ~, ge- agitate

ag(t) eight; oor 'n dag of ~ within a week

agte(r)lo'sig careless ook nala'tig

ag'ter behind, after; late; my horlosie is ~ my watch is slow; ~ die tralies in jail

ag'teraf backward; secretly; out-of-the-way; ~ men'se lowclass/backward people

agterbaks' -e; -er, -ste sly, underhand

ag'terbanker -s backbencher (parliament)

ag'terbeen ..bene hind leg

ag'terbly -ge- remain behind, straggle

ag'terbuurt -e/ag'terbuurte -s backstreet/ slum area ook krot'buurt

ag'terdeur -e backdoor; 'n ~ oophou keep a loophole open

ag'terdog suspicion ook suspi'sie; ~ koester harbour suspicion

agterdog'tig -e; -er, -ste suspicious

agtereenvol'gens successively, consecutively

ag'terent hind part, rear, backside, bum

ag'tergeblewe: ~ gemeen'skap deprived/dis= advantaged community

ag'tergrond background

ag'terhoede -s rearguard; backline

ag'terkant -e back, back part, reverse side

ag'terklas (s, b) lowclass (people)

ag'terkleinkind -ers great-grandchild

ag'terkom -ge- discover, find out

ag'terlaat -ge- leave behind; sy vrou onver= sorg ~ leave his wife unprovided for

ag'terlig -te tail light (car)

ag'terlik backward; (mentally) retarded ook sim'pel, vertraag'

ag'terlyf ..lywe hind quarters; abdomen (in= sect)

agtermekaar' in order, orderly; spick and span ook or'delik, puik; ~ kê'rel a fine/ smart fellow

agtermid'dag ..middae afternoon

agterna' after, later, subsequently; ~wys'heid hindsight

ag'terom round the back

agteroor' backward(s), supinely

ag'teros -se hind ox; ~ kom ook in die kraal slow but sure

ag'terpoot ..pote hind foot; gou op die ..pote wees be quick-tempered

ag'terplaas ..plase backyard

ag'terryer -s attendant on horseback; hench= man

ag'tersaal -s pillion

ag'terspeler -s back (football)

ag'terstaan -ge- be behind; by niemand ~ nie be inferior to nobody

agterstal'lig -e in arrear, overdue; sy rekening is drie maande ~ his account is three months overdue/outstanding

ag'terstand (s) arrears; backlog

ag'terste last, hindmost

ag'terstel (s) -le rear part (chassis)

agterstevoor' hind part foremost; topsyturvy ook a'weregs

ag'terstewe -ns stern (of ship); backside (of a person)

ag'tertoe astern; towards the back; staan asse= blief ~ please stand back

agteruit' backwards; die pasiënt gaan ~ the patient is getting worse

agteruit'gang deterioration, decline, decay

ag'tervoegsel -s suffix ook suf'fiks

agtervolg' ~ follow, pursue; ~ing pursuit, persecution; ~ingswaan' persecution ma= nia/complex

ag'terwiel -e back/rear wheel

ag(t)'hoek -e octagon

ag'ting regard, esteem, respect ook eer'bied, respek'

ag(t)'ste -s eighth

ag'(t)ien eighteen; ~**de** -s eighteenth

ag(t)'uur eight o'clock; breakfast; ~**werkdag** eight-hour working day

akade'mie -s academy; studies; academe

akade'mies -e academic(al); ~**e op'leiding** academic training

aka'sia -s acacia (tree)

akkedis' -se lizard

ak'ker[1] -s field; acre; *Gods water oor Gods ~ laat loop* let matters take their own course

ak'ker[2] -s acorn; ~**boom** *kyk* **ei'keboom**; ~**boon(tjie)** cowpea

akklimatiseer' ~, **ge-** acclimatise

akkommoda'sie accommodation *ook* **verblyf'**

akkoord' -e agreement, harmony; chord (mus.); ~ *gaan met* agree with

akkor'deon -s accordion *ook* **trek'klavier**

akkuraat' (b) accurate, exact

akkusatief' ..**tiewe** accusative

ak'nee acne, facial pimples *ook* **vet'puisie(s)**

akoestiek' acoustics *ook* **geluids'leer**

akrobaat' ..**bate** acrobat

aksent' -e accent *ook* **klem**; **tong'val**

aksep'bank -e merchant bank

aksepteer' **ge-** accept; *'n wissel ~* accept a bill (of exchange)

ak'sie -s action, suit; tiny bit; *'n ~ hê teen iem.* have a bone to pick with someone

aksyns' excise; ~**belas'ting** excise duty

ak'te -s deed; certificate; ~ **van oprigting** memorandum of association (of company), ~**tas** briefcase; ~~**uit'maker** conveyancer (person)

akteur' -s actor

aktief' active; ..**tie'we vulkaan'** active volcano

aktivis' -te activist (person)

aktiwiteit' -e activity

aktri'se -s actress

aktua'ris -se actuary (insurance)

aktueel' ..**tuele** actual, real, topical; vital

akupunktuur' (s) acupuncture

akuut' **akute** acute *ook* **skerp/he'wig**

akwa'rium -s aquarium

al[1] (b, telw) all, every; ~ *om die ander week* every other week; ~ *drie* all three; *in* ~*le geval* in any case

al[2] (bw) already; continually; ~ *hoe meer* more and more

al[3] (vgw) though, even if; ~ *is hy nog so arm* however poor he may be

alarm' -s alarm; ~ *blaas* sound the alarm

albas'ter -s marble (game); alabaster

al'batros -se albatross (bird)

al'bei both; *hulle is ~ siek* both of them are ill

albi'no -'s albino

al'bum -s album *ook* **gedenk'boek**

al'dag all day, every day; *nie ~ se kêrel nie* an outstanding fellow

aldus' thus, so

al'ewig -e continual, incessant; ~ *laat wees* be continually late

al'fa alpha; *die ~ en die omega* the beginning and the end

al'fabet -te alphabet

alfabe'ties -e alphabetic(al)

al'gar all, everybody *ook* **almal, ie'dereen**

al'ge algae *ook* **wier**

al'gebra algebra *ook* **stel'kunde**

al'geheel ..**hele** total(ly), entire(ly), overall; **al'gehele wen'ner** overall winner

algemeen' ..**mene**; ..**mener**, -**ste** general(ly), universal(ly), common(ly); *oor/in die ~* in general; **al'gemene jaar'vergadering** annual general meeting; **al'gemene praktisyn'** general practitioner *ook* **huis'arts**

alhoewel' (al)though *ook* **hoewel'**

a'lias (s) -se alias; (bw) alias, otherwise

a'libi -'s alibi; *sy ~ bewys* establish one's alibi

a'likreukel -s periwinkle

al'kant all sides; ~ *selfkant* six of the one and half-a-dozen of the other

al'kante on all sides

al'kohol alcohol

alkoholis' -te alcoholic (person); ~**me** alcoholism

al'ko: ~**me'ter** alcometer; ~**toet'ser** breathalyser

alledaags' (b) -e commonplace, ordinary

alleen' alone, single, lonely; sole/solo; ~**agent'** sole agent; ~**han'del** monopoly; ~**lik** only; ~**op'sluiting** solitary confinement; ~**praktyk'** solo practice; ~**spraak** monologue, soliloquy; ~**versprei'der** sole distributor

allegaar'tjie -s mixed grill; chow-chow, jumble, medley, hodge-podge

allegorie' -ë allegory *ook* **sin'nebeeld**

al'lemansvriend hail-fellow-well-met

alle'nig alone, lonely *ook* **alleen'**

allerbes'te very best

allereers'te very first

al'lerhande all sorts, all kinds, sundry

Allerhoog'ste the Supreme Being, God

allerlaas'te very last, ultimate

al'lerlei all kinds of, miscellaneous *ook* **diver'se**

allermins'te very least, least of all
al'lerweë everywhere, in all respects
al'les all, everything; a time for everything; ~ *en nog wat* one thing and another
al'les behalwe anything but, not at all
al'leswinkel -s hypermarket, bazaar
allitera'sie alliteration
allooi' alloy, standard, quality; *van die sui= werste* ~ of the finest quality
alluviaal' ..**viale** alluvial (diamonds)
al'mag omnipotence
almag'tig -e almighty, omnipotent; **die A~e God** the Almighty
al'mal all, everybody; *ons* ~ all of us
almanak' -ke almanac *ook* **kalen'der**
al'melewe always, the whole time; ~ *laat wees* be continually late
almiskie' nevertheless, notwithstanding; *dis nie* ~ *nie* it is quite certain
alom' everywhere; ~*bekend* known by all
alomteenwoor'dig -e omnipresent
alreeds' already *ook* **reeds**
alsien'de all-seeing; ~ **oog** all-seeing eye
alt -e contralto, alto
al'taar/altaar' altare altar
altans' at least, anyway, at any rate
al'te very; too; *ek voel nie* ~ *wel nie* I don't feel too well
altemit(s)' perhaps, maybe *ook* **miskien'**
alternatief' ..**tiewe** alternative
al'tesaam/al'tesame altogether, together
al'tyd always, ever
aluin' -e alum
alumi'nium aluminium
alum'nus ..**ni, -se** alumnus, graduate
alvo'rens before, until; ~ *hy aangestel word, moet hy* . . . before he is appointed he should . . .
al weer' once again
amalgama'sie amalgamation *ook* **sa'mesmel= ting**
aman'del -s almond
amaril' emery *ook* **skuur'steen**
amaso'ne -s amazon *ook* **man'netjiesvrou**
amateur' -s amateur *ook* **leek** (mens)
am'bag (s) **-te** trade, profession, handicraft, business; ~**skool** trade/industrial school; ~**sman** artisan
ambassa'de -s embassy
ambassadeur' -s ambassador
am'ber amber *ook* **geel** (verkeerslig)
ambi'sie ambition

ambisieus' ambitious *ook* **vooruitstre'wend**
ambulans' -e ambulance
a'men -s amen; *op alles ja en* ~ *sê* agree to everything
amendement' -e amendment *ook* **wy'siging**
Ame'rika America
Amerikaans' -e American
Amerika'ner -s American (person)
ameublement' -e set of furniture *ook* **meubel= ment'**
amfibie' (s) **-ë** amphibious animal
amfi'bies -e amphibious *ook* **tweeslag'tig**
amfitea'ter -s amphitheatre
ammoniak' ammonia
ammuni'sie ammunition
amnes'tie (s) amnesty *ook* **vry'waring**
amok' amok; ~ *maak* run amok *ook* **raserny'**
amp -te office, employment; duty, function; *'n* ~ *beklee* hold an office; ~**bekle'der/**~**be= kleër** officebearer, incumbent (of post)
am'per/am'pertjies nearly, almost; *amper maar nog nie stamper nie* a miss is as good as a mile
am'perbroekie -s scanty-panty, scanties
amp'genoot ..**note** colleague, official counter= part
amps: ~**bekle'ër** holder of office, incumbent; ~**gewaad'** robes of office; ~**hal'we** officially, ex officio, in attendance (meetings); ~**mo'tor** official car; ~**termyn'** term of office
amp: ~**telik'** official(ly); ~**tenaar'** official, officer, functionary
amusant' -e; -er, -ste amusing, entertaining *ook* **vermaak'lik**
anachronis'me -s anachronism *ook* **tyd'ver= skuiwing**
analfabeet' ..**bete** analphabete, illiterate (per= son)
anali'se -s analysis *ook* **ontle'ding**
analogie' -ë analogy *ook* **ooreen'koms**
anargie' anarchy *ook* **wet'teloosheid**
anargis' -te anarchist; ~**me** anarchism
anatomie' anatomy *ook* **ontleed'kunde**
an'der other, another; *aan die* ~ *kant* on the other hand; *met* ~ *woorde* in other words; ~**half** one and a half; ~**kant** across, on the other side
an'ders otherwise, else; failing which; ~ *as sy familie* not like his relations; *heeltemal iets* ~ something totally different; *maak gou,* ~ *is jy laat* hurry up, else you'll be late

andersden'kend (b) -e dissenting, of a differ=
ent opinion
an'dersins otherwise
an'dersom the other way about; *dis net* ~ just
the opposite
an'derste = anders
anekdo'te -s anecdote *ook* staal'tjie
ane'mies -e anaemic *ook* bloed'armoedig
anemoon'..mone anemone *ook* wind'blom
an'gel -s sting (of a bee)
angelier' -e carnation (flower)
Anglikaans' -e Anglican
angliseer' ge- Anglicise
Anglisis'me -s Anglicism
Anglo-Boe'reoorlog Anglo-Boer War; South
African War *ook* Twee'de Vry'heidsoorlog
angs -te anxiety, fear, agony, *dodelike* ~ *uit=
staan* be in mortal fear; ~knop'pie panic
button; ~sweet cold perspiration
ang'stig -e; -er, -ste afraid, terrified; ~e oom'=
blikke anxious moments
angswek'kend -e; -er, -ste alarming, fear=
some, horrifying
an'ker (s) -s anchor; *êrens* ~ *gooi* go courting
somewhere; *voor* ~ *lê* lie/ride at anchor
anna'le annals *ook* kroniek'e
anneksa'sie -s annexation *ook* in'lywing
annekseer' ~, ge- annex
annuïteit' annuity *ook* jaar'geld
anomalie' -ë anomaly *ook* ongerymd'heid
anoniem' -e anonymous *ook* naam'loos
anorek'sie (s) anorex'ia nervo'sa *ook* dieet'=
siekte *kyk* bulimie'
ansjo'vis anchovy
anten'ne -s aerial (wire) *ook* lug'draad
antibio'ties (b) -e antibiotic
antibio'tikum (s) -s, ..tika antibiotic
an'tichris antichrist
antiek' -e antique; ~win'kel antique shop
an'tiklimaks anticlimax
an'tiloop ..lope antelope
an'tirevolusionêr' (s) -e anti-revolutionist,
pacifist; (b) -e anti-revolutionary
an'ti-Semiet -e anti-Semite
antisep'ties -e antiseptic
antite'se antithesis *ook* teen'stelling
antitoksien' -e/antitoksi'ne -s antitoxin
An'tjie: ~ Somers bogeyman; ~ taterat gossip,
chatterbox (person)
antrasiet' anthracite
antropologie' anthropology
antropoloog' ..loë anthropologist

ant'woord (s) -e answer, reply; *in* ~ *op* in
reply to; (w) ge- answer, reply; *bevestigend
(ontkennend)* ~ reply in the affirmative
(negative); ~koevert' reply-paid envelope;
~masjien' answering machine (tel.)
anys' anise (plant); ~saad aniseed
apart' -e apart, separate; ~heid separateness;
apartheid (political system)
apokopee' -s apocope
apokrief'..kriewe apochryphal; Apokrie'we
Boeke Apochrypha
apologie' -ë apology *ook* versko'ning; ~
aanteken make/offer an apology
apos'tel -s apostle
aposto'lies -e apostolic
apostroof'..strowe apostrophe *ook* af'kap=
(ping)te'ken
apparaat'..rate apparatus
apparatuur' computer hardware *ook* har'de=
ware
ap'pel -s apple; pupil (eye); *die* ~ *val nie ver
van die boom nie* like father like son; *'n* ~
'n dag laat die dokter wag an apple a day
keeps the doctor away
appèl' -le appeal; ~ *aanteken* give notice of
appeal; ~hof court of appeal
appelkoos'..kose apricot; ~konfyt' apricot
preserve, apricot jam; ~siek'te diarrhoea
appellie'fie -s Cape gooseberry
ap'pelwyn cider
appendisi'tis appendicitis *ook* blindederm'=
ontsteking
applikant' -e applicant *ook* aan'soeker
applika'sie -s application (for a post); *'n* ~
indien/besorg submit an application
applous' applause *ook* toe'juiging
appresia'sie appreciation *ook* waarde'ring
apteek'..teke chemist's shop, pharmacy
apte'ker -s chemist, druggist
aptyt' appetite *ook* eet'lus
Ara'bië Arabia
Arabier' -e Arab (person)
Ara'bies (s) Arabian; (b) -e Arabian
ar'bei ge- work, labour, toil
ar'beid work, labour, toil; ~ *adel* labour en=
nobles; geskool'de ~ skilled labour; ~er
labourer, workman, worker; ~(s)intensief'
labour intensive
ar'beid(s): ~terapie' occupational therapy;
~veld sphere of action, field of activity;
~verhou'dinge industrial/labour relations
arbi'ter -s arbiter, arbitrator (person)

arbitra'sie arbitration
a'rea -s area *ook* gebied'
are'na -s arena *ook* stryd'perk
a'rend -e eagle
argaïs'ties -e archaic, obsolete
Argenti'nië Argentina (country)
Argentyn' -e (an) Argentinean; ~s (b) Argen=
tine
argeologie' archaeology *ook* oud'heidkunde
argeoloog' ..loë archaeologist
argief' argiewe archives
argipel' -le archipelago *ook* ei'landgroep
argitek' -te architect *ook* bou'meester
argitektuur' architecture
argiva'ris -se archivist
argument' -e argument, plea *ook* dispuut'
argumenteer' ~, ge- argue
arg'waan suspicion, mistrust
a'ria -s air, tune, song, aria
aristokraat' ..krate aristocrat *ook* edel'man
aristokra'ties -e aristocratic
ark -e ark; *uit die* ~ *se dae* from time im=
memorial; ~mark petshop
arka'de -s arcade *ook* deur'loop (s)
arm¹ (s) -s arm
arm² (b) -e; -er, -ste poor, indigent, needy
arm'band -e bracelet, bangle
arm'druk(wedstryd) arm/Indian wrestling
ar'mesorg care of the poor
arm'holte -s armpit *ook* ok'sel
armlas'tig -e; -er, -ste chargeable to the
parish; (s) ~e pauper (person)
ar'moede poverty, want
armoe'dig -e; -er, -ste poor, needy, indigent,
shabby; *'n* ~*e huisie* a shabby house
armsa'lig -e; -er, -ste pitiful, miserable
arm'stoel -e armchair *ook* leun'stoel
aro'ma -s aroma, fragrance
a'ronskelk -e arumlily *ook* vark'oor (blom)
arres'/arresta'sie arrest, custody *ook* aan'=
houding
arresteer' ~, ge- arrest, take prisoner
arseen' arsenic; ~vergif'tiging arsenic poi=
soning
arsenaal' ..nale arsenal *ook* wa'penhuis
arte'sies -e artesian; ~e bron/put artesian well
arties' -te artist *kyk* waag'arties
arti'kel -s article, clause; commodity
artikula'sie articulation
artillerie' artillery
artisjok' -ke artichoke
artistiek' artistic, tasteful; *die* ~*e gehalte* the
artistic quality
arts -e physician, doctor *ook* genees'heer *kyk*
tand'arts, vee'arts, huis'arts
artseny' medicine, medicament; ~kun'de phar=
macology
as¹ (s) ashes; ~ *is verbrande hout* if ifs and ans
were pots and pans; *in die* ~ *sit* repent
as² (s) -se axle, axis
as³ (bw, vgw) as, like, than; when, if; *so nim=
mer* ~*te nooit* never ever
asa'lea -s azalea *ook* berg'roos
as: ~baan dirt track, cinder track; ~bak'kie
ashtray
asbes' asbestos; ~sement' asbestos cement
a'sem (s) -s breath; *die laaste* ~ *uitblaas* expire;
(w) breathe; ~ha'ling breathing, respiration;
kunsma'tige ~ha'ling artificial respiration
asetileen' acetylene
as(se)gaai' -e assegai
as'hoop ..hope ash heap, dumping site
Asia'ties -e Asiatic
A'sië Asia
asiel' -e asylum, place of refuge, sanctuary
as'jas -se rascal; joker (cards)
as'koek -e ashcake; ne'er-do-well; ~ *slaan*
dance a reel
as'ma asthma
aspaai' I spy (hide-and-seek game)
aspek' -te aspect
asper'sie -s asparagus
aspirant' -e aspirant, applicant; ~onder=
wy'ser teacher in training
as'poestertjie -s cinderella
aspres'/aspris' deliberately, by design
asseblief' please, if you please; ~ *tog!* do
please!; *bly* ~ *aan* please hold the line
asses'sor -s, -e assessor, co-opted member
assimila'sie assimilation
assistent' -e assistant; ~re'kenmeester assis=
tant accountant
assosiaat' ..ate associate (of a society)
assosia'sie association *kyk* vere'niging
assuran'sie insurance, assurance *ook* verse'ke=
ring; ~agent' insurance agent; ~maat=
skappy' insurance company
as'ter -s aster, chrysanthemum; girl, girlfriend
astrant' -e; -er, -ste cheeky, impudent, bold
ook parman'tig
astrologie' astrology *ook* ster'rewiggelary'
astroloog' ..loë astrologer (person)
astrono'mies -e astronomic(al); ~e kos'te
astronomic/huge costs

astronoom′ ..**nome** astronomer *ook* **sterre=kun′dige** (mens)

as′tronout -e astronaut, spaceman *ook* **ruim′=tevaarder**

as′vaal ashen pale; *jou* ~ *skrik* become pale with fright

asyn′ vinegar

ateïs -te atheist *ook* **god′loënaar;** ~**me** atheism

ateljee′ -s studio, workshop *ook* **stu′dio**

ateljee′orkes -te studio orchestra

at′jar pickles

Atlan′ties -e Atlantic

at′las -se atlas

atleet′ atlete athlete

atletiek′ athletics; ~**baan** athletic track; ~**by=een′koms** athletic meeting

atle′ties -e athletic; ~**e figuur′** built like an athlete

atmosfeer′ ..**sfere** atmosphere

atoom′ atome atom; ~**bom** atom/atomic bomb; ~**fu′sie** atomic fusion; ~**oor′log** atomic war; ~**split′sing/**~**sply′ting** splitting of the atom, atomic fission

attaché -s attaché; ~**tas** briefcase *ook* **ak′tetas**

attent′ attentive; *iem. op iets* ~ *maak* draw someone's attention to

attributief′ ..**tiewe** attributive

Augus′tus August

Austra′lië Australia; ~**r** Australian (person)

Austra′lies (b) -e Australian

avoka′do -′s avocado

avonturier′ -s adventurer; fortune hunter

avontuur′ ..**ture** adventure; ~**lik** adventur=ous; ~**verhaal′** adventure story

a′wend -e evening, night (poetic)

A′wendmaal the Lord's Supper

a′weregs -e wrong *ook* **agterstevoor′**; purl (knitting)

a′wery average (at sea); ~**klousu′le** average clause (insurance)

B

ba! bah! pshaw! *nie boe of* ~ *sê nie* not say boo.to a goose

baad′jie -s coat, jacket

baai[1] (s) -e bay

baai[2] (w) ge- bathe *ook* **swem; -er** bather (person)

baal (s) bale bale; (w) **ge-** bale

baan (s) bane course, way; orbit (of a planet); court (tennis), lane (traffic);

baan: ~**bre′ker** pioneer; ~**sy′fer** par (golf, for course); bogey (for hole); ~**tjie** job, em=ployment; ~**tjies vir boeties** jobs for pals

baar (b) -der, -ste uncivilised, unskilled; (w) bear a child

baard -e beard

baar′moeder -s womb, uterus

baars -e bass; perch (fish)

baas base master, boss; crack, ace; ~**baklei′er** champion fighter; ~**raak** overcome, master

baat (s) profit, gain; **ba′te** assets; *ten bate van* in aid of

ba′ba/ba′batjie -s baby; **ba′bafol′tering** baby battering; ~**wag′ter** babysitter *ook* **kroos′=trooster**

bab(b)elas′ (s) hangover *ook* **win′gerdgriep**

bab′bel ge- tattle, chatter; ~**aar** tattler, chatterer; ~**bek/**~**kous** chatterbox

ba′ber -s barbel (fish)

baccalau′reus ..**rei, -se: B**~ **Artium** Bachelor of Arts

bad (s) -de, -dens bath; (swimming) bath/pool **baaie** mineral bath, hot spring; (w) **ge-** take a bath, bathe; ~**ka′mer** bathroom; ~**kos=tuum′** bathing costume

baga′sie baggage, luggage; ~**bak** boot (of car)

bag′ger ge- dredge; ~**boot/**~**masjien′** dredg=er, dredging machine

bai′c meer, meeste very, much, many; ~ *dankie* thank you very much; ~**maal/baie maal** many a time, frequently, often

bajonet′ -te bayonet

bak[1] (s) -ke basin, trough, bowl; body (of a car(t)); (b, bw), baggy; cupped

bak[2] (w) ge- bake, fry, roast; ~ *en brou* muddle; *'n poets* ~ play a trick

bak[3] (b) fine, first-rate, decent; *hy is 'n* ~ *ou* he is a first-rate chap

bakatel′ (s) -le trifle, bagatelle *ook* **klei′nig=heid**

bak′boord larboard, port (side); *iem. van* ~ *na stuurboord stuur* send someone from pillar to post

ba′ken -s beacon; buoy

bak′gat (b, tw) excellent/first-class; swanky

bak'ker -s baker; ~y bakery
bak'kie -s small dish (tray, basin, bowl); pickup van, bakkie; punnet
bak'kies -e face, phiz, mug, dial (idiom.)
bak'kopslang -e ringed cobra
baklei' ~, ge- fight, scrap, quarrel; ~ery' (s) fighting, scrap, brawl
bak'maat capacity, content (of a dam)
bak'oond -e (Dutch) oven
bak'oor ..ore large prominent ear
bak'sel -s batch, baking; ~ bro'de loaves in (out of) the oven
bak'steen ..stene brick
bakte'rie -ë, -s bacterium *ook* **kiem**
bak'vis -se/**bak'vissie** -s flapper, teenager (girl)
bal¹ (s) -le ball (e.g. tennis); (w) ge- clench (the fist)
bal² (s) -s ball (dance); **gemas'kerde** ~/ **mas'kerbal** fancy-dress ball
balakla'wa: ~**mus** balaclava/cap *ook* **klap'⸗ mus**
balans' -e balance, equilibrium; poise
balanseer' ~, ge- balance
balans'staat ..state balance sheet
balda'dig -e; -er, -ste mischievous; boisterous
ba'lie¹ -s bar; *tot die* ~ *toegelaat* admitted to the bar (legal)
ba'lie² -s tub; (water) barrel
baljaar' ~, ge- play noisily, gambol, frolic
balju' -'s messenger of the court, sheriff
balk¹ (s) -e beam, rafter; stave, bar (mus.)
balk² (w) ge- bray (donkey)
balkon' -ne, -s balcony
balla'de -s ballad
ballas' ballast; ~**mand'jie** large bushel basket
ballet' -te ballet; ~**dan'ser, ~danseres'** ballet dancer
bal'ling = **ban'neling**
ballon' -ne, -s balloon
bal'punt(pen)/bol'punt(pen) (s) ballpoint pen *ook* **rol'punt(pen)**
bal'sem (s) -s balm, balsam, ointment; (w) ge- embalm
bamboes' -e bamboo
ban (s) excommunication, banishment; *in die* ~ *doen* ban; excommunicate
banaal' ..nale; ..naler, -ste banal, vulgar
band -e band (for clothes); ribbon (for hair); tape, cord; girdle; tyre (for car)
bandelier' -e, -s bandoleer
bandiet' -e convict, prisoner

band: ~**opna'me** tape recording; ~**masjien'/ ~opne'mer** tape recorder; ~**oteek'** tape library; ~**sky'fiereeks** tapeslide sequence *kyk* **vi'deoband**
bang -e; -er, -ste afraid, frightened; *liewer* ~ *Jan as dooie Jan* discretion is the better part of valour; ~**broek** coward
banier' -e banner, standard
ban'jo -'s banjo
bank¹ (s) -e bench, form, desk; pew (church); *deur die* ~ on the average; throughout
bank² (s) -e bank; (w) ge- bank; ~**bestuur'der** bank manager
banket' confectionery; -te banquet; ~**bak'ker** confectioner
bankier' -s banker
bank: ~**kommis'sie** bank charges/rate; ~**noot** banknote; ~**re'kening** bank account
bankrot' (s) -te bankruptcy *ook* **bankrot⸗ skap**; ~ *speel* go bankrupt
bank: ~**staat** bank statement ~**wis'sel** bank draft
ban'neling -e exile, outcast *ook* **bal'ling**
ban'tamhoendertjie -s bantam fowl
barak' -ke barracks
barbaar' ..bare barbarian, savage (person)
barbaars' -e; -er, -ste barbarous, brutal person
barbier' -s barber *ook* **haar'kapper**
baret' -te beret; birette
ba'riton -s baritone
barmhar'tig -e; -er, -ste merciful, compassio⸗ nate; ~**e Samaritaan'** good Samaritan
ba'rometer -s barometer *ook* **weer'glas**
baron' -ne, -s baron
barones' -se baroness
bars¹ (s) -te burst, crack; (w) ge- burst, crack; *buig of* ~ bend or break
bars² (b, bw) -e; -er, -ste harsh, rough; *veg dat dit* ~ fight like mad
bas¹ -se bass (singer)
bas² -te bark, rind; body; *sy* ~ *red* save his skin; *tussen die boom en die* ~ betwixt and between
basaar' -s bazaar *ook* **ker'mis** (by skool)
baseer' ~, ge- base, ground
ba'sies -e basic *ook* **fundamenteel'**
ba'sis -se basis, base; foothold; **militê're** ~ military base
basket'bal basketball (men)
Baso'tho (s) Basuto (person)
bas'ta! enough! stop! ~ *nou met jou lollery!* stop bothering me!

bas'ter[1] (s) **-s** bastard, halfcaste; hybrid; (w) **ge-** hybridise

bas'ter[2] (bw) rather, somewhat; *ek voel ~ naar* I am feeling a little sick

bas'ter: ~**mie'lies** hybrid maize; ~**taal** barbarism (language); mixed jargon

bataljon' **-ne, -s** battalion

ba'te asset; credit; ~**s en las'te** assets and liabilities

ba'tig: ~**e sal'do** credit balance

battery' **-e** battery; *'n ~ laai* charge a battery

beamp'te **-s** (honorary) official; employee

beant'woord ~ answer, reply; *aan die doel ~* meet the purpose

bebloed' **-e** bloodstained, bloody

beboet' ~ fine; *iem. met R10 ~* fine someone R10

bebou' ~ cultivate, till; ~**de gebied'** built-up area

bed **-dens, -de** bed

bedaar' (w) ~ appease; subside, abate; ~**mid'del** tranquilliser *ook* **kalmeer'middel**

bedaard' **-e; -er, -ste** calm, sedate

bedags' during the day

bedag'saam (b) thoughtful, circumspect, considerate

bedank' ~ thank; decline, refuse; resign; *as lid ~* resign one's membership; *~ uit 'n komitee* resign from a committee; ~**ing** refusal; resignation; expression of gratitude; *die ~ing doen/uitspreek* propose a vote of thanks

bed'degoed bedding, bedclothes

bed'ding (s) river/flower bed

be'de **-s** prayer, petition; entreaty; ~**vaart** pilgrimage

bedees' **-de; -der, -ste** timid, bashful

bedek' (w) ~ cover up, conceal, hide; (b) hidden, covered; ~**te se'ën** blessing in disguise

be'del **ge-** beg, ask alms; ~**aar** beggar

bede'ling **-s, -e** endowment, supply; **nu'we ~** new dispensation/deal

beden'king **-e, -s** consideration, reflection, remark; ~**e teen iets hê** have doubts about something

bedenk'lik **-e; -er, -ste** critical, dangerous, serious; *hy lê in 'n ~e toestand* he is in a critical condition

bederf' (s) corruption, depravity; decay; (w) ~ spoil, corrupt, deprave, ruin; ~**ba're goe'dere** perishable goods

bedien' ~ serve, attend, wait upon; administer; ~**de** servant; domestic *ook* **huis'hulp**; attendant; ~**er** operator (of machine)

bed: ~**kus'sing** pillow; ~**laken** (bed)sheet; ~**lê'end** bedridden, confined to bed

bedoel' ~ mean; intend; purpose; *ek het dit nie so ~ nie* this is not what I meant; ~**ing** meaning, intention, purpose; *met goeie ~ings* with the best of intentions

bedom'pig **-e; -er, -ste** close; stuffy, sultry

bedor'we (b) spoiled; depraved; ~ **kind** spoilt child

bedra' ~ amount to; *die rekening ~ R5* the account/bill amounts to R5

bedrag' **bedrae** amount

bedreig' ~ threaten, menace; ~**de spe'sie** endangered species; ~**ing** threat, menace

bedre'we meer ~, **mees** ~ competent *ook* **bekwaam'**; skilled, experienced

bedrieër **-s** fraud, deceiver, cheat, conman

bedrieg' ~ cheat, deceive, defraud, con; ~**lik** deceptive, fraudulent, deceitful

bedroef' (w) ~ grieve, afflict; (b) sorrowful, sad, grieved *ook* **hart'seer**; ~ **min** precious little; ~ **wees oor** grieve at

bedroe'wend **-e** distressing, saddening

bedrog' **bedrieërye** deceit, deception, fraud; cheating; ~ **pleeg** commit fraud

bedruk' **-te; -ter, -ste** oppressed, dejected, downhearted *ook* **terneer'gedruk**

bedryf' (s) **bedrywe** (branch of) industry; (line of) business, profession, trade; act (play); *'n ~ beoefen* practise a trade; *in ~ kom* start operations; (w) ~ commit, perpetrate; ~**sielkunde** industrial psychology

bedryfs: ~**bates** current assets; ~**kapitaal'** working capital; ~**ken'nis** industrial art(s); ~**kos'te** working expenses; ~**las'te** current liabilities; ~**lei'er** executive *ook* **bestuurs'hoof**; ~**verhou'dinge** labour/industrial relations

bedry'wig **-e; -er, -ste** active, busy

bedui'dend significant, meaningful

bedui'e (w) ~ signify, mean, imply; point out, direct; *iem. die pad/rigting ~* explain the road/direction to someone

bedui'wel ~ make crazy, spoil *ook* **veron'geluk**; *hy het die hele saak ~* he has bungled the whole affair

bedwelm' (w) ~ stun, stupefy; drug; (b) benumbed, stunned, drugged; ~**ing** daze, stunned state; ~**mid'del** drug *kyk* **dwelms**

bedwing' ~ curb, check, restrain; *hy kon hom nie ~ nie* he could not restrain himself beë'dig (w) ~ swear to; put upon oath; *die burgemeester is* ~ the mayor was sworn in; (b) -de sworn; ~de verkla'ring sworn affi= davit

beef ge- tremble, shiver; quiver; ~ *soos 'n riet* tremble like an aspenleaf *ook* bewe

beëin'dig ~ finish off, terminate

beeld -e image, likeness, picture; statue; ~bou'er image builder

beeld'hou ge- sculpture, carve; ~er sculptor; ~kuns sculpture

beeld: ~ra'dio television; ~saai, ~send tele= vise; ~skoon beautiful as a picture; ~spraak figurative/metaphorical language

been bene bone; leg; *harde bene kou* suffer hardships; *deur murg en* ~ to the marrow of one's bones; ~af in love

beer bere bear (wild animal); boar (male pig)

bees -te beast; bovine (animal); cow; (mv) cattle

bees: ~boer stock/cattle farmer; ~melk cow's milk; ~vleis beef; ~wag'ter cowherd/herds= man

beet¹ bete beetroot

beet² bete bite; hold, grip; ~kry get hold of, seize

befoe'ter ~ spoil; bedevil; ~d (b) cantanker= ous, contrary *ook* beneuk'

begaaf' -de talented, gifted; ~de kind gifted child

begaan'¹ (w) ~ commit, perpetrate; *'n fout* ~ make a mistake

begaan'² (b) beaten, trodden; upset, worried; ~ *oor die uitslag* worried about the result

begeer' ~ desire, wish for, covet; ~lik desir= able; ~te desire, wish

begelei' ~ accompany, escort; ~de toer guided/conducted tour *ook* rond'leiding; ~ding accompaniment

begena'dig (w) ~ pardon, condone, reprieve

bege'rig -e; -er, -ste desirous; eager

begin (s) beginning, start, outset, commence= ment

begin'ner -s beginner, novice; ~s'kur'sus beginners' course

begin'sel -s principle *ook* grond'reël

begraaf' (w) ~ bury, inter *ook* begra'we; ~plaas graveyard, cemetery *ook* kerk'hof

begraf'nis -se burial, funeral; ~onderne'mer funeral undertaker; ~stoet funeral procession

begra'we ~ bury, inter

begrip' -pe idea, notion, conception; *traag van*

~ slow to understand, slow on the uptake

begroet' ~ greet, welcome

begroot' (w) ~ estimate, budget

begro'ting (s) -s estimate, budget

begryp' ~ understand, comprehend

behaal' ~ obtain, get, win, gain, score; *hy het sy graad* ~ he obtained his degree

beha'e delight, pleasure; ~ *skep in* delight in

behal'we except, save, besides; *alles* ~ any= thing but

behan'del ~ treat; handle; manage; ~ing treatment

behar'tig ~ have at heart; take care of *ook* hanteer'; *hy* ~ *die geldsake* he looks after the finances

beheer' (s) management, direction, control; (w) administer, control, manage; ~lig'gaam body corporate (sectional titles)

beheers' ~ rule, govern, manage, control

behels' ~ embrace, comprise; contain

behen'dig -e; -er, -ste dexterous, handy

behoed'saam cautious, circumspect, wary

behoef': ~te want, need, necessity; ~tig poor, needy

behoe'we on behalf of, in aid of; *die kollekte is ten* ~ *van die armes* the collection is in aid of the poor

behoor'lik (b) -e proper, fit, becoming

behoor(t)' ~ belong to; behove, ought; be proper; *die boek* ~ *aan my* the book belongs to me; *hy* ~ *tot/aan daardie kerk* he is a member of that church

behou' ~ keep, retain, preserve, save

behou'e (b) safe and well

behou'ering containerisation

behui'sing housing; ~ske'ma housing scheme

behulp' aid, help, shift; *met* ~ *van* with the aid of

bei'de both; *geen van* ~ neither of the two

beïnvloed (w) ~ influence, affect *ook* raak; bias

bei'tel (s) -s chisel; (w) ge- chisel

bejaard' -e aged, old, elderly; tehuis' vir ~es old-age home *ook* ou'etehuis

bejaar'desorg care of the aged

bejam'mer ~ deplore, lament, bewail; *ek* ~ *jou* you have my sympathy

beje'ën ~ treat, act towards; *met minagting* ~ treat with contempt

bek -ke beak (bird); snout (animal); muzzle (of firearm); mouth (animal); *'n dik* ~ *hê* sulk; *hou jou* ~! shut up! *met 'n* ~ *vol tande* without saying a word

bek: ~**af** downhearted, down in the dumps; ~**dry'wer** backseat driver

bekeer' ~ convert, proselytise

beken' ~ confess, acknowledge; ~**tenis'** confession

bekend' (b) -e; -er, -ste known, conversant with, noted, familiar

be'ker -s cup, jug, bowl, mug;. sports trophy ~**wed'stryd** cup match/final

beke'ring conversion

bek'ken -s pelvis; basin; catchment area

beklem'toon ~ emphasise, stress

beklink' ~ arrange, settle; *'n saak* ~ close a deal

beknop' -te; -ter, -ste succinct, concise, abridged; *'n* ~*te uitgawe van die boek* a condensed version of the book

bekom' (w) ~ obtain; recover from (fright)

bekom'mer ~ trouble, worry; *ek* ~ *my daaroor* I am worried about it; ~**nis** uneasiness; worry, anxiety

bekoor' ~ charm, enchant, fascinate, tempt; ~**lik** charming, fascinating *ook* **aanval'lig, fraai**

beko'ring charm, fascination

bekos'tig ~ afford; defray, pay; *ek kan dit nie* ~ *nie* I cannot afford it; ~**baar** (b) affordable *ook* **sak'pas**

bekrag'tig ~ ratify; confirm, sanction

bekrom'pe narrow-minded

bekro'ning crowning; reward of merit; award

bekroon' ~ crown; award; *met die eerste prys* ~ awarded the first prize

bekruip' ~ creep upon, steal upon, stalk

bekwaam' (w) ~ qualify; enable; train; (b) able, capable, competent, efficient; ~**heid** ability, capability, capacity

bekyk' ~ look at, view, inspect

bel (s) -le bell; wattle (bird); (w) **ge-** ring, 'phone *ook* **ska'kel**

belag'lik (b) ridiculous *ook* **bespot'lik**

beland' ~ land; get to; arrive

belang' -e importance; interest; concern; *in jou eie* ~ in your own interest

belang'rik -e; -er, -ste important, considerable; ~**heid** importance

belang'stel -ge-, **belang stel belang ge-** take an interest in, be interested in

belas' (w) ~ burden; tax; rate; assess; ~ *en belade* heavily laden; ~**te wins** profits after tax; ~**baar** taxable

belas'ting -s tax(ation); load; rate, duty; ~ *hef*

levy tax on; ~ **op toe'gevoegde waarde (BTW)** value added tax (VAT); ~**aan'slag** assessment; ~**beta'ler** taxpayer; ratepayer; ~**gaar'der** tax collector, receiver of revenue (state income) *ook* **Ontvang'er van In'komste**; ~**plig'tige** taxpayer; ~**vry** taxfree

belê' ~ convene, call (meeting); invest (money)

bele'dig ~ insult, offend; ~**ing** insult

beleef'[1] (w) ~ experience, witness, live to see *ook* **bele'we** (w)

beleef'[2] (b) -de; -der, -ste polite, civil, courteous *ook* **beleefd', hof'lik**

beleefd'heid civility, politeness, courtesy

bele'ër ~ besiege, lay siege to; ~**ing** siege

beleg' **beleëringe, beleërings** siege; *staat van* ~ state of siege; ~**ger** investor (of money)

beleg'ging -s, -e investment (of money, assets)

beleid' ~**e, beleidrig'tings** policy; ~**ma'ker** policy maker/shaper

belem'mer ~ hamper, obstruct; *die uitsig is* ~ the view is obstructed

bele'se well-read, widely read, erudite

belet' (w) ~ prohibit, forbid

bele'we ~ experience, witness, live to see *ook* **beleef'** (w)

bel'hamel -s bellwether; ringleader

belig' ~ lighten up; illuminate; expose

belig'ting exposure; illumination, lighting

belof'te -s promise; *'n* ~ *nakom* keep a promise

belo'ning -s, -e reward; *'n* ~ *uitloof* offer a reward

beloof'/belo'we (w) ~ promise

beloon' ~ reward, remunerate

belt (s) **bel'de** belt *ook* **gor'del**

bely' ~ confess, avow; ~**denis'** confession

bemaak' ~ bequeath (money in a will)

bemag'tiging empowerment (e.g. of women)

beman' (w) ~ man, equip; ~**ning** crew; manning (staff provision); **on'der**~ understaffed

bemark' (w) market; ~**ing** marketing

bemees'ter ~ overpower; master

bemerk' ~ observe, notice, perceive

bemid'delaar -s mediator, go-between *ook* **tus'senganger**

bemid'deld -e well-to-do, wealthy *ook* **wel'af**

bemin' ~ love, be fond of; ~**d'** loved, beloved; ~**de** loved one, lover

bemoei' ~ meddle, interfere; ~ *jou met jou eie sake* mind your own business; ~**siek** (b) meddlesome, officious

bemors' ~ soil, stain, begrime

bena'deel (w) ~ harm; hurt, injure

benader ~ approach; approximate, estimate; ~ing (s) approach; approximation, rough estimate; by ~ing approximately

bena'ming -s, -e name, title, term

benard' -e; -er, -ste distressed, trying; embar= rassed; in ~e omstandighede in straitened circumstances

ben'de -s band, troop, gang; ~lei'er gangleader; ~verkrag'ting gangrape ook groep'verkrag= ting

bene'de below, beneath, under; ~ my waar= digheid beneath my dignity

beneuk' (w) ~ damage, spoil, mar; (b) ook befoe'ter daft, cantankerous, unmanageable

bene'wel (w) ~ cloud, darken, obscure

bene'wel(d) (b) -de foggy, misty, hazy

bene'wens besides, in addition to

beno'dig(d)heid requirement

benoem' ~ nominate, appoint; ~ing appoint= ment, nomination

benoud' anxious, oppressed; stuffy, stifling

bensien'/bensi'ne benzine

benul' notion, idea; geen ~ nie not the slightest notion/idea

benut' (w) ~ utilise, avail oneself of

beny' ~ envy, grudge; ek ~ hom sy gesond= heid I envy him for his health

beoe'fen ~ study; practise; exercise; pursue (a profession); geduld ~ exercise patience

beoog' ~ aim at, have in view; ~de uit'brei= dings planned extensions

beoor'deel ~ judge, criticise, adjudicate

beoor'delaar -s adjudicator, judge; reviewer, critic

bepaal' ~ determine (date); define; stipulate

bepaald' (b) -e fixed, positive, definite

bepa'ling -s, -e stipulation; determination; provision; fixture (sport)

beperk' (w) ~ limit, confine, restrict; ~ tot restricted to; (b) limited, restricted; ~ing limitation, restriction

beplan' (w) plan; ~ning planning

bepleit' ~ plead, advocate

beproe'wing -s, -e trial, tribulation

beraad' deliberation, talk(s); ~slaag (w) deliberate, consult; ~sla'ging deliberation, consultation kyk bos'beraad/lekgot'la

beraam' ~ plan, contrive; frame; estimate; 'n plan ~ make a plan

bera'dene (s) -s counsellee (person being counselled)

bera'der (s) -s counsellor (psychology)

bera'ding (s) counselling

bera'ming -s, -e estimate; specification

bê're ge- store, save, put aside

bered'der ~ administrate, wind up (estate)

bere'de mounted; ~ poli'sie mounted police

beredeneer' ~ discuss, reason

berei' ~ prepare; dress; 'n maaltyd ~ prepare a meal

bereid' (b) ready, prepared, willing

bereidwil'lig -e ready, willing ook hulpvaar'= dig

bereik' (s, w) reach

bere'ken ~ calculate; compute; charge; ~aar estimator (person); calculator ook sak'reke= naar; ~ing calculation

bê'rekoop lay-by

bê'replek -ke storage space/room

berg¹ (s) -e mountain, mount; van 'n mols= hoop 'n ~ maak make a mountain out of a molehill

berg² (w) ge- salvage; store kyk op'berg

bergag'tig -e mountainous

berg: ~enier' mountaineer ook berg'klim= mer; ~hang mountain slope

berg'ie (s) (Table Mountain) tramp/loiterer

ber'ging salvage, salvaging (a ship); storing of; stowage (mealies); ~skip salvage vessel

berg: ~ket'ting mountain range; ~klim'mer mountaineer ook bergenier'; ~pas moun= tain pass; B~rede Sermon on the Mount; ~skool initiation school (tribal custom).

berig' (s) -te intelligence, news, report

beroemd' -e; -er, -ste famous, renowned, celebrated; ~heid fame, renown

beroep' (s) -e profession; calling, vocation; trade; appeal; 'n ~ beoefen follow a pro= fession; 'n ~ doen op appeal to; (w) call, nominate; appeal to; ~s'hal'we by virtue of one's profession; ~siek'te occupational dis= ease; ~s'keu'se choice of profession; ~s'= lei'er careers adviser; ~s'lei'ding career/ vocational guidance/counselling; ~s'man professional (person); ~s'op'leiding voca= tional training; ~spe'ler professional (player); ~sport professional sport; ~stoei pro= fessional wrestling; ~s'voor'ligting careers/ vocational guidance; ~wed'der bookie ook boe'kie

beroerd' (b) rotten, miserable, lousy

beroe'ring -e, -s commotion, disturbance

beroer'te (s) stroke; apoplexy, palsy

berok'ken ~ cause, create; *skade* ~ cause damage

beroof' ~ rob; deprive, bereave

berou' (s) repentance, regret, remorse; (w) repent, regret

berug' (b) **-te; -ter, -ste** notorious, infamous

berus' ~ rest upon, depend upon; acquiesce; *in die onvermydelike* ~ resign oneself to the inevitable

bes (s) best, utmost; quite; *sy uiterste* ~ *doen* do his utmost

besa'dig (b) **-de** composed, sedate, calm

beseer ~ hurt, injure (in accident)

besef' (s) idea, realisation; *tot die* ~ *kom* realise; (w) ~ realise, comprehend

be'sem -s broom

besen'ding -s, -e consignment (of goods)

bese'ring -s, -e injury

beset' ~ occupy (a place); engage; *die telefoon is* ~ the telephone is engaged

bese'tene -s possessed one; maniac; *hy gaan te kere soos 'n* ~ he carries on like a maniac/ madman

beset'ting -s, -e occupation; garrison

besiel' (w) ~ animate, inspire *ook* **inspireer'**

besie'ling inspiration, animation

besienswaar'dig -e worth seeing, remarkable; ~**heid** tourist attraction; curiosity

be'sig (w) ge- use, employ (words); (b) busy, engaged; ~**heid** business, occupation, employment

besig'tig ~ examine, inspect

besin' ~ reflect, come to one's senses; ~ *voor jy begin* look before you leap

besit' (s) possession; assets; *in* ~ *neem* take possession of; (w) own, possess, have; ~**lik** possessive; ~**reg** right of ownership; title; ~**ting** possession, property, estate

beskaaf' (w) ~ cultivate, civilise; (b) cultured, civilised *ook* **op'gevoed**

beska'dig (w) ~ damage, harm, injure

beska'wing -s, -e civilisation, culture

beskei'e meer ~, **mees** ~ discreet, modest; *na my* ~ *mening* in my humble opinion

beskerm' ~ protect; shelter; guard; ~**(e)'ling** protégé; ~**en'gel** guardian angel; ~**er** protector, patron; ~**heer** patron; ~**heilige** patron saint

besker'ming protection; patronage; auspices; *onder* ~ *van die nag* under cover of night

beskik' ~ manage; arrange; dispose; *die mens*

wik, God ~ man proposes, God disposes; ~**baar** available; ~**king** disposal, arrange‑ ment; *tot sy* ~**king hê** have at his disposal

besko're granted to, allotted; *dit was my nie* ~ *nie* I was not destined to . . .

beskou' ~ view, look at, behold; consider

beskryf'/beskry'we ~ describe, depict; draw up (in writing)

beskry'wing -s, -e description; ~**s'punt** point/ item for discussion (on the agenda)

beskuit' -e rusk

beskul'dig ~ accuse, charge with; ~ *van* accuse of; ~**de** accused, defendant (person); ~**ing** accusation, charge, indictment

beskut' ~ protect, shelter; ~**te beroep'/werk** sheltered occupation/employment

beslaan (w) ~ occupy, fill; cover (area)

besleg' ~ decide, settle; *hulle het die geskil* ~ they settled the argument

beslis' (w) ~ decide; (b) decided, positive; (bw) decidedly, positively; ~**send** decisive, final, conclusive; ~**sende stem** casting vote; ~**sing** decision, ruling, resolution

beslom'mering -s, -e, beslom'mernis -se vexation, trouble, cares (of office)

beslo'te korpora'sie (BK) close corporation (CC)

besluit' (s) **-e** resolution; decision; (w) resolve, decide; ~**e'loos** irresolute, wavering; ~**ne'‑ mer** decision maker

besmeer' ~ soil, smear, grease

besmet' ~ infect, contaminate, pollute

besmet'lik -e; -er, -ste contagious, infectious (disease)

besnoei' ~ curtail, retrench; cut; *uitgawes* ~ cut down on expenses

besny' ~ circumcise; ~**denis'** circumcision

besoe'del ~ stain, contaminate, pollute; ~**ing** contamination, pollution

besoek' (s) **-e** visit, call; ~ *aflê* pay a visit; (w) (~) visit, call on; try, afflict; ~**er** visitor; guest; ~**ing** visitation, affliction, trial

besol'dig ~ pay, remunerate; ~**ing** salary, remuneration, pay, wages

beson'der (s): *in die* ~ particularly; (b) particular, special, peculiar; (bw) exception‑ ally, particularly; ~**heid** detail, particular; *meer/nadere besonderhede* further details

beso'pe drunk, fuddled (with drink)

besorg' (w) ~ deliver (goods); procure; furnish (details); (b) anxious, concerned, uneasy; ~**d'heid** anxiety, worry

bespaar' ~ economise; save; ~ *jou die moeite*

save yourself the trouble; *geld/onkoste* ~ save costs/spending

bespa'ring saving; ~**s'rit** economy run (cars)

bespie'gel (w) ~ speculate, contemplate

bespoe'dig ~ accelerate; hasten; expedite

bespot' ~ mock, laugh at, ridicule; ~**lik** ridic=ulous; *hom ~lik maak* make an ass of himself; ~**ting** mockery, derision, ridicule

bespreek' ~ discuss, talk over/about; *ook* **beraad'slaag** (w); review (books); reserve, book (seats); *sitplekke* ~ book seats

bespre'king -s, -e discussion; conference; booking, reservation; review; ~**s'groep'** discussion group

besproei' ~ irrigate; ~**ing** irrigation

bes'sie -s berry; ~**sap** currant juice

bestaan' (s) existence, livelihood; (w) ~ exist, live, consist (of); ~ *uit* consist of; ~ *van* live on; ~**s'ekonomie'** subsistence econo=my; ~**s'jaar** year of existence, anniversary

bestand' proof (against), equal to; ~**deel** ingredient, component (part)

bes'te best, excellent; dear; *my (ou)* ~ my better half; *sy* ~ *vertoning nog* his best performance ever

beste'ding (s) expenditure *ook* **uit'gawes**

bestee' ~ spend; use; expend; *aandag* ~ *aan* give attention to

besteel' ~ rob

bestel' (w) ~ order, arrange, appoint

bestel'ling -s, -e order, delivery; appointment; *'n* ~ *plaas* place an order

bestel'vorm -s order form

bestel'wa ..waens delivery van; bakkie

bestem' ~ destine, fix, apportion; ~**ming** destination, destiny

bestem'pel ~ stamp; name, call (names); designate as

besten'dig (b) **-e** constant; consistent, stable; ~**e speler** safe/consistent player

bestier' (s) guidance; dispensation; ~**ing** act of Providence

bestook' ~ harass; batter, bombard; *met vrae* ~ bombard with questions

bestor'we deadly pale, livid; deceased; ~ **boe'del** deceased estate

bestraf' ~ rebuke, reprove, punish

bestry' ~ combat, contest; dispute

bestudeer' ~ study; investigate

bestuif'/bestui'we ~ cover with dust; pollinate

bestuur' (s) **..sture** management; directorate; board of control; (w) govern, rule, manage,

direct; drive, steer; **bestu'rende direkteur'** managing director; ~**der** manager, director; driver (car); ~**derslisen'sie** driver's-license *ook* **ry'bewys**

bestuurs': ~**hoof/**~**lei'er** executive *ook* **be=dryfs'hoof**; ~**komitee'** management com=mittee *ook* ~**raad**; ~**lid** board member

bestuur'skool ..skole driving school; school of management

bestuur'stel -le executive suite

bestuurs'vergadering -s, -e management meet=ing

besui'nig ~ economise, reduce expenses

beswaar' (s) **besware** objection, grievance, scruple; *besware maak/opper* raise objections

besweer' ~ swear; conjure; entreat; charm (snake)

bes'wil: *vir jou eie* ~ for your own good

beswyk' ~ succumb; yield; die *ook* **sterf**; *aan 'n siekte* ~ die of a disease

betaal' ~ pay, settle; **haal-en-**~ cash-and-=carry; **vooruit**~ paid in advance

beta'kel ~ dirty, besmear

beta'ling -s, -e payment

betas' ~ finger, feel; fondle *ook* **bevoel'** *kyk* **seksue'le teis'tering**

bete'ken ~ mean, signify, imply; spell; portend; serve; *dagvaarding* ~ *aan* serve summons on *ook: bestel aan*

bete'kenis -se meaning; sense, significance, importance *ook* **belang'rikheid**; *manne van* ~ men of note; ~**vol** significant, meaningful

be'ter better, superior; ~**skap** improvement, recovery; ~**we'ter** pedant, wiseacre, know-all (person)

beteu'el ~ restrain, check, bridle, curb

beteu'ter(d) -de perplexed, puzzled

beto'ger -s demonstrator (political)

beto'ging -s, -e demonstration (public) *ook* **protes'optog**

beton' concrete; **gewa'pende** ~ reinforced concrete

betoog' (s) **..toë** argument(ation); (w) demon=strate, argue, prove

beto'wer ~ enchant, charm, fascinate

beto'werend -e charming, fascinating, glam=orous *ook* **bekoor'lik**

betrap' ~ catch; surprise; trap; detect; *iem. heter daad op diefstal* ~ catch a thief redhanded

betree' ~ tread upon, enter, set foot upon; **onregma'tige betre'ding** trespassing

betref′ ~ concern, relate to, touch, affect; *wat my* ~ as for me; ~**fende** concerning, regarding *ook* **aangaan′de**

betrek′ ~ occupy; involve; ~**king -e** relation; ~**king -s** situation, job; *met* ~*king tot* with reference to

betreur′ (w) ~ regret, lament, deplore

betrok′ke cloudy, overcast; gloomy; concerned, involved; ~ **amp′tenaar** official concerned

betrou′ ~ trust; ~**baar** trustworthy, reliable; ~**baarheid** reliability

betuig′ ~ testify; declare; assure; show; express (thanks); *sy dank* ~ express his thanks

betwis′ ~ dispute; contest; *'n setel* ~ contest a seat (in election)

betwy′fel ~ doubt, question, query

betyds′ in time *ook* **op tyd**

beu′el -s bugle, trumpet

beul -e, -s hangman, executioner

beurs -e purse; bursary, scholarship; stock exchange; ~**note′ring** stock exchange listing

beur′sievryer -s sugardaddy *ook* **vroe′telvader, paai′pappie** (idiom.)

beurt -e turn; over (cricket); ~**e′lings** by turns, alternately, in rotation

beval′ling -s, -e confinement, delivery (of a child)

beva′re ~ **see′man** able seaman

bevat′ ~ contain, comprise, hold *ook* **behels′**; comprehend

beveel′ (w) ~ order, command, enjoin

beveg′ ~ combat, fight (against)

bevei′lig ~ shelter, protect, safeguard

bevel′ -e order, command; mandate; ~**voerder** commander; ~**voerende offisier** commanding officer

beves′tig ~ confirm, corroborate, bear out; ~**end** affirmative; ~**ende/reg′stellende ak′sie/optrede** affirmative action; ~**ing** confirmation, affirmation

bevind′ (w) ~ find, experience; ~**ing** (s) finding

bevlek′ ~ stain, defile, pollute

bevlie′ging -s, -e caprice, sudden fancy, whim; *'n* ~ *kry* act on a sudden impulse

bevoeg′ -de competent, qualified, able; ~**d′heid** competence, qualification; power

bevoel′ ~ feel; finger *kyk* **betas′**; touch

bevolk′: *dig* ~ densely populated; ~**ing** population; ~**ingsontplof′fing** population explosion

bevoor′deel (w) ~ favour, promote, advance

bevoor′oordeel(d) -de biased, prejudiced

bevoor′reg (b) **-te** privileged

bevor′der ~ promote, advance; ~**ing** promotion, rise

bevraag′teken (w) ~ query, doubt, question

bevre′dig ~ satisfy, appease, gratify; ~**end** satisfactory; ~**ende diens** satisfactory service

bevrees′ (b) afraid, anxious

bevriend′ -e friendly, on good terms; ~**e land** friendly country

bevries′ ~ freeze, congeal

bevro′re frozen; ~ **hoen′der** dressed chicken

bevrug′ ~ impregnate, fecundate; ~**ting** conception, impregnation; **kunsma′tige** ~**ting/insemina′sie** artificial insemination

bewaak′ ~ watch, guard

bewaar′ ~ keep, preserve; ~**der** keeper, warder; ~**kas** locker *ook* **sluit′kas**; ~**skool** infant school, crèche

bewa′pen (w) ~ arm, provide with arms

bewa′rea (s) nature reserve *ook* **bewaar′area**

bewa′ring keeping, custody; conservation *kyk* **natuur′bewa′ring**

be′we ge- tremble, shiver; quiver *ook* **beef**

beweeg′ ~ move, stir; persuade; ~**lik** movable, mobile; vivacious; ~**re′de** motive, rationale

beweer′ ~ assert, contend, allege

bewe′ging -s, -e movement, motion; ~**s′leer** eurythmics; kinetics

be′wer -s beaver

bewera′sie (s) trembling fit, shivering

be′werig -e; -er, -ste shaking, trembling, quivering; shaky

bewe′ring -s, -e assertion, contention, statement *ook* **stel′ling**; allegation *ook* **aan′tyging**

bewerkstel′lig ~ effect, cause, bring about

bewil′lig (w) grant, consent; *geld* ~ vote money/funds

bewind′ government, rule, administration; *aan die* ~ *kom* come to power; ~**heb′bende party′** ruling party; ~**heb′ber** governor, ruler

bewo′ë moved, affected; agitated

bewolk′ -te cloudy, overcast

bewon′der ~ admire; ~**aar** admirer, fan (person); ~**aars′pos** fan mail; ~**ing** admiration

bewo′ner -s inhabitant; occupier; ~ *van 'n huis* occupant of a house

bewoon′ ~ occupy, inhabit

bewoord′ ~ word, express (in words); ~**ing** wording, expression

bewus' -te aware, conscious; *ten volle* ~ *van* fully aware of; in question; ~**syn** con= sciousness

bewus'teloos . .lose unconscious

bewys' (s) -e proof, evidence; (w) prove, demonstrate; show; do (a favour)

bey'wer ~ endeavour, apply oneself; *hom* ~ *vir* work/strive for

bib'ber ge- shiver, tremble

bibliograaf' . .grawe bibliographer (person)

bibliografie' -ë bibliography *ook* **bron'nelys**

biblioteek' . .teke library

biblioteka'ris -se librarian

bid ge- pray, beseech, supplicate, ask a blessing; say grace; ~**stond** prayer meeting

bie ge- bid; tender

bied ge- offer, present; *teenstand* ~ offer resistance

bie'der -s bidder (at auction)

bief'stuk beefsteak *ook* **steak**

bieg (s) confession; (w) **ge-** confess; ~**poësie'** confessional poetry

bie'lie -s stalwart; whopper; *jy is darem 'n* ~! you're a brick!

bier beer; ~**brouer** brewer; ~**brou'ery** brew= ery; ~**saal** beer hall; ~**vat** beer cask, beer barrel

bies beestings, colostrum; ~**brui'lof** non-alco= holic wedding reception

bie'sie -s rush, reed; ~**pol** tussock of rush; peach of a girl

bie'tjie (s) a little bit; a moment; *alle* ~*s help* every little helps; (b) few; little; (bw) rather, slightly; *'n* ~ *baie* rather much; *gee* ~ *pad* just stand clear; *help* ~ please give me a hand

bifokaal' bifocal; . .kale **bril** bifocal specta= cles; (mv) bifocals

bigamis' -te bigamist *ook* **veel'wywer**

bilateraal' (b) . .ale bilateral *ook* **tweesy'dig**

bilhar'ziase bilharziasis (disease) *ook* **rooi'= water**

biljart' (s) billiards (game)

biljoen' (**miljoen miljoen**) billion (Eng 1 000 million = Afr **miljard'**)

bil'lik (b) -e; -er, -ste reasonable, fair, just, equitable; *nie meer as* ~ *nie* only fair

bil'likheid equity, justice, fairness

bil'tong -e biltong (dried meat); ~ *sny voor die bees geslag is* count one's chickens before they are hatched

bind ge- tie, bind, fasten; ~**geld** retaining fee, retainer; commitment fee

bin'ne in, within, into, inward, inside; ~ *'n paar dae* within a few days; *te* ~ *skiet* flash into one's mind; ~**aarse voe'ding** intrave= nous feeding; ~**band** tube; ~**brandmotor** internal combustion engine; ~**goed** intes= tines, entrails; *meer bek as* ~**goed** all talk; ~**-in** inside, within; ~**kant** inside; ~**kort'** shortly, soon, before long; ~**land** interior; ~**lands** inland, in the interior; ~**land'se sa'ke** home affairs (dept. of); ~**landse verbruik'** domestic consumption

bin'nens: ~**huis** indoors, in the house; ~**huise versie'ring** interior decorating *ook* **binne= versiering**

bin'ne(n)ste innermost; ~*buite* inside out

bin'ne: ~**pasiënt** -e in-patient; ~**versiering** interior decorating

bi'odata (s) curriculum vitae *ook* **CV, le'= wensprofiel'**

biografie' -ë biography *ook* **le'wensbeskry= wing**

biologie' biology

biolo'gies -e biological; ~**e na'vorsing** biolo= gical research

bio'nies (b): ~**e mens** bionic man; cyberman

bioskoop' . .skope bioscope, cinema, movie

bis'kop -pe bishop

bits/bit'sig -e; -er, ste harsh, sharp, biting

bit'ter [-e]; -der, -ste bitter, grievous; ~ *min* precious little; ~**einder** diehard, persister; ~**heid** bitterness; acerbity

blaad'jie -s leaflet *ook* **blad'skrif**

blaai ge- turn over pages; ~ *om (b.o.)* please turn over (p.t.o.); browse (comp.)

blaam blame, blemish

blaar[1] **blare** blister, bleb

blaar[2] **blare** leaf (of a plant)

blaas[1] (s) **blase** bladder

blaas[2] (s) **blase** bubble; (w) **ge-** blow, puff; ~**balk** bellows; ~**gom** bubblegum; ~**kans,** ~**tyd** break, time for a breather; ~**op'pie** -s toby (fish); ~**orkes'** brass band; ~**pyp** blowgun, blowpipe; ~**vlam** cutting torch

blad blaaie leaf (of a book); newspaper; blade (spring); shoulder (animal)

blad: ~**sak** knapsack; ~**skrif** leaflet, hand= out; ~**sy** page; ~**wy'ser** bookmark, index

blaf (s) **blawwe** bark; (w) **ge-** bark; *komman= deer jou eie honde en* ~ *self* do your own dirty work

bla'ker -s candlestick

blameer' ge-, ~ blame, slander

blan'ke -s white person; white (member of group or race)
blan'ko blank; ~ **tjek** blank cheque
blaps mistake, slip-up *ook* **fla'ter/glips**
blas -ser, -ste sallow, darkbrown
blat'jang chutney; relish, ketchup
bleek (w) ge- bleach; (b) pale, pallid, colour=
less; ~**siel** wimp *ook* **slap'gat** (*kru*)
bleik ge- bleach; ~**poei'er** bleaching powder
blêr ge- bleat; ~**fliek** talkie film; ~**kas** juke=
box
bles -se blaze; bald head; ~**bok** blesbuck;
~**hoender** whitefaced coot, moorhen;
~**perd** horse with a blaze
blie'per -s bleeper (for messages)
blik[1] (s) -ke glance, view; glance, look; *sonder
om te* ~ *of te bloos* without a blush
blik[2] (s) -ke tin; ~**brein** computer (idiom.);
~**kiesdorp'** shantytown; slum; ~**kieskos'**
tinned foodstuffs; ~**kiesmelk'** condensed/
tinned milk
blik'ker (w) glare, glitter, dazzle; ~**ing** (s)
glare (affecting vision)
Blik'oor ..ore nickname for Freestater
blik'sem (s) -s lightning *ook* **weer'lig**; scoun=
drel; (w) flash; ~**straal** flash of lightning
blik: ~**skêr -e** plate shears; tin opener;
~**skottel!** silly ass!; rascal!; ~**sla'er** tin=
smith; rascal; ~**sny'er** tin opener
blind -e blind; ~**e hoogte** blind rise; ~**e
vertrou'e** implicit faith; ~**doek** (s) eye
bandage; (w) blindfold
blin'dederm -s appendix *ook* **appen'diks**;
~**ontste'king** appendicitis
blin'de-instituut ..tute institute for the blind
blinde: ~**lings** blindly, implicitly, ~**mol'letjie**
blind man's buff (a game)
blin'der -s window blind
blin'de: ~**skool** school for the blind; ~**vlieg**
stingfly
blin'ding = blin'der
blind: ~**tik** touch typing; ~**tik'ster** touch
typist
blink (w) ge- shine, glitter; (b) shining, glitter=
ing; ~ **gedag'te** brainwave; ~ **toe'koms**
bright future
blits (s) -e lightning flash; (w) ge- flash;
~**aan'val** blitz, lightning attack; ~**debat'**
snap debate (parliament); ~**mo'tor** (flying)
squad car; ~**patrol'lie** flying squad; ~**ver=
ko'per** bestseller *ook* **tref'fer** (boek); ~**vin=
nig** like a flash

bloed blood; strain; *sy* ~ *kook* he is furious;
~**ar'moede** anaemia, chlorosis; ~**bad** blood=
bath; massacre
bloeddors'tig -e; -er, -ste blood-thirsty
bloed: ~**druk** blood pressure; ~**drup'pel** drop
of blood; ~**e'rig** bloody; *'n* ~*erige stuk
vleis,* meat dripping with blood; ~**hond**
bloodhound; ~**ig** bloody; scorching; *'n*
~*ige geveg* a bloody fight; ~**ige hit'te**
scorching heat; ~**ing** bleeding, haemor=
rhage; ~**jong/jonk** very young; ~**kan'ker**
leukemia; ~**min** precious little; ~**oortap'=
ping** blood transfusion; ~**rooi** bloodred;
~**skan'de** incest; ~**sken'ker** blood donor
bloeds'omloop circulation of the blood
bloed: ~**sui'er** leech, bloodsucker; extortioner;
~**vergie'ting** bloodshed; ~**vergif'tiging**/~**ver=
gif'ting** blood poisoning; ~**verwant'** rela=
tive; kinsman; ~**ve'te** blood grudge/feud,
vendetta
bloed'vint -e boil, furuncle
bloed: ~**vlek** bloodstain; ~**wei'nig** precious
little
bloei[1] (s) bloom, flourishing condition; *in die*
~ *van sy jare* in the prime of his life; (w)
ge- bloom (flowers); blossom (trees); flour=
ish; ~**ende be'sigheid** flourishing concern
bloei[2] (w) ge- bleed
bloei'sel -s blossom, bloom *ook* **bloe'sem**
bloc'kom bluegum
bloemis' -te florist
bloem'lesing -s anthology, selected writings
bloes(e) blouse
blok[1] (s) -ke block, log; clog; ~**bespre'king**
block booking; ~**fluit** recorder; ~ sjoko=
la'de slab of chocolate *ook* **sjok'kie**
blok[2] (w) ge- grind at, cram, swot
blok'huis -e blockhouse
blokka'de -s blockade; roadblock *ook* **pad'=
versperring**
blokkeer' ge- blockade; block
blok'kies: ~**raaisel** crossword puzzle *ook*
blok'raaisel; ~**vloer** parquet floor(ing)
blok'man -ne blockman
blom (s) -me flower, blossom; ~**bed'ding**
flower bed; ~**kool** cauliflower
blom'merangskikking -s flower arrangement
blom'meskou -e, blom'metentoonstelling -s
flower show
blom: ~**pot** flowerpot; ~**ryk** flowery; florid;
~**tuin** flower garden
blond -e; -er, -ste fair, light

blondi′ne -s blonde, fair-haired girl

bloos ge- blush, colour; ~ *tot agter die ore* blush to the roots of one's hair

bloot blote naked, bare; mere; *blote toeval* sheer coincidence; *met die blote oog* with the naked eye; ~**lê** (w) expose (crime ring) *ook* **oop′vlek**

bloots bareback(ed)

bloot′stel -ge- expose; *hom* ~ *aan gevaar* expose himself to danger

blos -se blush, bloom

blo′send -e; -er, -ste blushing, flushed; rosy, ruddy

blou -er, -ste blue; *bont en* ~ *slaan* beat black and blue

blou-blou: ~ *laat* let the matter rest

blou: ~**druk** blueprint; ~**kopkoggelman′der** blueheaded lizard; ~**kous** bluestocking, literary woman; ~**oog** blue-eyed; ~**reën** wistaria; ~**sel** (washing) blue; ~**skim′mel** -s bluish grey horse; ~**tjie:** *'n* ~*tjie loop* unsuccessful; refused by a girl; ~**wil′debees** blue wildebees, brindled gnu

bluf (s) bragging, boasting, bluff; (w) brag, bluff

blus (s): *sy* ~ *is uit* he is done for; (w) extinguish, quench, put out; slake (lime)

bly[1] (w) **ge-** stay, remain, live; ~ *aan* hold the line

bly[2] (b) glad, joyful, cheerful; ~ *u te kenne* how do you do, pleased to meet you *ook* **aan′genaam!**

bly′beurt (s) timeshare *ook* **tyd′deel**

blyd′skap joy, happiness

bly′er-vry′er live-in lover

blyk (s) -e proof, mark, token, sign; ~ *van waardering* token/mark of appreciation; (w) appear; seem, be evident; *dit sal gou* ~ we shall soon see

blyk′baar apparently, obviously, evidently

bly′kens according to; ~ *koerantberigte* judging from newspaper reports

blymoe′dig -e; -er, -ste joyful, glad, cheerful; joyous

bly′spel -e comedy *ook* **kome′die**

bly′wend -e lasting, permanent; fast; ~*e vrede* lasting peace

bo above; upstairs; up, upon; over; ~ *en behalwe* over and above; ~ *alle verwagting* beyond all expectations

bo: ~**aan** at the top, at the head; ~*aan die klas staan* be at the top of the class; ~**baas** topdog *ook* **uit′blinker**

bobbejaan′ . .**jane** monkey; baboon; *die* ~ *agter die bult/berg haal* create/pre-empt imaginary problems; ~**boud** old-fashioned musket; ~**spinnekop** tarantula, baboon spider; ~**stui′pe** hysterics, fits

bobo′tie curried mince, bobotie

bod/bot botte offer, bid

bud/der: *moenie* ~ *nie* don't bother

bo′de -s messenger

bo′dem -s bottom; soil

boe (tw) boo(h); *hy kan nie* ~ *of ba sê nie* he can't say boo to a goose

Boeddhis′ -te Buddhist (person); ~**me** Bud= dhism; ~**ties** Buddhistic

boe′del -s estate; ~ *oorgee* go bankrupt; give up; ~**belas′ting** estate duty; ~**bered′eraar** executor, administrator (of an estate)

boef boewe rogue, villain, knave *ook* **skurk, boos′wig**

boeg boeë bow, prow; ~**lam** tired out, fatigued, deadbeat

boe′goe buchu; ~**bran′dewyn** buchu brandy

boei (s) -e shackle; handcuff, fetter; (w) handcuff, chain, fetter, fascinate, capti= vate; ~**end** captivating, fascinating, inter= esting; ~**ende verhaal′** gripping story/ tale

boek (s) -e book; *anderman se* ~*e is duister*, the lives of others are a closed book; *te* ~ *stel* record; put on paper; (w) book, enter

boekanier′ -s buccaneer, pirate

boek: ~**beoor′delaar** reviewer, critic; ~**be= wys′** booktoken; ~**deel** volume, part; *dit spreek* ~*dele* it speaks volumes; ~**druk= kuns′** printing art, typography; ~**ekas** book= case; ~**ery′** library (private)

boeket′ -te bouquet *ook* **rui′ker**

boe′kevat -ge- observe divine service at home

boek′handel booktrade; bookshop; ~**aar** bookseller, stationer

boek′hou (s) bookkeeping; (w) keep books, keep accounts; ~**er** bookkeeper

boe′kie -s small book, booklet; bookie (horse racing)

boek′jaar . .**jare** financial year *ook* **geld′jaar**

boek: ~**rak** bookshelf, bookcase; ~**sak** school= bag, case, satchel; ~**staaf** (w) put on record, commit to paper; ~**win′kel** bookshop; ~**wurm** bookworm

boel crowd, lot, a great many; ~**hond** bulldog

boe′lie (w) bully *ook* **af′knou**; (s) bully *ook* **bul′lebak**

boe'mel ge- booze, spree; ~**aar** tramp, loafer; hobo; reveller; ~**trein** slow train

boe'merang -s boomerang

boen'der ge- scrub, rub, polish *ook* **boen**; bundle away

boen'doehof (s) kangaroo court *ook* **straat'hof**

bo'-ent -e topside; upper half

boe'pens -e paunch; potbelly

Boer[1] -e Boer (member of group or race); *die ~ met sy roer* the Boer and his (faithful) gun

boer[2] (s) -e farmer, peasant; jack, knave (cards); *die ~ die kuns afvra* try to find out a secret; (w) farm; stay; frequent; *hy ~ by daardie nooi* he is always off to that girl; *agteruit~* go downhill; ~**dery'** farm; farming; ~**(e)beskuit'** rusk; ~**boon(tjie)** broadbean; ~**pot** jackpot

boe're: ~**dag** agricultural/farmers' day; ~**matriek'** confirmation (church); ~**musiek'** popular music; ~**orkes'** traditional rural orchestra; ~**raat'** home remedy; ~**troos'** coffee (idiom.); ~**verneu'ker** conman; cheat; quack; ~**wors** boerewors; ~**kool** borecole, kale

boe'sem -s bosom, breast; *die hand in eie ~ steek* search one's own heart; ~**vriend'** chum, bosom friend

Boes'man -s Bushman *ook* **San**; ~**te'kening** Bushman drawing/rock painting

boet[1] (s) brother; *baantjies vir ~ies* jobs for pals; *boetie-boetie speel* be hand and glove together

boet[2] (w) ge- atone, expiate; *vir sy sondes ~* pay for his sins

boe'ta -s brother; old chap; *ek sal jou wys, ~ !* I'll show you, old chap!

boe'te -s fine; penalty; penance; *~ doen* do penance; *~ oplê* impose a fine; ~**bes'sie** metermaid; ~**bos'sie** burweed

boetiek' boutique *ook* **mo'dewinkel**

boe'we: ~**streek** villainy, roguery; ~**tro'nie** hangdog face

bof[1] (s) tee (golf); base (baseball); home (games)

bof[2] (w) ge- be lucky, have more success than expected

bof'bal baseball

bog (s) nonsense, trash, tripe; -**te** blighter, fool (person); *jou klein ~* you little fool/rascal; *dis pure ~* it's all bunkum

bo'gemiddeld above average

bog'gel -s hump, hunch; ~**rug** hunchback

bogh'er/bok'ker bugger (*vulgar*) *ook* **swer'noot**

bog: ~**rym'pie** limerick *ook* **limeriek'**; ~**praa'tjies** twaddle, trash, piffle

bohaai' fuss, hubbub, noise *ook* **kabaal'**

boi'kot (s) boycott; (w) boycott

bok[1] -**ke** goat, antelope, buck; trestle; *'n ou ~ is ook lus vir 'n groen blaartjie* old men like tender chickens; ~**kie** small buck; girlfriend

bok[2] -**ke** blunder; *'n ~ skiet* make a blunder

bok'baard billy goat (beard)

bok-bok-staan-styf' high cockalorum

bok: ~**haar** mohair; ~**hael** buckshot; ~**kapa'ter** castrated goat

bok'kem/bok'kom -s (dried) Cape herring; bloater

bok'kesprong -e caper, antic

bok'kie[1] -s kid; small trestle

bok'kie[2] -s buggy (cart)

bokmakie'rie -s bush shrike (bird)

bok: ~**melk** goat's milk; ~**ooi** she-goat; ~**ram** he-goat

bo'koste overhead costs, overheads

boks (w) ge- box; (s) boxing (sport); box, container *ook* **karton'doos**

bok'ser -s boxer

boks'handskoen boxing glove

bok'spring (s) -e caper, antic; (w) caper, prance

bok'veld goat pasture; *hy is ~ toe* he has gone west, has joined his forefathers

bok: ~**vet** goat suet; ~**wa** buckwagon; ~**wiet** buckwheat

bo'laag (s) upper layer; topdressing (lawn)

bol -**le** (s) ball; bulb; globe; (w) bulge; (b) convex, round

bo: ~**leer** upper leather, uppers; ~**lig** skylight, fanlight

bol'la -s chignon, bun (hair)

bol(le)makie'sie head over heels, somersault; *~ slaan* loop the loop

bol: ~**puntpen'** ballpoint pen *ook* **bal'puntpen**; ~**rond** convex, spherical

bol'werk (s) bulwark, rampart

bo'lyf . .lywe body above the hips

bom (s) -**me** bomb, shell; *die ~ het gebars* the fat is in the fire; (w) bomb; *die stasie is ge~* the station has been bombed

bombardement' -e bombardment

bombas'ties -e; -er, -ste bombastic

bom: ~**kombers'** bomb suppressor; ~**skok** shellshock; ~**wer'per** bomber (plane)

bo'natuurlik -e supernatural

bond -e confederation, association, union

bon'del -s parcel, bundle; ~**dra'er** pedlar, tramp; ~**transak'sie** package deal *ook* **pak= ket'akkoord**

bond'genoot ..note ally, confederate; ~**skap** alliance, confederacy

bon'dig -e; -er, -ste brief, terse, succinct, concise; *kort en* ~ short and to the point

bons (s) -e bump, bang, thud; (w) beat, palpitate, bounce (ball)

bont¹ (s) fur; ~**jas** fur coat *ook* **pels'jas**

bont² (b) -er, -ste odd-coloured, variegated, motley; *sy* ~ *varkie is weg* he has a screw loose; ~**e'bok** nunni, pied antelope, bonte= bok; ~**kwagga** Burchell's zebra; ~**lo'per** jaywalker; ~**lo'pery** jaywalking; ~**rokkie** stonechat (bird)

bo'nus -se bonus

bood'skap (s) -pe message, errand; *die blye* ~ the glad tidings/gospel; ~**per** messenger; courier *ook* **koerier'**

boog boë bow; curve, arch, arc; **pyl en** ~ bow and arrow; ~**skiet** archery; ~**skutter** archer

boom¹ bome bottom *ook* **bo'dem**

boom² bome tree; bar, beam; *tussen die* ~ *en die bas* betwixt and between

boom: ~**kap'per** treefeller (person); ~**sing'er= tjie** cicada, scissor grinder; ~**skil'padjie** ladybird

boom'skraap finished; empty; rock-bottom

boon bone bean; **grond'**~ peanut

boon'op moreover, besides *ook* **bowendien'**

boon'ste top, uppermost, highest

boon'tjie -s bean; ~ *kry sy loontjie* every dog has his day

boon'toe to the top, up(wards)

bo'-oor over the top, right over

bo'-op on top, atop of

boor (s) bore bore, drill; gimlet; (w) bore, drill

boord¹ -e orchard

boord² border, edge, brim; board (ship); *aan* ~ *gaan* go aboard; *oor*~ *gooi* throw to the winds

boord'jie -s collar

boor: ~**gat** borehole; ~**ling:** *'n* ~**ling** *v.d. Pêrel* born in Paarl; ~**man** driller; ~**masjien'** drilling machine

boor'suur boracic acid

boor'toring -s (oil) rig

boos [bose]; boser, -ste angry; wicked, evil; **bose kring'loop** vicious circle

boos: ~**doen'er** evildoer, villain, criminal;

~**wig** villain, criminal *ook* **skurk, boef**

boot bote boat *ook* **skuit**

bord -e plate; board

bordeel' ..dele brothel, house of ill-fame

bord'jie -s small plate; notice board; *die* ~*s is verhang* the tables are turned

bord'papier cardboard, paste board

borduur' (w) ge- embroider

borg -e surety, guarantee; sponsor; ~ *staan* become surety; stand bail; ~**skap** surety= ship; sponsorship; *op* ~*tog uit* released on bail; *hy* ~ *die byeenkoms* he is sponsoring the event

bor'rel (s) -s bubble; drop, tot; (w) bubble; tipple; ~**siek'te** air embolism; bends (diving)

bors -te breast; chest; thorax; *dit stuit my teen die* ~ it goes against the grain; ~**beeld** bust

bor'sel (s) -s brush; bristle; (w) brush

bors: ~**hemp** dress shirt; ~**lap** breastpiece; bib; ~**plaat** butterscotch; ~**speld** brooch; ~**suiker** sugarstick, lollipop; ~**rok** corset; foundation garment; ~**voe'ding** breast feed= ing (of baby)

bos¹ -se bundle, bunch

bos² -se forest, wood; shrub, bush; shock (hair); *om die* ~ *lei* lead by the nose; ~**aap** thick-tailed lemur; ~**a'pie** bushbaby; ~**be= raad'** bundu conference, bosberaad, lekgo= tla; ~**bou** forestry, afforestation; ~**buf'fer** bullbar *ook* ~**bre'ker**

bosga'sie/boska'sie -s copsewood, thicket; unkempt hair

bos: ~**god (s)** satyr *ook* **sa'ter, faun;** ~**lan'ser** unkempt country cousin; coward; ~**luis** bushtick

bos'sie -s shrub; *geld soos* ~*s* plenty of money

bo'staande above(-mentioned)

bos'tamboer grapevine (idiom.)

Bos'veld Bushveld

bos'wagter ranger, gamekeeper

bot¹ (s) -te fluke; flounder (fish); bid (auction) *ook* **bod**

bot² (s) -te sprout, bud; (w) bud, sprout

bot³ (b) -te; -ter, -ste blunt, dull, abrupt

bota'nies -e (b) botanic(al)

bota'nikus -se, ..ici botanist (person)

bo'tol (w, s) topspin (ball games)

bo'toon overtone; *die* ~ *voer* boss the show

bots (s) shock, collision; (w) collide, clash; ~**ing** collision, smash, clash

bot'stil stock-still, motionless

bot'tel (s) -s bottle, flask; *al bars die* ~ come

what may; (w) bottle; ~**nek** bottleneck *ook* **knel'punt**

bottelier' -s butler (bottlebearer)

bot'ter butter; *met die neus in die* ~ *val* have all the luck; ~**broodjie** scone *ook* **skon;** ~**pot** butterdish; ~**skors(ie)** butternut (veg= etable)

bou (s) build; structure; (w) build, construct; ~**aan'nemer** building contractor *ook* **bou= kontrakteur';** ~**bedryf'** building industry/ trade

boud (s) -e buttock; leg (of mutton)

bou'er -s builder

bou'kontrakteur -s building contractor

bou'kunde/bou'kuns architecture

boul (w) bowl; ~**beurt** over; **leë** ~**beurt** maiden over; ~**er** bowler

bou'rekenaar -s quantity surveyor

bout -e bolt, pin

bouval'lig -e; -er, -ste dilapidated, decayed, tottering, ramshackle

bou'vereniging -s building society

bo'we above; upon; over; upstairs; *te* ~ *kom* surmount difficulties

bowenal' above all (things)

bowendien' moreover, besides

bra' rather, really, actually; *hy is maar* ~ *dom* he is rather stupid

bra² (s) bra *ook* **buus'telyfie**

braaf brawe; brawer, ste honest, good, upright

braai ge- roast, fry, grill; scorch; ~**gereg'** grill; **gemengde** ~**gereg'** mixed grill *kyk* **allegaar'tjie;** ~**hoek** barbecue; ~**hoen'der/** ~**kui'ken** broiler; ~**huis/~restourant'** steakhouse *ook* **braais** (s); ~**rib'betjie** roast(ed) rib; ~**vleis** roasted meat, roast; ~*vleis hou* have a braai

braais = **braai'huis**

braak¹ (w) ge- vomit *ook* **op'gooi**

braak² (w) ge- break up; fallow

braam brame bramble

brab'bel (w) ge- jabber; mutter

brak¹ (s) -ke dog; cur, mongrel; **Brak'dag** Day of the Mutt

brak² (b) brackish, briny; ~**wa'ter** brack(ish) water

brak'kie -s small dog; small mongrel; ~**sak'kie** doggybag (idiom.)

brand (s) -e fire, conflagration; mildew, blight; *aan die* ~! on the go!; *aan die* ~ *steek* set on fire; (w) burn, scald, blaze, scorch, cauterise;

brand (cattle); ~**alarm'** fire alarm; ~**arm** indigent, destitute; ~**assuran'sie** fire in= surance; ~**baar** combustible; (in)flammable; ~**bestry'ding** fire fighting; ~**blus'ser** fire extinguisher; ~**bom** incendiary bomb

bran'der -s large wave, breaker; (mv) surf; ~**plank** surfboard; ~**ski** surf skiing

bran'dewyn brandy

brand: ~**hout** firewood; ~**kas** safe, strongbox; ~**kluis** strongroom; ~**ma'er** skinny, scraggy, as lean as a rake; ~**merk** (s) brand, stigma; (w) ge- brand, stigmatise; ~**po'lis** fire policy; ~**punt** focus; ~**sla'ner** firefighter; ~**spi'ritus** methylated spirits; ~**spuit** fire hose/hydrant; ~**sta'pel** stake, pile; pyre; ~**stig'ter** arsonist; ~**stig'ting** arson

brand: ~**stof** fuel; ~**stofbespa'ring** fuel econ= omy/saving; ~**stofverbruik'** fuel consump= tion; ~**trap** fire escape; ~**verseke'ring** fire insurance; ~**wag** guard, outpost; sentry, picket

brand'weer fire brigade

brava'de bravado, boast

bre'die stew (vegetables and meat), ragout

breed breë; breër, -ste broad, wide; *in breë trekke* in broad outline

breed'te -s breadth, width

breedvoe'rig -e; -er, -ste detailed, exhaustive

breek ge- break, smash, crush, snap, fracture; *maak en* ~ make and mar; ~**baar** break= able, fragile; ~**goed/~wa're** crockery

brei¹ ge- knit

brei² ge- prepare skins; coach, train

brei'er -s coach (sports); knitter

brein brain; intellect; ~**flou'te** black-out

brei'naald -e knitting needle

brein'spoeling brainwashing

breintas'ting (s) brainscan *ook* **breinskan= de'ring**

brek'fis (s) breakfast *ook* **ontbyt'**

breuk -e rupture, hernia; breach (peace); fracture; fraction

brief briewe letter, epistle; **aan'gehegte** ~ attached letter; **begelei'dende** ~ covering letter; **by'gaande** ~ accompanying letter; ~**hoof'** letterhead; ~**kaart** postcard *ook* **pos'kaart;** ~**wis'seling** correspondence *ook* **korresponden'sie**

bries¹ (s) -e breeze

bries² (w) ge- snort, fret; ~**end** (b) snorting, furious, wild with rage

brie'we: ~**bestel'ler** postman; ~**boek** letter= writer; ~**bus** posting box

brigadier′ -s brigadier (person)
briket′ -te briquette/bricket
bril (s) **-le** pair of spectacles; (w) **ge-** wear spectacles; ~**hui′sie** spectacle case
briljant′ (s) **-e** cut diamond; (b) brilliant *ook* **skit′terend**
bril′maker -s optician, optometrist
bring ge- bring, take, carry, convey; *te berde* ~ broach a matter; *iem. om die lewe* ~ kill a person
Brit -te Briton, Britisher; ~**s** (b) British
Brittan′je Britain
broe′der -s brother; ~**lief′de** brotherly love; ~**lik** brotherly, fraternal; ~**moord** fratri= cide; ~**skap** brotherhood
broei ge- brood, hatch; ~**kas** hothouse *ook* **kweek′huis**; ~**masjien′** incubator
broeis broody (hen)
broei′sel -s brood; clutch
broek -e (pair of) trousers, breeches; drawers, bloomers; ~**pak** slacksuit; ~**sak** trouser pocket
broer -s brother; ~**s′kind** nephew, niece
brok -ke piece, fragment; *stukkies en* ~**kies** odds and ends
brom (w) **ge-** grumble, mutter, growl
brom: ~**mer** grouser, grumbler; bluebottle, blowfly/drone fly; ~**po′nie** (motor) scooter; ~**pot** growler, grouser, grumbler; ~**vo′ël** ground hornbill
bron -ne spring; source, origin; ~ (*herkoms*) *en aanwending/besteding van fondse* source and application of funds; *uit betroubare* ~ from a reliable source
brongi′tis bronchitis
brons[1] (s) bronze, brass
brons[2] (s) rut, heat; ~**tig** ruttish, in/on heat
brood brode bread; loaf; *die een se dood is die ander se* ~ one man's meat is another man's poison; ~**boom** breadfruit tree, cycad; ~**lyn:** *onder die* ~**lyn leef** live under the breadline; ~**mes** bread knife; ~**mie′lie** variety of early mealies; ~**no′dig** indispensable, essential; ~**skry′wer** pen= ny-a-liner; ~**win′ner** breadwinner; ~**wor′=tel** cassava
brosju′re -s brochure, pamphlet *ook* **pamflet′**, **blad′skrif**
brou ge- brew; bungle, botch; ~**ery** brewery
brug[1] bridge (cards)
brug[2] **brûe** bridge; parallel bars; *'n* ~ *slaan oor* bridge; ~**hoof** bridgehead

bruid -e bride; ~**e′gom** bridegroom; ~**skat** dowry
bruids: ~**koek** wedding cake; ~**kom′buis′:** ~**kombuis** *hou* give a kitchen tea; ~**paar** bridal couple; ~**uit′set** trousseau
bruik′baar serviceable, useful
bruik′huur (s) leasing; lease; *ek het die (motor)kar op* ~ I am leasing this car
bruik′leen loan (for use); lease-lend; *in* ~ *afstaan* make a loan of (for use)
brui′lof -te wedding; **goue** ~ golden wedding
bruilofs: ~**gas** wedding guest; ~**pleg′tigheid** marriage ceremony
bruin -er, -ste brown; bay
bruin: ~**kapel′** brown cobra; ~**mense** co= loured people, coloureds *ook* **kleur′linge**
bruis ge- foam, froth, effervesce; ~**melk** milkshake; ~**poei′er** fruitsalts; ~**sui′ker** sorbit; ~**wyn** sparkling wine, champagne
brul (s) **-le** roar; (w) **ge-** roar; ~**pad′da** bullfrog
brunet′ -te brunette
brutaal′ ..**tale;** ..**taler, -ste** cheeky, impudent, insolent
bru′to gross; ~ **gewig′/mas′sa** gross weight/ mass; ~ **wins** gross profit
bry ge- roll the ''r'', speak with a burr
bud′jie -s budgie *ook* **parkiet′**
buf′fel -s buffalo; rude fellow
buf′fer -s buffer; bumper
buffet′ -te sideboard; bar; ~**e′te** buffet lunch/ supper
bui -e shower (of rain); whim, mood
bui′e/buig ge- bend, bow, stoop; curve
buig′baar ..**bare; -der, -ste** bendable; *daardie yster is* ~ you can bend that piece of iron
buig′saam ..**same;** ..**samer, -ste** flexible, pliable; yielding (person) *ook* **meegaan′de** ..*same rottang* flexible cane
buik -e stomach, belly; abdomen; ~**danseres′** bellydancer; ~**spraak** ventriloquy; ~**spre′=ker** ventriloquist; ~**vol** fed up *ook* **gat′vol** (*kru*)/**keel′vol**
buil -e boil; swelling; ~**epes′** bubonic plague
buis -e tube, pipe; duct; ~**lig** fluorescent light (tube)
buit (s) booty, loot, plunder; (w) rob, loot, pillage
bui′te outside; out of doors; ~ *geveg stel* disable; ~ **per′ke** out of bounds; ~**band** tyre; ~**eg′telik** out of wedlock, illegitimate (child); ~**baan** off-course (totalisator);

~**kans** unexpected advantage, windfall; outside chance; ~**kaŋt** (s) outside, exterior; (bw) outside; ~**klub** country club; ~**land** foreign country; ~**lan'der** foreigner; ~**lands** foreign; exotic *ook* **uitheems'**; ~**lug** open air; ~**muurs** extramural (studies)

bui'ten besides, except, beyond *ook* **behal'we**

buitendien' moreover, besides *ook* **bo'wendien**

bui'tengewoon ..wone extraordinary

buitenspo'rig extravagant, excessive; ~*e wins* exorbitant profit

bui'tenste outermost, exterior

bui'te: ~**pasiënt'** outpatient; ~**perd** outsider; ~**pos** outpost, outstation; ~**sintuig'like waar'neming** extrasensory perception; ~**stan'der** outsider; ~**ste'delik** peri-urban; ~**verkoop/** ~**verko'pe** off-sales

buit'maak (w) -**ge-** seize, capture, carry off

buk ge- stoop, bend, bow

buk'sie -s saloon rifle; smallish person

bul -le bull, steer *ook* **stier** (stiergeveg)

bul'der ge- roar, rage, boom

bulimie' (s) bulimia *ook* **geeu'honger**

bulk ge- low, bellow, moo

bulle'bak -ke bully *ook* **boe'lie**; lout

bulletin'/boeleticn' -s notice, bulletin

bult -e hillock, ridge, rising ground; hump, bump; *ons is amper oor die* ~ the worst is nearly over

bun'del (s) -s volume (book); bundle

burg -e gelded pig, barrow

bur'gemeester -s mayor; ~**es'** lady mayor; ~**s'vrou** mayoress

bur'ger -s citizen, civilian; burgher; ~**bandra'dio** citizen-band radio; ~**blin'de** civilian blind; ~**kle're** civilian clothes, civvies; *in* ~*drag/in* ~*klere* in plain clothes, in mufti; ~**kun'de** civics; ~**like** civilian (person); ~**like besker'ming** civil defence; ~**like onthaal'** civic reception; ~**lug'vaart** civil aviation; ~**oor'log** civil war; ~**sen'trum** civic centre; ~**wag** civic guard

buro' -'s office; (writing) desk; bureau

burokraat' ..krate bureaucrat (person)

bus[1] -se box, tin; bush (of a wheel)

bus[2] -se (omni)bus; ~**diens** bus service; ~**dry'wer** bus driver; ~**kaar'tjie** bus ticket

bus'kruit gunpowder

buur bure neighbour; ~**man** neighbour

buurt -e, buur'te -s neighbourhood, area, vicinity; ~**wag** neighbourhood watch

buur'vrou -e, -ens neighbour's wife

buus'te -s bust; ~**ly'fie** bra *ook* **bra**

by[1] (s) -**e** bee

by[2] (vs) at, near, by, with

by'behore accessories

By'bel -s Bible; ~**ken'nis** scriptural knowledge; (b) ~**s** biblical, scriptural; ~**verkla'ring** exegesis; ~**teks** text from Scriptures

byderhand' close by; handy

byderwets' with-it, trendy *ook* **bydertyds'**

by'dra -ge- contribute; ~**e** contribution

byeen' together; ~**roep** call together, convene (a meeting); ~**roe'pende kennis'gewing** notice calling a meeting

byeen'kom -ge- meet, gather, assemble; (s) ~**s** gathering, meeting, event (sport), assembly

by'e: ~**korf** beehive; ~**was** beeswax

by'gaande accompanying, enclosed; ~ **brief** accompanying letter

by'gebou -e annex; outhouse

by'geloof ..lowe superstition

bygelo'wig -e; -er, -ste superstitious

by'kans nearly, almost *ook* **by'na**

by'klank -e sound effect(s)

by'kom -ge- come up with; recover (from a faint); reach

by'komende additional, incidental; ~ **in'ligting** additional/further information

bykoms'tig -e accessory, minor, incidental; ~**e nala'tigheid** contributory negligence; ~**hede** accessories/parts; minor matters

byl -e axe, hatchet

by'lae -s appendix, annexure, supplement

by'lyn -e extension (telephone)

bymekaar' together

by'na nearly, almost; ~ *nooit* hardly ever

by'naam ..name nickname

by'nes -te beehive *ook* **bye'korf**

by'saak side issue, mere detail

bysien'de (b) short-sighted, myopic

by'sin -ne dependent/subordinate sentence

by'sit (w) -**ge-** add to; inter; help; *hand* ~ lend a hand

by'smaak ..smake aftertaste, peculiar flavour

by'staan -ge- assist, help, back up

by'stand assistance, aid, support; *op* ~ on standby (doctor); ~ *verleen* render assistance

byt (s) -**e** bite; (w) **ge-** bite, snap at

byt'soda caustic soda

by'vak -ke ancillary subject

by'val[1] (s) applause, approval, approbation; ~ *vind* meet with approval

by'val² (w) -ge- remember suddenly
by'verdienste sideline, extra income
by'voeg -ge- add, annex, append; ~'lik adjectival; ~like naam'woord adjective
byvoor'beeld for example
by'voordeel fringe benefit, perk (perquisite)

by'werk (w) update *ook* aan'vul/aan'suiwer
by'woner -s subfarmer; sharecropper
by'woon -ge- be present at, attend; ~regis'ter attendance register
by'woord -e adverb
by'wyf concubine, mistress *ook* hou'vrou

C

Calvinis' -te Calvinist (person); ~me Calvinism; ~ties Calvinistic
casi'no/kasi'no -'s casino *ook* dob'belplek
CD-ROM-aan'drywer CD-ROM drive (comp.)
chalet' -te chalet
cha'os chaos *ook* wan'orde
chao'ties -e chaotic
chauffeur' -s chauffeur; driver
chauvinis' -te chauvinist (person); ~me chauvinism; ~ties chauvinistic
chemie' chemistry
che'mies -e chemical; ~e on'kruidbeheer chemical weedcontrol
chemika'lie (s) -ë chemical
chev'ronteken -s chevron sign
Chi'na China
Chinees' ..nese Chinese *ook* Sjinees'
chiropraktisyn' -s chiropractor
chirurg'/sjirurg' -e surgeon *ook* sny'dokter; ~ie surgery; ~ies surgical; plas'tiese ~ie plastic surgery
chloor chlorine
chlo'roform chloroform
cho'lera/ko'lera cholera

choreograaf' ..awe choreographer
Chris'telik -e Christian(like); *die ~e jaar= telling* the Christian era
Chris'ten -e Christian; ~dom Christianity
Christin' -ne Christian (woman)
Chris'tus Christ; *na ~* Anno Domini (AD); *voor ~* before Christ (BC)
chro'nies/kro'nies -e chronic (illness)
chronolo'gies -e chronological, in order of time
chroom chromium
cochenil'le cochineal (dye, insect)
confet'ti/konfet'ti (s) confetti
con'tra/kon'tra contra, counter; ~produktief' counterproductive *ook* teenproduktief'
cot'tage cottage *ook* kot'huis
coun'try country (style of song)
cow'boy (s) cowboy (cattle herder on horseback)
crèche crèche *ook* bewaar'skool
cre'do credo; belief *ook* geloofs'belydenis'
crou'pier/kroepier' croupier (roulette master)
curri'culum vi'tae (v) curriculum vitae *ook* le'wensprofiel', bi'odata
cum: ~ lau'de with distinction

D

daad dade deed, action; *op heter ~ betrap* catch in the act
daag ge- summon; dawn; ~liks daily, every day; *vir ~likse gebruik* for daily use
daal ge- descend; sink; fall; ~spekulant' bear (stock exchange)
Daan'tjie: *tot by oom ~ in die kalwerhok* to the limit
daar (bw) there; (vgw) since, as, because; ~ag'ter behind that (it); ~bene'wens besides, in addition; ~by thereto, besides; ~deur thereby, by that means; through

(there); ~die that; those; daarente'ë/daar= enteen' on the other hand; *Piet is slim, Jan ~ is 'n bietjie dom* Peter is a clever boy, John on the other hand is not so bright *kyk* inteen'deel
daar: ~heen thither, there, to that place; ~in therein, in that; ~mee therewith, with that; ~na after that, afterwards; ~naas next to that
daar'om therefore, thus, for that reason *ook* dus, derhal'we
daar: ~on'der under that, down there, by that;

~**oor** about that; therefore; ~**op** thereupon, upon that; ~**so** there, yonder

daar: ~**teë/~teen** against that; ~**uit** thence, out of that; ~**van** of that, about that, thereof; ~**vandaan'** from there, thence; ~**voor** for that, therefore

da'del -s date (fruit)

da'delik immediately, at once, instantly

dag dae day; ~**bestuur'** executive/manage= ment committee; ~**boek** diary; ~**breek** daybreak

dag'ga dagga, Cape hemp, hashish, marijuana

da'gha clay (bricklaying), mortar

dag'lig daylight; ~**bespa'ring** daylight saving

dag: ~**lo'ner** daylabourer; ~**pak** lounge suit; ~**sê** good day, good morning/afternoon; ~**skolier** day scholar; ~**skool** day school; ~**taak** daily task; *sy ~taak is afgedaan* he has finished his day's work

dag'vaar ge- summon, subpoena; ~**ding** summons, warrant; *'n ~ding beteken/bestel aan* serve a summons on

dak -ke roof; ~**fees:** ~*fees vier* wet the roof; ~**geut** gutter; ~**pan** tile; ~**stel** penthouse suite

dak: ~**tuin** roof garden; ~**vink** roofclutcher (motorist), ~**wo'ning/~woon'stel** pent= house

da'ling descent; fall, drop, slump

dalk perhaps, maybe *ook* **miskien'/altemit'**

dam (s) **-me** dam, reservoir

dam'bord -e draughtboard *ook* **damspel':** draughts

da'me -s lady; ~*s en here!* ladies and gentle= men!

damp (s) **-e** vapour, steam; fume

dan[1] (bw) then

dan[2] (vgw) than; *al ~ nie* whether or not

dan'dy dandy, lounge lizard *ook* **laven'tel= haan**

da'nig (b) **-e** effusive, exuberant; (bw) much, awfully; over-friendly; *nie te ~ goed nie* not too wonderful; *hom ~ hou* give himself airs

dank (s) thanks, gratitude; ~ *betuig* express thanks; *mosie van ~* vote of thanks; *stank vir ~* get small thanks; *teen wil en ~* in spite of; (w) thank, give thanks; say grace; *te ~e aan* due to, thanks to; ~**baar** thankful, grateful; ~**brief** thank-you letter

dan'kie! thank you! thanks!; *jy kan ~bly wees* you can thank your lucky stars

dank: ~**of'fer** thanks offering; ~**seg'ging**

thanksgiving; ~**sy** thanks to; ~*sy Piet het ons dit oorleef* thanks to Peter we survived

dans (s) **-e** dance; (w) dance; *die poppe is aan die ~* the fat is in the fire

dan'ser -s dancer

dans: ~**les** dancing lesson; ~**party** ball, dance; ~**saal** ballroom; ~**skoen** dancing shoe, pump

dap'per brave, valiant, plucky, gallant; *met ~ en stapper reis* ride shanks's mare

da'rem though, all the same; surely; *hy is ~ nie te sleg nie* after all he is not too bad

dar'tel (w) gambol; (b) frisky, playful; ~**da'wie** (idiom.) playboy *ook* **swier'bol**

das[1] -se rockrabbit, das(sie)

das[2] -se tie (for the neck)

dat that, so that, in order that

da'ta data, facts; ~**bank** data bank; ~**ba'sis** database; ~**basisbedie'ner** database server; ~**verwer'king** data processing

da'tum -s date

Dawid David; *weet waar ~ die wortels graaf/ grawe* know what is what

dè! (w, imp.) take! here you are!; ~, *vat hier* here, take this

debat' -te debate

debiet' debit, ~**nota** debit note, ~**or'der** debit order; ~**sal'do** debit balance

debiteer' ge- debit, charge with

debiteur' -e, -s debtor

debutant' -e debutant; ~**e** debutante (tem.)

debuut' first appearance; debut *ook* **bui'ging**

deeg dough; ~**rol'ler** rolling pin

deeg'lik -e; -er, -ste solid, thorough, sound; ~**e on'dersoek** thorough investigation

deel (s) **dele** part, portion; share; division, section; (w) divide; participate; share

deel: ~**neem** participate in, take part in; ~*neem aan* participate in; ~**neemverband'** participation bond; ~**ne'mer** participant, contestant; ~**ne'ming** participation; sympa= thy; ~*neming/simpatie betuig* express sym= pathy

deels partly, in part

deel: ~**som** division sum; ~**te'ken** diaeresis; division sign; ~**ti'tel** sectional title; ~**woord** participle; *verle'de ~woord* past participle; ~**tyds/heeltyds** part-time/full- time; ~**wa're** shareware (comp.)

deemoe'dig -e; -er, -ste humble, meek

deer'nis compassion; commiseration, pity

defek' (s) **-te** defect; (b) defective

defini'sie -s definition *ook* **omskry'wing**
definitief' ..**tiewe** definite, decisive
def'tig -e; -er, -ste stately, grave, dignified; exclusive (suburb); ~ **informeel'** smart casual (clothing)
dein ge- heave, surge, swell; ~**ing** surge, (back)wash (waves); heave, swell
dek (s) -ke deck; (w) cover, clothe; be at stud, cover (horse); thatch (house); *die aftog* ~ cover the retreat; *tafel* ~ lay the table
dekaan' ..**kane** dean (university)
deka'de -s decade, ten (years)
dekadent' -e decadent, deteriorating
de'ken[1] -s counterpane, quilt, coverlet
de'ken[2] -s dean (church); doyen (ambassador)
dek: ~**gras** thatch (grass); ~**king** cover, shelter; coverage (news); guard
dek'mantel -s cloak; excuse, pretext; *onder die* ~ *van* under the cloak/guise of
dekodeer'der (s) decoder
de'kor/dekor' decor, (stage) scenery
dekora'sie -s decoration *ook* versiering; order (of knighthood), distinction
dekreet' dekrete decree, edict
dek'sel -s cover, lid
dek'sels (b) -e darned, confounded; *'n* ~*e gelol* a darned nuisance; (bw) confounded, darned; ~ *hard* dashed hard
dek'verband -e covering bond (on property)
delegeer' ge- delegate
de'ler -s divider; divisor; **groot'ste geme'ne** ~ greatest common factor
delf/del'we ge- dig, mine
delg ge- discharge, pay off, redeem; *jou skuld* ~ discharge one's debt
del'ging, redemption, amortisement: ~**(s)fonds** sinking fund, redemption fund
delikaat' delicate; tender; difficult (affair)
delikates'se -s delicacy, savoury bit
de'ling division; **lang** ~ long division
deli'ries -e delirious *ook* **ylhoof'dig**
del'ta -s delta
del'wer -s digger; ~**y** diggings
demobiliseer' ge- demobilise
demokraat' ..**krate** democrat (person)
demokrasie' (s) democracy
demokra'ties -e democratic
demonstreer' ~, ge- demonstrate *ook* **betoog'** (politiek)
demp ge- fill up with earth; quell (riot); quench (fire); dim (light); mute (sound)
den -ne fir (tree), pine (tree)

denk'baar ..**bare** imaginable, conceivable
denk'beeld -e idea, notion
denkbeel'dig -e imaginary
den'ke thought, (act of) thinking
denkvermo'ë (s) intellectual capacity
den'ne: ~**bol** fir cone; ~**boom** fir, pine; ~**bos** pine forest; ~**hout** pine (wood)
denomina'sie denomination *ook* **kerk'verband**
deo'dorant deodorant *ook* **reuk'weerder**
departement' -e department, office
deponeer' ~, ge- deposit, lodge
deporteer' ge- deport
depo'sito -'s deposit
depot' -s depot; dump
depresia'sie depreciation *ook* **waar'devermindering**
depresieer' ~, ge- depreciate
depres'sie -s depression
deputa'sie -s deputation *ook* **af'vaardiging**
der'de -s third; ~**dek'king** third-party cover (insurance); ~ **vloer/verdie'ping/vlak** third floor; ~**rangs** third-rate; ~**wê'reldland** third-world country
der'gelik -e such, the like, similar
der'halwe therefore, consequently, thus
derm -s intestine, gut; (mv) bowels, entrails; ~**ontste'king** enteritis
der'tien thirteen; ~**de** thirteenth
der'tig thirty; ~**ste** thirtieth
des: ~ *te beter* so much the better; *'n kind* ~ *doods* a dead man
Desem'ber -s December
desentralisa'sie decentralisation
de'ser: *die tiende* ~ the 10th instant
de'sibel -s decibel (unit of sound)
desimaal' ..**male** decimal; ..**male breuk** decimal fraction; ~**kom'ma** decimal comma; ~**stel'sel** decimal system
deskun'dig -e expert; ~**e getui'enis** expert evidence; (s) ~**e** expert (person)
des'nieteenstaan'de in spite of, notwithstanding
des'noods if need be, in case of need
desperaat' ..**rate** desperate *ook* **ra'deloos**
despoot' ..**pote** despot, tyrant
despo'ties -e despotic, tyrannic(al)
destabiliseer' ~, ge- destabilise
des'tyds at that time, then *ook* **in'dertyd**
detail' (s) detail *ook* **beson'derhede**; (w) detail
deten'sie detention; ~**kaser'ne** detension barracks

deug (s) **-de** virtue, excellence; *liewe* ~! good gracious! (w) be good for, serve a purpose, be of use; *potlood sal* ~ pencil will do; ~**niet** rascal, good-for-nothing *ook* **va'bond;** ~**saam** virtuous
deun'tjie -s air, tune, ditty
deur[1] (s) **-e** door, gate; *met die* ~ *in die huis val* come straight to the point
deur[2] (b) passed; (vs) through, by, throughout; ~ *die bank* all, without exception
deur'braak breach, burst; breakthrough
deur'bring -ge- pass; spend, squander; ~**er** spendthrift, waster
deur'dat because, as
deurdring' ~ permeate, pervade, impress; *die stank* ~ *die huis* the bad smell fills the house
deur'dring -ge- penetrate, pierce; *die waarheid het tot hom deurgedring* the truth dawned upon him
deurdrin'gend -e shrill, penetrating; searching *ook* **in'dringende** (b)
deur'druk -ge- press through; persist; *tot die end* ~ see it through to the end
deur en deur thoroughly, out and out
deur'entyd all the time
deur'gaans usually, invariably; generally
deur'gang -e passage; thoroughfare
deur: ~**glip** slip through; ~**gra'wing** cutting; ~**gren'del** doorbolt
deurgrond' ~ fathom, penetrate, understand
deur'haal -ge- delete; fetch/pull through
deur'hak -ge- cut through; solve, *die knoop* ~ cut the knot
deur'knop -pe doorknob
deur'kom -ge- get through; pass; survive; *hy het net-net deurgekom,* he just managed to pass
deur'kosyn -e doorframe
deur'kyk -ge- look over, skim, peruse; sum up
deur'laat -ge- let through, allow to pass
deurleef'/deurle'we ~ live through
deur'lees -ge- read through, peruse
deur'loop (s) **..lope** arcade *ook* **arka'de**
deur'loop[2] (w) **-ge-** move on; walk through; peruse; punish; *die stout seuns het almal deurgeloop* the naughty boys all had their punishment
deurlo'pend -e continuous, uninterrupted
deur'maak -ge- go through, experience
deur'mat -te doormat
deurmekaar' -der, -ste in confusion; ~**spul** mix-up, shambles

deur: ~**pad** freeway, motorway, throughway *ook* **snel'weg**
deur'reis[1] (s) passage; through-journey; (w) travel, pass through
deurreis'[2] ~ travel all over; *die wêreld* ~ globe-trotting
deur'settingsvermoë persistence; perseverance *ook* **volhar'ding**
deursig'tig -e transparent, lucid; ~**heid** transparency, openness *ook* **o'pen(lik)heid**
deur'skemer -ge- glimmer through; *laat* ~ hint at
deursky'nend -e transparent, translucent
deur'slaan -ge- strike/hit through; punch
deur'slag moist soil, boggy ground; decisive factor; **..slae** punch; ~**ge'wend** decisive *ook* **beslis'send**
deur: ~**slot** doorlock; ~**sluip** steal/sneak through; ~**smokkel** smuggle through
deur'snee/deur'snit section; diameter; average
deur'sneeprys average price
deur'snit = deur'snee
deur'soek -ge- examine, search; explore
deurspek' ~ interlard; intersperse; *sy proefskrif is* ~ *met aanhalings* his thesis is riddled with quotations
deurstaan' ~ endure, suffer, bear; stand
deur: ~**styl** doorpost; ~**suk'kel** struggle through, ~**sy'fer** trickle through, ~**sy'pel** ooze through
deurtas'tend -e decisive, resolute, vigorous, thorough; ~**e maat'reël** drastic measure
deur'tog passage; march through
deurtrap' -te sly, crafty, cunning; ~**te skelm** confounded rascal
deurtrek'[1] ~ pervade, permeate, imbue
deur'trek[2] **-ge-** pass through, pull through; ~**ker** spendthrift; pullthrough (rifle); loincloth; G-string *ook* **gena'delappie**
deur'voer -ge- carry out; *planne* ~ carry out/execute/implement plans
deur'wagter -s porter, janitor, doorkeeper; commissionaire
deurweek' ~ soak, moisten; ~ *van die reën* drenched with rain
deur'weg ..weë throughway *ook* **snel'weg**
devalueer' ~, **ge-** devaluate
diabe'tes diabetes *ook* **sui'kersiekte**
diabo'lies -e diabolic(al), devilish *ook* **dui'wels/sata'nies**
diagno'se -s diagnosis

diagnoseer' (w) **ge-** diagnose
diagonaal' ..**nale** diagonal
diagram' -**me** diagram
dia'ken -**s** deacon
dialek' -**te** dialect *ook* **streek'taal**
dialoog' ..**loë** dialogue *ook* **twee'gesprek**
diamant' -**e** diamond; sparkler; ∼**sly'per** diamond cutter
didak'ties (b) -**e** didactic *ook* **le'rend**
die (lw) the
dié (vnw) this; these
die'derik -e, -s golden cuckoo (bird)
dieet' diëte diet; ∼**kun'dige** dietician
dief diewe thief
dief'alarm burglar alarm
dief'stal -le theft, robbery; larceny; *skuldig aan* ∼ *van geld* guilty of theft of money
dief'wering burglar proofing; burglar guard
die'gene those
dien ge- serve, wait on; attend to; suit; *van advies* ∼/**bedien** advise; *hy* ∼ *in/op die adviesraad* he serves on the advisory coun=cil
die'naar -s; ..**nare** servant, valet; **werk'gewer en** ∼ master and servant
dien'lik -e; -er, -ste serviceable
dien'luik -e serving hatch
dien'ooreenkomstig accordingly
diens -te service; function, duty; *'n* ∼ *bewys* do a good turn; *in* ∼ *neem* engage; *op (aan)* ∼ on duty; *tot u* ∼ at your service; *van* ∼ *af* off duty; ∼**bus(sie)** service bus, courtesy bus; ∼**gelof'te** act of dedication *ook* **toe'wydingsformulier'**; ∼**in'gang** trades=man's entrance; ∼**le'weraar/**∼**verskaf'fer** service provider; ∼**mei'sie** domestic *ook* **huis'hulp**; ∼**plig** compulsory (military) service; ∼**reg** law of employment; ∼**ter=myn'** term of office; ∼**voor'waardes** con=ditions of service/employment; ∼**wei'eraar -s** conscientious objector
dienswil'lig -e; -er, -ste helpful, ready to serve; obedient
diens'woonstel -le serviced flat
dien'tafel -s dinner wagon
dien'tengevolge accordingly, consequently
diep -er, -ste deep; profound; ∼ *in gedagte* deep in thought; ∼/**bitter ongelukkig** ex=tremely unhappy; ∼**gaande on'dersoek** searching inquiry
diep'te -s depth; profundity; ∼**bom** depth charge; ∼**stu'die** in-depth study

dier -e animal; brute
diera'sie -s monster; vixen, (she)devil
dier'baar (b) dear, beloved, lovable
dier'bare (s) -s loved one, beloved (person)
die're: ∼**besker'ming** animal protection; **D**∼**besker'mingsvere'niging** Society for the Prevention of Cruelty to Animals (SPCA); ∼**her'berg** kennels *ook* **woe'fie=tuis'te**; ∼**kliniek'** veterinary clinic; ∼**ryk** animal kingdom; ∼**tuin** zoological gardens, zoo; ∼**win'kel** petshop *ook* **ark'-mark**
dier'lik (b) -**e** barbaric, brutal *ook* **wreed=aar'dig**
die'sel diesel; ∼**en'jin** diesel engine
dieself'de the same; *presies* ∼ exactly the same
die'we: ∼**ben'de** gang/pack of thieves; ∼**sleu'=tel** skeleton/master key; ∼**tra'lies** burglar bars
differensieer' **ge-** differentiate
dig[1] (w) **ge-** write poetry, compose, versify
dig[2] (b) tight; close; dense, compact; dull, stupid; ∼**bevolk'** (b) densely populated
dig'by digterby, digsteby nearby, close; ∼**-opname** close-up (photography)
dig: ∼**kuns** poetry *ook* **poësie'**; ∼**maat** metre, poetic measure
dig'ter -s poet (person)
dig'terlik -e; -er, -ste poetic(al); ∼**e vry'heid** poetic licence
digt'heid density, denseness
dik -ker,' -ste thick; bulky; stout, corpulent; satiated; ∼ *vir* fed-up with; *hulle is* ∼ *vriende* they are close friends; ∼**bek** (s) sulky person; pouter; (b) sulky; fed-up; ∼**melk** curdled milk
diktafoon' -s dictaphone
dikta'tor -s dictator
dik'te -s thickness, swollenness
diktee' -s dictation
dikteer' ∼, **ge-** dictate; ∼**masjien'** dictating machine, dictaphone
dik'wels often, frequently *ook* **baie'keer**
dilem'ma -s dilemma, predicament, quandary *ook* **verknor'sing**
dilettant' -s dilettante, amateur
dina'mies -e dynamic
dinamiet' dynamite
dinee' dinner (formal); ∼**pak** dinner jacket *ook* **aand'pak**
ding[1] (s) -**e** thing, object, affair, matter
ding[2] (w) **ge-** try for, compete *ook* **mee'ding**

din′ges what-do-you-call-it, thingumajig *ook* **wat′senaam/hoe′senaam**

dink ge- think, consider, ponder; *aan iets* ~ think of something; ~**skrum** thinktank

Dins′dag ..**dae** Tuesday

dip (s) **-pe** dip; (w) dip *ook* **diep** (beeste)

diplo′ma -s diploma, certificate; ~**pleg′tig= heid** graduation ceremony

diplomaat′ ..**mate** diplomat, diplomatist

diploma′ties -e diplomatic

direk′ (b) **-te** direct, straight *ook* **reg′streeks**

direk′sie -s direction; board of directors

direkteur′ -e, -s director; ~**-generaal** direc= tor-general

dirigeer′ ge- conduct (music); ~**stok** baton

dirigent′ -e (music) conductor

dis it is; ~ *te sê* that is (to say)

disket (s) **-te** computer disc/disk, diskette

diskon′to discount *ook* **af′slag, kor′ting**

diskoteek′ record library; discothéque, disco

diskre′sie discretion *ook* **goed′dunke**

dis′kus -se disc(us) *ook* **(werp)skyf**

diskusseer′ ge- discuss *ook* **bespreek′** ('n saak)

diskus′sie -s discussion, argument; ~**groep** discussion group *ook* **gons′groep**; news= group (Internet)

diskwalifika′sie -s disqualification

diskwalifiseer′ ~, **ge-** disqualify

dislek′sie dyslexia, (reading) impediment *ook* **leer′geremd′heid**

dis′nis: ~ *loop* run/knock someone flat

dispuut′ ..**pute** dispute, controversy, argument *ook* **konflik′**

dis′selboom (s) shaft, thill, beam (of wagon); pole (of cart)

disserta′sie -s dissertation, thesis

dissi′pel -s disciple; adherent

dissipli′ne discipline; *strenge* ~ *handhaaf* maintain rigid discipline; adherent

dissiplinêr′ (b) **-e** disciplinary; ~*e stappe neem/doen* take disciplinary action

dis′tel -s thistle

distilleer′ ge- distil (brandy)

distrik′ -te district; ~**s′geneesheer** district surgeon

dit this; it

divan′ -s divan, sofa; ottoman

diver′se sundries; incidental expenses; ~ **uitgawes** sundry/miscellaneous expenses

dividend′ -e dividend; *'n* ~ *uitkeer/uitbetaal* pay a dividend; *tussentydse* ~ interim dividend *ook* **tus′sendividend;** *'n* ~ *ver= klaar* declare a dividend

dob′bel gamble, play at dice; ~**aar** gambler; ~**huis** casino *ook* **kasi′no**; ~**ma′sjien** gam= bling machine, one-armed bandit; ~**steen** dice, cube; ~**wiel** roulette *ook* **roelet′**

dob′ber (s) **-s** float, buoy; (w) bob up and down, float, fluctuate

do′de: ~**dans** death dance; ~**lik** deadly, mortal, fatal; ~**mars** funeral march; ~**ryk** realm of death; ~**tal** number of deaths; ~**tol** death toll

doea′ne -s custom house; customs

doe′delsak bagpipe

doe′die -s (*verouderd*) girlie, cute (young) lass; **pronk**~ showgirl

doe′doe ge- sing to sleep; go to sleep; dormy (golf)

doek -e cloth; napkin (baby); canvas, painting

doel (s) **-e, -ein′des** purpose, aim, object; **-e** goal; *sy* ~ *bereik* attain one's goal/object; *die* ~ *heilig die middele* the end justifies the means; ~**ein′de** purpose, end, aim, goal; ~**gebou** (b) custom made; custo= mised; ~**loos** aimless, useless; ~**lyn** goal= line

doelma′tig -e; -er, -ste effective; appropriate

doel: ~**paal** goalpost; ~**punt** goal; ~**skop** goalkick, conversion

doeltref′fend -e; -er, -ste effective, efficient; effectual; ~**heid** effectiveness

doel: ~**wag′ter -s** goalkeeper; ~**wit** aim, goal *ook* **mik′punt/oog′merk**; ~**withestuur′** man= agement by objectives

doem ge- doom, condemn; ~**profeet′** prophet of doom

doen[1] (s): *ons* ~ *en late* our goings out and comings in

doen[2] (w) **ge-** do, make, effect, perform; *daar is niks aan te* ~ *nie* there is no help for it; ~**lik** feasible, practical; ~**likheidstu′die** feasibility study *ook* **haal′baar(heid)stu′die**

doe′pa love potion, charm *ook* **toor′goed**

dof dowwe; **dowwer, -ste** dull, faint, dim, indistinct; lack-lustre (eyes)

dog but *ook* **maar**; still, however; *hy is siek,* ~ *hy kom skool toe* he is ill, but he comes to school

dog′ma -s dogma *ook* **leer′stelling**

dogma′ties -e dogmatic(al)

dog′ter -s daughter; girl

doi′lie -s doily *ook* **be′kerlappie, kraal′doekie**

dok -ke dock; ~**geld** dock duties/dues
dok'ter (s) **-s** doctor, physician *ook* **genees'**=
heer; (w) **ge-** doctor, nurse; ~**es** female
doctor; ~**s'gelde** medical fees
dok'tor -e, -s doctor (of literature, law)
dok'torsgraad ..grade doctor's degree
dokument' -e document; ~**a'sie** documenta=
tion
dokumentêr' -e documentary; ~**e film** doc=
umentary (film)
dol -ler, -ste mad, crazy, frantic, ridiculous; *in*
~*le vaart* in headlong career
dolf/dolwe ge- dig deep, turn over (soil)
dolfyn -e dolphin
dol: ~**graag** very keen; ever so much; ~**heid**
madness
dolk -e dagger, poniard
dol'lar -s dollar
dol'leeg ..leë absolutely empty
dolomiet' dolomite
dol'os -se ball of anklejoint, astragulus, knuckle=
bone; ~ *gooi* throw the bones (witchcraft)
dol'verlief -de madly in love *ook* **smoor'ver**=
lief
dom[1] (s) **-me** dome, cathedral
dom[2] (b) **-mer, -ste** stupid; dull; *nie so* ~ *as*
hy lyk nie not as green as he is cabbage-
looking
domastrant' impudent, cheeky, insolent
dom'heid stupidity, dullness
dominant' (b) dominant *ook* **oorheers'end**
do'minee -s clergyman, minister, parson
domineer' ge- dominate, domineer
dom: ~**kop** blockhead/fathead, stupid, clod,
plonker; ~**krag** jackscrew, jack; *die kar*
opdomkrag jack up the car; ~**oor** dunce,
blockhead
domp (w) dim/dip (headlights)
dom'pel ge- plunge, dive, dip, immerse; *in*
ellende ~ plunge into misery
donateur' -s contributor; donor *ook* **sken'ker/**
borg
don'der (s) **-s** thunder; *jou* ~*!* you scoundrel!
(w) thunder, boom; fulminate; ~**bui** thun=
derstorm
Don'derdag ..dae Thursday
don'der: ~**slag** thunderclap; ~**storm** thunder=
storm; ~**weer** thundery weather; ~**wolk**
thundercloud
don'ga -s donga, gully
don'ker (s) darkness; *in die* ~ *tas* grope in the
dark; (b) dark; gloomy, obscure; ~**blou**

dark blue; ~**bruin** dark brown, dun; ~**te**
darkness; ~**vat** lucky dip; ~**werk:** ~*werk in*
konkelwerk bunglers work in the dark
don'kie -s donkey, ass; ~**long** concertina
(idiom.)
dons -e down, fluff; (b) ~**agtig,** ~**erig,** ~**ig**
fluffy, downy; ~**ha'el** fine shot'; dust;
~**kombers'** (eiderdown) quilt
dood (s) death, decease; demise; (w) kill; (b)
dooie dead, deceased, defunct; *liewer bang*
Jan as dooi(e) Jan discretion is the better part
of valour; *op sy dooie gemak* very leisurely;
so ~ *soos 'n mossie* as dead as a doornail;
~**(s)berig** death notice; ~**bloei** bleed to
death; ~**eenvou'dig** quite simple; ~**eer'lik**
quite honest; ~**gaan** die; ~**gebo're** stillborn;
~**gerus'** perfectly calm; ~**gewoon'** very
simple, very common; ~**goed** very kind;
~**(s)kis** coffin; ~**loop** come to a dead end;
peter out; ~**lui'ters** free and easy; ~**maak**
kill; ~**mak** quite tame; ~**mar'tel** torture to
death; ~**moeg** deadbeat, deadtired *ook* **poe'**=
gaai; ~**ongeluk'kig** utterly miserable; ~**ry**
ride to death; override, kill
doods -e desolate, dreary, deathlike; ~**e stilte**
deadly silence; ~**angs** agony, mortal fear;
~**berig'** death notice; ~**bleek** ghastly/dead=
ly pale; livid; ~**en'gel** angel of death; ~**ge**=
vaar' peril of death
dood: ~**siek** dangerously ill; ~**skiet** shoot dead
doods: ~**kleed** shroud; ~**klok** deathbell, knell
doods'kop[1] (n) **-pe** death's head, skull
dood'skop[2] (w) **-ge-** kick to death
dood: ~**skrik** be frightened to death; ~**snik**
last gasp
dood: ~**sonde** deadly sin; ~**steek** (s) death=
blow, coup de grace *ook* **gena'deslag;** *sy*
~*steek* his pet aversion; ~**steek** (w) stab to
death; ~**stil** very still, quiet as a mouse;
~**straf** capital punishment
doods: ~**von'nis** death sentence; ~**vy'and**
mortal enemy
dood: ~**swyg** ignore; ~**tevre'de** quite content;
~**verlief** madly in love *ook* **smoor'verlief;**
~**verwon'derd** quite astonished
dooie'punt (s) deadlock
doof[1] (w) **ge-** extinguish, put out *ook* **uit'doof**
doof[2] (b) **dowe, dower, -ste** deaf; (w) *so* ~
soos 'n kwartel as deaf as a post; ~**blind**
deaf and blind; ~**mid'del** anaesthetic,
drug(s) *kyk* **dwelm'middel/dwelm(s)**
doof'stom deafmute, deaf and dumb; ~**me**

deaf and dumb (person)
dooi ge- thaw (ice, snow)
dooi'e -s the dead, the deceased
dooi'emansdeur: *voor* ~ *kom* find nobody at home
dooi'epunt -e deadlock; stalemate
dooi'er -s yolk (of egg)
dooi'erig -e; -er, -ste lifeless, listless; slow
dooi'eskuld bad debts *ook* **sleg'te skuld**
dool ge- wander, roam; ~**hof** maze, labyrinth
doop (s) christening, baptism; (w) christen, baptise; dunk, dip; ~**formulier'** baptismal formulary; ~**gelof'te** baptismal vow; ~**naam** first name(s); ~**regis'ter** church register; ~**seel** baptismal certificate
Doops'gesind -e Baptist
doop: ~**vont** baptismal font, baptistry
doos do'se box *ook* **boks**; case; *uit die ou* ~ old-fashioned, antiquated
dop (s) **-pe** shell (eggs); peel, husk (seed); drink; *'n halwe eier is beter as 'n leë* ~ a bird in the hand is better than two in the bush; *'n* ~ *steek* have/take a drink; (w) shell, peel; fail (examination); ~**-ertjie** green pea
dop'hou -ge- keep an eye on
Dop'per -s Dopper, Calvinist-Reformed
dop'pie -s percussion cap; shell; tot; *sy* ~ *het geklap* he has had his chips
dor -re; -der, -ste dry, barren, withered
do'ring -s thorn, prickle, spine, topnotcher; crack (person); ~**draad** barbed wire
dorp -e village, town
dor'peling -e, dor'penaar -s; ..nare villager
dorps: ~**gek** village idiot; ~**ja'pie** ignorant/stupid chap from town; ~**ontwik'kelaar** town developer; ~**raad** village council
dors[1] (s) thirst; *die* ~ *les* quench the thirst; (w) thirst (for knowledge); (b) thirsty
dors[2] (w) **ge-** thresh
dors'masjien -e threshing machine
dos (s) attire, array, raiment; (w) attire, deck out; *spoggerig uitgedos* dressed to kill
doseer'[1] ~, **ge-** teach, lecture; ~**pos** lecturing post
doseer'[2] ~, **ge-** dose (animals)
dosent' -e teacher, lecturer
do'sie -s little box; ~ **vuur'houtjies** box of matches
do'sis -se dose; *te groot* ~ *(oordosis)* overdose; **skraag**~ booster dose
dossier' -s dossier, (personal) docket
dosyn' -e dozen

dot'jie -s little dear; dot; brimless hat
dou (s) dew; (w) dew; ~**trap'per** early bird (person); ~**voordag'** at the crack of dawn
do'yen doyen, senior member; dean
dra ge- carry; wear; bear
draad drade wire; thread, fibre; grain; fila= ment; fence; *kort van* ~ short-tempered; ~**loos** wireless *ook* **ra'dio**; ~**loosstasie** broadcasting station; ~**sit'ter** temporiser; ~**tang** wire pliers; ~**trek'ker** wirepuller; ~**trek'kery** wirepulling; intrigue; ~**werk** wire grate, filigree work; wiring; nonsense; *vol* ~*werk wees* be full of fads and fancies
draag'baar[1] (s) **..bare** bier, litter; stretcher *ook* **vou'katel(tjie)**; ~**dra'er** stretcher bearer
draag'baar[2] (b) **..bare; -der, -ste** portable, wearable; bearable; **..bare re'kenaar** por= table computer, laptop (computer)
draag: ~**lik** bearable, tolerable; ~**rak** carrier (on motorcar); ~**wyd'te** range; import
draai (s) **-e** turn, twist, corner, bend; whorl (shell); **Kaapse** ~ sudden sharp turn; **slap** ~ slight turn; (w) turn; revolve, twist, wind; tarry, linger *ook* **talm**, *stokkies* ~ play truant; ~**bank** lathe; ~**boek** scenario, script (film); ~**hek** turnstile; ~**jak'kals** long-eared fox; ~**kolk** whirlpool; ~**or'rel** barrel organ, ~**pot'lood** propelling pencil; ~**stan'der** lazy Susan (on dining table); ~**ta'fel** turntable
draak drake dragon; *met iem. die* ~ *steek* poke fun at somebody
draal ge- linger, dawdle *ook* **talm/sloer**
dra'er -s carrier, bearer; pallbearer *ook* **slip(pe)draer**
draf' (s) trot; (w) **ge-** trot; jog; ~**kar'retjie** sulky; ~**sport** jogging *ook* **pret'draf**
drag -te load, burden; dress, fashion
drag'tig -e pregnant, with young *ook* **swan'ger** (mens)
dra'ma -s drama; playwriting
drama'ties -e dramatic
dramatiseer' ge- dramatise
dramaturg' -e dramatist *ook* **toneel'skrywer**
drang -e urge; urgency, pressure
drank -e strong drink, liquor; beverage; potion; *'n* ~*ie maak* have/take a drink; *sterk* ~ alcoholic liquor; *aan die* ~ *verslaaf wees* be addicted to alcohol; ~**lisen'sie** liquor licence; ~**verslaaf'** (b) alcoholic; ~**win'kel** bottlestore
dra'radio portable radio
dras'ties -e drastic *ook* **ingry'pend**

dra'wiegie -s carrycot
draw'wer -s jogger ook pret'draw'wer; trotter (horse)
draw'wertjie -s trotter; courser (bird)
dreef: op ~ kom get into one's stride
dreig (w) ge- threaten, menace
dreigement' (s) -e threat, menace
drei'gend (b) -e threatening; imminent
dreineer' ~ ge- drain
drem'pel -s threshold (fig.) kyk drum'pel
drenk ge- drench, soak; allow to drink; ~e'ling drowned/drowning person
dren'tel ge- saunter, loiter
dresseer' ge- train, coach; drill, dress
dreun (s) rumble, roar, thud; (w) rumble, roar, roll, boom; ~strook rumble strip (on road)
drib'bel ge- dribble
drie -ë three; try (rugby)
Drie-een'heid Trinity
drie'ërlei of three kinds
drie'hoek -e triangle; ~ig triangular; ~s'me'ting trigonometry
drie: ~kuns hattrick (sport); ~kwart three fourths; threequarter (rugby); ~lettergre'pig trisyllabic; ~ling triplets; ~maan'deliks quarterly; ~manskap' triumvirate; ~poot tripod; ~sprong hop, skip and jump; ~sy'dig three-sided, trilateral; ~voet tripod; trivet; ~voud treble; triple; 'n verklaring in ~voud a statement in triplicate; ~wiel tricycle
drif¹ driwwe ford, drif(t)
drif² -te hot temper, passion; anger; sy ~ beteuel keep one's temper; ~tig passionate; hasty, quick-tempered
dril ge- bore; drill, exercise; train, coach; ~kol'lege cramcollege
dring ge- press, urge, throng; ~end (b) urgent, pressing
drink ge- drink; ~be'ker goblet, beaker
dro'ë (s) dry land; (w) dry, make dry; ~bek: ~bek sit wait in vain (for refreshments); be disappointed
droef droewe (b) sad, dejected
droefgees'tig -e; -er, -ste melancholy, dejected, gloomy ook verdrie'tig
droef'nis sadness, sorrow, affliction
droe'wig -e; -er, -ste sad, dismal, sorrowful; ~e afloop sorry end
drom (s) -me metal drum/container; (w) troop, crowd, throng; die mense ~ saam the people are flocking together
dro'merig -e; -er, -ste dreamy

drom'mel -s deuce, devil; wretch; arme ~ poor wretch; wat de/die ~ doen hy? what on earth is he doing?
dronk (b) -er, -ste drunk(en), intoxicated; ~aard drunkard; ~bestuur' drunken driving; ~en'skap drunkenness, inebriety; ~lap drunkard; ~slaan flabbergast, beat one's apprehension; dit slaan my ~ it gets me beat; ~verdriet' alcoholic blues
droog (w) ge- dry, make dry; (b) parched, arid; nie ~ agter die ore nie be a greenhorn; ~dok dry/graving dock; ~skoonmaker/ ~reiniger drycleaner; ~te drought
droom (s) drome dream; (w) dream; ~uit'lêer interpreter of dreams
drop liquorice ook soet'hout
dros ge- run away, abscond, desert
drosdy' -e landdrost's residence, residency
dros'ter -s runaway, absconder, deserter
druif druiwe grape; ~luis phylloxera
druip ge- drip, trickle, fall in drops; fail (in examination); ~eling failure (in examination); ~nat dripping wet, soaked; ~steen stalactite, stalagmite; ~stert sneaking; ~stert weggaan slink off; ~sy'fer failure rate (of students); ~vet dripping
druis ge- roar, swirl
drui'we: ~prieel' vinebower; ~sap grapejuice; ~stok vine; ~tros bunch of grapes
druk (s) pressure, weight; print; -ke edition; (w) press, print; squeeze; push; (b) busy, fussy, lively; ~fout printer's error; ~groep pressure group; ~kastrol' pressure cooker
druk'ker -s printer; ~s'duiwel printer's devil, literal ook set'satan; ~y printing works
druk: ~knoptelefoon' pushbutton/pressbutton telephone; ~kuns art of printing; typography; ~pers printing press; ~proef printer's proof; ~skrif typescript, print; ~stuk print-out; ~te (s) stir, bustle, fuss, ado
drum'pel -s threshold, doorstep
drup (s) eaves; drip (medical); (w) drip, drop
drup'pel -s drop; 'n ~ in 'n emmer a drop in the ocean; (w) drop, trickle
dryf ge- float; swim; impel, drive, conduct; handel ~ trade; die spot ~ mock; ~baan driving range (golf); ~krag motive power; force; drive; ~sand driftsand, quicksand; ~veer motive
dry'wer -s driver, wagon driver; fanatic
dub'bel -e double; twice; ~ en dwars verdien deserve over and over again; ~door double-

yolked egg; ~**gan'ger** double, second self, alter ego (person); ~**loop** double-barrel (gun); ~**pad** dual carriageway; ~**punt** colon

dubbelsin'nig -e; -er, -ste ambiguous

dub'beltjie -s devil's thorn; *loop voor die pad vol* ~*s is* be quick about it

duet' -te duet

dui'delik -e; -er, -ste clear, distinct, obvious; legible

duif duiwe pigeon, dove

duik[1] (s) **-e** dent; (w) **ge-** dent

duik[2] (w) **ge-** dive, plunge; ~**bom'werper** divebomber; ~**boot** submarine, U-boat; ~**er** diver; culvert; duiker (antelope); cormorant (bird); ~**long** aqualung; ~**plank** springboard; ~**weg** subway

duim -e thumb; inch; *iets uit die* ~ *suig* trump up a story; ~**gooi** hitchhike *ook* **ry'loop**; ~**gooier** hitchhiker; ~**pie** little thumb; **Klein D~pie** Tom Thumb; ~**ry** hitchhike; ~**ry'er** hitchhiker *ook* **ry'loper**; ~**spy'ker(tjie)** drawing pin; ~**stok** inch measure, footrule

duin -e dune

dui'nebesie -s beachbuggy (car)

dui'sel ge- grow giddy/dizzy, reel; ~**ig** giddy, dizzy *ook* **lighoof'dig**

dui'send -e thousand; ~**ja'rige ryk** millennium; ~**poot** millipede

duis'ter (s) dark(ness); (b) dark, dusky; obscure; ~**e poesie'** obscure poetry

Duits (s) German; (b) (language); ~**er** German (person); ~**land** Germany

dui'wehok -ke pigeon house, dovecot

dui'wel -s devil; *dank jou die* ~*!* well I never; *so bang soos die* ~ *vir 'n slypsteen* be as scared as the devil is of holy water; ~**s'kun'stenaar** sorcerer, magician; ~**spiraal'** vicious circle; ~**s** (b) devilish, diabolic *ook* **demo'nies**

duld ge- bear, tolerate, endure

dun (b) thin, rarefied; sparse; slender; washy

duplikaat' ..kate duplicate *ook* **twee'voud**

durf (s) pluck, daring, guts

dus thus, therefore *ook* **daar'om/derhal'we**

dus'kant this side of

dut'jie -s nap, snooze; *'n* ~ *doen* nap

duur[1] (s) duration; (w) last, continue; *dit* ~ *tien dae* it lasts ten days

duur[2] (b) **dure; -der, -ste** dear, expensive; *'n dure eed sweer* swear a solemn oath

duur'saam ..same; ..samer, -ste durable; lasting; wearing well

dwaal ge- err; wander, roam; ~**gees** wandering spirit; ~**koe'ël** stray bullet; ~**lig** will-o'-the-wisp; ~**spoor** false track

dwaas (s) **dwase** fool, silly fellow; (b) foolish, silly; ~**heid** folly, stupidity

dwang compulsion, coercion, force, constraint; ~**ar'beid** hard labour; ~**baad'jie** straitjacket; ~**voe'ding** force-feeding

dwar'rel ge- whirl; ~**wind** whirlwind *ook* **war'relwind**

dwars across, athwart; contrary; ~**boom** (w) thwart, obstruct; ~**lê'er** sleeper (railway); ~**straat** cross-street; ~**trek'ker** squabbler, thwarter (person)

dweep ge- rave about; ~**pos** fanmail *ook* **bewon'deraarspos**; ~**siek** fanatic(al)

dwelm: ~**afhank'likheid** drug dependence; ~**baas** drug lord; ~**han'delaar** drug trafficker; ~**mid'del** medical drug; ~**misbruik'** drug abuse; ~**slaaf** drug addict; ~**smous** drug pedlar/pusher; ~**toer** (drug) trip

dwelms drugs (non-medical)

dwe'per -s fanatic, bigot (person)

dwerg -e dwarf, pygmy, midget; ~**kees** toypom (dog); ~**ten'nis** tenniset

dwing ge- force, compel, constrain

dwin'geland tyrant *ook* **tiran'** (mens)

dy (s) **-e** thigh

dyk -e dike, bank

dyn'serig/dyn'sig -e; -er, -ste misty, hazy

dy'spier -e hamstring muscle

E

eb (s) ebb; ~ *en vloed* ebb and flow

e'del -e; -er, -ste noble, generous; **Sy E'dele** His Honour

edelag'baar ..bare honourable; Your/His Worship; **Sy Edelag'bare die Bur'gemeester** His Worship the Mayor

e'delman -ne, edellie'de nobleman

e'delsteen ..stene precious stone, gem

edik' -te edict, decree *ook* **dekreet'**

eed ede oath

eek'horinkie -s squirrel

eelt (s) **-e** horny skin, callus

een one, someone, a certain; *op* ~ *na* all but one; ~**ak'ter/**~**bedryf'** one-act play

eend -e duck

een'dag once, one day

een'dekker -s monoplane

een'ders/e'ners (b) similar, alike; *presies* ~ *lyk* look exactly alike

een'drag concord, union, unity, harmony; ~ *maak mag* union is strength

eend'stert -e ducktail (person)

een: ~**heid** unity; ~**ho'ring** unicorn; ~**kant** on one side, apart; ~**kleu'rig** monochrome; ~**lettergre'pig** monosyllabic; ~**lo'pend** un= married, single; ~**maal** once, one day; ~**ma'lig** once only

een'oog one-eye, one-eyed person

eenpa'rig -e unanimous; ~**e besluit'/beslis'**= **sing** unanimous decision

een'rigtingstraat one-way street

eens unanimous, of the same opinion; *ek is dit* ~ *met jou* I agree with you

een'saam . .**same;** . .**samer, -ste** solitary, lonely; **een'same op'sluiting** solitary con= finement; ~**heid** solitude, loneliness

eens'klaps suddenly, all of a sudden *ook* **skie'lik, plot'seling**

eenstem'mig -e unanimous *ook* **eenparig**

eensy'dig -e; -er, -ste onesided, unilateral; ~**e onafhanklikverkla'ring** unilateral declara= tion of independence (UDI)

een'talig (b) **-e** unilingual

een'tjie one; *op sy* ~ all by himself

eento'nig -e; -er, -ste monotonous, tedious *ook* **verve'lig**

eenvor'mig (b) **-e** uniform *ook* **u'niform**

een'voud simplicity

eenvou'dig (b) simple, easy; singular

eer¹ (s) honour, repute, credit; *die laaste* ~ *bewys* render the last (funeral) honours, pay the last respects; (w) honour, respect

eer² (vgw) before *ook* **voor'dat**

eer'baar . .**bare; -der, -ste** virtuous; chaste, honest; worthy

eer'betoon/eer'bewys tribute; homage, mark of honour/respect

eer'bied respect, regard, reverence

eerbie'dig (w) ~, **geëer-,** respect, revere; obey; *verkeersreëls* ~ obey traffic rules

eer'der sooner, rather; *hoe* ~ *hoe beter* the sooner the better

eer'gevoel sense of honour

eer'gister the day before yesterday

eerlang'/eerlank' before long, erelong

eer'lik -e; -er, -ste honest, upright, fair; ~**heid** honesty; ~**waar** honestly

eers first; formerly; only; even

eers'daags/eer'daags soon, shortly

eers'geboortereg birthright

eers'genoemde the former

eers'komende next, following

eer'ste first; *die* ~ *die beste boek* the first book at hand; ~**hands** firsthand; ~**hulp** first aid; ~**klas** first-class, first-rate *ook* **voortref'lik;** ~**ling** firstling, firstborn; ~**ns** firstly

eersug'tig ambitious *ook* **ambisieus'**

eer'tyds -e former(ly)

eer'vol -le honourable; ~**le vermel'ding** hon= ourable mention

eerwaar'de (s, b) reverend

eet geëet eat; ~**ka'mer** dining room; ~**le'pel** tablespoon; ~**lus** appetite; ~**luswek'**= **ker(tjie)** appetiser; ~**maal** meal *ook* **e'te** banquet; ~**plek** restourant, eatery; ~**ser**= **vies'** dinner service; ~**sta'king** hunger strike

eeu -e century; age; ~**wending** turn of the century

eeu'fees -te centenary

ef'fe even, level, flat, smooth; plain

effek' -**te** effect, result *ook* **uit'werking**

effek'te securities; gilts; ~**beurs** stock ex= change *ook* **aan'delebeurs;** ~**ma'kelaar** stockbroker; ~**trust** unit trust

effektief' . .**tiewe** effective *ook* **doeltref'fend**

ef'fens/ef'fentjies slightly; a moment; a little; just; *wag* ~ half a mo(ment)

eg¹ (s) marriage, wedlock; *in die* ~ *tree* enter into matrimony

eg² (s) **êe, eg'ge** harrow

eg³ (b) -**te; -ter, -ste** authentic, real, thorough, genuine; legitimate; ~**te diaman'te** genuine diamonds

ega'lig -e; -er, -ste level, smooth, even

eg'genoot . .**note** spouse, husband/wife *ook* **ga'de, we'derhelf** (mens)

eg'go - '**s** echo *ook* **weer'klank**

Egip'te Egypt; ~**naar** Egyptian (person)

e'go ego, self; *jou* ~ *streel* boost one's ego

egoïs' -**te** egoist; ~**me** egotism *ook* **self'sug**

eg'skeiding -s, -e divorce

eg'ter however; yet, notwithstanding; *die meeste leerlinge het geslaag, heelparty het* ~ *gedruip* most pupils passed, quite a few however failed

ei'e own; natural; peculiar, specific; familiar;

uit ~ *beweging* of one's own accord; ~**belang'** self-interest

eiegereg'tig (b) self-righteous, high-handed

eiehan'dig -e with one's own hand

ei'en geëien (w) recognise; appropriate, own

ei'enaar -s, . .nare proprietor, owner

eienaar'dig -e; -er, -ste peculiar, strange, odd

ei'endom -me property, belongings, posses= sion; **vaste** ~ real estate, fixed property; ~**ontwikkelaar** property developer

ei'endoms proprietary; ~**agent'** real estate agent; ~**reg** right of possession

ei'enskap -pe feature; trait, characteristic *ook* **ken'merk**

ei'er -s egg; *'n halwe* ~ *is beter as 'n leë dop* half a loaf is better than no bread at all; ~**dop** eggshell; ~**kel'kie** egg cup; ~**ko'**= **kertjie** eggboiler; sandglass; ~**stok** ovary; ~**vrug** brinjal

eiesin'nig (b) wilful, obstinate *ook* **kop'pig**

ei'etyds -e contemporary, with-it, trendy *ook* **bydertyds'**

eiewys' conceited, headstrong

ei'keboom (s) oak tree

ei'land -e island, isle

ei'na (b, bw) weak; painful; small, *sy kennis van Grieks is maar* ~ his knowledge of Greek is scanty; (tw) ouch! oh! ow! ~**broe'**= **kie** minipants; scantypanty

ein'de -s end, conclusion, termination

eind'eksamen -s final examination

ein'delik at last, finally, at length

ein'deloos . .lose endless, infinite

ein'dig (w) geëindig end, conclude, terminate; **boek'jaar** ~**ende 31 Maart** financial year ending 31 March

eind: ~**punt** terminus, end; ~**rond(t)e** final; ~**tel'ling** final score

ein'ste same; *die* ~ *man* the very same man

eint'lik (b) -**e** proper, real, actual; (bw) properly, actually; *nie* ~ *nie* not exactly

eis (s) -**e** demand, claim, requirement; (w) demand, claim

ei'ser -s plaintiff, claimant (person)

eistedd'fod -au, -s eisteddfod, song/singing festival *ook* **sang'fees** (Wallies)

ek I; ~ *en my vriend* my friend and I

ek'ke I (with stress); ~**rig** egotistic, self-= centred

ekologie' ecology *ook* **omge'wingsleer**

ekonomie' (s) economy; economics

ekono'mies (b) economic(al) *ook* **spaar'saam**

ekonoom' . .nome economist (person)

ekosisteem' ecosystem

ekotoeris'me (s) ecotourism

eksa'men -s examination; ~ *aflê (doen, skryf)* sit for an examination; *sy* ~ *sak (dop, druip)* fail his examination; *(in) sy* ~ *slaag* pass his examination; ~**vraag** examination question; ~**vra'estel** examination paper

eksamina'tor -s, -e examiner (person)

ekseem' eczema

eksekuteur' -s, -e executor (of an estate)

eksellen'sie -s excellency (person)

eksemplaar' . .plare specimen, copy

eksentriek' -e; -er, -ste eccentric, odd

eksklusief' . .siewe; . .siewer, -ste exclusive

ekskur'sie -s excursion, outing

ekskuus' . .kuse excuse, pardon; ~ *maak* apologise *kyk* **versko'ning**

ekskuus'! pardon me! sorry!

ek'sodus exodus *ook* **uit'tog**

ekso'ties -e exotic, foreign

ekspedi'sie -s expedition *ook* **(veld)tog**

eksperiment' (s) -**e** experiment; ~**eel'** experi= mental; ~**eer'** (w) experiment

eksta'se ecstasy; *in* ~ *raak* go into raptures

eksta'ties -e ecstatic

ekstern' -e extern; ~**e stu'die** external study *kyk* **af'standonderrig**

ek'stra extra, additional; spare

ekstremis' -te extremist (person)

ekume'nies (b) -**e** ecumenical, universal

ekwa'tor equator; ~**iale stil'tegordel** doldrums

ekwivalent' -e equivalent

el -le ell; **el'lelang verdui'deliking** too long an explanation

e'land -e eland (SA); elk (Europe); moose (America)

elas'ties (b) -**e** elastic; flexible *ook* **fleksiel'**

el'ders elsewhere

elegant' (b) elegant *ook* **sjiek** (mode)

elegie' -ë elegy *ook* **treur'sang**

elek'tries -e electric(al); ~**e stoel** electric chair; **elektrotegniese ingenieur'** electrical engineer

elektrisiën' -s electrician (person)

elektrisiteit' electricity

elek'trokardiogram (EKG) electrocardio= gram (ECG)

elektro'nies (b) electronic; ~**e beheer'** elec= tronic control; ~**e pos (e-pos)** electronic mail (e-mail/email); ~**e re'kenaar** computer

element' -e element; ~**êr'** (b) elementary
elf¹ (s) **elwe** elf, fairy
elf² (s) **elwe** shad, chard (fish)
elf³ eleven; *ter* ~*der ure* at the eleventh hour; ~**de** eleventh; ~**tal** team (cricket)
elimineer' (w) ~, **geël-** eliminate *ook* **uit'ska=kel**
elk -e each, every; ~**een** everybody, everyone *ook* **ie'dereen**
ellen'de misery, wretchedness, distress
ellen'dig -e; -er, -ste wretched, miserable
elm'boog ..**boë** elbow
eloku'sie elocution *ook* **spraak'kuns**
emal'je/enem'mel enamel; ~**verf** enamel paint *ook* **glans'verf**
embar'go -'s embargo, prohibition
embleem' ..**bleme** emblem
em'brio -'s embryo
emeritaat' ..**tate** clergyman's retirement
emigrant' -e emigrant (leaving country)
em'mer -s pail, bucket
emo'sie -s emotion *ook* **gevoel'**
emosioneel' (b) ..**nele** emotional
en and; *én* . . . *én* both . . . and
end ente end *ook* **ein'de**; termination; extremity
endosseer' (w) ~, **geën-** endorse
endossement' -e endorsement
e'ne one, a certain; ~ **mnr.** X a certain Mr X
energie' energy; ~**bespa'ring** energy saving
eng -er, -ste narrow, tight; narrow-minded
en'gel -e angel
En'geland England
en'gelebak -ke upper gallery, gods (theatre)
En'gels (s) English; *suiwer* ~ good English; the King's English; (b) English; ~**e sout** Epsom salts (idiom.)
En'gelsman Engelse Englishman
eng'te -s strait, defile, isthmus; difficulty; ~**vrees** claustrophobia
e'nig -e only, sole, any; unique; ~ *in sy soort* unique; the only of its kind
e'nigsins somewhat; *as dit* ~ *kan* if at all possible
e'nigste only, sole
enjambement' -e enjambment
en'jin -s engine; *die* ~ *kets* the engine backfires; *die* ~ *staak* the engine stalls; ~**dry'wer** engine driver
en'kel¹ (s) -s ankle
en'kel² (b) -e single
en'kel³ (bw) solely, merely, only
en'kel: ~**bed** single bed; ~**geslag'** unisex;

~**ing** individual (person); ~**reis** single journey; ~**spel** singles, single game; ~**voud** singular; ~**vou'dige ren'te** simple interest
enorm' -e enormous, immense *ook* **ys'lik**
ensiklopedie' -ë encyclopaedia
ent¹ (s) -e graft; (w) graft
ent² (s) distance, length; end; *dis 'n hele* ~ *hiervandaan* it is quite a distance from here
entoesias' -te enthusiast, fan (person); ~**me** (s) enthusiasm *ook* **gees'drif**
entomoloog' ..**loë** entomologist (person)
entrepreneur' (s) entrepreneur *ook* **onderne'=mer/sa'keman**
ent'stof ..**stowwe** serum, vaccine
epide'mie (s) -s epidemic
epide'mies -e epidemic; *kinderverlamming het* ~*e afmetings aangeneem* infantile paralysis (poliomyelitis) has assumed epidemic pro=portions
epigram' -me epigram *ook* **punt'dig**
epilep'sie epilepsy *ook* **val'lende siek'te**
episo'de -s episode *ook* **voor'val**
e'pos (s) epic (poem)
e-pos (s) e-mail/email (electronic mail)
erbarm' ~ have pity; *jou* ~ *oor* have pity on
er'de: ~**skot'tel** earthenware basin; ~**wa're** ceramics *ook* **keramiek'**; ~**werk** earthen=ware, pottery; crockery
erd: ~**vark** ant eater; ~**wurm** earthworm
e're honour; *ter* ~ *van* in honour of; ~**bur'ger** freeman; ~**bur'gerskap** freedom of the town/city; ~**diens** divine service; ~**graad** honorary degree; ~**lid** honorary member
ê'rens somewhere
e're: ~**sekreta'ris** honorary secretary; ~**wag** guard of honour; ~**woord** word of honour
erf¹ (s) **erwe** plot, stand
erf² (w) **geërf** inherit *ook* **er'we**; ~**enis'** in=heritance, heritage; **E~enisdag** Heritage Day (holiday); ~**geld** inherited money; ~**geld is swerfgeld** lightly come, lightly go; ~**genaam'** heir; ~**por'sie** inheritance, share of inheritance; ~**stuk** heirloom
erg (b) bad; evil; (bw) severely, extremely; *wat te* ~ *is, is te* ~ this is really too bad
er'gernis -se annoyance, nuisance; *al die* ~ all the annoyance/hassles
erg'ste worst; *op die* ~ *voorberei* prepare for the worst
erken' (w) ~ acknowledge, own up, admit; ~**ning** acknowledgment, admission

erkent'lik -e; -er, -ste grateful, thankful
erns earnest(ness), seriousness, gravity
ern'stig -e; -er, -ste serious, grave; earnest; *iets* ~ *opneem* take a serious view of
ero'sie erosion
ero'ties -e erotic; sensual
er'tappel -s potato; ~sky'fie (potato) chip *ook* aar'tappel
er'tjie -s pea; ~sop pea soup
erts -e ore; ~af'setting ore deposit
ervaar' (w) ~ experience, undergo
erva're experienced; skilled *ook* kun'dig
erva'ring -s, -e experience; ~ *opdoen* gain experience
e'sel -s ass, donkey; mule; easel; blockhead
eska'der -s squadron (navy, airforce)
eskadron' -ne, -s squadron (cavalry)
eskaleer' (w) ~ escalate, increasing progres= sively
essensieel' ..siële essential *ook* noodsaak'lik
este'ties -e aesthetic(al)
e'te -s meal, dinner *ook* maal(tyd); food
e'ter¹ -s eater
e'ter² ether, upper air; ~golf ether wave
etiket'¹ etiquette
etiket'² -te label; tag; docket
etimologie' -e etymology *ook* woord'afleiding
et'maal 24 hours, full day; ~diens 24-hour service
et'nies ethnic; ~e tale ethnic languages

ets (s) -e etching; (w) etch
et'ter (s) matter, pus; (w) fester
eufemis'me euphemism *ook* versagting
Eu'romark Euromart
Euro'pa Europe
Europeaan' ..peane/Europe'ër -s European (person)
Europees' ..pese European (a)
eu'wel -s evil *ook* boos'heid
evalueer' ~, geëv- evaluate, assess
evange'lie -s gospel, evangel
evangelis' -te evangelist (person)
evolu'sie/ewolu'sie evolution
e'we just as, even, equally; ~ *groot* of the same size
e'we: ~beeld likeness, counterpart; ~kan'sig random (stats.); ~knie equal, peer; counter= part *ook* amps'genoot
e'wenaar¹ (s) equator, line; (-s) differential (car)
ewenaar'² (w) geëw- equal, rival; *niemand kan hom* ~ *nie* no one can match/rival him
e'weneens similarly, in the same manner, like= wise
ewere'dig -e proportional, pro rata
e'wewig (s) equilibrium, balance; poise
ewewy'dig -e parallel, equidistant
e'wig (b) -e eternal, everlasting, perpetual
e'wigheid eternity *ook* hierna'maals

F

faal (w) ge- fail, be unsuccessful
fa'bel -s fable; legend, fiction
fabriek' -e factory
fabrieks': ~af'val factory waste/effluent; ~ar'beider factory hand; ~wer'ker factory worker
fabrikaat ..kate manufacture, make, brand; *ook* produk'; nuwe ~ mo'tor new make of car
fabrikant' -e manufacturer *ook* vervaar'diger (mens)
fak'kel -s torch; ~loop torchlight procession
faks (s, w) fax (facsimile)
fak'sie (s) faction, clique; ~geveg' faction fight
fakto'tum -s factotum, handyman *ook* nuts'= man

faktuur' ..ture invoice; bill
fakulteit' -e faculty (of university)
fami'lie -s family; relations, relatives; *aange= troude* ~ relations by marriage; *verlangs* ~ distantly related; ~kring family circle *kyk* (huis)gesin'; ~kwaal hereditary malady; ~lid member of a family; ~wa'pen family coat of arms
fantasie' -ë imagination, phantasy, fancy; ~kostuum' fancy dress
fantas'ties -e; -ste fantastic *ook* denkbeel'dig
farise'ër -s pharisee, hypocrite
farmaseu'ties -e pharmaceutical
fa'se -s phase, stage
faset' -te facet (of a diamond); ~ryk multi-facetted; versatile
fasiliteit' -e facility; comfort *ook* gerief'

fat (s) -te dandy, swell (person)
fatsoen′ -e shape, form; fashion, manners, good form
fatsoen′lik decent, respectable, proper
Fe′bruarie -s February
federa′sie -s federation
fee feë fairy; elf, pixie
feeks -e vixen, shrew, bitch (woman)
fe′ë: ∼**ryk** fairyland; ∼**verha′le** fairy tales
fees (s) -te feast, festival, fête; ∼ *vir die oë* a treat for the eyes; (w) ∼**vier** celebrate; feast; ∼**maal** banquet;· ∼**re′de** (festive) oration; inaugural speech
fees′telik -e festive; ∼ *onthaal* entertain lavishly
fees′vier -ge- feast, celebrate; ∼**ing** festival, feast; celebration, merrymaking
feit -e fact; *deur* ∼*e gestaaf* supported by facts
fei′te: ∼**ken′nis** knowledge of facts; ∼**materiaal′** body of facts; ∼**sen′ding** factfinding mission
feit′lik factual(ly); actually, practically; *hy het* ∼ *geen familie nie* he has practically no relatives; ∼**e gege′wens** factual details
fel (b) -le; -ler, -ste fierce, sharp, severe
ferm -e; -er, -ste firm, solid, strong; ∼**e op′trede** firm action
ferweel′ corduroy; ∼**broek** corduroy trousers *kyk* **fluweel′**
fias′ko -′s fiasco, wash-out; collapse, flop
fie′mies (s) capriciousness, freakishness; nonsense; *vol* ∼ *wees* finicky, fussy, faddish
fier -e; -der, -ste proud, bold
fiets (s) -e bicycle; (w) ge- cycle; ∼**ry′er,** cyclist; ∼**er** biker
figuur′ figure shape, figure; *'n droewige* ∼ *slaan* cut a sorry figure; ∼**lik** (b) figurative(ly)
fiks -e; -er, -ste healthy, robust, fit; *die rugbyspeler is nou weer* ∼ the rugby player is fit again; ∼**heidtoets′** fitness test
fik′sie -s fiction; **we′tenskap**∼ science fiction (sci-fi)
filet′ -te fillet (meat, fish)
filharmo′nies -e philharmonic (orchestra)
filatelie′ philately, stamp collecting
filiaal′ (s) **filiale** subsidiary; branch office; ∼**maatskappy′** subsidiary company
film (s) -s film; (w) film; ∼**er** film producer; ∼**oteek′** film library; ∼**ster′** film star
filosofie′ (s) philosophy *ook* **wys′begeerte**
filosoof′ ..**sowe** philosopher *ook* **wys′geer**

fil′ter -s filter, percolator
filtreer′ ge- filter; ∼**kof′fie** filter(ed) coffee
finaal′ finale final, total
fina′le: ∼ **wed′stryd** final match *ook* **eind′= wedstryd**
finansieel′ ..**siële** financial, monetary
finansier′ (s) -s financier, banker; (w) finance; *'n projek* ∼ finance a project
finan′sies finances *ook* **geld′sake**
finans′komitee -s finance committee
fineer′ (s, w) veneer
fir′ma -s firm; house; *die* ∼ *Brits & Bell* Messrs Brits & Bell; ∼**blad** house journal/ magazine; ∼**mo′tor** company car
firmament′ firmament, sky
fisant′ -e pheasant
fisiek′ (s) physique; (b) physical; *sy* ∼*e toe= stand* his physical/bodily condition
fi′sies -e physical; ∼**e aard′rykskunde** physical geography
fi′sika physics *ook* **natuur′kunde**
fisiologie′ physiology
fisioterapeut′ physiotherapist (person)
fisioterapie′ physiotherapy
fiskaal′ (s) ..**kale** fiscal; bailiff; butcherbird; ..**ka′le beleid′** fiscal/taxation policy
flad′der ge- flutter, flit, flap
flamink′ -e flamingo
flank -e flank, side; ∼**aan′val** flank attack
flankeer′ ∼, ge- flank; gad about; *met die nooiens* ∼ flirt with the girls
flap (s) -pe widowbird, sakabula; flap; iris (flower); (w) ge- flap
flap′pertjie -s crumpet, flapjack
flap′teks -te blurb (of a book)
fla′ter -s blunder,· mistake, slip-up *ook* **blaps;** *'n* ∼ *begaan* make a blunder
flen′nie flannel; ∼**bord** flannel graph/board
flen′ter (s) -s rag, tatter; *g'n* ∼ *omgee nie* not care a snap of the fingers
flen′ters in tatters; *iets fyn en* ∼ *slaan* smash to smithereens
fler′rie -s flirt, good-time girl
fles -se bottle, flask
fleur prime, bloom; *in die* ∼ *van sy lewe* in the prime of life
fliek (s) -e bioscope/movies/cinema *ook* **bioskoop′;** (w) go to the bio; *kom ons gaan* ∼ let's go to the movies/flicks; ∼**gan′ger** cinema goer; ∼**vlooi** flick fan (person)
flik′flooi (w) ge- coax, fawn, flatter
flik′ker ge- glitter, sparkle, twinkle; ∼**gram**

brainscan *ook* **breintas'ting**; ~**lig** flicker=
light, flashlight
flik'kers leaps (dancing); pranks; ~ *maak/gooi
by 'n nooi* dance attendance on a girl
flink (b) -e; -er, -ste energetic; brisk, vigor=
ous; (bw) soundly, vigorously, firmly
flits (s) -e (lightning) flash; (w) flash; ~**berig'**
news flash (radio); ~**lig** flashlight, torch
flon'ker ge- sparkle; twinkle; ~**ing** sparkling
flo'ra flora, plant life; vegetation
floreer' ~, ge- flourish, thrive
flore'rend flourishing, thriving (business)
flou (b) faint, weak, dead-tired; insipid; *geen
~e benul hê nie van* not have the vaguest
idea of; ~ *val* have a fainting fit
flous (w) ge- cheat, deceive, trick, fox
flou'te -s swoon, fainting fit, blackout *ook*
brein'floute
fluister ge- whisper
fluit (s) -e flute, whistle; (w) whistle, play on
the flute; zip (of bullets); piddle, urinate;
~**-fluit** easily; *hy het ~-~ (in) sy eksamen
geslaag* he passed his examination without
effort; ~**spe'ler** flutist
fluks -e; -er, -ste hardworking; willing
fluweel' velvet; *so sag soos ~* velvety soft/
smooth
foe'fie (s) trick; gimmick, ploy *ook* **truuk**
foe'lie tin(foil)
foen'dle (s) fundi, expert *ook* **ken'ner**
foe'ter (w) ge- bother; beat, thrash, wallop
fo'kus -se focus, focal point
folk (s) folk (music)
folk'lore folklore *ook* **volks'kunde**
fol'ter ge- torture, torment; **ba'bafoltering**
baby battering ~**ka'mer** torture chamber
fondament' -e foundation; bottom
fonds -e fund; ~**in'sameling** fundraising *ook*
geld'insameling
fonetiek' phonetics *ook* **klank'leer**
fone'ties -e phonetic
fontein' -e fountain, spring
fooi (s) -e tip; professional fee; gratuity
foon fone phone; ~**fler'rie/~snol** callgirl
fop (w) ge- hoax, cheat, fool; ~**dos'ser** (s)
drag queen (male transvestite); ~**myn**
booby trap; ~**-op'roep** hoax (telephone) call
fop'speen ..spene baby's dummy, comforter
forel' -le trout (fish)
formaat' ..mate size, shape; format
formaliteit' -e formality, matter of form
formeel' ..mele formal

formu'le -s formula
fors -e; -er, -ste robust, strong, powerful,
vigorous; ~ *gebou* sturdily built
forseer' ~, ge- force, compel *ook* **dwing**
fort -e fortress, fort *ook* **ves'ting**
fortuin' luck, fortune; wealth; ~**hou** hole-in-one
(golf); ~**le'ser** *kyk* **waar'sêer**; ~**soe'ker**
fortune hunter; adventurer
fossiel' -e fossil
fo'to -'s photo(graph); ~**al'bum** photo(graph)
album; ~**beslis'sing** photo finish (races);
~**ge'nies** (a) photogenic (person); ~**kopie'**
photocopy (s)
fotograaf' ..grawe photographer (person)
fotografeer ge- photograph, take a photo; *jou
laat ~* have one's photo taken
fotografie' photography
fout (s) -e mistake, error, fault *ook* **fla'ter, blaps**;
~**vry** foolproof *ook* **fla'tervry**
foutief' ..tiewe faulty, erroneous
fout'speurder -s troubleshooter
fraai (b) fine, handsome *ook* **sier'lik**
fragment' -e fragment, piece
frai'ing -s fringe, tassel
framboos' ..bose raspberry
Frank'ryk France
Frans (b) -e French
Frans'man Franse Frenchman
fra'se -s phrase
fraseer' ~, ge- phrase
frats -e freak, caprice, whim; *vol ~e wees* be
mischievous; ~**on'geluk** freak accident
fregat' -te frigate (skip)
frekwen'sie frequency; ~**modula'sie** fre=
quency modulation (FM)
fres'ko -'s fresco, mural (painting)
fret -te ferret (rodent)
frikkadel' -le minced-meat ball, rissole, frica=
del; ~**brood'jie** hamburger *ook* **ham'burger**
fris (b) cool; strong, stout, healthy; ~ *gebou*
well-built
frok'kiehemp ..de T-shirt *ook* **T-hemp**
from'mel (w) ge- fumble, crease, rumple
frons (s) -e frown; (w) ge- frown
front -e front; ~**bot'sing** head-on collision *ook*
kop-teen-kop-bot'sing; ~**li'niesta'te** front=
line states; (w) front (bv. noord)
frustra'sie -s frustration
frustreer' ~, ge- frustrate *ook* **dwars'boom**
fud'ge fudge (sweets)
fuif (s) -e spree, carousal; (w) carouse, spree;
~**party'** drinking/booze party

fundamenteel′ ..tele fundamental ~te′le reg′te fundamental/human rights
fungeer′ ~, ge- act, offiçiate, perform duties; **funge′rende voor′sitter** chairman/chairperson for the time being
funk′sie -s function *ook* **onthaal′** (s)
fusilleer′ ge- execute (by firing squad)
fut mettle, dash, vim, zip; *sy ~ is uit* he has lost his spirit

futiel′ -e futile *ook* **vrug′teloos**
fyn -e; -er, -ste fine, delicate; refined, subtle; ~ *en flenters breek* smash completely; ~ *oplet* pay careful attention
fyngevoe′lig -e; -er, -ste sensitive, delicate
fyn: ~**kam** search thoroughly; ~**proe′wer** connoisseur, epicure, gourmet; ~**stop** invisible mending; ~**tuin** herb/kitchen garden
fyt -e whitlow, felon

G

gaaf good, nice, pleasant; undamaged; *'n gawe kêrel* a fine fellow, a decent chap/guy
gaan ge- go; move; walk; *hoe ~ dit?* how do you do? *ook* **Aan′genaam!**
gaan′deweg gradually, by degrees
gaap (s) gape yawn; (w) yawn; gape; *so warm dat die kraaie ~* very hot
gaar (b) sufficiently cooked; done; dressed
gaar′der (s) receiver of revenue *ook* **belas′-tinggaarder**
gaas gauze, netting
ga′de -s spouse, consort *ook* **eg′genoot**
gal gall, bile
ga′la -s′ gala, festive show
gal: ~**bitter** bitter as gall; ~**blaas** gallbladder
galant′ (b) gallant, polite *ook* **hof′lik**
galery′ -e gallery; loft
galg -e gallows; *so slim soos die houtjie van die ~* as sharp as a needle
gal′gemaal last/parting meal
galm (s) -e, -s peal, clangour; (w) resound
galop′ (s, w) gallop
gal: ~**siek′te** gall sickness; ~**steen** gallstone
gang (s) -e gait, walk; pace (horse); course (meal); passage, corridor (in a house)
gang: ~**baar** passable, current; feasible; ~**baarheidstu′die** feasibility study *ook* **uit′voerbaarheidstudie**; ~**bare ken′nis** working knowledge
gangreen′ gangrene *ook* **kou′evuur**
gans[1] (s) -e goose; ~*e aanja* be tipsy
gans[2] (b) -e whole, entire, all; ~ *anders* totally different; *die ~e dag* the whole day
gans′loper -s jaywalker (person)
ga′ping -s, -e gap, hiatus; *die ~ vernou* narrow the gap
gara′ge -s garage *ook* **mo′torhawe/vul′stasie** (publiek); **mo′torhuis** (privaat)

garan′sie -s guarantee *ook* **waar′borg**
garde′nia -s gardenia *ook* **katjiepie′ring** (blom)
ga′re/ga′ring thread, yarn; **tol′letjie** ~ reel of cotton
garnaal′ ..nale shrimp; **steur**~ prawn
garnisoen′ -e garrison
gars barley; ~**kof′fie** barley coffee
gas[1] -te guest
gas[2] -se gas; *op ~ kook* cook by gas
gas′heer ..here host; *ons is ~ vir die geleentheid* we are hosting the event
gas: ~**lamp** gaslamp; ~**mas′ker** gas mask, respirator; ~**spre′ker** guest speaker *ook* **geleent′heidspreker**
gas′tehuis -e guesthouse, lodge
gas: ~**vrou** hostess; ~**vry′heid** hospitality
gat[1] -e hole, gap
gat[2] -te anus, arse (*vulgar*)
ga′we -s gift, donation; talent; *van gunste en ~ leef* live on charity
geag′ -te respected; esteemed; **Geag′te Heer** Dear Sir; **Geag′te Heer/Da′me** Dear Sir/Madam
gebaar′ ..bare gesture; gesticulation
gebak′ pastry, cake; *met die ~te pere bly sit* be left holding the baby
geba′ker: *kort ~ wees* be short-tempered
gebed′ -e prayer; *'n ~ doen* say/offer a prayer
gebed′(s)roeper -s muezzin (person)
gebeur′ ~ happen, occur, come to pass; *wat ook al ~* come what may; ~**likheid′** possibility; contingency; ~**likheidsplan′** contingency plan; ~**tenis′** event, occurrence
gebied′[1] (s) -e territory, area, domain
gebied′[2] (w) ~ command, order, direct; *iem. hiet en ~* order someone around
gebit′ -te set of teeth; dentures
gebod′ ..booie commandment; command,

order, decree; *iem. die tien gebooie voorlees* bring someone to book

gebooi'e marriage banns

geboor'te -s birth; ~**beper'king** birth control, family planning; ~**dag** birthday *ook* **ver= jaar'(s)dag;** ~**sy'fer** birth rate

gebo're born; née; ~ *en getoë* born and bred

gebou' -e building, construction

gebrek' -e defect, fault; lack, want; ~ *ly* suffer want; ~**kig** defective, faulty; *sy kennis van Engels is* ~*kig* his English is poor; ~**lik** disabled *kyk* **gestrem';** infirm; ~**like kind** crippled/deformed child

gebroe'ders brothers; ~ **Jones** Jones Bros

gebro'ke broken; ~ **gesin/huis** broken home

gebruik' (s) **-e** use; usage; practice, habit, custom; *in* ~ *neem* put into service; (w) use, employ, enjoy; ~**s'aanwysing** directions for use; ~**te mo'tor** used car; ~**ervrien'delik** userfriendly

gedaan' ..**dane** done, finished; exhausted; *gedane sake het geen keer nie* it is no use crying over spilt milk

gedag'te -s thought, idea, notion, opinion; ~*s wissel oor* exchange views on; ~**nis'** remembrance, memory; keepsake; *ter* ~*nis aan* in memory of

gedeel'te -s part, section, portion, share, instalment; ~**lik** partly, partially

gedek' -te covered (head); pregnant (animal); secured (debts)

gedemp' -te filled up; dim; *op* ~*te toon* in a muffled voice

gedenk' ~ remember, commemorate; *ons* ~ *sy geboorte* we commemorate his birth; ~**hoek** memorial volume, album; ~**diens** memorial service; ~**naald** obelisk; ~**pen'ning** me= dal(lion); ~**plaat** plaque; ~**skrif** memoir; ~**te'ken** monument, memorial

gedenkwaar'dig -e; -er, -ste memorable; ~**e dag** memorable day

gedig' -te poem

geding' -e lawsuit, case *ook* **hof'saak**

gedissiplineer' -de disciplined

gedoen'te -s fuss, noise; happening

gedra' ~ behave, conduct, act; *hy* ~ *hom goed* he behaves well

gedrag' (s) behaviour, conduct; ~**s'kode** code of conduct/ethics; ~**sielkunde** behavioural psychology; ~**s'lyn** line of conduct

gedrog' -te monster, monstrosity

gedug' -te formidable, tremendous, severe;

~**te span** formidable team

geduld' patience, forbearance; *my* ~ *is op* my patience is exhausted; ~**ig** (b) patient

gedu'rende during *ook* **ty'dens**

gedu'rig (b) **-e** constant, continual, incessant; (bw) constantly, continually

gedwee' (b) submissive, meek, docile

gedwon'ge compulsory, (en)forced; ~ **fout** forced error (tennis)

gee ge- give, confer, present with, yield; *dit gewonne* ~ yield the point; *te kenne* ~ notify, intimate

geëer' -de honoured; ~**de gas'te** honoured guests

geel yellow; ~**bek** Cape salmon; ~**hout** yellowwood; ~**slang** yellow cobra; ~**sug** jaundice; ~**vink** yellow finch; ~**wor'tel** carrot

geen[1] none; no; ~ *van beide* neither of the two

geen[2] (s) **ge'ne** gene *ook* **erf'likheidsbepa'ler** (biol.) *kyk* **gene'tiese manipule'ring**

geeneen' no one, not one

geen'sins by no means, not at all

gees -te spirit, ghost; mind, wit, intellect; *die* ~ *is gewillig maar die vlees is swak* the spirit is willing but the flesh is weak; *teenwoordigheid van* ~ presence of mind; ~**drif'** enthusiasm *ook* **entoesias'me**

geesdrif'tig (b) enthusiastic, keen

gees'telik -e spiritual; intellectual; religious; ~**e** clergyman/cleric, minister, parson

gees'tes: ~**gesteld'heid** state of mind, mental= ity; ~**we'tenskappe** human sciences

gees'tig (b) witty, bright, smart

gege'we given; *op 'n* ~ *uur* at a given hour

gege'wens data, information *ook* **da'ta, na= dere/meer** ~ further details

gegig'gel giggling, tittering

gegradueer'de -s graduate (person) *ook* **gra= duaat'**

gegroet'! greetings! hail! *ook* **groet'nis, dag'sê!**

gegrond' -e well-founded; ~**e re'des** sound reasons

gehal'te quality, standard *ook* **kwaliteit';** *hoë* ~ high standard; ~**beheer'** quality control

geha'wend (b) **-e** battered, dilapidated

geheel' (s) whole; entireness/entirety; *oor die* ~ on the whole; (b) whole, entire, complete; (adv) all, entirely; quite; ~ *en al* completely; ~**onthou'er** teetotaller

geheg' -te attached; fond of; ~ *aan* attached/ devoted to

geheim' (s) -e secret; *'n ~ verklap* let the cat out of the bag; (b) secret; ~**hou'ding** secrecy, concealment

geheimsin'nig mysterious *ook* **raaiselag'tig**; ~**heid** mystery

geheu'e -s memory; ~**verlies'** loss of memory; amnesia

gehoor' hearing; **..hore** audience; *die ~ toespreek* address the audience; ~**appa= raat'** hearing aid; ~**buis** receiver (tel.) *ook* **hoor'stuk**

gehoor'saam (w) ~ obey, submit; (b) obedi= ent, submissive

gehuud' gehude married; **on'gehude moe'der** unmarried mother

gei'gerteller -s geiger counter

geil -er, -ste rank; rich, fertile; lush *ook* **we'lig**; ~**jan** fatcat (person)

geïllustreer' -de illustrated; pictorial

geïnteresseer' -de interested; *hy is ~ (stel belang) in musiek* he is interested in music

gei'ser -s geyser

geit'jie -s small lizard; shrew (woman)

gek (s) -ke fool, madman, guy; *vir die ~ hou* make a fool of; *die ~ skeer* poke fun at; (b) foolish, mad, queer, crazy

gekeur'; ~**de spe'ler** seeded player (sport)

gek'heid folly, foolishness, madness; *alle ~ op 'n stokkie* all joking aside

gek'ke: ~**getal'** fool's number, number ele= ven; ~**paradys'** fool's paradise

gek'ko (s) gecko *ook* **boom'geitjie**

geklets' (s) tattle, twaddle

geklik'[1] (s) clicking; *sy kantoor is ~* his office is bugged

gek'lik[2] (b) silly, foolish

geknoei' (s) messing; plotting, scheming

gekompliseer' -de complicated

gekonfyt': ~ *wees in* be well versed in

gekon'kel (s) scheming

gekruis' -te crossed; ~**te tjek** crossed cheque

gek'skeer -ge- jest, joke, fool; *hy laat nie met hom ~ nie* he is not to be trifled with

gekwalifiseer' -de qualified, certificated

gekwes' -te wounded; disabled; ~**te bok** wounded buck

gekwets' -te hurt, offended; ~**te gevoe'lens** hurt feelings

gelaat' gelate face, countenance *ook* **gesig'**; ~**s'kleur** complexion

gelag'[1] (s) laughter, laughing

gelag'[2] score, bill; *die ~ betaal* pay the piper/bill

gelang: *na ~ van* according to

gelas' (w) ~ order, instruct, command; ~ *die soektog af* call off the search

geld[1] (s) -e money, cash; ~ *soos bossies* money like dirt; ~ *wat stom is, maak reg wat krom is* money works wonders

geld[2] (w) **ge-** be in force, be valid, concern, apply to

gel'delik -e monetary, financial, pecuniary; ~**e verknor'sing** financial dilemma

geldgie'rig covetous, miserly *ook* **hebsug'tig**

gel'dig -e legal, valid, binding; *die koepons is ~ vir een maand* the coupons are valid for one month; ~**e re'des** valid/acceptable reasons

geld: ~**in'sameling** fundraising; ~**stuk** coin; ~**trom'mel** moneybox/cashbox; ~**wolf** moneygrabber, miser

gele'de ago, past; (b) articulated (vehicle) *kyk* **kop'pellorrie**; *vyftig jaar ~* fifty years ago; *tot kort ~* until recently

gele'ë situated; convenient; *ter geleëner tyd* in due course

geleent'heid ..hede opportunity; occasion; ~**spre'ker** guest speaker *ook* **gas'spreker**

geleerd' (b) learned, scholarly; trained; ~**e** scholar, learned person

geleerd'heid learning, erudition

gelei': ~**delik'** gradually; ~**er** guide; conduc= tor (material)

gelid' geledere rank, file

gelief' -de dear, beloved; ~**de** beloved one, dearest, sweetheart

gelief'koosde favourite *kyk* **gun'steling**

gelie'we please; ~ *kennis te neem van 'n vergadering* notice is hereby given of a meeting; ~ *my te laat weet* please let me know

gelof'te -s vow, solemn promise

Gelof'tedag Day of the Vow (hist.)

geloof' (s) religion, faith; credo; trust; **..lowe** belief, creed

geloofs': ~**bely'denis** credo, confession of faith; ~**brie'we** credentials, letters of cre= dence; ~**gene'ser** faith healer; ~**vry'heid** freedom of faith/worship

geloofwaar'dig -e; -er, -ste trustworthy, credible, authentic; ~**heid** credibility

gelo'wig -e; -er, -ste believing, faithful, pious; ~**e** true believer (person)

geluid' -e sound, noise

geluk' (s) -ke joy, happiness; good luck; fortune; *veels ~* hearty congratulations;

veels ~ *met u/jou verjaardag* many happy returns; ~**brin'ger** mascot *ook* **ta'lisman**
geluk'kig -e; -er, -ste happy; fortunate, lucky
geluk': ~**skoot** windfall, fluke; ~**soe'ker** ad= venturer, fortune hunter; ~**s'pakkie** lucky dip/ packet
geluk'wens (w) congratulate; ~**ing** congratu= lation(s)
gelyk' (b) **-e; -er, -ste** equal, even, similar; deuce (tennis)
gely'ke -s equal, like; peer *ook* **po'rtuur'**; ~**nis** resemblance, likeness; parable
gelyk'heid equality; similarity, evenness *ook* **pariteit'**
gelyk'maak -ge- level; raze; equalise
gelyk'op equally, fifty-fifty; ~ *speel* play to a draw/tie; ~ *verdeel* divide equally
gelykty'dig -e simultaneous, concurrent
gemaak' -te affected, forced; *so* ~ *en so laat staan* beyond redemption; ~**t'heid** affecta= tion, pretence
gemak' ease, convenience, comfort; *op sy (dooie)* ~ at ease; ~**hui'sie** toilet, loo; ~**lik** easy; convenient; comfortable
gemas'ker -de masked; ~**de bal** masked (fancy dress) ball *ook* **mas'kerbal**
gema'tig (b) **-de** moderate (person); temperate (climate)
gemeen' (b) common; mean, vulgar, *niks* ~ *hê nie* have nothing in common, **geme'ne spel** foul play; ~**plaas** (s) commonplace; plati= tude, cliche; ~**skap** community; inter= course; *in/met* ~*skap van goed'* in com= munity of property
gemeen'skap: ~**sbou** community develop= ment; ~**sen trum** community centre
gemeen'te -s (church) congregation, parish
geme'nereg/geme'ne reg common law
gemeng' -de mixed, miscellaneous
gemeubeleer'/gemeubileer' furnished
gemid'deld (b) **-e** average, mean; ~**e tempe= ratuur'** mean temperature
gem'mer ginger; ~**bier** ginger beer; ~**lim= (ona'de)** ginger ale
gemoed' -ere mind, heart; *sy* ~ *lug* vent one's feelings
gemoe'delik (b) good-natured, genial
gemoeid' concerned, at stake; *baie geld is daarmee* ~ a big sum is involved
gemors' mess, waste; hash
gems'bok -ke gazelle, roebuck (Bible); gems= buck, oryx

gena'de mercy, grace, clemency; ~**brood** bread of charity; ~**dood** euthanasia/mercy killing; ~**lap'pie** G-string *ook* **deur'= trekker**; ~**slag** deathblow, coup de grâce
gena'dig -e; -er, -ste merciful, lenient
gene'ë meer ~, **mees** ~ inclined, disposed
genees' ~ cure, heal; recover; *iem.* ~ *van cure* a person of; ~**heer** physician, doctor, family practitioner *kyk* **huis'arts**
genees'kunde medical science, medicine
geneeskun'dig -e medical; ~**e on'dersoek** medical examination; ~**e** physician
genees'middel -s remedy, medicine, drug
geneig' inclined, prone; ~ *tot die verkeer= de* prone to wrong; **on'geluks~** accident prone
ge'ner: *van nul en* ~ *waarde* null and void
generaal' (s) **-s** general; **direkteur'-~** director-= general
genera'sie -s generation *ook* **geslag'**; ~**ga'ping** generation gap
gene'ries: ~**e medisy'ne** generic medicines
gene'sing recovery, restoration to health
ge'nesis genesis, origin *ook* **wor'ding**
gene'ties -e genetic; ~**e manipule'ring** genet= ic engineering
genie' -ë genius (person)
geniep'sig -e; -er, -ste underhand; spiteful, malicious *ook* **veny'nig**
genië'ring engineering (process)
geniet' ~ enjoy, possess; *ek het die aand* ~ I enjoyed the evening
genoe'ë -ns pleasure, delight; joy; *dit doen my* ~ it gives me pleasure
genoeg' enough, sufficient *ook* **voldoen'de**
genoot' ..**genote** fellow (of a society), ~**skap** society *ook* **vere'niging**
genot' (s) enjoyment, pleasure; ~**vol** delight= ful, enjoyable
genug'tig: *my goeie* ~! good gracious
geografie' geography *ook* **aard'rykskunde**
geologie' geology *ook* **aard'kunde**
geoloog' ..**loë** geologist (person)
geometrie' geometry *ook* **meet'kunde**
gepaard' -e coupled, in pairs; ~ *gaan met* coupled with, accompanied by
gepas' (b) **-te** becoming, suitable, seemly
gepensioeneer' -de pensioned; ~**de** (s) pen= sioner *ook* **pensioena'ris/pensioen'trekker**
gepeu'pel mob, populace, rabble
geraam'te -s skeleton, carcass; framework
geraas' noise; ~**bestry'ding** noise abatement

geraffineer′ -de refined; consummate; ∼de sui′ker refined sugar

gereed′ ready, prepared; ∼skap tools, imple= ments

gere′ël -de arranged, adjusted; *alles is* ∼ everything has been arranged

gereeld′ -e; -er, -ste regular, orderly; *hy kom* ∼ *laat* he is always late

gereg′[1] -te dish, course, meal *ook* maal′tyd

gereg′[2] justice; court; *voor die* ∼ *verskyn* appear before court; ∼s′bode messenger of the court; sheriff; ∼telik′ judicial, legal

gereg′tig -de entitled, qualified; ∼ *op* entitled to; ∼heid justice

gerei′: eet∼ cutlery; hen′gel∼ fishing tackle; huis∼ household appliances; skryf∼ sta= tionery *ook* skryf′ware/skryf′goed

gerf gerwe sheaf

gerief′ ..riewe comfort, convenience; facility; loo, closet; ∼lik convenient, comfortable; commodious; ∼s′hal′we for the sake of convenience

gering′ -e; -er, -ste small, slight, trifling; *weg van die* ∼ste *weerstand* line of least resistance

gerog′gel rattling (in throat); death rattle *ook* doods′roggel

geroos′ter -de roasted, toasted; ∼de brood toast *ook* roos′terbrood

gerug′ -te rumour, report; ∼te *versprei* spread rumours

gerui′me: ′n ∼ *tyd* a considerable time

gerus′ (b) -te quiet, calm, peaceful; (bw) safely, really; *jy kan dit* ∼ *doen* you can safely do it; *kom* ∼ do come

gerus′stel (w) -ge- reassure, soothe, relieve

gesaai′de -s crop(s) *ook* gewas′

gesag′ authority, power, influence; ∼voer′der commander *ook* bevel′hebber

gesa′mentlik (b) -e total (amount); collective; united (forces); joint (owners)

gesang′ (s) -e song, hymn

gesant′ -e ambassador; minister plenipoten= tiary; envoy, emissary

gese′ën -de blessed, fortunate; ∼de Kers′fees Merry Christmas

geseg′de (s) -s saying, expression

gesel′[1] (s) -le mate, companion; ∼lin′neklub escort agency

ge′sel[2] (s) -s scourge, whip; (w) scourge, whip; flagellate

gesel′lig -e; -er, -ste sociable, homelike, cosy,

comfy; ∼heid social function/party

gesels′ ∼ chat, talk

gesel′skap -pe company; party; (artistic) group; ∼sda′me hostess

geset′ (b) -te stout, corpulent, stocky

gesien′: ′n ∼e *man* an esteemed man

gesig′ -te face, sight, view; vision; eyesight; ∼gie little face; pansy (flower)

gesig′(s): ∼bedrog′ optical illusion; ∼ein′der horizon; ∼kuur facelift *ook* ontrim′peling; ∼punt viewpoint; ∼sne′sie facial tissue

gesin′ -ne household, family *ook* huis′gesin; ∼smoord family killing

gesind′ (b) -e disposed, minded; ∼heid atti= tude, disposition, inclination

gesins′beplanning family planning

Gesins′dag Family Day (holiday)

geskei′ (b) separated, parted; divorced

geskenk′ -e present, gift; ∼bewys gift voucher

geskied′ ∼ happen, occur, take place; *U wil* ∼ Thy will be done

geskie′denis -se history

geskiedkun′dig -e historical

geskied′skrywer -s historian

geskik′ -te; -ter, -ste fit, suitable *ook* bruik′= baar; proper; capable, appropriate

geskil′ -le quarrel, difference, dispute; ′n ∼ *besleg/bylê* settle a dispute

geskool′ -de trained, schooled, skilled; ∼de ar′beiders skilled labourers

geskree(u)′ shouting, crying, shrieking; *veel* ∼ *en weinig wol* much ado about nothing

geskrif′ -te writing, document

geskut′ cannon, artillery

geslaag′: ∼de kandidaat′ successful candi= date *ook* sukses′vol

geslag′[1] (s) -te gender, sex; lineage; race; generation; species; *die skone* ∼ the fair sex; ∼siekte venereal disease

geslag′[2] (b) -te slaughtered; butchered

geslags′: ∼drang/∼drif sex drive/urge; ∼gelyk′heid gender equity; ∼orga′ne geni= tals, sexual organs; ∼regis′ter genealogical register; ∼voor′ligting sex education

geslag′telik -e sexual

gesle′pe sly, cunning *ook* skelm, slu; cute

geslo′te closed, shut; reticent; *agter* ∼ *deure* privately, in camera; ∼ gele′dere closed shop (trade unions)

gesofistikeerd′ (b) sophisticated

gesog′ -te contrived, far-fetched; in demand

gesond′ -e; -er, -ste healthy, sound; whole=

some; sane; ~e **verstand'** common sense;
~**heid** health, soundness; ~**heidsorg'** health
care; ~**heid!** cheers!; *op iem. se* ~*heid
drink* drink to someone's health
gesout' -e salted; seasoned; immune (horse)
gespan'ne tense, strained
ges'pe (s, w) -s buckle, clasp
gespesifiseer' -de specified (account)
gespik'kel/gesprik'kel -de speckled, spotted
gesprek' -ke conversation, discourse; **ver=
trek'**~ exit interview
gespuis' rabble, scum, riffraff *ook* **gepeu'pel**
gestal'te -s build; stature, figure; size
gestel' (s) body, system; (vgw) supposing,
assuming
geste'wel -de booted; ~ *en gespoor* ready,
booted and spurred
gestig' -te institution, establishment; asylum
gestrem' (b) handicapped, disabled; ~**de** (s)
disabled/handicapped person
gesuk'kel botheration; bungling
geswel' -le swelling, tumour, growth
getal' -le number; **gely'ke** ~ even number
getjank' (s) yelping, whining
getrou' (b) faithful; true, reliable, trusty
getroud' -e married; **kwartie're vir** ~**es**
married quarters
getui'e (s) -s witness; ~**nis** evidence, testi=
mony; ~**nis aflê** give evidence
getuig' ~ testify, bear witness; give evidence;
~**skrif** testimonial, reference
gety' -e tide; *as die* ~ *verloop, versit 'n mens
die bakens* one must set one's sails to the
wind; ~**poel** tidal pool
geur (s) -e fragrance; scent, odour, aroma,
essence; flavour
geu'rig (b) fragrant *ook* **welrie'kend**
geut -e gutter; sewer, drain; duct
gevaar' **geva're** danger, peril, risk; *buite* ~ out
of danger (patient); ~**lik** dangerous, peri=
lous; ~**like af'val** toxic waste; -**te** colossus,
monster
geval' (s) -le case, event, matter; *in alle* ~ in
any case; ~**lestudie** case history
gevan'gene (s) -s prisoner, captive (person)
gevan'genis -se prison, jail, gaol
gevat' -te; -ter, -ste shrewd, clever, smart,
quick; ~*te antwoord* witty reply/retort
geveg' -te fight, battle, combat; *buite* ~ *stel*
put out of action; ~**s'linie** battle zone
geveins' -de feigned, false, pretending, hypo=
critical

gevoel' (s) -ens feeling, sentiment, sense, sen=
sation, emotion
gevoe'lig -e; -er, -ste tender, sensitive; ~**e
slag** severe blow
gevolg' -e consequence, result; retinue, fol=
lowers; suite; *ten* ~*e van* as a result of *ook*
weens; *die* ~*e dra* bear the consequences;
~**lik** consequently, hence
gevolg'trekking conclusion; deduction; *oor=
haaste* ~ *maak* jump to conclusions
gevolmag'tigde -s plenipotentiary; proxy
gevor'der -de advanced; *op* ~*de leeftyd* at an
advanced age
gevreet' gnawing pain; gorging; ..**vre'te** face,
mug, phiz *ook* **bak'kies**
gewaag (b) -de risky, dangerous, bold, hazar=
dous; ~**de stap** bold decision
gewaar'merk -te hallmarked; certified; ~**te
af'skrif** certified copy
gewaar'word -ge- become aware of, perceive,
notice; ~**ing** perception, sensation
gewa'pen -de armed, prepared
gewas' (s) -se crop(s), harvest; growth, tu=
mour; **kwaadaar'dige** ~ malignant growth
geweer' -s ..**were** rifle, firearm, gun; *pre=
senteer* ~ *!* present arms!
ge'wel -s gable; ~**huis** gabled house
geweld' force, violence
geweldda'dig -e violent; ~**e dood** violent death
gewel'dig (b) -e; -er, -ste violent, severe; (bw)
dreadfully, awfully; ~ *duur* extremely ex=
pensive
geweld'pleging (public) violence
ge'wer -s giver; donor *ook* **skcn'ker**; **donateur'**
gewer'skaf (s) bustle, to-do, fuss
gewe'se late, former; ex-; ~ **ko'ning** former
king *ook* **voorma'lige ko'ning**
gewe'te -ns conscience; *sy* ~ *kwel hom* his
conscience pricks him
gewe'tens: ~**beswaar'** conscientious scruple/
objection; ~**wroe'ging** qualms of con=
science
gewig' -te weight/mass; importance, moment;
soort'like ~ specific gravity; ~**op'teller**
weightlifter *ook* **krag'opteller**
gewild' -e wished-for, popular, in demand *ook*
populêr'
gewil'lig (b) willing, ready *ook* **bereid'**
gewis' (b) -se sure, certain; ~**se dood** certain
death; (bw) certainly, surely
gewoel' (s) bustle, tumult, stir; crowd
gewon'ne won; *dit* ~ *gee* yield the point

gewoon′ common, ordinary, usual; ∼**d′** accus=
tomed, used; ∼**lik** usually, ordinarily; ∼**te**
habit, custom, practice; *ouder* ∼*te* accord=
ing to custom
gewoon′temisdadiger habitual criminal
gewrig′ **-te** joint, wrist
gewyd′ **-e** sanctified, consecrated, sacred; ∼**e**
oom′blik sacred moment
ghan′tang **-s** suitor, lover *ook* **vry′er**
ghitaar′ **-s . .tare** guitar *ook* **kitaar′**
ghoen **-e, -s** shooting (big) marble
ghoe′roe (s) mentor, (spiritual) leader, guru
ook **leer′meester**
gholf golf; ∼**baan** golf course; ∼**jog′gie** cad=
die; ∼**klub′** golf club; ∼**stok** golf club
ghong **-s** gong
ghries (s) grease; (w) lubricate, grease
gids **-e** guide; directory; ∼**aan′leg** pilot plant;
∼**hond** guide dog
gier (s) **-e** fancy, whim, caprice *ook* **gril;** *die* ∼
kry get a sudden fancy
gie′rig **-e; -er, -ste** avaricious, miserly; ∼**aard**
miser (person)
giet ge- pour; cast, found; ∼**ende reën** pouring
rain; ∼**er** watering can; ∼**ys′ter** cast iron
gif[1] poison, venom *ook* **gif′stof**
gif[2] **-te** present, gift, donation *ook* **geskenk′**
gif: ∼**stof** poison; ∼**tand** poison fang; ∼**tig**
poisonous, venomous
gig′gel ge- giggle; snigger
gig′olo (s) gigolo, toyboy
gil (s) **-le** yell, scream, shriek; (w) yell, scream
gil′de **-s** guild; fraternity
gimka′na gymkhana *ook* **rui′tersport**
gimnas′ **-te** gymnast
gimna′sium **-s** gymnasium
gimnastiek′ gymnastics; ∼**verto′ning** gym=
nastics display
ginekoloog′ . .loë gynaecologist (doctor)
gips gypsum, plaster of Paris
giraf **-fe, -s** giraffe *ook* **kameel′perd**
gis[1] (s) yeast; (w) ferment, rise
gis[2] (w) ge- guess, conjecture
gis′ter yesterday; *nie* ∼ *se kind nie* no chicken
gisteraand′ yesterday evening, last night
gistermô′re/gistermo′re/gisterog′gend   yes=
terday morning
gits! *o* ∼*!* oh dear! oh my!
git′swart jet-black
glas′oog . .oë artificial eye
glad (b) **-de; -der, -ste** smooth; slippery *ook*
gly′erig; sleek; *so* ∼ *soos seep* very

slippery; (bw) quite, altogether; even; ∼
nie not at all
glans (s) gloss, lustre; brilliancy; (w) shine,
gleam, glitter; ∼**geleent′heid** glittering/
grand occasion; ∼**kring(e)** high society;
∼**punt** highlight, crowning feature; ∼**tyd′**=
skrif glossy magazine; ∼**verf** gloss/enamel
paint
glas **-e** glass, tumbler; **geslyp′te** ∼ cut glass;
∼**bla′ser** glassblower
glas′helder clear as crystal
glasuur′ enamel (teeth); glazing (pottery)
glet′ser **-s** glacier
gleuf gleuwe groove; slot; **tyd**∼ time slot
glib′berig **-e; -er, -ste** slippery, slimy
glim′lag (s) **-te** smile; (w) ge- smile
glim: ∼**drag** safety clothing; ∼**verf** luminous
paint; ∼**wurm** glowworm, firefly
glin′ster ge- glitter, glisten, sparkle
glip ge- slip, slide; **die** ∼**pe** the slips (cricket)
glips **-e** slip, slip-up, mistake *ook* **blaps**
glip′weg . .weë slipway, filter (traffic)
glo (w) ge- believe, credit, trust; ∼ *aan spoke*
believe in ghosts; ∼ *in God* believe in God
gloed glow, heat; ardour, fervour, passion
gloei ge- glow, be red-hot; ∼**end** glowing;
scorching; ∼**lamp** (electric) bulb
glo′rie glory, lustre, fame
gly ge- glide, slide, slip; ∼**erig′** slippery;
∼**ket′ting** choke chain (dog); ∼**skaal** slid=
ing scale
g'n no; not *ook* **geen**
God God; ∼ *sy dank* thank God; *as* ∼ *wil* God
willing
god **-e** idol, god
god: ∼**dank** thank God; ∼**delik′** divine,
sublime, glorious
goddeloos′ godless, wicked, sinful
godin′ **-ne** goddess
godlo′ënaar **-s** atheist, unbeliever
gods′diens **-te** divine worship, religion, faith;
∼**on′derrig** religious instruction
godsdiens′tig (b) religious, pious; devout
godslas′terlik **-e; er, -ste** blasphemous
gods′naam: *in* ∼ for Heaven's sake
godvre′send God-fearing; pious
goed[1] (s) **-ere** goods, stuff, property, things;
getroud in gemeenskap van ∼ married in
community of property
goed[2] (b) **goeie; beter, beste** good, kind, well,
proper; *iets* ∼*s* something good
goed: ∼**aar′dig** good-natured; ∼**bedeeld′**

buxom, full-bosomed (woman); ~**doen** do good; cheer up; ~**dun'ke** opinion, discre= tion; *na* ~*dunke* at will/discretion
goe'dere: ~**loods** goods shed; ~**trein** goods train
goed: ~**gaan!** goodbye, cheerio!; ~**guns'tig** well-disposed; ~**har'tig** kind-hearted; ~**heid** kindness, goodness
goe'dig -e good-natured, kind *ook* **meegaan'de**
goed'keur -ge- approve, confirm, consent; ~**ing** approval, consent; *sy* ~*ing wegdra* meet with his approval
goed: ~**koop** (b) cheap, inexpensive; ~*koop is duurkoop* a bad bargain is dear at a farthing
goed'vind -ge- think fit, approve of
goeie: ~**middag!** good afternoon! ~**môre!/** ~**mo're!** good morning! ~**nag'!** good night!
goei'en: ~**aand!** good evening *ook* **naand'sê**; ~**dag!** good day! ~**dag sê** greet; say good day *ook* **dag'sê!**
Goeie Vry'dag Good Friday
goei'ste: *my* ~*!* dear me! ~ *weet!* goodness knows!
go'ël ge- juggle, conjure; ~**aar** juggler, magician *ook* **kul'kunstenaar**
goewerment' **-e** government *ook* **rege'ring**
goewernan'te -s governess (lady)
goewerneur' -s governor
gog'ga -s insect, vermin; bogey
goi'ingsak -ke gunny/jute bag
golf¹ (s) **golwe** bay, gulf
golf² (s) **golwe** wave, billow; (w) wave; ~**leng'te** wavelength
gom gum, glue; ~**snuif** (w) glue sniffing
gomlastiek' Indiarubber, elastic
gom'pou -e kori bustard (bird)
gom'tor -re clodhopper, uncouth person, lout *ook* **ghwar, tak'haar**
gon'del (-s) gondola
gons ge- buzz, hum, drone; ~**er** buzzer; ~**groep** buzz/discussion group; ~**woord** buzz word *ook* **mo'dewoord/refrein'woord**
gooi (w) **ge-** throw, cast, fling
goor -der, -ste dirty; nasty; rancid (food)
gord (s) band, girdle, belt; (w) gird; ~ *vas!* belt/buckle up!
gor'del -s belt, girdle; zone (geography); ~**roos** shingles
gordyn' -e curtain, blind; *die* ~ *gaan op* the curtain rises; ~**kap** pelmet
gor'rel (s) -s throat; (w) gargle, gurgle; waffle (in exam.)

gort groats, grits; barley; *die* ~ *is gaar* the fat is in the fire
gou -er, -ste quick, rapid, soon
goud gold
gou'dief ..diewe pickpocket, sneak thief *ook* **gryp'dief, sak'keroller**
goud: ~**myn** goldmine; ~**prys** gold price; ~**rif** gold reef; ~**smid** goldsmith; ~**snee** gilt edge (of book); ~**vis** goldfish
gou'e golden, gold; ~ **brui'lof** golden wed= ding; ~ **ou'es** golden oldies
gou'-gou very soon, in a moment, quickly, in a trice/jiffy *ook* **tjop-tjop**
gous'blom -me calendula; **Namak'walandse** ~ Namaqualand daisy '
graad grade degree; stage, grade: **graad 12** grade 12 (former matric); ~**kur'sus** degree course
graaf¹ (s) **grawe** spade; (w) dig, burrow *ook* **gra'we/grou**
graaf² (s) earl (England); count; ~**skap** county, shire; earldom
graag liewer, liefste [graagste] gladly, read= ily, willingly; *ek wil* ~ *weet* I would like to know
graan grane grain, corn; cereal
graan: ~**kor'rel** grain seed; ~**si'lo** grain elevator *ook* ~**sui'er**; ~**sor'ghum** (grain) sorghum; ~**sui'er** grain elevator; ~**vlok= (kie)** cornflake
graat grate fishbone
graat'jiemeerkat -te true meercat; suricat
gra'de: ~**dag** honours day; ~**pleg'tigheid** graduation ceremony
gradueer' ge- graduate (at university)
graf -te grave, tomb
grafiek' -e graph
grafiet' graphite *kyk* **pot'lood**
graf: ~**kel'der** vault; ~**skrif** epitaph; ~**steen** tombstone
grag -te canal, ditch; moat (round castle)
gram -me gram
gramadoe'las rough country, outback, bundu *ook* **boen'doe**
gramma'tika -s grammar
grammofoon' ..fone gramophone; ~**plaat** gramophone record
granaat' ..nate pomegranate (fruit); grenade, shrapnel; garnet (gem)
graniet' granite
grap -pe joke, jest; fun; ~**jas** joker, merry andrew; ~**pig** (b) funny, comic(al), amusing

gras -se grass
gra'sie grace, favour; *by die* ~ *Gods* by the grace of God
grasieus' (b) graceful, elegant *ook* **sier'lik**
gras: ~**perk** lawn; ~**sny'er** lawnmower; ~**we'duwee** grass widow
gra'tis gratis, free; ~ **mon'ster** free sample
graveer' ~, **ge-** engrave
gravin' -ne countess
greep grepe grasp, grip; hilt; byte (comp.); *'n* ~ *uit die geskiedenis* a dip into history
grein -e grain; ~**tjie** particle; *geen* ~ *nie* not an atom
grenadel'la -s grenadilla (fruit)
gren'del (s) **-s** bolt, bar; (w) bolt, bar
grens[1] (s) **-e** boundary, border, limit, frontier; *aan die* ~ on the border; ~**oor'log** frontier war
grens[2] (w) **ge-** cry; ~**ba'lie** crybaby *ook* **tjank'balie**
grens: ~(e)**loos'** boundless, infinite; ~**oor'log** frontier war; ~**voor'dele** fringe benefits *ook* **by'voordele**
gre'tig (b) **-e; -er, -ste** eager, keen; greedy
grief (s) **griewe** grievance
griep (s) influenza, flu
grie'selig -e; -er, -ste creepy, gruesome, grisly
grif'fel grif'fie -s slate pencil
griffier -s registrar, recorder (in law)
gril[1] (s) **-le** caprice, whim, freak
gril[2] (w) **ge-** shudder; ~**lig** whimsical, fanci=ful; eerie, creepy
grimeer' ~, **ge-** make up (face)
grin'nik ge- sneer, mock, grin, snigger
groef (s) **groewe** groove, flute; *in 'n* ~ *raak* get into a rut
groei (s) growth; (w) grow; ~**fonds** growth fund; ~**koers** growth rate; ~**py'ne** growing pains; ~**sel** growth, tumour
groen green; verdant; unripe
groen'te -s vegetables, greens
groen'tjie -s fresher/freshette; novice
groep (s) **-e** group; ~**dina'mika** group dy=namics; ~**verkrag'ting** gang rape
groepeer' ~, **ge-** group, form groups; assort
groet (s) **-e** salute, greeting; (w) greet, salute, shake hands, say goodbye; ~**e/**~**nis'** re=gards, greetings; *groete van huis tot huis* love to all at home
grof growwe; growwer, -ste coarse; rough; rude, gruff; ~**smid** blacksmith
grom ge- grumble, growl, grouse
grond (s) **-e** ground, soil; reason; *te* ~*e gaan*

be ruined; *op* ~ *van* by virtue of; (w) found, ground, base; ~**belas'ting** land tax; ~**bewa'ring** soil conservation; ~**boon(tjie)** peanut, monkeynut; ~**gebied'** territory
gron'dig -e; -er, -ste thorough, searching; ~*e ondersoek* thorough investigation
grond: ~**laag** bottom layer; first coat (paint); ~**leg'ging** foundation; ~**reëls** constitution (of an association/club); ~**slag** foundation, basis; ~**stof** element, raw material
grond'waardin -ne ground hostess
grond'wet (written) constitution, fundamental law (of a country) *ook* **konstitu'sie**; ~**ge'wende verga'dering** constitutional as=sembly; ~**like hof** constitutional court
groot groter, -ste great, large, big, tall; vast; grown-up, adult; *grote genugtig!* good gra=cious!; *soos 'n* ~ *speld verdwyn* disappear on the sly; ~**bek** braggart; ~**boek** ledger
Groot-Brittan'je Great Britain
groot'handel wholesale trade; ~**aar** whole=saler
groothar'tig -e; -er, -ste magnanimous
groot'heid greatness, magnitude; grandeur; quantity (maths.); *die* ~ *van Napoleon* the greatness of Napoleon; ~**(s)waan'** mega=lomania, delusions of grandeur
groot'jie -s great grandmother/father; *loop na jou* ~ go to blazes
groot: ~**liks** greatly, to a great extent; ~**maak** rear, bring up; ~**man:** *jou* ~*man hou* pretend, show off; ~**mens** adult, grown-up (person); ~**moe'der** grandmother; ~**moe'dig** magnanimous; ~**oë:** ~*oë maak* show dis=approval; ~**ouers** grandparents; ~**pad** high=road, main road; ~**praat** brag, boast
groot: ~**skaals** on a large scale; extensive; ~**skeeps** grandiose; on a large/grand scale
groot'te -s size, extent; *die* ~ *van die kamer* the size of the room
groot: ~**va'der** grandfather; ~**wild** big game
gros gross; majority; ~**lys** shortlist
grot -te cave, grotto; ~**bewo'ner** cave dwell=er/troglodyte; ~**kun'de** speleology
gro'tendeels for the greater part, chiefly
gru ge- shudder; ~**moord** gruesome murder
gruis gravel; crushed mealies
gru'wel -s horror, abomination, crime; ~**daad** crime, atrocity, outrage; ~**grot** chamber of horrors
gru'welik -e; -er, -ste horrible, gruesome *ook* **afsku'welik, afgrys'lik**

gryns (s) **-e** grin, sneer; (w) grin, sneer; ~**lag** grin, sneer

gryp ge- seize, snatch, grab, clutch; ~**dief** snatch and grab thief, bag snatcher

grys -e; -er, -ste grey; *die* ~*e verlede* hoary antiquity, dim past; ~**aard** old man, grey= beard

guerril'la -s guerrilla (war)

guilloti'ne -s guillotine *ook* **val'byl**

gul'de (b) golden; *'n* ~/*goue geleentheid* a golden opportunity

gulp -e fly (of trousers)

gul'sig -e; -er, -ste gluttonous, greedy

gun ge- grant, allow; not grudge; *ek* ~ *jou dit* you are welcome to it

guns -te favour, goodwill; *'n* ~ *bewys* do a favour; *ten* ~*te van* in favour of; ~**bus(sie)** courtesy bus; ~**loon** kickback, unofficial commission; ~**teling'** favourite: *my gunste= lingskrywer* my favourite author; ~**tig** favourable, advantageous; ~**tige lig'ging** favourable site/situation

guur -der, -ste bleak, cold, harsh; **gu're weer** inclement/rough/foul weather

gy'selaar -s hostage; *vrylating van* ~*s* release of hostages (people)

H

haai[1] (s) **-e** shark (sea fish)

haai![2] (tw) heigh! I say!

haai[3] bleak, barren; *die* ~ *Karoo* the barren Karoo

haak (s) **hake** hook, hasp, bracket; (w) hook; heel (ball); *alles in die* ~ everything OK

haaks -e right-angled, square; *hulle is altyd* ~ they are continually at loggerheads

haak'speld -e safety pin

haal (s) **hale** stroke, lash; (w) fetch, reach, catch; *die trein* ~ catch the train; ~**-en= betaal'** cash-and-carry *ook* **koop-en-loop'**, ~**baar** (b) feasible, viable, attainable

haan hane cock, rooster; *geen* ~ *sal daarna kraai nie* nobody will be the wiser

haar[1] (s) hare hair; *hare kloof* split hairs

haar[2] (vnw) her

haar[3] (b) right; *hot en* ~ left and right

haard -e hearth, fireside

haar: ~**fyn** in detail *ook* **presies'**; ~**kap'per** barber, hairdresser; ~**knip'per** (pair of) hairclippers; ~**lint** hair ribbon; ~**lok** lock of hair; ~**mid'del** hair restorer; ~**naald** hairpin

haar: ~**sny'er** hairdresser *ook* **haarkap'per**; ~**sproei** hairspray; ~**stileer'der** hair stylist

haas[1] (s) haste, hurry; *hoe meer* ~ *hoe minder spoed* more haste, less speed

haas[2] (s) hase hare; rabbit *ook* **konyn'**

haas[3] (bw) almost, nearly *ook* **am'per**; *hy is* ~ *daar* he must have nearly arrived

haas: ~**bek** gap-toothed; ~**lip** cleft lip, harelip

haas'tig (b) **-e; -er, -ste** hasty, in a hurry

haat (s) hatred; (w) hate, detest

haat'draend revengeful, resentful

haat'lik -e; -er, -ste hateful, malicious

ha'el (s) hail; shot; (w) hail; ~**geweer'** shotgun; ~**kor'rel** grain of shot; hailstone; ~**steen** hailstone; ~**verse'kering** hail insurance/ cover

hak[1] (s) **-ke** heel; hock (animal)

hak[2] (w) **ge-** cut; mince; ~ *die knoop deur* cut the (Gordian) knot

ha'ker -s hooker (rugby)

ha'kie -s bracket; little hook; *tussen* ~*s* in brackets, in parenthesis; by the way

hak'kejag hot pursuit (military)

hak'kel ge- stammer, stutter *ook* **stot'ter**, ~**aar** stammerer

hak'skeen ..skene heel

half halwe half

halfag(t) half past seven

halfe'del (b) semiprecious; ~**ste'ne** semipre= cious stones

half'eindronde -s semifinal (sport)

halfmaan' ..mane crescent; semicircle

halfne'ge/halfne'ë half past eight

half: ~**pad** halfway; ~**slyt** partly worn (clothes); ~**stok** halfmast; ~**uur** half an hour; ~**vol** half-full

half'wekliks -e bi-weekly, twice weekly

hallelu'ja -s hallelujah

hallusina'sie -s hallucination *ook* **sins'bedrog**

hals -e neck; *jou iets op die* ~ *haal* bring trouble on oneself; ~**band** collar (dog); ~**doek** neckcloth; ~**ket'ting** necklace, neck= chain; ~**mis'daad** capital crime/offence; ~**oorkop'** head over heels, hurry-scurry;

~**horlo'sie**/~**oorlo'sie** pendant watch; ~**snoer** necklace; ~**snoermoord'** necklace murder
halsstar'rig -e; -er, -ste obstinate, headstrong, stubborn *ook* **kop'pig**
hal'te -s halt; siding
hal'ter -s halter
halveer' (w) ~, **ge-** halve, divide into halves
ham -me ham
ha'mel -s wether, hamel (sheep)
ha'mer (s) -s hammer; mallet (of wood); (w) hammer; *altyd op dieselfde aambeeld* ~ keep on harping on the same string
ham'burger -s hamburger
hand -e hand; *iets aan die* ~ *gee (doen)* suggest something; *die* ~*e uit die mou steek* put the shoulder to the wheel; ~**boei'e** handcuffs; ~**boek** manual, handbook, text=book *ook* **hand'leiding**
hand: ~**doek** towel; ~**druk** handshake, handclasp
han'dearbeid manual labour
han'del (s) trade, commerce, business; ~ *dryf (drywe)* carry on a trade; ~ *en wandel* conduct in life; (w) act; deal, carry on a business; ~**aar** merchant, dealer; ~**ing** action, conduct
han'dels: ~**arti'kel** commodity; ~**balans'** bal=ance of trade; ~**bank** commercial bank; ~**belan'ge** commercial interests; ~**betrek'=king** commercial relation, trade connection
han'delsender -s commercial transmitter (broadcasting)
han'delsfirma -s trading firm *ook* **sa'keonder=neming**
han'del: ~**skip** merchantman; ~**skool** com=mercial school
han'dels: ~**kor'ting** trade discount; ~**kuns'te=naar** commercial artist; ~**merk** trademark; ~**mis'daad** white-collar crime; ~**onder=ne'ming** commercial firm; commercial un=dertaking/venture; ~**reg** mercantile/com=mercial law; ~**rei'siger** commercial travel=ler; ~**re'kene/**~**re'kenkunde** commercial arithmetic
han'del(s)wyse procedure, line of action
hande-vier'voet on all fours
hand'gekeur handpicked; ~**de personeel'** handpicked staff
hand'gemeen (s) hand-to-hand fighting; (bw): ~ *raak* come to blows
hand: ~**granaat'** handgrenade; ~**haaf** main=tain, uphold; *standaarde* ~*haaf* maintain

standards
han'dig useful; skilful *ook* **knap** (mens)
hand: ~**ky'kery** palmistry; ~**lan'ger** helper, handyman; ~**lei'ding** textbook, manual (of instruction); ~**perd** led-horse; mistress; ~**pop** puppet; ~**rug** backhand (tennis); ~**skoen** glove: *met die* ~*skoen trou* marry by proxy; ~**skrif** handwriting; manuscript
hand: ~**tas** handbag; ~**te'kening** signature *ook* **naam'tekening;** ~**ves** charter; ~**wa'=pen** handgun; ~**werks'man** artisan, work=man; ~**woor'deboek** concise dictionary
ha'ne: ~**geveg'** cockfight; ~**spoor** cock's spur; ~**tree'tjie** short distance, stone's throw
hang (s) -e slope (of mountain); (w) hang, suspend
han'gar -s hangar *ook* **vlieg'tuigloods**
hang'brug ..**brûe** suspension bridge
hang: ~**kas** wardrobe; ~**mat** hammock; ~**slot** padlock; ~**sweef** hanggliding *kyk* **vlerk'=sweef;** ~**verband'** sling (broken arm)
hans orphan; ~ *grootmaak* bottle rearing; ~**lam** pet lamb, orphan lamb
hans'wors -te clown *ook* **nar**
hanteer' ~, **ge-** handle, manage, cope (with)
hap (s) -**pe** bite, piece; (w) bite, snap
haraki'ri harakiri; happy despatch (suicide)
hard hard; loud; stern; ~**e koeja'wel** tough customer (person) *ook* **har'dekwas**
har'der -s Cape herring; mullet
har'deskyf: ~**aan'drywer** hard drive (comp.)
har'deware hardware goods *ook* **ys'terware;** hardware (comp.)
hardhan'dig (b) rough, rude, hardhanded
hardho'rig/hardho'rend hard of hearing, deaf
hardkop'pig -e; -er, -ste obstinate, stubborn *ook* **hardnek'kig**
hard'loop ge- run, hurry, make haste
hardly'wig -e constipated, costive
hard'op aloud, in a clear voice; ~ *lees* read aloud
hardvog'tig callous, cruel, heartless
hardwer'kend -e hardworking, industrious
ha'rem -s harem, seraglio
ha'ring -s herring; **gerook'te** ~ kippered her=ring
hark (s) -e rake; (w) rake
harlekyn' -e harlequin, clown *ook* **hans'wors**
harmonie' -**ë** harmony; unison
harmo'nika -s harmonica, concertina
har'nas -se armour, cuirass; *iem. in die* ~ *ja(ag)* antagonise someone

harp -e harp
harpoen' -e harpoon
harpuis' resin, rosin (from fir trees)
hars resin, rosin ook **harpuis'**
har'sing: ~s cerebrum, brains; ~**skande'ring** brainscan; ~**skud'ding** concussion of the brain; ~**vliesontste'king** meningitis
hart -e heart, mind; core; courage; ~**aan'val** heart attack
har'te: ~**(ns)aas** ace of hearts; ~**(ns)boer** knave/jack of hearts
hart(e)'bees -te hartebees (antelope); ~**huis= (ie)** wattle-and-daub hut
har'te: ~**lus** heart's desire; *na* ~*lus* to one's heart's content
har'tens hearts (cards) ook **har'te**
har'tewens fondest wish
hart: ~**jie** little heart; darling; *in die* ~*tjie van die winter* in midwinter; ~**klop'pings** pal= pitations; ~**lam** darling, dearest ook **lief= ling, skat'(tie)**
hart'lik -e; -er, -ste hearty, sincere, cordial; ~*e groete* sincere greetings to all (at home)
hart: ~**om'leiding** heart/cardiac bypass; ~**oor'planting** heart transplant; ~**pas'= aangoër** heart pacemaker; ~**roe'rend** touching, pathetic; ~**'seer** (s) grief, sorrow; (b) heartsore, sad; ~**sken'ker** heart donor
harts'tog (s) **-te** passion ook **pas'sie, drif**
hartversa'king cardiac/heart failure
hartverskeu'rend -e heartrending
ha'sepad: *die* ~ *kies* take to one's heels
ha'we[1] goods, property, stock; *le'wende* ~ livestock
ha'we[2] -ns port, harbour; ~**hoof** pier, jetty
ha'wer oats; ~**mout** oatmeal
hê had, gehad have, possess
hè! oh! my!; not so! *jy kom bedel weer,* ~*!* you are begging again, you ..!
hcb'sug covetousness, greed, greediness
he'de[1] (s) the present, this day; *die* ~ *en die verlede* the present and the past; (bw) today, at present
he'de![2] (tw) *o* ~*!* oh my! oh goodness!
he'dendaags -e modern, presentday, nowa= days; trendy ook **bydertyds'**
heel[1] (w) **ge-** heal, cure
heel[2] (w) **ge-** receive (stolen property); *die heler is so goed as die steler* the receiver (of stolen goods) is as bad as the thief
heel[3] (b) **hele; heler, -ste** whole, entire
heel[4] (bw) very, quite; ~ *in die begin* at the

very outset; ~ *eenvoudig* quite simple; ~ *waarskynlik* most probably
heelal' universe
heel: ~**dag** the whole day; ~**huids** unscathed; *daar* ~*huids/ongedeerd van afkom* get off unscathed/unharmed
heel'temal quite, altogether, entirely, severely; ~ *alleen* all alone
heel'tyds fulltime ook **vol'tyds**
heel'wat quite a lot, a good deal
heen away, thither, thence; ~ *en weer* to and fro
heen: ~**gaan** go away, depart; die; ~**ko'me** refuge, escape; *êrens 'n* ~*kome vind* find a refuge somewhere
Heer[1] the Lord, God
heer[2] here gentleman; lord, master; *die* ~ *des huises* master of the house; *Geagte Heer/ heer* Dear Sir
heer'lik (b) glorious, delightful, delicious
heers ge- reign, govern, rule; prevail; ~**ende pry'se** ruling prices; ~**er** ruler
heerskappy' -e power, reign, authority
heerssug'tig imperious, despotic
hees (b) **heser, -ste** hoarse, husky
heet[1] (w) **ge-** be called; name; *hy* ~ *na sy pa* he is called after his father; *hy* ~ *hom welkom* he welcomes him
heet[2] (b) **hete; heter, -ste** hot, burning; ~**hoof** hothead (person) ook **ekstremis'**
hef[1] (s) **-te, hewwe** handle; *die* ~ *in hande hê* control a situation
hef[2] (w) **ge-** raise, lift; levy, impose; *belastings* ~ impose/levy taxes
hef'boom ..bome lever
hef'fing -s, -e levy; surtax
hef'tig violent, vehement ook **opvlie'ënd**
heg (w) **ge-** fasten, attach; *geen waarde* ~ *nie aan* attach no value to
heg: ~**pleis'ter** sticking plaster; ~**tenis'** cus= tody; detention; *in* ~*tenis neem* arrest/detain (a person)
hei'den -e, -s heathen, pagan ook **ongelo'wige**
heil welfare, good, bliss, prosperity; *alle* ~ *en seën!* best wishes!
Hei'land Saviour
heil'dronk -e toast; *die* ~ *instel* propose the toast
hei'lig (w) **ge-** sanctify, consecrate, hallow; (b) holy, sacred; ~**dom** sanctuary, holy shrine
hei'lige -s saint (person)
hei'lig: ~**sken'nis** blasphemy, sacrilege; ~**ver= kla'ring** canonisation

Heils'leër Salvation Army
heil'wens -e good wish(es) *ook* **seënwens(e)**
heim'wee (s) homesickness, longing
hei'ning -s fence, hedge, enclosure
hek -ke gate; railing; hurdle; turnpike
he'kel[1] (s) dislike, aversion; *'n ~ aan iem. hê*
    dislike someone intensely
he'kel[2] (w) ge- heckle; crochet; satirise;
    ~**dig'ter** satirist; ~**werk** crochet work
hek'geld gate money; admission
hek'kiesloop (s) ..**lope** hurdle race
heks -e witch, hag, vixen
hek'sluiter -s lastcomer; youngest child *ook*
    laat'lammetjie
hek'stormer -s gatecrasher *ook* **in'dringer**
hektaar' ..**tare** hectare
hek'to: ~**gram** hectogram; ~**li'ter** hectolitre;
    ~**meter** hectometre
hek'wagter -s gatekeeper
hel[1] (s) hell; inferno
hel[2] (w) ge- lean, slant, slope; incline
helaas'! alas! alack
held -e hero
hel'de: ~**ak'ker** heroes' acre; ~**daad** heroic
    deed; ~**dig** heroic poem; ~**dood** hero's
    death; ~**moed** heroic courage/heroism;
    ~**ontvangs'** hero's welcome
hel'der clear, bright, serene; (b) sonorous; *so
    ~ soos kristal* as clear as crystal; ~**sien'de**
    (b) clear-sighted; clairvoyant
heldhaf'tig -e; -er, -ste heroic, brave
he'ler[1] -s receiver (of stolen property)
he'ler[2] -s healer *ook* **heel'meester**
helf'te -s half; *die ~ minder* less by half
helikop'ter -s helicopter/chopper; ~**blad**
    heliport, helipad
hel'levaart descent into hell
hel'leveeg ..**veë** hellcat, termagant, shrew *ook*
    hel'pen (vrou)
hel'ling -s, -e slope, incline, declivity; gradient
    (of a road)
helm -s caul; helmet; *met die ~ gebore* born
    with a caul *kyk* **val'helm**
hel'met -s helmet (against sun)
help ge- help, assist, aid; *alle bietjies ~ many
    a mickle makes a muckle*; ~**er** helper;
    ~**-my-krap'winkel** junk shop
hels -e hellish, devilish, infernal; *'n ~e lawaai*
    a hell of a noise
he'mel (s) -e heaven, sky; ~**bed** fourposter;
    ~**lig'gaam** heavenly/celestial body; ~**poort**
    pearly gate; ~**ruim** sky; outer space

he'mels (b) -e heavenly, celestial; *in ~naam/
    om ~wil* for heaven's/goodness' sake
He'melvaart Ascension; ~**dag** Ascension Day
    (previously a holiday)
hemp hemde shirt; *die ~ is nader as die rok*
    charity begins at home
hen -ne hen; ~-**en-kui'kens** nest of tables
hends'op put up one's hands; surrender
hen'gel (w) angle, fish; ~**aar** angler; ~**gerei'**
    fishing tackle; ~**stok** fishing rod
hen'nep hemp
her: ~ *en derwaarts* hither and thither
heraldiek' heraldry *ook* **wa'penkunde**
her'berg (s) -e inn, hotel, tavern; (w) shelter,
    lodge, accommodate *ook* **huis'ves**
herbergier' -s innkeeper, host
herbo're (b) reborn, born again; regenerate
herdenk' ~ commemorate, remember; ~**ing**
    commemoration, remembrance
her'der -s shepherd, herd; clergyman; ~**staf**
    shepherd's crook; (bishop's) crosier
her'druk (s) -ke reprint; new edition; (w) ~
    reprint
He're the Lord, God, the Almighty
he'rehuis -e mansion, manor house
her'eksamen -s re-examination
here'nig ~ reunite
he'reregte transfer duty/dues
herfs -te autumn; ~**nage'wening** autumn equi=
    nox; ~**tint** autumnal tint *ook* **herfs'kleur**
herhaal' ~ repeat, recapitulate; ~**delik** re=
    peatedly, over and over
herha'ling -s, -e repetition; recurrence
herin'ner ~ remember, remind; ~ *aan* remind
    of; ~**ing** memory; remembrance, recollec=
    tion; *ter ~ing aan* in memory of
herken' (w) recognise; identify
herkies' ~ re-elect; ~**baar** eligible for
    re-election; *hy is en stel hom ~baar* being
    eligible he offers himself for re-election
her'koms (s) origin, descent; derivation
herkou' ~ chew the cud, ruminate; repeat; *'n
    saak ~* ponder over a matter
herlaai'baar (b) rechargeable
herlei' ~ reduce; convert; simplify
hermelyn' ermine, miniver (fur)
herneu'termes -se big hunting knife, bowie=
    knife
hernieu'/hernu'we/hernu' ~ renew (a sub=
    scription); renovate
hernu'wing renewal, renovation; ~**ken'nisge=
    wing** -s renewal notice

hero'ïes -e heroic; ~e stryd heroic struggle
her'oorweeg (w) ~ reconsider
her'open (w) ~ reopen
herout' -e herald ook bood'skapper
her'rie confusion, noise, rumpus, row; *iem. op sy ~ gee* thrash someone
herroep' ~ revoke, repeal, rescind, annul, recall, retract; *die ordonnansie is ~ the ordinance has been repealed*
her'senskim -me figment of the imagination; phantasm, chimera; hallucination
hersien' ~ revise, update; reconsider; ~ing revision, review
hersikleer' (w) ~ recycle ook herwin'
herskep ~, herskape re-create, regenerate, transform
her'soneer ~ rezone (a suburb)
herstel' (s) reparation; repair; redress; recov= ery; (w) rectify; restore; repair, mend; ~oord convalescent home; hospice ook hos'pies; ~verlof convalescent leave
hert -e stag, deer
her'tog hertoë duke
hertogin' -ne duchess
her'vestig resettle; ~ing resettlement
hervorm ~ reform, reshape; die H~de Kerk the Reformed Church; ~ing reformation; reform
hervul'ling refill (for pen)
herwin' ~ regain, recover, recycle; *sy bewus= syn ~ recover his consciousness*; ~ning recovery, recycling (glass, paper)
heterdaad'/heter daad: *(op) ~ betrap* catch redhanded
hetsy' either; whether; *~ warm of koud* either hot or cold
heug (s): ~like/gedenkwaar'dige dag memo= rable day
heu'ning honey; *~ om die mond smeer* softsoap a person
heup (s) -e hip; ~fles hipflask
heu'wel -s hill; mound
he'wel (s) -s siphon; (w) siphon; *petrol uit die tenk ~* siphon petrol out of the tank
he'wig -e; -er, -ste severe, violent, fierce, vehement; *~ ontstel* violently upset
hiasint' -e hyacinth ook na'eltjie (blom)
hiberneer' ~, ge- hibernate ook oorwin'ter
hidrou'lies -e hydraulic
hiel -e heel; bead(s) (of tyre); ~kus'sing heelpad
hië'na -s hyena

hiep-hiep-hoera'! hip, hip hurrah!
hier here; *~ te lande* in this country
hiërargie' hierarchy ook gesags'lyn
hier: ~bene'wens besides this, in addition to; ~by herewith; enclosed, included; ~die this, these; ~deur through this (means), by this; ~heen this way, to this side; ~in in this, herein
hier'jy! (s) lout; (tw) hallo! I say!
hier: ~mee with this, herewith; ~na after this, hereafter
hierna'maals (s) (the) hereafter, in the beyond
hier'natoe this way
hiëroglief' ..gliewe hieroglyph ook beeld'skrif
hier: ~oor about this, over this; ~so here, at this place; *kom ~so!* come here; ~teen against this; ~teenoor' opposite; against this; ~uit from this, out of this, hence; ~van herefrom, of this, about this; ~van= daan' from here; ~voor for this, in return (for this)
hiet ge- order; *iem. ~ en gebied* order someone about, push him around
higië'nies (h) -e hygienic
hik (s) -ke hiccup; (w) hiccup
him'ne -s hymn ook lof'sang
hin'der (s) trouble, impediment, obstacle; (w) hinder, annoy, hamper; ~laag ambush; ~lik annoying, troublesome; inconvenient; ~nis obstacle, obstruction; impediment; ~nis= wed'loop obstacle race
hings -te stallion, stud horse
hing'sel -s handle, hinge
hink ge- limp; halt, vacillate; *op twee gedagtes ~* halt between two opinions
hiperbool' ..bole hyperbole, exaggeration; hyperbola (geom.)
hi'perintelligent hyperintelligent
hi'permark -te hypermarket
hiperten'sie hypertension, high blood pressure ook hoë bloed'druk
hipno'se hypnosis
hipokon'ders/ipekon'ders (s) whims, caprices; imaginary ailments; *hy is 'n regte hipokon= der/ipekonder* he is a real hypochondriac
hip'pie -s hippie
histerektomie' hysterectomy, removal of womb ook baar'moederverwydering
histe'ries -e hysterical
histo'ries -e historic(al) ook geskiedkun'dig
histo'rikus ..rici, -se historian (person)
hit'te heat; *in die ~ van die stryd* in the heat of

battle; *op* ~ on heat (animal); ~**golf** heatwave; ~**steek** heatstroke

hit'tete: *so* ~*!* nearly, touch and go

hit'te-uitputting heat exhaustion

hob'bel ge- rock, go seesaw; (s) hump (speed= breaker); ~**perd** rocking horse

ho'bo -'s oboe (mus. instrument)

hoe how; what;· ~ *eerder* ~ *beter* the sooner the better

hoed[1] (s) **-e** hat, bonnet

hoed[2] (w) **ge-** guard, protect, tend

hoeda'nig -e how, what kind of; ~**heid** quality, capacity; *in die* ~*heid van* in the capacity of

hoe'de guard, care, protection; *op jou* ~ *wees* be on the alert/your guard

hoëdigt'heidsbehuising high-density housing

hoef[1] (s) **hoewe** hoof

hoef[2] (w) need; *jy* ~ *nie te kom nie* you need not come; *jy* ~ *nie te gekom het nie* you need not have come

hoef: ~**smid** farrier; ~**ys'ter** horseshoe

hoe'genaamd: ~ *niks* nothing whatever; ~ *geen voorraad nie* no stocks at all

hoek -e corner, angle; hook

hoe'ka: *van* ~ *se tyd af* from time immemorial *ook* **toe'ka**

hoe'kie -s little corner, nook; bar (shop); *uit alle* ~*s en gaatjies,* from every nook and corner

hoe'kig -e angular, rugged

ho'ëklas: ~ **buurt/voor'stad** upmarket suburb

hoe'kom why, for what reason, wherefore *ook* **waar'om**

hoek'steen **..stene** corner/foundation stone; ~**leg'ging** laying of the foundation/corner stone

hoe lank how long, till when

hoen'der -s fowl; chicken; *die* ~*s in wees* be furious; *mal Jan onder die* ~*s* a thorn among the roses; ~**kop** drunk, tipsy; ~**vel** gooseflesh: *ek kry* ~*vel daarvan* it gives me gooseflesh; ~**vleis** chicken; gooseflesh/pimples

hoe'pel -s hoop; ~**been** bandyleg

ho'ëpriester -s high priest

ho'ër higher; ~**hof** high court; ~ **on'derwys** higher/tertiary education; ~ **seun'skool/mei'=sieskool** boys'/girls' high school

hoer -e prostitute, whore, hooker *ook* **prosti=tuut'/seks'werker**

hoera'!/hoerê! hurrah!

ho'ërskool **..skole/hoër skool hoër skole** high/secondary school *ook* **sekondê're skool**

ho'ërskoolleerling -e high school pupil

hoes (s) cough; (w) **ge-** cough; ~**mid'del** cough remedy; ~**tablet'** cough lozenge

ho'ëskool **..skole** university, academy

ho'ëtrou high fidelity; ~**stel** hi-fi set

hoeveel' how much/many; ~**heid** quantity

hoe'veelste: *die* ~ *van die maand?* what day of the month? what is the date?

Ho'ëveld Highveld

hoever'/hoevêr'/hoever're: *in* ~ to what extent, (as to) how far

hoë'vlak (b): ~**sa'mesprekings** high-level talks

hoe'we -s smallholding *ook* **klein'hoewe**; plot

hoewel' though, although

hof' howe court; garden; *'n meisie die* ~ *maak* court a girl; **appèl**~ appeal court; ~**lewe=ransier'** purveyor (by royal appointment)

hof'lik -e; -er, -ste courteous, obliging, polite; ~**heidsbesoek'** courtesy visit

hof: ~**nar** court fool, jester; ~**saak** court case, lawsuit *ook* **regs'geding**

hok (s) **-ke** pen (fowl); sty (pig); hutch (rabbit); cage (bird); (w) enclose, shut in; gate (scholars); *die meisies is ge*~ the girls have been gated

hok'kie[1] hockey (game)

hok'kie[2] **-s** small shed, cubicle; pigeonhole

hol'[1] (s) **-e** cave, den; anus, arse (*vulgar*); (b) hollow, empty

hol[2] (s): *iem. op* ~ *jaag* distract/confuse some=one; (w) run, rush, bolt

holderstebol'der topsy-turvy, head over heals

Hol'land Holland, the Netherlands

Hol'lands (b) Dutch *ook* **Ne'derlands**

hom (vnw) him, it

hom(e)opaat' **..pate** hom(o)eopath

hom(e)opa'ties -e hom(o)eopathic

ho'mo (s, b) homosexual, gay

homogeen' (b) **..gene** homogeneous, of the same kind/level

homoniem' (s) **-e** homonym; (b) **-e** homo=nymous

homoseksueel' (s, b) homosexual; gay

hond -e dog, hound

hon'de: ~**berg** kennel; ~**hotel'** kennel *ook* **woe'fietuiste**; ~**le'we** wretched life

hon'derd -e hundred; ~**ja'rig** centennial, centenary; ~**ste** hundredth; ~**tal** a hundred; century (cricket)

hon'djie -s pup(py); *nie so erg vir die ~ as die halsbandjie nie* not as disinterested as it would appear .

honds -e brutal, churlish, cynic; **~dol'heid** rabies; hydrophobia (humans)

hon'ger (s) hunger; **~ ly** starve; *sy ~ stil* appease one's hunger; (w) hunger; (b) hungry; **~s'nood** famine, dearth; **~sta'= king** hunger strike *ook* **eet'staking**

honneurs' honours; **~graad** honours degree

honora'rium . .ria, -s honorarium, fee, royalty

honoreer' (w) **ge-** honour (a bill)

hoof -de head; chief, leader; principal (school); *die ~ van die gesin/die ~ des huises* the head of the family; *iets oor die ~ sien* overlook something; **~arti'kel** leader, editorial; **~be= stuur'** top management *ook* **top'bestuur;** **~bestuur'der** general manager; **~bestuurs'= leier** chief executive; **~bre'kens/~bre'kings** brainracking; **~doel** main object

hoof: **~kantoor'** head office; **~kwartier'** head= quarters; **~let'ter** capital letter; **~onder= wy'ser** headmaster, principal; **~pyn** head= ache; **~raamre'kenaar** mainframe computer; **~redakteur'** editor in chief; **~reg'ter** chief justice; **~re'kene/~re'kenkunde** mental ar= ithmetic; **~rol** leading role/part

hoof'saak main point, gist

hoofsaak'lik chiefly, mainly, principally

hoof: **~sekreta'ris** general secretary; **~sin** principal sentence/clause; **~stad** capital, metropolis; **~stuk** chapter; **~vak** main/ major subject

hoog hoë, hoër, -ste high, tall, lofty; *dit is ~ nodig* it is absolutely necessary; **~ag** (w) esteem highly, respect; **~agtend** *die uwe* yours faithfully; **hoë bloeddruk** high blood= pressure, hypertension

hoogdra'wend -e; -er, -ste bombastic, pom= pous, stilted, highflown

hooge'dele right honourable

hoogeerwaar'de right reverend

hooggeplaas'te (s) dignitary (person)

hoog'geregshof . .howe supreme court

hooghar'tig proud, haughty

hoog: **~land** highland, plateau; **~le'raar** professor *ook* **profes'sor**

Hoog'lied Song of Solomon, Canticles

hoogmoe'dig -e; -er, -ste proud, haughty

hoog: **~no'dig** most necessary, urgently needed; **~oond** blast furnace *ook* **smelt'= oond;** **~seisoen'** high season; **~span'ning**

high tension; **~ste** highest, senior; **~stens** at most, at best

hoogs' waarskynlik most probably

hoog'te -s height, altitude; hill; *op die ~ hou* keep posted; **~punt** highlight *ook* **glans'= punt;** zenith; pinnacle; **~vrees** acrophobia, fear of heights

hoog'ty: *~ vier* reign supreme

hoog: **~verraad'** high treason; **~waar'dig= heidsbekleër** dignitary, VIP *ook* **hoogge= plaas'te**

hooi hay; *te veel ~ op sy vurk* too many irons in the fire; **~koors** hay fever

hool hole hovel, den, unsavoury dwelling

hoop¹ (s) **verwagtings** hope; *~ koester* cherish hope

hoop² (s) **hope** heap; crowd

hoop'vol -le; -ler, -ste hopeful, confident

hoor (s): *'n lawaai dat ~ en sien vergaan* a deafening noise; (w) hear, listen, heed, learn; *horende doof wees* wilfully deaf; **~apparaat'** hearing aid; **~baar** audible; **~beeld** feature programme (radio)

hoor'spel . .ele radio play/drama

hoor'stuk -ke receiver (tel.) *ook* **hand'stuk**

hoort ge- belong, be proper, ought; *dit ~ nie so nie* it is not done

hop (w) bounce (ball, cheque) *ook* **bons**

ho'peloos hopeless; desperate

ho'ring -s horn; *die huis op ~s neem* create an uproar; **~oud** very old

ho'rinkie -s little horn; (icecream) cone

ho'rison -ne, -te horizon, skyline

horisontaal' . .tale horizontal, level; **. .ta'le kommunika'sie** horizontal communication

horlo'sie -s/oorlo'sie watch; clock *ook* **uur'= werk**

hormoon' (s) hormone

hor'relvoet -e clubfoot *ook* **klomp'voet**

hor'ries (s) delirium tremens (have the jumps)

hor'tjie -s wire blind, shutter; **~blin'der/ ~blin'ding** (Venetian) blind

hos'pies (s) hospice; convalescent home *ook* **herstel'oord**

hospitaal' . .tale hospital

hostel' -le (mine) hostel

hot left (team of animals); *~ en haar stuur* send from pillar to post; *dit ~agter kry* have a difficult time

hotel' -le, -s hotel; **~hou'er/~ier'** hotelkeeper; **~jog'gie** pageboy

hot'klou southpaw (lefthander)

hou¹ (s) **-e** blow, cut, stroke, lash; (w) cut, hack; strike

hou² (w) **ge-** keep, hold; contain; *links* ~ keep left; ~ *van* like; ~**ding** bearing, attitude, deportment; *'n* ~*ding aanneem* strike a pose; ~**er** container; ~**er'diens** container service *ook* **behou'ering**; ~**er'skip** container vessel

hout -e wood, timber; ~**han'delaar** timber merchant

hou'tjie -s bit of wood; *iets op eie* ~ *doen* do something off one's own bat

houts'kool charcoal

hout'snee . .**sneë** woodcut; ~**kuns/hout'sny= kuns** art of wood engraving

hu ge- marry, wed; ~**baar** marriageable

huid -e hide, skin

hui'dige present, current; modern; ~ *le'wens= duurte* present cost of living

hui'gel ge- pretend, feign, sham; ~**aar** hypo= crite

huigelary' hypocrisy/duplicity *ook* **skynhei'= ligheid**

huil ge- cry; weep; howl

huis -e house, dwelling, household; *die* ~ *op horings neem* turn the house upside down; *elke* ~ *het sy kruis* there is a skeleton in every cupboard; ~ *toe* home(wards); ~**arts** family practitioner; ~**braak'** housebreak= ing, burglary; ~**bre'ker** burglar; ~**dier** domestic animal; ~**dok'ter** family doctor *ook* **huis'arts**; ~**genoot'** house mate; inmate (of the same house); ~**gesin'** family, house= hold

huishou'delik -e economical, domestic; ~**e aan'geleentheid** domestic/internal affair

huis: ~**hou'ding** household, housekeeping; ~**houdkun'de** domestic science, home eco= nomics; ~**hulp** domestic/domestic servant; ~**huur** house rent; ~**in'wyding** house= warming

huis'lik -e; -er, -ste domestic, homely; ~**e plig'te** household duties/chores

huis'ves ge- house, lodge, board; ~**ting** accommodation *ook* **verblyf'**; ~**ting verskaf** provide boarding/accommodation

huis: ~**vlyt** home craft industry; ~**vrou** housewife; ~**werk** homework *ook* **tuis'werk**

hui'wer ge- shiver, tremble *kyk* **aar'sel**

hul (pers. vnw) they, them; (besit. vnw) their *ook* **hul'le**

hul'de homage, tribute; ~ *betuig/bring aan* pay homage to; ~**blyk** mark of respect

hul'le they; their, them; *Jan-*~ John and his party

hulp help, aid, support; assistant; ~ *verleen* render assistance; ~**bron** resource

hul'peloos helpless *ook* **mag'teloos**

hulp: ~**mid'del** aid, means; makeshift, ex= pedient; ~**troe'pe** auxiliary troops

hulpvaar'dig (b) helpful, obliging

hulp'werkwoord -e auxiliary verb

humeur' -e temper, mood; *jou* ~ *verloor* lose one's temper

hu'mor humour: ~**sin** sense of humour

humoris'ties (b) humorous *ook* **grap'pig**

hun'ker ge- long for, hanker for

hup'pel ge- skip, hop; gambol; ~**tuig** jolly jumper

hup'stootjie -s a helping push/shove

hur'ke haunches; *op sy* ~ *sit* squat

hus'se: *dis* ~ *met lang ore* curiosity killed the cat

hut -te hut, cabin, cottage; shanty, shack

huur (s) **hure** rent, hire, lease, tenancy; *die* ~ *opsê* give notice; (w) hire, rent, charter; *te* ~ to let; ~**der** tenant, lessee; ~**geld** rental, rent; ~**koop** hire purchase; ~**moor'denaar** hitman, assassin; ~**mo'tor** hired car, rent= a-car; ~**pag** leasehold; ~**soldaat'** mercen= ary; ~**tol** royalty *ook* **vrug'reg**; ~**vlug** chartered flight

hu'welik -e marriage, wedding, wedlock; *in die* ~ *tree* enter into matrimony

hu'weliks: *in die* ~*bootjie stap* get married; ~**bera'der** marriage counsellor

hu'weliks: ~**gebooie** banns; ~**onthaal'** wed= ding reception; ~**reis** honeymoon (trip); ~**voor'waarde(s)** antenuptial contract

hy he; it; ~ *self/hyself* he himself

hyg ge- pant, gasp for breath; ~**roman'** erotic fiction

hys ge- hoist; ~**bak** skip, lift; elevator; ~**er** lift, elevator; ~**kraan** crane; ~**vurk** front= loader

I

ideaal' ideale ideal
idealis' idealist (person); ~**me** idealism; *ook*
  doel'wit, stre'we; ~**ties** idealistic
idee' ideë, -s idea, notion, concept
iden'ties -e identical *ook* **e'ners**
identifiseer' ~, **geïd-** identify; *die probleme* ~
  identify the problems
identiteit' identity; ~**s'dokument'** identity
  document
idil'le -s idyll
idioma'ties -e idiomatic
idioom' idiome idiom *ook* **segs'wyse**
idioot' idiote idiot, imbecile *ook* **swaksin'nige**
ie'der -e each, every one, every; ~**een** every=
  body, everyone *ook* **elk'een**
ie'mand someone, somebody
iesegrim'mig surly, grumpy *ook* **knor'rig**
ietermago'/ietermagô'/ietermagog' pangolin,
  scaly anteater
iets something, anything; ~ *moois* something
  beautiful
ie'wers somewhere *ook* **ê'rens**
ignoreer' ~, **geïg-** ignore *ook* **verontag'saam**
illustra'sie -s illustration
imbesiel' -e imbecile *ook* **idioot'** (mens)
im'mer every, always; ~**groen** evergreen
im'mers yet, but, indeed; *hy behoort ~ beter*
  te weet he should have known better
immigrant' -e immigrant (person)
immigra'sie immigration
immoraliteit' immorality
immoreel' ..rele immoral
immuun' immune immune
imperialis' -te imperialist (person)
im'pie -s impi
implement' -e (s) (farm) machinery, tools *ook*
  plaas'gereedskap
implementeer' ~, **geïm-** (w) implement *ook*
  toe'pas, uit'voer
improviseer', geïm- improvise
impuls' -e impulse *ook* **stu'krag**
impulsief' ..siewe impulsive; impetuous
in¹ (w) **geïn** gather, collect; *belastings* ~
  collect taxes
in² (vs) in, into, within, during; ~ *stukke sny*
  cut to pieces
in ag neem in ag ge- consider, take account of
in'asem -ge- inhale, breathe in
in'begrepe included; *alles* ~ everything in=

  cluded, all told *ook* **altesa'me**
in'begrip inclusion; *met* ~ *van* including
in'bel: ~**program'** phone-in program(me)
in'boet -ge- plant in between; lose; *die lewe* ~
  pay with one's life
in'boorling -e native, aborigine
in'bors character, nature *ook* **aard/karak'ter**
in'bou -ge- build in; **in'geboude kas'te** built-in
  wardrobes
in'braak inbrake housebreaking, break-in;
  burglary *ook* **huis'braak**
in'breek -ge- break into, burgle
in'breker -s housebreaker, burglar
in'breuk infringement, transgression; ~ *maak*
  op encroach upon
in'deel -ge- divide, classify
in'deks -e index
in'deling -s -e division, classification
indemniteit' indemnity *ook* **vry'waring**
inderdaad' indeed, really, in fact
indertyd' at the time, formerly *ook* **des'tyds**
Indiaan' Indiane Indian (person, America)
in'dien¹ (w) **-ge-** hand in, lodge, tender, pre=
  sent, submit; *'n klag* ~ lay a complaint
indien'² (vgw) if, in case; *hy sal kom* ~ *dit nie*
  reën nie he will come if it isn't raining
indiens'-: ~**ne'mer** employer; ~**ne'ming** em=
  ployment; ~**op'leiding** inservice/incom=
  pany training; ~**pla'sing** job placement
In'diër -s Indian (person)
In'dies -e Indian; ~**-e rys** Indian rice
in'ding: *die* ~ the inthing, trendy thing (to do)
in'direk -te indirect *ook* **on'regstreeks**
individu'/indiwidu' individual (person)
individualis' -te individualist; ~**me** individu=
  alism; ~**ties** individualistic
indoe'na -s induna, tribal councillor
indoktrineer' (w) indoctrinate; brainwash
in'dring -ge- penetrate, intrude, force in; ~**er**
  intruder; gatecrasher
in'druk (s) **-ke** impression; *die* ~ *wek* create
  the impression
indrukwek'kend impressive *ook* **tref'fend**
industrieel' (b) **..riële** industrial
ineens' at once, suddenly *ook* **skie'lik**
ineen'stort -gestort fall in, collapse *ook*
  in'stort
in'ent ingeënt inoculate, vaccinate; ~**ing**
  vaccination, inoculation

infanterie' infantry *ook* **voet'soldate**

infanteris' **-te** infantryman, foot soldier

infek'sie infection *ook* **besmet'ting**; ~**siek'te** infectious disease *ook* **aansteek'like siek'te**

infinitief' **..tiewe** infinitive

inflamma'sie inflammation

infla'sie inflation; ~**spiraal'** inflation(ary) spiral

influen'sa influenza *ook* **griep**

informant' informer *ook* **verklik'ker**

informa'sie information *ook* **in'ligting**

informa'tika information studies

informeel' **..mele** informal; **..me'le drag** informal attire/dress; **..me'le sek'tor** informal sector

infrastruktuur' (s) infrastructure

in'gaan -ge- enter; go in for; ~ *op iets* consider/study/examine something

in'gang -e entrance, entry; doorway; *met* ~ *5 Junie* with effect from 5 June

in'gebore inborn, innate *ook* **aan'gebore**

ingedag'te (b) absent-minded *ook* **verstrooid'**

in'gee -ge- give in; inspire; administer; stop; yield, surrender

in'gelê ingelegde inlaid; canned, preserved; **ingeleg'de/ingemaak'te pers'kes** canned peaches

in'gelyf -de incorporated, embodied

in'gemaak -te canned (peaches)

ingenieur' **-s** engineer; **raadge'wende** ~ consulting engineer; ~**s'we'se** engineering (subject) *kyk* **genië'ring**

in'genome pleased, taken up with; *met jouself* ~ *wees* be pleased with oneself

in'geperk (b) restricted; confined

in'gerig -te arranged, prepared, organised; furnished; *hy het sy kantoor pragtig* ~ he has equipped his office beautifully

in'geskrewe enrolled; registered; conscript; ~ **klerk** articled clerk *kyk* **leer'klerk**; ~ **student'** registered student

in'geval in case; ~ *dit gebeur* if it should happen

ingevol'ge in terms/pursuance of, as a result, in consequence of

in'gewande (s) bowels, intestines, entrails

in'gewikkel(d) -de complicated, intricate

in'gewing -s, -e inspiration; suggestion; *skielike* ~ sudden (bright) idea *ook* **blink gedag'te**

ingrediënt' (s) ingredient *ook* **bestand'deel**

in'haal -ge- overtake, catch up with; make up for

inha'lig (b) greedy, covetous *ook* **hebsug'tig**

in'ham -me inlet, creek, bay

inheems' **-e** indigenous; native; home; endemic; ~**e taal** local/community language

inheg'tenisne'ming (s) arrest *ook* **arresta'sie**

inhibi'sie inhibition, hang-up, phobia

in'hou -ge- restrain, keep in check; contain; retain; *jou* ~ control one's temper

in'houd contents; capacity *ook* **volu'me**

in'houds: ~**maat** cubic measure; ~**op'gawe** table of contents, index

in'huldig -ge- inaugurate, install (mayor)

inisiatief' initiative

ink (s) ink; *skryf met* ~ write in ink

in'keep -ge- notch, indent (paragraph)

in'keer repentance; *tot* ~ *kom* repent

in'klaar -ge- clear in, clear (goods)

inkluis' included *ook* **in'begrepe**

inklusief'..siewe inclusive; *BTW* ~ VAT inclusive

in'kom -ge- come in(to), enter

in'komste (s) income, earnings; ~ **en uit'gawes** revenue and expenditure; ~**belas'ting** income tax; ~**diens'te** revenue services

in'koop (s) ..**kope** purchase(s); buying; (w) buy, purchase; ~**prys** cost price

in'kopie: ~*s doen* go shopping

in'kort (w) shorten, curtail; *sy uitgawes* ~/ *afskaal* reduce/curtail his expenses

in'laat (s) **inlate** inlet, intake; (w) let in, admit; *jou* ~ *met* have dealings with

in'lae -s enclosure (document) *ook* **by'lae**; deposit (money)

in'lê -ge- can (fruit) deposit, invest; inlay

in'leg ~**geld** stakes; entrance money; investment; ~**stro'kie** deposit slip

in'lei -ge- introduce, preface; usher in; ~**ding** introduction, preface, preamble

in'lewer -ge- deliver up, send in, hand in; submit; *taak* ~ hand in assignment

in'lig -ge- inform, enlighten

in'ligting information/info *ook* **da'ta**; intelligence; ~ *inwin* obtain information; **meer/na'der(e)** ~ further information

in'lyf -ge- incorporate; **in'gelyfde ver'eniging son'der wins'oogmerk** incorporated association not for gain

in'lynskaat'se in-line skates, rollerblades *ook* **(rol)lem'skaatse**

in'maak -ge- can, preserve; ~**bot'tel** canned-fruit bottle; ~**fabriek'** cannery

in'meng -ge- meddle, interfere; *in 'n ander se sake* ~ meddle in/with another's business

in'name (s) capture; collection
in'neem -ge- take, take in; conquer
inne'mend endearing, attractive (person)
in'nerlik -e inner; internal, intrinsic
in'nig (b) cordial, sincere, fond; intrinsic; ~e
meegevoel/simpatie sincere sympathy
in'pak -ge- pack; jou koffers ~ pack one's
suitcases/bags
in'palm -ge- haul in; grab (money, goods)
in'pas -ge- fit in
in'perk -ge- restrict, confine, ban
in'plof (w) implode; ~fing implosion
in'prent -ge- imprint, impress, inculcate; hom
allerlei bogstories ~ stuff his head with all
kinds of nonsense
in'rig -ge- arrange, organise; fit up, equip
in'rigting -s, -e arrangement; establishment,
institution ook in'stelling
in'roep -ge- call in ook ontbied'
in'ruil -ge- exchange, barter; ~waar'de tra=
de-in value (car)
in'ry -ge- ride/drive in; ~fliek drive-in flick
ook veld'fliek
in'sae inspection, perusal; ter ~ for perusal; on
appro(val)
in'samel -ge- gather, collect; ~ing collection;
ing(s)veld'tog fundraising campaign/drive
in'sek -te insect; ~do'der insecticide, pesti=
cide
in'sekte: ~-kun'de entomology; ~-kun'dige
entomologist (person)
insemina'sie insemination; kunsma'tige ~
(K.I.) artificial insemination (A.I.)
in'send -ge- send in, contribute
in'set -te stakes (gambling); pool; input; 'n ~
lewer make an input kyk uit'set
in'sien -ge- look into; understand, realise
in'sig -te insight, view, opinion; tem. met ~ a
man of discernment; ~ge'wend informative,
instructive ook leer'saam
in'sink -ge- sink in, sag, subside; ~ing
subsidence, collapse; relapse (illness)
in'sit -ge- strike up; begin (song); install; put
in; set in; be inside
in'skakel -ge- tune in (radio); insert; connect
up; put into gear; join
in'skep -ge- ladle into; dish up
in'skerp -ge- inculcate, impress; reinforce; die
oefening ~ repeat/drill the exercise
inskik'lik (b) -e; -er, -ste complying, yielding,
willing, affable ook toegeef'lik, meegaan'=
de

in'skink -ge- pour in
inskrip'sie -s inscription ook in'skrywing
in'skryf/in'skrywe -ge- inscribe; subscribe;
enrol, enlist, enter; tender; ~geld entrance
fee; ~vorm entry form
in'skrywing -s, -e subscription; enrolment,
registration, entry, tender
in'slaan -ge- drive in, smash, strike; ~ by die
publiek catch the popular fancy
in'sleep -ge- drag in(to); tow; ~diens break=
down service; tow-away service; ~wa break=
down van/lorry
in'sleutel (w) -ge- feed, key in (comp.)
in'sluimer -ge- doze off, fall asleep
in'sluit -ge- enclose; include, shut in, contain,
embrace; hierby ingesluit enclosed herewith
in'sluk -ge- swallow
in'smokkel -ge- smuggle/sneak in
insolvent' insolvent, bankrupt ook bankrot'
in'span -ge- exert; inspan; jou ~ exert oneself;
~ning exertion, strain, effort
inspek'sie (s) -s inspection, check-up
inspekteer' ~, geïn- inspect
inspekteur' -s inspector
inspira'sie inspiration ook besie'ling
inspireer' (w) ~, geïn- inspire ook besiel'
in'spraak dictate(s) (of one's heart), joint
consultation, participation ook me'deseg'=
genskap; hulle leiers wil ~ hê in landsake
their leaders want a say in national issues
in'spring -ge- jump in(to), indent (lines)
in'spuit -ge- inject; ~ing injection; skraag=
in'spuiting booster injection
in'staan -ge- guarantee, warrant, vouch for; vir
die waarheid ~ vouch for the truth
installa'sie -s installation, (factory) plant ook
aan'leg
installeer' geïn- install; inaugurate
instand'houding maintenance, upkeep
instan'sie instance; body, person (in power)
ook organisa'sie, lig'gaam; in eerste ~ in
the first place; verwys na ander ~s refer to
other bodies/parties
in'stel -ge- institute, establish, introduce;
on'dersoek ~ conduct an inquiry, investi=
gate; ~ling institution, establishment
in'stem -ge- agree, concur; tune in; ~mer
tuner (radio); ~ming agreement, accord;
assent; met algemene ~ming by common
consent
in'stink -te instinct ook natuur'drif
instinkma'tig/instinktief' (b) instinctive

instituut' (s) ..**tute** institute

in'stort -ge- collapse, tumble down; relapse; ~**ing** relapse; collapse

instruk'sie instruction, direction *ook* **op'drag**

instrukteur' -s instructor *ook* **leer'meester**

instrument' -e instrument, tool, implement; ~**paneel'** dashboard

in'studeer -ge- study; practise (songs)

insurgen'sie (s) insurgence *ook* **op'stand, op'=roer**

in'sypel -ge- infiltrate; ~**aar** infiltrator/insur=gent; ~**ing** infiltration

inteen'deel on the contrary; *hulle is nie arm nie;* ~, *hulle is skatryk* they are not poor; on the contrary, they are very well-off *kyk* **daarenteen'**

integra'sie integration, combination of parts

integriteit' integrity *ook* **eer'baarheid**

in'teken -ge- subscribe; *op 'n maandblad* ~ subscribe to a monthly (magazine); ~**aar** subscriber; ~**geld** subscription; ~**lys** sub=scription list

intellek' -te intellect *ook* **verstand'**

intellektueel' (s, b) ..**tuele** intellectual

intelligen'sie intelligence; ~**diens** intelligence service; ~**kwosiënt'** intelligence quotient

intelligent' -e; -er, -ste intelligent, bright *ook* **skran'der, slim**

intensief' intensive; **(intensie'we) sorg'een=heid/waak'eenheid** intensive care unit

interessant' -e; -er, -ste interesting *ook* **boei'end, tref'fend**

interesseer' geïn- interest, be interested in; *hy is geïnteresseer (stel belang) in tuinmaak* he is interested in gardening

in'terim interim *ook* **tus'sentyds** (dividend)

intermediêr' -e intermediate (bv. eksamen)

intern' -e intern, internal; ~**e beheer'** internal control; ~**e eksa'men** internal examination; ~**e kontro'le** internal check

internasionaal' ..**nale** international ..**na'le bemid'deling** international mediation

Internet Internet

internis' -te specialist physician

interplanetêr' -e interplanetary; ~**e vlug'te** interplanetary flights

interpreta'sie -s interpretation *ook* **vertol'king**

interprovinsiaal' ..**siale** interprovincial

interpunk'sie punctuation, interpunction

intiem' -e; -er, -ste intimate; ~**e vriend** close/intimate friend

intimida'sie (s) intimidation *ook* **vrees'aanjaging**

intona'sie -s intonation *ook* **stem'buiging**

in'trede entry, entrance; induction

in'tree (w) -**ge-** enter, go in; *hiermee het 'n nuwe tydperk ingetree* this marks a new era; ~**geld** admission/entrance fee; ~**preek** in=duction sermon; ~**re'de** inaugural address; maiden speech (parliament)

in'trek (w) move in (house); draw in (smoke); repeal (an act); cancel (leave); revoke (an edict); **nu'we** ~**kers** new occupants/neigh=bours

intri'ge -s intrigue, plot, scheme *ook* **komplot'**

introduk'sie -s introduction *ook* **in'leiding**

intuï'sie (s) intuition

intuïtief' ..**tiewe** intuitive *ook* **instinktief'**

intus'sen meanwhile, in the meantime

in'val (s) -**le** idea, thought; raid, invasion; (w) collapse; occur; join in

invali'de -s invalid (person)

inventa'ris -se inventory; *die* ~ *opmaak* take stock *ook* **voor'raadopname·**

in'vloed -e influence; ~**ryk** influential; ~**wer'wing** canvassing (for a job)

in'vloei -ge- flow in(to)

in'voeg -ge- put in, insert

in'voer (s) import(ation); (w) import; ~**der** importer (of); ~**reg** import duty

in'vorder (w) -**ge-** collect (taxes) *ook* **in'=samel**; demand (payment)

in'vul -ge- fill in, fill up; *'n vorm* ~ complete a form

in'wendig -e internal, inner; *nie vir* ~*e gebruik nie* not to be taken (medicine)

in'willig -ge- grant, consent, agree; accede

in'win -ge- obtain/gather (information)

in'wissel -ge- exchange, cash (a cheque)

in'woner -s inhabitant *ook* **bur'ger, on'der=daan**; resident (city)

in'woning (board and) lodging

in'wy -ge- open, initiate; ordain, consecrate; ~**ding** opening, inauguration

ipekon'ders/hipokon'ders whims, caprices; imaginary ailments

i'ris -se iris

iro'nies (b) -**e** ironical

isola'sie isolation *ook* **af'sondering**

i'tem item *ook* **nom'mer** (on programme)

ivoor' ivory; ~**to'ring** ivory tower

ja yes; *op alles* ~ *en amen sê* agree to every=
thing
ja(ag) ge- chase, pursue; race; *iem.
die skrik
op die lyf* ~ give someone a terrible fright
jaag: ~**dui'wel** helldriver, speed merchant;
~**strik** speed trap *ook* **snel'strik**
jaar jare year; ~**boek** yearbook ~**ein'de**
year-end; ~**geld** annuity; ~**gety'** season;
~**liks** yearly, annual; ~**sy'fer** year mark,
record
jaart -s yard (measure)
jaar: ~**tal** date; ~**tel'ling** era *ook* **tyd'vak**;
~**verga'dering** annual (general) meeting;
~**verslag'** annual report
ja'broer -s yes-man *ook* **krui'per**
jag[1] (s) -te yacht *ook* **seil'jag**
jag[2] -te hunt, chase (of game); *die* ~ *na
rykdom* the pursuit of wealth; (w) ge- hunt;
~**gesel'skap** hunting party
jag'ter -s hunter, huntsman
jakaran'da -s jacaranda
jak'kals -e jackal; sly person; ~ *prys sy eie
stert* he blows his own trumpet; *die* ~*e trou*
the fairies are baking; ~**draai'e** clever
excuses
jak'ker (w) gallivant, career along *ook* **rond**~
Ja'kob: *die ware* ~ the real Mackay
jakope'weroë protruding eyes
jaloers' (b) jealous, envious *ook* **afguns'tig**
jaloesie' jealousy, envy *ook* **af'guns**
jam'mer (s) pity; misery; (b) sorry; *hoe* ~!
what a pity!; ~**har'tig** (b) compassionate
jam'mer: ~**lap'pie** damp serviette/napkin;
~**lik** miserable, pitiable; ~**te** sorrow
Jan John; ~ **Bur'ger** John Citizen; ~ **Pam=
poen'** idiot, fool, dunce; ~ **Rap en sy maat**
rag-tag and bobtail; ~ **Sa'lie** stick-in-the-mud
ook **lam'sak**; ~ **Taks** Receiver of Revenue;
~ **Tuis'bly:** *met* ~ *Tuisbly se karretjie* have
to stay at home
ja-nee'! sure! indeed!
janfiskaal' butcherbird, fiscal shrike
janfre'derik Cape redbreast, robinchat
jangroen'tjie -s malachite sunbird
Jan'tjie/Jannetjie Johnie; ~ *wees* be jealous
Janua'rie -s January
ja'pie -s johnny; bumpkin, clodhopper
jap'piegriep yuppie flu *ook* **chro'niese uit=
puttingsindroom'**

japsnoet' -e inquisitive/impertinent child *ook*
snip; wise-acre, know-all
jap'trap: *in 'n* ~ in a jiffy, in two ticks
ja'relange long-continued; *ons* ~ *vriendskap*
friendship of many years' standing
jare lank for years (on end)
jas -se coat, greatcoat
jasmyn' jasmine
ja'vel/ja'fel lout, bumpkin *ook* **gom'tor**
ja'woord consent, permission, promise; *die* ~
kry be accepted (as lover)
jeans (s) jeans
jel'lie -s jelly
jene'wer gin
jeremia'de (s) -s jeremiad, woeful tale
Je'sus Jesus
Jeug'dag Youth Day (holiday)
jeug youth; *in sy prille* ~ in his early youth
jeug'dig -e young, youthful; ~**e** (s) youth;
juvenile (person)
jeug: ~**her'berg** youth hostel; ~**lektuur'**
juvenile literature; ~**mis'daad** juvenile
crime; ~**misda'digheid/**~**wan'gedrag** juve=
nile delinquency
jeuk/juk (w, s) itch
jig gout *ook* **wyn'toon**
jo'del ge- yodel (falsetto singing)
jo'dium (s) iodine
joernaal' journal, newspaper; logbook
joernalis' -te journalist, pressman; reporter
joernalistiek' journalism
jog'gie -s caddie (golf); lad(die)
jog'urt yoghurt
jok (w) ge- lie, tell stories/fibs
jo'ker (s) joker *ook* **as'jas** (kaartspel)
jok'kie -s jockey (horse racing)
jol ge- make merry, make fun; spree
jo'lig (b) -e jolly, merry, gay
jolyt' merry-making, revelry; ~**ma'ker** reveller
jong (s) -es young (animal); (w) bring forth
young; (b, attributief) young; *van* ~*s af*
from an early age; *die* ~*ste berigte* the latest
news/intelligence
jong'getroude -s newly married person; ~
paar newly-married couple
jong: ~**kêrel** bachelor *kyk* **ou'jongkêrel**;
young man; ~**leur** juggler *ook* **wig'gelaar**;
~**mei'sie** young girl, lass; ~**span** young
people *ook* **jong'klomp**

jonk[1] (s) -e junk (sailing vessel)
jonk[2] (b, predikatief) **jong'er, jong'ste** young
jon'ker -s squire; *hoe kaler* ~, *hoe groter pronker* great boast, small roast
Jood Jo'de Jew; *die wandelende* ~ the wandering Jew
jool jole (students') rag; fun, jollification; ~**blad** rag magazine; ~**koningin'** rag queen; ~**op'tog** rag procession
jou[1] (w) **ge-** boo *ook* **uit'jou, boe**
jou[2] (pers. vnw), you; (besit. vnw) yours
jou'e/jou'ne yours; *dis* ~ it is yours
joviaal' jovial, jolly, cheerful *ook* **op'gewek**
ju'bel (w) **ge-** rejoice, cheer, exult
jubile'um -s jubilee *ook* **gedenk'dag**
juf'frou miss, young lady; (lady) teacher
juig ge- rejoice, exult, cheer *ook* **ju'bel**

juis (b) -**te; -ter, -ste** exact, correct *ook* **presies'**; (bw) exactly, precisely; ~ *wat nodig is* exactly what is needed
juist'heid correctness, exactitude
juk'skei -e yokepin/yokeskey; jukskei (game); *'n orige* ~ a fifth wheel to the coach
Ju'lie -s July
jul'le (pers. vnw) you; (besit. vnw) your
Ju'nie -s June
ju'nior (s) -s junior; (b) junior
ju'rie -s jury
justi'sie justice *ook* **die reg, gereg'tigheid**
ju'te/juut jute *ook* **goi'ing**
juweel' juwele jewel, precious gem/stone
juwelier' -s jeweller; ~**s'wa're** jewellery
jy you; ~ *kan nooit weet nie* one never knows

K

kaai -e wharf, quay *ook* **ha'wehoof**
kaai'man -ne, -s alligator, cayman
kaak[1] **kake** jaw
kaak[2] **kake** pillory; *aan die* ~ *stel* expose to public contempt
kaal kale; kaler, -ste bald, bare, naked; *daar* ~ *van afkom* come off second best; ~**bas** nudist *ook* **naak'loper/hol'ler**; ~**baai'er** nude bather; ~**buus** topless; ~**hol** streak; ~**hol'ler** streaker *ook* **kaal'naeler, stry'ker**; ~**kop** baldpate, baldhead; *iem.* ~**kop** *die waarheid sê* go for a person baldheaded; ~**pers'ke** nectarine; ~**stroop** (w) clean(ed) out (housebreaking); ~**voet** barefoot
Kaap[1] Cape; Cape Town
kaap[2] (s) **kape** cape, promontory, headland
kaap[3] (w) **ge-** practise piracy, hijack/carjack *ook* **mo'torkaping; ontvoer'/skaak**
Kaaps -e Cape; *die* ~*se dokter* the south-~ easter; ~*e draaie maak* take sharp turns; *so oud soos die* ~*e wapad* as old as the hills; ~*e vlak'te* Cape Flats
Kaap'stad Cape Town
kaart -e map, chart; ticket; ~ **en transport'** title deed; ~**foon** card (tele)phone
kaar'tjie -s ticket; card
kaart: ~**man'netjie** jack-in-the-box; ~**speel** play cards
kaas kase cheese; ~**en-wyn'onthaal'** cheese and wine reception; ~**bur'ger** cheeseburger

kaat'jie: ~ *van die baan wees* be cock of the walk
Kaat'jie: ~ **Kek'kelbek** chatterbox
kaats ge- play (at) ball; ~**er** reflector
kabaal' noise, hubbub, clamour *ook* **her'rie, rumoer'**; ~ *maak/opskop* raise Cain
kabaret' -te cabaret; ~**lied'jie** cabaret song, ditty
kab'bel ge- babble, ripple
ka'bel (s) -s cable; *'n kink(el) in die* ~ a hitch; (w) cable
kabeljou' -e cod (fish); Cape salmon
ka'bel: ~**spoor** cableway *ook* **sweef'spoor**; ~**televi'sie** cable television
kabinet' -te cabinet, case; ministry, cabinet; ~**minis'ter** cabinet minister
kabou'ter -s gnome, elf, imp; ~**man'netjie** hobgoblin, elf
ka'der -s cadre; framework; skeleton; ~**per'soneel'** skeleton staff *ook* **ska'dupersoneel'**
ka'det -te cadet; trainee
kaf chaff; nonsense, tommyrot *ook* **bog, twak**; ~ *verkoop* talk nonsense; *iemand* ~*loop* knock spots off someone
kafee' -s café
kafete'ria -s cafeteria
kag'gel -s fireplace/chimney piece; range
kai'ing -s greave(s), browsel(s); crackling(s)
kajuit' -e cabin; ~**personeel'** cabin crew (airliner)

kak (*kru*) (s, w) shit (*vulgar*), dung
kaka'o cocoa
ka'kebeen jaw, jawbone; ~**wa** Voortrekker oxwagon
kaketiel'/kokketiel' cockatiel (bird)
ka'kie -s khaki; tommy; ~**bos** khakibos
kakkerlak' -ke cockroach *ook* **kokkerot'**
kak'tus -se cactus
kalan'der -s weevil
kalant' -e rogue, scamp; old hand, sly fox
kalbas' -se calabash, gourd; ~**kop** skinhead (person) *ook* **been'kop**
kalbas'sies orchitis *ook* **bal'ontsteking**
kalen'der -s calendar, almanac *ook* **almanak'**
kalf (s) **kalwers** calf; (w) calve
kalfs'vleis veal
kali'ber calibre; bore (of gun)
kalk lime; **geblus'te** ~ slaked lime
kalkoen -e turkey; *hy is nie onder 'n* ~ *uitgebroei nie* he is not as green as he looks
kalm -e; -er, -ste calm, quiet; composed
kalmeer' ge- calm, soothe, allay *ook* **sus, bedaar'** (w); ~**mid'del** sedative, tranquillis=er
kalorie' -ë heat unit, caloric
kal'wer: ~**hok** kraal for calves; *tot by oom Daantjie in die ~hok* go the whole hog, ~**lief'de** boy-and-girl-love, puppy love
kam (s) **-me** comb; crest; *almal oor dieselfde* ~ *skeer* treat all alike; (w) comb (your hair); card
kamas' -te gaiter, legging
kameel' kamele camel, ~**perd** giraffe *ook* **giraf'**
ka'mer -s room, chamber; *K* ~ *van Koop=handel* Chamber of Commerce; *K*~ *van Mynwese* Chamber of Mines
ka'mera -s camera; ~**man** cameraman (me=dia) *ook* **fotograaf'** (mens)
kameraad'..rade comrade, companion, mate; ~**skap** companionship
ka'mer: ~**jas** dressing gown; ~**musiek'** cham=ber music
kam'ma/kammakas'tig/kammalie'lies quasi, so-called, as if (it were); bogus; *hy het* ~ *geleer* he pretended to be studying
kam'mahortjie -s mock shutter
kam'makreef mock lobster
kamoefleer' (w) camouflage *ook* **vermom'**; ~**drag** camouflage uniform
kamp (s) **-e** camp, encampment; (w) camp *ook* **uit'kamp;** ~**bed** stretcher *ook* **vou'katel**

kampeer' camp *ook* **uit'kamp;** ~**terrein'** camping site; ~**wa** caravan *ook* **woon'wa**
kampioen' -e champion; ~**skap** championship
kam'pus -se campus
kamp'vegter -s fighter (for a cause), cham=pion; ~ *vir vryheid* champion/advocate of liberty/liberation
kan[1] (s) **-ne** can, jug; *die wysheid in die* ~ be tipsy
kan[2] (w) **kon** be able, can
kana'rie -s canary; ~**kou'(tjie)** (s) canary cage
kandidaat'..date candidate, applicant
kaneel' cinnamon
kan'fer camphor
kanferfoe'lie honeysuckle
kangaroe' -s kangaroo
kan'ker cancer, carcinoma *ook* **karsinoom'** (tumor)
kan'netjie -s small boy, kid, chappy; small jug, cannikin
kannibaal'..bale cannibal *ook* **mens'vreter**
kan'niedood (s) diehard; persister; variegated aloe; *hy is 'n regte* ~ he is everlasting; (b) indestructible
kano' -'s canoe; ~**wed'vaart** canoe race
kanon[1] **-ne** (big) gun; cannon (obsolete)
ka'non[2] canon (chain music)
kans -e chance, opportunity, prospect; *'n* ~ *waag* take a chance; ~**vat'ter** chancer
kan'sel -s pulpit; chancery
kanselier' -s chancellor (person)
kanselleer' (w) ~, **ge-** cancel
kant[1] (s) lace (fabric)
kant[2] (s) -e side, edge, brink; margin; *jou* ~ *bring* do one's share; ~ *kies* side with; ~ *en klaar* quite ready; *aan* ~ *maak* tidy (up)
kan'tel ge- topple, fall, capsize, tilt; ~**dem'per** anti-roll bar (car)
kantien' -e canteen; bar, pub *ook* **kroeg;** tin can
kant'lyn -e margin line; sideline
kantoor'..tore office; ~**u're** office hours
kant': ~**ruim'te** margin; ~**stro'kie** counter=foil; ~**te'kening** marginal note; ~**werk** lacework, lace
kap[1] (s) **-pe** shade; bonnet (of engine); cart hood; truss/principal of roof; hatch
kap[2] (s) cut, chop (with axe); (w) fell, cut wood, chop; paw (horse)
kap[3] (w) **ge-** cut, dress (hair)
kapasiteit' -e capacity *ook* **vermo'ë; in'houds=maat; bak'maat** (dam)

kapel'[1] **-le** chapel *ook* **be'dehuis**
kapel'[2] **-le** cobra *ook* **koperkapel'**
kapelaan' -s chaplain; padre
ka'per -s privateer, pirate, freebooter *ook* **see'rower**; hijacker, carjacker
kapitaal' (s) **..tale** capital; ~ *en rente* princi= pal and interest; (b) capital, splendid; ~**uit'= breiding** capital expansion
kapitalis'me capitalism
kapitalis'ties: ~**e stel'sel** capitalist system
kapituleer' ge- capitulate *ook* **oor'gee**
kapok' (s) snow; wadding; capoc; (w) snow; ~**gewig'** bantam weight ~**haan'tjie** bantam cock; cheeky fellow; ~**hoen'der** bantam fowl
kap'per -s hairdresser, barber
kap'pertjie -s nasturtium (flower)
kap'pie -s sunbonnet; canopy (of a bakkie); circumflex
kap'sel -s hairdress, coiffure; ~**para'de** hair= style parade
kap'sie: ~ *maak teen/op* raise objections
kap: ~**ste'wel** topboot, jackboot; ~**stok** hall stand, hat rack
kapsu'le -s capsule
kaptein' -s captain *ook* **gesag'voerder**; chief= (tain)
kap'werf chopshop (for stolen cars)
kar -re cart; (motor)car *ook* **mo'tor**
karaat' karate carat
karak'ter -s character, nature; ~**trek** trait; ~**(uit)beelding** portrayal of character
karavaan' caravan *kyk* **woon'wa**
karba' -'s wicker bottle, demijohn
kardinaal' (s) **..nale** cardinal (person); (b) cardinal, chief, vital
kardoes' -e paperbag; cartridge; ~**broek** plusfours, knickerbockers
ka'rig (b) sparing, skimpy, scanty; frugal; ~**e maal'tyd** scanty meal
kariljon' -s carillon, chimes *ook* **klok'kespel**
karkas' (s) **-se** carcass
karkat'jie -s sty (on the eye)
karnal'lie -s rogue, scamp, rascal (person)
karnaval' -s carnival *ook* **ker'mis**
karnuf'fel ge- hug, cuddle; manhandle/bully
karos' -se skin rug, kaross
karp(er) carp (fish)
kar'ring (s) **-s** churn; (w) churn; ~**melk** buttermilk
karton' cardboard, pasteboard; carton; ~**boks** cardboard box

karwats' -e riding crop, horsewhip *ook* **peits**
karwei' ge- ride transport, cart; ~**er** transport rider; cartage/removals contractor; carrier, haulier, trucker
kas[1] (s) **-te** box; case; cupboard, chest; cabinet
kas[2] (s) **-se** socket (eye) *ook* **oog'kas**
kas[3] cashbox/till; treasury; (w) deposit
kas'boek -e cashbook
kaser'ne -s barracks, (army) camp
kasi'no/casi'no casino *ook* **dob'belhuis**
kaska'de -s cascade
kas'kar (s) soapbox cart, go-cart
kaskena'de prank, mischievous trick, antic
kas'register -s cash register/till
kasset'speler -s cassette player
kassier' -s cashier; teller (in bank)
kastai'ing -s chestnut; ~**bruin** (b) auburn
kasteel' kastele castle, citadel *ook* **ves'ting**
kas'terolie castor oil
kastreer' (w) ~, **ge-** castrate *ook* **ontman'**
kastrol' -le stewpan, saucepan
kasty' **ge-** castigate, chastise, punish
kat -te cat; *die* ~ *uit die boom kyk* wait and see which way the cat jumps; *die* ~ *in die donker knyp* do things on the sly
kata'logus -se catalogue *ook* **prys'lys**
kat'apult (s) catapult *ook* **ket'tie**; slingshot
katar' catarrh
katarak' -te cataract
katastro'fe -s catastrophe *ook* **ramp**
katedraal' **..drale** cathedral *ook* **dom'kerk**
kategorie' -ë category
ka'tel -s bedstead *ook* **ledekant'**
katjiepie'ring -s gardenia (flower)
katkisant' -e candidate for confirmation
kat'lagter -s babbler (bird)
katoen' cotton
katoe'ter -s gadget *ook* **katot'ter**
Katoliek' -e (Roman) Catholic
katoliek' (b) universal, all-embracing
kat'oog ..oë cat's eye; reflectorised stud (on roads)
katrol' -le pulley; ~**stel** block and tackle
kats (s) **-e** cat-o'-nine-tails; (w) thrash, lash, whip
kats'wink dazed *ook* **dis'nis**; *slaan iem.* ~ knock someone unconscious
kat'te: ~**bak** dickey seat, rumble seat; ~**kroeg** milk bar; ~**kwaad** mischief, tricks; ~**ry** cattery (cat kennels)
keel kele throat; *sy eie* ~ *afsny* cut one's own throat

ke'ël -s cone; icicle; ∼**vor'mig** conical
keep (s) **kepe** notch, indentation, nick
keer (s) **kere** turn; time; *drie* ∼ three times;
(w) turn; prevent; ∼**dag** return day/date;
∼**kring** tropic (line); ∼**punt** turning point;
∼**sy** other/reverse side; ∼**tyd** return day/
date; ∼**weer** cul-de-sac, blind alley *ook*
dood'loopstraat
kees kese monkey; *dis klaar met* ∼ he is a
goner
ke'gel -s skittle, pin; ∼**spel** skittles; tenpin
bowling
kei'ser -s emperor
keiserin' -ne empress
kei'ser: ∼**ryk** empire; ∼**snee** Caesarian sec‑
tion
kek'kel ge- cackle; ∼**bek** chatterbox
kel'der (s) -s cellar; bottom of the sea; *na die*
∼ *gaan* go to Davy Jones's locker; (w) sink;
∼**verdie'ping** basement
kelk -e chalice, calyx; cup
kel'kie -s wineglass
kelkiewyn' -e Namaqua sandgrouse (bird)
kel'ner -s waiter, steward
ken[1] (s) -ne chin
ken[2] (w) **ge-** know; recognise; understand; *van*
buite ∼ know by heart; *te* ∼*ne gee* give to
understand; indicate
ken: -**letter(s)** designatory initials/title;
∼**merk** (s) characteristic; feature *ook* **ei'en‑**
skap; (w) **‑merk** characterise; ∼**ner** (s)
expert; fundi, boffin (person)
ken'nis knowledge; consciousness; acquain‑
tance; ∼ *gee* give notice; ∼ *maak met* make
acquaintance with; *in* ∼ *stel* notify;
∼**ge'wing** notice, announcement
ken: ∼**stro'kie** name tag (at conferences) *ook*
naam'plaatjie; ∼**te'ken** distinctive mark;
badge; ∼**wy'sie** theme/signature tune
keramiek' ceramics *ook* **er'dewerk**
ke're: *te* ∼ *gaan* make a fuss; rave
kê'rel -s fellow, chap; bloke, guy; *'n gawe* ∼ a
decent/fine chap; *haar* ∼ her suitor/boy‑
friend *ook* **vry'er**; *hulle is* ∼ *en nooi* they
are on courting terms; going steady
kerf (s) **kerwe** notch, incision; (w) notch; cut
(tobacco); ∼**stok** nickstick
kerk -e church, chapel; congregation; *die*
koeël is deur die ∼ the die is cast
ker'ker -s dungeon
kerk'hof ..**howe** churchyard, cemetery *ook*
begraaf'plaas

kerk: ∼**klok** church bell; ∼**muis** church
mouse: *so arm soos 'n* ∼*muis* as poor as a
church mouse; ∼**plein** church square; ∼**to'‑**
ring church tower, steeple
kerm (w) **ge-** lament, groan, whine
ker'mis -**se** fair, fête; carnival
kern -s kernel; core, pith; gist; nucleus; *die* ∼
van die saak the gist of the matter;
∼**aan'gedrewe** nuclear powered; ∼**af'val**
atomic waste
kernag'tig (b) pithy, terse
kern: ∼-**as** nuclear fallout; ∼**krag** nuclear
power; ∼**reak'tor** nuclear reactor, cyclo‑
tron; ∼**silla'bus** core syllabus; ∼**tyd** core
time *kyk* **skik'tyd** (kantoor)
ker'rie curry; ∼-**en-rys** curry and rice
kers -e candle; ∼ *opsteek* learn the tricks of
the trade
Kers: ∼**aand** Christmas evening/Eve; ∼**boom**
Christmas tree; ∼**dag** Christmas Day; ∼**fees**
Christmas; ∼**geskenk'** Christmas box/pres‑
ent
ker'sie -s cherry (fruit)
Kers'vader Father Christmas, Santa Claus *ook*
Va'der Kris'mis
Kers'vakansie Christmas holidays/vacation
ke'tel -s kettle; boiler (of engine)
ket'ter -s heretic, unbeliever (person)
ket'tie (s) catapult/catty *ook* **voëlrek(ker)**
ket'ting -s chain; ∼**reak'sie** chain reaction
keur (n) choice, selection; charter, *te kus en te* ∼
for the choosing; (w) test, try, judge; seed
(sport), *die eerste ge*∼*de* the first seed; ∼**der**
selector (sport); ∼**graad** choice grade (butter)
keu'rig (b) fine, exquisite, choice
keur: ∼**komitee'** selection committee; ∼**lys**
grading/seeding list (sport) *ook* **rang'lys**;
∼**toets** aptitude test *ook* **aan'legtoets**;
∼**troe'pe** elite troops
keu'se -s choice, selection; *uit vrye* ∼ of one's
own free will; ∼**vak** optional subject
ke'wer -s beetle
kiaat'hout teak (wood)
kib'boets (s) kibbutz *ook* **gemeen'skapplaas**
kib'bel ge- quarrel, squabble, bicker
kie'kie (s) -s snap, snapshot
kiel keel (of a ship); ∼**haal** (w) keelhaul, careen
kie'lie ge- tickle; ∼**bak** armpit *ook* **ok'sel**
kiem (s) -e germ; embryo; *in die* ∼ *smoor* nip
in the bud; (w) germinate
kie'persolboom ..**bome** umbrella tree
kie'piemielies popcorn *ook* **spring'mielies**

kie'rie -s (walking) stick; ~geld pension money (idiom); ~wis'selaar floorshift (car)
kies[1] (s) -e, -te cheek pouch; molar (tooth), grinder ook kies'tand
kies[2] (w) ge- choose, elect, pick
kies[3] (b) delicate, dainty ook keu'rig
kies: ~afdeling electoral division; constituency; ~baar eligible
kie'ser -s voter, elector; ~slys voters' roll
kieskeu'rig (b) particular, fastidious
kies'lys (s) menu (comp.)
kies'tand -e molar (tooth), grinder
kiet(s) quits, equal; ons is ~ we are quits
kiet'siesorg (s) cattery ook kat'tery
kieu/kief (s) gill (of fish)
kie'wiet -e lapwing, noisy plover (bird)
kil chilly, cold; ~(le) ontvangs' chilly reception
ki'lo -'s kilo; ~gram kilogram; ~li'ter kilolitre; ~me'ter kilometre
kind -ers child; infant, baby; 'n ~ des doods a doomed man; ~ nog kraai hê have neither kith nor kin; gerem'de ~ backward child; gestrem'de ~ handicapped child; vertraag= de ~ retarded child
kinderag'tig childish, silly ook laf, verspot'
kin'der: ~arts paediatrician ook pedia'ter; ~huis children's home ook kinderha'we kyk wees'huis; ~ja're childhood; ~lik childlike, innocent, filial; ~mishan'deling child abuse; ~molesteer'der child molester ook pedofiel'; ~rym'pie nursery rhyme; ~sorg child welfare; ~spe'letjies child's play; dis nie ~speletjies nie it is no joking matter; ~sterf'tesyfer infant mortality rate; ~verlam'ming infantile paralysis, poliomyelitis; ~wa'entjie perambulator (pram) ook stoot'waentjie
kinds (b) -e senile ook seniel'
kink (s) -e twist, knot, hitch; daar is 'n ~/kinkel in die kabel there is a hitch somewhere
kink'hoes (s) whooping cough
kiosk' kiosk, stall ook kraam'pie/stal(letjie)
kis (s) -te box ook boks; case, trunk; coffer; coffin; (w) coffin; ~hou winning shot, ace (sport) ook kol'hou (gholf); ~kle're Sunday best; Sunday-go-to-meeting
kitaar' -s; ..tare guitar ook ghitaar'
kits moment, trifle; in 'n ~ in a jiffy; ~bank automatic teller machine (ATM) ook OTM (outoteller); ~klaar ready in an instant; ~kof'fie instant coffee
kla/klae ge- complain; ek kan nie ~ nie things

are not too bad; ~ steen en been complain loudly
klaag: ~lied lamentation, dirge; ~muur wailing wall
klaar (b) ready, finished; clear
klaar: ~kom get finished; get along, manage; ek sal darem ~kom I'll be able to manage; ~maak get ready, finish; prepare
Klaas Vaak'/Klaas Va'kie Willie Winkie, the dustman, the sandman
klad[1] (s) -de blot, stain; (w) blot
klad[2] (s) rough draft; blemish/stain; ~werk rough work
kla'er -s plaintiff, complainant
klag -te/klag'te -s complaint; 'n ~ indien lodge a complaint; ~staat charge sheet
klam -mer, -ste damp, moist
klamp (s) -e clamp; bracket; (w) clamp
klandi'sie customers, patronage; clientele, custom; ~waar'de goodwill (business)
klank -e sound, tone; ~baan sound track; ~dem'per silencer (car); ~dig soundproof; ho'ë ~getrouheid high fidelity, hifi ook klank'trou/ho'ëtrou; ~grens sound barrier; ~ie suspicious smell (meat); ~na'bootsing onomatopoeia; ~verster'ker amplifier
klant -e customer; ~bus courtesy bus; ~esorg client/customer relations
klap (s) -pe slap, blow, crack; flap; (w) ge-smack, clap; crack
klap'per[1] -s cracker, explosive (sound)
klap'per[2] -s coconut
klap: ~roos corn poppy; ~mus balaclava cap
klarinet' -te clarinet
klas -se class, form; grade; category; eerste ~ first class; ~ka'mer classroom; ~kaptein' class captain; ~onderwy'ser class teacher
klassiek' -e classic(al); ~e musiek' classical music
klassifiseer' ge- classify ook in'deel
klassikaal' ..kale class; klassika'le on'derwys teaching by groups (classes)
klavier' -e piano ook pia'no
kla'wer[1] -s key (piano); lever (lock)
kla'wer[2] -s clover, shamrock; ~s clubs (cards)
klee(d) (w) ge- clothe, dress
kleed (s) klede garment, garb; ~ka'mer dress= ing room, cloakroom; ~repeti'sie dress/ fulldress rehearsal
kleef ge- cling, stick, adhere; ~band sticking tape; ~myn limpet mine; ~plastiek' cling/ glad wrap

klei clay; ~*trap*, flounder; ~**duifskiet'** clay-pigeon shooting *ook* **pie'ringskiet**
klein -er, -ste small, little; petty; *'n ~ bietjie* a tiny/little bit; ~**boer** small-scale (new) farm= er
klein'dogter -s granddaughter
Klein Duim'pie Tom Thumb
kleineer' (w) ~, **ge-** belittle, minimise
kleingees'tig -e; -er, -ste narrow-minded *ook* **bekrom'pe**
klein'geld small cash, change
klein'goed (s) small ones, children, kids
klein'handel retail trade; ~**aar** retail dealer; ~**prys** retail price
klein'hoewe (s) smallholding, plot
klein'huisie -s toilet, loo, lavatory
klei'nigheid trifle, small thing *ook* **nie'tigheid**
klein: ~**kind** grandchild; ~**kas** petty cash; ~**kry** understand, grasp; *ek kan dit nie ~ kry nie* I cannot understand/fathom it; ~**lik** petty, narrow-minded
klei'nood (s) ..**node** jewel, treasure, gem
kleinse'rig (b) touchy, sensitive, easily hurt
klein'seun -s grandson
klein: ~**span** little ones, youngsters, kids; ~**tjie** small/little one; ~**ton'getjie** uvula; ~**vee** small livestock; ~**wild** small game
klem (s) stress, accent *ook* **na'druk**; clamp, binding screw; ~ *in die kake* lockjaw, tetanus; ~ *lê op* stress; (w) clamp, clench
klep (s) -**pe** flap; valve
kle'pel -s tongue (of a bell)
kleptomaan' kleptomaniac *ook* **steelsug'tige** (mens)
klera'sie clothing; drapery
kle're clothes, clothing; ~**drag** fashion, dress, clothing; ~**kas** wardrobe; ~**ma'ker** tailor; ~**wer'ker** garment worker
klerikaal' ..**kale** of clergy; ..**ka'le drag** clerical garb (priest)
klerk -e clerk; ~**like werk** clerical work
klets ge- chatter, yap *ook* **bab'bel**; ~**kous** gossiper, chatterbox
klet'ter ge- clatter, patter, clash, clang
kleur (s) -**e** colour; ~ *beken* follow suit (cards); (w) colour, stain; tone; blush; ~**baad'jie** blazer
kleur'ling -e coloured *ook* **bruin'man;** (pl) coloured people *ook* **bruin'mense;** ~**ge= meen'skap** coloured community
kleur: ~**loos** colourless, drab; ~**serp** aca= demic hood; ~**sky'fie** colourslide; ~**stof**

pigment, dye
kleu'ter -s toddler; ~**skool** nursery school
kliek (s) clique, set; clan; (w) clique
kliënt -e client; ~**betrek'kinge** client rela= tions; ~**(e)lok'ker** tout (person); ~**vrien'= delik** client/customer friendly *ook* **gebrui'= kervriendelik**
klier -e gland
klik (s) -**ke** click (with tongue); (w) tell tales; click; bug; ~**bek/**~**spaan** telltale, tale= bearer; ~**ker** (electronic) bug; *my kantoor is geklik'* my office is bugged *kyk* **luis'= tervlooi;** ~**lig(gie)** warning light (in car); ~**toets** lie detector test
klim ge- climb, ascend, rise
klimaat' climate
kli'maks -e climax *ook* **hoog'tepunt**
klim: ~**baan** climbing lane (traffic); ~**op** ivy; creeper; ~**tol** yo-yo
kliniek' -e clinic; dispensary
kli'nies clinical; ~**e on'dersoek** clinical ex= amination; ~**e sielkun'dige** clinical psy= choloog (person)
klink ge- sound, ring; touch glasses; ~**er** vowel; army biscuit
klink'nael -s rivet; ~**broek** studded jeans
klip -pe, -pers stone, rock, pebble; *slaap soos 'n ~* sleeping like a top; *stadig oor die ~pe* go carefully; ~**hard** very hard
klits¹ (s) -**e** bur, burdock
klits² (w) **ge-** beat (eggs); whip (cream)
kloek (w) **ge-** cluck, chuck=
klok -ke clock, bell; (w) *'n toespraak ~* time a speech; ~**ke'spel** chimes; carillon; ~**reël** curfew; ~**slag** striking of the clock; (bw) exactly; ~*slag eenuur* one o'clock sharp
klomp¹ -e crowd, number, lot; lump; ~**voet** club foot *ook* **hor'relvoet**
klomp² -e wooden shoe, clog
klont -e lump (sugar); clod (earth); clot (blood)
kloof (s) **klowe** ravine, cleft, chasm, gorge; (w) cleave, split; *hare ~* split hairs; ~**paal** split pole
kloon (s) **klo'ne** clone (gene reproduction) *ook* **gene'tiese duplikaat';** (w) **kloneer'** clone
kloos'ter -s monastery; nunnery; cloister, convent; ~**skool** convent school
klop (s) -**pe** knock; beat; tap, rap; (w) knock; beat; throb, tap; balance, tally; defeat, lick; *dit gaan ~disselboom* everything is in top gear; ~**dan'ser** tap dancer; ~**jag** police raid/round-up

klos -se bobbin, spool, reel; coil (electr.)
klots ge- beat, clash (water)
klou (s) **-e** claw, paw; talon (bird of prey); (w) cling
klousu'le -s clause, paragraph; *ingevolge/ kragtens* ~ 6 in terms of clause 6
klou'tang -e vicegrip (pliers)
klou'ter ge- climb, clamber; ~**dief** cat burglar
klou'tjie -s hoof; *nie die* ~ *by die oor bring nie* unable to make a tale sound plausible
klub -s club
klug -te farce; joke, scream
kluif (w) **ge-** pick (~ a bone), gnaw
kluis -e hermitage; cell; strongroom; ~**e'naar** hermit, recluse (person)
kluit -e clod, lump
klui'tjie -s dumpling; lie; *iem. met 'n* ~ *in die riet stuur* put someone off with fair words
kluts: *die* ~ *kwyt raak* be at sea
knaag ge- gnaw; ~**dier** rodent (animal)
knaap knape lad, boy; chap
knab'bel ge- nibble, gnaw
kna'end (b) **-e** gnawing; nagging, boring
knak (s) **-ke** crack; (w) crack, snap; impair (health); ~**breuk** greenstick fracture; (w) ~**vou** jack-knife (articulated vehicle)
knal (s) **-le** report (of gun); clap, crack; (w) clap; explode; ~**dem'per** exhaust box, muffler, silencer; ~**dop(pie)** detonator
knap (b) clever, able, brainy *ook* **skran'der**; good-looking; ~**kaart** smartcard
kna'pie (s) **-s** small pulpit, lectern
knap'sak -ke knapsack *ook* **rug'sak**; kitbag
kneg -te servant; slave
knel (s) **-le** pinch, difficulty; (w) pinch; squeeze; press tightly; get jammed; ~**punt** bottleneck *ook* **verkeers'knoop, bot'telnek**; issue
kners ge- gnash, grind; ~**broek** ski-pants *ook* **kameel'kouse**
knet'ter ge- crackle (fire)
kneu'kel (s) **-s** knuckle
kneus (w) **ge-** bruise, contuse
kne'wel -s moustache; whopper, bouncer; *'n* ~ *van 'n leeu* a huge lion
knib'bel ge- haggle, higgle; quibble
knie[1] (s) **-ë** knee; *sy knieë dra* hurry away
knie[2] (w) **ge-** knead (dough)
knie: ~**broek** knickers, knee breeches; bloomers (for women); ~**bui'ging** genuflex= ion; curtsy; ~**diep** knee-deep; ~*diep in die moeilikheid* in real trouble; ~**hal'ter** knee= halter

kniel ge- kneel; ~**kus'sing** hassock
knik (s) **-ke** nod; rut (in a road); (w) nod; wink (at a girl)
knip (s) **-pe** bolt, clasp; clip; wink; (w) cut; clip; wink; ~**mes** pocket knife; *so gou as jy* ~*mes kan sê* before you can say Jack Robinson; ~**oog** (w) wink, blink; ~**pie** pinch (of salt); ~**sel** cutting, clipping; ~**seldiens** (press) cutting service; ~**speld** safety pin *ook* **haak'speld**
knoei ge- botch, bungle
knof'fel garlic
knol -le tuber, bulb; nag, hack; ~**skry'wer** hackwriter
knoop (s) **knope** button; knot, tie; curse; *die* ~ *deurhak* cut the Gordian knot; *daar sit die* ~ there's the rub; (w) tie, knot, swear; *iets in jou oor* ~ make a mental note of; ~**s'gat** buttonhole
knop -pe knob, pommel; bud; *'n* ~ *in die keel* a lump in the throat; ~**kie'rie** knobkerrie, club
knor (s) **-re** grunt, growl; (w) grumble, growl, grunt; ~**tjor** go-cart
knou (s) **-e** gnaw, snap, bite; injury; *'n* ~ *gee* impair (health); (w) hurt, injure
knup'pel (s) **-s** club, cudgel; ~**dik** gorged; ~**storm'loop** baton charge (police)
knut'sel (w) **ge-** tinker, trifle; ~**werk** pottering
knyp (s) **-e** pinch; *in die* ~ *sit* be in a fix; (w) pinch, squeeze; ~**bord** clipboard; ~**tang** (pair of) pliers/pincers
ko'bra -s cobra *ook* **koperkapel'**
kod'dig funny, comic; odd; quaint
ko'de -s code
koe'doe -s kudu (buck)
koëd'skool . .skole co-educational school
koe'ël (s) **-s** bullet (rifle); pellet (airgun); ball; *die* ~ *is deur die kerk* the die is cast; ~**vaste baad'jie** bulletproof vest/jacket
koei -e cow; *ou* ~*e uit die sloot haal* rake up old stories
koeja'wel -s guava; *har'de* ~ hard nut (person)
koek (s) **-e** cake; (w) knot, cluster
koekoek' -s cuckoo; ~**klok** cuckoo clock
koek: ~**poe'ding** cottage pudding; ~**struif** trifle
koel (w) **ge-** cool; vent; ~ *af, Jan!* cool it, John!; (b) cool, cold, fresh
koelbloe'dig (b) cold-blooded, savage
koel: ~**drank** cooldrink, soft/cold drink; ~**te** light breeze; shade; ~**to'ring** cooling tower; ~**trok** refrigerator truck

koem'kwat -te kumquat/cumquat (fruit)
koepee' -s coupé
koe'pel -s dome, cupola
koeplet' -te couplet, verse, stanza
koepon' -s coupon
koer (w) **ge-** coo
koerant -e newspaper *ook* **nuus'blad**; ~**berig'** newspaper report
koerier' courier/messenger; ~**diens** courier service
koers -e course, direction; exchange rate
koes/koets (w) **ge-** dodge, duck down
koesister/koeksis'ter -s cruller
koes'ter(tjie)[1] (s) **-s** pipit (South African lark)
koes'ter[2] (w) **ge-** cherish, pamper, nurse; *'n wrok* ~ bear a grudge
koets[1] (s) **-e** coach, carriage; **rou**~ hearse
koets[2] (w) **ge-** dodge, duck *ook* **koes**
koevert' -e envelope
koe'voet -e crowbar; lever
kof'fer -s trunk, travelling box, coffer; ~**dam** coffer dam
kof'fie coffee; ~**fles** vacuum/thermos flask
kog'gel (w) mimic, mock; ~**aar** mocking bird
koggelman'der -s black agama; rock lizard
kok -ke, -s cook; *te veel* ~*s bederwe die bry* too many cooks spoil the broth
koket' (s) **-te** coquette; flirt, vamp (girl); (b) coquettish; coy
kokketiel' -s cockatiel (bird)
kok'kedoor , dore big wig/shot (person)
kokkewiet' -e bush shrike
kokon' -s cocoon
ko'kosneut (s) coconut *ook* **klap'per**
kol -le bull's eye; spot, stain; star (of a horse)
ko'lera/cho'lera (s) cholera
kolf (s) **kolwe** butt end (rifle), bat (cricket); (w) bat; ~**beurt** innings; ~**blad** pitch
kol'hou -e hole in one (golf) *ook* **fortuin'hou/ kis'hou**
koliek' colic; ~**pyn** gripes
koljan'der coriander; *dis vinkel en* ~ six of the one and half a dozen of the other
kolk -e abyss; whirlpool, eddy
kollateraal' ..**rale** collateral; ..**ra'le sekuri= teit'** collateral security
kolle'ga -s colleague *ook* **amps'genoot**
kol'lege -s college; *op/aan* ~ at college
kollek'te -s collection (church, street)
kollekteer' **ge-** collect; ~**op'roep** collect call (tel.)
kollektief' ..**tiewe** collective; ~**ie'we beding'=**

ing collective bargaining
kolom' -me column, pillar
koloniaal' ..**niale** colonial
kolo'nie -s colony, settlement
kolon'ne -s (army) column; **vyf'de** ~ fifth column
kolossaal' (b) colossal, gigantic *ook* **enorm'**
kol'skoot bull's eye
kol'toets -e spot check *kyk* **steek'proef**
kom[1] (s) **-me** basin, bowl; dale, vale
kom[2] (w) **ge-** come, arrive
kombers' -e blanket
kombina'sie combination
kombuis' -e kitchen; ~**gerei'** kitchenware; ~**tee** kitchen tea *ook* **bruids'kombuis**
komediant' -e comedian, actor
kome'die -s comedy, farce *ook* **bly'spel/klug**
komeet' komete comet
ko'mies -e; -er, -ste comic(al), funny
komitee' -s committee; *hy dien in/op 'n* ~ he serves on a committee; **uitvoe'rende** ~ executive committee
komkom'mer -s cucumber
kom'ma -s comma
kommandant' -e commandant, commander
kommandeer' ~, **ge-** command, commandeer; ~ *jou eie honde en blaf self* do your own dirty work
komman'do -'s commando; ~**wurm** army worm
kom'mapunt -e semicolon (;)
kommentaar' ..**tare** commentary, comment; ~ *lewer op (maak oor)* comment upon
kommenta'tor -s, -e commentator (person)
kom'mer (s) trouble, distress, anxiety; *die toestand wek* ~ the situation is causing concern; ~**kra'le** worry beads; ~**nis** worry, care, anxiety
kommersieel' ..**siële** commercial; ..**ië'le reg** commercial law *kyk* **han'delsreg**
kommissa'ris -se commissioner; **K**~ **van E'de** Commissioner of Oaths
kommis'sie -s commission
kommoditeit' -e commodity, consumer article
kommu'ne -s commune
kommunika'sie -s communication; ~**kun'de/ ~leer** communication (subject)
Kommunis' -te Communist; ~**me** Commun= ism; ~**ties** (b) Communistic
kompak'skyf compact disc (CD) *ook* **la'serskyf**
kompanjie' -s company
komparatief' ..**tiewe** comparative
kompartement' -e compartment

kompas' -se compass
kom'per (s) computer *ook* **re'kenaar**; ~**druk= stuk** computer print-out
kompeteer' (b) compete *ook* **wed'ywer**
kompeti'sie -s competition
kompleet' ..**plete** complete *ook* **voltal'lig**
kompleks' (s) -e complex (cluster of houses/ shops); idea, obsession; (b) complicated
komplika'sie -s complication
kompliment' (s) -e compliment; *iem. 'n* ~ *maak* pay someone a compliment
kompli'menteer' (w) ~, ge- compliment
komplimentêr' -e complimentary; ~**e kaar'= tjie** complimentary ticket
komplot' -te plot, intrigue, conspiracy *ook* **sa'meswering**; *'n* ~ *smee* hatch a plot
komponeer' ge- compose (music)
komponis' -te composer (person)
komposi'sie -s composition *ook* **toon'setting**
kom'pos (s) compost
koms arrival, coming, advent
kondensa'sie condensation
kondi'sie -s condition *ook* **toe'stand**; **voor'= waarde**; state (of health)
kondoom' (s) condom
kondukteur' -s conductor, guard
konfedera'sie -s confederation
konferen'sie -s conference; ~**gan'ger** confer= ence delegate
konfidensieel' (b) ..**siële** confidential; **konfi= densië'le in'ligting** confidential information *ook* **vertrou'lik**
konfiskeer' ge- confiscate *ook* **beslag lê op**
konflik' -te conflict; ~**situa'sie** conflict situa= tion
konfronta'sie confrontation
konfyt'1 (s) -e jam; preserve
konfyt'2 (w): *ge*~ *wees in* be well versed in
kongres' -se congress
ko'ning -s king
koningin' -ne queen
ko'ninklik -e royal, regal, kingly; *van* ~*e afkoms* of royal descent
ko'ninkryk -e kingdom; empire
kon'ka -s empty (petrol) tin, drum, brazier; firetin
kon'kel (w) ge- plot, scheme *ook* **knoei**; botch; ~**aar** schemer (person)
kon'kelwerk muddling, botching; *donkerwerk is* ~ a bungler/schemer works in the dark
konklu'sie -s conclusion *ook* **gevolg'trekking**
konkreet ..**krete** concrete *ook* **tas'baar**

konkurren'sie competition, rivalry *ook* **me'= dedinging**; *strawwe* ~ stiff competition (in business)
konkurrent' -e competitor, rival
konnek'sie -s connection
konnekteer' (w) ge- connect
konsensieus' -e conscientious *ook* **pligs'ge= trou**
konsen'sus concensus, agreement, accord
konsentra'sie concentration; ~**kamp** concen= tration camp
konsen'tries -e concentric
konsep' -te draft, concept; ~**ordonnan'sie** draft ordinance; ~**wet'gewing** draft legisla= tion; ~**wets'ontwerp** draft bill
konsert' -e concert; recital
konserti'na -s concertina, squash-box; ~**hek** concertina (collapsible) gate
konservato'rium -s conservatoire, conservatory
konserwatief' ..**tiewe** conservative *ook* **be= hou'dend**
konses'sie -s concession *ook* **toe'gewing**; ~**kaar'tjie** concession ticket
konsisto'rie -s consistory, vestry (church)
konskrip'sie conscription
konsolida'sie consolidation
konsonant' -e consonant *ook* **me'deklinker**
konsta'bel -s constable
konstateer' (w) ~, ge- state, prove, declare
konstella'sie -s constellation; ~ *van state* constellation of states
konsterna'sie consternation, turmoil *ook* **op'= skudding**
konstitu'sie -s constitution *ook* **grond'wet/ grond'reëls**
konstrueer' ge- construe, construct
konstruk'sie -s construction
konsuis' quasi, as if (it were) *ook* **kam'(s)tig**
kon'sul -s consul
konsulaat' ..**late** consulate
konsul-generaal' consul-general
konsult' -e consultation; ~**ingenieur'** consult= ing engineer *ook* **raad'gewende ingenieur'**
konsulta'sie -s consultation *ook* **oorleg'ple= ging**
kontak' (s) -te contact; *in* ~ *bly met* keep in touch with; ~**lens** contact lens; (w) contact (a person)
kontamineer' ge- contaminate
kontant' (s) -e; ~ *by aflewering* cash on delivery; ~**stro'kie** cash slip; ~**vloei** cash flow

kontinent′ -e continent *ook* **vas′teland**
kontinentaal′ . .**tale** continental
kontoer′ -e contour
kontrak′ te contract; *'n* ~ *sluit/aangaan* enter into a contract; ~**breuk** breach of contract
kontrakteur′ -s contractor *ook* **aan′nemer** (mens)
kontras′ (s) -te contrast *ook* **teen′stelling**
kontrei′ -e region, area, (platteland) district *ook* **streek**
kontro′le (s) control *ook* **beheer′**
kontroleer′ ~, ge- control, check *ook* **na′gaan, moniteer′/mo′nitor** (w)
kontroleur′ -s controller, supervisor
konvensioneel′ . .**nele** conventional
konvoka′sie convocation (of a university)
konvooi′ (s) -e convoy
konyn′ -e rabbit, bunny *kyk* **haas**
kooi -e bed; cage; ~ *toe gaan* go to bed
kook[1] **ge-** boil, cook; do the cooking
kook[2] (w) falsify, cook (books); manipulate
kool[1] cabbage; *die* ~ *is die sous nie werd nie* the game is not worth the candle
kool[2] **kole** coal; *op hete kole sit* be on pins and needles
kool′stof carbon
koop (s) purchase, bargain; *op die* ~ *toe* into the bargain; (w) buy, purchase; ~**brief** deed of sale; ~**-en-loop** cash-and-carry; ~**-en-loop**′**-happies** take-aways
koöpera′sie/ko opera′sie ~ co-operative so-ciety (co-op)
koop: Kamer van K~**handel** Chamber of Commerce; ~**kontrak′** contract of sale; ~**krag** purchasing/buying power; ~**prys** cost, purchase price
koöpteer′/ko-opteer′ (w) ge- co-opt
koor kore choir (of singers); chorus (of a song); ~**lei′er** choirmaster
koord -e cord, rope; ~**dan′ser** tightrope walker; ~**ferweel′** corduroy
koördina′sie/ko-ordina′sie (s) co-ordination
koord′lose: ~ **telefoon′** cordless telephone
koors -e fever; ~**ag′tig** hectic, frenzied
koor′sang -e choral song; choral singing
koors: ~**blaar** blister; ~**(er)ig** feverish; ~**pen′netjie** clinical thermometer
kop[1] (s) -pe cob, ear (mealie)
kop[2] -pe head; mountain peak, summit; ~ *in een mus* be hand in glove (together); *op die* ~ *sesuur* exactly six o'clock; ~ **teen** ~ **bot′sing** head-on collision *ook* **front′**

botsing/tromp′opbotsing
ko′per[2] -s buyer
ko′per[2] copper; ~**draad** copper wire; ~**kapel′** yellow cobra
ko′pie[1] -s bargain *ook* **wins′kopie/keur′koop**
kopie′[2] -ë copy (of document); transcription
kopieer′ (w) ge- copy; transcribe
kopie′reg copyright
kop′krapper (s) brainteaser *ook* **breinboe′lie**
kop′pel (w) ge- couple, tie, connect; hyphen-ate; ~**aar′** coupler; match maker; pimp, procurer (prostitution) *ook* **pooi′er**; clutch (motor); ~**lor′rie** articulated vehicle; ~**te′-ken** hyphen; ~**uit′sending** simulcast trans-mission (TV); ~**vlak** interface
kop′penent -e head (of a bed)
kop′pesneller -s headhunter, scalphunter
kop′pie -s cup; hill(ock), koppie
kop′pig obstinate, stubborn, headstrong
kop: ~**seer** headache *ook* **hoof′pyn**; ~**speld** pin
koraal′ . .**rale** coral (reef); ~**boom** coral tree; ~**musiek′** choral music; ~**rif** coral reef
kordaat′ . .**dater, -ste** brave, undaunted, bold; **Jan K**~ brave fellow
kordon′ cordon; *'n* ~ *trek om 'n gebied* cordon off an area *ook* **af′sper**
korf korwe hive; ~**bal** basketball (women); ~**behuis′ing** cluster housing
ko′ring wheat; *ook groen* ~ *op die land hê* have fledglings of one's own; ~**kriek** corn/harvester cricket (Parktown prawn)
koronê′re trombo′se coronary thrombosis
korporaal′ -s corporal
korporaat′ corporate; ~**aanspreek′likheid** c. liability
korpora′sie -s corporation; **beslo′te** ~ close corporation
korps (s) -e corps
korrek′ -te correct, right; ~**sie** correction; ~**tlew′e diens′te** correctional services
kor′rel (s) -s grain; sight (rifle); bead; *met 'n* ~**tjie** *sout neem* take with a pinch of salt; (w) aim; pick off (grapes)
korrespondeer′ ~, ge- correspond
korresponden′sie correspondence; ~**kol′lege** correspondence college; ~**kur′sus** corre-spondence course *ook* **af′standonderrig**
korrespondent′ -e correspondent
korrigeer′ (w) ge- correct *ook* **reg′stel**
korrup′ -te corrupt; ~**sie** corruption
kors -te crust

korset′ -te corset; foundation garment
kor′sie -s crust (of bread)
kors′wel/kors′wil (s) jest, joke; (w) jest, joke; *ek ~ sommer* I'm only joking
kort (w) ge- shorten; (b, bw) short, brief; *~ en kragtig* short and sweet; *~af* abrupt, blunt; *~a′sem* short of breath *ook* **uita′sem**; *~golf*-sta′sie shortwave station; *~ing* discount, reduction *ook* **af′slag**; *~kuns* (modern) short prose; *~liks* briefly; *~om* in a word
kortsig′tig -e; -er, -ste short-sighted
kort′sluiting short-circuit
korston′dig short-lived, transitory; *~e vre′de* short-lived peace
kort: *~verhaal′* shortstory; *~wiek* (w) clip the wings; thwart *ook* **in′kort**
kos¹ (s) -se food; *~ en inwoning* board and lodging
kos² (w) ge- cost; *dit ~ niks* no charge
kos: *~baar* precious, dear; expensive; *~gan′ger* boarder, lodger; *~huis* boarding house
kosme′ties: *~e veran′dering* cosmetic/super-ficial change
kosmopoliet′ -e cosmopolitan *ook* **wêreldbur-ger**
kos′mos cosmos
kos: *~skool* boarding school; *~te* expenses, costs; *ten ~te van* at the cost of; *~te*-doeltref′fend/koste-effektief cost effective; *~telik′* precious, fine, excellent, *'n ~telike grap* a priceless joke; *~teloos′* free, gratis
kos′ter -s churchwarden, beadle, sexton
kostuum′ costume; *~bal* fancy-dress ball
kosyn′ -e frame, sill; doorpost
kot′huis -e cottage *ook* **cot′tage**
kots ge- vomit *ook* **braak, op′gooi**
kou¹ (s) -e cage *ook* **kou′tjie**
kou² (s) cold *ook* **kou′e**
kou³ (w) ge- chew, masticate; *harde bene om te ~* have a tough job
koud (b) cold, chilly
kou′e cold, chill; *~ vat* catch a chill; *~vuur* gangrene *ook* **gangreen′**
kou′gom chewing gum
kou′kus -se caucus (of political party); (v) confer, deliberate *ook* **beraad′slaag**
kous -e stocking, sock; *~broe′kie* pantihose
kraag krae collar
kraai (s) -e crow; *so maer soos 'n ~* as thin as a rake; (w) crow (rooster)
kraak (s) **krake** crack; *~been* cartilage
kraal¹ krale pen, kraal; tribal village; *agteros*

kom ook in die ~ slow but sure
kraal² **krale, ~tjie** -s bead
kraam¹ booth, stall *ook* **loket′/kiosk/stal**
kraam² labour (childbirth); *~in′rigting* mater-nity home; *~verlof′* maternity leave
kraan (s) **krane** tap, stopcock; crane
kraan′voël -s crane
krab′bel (w) ge- scratch, scrawl, scribble
kraf′fie -s waterbottle; decanter *ook* **karaf′**
krag -te strength, power, force, vigour; *van ~ word* come into force; *~boot* power boat
krag: *~fiets* buzz-bike, moped; *~mas* pylon; *~me′ting* match, contest; *~op′tel* power lifting; *~op′wekker* generator; *~prop* power plug; *~rem′me* power brakes
krag′sentrale -s power station *ook* **krag′stasie**
krag′tens by virtue of, in consequence of *ook* **ingevol′ge;** *~ die ordonnansie* in terms of the ordinance
krag′tig powerful, strong; *~e bom* powerful bomb
kram (s) -me clamp; staple; (w) clamp; staple; *~druk′ker/~bin′der* stapler
kram′metjie -s (wire) staple
kramp -e cramp, spasm; convulsion
krampag′tig -e convulsive, spasmodic
kranksin′nig -e insane, mad, crazy, lunatic; *~e* lunatic (person); *~e′gestig′* lunatic asylum
krans¹ (s) -e wreath; (w) festoon
krans² (s) -e rocky ridge, krans
krap¹ (s) -pe crab
krap² (s) -pe scratch; (w) scratch
kras (b) -ser, -ste vigorous; drastic: *~ optree teen* take drastic steps against
krat -te crate, holder/container
kra′ter -s crater
krediet′ credit; *~gerie′we* credit facilities; *~kaart* credit card; *~sal′do/~balans′* credit balance
krediteer′ ge- credit; *iem. ~ met* credit a person's account with
krediteur′ -e, -s creditor *ook* **skuld′eiser**
kreef krewe lobster; crayfish, crawfish
Kreefs′keerkring Tropic of Cancer
kremato′rium -s crematorium
kremetart′ cream of tartar; *~boom* baobab tree
krenk (w) ge- offend, hurt, mortify; slander
kreu′kel (s) -s crease, fold, ruck; (w) crease, fold; *~traag* crease-resistant; *~vry* non-creasing

kreun (s, w) groan, moan
kreu'pel (b) lame, limping *ook* **krup'pel**
kre'wel -s prawn *ook* **steur'garnaal**
kriek -e cricket (insect)
krie'ket cricket (game); ~**bal** cricket ball;
~**kolf** cricket bat; ~**spe'ler** cricketer
krie'wel ge- tickle, itch; fidget; ~**rig** itchy,
ticklish; fussy
krimineel' (b) **..nele** criminal; **krimine'le
aan'klag** criminal charge
krimp ge- shrink, diminish; ~ *van die pyn*
writhe with pain; ~**vry** shrinkproof;
~**ys'tervark** (Cape) hedgehog
kring -e circle; ring; circuit, orbit; *in sekere*
~*e* in certain quarters; ~**loop** cycle; *bo'se*
~*loop* vicious cycle/spiral; ~**televi'sie**
closed-circuit television
krin'kel (s, w) crinkle; ~**papier'** crêpe paper
krioel' ge- swarm, abound/teem with; *dit* ~
van die muise the place is overrun with mice
krip -pe manger, crib; *aan die* ~ *staan* have a
plush occupation
krisant' -e chrysanthemum *ook* **win'teraster**
kri'sis -se crisis
Kris'mis Christmas *kyk* **Kers'fees**
kristal' -le crystal; *so helder soos* ~ as clear as
crystal
krite'rium -s **krite'ria** criterion *ook* **maat'staf**
kritiek' (s) criticism, critique; flak; review (in
journal) *ook* **resen'sie**
kri'ties -e critical
kri'tikus -se, **kri'tici** critic (person)
kritiseer' (w) **ge-** criticise, slam, censure
kroeg kroeë pub, bar; tavern; ~**mei'sie/
~juf'fer** barmaid; ~**vlieg** barfly
kroepier' (s) -s croupier *ook* **roclet'meester**
kroes curly, frizzy (hair); crisp
krokodil' -le crocodile
krom (b) crooked, curved, bent; ~ *van die lag*
splitting one's sides with laughter; ~ *Afri=
kaans praat* speak faulty Afrikaans; ~**hout=
sap'** wine; ~**me** curve (maths.) *ook* **kur'we**
kroniek' -e chronicle
kro'nies/chro'nies (b) chronic (illness)
kro'ning coronation
kron'kel (w) ge- twist, kink, coil; meander;
~**pad** winding road
kroon (s) **krone** crown; (w) crown; ~**getui'e**
crown witness; ~**juwe'le** crown jewels;
~**prins** crown prince
kroos offspring, children; progeny, descendants;
~**troos'ter** babysitter; *ons gaan vanaand*

~*troos* we will be babysitting tonight
krop (s) -pe crop, gizzard; *dwars in die* ~
steek go against the grain
krot -te hovel, den, shanty; ~**buurt** slum
quarter; squatter camp (informal settlement)
krou'kie croquet (game)
kru (b) crude, coarse *ook* **grof/vulgêr**
krui (w) ge- spice, season
kruid kruie herb, spice *kyk* **krui'e**
kruidenier' -s grocer; ~**s'wa're** groceries
kruidjie-roer'-my-nie touch-me-not, sensitive
plant; touchy fellow
krui'e (s) spice; ~**dok'ter** herbalist
krui'er -s porter (person)
krui'e: (s)~**stel'(letjie)** cruet stand; ~**ry** con=
diment(s)
kruik -e pitcher, jug
kruin (s) -e top, crown, summit
kruip ge- creep, crawl; cringe
kruis (s) -e cross; affliction; sharp (mus.);
crux; *elke huis het sy* ~ there is a skeleton in
every cupboard; ~ *of munt* heads or tails;
(w) cross; cruise; crucify; intersect; inter=
breed; ge~**te tjek** crossed cheque; ~**bande**
(pair of) braces; ~**boog** crossbow
kruisement' mint
krui'sig ge- crucify; ~**ing** crucifixion
krui'sing -s, -e crossbreed(ing); crossing,
intersection
kruis: ~**pad** crossroad; ~**rid'der** crusader;
~**tog** crusade; ~**verhoor'** cross-examina=
tion; ~**verwy'sing** cross-reference; ~**vra**
cross-examine *ook* **ondervra'** (w)
kruit gunpowder; ~**bad** mineral baths; spa
krui'wa -ens wheelbarrow
kruk -ke crutch; stool; crank; ~**kelys'** ca=
sualty/injury list (sport)
krul (s) -le curl; scroll; (w) curl; wave (hair);
~**hare** curly hair; ~**tang** curling tongs
krum'mel (s) -s crumb; bit
krup'pel/kreu'pel -er, -ste lame, cripple(d)
kry ge- get, obtain, acquire, receive
krygs: ~**gevang'ene** prisoner of war; ~**raad**
court martial; ~**wet** martial law
krys (w) ge- crack, scream, screech
kryt[1] ring (for boxing), arena
kryt[2] chalk, crayon
ku'ber (b) cyber; ~**kuns** cyber art; ~**ruim'te**
cyberspace; ~**sluiper** cyberstalker
kubiek' -e cubic; ~**wor'tel** cube root
kud'de (s) -s herd, flock
kui'er (s) outing, visit, call; (w) visit, call; *hy*

het 'n maand lank by sy oom ge~ he stayed with his uncle for a month; ~**gas/**~**mens** visitor, guest; ~**koop** window shopping

kuif kuiwe crest, tuft

kui'ken -s chick, young chicken

kuil (s) **-e** pool, dam; bunker (golf)

kuil'tjie (s) **-s** dimple (in cheek, chin)

kuip (s) **-e** coop, tub; pit (motor racing); (w) cooper; ~**er** cooper (person)

kuis -e; -er, -ste chaste, pure, virtuous

kuit -e calf; ~**been** fibula

kul ge- cheat, deceive; ~**kun'stenaar** magi= cian *ook* **go'ëlaar**

kultureel' ..**rele** cultural

kul'tus cult, creed

kul'tuur culture, civilisation; cultivation

kun'dig (b) able, competent, skilful; ~**heid** skill, ability, expertise, know-how

kuns -te art, skill; knack; trick; *die beeldende* ~*te* the plastic arts; *die skone* ~*te* the fine arts; ~**aas** artificial bait, dummy; ~**galery'** art museum, picture gallery; ~**gebit'** den= ture, set of artificial teeth; ~**le'demate** artificial limbs

kunsma'tig -e artificial; ~**e insemina'sie (K.I.)** artificial insemination (A.I.)

kuns: ~**mis** fertiliser; ~**skil'der** artist, painter; ~**stop** invisible mending; ~**stuk** work of art; clever feat; ~**tenaar'** artist; ~**tig** ingenious, clever, artful; ~**vlieënier'** stunt flyer; ~**vlyt** arts and crafts; ~**wed'stryd** eisteddfod; ~**werk** work of art

kurk -e cork; ~**droog** (b) dry as a bone; ~**trek'ker** corkscrew

kur'per -s kurper, tilapia (fish)

kursief' ..**siewe** italic, in italics

kur'sus -se course; *'n* ~ *loop/volg* attend a course

kur'we -s curve *ook* **boog, ron'ding**

kus[1] (s) **-te** coast, shore

kus[2] (s) **-se** kiss *ook* **soen**; (w) kiss

kus[3] (s): *te* ~ *en te keur* for picking and choosing

kus'sing -s pillow, cushion; ~**sloop** pillow case; ~**tuig** hovercraft *ook* **skeer'tuig**

kuur (s) cure, remedy; **gesig(s)**~ facelift

kwaad (s) evil, mischief, wrong; ~ *wees vir* be angry with

kwaadaar'dig malignant; malicious, vicious; ~**e groei'sel/gewas'** malignant growth/tumour

kwaad: ~**doe'ner** evildoer; ~**geld** mischief; *vir* ~**geld** *rondloop* gad about

kwaai -er; -ste vicious, wild; hot-tempered; strict; ~ **hond** vicious dog

kwaaivrien'de bad friends

kwaak (w) ge- croak, quack

kwaal kwale ailment, complaint, malady

kwa'drupleeg ..**pleë** quadruplegic (person)

kwag'ga -s quagga; zebra

kwa'jong -ens mischievous boy, urchin; ~**streek** monkey trick, prank

kwak'salwer quack, charlatan, mountebank

kwalifika'sie -s qualification

kwalifiseer' (w) ~, ge- qualify

kwa'lik ill, amiss; hardly, scarcely; *hy kon* ~ *loop* he could hardly walk; *iem.* ~ *neem* blame someone

kwaliteit' -e quality *ook* **gehal'te**

kwansuis' quasi, as if (it were); so-called

kwantiteit' -e quantity *ook* **hoeveel'heid**

kwarantyn' (s) quarantine

kwart -e quart; quarter; ~ *oor/na agt* a quarter past eight

kwartaal' ..**tale** quarter, term

kwar'tel -s quail; *so doof soos 'n* ~ stonedeaf, as deaf as a post

kwartet' -te quartet

kwartier' -e quarter (of an hour, of the moon, battle); district; dwelling

kwarts quartz; ~**horlo'sie** quartz watch

kwas[1] (s) squash (drink)

kwas[2] **-te** brush; tuft; knot; tassel

kwa'sie quasi, as if

kweek[1] (s) couch/quick grass

kweek[2] (w) ge- cultivate, train; grow; *vrug= tebome* ~ grow fruittrees

kweek: ~**huis** hothouse; ~**huiseffek'** green= house effect; ~**pê'rel** cultured pearl; ~**skool** seminary

kwe'keling -e pupil teacher; cadet; trainee

kwe'kery -e nursery; seedplot

kwel ge- worry *ook* **bekom'mer**; trouble, harass, torment

kwe'la (w) kwela; ~**fluit** pennywhistle

kwe'per -s quince; ~**lat** quince cane

kwes ge- wound, injure; *'n bok* ~ wound a buck; ~**baar** vulnerable

kwes'sie -s question, matter; issue; *buite die* ~ out of the question

kwets (w) grieve, offend; *iem. se gevoelens* ~ hurt someone's feelings

kwê'voël grey lourie, go-away bird

kwik'silwer mercury, quicksilver

kwik'stertjie -s wagtail, Willie Wagtail

kwink'slag (s) witticism, quip
kwis'pel ge- wag the tail
kwis'tig lavish *ook* **rojaal'**; prodigal
kwitan'sie -s receipt (for money paid)
kwo'rum -s quorum; *geen ~ aanwesig nie* no quorum present
kwo'ta -s quota
kwota'sie -s quotation *ook* **prys'opgawe**
kwoteer' (w) **~, ge-** quote; estimate
kwyl (s) slaver, drivel; (w) slaver, drivel

kwyn ge- languish, pine away, wilt
kwyt (w) **ge-** discharge; acquit oneself; **~skeld** (w) waive; pardon
kyf ge- quarrel, dispute, argue *ook* **twis**
kyk (s) **-e** look, view; (w) look, see, view; pry; **~er** eye; looker-on; viewer (TV); **~kas(sie)** television set; **~rit** sightseeing tour; **~weer** replay (TV)
kys: *hy is my ~* he is my (steady) boyfriend; *ons is ge~* we are going steady

L

laaf/la'we refresh; help to recover from a swoon; **~nis/la'fenis** refreshment; relief
laag[1] (s) **lae** layer; coating; course (bricks)
laag[2] (b) **lae**; **laer**, **-ste** mean; low; vulgar; *teen 'n lae prys* at a low price
laag'te -s valley, dale, dell, dip
laag'water low tide *ook* **eb** (s)
laai[1] (s) **-e** drawer, till
laai[2] (s) **-e** trick, dodge; *dis sy ou ~* that's his old trick
laai[3] (w) **ge-** load; charge; **~graaf** front-end loader; **~kas** chest of drawers, tallboy; container
laai'meester -s checker (railways)
laan lane avenue, lane, alley
laas last; *die ~te (leste) een van julle* all of you; *ten ~te* at last; **~genoem'de** the latter; **~le'de** last, ultimo; **~te** last; **~tens** lastly
laat[1] (w) **ge-** let, allow, refrain from (doing); make (one) do; *in die steek ~* leave in the lurch
laat[2] (b) late; later, laatste late; **~lam'metjie** afterthought, late arrival (child)
laborato'rium -s, ..ria, laboratory
la'ding -s, -e cargo, load, shipment
la'er[1] (s) bearing (of engine) *ook* **koe'ëllaer**
la'er[2] (s) **-s** wagon encampment, laager
la'er[3] (b) lower, inferior
la'erskool/la'er skool ..skole primary school *ook* **primêre skool**
laf lawwe; lawwer, -ste insipid, flat; cowardly, silly; *law'we grap* silly joke; **~aard** coward *ook* **pap'broek**
lafhar'tig -e; -er, -ste cowardly
lag (s) laugh, laughter; *ek kon my ~ nie hou nie* I could not help laughing; *skater van die*

~ shake with laughter; (w) laugh; *lag-lag wen* win without effort
lagu'ne -s lagoon *ook* **strand'meer**
lagwek'kend -e; -er, -ste ludicrous
lai'tie (s) chappie *ook* **tjok'kertjie, buk'sie**
lak[1] (s) sealing wax, lacquer; (w) seal; japan; **~vernis'ser** French polisher
lak[2] (w) **ge-** tackle *ook* **laag'vat** (rugby)
lakei' -e footman, lackey; henchman; stooge
la'ken -s cloth, sheet
laks -e; -er, -ste lax, indolent, slack
lakseer' (w) purge, open (the bowels); **~mid'del** laxative, purgative
laks'man -ne hangman, executioner; butcher-bird, fiscal shrike
lam[1] (s) **~mers** lamb, (w) lamb
lam[2] (b) lame, paralysed; *~ geskrik* paralysed with fright
lamel'hout laminated wood
lamlen'dig lazy, indolent, miserable
lam'mer: **~ooi** ewe with lamb; **~van'ger** golden eagle, lammergeyer
lam'metjie/lammertjie little lamb
lamp -e lamp
lamp: **~kap** lampshade; **~o'lie** paraffin (oil)
lam'sak lazybones, weakling, shirker (person)
lam: **~siek'te** lameness, paralysis; botulism; **~slaan** (w) paralyse; *dit het my lamgeslaan* it knocked me sideways
land (s) **-e** land; country; field; *~ en sand (see) aanmekaar praat* talk without stopping; *hier te ~e* in this country; (w) disembark, arrive, land
land-af offshore (winds) *ook* **see'waarts**
land'bou agriculture; **~er** farmer
land: **~dros** magistrate *ook* **magistraat'**; **~e-**

lik' rustic, rural; ~*elike omgewing* rural environment; ~**genoot'** countryman, com=patriot; ~**goed** estate, country seat

lan'ding (s) landing; ~**strook** airstrip

land: ~**kaart** map; ~**loop** cross-country race; ~**lo'per** vagrant, tramp, vagabond; ~**merk** landmark; ~**me'ter** (land) surveyor; ~**myn** landmine; ~**skap** landscape

lands: ~**re'ën** general rain; ~**taal** vernacular, language of the country; ~**vlag** national flag

land: ~**streek** region, district; ~**verhui'ser** emigrant; ~**verraai'er** traitor; ~**(s)wyd** nationwide, countrywide; *landwye veldtog* national campaign

lan'fer crape (crêpe); mourning

lang (attributief) **-er, -ste** long, tall

langdra'dig long-winded, wordy, prolix

langdu'rig long-lasting, protracted; ~**e droog=te** prolonged drought

lang'saam slow, tardy

lang'samerhand gradually *ook* **gaan'deweg**

lang: ~**speelplaat/**~**spe'ler** LP record

langwer'pig -e oblong, rectangular

la'ning -s hedge, grove; avenue

lank (predikatief) **langer, langste** long, tall; ~**al** long ago; ~**laas** long time ago

lankmoe'dig -e; -er, -ste patient, clement

lans -e lance, spear

lanseer' ~, **ge-** launch (torpedo, spacecraft); start; lance, pierce (tumour); ~**blad** launch=(ing) pad *kyk* **loods** (w)

lantern' -s lantern

lap (s) **-pe** patch; cloth; rag; *op die* ~*pe bring* bring to light; (w) mend; patch; **ge**~**te broek'** patched trousers

la'pa (s) lapa, meeting place

lapel' -le lapel; ~**wa'pen** lapel badge

lar'we -s larva

las[1] (s) **-se** seam, joint, weld; (w) join, weld; pool funds

las[2] (s) **-te** burden, freight; charge, order; nuisance; **op** ~ by order (legal); **ba'tes en** ~**te** assets and liabilities

la'ser laser; ~**druk'ker** laser printer; ~**skyf** compact disk (CD) *ook* **laserplaat**; ~**straal** laser beam; ~**tas'ter** laser scanner

las'pos -te nuisance, troublesome person

las'ter (s) slander; defamation, libel; (w) slander; ~**lik** (b) libellous, defamatory

las'tig troublesome, annoying *ook* **hin'derlik**

las'wa articulated vehicle *ook* **kop'pellorrie**

lat -te lath; stick, cane; batten

la'ter later; *hoe* ~ *hoe kwater* the longer it lasts, the worse it becomes

Latyn' Latin

laven'tel lavender, scent; ~**haan** dandy (per=son)

la'wa lava

lawaai' (s) noise; hubbub, tumult

lê ge- place, put; lay (eggs); *dit* ~ *voor die hand* it goes without saying; *op sterwe* ~ be dying

le'degeld -e membership fee *ook* **lid'geld**

le'de: ~**lys** list of members *ook* **lid'lys**; ~**ma'te** (net in mv) limbs, parts of the body; ~**tal** number of members

le'dig (b) **-e** idle; vacant

le'digheid idleness; emptiness; ~ *is die duiwel se oorkussing* Satan finds some mischief for idle hands to do

leed (s) pain, sorrow, grief *ook* **verdriet'**

leef ge- live, exist, subsist; ~**tyd** lifetime; time of life, age; *op middelbare* ~*tyd* in middle life; ~**wy'se** manner of living, lifestyle *ook* **le'wenswyse**

leeg empty, void; vacant; ~**lê** (v) loiter; ~**lêer** vagrant, loafer

leek leke layman; novice

leem'te -s defect, gap, blank; lacuna

leen (w) **ge-** lend; borrow; *ek* ~ *van hom en hy* ~ *aan my* I borrow from him and he lends to me; ~**moe'der** surrogate mother

leer[1] (s) leather; (b) leather

leer[2] (s) **lere** ladder

leer[3] (s) **leerstel'linge** doctrine

leer[4] apprenticeship; (w) learn, study; teach; *van buite* ~ learn by heart

le'ër (s) **-s** army; lair, bed (animal)

lê'er -s file (for papers); layer (hen); register; leaguer (for wine); sleeper (railway)

leer: ~**der** learner; ~**gang** syllabus *ook* **silla'=bus**; ~**gie'rig** (b) studious

leer: ~**klerk** articled clerk; ~**krag** teacher; ~**ling** scholar, pupil; learner; ~**lingry'=bewys** learner driver's licence

leer'looier -s tanner; ~**y** tannery

leer: ~**mees'ter** teacher, tutor; ~**plan** curricu-lum; ~**saam** instructive, informative; ~**skap** articles (accountant, attorney); ~'**skool** prac-tice/demonstration school, workshop *ook* **slyp'skool**; ~**stoel** chair (university)

lees[1] (s) **-te** last; figure, waist; *op dieselfde* ~ *geskoei* cast in the same mould

lees[2] (w) **ge-** read; ~**baar** legible, readable;

~boek reader, reading book; ~gebrek' dyslexia; ~stof reading matter; ~te'ken punctuation mark *ook* interpunk'sie
leeu -s lion; ~bek'kie snapdragon, antirrhi= num (blom); ~e'aan'deel lion's share
leeu: ~hok lion's cage; ~kuil lions' den; ~man'netjie lion
leeu'rik -ke skylark *ook* le'werik (voëltjie)
leeu: ~tem'mer lion tamer; ~wy'fie lioness
legenda'ries -e legendary; ~e figuur' legend= ary figure
legen'de (s) -s legend
legioen' -e legion; ~soldaat' legionary
leg'kaart -e jigsaw puzzle
lei[1] (s) -e slate; ~ en grif'fel slate and slate pencil
lei[2] (w) ge- lead, conduct, guide; preside; ~band leash; *ook* lei'riem
lei'ding direction, management, guidance, leadership *ook* lei'erskap; conduit
lei'draad ..drade clue, lead, guide(line)
lei: ~er leader, guide; gebo're ~er born leader; ~ers'beraad' summit talks *ook* spits'beraad; ~erskap' leadership
lei'klip slate (stone)
lei'sel -s rein; *die* ~ *in hande neem* take charge
lek[1] (s) -ke leak(age), puncture; (w) leak
lek[2] (s) -ke lick; (w) lick
le'keprediker -s lay preacher
lek'ker[1] (s) -s sweet *kyk* lek'kergoed
lek'ker[2] (b) -der, -ste dainty, nice, sweet, palatable, savoury; tipsy; ~bek epicure, sweet tooth
lek'kergoed/lek'kers sweets, confectionery
lek'kerlyf (b) tipsy *ook* aan'geklam
lekkerny' -e titbit, delicacy
lek'sikon -s lexicon, dictionary *ook* woor'de= boek
lek'tor -e, -s lecturer *ook* dosent'
lektuur' reading matter *ook* lees'stof
lel -le lobe (of the ear); wattle (bird)
le'lie -s lily; ~wit lily-white
le'lik -e; -er, -ste ugly, unsightly, deformed; *so* ~ *soos die nag* as ugly as sin
lem -me blade (of a knife); ~skaat'se roller= blades, inline skates
lem'metjie[1] -s lime (fruit)
lem'metjie[2] -s (razor) blade; small blade; ~(s)draad razor wire
lemoen' -e orange; ~konfyt' orange jam/ preserve; ~kwas orange squash; ~sap orange juice

len'delam (b) hipshot, rickety; ~ ta'fel rickety table
le'ner -s borrower; lender *ook* uit'lener
leng'te -s length; longitude
le'nig (b) lithe, supple, agile
le'ning (s) loan
lens -e lens, optic glass
len'sie -s lentil; ~sop lentil soup
len'te -s spring; ~skool refresher course
leo'tard (s) leotard *ook* lyf'kous
le'pel -s spoon; ~ *in die dak steek* give up the ghost
le'pra (s) leprosy *ook* melaats'heid
le'raar -s minister (of religion), parson
les[1] (s) -se lesson
les[2] (w) ge- quench, slake; *jou dors* ~ quench one's thirst
les[3] (b): ~ *bes* last but not least
les'biër (s) -s lesbian
le'ser -s reader
les'sing -s lecture, reading *ook* referaat'
les'senaar -s desk *ook* skryf'tafel
let ge- heed, mind; ~ *wel* mind, note, N.B.
let'sel -s hurt, damage, injury; *sonder* ~ unscathed *ook* ongedeerd'
let'ter (s) -s letter; ~dief plagiarist (person)
let'tere literature; fakulteit' ~ faculty of arts
let'ter: ~greep syllable; ~kun'de literature *ook* literatuur'
letterkun'dig -e literary; ~e man of letters
let'ter ~lik literal(ly); *hulle is* ~lik *afgemaai* they were literally decimated; ~naam acronym, name compounded from initials (e.g. TELKOM, ISCOR)
leu'en -s lie, falsehood; *al is die* ~ *nog so snel, die waarheid agterhaal hom wel* a lie has short wings; ~aar liar (person)
leu'en: ~taal falsehood, untruth; ~ver= klik'ker lie detector
leukemie' leukemia *ook* bloed'kanker
leun ge- lean; ~stoel armchair; ~stoelpatat' (idiom.) couch potato (TV addict)
leu'ning -s support; back of a chair; rail
leu'se -s motto, device, slogan *ook* slag'= spreuk
Leviet' -e Levite; *iem. die L*~*e voorlees* rebuke a person
le'we (s) -ns life; *sy* ~ *lank* all his life; *die* ~ *skenk aan* give birth to; (w) live, exist, subsist
le'wend -e living, alive; ~e ha'we livestock; ~e uit'sending live broadcast

le'wendig alive (animal) *ook* **le'wend;** quick, lively (person); vivid (description)

le'wens: ~**beskry'wing** biography; ~**gehal'te** quality of life; ~**geskie'denis** life story; ~**gevaar'lik** very dangerous; ~**groot** life-size; full length

le'wenskets -e pen sketch (of person)

le'wens: ~*lange erelidskap* honorary life membership; *die* ~*lig aanskou* be born; ~**krag** vitality; ~**kwaliteit'** quality of life; ~**lang/** ~**lank** lifelong; indeterminate; ~**loop** career

le'wens: ~**lus** energy, vivacity; ~**nood-saak'lik** vital; ~**red'der** lifesaver *ook* **men'seredder, strand'wag**

lewensvat'baar (b) viable; ~**heidstudie** viability study *ook* **gangbaar(heid)studie**

le'wensversekering life insurance; ~**(s)maat-skappy'** life insurance company

le'wens: ~**verwag'ting** life expectancy; ~**wy'se** way/manner of life, lifestyle *ook* **leef'wyse**

le'wer[1] (s) **-s** liver

le'wer[2] (w) **ge-** furnish, supply; deliver

lewer ansier' -s furnisher, supplier

le'wer: ~**traan** cod-liver oil; ~**wors** liver sausage

liai'son (s) liaison *ook* **ska'keling**

liasseer' ~**, ge-** file; ~**kabinet'** filing cabinet

liberalis'me liberalism

lid lede member; limb; ~ *word van* become a member of; ~**geld** membership fee; ~**kaart(jie)** membership card

lid'maat ..mate member (of a church); ~**skap** membership *ook* **lid'skap** (van klub)

lid'woord -e article

lied -ere song; hymn

lie'derlik (b) filthy, dirty, debauched, dissolute

lief (s): *in* ~ *en leed* come rain, come shine; (b) dear, beloved, amiable; lovely, sweet; **lie'we mei'sie** sweet girl

liefda'dig -e charitable, benevolent; ~**heid** charity, benevolence

lief'de love; charity; *geloof, hoop en* ~ faith, hope and charity; ~**groete van** yours with love; ~**rik** loving, affectionate

lief'des: ~**ge'dig** love poem; ~**naam:** *in* ~*naam* for heaven's sake; ~**verhaal** love story; ~**wil:** *om* ~*wil* for heaven's sake

lief'hê ..gehad love, care for

liefheb'bend -e loving, affectionate; *u* ~*e niggie* your loving niece

lief'hebbery -e hobby, favourite pursuit *ook* **stok'perdjie**

lief: ~**koos ge-** caress, stroke; fondle; *my ge~koosde boek* my favourite book

lief'ling -e darling, pet, sweetheart; favourite; ~**s'boek** favourite book

lief'ste (s) **-s** sweetheart, dearest, darling *kyk* **lief'ling;** (b) dearest

lieg ge- lie, tell lies

lier -e lyre

lies -te groin; ~**band** athletic support

liet'sjie -s litchi (fruit)

lie'wer(s) rather, preferably; *ek wil* ~ *hierdie een hê* I'd prefer this one

lig[1] (s) **-te** light, give a light; ~**te verdof** dim lights; (b) light

lig[2] (w) **ge-** lift; ~ *op die klip!* pick up that stone!

lig[3] (b) **-te; -ter, -ste** easy; mild; slight; *te* ~ *in die broek* not equal to the task

li'ga -s league

lig'gaam ..game body; *met* ~ *en siel* body and soul

lig'gaams: ~**bou** build of body, stature; ~**oe'fening** physical exercise; ~**op'voe-ding** physical education; ~**taal** body language *ook* **lyf'taal**

liggelo'wig -e; -er, -ste gullible, credulous

lig'ging -s, -e site, position; location

lig'straal (s) **..stra'le** ray of light

lig'telaaie: *in* ~ ablaze, in a blaze; on fire

likeur' -s, -e liqueur

likied' liquid; ~**e ba'tes** liquid assets

likkewaan' ..wane iguana, leguan

likwida'sie liquidation

lim'bier (s) shandy *ook* **lim(ona'de)bier**

limeriek' limerick *ook* **bog'rympie**

limona'de lemonade

linguis' -te linguist *ook* **taal'geleerde**

liniaal' liniale ruler

linieer' (w) **ge-** rule (lines)

lin'ker left; ~**arm** left arm; ~**kant** left side; ~**stuur** lefthand drive

links left-handed; to/on the left; ~ *af* to the left; *iets* ~ *laat lê* leave something undone; ~**gesind'** leftwing (politics)

lin'ne linen; ~**goed** linen

lint -e ribbon; tape; ~**reën** (s) ticker-tape parade/procession; ~**wurm** tapeworm, taenia

lip -pe lip; ~**pe'diens** lip service; ~**stif'fie** (s) lipstick

liriek' (s) lyric poetry; lyrics

lirie'ke lyrics *ook* **(li'riese) teks/woor'de**

li'ries -e lyric(al) *ook* **melodieus'**
lis[1] -te trick, ruse, cunning, artifice
lis[2] -se noose, loop *ook* **lus** (s)
lisensiaat' licentiate
lisen'sie -s licence *ook* **liksens'**
lis'tig -e; -er, -ste cunning, artful, wily *ook* **slu, gesle'pe**
lit -te joint; internode; *uit* ~ out of joint
li'ter -s litre; *twee* ~ *melk* two litres of milk
litera'tor -e, -s literator, man of letters
literatuur' ..**ture** literature
literêr' -e literary
lit'teken -s scar, flesh mark
loei (w) ge- low, bellow, moo; ~**er** siren
loer ge- spy, watch, lurk; *op die* ~ *lê* lie in wait; ~**gaat'jie** peephole
loe'rie -s lourie (bird)
loer: ~**koop** window shopping; ~**ky'ker** seeing eye; ~**vink** Peeping Tom
loe'sing -s thrashing, hiding; *iem. 'n afgedankste* ~ *gee* give someone a sound thrashing
lof praise, eulogy; *met* ~ *slaag* pass with honours/distinction; ~**re'de** panegyric, eulogy; ~**san'ger** praise singer (imbongi); ~**waar'dig** praiseworthy
logarit'me -s logarithm
lo'gies (b) e logical
lojaal (b) **lojale** loyal *ook* **trou**
lojaliteit' loyalty
lok[1] (s) -ke curl, lock; coil
lok[2] (w) ge- decoy, entice, lure
lokaal' (s) **lokale** hall, room *ook* **saal, vertrek'**; (b) **lokale** local
lok'aas ..**ase** bait, allurement, decoy
loket' -te ticket window, box office; ~**tref'fer** box office success
lok'film trailer
lokomotief' ..**tiewe** locomotive, engine
lok'val -le ambush, trap *ook* **hin'derlaag**
lok'vink -e police trap; decoy
lol ge- bother, trouble; *moenie heeldag met my* ~ *nie* don't pester me always; **kin'derlol'ler** child molester *ook* **pedofiel'**
lomp -e; -er, -ste clumsy, awkward
lom'pe: ~ *tot luukse* rags to riches
long -e lung; ~**kan'ker** lung cancer; ~**ontste'king** inflammation of the lungs, pneumonia; ~**te'ring** phthisis
lont -e fuse; ~ *ruik* smell a rat
lood lead; plumb, plummet; ~**gie'ter** plumber; ~**reg** perpendicular, vertical; ~**vry(e) pet'rol** unleaded petrol

loods[1] (s) -e shed; hangar (aircraft)
loods[2] (s) -e pilot (harbour); (w) pilot; launch (a scheme/project)
loof (w) ge- praise, extol, glorify *ook* **prys** (w)
looi ge- tan; beat, thrash; ~**bas** wattle bark; ~**ery** tannery
loon (s) **lone** reward; pay; wages; *hy kry sy verdiende* ~ it serves him right; (w) pay, reward; *dit sal die moeite* ~ it will be worth the trouble; ~**ga'ping** wage gap
loop (s) **lope** course, run; walk; stream; barrel (gun); (w) walk; go; ~**baan** career; ~**dop** last drink, one for the road; ~**gesel'ser** walkietalkie; ~**graaf** trench; ~**plank** gangway, footboard; ~**ring** walking ring (for child)
loops -e ruttish; on heat *ook* **op hit'te**
loop: ~**tyd** duration (of loan, etc.); currency (of bill, etc.)
loot[1] (s) **lote** shoot; descendant, offspring
loot[2] (w) ge- draw lots, raffle; ~**jie** lottery ticket; *die cc*~ *wen* win the toss (sport)
lo'pend -e current, present, running; ~**e belas'tingstelsel (LBS)** Pay As You Earn (PAYE); ~**e re'kening** current account
lo'per -s runner, staircarpet; walker; masterkey/skeleton key
lu'pie -s little stream; run (cricket)
lor'rie -s lorry; ~**dry'wer** lorry driver
los (w) ge- loosen; free; redeem; let go; *laat my* ~! let me go!; (b) loose, free; ~ **wer'ker** casual worker
lusban'dig -e; -er, -ste dissolute, licentious
los'bol -le rake, libertine, playboy (person)
los'brand -ge- discharge, fire off
los'breek -ge- break loose/away
loseer' ~, ge- lodge, board, stay at; ~**der** lodger, boarder
los'geld ransom money *ook* **los'prys**
los'goed movable property *ook* **roe'rende goed**
lo'sie -s lodge (Freemason); (private) suite
losies' lodging, boarding; ~**huis** boarding house
los'loop -ge- run loose, be at large; **los'loperhond/los'loophond** stray dog
los'lootjie -s bye (in the draw)
los'pitperske -s freestone peach
los'prys ransom *kyk* **los'geld**
lot[1] fate, destiny; *hom aan sy* ~ *oorlaat* leave him to his fate
lot[2] -te lot/batch (at sale)
lot[3] lot; *die* ~ *laat beslis* decide by casting lots
lo'tery -e lottery, raffle
lo'ting draw, drawing of lots; ballot

lot'jie: *van* ~ *getik* mad, daft, crazy (person)
lou -er, -ste lukewarm, tepid
lou'ere laurels; *op sy* ~ *rus* rest on one's laurels
lourier' -e laurel, bay; ~**krans** laurel wreath
lo'wer/loof (s) foliage; ~**groen** quite (very) green; **lo'werstad** arbor city
lug (s) **-te** air, sky; smell; (w) air, ventilate; *sy gevoelens* ~ vent one's feelings; *die* ~ *suiwer* clear the air; ~**aan'val** air attack; ~**akrobaat'** stunt flyer; ~**ballon'** hot-air balloon; ~**bombardement'** air raid; ~**band** tubeless tyre; ~**diens** airways/airline; ~**dig** airtight; ~**draad** aerial; ~**druk** atmospheric pressure; ~**duik** skydiving; ~**fil'ter** air filter; ~**fo'to** aerial photograph
lughar'tig -e; -er, -ste light-hearted
lug: ~ **ha'we** airport; ~**le'dig** void of air; ~**leë ruim'te** vacuum; ~**mag** air force; ~**pos** airmail; ~**redery'** airline; ~**ruim** atmosphere; ~**sak** airbag (car); ~**skip** airship, dirigible; ~**spie'ëling** mirage; fata morgana; ~**sui'weraar** air filter
lug'tig -e airy, lightly, light-hearted; afraid; *hy is maar* ~ *vir my* he takes no liberties with me
lug: ~**vaart** aviation, aeronautics; ~**ver= fris'ser** air freshener; ~**versor'ging** air= conditioning; *die winkel is lugversorg* the shop is airconditioned; ~**waardin'** air hostess (cabin crew)
lui[1] (w) **ge-** sound, ring, toll, peal; *hoe* ~ *die brief?* how does the letter go?
lui[2] (b) **-er, -ste** lazy, idle; slothful; ~**aard** sluggard, lazybones, laggard *ook* **lui'lak**; ~**dier** sloth *ook* **ai** (indien drietoon)
luid'keels (b) at the top of one's voice
luid'roeper -s loudhailer; megaphone
luidrug'tig -e; -er, -ste noisy, clamorous
luid'spreker -s loudspeaker; ~**stel'sel** public address system
lui'er[1] (s) **-s** swaddling cloth, napkin (baby); ~**diens** napkin service
lui'er[2] (w) **ge-** laze about; idle (engine)
luik (s) **-e** shutter; manhole; trapdoor; hatch (ship); ~**rug** hatchback (car)
lui'lak -s -ke sluggard, lazybones (person)
luilek'kerland (land of) Cocagne, fool's para= dise, happy valley
luim (s) **-e** whim, mood; *in ligter* ~ in lighter vein
lui'perd -s leopard; panther
luis -e louse, vermin; *jou lae* ~*!* you cad!

lui'slang -e python, boa constrictor
lui'ster[1] (s) lustre, glory, splendour
luis'ter[2] (w) **ge-** listen, hear; obey; *na goeie raad* ~ follow good advice; ~**lied'jie** light modern song; ~**aar** listener (radio); ~**vink** eavesdropper; ~**vlooi** electronic bug *ook* **klik'apparaat**
luit -e lute
luitenant' -e, -s lieutenant
lukwart' -e loquat (fruit)
lum'mel -s boor, lout, simpleton (person)
lus (s) **-te** desire, appetite, inclination
lusern' lucerne
lus: ~**hof** pleasure garden; ~**teloos'** listless, dull; ~**tig** cheerful
luuk'se (s) luxury; *nie gewoond aan sulke* ~*s nie* not used to such luxuries; ~ **arti'kel** luxury article; ~ **bus** luxury bus; ~ **mo'tor** luxury car *ook* **weel'demotor**
ly ge- suffer, bear, endure; *skipbreuk* ~ be shipwrecked; *dit* ~ *geen twyfel nie* there is no doubt
ly'delik -e passive, submissive; ~**e verset'** passive resistance
ly'dend -e suffering, passive; ~**e vorm** passive voice
ly'ding suffering *ook* **pyn, ellen'de;** *'n dier uit sy* ~ *verlos* put an animal out of its pain
lyf lywe body; ~**blad** house journal; ~**braai** (w) tan; ~**straf** corporal punishment; ~**taal** body language; ~**wag** bodyguard
lyk[1] (s) **-e** corpse, cadaver
lyk[2] (w) **ge-** resemble, appear, seem to be; *baie na mekaar* ~ resemble each other
lyk: ~**besor'ger** undertaker; ~**skou'ing** au= topsy, postmortem (examination); ~**stoet** funeral procession; ~**verbran'ding** crema= tion *ook* **veras'sing**
lyks: ~**huis** mortuary, morgue; ~**wa** hearse *ook* **rou'koets**
lym (s) glue; (w) glue/gum, paste
lyn -e rope, line, string; track (railway); *in* ~ *met* in line with
lyn: ~**o'lie** linseed oil; ~**reg** straight, perpen= dicular; ~**reg'ter** linesman, line judge; ~**staan** line-out (rugby)
lys -te list, catalogue; frame, rail; ledge; (w) list; ~ *jou vrae* list your questions
lys'ter -s thrush (bird)
ly'wig -e; -er, -ste corpulent, fat, thick; bulky; ~**e verhan'deling** comprehensive thesis/ dissertation

M

ma -'s mother; mummy; ma (informal) *ook* moe'der

maag mae, mage stomach; *jou oë is groter as jou ~ you* ask for more than you can eat

maagd (s) -e virgin, maiden

maag: ~kan'ker cancer in the stomach; ~koors gastric fever; ~pyn stomach ache; ~seer (s) gastric/duodenal ulcer

maai (w) ge- mow, reap; *~ waar hy nie gesaai het nie* reap where he has not sown

maak (s) make *ook* fabrikaat'; (w) make, do, shape; *dit ~ geen/nie saak nie* it doesn't matter

maal^1 (s) male time *ook* keer; *drie ~ vier* three times four

maal^2 (s) male meal *ook* maal'tyd, e'te

maal^3 (w) ge- grind; paint; circle round and round; ~stroom whirlpool; ~tyd meal; ~vleis minced meat, mince

maan (s) mane moon

maand -e month; *die ~ Maart* the month of March

Maan'dag ..dae Monday; *blou ~* blue Monday

maand: ~blad monthly magazine; ~e'liks monthly; ~ston'de menstruation

maan: ~lan'ding moon landing; ~lig moonlight; ~sak moonbag *ook* pens'portefeul'je; ~s'verduis'tering eclipse of the moon; ~vlug lunar flight

maar but, merely, only, yet, just; *toe ~!* don't mention it

maar'skalk -e marshal

maat^1 mate measure; dimension, size; *die ~ hou* beat time; ~band tape measure

maat^2 -s, maters chum, mate, comrade, partner; *Jan Rap en sy ~* ragtag and bobtail

maat'reël -s measure; *~s tref* take steps

maatskap'lik -e social; *~e werk* social work; *~e wer'ker* social worker

maatskappy' -e company; society

maat'staf ..stawwe criterion, standard, gauge

ma'deliefie -s daisy *ook* gous'blom

ma'er -der, -ste lean, thin; meagre; *so ~ soos 'n kraai* as thin as a lath; ~mer'rie shin

mag$^1_2$ (s) -te power, might, strength

mag^2 (w) mog may; *jy ~ nie steel nie* thou shalt not steal

magasyn' -e shop, warehouse; ~mees'ter storeman

magis'ter -s master's degree

magistraat' ..strate magistrate *ook* land'dros

magnaat' ..na'te magnate; tycoon (person)

magneet' ..nete magnet

magne'ties -e magnetic

mags: ~de'ling power sharing; ~vertoon' show of force/strength

mag'teloos ..lose powerless, helpless

mag'tig (w) ge- authorise, warrant, empower; (b) powerful, mighty; skrif'telike ~ing written authority/mandate

ma'-hulle mother and the rest, mum and co(mpany)

ma'jesteit -e majesty; splendour

majestueus' -e majestic (view); august

majoor' -s major (person)

mak -ker, -ste tame, docile, gentle; *so ~ soos 'n lam(metjie)* as gentle as a lamb

makeer' ~, ge- ail, lack, matter; be wanting; *wat ~ jou?* what are you suffering from?; *wat ~ jy?* what has come over you, what are you up to?

ma'kelaar -s broker (person)

ma'ker -s maker; creator

makie'tie -s feast, festivity, celebration *ook* fees(vie'ring), jolyt'

mak'lik -e; -er, -ste easy

mak'rostraler -s jumbo jet

mak'simum -s maximum

mal -ler, -ste mad, foolish, silly

mala'ria malaria; ~muskiet' anopheles

mal'beessiekte mad cow disease

Malei'er -s Malay (person)

mal: ~heid madness, nonsense, foolishness; ~huis madhouse; lunatic asylum

mal'jan: *~ onder die hoenders* a thorn among the roses

mal: ~kop madcap, tomboy *ook* mal'trap; ~lemeule merry-go-round, carousel

mals -e; -er, -ste soft, juicy, tender

mal'va -s geranium; ~lek'ker marshmallow

mam'ba -s mamba

mam'ma -s mamma

mam'mie -s mummy (mother)

mampar'ra -s ass, clot, fool

mampoer' peach brandy *ook* per'skebran'dewyn; wit'blits (van druiwe)

man -ne, -s man; husband; *aan die ~ bring* sell, dispose of; *met ~ en muis vergaan* lost with all hands on board

mandaat' ..**date** mandate, power to act

mand'jie -s basket, hamper

manel' -le dress coat, frock coat; *so waar soos padda* ~ *dra* as true as faith

maneu'ver -s manoeuvre

manewa'le -s antics, capers *ook* **kaskena'des**

man'gel -s tonsil; ~**ontste'king** tonsillitis

man'go ~'s mango (fruit)

manhaf'tig -e; -er, -ste brave, courageous

maniak'/ma'niak -ke maniac; crank (person)

manier' -e manner, fashion, way; *op hierdie* ~ in this way

manifes' -te manifest(o) *ook* **cre'do**

manipuleer' ~, ge- manipulate

mank -er, -ste limping, lame, crippled

man'lik -e manly; masculine; *alle* ~*e afstam= melinge* all male descendants

manmoe'dig (b) brave, manly, courageous

man'na manna; ~**wa'** gravy train *ook* **sous'= trein/stroop'trein**

man'nekrag manpower/fempower; labour force

mannekyn' -e mannequin

mans'hemp ..**hemde** man's shirt

mansjet' -te cuff; ~**knoop** cuff link

man: ~**skap** crew; man, soldier; ~**slag** manslaughter, homicide *ook* **dood'slag**

man'tel -s mantle, cloak, cape; ~**draai'er** turncoat; ~**pak** coat and skirt (costume)

manuskrip' -te manuscript

mar'at(h)on (s) marathon

mar'ge (s) margin *ook* **spe'ling**

marionet' -te puppet; ~**spel** puppet show *ook* **pop'pekas**

mark -e, -te market; ~**aan'deel** market share

markeer' (w) mark; *die pas* ~ mark time

markee'tent/markies'tent marquee (tent)

mark: ~**na'vorsing** market research; ~**plein** market square

marmela'de marmalade *ook* **lemoen'konfyt**

mar'mer marble

marmot'jie -s guinea pig

maroen' maroon (colour) *ook* **bruin'rooi**

mars (s) -e march

marsjeer' (w) ~, ge- march

mar'tel ge- torment, torture, rack; ~**aar** martyr (person); ~**ka'mer** torture chamber

mas -te mast, pole

ma'sels measles; **Duit'se** ~ German measles

masjien' -e machine; engine

masjinis' -te machinist; mechanic; engineer; engine driver *ook* **trein'drywer**

maskeer'band (s) masking tape

mas'ker (s) -s mask, disguise; (w) mask; screen; ~**bal** fancydress ball

mas'sa -s mass, crowd; bulk, lump; mass/ weight; ~**me'dia** mass media

mas'sa: ~**-op'trede** mass/industrial action *ook* **protes'optrede**; ~**produk'sie** mass produc= tion; ~**verga'dering** mass meeting *ook* **mon'= sterverga'dering**; ~**versen'ding** bulk posting

masseer' (w) ~, ge- massage; ~**salon'** mas= sage parlour

massief' ..**siewe** massive, solid

mas'tig! good gracious!; *ook* **gro'te genug'tig!**

mat (s) -te (door)mat; carpet; *deur die* ~ *val* flop (a plan/project); take a tumble

ma'te measure, degree, extent; *in 'n groot* ~ to a large extent

materiaal' ..**riale** material; fabric

materialis' -te materialist; ~**ties** materialistic

ma'ters companions, chums/pals *ook* **tjom'= mies**

mate'sis mathematics *ook* **wis'kunde**

mat'glas frosted glass

ma'tig (b) moderate; temperate; sober; *iets* ~ *gebruik* use/consume in moderation

matinee' -s matinee *ook* **mid'dagvoorstel= ling**

mat'jie -s rug, little mat

matras' -se mattress

matriek' matriculation, matric

matro'ne -s matron, housemother

matroos' ..**trose** sailor

me'bos dried and sugared apricots, mebos

medal'je -s medal; ~**wen'ner** medallist

medaljon' -s medallion; locket

me'de (together) with, co-; ~**bestuurder** joint manager; ~**bestuurs'hoof** joint executive; ~**bur'ger** fellow citizen

mededeel'saam ..**same** generous, charitable

me'de: ~**de'ling** communication; ~**din'ger** competitor, rival *ook* **teen'stander**; ~**klin'= ker** consonant

medely'de sympathy *ook* **simpatie'**

medeplig'tig -e accessory to, concerned in; ~**e** accomplice, collaborator (person)

me'de: ~**wer'king** co-operation, collabora= tion; ~**we'te** knowledge: *sonder die* ~*wete van A* without A's knowledge

me'dia (s) (mv) media; ~**beamp'te** public relations officer; ~**gebrui'ker** media user; ~**sen'trum** media centre *ook* ~**teek**; ~**ska'= kel** media officer

me'dies (b) -e medical *ook* **geneeskun'dig**; ~e **on'dersoek** medical examination
medika'sie (s) medication, drugs
me'dikus -se, ..**dici** physician, doctor, medical/family practitioner *ook* **genees'heer**
medisy'ne medicine
me'dium ..**dia, -s** medium
mee with, together *ook* **saam**; also, likewise
mee'deel -ge- inform, impart (facts)
mee'ding -ge- compete *ook* **wed'ywer**
meegaan'de sympathetic, tolerant (person)
mee'gevoel sympathy *ook* **me'delye**
meel meal; flour; ~**blom** flour
mee'luister -ge- listen together; monitor; tap (telephone); ~**apparaat'** bugging device *ook* **luis'tervlooi**
meen ge- mean, intend, think; ~ *jy dit regtig?* do you really mean it?
meent (s) commonage *ook* **dorps'grond**; ~**huis** townhouse
meer[1] (s) **mere** lake
meer[2] (b) more; *niks ~ as billik nie* only fair; ~**dere** superior (person)
meer'derheid majority, superiority; ~**s'rege'= ring** majority government
meerderja'rig -e major, of age; ~e major (person) *ook* **volwas'sene**
meer'kat -te, ..**kaaie** meercat, suricate
meer'min -ne mermaid *ook* **see'vrou**
meer'voud -e plural
mees (b) most; (bw) mostly
mees'(t)al generally, as a rule, mostly
mees'te most, greatest; *die ~ mense* most people
mees'ter -s master; teacher; *hy is ~ van sy vak* he knows his trade/profession thoroughly
mees'terbrein mastermind
mees'ter: ~**lik** excellent, masterly; *hy het hom ~lik van sy taak gekwyt* he made an excellent job of it; ~**stuk** masterpiece
meet (w) ge- measure, gauge; ~**band** tape measure; ~**kun'de** geometry
meeu -e seagull
mee'val -ge- cause surprise, succeed (beyond expectation); ~**ler(tjie)** windfall, stroke of luck, bonanza
mee'werk -ge- co-operate, collaborate
me'gagreep (s) megabyte (Mb, comp.)
mega'nies -e mechanical
Mei May
mein'eed perjury; ~ *pleeg* commit perjury
mei'sie -s girl, maiden
mei'sieskool girls' school; **Ho'ër Mei'sieskool**

Boks'burg Boksburg Girls' High School
mejuf'frou -e miss *kyk* **juf'frou**
mekaar' each other, one another; *na ~* one after the other
melaats' -e leprous; ~**heid** leprosy *ook* **le'pra**; ~e (mens) **le'per** *ook* **le'pralyer**
melancho'lies (b) melancholic *ook* **neerslag'tig**
meld ge- mention, inform, communicate; ~ *jou môre aan* report tomorrow
mel'ding mention; ~ *maak van* make mention of; mention (v)
melk (s) milk; (w) ge- milk
melk: ~**baard** down (on the chin), soft beard; ~**ery** dairy, dairy farm; milking; ~**koei** milch cow; ~**sak'kie** milk sachet; ~**tert** milktart; M~**weg** Milky Way
melodie' -ë melody, tune
melodieus' -e melodious
memoran'dum ..**da, -s** memorandum
memoriseer' (w) ~, ge- memorise
mena'sie -s mess (club for soldiers/sailors)
meneer' menere sir, mister; gentleman; **(Meneer die) Voor'sitter** Mr Chairman, Chairperson *ook* **Ag'bare Voor'sitter**
meng ge- mix, blend; mingle; ~ *jou met semels, dan vreet die varke jou op* touch pitch and you will be defiled
men'gel mingle, mix; ~**dran'kie** cocktail; ~**moes** hotchpotch, hash
meng'sel -s mixture, blend; mix
me'nige many, several
me'nig: ~**een** many, several, many a one; ~**maal** often; ~**te** multitude, crowd
me'ning -s, -e opinion, belief, view; *'n ~ huldig* hold a belief; *na my ~* in my opinion; ~**(s)op'name** opinion poll, survey; ~**vor'mer** opinion former/maker
me'ningverskil -le difference of opinion
me'nopouse menopause, change of life
mens (s) -e human being, person; *die ~ wik, God beskik* man proposes, God disposes; (vnw) one, you; ~**dom** humanity, mankind
men'se: ~**bron'ne** human resources *ook* **mens'= like hulp'bronne**; ~**ken'nis** knowledge of people/human nature; ~**materiaal** human resources; ~**reg'te** human/fundamental rights
Men'seregtedag Human Rights' Day (holiday)
men'severhoudinge human relations
menslie'wend (b) humane, philanthropic(al)
mens'lik -e human; ~**e hulp'bronne** human resources *ook* **men'sebronne**
mens'likheid humanity; human kindness

menstrua'sie menstruation *ook* **maand'stonde**
mens: ~**vre'ter** cannibal, maneater; ~**waar'=
dig** worthy of a human being; ~**waar'=
digheid** human dignity
mentaliteit' mentality
men'tor (s) adviser, teacher *ook* **leer'meester**
me'rendeel majority; ~**s** mostly, for the
greater part
meridiaan' ..**diane** meridian
merie'te merits; *derde op die* ~*lys* graded/
ranked third
merk (s) **-e** mark; sign; token; brand; (w) ge-
mark; observe, notice
merk: ~**arti'kel** brand(ed) article/goods;
~**baar** perceptible, noticeable
merkwaar'dig remarkable, noteworthy
mer'rie -s mare; ~**vul** filly
mes -se knife; *voor jy* ~ *kon sê* before you
could say Jack Robinson
mes'sel ge- lay bricks, build; ~**aar** bricklayer
mes'sestel (s) set of cutlery
met with; ~ *geweld* by force; ~/*op vakansie
(sake)* on holiday (business)
metaal' metale metal; ~**verklik'ker** metal
detector; ~**verswak'king** metal fatigue
metafoor' ..**fore** metaphor *ook* **beeld'spraak**
meteen' at the same time
meteens' all of a sudden, all at once, suddenly
ook **skie'lik/plot'seling**
meteoor' meteore meteor
me'ter -s meter, gauge; metre
met'gesel -le companion, mate; consort
me'ting -s, -e measuring, reading
meto'de -s method, manner
metodiek' method(ics)
meto'dies -e methodical
metriek' (b) **-e** metric; ~**e stel'sel** metric system
metrise'ring metrification
metronoom' ..**nome** metronome *ook* **maat'=
meter**
metropolitaan' ..**tane** metropolitan; ~**se
sub'struktuur** metropolitan substructure
me'trum -s ..**tra** metre *ook* **vers'maat**
mettertyd' in course of time *ook* **gaan'deweg**
meu'bel -s piece of furniture
meubileer'/meubeleer' ge- furnish; ~**der**
furnisher *ook* **meubelier'** (mens)
meul -e/meu'le -ns mill; *water op sy* ~ grist
to his mill; ~**e'naar** miller
mevrou' -e, -ens Mrs (when addressed with
surname); madam, mistress; *is* ~ *tuis?* is
your wife at home?

mid'byt (s) brunch
mid'dag ..**dae** midday, noon; *'n vry* ~ an
afternoon off; ~**e'te** lunch, luncheon; (mid=
day) dinner; ~**verto'ning** matinee
mid'de middle, midst; *te* ~ *van gevaar* in the
midst of danger
mid'del[1] **-s** waist; centre, middle
mid'del[2] **-e, -s** means, instrument, remedy;
product; *deur* ~ *van* by means of; ~**aar**
mediator, go-between *ook* **tus'senganger**
(mens)
mid'delbaar ..**bare** secondary; moderate,
middle; ..**ba're on'derwys** secondary edu=
cation
middeldeur' (b) in two, asunder
Mid'deleeue Middle Ages
mid'del: ~**lyn** diameter; equator; halfway
line; ~**man'netjie** hog's back (road)
middelma'tig -e mediocre; only average
middelpuntsoe'kend -e centripetal
middelpuntvlie'dend -e centrifugal
mid'de(l)weg the golden mean
mid'delvinger -s middle finger
mid'dernag midnight; ~**son** midnight sun
mied -e pile, heap; stack (hay)
mie'lie -s mealie, maize; ~**boer** maize farmer;
~**meel** mealie meal; ~**pap** mealie/maize
porridge; ~**stronk** mealie cob/stalk
mier -e ant; ~**hê** be fidgety
miershoop ..**hope** antheap
migraine' migraine *ook* **skeel'hoofpyn**
mik (s) **-ke** forked stick; gibbet; (w) aim
mik'punt aim, target; objective *ook* **doel'wit**
mikrochirurgie' microsurgery
mi'krofilm microfilm
mikrofoon' ..**fone** microphone
mi'krogolf ..**golwe** microwave; ~**oond** mi=
crowave oven
mi'kroligte: ~ **vlieg'tuig** microlight aircraft/
plane *ook* **mi'krotuig**
mikroskoop' ..**skope** microscope
mi'kroskyfie/mi'krovlokkie -s microchip
mik'stok -ke forked stick
mild (b) **-e; -er, -ste** generous, liberal, soft
militant' militant *ook* **veglus'tig**
militêr' (s) **-e** military man; (b) military; ~**e
diens** military service, national service
miljard' -e billion (1 000 million) *kyk* **biljoen'**
miljoen' -e million
miljoenêr' -s millionaire (person)
mil'li: ~**gram** milligram; ~**li'ter** millilitre;
~**me'ter** millimetre

mimiek' (s) mimicry; mimic art
min[1] (s) love; (w) **ge-** love
min[2] (b) **-der, -ste** little, few; (bw) minus, less; ~ *of meer* more or less
min'ag ge- disdain, slight; ~**ting** disrespect; ~*ting van die hof* contempt of court
min'der less, fewer, inferior; ~**bevoor'reg** underprivileged; ~**bevoor'regte gemeen**=**skap** disadvantaged community
min'derheid minority; inferiority
min'derja'rig -e under age, minor
minderwaar'dig -e inferior; ~**heid(s)kom**=**pleks'** inferiority complex
mineraal' (s)..**rale** mineral; (b) mineral;..**rale** **bad/bron** mineral baths *ook* **kruit'bad**
mineur' minor (mus.)
mi'ni (s) **-'s** mini; ~**bustax'i** minibus taxi
miniatuur'..**ture** miniature
mi'nimum -s,..**ma,** minimum
minire'kenaar (s) minicomputer
mi'nirok -ke/mi'niromp -e miniskirt
minis'ter -s minister
ministe'rie -s ministry; cabinet
min'naar -s lover
minnares' -se ladylove, mistress
min'ne: *in der* ~ *skik* settle amicably; ~**brief** love letter; ~**dig** love poem, ~**lied** love song; ~**san'ger** minstrel
min'ste least, smallest; *op sy* ~ (at) the least; *sy is ten* ~ *eerlik* at least she is honest
min'stens not less than, at least; *sy is 'n veertig* she is forty if she is a day; *dit weeg* ~ *tien kilogram* it weighs at least ten kilograms
mi'nus minus, less
minuut'..**nute** minute; ~**wys'(t)er** minute hand
mira'kel -s miracle, wonder *ook* **won'derwerk**
mis[1] (s) **-se** mass (in church)
mis[2] (s) te mist, fog; vapour
mis[3] (s) manure, dung
mis[4] (w) **ge-** miss; ~ *die trein* miss the train; (b, bw) amiss, wrong
mis'bruik (s) **-e** abuse, misuse; ~ *maak van* take advantage of
misbruik' (w) ~ abuse, misuse
mis'daad..**dade** crime, offence, misdeed; *'n* ~ *begaan/pleeg* commit a crime; ~**voor**=**ko'ming** crime prevention
misda'dig (b) **-e** criminal, felonious; ~**er** criminal, evildoer *ook* **boos'wig, skurk**
mis'dryf (s)..**drywe** crime, offence
misera'bel (b) miserable *ook* **ellen'dig**
mishan'del ~ ill-use, maltreat, abuse

misken' ~ misjudge, fail to appreciate; ~**de genie'** neglected/disregarded genius
miskien' perhaps, maybe *ook* **dalk**
mis'kraam..**krame** miscarriage, abortion
mis'kruier -s tumblebug, dung beetle
mis'lik -e; -er, -ste sick, qualmish, nauseous; disgusting; ~**heid** sickness, nausea
misluk' ~ fail, miscarry; ~*te poging* vain attempt; ~**keling** misfit; dropout; ~**king** failure, miscarriage
mismaak' (w) ~ deform, disfigure; (b) de=formed
mismoe'dig (b) **-e** discouraged, dejected
misnoe'ë discontent, displeasure; *sy* ~ *te kenne gee* express his displeasure
misre'ken ~ be mistaken, meet with disap=pointment; *hy het hom* ~ he backed the wrong horse
mis'sie (s) mission *ook* **op'drag, sen'ding**
missiel..**e** missile
mis: ~**slaan** miss (when hitting); ~**stap** false/wrong step
mis'stof..**stowwe** manure; fertiliser
mis'tel[1] (s) **-s** mistletoe
mis'tel[2] (w) **-ge-** count wrongly, miscount
miste'rie -ë, -s mystery *ook* **gehei'menis**
mis'tig -e foggy, misty
mis'verstaan ~ misunderstand
mis'verstand (s) **-e** misunderstanding, error
misvorm' (b) **-de** deformed, disfigured
mi'te -s myth
mitologie' mythology
mits provided (that); on condition (that); *ek sal jou help,* ~ *jy my vertrou* I shall help you if you trust me
mobiel' -e mobile *ook* **beweeg'baar**
mod'der mud, mire, sludge; ~**ig** muddy; ~**skerm** mudguard, fender
mo'de -s fashion, mode, vogue; *uit die* ~ *raak* go out of fashion; ~**gier** whim of fashion
model' -le pattern, example; model
mo'de: ~**maak'ster** dressmaker *ook* **kle're**=**maakster;** ~**ontwer'per** fashion designer; ~**pop** fop, dandy; dressy woman
modereer' ~, **ge-** moderate; ~**komitee'** com=mittee/panel of moderators
modern' -e; -er, -ste modern, fashionable, trendy *ook* **by'dertyds**
mo'de: ~**skou** fashion show; ~**woord** buzz word
modieus' -e fashionable, stylish; trendy
modis'te -s dressmaker, modiste, milliner

moed courage, heart, spirit; *hou goeie* ~ never say die! be of good cheer!

moe'deloos (b) dejected, disheartened

moe'der -s mother; ~**lief'de** motherly/mater= nal love; ~**maatskappy'** holding company *ook* **hou'ermaatskappy**; ~**o'werste** Mother Superior; ~**sielalleen'** quite alone; ~**taal** mother tongue/language, vernacular

moe'dig -e; -er, -ste brave, courageous

moedswil'lig (b) wilful, mischievous, petulant *ook* **opset'lik**

moeg moeë; **moeër**, -ste tired, weary

moei'lik -e; -er, -ste difficult, hard, arduous, hard to handle; ~**heid** difficulty, trouble; *jy soek* ~*heid* you are looking for trouble

moei'te trouble, difficulty, pains, hassle; *nie die* ~ *werd nie* not worth while

moe'nie! don't!

moer -e nut (with bolt)

moeras' -se marsh, morass, swamp

moer'bei -e mulberry

moe'sie -s mole; beauty spot (on face)

moet (w) moes must, ought, be obliged, have to; *ek moes lag/ek kon my lag nie hou nie* I couldn't help laughing

moe'tie (s) muti *ook* **toor'medisyne**

mo'ker ge- strike, beat, hammer

mol[1] flat (mus.)

mol[2] mole; *so blind soos 'n* ~ as blind as a bat

moles' -te trouble, harm; rumpus; ~ *maak* cause trouble, harm; ~**ma'ker** hooligan

molesteer' ~, ge- molest (e.g. a child)

mol'lig (b) soft, plump, cuddlesome (girl)

mols'hoop ..hope molehill

mol'trein -e tube, underground train

mom'bakkies mask (false face)

moment' -e moment *ook* **oom'blik**

mom'pel ge- mutter, mumble, grumble

monarg' -e monarch; potentate

monargie' -ë monarchy

mond -e mouth; estuary (of river); *by* ~*e van* as cited/stated by; *nie op sy* ~ *(bek) geval wees nie* have a ready tongue; *hou jou* ~! shut up!

mon'deling(s) (b) -e verbal, oral; **mon'delinge eksa'men** oral examination

mond'fluitjie -s mouth organ

mon'dig -e of age, major; ~**wor'ding** coming of age

mond'jie vol mondjies vol tiny bit; smattering; *hy ken 'n* ~ *Engels* he knows a little English

monetêr -e monetary; **Interna'sionale M~e**

Fonds (IMF) International Monetary Fund (IMF)

moniteer' (w) monitor *ook* **mon'itor** (w), **kontroleer'**

mon'itor (s) -s monitor; prefect (person)

mon'nik -e monk, friar

monoloog' (s) ..loë monologue, soliloquy *ook* **alleen'spraak**

monopolie' -ë, -s monopoly *ook* **alleen'handel**

mon'ster[1] (s) -s monster, brute

mon'ster[2] (s) -s sample; **volle'dige stel** ~s complete range of samples; (w) ge- com= pare; muster (army)

mon'steragtig -e monstrous

mon'ster: ~**ne'ming** sampling; ~**verga'de= ring** mass meeting

monteer' (w) ~, ge- mount, assemble, set; ~**aan'leg** assembly plant; ~**baan** assembly line; ~**huis** prefabricated house

monument' -e monument *ook* **gedenk'teken**

mooi -er, -ste handsome, nice, fine, pretty; ~ *broodjies bak* eat humble pie; ~**maakgoed** cosmetics; ~**praat'jies** flattery, softsoaping; ~**weersvriend'** no friend in need

moond'heid (s) power, state *ook* **rege'ring**

moont'lik -e possible *ook* **haal'baar**; ~**heid** possibility, likelihood

moor (w) ge- kill, commit murder; maltreat; *jouself* ~ flog oneself

moord -e murder; ~**ben'de** hit squad

moor'denaar -s murderer; killer

moord: ~**lys** hitlist; ~**toneel'** scene of murder

moraal' moral; *hierdie storie hou 'n* ~ *in* this story has a moral lesson

moraliteit' morality; morality play/drama

mô're/mo're (s) -s morning; ~ *is nog 'n dag* tomorrow is another day; (bw) tomorrow; ~**aand** tomorrow night; ~**sê!** good morn= ing!

moreel' (s) morale *ook* **gees'teskrag**; (b) moral; *sy soldate se* ~ *verstewig* improve the morale of his soldiers; *jou morele plig* one's moral duty; ~**kik'ker** morale booster

mô're=/moreog'gend tomorrow morning

mô're=/mo'repraatjies: *sy aand- en môrepraat= jies kom nie ooreen nie* his word is unreliable

morfien/morfi'ne morphia, morphine

moroon/mo'ron moron, mentally deficient person

mors (w) ge- dirty, make a mess; waste, spill; ~**dood** stone-dead

mors: ~**jors** litterbug *ook* **rom'melstrooier;**

~**jur'kie** overall (for little girl); ~**pot** dirty person, messer
mortier' -e mortar
mos[1] (s) -se moss
mos[2] (s) must; new wine
mos[3] (bw) indeed, at least; *ek het ~ gesê hulle sal verloor* didn't I say they would lose?
mosaïek' mosaic
mo'ses match, superior; *sy ~ teëkom* meet one's match
mo'sie -s motion, vote; ~ **van wan'troue** motion of no confidence
moskee' -s, ..**keë** mosque
mos'konfyt moskonfyt, grape syrup
Mos'lem/Moes'liem Muslim (person)
mos'sel -s mussel
mos'sie -s Cape sparrow, mossie
mos'terd mustard; ~ *na die maal* too late
mot -te moth; ~**bestand'** mothproof
motel' -le, -s motel
motief' ..tiewe motive *ook* **dryf'veer**
motiveer' ge- motivate *ook* **staaf** (w); ~**praat'jie** peptalk
mo'tocross motocross (motorbike off-road racing)
mo'tor (s) -s, -e motorcar; motor (engine); ~**bestuur'der** car driver; chauffeur; ~**bom** car bomb; ~**fiets** motorcycle; ~**ha'we** garage; ~**huis** garage (private); ~**is'** motorist *ook* **motorry'er**; ~**ka'per** car hijacker, carjacker; ~**ka'ping** carjacking; ~**afrui'ling** carport; ~**voer'tuig** motor vehicle
mot'reën drizzle
mou -e sleeve; *die hande uit die ~ steek* put the shoulder to the wheel; ~**ska'kel** cuff link *ook* **mansjet'knoop**
muez'zin/mued'zin muezzin *ook* **gebeds'roeper** (Moslem)
muf (b) musty, mouldy, fusty
mug'gie -s gnat, midge; *van 'n ~ 'n olifant maak* make a mountain of a molehill
muil[1] -e mule
muil[2] -e mouth (animal) *ook* **bek**; ~**band** (s) muzzle; (w) ge- muzzle
muis -e mouse; ball (thumb); fetlock (of horse); *klein ~ies het groot ore* little pitchers have long ears; ~**hond** skunk, polecat; mongoose; ~**nes** mousenest; (mv) musings; *die kop vol ~neste hê* have a mind full of cobwebs

(when in love); ~**val** mousetrap
muit (w) ge- mutiny, revolt, rebel; ~**ery'** mutiny, sedition *ook* **op'stand**
mul'ti: ~**dissiplinêr** (b) multidisciplinary; ~**me'dia** multimedia (comp.); ~**miljoenêr** multimillionaire
mum'mie -s mummy (embalmed body)
munisipaal' ..**pale** municipal; ..**a'le veror'deninge** municipal by-laws
munisipaliteit' -e municipality
munt (s) -e mint, coin; (w) **ge-** mint, coin; ~**kun'de** numismatics; ~**outomaat'** vending machine; ~**stuk** coin; ~**was'masjien** launderette *ook* **wasseret'**
mura'sie -s old walls, ruins (of a house)
murg marrow; *deur ~ en been gaan* penetrate to the marrow
mur'mel (w) **ge-** murmer, babble; gurgle
murmureer' **ge-** grumble, grouse
mus -se cap; nightcap; teacosy; *kop in een ~* in cahoots
muse'um -s museum
musiek' music; ~ *van die meesters/klassieke ~ classical music*; ~**bly'spel** musical (n); ~**sen'trum** music centre; ~**stuk** piece of music, musical composition
musikaal' ..**kale** musical; *'n musikale gehoor hê* have an ear for music
musikant' -e member of a band; music maker
mu'sikus -se, ..**ci** musician, musical expert
muskeljaat'kat/mussel jaat'kat -te genet
muskiet' -e mosquito
muur mure wall; *oor die ~ wees* be done for; ~**tapyt'** tapestry *ook* **tapisserie'**
my (pers. vnw) me; *dis vir ~ te duur* I can't afford it, *ek het ~ vergis* I was mistaken; (besit. vnw) my, mine
myl -e mile; ~**paal** milestone; landmark
my'mer (w) **ge-** ponder, meditate, muse
myn (s) -e mine; (w) **ge-** mine (e.g. gold)
my'ne mine; *dis ~!* it's mine!
myn: ~**bou** mining (industry); ~**er** miner *ook* **myn'werker**; ~**ingenieur'** mining engineer; ~**skag** shaft; ~**te'ring** miner's phthisis, pneumoconiosis; ~**veër** minesweeper; ~**werkersbond'** miners' union
myself' myself; *ek praat net vir ~* I speak only on my own behalf
my'ter -s mitre; bishop's hat

N

'n a, an; ~ *mens* one, you
na[1] (b, bw) **nader, naaste** close, near
na[2] (vs) after; to; according to; on; *op een* ~ *die laaste* the last but one; ~ *my mening* in my opinion; ~ *skool* after school (hours); *tien* ~/*oor nege* ten past nine
naaf nawe nave, hub; ~**dop** hubcap
naai ge- sew; ~**masjien'** sewing machine
naak (b) naked, nude; ~**danseres'** stripteaser/stripper; ~**lo'per** nudist; naturist
naakt'heid nudity, nakedness
naald -e needle; spire; obelisk; ~ *en garing* needle and cotton; ~**eko'ker** needlecase; dragonfly; ~**werk** needlework
naam name name; ~**bord** signboard; ~**kaar'**=**tjie** visiting/business card
naam'lik namely, to wit
naam'loos ..**lose** nameless, anonymous
naam'plaatjie name tag *ook* **ken'strokie**
naam'tekening signature *ook* **hand'tekening**
naam'val -le case
naam'woord -e nomen (noun, pronoun or adjective); **byvoeg'like** ~ adjective; **self**=**stan'dige** ~ noun
naand! good evening! *ook* **naandsê!**
na'-aper -s imitator
naar (b) sick *ook* **mis'lik**; dreary, sad; ~**sak'kie** air/sea-sickness bag
naas next to, beside, alongside of; ~**bestaan'de** next of kin, nearest relative; ~**beste** second best; ~**eergis'ter** three days ago; ~**links** second from left (photo); ~**oormô're**, ~=**oormo're** three days hence
naas'te (s) -s neighbour, fellowman; (b) nearest
naas'te(n)by approximately, more or less
naas'teliefde love of one's fellowmen
naas'wenner (s) runner-up (competition/sport)
naas'wit off-white
naat nate seam; joint; suture; *op die* ~ *van jou rug lê* lie flat on your back; ~**bou'ler** seam bowler (cricket)
na'boots -ge- imitate, mimic; simulate, copy; ~**er** simulator (trainee pilots)
na'by nader, naaste near, close to; ~ *die dood omdraai* have been at death's door; ~ **fo'to** close-up photograph
naby'geleë adjacent, neighbouring
na'dat after, when
na'deel na'dele disadvantage; loss

nade'lig (b) detrimental, disadvantageous; ~**e sal'do/balans'** debit balance
na'der (w) ge- approach, come nearer; (b, bw) nearer; ~**e (meer) beson'derhede** further particulars
na'dink -ge- reflect, consider *ook* **oorweeg'**
na'doods after death; posthumous; ~**e on'der**=**soek** postmortem, autopsy
na'draai aftereffects, sequel, aftermath
na'druk emphasis, stress *ook* **klem**; ~ *lê op* emphasise
na'el[1] (s) -s nail; *sy* ~*s byt* bite one's nails
na'el[2] (s) -s navel
na'el[3] (w) ge- nail; sprint; *hy het laat* ~ he took to his heels
na'el: ~**lo'per** sprinter (athlete); ~**ren** cycle race/sprint; ~**skraap** by the skin of the teeth: *dit het* ~*skraap gegaan* it was touch and go; ~**string** umbilical cord
na'eltjies cloves; ~**o'lie** oil of cloves
na'elwedloop ..**lope** sprint (sport)
nag -te night; *so lelik soos die* ~ as ugly as sin
na'gaan -ge- trace, check *ook* **tjek** (w); run over (with the eye); monitor; *die inskry*=*wings* ~ check the entries
nag: ~**aap** bushbaby; ~**ad'der** night adder
na'gedagtenis memory, remembrance; *ter* ~ *aan* in memory of
na'gemaak -te forged, false, imitated
na'gereg -te dessert (course)
na'geslag -te descendants, offspring
Nag'maal Holy Communion
nag: ~**klub** night club; ~**mer'rie** nightmare
na'graads (b) -e postgraduate
nag'tegaal ..**gale** nightingale (bird)
nag: ~**te'lik** nocturnal, nightly; ~**wag** night watchman
naïef' (b) naive/naïve, simple, artless
na'jaar autumn *ook* **herfs**
na'kend -e naked, nude, in the buff
na'kom -ge- fulfil; carry out; meet (obligation); *beloftes* ~ keep promises
na'komeling -e descendant, offspring
na'kyk -ge- look after; examine, revise, check; eye
na'laat -ge- bequeath (an inheritance); *sy oom het hom R1 000 nagelaat* he inherited R1 000 from his uncle; neglect; omit
nala'tig negligent, careless *ook* **agte(r)lo'sig**

na'maak -ge- imitate, copy; ~sel imitation, counterfeit

nama'te as, in proportion to; ~ hy aansterk, eet hy beter as he improves/recuperates he has a better appetite

na'mens in the name of, on behalf of, for

Nami'bië Namibia; ~r Namibian (person)

na'middag ..dae afternoon

nar -re fool, jester ook harlekyn'/hans'wors

narko'se anaesthetic ook (ver)doof'middel

narko'tikaburo narcotics bureau

narkotiseur' -s anaesthetist (specialist)

nar'tjie -s mandarin (orange), tangerine, naar= tjie

na'saat nasate descendant ook na'komeling

na'sie -s nation; Vere'nigde N~s United Nations

na'sien -ge- correct; mark; examine; revise, check; ~er marker (of scripts)

nasionaal' ..nale national; ..nale pad national road

Nasiona'le: ~ Raad van Provinsies National Council of Provinces; ~ Vroue'dag Na= tional Women's Day (holiday)

nasionalis' -te nationalist; ~me nationalism

nasionaliteit' -e nationality

na'skrif -te postscript

na'slaan -ge- look up, consult (a book); ~biblioteek' reference library; ~werk ref= erence book/work

na'sorg aftercare, follow-up

nat ter, nte wet, moist; ~ agter die ore still a greenhorn

nat: ~heid moistness, wetness; ~lei/~maak water (garden); wet

naturel' (b) natural (mus.)

natuur' nature nature; temper, temperament; van nature by nature; ~bewa'ring nature conservation; ~bron'ne natural resources; ~frats freak of nature; ~le'wevere'niging wildlife society

natuur'lik (b) natural; ~e aan'leg natural bent; (bw) of course, naturally; hy sal ~ kom of course he will come

natuur': ~oord nature resort; ~skoon (nat= ural) scenery; ~toneel' scenic beauty

natuurwetenskap'lik (b) scientific, pertaining to natural science

na'uurs part-time (studies); after hours

na'volg -ge- follow, imitate

na'vors -ge- research; ~er researcher; ~ing (s) research

na'vraag navrae enquiry; query; ~ doen seek information

na'week naweke weekend

na'wel -s navel; ~lemoen' navel orange

nè? is it not? isn't it? yes? dink 'n bietjie ~! just fancy!

ne'derig -e; -er, -ste humble, modest

Ne'derland: ~er Dutchman, Hollander

ne'dersetter -s settler ook set'laar

ne'dersetting -s, -e settlement, colony

nee no; ~ sê say no; refuse

neef -s (male) cousin; nephew

neem ge- take, receive, accept

neer down, downwards; ~kniel' kneel down

neer'kom -ge- come down, fall on; dit kom alles op dieselfde neer it works out to the same thing

neer'laag/ne'derlaag ..lae defeat, reverse; die ~ ly suffer defeat

neer'lê -ge- lay down, abdicate, resign

neerslag'tig depressed, gloomy, despondent

negatief' (s, b) ..tiewe negative

ne'ge nine; ~ maal ~ nine times nine; ~ keer nine times

ne'gentien/ne'ëntien nineteen

neig ge- bend, incline; mense is ge~ om people are apt to

nei'ging -s, -e inclination, tendency; trend; predisposition

nek -ke neck; mountain pass; op iem. se ~ lê abuse someone's hospitality; ~slag death= blow

neologis'me -s neologism ook nuut'skepping

nerd (s) nerd (asocial, bookish young man) ook vaal'jan, bleek'siel, nof'fie

nê'rens nowhere; ~ voor deug nie serve no earthly purpose

nes[1] (s) -te nest

nes[2] (bw) just as, just like; ~ hy kom, sluit ons die deur as soon as he arrives we'll lock the door

net[1] (s) -te net

net[2] (b) neat, clean ook net'jies

net[3] (bw) only, just; ~ genoeg just enough

net: ~heid tidiness, neatness; ~jies (b) neat, tidy, clean, trim; (bw) neatly, nicely; jou werk ~jies doen produce tidy work; ~nou in a moment; ~werk (s) network

net'to net; ~ gewig'/mas'sa net weight/mass; ~ wins net profit

neuk (kru) (w) ge- hit ook foe'ter; bother, trouble; ~ery annoyance, fine how-do-you-do

neul (w) ge- nag, bother, pester ook sa'nik

neu'rie ge- hum, croon; ~san'ger crooner

neus (s) -e nose; *met sy ~ in die botter val* strike oil/be in clover; ~ *in die lug con=* ceited; haughty

neut -e nut; ~kra'ker pair of nutcrackers

neutraal' ..trale neutral

ne'wel -s mist, fog

ne'weproduk -te byproduct

nie not; *so ~* if not, failing which; *dis ~ so ~* it isn't true; ~aan'valsverdrag non-aggres= sion pact; ~beta'ling non-payment *ook* wan'betaling

nie'fiksie non-fiction

nie'mand nobody, none, no one; ~ *anders nie as* no other than

nie'amptelik -e unofficial

nier -e kidney

nierassis'ties (b) nonracial

nies (s) -e sneeze; (w) ge- sneeze

nie'teenstaande notwithstanding

nie'temin nonetheless *ook* nog'tans

nie'tig insignificant *ook* onbedui'dend; void

nig -te/nig'gie -s (female) cousin; niece

nikotien'/nikoti'ne nicotine

niks nothing; ~nuts good-for-nothing (per= son); ~werd worth nothing, worthless

nimf -e nymph; ~omaan' nymphomaniac, highly-sexed female

nim'mer never, never ever *ook* nooit

nip'pel (s) -s nipple

nip'pertjie: *op die ~* in the nick of time

no'ag: ~kar/~mo'tor vintage/veteran car

no'dig (b) -e; -er, -ste necessary

noem ge- call, name, mention

noen noon; ~byt brunch *ook* mid'byt; ~maal luncheon (formal)

nog[1] (b, bw) still, yet; ~ *iets?* anything else? ~ *'n keer* once again

nog[2] (bw) now; *tot ~ toe* up till now

nóg .. nóg (vgw) neither . . . nor; *nóg die een, nóg die ander* neither the one, nor the other

nog: ~al rather, quite (so); ~maals once more; ~*maals hartlik bedank* once again many thanks; ~tans yet, nevertheless

nok -ke ridge (of the roof); cam (of wheel); ~as camshaft

nomina'sie -s nomination

nominéer' ~, ge- nominate *ook* benoem'

nom'mer (s) -s number; size (shoe); item (concert); ~pas perfect fit; ~plaat number plate; (w) number

non -ne nun

nood need, want; distress; danger; *in geval van* ~ in case of emergency; ~berig' emer= gency/distress message; ~deur emergency door, fire escape

nood: ~hulp first-aid; makeshift; ~lan'ding emergency/forced landing; ~len'iging(s)= fonds relief fund; ~leu'en white lie; ~lot fate, destiny

noodlot'tig -e; -er, -ste fatal; disastrous

nood: ~maatreël emergency measure; ~op'= roep emergency/distress call

noodsaak'lik (b) -e essential, imperative

nood'toestand state of emergency

nood'weer self-defence *ook* selfverde'diging

nood'wiel -e spare wheel

nooi[1] (s) -ens young lady; sweetheart; *by 'n ~ vlerksleep* court a girl

nooi[2] (w) ge- invite; *ook* uit'nooi; *ek ~ jou vir Saterdag* I am inviting you for Saturday

nooi: ~ens'toe'spraak maiden speech (parlia= ment) *ook* nu'welingtoespraak; ~ens'van maiden name

nooit never; *so ~ aste nimmer!* never!

noord north

Noor'delike Provin'sie Northern Province

noor'der: ~breedte northern latitude; ~lig aurora borealis

noor'dewind north wind

Noord-Kaap (provinsie) Northern Cape

noord'pool north pole

noordwes' northwest; N~(-provin'sie) North West (Province); ~te north-west

Noor'weë Norway; ~r Norwegian (person)

noot note note

nop'pies: *in sy ~* as pleased as Punch

normaal' ..male normal; ~kol'lege normal college *ook* on'derwyskollege

nors -e; -er, -ste surly, grumpy; peevish

nos'sel (s) -s nozzle *ook* spuit'kop

noteer' ~, ge- jot down; quote (prices)

note'ring -s, -e quotation; ~ *op die beurs* stock exchange listing

no'tule/notu'le -s minutes; *die ~ lees en goed= keur* read and approve the minutes

notuleer' (w) ge- record; minute; take down

nou[1] (b) [-e]; -er, -ste narrow, tight

nou[2] (bw) now; ~ *of nooit* now or never

nou'geset (b) conscientious, painstaking

noukeu'rig exact, accurate, precise

nou'-nou just now, in a moment *ook* net'nou

nou'strop: ~ *trek* be under pressure

nou'te -s narrowness; narrow pass; ~**vrees** claustrophobia *ook* **eng'tevrees**
novel'le -s short novel, novelette
nudis' -te nudist, naturist; ~**me** nudism
nug'ter [-e]; -der, -ste sober, clearheaded; *op sy* ~ *maag* on an empty stomach
nuk -ke freak, whim, caprice, mood; ~**ke'rig** moody *ook* **nors/knor'rig**
nul -le nil, zero, nought, cipher; *van* ~ *en gener waarde* null and void
numeriek' -e numerical; ~**e volg'orde** numerical order
nut (s) use, benefit, avail
nuts'man handyman *ook* **fakto'tum**
nuts'meisie Girl Friday (in office)
nut'teloos ..lose; ..loser, -ste useless

nut'tig[1] (w) ge- partake of (meal)
nut'tig[2] (b) -e; -er, -ste useful, serviceable
nuus news, tidings; *die jongste* ~ the latest news; ~**berig'** news item; ~**blad** newspaper; ~**brief** newsletter; ~**bulletin'** newscast
nuuskie'rig (b) inquisitive, curious; ~**e agie** nosy parker; ~**heid** curiosity
nuut new, recent; ~**skep'ping** neologism
Nuwejaars': ~**dag** New Year's Day (holiday); ~**voor'neme** New Year's resolution
nuwerwets' -e modern; with-it, trendy *ook* **bydertyds'**
nu'wigheid ..hede novelty; innovation
nyd (s) envy, jealousy; ~**ig** angry, cross
ny'weraar -s industrialist (person)
ny'werheid ..hede industry *ook* **bedryf'**

O

oa'se (s) -s oasis
obelisk' -e obelisk *ook* **gedenk'naald**
objektief' (b) ..tiewe objective (e.g. opinion)
oblie'tjie -s (rolled) wafer
obliga'sie -s debenture (of a company) *ook* **skuld'brief**; obligation; bond
obses'sie obsession *ook* **behept'heid**
obstruk'sie -s obstruction *ook* **versper'ring**
o'de -s ode *ook* **lof'sang**
oe'fen ge- exercise, practise; train, coach; ~**baan** practice court/track; ~**ing** exercise, practice; ~**lo'pie** trial run; ~**skrif** exercise book *ook* **skryf'boek**
o'ënskou: *in* ~ *neem* inspect; survey
oënskyn'lik (b) -e apparent, ostensible; (bw) apparently, seemingly
oer: ~**knal** big bang (astronomy); ~**mens** first/primeval man; ~**woud** virgin forest; jungle
oes' (s) -te harvest, crop; ~**jaar** vintage year; yield *ook* **op'brengs**; (w) harvest, reap
oes'ter -s oyster
o'ëverblindery make-believe, eyewash; magic, optical illusion
oe'wer -s riverbank; ~**bewo'ner** riparian (dweller)
of or; but, if, whether; *min* ~ *meer* more or less; *ek weet nie* ~ *dit waar is nie* I don't know whether it is true
óf .. óf either .. or; ~ *Jan* ~ *Piet* either John or Peter

offensief' (s) ..siewe offensive
of'fer (s) -s sacrifice, offering; (w) devote, sacrifice; ~**ande** offering, sacrifice
offisier' -e, -s (military or naval) officer
ofskoon' although, though *ook* **hoewel'**
of'te: *nooit* ~ *nimmer* never (ever)
oftewel' that is (to say), namely
og'gend -e morning; ~**blad** morning paper; ~**e'te** breakfast *ook* **ontbyt'**
o'gie -s eyelet; ~*s maak* wink, give the glad eye, ogle
o'giesdraad wire netting
oka'pi -'s okapi (buck)
o'ker ochre, red clay *ook* **geel'klei**
okkerneut' -e walnut
oktaaf' ..tawe octave
oktrooi' (s) -e charter, patent
oktrooieer' (w) ~, ge- charter, patent; **geoktrooieer'de re'kenmeester** chartered accountant
o'lie (s) -s oil; (w) oil; ~**bak** sump; ~**bol** doughnut; ~**boor'toring** oil rig; ~**kan** oilcan
olien'hout wild olive
o'lie: ~**pyp'leiding** oil pipeline; ~**slik** oil slick; ~**to'ring** derrick; ~**verbruik'** oil consumption; ~**verfskildery'** oil painting
o'lifant -e elephant
o'lifant(s)tand -e elephant's tusk; ivory
o'lik (b) unwell, seedy, out of sorts; ~**heid** seediness: *na vrolikheid kom* ~*heid* after laughter come tears

Olim'piese spe'le Olympic games
olm -s elm (tree)
olyf' olywe olive
om (bw) out; round; over, up; ~ en ~ round and round; (vs) at, about, round; ~ agtuur at eight o'clock; ~ die hoek round the corner
om'blaai -ge- turn over (leaves of a book)
om'budsman (s) ombudsman
om'dat because, since, as ook aan'gesien
om'draai -ge- turn round, turn back; twist; revolve; nie doekies ~ nie not mince matters
omelet' -te omelette
om'gaan -ge- mix with, associate; go round
om'gang (s) intercourse, association
om'gangstaal colloquial language, common way of speaking ook spreek'taal
om'gee -ge- care; nie ~ nie not care/mind
om'gekeerd (b) -e turned upside down, re= versed
omge'wing -s, -e surroundings, environment, vicinity
omge'wings: ~bewa'ring environmental con= servation; ~leer ecology; environmental stud= ies; ~vrien'delik environmentally friendly
omhels' (w) ~ embrace, hug
om'kom -ge- die, perish; come round; in 'n ongeluk ~ die in an accident
om'koop -ge- bribe, corrupt; 'n getuie ~ bribe a witness; ~geld bribe/hush money
om'krap -ge- bring in disorder, upset; omge= krap voel be upset
om'kyk -ge- look back, look around
om'leiding -s bypass (heart operation)
omlig'gende surrounding, neighbouring; ~ pla'se neighbouring/adjacent farms
om'loop (s) circulation; omlope ringworm, cutaneous disease
om'mesientjie: in 'n ~ in a trice/jiffy
om'pad ompaaie detour
om'praat (w) -ge- persuade; dissuade
omring' ~ surround, encircle
om'roep -e broadcasting station; ~er (town)= crier; announcer (radio)
om'ruil -ge- exchange, swap/swop
om'ry -ge- drive down; drive/ride round; knock down, run over
om'sendbrief ..briewe circular (letter)
om'set turnover; jaar'likse ~ annual turnover (sales)
omsin'gel ~ surround, encircle; hulle het die vyand ~ they surrounded the enemy
om'skep -ge- change, convert; die tennisbaan

word in 'n tuin omgeskep the tennis court is being changed into a garden
omskep' ~ transform, recreate; dit het hom ~ tot 'n nuwe mens it transformed him into a new person
omskry'wing -s, -e description, definition
om'slag ..slae hem, border, cuff; wrapper; fold-over; brace
omslag'tig (b) wordy/verbose, digressive
om'stander -s bystander, onlooker
omstan'digheid ..hede circumstance; onder geen ..hede nie in/under no circumstances; versag'tende ..hede extenuating circum= stances
omstre'de (b) controversial, contentious, dis= puted; ~ boek controversial book
om'streke (mv) vicinity, neighbourhood
om'trek (s) -ke outline, circumference; vicin= ity; in die ~ in the neighbourhood
omtrent' about, almost, nearly; dis ~ tyd it is just about time
om'val -ge- fall over/down, topple over
om'vang extent; scope; size; ambit
omvat' (w) ~ embrace, enclose, comprise; ~tende verse'kering comprehensive insur= ance
om'wenteling -s, -e revolution; rotation; 'n ~ teweegbring revolutionise; dertig ~e per minuut thirty revolutions a minute
onaan'genaam unpleasant, disagreeable
onaantrek'lik -e unattractive
onaf'gebroke uninterrupted, continuous; ~ vlug nonstop flight
onafhank'lik -e independent; ~heid indepen= dence; ~verkla'ring declaration of inde= pendence
onafskei(d)'baar ..bare/onafskei'delik -e in= separable
onbaatsug'tig (b) unselfish; disinterested
onbarmhar'tig (b) merciless, unmerciful
onbeant'woord -e unanswered; unreturned (love)
onbedag'saam ..same thoughtless, inconsider= ate
onbedui'dend (b) insignificant, trifling
onbegaan'baar ..bare impassable (road)
onbegon'ne impossible; ~ taak impossible task
onbegryp'lik inconceivable, incomprehensible
onbehol'pe awkward, clumsy (person)
onbehoor'lik -e improper, unseemly (behav= iour); indecent
onbekend' -e unknown; unacquainted; unfa= miliar; ~ maak onbemind unknown, unloved

onbekom'merd -e unconcerned, unworried
onbekwaam' incapable, incompetent *ook* **on=**
bevoeg'; unfit
onbelang'rik -e unimportant; immaterial
onbeleef' impolite, uncouth, uncivil
onbelem'mer -de unhindered, unimpeded;
~**de uit'sig** unrestricted/unobscured view
onbenul'lig -e fatuous; trifling; *dis 'n* ~*heid* it
is of no importance
onbepaald' -e indefinite, unlimited; *vir 'n* ~*e*
tyd indefinitely
onbeperk' -te unlimited, boundless
onbere'kenbaar ..bare incalculable; **..bare**
ska'de incalculable harm/damage
onberis'pelik -e faultless; impeccable; ~**e**
gedrag' exemplary behaviour
onbeskaaf' uncivilised, uncouth, rude
onbeskof' insolent, ill-mannered, impudent
onbeskryf'lik -e beyond description; ~**e**
ellen'de indescribable suffering
onbeskut' -te unprotected; unsheltered
onbeslis' -te undecided; pending; sub judice
(suit); drawn (game): *die wedstryd het* ~
geëindig the match was drawn
onbeson'ne thoughtless, inconsiderate, fool=
ish; ~ **daad** rash deed
onbespro'ke irreproachable; ~ **karak'ter** high
integrity/character
onbestre'de undisputed, unopposed; ~ **se'tel**
unopposed seat (election)
onbetaald(d)' de unpaid, ~e re'kening un=
paid/unsettled account
onbetrou'baar (b) unreliable, untrustworthy
onbevlek' -te undefiled, untainted; ~**te ont=**
van'genis immaculate conception
onbevoeg' (b) -de incompetent, unfit
onbevoor'oordeeld -e unprejudiced, unbiased
onbevre'digend unsatisfactory
onbewoon' -de uninhabited, desolate
onbewus' -te ignorant, unaware; unconscious
onbil'lik -e; -er, -ste unfair, unjust
on'dank ingratitude, thanklessness; ~ *is*
wêreldsloon the world pays with ingratitude
ondank'baar ..bare ungrateful, thankless
on'danks in spite of, notwithstanding; ~ *al sy*
pogings in spite of all his efforts
on'der under; down; among; below; ~ *andere*
inter alia; ~ *vier oë* in private; ~**aan** at the
foot, at the bottom
on'der: ~**af'deling** subdivision; ~**baad'jie**
waistcoat; ~**beklem'toning** understatement;
~**beman'** shortstaffed; ~**bevoor'reg** disad=

vantaged (community)
on'derbewus (b) **-te** subconscious; ~**syn** sub=
consciousness *ook* **onderbewus'te**
onderbreek' ~ interrupt
onderbre'king -s, -e interruption, break
on'derbroek -e pair of underpants/drawers
on'derdaan ..dane subject (person); national
(of a country) *ook* **bur'ger**
onderda'nig submissive, obedient, humble
on'derdeel ..dele subdivision; spare part
on'derdompel -ge- immerse
on'derdorp (s) poorer part of town
on'derdruk¹ -ge- press down or under
onderdruk'² ~ oppress (a nation); suppress
(feelings); repress; quell (riot)
onderduims' -e underhand *ook* **agterbaks'**
on'derent -e bottom/lower end
ondergaan'¹ ~ undergo, suffer; *behandeling*
~ receive treatment
on'dergaan² -ge- go under; sink (ship); set
(sun); be ruined; ~ *in die stryd* perish in the
struggle
on'dergang (s) ruin, decline; setting (sun)
on'dergeskik -te subordinate, inferior; *van*
~*te belang* of minor importance; *jou* ~*tes*
your subordinates (people)
on'dergetekende -s undersigned (person)
ondergronds' -e underground, subterranean;
~**e spoorweg** underground railway, tube
ook **mol'trein**
onderhan'del ~ negotiate, bargain; ~**aar**
negotiator; ~**ing** negotiation *ook* **beraad'=**
(slaging), oorleg'pleging; ~*inge aanknoop*
open negotiations; *salaris* ~*baar/reëlbaar*
salary negotiable
on'derhemp ..hemde vest *ook* **frok'kie**; sin=
glet; chemise (woman's)
onderhe'wig liable to, subject to *ook* **onder=**
wor'pe (aan)
on'derhoof -de vice-principal
onderhou'¹ (w) ~ support, maintain; feed
on'derhou² -ge- hold down or under
on'derhoud¹ maintenance, support, upkeep;
betaal ~ *vir kind* pay alimony for child
on'derhoud² -e interview *ook* **vraag'gesprek**;
'n ~ *hê/voer met iem.* interview someone;
~**voe'ring** interviewing
on'derklere underclothing
on'derkomitee -s subcommittee
on'derlaag ..lae bottom layer, substratum;
undercoat (paint)
on'derling -e mutual; *tot* ~*e voordeel* to

mutual advantage/gain

ondermyn' ~ undermine, *ook* **dwars'boom** (w)

onderne'mer -s undertaker; originator, entre=preneur; **begrafnis**~ funeral undertaker

onderne'merskap: vrye ~ free enterprise

onderne'ming -s, -e enterprise, undertaking, venture; **~s'gees** spirit of enterprise; **~s'vry=heid** free enterprise

on'deroffisier -e, -s non-commissioned offi=cer, petty officer

on'derpresteerder underachiever (student)

on'derrig (s) instruction, tuition *ook* **op'lei=ding**

onderrig' (w) ~ instruct, teach

onderskat' ~ undervalue, underestimate

onderskei' ~ distinguish, differentiate

on'derskeid difference, distinction; ~ *maak tussen* distinguish between

onderskei'delik respectively

onderskei'ding -s, -e distinction; *slaag met* ~/ *lof* pass with distinction

onderskei'e various, different; respective

on'dersoek (s) examination, inquiry, investi=gation, probe; ~ *instel* inquire into; *by nader* ~ on closer examination; **kommis'sie van** ~ commission/board of inquiry; **~be=amp'te** investigating officer (police)

ondersoek' (w) ~ examine; scrutinise; in=quire, investigate, probe; *die oë* ~ test the eyes

on'derspit: *die* ~ *delf* come off second best

on'derstaande subjoined, following

on'derste (s) **-s** bottom; (b) lowermost, lowest

onderstebo' upside-down, higgledy-piggledy; upset; *hy sit kop* ~ he feels depressed

on'derstel (s) **-le** undercarriage (railway truck); chassis (motorcar)

ondersteun' (w) ~ support, assist; sponsor; **~er** supporter; **~ing** support, relief

onderte'ken (w) ~ sign *ook* **te'ken**; *'n brief* ~ sign a letter; **~aar** signatory (of document); subscriber; **~ing** signature *ook* **hand'teke=ning/naam'tekening**

on'dertoe lower down, to the bottom

ondertus'sen meanwhile, in the meantime

on'derverhuur (w) ~ sublet

ondervind' ~ experience; **~ing** experience; *~ing is die beste leermeester* experience is the best teacher

ondervoed' (b) **-e** underfed; **~ing** malnutri=tion, underfeeding

on'dervoorsitter -s vice-chairman

ondervra' ~ interrogate, question, examine; *aangehou vir ~ging* detained for questioning

onderweg' on the way; in transit

on'derwerp¹ (s) **-e** subject, topic, theme

onderwerp'² (w) ~ subdue, subject; *aan Gods wil* ~ resign to God's will

onderwor'pe subject to; submissive; ~ *aan goedkeuring* subject to approval

onderwys' (w) ~ teach, instruct, inform

on'derwys (s) education, tuition, instruction; ~ *buite skoolverband* adult education; ~ *gee* teach; *hoër* ~ higher (university) education; *middelbare (sekondêre)* ~ secondary educa=tion; ~ *vir volwassenes* adult education; **~departement'** department of education; **voort'gesette** ~ continuing education

onderwy'ser -s teacher

on'derwys: ~kol'lege college of education; **~personeel'** teaching staff

on'deug -de vice, mischief, depravity; imp, bounder; *'n klein* ~ a little bounder/rascal (child)

ondeund' mischievous, naughty *ook* **onnut'sig**

ondeursky'nend -e opaque

on'dier (s) **-e** monster, brute; beast

ondraag'baar ..bare too heavy to be carried; unwearable

ondraag'lik -e intolerable, unbearable; **~e py'ne** excruciating pains

ondubbelsin'nig (b) **-e** unambiguous

ondui'delik -e; -er, -ste indistinct; not clear (meaning); illegible (handwriting)

one'del -e ignoble, mean; base; **~e meta'le** base metals

oneerbie'dig (b) disrespectful, irreverent

oneer'lik -e; -er, -ste dishonest, unfair, fraudu=lent; **~e prakty'ke** sharp practices; **~heid** dishonesty, bad faith

oneg' -te falsified, spurious; **~te diamant'** imitation diamond

onein'dig -e infinite, endless; ~ *dankbaar* extremely grateful

one'nig at variance, discordant; **~heid** dis=cord; **~heid kry/haaks wees** quarrel

onerva're inexperienced; unskilled

one'we unequal, uneven; ~ *getal'* odd number

onewere'dig -e disproportionate

onfatsoen'lik (b) **-e** indecent, improper

onfeil'baar ..bare infallible

ongeag' -te unesteemed, unnoticed; irrespec=tive of; ~ *die koste* regardless of expense/costs

ongedeerd' -e uninjured; unharmed, un=
scathed; *daar ~ van afkom* escape unhurt
ongedul'dig -e; -er, -ste impatient
ongeërg -de imperturbed, calm, nonchalant;
~**de hou'ding** don't care attitude
ongeëwenaard' -e unequalled, unparalleled;
unrivalled
ongegrond' -e false, unfounded; ~e **aan'ty=
gings/bewe'rings** unbased accusations
ongehoor'saam disobedient; ~**heid** disobe=
dience
ongehuud' ..**hude** unmarried; **ongehu'de
moe'der** unmarried mother
on'gekeur unseeded; ~**de spe'ler** unseeded
player (sport)
ongel'dig -e invalid, null and void
ongeleer(d)' uneducated, illiterate *ook* **onge=
let'terd;** not broken in (horse)
ongelet'ter(d) -**de** illiterate
on'gelode: ~ **pet'rol** unleaded petrol
ongeloof'lik incredible, unbelievable
ongelo'wig unbelieving, sceptical, incredu=
lous; ~**e** unbeliever (person); infidel
on'geluk -**ke** accident, mishap, misfortune; *per*
~ by accident/mistake
ongeluk'kig unhappy; unfortunate, unlucky
ongelyk' (b) -e unequal, uneven; diverse
on'gemak -**ke** inconvenience, discomfort;
~**sy'fer** discomfort index (climate), humi=
ture (hot, humid)
ongemak'lik -**e; -er, -ste** uncomfortable; ill at
ease; uneasy, inconvenient
ongemanierd' -**e** rude, uncivil, ill mannered
ook **onbeskof'**
ongena'dig -**e** merciless, cruel; violent
ongene'ë disinclined; unwilling; *sy is hom nie*
~ *nie* she rather likes him
ongenees'lik -**e** incurable (illness)
ongepoets' uncouth, ill-mannered
ongereeld' -**e; -er, -ste** irregular, disorderly;
op ~**e** *tye* at odd times
on'gerief ..**riewe** inconvenience, discomfort;
~ *veroorsaak* inconvenience (v)
ongerus' -**te; -ter, -ste** uneasy, anxious; ~ *oor*
iem. anxious/worried about a person
ongeskik' unsuitable, unfit; rude/ill-mannered
ongeskon'de uninjured, intact
ongeskool' -**de** untrained, unskilled; ~**de ar'=
beid** unskilled labour
ongesond' unhealthy, unhygienic *ook* **onhigië=
nies;** unsound
ongetwy'feld undoubtedly, doubtless

on'geval -**le** accident, mishap; casualty
on'gevalleverse'kering accident insurance
on'geveer roughly, approximately, about
ongevraag' -**de** uncalled for; ~**de advies'**
unasked for advice
ongewens' -**te** undesired, undesirable; ~**te**
publika'sie undesirable publication
ongewoon' ..**wone;** ..**woner, -ste** unusual,
uncommon; *iets* ~**s** something out of the
ordinary; ~**d'** unaccustomed
ongrondwet'lik -**e** unconstitutional
on'guns disfavour, disgrace; *in* ~ *raak* fall
into disfavour
onguns'tig -**e; -er, -ste** unfavourable; ~**e**
rapport' unfavourable report
onguur' **ongure** rough, coarse, repulsive;
..**gu're vent** unsavoury fellow
onheilspel'lend (b) ominous, sinister
onherstel'baar ..**bare** irreparable, irretrieva=
ble; ..**bare verlies'** irreparable loss
o'niks (s) onyx (form of agate)
on'juis -**te** incorrect, erroneous
on'kant offside (sport)
on'klaar out of order, defective; ~ *raak* break
down (car)
on'koste expenses, charges; *na aftrek van* ~
all charges deducted
on'kruid -**e** weeds; ~ *vergaan nie* ill weeds
grow apace; ~**do'der** weedkiller, herbicide
on'kunde ignorance; *sy* ~ *openbaar* display
his ignorance
on'langs (b) -**e** recent; (bw) recently/lately
on'lus dislike; disturbance, riot; ~**een'heid**
riot squad/unit
onmens'lik -**e** inhuman, cruel, brutal
onmid'dellik -**e** immediate(ly), direct(ly)
on'min disagreement, discord *ook* **on'vrede**
on'misbaar ..**bare** indispensable, essential
onmoont'lik -**e; -er, -ste** impossible
onnatuur'lik -**e** unnatural, artificial
onno'dig -**e** unnecessary
onno'sel -**e** silly; stupid *ook* **dom, dwaas;** ~**e**
vent simpleton, Simple Simon
onomatopee' ..**peë** onomatopoeia *ook* **klank=
nabootsing**
onop'gevoed -**e** uneducated, ill-bred
onopset'lik -**e** unintentional
on'paar odd, unmatched; ~ *kou'se* odd stockings
onparty'dig (b) impartial, unbiased
onplesie'rig unpleasant, disagreeable
on'raad (s) danger, trouble; ~ *merk* smell a
rat, scent danger

onre'delik (b) unreasonable, unfair
onreëlma'tig -e irregular
on'reg wrong, injustice; skrei'ende ~ glaring injustice
onregver'dig -e; -er, -ste unjust, unfair
onroe'rend -e immovable; ~e goed'(ere) immovable property *ook* vas'goed
on'rus unrest, anxiety; disquiet, disturbance; ~ stook create alarm, incite
onrusba'rend disquieting, alarming
on'russtoker -s mischief maker; agitator
onrus'tig -e; -er, -ste restless, uneasy, anx=ious; turbulent; ~ slaap sleep uneasily
ons¹ (s) -e ounce
ons² (pers. vnw, mv), we, us; ~ s'n ours
onse'ker -e uncertain; unsafe, insecure
onsig'baar ..bare invisible, unseen; onsig=bare op'rit/in'rit concealed onramp/entry
on'sin nonsense *ook* kaf, snert; ~ praat talk rubbish
onska'delik -e harmless, innocuous
onskat'baar ..bare invaluable, inestimable; ..bare waar'de inestimable value
on'skuld (s) innocence
onskul'dig -e; -er, -ste innocent; harmless
onsterf'lik -e immortal; ~heid immortality; ~e roem immortal/lasting fame
onstui'mig turbulent, boisterous; rough (weather); ~e verga'dering unruly meeting
onsy'dig -e impartial; neuter (gender)
ontbied' (w) ~ send for, summon (doctor)
ontbind' ~ dissolve; decay, untie, undo; 'n vennootskap ~ dissolve a partnership
ontbloot' (w) ~ strip, deprive; lay bare; (b) devoid; uncovered; ~ van alle waarheid devoid of all truth; ontblo'te hoof bare=headed; ontblo'ter (man) exposer/flasher
ontbon'del (w) unbundle (a company) *ook* ontknoop'
ontbreek' ~ be wanting, be missing
ontbyt' (s) -e breakfast; ~ nuttig have break=fast; (w) ~ have breakfast
ontdek' ~ discover, find out; ~king discov=ery; ~kingsrei'siger explorer
ontdooi' ~ thaw (snow); unbend
ontduik' ~ evade, dodge; escape; die wet ~ evade the law; ~er dodger
ontevre'de -ner, -nste of meer ~, mees ~ discontented, dissatisfied
ontgroen' ~ initiate; ~ing initiation; induc=tion *ook* in'burgering/induk'sie
onthaal' (s) ..hale reception; (w) ~ entertain;

gaste ~ entertain guests
onthei'lig (w) ~ desecrate, profane *ook* skend
onthoof' (w) ~ behead, decapitate
onthou' ~ remember; recall; abstain, refrain; help my ~ remind me, please; ~er abstain=er, teetotaller (person)
onthul' ~ unveil; reveal; disclose
ontken' ~ deny; ~nend negative
ontken'ning -s, -e denial; dubbele ~ double negative
ontklee' ~ undress; ~dans striptease (act) *ook* lok'dans; ~danseres' stripper
ontknoop' (w) unbundle (company) *ook* ont=bon'del
ontle'ding (s) analysis *ook* anali'se
ontlont' (w) ~ defuse (crisis)
ontluik' ~ open, unfold; ~ende talent' bud=ding talent
ontman' ~ castrate, emasculate
ontmoet' ~ meet (with); encounter
ontnug'ter (b) disillusioned, disenchanted
ontplof' ~ explode, detonate; ~fing explo=sion, blast, detonation
ontplooi' ~ unfurl; deploy (troops)
ontrim'peling facelift *ook* gesigs'kuur
ontroer' ~ move, touch, affect; ~ende ton'ele stirring/moving scenes
ontrou' (b) -e; -er, -ste disloyal; faithless
ontruim' ~ evacuate; vacate; die gebou ~ evacuate (the people in) the building
ontsag' awe, respect; ~ inboesem stand in awe of; command respect; ~lik (b) formidable, huge *ook* gewel'dig
ontset' (b) -te appalled, aghast; ~tend terrible, awful, appalling; (w) relieve (a town)
ontsien' ~ respect, stand in awe of; geen moeite ~ nie spare no pains
ontslaan' ~ dismiss, discharge/axe; retrench; iem. uit sy betrekking ~ dismiss someone
ontsla'e rid; ~ raak van get rid of
ontslag' (s) release; dismissal, discharge
ontsla'pe dead, deceased *ook* oorle'de
ontsmet' ~ disinfect; ~ting disinfection; ~(tings)mid'del disinfectant, antiseptic
ontsnap' (w) escape; ~ping escape; jailbreak
ontspan' ~ relax, divert; unbend; tyd om te ~ time to relax; ~gerie'we recreational facil=ities/amenities
ontspoor' ~ derail
ontstaan' (s) origin; (w) ~ begin, originate, arise; hoe het die rusie ~? what was the cause of the argument?

ontstel' (w) ~ startle, upset, disturb
onttrek' ~ withdraw; **~king'simptoom** with=drawal symptom
on'tug prostitution, immorality
on'tuis ill at ease; ~ *voel* be ill at ease
ontvang' ~ receive; conceive; **~er** recipient, receiver; **~er van in'komste** receiver of revenue; **~s'** receipt; reception; takings; **~s'da'me** receptionist
ontvoer' ~ abduct, kidnap; **~der** kidnapper *ook* **ka'per/ska'ker**
ontvolk' ~ depopulate
ontwa'pen ~ disarm; **~ing** disarmament
ontwa'semer -s demister
ontwerp' (s) **-e** draft, sketch, design; project; (w) ~ project, plan, design; draft
ontwik'kel ~ develop, evolve; **~d** developed; educated; **~aar** developer (of property); **~ende lan'de** developing countries
ontwik'keling development; evolution
ontwil' sake; *om my* ~ for my sake
ontwrig' ~ dislocate; disrupt; *die klas* ~ disrupt the class
ontwyk' ~ evade, shun; **~end** evasive
o'nus onus, obligation; duty
onvanpas' (b) out of place, unsuitable
onverantwoor'delik (b) irresponsible
onverbe'terlik -e incorrigible (child)
onverdraag'saam (b) intolerant
onvergank'lik -e imperishable, undying, ever=lasting; **~e roem** immortal fame
onvergeef'lik -e unpardonable
onvergeet'lik -e memorable, unforgettable
onverhoeds' unexpectedly, unawares; ~ *be=trap* caught unawares
onverkry(g)baar ..**bare** unobtainable
onvermy'delik -e unavoidable; inevitable
onversig'tig careless; imprudent
onverskil'lig -e; -er, -ste indifferent; rash, reckless, heedless; ~ *ry* drive recklessly
onverskrok'ke bold, undaunted *ook* **vrees'=loos**; ~ **jag'ter** fearless hunter
on'versoet unsweetened
onverstaan'baar ..**bare** incomprehensible, unintelligible
onverstan'dig -e; -er, -ste unwise, foolish
onverwag' **-te** unexpected; **~s'** unexpectedly, unawares, suddenly *ook* **skie'lik**
onvoldoen'de insufficient, inadequate
onvoltooi' **-de** imperfect, incomplete; **~de simfonie'** unfinished symphony
onvoorwaar'delik -e unconditional; **~e oor'=**

gawe unconditional surrender
on'vrede discord, feud; *in* ~ *lewe* lead a cat-and-dog life
onvrien'delik unkind, unfriendly
onvrug'baar sterile, barren, infertile
onwaar' ..**ware** untrue; false
onwaarskyn'lik -e; -er, -ste improbable
on'weer (s) unsettled/stormy weather
onweerstaan'baar ..**bare** irresistible
onwet'tig -e unlawful, illegal; **~e immigrant'** illegal immigrant
onwil'lig -e unwilling; loath, reluctant
oog oë eye; fountain, source; *met die blote* ~ with the naked eye; *uit die* ~, *uit die hart* out of sight, out of mind; **~ap'pel** eyeball; darling; **~arts** eye specialist, ophthalmolo=gist; **~getui'e** eyewitness; **~haar** eyelash: *nie ~hare hê vir* not fancy (someone/something); **~knip** wink; **~kun'dige** optometrist; **~lid** eyelid; **~lo'pend** (b) obvious
ooglui'kend stealthily, on the sly; close an eye to; ~ *toelaat* connive at
oog: ~merk aim, intention; **~punt** viewpoint; **~wenk/~wink:** *in 'n* ~ in a moment/jiffy; **~wim'per** eyelash
ooi -e ewe
ooi'evaar -s, ..**vare** stork; **~s'drag** maternity wear; **~s'tee** stork party/babyshower
ooit ever, at any time
ook also, too
oom =s uncle, *Liewe ~ Piet* Dear uncle Peter
oom'blik -ke moment, instant
oomblik'lik -e immediate(ly), instantly
oond -e oven; furnace; kiln
oop open; vacant; **~staan** be open (door); **~stel** throw open; *geriewe* ~ *vir almal* open (the) facilities for all
oor¹ (s) **ore** ear; *iem. ore aansit* outdo/out=smart someone
oor² (bw) over, past; ~ *en weer* to and fro, mutually; **tien ~/ná elf;** (vs) over, via, be=yond, across; ~ *die geheel* on the whole
oor³ (vgw) because; *hy vorder* ~ *hy werk* he makes progress because he works
oor: ~beklem'toning overstatement; **~bel** earring; earlobe; **~bevolk'** overpopulated
oorbluf' ~ disconcert, strike dumb; *heeltemal* ~ completely dumbfounded
oorbo'dig -e superfluous *ook* **oortol'lig**
oorbrug' ~ bridge (over); *probleme* **~/uitstryk** solve (the) problems
oord (s) **-e** region, locality; resort

oor'daad (s) excess, extravagance

oor'deel (s) ..**dele** judgment; verdict; ~ *vel* pass judgment/sentence; (w) judge

oordeelkun'dig (b) **-e** judicious

oorden'king (s) meditation; epilogue

oordraag'baar ..**bare** transferable

oor'drag transfer, cession

oordre'we (b) exaggerated; overdone

oordryf' oordry'we ~ exaggerate, overstate, overdo

ooreen' in agreement; *hulle kom* ~ they agree *ook* **akkordeer'** (w)

ooreen'koms resemblance, conformity; agreement, treaty; *'n* ~ *aangaan/sluit/tref* enter into an agreement

ooreenkoms'tig -e in accordance with, in terms of *ook* **vol'gens/ingevol'ge**

ooreen'stem -gestem agree, concur

oorerf'lik -e hereditary

oor'gang (s) transition; **-e** crossing, passage

oor'gawe -s surrender; transfer, cession

oor'gee -ge- surrender, yield; *hom* ~ *aan* surrender himself to

oor: ~**genoeg** more than enough; ~**gerus** over= confident; ~**gevoe'lig** oversensitive, hyper= sensitive; ~**gewig'** overweight; obese/obe= sity; excess weight

oor'groot: ~**moe'der** great-grandmother; ~**ou'ers** great-grandparents; ~**va'der** great-grandfather

oor'haal -ge- fetch across; persuade *ook* **oorreed'**; cock (rifle); induce

oorhan'dig ~ hand over, deliver; present; ~**ing** handing over, delivery; presentation (of prizes)

oorheers' ~ dominate *ook* **domineer'**; ~**ing** domination

oor'hou -ge- save, have left

oor'kant (s) other/opposite side; *(aan die)* ~ *(van) die straat* on the other side of the street

oor'klank -ge- dub; ~**ing** dubbing (radio/TV)

oor'klere overall(s) *ook* **oor'pak**

oorkoe'pel ~ cover, vault, arch; ~**ende organisa'sie** umbrella organisation

oor'kussing pillow; *ledigheid is die duiwel se* ~ Satan finds mischief for idle hands to do

oorlaai'[1] ~ overload, overcharge, overburden; *hy is met presente* ~ presents were heaped upon him

oor'laai[2] **-ge-** reload; transship

oor'laat -ge- leave over, leave (to others); *aan*

sy lot ~ leave to his fate

oorlams' (b) **-e** clever, handy; cunning, crafty, wily, shrewd; trained

oor'las (s) nuisance, trouble

oorle'de deceased, late; ~ *Jan* the late John

oorle'dene -s the deceased, the departed

oorleg' deliberation, counsel, consideration, judgment; ~**komitee'** liaison committee *ook* **ska'kelkomitee**; ~**ple'ging** consultation, talks/negotiations

oor'lel -le lobe of the ear

oorle'wing survival *ook* **voort'bestaan**; ~ *van die sterkste* survival of the fittest; ~(s)**kur'= sus** survival course

oor'log ..**loë** war; ~ *verklaar* declare war; ~ *voer* wage war

oor'logverklaring declaration of war

oor'loop (s) overflow; ..**lope** spillway; (w) desert; overflow (dam); *na die vyand* ~ defect/desert to the enemy

oorlo'sie -s watch, clock *ook* **hor'losie**; *my* ~ *is agter* my watch is slow; *my* ~ *is voor* my watch is fast; ~**ma'ker** watchmaker

oormees'ter (w) overpower; master

oor'môre day after tomorrow

oor'nag (w) ~ stay overnight; (b, bw) over= night

oor'name (s) **-s** takeover (of company)

oor'neem -ge- take over (management); as= sume; copy; borrow

oor'pak -ke overall

oor'plant (w) **-ge-** transplant (heart)

oor'pyn earache

oorreed' ~ persuade, prevail on *ook* **om'praat**

oorrom'pel ~ surprise, overwhelm

oor'saak ..**sake** cause, reason; ~ *en gevolg* cause and effect

oorsees' ..**sese** oversea(s), transmarine; **oor= se'se han'del** overseas/foreign trade

oor'sig -te survey; review, summary; view

oor'sit -ge- put over; translate; move up (pupils)

oorskat' (w) overestimate, overrate

oor'skiet (s) remains; rest; remnant; (w) remain; ~**kos** leftovers

oor'skot -te remainder, residue; remnant; sur= plus; **stof'like** ~ mortal remains; ~**waar'de** scrap value; **handels**~ trade surplus

oorskry' ~ exceed; surpass; *uitgawes* ~ *inkomste* expenditure exceeds income/rev= enue

oor'sprong (s) origin, cause, root, source

oorspronk'lik -e original, primary; primor=
dial; ~heid originality
oor'steek -ge- cross (a street)
oorstroom' ~ overflow, inundate
oortol'lig -e superfluous; redundant (staff)
oortre'der -s trespasser, transgressor; delin=
quent, offender; ~s word vervolg trespas=
sers will be prosecuted
oortref' (w) surpass, outclass, excel
oortrek' (w) ~ cover; pull over; trace (draw=
ing); ~king overdraft (bank account)
oor'trektrui -e pull-over, sweater
oortuig' (w) ~ convince ook oorreed'; ~end
convincing
oortui'ging (s) conviction
oor'tyd overtime; ~beta'ling overtime pay
oor'vloed abundance, plenty
oorvra' ~ overcharge (for article); surcharge
oorweeg' ~ consider, deliberate; 'n voorstel ~
consider a proposal/suggestion
oor weg ..weë level crossing; crossroad
oorwe'ging -s, -e consideration
oorwel'dig (w) ~ overpower, overwhelm;
~end overpowering, overwhelming
oorwin' ~ conquer, overcome; ~naar con=
queror, victor
oorwin'ning -s, -e victory, conquest ook
triomf'; die ~ behaal gain the victory
oorwin'ter ~ spend the winter, hibernate
oorwo'ë considered; contemplated; ~ me'ning
considered opinion
oos east, ~ wes, tuis bes there is no place like
home
Oos-Kaap (provinsie) Eastern Cape
Oos'te Orient, the East; Ver're ~ Far East
Oos'tenryk Austria; ~er Austrian (person)
oos'tewind -e eastwind
op (b) finished; (bw) up, on; (vs) on, upon; at,
in; almal ~ een na all but one; ~ gereed=
heidgrondslag on alert; ~ skool at school; ~
tyd on time ook betyds'
opaal' opale opal
op'bel (w) -ge- ring up, phone ook bel/ska'kel
op'berg -ge- store, stock; stockpile
op'beur (w) -ge- cheer up ook opkik'ker
op'blaas -ge- blow up; inflate
op'bou (w) -ge- build up; ~end constructive;
~ende kritiek' constructive criticism
op'brengs/op'brings -te output, yield, return
(econ.); proceeds
op'daag -ge- turn up, arrive
op'doen -ge- gain, acquire, obtain; overhaul

ook op'knap; kennis ~ acquire knowledge
op'dok -ge- pay, foot the bill; cough up
op'domkrag opge- jack up (a car)
op'dons -ge- go about carelessly, bungle; treat
severely ook op'foeter/op'neuk; iem. goed
~ give someone a drubbing
op'draand (s) -e/op'draande -s rise, slope,
rising ground, uphill; acclivity
op'drag -te instruction, order; commission;
terms of reference; dedication; in ~ van die
bestuur by order of management
o'pe open; vacant; blank (line); dis 'n ope vraag
it is a moot point; ~/oop dag open day
opeens' suddenly ook skie'lik
opeen'volg -gevolg follow each other; ~end
successive, consecutive; tien ~ende dae ten
consecutive days/ten days running
op'eet opgeëet eat up, finish; alles vir soetkoek
~ believe everything
o'pelug open-air; ~muse'um open-air mu=
seum
opelyf' evacuation/movement of the bowels
o'pen (w) ge- open; ~heid transparency
openbaar' (s) public; in die ~ in public; (w)
make public, disclose, reveal
openba're: ~besker'mer public protector ook
om'budsman; ~ betrek'kinge public rela=
tions; ~ska'kelamptenaar public relations
official/officer ook me'diaskakel; ~ vakan'=
siedag public holiday
openhar'tig -e open-hearted, frank, candid
o'pening -s, -e opening; gap; vacancy
o'penlik -e openly, publicly
o'pera ~s opera; ~gebou' opera house
opera'sie -s operation; 'n ~ ondergaan under=
go an operation; ~tea'ter operating theatre
operateur' -s operator (of machine)
opereer' ~, ge- operate (on)
operet'te -s operetta; light opera
op'foeter (w) let someone have it; bungle
along ook op'dons
op'gaan -ge- go up, ascend, rise
op'gawe/op'gaaf -s task, assignment, brief;
statement ook voor'legging; return (income)
op'geruimd (b) cheerful, gay, bright
op'geskeep -te saddled (with); at a loss
op'geskort -e suspended (sentence)
op'gevoed (b) educated; cultured
op'gewasse equal (to); nie ~ vir die taak nie
not equal to the task
op'gewek lively, cheerful, bright ook op'ge=
ruimd; ~te musiek' bright/lively music

op'gewonde (b) excited, thrilled; ~n'heid ex= citement

op'gooi -ge- throw up; chuck up; vomit ook braak; tou ~ throw in the towel

op'gradeer (w) upgrade, improve quality

op'hang -ge- hang; suspend

op'hef (s) fuss; 'n groot ~ maak van make a fuss about; (w) abolish, waive

op'hoop -ge- accumulate; heap up; opge= hoop'te verlies'e accumulated losses

op'hou -ge- keep up, support; keep on; uphold; cease, stop; die reën sal nou ~ it will stop raining now; hou op! stop it!

opi'nie -s opinion; ~pei'ling opinion poll

op'kikker -ge- cheer up; pep up; ~tablet' pep pill ook verbo'de stimulant'; ~s steroids

op'kikpraatjie (s) peptalk

op'klaar -ge- brighten; clear (up) (weather)

op'knap -ge- tidy up; recondition; renovate; ~kur'sus refresher/crash course

op'kom -ge- come up, rise; occur; crop up; ~s rise; attendance (at meeting)

op'laag ..lae edition (of a book); circulation (newspaper)

op'laai -ge- give a lift; load

op'lê -ge- impose (a fine); charge

op'lei -ge- instruct, educate, train; ~er trainer; ~kur'sus training course

op'leiding education, training

op'let -ge- pay attention, take notice

oplet'tend (b) -e; -er, -ste attentive, observant

op'lewing revival; ~ van die ekonomie revival/upswing of the economy

op'loop (w) -ge- accumulate, accrue, increase; op'geloopte ren'te accrued interest

op'los -ge- dissolve; solve (problem)

op'lossing -s, -e solution; explanation

op'meet -ge- survey; measure

op'merk -ge- notice; observe; remark; ~ing remark, observation

opmerk'lik -e; -er, -ste remarkable; strange

op'meter -s mine surveyor

op'name -s recording (on tape); survey

op'neem -ge- take up; record; receive; shelter; voorraad ~ take stock

op'offering -s, -e sacrifice

op'onthoud (s) delay, stoppage ook vertra'= ging

op'pas -ge- be careful, beware, mind; attend to, care for/nurse; pas op! be careful! look out!

op'passer -s caretaker, attendant/orderly; nurse

op'per (w) ge- suggest, moot; besware ~ raise objections

op'perbevel high/supreme command

op'perhoof -de (paramount) chief, chieftain

op'perste uppermost, highest; ~ va'bond archscoundrel

op'pervlak (s) surface; die swemmer verdwyn onder die ~ the swimmer disappears under the surface

oppervlak'kig (b) superficial, shallow; ~e kennis superficial knowledge

op'pervlakte -s area; die wandellaan beslaan 'n ~ van 3 hektaar the mall covers an area of 3 hectares

Op'perwese Supreme Being, God

opportunis' -te opportunist (person)

opposi'sie opposition ook teen'stand

opreg' sincere, genuine; ~ die uwe yours sincerely

op'rig -ge- erect; found; raise; establish; 'n maatskappy ~ form/float a company

op'rit -te onramp (traffic) ook in'rit; driveway

op'roep (s) -e summons; (telephone) call; (w) call up, commandeer

op'roer -e revolt, insurrection, riot

op'roermaker -s rioter, insurgent (person)

op'ruim -ge- clear away, tidy; ~verko'ping clearance sale

(op)rylaan driveway ook in'rit

op'sê -ge- recite; dismiss, give notice

op'set (s) plan; purpose, intention; met ~ on purpose

opset'lik -e on purpose, deliberate(ly)

op'sie -s option ook keu'se

op'siener -s overseer, supervisor; invigilator ook toe'sighouer (eksamen); commissioner

op'sig -te supervision; respect; in alle ~te in all respects; ~ter supervisor; caretaker

op'skeep -ge- saddle with

op'skop[1] -ge- kick up; 'n lawaai ~ make a fuss

op'skop[2] (s) -pe informal dance/party

op'skort -ge- suspend (a sentence); op'ge= skorte von'nis suspended sentence

op'skrif -te inscription, title, heading

op'skudding agitation, sensation, alarm

op'slaan -ge- raise; pitch (tent); lift (eyes); ~huis prefabricated house

op'slag opslae rise; glance; self-sown plants; bounce; ~koe'ël ricochet shot; ~plek supply dump/depot; ~so'mer Indian summer

op'som -ge- summarise, sum up; ~ming summary ook sa'mevatting; résumé

op'spoor -ge- track down, trace
op'spraak sensation, commotion; ~wek'kend sensational
op: ~staan stand up; get up; revolt; ~stal premises (farm), homestead
op'stand -e revolt, insurrection *ook* op'roer
op'standing resurrection
op'steek -ge- raise, put up; light; incite; prick up; *stem per/met* ~ *van hande* vote by show of hands
op'stel (s) -le essay, composition; (w) com= pose; draft; compile
op'stoker -s inciter, instigator, agitator
op'stop -ge- fill up; stuff, mount; ~per punch, smack; taxidermist
op'styg -ge- rise, ascend; ~ing ascent, rising; lift-off (spacecraft)
op'sweep -ge- whip up, incite; *die gemoedere* ~ rouse the feelings/passions
op'swel -ge- swell; inflate
op'tel -ge- enumerate; add; lift; ~fout adding error; casting error; ~som addition sum
op'ties -e optic(al)
optimis' -te optimist (person); ~me optimism
op'tog -te procession; histo'riese ~ historical pageant
op'tree -ge- appear, take action/steps, *as voorsitter* ~ act as chairman; ~fooi appear= ance fee (sport, social)
opval'lend conspicuous, noticeable, striking
op'vang -ge- intercept, catch up, overhear; ~gebied' catchment area (water)
op'vat -ge- understand, take up; *iets ernstig* ~ regard something seriously; ~ting opinion, idea, conception, view
op'veil -ge- sell by auction
opvlie'ënd -e quick-tempered, irascible
op'voed -ge- educate, rear, bring up; ~e'ling educant; ~er educator, educationist; ~ing education; ~kunde pedagogy
opvoedkun'dig pedagogic, educative, educa= tional; ~e educationist (person)
op'voer -ge- lead up to; perform, act; ~ing performance; production (play)
op'volg -ge- follow; succeed; ~aan'val hot pursuit *ook* hak'kejag; ~on'dersoek check-up
op'vra -ge- call in, demand back; withdraw; ~ging withdrawal (money)
op'vreet -ge- devour (animal); put up with
op'was (w) wash the dishes; (s) ~ser dishwasher
op'wek -ge- awake, stimulate, rouse; generate (electricity; steam) *kyk* krag'opwekker

op'wen (w) wind up (watch); get excited
op'wipkieslys (s) pop-up menu (comp.)
o'ral(s) everywhere
orangoe'tang -s orangutan
oran'je orange (colour)
or'de order, arrangement; ~lik orderly
ordent'lik (b) decent, reasonable, fair
or'der -s command, order
ordinan'sie -s ordinance (Church ruling/ritual)
ordonnan'sie -s ordinance (of a province)
orent' upright, straight up
orgaan' organe organ; ~sken'ker organ donor
organisa'sie -s organisation *ook* fir'ma
organiseer' ~, ge- organise; ~der organiser, promoter
orgidee' ..deë orchid (flower)
orgie' -ë orgy, debauching *ook* fuif'party
oriënta'sie/oriënte'ring orientation; induction (students, staff)
o'rig superfluous; meddlesome; flirtatious
orkaan' orkane hurricane *ook* storm'wind
orkes' -te orchestra, band; ~lei'er bandleader
ornament' (s) -e ornament *ook* sie'raad
or'rel -s organ; ~draai'er organ grinder
orrelis' -te organist
ortodontis' -te orthodontist (dental specialist)
ortopeed' ..pede, ortopedis -te orthopaedic surgeon
os -se ox; *van die* ~ *op die esel/jas* switching the conversation
os'braai -e ox-braai
oseaan' oseane ocean
osoon' ozone; ~vrien'delik ozone friendly
ot'jie -s young pig; grunter (fish)
ot'ter -s otter
ot'tery -e piggery
ou (s) -ens chap, fellow, guy; *ek het nie oog= hare vir daardie* ~ *nie* I do not fancy that guy/chap
ou'boet -e/ou'boetie -s eldest brother
oud (b) old, aged; ~ *maar nog nie koud nie* there is still a kick left in the old horse
oud- ex; former; retired; ~leer'ling ex-pupil
ou'dergewoonte/ou'der gewoonte as usual
ou'derdom -me age; ~ga'ping generation gap *ook* genera'siegaping
ou'derling -e, -s elder (in church)
ouderwets' -e old-fashioned *ook* ou'tyds; for= ward, precocious (child)
oudiovisueel' (b) audiovisual; ..visue'le hulp'= middels audiovisual aids

ou'dit (s, w) audit *ook* **ouditeer'** (w)
ouditeur' -e, -s auditor
ou'ditkunde (science of) auditing
oudleerling -e ex-pupil, old boy/girl (of a school)
oud'ste -s eldest, oldest, doyen
oud'student' -e ex-student, alumnus
ou'e -s old one; chap; *die* ~*s van dae* the aged; *haai, julle* ~*(n)s!* I say, chaps!
ou'er -s parent; ~*s vra* ask parents' consent (to get married)
ou'etehuis -e old-age home, home for senior citizens *ook* **tehuis' vir bejaar'des**
Ou'jaar Old Year's Day; ~**s'aand** New Year's Eve
ou'jong; ~**kêrel** (old) bachelor *ook* **vry'gesel;** ~**nooi** spinster, old maid
Ou'kersaand -e Christmas Eve
ou'laas: *vir* ~ for the last time
ou'lik precocious (child); tricky, nice; smart, cute; ~**e kê'reltjie** smart little chap

ou'ma -s grandmother; ~**groot'jie** great= grandmother
ou'pa -s grandfather; ~**groot'jie** great-grand= father
outeur' -s author *ook* **skry'wer**
ou'tjie -s (old) fellow, chum, chap, chappie; *die klein* ~*s* the tiny tots
outobiografie' -ë autobiography
outoma'ties -e automatic
ou'totel'ler (s) automatic teller machine (ATM) *ook* **kits'bank**
ou'tyds -e old-fashioned, old-fangled
ou'volk spiny-tailed lizard *ook* **son'kyker**
ou'vrou-onder-die-kombers' toad-in-the-hole
ovaal' ovale oval
o'werheid . .hede authority; ~**beste'ding** pub= lic/state expenditure/spending; ~**sek'tor** public sector
o'werspel adultery *ook* **eg'breuk**
o'werste -s chief, head; superior (person)

P

pa -'s pa, dad
paad'jie footpath, small path; parting (hair)
paai ge- appease, coax, soothe; ~**boe'lie** bug= bear, golliwog; ~**pap'pie** sugardaddy
paaiement' -e instalment
paal pale pole, stake, standard; *die* ~ *nie haal nie* unable to make the grade; ~**tjie'wag'ter** wicketkeeper
paar (s) **pare** couple, pair; a few; (w) match, mate, copulate; pair off
Paas: ~**fees** Easter; Passover; ~**maan'dag** Easter Monday *nou* **Gesins'dag**
pad paaie path, road; way; *iem. in die* ~ *steek* send someone packing; ~**blokka'de/**~**ver= sper'ring** roadblock
pad'da -s frog, toad; *so waar as* ~ *manel' dra* truly; ~**slag'ter** blunt knife; ~**stoel** toad= stool; mushroom
pad: ~**kafee'** roadhouse; ~**kos** provisions (for a journey)
pad'langs straight *ook* **openhar'tig**
pad: ~**loop** roadrace; ~**skra'per** grader; ~**stal** farmstall; ~**te'ken** roadsign; ~**vaar'= dig** ready for the road; ~**vark** roadhog (motorist); ~**vei'ligheid** road safety; ~**ver= leg'ging** deviation (of road); ~**versper'ring** roadblock; ~**vin'der** boy scout; pathfinder;

~**waar'dig** (b) roadworthy
pa'-hulle father and close relatives; dad and company
paja'ma -s pyjamas
pak (s) -ke suit (of clothes); pack, bundle; thrashing, licking; *'n* ~ *klere* a suit of clothes; *'n* ~ *slae* a thrashing; (w) pack up; seize, grasp; ~**huis** warehouse
pak'kend (b) gripping, thrilling *ook* **boei'end**
pakket' -te parcel, packet; package; ~**ak= koord'** package deal; ~**pos** parcel post
pak'kie -s parcel, packet
pak: ~**stap'per** backpacker; ~**stuk** gasket (engine)
paleis' -e palace
pa'ling -s eel (fish)
palm[1] -s palm; ~**boom** palm (tree)
palm[2] (s) palm (of the hand)
palmiet' bulrush
pamflet' -te pamphlet; brochure, handout
pampoen' -e pumpkin; *vir koue* ~ *skrik* afraid of one's own shadow; ~**tjies** mumps, parotitis
pan -ne pan; tile; small lake
pand -e pledge, pawn, forfeit
pan'dak -ke tiled roof
pand: ~**jies'baas** pawnbroker; ~**jies'win'kel** pawnshop

paneel' panele panel; *die* ~ *beoordelaars* the panel of adjudicators; ~**kas'sie/kis'sie** cub= byhole/glove box; ~**wa** panel van
paniek' -e panic, stampede; ~**bevan'ge** pa= nic-stricken, panicky; ~**knop'pie** panic button *ook* **angs'knoppie**
pan'nekoek -e pancake
pantof'fel -s slipper; ~**held** henpecked husband
pap^1 (s) porridge; -**pe** poultice
pap^2 (b) -**per**, -**ste** soft, weak; deflated; ~ **band** deflated/flat tyre
papa'ja -s papaw (fruit)
papa'wer -s poppy *ook* **klap'roos**
pap'broek -e milksop, coward (person)
papegaai' -e parrot, polly; popinjay
papier' -e paper; ~**lint** streamer
pap'nat dripping wet *ook* **sop'nat**
pap'pa -s papa, dad
pap'pie -s daddy
paraat' (b) **parate** ready, prepared
para'de -s parade; ~**pas** goose step
paradys' (s) -e paradise
parafeer' ~, **ge-** initial; ~ *elke bladsy* initial every page
paraffien' paraffin oil *ook* **lamp'olie**
parafra'se -s paraphrase
paragraaf' ..**grawe** paragraph
parallel' -**le** parallel
parame'dies paramedical; **parame'dikus** para= medic (person) *ook* **me'diese ordonnans'**
parapleeg' ..**pleë** paraplegic (person)
parasiet' -e parasite; sponger
parfuum' -s scent, perfume *ook* **laven'tel**
pa'ri par; *onder* ~ below par
park -e park; ~**a'de** parkade
parkeer' (w) park; ~**me'ter** parking meter
parkiet' -e parakeet; ~**tjie** budgerigar (budg= ie) *ook* **bud'jie**
parlement' -e parliament
parman'tig (b) impudent, impertinent, cheeky
parodie' -ë parody, travesty
parool' parole; watchword
part -e part, portion, share; trick
party'^{1} (s) -e party; faction; ~ *kies* take sides
party'^{2} (b) some, a few
party'dig -e; -**er**, -**ste** partial, biassed
party'keer/party'maal sometimes
Parys^1 Paris (France); Parys (SA)
pas^1 (s) -**se** pass; passage; step, gait; *die* ~ *aangee* set the pace; ~**aange'ër** pacemaker (heart); go-getter (person)
pas^2 (s) place; fit; (w) fit, suit, try on, be proper;

nie bymekaar ~ *nie* not match; ~**geweer'** custom-made gun/rifle
pas^3 (bw) just, only; hardly; ~ *aan'gestelde* hoof newly appointed head/principal
Pa'se Easter *ook* **Paas'fees**
pasiënt' -e patient
pasifis' -**te** pacifist; ~**me** pacifism
pas'klaar (b) ready for fitting; ready-made
pas'lik -e fitting, suitable, becoming
pas'poort -e passport
passaat' passage; ~**wind** trade wind
passa'sie -s passage; ~ *uit 'n roman* fragment/ passage from a novel
passasier' -s passenger; **blin'de** ~ stowaway *ook* **verste'keling**; ~**stra'ler** jetliner
pas'send -e fitting; proper, appropriate; *daarby* ~*e skoene* shoes to match
pas'ser -s pair of compasses; ~ **en draai'er** fitter and turner (person)
pas'sie passion, craze
passief' passive; inactive
pas'siespel -e passion play
pas'stuk -ke adaptor *ook* **aan'passer** (elektr.)
pastei' -e pie, pastry
pastel' -**le** crayon, pastel
pastoor' -**s**, ..**tore** pastor; priest
pas'tor -s clergyman, pastor
pastorie' -ë parsonage, vicarage, rectory
patat'(ta) -s sweetpotato *ook* **soet'patat'**
patent' (s) -e patent
pate'ties pathetic *ook* **aandoen'lik**
pa'tio (s) -'s patio, stoep *ook* **bui'testoep**
patrio'ties (b) -e patriotic
patrol'lie -s patrol
patroon'^{1} **patrone** pattern, model, design
patroon'^{2} **patrone** cartridge (of firearm)
patrys' -e partridge; ~**poort** porthole (ship)
paviljoen'/pawiljoen' -e pavilion, stand
pê tired, worn out; *hy kan nie* ~ *sê nie* he can= not say boo to a goose
pedaal' **pedale** pedal
pedan'ties -e; -**er**, -**ste** pedantic
pedia'ter paediatrician *ook* **kin'derarts**
pedofiel' child molester, paedophile
peer pere pear; *met die gebakte pere bly sit* be saddled with something
peet pete sponsor, godparent; ~**tjie:** *loop na jou* ~*jie* go to the devil; ~**kind** godchild; ~**ou'ers** godparents
peil (s) mark, gauge; standard, level; (w) sound, fathom, gauge, plumb
peins (w) **ge-** meditate; ponder

pe'kel (s) brine; difficulty; ~**wa'ter** brine
pel'grim -s pilgrim; ~**s'reis** pilgrimage
pelikaan' ..**kane** pelican
peloton' -s squad, platoon; **vuur**~ firing squad
pels -e fur; ~**er** pilchard *ook* **sardyn'** (vis);
　~**jas** furcoat
pen (s) -ne pen; nib, quill; peg (tent)
pena'rie difficulty, predicament, fix
pen'del (w) ge- commute; ~**aar** commuter;
　~**diens** shuttle service; ~**tuig** space shuttle
pendu'le -s pendulum *ook* **pendu'lum**
pe'nis (s) penis *ook* **fal'lus**
pen'kop -pe youngster, inexperienced youth
pen'nelekker -s clerk, penpusher
pen'ning -s medal, penny; ~**mees'ter** treasurer
　ook **tesourier'**
pen: ~**orent'** erect, straight up; ~**punt** nib;
　upright; ~**reg'op** perpendicular
pens -e belly, stomach, paunch (animal); ~ *en*
　pootjies bodily
pensioen' -e pension; retiring pay; *met* ~
　aftree retire on pension; ~**a'ris** pensioner;
　~**fonds** pension fund; ~**trek'ker** pensioner
pens: ~**klavier'** accordion; ~**win'keltjie** ped=
　lar's tray
pe'per (s) pepper; ~**duur** sinfully dear
peperment'/pipperment' -e peppermint
per by, via, per; ~ *abuis* by mistake; ~ *adres*
　care of; ~ *kerende pos* by return of post
perd -e horse
per'de: ~**by** wasp; hornet; ~**krag** horsepower;
　~**rui'ter** horseman, equestrian; ~**sport** show=
　jumping *ook* **rui'terkuns**
perd: ~**fris** hale and hearty; ~**jie** small horse,
　pony; *gou op sy* ~*jie wees* quickly steamed
　up
pê'rel -s pearl; ~*s voor die swyne werp/gooi*
　cast pearls before swine; **gekweek'te** ~
　cultured pearl; ~*snoer* string of pearls
perfek' -te perfect; ~**sie** perfection
perio'de -s period *ook* **tyd'perk, termyn'**
periodiek' periodic(al), from time to time
perk -e limit; ~**tyd** deadline *ook* **sper'tyd**
perlemoen' mother of pearl, abalone
permanent' -e permanent *ook* **bly'wend**
permissiwiteit' permissiveness
permit' -te permit, pass
perron' platform (railway) *ook* **plat'form**
pers[1] (s) printing press; ~**fotograaf'** press photo=
　grapher (person)
pers[2] (b) purple (colour)
perseel' ..**sele** lot; plot, stand; premises

persent' per cent; 10 ~ **sty'ging** 10 per cent
　increase
persenta'sie -s percentage
persep'sie (s) perception *ook* **idee'**
pers'ke -s peach; ~**bran'dewyn** peach brandy
　ook **mampoer'**
personeel' ..**nele** staff, personnel; ~**agent'skap**
　employment agency
personifika'sie -s personification
persoon' ..**sone** person; *die aangewese* ~ the
　right person; ~**lik** personal; ~**like re'kenaar**
　personal computer (PC); ~**likheid'** person=
　ality; **gesple'te** ~**likheid** split personality
pers: ~**verkla'ring** press release; ~**vry'heid**
　press freedom
pervert' (s) pervert (person); (a) perverted
pes (s) -te pest, plague
pessimis' -te pessimist; ~**me** pessimism; ~**ties**
　pessimistic *ook* **neerslag'tig**
pet -te cap
petal'je (s) -s affair *ook* **bohaai'**; to-do
peti'sie -s petition *ook* **versoek'skrif**
pe'trol petrol; ~**jog'gie** pump attendant; ~**pomp**
　petrol pump, bowser; ~**tenk** petrol tank
petro'leum petroleum, rock oil
peul (s) -e pod, husk, shell
peu'sel ge- nibble, pick; piffle; ~**hap'pie** snack;
　~**kroeg** snackbar; ~**wer'kie** odd job
peu'ter (s) toddler *kyk* **kleu'ter**; ~**vry** (b)
　foolproof; tamperproof
pianis' -te pianist *ook* **klavier'speler**
pia'no -'s piano/klavier
piek -e peak, pinnacle; (w) peak
piek'fyn spick-and-span; grand, snazzy
piek'niek -s picnic; ~**oord** picnic/pleasure resort
pienk (b) pink (colour) *ook* **ligroos'**
piep'erig (b) sickly, weak, thin, squeaky
pie'pie (w) ge- make water (nursery term);
　pee, piddle
piep'jong/piep'jonk very young, tender
pie'rewaaier -s playboy, goodtimer *ook* **swier** =
　bol; dar'teldawie (idiom.)
pie'ring -s saucer; ~**skiet** clay pigeon/skeet
　shooting
pie'sang -s banana
pietersie'lie parsley
piet-my-vrou' -e red-chested cuckoo
piets (w) ge- whip lightly, flick
pigmee' ..**meë** pygmy (dwarf)
pik (s) pitch; (w) peck; nag, find fault; bite
　(snake); ~**don'ker** pitch dark
pikkewyn' -e penguin

pik'swart black as pitch, pitch black
pil -le pill; *die* ~ *verguld* sugar a pill
pilaar' pilare pillar, column
Pila'tus Pilate; *van Pontius na* ~ from pillar to post
pim'pel: ~ *en pers* black and blue
pin'kie -s little finger
Pink'ster: ~**fees** Whitsuntide, Pentecost
pinset' (s) **-te** forceps; tweezers *ook* **haar'= tangetjie**
pint -e pint
pion' -ne pawn (chess); stooge (person)
pionier' -s, -e pioneer *ook* **baan'breker**
piou'ter (s) pewter
pirami'de/piramied' pyramid
pis (s) piss, urine; (w) urinate, piss, piddle
pistool' pistole pistol
pit -te kernel (nut); core (tree); stone (peach); pip (orange); wick (lamp)
pit'tig (b) **-e; -er, -ste** pithy; terse, snappy
pla (w) **ge-** tease, annoy, vex, worry
plaag (s) **plae** plague, pest; affliction; ~**be= heer'** pest control; ~**do'der** pesticide, in= secticide, herbicide; ~**gees** tease *ook* **terg'gees;** tormenting fiend (person)
plaak plaque (teeth); fatty deposit
plaas (s) **plase** place; farm; (w) put, place, locate; ~**ja'pie** (country) bumpkin, yokel; ~**kiosk'** farm stall *ook* **pad'stal;** ~**lik** local; ~*like bestuur* local government; ~*like ower= heid* local authority, ~**ver van'ger** substitute, deputy; proxy
plaat plate plate; slab; sheet; stake (races); ~**kompeti'sie** plate event (sport)
plafon' -ne ceiling
plagiaat' plagiarism *ook* **let'terdiefstal**
plak¹ (s) **-ke** ferule; slab; ~ *sjokola'de* slab of chocolate *ook* **blok sjokola'de**
plak² (w) **ge-** paste, paper, stick; squat (on land); ~**boek** scrapbook
plakkaat' ..kate placard, poster, billboard
plak: ~**ker** paper hanger; sticker; squatter (per= son); ~**papier'** wallpaper; ~**ers'kamp'** squat= ter camp, informal settlement; ~**kery'** squatting
plak'kies (s) beach thongs, slip-slops
plan -ne plan, scheme, project, intention
planeet' ..nete planet
planeta'rium -s planetarium
plank -e plank, board; ~**e'vrees** stage fright
plant (s) **-e** plant; (w) plant
planta'sie -s plantation

plant: ~**egroei** vegetation; ~**e'tend** herbivo= rous; ~**kun'de** botany
plas (s) **-se** pool, puddle; (w) paddle, splash; ~**poel** paddling pool
plastiek' plastic; plastic art; ~**be'ker** plastic mug; ~**sak'kie** plastic bag; (milk) sachet
plas'ties -e plastic; ~**e** sny'kunde/~**e** chirur= gie' plastic/cosmetic surgery
plat -ter, -ste flat, level; slangy, vulgar
plataan' platane plane tree
platan'na -s spur-toed frog, platanna
pla'tejoggie disc jockey (radio)
plat'form -s platform (at station); stage *ook* **verhoog'**
plat'jie -s rogue; mischievous fellow
plato' -'s plateau *ook* **hoog'land**
plato'rand -e escarpment
plat'riem -e ferule, strap
plat'sak (b) hard up, broke, penniless
plat'teland country, rural districts, platteland
plat'voet -e flat foot
plavei' ge- pave; ~**sel** pavement
pleeg ge- commit, perpetrate; *selfmoord* ~ com= mit suicide; ~**ou'ers** foster parents; ~**sorg** foster care
pleg'tig -e; -er, -ste solemn, ceremonious
pleidooi' (s) **-e** plea, argument, defence
plein -e square
pleis'ter¹ (s) **-s** poultice
pleis'ter² (s) **-s** plaster; (w) plaster, stucco, ~**aar'** plasterer
pleit (s) plea; (w) plead; intercede
plek -ke place; spot; room, space; position; ~**bespre'king** booking/reservation
pleks instead of
plesier' -e pleasure, enjoyment, fun; ~**kie'rie** (idiom.) floorshift (car)
plesie'rig (b) pleasant, happy; merry, jolly
plesier'oord pleasure resort
plig -te duty, obligation; ~**s'getrou** dutiful
ploeg (s) **ploeë** plough; gang, shift
plof (s) thud, thump
plof'stof (s) **..stowwe** explosives; ~**deskun'= dige** explosives expert
plomp (b) stout, awkward, clumsy
plons (s) **-e** splash; (w) splash; ~**lan'ding** splash landing (spacecraft)
plooi (s) **-e** fold, wrinkle, crease; plea; (w) fold; ~**baar** amenable (person)
plot'seling (b) sudden, abrupt *ook* **skie'lik;** (bw) suddenly, all of a sudden
pluim -e plume, feather; ~**bal** badminton;

~**pie** plumelet; compliment: *'n ~pie kry* be complimented; ~**vee** poultry
pluis: (s) ~**ie** plug, wad; ~**keil** tophat; (w) ~**kam** tease (girl's hair); (b) in order
pluk ge- pick, gather
plun'der ge- plunder, ransack, loot
plus plus; ~**mi'nus** about, more or less
poe'del -s poodle; ~**hond** poodle; ~**naak/** ~**na'kend** stark-naked; ~**prys** booby prize
poe'ding -s pudding
poei'er (s) -s powder; (w) powder
poel -e pool; puddle; pond; (w) pool (funds)
poe'ma -s puma *ook* **berg'leeu**
poens'kop -pe hornless animal
poësie' poetry *ook* **dig'kuns**; ~**waarde'ring** poetry appreciation
poë'ties -e poetic(al)
poets[1] (s) -e trick, prank; *iem. 'n ~ bak* play a trick on someone
poets[2] (w) ge- polish, rub; ~**katoen'** cottonwaste
pof: ~**ad'der** puff adder; ~**broek** plusfours; ~**fer'tjie** fritter, puffcake
po'ging -s, -e effort, attempt, endeavour; *'n ~ aanwend* make an attempt
pok'ke/pok'kies smallpox
pol -le tuft of grass
po'lis -se insurance policy
poli'sie police; *die ~ ontbied* call the police; ~**beamp'te** police officer; ~**dien'ste** police services; ~**hond** police dog; ~**kantoor'** charge office; ~**man** policeman, constable; ~**-on'dersoek** police investigation; **polisië'=ring** policing; ~**soek'tog** manhunt
politiek' (s) politics; (b) political; politic
poli'tikus ..**tici,** -se politician (person)
politoer' (s) -e polish; (w) polish
po'lo polo; ~**nek'trui** polo-neck sweater
pols (s) -e pulse; (w) feel the pulse; sound; *iem. ~* sound someone; ~**horlo'sie/~oor-lo'sie** wristwatch
pome'lo -'s grapefruit, pomelo
pomp (s) -e pump; (w) pump; ~**jog'gie** pump attendant; ~**sto'fie** pressure stove
pond -e pound, sovereign
pondok' -ke hovel, hut; shack (squatters)
po'nie -s pony; ~**koerant'** tabloid newspaper
pons (s, w) punch
pont -e ferryboat *ook* **veer'boot**; pontoon, pont
Pon'tius Pontius; *iem. van ~ na Pilatus stuur* send someone from pillar to post
poog ge- try, attempt *ook* **probeer'**
pooi'er -s pimp, procurer *ook* **kop'pelaar** (vir prostitute)

pook (s) **poke** poker *ook* **vuur'yster**; (w) poke
pool[1] **pole** pole (of earth; battery)
pool[2] (s) pile (of carpet)
poort -e gate, gateway; poort, defile
poot pote foot, leg, paw; *op eie pote staan* be independent
poot'jie (w) ge- trip someone
poot'uit down, done for; deadbeat
pop[1] -pe doll; puppet; *die ~pe is aan die dans* the fat is in the fire
pop[2] pop, popular; ~**musiek'** pop music
pop'pekas -te puppet show, Punch and Judy show
populariteit' popularity *ook* **gewild'heid**
populêr' popular *ook* **gewild'**
populier' (s) -e poplar (tree)
por (w) ge- poke, jab; urge, egg on
por'noboek/~film porn book/film
pornogra'fies -e pornographic *ook* **obseen'**
porselein' (real) china; porcelain
por'sie -s portion, share; helping (of food)
portaal' ..**tale** porch, lobby; (entrance) hall
portefeul'je -s portfolio; wallet
portier' doorman, commissionaire *ook* **deur'=wagter**
portret' -te portrait, picture
portuur' **porture** match, equal, peer; ~**groep** peer group
pos[1] (s) -te post (office); (w) post
pos[2] (s) -te entry; (w) enter; *in die grootboek ~* enter in ledger
pos[3] (s) -te job, post, position
pos: ~**beskry'wing** job description; ~**bestel=ler** postman; ~**bus** Post Office box; letter=box; ~**diens** postal service; ~**duif** homing/carrier pigeon
poseer' ~, ge- pose (for photo)
pos: ~**geld** postage; ~**gids** postal guide
posi'sie -s position
positief' ..**tiewe** positive
pos: ~**kantoor'** post office; ~**lo'tery** sweep=stake; ~**mees'ter** postmaster; ~**or'der** post-al order; ~**seël** postage stamp; ~**seëlver-sa'melaar** philatelist; ~**tarief'** postal rates
postuur' ..**ture** posture, figure; ~**drag** foun=dation garment *ook* **vorm'drag**
pot -te pot; jar; game (tennis); *die ~ aan die kook hou* be able to make ends meet
pot: ~**dig** airtight; very reserved; ~**doof** stonedeaf
potensiaal' ..**siale** potential

pot'jiekos (s) potjiekos, iron-pot stew *ook* ys'terpotbre'die
pot'lood (lead) pencil; ~skerp'maker pencil sharpener
potsier'lik (b) farcical, droll *ook* kod'dig
pot'tebakker -s potter, ceramist; ~y pottery
pot'yster cast iron *ook* giet'yster
pou -e peacock
pous -e pope, pontiff; ~dom papacy
pou'se -s interval, pause, break, recess
po'wer -e poor, miserable *ook* armsa'lig
praal (s) pomp, magnificence; ~graf mauso= leum
praat ge- talk, chat, converse
prag (s) splendour, magnificence; ~stuk stunningly beautiful (object); ~tig beauti= ful, magnificent; ~werk thing of beauty
prakseer' ~, ge- think, consider, plan
prak'ties (b) practical; (bw) practically, vir= tually
praktiseer' (w) ~, ge- practise
praktisyn' -s practitioner; al'gemene ~ gen= eral practitioner *ook* huis'arts
praktyk' -e practice; procedure
predikant' -e minister, parson *ook* le'raar
pre'diker -s preacher
preek (s) preke sermon; (w) preach; ~stoel pulpit
prefek' -te prefect *ook* klas'voog
pre'mie -s premium; bounty; bonus
premier' -s premier, prime minister
prent -e picture; illustration, ~e'boek picture-book; ~(e)stro'kies comic strips
presen'sie (s) presence; ~lys attendance register
present' (s) -e present, gift *ook* geskenk'
president' -e president; staatshoof
presies' (b) exact, precise; particular *ook* nou= keu'rig; (bw) precisely
presta'sie -s performance, achievement; feat; ~me'ting performance appraisal
presteer' (w) ~, ge- achieve, perform; ~der achiever (person)
presti'ge prestige, influence *ook* aan'sien (s)
pret pleasure, fun; ~beder'wer spoilsport, killjoy; ~draf jogging; ~loop funrun; ~park amusement park
preuts -e; -er, -ste coy, prudish, pert
pre'wel (w) ge- mutter; mumble
prieel' priële pergola, arbour, bower
pries'ter -s priest
prik (s) -ke prick; puncture; (w) prick
prik'kel (s) -s stimulus; (w) irritate, excite;

stimulate; ~baar irritable; ~end irritating; stimulating; ~lektuur' soft pornography; ~pop glamour girl, pin-up
pri'ma prima, first-rate; ~ uit'leenkoers prime lending rate
primêr' -e primary; ~e gesond'heidsorg pri= mary health care; ~e on'derwys primary education
primitief' (b) primitive
prins -e prince
prinses' -se princess
prinsipaal' ..pale principal, head(master)
prioriteit' priority; top~ top priority
pris'ma -s prism
prisonier' -s prisoner *ook* gevang'ene
privaat[1] (s) ..vate lavatory, privvy, loo
privaat[2] (b) ~, ..vate private; ~ sek'tor pri= vate sector; ~ skool private school
privatise'ring privatisation
probeer' ~, ge- try, attempt; ~ *is die beste ge= weer* there is nothing like trying
probleem' ..bleme problem; ~ oplos/uitstryk solve a problem
produk' -te product, produce; ~sie produc= tion, output/yield *ook* op'brengs
produktiwiteit' productivity
produsent' -e producer
proe ge- taste, sample; *hy ~ die wyn en dit smaak lekker* he tastes the wine and it tastes nice
proef (s) proe'we experiment, test, trial; spe= cimen, proof, sample; ~arts houseman; ~balans' trial balance; ~beamp'te proba= tion officer; ~buisba'ba testtube baby; ~ne'ming experiment; ~konyn' experi= mental guinea pig; ~on'derwys practical teaching; ~plaas experimental farm; ~skrif dissertation/thesis
proes ge- sneeze aloud, snort
profeet' ..fete prophet
profesie' -ë prophecy *ook* voorspel'ling
profes'sie -s profession *ook* beroep'
professioneel' ..nele professional
profes'sor -e, -s professor
profiel' -e profile; le'wens~, CV *ook* bioda'ta
profyt' -e profit, gain *ook* wins
program' -me programme; ~matuur' com= puter software *ook* sag'teware; ~meer'der programmer (comp.)
progressief' ..siewe progressive
projek' (s) -te project; ~tor projector
proklama'sie -s proclamation

prokura'sie -s power of attorney *ook* **vol'mag**
prokureur' -s solicitor, attorney
promes'se -s promissory note, IOU
promo'sie -s promotion/product launch; gra=
duation
promo'tor -s promoter; sponsor *ook* **borg**
pronk (w) show off, display; ~**er'tjie** sweet=
pea; ~**poppie** show/chorus girl
pront exact, pure; ~**uit** straight out
prooi -e prey; *ten* ~ *val* fall prey to
prop -pe stopper, plug, cork, gag, wad
propagan'da propaganda
pro'sa prose *ook* **roman'kuns**
prosaïs' -te/pro'saskrywer -s prose writer
prosedu're -s procedure *ook* **werk'wyse**
proses' -se process; ~**sie** procession
prospekteer' (w) ge- prospect; ~**der** prospec=
tor (person)
prospek'tus -se prospectus
prostituut' ..**tute** prostitute, hooker *ook* **straat'=
hoer, seks'werker**
proteïen'/proteï'ne protein
protes' -te protest; ~**op'trede** industrial action,
mass action; ~**verga'dering** protest meeting
provinsiaal' ..**siale** provincial
provin'sie -s province
pruik -e wig, peruke; hairpiece
pruim[1] (s) -e plum; prune
pruim[2] (s) -e quid; (w) chew (tobacco)
pruim'boom ..**bome** plum tree
pruimedant' -e prune
prul -le trifle, trash, rubbish; ~**kos** junk food
prut'kis(sie) haybox *ook* **hooi'kis**
pryk (w) ge- shine, look fine, show off
prys[1] (s) -e price, value; *tot elke* ~ at all costs;
op ~ *stel* esteem, value; (w) price; ~**be=
heer'** price control
prys[2] (s) -e prize, award
prys[3] (s) praise; (w) praise
prysenswaar'dig -e; -er, -ste praiseworthy
prys: ~**fees** sale (for shoppers); ~**gee** abandon,
give up; ~**geld** prize money; ~**lys** price list;
~**skiet** bisley; ~**sty'ging/**~**verho'ging** price
increase; ~**uit'deling** prize-giving, awards
ceremony; ~**vraag** competition
psalm -s psalm; ~**boek** psalm book/psalter

psigia'ter -s psychiatrist (person)
psigologie' psychology *ook* **siel'kunde**
psigopaat' ..**pate** psychopath (person)
puberteit' puberty; ~**s'jare** age of puberty
publiek' (s) public; (b) -e public
publika'sie -s publication
publiseer' (w) ~, ge- publish *ook* **uit'gee**
publisiteit' publicity; ~**s'buro** publicity bu=
reau
puik (b) excellent, splendid, choice; ~ **diens**
sterling service
puim'steen pumice
puin ruins, debris
puis -te pimple, pustule; ~**ie** -s pimple
punt[1] -e point, tip; ~*e aanteken* score points;
hoë ~*e in die eksamen* good marks in the
examination; ~**diens** point duty (traffic
officer)
punt[2] -e stop, fullstop; period
pun'telys -te marksheet *ook* **pun'testaat**; log
puntene'rig/punteneu'rig (b) touchy, easily
offended; particular
pun'tetelling score
pupil' -le pupil (of eye) *ook* **ky'ker**
purgeer'mid'del purgative, laxative
pur'per purple *ook* **pers**; ~**win'de** morning
glory (flower)
put (s) -te well; pit; cesspool; (w) draw
(knowledge); ~**tjie** hole (golf)
puur (b) pure, excellent; *pure onsin* sheer/
absolute nonsense
pyl -e (s) arrow, dart; *soos 'n* ~ *uit die boog*
like an arrow from a bow; (w) dart, go
straight; ~**reg'uit** straight as an arrow; ~**tjie**
dart (game); ~**tjiebord'** dartboard; ~**vak**
home stretch/straight (athletics)
pyn[1]₂ (s) -e pine/fir tree *ook* **den'neboom**
pyn[2]₂ (s) -e pain, ache; *ineenkrimp van* ~
writhe with pain; (w) ache, smart; ~**do'der**
painkiller *ook* **pyn'stiller**; ~**lik** painful;
distressing; ~**stil'ler** analgesic
pyp -e pipe; leg (of trousers); *na iem. se* ~*e
dans* dance to someone's tune; ~**kan** (s)
feeding bottle; (w) cheat, fool; (sell a)
dummy (rugby); ~**lei'ding** pipeline; ~**steel**
pipe stem; panhandle (street)

Q

quidproquo' something for something, coun=
ter-performance, quid pro quo

quis'ling -s quisling, traitor *ook* (land)ver=
raai'er

R

raad[1] **rade** council, board *ook* **bestuurs'lig=
gaam**; ∼(s)ka'mer boardroom
raad[2] **-gewinge, -gewings** advice, counsel;
met ∼ *en daad* with words and deeds; *ten
einde* ∼ *wees* be at one's wits' end; ∼**ge'=
wend** advisory; consulting (engineer); ∼**op**
at one's wits' end; ∼**pleeg** consult, take
counsel with; *die dokter* ∼*pleeg/sien* con=
sult/see the doctor
raad'saal ..**sale** council chamber
raads: ∼**'besluit'** decision/resolution of the
council; ∼**heer** alderman *ook* **ol'derman**;
∼**lid** councillor
raai ge- guess; advise; spot (a question)
raai'sel -s riddle, puzzle, enigma; ∼**ag'tig**
mysterious
raak (w) **ge-** hit; touch; concern
raam[1] (s) **rame** window frame; (w) frame
raam[2] (w) **ge-** estimate, calculate; *hy* ∼ *die
koste op* he estimates the cost at
raap[1] (s) **rape** turnip; rape, cole
raap[2] (w) **ge-** gather, pick up; ∼ *en skraap*
scrape together
raar [rare] funny, strange, odd, queer; ∼
maar waar believe it or not
raas (w) **ge-** make a noise, scold; rave
raat rate (traditional) remedy; **boe're**∼ home
medication
rabar'ber rhubarb
rabbedoe' (s) tomboy; don't care (person)
rab'bi -'s/rabbyn' -e rabbi
ra'dar radar, radio location
ra'dio -'s radio, wireless; broadcasting; ∼**ak=
tief'** radio-active; ∼**dra'ma** radio drama/
play
radioloog' ..**loë** radiologist (person)
ra'dio: ∼**om'roeper** announcer; ∼**program'**
radio program(me)
radys' -e radish
ra'fel (s) **-s** fray, thread; (w) fray out
raffina'dery -e refinery (sugar, oil) *ook*
raffineer'dery

rak -ke rack, shelf; web
raket' -te racket (tennis) *ook* **spaan**
rak'ker -s little bounder, rascal *ook* **va'bond**
rak'leeftyd (s) shelf life (fruit)
ram -me ram
ra'ming -s, -e estimate, forecast
ram'mel ge- rattle, clatter, clank
ramp -e disaster, calamity, catastrophe
ram'party -e stag party
rampok'ker -s gangster, gunman; racketeer
rand[1] (s) rand (monetary unit); *dit kos twaalf*
∼ it costs twelve rand(s)
rand[2] (s) **-e** brim (hat); edge, margin; verge
(disaster); ∼**apparatuur'** peripherals (comp.);
∼**ei'er** outsider; ∼**sny'er** weedeater; ∼**steen**
kerb, kerbstone
rang -e rank, class, grade; ∼**lys** ladder (sport),
grading, order of merit; *derde op die* ∼*lys*
ranked/seeded third
rang'skik ge- arrange, tabulate, classify,
∼**king** (flower) arrangement; classification
rang'telwoord -e ordinal number
rank (s) **-e** tendril; shoot, sprout; (w) sprout;
reach high (rugby); ∼**boon(tjie)** runnerbean
rant' -e hill, ridge; reef
rantsoen' -e ration, allowance
rapport' -e report, statement; dispatch
rapport'ryer -s dispatch rider
raps (s) **-e** blow, flick; (w) strike, flick
rap'sie -s a little, a bit; slight blow/cut
rapsodie' -ë rhapsody
rariteit' -e curiosity, rarity; curio
ras (s) **-se** race; breed; *van suiwer* ∼ *(perd)*
thoroughbred
ras'eg -te pure bred, thoroughbred
ra'send (b) **-e** furious, raving *ook* **brie'send**
ra'sieleier -s cheerleader (sport meeting)
ras'se: ∼**haat** race hatred, racialism; ∼**ha'ter**
racialist (person)
ras: ∼**sis'** racist; ∼**sis'ties** racial (a)
rat -te gear, (cog)wheel
ra'tel[1] (s) **-s** rattle; (w) rattle

ra'tel² (s) -s Cape (honey) badger
ra'telslang -e rattlesnake, rattler
rat'kas -se gearbox
rats -er, -ste nimble, swift, quick, agile
ravyn' -e gorge, canyon, ravine
reageer' ~, ge- react
reak'sie -s reaction; ~maatskappy' reaction company (security)
realis'ties -e realistic
rebel' -le rebel ook op'standeling
red (w) ge- save, rescue
redak'sie -s editorial staff
redakteur' -s editor (both sexes)
red'dings: ~boei lifebuoy; ~boot lifeboat; ~vlot life raft
re'de -s sense; speech; address, oration; reason, cause; sonder (enige) ~ without any reason; iem. in die ~ val interrupt someone; direkte ~ direct speech
re'dedeel ..dele part of speech
re'dekawel ge- argue, reason
re'delik reasonable, tolerable, fair
re'denaar -s orator; ~s'kuns public speaking
redeneer' ~, ge- reason, argue
re'dery -e shipping/airline/transport firm; air= line ook lug'diens
re'devoering (s) public speaking; discourse
red'gordel -s safety belt; life belt
reduplika'sie reduplication
reeds already; ~ jare gelede many years ago
reëel reële real, genuine; reë'le groei real growth
reeks -e series, row, sequence; ~moor'denaar serial killer
re'ël (s) -s rule; line; 'n gulde ~ a golden rule; tussen die ~s lees read between the lines; (w) regulate, arrange; ~aar governor (en= gine); ~baar negotiable (salary)
re'ëling -s, -e regulation, adjustment; ~(s)ko= mitee' organising/steering committee
reëlma'tig -e; -er, -ste regular
re'ën (s) -s rain; (w) rain; dit ~ dat dit giet it is raining cats and dogs; ~boog rainbow; ~bui shower (of rain); ~jas raincoat, mack= intosh; ~me'ter rain gauge
reep repe string, strip; ~/blok sjokola'de slab of chocolate
referaat' ..rate lecture, paper, treatise
referen'dum referendum ook volk'stemming
referent' -e lecturer; reporter, informer; ref= eree' (for testimonial)
refleks' -e reflex; ~bewe'ging reflex action

refrein' -e chorus, refrain
reg¹ (s) -te right, title; claim; law, justice; in die ~te studeer study/read law
reg² (b) -te right, correct, straight; ~af straight down; sheer
regat'ta (s) regatta ook roei'wedstryd/wed'= vaart
regeer' ~, ge- rule, govern, reign ook heers
rege'ring -s, -e government ook staat; regime, reign (of)
reghoe'kig -e rectangular
regie' stage management; onder ~ van pro= duced by
regiment' -e regiment
regisseur' -s stage manager; producer (of a play, film)
regis'ter -s register, record, index
registra'sie registration
registrateur' -s registrar (person)
registreer' ~, ge- register ook in'skryf
reglement' -e rules, regulations, by-laws; ~ van or'de standing orders
reg'maak -ge- put right; square up; repair; castrate (male animal); spay (female ani= mal); neuter (cat); sterilise
regma'tig -e rightful, lawful, fair; ~e ei'enaar rightful/legal owner
reg'op erect, perpendicular, straight (up)
regs (b) right-handed; of the right; (bw) to the right
regs: ~advies' legal advice; ~geleer'de jurist, lawyer
regska'pe righteous, honest (person)
reg'soewereiniteit' rule of law
regs: ~persoon'likheid body corporate; in= corporation; ~ple'ging administration of justice; ~praktyk' legal practice
reg'stel (w) rectify, amend, adjust; ~ak'sie, ~lende/beves'tigende/herstellende optre= de affirmative action; ~ling correction
regs'term law/legal term
reg'streeks (b) -e direct; ~e bewys' direct evidence; ~ en on'regstreeks direct(ly) and indirect(ly)
reg'te¹ (s) rights; law; in die ~ studeer study/ read law
reg'te² (bw) truly, quite so, really; na ~ really, by right(s)
reg'te³: ~ hoek right angle
reg'ter¹ (s) -s judge, justice
reg'ter² (b) right; ~hand right hand; ~kant right side

reg'tig (b) -e true; (bw) really *kyk* **rê'rig**
reg'uit (b) straight, honest, candid; (bw)
straight, openly, candidly
regula'sie -s regulation; by-law (local govt.)
regver'dig (w) ~, ge- justify; (b) just, fair,
righteous
reg voor right in front
rehabiliteer' ~, ge- rehabilitate; discharge
rei'er -s heron, egret
reik ge- reach, extend to; *iem. die hand* ~ lend
someone a helping hand; ~af'stand range
ook ~wyd'te
rein (s): *in die* ~e *bring* put right; (b) pure,
clean, chaste; *die* ~e *waarheid* the gospel
truth
rei'nig (w) ge- purify, cleanse; ~ing purifica=
tion, cleaning/cleansing; ~ingsdiens' sani=
tary department, street cleaning
reïnkarna'sie (s) reincarnation
reis (s) -e journey, trip, voyage; (w) ge- travel;
~ *en verblyf* transport and subsistence;
~agent'skap/~buro' travel agency; ~be=
skry'wing account of a journey, travelogue;
~de'ken (travelling) rug; ~genoot' fellow
traveller; ~gids traveller's guide *ook* toer'=
gids
rei(i)'sies races; ~baan racecourse; ~perd
racehorse *ook* ren'perd
rei'siger -s traveller; tourist
reis: ~in'drukke impressions of travel;
~plan itinerary; ~tjek traveller's cheque
reis'verhaal ..hale account of (one's) travels;
travelogue (in book)
rek (s) elasticity; -ke catapult, elastic; (w)
stretch, extend; protract; *jou bene* ~ stretch
one's legs
re'ken (w) ge- calculate, compute; reckon; do
sums; ~aar computer; reckoner; ~aar'=
bedre'we/~aarvaar'dig/~aarbevoeg' com=
puter literate; ~aarstu'die/~aarwe'tenskap
computer science
re'kene arithmetic *ook* re'kenkunde
re'kening -e, -s bill, account; statement;
lo'pende ~ current account; ~kunde ac=
counting/accountancy; ~kun'dige accoun=
tant *ook* re'kenmeester
re'kenkunde arithmetic
re'ken: ~mees'ter accountant; ~skap ac=
count: ~skap gee van account for
rekla'me advertising *ook* adverteer';
~agent'skap advertising agency/firm
rekonsilia'sie reconciliation *ook* versoe'ning

re'kord -s record; *die* ~ *slaan/verbeter/breek*
beat/break the record (sport); ~hou'ding
keeping of records; ~s office records/
documents
rekruut' rekrute recruit (person)
rek'spring (w) bungee jump(ing); ~er bungee
jumper
rek'stok -ke horizontal bar (gymnastics)
rek'tor -e, -s rector; principal (university)
religieus' -e religious *ook* godsdiens'tig (b)
re'ling -s railing
rem (s) -me brake; (w) brake; ~pedaal' brake
pedal; krag~ power brake(s)
remedië'rend remedial; ~e on'derwys reme=
dial education
ren ge- race, run; ~baan racecourse, race=
track; speedway; ~bo'de courier *ook* koe=
rier'; ~dier reindeer
renegaat' renegade *ook* oor'loper (mens)
ren'jaer -s racing driver
ren'motor -s racing car
renons' (s) dislike, antipathy *ook* teen'sin
renos'ter -s rhinoceros
ren'perd -e racehorse
rens (b) sour, rancid *ook* gal'sterig
ren'stel -le dragster; ~ja'ery drag racing *kyk*
versnel'renne
ren'te -s interest; ~koers rate of interest
rep (s) commotion; *in* ~ *en roer* in commo=
tion; (w) hurry up; mention; *niks daarvan* ~
nie keep mum about it
repara'sie -s repair; ~ko'ste cost of repair *ook*
herstel'koste
repatrieer' (w) repatriate (to own country)
repeteer' ge- repeat, recur; rehearse
repeti'sie -s repetition; rehearsal (stage)
reptiel' -e reptile
republiek -e republic
republikein -e republican (person)
reputa'sie -s reputation *ook* aan'sien; ge=
ves'tigde ~ established reputation
rê'rig really, truly *kyk* reg'tig
res (s) -te rest, remainder
resensent' -e reviewer; critic (person)
resen'sie -s review (books, plays) *ook* (boek)=
bespre'king
resep' -te, -pe recipe; prescription *ook* voor'=
skrif; ~te'rende dok'ter dispensing doctor
reservoir' -s reservoir *ook* op'gaartenk/dam
reser'we -s reserve; ~fonds reserve fund
reses' -se recess; termyn'~ mid-term break
reses'sie -s recession, economic slump

resita'sie recitation; ~ *opsê* recite (a poem)
resiteer' (w) ~, ge- recite (a poem)
respek' (s) respect, esteem *ook* ag'ting
respekta'bel -e; -er; -ste respectable
respekteer' ~, ge- respect, hold in respect
restourant'/restaurant' -e, -s restaurant
resultaat' ..tate result, outcome
retoer' -e return; ~reis return journey
reto'ries -e rhetorical
reuk -e scent, smell, odour; ~orgaan' olfactory
    organ; ~wa'ter perfume, scent; ~weer'der
    deodorant
reun -s, -e male dog; gelding (horse)
reünie/reu'nie -s reunion
reus -e giant
reusag'tig gigantic *ook* enorm'
reu'se: ~gebou' huge building; ~krag strength
    of a giant
reu'se: ~skre'de giant stride; *met* ~*skredes*
    vooruitgaan progress by leaps and bounds;
    ~taak gigantic task
revolu'sie/rewolu'sie -s revolution
rewol'wer -s revolver
rib -bes rib; ~be'been rib; ~be'kas thorax,
    thoracic skeleton; ~be'tjie rib; cutlet;
    ~stuk rib, chop *ook* tjop
rid'der -s knight, chevalier; *tot* ~ *slaan* knight
    (v); ~or'de order of knighthood; ~spoor
    larkspur; ~roman'/~verhaal' tale of chiv=
    alry
riel -e reel, old-fashioned dance
riem[1] -e oar (rowing)
riem[2] -e ream (paper)
riem[3] -e strap, thong; riem; belt; *'n* ~ *onder*
    die hart steek put fresh heart into someone;
    hy het sy ~*e styfgeloop* he has come to the
    end of his tether; ~spring skip; *iem. laat*
    ~*spring* give someone a hiding; ~tele=
    gram' unfounded rumour *kyk* bos'tamboer'
riet -e reed, rush; cane; thatch; ~blits cane
    spirits; ~dak thatched roof; ~skraal as thin
    as a rake; ~stoel wicker chair; ~sui'ker
    cane sugar
rif riwwe reef
rif'fel (s) -s ripple, wrinkle; corrugation (road);
    (w) wrinkle; corrugate; ~strook jiggle bar
    (on road)
rif'rug ridgeback (dog)
rig ge- direct, address; aim; *die woord* ~ *tot*
    address (an audience)
rig: ~lyn guideline; ~prys recommended
    price; ~snoer rule of conduct; ~ting

direction; trend; ~tingflits'er/~tingwy'ser
    flash indicator
ril ge- shiver, shudder; ~ler thriller (book,
    film) *ook* sensa'sieverhaal
rim'pel (s) -s wrinkle, fold, crease; (w) wrinkle,
    ripple; ~effek' ripple effect
ring -e ring; circle; church district
ring: ~muur · circular wall; ~vinger ring
    finger
rin'kel ge- jingle, tinkle
rink'halsslang -e ringed cobra, rinkhals
rinkink' (w) ~, ge- gambol, make merry *ook*
    baljaar'/ravot'
rinneweer' ~, ge- ruin, destroy
riole'ring sewerage, drainage
riool' riole drain, sewer; ~slyk sludge
ri'siko -'s risk; venture; *op jou* ~ at your
    risk
ris'sie -s cayenne pepper, chilli
rit -te (s) ride, drive, spin
rit'mies -e rhythmic(al)
rits -e string, series; zip fastener; *'n hele* ~
    name a whole string of names
rit'sel ge- rustle; ~ing rustling, rustle
rits'sluiter -s zip fastener
rit'tel ge- shake, shiver, tremble, quiver; ~dans
    (s) jive session
ritteltit': *die* ~*(s) kry* go into hysterics
ritueel' ritual; ritue'le moord ritual murder
rivier' -e river; ~bed'ding river bed; ~mond
    estuary, river mouth
rob -be seal
ro'bot -s robot; mechanical man
robyn' -e ruby
rock (s) rock (mus.)
roe'de -s rod, birch *ook* rot'tang; rood; *wie die*
    ~ *spaar, bederf die kind* spare the rod and
    spoil the child
roei (w) ge- row; ~ *met die rieme wat jy het*
    manage with the tools at one's disposal
    ~boot'jie rowing boat; ~er rower; ~spaan
    riem oar; ~wed'stryd boatrace, regatta
roe'keloos reckless, rash; dare-devilish; roe'=
    kelose bestuur'der reckless driver
roelet'/roulet'te roulette *ook* dob'belwiel
roem (s) glory, renown, fame *ook* faam; (w)
    praise, extol, laud; ~ryk glorious, famous
roep ge- call, cry, shout; *om hulp* ~ cry for
    help; ~baar/op roep on call (doctor)
roep'radio (s) radio pager *ook* spoor'der
roep'soek (w) page (someone) *ook* spoor

roer[1] (s) -s gun, rifle *ook* **geweer**
roer[2] (w) ge- stir, move; ~ *jou (riete)* get a
move on; ~**ei'ers** scrambled eggs; ~**end**
touching; movable; ~**ende goed** movables
ook **losgoed**; ~**ende verhaal'** moving/poign=
ant story; (bw) quite; *hulle is dit* ~*end eens*
they agree in all respects
roer[3] (s) rudder (ship); helm
roer'loos . .**lose** motionless
roes[1] (s) rust; blight; (w) rust; *ou liefde* ~ *nie*
first love never dies
roes[2] (s) drunken fit; ecstasy, frenzy
roes: ~**vlek** rust stain; ~**vry** rustproof, stain=
less; ~**we'rend** (b) rust resistant
roet soot
roe'te -s route, road
roeti'ne routine; ~**-on'dersoek** (medical)
check-up; ~**taak** chore(s)
rof'stoei (s) all-in wrestling; ~**er** all-in
wrestler
rog rye; ~**brood** rye bread
rog'gel (s) -s ruckle; rattle, phlegm; (w) rattle
(in the throat); ruckle
rojaal' royal; generous, lavish, ~ *lewe* live
extravagantly
rok -**ke** skirt *ook* **romp**; costume, dress; *die
hemp is nader as die* ~ charity begins at
home; ~**band** waist band; apron strings
(idiom.); ~**jag'ter** womaniser
ro'ker -s smoker (person)
rol (s) le roll, list; roller; part, role, scroll, *van
die* ~ *skrap* strike off the roll; '*n* ~ *speel*
play/act a part, (w) ge- roll
rol: ~**bal** bowls; ~**beset'ting** cast (of a play);
~**lem'skaatse** rollerblades *ook* **in'lynskaat-
se;** ~**lo'per** travelator (airport), ~**prent**
film, motion picture, movie; ~**prentster'**
film star; ~**saag** circular saw; ~**skaats**
roller skate; ~**spe'ler** role player; ~**stoel**
wheelchair *ook* **ry'stoel;** ~**tabak'** rolled
tobacco; ~**trap** escalator; ~**verde'ling** cast
roman' -s novel (book)
roman': ~**se** romance; ~**skry'wer** novelist
(both sexes)
roman'ties -e romantic; glamorous
Romein' (s) -e Roman; ~**s'** (b) Roman;
Romeins'-Hol'landse Reg Roman-Dutch
Law; ~**se sy'fers** Roman numerals
rom'mel[1] (s) lumber; rubbish; junk, litter
rom'mel[2] (w) ge- rumble
rom'mel: ~**strooi'er** litterbug *ook* **mors'jors;**
~**veld'tog** anti-littering campaign; ~**verko'** =

ping jumble sale
romp -e trunk, torso; hull; fuselage; skirt
romp'slomp red tape (official); fuss/bother
rond -e; -er, -ste round; ~e **jaar** a full year;
~e **som** lump sum; round figures
ronda'wel -s round hut, rondavel
ron'de -s round (boxing) *ook* **rond'te;** *die
gerug doen die* ~ there is a rumour abroad
rond'gaan -ge- go about; ~**de hof** circuit
court
rond: ~**jak'ker** (w) gallivant *ook* **rondrits';**
~**kyk** look about; ~**lei'ding** guided tour
(museum); ~**loop** stroll, loaf; ~**lo'per** tramp,
vagrant; gadabout; ~**lo'perhond** stray dog
rond'om all round, on every side
rondomta'lie round about, merry-go-round
ook **mal'lemeule;** round robin (sport)
rond'reis (w) -ge- travel about, tour
rond: ~**strooi** scatter/strew about; ~**swerf/**
~**swer'we** roam/wander about
rond'te -s round; circumference; lap (motor
sport); *die* ~ *van Vader Cloete doen* do the
rounds; *in die* ~ in a circle
rond'vaar (w) -ge- cruise; ~**t** (s) cruise
roof (s) plunder, booty; scab *ook* **ro'fie;** (w)
rob, loot; ~**bou** overcropping; ~**dier** beast
of prey, predator, ~**ky'ker** pirate viewer;
~**on'derdeel** pirate part (motor trade); ~**tog**
heist (bank); robbery; marauding/looting
expedition; ~**voël** bird of prey, raptor
rooi -**er**, -**ste** red; ~**bek'kie** waxbill; ~**bok**
impala; ~**bor'sie** robin redbreast; ~**bostee'**
redbush/rooibos tea
Rooi'kappie Little Red Riding Hood
Rooi'nek -**ke** Englishman (nickname from
Anglo-Boer War)
rooi: ~**vonk** scarlatina, scarlet fever; ~**wa'ter**
redwater (cattle); bilharziase (humans)
rook (s) smoke; fume(s); ~**mis** smog; ~**skerm**
smokescreen; ~**(ver)klik'ker** smoke detec=
tor; ~**wors** smoked sausage
room cream *ook* **ro'mer;** ~**afskei'er** (cream)
separator; ~**kan** cream can
Rooms-Katoliek' -**e** Roman Catholic
room: ~**tert** cream tart; ~**ys** icecream
roos[1] erysipelas, eczema (skin disorder)
roos[2] rose rose; '*n* ~ *tussen die dorings* a rose
among thorns
roos: ~**kleu'rig** rose-coloured; ~**kleu'rige
toe'koms** bright future; ~**knop** rosebud
roos'ter -s gridiron, grate, griller; timetable;
~**brood** toast: ~*brood met kaassous* rarebit;

~**vlug** scheduled flight

roos'tuin -e rose garden

ro'sekrans -e rosary *ook* **bid'snoer**

roset' -te rosette *ook* **kokar'de/strik'kie**

ros'kam (w) **ge-** currycomb (horse); criticise severely

rosyn¹ -e raisin

rot¹ -te rat

rot² (bw): *iem.* ~ *en kaal steel* strip someone bare

Rota'riër -s Rotarian (person)

roteer' (w) ~**, ge-** rotate *ook* **wen'tel**

rot'ren (s) **-ne** rat race, hectic rush

rots -e rock, cliff

rotsag'tig -e; -er, -ste rocky

rots: ~**stor'ting** rockfall; ~**tuin** rockery; ~**vas** firm as a rock

rot'tang -s cane, rattan; wicker

rot'te: ~**gif** rat poison; ~**kruid** arsenic, ratsbane; ~**plaag** rat plague

rot'(te)vanger -s rat catcher; ~ **van Hameln** Pied Piper of Hamelin; rodent eradicator

rou¹ (s) mourning; (w) **ge-** mourn *ook* **treur**; ~**bekla'er** mourner

rou² (b) **-er, -ste** raw; hoarse

rou: ~**brief** death notice; ~**diens** memorial service *ook* **gedenk'diens**; ~**dig** elegy; ~**koets** hearse *ook* **lyk'wa**

ro'wer -s robber, pirate, highwayman; ~**ben'**= **de** band of robbers

ru (b) **-we; -wer, -uste** rough, rude, crude

rub'ber rubber; ~**boot'jie** dinghy

rubriek' -e column, rubric, category; ~**skry'**= **wer** columnist

rug rûe back; *dis gelukkig agter die* ~ fortunately that is over

rug'by rugby; ~**spe'ler** rugby player; ~**wed'**= **stryd/kragme'ting** rugby match

rug'graat ..grate backbone, spine

rug: ~**murg** spinal cord; ~**pyn** backache; ~**sak** rucksack; ~**steun** (s, w) support; back (up)

ruig (b) bushy, shrubby; ~**ryp** hoarfrost; ~**te** undergrowth, copse, jungle

ruik (s) = **reuk**; (w) smell, scent; *sterk* ~ *na drank* smell strongly of liquor; *lont* ~ smell a rat

rui'ker -s bouquet; nosegay; ~**tjie** posy; button= hole

ruil (w) **ge-** exchange, swop; barter

ruim (s) **-e** hold (ship) *ook* **vrag'ruim**; (b, bw) ample, wide, spacious; ~**(e) keu'se** wide choice

ruim'te -s room; scope; space; ~**rom'mel** space debris; ~**tuig** spacecraft; ~**vaar'der** spaceman, astronaut; cosmonaut; ~**vaart** space travel

ruï'ne -s ruins *ook* **bou'val(le)**

ruis ge- rustle, murmur

ruit -e (window)pane; rhombus

rui'tens diamonds (cards)

rui'ter -s horserider, equestrian; ~**lik** frank, straight out, chivalrous; ~**sport** showjump= ing, (horse) riding competition; ~**(stand)'**= **beeld** equestrian statue; ~**y** cavalry

ruit'veër -s windscreen wiper

ruk (s) **-ke** pull, tug, jerk; while; (w) pull, tug, jerk; ~**kie** little while; ~**stopgor'del** inertia reel safety belt; ~**wind** squall, gust

rum rum

rumatiek' (s) rheumatism; ~**koors** rheumatic fever

rumoer' (s) **-e** uproar, turmoil; noise

run'nik (w) **ge-** neigh, whinny (horse)

ru'olie -s crude oil

rus (s) rest, repose; calm; rest (mus.); ~ *roes* to rest is to rust; (w) rest, repose; ~**bank** couch, sofa

ru'sie -s quarrel, dispute, brawl; ~**ma'ker/** ~**soe'ker** brawler, troublemaker; bully

rus'kamp -e rest camp

rus'pe(r) -s caterpillar; ~**trek'ker** caterpillar tractor

rus'teloos restless *ook* **ongedu'rig**

rus'tend -e retired; ~**e vennoot'** retired/in= active partner

rus: ~**tig** calm, placid; ~**tyd** time of rest; interval, halftime; ~**versteu'ring/**~**versto'**= **ring** breach of the peace

ry¹ (s) **-e** row, series; *almal in 'n* ~ all in a row

ry² (w) **ge-** ride, drive; ~**bewys'** driver's licence

ryk¹ -e empire, kingdom, realm

ryk² (b) rich, wealthy *ook* **wel'af**; ~**dom** wealth, riches; profusion

ry: ~**laan** drive; ~**loop** hitchhike *ook* **duim'**= **gooi**; ~**lo'per** hitchhiker

rym (s) **-e** rhyme; (w) rhyme; tally, agree; *dit* ~ *nie met die feite nie* this does not tally with the facts

ryp¹ (s) (hoar)frost; (w) frost

ryp² (b) **-e; -er, -ste** ripe, mature

ry'perd (s) **-e** riding/saddle horse; (tw) splendid!

ry'plank -e surfboard *ook* **bran'derplank**; scooter

rys¹ (s) rice

rys[2] (w) **ge-** rise; ferment
ry'skool ..**skole** riding school
rys: ~**kor'rel** grain of rice; ~**kultuur'** rice culture

rys'mier (s) -**e** white (flying) ant; termite; (w) undermine, infiltrate
ry: ~**tuig** (railway) coach; vehicle, carriage; ~**wiel** bike, bicycle *ook* **(trap)fiets**

S

sa! catch him! tally-ho!
saad (s) semen (human); sperm (animals); progeny, offspring; germ; **sa'de** seed (plants) *ook* **saat**
saag (s) sae saw; (w) ge- saw, cut; *balke* ~ snore loudly; ~**meul/meule** sawmill; ~**sel** sawdust
saai[1] (w) **ge-** sow; scatter; ~**boer** grain/crop farmer
saai[2] (b) -**e; -er, -ste** dull, tedious, drab
saak sake affair, thing, matter; business, concern; action, case; *bemoei jou met jou eie sake* mind your own business; *dit maak geen* ~ *nie* it does not matter
saak'lik (b) businesslike, precise, succinct
saal[1] sale hall; *vol sale trek* draw full houses
saal[2] -s saddle; *tem. uit die* ~ *lig* oust (from a post); ~**ma'ker** saddler
saam together, (con)jointly, between them
saam'gaan -ge- go with, accompany; agree
saam'gesteld ~*e* ren'te compound interest
saamho'righeid solidarity, coherence
saam'ryklub -**s** liftclub
saam: ~**smelt** merge, amalgamate; ~**span** conspire, plot together; unite; ~**stel** compose; compile; ~**stem** agree, concur
saam'trek (s) -**ke** rally; gathering
saam: ~**val** happen simultaneously, synchronise; ~**werk** co-operate, work in concert
saans in the evening, at night
Sab'bat -te Sabbath; *die* ~ *ontheilig* desecrate the Sabbath
sa'bel[1] -**s** sword *ook* **swaard**; sabre
sa'bel[2] -**s** sable (animal); ~**bont** sabeline
sabota'sie sabotage *ook* **ondermy'ning**
saboteur' -**s** saboteur (person)
sadis'me sadism
safa'ri -**'s** safari, hunting trip
saffier' -**e** sapphire
sag -te; -ter, -ste soft; ~**te tei'ken** soft target; low; mild; sweet
sa'ga -**s** saga (Scandinavian epic tale of heroism)

sa'ge -s legend, myth; romantic folktale
sag'geaard -e gentle, kind, meek
sag'gies gently, softly, quietly
sagmoe'dig -e; -er, -ste sweet, mild
sag'te: ~**bal** softball (game); ~**wa're** soft goods; software (comp.)
sak[1] (s) -**ke** bag, sack; pocket; pouch; *sy hand in sy* ~ *steek* bear the expense; ~ *Sarel!* less exaggeration, please!
sak[2] (w) ge- sink, subside; fail (in examination) *ook* **dop/druip**; go flat
sak: ~**boek** pocket book; ~**doek** handkerchief, hanky
sa'ke: *ter* ~ to the point, relevant; ~**brief** business letter; ~**ka'mer** chamber of commerce; ~**kern** central business area/district; ~**lui** business men (pl), ~**lys** agenda *ook* **agen'da**; ~**man** businessman; ~**vernuf** expertise, know-how
sak: ~**ke'roller** pickpocket; ~**mes** pocket knife *ook* **knip'mes**; ~**horlo'sie** pocket watch; ~**pas** (b) pocket-size *ook* **sak'formaat**; affordable; ~**re'kenaar** calculator
sal (w) **sou** shall, will; *hy sou dit agterlaat* he was to have left it behind
sala'ris -se salary; ~**kerf** salary notch; ~**pakket'** salary package; ~**skaal** salary scale; ~**verho'ging** increment, salary increase
sal'do -'s balance (of account) *ook* **balans'**
salf (s) **salwe** ointment, salve; balm
sa'lie salvia, sage (plant)
sa'lig (b) -**e; -er, -ste** blessed, blissful
Sa'ligmaker Saviour (Christ)
salm -s salmon
salon' -s, -ne drawing room, saloon; **skoon'heid**~ beauty parlour
salpe'ter (s) saltpetre; ~**suur** nitric acid
salueer' (w) ~, **ge-** salute
saluut' (s) **salute** salute
sambok' (s) -**ke** sjambok
sambreel' ..**brele** umbrella
sa'me: ~**koms** gathering, meeting; ~**le'wing**

society, community *ook* **gemeen'skap**
sa'meloop (s) concourse (of people); conflu=
ence (rivers)
sa'me: ~**roe'per** convener; ~**smel'ting** fusion,
union; amalgamation; ~**span'ning** collusion
sa'mespreking -s, -e interview, talk(s), con=
ference, discussion *ook* **beraad'slaging**;
~**(s)** *voer* confer, deliberate, discuss
sa'meswering -s, -e conspiracy, plot
sa'me: ~**vat'ting** resumé, summary *ook* **op'**=
somming; ~**vloei'ing** confluence; concourse;
~**voe'ging** union, junction; ~**wer'king** co-
operation; collaboration
sampioen' -e mushroom *ook* **pad'dastoel**
sanato'rium -s ..ria sanatorium
sand (s) sand
sandaal' ..dale sandal
sand: ~**korrel** grain of sand; ~**lo'per(tjie)**
eggtimer *ook* **uur'glas**; ~**sui'ker** crystal=
lised sugar
sang (s) **-e** song, tune, singing; canto
san'ger -s singer, vocalist (both sexes)
sang: ~**les** singing lesson; ~**spe'letjie** action
song; ~**stuk** song
sa'nik ge- worry, bother; nag *ook* **neul**
sank'sie (s) sanction/approval; ~**s** punitive
measures
sap -pe juice, sap
sardien'(tjie) -s sardine
sar'dyn -e pilchard (fish) *ook* **pel'ser**
sarkas'ties (b) sarcastic *ook* **by'tend**
sar'sie -s volley (of shots)
sat (b) sick, satiated; fed-up with
sata'nies -e satanic(al), diabolical
satelliet' -e satellite; ~**fo'to** satellite photo=
graph; ~**-TV** satellite TV
Sa'terdag ..dae Saturday
sati'ries -e satirical *ook* **by'tend**
satyn' satin
saxofoon'/saksofoon' ..fone saxophone
se of; *pa* ~ *hoed* father's hat
sê (s) say; (w) **ge-** say, speak, tell, order, state;
so ge~, *so gedaan/gedoen* no sooner said
than done
sean'ce -s seance (spiritualist meeting)
se'bra -s zebra; ~**oor'gang** zebra crossing
se'de -s habit, custom, morals, manners
se'der -s cedar; ~**boom** cedar
se'dert since; ~ *verlede maand,* since last
month
se'dig (b) demure, prim, coy *ook* **preuts**
see seë sea, ocean; *oor*~ *gaan* go abroad

see: ~**geveg'** naval battle; ~**juf'fer** Swan
(fleet); ~**kaptein'** sea captain; ~**kat** octopus
ook **ok'topus**
see'koei -e hippopotamus; ~**gat** hippo pool;
~**koei** hippopotamus cow
see: ~**kus** coast, seashore; ~**kwal** jellyfish
se'ël (s) **-s** seal; stamp; sanction; (w) seal;
~**belas'ting** stamp duty
see'leeu -s seal; sea lion
se'ël: ~**lak** sealing wax; ~**ring** signet ring
see: ~**man ..liede, ..lui** sailor, marine(r);
~**meeu** seagull; ~**moond'heid** naval power
seems'leer shammy, chamois leather
see'myl -e nautical mile (1 852 m)
se'ën (s) **-ings, -inge** benediction, blessing;
bedekte ~ blessing in disguise; (w) bless;
~**wens** blessing, good wishes
seep soap; ~**bel** soap bubble; ~**so'da** caustic
soda
seer (s) **sere** sore, wound; (b) painful, sore;
~**keel** sore throat
see'rower -s pirate, buccaneer *ook* **ka'per**
see: ~**siek** seasick; ~**skil'pad** sea turtle; ~**slag**
naval battle; ~**soldaat'** marine; ~**spie'ël** sea
level *ook* **see'vlak**; ~**strand** beach, seashore
see: ~**vaar'der** navigator; ~**verse'kering**
marine insurance
se'ëvier (w) **ge-** triumph *ook* **wen, triomfeer'**
see: ~**vlak** sea level; ~**wier** seaweed
se'ge victory, triumph
seg'genskap say, authority; ~ *hê in die saak*
have a say in the matter
segment' -e segment
segrega'sie segregation *ook* **skei'ding**
segs'man spokesman/spokesperson *ook* **woord'**=
voerder
seil (s) **-e** tarpaulin, sail, canvas; (w) sail;
~**boot** sailing boat; ~**jag** (sailing) yacht;
~**plankry'** windsurfing; boardsailing; ~**skip**
sailing vessel; windjammer; ~**skoen** tackie
sein (s) **-e** signal; (w) signal; ~**fak'kel** flare
seis -e scythe *ook* **sens**
seismograaf' ..grawe seismograph
seisoen' -e season; *buite die* ~ out of season;
~**aal** (b) seasonal; ~**kaar'tjie** season ticket
se'kel -s sickle
se'ker (b) certain; sure, positive; (bw) cer=
tainly, surely; (w) make safe; ~ *die pistool*
put the pistol on safety
se'kerheid certainty; ~**s'verkla'ring** security
clearance; ~**s'personeel'** security staff
se'kering -s, -e safety (cut-out) fuse

se'kerlik certainly, decidedly
sekondant' -e second(er) (person)
sekon'de -s second (time)
sekondeer' (w) ge- second (a proposal)
sekondêr -e secondary; ~e skool secondary/
   high school
sekon'dewyser -s second hand (watch)
sekretares'se -s female secretary
sekreta'ris -se secretary; ~-generaal' secre=
   tary-general; ~vo'ël secretary bird
seks (s) sex; sensuality; (w) sex; ~is'me sexism;
   ~ka(a)tjie sex kitten; ~trek sex appeal;
   ~wer'ker sex worker, prostitute
sek'sie -s section ook af'deling
seksueel' ..suele sexual; seksue'le teis'tering
   sexual harassment/intimidation
sek'te -s sect ook splin'tergroep
sek'tor -s sector
sekuriteit' -e security; kollatera'le ~ collat=
   eral security; ~s'wag security guard
sekuur' (b) secure, accurate
sel -le cell, ~vor'mig cellular
sel'de minder, minste seldom, rarely; ~ of
   (n)ooit hardly ever
sel(d)ery' celery
seld'saam rare, scarce; ..sa'me versa'meling
   rare collection
self self; ~aan'sitter self-starter; ~beeld self-=
   esteem; ~bedien'ing self-service; ~beskik'=
   king self-determination; ~bestuur' self-
   government, home rule; ~bewus' self-
   assuring; self-conscious; ~dien self-service
self'moord -e suicide; ~ pleeg commit suicide
self: ~op'offering self-sacrifice; ~respek'
   self-respect; ~sorg self-catering (on holi=
   day)
sel'foon (s) cellphone, cellular 'phone
selfs even; ~ Piet het geslaag even Peter passed
selfstan'dig independent, self-supporting, un=
   aided; ~e naam'woord noun, substantive;
   ~heid independence
selfsug'tig (b) selfish, egotistic
self: ~verde'diging self-defence; ~vertrou'e
   self-confidence
se'mels: bran; meng jou met ~s, dan vreet die
   varke jou touch pitch and you will be defiled
sement' cement
semes'ter -s semester; halfyear; ~kur'sus
   semester course; ~punt' halfyearly mark
semifinaal' ..ale semifinal (game) ook half=
   eindronde
seminaar' (s) seminar, course, workshop

senaat' senate senate
send ge- send; ~brief letter, epistle; ~e'ling
   missionary; ~er sender; transmitter (person;
   radio)
sen'ding consignment; mission; fact-finding
   mission; ~genoot'skap missionary society;
   ~sta'sie mission station
seniel' (b) senile ook kinds
se'ning -s sinew
se'nior senior; superior; ~ bur'ger senior citizen
sensa'sie -s sensation ook op'spraak
sensasioneel' ..nele sensational
sensitief' ..tiewe sensitive ook gevoe'lig
sen'sor censor (person); sensor
sen'sus -se census ook volks'telling; ~op'=
   gawe census return
sensuur' censure; censorship
sent -e cent
sentimenteel' sentimental
sen'timeter -s centimetre
sentraal' ..trale central; sentra'le sa'kegebied
   central business district (CBD) ook sa'ke=
   kern; sentra'le verwar'ming central heat=
   ing
sentra'le -s power station ook krag'sentrale;
   (telephone) exchange ook ska'kelbord
sentralisa'sie centralisation
sen'trum -s centre; win'kel~ shopping centre
se'nuaanval -le nervous attack
se'nu; ~siekte neurosis; ~stel'sel nervous
   system; ~ter'gend nerve-racking
se'nuwee -s nerve; op sy ~s kry be all nerves;
   ~aan'doening nervous attack
senuweeag'tig (b) -e; -er, -ste nervous
se'pie (s) soapie/soap opera ook strooi'sage
sep'ter -s sceptre; die ~ swaai rule
serebraal' ..brale cerebral; ~gestrem' cerebral palsied
seremo'nie -s ceremony ook pleg'tigheid
seremo'niemeester -s master of ceremonies
   ook ta'felheer
serena'de -s serenade
serfyn' -e harmonium ook huis'orrel
se'rie -s series; ~nom'mer serial number ook
   volg'nommer; ~poort serial port (comp.)
sering' -e lilac; ~boom lilac tree
serp -e scarf, muffler ook hals'doek
sersant' -e sergeant; ~-majoor' sergeant-major
sertifikaat' ..kate certificate
se'rum -s serum ook ent'stof
servet' -te serviette, napkin
servies' -e service, set; eet'~ dinner service

ses -se six
ses'de -s sixth
ses: ~**hoe'kig -e** hexagonal; ~**maan'deliks** halfyearly
sessie -s cession (in law); sitting, session
sestet' -te sestet (part of a sonnet)
ses'tien -e sixteen; ~**de** sixteenth
ses'tig -s sixty; ~**ste** sixtieth; *op sy* ~*ste verjaar(s)dag* on his sixtieth birthday
ses: ~**uur** six o'clock; ~**voud** multiple of six
set (s) **-te** move; push, trick; putt (golf); (w) set up (in type); putt (golf) *ook* **put** (w)
se'tel (s) **-s** seat (government); chair
set'laar -s settler *ook* **ne'dersetter**
set: ~**perk** (putting) green (golf); ~**ter** compositor (person); putter (golf)
seun -s son, boy; **verlo're** ~ prodigal son
se'we -s seven; ~**jaar'tjie** everlasting (flower)
se'wende -s seventh
se'wentien -e seventeen
se'wentig -s seventy; ~**ste** seventieth
sex'y (b) sexy
sfeer sfere sphere *ook* **bol**; **gebied'**
sfinks -e sphinx
shan'dy shandy (beer) *ook* **lim'bier**
sianied' cyanide
sid'der (w) **ge-** shudder, tremble
siek -er, -ste ill, sick; *so* ~ *soos 'n hond* as sick as a dog; *jou* ~ *lag* rock with laughter; ~**bed** sickbed; illness; ~**bedsjar'me** bedside manners
sie'ke (s) **-s** patient, invalid; ~**boeg** sickbay; ~**fonds** medical aid fund
siek'lik -e; -er, -ste ailing, sickly
siek'te -s illness, malady, sickness, disease; **aansteek'like** ~ infectious disease; **besmet'like** ~ contagious disease; ~**simptoom'** symptom, syndrome *ook* **sindroom'**; ~**verlof'** sick leave: *met* ~*verlof* on sick leave
siel -e soul; mind, spirit
siel'kunde psychology *ook* **psigologie'**
sielkun'dig -e psychological; ~**e oor'logvoering** psychological warfare; ~**e** psychologist (person) *ook* **psigoloog'**
siel'siek mentally deranged, psychopathic; ~**e** mental patient, psychopath
siel'siekehospitaal' mental hospital
sien ge- see, look, view, observe; interview; *oor die hoof* ~ overlook mistakes; pass someone over (for promotion)
sie'ner -s seer, prophet
siens: *tot* ~*!* so long!, bye-bye! *ook* **goed'gaan!**

siens'wyse -s opinion, view(point) *ook* **ge-sig'(s)punt**
sie'raad ..**rade** trinket, ornament
sier: ~**boom/struik** ornamental tree/shrub; ~**duik** display diving
sier'lik (b) ornamental; elegant, graceful
sier: ~**steen** facebrick; ~**struik** ornamental shrub; ~**wa** float (rag); ~**wa're** fancy goods
sies! fie! for shame! bah! pooh!; **sies tog!** shame! what a pity! *ook* **foei tog/foei'tog**
sif (s) **siwwe** sieve; (w) sift; ~**draad** wire netting, gauze
si'filis syphilis *ook* **vuil'siekte**
sig (s) sight; visibility; ~**blad** spreadsheet (comp.)
sigaar' ..**gare** cigar; ~**ko'ker** cigar case
sigaret' -te cigarette
sig'baar ..**bare** visible; ~**heid** visibility
sigeu'ner -s gipsy
sigorei' chicory
sig'sag zig-zag
sikadee' sikadeë cycad *ook* **brood'boom**
sik'kel -s shekel
sikloon' siklone cyclone
si'klus -se cycle *ook* **kring'loop**
silhoeët -te silhouette *ook* **ska'dubeeld**
silin'der -s cylinder
silla'be -s syllable *ook* **let'tergreep**
silla'bus -se syllabus *ook* **leer'gang**
si'lo -'s silo *ook* **kuil'toring**
sil'wer silver; ~**brui'lof** silver wedding; ~**doek** (cinema) screen; ~**kollek'te** silver collection; ~**smid** silversmith
simbaal' ..**bale** cymbal
simbool' ..**bole** symbol *ook* **sin'nebeeld**
simfonie' -ë symphony
simme'tries -e symmetric(al)
simpatie' -ë sympathy *ook* **mee'gevoel/me'delye;** ~ *met jou verlies* sincere sympathy
sim'pel -e; -er, -ste simple, silly; plain
simptoom' ..**tome** symptom
simuleer' (w) simulate *ook* **na'boots**; pretend
sin[1] (s) **-ne** sense, mind; inclination; meaning; taste, fancy; ~ *vir humor* sense of humor *ook* **hu'morsin**; (a) ~**(ne)loos** senseless, futile; mad, demented
sin[2] (s) **-ne** sentence
sinago'ge -s synagogue
sin'delik (b) clean, tidy; housetrained (animal)
sindikaat' ..**kate** syndicate
sindroom' syndrome (disease symptoms)
sing ge- sing; twitter, warble

sin'gel -s crescent; moat
si'nies -e cynic(al) *ook* **sma'lend**
sinjaal' ..jale signal *ook* **sein**
sink[1] (s) zinc; sheet iron *kyk* **sink'plaat**; galvanised/corrugated iron
sink[2] (w) ge- sink; ~**dal** rift valley *ook* **slenk'dal**; ~**gat** sinkhole
sin'kings rheumatic pains, neuralgia
sink'plaat ..plate sheet of galvanised iron; iron sheeting
sin'nigheid (s) liking, inclination
sino'de -s synod
sinoniem' (s) -e synonym; (b) synonymous
sinop'ties synoptic; ~**e kaart** synoptic chart
sins'bou construction of a sentence; syntax
sins'ontleding analysis (sentence)
sint -e saint
sintak'sis syntax *ook* **sins'bou**
sinterklaas' Santa Claus; Father Christmas
sinte'ties (b) -e synthetic(al)
sin'tuig ..tuie sense organ
sin'vol (b) meaningful *ook* **sin'ryk**
sipier' -s, -e jailer *ook* **tronk'bewaarder**; turnkey
sipres' -se cypress (tree)
sire'ne -s siren; ~**sang** siren's song
sir'kel -s circle; ~**gang** circular course; circuit; ~**saag** circular saw
sirkoon' ..kone zircon, near diamond
sirkula'sie circulation *ook* **om'set**; *in ~ bring* bring/put into circulation
sirkuleer' ge- circulate
sirkulê're -s circular *ook* **om'sendbrief**
sir'kumfleks -e circumflex *ook* **kap'pie** (^)
sir'kus -se circus
sistema'ties -e systematic *ook* **stelselma'tig**
sit[1] ge- sit; *aan tafel ~* sit at table; ~**beto'ging** sit-in
sit[2] ge- put, place; *op loop ~* chase away
sit[3] (s) sitting down; *kry jou ~!* do sit down now!
si'ter -s zither
sit: ~**ka'mer** lounge; ~**kie'rie** shooting stick; ~**kom(edie)** sitcom(edy); ~**plek** seat; ~**plek= gor'del** seatbelt
si'trus citrus
sit-'sit' sitting for a while; ~ *slaap* sleep in a sitting posture
sit'ting -s, -e session, sitting *ook* **ses'sie**; seat
situa'sie -s situation
siviel' -e civil; ~**e ingenieur'** civil engineer
sjaal -s shawl *ook* **tja'lie**

sjampan'je champagne *ook* **von'kelwyn**
sjampoe' shampoo
sjarmant' -e; -er, -ste charming
sjar'me (s) charm; ~**skool** charm/finishing school; **siek'bed**~ bedside manners
sjebien' -s shebeen *ook* **smok'kelkroeg**
sjef -s chief; chef *ook* **mees'terkok**
sjeik -s sheik; woman charmer
sjer'rie -s sherry
sjiek (b) chic, smart *ook* **uit'gevat**
sjimpansee' -s chimpanzee
sjoe'broekie -s scanty-panty; hot pants, mini= pants *ook* **am'perbroekie/ei'nabroekie**
sjoe'sjoe (s) shu-shu (creeper)
sjokola'de -s chocolate *ook* **sjok'kie**; **blok ~** slab of chocolate
skaaf (s) **skawe** plane; (w) plane; chafe; scrape
skaai (w) pilfer, pinch *ook* **vas'lê**
skaak[1] (s) chess; *potjie* ~ a game of chess
skaak[2] (w) ge- elope (with girl); kidnap, carry off; hijack (plane/car) *ook* **kaap** (w)
skaak: ~**bord** chessboard; ~**mat** checkmate; ~**toernooi'** chess tournament
skaal skale scale, balance
skaam (w) ge- be ashamed; ~ *jy jou nie?* are you not ashamed of yourself?; ~ *jou!* fie!, shame on you! (b) shy, bashful, timid; ~**de'le** genitals
skaam'te shame, modesty; ~**loos** shameless
skaap skape sheep; ~**boud** leg of mutton; ~**skêr** (pair of) shears; ~**tjop** mutton chop
skaaps'klere: *(wolf) in ~* in sheep's clothing
skaap: ~**vel** sheepskin; ~**wag'ter** shepherd; ~**wag'tertjie** capped wheatear (bird)
skaars (b) scarce, scanty; (bw) hardly, scarcely
skaats (s) -e skate; (w) skate; ~**haan** skating rink; ice rink; ~**bord/~plank** skateboard
skade -s damage, loss; ~ *aanrig/berokken* cause damage; *deur ~ en skande wys word* experience makes fools wise; ~**lik** harmful, injurious; ~**loosstel'ling** compensation, in= demnification; ~**vergoe'ding** compensation
ska'du -'s shadow, shade; ~**kant** shady/dark side; ~**personeel'** skeleton staff
ska'duwee -s shade, shadow
skag -te shaft; ~**gra'wer** shaft sinker
ska'kel -s link; shackle; (w) dial (tel.); link; connect; liaise; switch (electr.); ~**aar** switch; ~**amp'tenaar** public relations (liaison) officer; media liaison; ~**bord** switchboard; ~**huis** semi-detached house; ~**komitee'** liai= son committee; ~**toon** dialling tone

ska'ker[1] **-s** chess player

ska'ker[2] **-s** seducer; kidnapper; hijacker *kyk* **ka'per**

skake'ring -s, -e tint, shade, variegation

skandaal' ..dale (public) scandal, disgrace

skan'de -s shame, disgrace, dishonour

skan'delik shameful, disgraceful, outrageous *ook* **skanda'lig**

skande'ring scansion (poetry); scanning (radiation) *ook* **(af)tas'ting**

skans -e bulwark; trench

ska're -s crowd, multitude, host; mob

skarla'ken scarlet; ~**koors** scarlet fever

skarnier' -e hinge; (w) hinge

skar'rel ge- rummage; ransack; scatter

skat[1] **(s) -te** treasure; darling, dearest

skat[2] **(w) ge-** estimate; esteem, appraise; *die waarde te hoog/laag* ~ overestimate/underestimate the value

ska'ter ge- burst out laughing; ~**lag (s)** loud laugh; (w) laugh heartily

skat: ~**kis** treasury, exchequer; ~**ryk** very rich

skat'tebol: *my* ~ my darling/heartbeat/sweetie

skat'tejag treasure hunt

skat'ting -s, -e estimate, estimation; **globa'le** ~ rough estimate

skavot' -te scaffold (for executions)

ske'del -s skull, cranium; ~**breuk** fracture of the skull

skeef skew; crooked; slanting; distorted

skeel[1] **(w) ge-** matter; lack, ail; *wat kan dit my* ~? what does it matter to me?

skeel[2] **(b)** squinting; ~**hoof'pyn** migraine

skeen skene shin *ook* **ma'ermerrie**

skeeps: ~**beman'ning** crew; ~**kaptein'** skipper, ship's captain; ~**la'ding** cargo; ~**re'dery** shipping line; ~**ruim** ship's hold; ~**werf** dockyard

skeep'vaart navigation, shipping

skeer ge- shave, shear, trim; skim (over water); ~**boot** hydrofoil/jetfoil craft; ~**kwas** shaving brush; ~**mes** razor

skeer'tuig ..tuie hovercraft *ook* **skeer'boot**

skeet skete imaginary ailment; whim; *vol skete* have all kinds of ailments

skei (w) ge- separate; divide; sever, disconnect; divorce

skeids'regter -s referee; arbitrator, umpire

skei'kunde chemistry *ook* **chemie'**

skeld'woord abusive word/name *ook* **vloek'woord**

skelm (s) -s rogue, knave, rascal, crook; (b) crooked, furtive; ~**streek** sly/underhand trick

skel'vis -se haddock, whitefish

ske'ma -s scheme; sketch, outline; ~**huis** subsidised house (of housing scheme)

ske'mer (s) twilight, dusk; (w) grow dusky; ~**kel'kie** sundowner, cocktail; ~**party'/~onthaal'** cocktail party/reception

skend ge- violate, desecrate; mutilate; ~**ing** breach; violation; desecration (of graves)

skenk ge- give, endow, present, grant

skenk: -er donor (person); ~**ing** endowment, grant, donation

skep[1] **(s) -pe** scoop; spoonful; spadeful; (w) dip out, scoop

skep[2] **(w) geskape** create; ~**pende werk** creative work

skep'doel -e drop goal (rugby)

Skep'per Creator

skep ~**ping** creation; ~**sel** creature, human being; ~**skop** drop kick (rugby)

skep'ties -e sceptical *ook* **si'nies**

skêr -e (pair of) scissors/shears

skerf (s) skerwe shard, morsel, bit

skerm[1] **(s) -s** curtain, screen; *agter die* ~s behind the scenes

skerm[2] **(w) ge-** fence, spar, parry; ~**drag** protective clothing; ~**kuns** (art of) fencing; ~**maat** sparring partner (boxing)

skermut'sel (w) ge- skirmish; ~**ing** skirmish

skerp (b) sharp, keen, acute; severe

skerpioen' -e scorpion

skerp: ~**puntkoeëls** live ammo; ~**sin'nig** sharp-witted; ~**skutter** sniper, sharpshooter

skerts (s) fun, joke; legpulling *ook* **gek'skeerdery**; (w) jest, joke *ook* **kors'wel/gek'skeer**

skets (s) -e sketch, draft; (w) sketch, draw roughly; *in breë trekke* ~ sketch in broad outline; ~**boek** sketchbook

skeur (s) -e tear, rend; crack; fissure; (w) tear, rend; *die wêreld* ~ run away very quickly; ~**buik** scurvy; ~**ing** division; split; ~**kalen'der** tear-off calender; ~**stro'kie** tear-off slip

ske'webek wry face; ~ *trek* pull faces

ski -'s ski; ~**boot** skiboat; **ski'ër** skier

skie'(r)lik sudden(ly), unexpected(ly) *ook* **plot'seling**

skier'eiland -e peninsula

skiet[1] **(s):** ~ *gee* give more rope

skiet[2] **(w) ge-** shoot, fire; dart; blast; *met spek* ~/*spekskiet* tell tall stories

skiet: ~**baan** rifle/shooting range; ~**geveg'** shootout *ook* **skie'tery;** ~**lus'tig** (b) trig=ger-happy; ~**sta'king/**~**stil'stand** ceasefire
skik[1] (s) liking; pleasure; *in sy* ~ *wees* be delighted *ook* **in sy noppies**
skik[2] (w) ge- arrange, order, settle; ~ *na omstandighede* adapt to circumstances
skik: ~**king** agreement, settlement *ook* **ak=koord';** ~**plan** settlement plan; ~**tyd** flexi=time/flextime, staggered hours
skil (s) **-le** peel, skin, shell, rind; (w) peel, skin; *'n appeltjie met iem.* ~ pick a bone with someone
skild -e shield, buckler; aegis
skil'der (s) **-s** painter (artist) *ook* **ver'wer** (ambag); (w) paint
skilderag'tig (b) picturesque *ook* **kleur'ryk**
skil'der: ~**kuns** (art of) painting: ~**kwas** paint-brush; ~**(s)'esel -s** painter's easel; ~**stuk** picture, painting
skildery' -e picture, painting (art)
skild: ~**vel** rawhide shield; ~**wag** sentry, guard *ook* **brand'wag** (mens)
skil'fer(s) (s) **-s** dandruff; mould; scab, flake, scale
skil'pad skilpaaie tortoise (on land); turtle (in water)
skim -me shadow; apparition, ghost; ~**skry'=wer** ghost writer/author
skim'mel (s) mould, mildew; fungus
skimp (s) **-e** mockery, gibe, jeer, scoff; ~*e gooi* throw hints; (w) mock, jeer, scoff
skin'der (w) ge- gossip, slander *ook* **kwaad'=stook;** ~**bek** gossiper, slanderer; ~**praat=jies** gossip
skink ge- pour in; *koffie* ~ pour coffee; ~**bord** tray, salver; ~**juffer/**~**juffie** barmaid
skip skepe ship, vessel, boat; skip (mining); ~**breuk** shipwreck; ~*breuk ly* be wrecked; ~**breu'keling** shipwrecked person
skip'per (s) **-s** captain, skipper; skip (bowls)
ski'roei paddle skiing; ~**er** paddle skier
skit'ter ge- glitter, shine, sparkle; ~ *deur sy afwesigheid* conspicuous by his absence; ~**end** brilliant *ook* **uitmun'tend** (skoolre=kord); sparkling, radiant
skob'bejak -ke rascal, scamp, rogue, lout
skoei ge- shoe; tread (tyre); ~**sel** footwear
skoen -e shoe, boot; (mv) footwear; *die stoute* ~*e aantrek* screw up one's courage
skoe(n)lapper -s butterfly *ook* **vlin'der**
skoen: ~**lees** (boot) last; ~**ma'ker** cobbler,

shoemaker; ~**riem** shoe lace (leather); ~**ve'ter** shoe lace; ~**waks** boot polish; *die stoute* ~*e aantrek* pluck up courage
skof[1] **skowwe** shoulder (ox); withers
skof[2] **-te** stage; shift; lap; distance covered in one trek
skof'fel (s) **-s** hoe; (w) clear (weeds), hoe; dance; ~**ploeg** cultivator
skok (s) **-ke** shock; (w) shock, frighten; ~**dem'per** shock absorber; ~**granaat'** stun=grenade
skok'kend (b) **-er, -ste** shocking
skolier -e scholar, pupil *ook* **leer'ling;** ~**pa=trol'lie** scholar patrol
skol'lie -s thug, hooligan; skollie
skom'mel ge- rock, shake, swing, wobble; fluctuate; ~**stoel** rocking chair
skon -s scone *ook* **bot'terbroodjie**
skool' (s) **skole** school; *die* ~ *sluit* the school breaks up; *op* ~ at school; (w) train; **ge~de ar'beid** skilled labour
skool[2] (s) **skole** shoal (of fish)
skool: ~**biblioteek'** school library; ~**blad** school magazine
skooleind'sertifikaateksamen -s schoolleaving certificate examination
skool: ~**geld** school fees; ~**hoof** school princi=pal; ~**hou** teach; ~**ker'mis** school bazaar; ~**kind** schoolchild, pupil; ~**raad** school board; ~**verla'ter** school leaver; ~**woor'de=boek** school dictionary
skoon[1] (s) the beautiful; *die skone geslag* the fair(er) sex; (b) clean; beautiful; ~ **gewe'te** clear conscience; ~ **stel'le** straight sets (ten=nis)
skoon[2] (bw) quite, altogether; ~ *vergeet* for=got completely
skoon'dogter -s daughter-in-law
skoon'heid ..hede beauty; ~**salon'** beauty parlour
skoon: ~**maak** clean; ~**ma'ker** cleaner; ~**moe'=der** mother-in-law; ~**ou'ers** parents-in-law/in-laws; ~**va'der** father-in-law; ~**vang** mark (rugby); ~**veld** (s) fairway (golf); (b) clean gone, out of sight
skoor (s): ~ *soek* look for trouble; ~**soe'ker** troublemaker
skoor'steen ..stene chimney, flue; ~**man'tel** mantelpiece; ~**ve'ër** chimney sweep
skoot[1] **skote** shot; report (of gunshot)
skoot[2] **skote** lap, bosom; fold; ~**hond'jie** lapdog; ~**re'kenaar** laptop computer

skop (s) **-pe** kick; (w) kick; recoil (rifle); ~**boks** kickboxing

skop'graaf ..**grawe** shovel

skoppelmaai' (s) swing *ook* **swaai** (s)

skop'pens spades (playing cards)

skorriemor'rie rabble, riff-raff, hooligans

skors (w) **ge-** suspend (from school/member= ship); ~**ing** suspension; ~**ie** (s) gem squash

skots (b): ~ *en skeef* topsy-turvy

skot'tel -s dish, basin; satellite dish (TV); ~**goed** dishes, crockery; ~**goedwas'ser** dishwasher *ook* **op'wasser**

skot'vry (b) unpunished, untouched, scot-free

skou -e show, exhibition; (w) exhibit, put on show; view, inspect

skou'burg -e theatre, cinema; **stad**~ civic theatre

skou'er -s shoulder

skou: ~**huis** showhouse *ook* **toon'huis;** ~**put** manhole; ~**spel** spectacle, sight

skraag ge- prop, support, buttress up *ook* **stut;** ~**do'sis** booster dose

skraal (b) meagre, thin, scanty; bleak

skraap (s) **skrape** scratch; (w) scrape, scratch; *raap en* ~ pinch and scrape

skram'skoot ~**skote** grazing shot; graze

skran'der intelligent; shrewd, clever; ~ **leer'** = **ling** bright pupil

skrap ge- erase, delete, strike off; scratch out; ~ *waar nodig* delete which is not applic= able; ~**nel** shrapnel

skraps (b) poorly, scarcely, skimpy; ~ *ge= kleed* scantily dressed

skre'de -s step, tread, stride; pace

skree(u) (s) shout, scream; (w) scream, cry, shout; *moord en brand* ~ cry murder; ~ *soos 'n maer vark* squeal like a pig; ~**ba'lie** crybaby *ook* **tjank'balie;** ~**le'lik** very ugly; ~**snaaks** hilariously funny

skre'fie -s little opening, slit; *die deur staan op 'n* ~ the door stands ajar

skrei ge- weep; ~**ende skan'de** crying shame

skri'ba -s secretary of the church council; scribe

skrif handwriting; **-te** exercise book; ~**ge= leer'de** learned person; scribe; ~**le'sing** prayers; reading of the lesson; ~**te'like eksa'men** written examination

Skrif: *die Heilige* ~ the Scriptures, Holy Writ

skrik (s) fright, terror; *die* ~ *op die lyf ja(ag)* give someone a fright; (w) be startled, be frightened; *hy het groot ge*~ he got a big fright; ~**beeld** scarecrow, bugbear, bogey;

~**bewind'** reign of terror

skrik'keljaar ..**jare** leap year

skrikwek'kend (b) alarming, terrifying

skril -le; -ler, -ste shrill, piercing; glaring

skrobbe'ring -s, -e scolding, reprimand; dres= sing down

skroef (s) **skroewe** screw, vice; propeller (aero.); ~**sleu'tel** shifting spanner

skroei ge- scorch, burn, singe, sear

skroe'wedraaier -s screwdriver

skroom (s) timidity, modesty; (w) hesitate; *hy sal nie* ~ *om moord te pleeg nie* he won't stop at committing murder

skroot grapeshot; scrap, scrap iron; ~**werf** scrapyard *ook* **wrak'werf**

skrop (s) **-pe** dam scraper; (w) scrub; scratch (poultry); work (odd/casual jobs); ~**bor'sel** scrubbing brush; ~**hoen'der** free-range chicken *ook* **werf'hoender**

skrum (s, w) scrum; ~**ska'kel** scrumhalf

skryf ge- write; *met ink* ~ write in ink; ~**behoef'tes** stationery *ook* **skryf'ware/ skryf'goed;** ~**blok** writing pad; ~**boek** exercise book; writing pad; ~**goed** stationery; ~**ta'fel** writing table, desk *ook* **les'senaar;** ~**wa're** stationery

skry'we (s) letter, minute; (w) write *ook* **skryf**

skry'wer -s writer, author *ook* **outeur'**

sku (b) **-(w)er, -uste** shy, timid

skud ge- shake; shuffle; *hy* ~ *soos hy lag* he is convulsed with laughter; *kaarte* ~ shuffle the cards; ~**ding** shaking; tremor *kyk* **aard'= skudding;** concussion

skug'ter -der, -ste shy, timid, bashful; coy

skuif (s) **skuiwe** bolt; move; puff (pipe); (w) shove, move, push; ~**deur** sliding door; ~**leer** extension ladder; ~**meul(e)** noughts and crosses (game); pretext, excuse; ~**raam** sash window; ~**speld** paperclip; ~**trompet'** trombone, sliding trumpet

skuil (w) **ge-** hide, take shelter; ~**kel'der** air-raid shelter; ~**naam** pseudonym; ~**plek** hiding place, hide-out; retreat

skuim (s) foam, scum, froth; (w) foam; ~**rub'**= **ber** foam rubber; ~**wyn** sparkling wine *ook* **von'kelwyn**

skuins -er, -ste sloping, slanting, oblique

skuit (s) **-e** boat *ook* **boot**

skui'wergat -e drainhole; loophole

skuld -e debt; fault; guilt; *agterstallige* ~ arrears; *oninbare/dooie* ~ bad debts; (w) owe; ~**beken'tenis** confession of guilt;

~**brief** debenture; ~**ei'ser** creditor; ~**enaar'** debtor; ~**erken'ning** admission of guilt
skul'dig -e guilty; convicted; ~ *bevind aan* found guilty of; ~ *pleit* plead guilty; ~**e** guilty person; offender
skulp (s) -e shell, conch
skurf scabby; chapped (hands); dirty (joke)
skurk -e rascal, rogue, scoundrel *ook* **boef**
skut¹ (s) -s shot, marksman, rifleman
skut² (s) -te protection; guard; pad (cricket); (w) protect
skut³ (s) (animal) pound; ~'**blad** flyleaf
skuur¹ (s) **skure** barn, shed; hangar
skuur² (w) **ge-** polish, rub, scour; ~**papier'** sandpaper, emery paper
skyf skywe slice, disc, quoit; target; quarter (of an orange); ~**ie** (s) film slide; disc (sticker); ~**let'sel** slipped disc; ~**skiet** gun/ rifle practice; bisley; ~**spa'sie** disc space (comp.)
skyn (s) light, glow; pretence; ~ *bedrieg* appearances are deceptive; (w) shine; seem, appear; ~**aan'val** mock attack; ~**baar** apparent(ly); ~**geveg'** mock fight
skynhei'lig (b) sanctimonious; hypocritical *ook* **vals, huigelag'tig**
slaaf (s) **slawe** slave; (w) slave, drudge, toil
slaag ge- succeed; pass; *ek het daarin ge~* I succeeded in . . .; ~**punt** passmark
slaags fighting, engaged; ~ *raak* come to blows
slaai lettuce; salad; *in iem. se ~ krap* meddle with someone else's girl; **vrug'te~** fruit salad
slaak ge- heave, utter, breathe; *'n sug (van verligting)* ~ heave a sigh (of relief)
slaan ge- beat, strike; *'n slag ~* make a bargain; *op die vlug ~* take to flight; ~**krag** punch(ing) power; ~**sak** punchbag
slaap¹ (s) **slape** temple (anat.)
slaap² (s) sleep; *aan die ~ raak* fall asleep; (w) sleep; ~**ka'mer** bedroom; ~**kle're** pyjamas *ook* **paja'mas**; ~**saal** dormitory; ~**sak** sleeping bag; ~**siek'te** sleeping sickness; lethargy; ~**wan'delaar** somnam= bulist
sla'e thrashing, hiding; **pak** ~ thrashing
slag¹ (s) **slae** battle; loss; beat (pulse); clap (thunder); blow, stroke; *'n ~ hê* have the knack; *op ~ dood* killed instantly; *'n swaar ~* a severe blow
slag² (w) **ge-** slaughter, kill; ~**aar** artery

slag: ~**gat** pothole; ~**huis** butchery; ~**kreet** slogan *ook* ~**spreuk**; ~**of'fer** victim: ~**orkes'** percussion band; ~**pa'le** slaughter= ing place; ~**plaas** abattoir *ook* **ab'attoir**; ~**room** whipped cream; ~**spreuk** slogan; ~**tand** tusk (elephant); fang; eye tooth; ~**ter** butcher; ~**ting** slaughter, massacre; ~**veld** battlefield; ~**yster** spring trap
slak -ke snail; slag (ore smelting waste); *op 'n* ~*kegang* at a snail's pace
slampam'per (w) **ge-** revel; stroll; ~**lied'jie** carousal song; vagrant song/ditty
slang -e snake; serpent; hosepipe (garden); ~**besweer'der** snake charmer; ~**kuil** snake pit
slank (b) slender, slim *kyk* **verslank'** (w)
slap -per, -ste loose; slack, dull; supple; ~**band(boek)** paperback
sla'per -s sleeper, dreamer
slap: ~**gat** (*plat*) spineless fellow; ~**skyf** floppy disc/disk; ~**tjips** chips (with fish); ~**verkeer'** off-peak traffic
slawerny' slavery
slee sleë sledge; sleigh (for person)
sleep (s) **slepe** retinue; (w) drag, trail; tow; *slepende siekte* lingering disease; ~**boot** tug; ~**haak** towbar *ook* **trek'stang**; ~**hel'ling** slipway (boating); ~**ren** drag racing; ~**tou** towing rope; ~**wa** trailer *ook* **trei'ler**
sleg (b, bw) bad, evil, base; foul, wicked; ~**te humeur'** bad temper
slegs only, merely; ~ *volwassenes* adults only
sleng/slang (s) slang (language) *ook* **jar'gon**
slenk'dal rift valley
slen'ter (s) trick, bluff, ploy; (w) saunter; ~**broek** slacks; ~**drag** casual dress/wear
slet -te slut, bitch (woman) *ook* **sloe'rie, snol**
sleur (s) humdrum way, rut, routine; (w) drag; ~**fak'tor** drag factor (aerodynamics); ~**werk** routine work, chores
sleu'tel -s key (door); clef (mus.); register; wrench, spanner; ~**been** collarbone; ~**gat** keyhole; ~**pos** key position (work)
slik (s) silt, mire, slime *ook* **slib**
slim clever, intelligent; crafty, sly; *Slim het sy baas gevang* (he was) too clever for his own good; ~**kop** bright student/person; ~**praat** = **jies** claptrap, glib/evasive talk
slin'ger (s) -s pendulum (clock); sling; handle; crank (motorcar); (w) sling, oscillate, reel; ~**plant** creeper; ~**vel** sling(shot)

slinks sly, crafty, treacherous, underhand *ook*
slu, gesle'pe
sloer ge- loiter, linger, dawdle; ~**sta'king**
go-slow strike
sloop[1] (s) **slope** pillowcase
sloop[2] (w) ge- demolish; dismantle
sloot slote ditch, furrow, trench
slor'dig -e; -er, -ste careless, untidy
slot[1] **-te** lock; clasp; *agter* ~ *en grendel* under
lock and key
slot[2] end(ing), conclusion; *per* ~ *van rekening*
after all; *ten* ~*te* in conclusion
slot[3] **-te** castle, citadel *ook* **kasteel'/ves'ting**
slot: ~**ma'ker** locksmith; ~**knip'per** bolt
cutter; ~**sang** final song/hymn; ~**som** result,
conclusion, bottomline *ook* **somtotaal'**
slu (b) sly, cunning, wily *ook* **slinks**
slui'er (s) **-s** veil; mask
sluik: ~**han'del** black market *ook* **swart'mark;**
~**werk** moonlighting, double-jobbing
slui'mer (s) slumber; (w) slumber
sluip ge- steal along, sneak away; ~**moord**
assassination; ~**moor'denaar** assassin; ~**sla'-**
per yard sneaker, sly lodger
sluis -e sluice, lock, floodgate
sluit ge- lock, close, shut; conclude; *die skole*
~ the schools are breaking up; *vrede* ~
conclude/make peace; ~**da'tum** closing
date *ook* **sper'datum;** ~**kas** locker
sluk (s) **-ke** epiglottis; gulp, swallow; (w)
swallow, gulp; ~**derm** gullet, esophagus
slum -s slum *ook* **krot'buurt**
slurp (s) trunk (elephant); (w) lap, gobble
slyk mud, mire, sludge *ook* **slik**
slym slime, phlegm, mucus
slyp ge- sharpen, whet, grind; polish; *sy tande*
vir iets ~ look forward to with keen anticipation; ~**skool** workshop, finishing school;
~**steen** grindstone, hone; ~**wiel** emery wheel
slyt ge- wear away, diminish
slyta'sie wear, wastage; **bil'like** ~ fair wear
and tear
smaak (s) **smake** taste, relish, flavour; *na my*
~ to my liking; (w) taste, savour; *ek proe dit*
en dit ~ *goed* I taste it and it tastes nice
smaak'lik tasty, palatable; ~*e ete!* enjoy your
meal!
smaak'vol -le tasteful, elegant; *sy is* ~
aangetrek she is dressed elegantly/smartly
smal -ler, -ste narrow, thin
smarag' -de emerald
smart (s) **-e** grief, sorrow *ook* **verdriet'**

smee(d) ge- weld, forge; coin, devise; *'n*
komplot ~ hatch a plot
smeek ge- pray, beg, beseech, entreat, implore; *om genade* ~ plead for mercy
smeer ge- grease, smear, oil, lubricate; ~**kaas**
cheese spread; ~**veld'tog** smear campaign
smee'yster wrought iron
smelt ge- melt, dissolve; fuse (wire); ~**ery'**
foundry; ~**oond'** furnace
sme'rig greasy, squalid, dirty *ook* **mor'sig**
smet (s) **-te** blot, stain, blemish
smeul ge- smoulder; ~**stoof** slow-combustion
stove
smid smede (black)smith
smid'dags in the afternoon, midday
smok'kel (s) smuggling; (w) smuggle; ~**aar**
smuggler; bootlegger; ~**kroeg** shebeen *ook*
sjebien'
smoor (w) **ge-** suffocate, smother; ~**dronk**
dead drunk; ~**klep** choke (engine); ~**ver-**
lief' head over heels in love
smo'rens/smô'rens in the morning
smous (s) **-e** hawker, pedlar; (w) barter; hawk;
~**pos** junk mail
smuk: ~**spie'ëltjie** vanity mirror; ~**tas'sie**
vanity case *ook* **tooi'tassie**
smul (w) feast, junket; ~**paap** gastronome,
gourmand; belly worshipper; ~**party'** carousal, feast
s'n 's, of; *hulle* ~ theirs; *pa* ~ father's
snaaks funny, queer, strange; comical
snaar snare string, cord; chap, guy; lover
snags during the night, by night
snap ge- understand, comprehend, catch
snaps (s) **-e** drop, drink, tot *ook* **so'pie/dop**
sna'ter (s) **-s** mouth, mug; beak; *hou jou* ~!
shut up!; (w) chatter, jibber
sna'wel -s beak, bill
sneeu (s) snow *kyk* **kapok'**; (w) snow; ~**vlok'-**
kie snowflake; ~**wit** snow white; **Sneeuwit'-**
jie Little Snowwhite
snel (w) **ge-** rush, hurry; (b) rapid, quick *ook*
vin'nig; fleet, swift; ~**heid** velocity
snel'ler -s trigger; sprinter *ook* **na'elloper**
snel: ~**rat** overdrive; ~**sêer** tongue twister;
~**skrif** shorthand, stenography; ~**skriftik'-**
ster shorthand typist; ~**strik** speed trap *ook*
jaag'strik; ~**trein** express train; ~**vuur**
rapid fire; ~**weg** freeway (rural), highway
(Am); speedway, expressway
sner'pend -e painful, biting, smarting *ook*
y'sig; ~ *koud* bitterly cold

snert small talk, trash, tripe *ook* **kaf, bog**

sne'sie -s tissue; *kry 'n ~ en snuit jou neus* get a tissue and blow your nose

sneu'wel ge- perish, be slain, fall (in battle)

snik (s) **-ke** sob; (w) sob, sniffle; ~**heet** (b) sweltering; ~**san'ger** crooner, sobsinger

snip'per: ~**aar** shredder; ~**jag** paperchase; ~**mand'jie** wastepaper basket

snob -s snob *ook* **ploert, in'kruiper** (mens)

snobis'me snobbery

snoei ge- prune, clip, lop; ~**skêr** garden/ pruning shears, pruner

snoek -e snoek (SA); barracuda; sea pike

snoe'ker (s) snooker (game)

snoep (w) **ge-** eat dainties secretly; withhold; (b) tight-fisted; ~**e'rye** snacks, dainties *ook* **peu'selhappies;** ~**hoe'kie** snackbar; ~**win' kel(tjie)** tuckshop

snoer (s) **-e** string, cord; ~ **pê'rels** string of pearls; (w) silence someone

snoet -e snout, muzzle

snor (s) **-re** moustache, whisker

snork (s) **-e** snore; (w) **ge-** snore, snort

snot mucus, snot; ~**neus** snotty nose (child); brat, little minx

snou (w) **ge-** snarl *ook* **af'snou'**; gnarl; rebuke

snuf''fel ge- sniff, sniffle, smell (out), ferret (out); search, investigate; ~**hond** sniffer dog; ~**mark** browser's market, fleamarket *ook* **vlooi'mark**

snuif (s) **snuiwe** snuff; (w) take snuff, sniff; ~**doos** snuff box

snuis'tery -e novelty, trinket, bric-a-brac

snuit (s) **-e** snout, nose; nozzle; (w) blow the nose; ~**er** little fellow/youngster; snuffer

sny (s) **-e** slice; cut, gash; (w) cut; castrate/ geld; operate; ~**dok'ter** surgeon *ook* **chirurg'/sjirurg';** ~**er** tailor; ~**kunde** surgery; **plas'tiese** ~**kunde** plastic/cosmetic surgery

so so, thus, like this

so'ber sober; temperate; austere

soda'nig -e such like; *die toestand is* ~ *dat* the position is such that

so'dat so that, in order that

so'doende thus, in that manner

sodomie' (s) sodomy, homosexual intercourse

sodra' as soon as; the moment that

soe'bat ge- beg, entreat, plead *ook* **smeek**

soek (s): *op* ~ *na* in search of; (w) seek, look for, search; ~**gesel'skap** search party; ~**lig** searchlight/spotlight

soen (s) **-e** kiss; (w) **ge-** kiss *ook* **kus**

soe'pel -er, -ste supple *ook* **le'nig;** flexible

soet (s) the sweet; *die ~ en suur van die lewe* the ups and downs of life; (b) sweet; well-behaved; ~**igheid** sweetness; sweet; ~**jies** gently, noiselessly; ~**koek** sweet cake: *alles vir* ~**koek opeet** swallow everything you are told; ~**lief** sweetheart; ~**ris'sie** green pepper; ~**skeel** slightly squinting

soewenier' -s souvenir *ook* **aan'denking**

soewerein' (b) **-e** sovereign, supreme

so'fa -s sofa *ook* **rus'bank**

sog -ge, sôe sow (pig)

so'genaamd/so'genoemd (b) **-e** so-called

sog'gens in the morning

so'heen thither, there; ~**toe** thither, that way *ook* **soontoe**

so'jaboon(tjie) -s soybean

sok'ker soccer, football; ~**boe'we** soccer hooligans

sok'kie -s sock; ~**jol** informal dance *ook* **op'skop** (s)

solank' for the time being, meanwhile

soldaat' ..date soldier

soldeer' (w) solder; ~**bout** soldering iron

sol'der -s garret, loft

soldy' soldier's pay/wages

solidariteit' solidarity *ook* **saamho'righeid**

solied' -e; -er, -ste solid; reliable

solis -te soloist, solo vocalist (both sexes)

som -me sum, amount; problem

som'ber (b) **-der, -ste** sombre, gloomy

so'mer -s summer; *in die ~* in/during summer; ~**vakan'sie** summer holidays

som'mer just, for no reason; *ag* ~! oh, just because; ~ *huil* cry for no reason

som'mige some *ook* **party'** (mense)

soms/som'tyds sometimes *ook* **party'keer**

son -ne sun; *die ~ kom op/gaan onder* the sun rises/sets

sona'te -s sonata

son: ~**be'sie** cricket (cicada); ~**bruin** (s) tan; (w) tan *ook* **lyf'brand**

son'daar -s, ..dare sinner; offender

Son'dag ..dae Sunday; ~ *oor agt dae* next Sunday week

son'de -s sin, trespass; probe (instrument); ~**bok** scapegoat, guiltless person; whipping boy

son'der without; ~ **winsoogmerk** not for gain/ profit; ~**ling** (b) peculiar, queer

sond'vloed deluge, great flood

so'ne -s zone

son: ~**krag** solar power; ~**lig** sunlight; ~**ne**ʹ= **blom** sunflower

sonnetʹ **-te** sonnet *ook* **klink**ʹ**dig**

sonʹ**onder** (s) sunset; (bw) at sunset

sonoorʹ **sonore** sonorous

sonʹ**op** (s) sunrise; (bw) at sunrise

son: ~**steek** sunstroke; ~**straal** sunbeam

sonsʹ**verduistering -s, -e** solar eclipse

son: ~**verhit**ʹ**ting** solar heating; ~**verwar**ʹ= **mer** solar heater; ~**vlek** sunspot, solar spot; ~**wy**ʹ**ser** sundial

soog ge- suckle, nurse; ~**dier** mammal; ~**vrou** wet nurse *ook* **voed**ʹ**ster**

sooi -e sod; ~**brand** heartburn; ~**merk** divot (golf)

sool sole sole; ~**leer** sole leather

soölogieʹ zoology *ook* **dier**ʹ**kunde**

soom (s) some seam, hem; edge, border

soonʹ**toe** thither, that way

soort -e kind, sort; *enig in sy* ~ the only one of its kind; ~ *soek* ~ birds of a feather flock together; ~**gelyk**ʹ similar; ~**lik** specific: ~*like gewig* specific gravity; ~**naam** com= mon name

soos as, like; *so siek* ~ *ʹn hond* very ill/ miserable; ~ *volg* as follows

sop soup; ~**le**ʹ**pel** soup spoon/ladle

soʹ**pie -s** glass of liquor; drink, tot *ook* **dop** (s)

sopraanʹ **soprane** soprano (singer)

sorg (s) **-e** care, charge; trouble, anxiety; (w) care for, look after, provide for; ~ *vir die oudag* provide for one's old age; ~**een**ʹ**heid** intensive care unit *ook* **intensie**ʹ**we** ~**een**ʹ= **heid**; ~**sen**ʹ**trum** frailcare unit

sorʹ**ghum** (grain) sorghum

sorg: ~**vul**ʹ**dig** careful, thorough; ~**wek**ʹ**kend** alarming

sorteerʹ ~, **ge-** sort, select, grade

sosaʹ**tie -s** sosatie, grilled curried meat, kebab

sosiaalʹ **sosiale** social; **sosia**ʹ**le vlin**ʹ**der** social climber/socialite

sosialietʹ **-e** socialite (person)

sosialisʹ **-te** socialist; ~**me** socialism

sosiologieʹ sociology (subject)

sot (s) **-te** fool *ook* **idioot**ʹ (mens); (b) foolish

soul soul (mus.)

sous (s) **-e** sauce, gravy; ~**trein** gravy train *ook* **stroop**ʹ**trein/man**ʹ**nawa**

sout (s) **-e** salt; *ʹn sak* ~ *saam opeet* know someone intimately; (w) salt, cure; initiate; (b) briny, salt; ~**hap**ʹ**pies** savouries

soʹ**veel** so much, so many; ~**ste** umpteenth

soverʹ**/so vêr** so far; ~ *ek weet* as far as I know

soʹ**ver** so far, thus far; *tot* ~ as far as this

sowaarʹ truly; indeed, really *ook* **reg**ʹ**tig**

soʹ**wat** about *ook* **ongeveer**ʹ; ~ *vyftig rand* fifty rands odd

sowelʹ both . . . and; as well (as); ~ *hy as sy* both he and she

spaan (s) **spane** skimmer; oar; racket (tennis)

spaanʹ**der** (s) **-s** chip of wood; (w) run away; ~**bord/**~**hout** chipboard

spaar ge- save, economise; spare; ~**bank** savings bank; ~**bankboe**ʹ**kie** deposit book; ~**re**ʹ**kening** savings account; ~**var**ʹ**kie** pig= gybank *ook* **ot**ʹ**pot** (idiom.)

spaarʹ**saam** thrifty

spalk (s) **-e** splint; (w) splint; set (leg or arm)

span (s) **-ne** span; team; (w) stretch; brace; hobble; cock (gun); ~**broek** pair of tights

spandaʹ**bel** (b) spendthrift, extravagant

spandeerʹ ~, **ge-** spend *ook* **uit**ʹ**gee** (geld)

spanʹ**doek -e** wide banner/streamer

spanʹ**gees** team spirit, esprit de corps

spanʹ**nend** tight; exciting, thrilling

spanʹ**ning** tension, stress; suspense; voltage

spanspekʹ **-ke** muskmelon, spanspek

sparʹ**tel ge-** sprawl, twitch; struggle

spaʹ**sie -s** space, opening *ook* **ruim**ʹ**te**

spat (w) **ge-** splash, spatter

speaʹ**ker -s** speaker (of parliament)

speek speke spoke (of wheel)

speekʹ**sel** spittle, saliva

speel ge- play; trifle with; perform, act; *ek* ~ *maar* I am only joking; *jy* ~ *met vuur* you are playing with fire; ~**ding** toy; ~**goed** toys

speels -e; -er, -ste playful; merry

speel: ~**tyd** playtime; recess, interval; ~**vak** season, run (theatre); ~**veld:** *die* ~ *gelyk maak* level the playing field

speen (s) **spene** teat; nipple; (w) wean; ~**vark** sucking pig

speer spere spear *ook* **spies**

spei (w) spay (a bitch), neuter (a cat)

spek (smoked) bacon; ~ **en ei**ʹ**ers** bacon and eggs; *met* ~ *skiet/spekskiet* draw the long bow

spektaʹ**kel -s** scene; row; sight *ook* **skou**ʹ**spel**

spekuleerʹ **ge-** speculate; stag (stock ex= change) *ook* **bespie**ʹ**gel** (w)

spek: ~**vark** baconer, porker; ~**vet** very fat

spel[1] (s) **-e** game, play; *daar is baie op die* ~ there is much at stake

spel[2] (w) **ge-** spell; foretell

spel: ~**beder'wer/**~**bre'ker** killjoy, spoilsport
speld (s, w) pin
spe'ler -s player, actor
spe'letjie -s game, fun
spel'fout -e spelling error
spe'ling play, scope, range; clearance
spel'letjie -s game; *'n* ~ *kaart* a game of cards
spel'ling (s) spelling, orthography
spelonk' -e cave, cavern *ook* **grot**
spens -e pantry
sper: ~**streep** barrier (solid white) line; ~**tyd** deadline *ook* **perk'tyd**
spesery' -e spice; ~**han'del** spice trade
spesiaal' ..**siale** special *ook* **beson'der**
spesialis' -te specialist (medicine, etc.)
spesialiseer' ~, ge- specialise
spesialiteit' -e speciality; *brei is haar* ~ she excels in knitting
spesifika'sie -s specification *ook* **op'gawe**
spesmaas' idea, notion, inkling; *ek het 'n* ~ *dat . . .* I have an idea/feeling that . . .
speur ge- track, trace, spy, ferret out; ~**der** detective; ~**hond** tracker dog, police dog; ~**verhaal'** detective story
spie'ël (s) -s mirror, looking glass; (w) mirror; ~**kas** wardrobe; ~**ta'fel** dressing table
spier -e muscle; *geen* ~ *vertrek nie* without batting an eyelid; ~**bou'er** bodybuilder; ~**krag** muscular force; ~**verslap'per** muscle relaxant; ~**wit** snow-white, lilywhite
spies -e spear, lance; ~**hengel** spearfishing
spiet'kop -s speedcop *ook* **pad'valk**
splk'splinternuut ..**nuwe** brand-new
spil (s) -le pivot, axis; swivel; spindle
spin ge- spin, purr (cat)
spina'sie spinach
spin'ne: ~**kop** spider; ~**rak** cobweb
spioen' (s) -e spy; scout, secret agent
spioena'sie espionage, spying
spioeneer' ge- spy, pry
spiraal' ..**rale** spiral; ~**veer** coil spring
spiritis' -te spiritualist (person); ~**me** spiritualism
spi'ritus spirit(s); alcohol
spit[1] (s) -te spadeful; spade depth; *die* ~ *afbyt* bear the brunt; (w) dig
spit[2] (s) -te spit (for roasting)
spits (s) -e point, top, tip, peak; spire, pinnacle; (w) point; *die ore* ~ prick up the ears; (b) pointed, sharp; ~**beraad'** summit talks; ~**tyd** peak period; ~**uur** peak hour/period, rush hour; ~**verkeer'** peak traffic

spitsvon'dig subtle, quick-witted
spleet splete crevice, slit, fissure, chink
splin'ter (s) -s splinter; (w) splinter; ~**nuut'** brand-new; ~**vry** shatterproof
splits ge- split, divide; splice
splyt ge- cleave, split; *gesple'te lip* harelip; ~**ing** splitting (atom)
spoed (s) **snelhede** speed, progress, haste; *hoe meer haas hoe minder* ~ the more haste the less speed; (w) speed, hasten; ~**hob'bel** speed hump; ~**ig** soon, speedy/speedily, quick(ly)
spoeg/spuug/spu (s) spittle, saliva; (w) spit, expectorate *ook* **spu** (w)
spoel[1] (s) -e shuttle, spool
spoel[2] (w) ge- rinse, wash; flow; ~**bak** washtub; cistern; ~**diamant'** alluvial diamond
spog ge- boast, show off, brag
spons (s) ge- sponge; (w) sponge; ~**rub'ber** foam rubber
spontaan' (b) spontaneous *ook* **ongedwon'ge**
spook (s) **spoke** ghost, apparition, spectre; (w) be very active, struggle, haunt; ~**a'sem** candyfloss; ~**sto'rie** ghost story
spoor (s) **spore** track, footprint; trail; scent; rail(way); spore; *per* ~ by rail; (w) align (wheels) *kyk* **wiel'sporing**
spoor: ~**brug** railway bridge; ~**loos** (b) trackless; (bw) completely; ~*loos verdwyn* vanish into space; ~**lyn** railway line; ~**sny'er** tracker
spoor'weg ..**weë** railway; ~**kaar'tjie** railway ticket
spo'ring wheel alignment
sport[1] -e rundle, step, rung (ladder)
sport[2] -e, -soor'te sport; ~**baad'jie** sports jacket; ~**grond** recreation/sports ground(s)
sportief' ..**tiewe** sportive, sportsmanlike
sport: ~**klub** sports club; ~**manskap'** sportsmanship
spot (s) scorn, mockery; (w) jest; deride, mock, jeer; ~**goedkoop'** dirt-cheap; ~**prent** cartoon; caricature (newspaper)
spraak speech, language, tongue; ~**gebrek'** speech impediment; ~**saam** talkative
spra'ke rumour, talk; *ter* ~ *bring* broach a subject; *geen* ~ *van* no question about it; ~**loos** speechless, dumb
sprankel (w) ge- spark(le); scintillate
spreek ge- speak, talk, converse; *kan ek die hoof* ~*/(sien)?* may I see the principal?; *dit* ~ *vanself* it goes without saying; ~**ka'mer** consulting room; ~**woord** proverb, saying
spreeu -s starling; **In'diese** ~ (Indian) mynah

sprei[1] (s) **-e** counterpane; bedspread, quilt
sprei[2] (w) **ge-** scatter, spread out; ~**lig** flood=
light
spre'kend -e speaking; lifelike; *'n* ~*e gelyke=*
nis an exact/striking likeness
spre'ker -s speaker; orator
spreuk -e proverb, aphorism, maxim
spriet -e blade (grass); feeler (insect)
spring (s) **-e** leap, jump, hop; (w) jump, leap;
~**bok** springbok
spring: ~**jurk** gym, gymnastic costume; tunic;
~**kasteel'** jumping/bouncy castle; ~**le'wen=**
dig very much alive, sprightly; ~**mat**
trampoline *ook* **wip'mat**; ~**mes** flick-knife;
~**mie'lies** popcorn; ~**stof** explosive(s) *ook*
plof'stof; ~**tou** skipping rope; ~**ty** spring=
tide; ~**wer'ke** blasting operations
sprin'kaan ..kane locust, grasshopper; ~**vo'ël**
locust bird; stork (large)
sprin'kel ge- sprinkle; ~**besproei'ing** spray/
sprinkler irrigation
sproei (w) **ge-** spray, irrigate; (s) ~**er** sprayer;
jet; ~**kop** nozzle *ook* **nos'sel**
sproet -e freckle; ~**gesig'** freckled face
spro'kie -s fairytale; fable
sprong -e jump, leap; caper, hop
spruit (s) **-e** shoot; offshoot; brook, stream=
(let); (w) sprout; arise
spuit (s) **-e** syringe; squirt; sprayer; (w) inject;
spout, spray, squirt; ~**fontein'** leaping foun=
tain/waterfountain; ~**kan(netjie)** spray/aero=
sol can; ~**stof** vaccine; ~**verf** spray paint
spul affair; lot; *die hele* ~ the whole lot
spy'ker -s nail; brad, tack; ~**skoen** (mv)
spikes (athletics); ~**ta'fel** pintable
spys -e food, victuals; ~**e'nier'** caterer;
~**e'neer/e'nier** (w) cater; ~**e'ne'ring** cater=
ing; ~**kaart** menu; ~**verte'ring** digestion:
slegte ~*vertering* indigestion
spyt (s) regret, sorrow; *ten* ~*e van* in spite of;
(w) regret, be sorry; *dit* ~ *my* I am sorry
ook: ek is jammer
staaf[1] (s) **stawe** bar, rod, stave
staaf[2] (w) **ge-** confirm, ratify; ~ *u antwoord*
met support your answer with
staaf'goud bar gold, bullion
staak ge- strike, cease work; discontinue; stall
(car); ~**wag** picket (person)
staal steel; *jou* ~ *toon* show one's mettle
staal'tjie -s yarn, yoke; anecdote
staan ge- stand; *duur te* ~ *kom* pay dearly for;
~**de mag** permanent force

staan'der -s standard; stand (for hats)
staan: ~**horlo'sie** grandfather clock; ~**plek**
standing room; parking area/bay
staan'spoor start, beginning; *uit die* ~/*van die*
~ *af* from the outset
staar (w) **ge-** gaze, stare
staat[1] state statement; return
staat[2] condition; *in* ~ *wees* be able
staat[3] state state; government
staat'kunde politics, statemanship
staat: ~**maak** rely (up)on; ~**ma'ker** main=
stay, stalwart, reliable person
staats: ~**aan'klaer** public prosecutor; ~**amp'=**
tenaar civil servant; ~**diens** civil service;
~**greep** coup (d'état); ~**hoof** head of state
staat'sie pomp; state; *in* ~ *lê* lie in state
staats: ~**koerant'** government gazette; ~**leer**
political science; ~**lotery'** state lottery; ~**man**
statesman, diplomat
stabiel' -e solid, firm, stable *ook* **ste'wig**
stad stede city; ~**huis** town/city hall, muni=
cipal complex
sta'dig slow; ~**e ak'sie** slow motion
sta'dion -s stadium; **S~ Boland** Boland Stadium
sta'dium -s ..dia stage, phase; *in hierdie* ~ at
this point *ook: op hierdie tydstip*
stad'saal ..sale town hall, city hall
stads: ~**huis** house in town; ~**kalant'** city
slicker; ~**klerk** town clerk
stad'skouburg -e civic theatre
stads: ~**raad** town council; ~**wa'pen** coat-
of-arms; ~**wyk** municipal ward
staf stawe staff; mace (parliament); baton
(marshall); crozier (bishop)
sta'ker -s striker; ~**(s)wag** picket
sta'king -s, -e strike; suspension, cessation; ~
van stemme equality of votes
stal -le stable; (w) stable; ~**kneg** stablehand
stal'letjie -s (display) stall *ook* **kiosk'**; booth
stam (s) **-me** trunk, stem; tribe, clan; ~**boom**
genealogical tree, family tree, pedigree
sta'mel (w) **ge-** falter; stammer
stam: ~**geveg** faction fight; ~**oor'log** tribal war
stamp (s) **-e** knock, stamp, bump; *met* ~*e en*
stote by fits and starts; (w) pound, stamp,
bump; ~**mo'tor** stock car; ~**vol** chockful,
packed (hall)
stand -e standing, position; rank; stance; ~
van sake state of affairs
standaard' -e standard, criterium *ook* **maat'=**
staf, norm; ~**werk** standard work

stand'beeld -e statue
stan'derd -s standard (class in school); grade
stand: ~**plaas** stand, erf; ~**punt** standpoint; point of view/viewpoint *ook* **siens'wyse**
standvas'tig -e firm, constant, steadfast
stang -e bit (of bridle); bar
stank -e stench, bad smell, stink; ~ *vir dank kry* not get as much as a "thank you"
stan'sa -s stanza *ook* **stro'fe**
stap (s) -pe step, pace, stride; move; ~*pe doen* take action; (w) walk; step, stride; hike; *'n entjie gaan* ~ go for a walk
sta'pel (s) -s pile, heap, stack; *die skema van* ~ *laat loop* launch the scheme *ook* **loods**; (w) heap up, pile, stack; ~**gek** insane, raving/stark mad; ~**kos** staple food; ~**kur'sus** crash/sandwich course
stap: ~**per** -s walker, hiker; *met dapper en* ~*per* on foot; ~**roe'te** hiking trail *ook* **voet'slaanpad**; ~**toer** hiking trip
sta'sie -s station; ~**wa** station wagon
sta'tebond commonwealth
sta'ties (b) -e static
sta'tig stately, elegant; dignified
statistiek' -e statistics *ook* **da'ta**
statuut' statute statute *ook* **wet**
steak (s) steak *ook* **bief'stuk**
ste'de stead; *in* ~ *van* instead of; ~**like bevol'king** urban population; ~**like terroris'me** urban terrorism; ~**ling** townsman, city dweller
steeds (bw) constantly, always; ~ *kouer* colder and colder
steeg stege lane, alley; **blin'de** ~ blind alley
steek (s) **steke** prick (pin), stitch (needle), sting (bee); bite; stab; *in die* ~ *laat* leave in the lurch; (w) prick; sting; stab; ~**proef** random sample, spot check
steeks (b) obstinate *ook* **kop'pig**
steel¹ stele handle; stalk (flower); stem (pipe); shaft
steel² (w) ge- steal, thieve
steel'kant blind side (rugby)
steen stene brick; stone; bar (soap)
Steen'bokskeerkring Tropic of Capricorn
steen: ~**groef** quarry; ~**kool** coal
steg'gie cutting *ook* **stig'gie**
stei'er¹ (s) -s scaffold(ing)
stei'er² (w) ge- stagger, prance, rear
steil (b) steep, precipitous; sheer; ~**te** gradient, rise/slope, steepness
stel¹ (s) -le set (tennis); (dinner) service; suite

(of rooms)
stel² (w) ge- fix; draw up; adjust; set; compose; *gestel dat* supposing that; *die wekker* ~ set the alarm (clock)
stel'ling -s, -e doctrine, thesis, statement; *bespreek hierdie* ~ discuss this statement/ assertion
stel'sel -s system; **metrie'ke/tiende'lige** ~ metric system
stelselma'tig -e systematic(al)
stel'skop -pe place kick
stelt -e stilt; ~**lo'per** stilt walker
stem (s) -me voice; vote; ~*me uitbring* cast votes, poll; (w) tune; vote; ~**band** vocal chord; ~**brief(ie)** ballot paper; ~**bui'ging** modulation, intonation; ~**bus** ballot box; ~**lokaal'** polling station; ~**mig** sedate, sober, quiet
stem'ming -e, -s ballot, election, voting, poll *ook* **stem'mery**; mood; *in 'n goeie* ~ *bring* put in a good mood; *tot* ~ *oorgaan/bring* proceed/put to the vote
stem'opnemer -s polling officer, returning officer, scrutineer
stem'pel -s seal, stamp
stem: ~**reg** franchise; right to vote; ~**vurk** tuning fork
ste'nig (w) ge- stone
ster -re star; luminary
ste'reo stereo; ~**tiep'** stereotype
sterf ge- die, expire *ook* **ster'we**; ~**geval'** death; ~**-lik** (b) mortal; ~**ling** mortal (being); *geen* ~*ling nie* not a living soul; *aan 'n siekte* ~ *die* of a disease/illness; ~**te'syfer** death rate
steriel' -e sterile
steriliseer' (w) sterilise; castrate; spay *ook* **spei** (w)
sterk (w) ge- strengthen; *iem. in sy kwaad* ~ encourage a person in wrongdoing; (b) strong, powerful; ~**te** strength; ~**te!** good luck to you!
ster're: ~**beeld** constellation; ~**kunde** astronomy
sterrekun'dig (b) astronomical; ~**e** astronomer (person)
ster're: ~**tjie** little star; asterisk; ~**wag** observatory; ~**wig'gelaar** astrologer
stert -e tail; ~**riem** loin skin
steun¹ (s) -e groan, moan; (w) groan
steun² (s) support, aid; (w) support, aid, stay; *geldelik* ~ finance (v); ~**pilaar'** pillar of support; ~**sool** arch support

steur[1] (s) -s sturgeon; ~**garnaal**' prawn *ook* (swem)**kre**'**wel**

steur[2] (w) ge- disturb, trouble; care for, mind; *moenie jou daaraan* ~ *nie* don't mind that; *atmosferiese* ~**ings** atmospherics; ~**end** (b) disturbing

ste'**wel** -s boot; *vier* ~**s** *in die lug lê* lie flat on the back

ste'**wig** (b) firm; thorough; solid, sound

stie'**beuel** -s stirrup

stief step; ~**broer** stepbrother; ~**moe**'**der** stepmother; ~**moe**'**derlik** stepmotherly

stier -e bull *ook* **bul**; ~**geveg**' bullfight

stif'**fie** (s) stiffy, diskette (comp.)

stig ge- found, establish, raise; form (a company); edify; *brand* ~ raise a fire; '*n fonds* ~ establish a fund

stig'**ma** -s stigma, brand *ook* **smet** (s)

stig: ~**ter** founder; ~**ters**'**lid** founder member; ~**ting** foundation; institution

stik[1] ge- embroider; stitch (by machine)

stik[2] ge- choke, suffocate; ~**sie**'**nig** short-sighted, myopic; ~**stof** nitrogen

stil (w) ge- calm, soothe, allay, satisfy; *honger* ~ appease hunger; (b, bw) quiet, calm, peaceful; ~**bly** keep quiet

stil'**hou** -ge- stop, pull up

stil: ~**letjies** quietly, on the sly, secretly; ~**le**'**we** still-life (painting); ~**stand** truce, cessation, standstill; *tot* ~*stand kom* come to a stop; ~**swy**'**e** silence: *die* ~*swye bewaar* keep silent

stil'**te** quietness, calm, silence; *die* ~ *voor die storm* the lull before the storm

stimuleer' ge- stimulate *ook* **aan**'**spoor; op**'**= wek**

sting'**el** -s stalk, stem

stink (w) ge- stink, reek; (b) stinking; ~**hout** stinkwood

stip[1] (s) -**pe** spot, dot, speck

stip[2] (b, bw) strict; punctual; ~**te beta**'**ling** prompt payment

stip'**pel** (s) -s spot, dot, speck; (w) spot, dot; ~**streep** dotted/broken line (traffic)

stip'**telik** -e punctually, promptly

stoei ge- wrestle; romp; ~**er** wrestler; ~**kryt** wrestling ring; ~**promo**'**tor** wrestling promoter

stoel (s) -e chair, seat, stool

stoep -e stoep; patio

stoet[1] -e procession; retinue, train

stoet[2] -e stud; ~**bees**'**te** stud/pedigree cattle; ~**ery**' stud farm

stof[1] **stowwe** material, matter, stuff; **plof**'~ explosives

stof[2] **stowwe** dust; powder

stoffeer' (w) upholster; ~**der** upholsterer

stof'**fer** -s duster *ook* **stof**'**lap**

stof: ~**lik** mortal; material; ~**like oor**'**skot** mortal remains; ~**sui**'**er** vacuum cleaner

stok -**ke** stick, cane, staff; ~**doof** stone-deaf

sto'**ker** -s stoker, fireman; distiller

stok: ~**kie** little stick; ~**kies draai** play truant; ~**kie**'**lekker** lollipop; ~**kiesdraai**'**er** truant; ~**oud** very old, hoary with age; ~**perd**'**jie** hobby; fad; ~**sielalleen**' all alone; ~**styf** stiff as a poker; ~**vel** stokvel, savings/burial society

stol ge- congeal, coagulate; freeze (TV)

stom [-**me**] dumb, mute; stupid; *die* ~*me diere* the poor animals

stomp (b) -**er**, -**ste** blunt, dull, obtuse

stom'**pie** -s cigarette end, fag-end, stub

stonk (w) ge- stump (cricket)

stoof (s) **stowe** stove, range; (w) warm, stew, braise, simmer

stook ge- stoke, fire; distil; *kwaad* ~ stir up strife; instigate; ~**ke**'**tel** still

stoom (s) steam; (w) steam; ~**boot** steamship; ~**ke**'**tel** boiler; ~**pot** pressure cooker

stoor (w) ge- disturb *ook* **steur**; interrupt; store (away) *ook* **op**'**berg**; (s) storeroom *ook* **pak**'**kamer/skuur**

stoot (s) **stote** stab; poke; push; (w) poke, butt; push; thrust; ~**kar**'**retjie** handcart, pushcart; ~**skra**'**per** bulldozer

stop[1] (s) -**pe** pipe-fill; (w) darn; fill

stop[2] (w) ge- stop, halt

stop'**horlosie/stop**'**oorlosie** stopwatch

stop: ~**sel** -s filling (pipe; tooth) *ook* **vul**'**sel**; ~**straat** stopstreet; ~**verf** putty

sto'**rie** -s story, tale

storm (s) -s storm, tempest; (w) attack, storm

stormag'**tig** stormy, tempestuous, tumultuous

storm: ~**ja**'**er** dumpling; doughnut; assailant; ~**lantern**' hurricane lamp; ~**loop** (s) rush, onslaught; (w) attack, rush at; ~**wind** gale, hurricane

stort ge- pour, spill, shed; deposit; (take a) shower; *trane* ~ shed tears; ~**bad** shower bath; ~**bui** rainstorm *ook* **stort**'**reën**; ~**ing** deposit; shedding; **geen** ~**ing** no dumping; ~**reën** (s) heavy shower, downpour; ~**vloed** flood, deluge; (w) come down in torrents

stot'**ter** (w) ge- stutter *ook* **hak**'**kel**

stout naughty; bold, brave; *die ~e skoene aantrek* take a bold step; ~erd naughty child
stow'werig (b) -e; -er, -ste dusty
straal (s) strale beam, ray; radius (circle); jet, spurt (water); (w) beam, radiate; ~draal jetlag *ook* vlieg'voos; ~ja'er/~veg'ter jet fighter; ~jak'ker jetsetter; ~laag radial ply (tyres); ~vlieg'tuig jet aircraft/plane
straat (s) strate street; strait; (w) pave; ~boef hooligan; ~geweld' (street) violence; ~roof mugging; ~smous street vendor/informal trader; ~verlig'ting street lighting; ~vrou prostitute
straf[1] (s) strawwe punishment, penalty; (w) punish
straf[2] (b) severe, rigid, stern; straw'we droog'= te severe drought
straf: ~baar punishable; ~ba're man'slag culpable homicide, manslaughter; ~skop penalty kick; ~werk punishment, detention work
strak (b) tight, taut, stiff; ~ gesig' pokerface
straks perhaps; presently
stra'lend -e beaming, radiant; ~ *van geluk* radiant with happiness
stra'ler -s jet (of engine); jet (plane); jetliner; ~jak'ker jetsetter; ~kliek jetset
stram -mer, -ste stiff, hard, rigid
strand (s) -e beach, shore, seaside; (w) strand, run ashore/aground; ~huis beach cottage; ~jut (s) brown hyena; beachcomber; ~meer lagoon *ook* lagu'ne; ~oord seaside resort; ~wag lifesaver, lifeguard
strategie' strategy *ook* krygs'kuns
streef/strewe ge- strive, endeavour
streek streke district, region; line; tract; artifice, trick; ~nuus regional news; ~spraak dialect
streel (w) ge- caress, stroke; fondle; flatter
streep (s) strepe line, stroke; dash; (w) streak, line; hit; ~sui'ker thrashing, strap oil; ~vis seventyfour
strek ge- stretch, extend, reach; *dit ~ jou tot eer* it does you credit; ~king tendency, drift; moral
stre'lend -e pleasant, soothing; flattering; ~e musiek' soothing music
streng (b) strict, stern, rigorous; ~ vertroulik strictly confidential
stres (s) stress, anxiety, tension *ook* (werk)= span'ning; ~hante'ring stress management
strik[1] (s) -ke bow
strik[2] (s) -ke trap, snare *ook* wip

strik[3] (b) strict; accurate, exact
strik: ~das bow tie; ~vraag tricky question
string -e string (of pearls); trace, skein, strand
stroef gruff, harsh, grim
stro'fe -s stanza, verse; strophe
stro'kies: ~film strip film; ~prent/~verhaal comic (strip)
stronk -e stalk; cob (mealie)
stront (*kru*) shit, dung; rotter (person)
strooi[1] (s) straw
strooi[2] (w) ge- distribute, scatter; strew; sprinkle
strooi'biljet -te handbill/handout; pamphlet
strooi: ~dakhuis' house with thatched roof; ~jon'ker best man; ~lektuur' light read= ing; ~mei'sie bridesmaid; ~pop puppet/ stooge; ~pos junk mail; ~sa'ge soapie *ook* se'pie
strooi hut *ook* struis
strook (s) stroke strip; band; (w) agree, tally
stroom (s) strome stream, current; (w) flow, stream; ~ys (s) soft serve
stroop[1] (s) syrup; treacle, molasses; ~trein gravy train *ook* sous'trein/man'nawa
stroop[2] (s) love (in tennis)
stroop[3] (w) ge- pillage, plunder; rustle (cattle); ~tog raid, invasion
stroop (s) -pe strap, halter; ~das stock tie/ cravat
stro'per -s poacher (of game); plunderer; combination harvester (farming)
strot -te throat; ~te'hoof larynx
strug'gle (s) struggle *ook* (vryheid)stryd; strife, conflict
struik -e bush, shrub
strui'kel ge- stumble; ~blok stumbling block, obstacle *ook* hin'dernis
struik: ~gewas' shrubs, undergrowth; brush; ~ro'wer highwayman, bandit; hijacker
stru'weling (s) dispute, wrangle *ook* twis
stry (w) ge- dispute, contradict, argue
stryd (s) fight, strife, struggle, conflict, com= bat; ~byl hatchet: *die ~byl begrawe* bury the hatchet (make peace); ~dag party rally
stry'der -s warrior, fighter, combatant
stryd: ~kreet warcry; slogan; ~vraag ques= tion at issue, point in dispute
stryk[1] (s) stroke; pace (of horse); *op ~ kom* get into form; *van ~ wees* be out of form; (w) walk, stride; ~er fiddler (violin); streaker
stryk[2] ge- iron (clothes); stroke; strike (flag)
stryk: ~orkes' string orchestra; ~stok fiddle

stick; bow; ~**ys'ter** flat iron

stu ge- push, propel; prop; ~**dam** weir, barrage

studeer' ~, ~, **ge-** study; ~ *vir onderwyser* study to become a teacher; ~**ka'mer** study

student' -e student (both sexes)

studen'te: ~**blad** students' magazine; ~**raad** students' (representative) council

stu'die -s study; ~**beurs** scholarship, bursary

stug (b) stubborn, surly, sullen, obstinate

stuif stuiwe ge- make dust; drizzle; ~**meel** pollen; ~**sand** drift sand

stui'pe convulsions; *die ~ kry* be violently up= set, become livid with anger

stuit ge- stop, check *ook* **stop, keer** (w); ~**bed'ding** arrestor bed (heavy vehicles downhill)

stui'tjie -s rump, tailbone; pope's nose (fowl)

stuk -ke piece, fragment, oddment; document; play; part

stuk'kend (b) broken, torn; drunk

stuk'kie -s small piece, bit, morsel

stut (s) -te support, prop; truss; (w) support, prop; ~**muur** retaining wall; ~**prys** support price

stuur (s) **sture** steering gear, rudder, helm (ship); handle; (w) send; steer; ~**boord** starboard; ~**kajuit'** cockpit; ~**man** helms= man, chief mate; pilot; ~**outomaat'** auto= matic pilot

stuurs (b) surly, sulky, sullen *ook* **knor'rig, stug**

stuur'wiel -e steering wheel

stuwadoor' stevedore, docker

styf (w) **ge-** starch; stiffen; strenghten *ook* **sty'we;** (b) stiff, tight; rigid, formal

styfkop'pig obstinate, headstrong

styg ge- ascend, mount, climb, rise; ~**baan** runway *ook* **aan'loopbaan;** ~**ing** rise; in= crease; ascension; ~**spekulant'** bull (stock exchange)

styl style, manner; ~**figuur'** figure of speech; ~**e** doorpost, bedpost

sty'sel starch

subjektief' ..**tiewe** subjective

sub'komitee -s subcommittee *ook* **on'derko= mitee**

subsi'die -s subsidy, grant-in-aid

subskrip'sie -s subscription *ook* **in'tekengeld, lid'geld**

sub'struktuur (s) substructure (metropolitan)

subtiel' -e; -er, -ste subtle *ook* **fynsin'nig**

sub'tropies -e subtropical

suf (w) **ge-** dote; (b) dull, stupid, beef-witted

sug (s) -te sigh; passion; *'n ~ slaak (van verligting)* heave a sigh (of relief); (w) sigh

sugges'tie -s suggestion *ook* **voor'stel**

suid south

Suid-A'frika South Africa (SA); ~**ner/**~**an'** (mens) South African

sui'de south; ~**lik** southern, southerly; ~**like half'rond** southern hemisphere

Sui'der-A'frika Southern Africa

sui'derbreedte south latitude

Sui'derkruis Southern Cross

sui'dewind -e south wind

suid'kus -te south coast

suidoos' (-te) south-east

Suid'pool (s) South Pole

suidwes'telik -e south-westerly

sui'er -s piston; sucker; off-shoot, sprout

suig ge- absorb; suck, suckle

sui'ker (s) -s sugar; (w) sugar, sweeten; ~**bek'kie** sugarbird/sunbird *ook* **jangroen'= tjie;** ~**bedryf'** sugar industry; ~**klon'tjie** lump of sugar; ~**oom'pie** (idiom.) sugardad= dy; ~**riet** sugar cane; ~**siek'te** diabetes

suil -e column, obelisk *ook* **gedenk'naald**

sui'nig sparing, stingy; frugal, economical

suip ge- drink (animals); booze; ~**lap** tippler, boozer; ~**party'** binge, spree

suis ge- rustle, buzz; tingle (in ears)

sui'te (uitspr. *swiete*) suite (rooms, offices)

sui'wel butter and cheese, dairy products

sui'wer (w) **ge-** purify, refine, cleanse; purge; (b) pure (gold); clean (hands); sheer (nonsense)

suk'kel ge- progress poorly; trudge along; annoy someone; *hy ~ met sy gesondheid* he is in indifferent health; ~-~ struggling all along; ~**aar** bungler, stick-in-the-mud; ~**veld** rough (golf) *ook* **ru'veld**

sukses' -se success; *ek wens jou ~!* good luck to you!; ~**boek** bestseller *ook* **tref'ferboek/ blits'verko'per;** ~**jag** rat race *ook* **rot'ren**

sukses'vol -le; -ler, -ste successful

sul'ke such; ~ *domkoppe!* such fools!

sult brawn (meat dish) *ook* **hoof'kaas**

summier' -e summary, without formalities; ~**e ontslag'** summary/instant dismissal

superintendent' -e superintendent

superlatief' ..**tiewe** superlative

su'permark -te supermarket

superso'nies -e supersonic

su'ring sorrel (plant)

sur'plus surplus, excess *ook* **oor'skot**

surrogaat': ~**moe'der** surrogate mother *ook* **leen'moeder**
sus (w) ge- hush, quiet (a child); pacify; soothe; *sy gewete* ~ silence his conscience; ~**mid'del** tranquilliser
suspi'sie suspicion *ook* **ag'terdog**
sus'sie -s little sister
sus'ter -s sister; ~**lik** sisterly
suur (s) sure acid; (b) sour, acid, acetous; ~**deeg** yeast, leaven; ~**knol** sourpuss; ~**lemoensap'** lemon juice: *daar loop* ~*= lemoensap deur* there is something fishy about it; ~**reën** acid rain; ~**stof** oxygen
suut'jies = soetjies
swaai (s) -e swing *ook* **skoppelmaai'**; (w) swing; wave; *die septer* ~ rule the roost
swaan swane swan
swaap swape blockhead, fool, clot, idiot
swaar (b) heavy; ponderous; difficult
swaard -e sword, rapier
swaar'gewig heavyweight (boxer)
swaarly'wig corpulent, obese *ook* **geset'/vet**
swaarmoe'dig melancholy, dejected
swaar'te weight, heaviness; ~**krag** gravita= tion, gravity; ~**punt** centre of gravity
swa'el[1] (s) sulphur *ook* **swa'wel**
swa'el[2] (s) -s swallow (bird); ~**stert** dovetail (joint)
swa'el[3] (w) **ge-** drink, booze; *hy was lekker ge-* he had one too many
swa'elsuur/swa'welsuur sulphuric acid
swa'er -s brother-in-law
swak (s) weakness; (b) weak, infirm, delicate, feeble; faint; ~**ke'ling'** weakling
swaksin'nig -e mentally deficient, feeble= minded; ~**e** mentally deficient person
swam -me fungus *ook* **skim'mel**; agaric
swa'nesang -e swan song, death song
swang vogue; *in* ~ *wees* be in fashion
swan'ger pregnant *ook* **verwag'tend**; ~**skap** pregnancy
swart (s) black; (b) black
swartgal'lig (b) melancholy, morose
swart: ~ **man/vrou/kind** black (person); ~**mark** black market; ~**smeer** (w) slander
swartwit'pens -e sable antelope
sweef/swe'we ge- hover, glide; **sweef'arties** trapeze artiste; ~**stok** trapeze; ~**tuig** glider
sweep swepe whip, lash *ook* **karwats'**, **peits**
sweer[1] (s) swere abscess, sore, boil; ulcer *ook* **maag'seer**; (w) fester, ulcerate
sweer[2] (w) ge- vow; swear, take an oath; *hoog*

en laag ~ swear by all that is holy
sweet (s) perspiration; (w) perspire, sweat; ~**pak** tracksuit
sweis ge- weld; ~**er** welder
swel ge- swell, expand; ~**sel** swelling; tumour
swelg ge- gorge, swill; guzzle (food); ~**party'** booze party *ook* **dronk'nes** (s)
swem ge- swim; *gaan* ~ go for a swim; ~**bad** swimming bath; pool; ~**broek** swimming trunks; ~**duik** skindiving, findiving; ~**mer** swimmer; ~**pak** swimming costume/trunks
swen'del (w) swindle; ~**aar** swindler, racket= eer, conman; ~**ary'** scam (n) *ook* **be= drog(spul)/verneuk'spul**
swenk ge- swerve; sidestep (rugby)
swerf/swerwe ge- roam, wander, rove
swerm -s swarm (birds, bees); flock, throng
swer'noot ..note rascal, rogue (person)
swer'wer -s wanderer, vagabond, rover; ~**s'= drang** wanderlust, roaming spirit
swets (b) ge- swear, curse *ook* **vloek**
swetterjoel' -e crowd, caboodle, lot
swier (s) elegance, gracefulness; swagger; (w) loaf, be on the spree; ~**bol** wild spark; playboy *ook* **pie'rewaaier**, **dar'teldawie** (idiom.); ~**ig** elegant, stylish
swig ge- yield, give in
swik ge- sprain (ankle); twist
swoeg ge- drudge, toil and moil
swoel sultry, close, oppressive (climate)
swoerd (s) crackling
swyg (w) **ge-** be silent, keep quiet/mum; ~ *soos die graf* remain silent as the grave; ~**geld** hush money
swyn -e hog, pig *ook* **vark**; swine; *pêrels voor die* ~*e werp/gooi* cast pearls before (the) swine
sy[1] (s) silk; ~ *dra* ~ she wears silk
sy[2] (s) -e side; *met die hande in die* ~*e* with arms akimbo; ~ ~ *is seer* his side is aching/ sore
sy[3] (pers. vnw) she; (besit. vnw) its, his
sy'fer[1] (s) -s figure, number; par, bogey (golf); ~**horlo'sie** digital watch
sy'fer[2] (w) **ge-** ooze (through); ~**put** French drain *ook* **sy'pelput**
syg ge- strain, percolate, filter
sy'ne his, 's; *dis Piet* ~ *(s'n)* that is Peter's; *dis* ~ that is his
sy'paadjie -s sidewalk, pavement
sy'pel ge- seep, drain; ~**put/**~**riool'** French drain
sy'sie -s seed eater, siskin (small bird)
sy'wurm -s silkworm

T

't: *aan* ~ *speel* playing; *as* ~ *ware* as it were
taai tough, wiry; sticky; *so* ~ *soos 'n ratel* as
tough as nails; ~ **wed'stryd** hard/tough
match; ~**pitper'ske** clingstone peach
taak take task, job, duty; assignment; ~**groep**
task group; ~**mag** task force
taal tale language, speech; ~**kunde** grammar;
linguistics
taalkun'dig -e grammatical, linguistic
taal: ~**laborato'rium** language laboratory;
~**onderwy'ser** language teacher; ~**skat**
vocabulary (of a language) *ook* **woor'deskat**
taam'lik (b) **-e** fair, tolerable; (bw) rather,
fairly; ~ *goed* fairly good
taan tan (colour) *ook* **geel'bruin**
T-aan'sluiting T-junction
tabak' tobacco; ~**boetiek'** tobacconist's shop,
smoker's emporium; ~**sak** tobacco pouch
tab'berd -s dress, frock *ook* **rok/japon'**
tabel' -**le** table; index
tablet' -**te** tablet, lozenge
tablo' -**'s** tableau
taboe' taboo *ook* **verbo'de**
tabuleer'/tabelleer' ge- tabulate
ta'fel -s table; ~ *dek* lay the table
ta'fel: ~**geld** service charge (restaurant); ~**heer**
master of ceremonies *ook* **seremo'niemees=
ter**; ~**re'de** after-dinner speech; ~**ten'nis**
table tennis
tafereel ..**rele** scene, picture *ook* **toneel'**
tag'tig eighty; *die jare T*~ the Eighties
tag'tigjarige -s octogenarian (person)
tag'tigste -s eightieth
tak -ke branch, bough; tine (antler); *van die
hak op die* ~ *spring* jump from one subject
to another; *hoog in die* ~*ke wees* be three
sheets in the wind
tak'bok (n) stag, deer *ook* **hert**
ta'kel (s) **-s** tackle; (w) maul; rig; knock about,
confront; ~**aar** rigger (person)
tak'haar (s) backvelder *ook* **gom'tor**
taks estimate, rate, share; **Jan Taks** Receiver
of Revenue *ook* **Ontvan'ger van In'komste**
takseer' ~, **ge-** estimate, value, appraise
taksidermis' (s) taxidermist
takt tact; ~ *gebruik* exercise tact
taktiek' tactics
takt'vol tactful, judicious, discreet
tal number; ~**le voor'beelde** many examples

talent' -**e** talent, natural gift, ability *ook* **aan=
leg**; (b) talented, gifted
talm ge- linger, loiter, dawdle; ~**lont** delayed-
action fuse
tam tired, exhausted *ook* **uit'geput**
tamaai' (b) huge, colossal, enormous
tama'tie -s tomato; ~**pruim** persimmon
tamboer' -**e** drum, tambour; ~**nooi** drum
majorette *ook* **trom'poppie**
tand -**e** tooth; cog; tine; ~**arts** dentist
tan'de: ~**bor'sel** toothbrush; ~**pas'ta** tooth=
paste; ~**vlos** dental floss
tand: ~**rat** cogwheel; ~**vleis** gum; ~**vul'ling**
stopping, filling, plugging
tang -e (pair of) pliers, tongs; forceps
tan'nie -s auntie
tans now, at present; ~ *van Pretoria* presently
living in Pretoria
tant aunt (when followed by proper name);
Liewe ~ *Hester* Dear aunt Hester
tan'te -s aunt
tap (s) -**pe** tap (of a barrel); bung, spigot
(hole); (w) tap, draw
tapisserie' tapestry *ook* **muur'tapyt**
tap'toe tattoo (mil.); last post
tapyt' -**e** carpet *ook* **mat**; tapestry
tarentaal' ..**tale** guinea fowl
tarief' tariewe tariff; rate
tart (w) ge- taunt, provoke, challenge, defy
tas[1] (s) -**se** bag; pouch; scan
tas[2] (w) ge- feel, touch, grope; *in die duister* ~
grope in the dark
tas'baar (b) tangible, palpable; **tas'bare
bewys'** tangible token/proof
tatoeëer' (w) ge- tattoo
ta'xi -'s taxi
te (bw) too; ~ *sleg* too bad; (vs) to, at, on, in;
~ *huur* to let; ~ *alle tye* at all times
teak (s) teak *ook* **kiaathout**
tea'ter -s theatre *ook* **skou'burg**
ted'diebeer (s) teddybear
tee tea
te'ë against; tired of
teef (s) **tewe** bitch
te'ëhanger -s counterpart, opposite number
ook **amps'genoot** (mens)
te'ël -s tile
teel ge- breed, rear, raise (animals)
tee'lepel -s teaspoon

teen against, to, towards, versus
teen': ~**aan'val** counterattack; ~**deel** contrary; *die* ~*deel is waar* the contrary is true; ~**gif** antidote; ~**maat'reël** countermeasure; ~**mid'del** antidote, remedy; ~**offensief'** counteroffensive
teenoor'gestel(d) -de opposite, contrary
teen: ~**produktief'** counterproductive; ~**reak'sie** backlash; ~**spoed** adversity, ill-fortune; breakdown; ~**spoedwa** breakdown van; ~**staan** resist; ~**stand** resistance, opposition: ~*stand bied* offer resistance; ~**stan'der** adversary, opponent (person)
teen'stelling -s, -e contrast, set-off; *in* ~ *met sy broer* unlike his brother
teen: ~**stem** (s) dissenting/negative vote; ~**strib'bel** kick against, resent
teenstry'dig (b) -e contradictory, conflicting
teenswoor'dig -e nowadays, at present; *kos is* ~ *baie duur* food these days is expensive
teen'verkeer approaching/oncoming traffic
teenwoor'dig (b) -e present; *veertien lede is* ~*/ aanwesig* there are fourteen members present; ~**e tyd** present tense; ~**heid** presence: ~*heid van gees* presence of mind
te'ëpraat -ge- contradict
teer¹ (s) tar; (w) tar; *iem.* ~ *en veer* tar and feather someone
teer² (w) **ge-** consume; live/sponge on
teer³ (b) **-der, -ste** tender; slender; delicate; *'n* ~ *punt* a sore point
teer: ~**pad** tarred road; ~**straat** tarred/asphalt street; ~**tou** dirty fellow *ook* **tak'haar**
te'ësin aversion, dislike
te'ëspoed = **teen'spoed**
te'ëvoeter -s antipode; opposite (of)
tef teff (grass)
tegelyk' together, at the same time; *almal* ~ all together; ~**ertyd'** simultaneously, concurrently
tegemoet'kom -gekom meet halfway; ~**ing** partial compensation; willingness to accommodate
tegniek' technique
teg'nies -e technical; ~**e bena'minge/ter'me** technical terms; ~**e uit'klophou** technical knockout (k.o.)
teg'nikus -se technician (person)
tegnologie' technology
tehuis' -e hostel, home; ~ *vir bejaardes* old-age home, home for senior citizens
tei'ken -s target *ook* **doel'wit**; *sagte* ~ soft

target; ~**da'tum** target date; ~**skiet** rifle practice
teis'ter (w) **ge-** afflict, ravage, scourge
teken (s) **-s** sign; token; signal; mark; (w) sign; draw; ~**aar** draftsman, designer; ~**ing** drawing, sketch; ~**kryt** crayon; ~**prent** comics *ook* **prent'verhaal**
tek'kie -s (pair of) tackies
tekort' -e deficit, shortage; ~**ko'ming** shortcoming, imperfection
teks -te text; ~**boek** textbook, manual
tekstiel': ~**goe'dere** soft goods; ~**ny'werheid/** ~**bedryf'** textile industry
teks'verwerker -s word processor *ook* **woord'verwerker**
tel (w) count; ~**bord** scoreboard
telefaks telefax
telefoneer' (w) ~, **ge-** telephone *ook* **(op)bel**
telefonis' -te telephone operator
telefoon' ..**fone** telephone; ~**gids** telephone directory; ~**nom'mer** telephone number; ~**op'roep** telephone call; ~**sentra'le** telephone exchange
telegram' -me telegram, wire
telekommunika'sie telecommunication
te'leks (s) -e telex; (w) telex
telepatie' telepathy *ook* **gedag'te-oordrag**
teleskoop' ..**skope** telescope *ook* **vêr'kyker**
teleur'gestel(d) -de disappointed
teleur'stel -gestel disappoint, baffle; ~**ling -s, -e** disappointment
televi'sie television
tel'kens every time, ever and anon
tel'ler (s) -s counter; scorer; teller (bank)
tel'ling -s, -e score (games); census; numeration, counting
tel'raam ..**rame** abacus, ballframe *ook* **ab'akus**
tel'woord -e numeral
tem (w) **ge-** tame, break in, subdue
te'ma -s theme, subject
tem'pel -s temple; shrine
temperament' -e temperament, temper
temperatuur' ..**ture** temperature; **aan'voel**~ wind-chill factor
tem'po -'s tempo, pace, rate; *die* ~ *versnel* quicken the pace
ten at, in; ~ *behoewe van* in aid of; ~ *einde (aflewering te bespoedig)* in order to (expedite delivery); ~ *opsigte van* with respect to; ~ *spyte van* in spite of; ~ *tye/ tyde van* at the time of

ten'der (s) -s tender; offer; (w) tender
tenk -s, -e tank; cistern
ten min'ste/tenmin'ste at least
ten'nis tennis; ∼**baan** tennis court; ∼**bal** tennis ball; ∼**spe'ler** tennis player
tenniset' tennisette *ook* **dwerg'tennis**
tenoor' tenore tenor (male singer)
tensy' unless
tent -e tent; hood; ∼ *opslaan* pitch tent; ∼**ma'ker** parttime church minister
tentoon'stelling -s show, exhibition *ook* **skou**
teolo'gies -e theological; ∼**e skool** theological seminary
teore'ties -e theoretical
teorie' -ë theory
te'pel -s nipple, teat *ook* **tet/tiet, speen**
ter at, to, in; ∼ *dood veroordeel* sentence to death; ∼ *wille van* for the sake of
terapie' therapy *ook* **genees'wyse**
terapeut' -e therapist (person)
terde'ë thoroughly, duly
tereg' rightly, justly, in good reason; ∼**stel'ling** execution; ∼**wys** admonish
terg ge- tease, annoy, nag; ∼**gees** nagging fellow, tease *ook* **plaag'gees**
te'ring consumption (phthisis, tuberculosis, pneumoconiosis, silicosis)
terloops' (b) -e casual, incidental; (bw) in= cidentally; ∼, *wat doen ons môre?* by the way, what are our plans for tomorrow?
term -e term; *nuwe* ∼*e vir* new terms/names for
termiet' -e termite, white ant
terminaal' ..ale terminal; ..ale **pasiënt'** term= inal patient
terminologie' terminology, nomenclature
ter'minus -se, ..ni terminus *ook* **eind'halte**
ter'mometer -s thermometer
termyn' -e term, time, period; *binne die vasgestelde* ∼ within the appointed time; ∼**reses'** midterm break
terneer'gedruk (b) depressed, downhearted
ternou'ernood scarcely, hardly
terpentyn' turpentine, oil of terebinth
terras' -se terrace
terrein' -e building site; ground; sphere, domain; area
terreur' terrorism *ook* **skrik'bewind**
terroris' -te terrorist (person)
tersiêr -e tertiary; ∼**e on'derwys** tertiary education
tert -e tart; ∼**pan** pastry pan, pie plate

terug' back, backwards; ∼**gaan** go back, retrace; ∼**gee** return, restore, give back; ∼**keer** return; ∼**kom** come back; return; ∼**reis** return journey; ∼**slag** recoil; setback, reverse; ∼**trek** retreat, withdraw, retract; ∼**voer(ing)** feedback; ∼**wer'kend:** ∼*wer= kend van* retrospective/retroactive from
terwyl' while, as
te'sis -se thesis *ook* **proef'skrif**
tesourie' treasury; ∼**r'** treasurer (person)
testament' (s) -e testament, will
te'tanus tetanus *ook* **kaak'klem**
teu'el -s bridle, rein
tevergeefs' in vain, futile
tevo're before, previously
tevre'de (b) satisfied, content(ed); ∼ *stel* satisfy, please; ∼**nheid** satisfaction
tien -e ten; ∼**de** tenth; ∼**des betaal** pay tithes; ∼**de'lig** decimal; ∼**er/∼derja'rige** teenager; ∼**er'drag** teenage dress/clothes; ∼**kamp** decathlon; ∼**keg'elbaan** tenpin (bowling) alley; ∼**tal** decade; ∼**uur** ten o'clock; ∼**voud** tenfold
tier[1] (s) -e, -s tiger; SA leopard
tier[2] (w) ge- thrive, flourish; rage
tierlantyn'tjie (s) -s flourish; trifle
tier: ∼**melk** strong drink; *hy is ge*∼ he is in= toxicated; ∼**wy'fie** tigress; hellcat (woman); *so kwaai soos 'n* ∼*wyfie* a veritable shrew
tifoon' tifone typhoon
ti'fus typhus fever *ook* **luis'koors**; camp fever
tik (s) -ke pat, touch, rap; (w) tap, rap; type; *van lotjie ge*∼ have a screw loose; *op die vingers* ∼ reprimand; ∼**masjien'** typewriter; ∼**skrif** typing, typewriting; ∼**poel** typing pool; ∼**ster** typist
tim'mer ge- build, construct (by carpentry); ∼**hout** timber; ∼**man** carpenter
tin tin; pewter *ook* **piou'ter**; ∼**erts** tin ore
tin'gel ge- tinkle, jingle
tin'ger/ten'ger (b) slender, frail, delicate
tinktin'kie (s) -s (Cape) warbler, wren, tink= tinkie
tint -e tinge, hue, tint
tin'tel (w) ge- twinkle, sparkle
tip -pe tip; point (of leaves)
ti'pe -s type, character
tipeer' (w) ∼, ge- typify
ti'pies -e typical *ook* **kenmer'kend**
tiran' -ne tyrant *ook* **despoot'** (mens)
ti'tel -s title; heading; ∼**ak'te** title deed; ∼**rol** title role/part

tja'lie -s shawl, wrap *ook* **serp**

tjank ge- yelp, howl; ~**ba'lie** crybaby

tjek[1] (s) -s cheque; *gekruis'te* ~ crossed cheque; ~**boek** cheque book

tjek[2] (w) check; ~ *daardie syfers* check those figures; ~**lys** check list

tjel'lo -'s (violin)cello

tjienkerientjee' -s chinkerinchee (flower)

tjips (s) crisps (in packet); chips (with fish) *ook* **slap'tjips/sky'fies**

tjoep'stil very quiet, absolutely silent

tjok'ker(tjie) young chappie *ook* **kan'netjie**

tjom/tjom'mie chum, pal

tjop chop (meat)

tjop-tjop in no time, in a jiffy

tjor(rie) jalopy, old/dated motorcar

tjor'lapper -s backyard mechanic

toe[1] (b) closed; dumb, fuzzy-brained, stupid; *die winkels is* ~ the shops are closed; *hy is darem* ~ isn't he stupid?

toe[2] (bw) then; in those days; *van* ~ *af* since then

toe[3] (bw) to, towards; *sleg daaraan* ~ *wees* be badly off

toe[4] (vgw) when; while; ~ *ek daar kom, was hy in die bed when I got* there he was in bed

toe[5] (tw) do! please! ~ *maar!* never mind!; *help my,* ~? won't you please help me?

toe'behore (s) accessories *ook* **by'behore**; adjuncts, fittings

toe: ~**brood'jie** sandwich; ~**doen** assistance; aid; *deur jou* ~*doen was ek laat* through your doing I was late; ~**draaipapier'** wrapping paper; ~**drag** particulars, circumstances; *ware* ~*drag van sake* the ins and outs of the affair; ~**gang** entrance, admission; access; ~**geete'ken** yield sign; ~**gene'ë** kindly disposed, affectionate; *jou* ~**geneë** *vriend* yours sincerely/affectionately; ~**gepas'** applied; ~**gepas'te wis'kunde** applied mathematics; ~**ge'wing** concession; ~**gif** bonus; encore; ~**hoor'der** hearer; ~**hoor'ders** audience; ~**juig** cheer, applaud, approve; ~**jui'ging** (s) applause, cheer

toe'ka very remote; *van* ~ *se dae (af)* from time immemorial; ~**mo'tor** vintage/veteran car

toe'ken -ge- award; allot; ~**ning** award, prize; grant

toe'komend -e next, future; ~**e tyd** future tense

toe'koms future; *in die* ~ in future

toe'kring-TV closed-circuit TV *kyk* **kring'televisie**

toe: ~**laag/**~**'lae** gratification, subsidy; bonus, allowance; ~**laat** admit, permit, allow

toe'lating admission/admittance; permission; ~**(s)eksa'men** entrance examination

toe'lig -ge- illustrate, elucidate, explain

toe'nader (w) approach; ~**ing** friendly advance, reconciliation; ~**ing soek** make friendly overtures; compromise

toe'name increase *ook* **sty'ging**

toe'neem -ge- increase; become worse; *toenemende belangstelling* growing interest

toen'tertyd then *ook* **des'tyds**

toe'pas -ge- put into practice, implement

toepas'lik suitable, appropriate, fitting, applicable; relevant

toer (s) -e tour, excursion; trick; (w) tour, travel; ~**bus** tourbus, motor coach

toe'reteller -s rev(olutions) counter

toeris' -te tourist (person); ~**me** tourism

toernooi' -e tournament

toe'rus -ge- equip; ~**ting** equipment

toe'sig supervision; surveillance; care; ~ *hou* supervise; invigilate; ~**hou'er** invigilator (exam.), supervisor (factory)

toe: ~**skou'er** spectator, onlooker; ~**skryf/** ~**skrywe** ascribe/attribute to; ~**sluit** lock up; close; ~**spits:** ~*spits op* concentrate on; ~**spraak** address, speech; *'n* ~*spraak lewer/ hou* deliver a speech; *'n* ~*spraak klok* time someone's speech; ~**spreek** address; ~**staan** allow, permit, grant; ~**stand** state, condition, circumstances; ~**stel** apparatus, appliance, device

toe'stem grant, consent, agree; ~**ming** consent, permission, approval

toet (w) ge- blow a horn, hoot *ook* **toe'ter**

toe'ter (s) -s horn, hooter; (w) hoot

toets (s) -e key (piano); test; trial; ~**bord** keyboard; (w) test, try; ~**rit** trial run; ~**saak** test case; ~**vlug** test flight; ~**wed'stryd** test match ·

toe'val[1] (s) accident, chance, coincidence; *blote* ~ (mere) coincidence

toe'val[2] (s) -le fainting fit

toe'val[3] (w) -ge- fall to the lot of; cave in

toe'val[4] (w) -ge- accrue to (interest)

toeval'lig (b) casual, accidental; (bw) accidentally, by chance

toe'vertrou ~ entrust; confide; *iem. 'n geheim* ~ confide a secret to a person toe'vlug refuge, recourse; ~ tot 'n vriend neem seek a friend's aid; ~(s)oord' refuge, sanctuary

toe'voer (s) supply; (w) supply; ~diens feeder service; ~pad access road

toe'wy -ge- dedicate, consecrate, devote; ~dings= formulier' act of dedication ook diens'gelofte

tof'fie (s) toffee; ~-ap'pel toffee apple

tog[1] (s) -te draught, current of air; expedition, journey, trip

tog[2] (bw) yet, still, all the same; hy is siek, ~ kom hy skool toe he is ill, yet he comes to school

to'ga -s gown, robe, toga (academic)

tog'snelheid ..hede cruising speed

toi'ings rags, tatters

toilet' -te toilet; ~papier' toilet paper

toi-toi (w) toyi-toyi(ng)

tok'kel ge- touch (string of a musical instru= ment), strum, twang; ~klavier' honkytonk piano

tokkelok' -ke theological student (sl)

toktok'kie -s tapping beetle; tick-tock (boys' prank)

tol[1] -le top; (w) spin, turn; ~dro'ër spindrier

tol[2] tribute, customs; toll; ~geld toll, customs; ~hek tollgate; ~pad tollroad; ~vry tollfree

tolk (s) -e interpreter (person); (w) interpret

tol'lenaar -s, ..nare publican

tol'letjie -s reel, bobbin

tom'be -s tomb ook graf'kelder

ton -ne cask, tub; ton (weight); ~ne geld tons of money

toneel' tonele scene; stage; ~gesel'skap/~groep theatrical company, performing group; ~in= kleding decor; ~op'voering dramatic perfor= mance; ~skry'wer dramatist ook dramaturg'; ~spe'ler actor; player; ~stuk play

tong -e tongue; sole (fish); ~kno'per tongue twister ook snel'sêer; ~vis sole

to'nikum ..ka tonic (medication)

ton'nel (s) -s tunnel; subway; (w) tunnel

ton'nemaat tonnage

tonsilli'tis tonsillitis ook man'gelontsteking

tooi (w) ge- adorn, decorate, array, trim; ~tas'sie vanity case ook smuk'tassie

toom -s, tome bridle

toon[1] (s) tone toe; van kop tot ~ from head to foot

toon[2] (s) tone pitch (of voice); tone

toon[3] (s): ten ~ stel exhibit; (w) show, in= dicate, demonstrate

toon: ~bank counter; ~beeld model, exam= ple; ~kas display case/cabinet; ~lad'der scale, gamut; ~lokaal' showroom

toon'set ge- put to music, compose; ~ting (musical) composition

toon'venster -s display window

toor ge- conjure, practise witchcraft; ~dok'ter witchdoctor; ~kuns sorcery, magic, witch= craft; ~kuns'tenaar magician ook kul'= kunstenaar; ~medisy'ne muti ook moe'tie/ doe'pa

toorn (s) anger, wrath

toorts -e torch (flame)

top[1] (s) -pe summit, peak, top, tip

top[2] (w) ge- top, trim

top: ~bestuur' top management; ~punt summit, peak; zenith; ~swaar top-heavy; ~verko'per bestseller ook blits'verko= per

tor -re beetle; clodhopper (person)

to'ring -s tower, steeple

torna'do -'s tornado, whirlwind

torpe'do -'s torpedo

tor'ring (b) ge- rip up, unpick; pester/bother

tor'telduif ..duiwe turtle dove

tot to, until, till; ~ dusver/dusvêr up till now; ~ en met up to and including; ~ siens!/ totsiens'! so long! ook goed'gaan!

totaal' (s) tota'le total amount; (bw) altogether

tot'dat until, till

tou[1] (s) -e string, twine, cord; rope

tou[2] (s) -e queue; (w) straggle after; walk in tandem; queue up

tou: ~spring skip; ~staan form a queue

tou'trek (s) tug-of-war; (w) pull at tug of war; wrangle

tou'wys: iem. ~ maak show someone the ropes

to'wenaar -s sorcerer, wizard; magician

to'wer ge- enchant, charm; ~heks witch; ~staf magic wand

town'ship (s) township ook woon'buurt

traag slow, indolent, inert; dull

traak concern; dit ~ my nie I don't care

traan (s) trane tear; trane stort shed tears; (w) water (eyes)

traan'rook tear smoke ook traan'gas

tradi'sie -s tradition ook oor'lewering

tra'gies -e; -er, -ste tragic

trajek' -te trajectory; stretch, stage

traktaat' ..tate treaty, tract

trakteer' ~, ge- treat, entertain; iem. op 'n drankie ~ stand someone a drink

tra'lie -s trellis, lattice; *agter die* ~**s** *sit* be be=
hind bars/in jail
trampolien -s trampoline *ook* **wip'mat**
tra'ne: ~**dal** vale of tears; ~**trek'ker** tearjer=
ker (film, book)
transak'sie -s transaction, deal *ook* **akkoord',**
ooreen'koms
transforma'sie -s transformation
transport' -e transport; ~**ak'te** deed of transfer;
title deed (property)
trant manner, style; *op die ou* ~ as usual
trap[1] (s) **-pe** trample, kick; (w) kick, tread;
flee, go away, scoot; thresh
trap[2] (s) **-pe** staircase; step; degree; pedal;
stellende, vergrotende en oortreffende ~
positive, comparative and superlative degree
trap: ~**fiets** pushbike; ~**kar** pedal car; ~**leer**
stepladder
trapsoe'tjies/trapsuut'jies -e chameleon; slow=
coach (person)
tras'sie -s hermaphrodite; freemartin
trau'ma/trou'ma trauma; *'n* ~*tiese ondervin*=
ding a traumatic experience
tred pace, tread, step; *(gelyke)* ~ *hou met* keep
abreast of
tree (s) **treë** pace, step; (w) pace, tread, step;
in diens ~ enter service; *in die huwelik* ~
marry; ~**plank** running board, footboard
tref ge- hit, strike; fall in with, come across;
maatreels ~ take steps; ~**af'stand** effective
range: *binne* ~*afstand* within range; ~**-en-**
trap'voorval hit and run case; ~**fend** (b)
striking, stirring, touching; ~**fer(boek)** best=
seller; ~**ferpara'de** hit parade (radio)
treg'ter -s funnel
treil ge- tow; ~**er** trawler *ook* **vis'treiler**
trein -e train; *die* ~ *haal* catch the train; *die* ~
mis/verpas miss the train; ~**dry'wer** train
driver
trei'ter ge- tease, taunt, torment *ook* **tart**
trek (s) **-ke** pull; migration; stage (bus);
draught; *in breë* ~*ke* in broad outline; (w)
pull, draw, haul; move; migrate; be draughty;
in twyfel ~ doubt; ~**ar'beid** migrant labour;
~**ker** puller; trekker, emigrant; tractor;
~**klavier'** accordion; ~**pas** dismissal: *die*
~*pas kry* be discharged/sacked; ~**pleis'ter**
drawcard; lover; ~**skaal(tjie)** spring balance;
~**slui'ter** zip fastener *ook* **rit(s)slui'ter;**
~**vo'ël** bird of passage
trem -s, -me tram; ~**bus** trolleybus
treur ge- mourn, grieve for; ~**ig** sad, mournful,

gloomy; ~**ige** verto'ning miserable perfor=
mance; ~**mars** funeral march; ~**sang** elegy,
dirge; ~**spel** tragedy; ~**wilg(er)** weeping
willow
tries'tig -e; -er, -ste gloomy, sad; dismal
tril'ling -s, -e vibration *ook* **vibra'sie;** tremor
trim'park -e trimpark
triomf' -e triumph, victory *ook* **oorwin'ning**
tri'plo -'s triplicate *ook* **drie'voud**
trip'pel ge- trip along; tripple (horse)
troebadoer' -s troubadour *ook* **min'nesanger**
troe'bel -er, -ste muddy, turbid *ook* **mod'derig**
troef (s) **troewe** trump; (w) trump
troep -e troop, group; troupe (actors)
troe'pe troops, forces; ~**dra'er** troop carrier;
~**mag** military force
troe'tel (w) ge- pet, fondle, caress, coddle *ook*
lief'koos; pamper; ~**dier** pet animal; ~**dier-**
win'kel petshop *ook* **ark'mark** (idiom.)
trofee' trofeë trophy *ook* **be'ker**
trof'fel -s trowel
trog trôe, -ge trough; manger
troglodiet' -e cave dweller, troglodyte
trok -ke truck
trol'lie -s trolley *ook* **dien'wa(entjie)**
trom -me drum (music)
trombo'se thrombosis *ook* **aar'verstopping**
trom'mel -s (steel) trunk; canister; tympanum,
eardrum; ~**dik** quite filled, with a full
stomach
trompet' -te trumpet; ~**bla'ser** trumpeter
trom'pie -s mouth harp, jew's-harp
tromp'op point-blank; close; *iem.* ~ *loop*
rebuke someone unceremoniously; ~**bot'-**
sing head-on collision *ook* **front'botsing**
trom'poppie -s drum majorette
tronk -e prison, jail; *van nuuskierigheid is die*
~ *vol* curiosity killed the cat; ~**bewaar'der**
prison warder *ook* **korrektie'we beamp'te;**
~**vo'ël** jailbird; habitual criminal
troon (s) **trone** throne; ~**op'volger** heir to the
throne
troos (s) comfort, consolation; (w) console,
comfort; *skrale troos* cold comfort; ~**prys**
consolation/booby prize
trop -pe flock (sheep); troop (baboons); herd
(cattle); pride (lions)
tro'pies -e tropical
trop'sluitertjie -s youngest child *ook* **laat'-**
lammetjie
tros (s) bunch, cluster; (w) cluster; ~**behui'-**
sing cluster housing *ook* **korf'behui'sing**

trots (s) pride, haughtiness; (b) proud, haughty
trotseer' (w) ~, **ge-** go against, defy, with=
stand, challenge; brave
trou[1] (s) fidelity, faith; *te goeder* ~ in good
faith; ~ *sweer aan* swear allegiance to; (b)
faithful, true
trou[2] (w) **ge-** marry, wed; *met iem.* ~ marry
someone; **pas'getroude paar'tjie** newly-
wed couple; ~**dag** wedding day
tru'beeld -e replay (TV)
trui -e jersey
tru: ~**kaat'ser** reflector; ~**knal** backfire;
~**projek'tor** overhead projector; ~**rat** re=
verse gear; ~**spie'ël(tjie)** rearview mirror
trust -e trust (person); ~**ee** trustee
tru'tol backspin (of a ball)
truuk -s trick, gimmick
tset'sevlieg..vlieë tsetse fly
tug (s) discipline, punishment; (w) punish;
~**komitee'** disciplinary committee; ~**maat'**=
reël disciplinary measure; ~**mees'ter** dis=
ciplinarian (person)
tuig tuie harness; rigging
tui'mel ge- tumble, topple over; ~**dro'ër** tumble
dryer; ~**kar'retjie** roller coaster *ook* **wip'**=
waentjie
tuin -e garden; ~**beplan'ner/argitek'** landscape
gardener; ~**bou** horticulture; ~**hulp/**~**ier**
gardener; ~**slang** garden hose; ~**woon'stel**
granny flat
tuis at home; ~**blad** home page (Internet);
~**land** homeland; ~**ny'werheid** home indus=
try; ~**werk** (school) homework *ook* **huis'werk**
tulp -e tulip; ~**bol** tulip bulb
turf peat, turf
turksvy' -e prickly pear; tricky problem
tus'sen among, between; ~ *die reëls lees* read
between the lines
tus'senganger -s (inter)mediator, go-between
ook **bemid'delaar**
tussenin' in between, in among
tus'sen: ~**po'se** interval, pause; ~**tyd'se divi**=

dend' interim dividend; ~**verkie'sing** by-
election; ~**vloer** mezzanine; ~**werp'sel** in=
terjection
twaalf twelve; ~**de** twelfth; ~**uur** twelve
o'clock; lunch/dinner time
twak tobacco *ook* **tabak**; nonsense; piffle
twee tweë, -s two; ~ *maal/keer* twice
twee'de second; **T~ Kersdag (Welwil'lend**=
heidsdag) Day of Goodwill (Boxing Day);
~**hands** secondhand; ~**ns** secondly, in the
second place; ~**rangs** second rate; ~ **vloer/**
vlak second floor
twee: ~**drag** discord: ~*drag saai* sow the
seeds of discord; ~**geveg'** duel; ~**klank**
diphthong; ~**lettergre'pig** disyllabic;
~**ling** twin(s); ~**rom'per** catamaran (sail=
ing boat); ~**stryd** indecision; inward con=
flict; ~**ta'lig** bilingual; ~**uur** two o'clock;
~**voud** multiple of two: *in* ~*voud* in dupli=
cate
twin'tig twenty; ~**ste** twentieth
twis (s) -**te** quarrel, dispute, row *ook* **ru'sie**;
(w) quarrel; ~**ap'pel** apple of discord
twy'fel (s) doubt; (w) doubt
twyfelag'tig (b) dubious, doubtful
tyd tye time; tense; *te eniger* ~ at any time;
ten tye/tyde van at the time of; ~**(s)bere'**=
kening timing; ~**bom** time bomb; ~**deel** (s)
timeshare
tyd'delik (b) -**e** temporary (job)
ty'dens during *ook* **gedu'rende**
tyd: ~**genoot'** (s) contemporary (person);
~**gleuf** time slot
ty'dig timely, betimes; ~ *en ontydig* in season
and out (of season)
ty'ding -s, -e news, tidings *ook* **berig'**
tyd: ~**perk** period; ~**ren** rally (cars)
tydro'wend -e time consuming
tyd: ~**skrif** periodical/magazine; ~**stip** point
(of time): *op hierdie* ~*stip* now; at this point
in time; ~**ta'fel** timetable *ook* **roos'ter**;
~**verdryf'** pastime *ook* **stok'perdjie**

U

u (pers. vnw) you; (besit. vnw) your (singular
and plural); *ek waardeer* ~ *hulp* I appreciate
your help *kyk* **die u'we**
ui -e onion
ui'er (s) -**s** udder

uil -e owl; *soos 'n* ~ *op 'n kluit* alone and
perplexed; *'n* ~*tjie knyp/knip* take a nap;
~**s'kuiken** dunce, stupid, numskull *ook* **dom'**=
kop, skaap
uil'spieël -s clown, wag; rogue

uin'tjie -s nutgrass, nutsedge, uintjie(s)
uit (w) **ge-** utter, voice *ook* **ui'ter**; (b, bw) over, out, off; (vs) out, out of, from
uit'asem/uit'adem (w) **-ge-** exhale
uita'sem (b, bw) out of breath
uit'bars -ge- burst out; explode; erupt (volca= no); ~**ting** eruption
uit'beeld -ge- sketch, draw; depict
uit'betaal ~, pay out, disburse; *'n dividend* ~ pay a dividend
uit: ~**blaas** blow out; ~**bla'ker** blurt out; ~**blink** outshine, surpass, excel *ook* **pres= teer'**; ~**blinker** ace, crack, topdog
uit'braak (s) outbreak (of epidemic) *ook* **uit'= bre'king**
uit'breek -ge- break out; erupt, burst out
uit'brei -ge- extend, enlarge; spread; ~**ding** extension, enlargement
uit'broei -ge- hatch
uit'buit exploit, rip-off; take advantage of
uitbun'dig excessive; clamorous; ~**e vreug'de** hilarious joy
uit'daag -ge- challenge, defy; ~**be'ker** chal= lenge cup
uit'daging -s, -e challenge
uit'deel -ge- distribute, mete out, portion
uit'deler (s) dispenser (apparatus)
uit: ~**delg** exterminate; ~**dos** trim out, deck out; ~**draai** turn aside; turn out; ~**draaipad** turn-off
uit'druk -ge- express, squeeze out, ~**king** ex= pression *ook* **geseg'de**
uitdruk'lik (b) -e emphatic, explicit
uit'dun -ge- thin out; eliminate; cull (animals); ~**ron'de** elimination round/bout; ~**wed'= loop** heat (athletics)
uiteen' asunder, apart; ~**lo'pend** divergent, different; ~**set'ting** explanation; ~**sit** ex= plain, expound
uitein'delik finally, at last, ultimately
ui'ter ge- utter, voice *ook* **uit** (w)
uiteraard' by the nature of *ook* **uit die aard van**
ui'terlik (s) outward appearance, exterior; (b, bw) outward(ly), external(ly); ~ *30 Mei* not later than 30 May/May 30
ui'ters exceedingly, extremely; *dis* ~ *jammer* it is a great pity; ~ *dertig mense* thirty people at the most
ui'terste (s) -s death; extreme limit; (b) extreme, utmost, last; *jou* ~ *bes doen* do one's utmost
uit'faseer ~ phase out

uit'gaan -ge- go out; end in; emanate from
uit'gang -e exit, way out; ending; ~**s'punt** starting point *ook* **begin'punt**
uit'gawe -s expenditure, expenses; cost; edi= tion (of book); issue, impression
uit'gelate elated, exuberant, boisterous
uit'gelese choice, picked; ~ **gesels'kap** select/ distinguished company
uit: ~**gesla'pe** sly, cunning; wide awake; ~**ge= son'der** except, excluding; ~**gewe'kene** refugee, fugitive; expatriate (person)
uit'gewer -s publisher
uit'gif -te hand-out *ook* **strooi'biljet'; aan'de= le-uit'gifte** shares issue
uit'grawing -s, -e excavation; exhumation (corpse); cutting
uit'haler (s) -s ace; showy person *ook* **uit'= blinker**; (b) smart, showy; first-rate, crack; ~**spe'ler** crack player
uitheems' -e foreign, exotic
uit'hou -ge- bear, stand, endure; ~**vermo'ë** en= durance; ~**wed'ren** endurance race
ui'ting -e, -s saying, utterance; *tot* ~ *kom* find expression
uit: ~**jou** boo, barrack, hiss at; ~**kamp** camp= (out) *ook* **kampeer'**
uit'keer -ge- pay out, pay back, pay (divi= dend); ~**po'lis** endowment policy
uit'ken recognise, identify; ~**para'de** identi= fication parade
uit'klaar check out (of army); clarity, explain
uit'klop (w) beat out (dent); knockout (box= ing)
uit'kyk: *op die* ~ on the lookout; (w) look out
uit'laat (s) ..**late** outlet; exhaust (engine); (w) omit, skip, leave out; let out; express; ~**pyp** exhaust pipe
uit'lê (w) explain, elucidate *ook* **verklaar'**
uit'leen -ge- lend (out); ~**koers** lending rate
uit'leg layout, plan; explanation
uit'lek (w) leak (information)
uit'lewer -ge- extradite; hand over, surrender
uit'lok -ge- tempt, solicit; decoy; *baie kritiek* ~ arouse a great deal of criticism
uit'loof -ge- offer (a reward); institute/prom= ise/sponsor a prize
uit'loop (s) ..**lope** spillway; (w) walk out; result in; *op niks* ~ come to nothing
uit'loot (w) draw; raffle
uit'maak -ge- make out, settle; break off
uit: ~**mond in die oseaan** flow/discharge into

the ocean (a river); ∼**moor** massacre, butcher; ∼**munt** excel, surpass

uitmun'tend (b) excellent *ook* **voortref'lik**

uitne'mend excellent; *by* ∼*heid* par excel= lence

uit'nodiging -s, -e invitation

uit'nooi -ge- invite *ook* **nooi** (w)

uit'oefen -ge- practise, exercise; discharge (duties); exert *kyk* **be'oefen**

uit: ∼**oorlê** outmanoeuvre, get the better of, outwit; ∼**peul** protrude, bulge (eyes); ∼**plant** plant out; transplant; ∼**pluis** pick out, sift, ferret out; unravel

uit'put -ge- exhaust, deplete; ∼**ting** exhaus= tion; ∼**(tings)oor'log** war of attrition

uit'reik -ge- hand out, issue; *sertifikate* ∼ issue certificates; ∼**fonds** outreach fund; ∼**program'** outreach program(me)

uit'roei -ge- uproot; exterminate; *met wortel en tak* ∼ destroy altogether

uit'roep (s) **-e** exclamation, shout, cry; (w) call out, exclaim; *'n staking* ∼ call a strike; ∼**(ings)te'ken** exclamation mark

uit'ruil (w) exchange; ∼**student'** exchange student

uit'rus[1] **-ge-** repose, rest

uit'rus[2] **-ge-** equip, fit out; ∼**ter** outfitter; ∼**ting** outfit; equipment

uit'saai -ge- broadcast; ∼**sta'sie** broadcasting/ radio station

uit'sak -ge- bulge out; fall (rain); lag behind; ∼**ker** dropout (student) *ook* **skoolsta'ker**

uit'set -te marriage outfit, trousseau; output, yield; ∼**ting** expulsion (school); eviction (from house/flat); expansion (of joints)

uit'sien -ge- look out for; look forward to

uit'sig -te view; prospect; **onbelem'merde** ∼ unobstructed view; *met* ∼ *op die see* facing the sea; ∼**pad** scenic road

uit'sit -ge- expand, dilate; eject; evict, expel; *iem. by sy nooi* ∼ oust a rival; *'n dier* ∼ put down an animal; ∼**voeg** expansion joint

uit'skakel eliminate; cut out, disconnect

uit'skei -ge- cease, stop; *met/teen* ∼*tyd* at the close of play (cricket)

uit: ∼**skel** (w) scold, call names, abuse; ∼**skietstoel** ejection seat (aircraft); ∼**skop= ska'kelaar** trip switch

uit'skot rejects; rabble, riff-raff

uit'slag[1] rash (skin)

uit'slag[2] **..slae** result, issue; *die* ∼ *van die*

eksamen the examination results

uitslui'tend/uitsluit'lik exclusive(ly); solely

uit'smyt -ge- eject, chuck out; ∼**er** chucker-= out, bouncer (person)

uit: ∼**soek** select, choose, have one's pick; ∼**sonder** (w) except, exclude

uit'sondering -s, -e exception; ∼ *op die reël* exception to the rule

uit'span -ge- unharness, outspan, unyoke; ∼**ning** outspan place

uitspat'tend/uitspat'tig dissipated; ornate/ flamboyant *ook* **swie'rig**

uit'spraak ..sprake pronunciation; sentence, verdict; award; ∼ *voorbehou* reserve judg= ment

uit: ∼**spreek** pronounce, express; ∼**spring** jump out; bail out (from aircraft)

uit'staan -ge- endure, withstand; stand out; bulge out; *ek kan hom nie* ∼ *nie* I cannot bear him; ∼**de** outstanding (debt; achieve= ment); projecting (rock)

uit'stal -ge- display, exhibit; ∼**ling** display, exhibit; ∼**ven'ster** show window *ook* **toon'= venster**

uit'stap -ge- alight, step out; ∼**pie** excursion, trip, outing

uitste'dig -e out of town

uit'stek: *by* ∼ pre-eminently

uitste'kend -e excellent, superb *ook* **puik**

uit'stel (s) delay; postponement; *van* ∼ *kom afstel* procrastination is the thief of time; ∼ *gee* grant an extension of time; (w) delay, postpone

uit'sterf/uit'sterwe -ge- become extinct, die out

uit: ∼**stra'ling** radiation; emission; ∼**stryk** iron out; settle problem; ∼**tart** provoke, defy; ∼**teer** pine away, emaciate

uit'tog departure, exodus; flight

uit'trede/uit'treding retirement (from board)

uit'tree -ge- retire (as chairman); withdraw; ∼**pakket'** severance package *ook* **skei'= ding(s)pakket'**

uit'trek -ge- undress; march out (soldiers); extract, pull out (tooth)

uit'vaagsel scum, riff-raff *ook* **skuim** (mense)

uit'val (s) **-le** sally; sortie; clash/quarrel; outburst; (w) fall out

uit: ∼**veër** eraser, rubber; ∼**verkie'sing** pre= destination

uit'verkoop (w) sell out; *dit is* ∼ it is sold out

uit'verkoping -s, -e (clearance) sale

uit'verkore elect, select; *die* ~ *volk* the chosen people; ~**ne** favourite, chosen one (person)
uit'vind -ge- invent, find out; ~**ing** invention; ~**sel** contrivance, contraption
uit'vloei -ge- flow out; ~**sel** outcome, result
uit'voer (s) export; (w) execute; implement; perform; (s) ~**ing** performance (music)
uitvoer'baar **..bare** feasible, practicable *ook* **haal'baar**; ~**heidstu'die** feasibility study
uit'voerend -e executive; ~**e komitee'** executive committee; ~**e kun'ste** performing arts; ~**e oor'gangsraad** transitional executive council
uit'waarts outward; ~**e beleid'** outward policy
uit'weg **..weë** outlet, escape, way out
uitwen'dig -e external; outward; *vir* ~*e ge= bruik* not to be taken (medicine)

u'nie (s) union *ook* **een'heid**
uniek' **-e** unique *ook* **e'nig**
u'niform (s) **-s** uniform; (b) uniform *ook* **een= vor'mig**
universeel' **..sele** universal, all-embracing
universiteit' **-e** university; *op/aan* ~ at uni= versity; ~**s'graad** university/academic de= gree
uraan' uranium; ~**verry'king** uranium enrich= ment
uri'ne (s) urine *ook* **urien'**
uur ure hour; *om vyf*~ at five o'clock; *ter elfder ure* at the eleventh hour; ~**werk** timepiece, clock; ~**wy'ser/wys'ter** hour hand
u'we yours; **(hoog'agtend/opreg) die** ~ yours faithfully/sincerely

V

vaag (b) vague *ook* **ondui'delik**
vaak (b) **vaker, -ste** sleepy, drowsy; **Klaas Va'kie** Willie Winkie, sandman
vaal valer, -ste tawny; pale, sallow; drab
vaal'pens -e nickname for Transvaaler
vaan'del -s standard, flag, banner
vaar (w) ge- sail, navigate
vaar'dig (b) skilled, handy, dexterous
vaart **-e** cruise, navigation, leap, speed; ~**be= lyn'** streamlined
vaar'tjie: *uurdjie na sy* ~ like father like son
vaar'tuig **..tuie** vessel; (mv) watercraft
vaarwel' farewell, goodbye
vaas vase vase, flowerpot
vaat'jie -s barrel, tub; fatty (person)
va'bond -e rogue, (little) rascal; vagabond
va'dem -s fathom *ook* **vaam**
va'der -s father; sire (animal)
va'derland -e native country, fatherland, ~**er** patriot; ~**sliefde** patriotism
va'der: ~**lik** paternal, fatherly
va'dersnaam: *in* ~ for God's sake
va'doek -e dishcloth
vag -te fleece, pelt; fell, clipping (wool)
vak -ke subject; compartment, partition, pigeon hole; vocation, trade
vakan'sie -s holiday(s), vacation; ~ *hou* be on holiday; *met/op* ~ on holiday; ~**oord** holi= day resort
vakant' **-e** vacant; empty; ~**e pos** vacancy

vakatu're -s vacancy
vak'(ver)bond trade union *ook* **vak'unie**
vak: ~**ken'nis** vocational/technical knowl= edge; know-how, expertise; ~**leer'ling** ap= prentice; ~**man** expert, specialist artisan; ~**manskap'** workmanship; ~**on'derwys** technical/vocational education/instruction; ~**praat'jies** shop talk
val¹ (s) **-le** trap *ook* **strik**
val² (s) **-le** fall, downfall; gradient; (w) fall, drop; succumb; *in die oog* ~ catch one's eye; *in die rede* ~ interrupt; ~**byl** guillo= tine; ~**bylpot'** tiebreaker game (tennis)
val: ~**hek** boom; ~**helm** crash helmet
valk -e falcon, hawk; ~**e'nier'** falconer
vallei' -e valley, dale, vale
vall'end -e falling; ~**e siek'te** epilepsy
val'luik -e trapdoor; drop (gallows)
vals (b) false, phoney; forged, faked, artificial
val'skerm -s parachute; ~**troe'pe** para(chute) troops, parabats; ~**sprin'ger** (para)chutist
val'strik -ke trap, snare, pitfall
valueer' ~, **ge-** valuate, value, assess
valu'ta (foreign) currency; **bui'telandse** ~ foreign exchange
vampier' -e, -s vampire *ook* **bloed'suier**
van¹ (s) **-ne** surname, family name
van² (vs) of, from, with, by, for; ~ *jongs af* since childhood
vanaand' this evening, tonight

vanaf from
vandaal' ..dale vandal *ook* **verwoes'ter**
vandaan' from
vandaar' hence, that is why
vandag' today
vandalis'me vandalism *ook* **verniel'sug**
vandees'jaar this year
vandees'maand this month
vandees'week this week
vandi'sie/vendu'sie auction (sale/mart) *ook* **vei'ling**
vang ge- catch, seize, capture, trap; ~s catch, haul
vanjaar' this year
vanmekaar' asunder, separated; to pieces
vanmele'we/vansle'we in earlier times, in days of yore *ook* **toe'ka se dae/tyd**
vanmo're/vanmôre this morning
vannag' tonight; last night
vanself of its own accord; ~spre'kend obvious, self-evident, implied
vantevo're previous(ly), before *ook* **voor'heen**
vanweë on account of, because of, owing to
varia'sie -s variation *ook* **wis'seling**
varieer' ~, **ge-** vary, change
va'ring -s fern
vark -e pig, hog, swine; ~oor pig's ear; arum lily *ook* **a'ronskelk**; ~sog sow; ~vleis pork
vars -er, -ste fresh; ~ ei'ers new-laid eggs
vas¹ (w) **ge-** abstain from food, fast
vas² (b) firm, fixed; permanent; ~te ei'endom immovable property; (bw) firmly; soundly
vas'berade (b) resolute, strong-minded
vas: ~beslo'te determined; ~brand run dry, seize; get into difficulty
vas'goed immovable/landed property
vas'golf permanent wave; *sy laat haar hare* ~ she is going to have a perm
vas'keer (w) **-ge-** corner; drive into a corner
vas: ~klou cling to; ~lê steal, pinch; pilfer; ~maak fasten, tie
vas'pen -ge- control; *pryse* ~ peg prices
vas'stel -ge- fix, establish, ascertain, stipulate; *die skade* ~ assess the damage
vas'teland continent *ook* **kontinent'**
vas'trap (s) popular folk dance; (w) stand firm, persevere
vas'vra -ge- corner, quiz; ~wed'stryd quiz
vat¹ -e tub, barrel; vessel; vat; cask
vat² (s) grip, hold; (w) grip, take, catch, seize; grasp, understand; *koue* ~ catch a chill; *vlam* ~ catch fire

vee¹ (s) livestock; cattle, sheep
vee² (w) **ge-** sweep, wipe *ook* **veeg**
vee'arts -e veterinary surgeon
vee'boer -e livestock farmer, cattle farmer, sheep farmer; ~dery' stock farming
vee'dief cattle/stock thief, rustler; ~stal cattle/ stock rustling/raiding
veel (b, bw) **meer, meeste** much, many, frequently; *te* ~ too much
veel: ~belo'wend promising, hopeful; ~bete'= **kenend** significant *ook* ~seg'gend; ~ei'= **send** demanding, exacting
veelkeu'sig multiple choice; ~e vra'e multiple-choice questions *ook* **veel'keusevrae**
veels: ~ *geluk* hearty congratulations; ~ *te veel* altogether too much
veelsy'dig -e many-sided; versatile, all-round
veelvol'kig multinational, multiracial
veer¹ (s) **vere** spring; (w) spring
veer² (s) **vere** feather; (w) feather; ~boot ferry; ~gewig' featherweight; ~kombers' eiderdown (quilt) *ook* **ve'rekombers**
veer'kragtig -e elastic, resilient
veer'pyltjie -s dart(s) (game)
veer'tien -e fourteen; ~ dae a fortnight; ~de fourteenth
veer'tig -s forty; ~ste fortieth
vee: ~sta'pel (live)stock; ~teelt stock breed= ing; ~vei'ling cattle auction
veg (w) **ge-** fight, contend *ook* **baklei'**; ~bul= ter'riër pitbullterrier
vegeta'riër -s vegetarian (person)
veg: ~gees fighting spirit; ~kno'per promoter (boxing, wrestling); ~vlieg'tuig fighter plane
veg'ter -s fighter, combatant
vei'lig (b) **-e; -er, -ste** safe, secure
vei'ligheid (s) safety, security; ~s'gor'del safety belt *ook* **sit'plekgordel**; ~s'hal'we for safety's sake; ~s'raad Security Council (UN)
vei'ling -s, -e auction, sale *ook* **vandi'sie**
vel¹ (s) **-le** skin, hide; sheet
vel² (w) **ge-** pass (sentence); fell, cut down; *vonnis* ~ pass sentence
veld -e field, plain; ~fiets scrambler (bike); ~fliek drive-in theatre; ~maar'skalk field marshal; ~ren'ne scrambling; off-road ra= cing (cars); ~skoen home-made shoe, vel= skoen; ~slag battle; ~stoel folding stool, campstool; ~tog campaign
vel'ling -s felly, rim
vendu'sie -s auction, sale *ook* **vandi'sie**

vene'ries -e venereal (disease)

vennoot' ..note partner; ~skap partnership; die ~skap ontbind dissolve the partnership

ven'ster -s window; ~bank window sill; ~koevert' window envelope

vent[1] (s) -e fellow, chap, guy, bloke; 'n gawe ~ a decent chap; 'n snaakse ~ a funny guy/bloke

vent[2] (w) ge- hawk, peddle; ~er pedlar, hawker ook smous; informal trader

ventila'sie ventilation ook lug'vervarsing

venyn' venom, poison; ~ig (b) venomous ook bit'sig

ver/vêr far, remote, distant

ver'af/vêr'af far away, remote; ~ geleë remote

veraf'sku (w) ~ abhor, loathe, detest

verag' (w) ~ despise, disdain; ~telik' (b) despicable, contemptible

veral' especially; ~ hy he of all people

veran'der ~ change, modify; ~ing change, alteration; ~lik variable; fickle

verantwoor'delik (b) -e responsible, accountable; ~heid responsibility

veras' ~ cremate; ~-sing cremation

verbaal' verbale verbal; verba'le kommunika'sie verbal communication

verbaas' (w) ~ astonish, amaze; (b) astonished, amazed

verban' ~ banish, exile; expel (a person)

verband'[1] bandage (for an arm); dressing

verband[2] (s) -e bond, mortgage; eerste ~ first mortgage bond; (w) bond; (b) bonded; ~e ei'endom bonded property; ~ge'wer mortgagor; ~hou'er mortgagee

verband[3] connection, context; relation; in ~ met in connection with

verba'sing astonishment, amazement

verbas'ter ~ degenerate; hybridise

verbeel' ~ imagine; represent; be proud, fancy; hy ~ hom baie he is very conceited; ~ jou! just fancy!; ~ding fancy, imagination; pure ~ all imagination

verbe'ter ~ correct, improve, mend, rectify; ~(ing)skool reformatory; ~ing improvement, correction ook regstelling

verbeur' ~ forfeit; punte ~ lose marks

verbied' ~ prohibit, forbid; 'n boek ~ ban a book; rook ~/verbode no smoking

verbind' (w) ~ join; connect; combine; commit; bandage; ~ tot verandering committed to change

verbin'ding -s, -e connection, junction, com

bination; communication

verbin'tenis -se union, contract, agreement; ~student' agreement/contract student

verbit'ter(d) (b) embitter(ed), exasperate(d)

verblind' (w) dazzle, blind; ~end (b) glaring

verbloem' ~ disguise, conceal ook verslui'er

verbly' ~ gladden, please; ~dend joyous, gladdening; ~dende te'ken hopeful sign

verblyf' ..blywe residence, abode; ~permit' resident's permit; reis en ~ transport and subsistence

verbod' (s) prohibition; ban (on books); embargo (on imports)

verbo'de prohibited, forbidden; toegang ~ no admittance; ~ boek banned book

verbo'ë declined, inflected

verbond' -e treaty, league, covenant

verbon'de connected, linked, attached

verbouereerd' -e perplexed; flabbergasted

verbrand' (w) ~ burn; cremate (corpse); (b) burnt, charred; sunburnt/tanned

verbrands'! hang it all!; confound it!

verbreek' ~ break, bust; violate; 'n verlowing ~ break off an engagement

verbrou' ~ bungle, muddle; make a mess

verbruik' (s) consumption; (w) consume

verbrui'ker -s consumer; ~-(s)prysin'deks consumer price index; ~vrien'delik/~gun'stig consumer friendly

verbruiks'artikel -s consumer article

verby' past, beyond, dis alles ~ it is all over; ~gaan pass, go past; neglect; ~pad bypass

verby'praat -ge-: sy mond ~ let the cat out of the bag

verby'steek overtake (a car); (by)pass

verby'ster(d) perplexed, bewildered

verdaag' ~ adjourn (a meeting); postpone, prorogue

verdag' (b) -te suspicious, suspected; ~te (s) suspect (person/criminal)

verdamp' evaporate; ~ing evaporation

verde'dig ~ defend, stand up for; ~er defender; counsel for the defence

verde'diging defence

verde'digingsmag defence force ook weer'mag

verdeel' (w) divide, distribute; apportion

verdeeld -e divided; ~heid discord, strife

verden'king suspicion; mistrust; in/onder ~ under suspicion

ver'der/vêr'der farther, further; again

verderf' (s) ruin, destruction; perdition

verdien' ~ earn (salary); deserve, merit

verdien(d)′ (-de) deserved; *dis jou ∼de loon* that serves you right

verdien′ste merit; wages, earnings; **sertifi=kaat′ van** ∼ certificate of merit; **∼lik** meritorious, deserving, creditable

verdiep′ ∼ deepen; **∼ing** storey, floor; deepening; **onderste ∼ing** ground floor; **tweede ∼ing** second floor *ook* **tweede vloer/vlak**

verdink′ ∼ suspect; distrust

verdoel′ ∼ convert a try (rugby)

verdoem′ ∼ curse, damn; slam

verdof′ (w) ∼ dim; *jou ligte* ∼ dim one's lights *kyk* **domp**

verdoof′ (w) drug (anaesthetic); stun; deafen; **∼mid′del** anaesthetic *ook* **narko′se**

verdor (w) ∼ wither; (b) shrivelled up, parched, withered

verdo′wing stupor, numbness; anaesthesia

verdo′wingsmiddel anaesthetic

verdra′ ∼ bear, endure, tolerate, suffer; *ek kan hom nie* ∼ *nie* I can't bear him

verdraag′saam (b) tolerant, patient

verdraai′ ∼ twist, distort, contort

verdrag′ . .drae treaty, convention, pact

verdriet′ grief, sadness; **∼ig** (b) sad

verdrink′ ∼ drown; be drowned

verdruk′ ∼ oppress; **∼king** oppression

verdub′bel ∼ double; redouble; *jou winste* ∼ double your profits

verdui′delik ∼ elucidate, explain; clarify *ook* **verklaar′**; **∼ing** explanation

verduis′ter (w) ∼ eclipse (sun); obscure, dim; embezzle, defalcate (money); **∼ing** eclipse

verdwaal′ ∼ go astray, lose the way, get lost; *ek het skoon* ∼ I got lost completely

verdwyn′ (w) disappear, vanish

vereensel′wig ∼ identify (with)

vereer′ (w) honour (a person); respect, revere

veref′fen settle (a debt); pay up; adjust

vereis′ ∼ require, demand; **∼te** requirement, requisite; *aan alle ∼tes voldoen* satisfy all the requirements

ve′rekombers (s) eiderdown (quilt) *ook* **veer′=kombers**

vere′nig ∼ unite; reconcile; merge, amalgamate; **V∼de Na′sies** United Nations (UN); **∼baar** compatible (computers); **∼ing** society, association; combination

ver′erg (w) ∼ grow angry; *ek* ∼ *my vir hom* he annoys me; (b) angry

verf (s) **verwe** paint, dye; (w) paint; **∼kwas** paintbrush; **∼stro′per** paint remover

verfris′ ∼ refresh; **∼send** refreshing

verfyn′ (w) refine; **∼d** (b) refined, cultured

vergaan′ ∼ perish, decay; be wrecked (ship) *ook* **strand**

vergaap′ ∼: *hom* ∼ *aan* stare in wonderment

vergaar′ ∼ collect, gather *ook* **versa′mel**

verga′der ∼ meet, gather; assemble; **∼ing** meeting, assembly; gathering; *'n ∼ing (af)=sluit* close a meeting; *'n ∼ing belê* convene/call a meeting; *'n ∼ing verdaag* adjourn a meeting; **openba′re ∼ing** public meeting

vergas′ser -s carburettor

vergeef′/verge′we (w) forgive, pardon

vergeefs′ (b) **-e** futile *ook* **tevergeefs′**; idle; **∼e po′ging** abortive attempt; (bw) in vain

vergeet′ ∼ forget; *ek het skoon* ∼ I quite forgot; **∼ag′tig** forgetful

vergel′ding (s) reprisal, retaliation, retribution

vergele′ke compared; ∼ *met* in comparison with *ook: in vergelyking met*

vergelyk′ (s) **-e** compromise; arrangement, agreement; (w) compare

vergely′king -s, -e comparison; equation

vergesel′ (w) ∼ accompany (a person); attend

ver′gesig/vêr′gesig view, vista

ver′gesog/vêr′gesog (b) far-sought, far-fetched

verge′telheid oblivion

verge′we[1] ∼ forgive, forgave; ∼ *en vergeet* forgive and forget

verge′we[2] ∼ poison *ook* **vergif′tig**

vergif′nis pardon, forgiveness, indulgence

vergif′tig (w) ∼ poison; (s) **∼ing** poisoning

vergis′ ∼ mistake, be mistaken; **∼sing** mistake, error, slip (up)

vergoed (w) ∼ compensate; indemnify, reimburse; *skade* ∼ compensate; **∼ing** compensation; indemnification; reimbursement

vergroot′ ∼ enlarge, magnify, increase; **ver=gro′tende trap** comparative degree; **∼glas** magnifying glass

vergro′ting -s, -e enlargement; increase

vergun′ning -s, -e permission; concession, licence; *met vriendelike* ∼ *van* by courtesy of, with kind permission of

verhaal (s) **..hale** narrative, story, account; (w) narrate, tell, relate; recover (a debt)

verhe′melte palate *ook* **gehe′melte**; **gesple′te** ∼ cleft palate; **har′de/sag′te** ∼ hard/soft palate

verheug′ (w) ∼ rejoice, delight; *hom* ∼ *oor* rejoice at; (b) delighted

verhe′we exalted, sublime

verhin′der (w) ∼ prevent, hinder *ook* **verhoed′**

verhit' (w) heat; (b) heated, hot; ~**ting** heating *kyk* **son'verhitting**

verhoed' ~ prevent, ward off *ook* **voorkom'**

verho'ging -s, -e elevation, promotion, increment, increase, rise (in salary)

verhoog' (s) ..**hoë** stage, platform; (w) raise, elevate; enhance; ~**kun'stenaar** stage performer/entertainer

verhoor' (s) ..**hore** examination; hearing; trial (in court); (w) interrogate, examine; *sy gebed is* ~ his prayer was answered; ~**af'wagtende** (s) person awaiting trial

verhou'ding -s, -e relation, proportion, ratio; (love) affair

verhuis' ~ move/relocate; die; ~**ing** moving; migration; ~**wa** removal van; pantechnicon

verhuur' (w) let, hire; ~**der** landlord/lessor

verjaar' ~ celebrate one's birthday; prescribe (a debt); ~**(s)'dag** birthday; ~**s'geskenk'/**~**s'present** birthday present

verjong' (w) rejuvenate; ~**ing(s)kuur'** facelift *ook* **ontrim'peling**

verkeer' (s) traffic; communication; (w) have intercourse; keep company with; ~**beheer'** traffic control; ~**dem'ping** traffic calming

verkeerd' (b) wrong; unreasonable

verkeers': ~**beamp'te** traffic officer *vgl.* **spiet'-kop**; ~**boe'te** traffic fine; ~**diens** point duty; ~**knoop** traffic jam; ~**lig** traffic light, robot; ~**te'ken** traffic sign/signal; ~**wis'-selaar** traffic interchange

verken' ~ reconnoitre, spy; ~**ner** scout

verkies' ~ elect; choose, prefer; *tot die raad* ~ elected to council; *tot voorsitter* ~ elected *as* chairman; ~**baar** eligible, ~**ing** election; ~**lik** preferable/desirable

verklaar' (w) ~ explain, clarify; declare

verklap' ~ tell tales, tell a secret

verkla'ring -s, -e explanation, statement; evidence; declaration; *'n* ~ *aflê* make a statement; **be'ëdigde** ~ (sworn) affidavit

verklein'woord -e diminutive

verkleur' ~ lose/change colour; discolour; ~**man'netjie** chameleon *ook* **trapsuut'jies**; turncoat

verklik' ~ disclose, give away (secret); ~**ker** detector (metal, smoke)

verkluim' ~ grow stiff/numb with cold

verknoei' ~ spoil, make a mess, bungle

verknor'sing fix, quandary, dilemma

verkoel' ~ cool, refrigerate; ~**er** radiator

verkon'dig ~ announce, proclaim

verkoop' (s) sale; ~**(s)bestuur'der** sales manager; ~**kuns** salesmanship

verko'per -s seller; vendor, salesman

verko'ping -s, -e sale, auction

verkort' (w) ~ shorten, abridge, abbreviate; (b) **-e** abridged

verko'se returned, elected; ~ **president'** president-elect

verkou'e -s cold, chill; *'n* ~ *kry* catch a cold; ~ *wees* have a cold

verkrag' (w) violate; rape; ~**ter** rapist (person); ~**ting** (s) rape

verkramp' unenlightened, verkramp

verkry' (w) obtain, acquire; ~**(g)'baar** obtainable

verkwik' ~ refresh; ~**kend** (b) refreshing

verkwis' ~ waste, squander, dissipate

verkyk' ~ stare in amazement

vêr'kyker -s (pair of) fieldglasses, telescope, binoculars *kyk* **teleskoop'**

verlaat' ~ leave, abandon, quit; forsake

verlam' ~ paralyse; (b) lame, cripple; ~**ming** paralysis; lameness

verlang' ~ desire, long for; *vurig* ~ *na* yearn for; ~**e** (s) desire, wish, longing

ver'langs/vêr'langs: ~ **fami'lie** distant relative(s)

verla'te (b) abandoned, lonely, forsaken

verle'de (s) past; *die grys(e)* ~ the distant past; *die* ~, *hede en toekoms* the past, present and future; (b) past; last; ~ **deelwoord** past participle; ~ **maand** last month

verle'ë timid, bashful, self-conscious *ook* **bedeesd'/ska'merig**

verleen' ~ grant, give, confer, bestow

verleent'heid embarrassment, quandary

verleg'ging deviation; detour (road)

verlei' ~ seduce, tempt; mislead

verleng' ~ lengthen, prolong, extend; ~**koord** extension cord

verlep' (w) fade, wilt; (b) withered

verlief' -**de** in love, fond of, sweet on; amorous; ~ *raak op* fall in love with

verlief'de -s person in love, lover

verlies' -**e** loss, defeat; bereavement

verlig¹ (w) ~ relieve; (b) relieved

verlig² (w) ~ illuminate; (b) enlightened; lit up; *die* ~**te** *eeu* the enlightened age; ~**ting** lighting (streets), illumination

verlof' leave; permission *ook* **toe'stemming**

verloof' ~ become engaged/betrothed; ~ *raak aan* become engaged to; ~**de** fiancé (man), fiancee (woman)

verloop' (s) course, lapse, sequel; progress

verloor' (w) ~ lose

verlos' ~ deliver; release, liberate; redeem; **~kunde** midwifery, obstetrics *ook* **obstetrie'**

Verlos'ser Redeemer, Saviour

verlos'sing deliverance; redemption; delivery

verlo'wing -s, -e engagement, betrothal

vermaak' (s) ..**make** pleasure, amusement, entertainment; (w) enjoy, amuse; mock/ridicule (someone)

vermaak'lik enjoyable, amusing, entertaining; **~heid** amusement, entertainment

vermaan' (w) ~ admonish, warn; caution

vermeen'de alleged, supposed, reputed

vermeer'der ~ increase, enlarge, augment; **~ing** increase

vermenigvul'dig ~ multiply; ~ *met* multiply by; **~ing** multiplication

verme'tel audacious, daring *ook* **astrant'**

vermin'der ~ lessen, diminish, decrease; slacken (speed); **~ing** reduction, decrease

vermink' (w) ~ mutilate, maim; deface

vermis' ~ miss; *as* ~ *aangegee* reported missing

vermoed' ~ suspect: *geen kwaad* ~ *nie* suspect no evil; presume, suppose

vermoe'de -ns suspicion, presumption

vermo'ë -ns fortune, wealth; ability; **~nd** (b) wealthy, rich; influential

vermoei' ~ tire, weary, fatigue; **~end** (b) tiring, wearisome

vermom' ~ disguise, mask

vermoor' ~ murder, kill

vermors' ~ squander, spend, spill

vermy' ~ avoid, shun, evade

vernaam' (b) important, prominent, distinguished; (bw) especially; **~lik** especially, mainly

verne'der (w) humiliate, degrade, humble; **~end** humiliating; **~ing** humiliation

verneem' ~ understand, learn; enquire

verneuk' ~ cheat, defraud, swindle *ook* **kul**; **bedrieg'**

verniel' ~ destroy, wreck (items owned)

verniet' in vain; free (of charge); unnecessarily

vernie'tig ~ annihilate; destroy (a letter)

vernis' (s) **-se** varnish; (w) varnish

vernou' ~ grow narrower, narrow; *die loongaping* ~ narrow the wage gap

vernuf' **-te** intelligence, talent; expertise; genius; **~tig** ingenious, innovative

vernu'wing -s, -e renewal; renovation

veron(t)ag'saam (w) ~ ignore, disregard; neglect

veronderstel' ~ suppose, assume *ook* **gestel'** (w); **~ling** assumption, supposition

veron'geluk ~ fail, miscarry; lose one's life in an accident; jeopardise (one's chances)

verontwaar'dig -de indignant, grieved

veroor'deel ~ condemn, sentence; *ter dood* ~/ *tot die dood* ~ condemn to death

veroor'saak ~ cause, bring about; trigger; *moeite* ~ cause/give trouble

veror'den ~ order, enact, decree; **~ing** (municipal) by-law; decree, ordinance, statute

verou'der ~ grow old; become obsolete

vero'wer (w) conquer, capture; **~aar** victor

verpand' ~ pawn; pledge; mortgage

verplaas' ~ remove, displace; transfer (to another post/town)

verpla'sing -s, -e transfer, displacement

verpleeg' (w) ~ nurse, tend; **~kun'de** nursing; **~personeel'** nursing staff; **~ster** nurse; **~sus'ter** nursing sister

verple''ër -s male nurse

verple'ging/verpleegkun'de nursing

verplet'ter ~ crush, smash *ook* **verbry'sel**

verplig' (w) ~ oblige, compel; (b, bw) obliged, bound; compulsory; **~te on'derwys** compulsory education; **~tend** compulsory, obligatory; **~ting** obligation; liability; *sonder* **~ting** without obligation

verraad' treason, treachery

verraai' ~ betray; **~er** traitor

verras' ~ surprise, startle; **~send** surprising; **~sing** (s) surprise; eye-opener

ver'regaande outrageous, scandalous

ver'reikend -e far-reaching; **~e gevolge** far-reaching consequences

ver'reweg by far; ~ *die beste plan* by far the better plan

verrig' ~ do, perform, execute; **~tinge** proceedings (at a meeting)

verroes ~ rust away; corrode

verrot' (w) ~ decay, putrefy, decompose; (b) rotten *ook* **vrot**

verryk' ~ enrich; **~te uraan** enriched uranium

vers[1] **-e** heifer

vers[2] **-e** stanza, verse; *met* ~ *en kapittel bewys* quote chapter and verse

versa'dig (w) satisfy; (b) satisfied (appetite)

versag' ~ soften, relieve; mitigate; **~tend** extenuating, mitigating: **~tende omstandighede** extenuating circumstances

versa'mel ~ collect, gather, mass; ~ing col=
lection; compilation; gathering
versap'per -s liquidiser; juicer, blender
verseg' ~ refuse point-blank/flatly
verse'ker (w) ~ insure, assure; affirm; (b)
assured/insured
verse'kering assurance, insurance; ~ teen
brand fire insurance; ek gee julle die ~ I
give you the assurance; ~maatskappy' in=
surance company; ~po'lis insurance policy
versend' ~ dispatch/despatch, consign
ver'sene: die ~ teen die prikkels slaan kick
against the pricks
verset' (s) resistance; ly'delike ~ passive re=
sistance; (w) resist
versien' (w) ~ service (of car) ook diens (w)
ver'siende far-seeing; long-sighted
versier', ~ adorn, decorate; ~ing decoration,
ornament; ~sui'ker icing sugar ook sier'=
suiker
versig'tig careful, cautious; prudent
verskaf ~ supply, furnish, provide; ~fer supplier
verskei'denheid variety, assortment, diversity
verskei'denheidskonsert' variety concert
verskei'e several, sundry, various
verskeur' ~ tear to pieces, lacerate
verskil (s) -le difference, disparity, discrep=
ancy; ~ van mening difference of opinion;
(w) differ, vary; ~lend different; unlike
versko'ning -s, -e excuse, apology
verskoon' ~ excuse, pardon; ~ my pardon/
excuse me
verskrik' ~ terrify; ~king horror, terror; ~lik
(b) terrible, horrible, dreadful
verskroei' ~ scorch, singe
verskul'dig (b) -de due, indebted, owing
verskyn' ~ appear; be published; ~ing
appearance; publication
verslaaf (w) ~ enslave; ~ raak aan become
addicted to; hooked on ook: versot op; (b)
addicted
verslaan ~ defeat (in war); conquer; beat (sport)
verslaap' ~ oversleep (oneself)
versla'e dismayed, dejected
verslag' ..slae report, account; ~ doen/lewer
give an account; (submit a) report; ~ge'wer
reporter ook joernalis'
verslank' (w) slim; ~ing slimming
versleg' ~ deteriorate, grow worse
versmaai' ~ scorn, despise, slight; dis nie te ~
nie it is not to be scorned/sneezed at
versmoor ~ smother, suffocate, stifle

versna'pering (s) delicacy, dainty, titbit, light
refreshment; ~s snacks
versnel' ~ accelerate, quicken; ~ling accel=
eration; speed; ~ren'ne drag racing
versoek' (s) -e request, petition; (w) request,
ask, invite
versoe'king -s, -e temptation
versoek'skrif -te petition ook peti'sie
versoen' ~ reconcile, conciliate, placate
Versoe'ningsdag Day of Reconciliation (holi=
day)
versoet' ~ sweeten; (s) -er sweetener
versool' ~ resole (shoe); retread/recap (tyre)
versorg' ~ care for; ~ing maintenance, care
versper' ~ block, obstruct, bar, barricade; ~
die uitsig obscure the view; ~ring barri=
cade, roadblock
verspil' ~ squander, waste ook (ver)mors
verspoel' ~ wash away; ~ing flood
verspot' (b) ridiculous, silly ook laf (b)
versprei' ~ spread, disperse, scatter
ver'spring/vêrspring (s) long jump
verstaan' ~ understand, comprehend; rede ~
listen to reason; ~baar intelligible, com=
prehensible
verstand' sense, intellect, intelligence, gesond'=
de ~ common sense
verstan'de: met dien ~ provided that; ~lik
vertraag/gestrem mentally retarded
verstan'dig (b) intelligent, sensible, wise
verste'delik ~ urbanise; ~ing urbanisation
versteek' ~ hide (away), stow away
versteen' (w) ~ petrify, turn to stone
verste'keling -e stowaway (on ship, plane)
verstel' ~ mend; readjust; change gears;
~baar adjustable
versterk' ~ fortify, strengthen, reinforce; ~ing
support, reinforcement; ~mid'del tonic
versteur'/verstoor' (w) disturb, upset; die
(openbare) rus ~ disturb the peace
verstom' (w) become/strike dumb; (b) speech=
less ook spra'keloos
verstoot' ~ disown; reject; cast out, repudiate
verstop' ~ plug, clog; constipate; ~ping -s, -e
obstruction/stoppage
versto'teling -e outcast, pariah (person)
verstout' ~ make bold, take courage; jou ~
om make bold to
verstrek' ~ furnish, supply, provide; beson=
derhede ~ give details
verstrooi' ~ scatter, disperse; ~(d)' scattered;
~de profes'sor absent-minded professor

verstryk' ~ elapse, expire; terminate; **~da'=tum** expiry date *ook* **verval'datum**
verstuit' ~ dislocate, sprain (wrist/ankle); twist
versuim' (s) omission, neglect; default; (w) neglect; omit; *sy plig* ~ neglect one's duty
versuip' (w) ~ drown (animal)
verswaar' ~ aggravate; **verswa'rende om=stan'dighede** aggravating circumstances
verswak' (w) weaken; **~te bejaar'des** frail aged; **~te'sorg** frailcare
verswik' ~ sprain (ankle) *ook* **verstuit'** (w)
verswyg' ~ suppress, conceal, keep silent; *die feite* ~ withhold the facts
vertaal' ~ translate; *letterlik* ~ translate literally
verta'ler -s translator; **beë'digde** ~ sworn trans=lator
verta'ling -s, -e translation, version
verteenwoor'dig ~ represent; **~end** repre=senting; **~er** representative (person)
verteer' ~ digest; spend (wastefully)
vertel' ~ tell, relate, narrate; **~ler** narrator, storyteller; **~ling** narrative, tale
vertikaal' **..kale** vertical
vertoef' ~ stay, linger, tarry *ook* **aan'bly**
vertolk' ~ interpret, explain; **~ing** interpreta=tion, rendering
verto'ning -s, -e show, display; performance (of the economy)
vertoon' (s) show, sight; (w) show; expose; perform; exhibit, display; **~kas** display cabinet *ook* **toonkas**; **~wed'stryd** exhibi=tion match
vertraag' ~ delay, slacken; retard; **~de/gestrem'de kin'ders** retarded children
vertrek¹ (s) **-ke** room, apartment *ook* **lokaal'**
vertrek² (s) departure; *dag van* ~ day of departure; (w) leave, depart
vertrek³ (w) ~ distort; *sy gesig* ~ *van die pyn* his features are twisted with pain
vertroe'tel spoil, (over)indulge; pamper
vertrou' ~ trust, confide in, rely upon; **~baar** reliable, dependable
vertrou'e confidence, trust; **~ling** confidant
vertrou'ensgaping credibility gap
vertrou'eswendelaar confidence trickster, conman, spiv
vertrou'lik (b) **-e; -er, -ste** confidential; private; *streng* ~ strictly confidential
vervaar'dig ~ make; manufacture; **~er** manu=facturer *ook* **fabrikant'**
verval' (s) decay, decline; maturity; (w) de=cline, decay; fall due, expire, mature; *die wissel* ~ *(op) 21 Maart* the bill (of ex=change) matures on 21 March; **~dag** due/expiry date
vervals' ~ adulterate; falsify, fake; forge; **~ing** fake; falsification, forgery
vervang' (w) ~ replace, substitute
verveel' ~ bore, weary; *jou* ~ be bored
verveer' ~ moult (birds)
vervel' ~ cast the skin, slough (snake)
verve'lend (b) boring, tedious *ook* **verve'lig** *'n* ~*e* vent a regular bore
verve'lens: *tot* ~ *toe* ad nauseam
verver'sing -s, -e refreshment
vervlaks'!/vervloeks! confound it!; damn it!; dash it!
vervoer' (s) transport, transportation; convey=ance, traffic; (w) convey, carry; **~diens'te** transport services; **~ing** enthusiasm, rap=ture, ecstasy: *in* ~*ring raak* go into raptures; **~toe'lae** transport/locomotion allowance
vervolg' (s) continuation, sequel, future; (w) continue; pursue; proceed against; *oortre=ders word* ~ trespassers will be prosecuted; *word* ~ to be continued; **~ingswaan'** persecution mania; **~verhaal'** serial
vervolmaak' (w) ~ perfect; *hy het die proses* ~ he perfected the process
verwaand' (b) conceited, pedantic, stuck up
verwaar'loos (w) neglect; (b) neglected
verwag' ~ expect; look forward to; **~tende moe'der** expectant mother
verwag'ting -s, -e expectation, hope
verwant' (s) **-e** relative, relation; (b) akin, allied; related; **~skap** relationship
verwar(d) (b) confused, disordered
verwarm' (w) ~ warm, heat; **~ing** heating
verwar'ring confusion, perplexity
verweer (s) defence; resistance; (w) defend, resist
verwel'kom ~ welcome (someone); **~ing** wel=coming, welcome
verwens' ~ curse, execrate
ver'wer -s painter (by trade) *kyk* **skil'der**
verwerf' ~acquire, obtain (degree), gain
verwerk' ~ work up; process; digest; revise; **~er** processor (data, words)
verwerp' ~ reject; discard; refuse; *'n voorstel* ~ reject a motion
verwe'se (b) disconcerted; dazed, stunned
verwe'senlik ~ substantiate, realise, materi=alise; *ambisies* ~ realise ambitions

verwil'der ~ grow wild; chase away
verwis'sel ~ exchange; alternate; commute; *die tydelike met die ewige* ~ die, pass away
verwit'tig ~ notify, acquaint, inform
verwoes' (w) ~ destroy, ruin, devastate, lay waste; (b) destroyed; ~**ting** destruction, devastation; ~*ting aanrig* play havoc
verwon'der ~ astonish, amaze, surprise; *jou* ~ *oor* be surprised at
verwurg' ~ strangle, throttle
verwy'der ~ remove, withdraw; alienate
verwys' ~ refer; ~**ing** reference; *met* ~*ing na* with reference to; ~**nom'mer** reference number
verwyt' (s) -e reproach, reproof; (w) reproach, blame
very'del ~ frustrate, baffle, shatter, foil
ve'sel (s) -s fibre, thread, filament; ~**glas** fibreglass *ook* **glas'vesel**
ves'tig ge- establish; settle; *die aandag op iets* ~ draw attention to something; *nywerhede* ~ establish industries
ves'ting (s) fortress, stronghold
vet (s) -te fat, lard, grease, suet; rich, fertile, fat, corpulent; *so* ~ *soos 'n vark* as fat as a pig; *so waar soos* ~ upon my word
ve'te -s quarrel; feud; vendetta *ook* **bloed'vete**
ve'ter -s lace, bootlace
veteraan' ..rane veteran; ~**mo'tor** vintage car; veteran car
vet: ~**plant** succulent; ~**sug** obesity
vi'a via, per
vibreer' ~, ge- vibrate *ook* **tril**
vi'deo: ~**band** video tape; ~**kasset'opnemer** video cassette recorder; ~**teek** video library
vier[1] (s) -e four
vier[2] (w) ge- celebrate (birthday); observe
vier: ~**de** fourth; ~**dens** in the fourth place
vier'kant -e square; ~**ig** (b) square; ~**s'wortel** square root
vier'rigtingstop'(straat) fourway stop (street)
vier'uur four o'clock
vier'wieldryf four-wheel drive
vies (b) nasty, offensive, filthy; fed-up; ~ *maak* annoy, vex
vies'lik dirty, filthy; smutty (joke)
viets spruce, smart; ~**e nooi** smart-looking girl
vigs (s) Aids; ~**ly'er** Aids sufferer
vilt/velt felt; ~**hoed** felt hat
vin -ne fin; *geen* ~ *verroer nie* not lift/stir a finger
vind ge- find, come across, meet with

vin'dingryk resourceful, inventive, innovative
vin'duik skindiving/findiving
vin'ger -s finger; *iets deur die* ~*s sien* overlook a mistake; ~**af'druk** fingerprint; ~**hoed** thimble; ~**spraak** sign language; ~**wy'sing** hint; pointer
vink -e finch, weaverbird
vin'kel fennel; *dis* ~ *en koljander* it is six of the one and half a dozen of the other
vin'nig -e; -er, -ste quick, fast, speedy
viool' viole violin; fiddle; *tweede* ~ *speel* play second fiddle; ~**spe'ler** violinist *ook* **violis'**; ~**tjie** violet (flower)
vir for, to; ~ **goed** permanently, for good
virtuoos' virtuose virtuoso
vis (s) -se fish
vi'sekanselier -s vice-chancellor
vi'seprinsipaal ..pale vice-principal
vis: ~**gerei'** fishing tackle; ~**graat** fishbone; ~**hoek** fish hook
visier' -e, -s visor (of helmet); elevating sight (rifle)
visioen' -e vision
vis'ser -s fisher, fisherman *ook* **vis'serman/ vis'terman**
vis'terman -ne angler *ook* **heng'elaar**
vi'sum (s) -s visa
vis'vang (w) -ge- catch fish; nod, doze
vitaliteit' vitality *ook* **le'wenskrag**
vitamien'/vitami'ne vitamine
vla -'s custard
vlaag vlae *'n* ~ *van woede* a fit of anger; sudden squall, gust (of wind)
vlag vlae flag; standard; vane; *die* ~ *hys* hoist the flag; *die* ~ *stryk* strike one's colours; ~**hy'sing** flag-hoisting (ceremony)
vlak (s) -ke plane; level, floor; surface
vlak'te -s plain, flats
vlak: ~**vark** warthog; ~**vo'ël** spike-heeled lark
vlam (s) -me flame, blaze; *ene vuur en* ~ very enthusiastic; (w) blaze, burn; ~**baar** flammable *ook* **brand'baar**
vlas flax
vlees flesh, meat; pulp *kyk* **vleis**; ~**lik** carnal, sexual/sensual
vleg (w) ge- plait, wreathe, twine; ~**sel** string, tress, braid
vlei[1] (s) -e valley, vale, meadow; vlei
vlei[2] (w) ge- flatter; cringe, coax
vleis meat; ~**braai(ery)** braai, barbecue, braaivleis; ~**pastei'** meat pie/patty
vlek (s) -ke blot, spot, stain; blemish; (w) soil,

blot, stain; ~**vrystaal'** stainless steel

vlerk -e wing, pinion; ~**sleep** (w) impress; court a girl; ~**sweef** hang gliding; ~**swe'= wer** hang glider

vler'muis -e bat, flitter mouse

vleu'el -s wing; pinion, vane; grand piano; wing threequarter; side aisle; ~**klavier'** grand/ concert piano

vlie'ënd -e flying; ~**e pie'ring** flying saucer

vlieënier' -s pilot; aviator, airman

vlie'ër -s kite

vlieg[1] (s) **vlieë** fly

vlieg[2] (w) **ge-** fly; aviate; ~**dekskip'** aircraft carrier; ~**masjien'** aeroplane/aircraft *kyk* **vlieg'tuig**

vlieg'tuig ..**tuie** aircraft; (jet) plane; airliner (passenger service)

vlieg'veld -e aerodrome *kyk* **lug'hawe**

vlin'der -s butterfly *ook* **skoe(n)'lapper**

vloed -e flood, inundation; ~**golf** tidal wave; ~**ramp** flood disaster

vloei **ge-** flow, stream; ~**baar** fluid, liquid; ~**end** flowing, fluent, smooth, easy: ~**end Engels praat** be fluent in English; ~**kaart** flowchart; ~**stof** liquid, fluid

vloek (s) -e curse, oath; (w) swear, curse; ~ *soos 'n matroos/ketter* swear like a trooper; ~**woord** swearword; curse

vloer -e floor; *derde* ~/*vlak* third floor; ~**kie'rie** floorshift (car) *ook* **plesier'kierie**

vlooi -e flea; ~**byt** fleabite; ~**e'spel** tiddly= winks; ~**mark** fleamarket; ~**poei'er** insect powder

vloot **vlote** fleet, navy; ~**ei'enaar** fleet owner (cars); ~**soldaat'** marine

vlot (s) -te raft; float (cash); (w) succeed, go smoothly; (b, bw) fluent; afloat; ~ *praat* speak fluently; ~ *verloop* proceed smoothly; ~**ter** float (fishing)

vlug[1] (s) covey; bevy; *'n* ~ *patryse* a covey of partridges

vlug[2] (s) flight; escape; *op die* ~ *slaan* take to flight; (w) flee; **huur**~ chartered flight

vlug[3] (b) quick; nimble; agile; ~ *van begrip* quick-witted

vlug: ~**bal** volleyball; ~**heu'wel** traffic island; ~**hou** volley (tennis); ~**op'nemer** flight data recorder (black box); ~**roos'ter** flight plan; ~**skop** punt(ing); ~**skrif** leaflet; hand-out; ~**sout** volatile salts; ~**te'ling** fugitive/refugee

vlug'tig (b) hasty, cursory, fleeting

vly **ge-** lay down, nestle *ook* **neer'vly**

vlym -e lancet; fleam; ~**skerp** razor-edged

vlyt diligence, industry; ~**ig** (b) diligent

voed (w) **ge-** feed, nourish

voe'ding feeding, nourishment, nutrition

voed'saam nutritious, nourishing

voed'sel food, nutriment; ~**vergif't(ig)ing** food poisoning

voeg' (s) **voeë** joint, seam; (w) join; seam; point (bricks); ~**woord** conjunction

voel **ge-** feel, touch, grope; *tuis* ~ feel at home

vo'ël -s bird; ~**kyk** birdwatching/birding; ~**ky'ker** birdwatcher/birder/twitcher; ~**ver= skrik'ker** scarecrow; ~**vlug** bird's-eye view

vo'ëlvry -e outlawed; free as a bird; ~ *verklaar* outlaw a person

voer[1] (s) fodder, forage; (w) feed

voer[2] (w) **ge-** conduct; wage (war); transport; *briefwisseling* ~ conduct correspondence; *samesprekings* ~ have talks; ~**band** con= veyor belt; ~**ing** lining; ~**kraal** feedlot; ~**kuil** silo; ~**taal** language medium

voert'sek! get away!; be off!; foot'sack!; scram!

voer'tuig vehicle, carriage *ook* **ry'tuig**

voet -e foot; footing; ~ *in die wind slaan* take to one's heels; ~**boei** leg-iron

voet'bal football; ~**wed'stryd** football match

voet'brug footbridge

voe'tenent -e foot, lower end (bed)

voet'ganger -s pedestrian; hopper (wingless locust)

voe'tjie-voe'tjie slowly, cautiously

voet: ~**heelkun'dige** chiropodist; ~**pad** foot= path; ~**skim'mel** athlete's foot; ~**slaan** hike/ tramp; footslog; ~**slaanpad'** hiking/tramping trail *ook* **stap'roete**; ~**sla'ner** hiker, back= packer *ook* **pak'stapper**; ~**soolvlak'** grass= roots (level) *ook* **grond'vlak**; ~**spoor** footprint

vog -te liquid, moisture; ~**tig** damp, moist

vokaal' (s) **vokale** vowel *ook* **klin'ker**

vol full, filled; *ten* ~**le** completely, fully; ~**bloed** thoroughbred *ook* **ras'eg**

voldoen' ~ satisfy; pay; comply with; *aan 'n versoek* ~ comply with a request

volg **ge-** follow, succeed; shadow; ~**afstand** following distance (cars); ~**ens** according to; ~**ens artikel 137** under section 137; ~**e'ling** follower/adherent; ~**or'de** consecu= tive order, sequence

volhard' (w) ~ persevere, persist

vol'hou -**ge-** persevere, maintain, endure

volk -e, -ere people, nation; *die uitverkore* ~

the chosen people
vol'ke: ~**kun'de** anthropology, ethnology; ~**reg** international law
volko'me complete, quite, perfect, absolute
volks: ~**etimologie'** popular etymology; ~**kun'**= **de** folklore; ~**lied** national anthem; ~**mond:** *in die* ~*mond* in the language of the people
volk'spele folk dances *ook* **volks'danse**
volks: ~**tel'ling** census; ~**wel'syn** social welfare
volle'dig -e; -er, -ste complete, entire
vol'maak (w) **vol ge-** fill
volmaak' (b) perfect; ~**te geluk'skoot** perfect fluke (golf) *ook* **kolhou;** ~**t'heid** perfection
vol'maan full moon
vol'mag -te power of attorney, proxy
vol'op in abundance, plentiful
volstrek' -te absolute; ~**te meer'derheid** absolute/clear/overall majority
vol'struis -e ostrich; ~**skop** flying kick; mule kick
voltooi' ~ complete, finish; ~**d teenwoor'dige tyd** perfect tense
vol'treffer -s direct hit
vol'tyds (b) full-time (job) *ook* **heel'tyds**
volu'me -s volume, bulk
vol'vloertapyt -e wall-to-wall carpet(ing)
volwas'se (b) adult, full-grown; ~**ne** (s) full-= grown person, adult
vo'meer' ~, **ge-** vomit *ook* **op'gooi, braak**
von'deling -e foundling (baby)
vonds (s) **-te** find, discovery
vonk -e spark
von'kel ge- sparkle, emit sparks; ~**ontbyt'** champagne breakfast; ~**wyn** champagne
vonk'prop -pe spark plug
von'nis (s) **-se** sentence, judgment; (w) sentence, pass judgment
voog -de guardian; curator (both sexes)
voor[1] (s) **vore** furrow, ditch
voor[2] (bw, vgw, vs) before; in front of; previous to; *een putjie* ~ one hole up (golf); *jou horlosie is* ~ your watch is fast; ~**aand** eve; early evening; ~**af** previously, beforehand; *jy moet hom* ~*af waarsku* you should warn him beforehand; ~**arm** forehand (tennis)
voor'baat advance; *by* ~ *dank* thank(ing) you in anticipation
voor'beeld -e example, instance; *by*~ for example
voorbeel'dig -e; -er, -ste exemplary (conduct)
voor'behoedmiddel -s contraceptive; prophy= lactic

voor'behoedpil -le contraceptive pill
voor'behou: *all regte* ~ all rights reserved
voor'berei ~ prepare; coach; ~**ding** prepara= tion; ~**d'sels** arrangements, preliminaries
voor: ~**bladnooi'** cover girl (magazine); ~**bode** forerunner; omen, foreboding; ~**bok** bell= wether; ringleader
voor'brand -e firebreak; ~ *maak* prepare, pave the way
voor'dat before
voor'deel (s) advantage, gain, benefit; ~ *van die twyfel* benefit of the doubt; ~**trek'ker** beneficiary *ook* **beguns'tigde** (mens)
voorde'lig profitable, beneficial
voor: ~**deur** front door; ~**dra** recite; ~**drag** address, speech; delivery, recital; ~**eergis'**= **ter** three days ago; ~**gan'ger** predecessor
voor: ~**gee** pretend, profess to be; give odds; give a start, handicap; ~**geweed'loop** handi= cap race
voor'(ge)meld -e/voor'(ge)noem -de above-= mentioned, aforesaid
voor'gereg -te first course, entrée
voor'geskrewe: ~ **boe'ke** prescribed books
voor'gestel -de proposed; introduced
voor: ~**geveg'** preliminary bout, curtain-raiser; ~**geslag** ancestors, forefathers; ~**gevoel'** presentiment, suspicion, foreboding; ~**graads** undergraduate (student); ~**grond** foreground; ~**ha'ker** mechanical horse
voor'heen formerly, late; ~ *van die firma X* formerly of X's
voor: ~**hoe'de** vanguard, advance guard; ~**hoof** forehead; ~**huis** lounge *ook* **sit'ka**= **mer;** ~**jaar** spring; ~**kant** front, face; ~**keer** (w) prevent; bar, block
voor'keur preference; ~**aan'deel** preference share; ~**pos** priority/fast mail
voorkom' (w) ~ forestall, prevent (accident)
voor'kome appearance, looks; bearing
voor: ~**laai'er** muzzleloader (rifle); front-end loader (machine); ~**laaste** last but one, penultimate
voor'land fate, destiny; *dis jou* ~ that is in store for you
voor'lê -ge- submit *ook* **in'dien;** lie in ambush
voor'lees -ge- read to; *iem. die leviete* ~ reprimand someone
voor'legging submission (report, memorandum)
voor: ~**letter** initial (letter); ~**liefde** special liking, preference; ~**lig** enlighten; give information *ook* **in'lig**

voorlo′pig (b) preliminary, provisional(ly)
voorma′lig -e former, sometime; **~e presi=dent′** former president
voor: ~man leader, foreman; **~mid′dag** forenoon, morning; **~naam** first name/forename; **~naamwoord** pronoun; **~neem** resolve, make up one's mind; **~neme** intention; resolve: **~nemens wees** intend
voor′oordeel ..dele prejudice, bias
voor: ~ou′ers ancestors; **~portaal′** porch, lobby; foyer; **~pos** outpost
voor′raad ..rade stock, provisions, supply; **~op′name** stocktaking
voor: ~reg privilege, prerogative; **~ruit** windscreen (car); **~sê** (w) prompt, whisper to; **~set′sel** preposition
voorsien′ (w) ~ provide, furnish; foresee; anticipate; *in 'n behoefte* ~ meet a need; ~ *van* provide/supply with
Voorsie′nigheid Providence
voorsie′ning provision; ~ *maak vir* make provision for
voor′sit -ge- preside, take the chair; **Ag′bare ~ter/~ster** Madam Chair, Chairperson; **~ter** chairman/chairperson/chair
voor: ~skiet (w) advance (money); **~skoot′** apron, pinafore; **~skot** advance/loan; **~skrif** prescription; direction
voor′skyn *te* ~ *bring* produce; bring to light; *te* ~ *kom* appear *ook* **verskyn′**
voor: ~smaak foretaste; **~snybuffet′** carvery; **~sorg** precaution, provision
voor′spel¹ (s) **-e** prelude, overture (mus.)
voorspel′² (w) predict, prophesy, foretell, forecast
voor′speler -s forward (football)
voorspel′ling -s, -e prophecy, prediction
voor′spoed prosperity *ook* **wel′vaart**
voorspoe′dig prosperous, flourishing
voor′sprong start, advantage; *sy* ~ *behou* retain one's lead
voor: ~stad suburb; **~stan′der** advocate (for), proponent, upholder; **~ste′delik** (b): **~stedelike trein** suburban/commuter train *ook* **pen′deltrein**; **~stel** (s) proposal; (w) propose, move; **~stel′ling** presentation
voort′bestaan (s) survival *ook* **oorle′wing**
voortdu′rend -e continuous, incessant
voor′teken -s omen, augury, foretoken
voort′gaan -ge- continue, proceed; go on
voort′gesette: ~ **on′derwys** continuing/ongoing education

voor′tou lead: *die* ~ *neem* take the lead
voort′plant -ge- spread, multiply *ook* **kweek**; propagate, transmit
voortref′lik excellent, first rate *ook* **uitmun′tend**
voor′trek (w) be partial to; treat with favour
voorts moreover, further(more), besides
voort′spruit -ge- arise, spring from
voortva′rend (b) impulsive, impetuous
vooruit′ beforehand, in advance; in front of, before; **~gedateer′de tjek** postdated cheque; **~betaal′baar** payable in advance; **~gang** progress, advancement
vooruit′sig (s) **-te** prospect, outlook
vooruit′skat -ge- forecast; **~ting** forecast *ook* **projek′sie**
vooruit′streef/vooruit strewe -ge- forge ahead, strive forward
voor: ~val (s) incident, event; (w) take place, occur; **~verto′ning** preview (of show, event); **~vin′ger** index finger; **~voeg′sel** prefix
voorwaar′ indeed, truly, surely
voor′waarde -s condition, stipulation; *op* ~ *dat* on condition that; *onder daardie* ~ on that condition
voorwaar′delik -e conditional
voor′waarts =e forward; ~ *mars!* quick march!
voor′wedstryd -e curtain-raiser
voor′wend -ge- pretend, make believe; **~sel** pretext, pretence; subterfuge
voor′werp -e object, thing
voor′wiel -e front wheel; **~aan′drywing** front-wheel drive *ook* **dryf′**
voor′woord -e foreword, preface
vor′der (w) **ge-** make progress; demand; **~ing** (s) progress; claim, demand
vo′rentoe to the fore, forward; ~ *boer* forge ahead; *dit smaak* ~ it tastes good
vo′rige former, past, last; *die* ~ *dag* the day before
vorm (s) **-s, -e** form, mould, shape; (w) shape, form, mould; *lydende en bedrywende* ~ passive and active voice; **~brief** stock letter; **~drag** foundation garment
vors′telik: ~e belo′ning princely reward; **~e ontvangs′** red-carpet welcome/reception
vort away, gone
vos -se fox *ook* **jak′kals**
vou (s) crease, fold, ruck, pleat; (w) fold, pleat; **~blad** folder; **~ka′tel** stretcher *ook* **kamp′bed**; **~stoel** folding chair/stool
vra ge- ask, question, enquire

vraag vrae question, query, request; ~ *en aanbod* demand and supply; *'n groot* ~ *na a* big demand for; ~**bank** question bank; ~**stuk** problem; ~**te′ken** question mark

vraat vrate glutton (person); ~**sug** gluttony

vra′e ~**lys** questionnaire; ~**stel** (examination) paper; set of questions

vrag -te load, cargo, freight; carriage; ~**brief** consignment note (rail), bill of lading (boat); ~**karwei′er** haulier, cartage contrac= tor; ~**mo′tor** lorry, truck; ~**skip** cargo vessel, freighter

vrat -te/~jie -s wart

vrede peace, calm; *rus in* ~ rest in peace

vredelie′wend -e; -er, -ste peace-loving

vre′de: ~**reg′ter** justice of the peace; ~**s′= voor′waardes** peace terms, conditions of peace

vreed′saam peaceful, calm; ..**same naas′be= staan** peaceful coexistence

vreemd strange, queer, foreign, alien; *in die* ~*e* in foreign parts, abroad; ~**e′ling** stran= ger, foreigner (person)

vrees (s) fear, apprehension; (w) fear, dread, apprehend; *ek* ~ *dat . . . I am afraid that . . .* ; ~**aanja′(g)end** terrifying

vrees′lik (b) e; er, -ste terrible, horrible, dreadful; (bw) terribly, awfully

vreet ge- eat (animals), gorge

vrek¹ (s) -**ke** miser (person) *ook* **gie′rigaard**

vrek² (w) **ge-** die (animals)

vrek³ (bw) extremely; *jou* ~ *werk* work oneself to death; ~**ma′er** terribly thin

vrek′kerig/vrek′kig miserly, avaricious, stingy *ook* **gie′rig**

vreug′(de) joy, gladness *ook* **blyd′skap**

vriend -e friend; *dik* ~*e wees* be inseparable friends

vrien′delik -e; -er, -ste kind, friendly

vriendin′ -ne lady friend

vriend′skap friendship; favour

vriendskap′lik friendly, amicable, ~**e wed′= stryd/brief** friendly match/letter

vries ge- freeze; ~**brand** frostbite; *hy het ge~brand* he was frostbitten; ~**punt** freez= ing point

vroed′vrou midwife *ook* **kraam′verpleegster**

vroe′ër (b) former, late; (bw) formerly, earlier; ~ *of later* sooner or later

vroeg vroeë; vroeër, -ste early, timely; *'n vroeë dood* an untimely death; *smôrens* ~ early in the morning

vroe′tel (w) wallow, scratch up soil, burrow

vro′lik -e; -er, -ste merry, gay, cheerful

vro′likheid cheerfulness, gaiety, mirth; *na* ~ *kom olikheid* after laughter come tears

vroom (b) pious; devout, saintly, religious

vrot (w) **ge-** rot, putrefy, decay; (b) rotten, decayed, putrid; ~**sig** inefficient, lousy

vrou -e, -ens woman, wife

vrou′e: ~**dokter** female doctor; gynaecologist *ook* **ginekoloog′;** ~**ha′ter** woman hater, misogynist; ~**krag** woman/fem power; ~**sla′ner** wife beater (man); ~**vry′heid** women's lib(erty)

vrou: ~**lik** womanly; feminine; ~**mens** female

vrug result, effect; **-te** fruit; ~**afdry′wing** abortion *ook* **abor′sie;** ~**baar** fruitful, prolific, fertile; ~**gebruik** usufruct; ~**reg** royalty (mining)

vrug′te fruit; results; ~**sap** fruit juice; ~**slaai** fruit salad, angels' food

vry¹ (w) **ge-** woo, court, flirt; *hy* ~ *na die nooi* he is courting the girl

vry² (b) free, unconstrained; off duty; ~**bel= nom′mer** tollfree number; ~**e mark′stelsel** free enterprise

vry′buiter -s privateer, freebooter, buccaneer

Vry′dag ..dae Friday; **Goeie** ~ Good Friday

vry′er -s lover, suitor, wooer

vry′etyd(s)beste′ding recreational activities

vryf/vry′we ge- rub; massage; polish

vrygesel′ bachelor *ook* **ou′jongkêrel**

vryge′wig -e; -er, -ste generous; liberal

vry′heid ..hede liberty, freedom

Vry′heidsdag Freedom Day (holiday)

vry: ~**heidsveg′ter** freedom fighter; ~**hoog′te** clearance; ~**la′ting** release, emancipation, liberation; ~**lating van gyselaars** release of hostages

Vrymes′selaar -s Freemason

vrymoe′dig -e; -er, -ste candid, frank

vry′pos (s) freepost

vrypos′tig (b) impudent, forward *ook* **astrant′**

vry′skut freelance; ~**werk doen** freelancing

Vry′staat¹ (provinsie) Free State

Vrystaat′!² (tw) press on regardless!; well done!

vry′stel -ge- exempt, let off; ~**ling** exemption

vry′waar (w) indemnify; protect, guard, guarantee; *iem. vrywaar van/teen siekte* safeguard someone against illness

vry′wil (w) **ge-** volunteer (for service, etc.)

vrywil′lig voluntary; ~**er** volunteer (person)

vuil dirty, nasty, smutty, foul, obscene; ~ *spel*

foul/dirty play; ~ *taal gebruik* use dirty language; ~**goed** dirt; rubbish *ook* **vul'lis**; dirty person; weeds *ook* **on'kruid**
vuis -te fist; *uit die* ~ *praat* speak extempore; ~**geveg'** boxing match; fisticuffs; ~**ys'ter** knuckle duster
vul[1] (s) foal; colt (male); filly (female); (w) foal
vul[2] (w) **ge-** fill, stuff
vulgêr' -e vulgar *ook* **grof, plat**
vulkaan' ..kane volcano; **uitgedoof'de/uitge= werk'te** ~ extinct volcano
vul'lis rubbish, refuse, trash
vul: ~**pen** fountain pen; ~**sta'sie** filling station
vu'rig fiery; spirited, fervent, ardent
vurk -e fork; ~**hy'ser** forklift
vuur (s) **vure** fire, flame; ardour; (w) fire
vuur: ~**doop** baptism of fire; crucial test; ~**hout'jie** match; ~**maakplek'** fireplace; comprehension: *dis bo(kant) my* ~*maakplek* it is beyond me; ~**peloton'** firing squad; ~**proef** crucial test, acid test, ordeal: *die* ~*proef deurstaan* stand the test; ~**pyl** sky

rocket; ~**slag** flint, steel and tinder; (cigar= ette) lighter; ~**spu'wend** belching fire; volcanic: ~*spuwende berg* volcano; ~**to'= ring** lighthouse; ~**vas** fireproof; refractory; ~**vre'ter** fire-eater, hothead/firebrand (per= son); ~**wa'pen** firearm; ~**warm** very hot; ~**werk** fireworks, pyrotechnics
vy -e fig
vy'and -e enemy, foe; **geswo're** ~ sworn enemy/ foe
vyan'delik hostile; ~**e gebied'** enemy territory
vyan'dig antagonistic, inimical/harmful; ~**e hou'ding** hostile attitude
vyf vywe five; ~**de** fifth; ~**de kolon'ne** fifth column; ~**kamp** pentathlon (sport); ~**tien** fifteen; ~**tig** fifty; ~**uur** five o'clock; ~**vou'= dig** fivefold, quintuple
vy'gie -s several species of *Mesembryanthemum*, vygie
vyl (s) file (tool); (w) file (one's nails)
vy'sel -s mortar; ~**stam'per** pestle
vy'wer -s pond, ornamental pool

W

wa -ens wagon; carriage; truck
waag (w) **ge-** venture, risk, hazard; *'n kans* ~ take a chance; ~**arties'** stuntman; ~**hals** daredevil
waaghal'sig (b) daredevilish, reckless
waag: ~**hans** chancer; ~**stuk** daring feat; hazardous undertaking
waai (w) **ge-** blow, fan; ~**er** fan; ~**erband'** fanbelt
waak ge- watch, be awake; ~**een'heid** in= tensive care unit *ook* **intensie'we sorg'= eenheid**
waansin'nig (b) insane, deranged, demented
waar[1] (b, bw) **ware** true, real, genuine; *die ware Jakob* the real Mackay; *so* ~ *soos padda manel dra* as true as faith
waar[2] (bw) where; ~**aan?** by what?; to which?; ~*aan dink jy?* what are you thinking about?
waar[3] (vgw) since, seeing that, whereas
waarag'tig (b) true, real, genuine; (bw) really, truly, veritably
waar'borg (s) **-e** guarantee, warranty
waarda'sie assessment, valuation
waar'de (s) **-s** worth, value; *ter* ~ *van* to the

value of; ~**bepa'ling** assessment, evalua= tion *ook* **evalue'ring**
waardeer' ~**, ge-** value, estimate; esteem; appreciate; assess, appraise; ~**der** valuator, assessor *ook* **asses'sor**
waarde'ring (s) regard, appreciation, esteem; *blyk van* ~ token of appreciation
waar'de: ~**vermin'dering** depreciation, deval= uation; ~**vol** valuable
waar'dig (b) worthy, dignified; *benede sy* ~**heid** beneath his dignity, infra dig
waar'heen/waar heen whither, where to
waar'heid ..hede truth; reality; truism; *van alle* ~ *ontbloot* devoid of all truth
waar'in? wherein?; in what/which?
waar'mee?/waar mee? with what/which?
waar'merk (s) **-e** stamp, hallmark; (w) certify, authenticate/validate
waarna' after what/which, whereafter
waar'natoe? where to?; whither?
waar'neem (w) **-ge-** observe; perform; depu= tise *ook* **ageer'** (w)
waar'nemend -e acting; ~**e direkteur'** acting/ deputy director *ook* **adjunk'direkteur'**
waar'om? why?; wherefore? *ook* **hoe'kom?**

waar'onder? among which/whom?
waar'oor? about what?; why?
waar'op on what; ~ *staan jy?* what are you standing on?
waarop' on which, whereupon; *die stoel ~ hy sit* the chair he is sitting on
waar'sê -ge- tell fortunes, foretell; **~er** fortune teller, clairvoyant, soothsayer
waar'sku ge- warn, caution; alert; **~wing** warning; admonition
waarskyn'lik probable, likely; *na alle ~heid* in all probability
waar'sonder/waar son'der without which
waar'teen against what/which
waar'uit? out of which/what?
waar'van¹ from where?; of/about what? ~ *het jy gepraat?* what were you talking about?
waarvan'² of which, whose; *die motor ~ die band pap is* the car with a flat tyre
waar'voor? wherefore?; why?; for which?
waat'lemoen -e watermelon
wa'enhuis -e wagon house, coach house
wa'fel -s waffle, wafer
wag (s) **-te** watch; guard, sentry; (w) wait, stay; ~ *hou* be on guard
wag'gel ge- totter, stagger, reel
wag: **~hond** watchdog; **~ka'mer** waiting room *kyk* **spreek'kamer**; **~lys** waiting list; **~woord** watchword, password
wa'kend -e wakeful, vigilant; *'n ~e oog hou op* keep a watchful eye on
wak'ker (b) awake; alive, vigilant, alert
waks (boot) polish; (w) polish
wal -le bank (of river); shore, embankment
wal'rus -se walrus
wals (s) **-e** waltz; roller; (w) waltz, dance; roll (steel); **~meu'le** rolling mill
wal'vis -se whale
wan: **~aan'gepas** maladjusted; **~bestuur'** mismanagement; **~beta'ling** non-payment, default
wand -e wall; **~tapyt'** tapestry *ook* **muur'tapyt'**
wan'daad ..dade misdeed, atrocity; outrage
wan'del (s) walk; conduct, behaviour; *sy handel en ~* his conduct of life; (w) walk; take a walk; *gaan ~* go for a walk/stroll; **~aar** walker, pedestrian; **~ing** walk, stroll; **~laan** (pedestrian) mall; **~pad** hiking trail *ook* **voet'slaanpad/stap'roete**
wang -e cheek
wan'gedrag (s) misconduct, misbehaviour

wan'hoop (s) despair; (w) despair
wan'neer when; if
wan'orde disorder, confusion; **~lik'** disorderly, chaotic
wanska'pe monstrous, deformed (person)
want¹ (s) rigging (sailing vessel)
want² (vgw) for, because *ook* **omdat'**
wan'trou (w) ge- distrust, suspect; **~e** distrust, mistrust, suspicion; *mo'sie van ~e* motion of no confidence
wa'pen (s) **-s** weapon, arm(s); coat of arms, crest, badge; (w) arm; **~geklet'ter** sabre rattling; **~op'slagplek** arms cache; **~stilstand** armistice, truce; **~tuig** arms, weaponry; **~wed'loop** armaments race
wap'per ge- fly out, float; flutter (flag)
war (s) confusion, muddle; **~boel** confusion, muddle, mixup *ook* **deurmekaar'spul**
wa're wares, goods, commodities
warm (w) ge- warm; (b) warm/hot; **~bad** hot/thermal spring(s) *ook* **kruit'bad**; **~lugballon'** hot air balloon
warm'te heat, warmth; ardour
war'rel ge- whirl, swirl; reel; **~wind** whirlwind *ook* **dwar'relwind**
was¹ (s) washing; (w) wash; *iem. se kop ~* give someone a bit of one's mind
was² (s) **-se** wax; **~muse'um** wax museum, chamber of horrors *ook* **gru'welgrot**
was³ (w) ge- grow, wax; **~sende maan** waxing moon
was'bak -ke sink, wash basin/tub
wa'sem -s vapour, steam
was'goed washing; **~mand'jie** laundry basket; **~masjien'** washing machine; **~pen'netjie** clothes peg *ook* **was'pennetjie**; **~poei'er** washing powder
wasseret' -te launderette, laundromat
was'ter -s washer (ring) *ook* **was'ser**
wat (vr. vnw) what; *alles en nog ~* all sorts of things; (betr. vnw) who, that, which, what; (onbep. vnw) whatever, something
wa'ter (s) **-s** water; *te ~ laat* launch (ship); (w) water; **~bestand'** water resistant; **~blom'metjie** Cape pond weed; **~dig** waterproof; **~dra'er** drone; water carrier
wa'ter: **~hoof** hydrocephalus; **~hoos** water spout (in ocean); **~nood** need/shortage of water; **~pas** (s) spirit level; (b) level; **~pok'kies** chicken pox; **~po'nie** wetbike; ski-jet/jetski
wa'tersnood inundation, floods/flooding

wa'ter: ~ste'wel gum/rubber boot; ~stof hydrogen; ~stofbom' hydrogen bomb; ~tand make the mouth water; ~val water=fall, cataract

wa'terverf water colour; ~skildery' water=colour painting

wa'ter: ~vloed flood(s), deluge; ~we'rend water resistant; ~wy'ser water diviner, dowser (person)

wat'te wadding; cotton wool

wat'ter which; ~ een which (one)?

wa'wyd ..wye very wide; ~ oop wide open; ~ wakker wide-awake

web -be web ook weef'sel, spin'nerak

web'blad/web'tuiste (s) website (comp.)

wed ge- wager, bet; ek ~ jou I bet you; ~denskap' wager, bet; ~der' punter (horse racing) ook wed'renganger

we'derhelf(te) (s) spouse, better half; half=section

wederke'rig -e reciprocal; mutual

wederop'standing (s) resurrection

we'dersyds mutual, reciprocal

wederva'ring -s, -e occurrence; adventure

wed: ~loop race (athletics); ~ren race (cars, horses); ~stryd match, competition, contest ook krag'meting; ~strydpunt' match point; ~vaart boat race; ~vlug air race

we'duwee -s widow

wed'ywer (w) ge- compete, contest

weef ge- weave

weeg ge- weigh, balance; ~skaal balance, (pair of) scales

week[1] (s) weke week; oor 'n ~ this day week

week[2] (w) ge- soak, steep in

week[3] (b) weker, -ste soft, tender

week'blad ~blaaie weekly (newspaper)

week: ~liks weekly; ~loon weekly wages; ~s'dag weekday

weel'de luxury; profusion; ~arti'kel luxury article; ~mo'tor luxury car

wee'luis -e (bed) bug

weemoe'dig sad, melancholy ook droe'wig

ween ge- weep, cry

weens (vs) owing to; on account of; ~ gebrek aan geld for want of money

weer[1] (w) weather; swaar ~ thunder and lightning

weer[2] (w) ge- defend; exert oneself

weer[3] (bw) again, a second time; ~ eens/weereens (once) again; heen en ~ to and fro

weer: ~berig' weather report; ~buro' weather bureau

weergalm' (w) ~ echo, resound ook eg'go

weer: ~glas barometer ook ba'rometer; ~haan weathercock

weerkaats' ~ reflect; re-echo; ~ing reflection

weer: ~klank echo, resonance; ~kun'de meteorology; ~lig (s) lightning; ~loos defenceless; ~mag armed forces; defence force; ~profeet' weather prophet

weer'sien -ge- meet again; ~s: tot ~s! so long!; till we meet again!

weer'sin repugnance, antipathy, dislike

weers'kante both sides

weerspie'ël (w) ~ mirror, reflect; ~ing reflection (in water)

weerspreek' ~ contradict, gainsay; belie

weer'stand resistance, opposition; die weg van die geringste ~ the line of least resistance

weer'standsbewe'ging resistance movement

weer'vas all-weather; ~te baan all-weather court

weer'voorspelling -s weather forecast

weer'wil: in ~ van in spite of, despite

weer'wraak (s) retribution, reprisal ook ver=gel'ding

wees[1] (s) wese orphan ook wees'kind

wees[2] (w) is, was, ge- to be

wees: ~huis orphanage; ~kind orphan

weet wis, ge- know, be conscious of, have knowledge of

weetgie'rig eager to learn; inquisitive

weg[1] (s) weë way, road ook pad

weg[2] (b, bw) away, off, gone

weg'breekvakansie break-away holiday

weg'doen -ge- dispose (of); ~baar disposable (e.g. syringe)

weg'kom -ge- get away; maak dat jy ~! be gone; ~mo'tor getaway car

weg'kruip -ge- hide oneself; ~ertjie' hide-and-seek (children's game); bo-peep

weg'neem -ge- take away; ~e'te take-away (food)

weg: ~skram flinch away; evade; ~slaan strike/beat away; swallow (a drink)

weg'spring -ge- jump away; start off; on=gelyke ~ false start; ~blok starting block

weg: ~steek hide; retain; ~sterf die away

wei (w) feed, graze; ~ding pasturage, grazing ook wei'veld

wei'er ge- decline, refuse; ~ing refusal

wei'fel ge- waver, vacillate ook aar'sel

wei'nig -e; minder, minste little, few

wei'veld **-e** pasture land, meadow; grazing

wek **ge-** wake, rouse, stir; ∼**ker** alarm clock; ∼**roep** clarion call; slogan

wel¹: (s) *die ∼ en wee* the weal and woe; (bw) **beter bes(te)** well, all right; ∼ *te ruste!* good night! sleep well!

wel² (tw) well!

wel: ∼**beha'e** feeling of comfort, pleasure; ∼**bekend'** well-known, noted; ∼**daad** kind= ness, kind action; ∼**doen'er** benefactor

weleerwaar'de (right) reverend

wel: ∼**geska'pe** well-formed, well-made; ∼**ge= steld'** affluent, well-to-do *ook* **welaf'**

we'lig luxuriant, exuberant *ook* **geil**

wel'ke which, what *ook* **wat'ter**

wel'kom **-e** welcome; acceptable; ∼ *heet* extend a welcome; ∼ *in Welkom* welcome to Welkom; ∼ *tuis!* welcome home!

wellui'dend **-e; -er, -ste** melodious

wel'lus **-te** sensual pleasure, lust; bliss

welp **-e** cub, whelp (animal)

welrie'kend (b) fragrant *ook* **geu'rig**

wel'sand quicksand *ook* **dryf'sand**

wel'slae success; *met ∼ voltooi* complete successfully

welspre'kend (b) eloquent, articulate

wel'syn wellbeing; welfare; *na sy ∼ verneem* enquire after his wellbeing

wel'vaart (s) prosperity *ook* **voor'spoed**

welva'rend prosperous, thriving; affluent

welwil'lend kindly disposed, favourable; ∼**heids'besoek** courtesy visit *ook* **hof'lik= heldsbesoek**

Welwil'lendheidsdag Day of Goodwill

we'mel **ge-** swarm, teem with; *dit ∼ van foute* it bristles with mistakes

wen (w) **ge-** win, gain; outdistance; *'n wed= stryd ∼* win a match

wend (w) **ge-** turn; *jou tot iem. ∼ om raad* turn to someone for advice

wen'ding **-s, -e** turn; *'n gunstige ∼ neem* take a turn for the better

wenk **-e** hint, sign, nod, tip; tip-off; ∼**brou** eyebrow

wen'ner **-s** winner

wens (s) **-e** wish, desire; (w) wish, desire; ∼**den'kery** wishful thinking

wens'lik **-e; -er, -ste** desirable

wens'put **-te** wishing well

wen'streep **..strepe** finishing line (in a race)

wen tel **ge-** roll over; welter, revolve, rotate; orbit; ∼**baan** orbit; ∼**krediet'** revolving

credit; ∼**trap** spiral/winding staircase

werd worth; *nie die moeite ∼ nie* not worth= while

wê'reld **-e** world; ∼**beroemd'** world famous; ∼**deel** continent *ook* **vas'teland**

wêrelds **-e** worldly, secular

wê'reld: ∼**stad** metropolis; ∼**wyd** worldwide; ∼**wye** web worldwide web (comp.)

werf¹ (s) **werwe** (farm)yard; shipyard; pre= mises; ∼**hoen'der** free-range chicken

werf² (w) **ge-** enlist, enrol, recruit; *stemme ∼* canvass (for) votes

werk (s) **-e** work, labour, employment; ∼**blad** spreadsheet (comp.); (w) work, labour, oper= ate, function; ∼ *soos 'n esel* work like a slave

wer'ker **-s** worker; ∼**ska'kel** shop steward (in trade union) *ook* **vloer'leier**

Wer'kersdag Workers' Day (holiday)

werk: ∼**geleent'heid** job opportunity; ∼**ge'= wer** employer

wer'king **-e, -s** action, working, operation; *buite ∼ stel* put out of action; *in volle ∼* in full swing/production

werk'lik **-e** real, true, actual; ∼ *waar* actually; truly; ∼**heid** reality

werk'loos **..lose** unemployed; out of work; inactive; ∼**heid** unemployment

werk: ∼**man** workman, labourer, artisan *ook* **vak'man**; ∼**ne'mer** employee; ∼**saam** ac= tive, industrious, effective

werk(s)'bevre'diging job satisfaction

werk'sku **-we** workshy

werk: ∼**skep'ping** job creation; ∼**slaaf** work addict; workaholic; ∼**soe'ker** job seeker; ∼**sta'king** strike; ∼**tuig** tool, implement

werktuigkun'dige (n) mechanic(ian)

werk: ∼**verrig'ting** performance (of work); ∼**verskaf'fing;** job creation *ook* **werkskep'= ping;** ∼**(s)win'kel** workshop *ook* **werk'ses'sie;** ∼**woord** verb; ∼**wy'se** method/manner of operation *ook* **han'del(s)wyse**

werp **ge-** cast; throw; ∼**skyf** quoit; discus; ∼**spies** javelin; dart

wer'skaf (w) **ge-** do, make, be busy; *waaraan ∼ jy?* what are you busy on?

wes west

we'se **-ns** being, nature, essence; *geen lewende ∼ nie* not a living soul

we'sel **-s** weasel, mink (animal)

wes'kus **-te** west coast

Wes-Kaap (provinsie) Western Cape

wesp -e wasp *ook* **per'deby**

wes'tergrens -e western boundary

wes'tewind -e west wind

wet (s) **-te** law; act; *'n ~ oortree* contravene a law; *die ~ toepas* enforce the law

we'te knowing, knowledge; *teen jou beterwete in* against one's better judgment; *na my beste ~* to the best of my knowledge

we'tenskap -pe science; knowledge; **~fik'sie** science fiction, sci-fi

wetenskap'lik -e scientific; **~e** scientist (person)

wet: **~geleer'de** lawyer, jurist *ook* **regs'-geleerde**; **~ge'wend** legislative; **~ge'wende verga'dering** legislative assembly; **~ge'-wing** legislation

wet'lik -e legal; *hulle is ~ geskei* they are legally divorced; **~e voor'skrif** legal prescription/requirement

wets: **~gehoor'saam** law abiding; **~ontwerp'** bill, draft act; **~toe'passing** law enforcement

wet'tig (w) **ge-** justify; legalise; (b) lawful, legitimate; **~e eg'genoot** lawful spouse; **~e erf'genaam** heir-at-law

we'wenaar -s widower; blackjack (weed)

we'wer -s weaver; **~y** weaving/textile mill, cotton factory

whis'ky whisky (Scotch); whiskey (Irish)

wie who; whom; *~ se hoed?* whose hat?

wieg (s) **wieë** cradle, cot

wie'gelied -ere lullaby, cradle song

wie'gie (s): **~sterfte/dood** cot death; **~wag'-ter** babysitter *ook* **kroos'trooster**

wiel -e wheel; *iem. in die ~e ry* put a spoke in someone's wheel; **~dop** hub cap

wiel(i)ewa'lie merry-go-round (game)

wiel'sporing wheel alignment

wier -e seaweed; alga

wie'rook incense; **~vat** thurible/censer

wig (s) **wîe** wedge

wik ge- reflect, poise; *die mens ~, maar God beskik* man proposes, God disposes

wik'kel (w) **ge-** wrap, wind round; wobble; *ge~ raak in* get involved in

wil[1] (s) will, wish, desire; *teen ~ en dank* in spite of oneself; *ter ~le van* for the sake of

wil[2] (w) **wou, ge-** wish, want to

wild (s) game; (b) wild, savage, fierce; **~dief/stro'per** game poacher

wil'de (b) savage; **~bees'** wildebees, gnu; **~makou'** spur-winged goose

wil'dernis -se wilderness, waste

wildewrag'tig wild-looking/scary person

wild: **~stro'per** poacher; **~s'vleis** venison, game; **~tuin** game reserve; **~vreemd** quite strange; totally unknown

wilg/wil'ger/wil'gerboom willow tree, weeping willow *ook* **treur'wilger**

wils'krag willpower

wim'pel -s pennant, pennon, streamer

wim'per -s eyelash *ook* **oog'haar**

wind ,-e wind, breeze; flatulence; *die ~ van voor kry* run into difficulties; **~buks** airgun, pellet gun; **~erig** windy; **~hoos** windspout, whirlwind (in ocean); **~jek'ker** windbreaker; **~lawaai'** braggart, gasbag (person); **~me'ter** wind gauge; **~meul/meu'le** windmill: *'n klap van die ~meul weg hê* have bats in the belfry; **~skeef** (b) skew, lopsided; **~stil'te** calm; *streek van ~stilte* doldrums; **~weer'stand** wind resistance

win'gerd -e vineyard; **~griep** hangover

wink (s) **-e** wink; (w) wink, beckon; ogle

win'kel -s shop, store; **~dief'stal** shoplifting; **~haak** set square, try square

winkelier' -s shopkeeper, dealer

win'kel: **~sen'trum** shopping centre; **~slyt** shop-soiled; **~tan'de** dentures, false teeth; **~ven'ster** shop window *ook* **toon'venster**

wins -te profit, gain; *~ afwerp/oplewer* yield a profit; **~drem'pel** break-even point

wins-en-verlies'-rekening -e, -s profit and loss account

wins: **~ge'wend** lucrative, profitable; **~grens** profit margin; **~ko'pie** bargain; **~oog'merk** profit motive: *vereniging sonder ~oogmerk* association not for gain

win'ter -s winter; *in die ~* in winter; **~s'han'de** chilblained hands; **~slaap** hibernation

wip (s) **-pe** seesaw; snare, trap; (w) hop; seesaw; tilt; turn cheeky; **~mat** trampoline *ook* **trampolien'**; **~plank** seesaw; **~tuig** jolly-jumper *ook* **hup'peltuig**

wis'kunde mathematics *ook* **mate'sis**

wiskun'dig -e mathematical; **~e** mathematician (person)

wispeltu'rig (b) fickle, inconsistent

wis'sel (s) **-s** bill, draft; points, switch (railway); *'n ~ akspeteer* accept a bill; *'n ~ honoreer* honour a bill; (w) exchange, change; shed (teeth); **~aar** traffic interchange; **~bou** crop rotation; **~fonds** cash float; **~koers** rate of exchange; **~stroom**

alternating current; ~**trofee'** floating trophy
wisselval'lig (b) variable, uncertain, unsteady
wis'ser -s wiper, sponge; eraser (rubber)
wit (w) **ge-** whitewash; (b) white; blank;
~**blits** grape brandy *kyk* **mampoer'**
wit'man ..mense white South African, white
wit: ~**seerkeel'** diphtheria; ~**tebroods'dae**
honeymoon; ~**voet** whitefooted: ~*voetjie
soek* curry favour
woed ge- rage, wreak havoc; ~**e** fury, rage;
~**e'bui** (temper) tantrum; ~**end** furious,
violent, infuriated
woe'fie -s (pet name for) dog; ~**boetiek'** pooch
parlour; ~**tuis'te** (boarding) kennels
woek'er (w) **ge-** make the most of; ~**wins**
exorbitant/usurious profit
woel ge- bustle; fidget; work hard; toss about;
~**wa'ter** restless person, bustler; over-active
child
woe'ma (s) vim, zest, muscle *ook* **fut, oemf**
Woens'dag ..dae Wednesday
woes (b) **-te; -ter, -ste** desolate, waste, wild;
furious, savage, fierce, ferocious
woestyn' -e desert, wilderness
wol wool; ~**beurs** wool exchange
wolf wolwe wolf
wolk -e cloud; ~**breuk** cloudburst
wol'kekrabber (s) **-s** skyscraper
wol'wegif strychnine
wond (s) **-e** wound; (w) wound
won'der (s) **-s** wonder, (w) wonder
won'der: ~**kind** wonder child, infant prodigy;
~**lik** marvellous, wonderful; strange, cu=
rious; ~**werk** miracle
wo'ning -s dwelling, residence
woon: ~**buurt** residential area; ~**huis** dwell=
ing house, residence; ~**stel** flat, maisonette;
~**stelverhuur'der** landlord; ~**vertrek'** liv=
ing room; ~**wa** caravan
woord -e word; term; message
woor'de: ~**boek** dictionary; ~**lik** literal, verba=
tim; ~**skat** vocabulary; ~**wis'seling** dispute,
argument
woord: ~**spe'ling** pun, quibble; ~**verwer'ker**
word processor *ook* **teks'verwerker;** ~**ver=
wer'king** word processing (comp.); ~**voer=
der** spokesman/spokesperson; mouthpiece
word ge- become, take place; *dronk* ~ get
drunk; *siek* ~ take ill
wors -e, -te sausage; ~ *in 'n hondestal soek*
look for a needle in a haystack; ~**brood'jie**
hot dog; ~**rol'letjie** sausage roll

wor'stel ge- wrestle; struggle; ~**stryd** struggle
for life
wor'tel (s) **-s** root; carrot *ook* **geel'wortel**
woud -e forest *ook* **bos**
wou'terklouter jungle-gym (play apparatus)
ook **klim'raam**
wraak (s) revenge, vengeance; ~ *neem* take
revenge *ook* **weer'wraak**
wrag'tie indeed, surely, truly; *hy is* ~ *weg!* he
is actually gone!
wrak -ke wreck, derelict; **liggaam'like** ~
physical wreck; ~**werf** scrap yard *ook*
skroot'werf
wreed wrede; wreder, -ste cruel, barbarous;
~**aard** brute; cruel person
wreedaar'dig -e; -er, -ste cruel, inhuman
wreek ge- take revenge, avenge
wre'wel (s) resentment, rancour, spite
wring ge- wring, wrench; ~**krag** torque
wrin'tigwaar really, surely, truly
wroeging -e, -s remorse, self-reproach
wrok -ke grudge, rancour; *'n* ~ *koester* bear a
grudge
wry'wing -s, -e friction; rubbing
wuif/wui'we ge- wave, beckon; *vriende tot
siens* ~ wave goodbye to friends
wulps (b) **-e; -er, -ste** lascivious, sexy
wurg ge- strangle, throttle, choke; ~**greep**
stranglehold; ~**ket'ting** choke chain *ook*
gly'ketting; ~**roof** mug(ging) *ook* **straat'=
roof;** ~**ro'wer** mugger *ook* **straat'rower**
wurm -s worm; maggot, grub
wyd wye; wyer, -ste wide, broad, spacious,
ample; ~ *en syd* far and wide
wyds'been astraddle, astride
wyd'te -s width, breadth
wyf wywe mean woman, vixen, shrew
wy'fie -s female (animal); hen (birds); ~**-eend**
duck
wyk[1] (s) ward, quarter; area, district
wyk[2] (w) **ge-** withdraw, yield, give way; *geen
duimbreed* ~ *nie* not budge an inch
wy'le late, deceased; ~ **mnr. X** the late Mr.
X
wyn -e wine; ~**bou** viticulture; wine growing;
~**kel'der** wine cellar; winery; ~**koek** tipsy
cake; ~**kraf'fie** wine decanter; ~**proe=
(wery)** wine tasting; ~**vaat'jie/**~**vat** wine
barrel/cask
wys[1] (s) **-e** way, manner *ook* **wy'se;** mood
(grammar); *by* ~*e van* by way of
wys[2] (w) **ge-** show, demonstrate, indicate;

direct; *iem.* ~ *waar Dawid die wortels ge=
grawe het* teach someone a thing or two
wys[3] (b) wise; prudent; obstinate
wys'begeerte philosophy *ook* **filosofie'**
wy'se -s way; mood (gram.)
wy'ser/wys'ter (s) index hand (of a clock);
pointer
wys'geer ..**gere** philosopher *ook* **filosoof'**
wys'heid wisdom *ook* **in'sig/ken'nis**

wy'sie (s) -s melody, tune, air
wy'sig ge- modify, amend, alter; ~**ing** amend=
ment, modification; *die grondreëls/konstitu=
sie* ~ amend the constitution
wys'maak -ge- make believe; impose on; *iem.
iets* ~ spin someone a yarn
wys'vinger -s index finger, forefinger
wyt ge- impute, accuse, blame; *te* ~*e aan*
owing to *kyk: te danke aan*

X

X'-bene knock-knees *ook* **aan'kapknieë**
xenograaf' ..**grawe** xenographer
Xho'sa Xhosa

xilofoon' ..**fo'ne** xylophone *ook* **hout'harmo=
nika**
X'-stra'le X-rays, röntgen rays

Y

y'del idle, useless, vain, conceited; ~**heid**
vanity
yk ge- test, assize; **geyk'te uit'drukking**
standing phrase
yl' (b) -**er, -ste** thin, rarefied (atmosphere)
yl' (w) be delirious *ook* **koor'sig** (b)
ylhoof'dig -e delirious, light-headed
ys[1] (s) *op gladde* ~ *staan* be in danger; (w)
freeze, ice
ys[2] (w) **ge-** shudder, shiver; *ek* ~ *as ek dink
aan* I shudder to think of
ys: ~**baan** ice/skating rink; ~**beer** polar bear;
~**berg** iceberg; ~**ig** ice-cold; ~**kas** refrig=
erator *ook* **koel'kas**; icebox; ~**koud** cold as

ice; *dit laat my* ~*koud* it leaves me cold
y'sig (b) freezing
ys'lik (b) -**e** enormous, tremendous *ook* **tamaai'**
ys: ~**reën** sleet; ~**sak** coolbag; ~**skaats** ice
skating
Ys'see Arctic Ocean
ys'ter -s iron
ys'terklou: ~ *in die grond slaan* take to one's
heels; dig in one's heels
ys'ter: ~**paal** iron standard/pole; ~**saag** hack=
saw; ~**vark** porcupine; ~**wa're** hardware
ook **har'deware**; ironmongery
y'wer (s) diligence, zeal *ook* **vlyt**; ~**ig'** (b)
diligent *ook* **vly'tig**

Z

ze'ro zero, naught
Zimbab'we Zimbabwe; **Zimbab'wiese eko=
nomie'** Zimbabwe (Zimbabwean) economy
Zimbab'wiër -s Zimbabwean (person)
Zoe'loe -s Zulu *ook* **Zu'lu**; ~**-im'pie** Zulu
regiment; ~**land** Zululand

zoem (s) buzz(ing), drone; (w) buzz, zoom,
whizz, drone; ~ *in* zoom in (phot.); ~ *weg*
zoom away; ~**er** buzzer *ook* **gon'ser**;
~**lens** zoom lens; ~**pie** blue duiker (ante=
lope)
zom'bi (s) zombi *ook* **le'wende lyk**

Afkortings/Akronieme

A

AA[1] Alkoholiste Anoniem □ Alcoholics Anonymous **AA**

AA[2] Automobiel-Assosiasie □ Automobile Association **AA**

aa afskrif(te) aan □ carbon copy to **cc**

aanget. aangeteken □ registered **regd.**

a.asb. antwoord asseblief □ *Répondez s'il vous plaît* please reply **RSVP**

AD *Anno Domini* in die jaar van ons Here □ *Anno Domini* in the year of our Lord **AD**

ad inf. *ad infinitum* tot die oneindige □ *ad infinitum* to infinity **ad inf.**

admin. administrateur/administrasie □ administrator/administration **adm.**

adm. admiraal □ Admiral **Adm.**

adv. advokaat □ Advocate **Adv.**

ad val. *ad valorem* volgens waarde □ *ad valorem* according to value **ad val.**

Afr. Afrikaans; Afrikaner; Afrikaan □ Afrikaans; Afrikaner; African **Afr.**

AGS Apostoliese Geloofsending □ = **AGS**

AHI Afrikaanse Handelsinstituut □ = **AHI**

ANC – □ African National Congress **ANC**

antw. antwoord □ answer/reply **ans.**

AOTH Algemene Ooreenkoms op Tariewe en Handel □ General Agreement on Tariffs and Trade **GATT**

Apr. April □ April **Apr.**

Arab. Arabies □ Arabian/Arabic **Arab.**

art. artikel □ article **art.**

as. aanstaande □ *proximo* next **prox.**

asb. asseblief □ please/*s'il vous plaît* **please/s.v.p.**

Aug. Augustus □ August **Aug.**

ATKV Afrikaanse Taal- en Kultuurvereniging □ – **ATKV**

a.w. aangehaalde werk □ *opere citato* in the work quoted **op. cit./loc. cit.**

AWB Afrikaner-Weerstandbeweging □ – **AWB**

AWS Afrikaanse Woordelys en Spelreëls □ – **AWS**

AZAPO – □ Azanian People's Organisation **AZAPO**

B

B.A. *Baccalaureus Artium* □ *Baccalaureus Artium* Bachelor of Arts **B.A.**

BBP baie belangrike persoon □ very important person **VIP**

B.Com. *Baccalaureus Commercii* □ *Baccalaureus Commercii* Bachelor of Commerce **B.Com.**

B.D. *Baccalaureus Divinitatis* □ *Baccalaureus Divinitatis* Bachelor of Divinity **B.D.**

BD besturende direkteur □ managing director **MD**

bd. boulevard □ boulevard **Bd.**

B.Ed. *Baccalaureus Educationis* □ *Baccalaureus Educationis* Bachelor of Education **B.Ed.**

bet. betaal □ paid **pd.**

bg. bogenoemd(e) □ above-mentioned

bio biografie/biografies *ook* **CV** □ Curriculum vitae **CV** *also* **biodata**

B. Jur. *Baccalaureus Juris* □ *Baccalaureus Juris* Bachelor of Law **B. Jur.**

BK beslote korporasie □ close corporation **CC**

B.Mus. *Baccalaureus Musicae* □ *Baccalaureus Musicae* Bachelor of Music **B.Mus.**

bn biljoen □ billion (Afr. miljard) **bn**

b.nw. byvoeglike naamwoord □ adjective **adj.**

BO bevelvoerende offisier □ commanding officer **CO/OC**

b.o. blaai om □ please turn over **PTO**

Bpk Beperk □ Limited **Ltd**

bpm bladsye per minuut □ pages per minute **ppm**

B.Sc. *Baccalaureus Scientiae* □ *Baccalaureus Scientiae* **B.Sc**

BSW buitesintuiglike waarneming □ extrasensory perception **ESP**

BTW belasting op toegevoegde waarde □ value added tax **VAT**

bv. byvoorbeeld □ *exempli gratia* for example/instance **e.g./eg**

b.v.p./bvp been voor paaltjies □ leg before wicket **lbw**

B.V.Sc. *Baccalaureus Veterinariae Scientiae* □ *Baccalaureus Veterinariae Scientiae* Bachelor of Veterinary Science **B.V.Sc.**

bw. bywoord □ adverb **adv.**

byl. bylae/bylaag □ enclosure/annexure **encl./ annex.**

C

C Celsius □ Centigrade/Celsius **C/Cels.**
c sent □ cent **c**
ca. *circa* ongeveer □ *circa* about **circa/c**
cc kubieke sentimeter □ cubic centimetre **cc**
CD/cd laserplaat/laserskyf □ compact disc **CD/cd**
cg sentigram □ centigram(s) **cg**
Ch.B. *Chirurgiae Baccalaureus* □ *Chirurgiae Baccalaureus* Bachelor of Surgery **Ch.B.**
CJMV Christelike Jongmannevereniging □ Young Men's Christian Association **YMCA**
cℓ sentiliter □ centilitre **cℓ**
cm sentimeter □ centimetre **cm**
Contralesa – □ Congress of traditional leaders of SA **Contralesa**
Cosas – □ Congress of SA Students □ **Cosas**
Cosatu – □ Congress of SA Trade Unions □ **Cosatu**
CSV Christenstudentevereniging □ Student's Christian Association **SCA**
CV *Curriculum vitae* (lewensprofiel, biodata) □ *Curriculum vitae* **CV**
cwt sentenaar □ hundredweight **cwt**

D

d. *denarius* pennie □ *denarius* penny **d.**
D Romeinse 500 □ Roman numeral 500 **D**
Dalro Dramatiese, Artistieke en Letterkundige Regte-Organisasie □ Dramatic, Artistic and Literary Rights Organisation **Dalro**
DBV Dierebeskermingvereniging/Dieresorg □ Society for the prevention of cruelty to animals **SPCA**
d.d. *de dato* gedateer □ *de dato* dated –
D.D. *Doctor Divinitatis* □ *Doctor Divinitatis* Doctor of Divinity **D.D.**
DDS doen dit self □ do it yourself **DIY**
deelw. deelwoord □ participle **part.**
def. definisie □ definition **def.**
dept. departement □ department **dept.**
des. deser □ instant **inst.**
Des. Desember □ December **Dec.**
dg desigram □ decigram **dg**
Dg dekagram □ decagram(s) **Dg**
D.G. *Dei Gratia* deur Gods genade □ *Dei*

Gratia by the grace of God **D.G.**
DG direkteur-generaal □ Director-General **DG**
dgl. dergelike □ such –
d.i. dit is □ *id est* it is **i.e./ie**
di *domini* predikante □ (the) Reverends **Revs.**
Di. Dinsdag □ Tuesday **Tu(es)**
DIN Duitse Industrienorm □ (German Industrial Standard) **DIN**
dist. distrik □ district (of) **dist.**
div. dividend □ dividend **div.**
dℓ desiliter □ decilitre **dℓ**
dl. deel □ volume (of book) **vol.**
Dℓ dekaliter □ Decalitre **Dℓ**
D.Litt. *Doctor Literarum* □ *Doctor Literarum* Doctor of Literature **D.Lit(t).**
dm. duim □ inch **in.**
dm desimeter □ decimetre(s) **dm**
Dm dekameter □ Decametre(s) **Dm**
dnr. dienaar □ servant **serv.**
do. *ditto* dieselfde □ *ditto* the same **do.**
Do. Donderdag □ Thursday **Thurs.**
dos. dosyn □ dozen **doz.**
DP Demokratiese Party □ Democratic Party **DP**
D.Phil. *Doctor Philosophiae* □ *Doctor Philosophiae* Doctor of Philosophy **D.Phil.**
dr debiteur □ debtor **Dr**
dr(.) doktor/dokter □ doctor **Dr**
drr(.) dokters/doktore □ doctors **Drs**
ds(.) *dominus* dominee □ reverend **Rev.**
D.Sc. *Doctor Scientiae* □ *Doctor Scientiae* Doctor of Science **D.Sc.**
dt. debiet □ debit **Dr/Dt**
DV *Deo Volente* as God wil □ *Deo Volente* God willing **DV**
DVD Dekorasie vir Voortreflike Diens □ Decoration for Meritorious Service **DMS**
dw. dienswillig □ obedient **obed.**
d.w.s./dws dit wil sê □ *id est* that is **i.e./ie**
dwt pennyweight □ *denarius* weight **dwt**

E

e.a. en ander(e) □ *et alii* and others **et al.**
e.d. en dergelike □ *et cetera* and so forth **etc.**
Ed. Edele □ Honourable **Hon.**
Ed.Agb. Edelagbare □ the Honourable/Your Honour (in court) **Hon./Your Hon.**
e.d.m. en dergelike/dies meer □ *et cetera* and so forth **etc.**
Edms. Eiendoms □ Proprietary **Pty**

EG Europese Gemeenskap *kyk* EEG ☐
European Community EC
eerw. eerwaarde ☐ Reverend **Rev.**
e.g. eersgenoemde ☐ the former –
EEG Europese Ekonomiese Gemeenskap ☐
European Economic Community EEC
ek. eerskomende ☐ *proximo* next **prox.**
EKG elektrokardiogram ☐ electrocardiogram
ECG
Eks. Eksellensie ☐ Excellency **Exc.**
Eng. Engels ☐ English **Engl.**
ens. ensovoorts ☐ *et cetera* and so forth **etc.**
e-pos elektroniese pos ☐ electronic mail
e-mail/email
eresekr. eresekretaris ☐ Honorary Secretary
Hon. Sec.
Eskom – ☐ Electricity Supply Commission
Eskom
e.s.m. en so meer ☐ *et cetera* and so forth **etc.**
EU Europese Unie *kyk* EG ☐ European
Union **EU**

F

F Fahrenheit ☐ Fahrenheit **F**
f *forte* luid ☐ *forte* loud **f**
FAK Federasie van Afrikaanse Kultuurvereni-
gings ☐ – **FAK**
faks faksimilee ☐ facsimile **fax**
fakt. faktuur ☐ invoice **inv.**
Feb(r) Februarie ☐ February **Feb**
fig. figuur(lik) ☐ figure/figurative **fig.**
Finrand finansiële Rand ☐ financial Rand
Finrand
FM frekwensiemodulasie ☐ frequency mod-
ulation **FM**
Frelimo Frente de Libertação de Moçambique
☐ – **Frelimo**
F en WU foute en weglatings uitgesonder ☐
errors and omissions excepted **E & OE**
Fr. Frankryk/Frans ☐ France/French **Fr.**
fr. frank ☐ franc(s) **fr.**

G

g gram ☐ gram **g**
Gasa – ☐ Gay Association of SA **Gasa**
gall./gell. gallon/gelling ☐ gallon(s) **gal.**
geb. gebore ☐ born, née; *natus* **b./n.**
(ge)b. geb. geboul ☐ bowled **b.**

gebrs. gebroeders ☐ Brothers **Bros**
geïll. geïllustreer ☐ illustrated **illus.**
gell./gall. gelling/gallon ☐ gallon(s) **gal.**
genl. generaal ☐ General **Gen.**
Geref. Gereformeerd ☐ Reformed **Ref.**
get./w.g. geteken/was geteken ☐ signed **sgd.**
(ge)v. gevang (krieket) ☐ caught **c.**
GIS Instituut van Geoktrooieerde Sekretarisse
en Administrateurs ☐ Institute of Chartered
Secretaries and Administrators **CIS**
GKC Genoot v.d. Kollege van Chirurgie ☐
Fellow of the College of Surgeons **FCS**
Glow – ☐ Gay and Lesbian Organisation
Glow *see* **Gasa**
gr. graad (vir standerd) ☐ grade (new school
years) **gr.**
GRA Genootskap van Regte Afrikaners ☐ –
GRA
GR Geoktrooieerde Rekenmeester ☐ Char-
tered Accountant **CA**
GRS Gesagvereniging vir Reklamestandaarde
☐ Advertising Standards Authority **ASA**
GV Grondwetgewende Vergadering ☐ Con-
stitutional Assembly **CA**

H

ha hektaar ☐ hectare(s) **ha**
H.d.L. Heil die Leser ☐ *Lectori Salutem* hail
the reader **L.S.**
H.Ed. Hoogedele ☐ Right Honourable **Rt.**
Hon.
H.Eerw. Hoogeerwaarde ☐ Right Reverend
Rt. Rev.
Herv. Hervormd ☐ Reformed **Ref.**
hfst. hoofstuk ☐ chapter **c/ch.**
hg hektogram ☐ hectogram(s) **hg**
HKH Haar Koninklike Hoogheid ☐ Her Royal
Highness **HRH**
hℓ hektoliter ☐ hectolitre(s) **hℓ**
HM Haar Majesteit ☐ Her Majesty **HM**
hm hektometer ☐ hectometre(s) **hm**
HNP Herstigte Nasionale Party ☐ – **HNP**
HOD Hoër Onderwysdiploma ☐ Higher Diplo-
ma in Education **HDE**
HOP Heropbou- en Ontwikkelingsprogram
☐ Reconstruction and Development Pro-
gramme **RDP**
hs./ms. handskrif/manuskrip ☐ manuscript
MS
h.v. hoek van ☐ corner **cor./cnr.**

I

ID identiteitsdokument □ identity document **ID**

id. *idem* dieselfde □ *idem* the same **id.**

i.e. *id est* dit is □ *id est* that is **i.e.**

IK intelligensiekwosiënt □ intelligence quotient **IQ**

IMF Internasionale Monetêre Fonds □ International Monetary Fund **IMF**

in'fo informasie/inligting □ information **info**

infra dig. *infra dignitatem* benede sy waardigheid □ *infra dignitatem* beneath his dignity **infra dig.**

INMDC – □ Interim National Medical and Dental Council **INMDC**

Interpol Internasionale Kriminele Polisiekommissie □ International Criminal Police Commission **Interpol**

IOK Internasionale Olimpiese Komitee □ International Olympic Committee **IOC**

i.p.v./ipv in plaas van □ instead of –

IRL Ierse Republikeinse Leër □ Irish Republican Army **IRA**

is. in sake/insake □ regarding **re**

ISBN Internasionale standaardboeknommer □ International standard book number **ISBN**

Iscor – □ (SA) Iron and Steel Corporation **Iscor**

i.v.m./ivm in verband met □ regarding **re**

IVP Inkatha Vryheidsparty □ Inkatha Freedom Party **IFP**

J

JA Johannesburgse Aandelebeurs □ Johannesburg Stock Exchange **JSE**

Jan. Januarie □ January **Jan.**

J.C. Jesus Christus □ Jesus Christ **JC**

jl. jonglede □ *ultimo* last **ult.**

jap'pie jong opkomende professionele persoon □ young upwardly mobile professional (person) **yup'pie**

jr. jaar/junior □ year/junior **yr./Jun.**

juf. juffrou □ Miss –

Jul. Julie □ July **Jul.**

Jun. Junie □ June **Jun.**

K

kapt. kaptein □ captain **Capt.**

kar. karaat □ carat(s) **car./ct.**

k.a.v. koste, assuransie, vrag □ cost, insurance, freight **c.i.f.**

k.b.a./kba kontant by aflewering □ cash on delivery **C.O.D./COD**

KEEM Kantoor vir ernstige ekonomiese misdrywe □ Office for serious economic offences **OSEO**

kg kilogram □ kilogram(s) **kg**

KI kunsmatige inseminasie □ artificial insemination **AI**

km/h kilometer per uur (hora) □ kilometres per hour **km/h**

Kie. kompanjie □ company **Co.**

kℓ kiloliter □ kilolitre(s) **kℓ**

km kilometer □ kilometre(s) **km**

k.m.b./kmb kontant met bestelling □ cash with order **C.W.O./CWO**

kmdt. kommandant □ Commandant **Comdt.**

kol. kolonel □ Colonel **Col.**

koöp./ko-op. koöperasie □ co-operative **co-op**

KP Konserwatiewe Party □ Conservative Party **CP**

kpl. korporaal □ Corporal **Cpl.**

kr. krediteur/krediteer □ creditor/credit **Cr.**

KSOK Kleinsake-Ontwikkelingskorporasie □ Small Business Development Corporation **SBDC**

kt. krediet □ credit **Cr.**

kub. kubiek(e) □ cubic **cub.**

kW kilowatt □ kilowatt(s) **kW**

KWV Koöperatiewe Wynbouersvereniging □ – **KWV**

KZN KwaZulu-Natal □ KwaZulu/Natal **KZN**

L

£ pond (geld) □ *libra* (pound, money) **£**

l. *lira*/links □ *lira*/left **l.**

ℓ liter □ litre(s) **ℓ**

ℓ/100 km liter per 100 km □ litres per 100 km **ℓ/100 km**

L Romeinse 50 □ Roman numeral 50 **L**

L. Akad. (SA) Lid van die SA Akademie vir Wetenskap en Kuns □ – **L. Akad. (SA)**

LAN lokaleareanetwerk □ local area network **LAN**

Lat. Latyn □ Latin **Lat.**

l.a.w./LAW ligte afleweringswa ☐ light deliv= ery van **LDV**
lb. *libra* pond, gewig ☐ *libra* pound, weight **lb.**
LBS lopende betaalstelsel ☐ pay-as-you-earn **PAYE**
lg. laasgenoemde ☐ the latter –
ll. laaslede ☐ *ultimo* last **ult.**
LL.B. *Legum Baccalaureus* ☐ *Legum Bacca= laureus* Bachelor of Law **LL.B.**
l.n.r. links na regs ☐ left to right **l. to r.**
LP Lid van die Parlement ☐ Member of Parliament **MP**
LS langspeler (plaat) ☐ long-playing (record) **LP**
L.S./H.d.L. *Lectori Salutem* heil die leser ☐ *Lectori Salutem* hail to the reader **L.S.**
LSD lisergiensuur-diëtielamide ☐ lysergic acid diethylamide **LSD**
lt. luitenant ☐ lieutenant **Lt.**
lt.kol. luitenant-kolonel ☐ Lieutenant-Colonel **Lt. Col.**
lw. lidwoord ☐ article (gram.) **art.**
LW let wel ☐ *nota bene* mark well **NB**

M

m meter; myl ☐ metre(s); mile(s) **m**
m. manlik ☐ masculine **m./masc.**
Ma. Maandag ☐ Monday **Mon.**
M.A. *Magister Artium* ☐ *Magister Artium* Master of Arts **M.A.**
maj. majoor ☐ Major **Maj.**
m.a.w./maw met ander woorde ☐ in other words –
Mb megagreep ☐ megabyte **Mb**
MBA/MBL Magister in Besigheidsadminis= trasie/Bedryfsleiding ☐ Master(s) (degree) in Business Administration/Leadership **MBA/MBL**
m.b.t./mbt met betrekking tot ☐ with refer= ence to –
M.B. *Medicinae Baccalaureus* ☐ *Medicinae Baccalaureus* Bachelor of Medicine **M.B.**
M.D. *Medicinae Doctor* ☐ *Medicinae Doctor* Doctor of Medicine **M.D.**
Me/me. (mv. **mee.**) Me(juffrou)/Me(vrou) ☐ Miss **Ms**
M.Ed. *Magister Educationis* ☐ *Magister Educationis* Master of Education **M.Ed.**
Medun'sa Mediese Universiteit van Suider-Afrika ☐ Medical University of Southern

Africa **Medun'sa**
mej(.)/mejj(.) mejuffrou(e) ☐ Miss/Misses –
memo. memorandum ☐ memorandum **memo.**
mev(.) mevrou ☐ mistress/madam **Mrs**
mevv(.) mevroue ☐ mesdames **Mmes**
mg milligram ☐ milligram(s) **mg**
m.i. myns insiens ☐ in my view –
mil. militêr(e) ☐ military **mil.**
min. minister/minuut/minimum ☐ minister/minute/minimum **Min./min.**
Min'tek Raad vir Mineraaltegnologie ☐ Council for Mineral Technology **Min'tek**
MIV/HIV menslike immuniteitsmorende virus ☐ human immunosuppressive virus **HIV**
MK – ☐ Umkhonto we Sizwe **MK**
mℓ – milliliter ☐ millilitre(s) **mℓ**
mm millimeter ☐ millimetre(s) **mm**
M.Net. Elektroniese Medianetwerk ☐ Elec= tronic Media Network **M-Net**
MNR Mediese Navorsingsraad ☐ Medical Research Council **MRC**
mnr(.) meneer ☐ Mister **Mr**
mnre(.) menere ☐ Messieurs **Messrs**
m.p.u./mpu myl per uur ☐ miles per hour **mph**
MR Metropolitaanse Raad ☐ Metropolitan Council **MC**
Mrt. Maart ☐ March **Mar.**
ms. manuskrip ☐ manuscript **MS**
MSS Metropolitaanse substruktuur ☐ Metro= politan substructure **MSS**
MTN – ☐ Mobile Telephone Network **MTN**
mus. musiek/musikaal ☐ music/musical **mus.**
mv. meervoud ☐ plural **pl.**
MVSA Mediese Vereniging van Suid-Afrika ☐ Medical Association of South Africa **MASA/Masa**
MWU Mynwerkersunie ☐ Mineworkers' Union **MWU**
My./Mpy maatskappy ☐ company **Co.**

N

N. noord ☐ North **N.**
n. namens ☐ for; on behalf of –
Nasrec Nasionale sport-, ontspan- en uitstal= sentrum ☐ National sport, recreation and exhibition centre **Nasrec**
Nat. Natuurkunde ☐ Physics **Phys.**
n.a.v./nav na aanleiding van ☐ with reference to **w.r.t.**

Navo Noord-Atlantiese Verdragorganisasie
□ North Atlantic Treaty Organisation **Nato**
NB *Nota Bene* let wel □ *Nota Bene* mark well
NB
n.C./nC na Christus □ *Anno Domini* of the
Christian era **AD**
Ndl. Nederland(s) □ Netherland(s)/Dutch
Neth./Du.
N(ed). G(eref). Nederduitse Gereformeerde
□ Dutch Reformed **DR**
N(ed). Herv. Nederduits Hervormd □ Neder=
duits Hervormd **NH**
NGK Nederduitse Gereformeerde Kerk □
Dutch Reformed Church **DRC**
nl. naamlik □ *videlicet* namely **viz.**
nm(.) namiddag □ *post meridiem* in the after=
noon **pm**
no./nr. *numero* nommer □ *numero* number
No.
NOIK Nederlandse Oos-Indiese Kompanjie
□ Dutch East India Company **DEIC**
NOK Nywerheidontwikkelingskorporasie □
Industrial Development Corporation **IDC**
NOKSA Nasionale Olimpiese Komitee van
SA □ National Olympic Committee of SA
NOCSA
Nov. November □ November **Nov.**
NP Nasionale Party □ National Party **NP**
nr./no. *numero* nommer □ *numero* number **No.**
NRP Nasionale Raad van Provinsies □
National Council of Provinces **NCOP**
Ns. naskrif □ *post scriptum* postscript **PS**
NT Nuwe Testament □ New Testament **NT**
NUM Nasionale Unie van Mynwerkers □
National Union of Mineworkers **NUM**
nv. naamval □ case **c.**
n.v.t./NVT nie van toepassing □ not appli=
cable **n.a./NA**
nw. naamwoord □ noun **n.**

O

o./ons. onsydig □ neuter **n./neut.**
O. oos □ east **E.**
o.a. onder ander(e) □ *inter alia* –
OAE Organisasie vir Afrika-Eenheid □
Organisation for African Unity **OAU**
OB Openbare Beskermer □ Public Protector
PP
OBSA Ontwikkelingsbank van Suider-Afrika
□ Development Bank of Southern Africa

DBSA
oef. oefening □ exercise **ex.**
o.i. onses insiens □ in our view
Okt. Oktober □ October **Oct.**
OLP ongelode (loodvrye) petrol □ unleaded
petrol **ULP**
o.l.v./olv onder leiding van □ under direction
of **u.d.o.**
o.m. onder meer □ *inter alia* –
ong. ongeveer □ *circa* about **c.**
oorl. oorlede □ *obiit* died, late **d.**
opm. opmerking(e) □ remark(s) **rem.**
OPUL/OPEC Organisasie van Petroleum=
Uitvoerlande □ Organisation of Petroleum
Exporting Countries **OPEC**
ord. ordonnansie □ ordinance **Ord.**
ost. onderstaande □ following **fol.**
OT Ou Testament □ Old Testament **OT**
OTM outomatiese tellermasjien/kitsbank □
automatic teller machine **ATM**
Oudl. ouderling □ elder –
OUO Onafhanklike uitsaai-owerheid □ In=
dependent broadcasting authority **IBA**
OW/ow ontvangwissel □ Bill Receivable **B/R**
oz ons □ ounce(s) **oz**
Oz Australië (doeronder) □ Australia (down
under) **Oz**

P

p./bl. *pagina* bladsy; *per* vir; met □ page; per
p.
p. paaltjie (krieket) □ wicket **w.**
p *piano* sag □ *piano* softly **p**
p.a./p.j. *per annum* (per jaar) □ *per annum*
(per year) **p.a.**
p.a. per adres □ care of **c/o**
PAC – □ Pan Africanist Congress **PAC**
par. paragraaf □ paragraph **par.**
PANSAT Pan-Suid-Afrikaanse Taalraad □ Pan
South African Language Board **PANSAT**
PBO Palestynse Bevrydingsorganisasie □
Palestinian Liberation Organisation **PLO**
pd. pond gewig; geld □ *libra* pound weight **lb**
PG/prok.genl. prokureur-generáal □ Attor=
ney-General **AG**
Ph.D. *Philosophiae Doctor* □ *Philosphiae
Doctor* Doctor of Philosophy **Ph.D.**
p.j./p.a. per jaar/annum □ *per annum* yearly
p.a.
pk perdekrag □ horse power **h.p.**

Pk. poskantoor ☐ Post Office **PO**
p.m. per maand/per minuut ☐ *per mensem* per month; per minute **p.m.**
POPCRU – ☐ Police and Prisons Civil Rights Union **POPCRU**
pp *pianissimo* baie sag ☐ *pianissimo* very softly **pp**
p.p./per pro. *per procurationem* by volmag ☐ *per procurationem* by procuration **p.p./ per pro.**
PR persoonlike rekenaar ☐ personal computer **PC**
pres. president ☐ President **Pres.**
prof. professor ☐ Professor **Prof.**
PS *post scriptum* (naskrif) ☐ *post scriptum* postscript **PS**
Ps. psalm ☐ Psalm **Ps.**
ps. privaat(pos)sak ☐ private/postal bag **P/B**
PU vir CHO Potchefstroomse Universiteit vir Christelike Hoër Onderwys ☐ Potchefstroom University **PU**

Q

q.e.d. *quod erat demonstrandum* wat bewys moes word ⊔ *quod erat demonstrandum* which was to be demonstrated **QED**

R

R Rand ⊔ Rand(s) **R**
RAU Randse Afrikaanse Universiteit ☐ Rand Afrikaans University **RAU**
rdh(.) raadsheer ☐ alderman **ald.**
rdl(.) raadslid ☐ councillor **clrs(.)**
red. redakteur/redaksie ☐ editor **Ed.**
rek. rekening ☐ account **a/c**
RGN Raad vir Geesteswetenskaplike Navorsing ☐ Human Sciences Research Council **HSRC**
RGO/RO rekenaargesteunde onderrig ☐ computer-aided instruction **CAI**
RIP *requiescat in pace* rus in vrede ☐ *requiescat in pace* rest in peace **RIP**
RK Rooms-Katoliek ☐ Roman Catholic **RC**
rln. rylaan ☐ drive **dr.**
r/min (opm) omwentelinge per minuut ☐ revolutions per minute **r/min**
RNE Regering van Nasionale Eenheid ☐ Government of National Unity **GNU**

ROEP red ons eensame platteland ☐ rescue our endangered platteland **ROEP**
RSA Republiek (van) Suid-Afrika ☐ Republic of South Africa **RSA**
RSVP/a.asb. *rèpondez s'il vous plaît* antwoord asseblief ☐ *rèpondez s'il vous plaît* please reply **RSVP**
RU Rhodes Universiteit ☐ Rhodes University **RU**

S

S. suid(elik) ☐ south(ern) **S.**
SA Suid-Afrika ☐ South Africa **SA**
Sa. Saterdag ☐ Saturday **Sat.**
SAA – ☐ South African Airways **SAA**
SABC – ☐ South African Broadcasting Corporation **SABC**
SABEK SA Besigheidskamer ☐ SA Chamber of Business **SACOB**
SABS Suid-Afrikaanse Buro vir Standaarde ☐ South African Bureau of Standards **SABS**
SAGTR kyk **INMDC**
SAID SA Inkomstedienste ☐ SA Revenue Services **SARS**
SAKD Suid-Afrikaanse Kommunikasiedienste ☐ South African Communication Services **SACS**
SAKP SA Kommunisteparty ☐ SA Communist Party **SACP**
SAL kyk **SAA**
SALM Suid-Afrikaanse Lugmag ⊔ South African Air Force **SAAF**
Samro SA Musiekregte-Organisasie ☐ SA Music Rights Organisation **Samro**
SANW Suid-Afrikaanse Nasionale Weermag ☐ South African National Defence Force **SANDF**
SAPD Suid-Afrikaanse Polisiedienste ☐ South African Police Services **SAPS**
Sapa Suid-Afrikaanse Pers-Assosiasie ☐ South African Press Association **Sapa**
Sasol Suid-Afrikaanse Steenkool-, Olie- en Gaskorporasie ☐ South African Coal, Oil and Gas Corporation **Sasol**
SAUK kyk **SABC**
SBSS Skielike Babasterftesindroom ☐ Sudden Infant Death Syndrome **SIDS**
S. Ed. Sy Edele ☐ the Honourable **the Hon.**
S. Ed. Agb. Sy Edelagbare ☐ the Honourable **the Hon.**

sek. sekonde(s) □ second(s) **sec.**
sekr. sekretaris □ secretary **Sec.**
S. Eks. Sy Eksellensie □ His Excellence **HE**
sen. senator/senaat □ senate/senator **Sen.**
Sep(t). September □ September **Sep(t).**
sers. sersant □ Sergeant **Sgt.**
sert. sertifikaat □ certificate **cert.**
s.g. soortlike gewig □ specific gravity **sp. gr./SG**
sg. sogenaamd(e)/sogenoemd(e) □ so-called
SH Sy Heiligheid/Hoogheid □ His Holiness/Highness **HH**
S.H. Ed. Sy Hoogedele □ the Right Honour= able **the Rt. Hon.**
sitkom situasiekomedie □ situation comedy **sitcom**
SKH Sy Koninklike Hoogheid □ His Royal Highness **HRH**
sktr. skutter □ gunner/rifleman **gnr./rfn.**
s.nw. selfstandige naamwoord □ noun **n.**
So. Sondag □ Sunday **Sun.**
Soekor Suidelike Olie-Eksplorasiekorporasie □ Southern Oil Exploration Corporation **Soekor**
sos sien ommesy □ please turn over **PTO**
SOS internasionale noodsein □ international distress signal **SOS**
SR Studenteraad □ Students' Representative Council **SRC**
sr. senior □ senior **Sen.**
SSG Sentrale Sakegebied *ook* **sa'kekern** □ Central Business District **CBD**
st. standerd (nou graad) □ Standard (now grade) **Std.**
St. *Sint* Heilige □ Saint **St.**
str. straat □ street **St.**
subj. subjek/subjunktief □ subject/subjunc= tive **subj.**
supt. superintendent □ Superintendent **Supt.**
s.v.p. *s'il vous plaît* asseblief □ *s'il vous plaît* please **s.v.p.**
Swapo – □ South West African People's Organisation **Swapo**

T

t ton (metriek) □ ton(s) **t**
t. *tarra* eiegewig □ *tare* own weight **t.**
t.a.p. ter aangehaalde plaatse □ *loco citato* in the place cited **loc. cit.**
t.a.v. ten aansien van □ in respect of **i.r.o**

tel. telefoon □ telephone **tel.**
Telkom telekommunikasiedienste □ telecom= munication services **Telkom**
telw. telwoord □ numeral **num.**
t.o.v./tov ten opsigte van □ with regard to –
t.t. *totus tuus* geheel die uwe □ *totus tuus* faithfully yours **t.t.**
TV televisie □ television **TV**
tw. tussenwerpsel □ interjection **int(erj).**
t.w. te wete □ *vedelicet* namely **viz.**

U

U Ed. U Edele □ Your Honour **Yr. Hon.**
uitbr. uitbreiding □ extension **ext.**
UK Universiteit (van) Kaapstad □ University of Cape Town **UCT**
ult. *ultimo* laaste □ *ultimo* last **ult.**
UN Universiteit (van) Natal □ University of Natal **UN**
Unesco – □ United Nations Educational, Scientific and Cultural Organisation **Unesco**
Unisa Universiteit van Suid-Afrika □ Uni= versity of South Africa **Unisa**
Unita – □ União Nacional para a Indepen= dencia Total de Angola **Unita**
Unitra – □ University of the Transkei **Unitra**
UP Universiteit (van) Pretoria □ University of Pretoria **UP**
UPE Universiteit (van) Port Elizabeth □ University of Port Elizabeth **UPE**
US Universiteit (van) Stellenbosch □ Uni= versity of Stellenbosch **US**
UVS Universiteit van die Vrystaat □ Uni= versity of the Free State **UFS**
UW Universiteit van die Witwatersrand □ University of the Witwatersrand **UW/Wits**
UWK Universiteit Wes-Kaap □ University of the Western Cape **UWC**
UZ Universiteit (van) Zoeloeland □ Univer= sity of Zululand **UZ**

V

v./vr. vroulik □ feminine **f(em).**
VAE Verenigde Arabiese Emirate □ United Arabic Emirates **UAE**
vb. voorbeeld □ example **ex.**
v.C. voor Christus □ before Christ **BC**
v.d. van die; van der; van den □ of the –

veldm. veldmaarskalk ☐ Field Marshal **FM**
verklw. verkleinwoord ☐ diminutive **dim.**
verl. verlede ☐ past –
verl.dw. verlede deelwoord ☐ past participle **p.p.**
verw. verwysing ☐ reference **ref.**
Vetsak Vrystaatse en Transvaalse Sentrale Aankoopkoöperasie ☐ – **Vetsak**
VF Vryheidsfront ☐ Freedom Front **FF**
VGA videografika-aanpasser ☐ videographics adapter **VGA**
vgl. vergelyk ☐ *confer(atur)* compare **cf./cp.**
vgw. voegwoord ☐ conjunction **conj.**
vh. voorheen ☐ late/former(ly) –
vigs verworwe immuniteitgebreksindroom ☐ acquired immunodeficiency syndrome **Aids**
vk. vierkant ☐ square **sq.**
VK Verenigde Koninkryk ☐ United Kingdom **UK**
VKV Veelkeusevraag ☐ Multiple Choice Question **MCQ**
vlg. volgende ☐ following **seq./fol.**
vm. voormiddag ☐ *ante meridiem* before noon **am/a.m.**
VN Verenigde Nasies ☐ United Nations **UN**
vnw. voornaamwoord ☐ pronoun **pron.**
v(oe)gw. voegwoord ☐ conjunction **conj.**
Vodacom – ☐ Voice and data communication **Vodacom**
vol. volume ☐ volume **vol.**
v(oor)s. voorsetsel ☐ preposition **prep.**
voorv. voorvoegsel ☐ prefix **pref.**
voorw. voorwerp ☐ object **obj.**
VR vrederegter ☐ Justice of the Peace **JP**
vr./v. vroulik ☐ feminine **f(em).**
Vr. Vrydag ☐ Friday **Fri.**
VS Vrystaat ☐ Free State **FS**
vs./v. *versus* teen ☐ *versus* against **v./vs.**
VSA Verenigde State van Amerika ☐ United States of America **USA**
VSR Verteenwoordigende Studenteraad ☐ Students' Representative Council **SRC**
vt. voet ☐ foot, feet **ft.**
VT verwys na trekker ☐ refer to drawer **R/D**
VVV vreemde vlieënde voorwerp ☐ unidentified flying object **UFO**

W

w. woord; week ☐ word; week **w.**
W. Wes(te)/westelik(e) ☐ West **W.**
WAT Woordeboek van die Afrikaanse Taal ☐ – **WAT**
wdb. woordeboek ☐ dictionary/lexicon **dict./lex.**
wed. weduwee ☐ widow –
w.g./get. was geteken/geteken ☐ signed **sgd.**
wisk. wiskunde ☐ mathematics **maths.**
wnd. waarnemende ☐ acting (deputy) **actg.**
WNNR Wetenskaplike en Nywerheidnavor=singsraad ☐ Council for Scientific and Industrial Research **CSIR**
Wo. Woensdag ☐ Wednesday **Wed.**
WRK Wêreldraad van Kerke ☐ World Council of Churches **WCC**
Wo. Woensdag ☐ Wednesday **Wed.**
WV Wetgewende Vergadering ☐ Legislative Assembly **LA**
WVK Waarheid- en Versoeningskommissie ☐ Truth and Reconciliation Commission **TRC**
ww. werkwoord ☐ verb **v./vb**
WWW Wêreldwye Web ☐ Worldwide Web **WWW**

X

X Romeinse 10 ☐ Roman numeral 10 **X**

Y

Yskor (SA) *kyk* Iscor

Z

Zim. Zimbabwe ☐ Zimbabwe **Zim.**

Provinsies van Suid-Afrika

Gauteng ☐ Gauteng
KwaZulu-Natal ☐ KwaZulu-Natal
Mpumalanga ☐ Mpumalanga
Noordelike Provinsie ☐ Northern Province
Noord-Kaap ☐ Northern Cape
Noordwes ☐ North West
Oos-Kaap ☐ Eastern Cape
Vrystaat ☐ Free State
Wes-Kaap ☐ Western Cape

Ampstale van Suid-Afrika

Die **vet gedrukte** vorme is só in die Grondwet van die Republiek van Suid-Afrika (1994) aangegee. Dié tussen hakies is die algemeen gebruikte vorme.

Afrikaans ☐ **Afrikaans**
Engels ☐ **English**
isiNdebele (Ndebele) ☐ **isiNdebele** (Ndebele)
Sepedi/Sesotho sa Leboa (Noord-Sotho) ☐ **Sepedi/Sesotho sa Leboa** (Northern Sotho)
Sesotho (Suid-Sotho) ☐ **Sesotho** (Southern Sotho)
Setswana (Tswana) ☐ **Setswana** (Tswana)
siSwati (Swazi) ☐ **siSwati** (Swazi)
Tshivenda (Venda) ☐ **Tshivenda** (Venda)
isiXhosa (Xhosa) ☐ **isiXhosa** (Xhosa)
Xitsonga (Tsonga) ☐ **Xitsonga** (Tsonga)
isiZulu (Zulu, Zoeloe) ☐ **isiZulu** (Zulu)

ENGLISH – AFRIKAANS

Abbreviations and signs

The following abridged abbreviations appearing after a headword indicate its part of speech:

(a)	= adjective	(num)	= numeral
(adv)	= adverb	(prep)	= preposition
(conj)	= conjunction	(pron)	= pronoun
(interj)	= interjection	(v)	= verb
(n)	= noun		

Other abbreviations used in this dictionary include: (aero.) aeronautics; (Am.) America/≠n; (anat.) anatomy; (biol.) biology; (comp.) computer/computer science; (derog.) derogatory; (econ.) economy; (e.g.) for example; (electr.) electricity/electrical; (exam.) examination(s); (fem.) feminine; (fig.) figurative; (govt.) government; (gram.) grammar.grammatical; (hist.) historical; (idiom.) idiomatic; (maths.) mathematics; (mil.) military; (mus.) music; (phot.) photography; (pl) plural; (pron.) pronounced/pronunciation; (Prot.) Protestant; (R.C.) Roman Catholic; (SA) South Africa/≠n; (S.Am.) South America/≠n; (sing) singular; (stats.) statistics; (sl) slang; (tel.) telephone

1. **Tilde** or **swung dash** (∼) replaces the headword as it stands:
   a) **acid:** as a separate word: ∼ **test** means: **acid test.**
   b) **ill:** with a hyphen: ∼**-tempered** means **ill-tempered.**
   c) **bush:** when joined: ∼**baby** means **bushbaby.**
2. **Double dots (..)** are used where the last syllable of a word changes for the plural: **agency ..ies** means **agency, agencies.**
3. **Hyphen (-):**
   South African English has a strong tendency to diminish hyphens. The trend is **jaw bone > jaw-bone > jawbone**, but:
   a) Avoid ambiguity, therefore: **rugby-mad** schoolboy.
   b) Use hyphens in linked adjectives: **red-tailed** jack; **well-meant** effort.
   c) Words starting wih **self-** are always hyphenated: **self-satisfied; self-control; self medication.**
4. **Semicolon (;):** While a comma in the initial translated version separates words/phrases of similar meaning, a semicolon denotes a secondary or quite different meaning.
5. **Double hyphens (=)** are used at the end of a line to denote that the word must be written as one word and not hyphenated.
6. The **stress mark** (′) indicates that in pronouncing the word the stress falls on the syllable preceding the mark: **ab′dicate; jet′set; reconcilia′tion.**
7. The **solidus** or **slash** (/) denotes optional use: **wish** or **want** in **wish/want; revamp** or **refurbish** in **revamp/refurbish; hijacking** or **carjacking** in **hijacking/carjacking.**

A

a, an 'n
aback' terug, agteruit; *taken* ~ oorbluf, ver=
stom, verras
ab'acus . .ci telraam, rekenbord; abakus
ab'alone (n) perlemoen *also* **perlemoen'**
aban'don (n) oorgawe; onverskilligheid; (v)
opgee; verlaat; in die steek laat *also* **desert'**
(v); ~**ed** verlate, oorgegee; losbandig
ab'attoir (n) -s abattoir, slagplaas
abb'ey -s abdy, klooster(kerk)
abb'ot ab, kloostervoog
abbre'viate afkort *also* **abrid'ge**
abbrevia'tion afkorting, verkorting
ab'dicate afstand doen (van die troon), abdikeer
abdom'en buik, onderbuik, abdomen
abduct' (v) ontvoer, kaap *also* **kid'nap/hi'jack**
abey'ance opskorting, stilstand; *in* ~ opgeskort,
oorgestaan *also* **pen'ding**
abid'ing duursaam, ewig; ~ **love** ewige/duren=
de liefde
abil'ity . .ties bekwaamheid, vermoë, knapheid;
(pl) geestesgawes, talente; *to the best of my*
~ na my beste vermoë
ablaze' aan die brand, in ligte laaie
a'ble bekwaam, knap; bevoeg; ~ **sea'man** be=
vare/vol matroos
ablu'tion reiniging; ~ **block** ablusieblok
abnorm'al abnormaal, onreëlmatig; gestrem
abol'ish afskaf, ophef, intrek *also* **can'cel**
abom'inable afskuwelik, gruwelik, walglik
abori'ginal (n) inboorling (mens)
abort'ion (n) miskraam; vrugafdrywing/abor=
sie; misgewas (mens)
about' (adv, prep) ongeveer, omtrent; aan=
gaande, rakende, met betrekking tot
above' (adv, prep) bo, meer; bokant; ~ *all* bo=
wenal, veral; ~*-average intelligence* boge=
middelde intelligensie; ~**men'tioned** boge=
noemde
abracadab'ra abrakadabra; wartaal
abra'sive (n) skuurmiddel; (a) skurend; kwet=
send (iem. se houding)
abreast' langs mekaar, in gelid; ~ *of* op (die)
hoogte van
abridge' verkort, beperk; beknopter maak
abroad' buitekant; buitelands, oorsee
abrupt' (a) afgebroke; plotseling, kortaf
ab'scess -es geswel, ettersweer, abses
ab'seil (v) abseil; ~**er** abseiler (mens)

ab'sence afwesigheid; gebrek
absent'[1] (v) (jou) verwyder; wegbly
ab'sent[2] (a) afwesig; verstrooid; ~**ee'** afwe=
sige; ~**-min'ded** afgetrokke; ~**-min'ded**
profes'sor verstrooide professor
ab'solute volstrek, onbeperk, volkome; abso=
luut; ~ **majo'rity** volstrekte meerderheid
absorb' opsuig, absorbeer; ~**ing** (a) boeiend
abstain' afskaf; ~**er** onthouer, afskaffer; **to'tal**
~**er** geheelonthouer (van drank)
ab'stract[1] (n) uittreksel; opsomming; (a) diep=
sinnig; abstrak
abstract'[2] (v) aftrek, abstraheer; ~**ion** abstraksie
absurd' (a) verspot, dwaas, absurd *also* **cra'zy**
abun'dant oorvloedig, volop *also* **am'ple**
abuse' (n) mishandeling; **child** ~ kindermishan=
deling/kindermolestering; (v) mishandel; uit=
skel, beledig
abus'ive beledigend, lasterend
abyss' -**es** afgrond; (bodemlose) poel/kolk
aca'cia -s akasia, doringboom/struik
academ'ic(al) akademies; onprakties
aca'demy akademie; studie; genootskap
accede' toestem; toestaan, instem, toegee
accel'erate versnel; verhaas; bespoedig
accel'erator versneller (motor); dryfspier
ac'cent (n) nadruk, klem(toon); stembuiging,
tongval; aksent, klemteken
accept' (v) aanneem, aanvaar; aksepteer (wis=
sel); ~**able** (a) aanneemlik, aanvaarbaar
ac'cess toegang; ~ **con'trol** toegangbeheer; (v)
~ **informa'tion** inligting bekom
acces'sible (a) toeganklik; genaakbaar
acces'sion toetrede/toetreding; aanwins; amps=
aanvaarding; troonbestyging
acces'sory (n) . .ries medepligtige (mens); by=
komstigheid; (pl) toebehore, bybehore; (a)
bykomstig; medepligtig
ac'cident ongeluk, ongeval; toeval; ~ **insur'=**
ance ongevalleversekering; ~ **prone** onge=
luksgeneig
acclama'tion toejuiging; byval, akklamasie
accom'modate (v) aanpas, skik; akkommo=
deer; huisves, herberg *also* **board**
accommoda'tion skikking; huisvesting, ver=
blyf(plek); akkommodasie
accom'paniment begeleiding (op klavier)
accom'pany (v) vergesel, begelei; saamgaan;
~**ing let'ter** bygaande brief

accom'plice (n) medepligtige (in misdaad); handlanger

accom'plish uitvoer, tot stand bring; ~ed voltooid; bedrewe; begaaf *also* **tal'ented**

accord' (n) ooreenstemming; verdrag; harmonie; akkoord; (v) ooreenstem; akkordeer; ~ance ooreenstemming: *in* ~*ance with* ooreenkomstig; ~ing volgens, namate, ooreenkomstig: ~*ing to* volgens, ingevolge; ~ingly' ooreenkomstig, gevolglik, dus

accor'dion akkordeon, trekklavier

account' (n) rekening; berig, verslag; rekenskap; ~ *rendered* gelewerde rekening; *on* ~ *of* weens, vanweë; (v) rekenskap gee, verantwoord

accoun'tancy rekeningkunde

accoun'tant rekenmeester

accoun'ting rekeningkunde; ~ **po'licy** reken(ing)kundige beleid, boekhoubeleid

accounts' exec'utive (n) kliënteskakel (reklamewese)

accrue' aangroei, toeneem; oploop; ~d **in'terest** opgeloopte rente

accu'mulate ophoop, opgaar; oploop; ~d **lea've** opgehoopte/opgegaarde verlof

acc'uracy (n) noukeurigheid, stiptheid, juistheid, presiesheid, akkuraatheid

acc'urate (a) noukeurig, nougeset, akkuraat

accusa'tion beskuldiging; aantyging

accuse' beskuldig, aankla; verkla; ~d' beskuldigde, aangeklaagde (mens)

accus'tom gewoon(d) maak; ~*ed to* gewoond aan

ace bobaas, uitblinker; aas; kishou (sport)

ache (n) pyn; (v) pyn, seer wees, pyn ly

achieve' behaal, verrig, presteer *also* **accom'plish;** ~r presteerder; ~ment prestasie

a'cid (n) suur; (a) suur, bitter, wrang; ~ **drop** suurklontjie; ~ **rain** suurreën; ~ **test** vuurproef

acknow'ledge erken, beken; berig; beantwoord; ~ *receipt of* ontvangs erken van

acknow'ledgment erkenning; berig; dankbetuiging *also* **apprecia'tion**

ac'me toppunt *also* **peak, sum'mit**

ac'ne (vet)puisie, aknee; puisiesiekte

ac'orn akker (aan eikeboom)

acous'tics (n) geluidsleer, akoestiek

acquaint' bekend maak, berig, meedeel; ~ance bekendheid; kennis (mens)

acquire' verkry, verwerf; aanleer; aankoop; ~d **tas'te** aangeleerde smaak

acquisi'tion aanskaffing; aanwins (vir biblioteek)

acquit' vryspreek; kwytskeld

a'cre acre (± 4 000 m²); ~age oppervlakte; grootte in acres

ac'robat akrobaat; ~ic/stunt **flier** kunsvlieënier

ac'ronym letternaam (bv. SANLAM)

ac'rophobia hoogtevrees

across' (adv) dwars; (prep) oor; dwars; oorkruis; *come* ~ teëkom, ontmoet

act (n) daad, handeling; akte; wet; bedryf (toneelstuk); *caught in the* ~ op heter daad/heterdaad betrap; ~ **of dedica'tion** toewydingsformulier/diensgelofte;   (v)   handel, doen, te werk gaan; optree

act'ing (n) voordrag; (toneel)spel; (a) waarnemend, agerend; ~ **reg'istrar** waarnemende registrateur

act'ion handeling, verrigting; geveg, aksie; *killed in* ~ gesneuwel; ~ **song** sangspeletjie

act'ive werksaam, bedrywig, besig; ~ **voice** bedrywende vorm

ac'tivist (n) aktivis (mens)

activ'ity ..ties werksaamheid, bedrywigheid, doenigheid, aktiwiteit

ac'tor toneelspeler, akteur; bewerker

ac'tress -es toneelspeelster, aktrise

ac'tual (a) werklik, wesenlik, feitlik

ac'tually regtig, werklikwaar; eintlik

ac'tuary ..ries aktuaris; griffier

acute skerp; fyn; vlug; gevat, skerpsinnig

acupunc'ture akupunktuur, naaldprikking

Ad'am Adam; ~'s **ap'ple** adamsappel

ad'amant onwrikbaar *also* **firm**

adapt' aanpas; aanwend; ~able plooibaar; aanwendbaar; ~er passtuk; aanpasser (elektrisiteit)

add byvoeg, optel, vermeerder

adden'dum ..denda bylae, toevoegsel *also* **appen'dix/an'nexure**

add'er adder, pofadder

add'ict (n) verslaafde (mens)

addict' (v) toewy, oorgee aan; ~ed verslaaf; ~*ed to drink* aan drank verslaaf

addi'tion byvoeging, optelling; *in* ~ *to* boonop; behalwe, benewens; ~al bykomend, addisioneel; ~ **sum** optelsom

address' (n) adres; toespraak, rede; (v) adresseer; wend/rig (tot); ~ *a problem* 'n probleem aanpak/aanspreek; ~ee' geadresseerde (mens)

ad'equate (a) voldoende *also* **suffi'cient**
adhere' aanhang, bly by; ~ *to, the rules* die reëls nakom/eerbiedig
adhe'sive vasklewend; ~ **plas'ter** hegpleister; ~ **tape** kleefband
adja'cent aangrensend, naasgeleë, naby; ~ **inte'rior** aangrensende binneland
ad'jective (n) byvoeglike naamwoord; (a) byvoeglik; ondergeskik
adjoin' aanheg; grens aan
adjourn' opskort, verdaag; ~ *a meeting* 'n vergadering verdaag; ~**ment** verdaging
adju'dicate (be)oordeel, uitspraak gee *also* **jud'ge** (v)
adju'dicator beoordelaar
adjust' in orde bring, reël, vereffen; aansui= wer; ~**able** verstelbaar; ~**ment** skikking/ reëling; aansuiwering (boekhou)
ad'jutant adjudant; hulp
admin'ister bestuur, beheer; toedien
administra'tion beheer; administrasie
admin'istrative besturend, administratief; ~ **staff** klerklike personeel
admin'istrator administrateur; administreer= der, administrator (mens)
ad'mirable (a) bewonderenswaardig
ad'miral admiraal
admira'tion bewondering, verering *also* **praise**
admire' bewonder, vereer; ~**r** bewonderaar, aanhanger/aanbidder
admis'sion toelating, toegang; erkenning; ~ *free* vry(e) toegang; ~ *of guilt* skulderken= ning; ~ **tick'et** toegangskaartjie
admit' toelaat; opneem (hospitaal); ~**tance** toegang; toelating
admon'ish vermaan, teregwys *also* **reprimand'**
ado' ophef, gedoente; *much* ~ *about nothing* veel geskree(u) en weinig wol
adoles'cence puberteitsjare, adolessensie
adoles'cent (n) jongeling/jongmeisie; jeugdi= ge; (a) jeugdig; opgroeiend, adolessent *also* **ju'venile** (a)
adopt' aanneem, aanwend; ~**ed** aangenome: ~**ed** *child* aangenome kind
adore' aanbid, vereer; vurig liefhê
adorn' versier, verfraai *also* **dec'orate**
adren'alin(e) adrenalien, bynierstof
ad'ult (n) grootmens, volwassene; (a) volwas= se
adul'terer egbreker, owerspeler (mens)
adul'tery owerspel, egbreuk; ontug
advance' (n) vooruitgang; voorskot; (v) be=

vorder; voorskiet (geld); ~ *money* geld voorskiet; ~ *the date* die datum vervroeg; ~**d** gevorder(d); ver
advan'tage (n) voordeel *also* **ben'efit;** baat
adven'ture (n) avontuur; waagstuk; (v) waag, onderneem; ~**r** waaghals *also* **da'redevil**; avonturier, geluksoeker
adven'turous avontuurlik, ondernemend
ad'verb bywoord
adver'bial bywoordelik
ad'versary (n) ..ries teenstander, opponent
ad'verse teenstrydig; vyandig; ongunstig; ~ **com'ment** ongunstige kommentaar
adver'sity teenspoed, ongeluk
ad'vertise adverteer; bekend maak
adver'tisement advertensie, reklame
ad'vertiser adverteerder; aankondiger
ad'vertising reklamewese; ~ **a'gency** rekla= meagentskap, advertensieburo
advice' (n) raad; advies *also* **coun'sel**
advi'sable (a) raadsaam, gerade
advise' (v) aanraai, adviseer; ~**r** raadsman/ raadgewer; berader
advi'sory raadgewend, adviserend; ~ **coun'cil** adviesraad
ad'vocate (n) advokaat; pleitbesorger; (v) be= pleit, verdedig
ae'rial (n) lugdraad, antenne; ~ **pho'tograph** lugfoto; ~ **rail'way** lugspoor
a'erobat kunsvlieenier, fratsvlieer
a'erodrome vliegveld, vliegbaan *see* **air'port**
a'eronaut ruimtevaarder *also* **as'tronaut**
a'eroplane (obsolete) *see* **air'craft**
a'erosol aerosol; ~ **can/contai'ner** spuitkan= (=netjie)
aesthet'ic(al) esteties, skoonheids=
aff'able vriendelik, minsaam, inskiklik
affair' saak, aangeleentheid, besigheid, affère; (liefdes)verhouding
affect' (v) werk op, aantas; raak, affekteer
affec'ted aangedaan, aanstellerig; aangetas
affec'tionate toegeneë, liefhebbend; hartlik
affida'vit (n) beëdigde verklaring
affilia'tion aansluiting, affiliasie
affirm' bevestig; bekragtig; ~**ative** bevesti= gend: *answer in the* ~*ative* bevestigend antwoord; ~**ative ac'tion** regstellende/be= vestigende/herstellende aksie/optrede, reg= stelaksie
af'fluence oorvloed, rykdom, weelde
af'fluent (a) oorvloedig; ryk, welgesteld; ~ **soci'ety** welvarende/gegoede gemeenskap

afford' bekostig, bybring; *he can* ~ *to* hy kan dit bekostig; ..**able** bekostigbaar, sakpas
afoot' te voet; op die been; op tou
afore' (adv, prep) voor, vantevore; ~**going** voorgaande; ~**men'tioned** voorgenoemd, voorgemeld; ~**said** voorgenoemd
afraid' bang, bangerig, bevrees; ~ *of* bang vir; ~ *to* bang om
afresh' opnuut, van voor af, weer
Af'rica Afrika
Af'rican (n) Afrikaan (mens van Afrika); (a) van Afrika; Afrikaans; ~ **lan'guages** Afri=katale; **South** ~ Suid-Afrikaner
Africa'na Africana
Afrikaans' Afrikaans (taal)
Afrika'ner (n) -s Afrikaner; afrikanerbees; (a) Afrikaans
Af'ro-A'sian Afro-Asiaties
af'ter[1] (a) later; (prep) agter; naderhand; na, daarna, later; ~ *all* tog, darem, per slot van rekening, op stuk van sake; *enquire* ~ vra na; *look* ~ kyk na, sorg vir
af'ter[2] (conj) nadat
af'ter: ~**care** nasorg; ~**-dinner speech** tafelre=de; ~**-effect** nawerking, gevolg; ~**noon'** namiddag, agtermiddag; ~**thought** nagedag=te; laatlammetjie, heksluiter (kind); ~**wards** naderhand, daarna
again' weer, opnuut; aan die ander kant; vir die tweede maal; *now and* ~ af en toe; *time and* ~ herhaaldelik
against' teen, strydig met
age (n) ouderdom, leeftyd, eeu; *coming of* ~ mondig; **Middle A~s** Middeleeue; (v) oud word, verouder; ~**d** oud, bejaard; afgeleef; ~ **lim'it** ouderdomsgrens
a'gency ..**cies** agentskap; bemiddeling; **ad'ver=tising** ~ reklameagentskap; **employ'ment** ~ personeelagentskap; **tra'vel** ~ reisburo, reis=agentskap
agen'da (n) agenda, sakelys
a'gent agent; rentmeester; bewerker; middel
agg'ravate (v) verswaar, vererger; verbitter; terg; **ag'gravating cir'cumstances** verswa=rende omstandighede
agg'regate (n) totaal, geheel; aggregaat; (v) versamel; beloop; (a) gesamentlik
aggress' aanval; ~**ion** aanval, aggressie; ~**ive** strydlustig, aggressief *also* **hos'tile**; ~**or** aggressor, aanvaller
ag'ile rats, lenig, behendig *also* **nim'ble**
agita'tion opskudding, agitasie

ag'itator opruier, oproermaker, agitator (mens)
ago' gelede; *a week* ~ 'n week gelede
ag'ony (n) doodsangs; kwelling *also* **an'guish**
agree' ooreenstem; toestem; ~ *on* saamstem; ~ *with* akkordeer met; ~**able** aangenaam, welgevallig, behaaglik; ~**d**'! top!, afge=spreek! ~**ment** ooreenkoms; verdrag; ver=gelyk; akkoord; ~**ment stu'dent** verbinte=nisstudent
agricul'tural landboukundig, landbou-; ~ **day** boeredag; ~ **jour'nal** landboutydskrif, land=boublad
agricul'ture landbou
ahead' vooruit, vooraan; voorwaarts
aid (n) hulp, bystand; subsidie; hulpmiddel; *in* ~ *of* ten bate van, ten behoewe van; (v) help, steun; bydra; **hea'ring** ~ hoortoestel
Aids (n) vigs; ~**sufferer** vigslyer
ail makeer, sukkel, siek wees; ~**ing** sieklik; ~**ment** siekte, kwaal *also* **disor'der**
aim (n) doel(wit), oogmerk, doelstelling, plan; *take* ~ korrelvat op; (v) doel; korrel; beoog, mik; ~ *at* mik op; ~**less** doelloos
air (n) lug, windjie; lied, melodie; *on the* ~ oor die radio, uitgesaai (word); (v) lug; ~ *one's views* jou mening gee; (a) lugwind-; ~ **alarm'** lugalarm, koe(t)stoeter; ~ **ap=pren'tice** lugvakleerling; ~**bag** lugsak (mo=tor); ~**brick** lugrooster; ~**condi'tioning** lugversorging: *these premises are aircondi=tioned* hierdie winkel is lugversorg
air'craft vliegtuig, vliegmasjien; ~ **car'rier** vliegdekskip
air: ~**filter** lugsuiweraar, lugfilter; ~ **force** lugmag; ~ **fresh'ener** lugverfrisser; ~**gun** windbuks; ~ **hos'tess** lugwaardin (kajuit=personeel); ~**lift** lugbrug; ~**line** lugrede=ry; ~**li'ner** passasierstraler; ~**mail** lugpos; ~ **mechan'ic** lugwerktuigkundige; ~ **pi'lot** vlieënier; ~**port** lughawe; ~ **raid** lugaanval; ~**shel'ter** skuilkelder; ~**ship** lugskip; ~**-sick'ness bag** naarsakkie; ~**strip** landingstrook; ~**tight** lugdig; ~**ways** lugdiens/lugredery *also* **air'line**; ~**y** vrolik; yl
aisle vlerk, vleuel (van 'n gebou); paadjie (tussen stoele of banke) *also* **cor'ridor**
ajar' half oop, op 'n skrefie
akin' verwant *also* **rela'ted**
alarm' (n) alarm; ~ **clock** wekker; ~**ing** ver=ontrustend; onrusbarend
alas'! helaas! *also* **alack!**

al'batross -es albatros, stormvoël
albe'it alhoewel, hoewel
albi'no -s albino
al'bum album; gedenkboek
al'cohol alkohol, wyngees
alcohol'ic alkoholies, bedwelmend; dranksug=
tig; (n) alkoholis; ~ **blues** dronkverdriet
al'coholism alkoholisme
al'cometer alkometer, asemtoetser *also* **breath'=
alyser**
al'derman raadsheer, olderman (in stadsrade)
ale Engelse bier; ~ **house** tappery
alert' (n) alarm(sein); (v) aansê, waarsku; (a)
waaksaam, wakker; *on* ~ op gereedheid=
grondslag
al'ga (n) **-e** seegras, seewier, alge
al'gebra algebra, stelkunde
al'ibi alibi; uitvlug
al'ien (n) vreemdeling, uitlander; (a) vreemd,
uitlands; ~**ate** vervreem; afkonkel; ~**a'tion**
vervreemding
align' rig, op een lyn bring; spoor (wiel);
~**ment** linie, riglyn; sporing (van wiele)
alike' gelyk, eenders/eners
alive' (a) lewend; lewendig/wakker; gevoelig;
wemelend
all (pron) almal, algar; *not at* ~ glad nie, geen=
sins; ~ *day* heeldag; (adv) heeltemal, totaal;
~ *the better* des te beter; ~ *the same* darem,
tog, ~**see'ing eye** alsiende oog
all'-bran volsemel
all'-comers almal; iedereen
allega'tion aanklag/aantyging; beskuldiging
allege' (v) aanvoer, beweer; ~**d mur'derer**
beweerde/vermeende moordenaar
alle'giance getrouheid, onderdanigheid
al'legory ..ries sinnebeeld, allegorie
all'-embracing alomvattend
aller'gic allergies *also* **suscep'tible**
al'ley -s steeg, laning; gang
alli'ance (n) verbond, bondgenootskap, alli=
ansie *also* **u'nion, pact**
al'ligator kaaiman, alligator
all'-in: ~ **wrest'ling** rofstoei
allit'era'tion alliterasie, stafrym
all'ocate (v) aanwys, toewys, toedeel
alloca'tion plekaanwysing; toewysing
allot' aanwys, toemeet, toeken
all'-out uit alle mag
allow' (w) toelaat; bewillig; ~**ance** toelating;
toelae; *make* ~*ance(s) for* in aanmerking
neem; rekening hou met

al'loy/alloy' (n) mengsel; gehalte; allooi
all'right goed, reg, in orde; *I am* ~ ek is
orraait
all'round (a) veelsydig *also* **ver'satile**; (adv)
oor die algemeen; ~**er** veelsydige sport=
man/sportvrou
alluv'ial uitgespoel, alluviaal, spoel=; ~ **di'a=
monds** spoeldiamante
all'-weather weervas; ~ **ten'nis court** weer=
vaste tennisbaan
al'ly (n) **allies** bondgenoot, geallieerde
al'manac almanak, kalender
Almi'ghty: *the* ~ *God* die Almagtige
alm'ond amandel
al'most amper, byna
alms (n) aalmoes, liefdegawe
al'oe -s aalwyn/aalwee, garingboom
alone' (a) alleen; eensaam; (adv) net, enkel,
alleen; *leave* ~ alleen laat, uitlos
along' langs, deur; met; *all* ~ die hele tyd;
~**side** naas, langsaan
aloof' afsydig (mens); op 'n afstand
aloud' hardop; *read* ~ hardop lees, luidlees
al'pha alfa
al'phabet abc, alfabet
alread'y al, reeds, alreeds
al'so ook, eweneens *also* **as well as**
alt alt, hoë noot
al'tar altaar
al'ter (v) verander, wysig; ~**a'tion** verande=
ring, wysiging *also* **amend'ment**
alter'nate (n) plaasvervanger (mens); (a)
(af)wisselend, alternatief
al'ternate (v) (af)wissel; verwissel
al'ternating (af)wisselend; ~ **cur'rent** wissel=
stroom
altern'ative (n) keuse, alternatief *also* **op'tion**
although' hoewel, alhoewel
al'titude hoogte (bo seespieël); diepte; **high** ~
ten'nis balls hoëvlak-tennisballe
altogeth'er almal; heeltemal, tesame; *in the* ~/
buff poedelnakend
altruis'tic (a) onbaatsugtig, altruïsties
al'lum aluin
alumin'ium aluminium
al'ways altyd, gedurig *also* **fore'ver**
amalgama'tion samesmelting, amalgamasie
also **mer'ger**
am'ateur amateur, beginner *also* **lay'man**
amaze' verbaas; ~**d** verbaas *also* **aston'ished**
amaz'ing (a) verbasend, wonderlik
Am'azon Amasone; manhaftige vrou

ambass'ador ambassadeur; gesant (mens)
am'ber amber, barnsteen; ~ **traf'fic light** amber/geel verkeerslig
ambidex'trous (a) ewehandig, gelykhandig
ambig'uous (a) dubbelsinnig; duister
ambi'tion eersug, ambisie
ambi'tious eersugtig, eergierig, ambisieus
am'bulance ambulans
am'bush (n) hinderlaag; lokval, strik
amen'/a'men amen
amend' (v) verbeter, wysig; ~**ment** wysiging; amendement (op 'n mosie)
amends' vergoeding; *make* ~ goedmaak
amen'ity minsaamheid, innemendheid; **..ties** geriewe, fasiliteite; beleefdhede
Amer'ica Amerika; ~**n** Amerikaner (mens)
am'iable (a) beminlik, lief, lieftallig
am'icable (a) vriendelik, vriendskaplik
ammon'ia ammoniak
ammuni'tion ammunisie, skietgoed; ~ **dump** ammunisieopslagplek
am'nesty vrywaring, kwytskelding, amnestie; *grant* ~ amnestie verleen
amok' amok; *run* ~ amok maak
among' onder, tussen, by; ~ *ourselves* onder ons
am'orous verlief, liefdes=, minne=
amount' (n) bedrag, opbrengs; hoeveelheid; *expenses* ~*ing to* uitgawes ten bedrae van; (v) bedra
amphib'ia amfibieë, tweeslagtige diere
am'phitheatre amfiteater; strydperk
am'ple ruim; oorvloedig *also* **plen'tiful**
am'plifier klankversterker; vergroter
am'plify (v) uitbrei; toelig, vergroot, versterk
am'putate (v) afsit, amputeer (been)
am'ulet amulet, geluksteentjie *also* **charm** (n)
amuse' vermaak, amuseer; ~**ment** vermaak; ~**ment park** pretpark *also* **fun fair**
amus'ing (a) vermaaklik, onderhoudend, amusant
an 'n
anabol'ic ste'roid (n) (op)kikker, sluipkikker *also* **pep pill**
anach'ronism tydteenstrydigheid, tydverskuiwing, tydverrekening, anachronisme
anaem'ic bloedloos, bloedarm
anaesthet'ic (n) (ver)doofmiddel/narkose
anaes'thetist narkotiseur (mediese spesialis)
analges'ic (a) pynstillend; (n) pynstiller
analphabete' ongeletterde, analfabeet (mens)
an'alyse (v) ontleed, oplos, analiseer

anal'ysis ..lyses ontleding, analise
an'archist anargis, oproermaker
an'archy regeringloosheid, anargie
anat'omy ontleedkunde, anatomie
ances'tral (a) voorvaderlik (bv. geeste)
an'cestry voorouers, afkoms, afstamming
an'chor (n) anker (skip); steun; (v) anker
anchov'y ansjovis
an'cient oud, outyds; antiek *also* **archa'ic**
ancill'ary ondergeskik; ~ **sub'jects** byvakke
and en
an'ecdote anekdote, staaltjie *also* **yarn**
anem'one anemoon *also* **wind'flower**
anew' opnuut; weer
an'gel engel; serafyn
an'ger (n) toorn, gramskap *also* **fu'ry/rage**; (v) vertoorn, vererg, kwaad maak
an'gle¹ (n) vishoek; haak; (v) visvang, hengel
an'gle² (n) hoek; gesig(s)punt; ~ **i'ron** hoek= yster
an'gler hengelaar; visvanger
An'glicism Anglisisme, Engelse uitdrukking
An'glo- Engels, Anglo-; **A~-Boer War** Anglo-Boereoorlog, Engelse Oorlog, Twee= de Vryheidsoorlog *also* **South Af'rican War**
angor'a: ~ **goat** angorabok, sybok
an'gry kwaad, boos *also* **annoy'ed**; ~ *about* kwaad oor; ~ *with* kwaad vir
an'gular hoekig, hoek=, puntig
an'imal (n) dier, bees; (a) dierlik; sinlik; ~ **hus'bandry** veeteelt; ~ **king'dom** die diere= ryk; ~ **lov'er** diereliefhebber
animos'ity verbittering, wrok *also* **grud'ge**
an'iseed anyssaad
an'kle enkel; ~ *deep* tot aan die enkels
ann'als jaarboeke, annale, kronieke
annex' (v) annekseer; inlyf; ~**a'tion** inlywing, anneksasie
ann'ex (n) aanhangsel, bylae; bygebou
an'nexure aanhangsel, bylae *also* **appen'dix**
anni'hilate (v) vernietig, verdelg, uitdelg
anniver'sary ..ries verjaardag; jaarfees; ge= denkdag; bestaansjaar (organisasie)
announce' aankondig, bekend maak; aanmeld; ~**ment** aankondiging; bekendmaking; ~**r** omroeper (radio); aankondiger
annoy' (v) lastig val, hinder, pla; ~**ed** omge= krap, vererg; ontstig; ~**ing** lastig, vervelig, hinderlik
ann'ual (n) jaarboek; eenjarige plant; (a) jaar= liks, jaar=; eenjarig; ~ **gen'eral meet'ing**

algemene jaarvergadering

annu'ity ..ties jaargeld, annuïteit; **reti'rement** ~ aftree-annuïteit

anom'aly ..lies ongerymdheid, anomalie

anon'ymous naamloos, anoniem

anorex'ia nervo'sa aptytverlies, anoreksie

anoth'er 'n ander; nog een; ~ *year of inflation* nog 'n inflasiejaar; *one* ~ mekaar

an'swer (n) antwoord; oplossing; (v) antwoord, beantwoord; ~ *the telephone* die telefoon beantwoord; ~**able** verantwoordelik, aanspreeklik; ~**ing machi'ne** antwoordmasjien

ant mier

antag'onism vyandskap, antagonisme

antag'onist teenstander, teenparty

Antarc'tic suidelik; Suidpool-; ~ **Cir'cle** Suidpoolsirkel; ~ **O'cean** Suidelike Yssee

Antarc'tica Suidpoolstreek, Antarktika

ant: ~**bear**/~**ea'ter** erdvark, miervreter

an'telope wildsbok, antiloop

anten'na -e voelhoring, voelspriet; lugdraad, antenne

antenup'tial van voor die huwelik, huweliks=; ~ **con'tract** voorhuwelikse kontrak

an'them lofsang; **nat'ional** ~ volkslied

ant'hill mier(s)hoop *also* **ant'heap**

anthol'ogy ..gies bloemlesing (van gedigte)

an'thracite antrasiet

anthropol'ogist antropoloog (mens)

anthropol'ogy menskunde, antropologie

an'ti teen=, anti=, strydig met

an'ti-aircraft gun lugafweergeskut

antibiot'ic (n) antibiotikum; (a) antibioties

antic'ipate verwag; voorsien/vooruitloop

anticipa'tion voorgevoel, verwagting; voorsmaak; *in* ~ by voorbaat

anticlim'ax antiklimaks

anti-clock'wise linksom, antikloksgewys

an'tics (pl) kaskenades, manewales

an'tidote teengif, antidoot

an'ti-littering campaign' rommelveldtog

antip'athy teensin, renons, antipatie

antiquar'ian (n) oudheidkenner (mens); (a) oudheidkundig, antikwaries

antique' (n) antieke kunswerk; (a) antiek; ~ **dea'ler (shop)** antiekwinkel

antisep'tic antisepties, ontsmettend

an'us (n) anus, aars, agterent

an'vil aambeeld

anxi'ety angs, kommer, besorgdheid, stres *also* **distress'**

an'xious bekommerd, besorg; verlangend; ~ *to help* gretig om te help

an'y elke, enige; iedereen, elkeen, enigiemand; *applicants for the post, if any* aansoekers om die pos, as daar is; *in* ~ *case/at* ~ *rate* in alle geval; ~ *person who* elkeen wat

an'ybody enigeen, elkeen, iedereen

an'yhow (adv) in elk geval; hoe dan ook

an'yone enigeen, iedereen *also* **an'ybody**

an'ything enigiets; ~ *but* alles behalwe

an'ywhere oral, op enige plek

apart' afsonderlik, alleen; apart; ~ *from* afgesien van; *jesting* ~ gekheid op 'n stokkie; ~**heid** apartheid (politieke stelsel)

apart'ment vertrek, apartement

ap'athy onverskilligheid, apatie *also* **indiffe= rence**

ape (n) aap; koggelaar; (v) na-aap, (uit)koggel

aph'orism (n) aforisme, (leer)spreuk

a'piary (n) byeboerdery/byery *also* **bee farm**

ap'iculture byeteelt

apoc'alypse openbaring, apokalips

apol'ogise (v) verskoning maak vir; verontskuldig; apologie aanteken

apol'ogy ..gies verskoning, apologie

apos'tle apostel, godsgesant

apostol'ic apostolies

apos'trophe afkap(pings)teken, apostroof

appal' verskrik, ontstel; ~**ling** verskriklik, ontsettend *also* **hor'rifying**

apparat'us -es toestel, apparaat; orgaan

appar'ent blykbaar, duidelik; skynbaar; ~**ly** klaarblyklik, vermoedelik; oënskynlik

appari'tion spook; gedaante *also* **phan'tom**

appeal' (n) appèl, hoër beroep; aantreklikheid; (v) appelleer; ~ *to* 'n beroep doen op

appear' verskyn, optree; lyk, blyk

appear'ance verskyning; skyn, voorkoms; ~ **fee** optreefooi (sport, sosiaal)

appease' bevredig; paai; bedaar; ~**ment** versoening; *policy of* ~**ment** paaibeleid

appendicit'is blindedermontsteking, appendisitis

appen'dix -es, ..ices aanhangsel, bylae/bylaag *also* **an'nexure**; blindederm

app'etiser eetluswekker(tjie)

app'etite eetlus, aptyt; begeerte, lus

applaud' (v) toejuig; prys, apploudeer

applause (n) toejuiging, applous

a'pple appel; oogappel; ~ *of discord* twisappel; *an* ~ *a day keeps the doctor away* 'n appel 'n dag laat die dokter wag

appli'ance (n) toestel, apparaat; **hou'sehold** ~**s** (pl) huisbehore, huisgerei

applic'able (a) toepaslik

app'licant aansoeker, applikant

applica'tion aanwending, toepassing; applika= sie; aansoek; ~ **form** aansoekvorm

applied' toegepas; ~ **mathema'tics** toegepaste wiskunde

apply' aanwend; toepas/implementeer; aan= soek doen; ~ *for a post* aansoek doen om/ vir 'n betrekking

appoint' bepaal, vasstel; aanstel, benoem

appoint'ment afspraak; aanstelling, benoe= ming; *keep an* ~ 'n afspraak hou/nakom; ~s **reg'ister** aanstellingregister, vakaturelys

apprec'iable merkbaar; aansienlik

appre'ciate (v) waardeer, op prys stel; appre= sieer/styg (aandele)

apprecia'tion waardering; waardevermeerde= ring, appresiasie (boekhou); *token of* ~ blyk van waardering

apprehend' (v) aanhou, gevange neem; begryp

appren'tice (n) vakleerling; leerklerk; (v) inboek; ~**ship** leerskap, leerjare

approach' (n) nadering; **-es** toegange; (v) nader, naderkom; benader; ~**able** toegank= lik *also* **access'ible**; genaakbaar

appro'priate¹ (v) toewys, toedeel; afsonder

appro'priate² (a) gepas, paslik; geskik

appropria'tion toewysing; ~ **account'** (wins)= verdelingsrekening

appro'val goedkeuring, byval; *on* ~ op sig

approve' goedkeur; bevestig; bekragtig

approx'imate (v) benader; (a) by benadering, naaste(n)by; ~**ly** omtrent, naaste(n)by

ap'ricot appelkoos

Ap'ril April, Aprilmaand

Ap'ril fool Aprilgek

ap'ron voorskoot; deklaag; *tied to the* ~ *strings of* onder die plak van

apt geskik, paslik; geneig; onderhewig aan

ap'titude geskiktheid; bekwaamheid, aanleg; ~ **test** aanlegtoets

aq'ua: ~**lung** duiklong; ~**plane** ski/brander= plank

aquar'ium ..ria, -s akwarium

aq'ueduct (n) watergang, akwaduk

Ara'bia Arabië; ~**n** (a) Arabies

arbitra'tion arbitrasie

ar'bitrator skeidsregter, arbiter (mens)

ar'bor: ~ **city** lowerstad; ~ **day** boomplantdag

arc boog

arcade' deurloop, arkade *see* **mall**

arch¹ (n) **-es** boog, gewelf/verwelf; (v) buig,

krom (rug); ~ **support'** steunsool

arch² (a) aarts=, opperste (vyand, skelm)

archaeol'ogist oudheidkundige, argeoloog

arch'angel aartsengel

arch'bishop aartsbiskop

arch'en'emy ..mies aartsvyand

arch'er boogskutter; ~**y** boogskiet

arch'itect argitek, boumeester

architec'ture boukunde, argitektuur

ar'chives argief (bewaarplek)

Arc'tic noordelik; Noordpool

ard'ent (a) gloeiend; ywerig; hartstogtelik

ard'uous steil; moeilik, opdraand, swaar

are *see* **be**

ar'ea -s oppervlakte; streek, wyk, gebied; area; ~ **commit'tee** streekkomitee

aren'a -s strydperk, arena

Argenti'na (n) Argentinië; **Ar'gentine** (a) Ar= gentyns

ar'gue redeneer; stry; betoog, argumenteer

ar'gument bewysgrond/beweegrede; argument *also* **quar'rel**; debat; stelling

ar'ia aria, lied; melodie

ar'id dor, droog

arise' oprys, ontstaan; opstaan; herrys; ~ *from* (voort)spruit uit

aristoc'racy aristokrasie, adelstand

ar'istocrat aristokraat (mens)

arith'metic rekenkunde, rekene

ark ark; *A*~ *of the Covenant* Verbondsark; *Noah's* ~ Noag se ark

arm¹ (n) (pl) wapens; wapentuig; *take up* ~s die wapens opneem; (v) wapen; ~**ed rob'=** **bery** gewapende roof; ~**s cache** wapenop= slagplek

arm² (n) arm; been (van 'n hoek); *infant/baby in* ~s suigeling; ~**pit** oksel

arm'ament bewapening, krygstoerusting; swaargeskut; ~**s race** wapenwedloop

arm'chair leunstoel, armstoel

arm'/In'dian: ~ **wrest'ling** armdruk (wedstryd)

arm'istice wapenstilstand *also* **truce**

arm'oured gepantser, pantser=; ~ **car** pantser= motor; ~ **divi'sion** pantserdivisie

arm'oury ..ries arsenaal, wapenhuis, wapen= kamer; magasyn

arm'y armies leër; weermag/krygsmag; ~ **pay** soldy; ~ **worm** kommandowurm

aro'ma -s geur, aroma *also* **fra'grance**

around' om, rondom, in die rondte

arouse' (v) opwek, aanspoor *also* **inci'te**

arrange' skik, rangskik; reël, inrig; ~**ment**

skikking, rangskikking; **flo'wer/flor'al** ~**ment** blommerangskikking

arrear'(s) agterstallige gelde; **arrear' instal=ments** agterstallige paaiemente

arrest' (n) inhegtenisneming, arres; *under* ~ onder arres; in aanhouding; (v) in hegtenis neem, arresteer; aanhou; **car'diac** ~ hart=staking

arres'tor: ~**bed** stuitbedding (swaar voertuie)

arriv'al aankoms; aangekomene (mens)

arrive' aankom, land, arriveer; bereik

a'rrogant aanmatigend, verwaand, arrogant

a'rrow (n) pyl

ars'enal wapenhuis, magasyn, arsenaal

ars'enic (n) arseen, rottekruid/rotgif

ars'on (moedswillige) brandstigting; ~**ist** brandstigter (mens)

art kuns; lis, bedrog; (pl) lettere, kunste; ~**s and crafts** kunsvlyt; bedryfskennis; **com=mer'cial** ~ handelskuns; **fine** ~**s** skone kunste

art'ery ..**ries** slagaar

art: ~**ful** kunstig; listig *also* **craf'ty, cun'=ning;** ~ **gal'lery** kunsgalery

arthri'tis gewrigsontsteking, artritis

art'icle (n) lidwoord; artikel; voorwaardes; klousule; *serve one's* ~**s** jou leerskap uit=dien; ~**d clerk** leerklerk (prokureur)

artic'ulate[1]: ~**d truck/ve'hicle** koppellorrie

artic'ulate[2] (a) welsprekend

articula'tion (n) stembuiging, artikulasie

artifi'cial kunstig; kunsmatig; vals; oneg; ~ **insemina'tion (A.I)** kunsmatige insemina=sie/bevrugting (K.I.); ~ **limbs** kunsledema=te; ~ **teeth** kunsgebit; winkeltande

artill'ery geskut, artillerie

ar'tisan ambagsman; vakman *also* **crafts'man**

art'ist kunstenaar; arties

artis'tic kunsvol, artistiek, kunssinnig

as (adv, conj) as, soos; net soos; aangesien; namate; terwyl; ~ *soon* ~ sodra; ~ *the population increases* namate die bevolking aangroei

asbes'tos gareklip, asbes

Ascen'sion Day Hemelvaartdag (voorheen vakansiedag)

ascertain' (v) bepaal, vasstel *also* **deter'mine**

ascribe' toeskryf (aan)

asep'tic (n) ontsmetmiddel; (a) ontsmettend, asepties, kiemvry

ashamed' beskaam, skaam; *are you not* ~ *of yourself?* skaam jy jou nie?

ash'es as

ash'tray -s asbakkie

A'sia Asië; ~**tic** Asiaties

ask vra; versoek *also* **request**; eis; ~ *for trouble* moeilikheid/skoor soek

asleep' aan die slaap; *fall* ~ aan die slaap raak

aspa'ragus aspersie; **wild** ~ katdoring

as'pect aspek; kant; gesig(s)punt; uitsig

as'phalt (n) asfalt; (v) asfalt lê, teer

as'pirant aspirant, kandidaat

ass -es esel, donkie; *make an* ~ *of* 'n gek maak van

assass'in sluipmoordenaar *also* **hit'man;** ~**ate** vermoor; ~**a'tion** (sluip)moord

assault' (n) aanval, aanranding; (v) aanrand; bestorm, aanval

ass'egai -s asgaai/assegaai

assem'ble versamel, vergader *also* **con'ge=grate;** inmekaarsit, monteer

assem'bly ..blies byeenkoms, vergadering; montering (masjien); **Leg'islative A**~ Wet=gewende Vergadering; ~ **line** monteerlyn; ~ **plant** monteeraanleg

assent' (n) toestemming, goedkeuring

assert' (v) laat geld; handhaaf; bevestig

assess' skat; belas, aanslaan, bepaal, evalueer; ~**ment** skatting, waardebepaling, evalue=ring; ~**ment rate** eiendomsbelasting, erfbe=lasting; ~**or** taksateur, waardeerder; asses=sor (mens)

ass'et besit, bate; aanwins; ~**s** bates; boedel, nalatenskap; ~**s and liabil'ities** bates en laste

assign'ment opdrag; werkstuk, studiestuk, op=gaaf/opgawe; taak; bestemming

assist' (v) help, bystaan, steun; ~**ance** hulp, bystand *also* **help, aid** (n); ~**ant** (n) helper; assistent; (a) behulpsaam

asso'ciate (n) maat; assosiaat (van 'n vereni=ging); vennoot; medepligtige; (v) verenig; omgaan met, assosieer; ~**d** bybehorende; gepaardgaande; ~ **mem'ber** assosiaatlid

associa'tion vereniging; assosiasie; ~ **foot'=ball** sokker(voetbal)

assort' uitsoek, sorteer; ~**ment** verskeiden=heid *also* **vari'ety**

assume' aanneem; aanvaar; veronderstel; ~ *responsibility* verantwoordelikheid aanvaar

assump'tion veronderstelling

assur'ance versekering; assuransie

assure' verseker; ~**d** versekerde (persoon); ~**r** versekeraar/onderskrywer *also* **un'derwriter**

as'ter aster (blom)
as'terisk (n) sterretjie, asterisk
asth'ma asma; ~t'ic aamborstig
aston'ish verbaas, verwonder; ~ing verba=
send; ~ment verbasing *also* ama'zement
astray' verdwaal; *lead* ~ verlei; op 'n dwaal=
spoor bring
astrol'oger sterrewiggelaar, astroloog (mens)
as'tronaut ruimtevaarder, ruimtereisiger
astron'omer sterrekundige, astronoom (mens)
astronom'ical astronomies; sterrekundig
astron'omy sterrekunde, astronomie
astute' skerpsinnig *also* sharp; geslepe; slu
asyl'um -s toevlugsoord; skuilplek, asiel; ge=
stig; men'tal ~ sielsiekegestig
at tot; te, op, in; aan, by; teen, met; na; oor; *not*
~ *all* glad nie, heeltemal nie; ~ *present*
teenswoordig, nou; ~ *school, college and*
university op skool, op/aan kollege en op/
aan universiteit
ath'eist godloënaar, ateïs (mens)
ath'lete atleet, sportman; ~'s **foot** voetskim=
mel
athlet'ic frisgebou(d), sterk, atleties; ~ sup=
port' liesband
at'las -es atlas
at'mosphere atmosfeer, dampkring
atmospher'ic (n, pl) lugsteuring; (a) atmos=
feries
at'om atoom; ~/atom'ic bomb atoombom
atom'ic atomies, atoom; ~ **age** atoomeeu; ~
fis'sion atoomsplitsing, atoomsplyting; ~
fu'sion atoomfusie
atro'cious (a) gruwelik, afgryslik *also* hor'ri=
ble, ter'rible
atro'city ..ties gruweldaad, afgryslikheid
attach' vasmaak, aanheg; in beslag neem
atta'ché (gesantskaps)attaché; ~ **case** briewe=
tas, aktetas *also* **brief'case**
attack' (n) aanval; (v) aanval; **mock** ~ skyn=
aanval
attain' bereik; verkry; ~able haalbaar, be=
reikbaar; ~ment bereiking *also* accom'=
plishment
attempt' (n) probeerslag, poging; (v) probeer/
poog *also* **try** (v); onderneem
attend' ag gee, oppas; bywoon; oplet; ~
clas'ses klasloop; ~ *to* aandag gee aan; let
op; oppas
attend'ance bywoning, teenwoordigheid; *in* ~
ampshalwe teenwoordig (vergaderings); ~
reg'ister presensielys

atten'tion aandag, oplettendheid, sorg; *pay* ~
to aandag gee aan
atten'tive oplettend *also* **alert**; beleefd
att'ic solderkamer, dakkamer
att'itude gesindheid; gestalte, houding
attor'ney -s prokureur; regsverteenwoordiger;
po'wer of ~ volmag, prokurasie
attract' (v) aantrek; aanlok; boei
attrac'tion aantreklikheid; aantrekkings(krag);
next ~ volgende vertoning
attrac'tive aantreklik, aanvallig; bekoorlik
att'ribute[1] (n) eienskap, hoedanigheid; ken=
merk, attribuut
attrib'ute[2] (v) toeskryf; wyt; *attributable to*
toeskryfbaar aan
au'burn donkerbruin, goudbruin
auc'tion vandisie/vendusie, veiling; *sell by* ~
opveil
auctioneer' afslaer (by vandisie)
aud'ible hoorbaar
aud'ience gehoor, toehoorders; oudiënsie
aud'io-visual (a) oudiovisueel; ~ **educa'tion**
oudiovisuele onderwys/onderrig
aud'it (n) oudit, ouditering; (v) oudit, ouditeer;
~ing ouditkunde (vak)
aud'itor ouditeur (mens)
auditor'ium gehoorsaal, ouditorium
augment' (v) vermeerder, vergroot, aanvul
Au'gust[1] Augustus
august'[2] (a) verhewe, groots, vernaam
aunt tante, tannie; tant (voor haar naam)
aus'pices bystand, beskerming; *under the* ~ *of*
onder beskerming van
auster'ity strengheid; eenvoud, soberheid
Austra'lia Australië
Aus'tria Oostenryk
authen'tic eg, opreg, outentiek *also* **gen'uine**
auth'or skrywer, outeur (albei geslagte)
autho'rity ..ties gesag; mag; mandaat, ver=
gunning; outoriteit
auth'orise magtig; wettig; ~d **cap'ital** ge=
magtigde kapitaal
autobiog'raphy ..phies outobiografie
aut'ograph (n) eie handskrif/outograaf; (v) teken,
outografeer; ~ **hun'ter** handtekeningjagter
automat'ic (n) outomatiese pistool; (a) outo=
maties; ~ **pi'lot** stuuroutomaat; ~ **tel'ler**
machine' (**ATM**) outoteller, kitsbank (OTM)
auton'omous selfbesturend, outonoom
autop'sy ..sies lykskouing, outopsie
aut'umn herfs, najaar
auxil'iary (n) helper, bondgenoot; ..ries hulp=

troepe; (a) hulp=; ~ **ser'vice** hulpdiens; ~ **verb** hulpwerkwoord

avail' (n, v) baat, nut; ~**able** verkry(g)baar, beskikbaar

av'alanche sneeustorting, lawine

avari'cious (a) gierig, hebsugtig, vrekkerig

avenge' wreek, wraak neem; ~**r** wreker

av'enue laning, laan; toegang

av'erage (n) gemiddelde; awery (skeepvaart); (a) gemiddeld

aver'sion afkeer (van); teensin; walging

a'viary aviaries voëlhok

avia'tion lugvaart; vliegkuns

avoca'do -s avokado(peer)

avoid' (v) vermy; ontwyk

await' verwag, afwag; ~*ing trial* verhooraf= wagtend

awake' (v) wek; ontwaak, wakker word; (a) wakker; opgewek, lewendig; *be ~ to* besef;

op die hoede wees teen

award' (n) uitspraak, beslissing; beloning; toekenning, prys, bekroning *also* **pri'ze**; (v) toeken; bekroon *also* **confer'/bestow'**

aware' bewus; versigtig; bedag; *be ~ of* be= wus wees van

away' weg; vo(o)rt; **right** ~ dadelik, onmiddel= lik/oombliklik *also* **imme'diately/in'stantly**

awe (n) ontsag, eerbied; vrees

aw'ful vreeslik; verskriklik; ontsettend, skrik= wekkend *also* **ter'rible**

awk'ward onhandig, lomp *also* **clum'sy**

awl (n) els (gereedskap)

awn'ing seilkap, sonskerm; agterdek

axe byl; hatchet; *have an ~ to grind* bybedoe= lings ('n grief) hê; eiebelang soek

ax'le as; ~ **pin** luns, lunspen

aza'lea -s asalea, bergroos

az'ure (a) hemelsblou, asuur

B

baa (n) geblêr; (v) blêr *also* **bleat**

bab'ble (n) gepraat, gebabbel, geklets; (v) bab= bel; murmel (water); ~**r** babbelaar; verklikker

babe kindjie, babatjie *also* **ba'by**

baboon' bobbejaan

bab'y babies baba(tjie); ~ **bat'tering** baba= foltering; ~ **sho'wer** ooievaarstee; ~**sit'ter** babawagter, kroostrooster; *she will be ~sit= ting tonight* sy gaan vanaand kroostroos

bach'elor vrygesel; oujongkêrel; ~ **flat** een= persoonwoonstel; ~ **girl** jong selfstandige, ongetroude vrou

back (n) rug, agterkant; agterspeler; (v) wed op; ondersteun; ~ *a horse* op 'n perd wed; ~ *up* ondersteun, rugsteun; (a) agterste; agterstallig; (adv) terug, agteruit; gelede; ~**fire** truknal/truplof (enjin); ~**ground** ag= tergrond; ~**hand** handrug (tennis); ~**lash** teenreaksie; ~**log** agterstand, ophoping; ~**pac'ker** pakstapper; rugsaktoeris; ~**seat dri'ver** bekrydwer; ~**spin** trutol (bal); ~**-up** (nood)bystand; ~**veld** agterveld; ~**ward** agterlik; dom; ~**wash** terugspoeling; ~**yard mechan'ic** tjorlapper

bac'on (n) (vark)spek; ontbytspek/bacon

bad (a) **worse, worst** sleg; stout; nadelig; ~ **debts** dooieskuld, oninbare skuld; ~ **luck** teen= spoed; ~ **tem'per** slegte bui, kwaai humeur

badge (n) kenteken, wapen; kleurteken

badg'er (n) ratel (dier)

bad'minton pluimbal

bag (n) sak, tas; *in the ~* uitgemaakte saak

bagg'age bagasie, reisgoed *also* **lug'gage**

bag'pipe doedelsak; *play the ~* doedel

bag snat'cher handsakrower

hail (n) borg, borgtog; *released on ~* op borg= tog vrygelaat; (v) borg staan; ~ *out* uitborg

bait (n) aas (vis); lokaas (mense/diere); (v) aanhits; terg; **artifi'cial** ~ kunsaas

bake bak; hard word; ~**r** bakker; ~**r's dozen** dertien; ~**ry** bakkery

bak'ing baksel; ~ **pow'der** bakpoeier

bak'kie bakkie, ligte bestelwa *also* **light deliv'ery van (LDV)**

balacla'va: ~**cap** klapmus, balaklawamus

bal'ance (n) balans, ewewig; saldo; (weeg)= skaal; (v) weeg; vereffen, balanseer, saldeer (boeke), klop (syfers); ~ **of po'wer** mags= ewewig

bal'cony ..nies balkon

bald (a) kaalkop; ~ **facts** naakte feite

bal'derdash geklets, onsin, kaf(praatjies)

bale[1] (n) baal; (v) in bale pak

bale[2] (v) uitskep (water uit bootjie)

ball[1] dansparty, bal

ball[2] koeël, bal, bol; kluit; oogappel

ball'ad ballade; lied (in digvorm)
ball'bearing (koeël)laer
ball'et ballet, toneeldans; ~ **dan'cer** balletdanser
balloon' (lug)ballon; ~ **tyre** kussingband
ball'ot (n) stembrief; stemming; *vote by* ~ met/per geslote stembrief stem
ball'point pen balpunt(pen), rolpunt(pen)
ballroom danssaal, balsaal; ~ **dan'cing** baldans
balm (n) balsem; ~**y** mild (weer); simpel, getik *also* **cra'zy**
bamboo' **-s** bamboes
bamboo'zle (v) kul, verneuk *also* **swin'dle/con**
ban (n) ban; verbod; (pl) huweliksgebooie; (v) verban, ban; inperk; ~ *a book* 'n boek verbied; ~ *a person* iem. verban/inperk
ban'al (a) banaal, afgesaag, alledaags
bana'na **-s** piesang
band (n) bende; orkes; band
ban'dage (n) verband; (v) verbind
ban'dit voëlvryverklaarde, rower; **ar'med** ~ gewapende rower
band'master kapelmeester, orkesdirigent
bandoleer' (n) bandelier
band'saw bandsaag, lintsaag
band'wagon: *jump on the* ~ oorloop na die wenparty
ban'dy: ~ *about with someone's name* met iem. se naam smous; ~**-legged** hoepelbeen=
bang (n) slag, knal; *go* ~ ontplof
ban'gle armband *also* **bra'celet**
ban'jo **-s** banjo
bank (n) bank; (v) geld in die bank sit (deponeer); **commer'cial** ~ handelsbank; **mer'chant** ~ aksepbank; ~ *on* staatmaak op; ~**er** bank, bankier; ~**ing** bankiersake, bankwese; ~**note** banknoot; ~ **rate** bank= koers; ~ **rob'bery** bankroof *also* **heist**
bank'rupt (a) bankrot, insolvent; *go* ~ ban= krot speel; ~**cy** bankrotskap
bann'er banier, vaandel; spandoek
banns huweliksgebooie
ban'quet (n) feesmaal, banket
ban'tam kapokhoendertjie; ~ **weight** bantam= gewig (boks)
ba'obab kremetartboom, baobab
bap'tise (v) doop; onderdompel
bap'tism doop; ~ *of fire* vuurdoop
bap'tist (n) doper; wederdoper
bar (n) regbank, balie; kantien, kroeg; maatstreep (mus.); (v) uitsluit, belet; ~ *one* op een na
barb (n) weerhaak; ~**ed wire** doringdraad

barbar'ian (n) barbaar; wreedaard
barbar'ic (a) barbaars *also* **bar'barous**
bar'becue braaihoek, braaiplek, braaistel
barb'el baber (vis)
barb'er haarsnyer, haarkapper; barbier
bare (v) ontbloot; (a) bloot, kaal; ~**fa'ced lie** onbeskaamde leuen; ~**foot(ed)** kaalvoet; ~**ly** ternouernood, skaars
bar'fly kroegvlieg
bar'gain (n) winskoop, (wins)kopie, keur= koop; *into the* ~ op die koop toe; *strike a* ~ 'n slag slaan; (v) kwansel, knibbel; ~**ing po'wer** bedingingsmag/bedingvermoë
barge (n) trekskuit, sloep; (v) bons
ba'ritone bariton
bark[1] (n) bas; (v) bas afmaak; 'n kors vorm
bark[2] (n) bark, skuit
bark[3] (n) geblaf; (v) blaf
bar'keeper kroegbaas, kroeghouer
bar'ley gars; ~ **wa'ter** gortwater
bar'maid skinkjuffie, kroegjuffrou, tapster
bar'man kroegman, tapper
barn skuur, loods *also* **shed**
barom'eter weerglas, barometer
ba'ron baron, vryheer
ba'rrack (n) barak; hut; leërkamp; (pl) kaser= ne, barakke; (v) uitjou
ba'rrage (n) studam, keerwal, afsluitdam; spervuur (mil.)
ba'rrel (n) vaatjie; geweerloop; (v) inkuip; ~ **or'gan** draaiorrel
ba'rren bar, dor; onvrugbaar; kaal; skraal
barricade' (n) versperring; (pad)blokkade *also* **road'block**; (v) versper, verskans
ba'rrier (n) slagboom, verskansing, versper= ring; (v) afsluit; ~ **line** (solid white line) sperstreep; ~ **reef** koraalrif
ba'rrow burg (vark)
bart'er (n) ruilhandel; (v) (uit)ruil, verruil
base[1] (n) grondslag, basis; voetstuk; (v) ba= seer, grond; ~ *their opinion on* grond hulle mening op
base[2] (a) sleg, laag *also* **depra'ved**; onedel (metale)
base'ball bofbal
base'ment kelder(verdieping)
bash'ful skaam; verleë *also* **tim'id, shy**
bas'ic basies, grond=; ~ **En'glish** basiese Engels; ~ **prin'ciples** grondbeginsels
bas'in kom, skottel, wasbak; hawekom
bas'is bases grondslag; basis
bask (v) koester, stoof/stowe (in die son)

bas'ket mandjie, korf; ~ball korfbal

bass -es basstem, bas; basviool

bast'ard (n) baster; vuilgoed (mens); onegte kind (veroud.); (a) baster=; buite-egtelik; ~ise verbaster

bat[1] (n) vlermuis

bat[2] (n) knuppel; krieketkolf; *off his own* ~ op eie houtjie; (v) kolf, slaan (bal)

batch -es klomp; baksel (brood); broeisel (eiers); besending (goed); lot (veiling)

bath (n) bad; badkamer; (v) bad

bathe (v) bad, baai; besproei

bath'ing: ~ cos'tume baaikostuum; ~ trunks swembroek(ie)

bat'on dirigeerstok; knuppel; ~ charge knup= pelstormloop

bats'man ..men kolwer, slaner

battal'ion bataljon

batt'ery (n) ..ries battery; aanranding; ~ chic'kens batteryhoenders

batt'le (n) veldslag, stryd; (v) veg; ~-axe strydbyl; kwaai vroumens, feeks; ~ dress gevegstenue, vegklere; ~field slagveld

bay[1] (n) baai; inham (see)

bay[2] (n) blaf, geblaf (hond); *keep at* ~ op 'n afstand hou; (v) blaf, aanblaf

bay[3] (n) nis *also* **ni'che, recess'**; uitbousel

bay[4] (n) bruin perd; (a) bruin

bay'onet (n) bajonet

bazaar' basaar/bazaar; markwinkel *also* **mart**

be wees, bestaan, ~ *gone!* trap!; *don't* ~ *long* moenie lank wegbly nie

beach -es kus, strand; wal; ~bug'gy duinebesie; ~com'ber lang golf (strand); strandsnuffelaar (vir wrakgoed); strandjut (aaswolf), ~ cot'tage strandhuis; ~ thongs plakkies *also* **slip-slops**

beac'on (n) baken; vuurtoring; (v) afbaken

bead (n) kraal; pêrel; sweetdruppel; blasie; korrel (geweer); (pl) rosekrans; (v) inryg

bea'gle jaghond; speurhond; spioen

beak bek, snawel; kromneus, tuit (ketel)

beak'er (n) beker

be'-all einddoel; alles; wese; *the* ~ *and end-all* die begin en die einde

beam (n) balk; juk (skaal); straal; (v) straal; skyn; ~ing (a) stralend (van geluk)

bean boon(tjie); (pl) pitte, geld; *full of* ~s op sy stukke; ~stalk boontjierank

bear[1] (n) beer (dier); lomperd

bear[2] (n) daalspekulant (effektebeurs)

bear[3] (v) bore, born baar, voortbring; dra; ver= dra, duld; ~ *in mind* onthou asseblief; ~able

draaglik, redelik

beard baard; weerhaak

bear'er draer, bringer; toonder (tjek); lyk= draer; ~ certi'ficate toondersertifikaat

bear'ing houding; gedrag; peiling; ~s rigting

beast bees, dier; ~ly beesagtig, dierlik

beat (n) patrollie, rondte; slag; tik; ritme; (v) klop, slaan; kneus; uitklop; oortref, wen; *that* ~s *me* dit slaan my dronk; ~ *your opponent* jou teenstander klop/wen

beat'ing slanery, kloppery; loesing *also* **hi'ding**

beauti'cian (n) skoonheidkundige

beaut'iful mooi, pragtig, fraai, sierlik

beaut'y skoonheid; ~ par'lour skoonheid= salon; ~ queen skoonheidskoningin; ~ spot moesie; pronkpleistertjie; mooi plekkie

beav'er bewer (dier)

because' omdat, want, daar (vgw)

beck'on (v) wink, knik, wuif

become' (v) word; betaam; pas

becom'ing (a) betaamlik; netjies, passend

bed bed, kooi; bedding (rivier); ~ *and break= fast* bed en ontbyt

bed'lam deurmekaarspul *also* **cha'os**

bed: ~rid'den bedleënd; ~room slaapkamer; ~side man'ners siekbedsjarme

bee by, byeenkoms

beef beesvleis; ~steak biefstuk, steak

bee: ~hive byekorf, by(e)nes; ~line reguit lyn, luglyn; ~kee'per byeboer

beer bier; ~hall biersaal; taphuis

beet'le (n) kewer, tor

beet'root beet; ~ su'gar beetsuiker

before' voor, vooruit, vantevore; vooraf, vroeër; ~ *long* binnekort

before'hand vantevore, vooraf

beg versoek; smeek/soebat; bid; bedel; ~ *par= don* verskoning vra

begg'ar (n) bedelaar; *little* ~ klein vabond

begin' begin, 'n aanvang neem; ~ner begin= ner; leerling; groentjie

begin'ning begin, aanvang; aanhef; *from the* ~ uit die staanspoor, van meet af

begone'! voort!; trap!; voert!

behalf' ontwil; namens; *in/on* ~ *of* ten be= hoewe van; namens

behave' gedra; ~ *oneself* jou gedra

behav'iour gedrag, houding

behead' onthoof *also* **decap'itate** (v)

behind' agter; van agter, agteraan

behold' (v) aanskou, sien, beskou

be'ing aansyn, bestaan; wese; skepsel; *for the*

time ~ voorlopig, intussen
belch (v) wind opbreek *also* **burp**; uitbraak
bel'fry belfries kloktoring
belief' (n) geloof *also* **faith**; mening
believe' (v) glo, vertrou, meen; ~ *it or not* raar
maar waar; **make-**~ (n) skyn, wysmakery
believ'er gelowige *also* **disci'ple**
belit'tle (v) verklein, verkleineer; gering ag
bell klok, bel; *answer the* ~ maak die deur oop
bell'buoy klokboei, belboei
bell'ow (n) geblêr; gebulk; (v) blêr; bulk
bell'ows (n) blaasbalk
bell: ~**ring'er** klokluier; ~**weth'er** belhamel,
voorbok
bell'y (n) buik, maag *also* **abdo'men**; ~**dan'cer**
buikdanseres
belong' behoort; *he* ~*s to a church* hy behoort
tot 'n kerk; ~**ing** behorend; ~**ings** (pl) be=
sittings, goed
beloved' (n) beminde, geliefde; (a) bemind
below' onder, benede, omlaag
belt (n) lyfband/belt; gordel; dryfband; (v)
omgord; ~ *up!* gord/gespe vas!; **fan**~
waaierband; **seat**~ sitplekgordel
bench -es bank, sitbank; regbank
bend (n) buiging; (v) buig; draai
bends (n) borrelsiekte
beneath' onder, benede, onderaan
benedic'tion (n) seëning; gebed, seënwens
benefac'tor weldoener (mens)
benefi'ciary begunstigde (in 'n erflating)
ben'efit (n) voordeel; voorreg; ~ *of the doubt*
voordeel van die twyfel; **fringe** ~ byvoor=
deel *also* **perk(s)**; (v) bevoordeel; bevorder;
~ **socie'ty** bystand(s)vereniging
benev'olent (a) welwillend; goedgunstig; wel=
dadig; ~ **fund** bystand(s)fonds
benign' (a) goed, minsaam, goedaardig
bequeath' (v) bemaak, nalaat (in testament)
bequest' (n) bemaking, erfporsie, erflating
berea've berowe; ontneem; *the* ~*d parents* die
bedroefde ouers; ~**ment** sterfgeval; verlies
be'ret baret
berg berg, ysberg; ~**wind** bergwind
be'riberi berrie-berrie
ber'ry bessie; viseier
ber'serk rasend; ~**er** berserker (mens)
berth (n) ankerplek; kajuit; (v) vasmeer (skip)
besi'de langs, naas; by; behalwe, buiten; ~ *the*
point/question nie ter sake nie
besi'des bowendien, behalwe, buiten
besiege' (v) beleër (stad)

best beste; *do your* ~ jou beste doen/lewer; *to*
the ~ *of my ability/knowledge* na my beste
vermoë/wete
bes'tial (a) dierlik, beesagtig; sinlik
best'man strooijonker
bestow' (v) skenk, bestee, verleen
best'seller (n) topverkoper, blitsverkoper; tref=
fer(boek)
bet (n) weddenskap; (v) wed, verwed; *you* ~!
dit kan jy glo!
betray' (v) verraai; mislei, bedrieg; ~**al** ver=
raad, troubreuk
betroth' verloof; toesê; ~**al** verlowing *also*
enga'gement; ~**ed'** verloofde (mens)
bet'ter (n) voordeel; oorhand; meerdere; *for*
~, *for worse* in lief en leed; (v) verbeter; (a)
beter; *you had* ~ *go* jy moet liewer gaan; ~
half (n) wederhelf
between' tussen, tussenin; ~ *ourselves* onder
(ons)
beware' oppas; op jou hoede wees
bewil'der verwar, verbyster; ~**ed** deurmekaar
beyond' (n) oorkant; (adv, prep) bo; buite;
verby; oorkant; anderkant; *that is* ~ *me* dis
bokant my vuurmaakplek
bi'as (n) oorhelling; neiging; ~**sed** (a) be=
vooroordeel(d), partydig
bib (n) borslappie
Bi'ble Bybel *also* **Scriptures**
bib'lical Bybels, Bybel=
bibliog'raphy . .phies bronnelys, bibliografie
bi'ceps -es biseps, boarmspier
bick'er (v) kibbel, twis; flikker (skerp lig)
bi'cycle (n) fiets, rywiel; (v) fiets, fiets ry
bid (n) bod; (v) beveel; nooi; sê; bie; ~**der**
bieër (veiling); ~**ding** bieëry (vandisie)
bifo'cal bifokaal; ~ **spec'tacles/bifo'cals** bifo=
kale bril, dubbeldoorbril
big groot, swaar, dik; ~ **bang** oerknal (sterre=
kunde); ~ **shot** groot kokkedoor; ~ **stick**
magsvertoon
big'amist bigamis, tweewywer
bi'ker (n) fietser (wedrenne)
bile (n) gal; humeurigheid
bilhar'zia bilharzia-parasiet, slakwurm
bilharzias'is bilharziase, rooiwater (siekte)
bil'iary (n) gal=; ~ **fe'ver** galkoors
bilin'gual tweetalig; ~**ism** tweetaligheid
bil'ious (a) gallerig, mislik
bilk bedrieg, fop; **hotel'** ~**er** glyjakkals
bill[1] (n) wetsontwerp
bill[2] (n) bek; snawel; (v) met die bek streel

bill[3] (n) rekening *also* **account'**; bewys; plakkaat; ~ **of exchan'ge** wissel; ~ **pay'**= **able** betaalwissel; skuldwissel; ~ **recei'v**= **able** ontvangwissel
bill'iard: ~ **cue** biljartstok; ~**s** biljart(spel)
bill'ion miljard (1 000 miljoen)
bill'ygoat bokram
bin meelkas, kis; bak, bien
bind (v) **bound, bound** verbind (wond); bind; verplig; ~**er** binder; verband
bin'ge (n) fuifparty, dronknes *also* **spree**
binoc'ular (pl) verkyker/vêrkyker
biochem'istry biochemie
bi'odata (n) biodata, lewensprofiel *also* **curri'**= **culum vitae (CV)**
biodegra'dable bio-afbreekbaar
biog'raphy . .**phies** lewensbeskrywing, biogra= fie *also* **life story/pro'file**
biol'ogy biologie
bio'nic: ~ **man** bioniese mens
bi'oscope bioskoop *also* **cin'ema/mo'vie**; *going to* ~ bioskoop toe gaan, gaan fliek
bird voël; ~ *of prey* roofvoël; ~**ie** voëltjie (ook gholfterm); ~**lime** voëllym, voëlent; ~**watch'er** voëlkyker *also* **bir'der/twit'**= **cher;** ~**watch'ing** voëlkyk *also* **bir'ding**
birth geboorte; ontstaan; *give* ~ *to* die lewe skenk aan; ~ **certi'ficate** geboortebewys; ~ **control'** geboortebeperking *also* **fam'ily plan'ning;** ~**day** verjaar(s)dag; ~**mark** moe= dervlek/geboortemerk, ~**rate** geboortesyfer
bis'cuit soetkoekie, droëkoekie
bisex'ual (a) dubbelslagtig, biseksueel
bish'op biskop; raadsheer (skaak)
bis'ley (n) prysskiet; bisley
bit[1] (n) bietjie, stukkie; bis (rek.)
bit[2] (n) stang; (v) 'n toom aansit
hitch -es teef (wyfiehond); feeks; hoer; ~**y** (a) katterig, venynig *also* **nas'ty, spi'teful**
bite (n) byt; hap; (v) byt; kwes; bedrieg
bitt'er (a) bitter; skerp
black (n) swart, rouklere; *in* ~ *and white* swart op wit; (v) swart maak; ~**ball** (v) uitstem, veto; ~**board** skryfbord, skoolbord; (v) ~**mail** afdreig; afpers; swartsmeer; ~ **man/woman/ child** swart man/vrou/kind; ~**mar'ket** (n) swartmark/sluikhandel; ~**-out** verdonkering; breinfloute; ~**smith** grofsmid; ~**wattle** wat= telboom/looibasboom
blad'der (n) blaas; windsak; binnebal
blade lem, skeerlemmetjie; halm; blaadjie
blame (n) blaam; (v) blameer, verkwalik

blank (n) leegte, leemte; nul; (a) wit; blank, bleek; onbeskrewe; rymloos (verse); ~ **cart'**= **ridge** loskruitpatroon
blank'et (n) kombers; **wet** ~ pretbederwer
blas'phemous godslasterlik *also* **profa'ne**
blas'phemy godslastering; heiligskennis
blast (n) wind, rukwind; ontploffing; (v) uitbars; skiet (dinamiet); vervloek; ~**ed fellow** ver= vloekte vent; ~**er** (dinamiet)skieter; ~**-fur'**= **nace** smeltoond; hoogoond; ~**ing certif'icate** skietsertifikaat; ~**ing opera'tions** springwerke
blaze[1] (n) bles (van perd); ~ *a trail* die weg baan
blaze[2] (n) vlam, vuurgloed; gerug; *in a* ~ in ligte laaie; (v) vlam, brand; skitter
blaz'er kleurbaadjie, sportbaadjie
bleach bleik; ~**ing pow'der** bleikpoeier
bleak (a) kaal, verlate, koud *also* **bar'ren**
bleat (n) geblêr; (v) blêr, bulk
bleed bloei; bloedlaat; ~**er** bloeier
bleep'er -s blieper (vir boodskappe)
blem'ish (n) -es vlek, smet *also* **blot**; skande
blend (n) mengsel; (v) meng, vermeng
bles'bok blesbok
bless (v) seën, loof; wy
bless'ed (a) geseën, gelukkig; saliger; *of* = *memory* saliger nagedagtenis
bless'ing (n) seën, seëning; (tafel)gebed; ~ *in disguise* bedekte seën
blind[1] (n) (rol)gordyn, blinding/blinder; skerm
blind[2] (v) verblind, blind maak; (a) blind, don= ker; verborge, ~ **al'ley** blinde steeg, keer= weer; doodloopstraat; ~ **date** blinde af= spraak/ontmoeting; ~ **rise** blinde hoogte; ~ **side** skeelkant; steelkant (rugby); ~**fold** (v) blinddoek; (a) geblinddoek; ~**ly** blinde= lings; ~**man's buff** blindemannetjie, blin= demolletjie (kinderspel)
blink (n) flikkering; (v) knipoog, gluur
blink'ers oogklappe
bliss (n) saligheid, geluk, heil; ~**ful** salig
blis'ter (n) blaar; blaas (aan voete, hande); (v) afdop (verf)
blizz'ard (n) sneeustorm, sneeujag
block (n) blok; hindernis; (v) afsluit, versper; dwarsboom; ~ **and tack'le** katrol(stel)
blockade' (n) blokkade *see* **roadblock**; (v) blokkeer
block: ~**head** domkop, uilskuiken; ~**house** blokhuis; ~**man** blokman (in slaghuis)
blo'ke kêrel, vent, ou *also* **guy**
blond (a) blond, lig

blonde (n) blondine, witkop (vrou)

blood (n) bloed; verwantskap; *blue* ~ aristo=
kratiese bloed; *in cold* ~ koelbloedig; ~**bath**
bloedbad; ~ **do'nor** bloedskenker; ~ **poi'=
soning** bloedvergift(ig)ing; ~ **pres'sure**
bloeddruk; ~ **transfu'sion** bloedoortapping;
~**y** bloeddorstig, bloederig; vervloekte, ver=
vlakste

bloom (n) bloeisel, blom; fleur, bloei; (v) bloei,
voorspoedig wees *also* **flou'rish**; blom

bloom'ing bloeiend; blosend; vervlakste

bloss'om (n) bloeisel; (v) bloei, blom

blot (n) klad, vlek; skandvlek; (v) beklad

blott'ing paper vloeipapier; kladpapier

blouse (n) bloes(e); hempbaadjie

blow[1] (n) slag, klap; hou, raps; ramp; *come to*
~*s* handgemeen raak

blow[2] blaas, waai; ~**gun/**~**pipe** blaaspyp

blue (n) blousel; blou, lug; (a) blou; neerslag=
tig; *out of the* ~ uit die bloute; ~**gum** bloe=
kom(boom); ~**stock'ing** bloukous, geleerde
vrou

bluff[1] (n) grootpratery, bluf *also* **preten'ce**; (v)
uitoorlê, wysmaak; grootpraat

bluff[2] (n) steil voorgebergte; (a) grof; steil

blun'der (n) flater, blaps; fout; ~**er** knoeier,
ploeteraar, sukkelaar

blunt (v) stomp/ongevoelig maak; afstomp;
(a) stomp; bot; nors, kortaf

blur (n) vlek, smet; (v) beklad

blurb (s) flapteks (boek); reklameteks

blurt: ~ *out* uitblaker, uitflap, uitbasuin

blush (n) **-es** blos; gloed; ~**ing** blosend

bo'a -s boa; ~ **constric'tor** (S. Am.) luislang

boar beer; wilde swyn

board (n) plank; tafel; boord (skip); raad;
kommissie; losies; karton; ~ **of inqui'ry**
ondersoekraad; ~ **and lod'ging** kos en in=
woning; (v) inwoon, loseer; ~**er** loseerder;
~**ing** losies; ~**ing house** losieshuis; ~**ing
school** kosskool; ~ **mee'ting** direksiever=
gadering; ~**room** raad(s)kamer, raadsaal;
~**sail'ing** seilplankry

boast (n) grootpratery; (v) spog *also* **brag**;
~**er** grootprater

boat (n) boot, skuit, skip; ~**race** wedvaart

bobb'y bobbies konstabel (polisie)

bob'tail stompstert; *ragtag and* ~ Jan Rap en
sy maat

bod'y (n) **bodies** liggaam, lyf; persoon; lyk/
stoflike oorskot; bak(werk) (motor); ~ **cor=
porate** beheerliggaam (deeltitels); (v) belig=

gaam; ~**buil'der** liggaamsbouer, spierbouer;
~**guard** lyfwag; ~ **lan'guage** lyftaal

bof'fin uitvinder; kenner *also* **ex'pert**

bog (n) moeras, vlei; (v) ~ **down** vasval

bog'ey -s baansyfer (gholf)

bog'us vals, oneg; ~ **collec'tor** kammakollek=
tant; ~ **com'pany** swendelmaatskappy

bog'y bogies paaiboelie, spook, skrikbeeld

boil[1] (n) pitsweer, bloedvin(t) *also* **furun'cle**

boil[2] (v) kook; ~**er** (stoom)ketel; ~**erma'ker**
ketelmaker; ~**ing point** kookpunt

bois'terous onstuimig, wild *also* **noi'sy**

bold vrypostig; dapper; vermetel; *I make* ~ *to
say* ek verstout my om te sê

bol'ster (n) kussing; stut; (v) ondersteun/
rugsteun; opvul; ~ *up* steun, stut

bolt[1] (n) pyl; grendel; bout; skuif; bliksem=
straal; ~ **cut'ter** boutknipper

bolt[2] (v) weghol; op loop sit (perd)

bomb (n) bom, granaat; **at'om(ic)** ~ atoombom;
~ **blast** bomontploffing; (v) bombardeer

bombard' bombardeer; ~**ment** bombardement

bomb: ~**er** bomwerper (vliegtuig); ~ **shel'ter**
bomskuiling

bonan'za meevaller(tjie), gelukslag

bond (n) band; verband; obligasie; verbinte=
nis; ooreenkoms; (v) verpand; verband,
beswaar; ~**ed prop'erty** verbande/beswaar=
de eiendom; ~**hol'der** verbandhouer; ~**s**
skuldbriewe, obligasies

bone (n) been; (pl) gebeente; ~ *of contention*
twisappel; *pick a* ~ *with* 'n appeltjie skil
met (iem.)

bon'fire vreugdevuur

bonn'et mus, kappie, hoedjie; kap (motor)

bonn'y (a) lief, aanvallig, fraai; vrolik, dartel

bon'us -es bonus, premie

bon'y (a) benerig, beenagtig; vol grate (vis)

boo (v) uitjou, boe *also* **bar'rack**

boob'y boobies lummel, domoor; ~ **prize**
poedelprys, troosprys; ~ **trap** fopmyn

book (n) boek; geskrif; Bybel; ~ *of reference*
naslaanboek; bewysboek; (v) inboek; op=
skryf; ~**ie** beroepswedder; boekie/boekma=
ker; ~**ing of'fice** loket, kaartjieskantoor;
~**kee'ping** boekhou; ~**mark** bladwyser;
~**sel'ler** boekhandelaar; ~**to'ken** boekbewys

boom[1] (n) sluitboom, valhek

boom[2] (n) gedreun; gebulder (kanon); (v)
bulder, dreun

boom[3] (n) welvaart; oplewing, boom (in eko=
nomie)

boom'erang boemerang, werphout
boon (n) geskenk; guns; genade; uitkoms; (a) vrolik, vriendelik; weldadig (mens)
boor lummel, lomperd (mens); ~**ish** onbeskof
boost (v) ophemel; aanjaag; versterk; ~ *one's ego* jou ego streel; ~**er** aanjaer; ~**er ca'ble** aansitkabel *also* **jum'per lead**; ~**er dose** skraagdosis
boot[1] (n) stewel; bagasieruim; *get the* ~ uit= geskop word; (v) uitskop
boot[2] (n) wins, voordeel; *to* ~ op die koop toe
booth hut; stalletjie/kraampie; afskorting
boot: ~**lace** skoenveter/skoenriem; ~**leg'ger** (drank)smokkelaar; ~**po'lish** waks, skoen= smeer; ~ **spoi'ler** drukvin, blitsvlerk (mo= tor); ~ **tree** skoenlees
boot'y (n) **booties** buit, roof *also* **loot**
booze (n) drinkgoed; *on the* ~ aan die fuif; (v) suip, swier, boemel
bord'er (n) rand; kant; grens (land); soom; (v) omsoom; begrens; ~ *on* grens aan; *on the* ~ aan die grens; ~**line case** grensgeval
bore[1] (n) boor; boorgat; kaliber (geweer); wydte; (v) boor; uitboor
bore[2] (n) vervelende mens of saak; (v) ver= veel, neul
bor'ing (a) vervelend/vervelig; saai
born gebore; ~ *and bred* gebore en getoë; ~ *in the Karoo* 'n boorling v.d. Karoo
borne gedra *see* **bear**
bo'rough stad, dorp; munisipaliteit
bo'rrow (v) leen (van iem.); ~**er** lener
bos'beraad bosberaad *also* **bun'du con'fer= ence/lekgot'la/inda'ba**
bo'som (n) boesem, bors; ~ **friend** boesem= vriend
boss (n) **-es** haas, meester; (v) bestuur, baas= speel; (a) ~**y** baasspelerig, dominerend
bot'any plantkunde, botanie
both beide, albei, altwee; ~ *Ann and Mary* sowel Ann as Mary; ~ *languages* albei tale; ~ *of us* ons albei
both'er (n) moeite, kwelling; (v) neul, lastig val; moeite maak; bodder
bot'tle (n) bottel, fles; (v) bottel; inlê; ~**neck** knelpunt/bottelnek; ~**store** drankwinkel
bott'om (n) boom; grond(slag); onderkant; (v) grondves; steun; (a) onderste; ~**less pit** bodemlose put; ~**line** slotsom/konklusie/ deurslaggewende faktor *also* **fundamen'tal factor, gist**; wins/verlies (boekhou)
bought *see* **buy**

boul'der rotsblok, groot klip
bounce (n) slag, opslag, hou; grootpraat; (v) (op)spring; bons; hop (ook 'n tjek); ~**r** uit= smyter *also* **chuck'er-out**; windmaker; lig= ter (krieket)
bound[1] (n) grens; *out of* ~s buite perk(e)
bound[2] (a) verbonde, verplig; bestem; ~/*com= mitted to* verbind tot
boun'dary grens; grenshou (sport)
bout beurt; wedstryd; ronde *also* **round** (boxing)
bouti'que boetiek
bow[1] (n) buiging; (v) buig, buk
bow[2] (n) boeg (van skip)
bow[3] (n) strykstok; strik (strikdas)
bow'els ingewande; gevoel
bowl (n) skaal; kom; beker
bow'legged hoepelbeen=
bow'ler bouler (krieket)
bow'ling: ~ **al'ley** kegelbaan; ~ **green** rolbal= baan
bowls rolbal
bow'string boogsnaar, boogpees
bow'tie (n) strikdas, vlinderdas
box[1] (n) opstopper, klap; boks; (v) boks
box[2] (n) **-es** boks, houer; kas, kis; (pos)bus; briewebus; ~**er** bokser/vuisvegter *also* **pu'= gilist**; ~**ing** boks, ~**ing glo'ves** bokshand= skoene; ~ **of'fice** loket; ~ **of'fice success'** lokettreffer
boy -s seun, knaap, jongetjie *also* **lad**
boy'cot (n) boikot; (v) boikot
boy: ~**s' high school** hoër seunskool; ~ **scout** padvinder
bra (n) buustelyfie, bra
braai/braai'vleis (n) braaivleis
brace'let armband *also* **ban'gle**
brac'es kruisbande
brack'et (n) klamp; (v) klamp; *in* ~s tussen hakies
brack'ish (a) brak, souterig
brag (v) spog, grootpraat *also* **show off, boast**; ~**gart** grootprater, grootbek; ~**ging** (n) grootpraat
braid (n) vleg, haarvleg; koord, omboorsel
braille puntskrif, blindeskrif, brailleskrif
brain brein, harsings; verstand; ~**child** uit= vindsel, geesteskind; ~**drain** breinerosie; ~**scan** breintasting/breinskandering; ~**tea'= ser** kopkrapper/breinboelie; ~**wash'ing** brein= spoeling; ~**wave** blink gedagte; ~**y** skrander, knap, slim
brake (n) remskoen, rem, briek; (v) rem,

briek; ~ **li'ning** remvoering
bram'ble braam (struik)
bran semels
branch (n) **-es** tak; vertakking; takkantoor; (v) vertak
brand (n) merk, brandmerk; handelsmerk; (v) brandmerk; kenmerk; ~**ed goods** merk= artikels
brand'-new (spik)splinternuut
bran'dy ..**dies** brandewyn, hardehout (idiom.)
brass geelkoper; geld; skaamteloosheid; ~ **band** blaasorkes
brass'ière buustelyfie, bra *also* **bra**
brava'do (n) grootpratery, bluf, bravade
brave (v) uitdaag; tart; (a) dapper, moedig
bra'vo (interj) bravo!; mooi skoot!; skote P(r)etoors! *also* **well done!**
brawl (n) rusie, bakleiery; (v) twis, rusie maak; ~**er** molesmaker (mens)
brawn sult, hoofkaas (vleisgereg); ~**y** gespier(d)
bray (v) balk (donkie); runnik
braze (v) sweissoldeer, braseer; hard maak
braz'en-faced onbeskaamd
breach (n) **-es** breuk, verbreking; bres, skeur; oortreding; ~ *of contract* kontrakbreuk; ~ *of the peace* rusverstoring
bread brood; *quarrel with your* ~ *and butter* in jou eie lig staan
breadth breedte, wydte
bread'winner broodwinner (mens)
break (n) steuring; breuk; pouse; blaaskans; (v) breek, verbreek; vernietig; ~ *off an engagement* 'n verlowing verbreek; ~ *a record* 'n rekord slaan/oortref; ~**-away holiday** wegbreekvakansie; ~**down** instor= ting; onklaarraking; ongeluk; ontleding (van syfers); ~**down lor'ry** insleepwa; ~**down ser'vice** insleepdiens
break'er brander (see)
break-e'ven point winsdrempel, gelykbreek= punt
break'fast ontbyt, oggendete; **champag'ne** ~ vonkelontbyt
break: ~**-in** inbraak, huisbraak; ~**through** deurbraak; ~**wa'ter** hawehoof; golfbreker
breast (n) bors; boesem, skoot; ~ **fee'ding** borsvoeding (baba)
breath asem; luggie, windjie; *out of* ~ uit= asem; ~**aly'ser** alkotoetser
breathe (v) asem, asemhaal; adem (fig.); ~**r** blaaskans
breed (n) geslag, ras, soort; (v) (aan)teel; (uit)=

broei; voortbring; ~**er** teler; ~**ing** teelt; beskawing, verfyndheid
breeze (n) luggie, windjie, bries
brew (n) brousel; (v) brou, gis; ~**ery** brouery
bri'ar wilde roos; rooshout
bribe (n) omkoopgeld; (v) omkoop; ~**ry** om= kopery
brick (n) baksteen; staatmaker (mens); (a) baksteen=; ~**lay'er** messelaar
brid'al (a) bruids=; ~ **coup'le** bruidspaar
bride bruid; ~**groom** bruidegom; ~**smaid** strooimeisie; ~**sman** strooijonker *also* **best'= man**
bridge[1] (n) brug (kaartspel); (v) brugspeel
bridge[2] (n) brug; vioolkam; rug (neus); (v) oorbrug; ~**head** brughoof
brid'ging: ~ **cap'ital** oorbruggingskapitaal; ~ **course** oorbruggingskursus
bri'dle (n) toom, teuel; (v) beteuel
brief[1] (n) **-s** samevatting; opdrag, voorskrif, volmag, mandaat; ~**case** aktetas, briewetas
brief[2] (a) kort, beknop
brigadier' brigadier; ~**-gen'eral brigadiers-general** brigade-generaal
bright (a) helder, skitterend; skrander; ~ **fu'ture** blink toekoms; ~ **stu'dent** slimkop, knap student
brill'iant (a) glinsterend, skitterend; briljant
brim (n) rand, kant
brine (n) pekel; (v) insout
bring (v) bring, saambring; veroorsaak; ~ **about** teweegbring; ~ *down the house* algemene byval vind
brin'jal (n) eiervrug, brinjal
brink rand; waterkant; *on the* ~ *of* aan die rand van
brisk (a) lewendig, wakker; kragtig
bris'tle (n) varkhaar, borsel; ~ *with* wemel/ krioel van
Brit'ain Brittanje
Brit'ish (a) Brits
brit'tle bros, breekbaar
broach (v) ter sprake bring, opper; ~ *a subject* 'n saak aanroer/opper
broad breed, wyd; ~**bean** tuinboon, boer= boon(tjie)
broad'cast (v) uitsaai
broad'casting uitsaaiwese; ~ **corpora'tion** uitsaaikorporasie; ~ **pro'gramme** radiopro= gram; ~ **sta'tion** radio-omroep
broad: ~**en** breed maak, verbreed; ~**-mind'= ed** onbekrompe, verlig

bro'chure (n) brosjure; pamflet, bladskrif
broil'er (n) braaihoender, braaikuiken
broke (a) gebreek; platsak, bankrot
brok'en gebreek, stukkend; verslae, moede=
loos; gebroke (hart); ~ **home** gebroke gesin/
huis; ~ **line** stippelstreep (pad)
bro'ker makelaar (mens, firma)
bronchi'tis lugpypontsteking, brongitis
bronze (n) brons; bronsfiguur; (v) (ver)brons
brooch -es borsspeld
brood (n) broeisel; gespuis; (v) broei, uitbroei;
~y broeis (hen)
brook (n) spruit(jie), driffie *also* **stream**
broom besem; veër; **hard** ~ skropbesem
broth dun vleissop, kragsop; *too many cooks
spoil the* ~ baie koks bederf die bry
broth'el (n) bordeel, hoerhuis
broth'er -s, brethren broer, boet; ~**hood** broe=
(de)rskap; ~**in-law brothers-in-law** swaer
brow winkbrou, wysbrou
brown bruin; donker
browse rondkyk, rondblaai; (deur)blaai (van
Internet); ~**r's mar'ket** snuffelmark
bruise (n) kneusplek; (v) kneus
brunch (s) noenbyt, midbyt, brunch
brunette' brunet, swartkop (vrou)
brunt skok, heftigheid, skerpte; *bear the* ~ *of*
die spit afbyt
brush (n) **-es** borsel, kwas; (v) borsel
bru'tal wreedaardig, dierlik, onmenslik
brute (n) redelose dier; onbeskofte mens; (a)
dierlik, ru, onbeskof
bub'ble (n) lugbel, borrel; (v) (op)borrel;
blaas; ~**gum** blaasgom, borrelgom
bubon'ic pla'gue builepes
buccaneer' seerower, vrybuiter, boekanier
buck (n) bokram; modegek
buck'et emmer; bak; *kick the* ~ lepel in die
dak steek
buc'kle (n) gespe; (v) vasgespe; ~ *up!* gord vas!
bud (n) knop, bot; ent; *nip in the* ~ in die kiem
smoor; (v) bot, uitloop
budge (v) wyk, verroer, beweeg
bud'ge(rigar)' parkietjie, budjie (voël)
budg'et (n) begroting; leersak; (v) begroot
buff'er stootkussing, buffer
bug[1] (n) luis, weeluis; (elektroniese) klikker/
klikapparaat, luistervlooi
bug[2] (v) meeluister/afluister *also* **tap** (v) (tel.);
his office was bugged sy kantoor was geklik
bug'bear skrikbeeld; paaiboelie; wildewragtig
(mens) *also* **bugaboo'**

bu'gle beuel; horing; ~**r** trompetter
build (n) bou, vorm, liggaamsbou; (v) bou;
stig; oprig
buil'der bouer; boumeester
buil'ding (n) gebou; bouery; ~ **contrac'tor**
bouaannemer, boukontrakteur; ~ **socie'ty**
bouvereniging
built-up area beboude gebied
bulb bol; gloeilamp(ie); blombol
bulge (n) knop; (v) swel, uitsit; uitpeul (oë)
buli'mia bulimie, geeuhonger *see* **anorex'ia**
bulk (n) omvang, grootte, klomp; ~ **pos'ting**
massapos; ~**y** lywig
bull[1] stygspekulant (effektebeurs)
bull[2] bul; ~**bar** bosbreker/bosbuffer; ~**calf**
bulkalf; ~**dog** boelhond; ~**do'zer** stootskra=
per
bull'et koeël; ~**proof** koeëlvas
bull'etin daaglikse verslag, bulletin/boeletien
bull'fight stiergeveg
bull'terrier bulterriër (hond)
bull'y (n) **bullies** afknouer, boelie, bullebak;
(v) treiter, baasspeel; afknou, boelie
bum (n) agterent, agterste; skobbejak (mens)
bump (n) slag, stamp; (v) stamp
bum'per (n) stamper, buffer; ligter/opslagbal
(krieket); (a) oorvloedig; ~ **crop** rekordoes
bump'kin lummel, lomperd, (plaas)japie
bun[1] bolletjie; **must** ~ mosbolletjie
bun[2] bolla (hare)
bunch -es bos, bondel; tros
bun'dle (n) bondel, gert; (v) saambind
bun'du gramadoelas, agterveld, boendoe; ~
bash'ing boendoebaljaar; ~ **con'ference/
sum'mit** bosberaad *also* **lekgot'la**
bung'alow bungalow; **sea'side** ~ strandhuis
bun'gle (v) knoei; konkel; ~**r** knoeier, ploe=
teraar, sukkelaar (mens)
bun'gee: ~ **jum'ping** rekspring; ~ **jum'per**
rekspringer
bun'ion eelt
bunk[1] (n) slaapbank, kooi
bunk[2] (n) kaf, twak, onsin *also* **trash**
bunk[3] (v) stokkies draai, wegbly (van skool)
bun'ker (n) kolehok; hindernis; bunker; (sand)=
kuil (gholf); (v) kole laai, bunker
bunk'um onsin, bog, kafpraatjies
bun'ny troetelnaam vir hasie/konyntjie
buoy (n) **-s** baken (in see); boei
burd'en (n) las, vrag, pak; refrein (lied);
hooftema; **beast of** ~ lasdier
bureau' -x kantoor, buro

bu′reaucrat burokraat (mens)

burg′lar inbreker, huisbreker *also* hou′se= breaker; ~y inbraak; huisbraak; ~ alarm′ diefalarm; ~ bars diewetralies; ~ guard/~ proo′fing diefwering

bu′rial begrafnis; ~/memo′rial ser′vice rou= diens; ~ socie′ty begrafnisklub, stokvel

burn (n) brandplek; (v) brand; gloei

burs′ar penningmeester; beurshouer; ~y stu= diebeurs

burst (n) bars, skeur; (v) bars

bu′ry (v) begrawe; ~ the hatchet die strydbyl begrawe, vrede maak

bus -es bus; *catch the* ~ die bus haal; *miss the* ~ die bus mis; ~ dri′ver busdrywer/ busbestuurder; ~ ser′vice busdiens

bush -es bos, bossies; bosveld; ~ba′by nag= apie; ~ ran′ger boswagter; ~ shrike bok= makierie; ~tick bosluis

bus′iness -es besigheid, sakeonderneming, be= dryf; ~ col′lege handelskollege; ~ lea′der= ship bedryfsleiding; ~ let′ter sakebrief; ~man sakeman (mv. sakelui, sakemanne)

bust (n) borsbeeld; buuste, bors

bu′stle (n) gewoel, lewe, rumoer

bus′y (a) besig, woelig, bedrywig; ~bod′y be= moeial, kwaadstoker (mens)

but (n) maar; (prep) maar, dog, egter; behal=

we; *the last* ~ *one* die voorlaaste

butch′er (n) slagter; (v) slag; vermoor; ~bird laksman; ~y slaghuis

but′ler (oorspr.) bottelier; hoofbediende

butt′er (n) botter; (v) met botter smeer; ~fly skoe(n)lapper, vlinder; ~milk karringmelk

butt′ock boud, agterste/agterstewe

butt′on (n) knoop, knop; (v) toeknoop; ~hole knoopsgat; ruikertjie

bux′om (a) lewendig; goedbedeeld, mollig (meisie)

buy koop, inkoop; ~er koper; aankoper (vir firma)

buzz (v) gons, brom; ~ bike kragfiets; ~er gonser; zoemer (tegn.); ~ group gonsgroep; ~ word gonswoord/modewoord/refreinwoord

by deur; tot, met; na; by, op; ~ *far the best dictionary* verreweg die beste woordeboek; ~ *mistake* per ongeluk/abuis; ~ *no means* glad nie

bye loslopie (krieket)

bye-bye! wederom!; tot siens!; goedgaan!

by′-election tussenverkiesing

by′-law munisipale verordening

by: ~pass (n) verbypad; omleiding (hart); (v) verbysteek; ~pro′duct neweproduk; ~stan′= der omstander, toeskouer

byte (n) greep (rek.)

C

cab′aret (n) kabaret

cabb′age (kop)kool

cab′in (n) kajuit; hut; ~ crew kajuitpersoneel

cab′inet kabinet, ministerie; kas; display′ ~ toonkas

ca′ble (n) kabel; kabeltou; (v) kabel; vasmaak; ~way kabelspoor/sweefspoor

cac′kle (n) gekekkel; (v) kekkel

cac′tus -es ..ti kaktus

cad gemene vent, ploert, skobbejak *also* bum

cadd′ie joggie (gholf)

cadd′y caddies teebus

cadet′ kadet

ca′dre (n) kader, soldate-eenheid

Caesa′rean section keisersnee (med.)

caf′é kafee; koffiehuis

cafeter′ia kafeteria

cage (n) koutjie, kooi, voëlhok; kooi (myn= bou), hysbak, hyshok; (v) opsluit

cake (n) koek

cal′abash -es kalbas

calam′ity (n) ramp, onheil *also* disas′ter

cal′culate (v) bereken, reken; ~d voorbedag, berekend, koelbloedig; ~d in′sult bereken= de affront

calcula′tion berekening

cal′culator sakrekenaar; berekenaar

cal′ender (n) kalender, almanak; rol

calen′dula gousblom

calf[1] calves kuit (been)

calf[2] calves kalf; ~ love kalwerliefde

cal′iber deursnee; gewig; gehalte, kaliber

call (n) beroep; kuier; gefluit; oproep (foon); vraag; lokstem; bod (kaarte); (v) roep; noem; beroep (predikant); besoek; kuier; bel, lui, skakel (foon); ~ *off* afgelas; *on* ~ op roep; ~er roeper; besoeker; ~girl foon= snol/loknooi

call'ing (n) roeping; beroep; geroep

call'us (n) -es eelt

calm (n) kalmte, windstilte; (v) kalmeer, be= daar; (a) kalm, rustig, stil

cal'orie kalorie, warmte-eenheid

cam nok; ~**shaft** nok-as (enjin)

cam'el kameel

camell'ia japonika, kamelia (blom)

ca'meo kamee

cam'era -s kamera (fot.); *in* ~ in camera (hofsaak); agter geslote deure

cam'ouflage (n) kamoeflage; vermomming; ka= moefleerdrag; (v) vermom, kamoefleer; ~ **u'niform** kamoefleerpak/kamoefleerdrag

camp (n) kamp; (v) kampeer, uitkamp

campaign' (n) veldtog, kampanje

campanile' kloktoring

camp: ~**bed** veldbed, voukatel; ~**fire** kamp= vuur

cam'phor kanfer; ~**ated** kanfer=

cam'ping: ~ **site** kampeerterrein

cam'pus kampus, (universiteits)terrein

can[1] (n) kan, blik; (v) inmaak (in bottels); inlê; ~**ned fruit** ingemaakte/ingelegde vrugte

can[2] (v) **could** kan

canal' kanaal; buis; groef; ~**ise** kanaliseer

canar'y ..**ies** kanarie (voëltjie)

can'cel kanselleer; herroep; skrap; ~ **an ap=** *pointment* 'n afspraak afsê/afstel; ~**la'tion** kansellasie

can'cer[1] kanker/karsinoom; ~**ous** kankeragtig

Can'cer[2] Kreef; **Trop'ic of** ~ Kreefskeerkring

can'did (a) eerlik, opreg, openhartig, padlangs

can'didate kandidaat; aansoeker

can'dle kers; ~**stick** blaker, kandelaar; ~**wick** kerspit

can'dy (n) ..**dies** kandy, sukade; suikerklont= jie; ~**floss** spookasem

cane (n) riet, rottang, lat; suikerriet; kierie, wandelstok; (v) slaan, pak gee; mat (stoel); ~ **spir'its** rietblits/rietsnaps

can'ned ingelê, ingemaak; ~-**fruit bott'le** in= maakbottel; ~ **pea'ches** ingelegde/inge= maakte perskes

cann'ibal mensvreter, kannibaal

cann'on kanon, geskut *see* **gun**

cann'ot kan nie

cann'y (a) versigtig, slim, oulik; uitgeslape

canoe' -s kano; ~**ist** kanovaarder; ~ **ra'ce** kano= (wed)vaart

can'on (n) kanon, kerkwet; reël

can'opy (troon)hemel; kap(pie) (op bakkie)

cantank'erous (a) vitterig, prikkelbaar, suur

canteen' kantien, kroeg; verversingslokaal; veldkombuis; ~ **of cut'lery** messestel

can'ter (n) kort galop, handgalop; *win in a* ~ fluit-fluit wen; (v) op 'n kort galop ry

can'tilever vrydraer, vrydraend

can'tor kantor, voorsinger (Joods)

can'vas (n) seil(doek); skilderdoek; *under* ~ in tente

can'vass (v) (stemme) werf; kolporteer; ~**er** (stemme)werwer; ~**ing** invloedwerwing (vir 'n betrekking)

can'yon bergkloof, ravyn *also* **gorge**

cap (n) mus, hoed, pet, baret; *a feather in his* ~ 'n pluimpie; *if the* ~ *fits* as die skoen pas

cap'able (a) bekwaam, geskik; vatbaar

capa'city (n) bekwaamheid, bevoegdheid; vermoë, lewering; bakmaat (dam); kapasi= teit; *in the* ~ *of* in die hoedanigheid van

cape[1] (n) mantel; kraag

cape[2] (n) kaap

cap'er sprong, kaperjol; *cut a* ~ flikkers gooi; (v) rondspring; bokspring

Cape Town Kaapstad

cap'ita: *per* ~ per hoof/kop/capita

cap'ital (n) hoofstad; kapitaal; hoofletter; (a) belangrik; hoofs; ~ **crime/offen'ce**, hals= misdaad; ~ **let'ter** hoofletter; ~ **punish=** **ment** doodstraf

cap'italism kapitalisme

capitula'tion kapitulasie, oorgawe

caprice' luim, gril, gier, nuk; fiemies

Cap'ricorn Steenbok; **Trop'ic of** ~ Steenboks= keerkring

capsize' omval, omslaan (boot)

cap'sule saadhuisie; kapsule; omhulsel

cap'tain (n) kaptein; aanvoerder

cap'tion (n) opskrif, byskrif; titel

cap'tivating (a) betowerend; boeiend, pakkend

cap'tive (n) gevangene; (a) gevang; geboei; ~ **au'dience** gedwonge/vasgekeerde gehoor

captiv'ity gevangenskap

cap'ture (n) vangs, roof; inname; gevange= neming; buit; (v) vang; buitmaak

car (motor)kar, kar; *by* ~ per motor, met die kar; ~ **bomb** motorbom; ~**jack'er** motorkaper; ~**jack'ing** motorkaping *see* **hi'jacking; com'pany** ~ firmamotor

ca'rat karaat

ca'ravan karavaan; woonwa, kampeerwa

carb'ide karbied

carb'on koolstof; ~ **pa'per** koolpapier

carb'uncle karbonkel, negeoog, steenpuis

carb'urettor vergasser (motor)

car'cass karkas, geraamte, romp

card (n) kaart; program; spyskaart; ~board karton, bordpapier; ~board box karton= boks; ~ 'phone kaartfoon

card'iac kardiaal, hart=; ~ by'pass hartomlei= ding; ~ fail'ure hartversaking; ~ pa'tient hartpasiënt

card'iogram kardiogram (lesing)

card'iograph kardiograaf (apparaat)

card'inal (n) kardinaal (mens); (a) kardinaal, vernaamste, hoof=

care (n) sorg; oplettendheid, sorgvuldigheid; bekommernis; ~ of the aged bejaardesorg; ~ of per adres; take ~ oppas; (v) sorg dra, omgee; besorg wees; pri'mary health ~ primêre gesondheidsorg

career' (n) loopbaan; beroep; (v) rondhard= loop, kerjakker; ~s advi'ser beroepsvoor= ligter; ~s exhibi'tion loopbaanuitstalling; ~ gui'dance/coun'selling beroepsleiding, loop= baanvoorligting; ~ path beroepsbaan

care: ~ful versigtig, oppassend; ~less nalatig, agte(r)losig

caress' (v) liefkoos, streel

care: ~ta'ker opsigter, oppasser; ~worn uit= geput, afgesloof

carg'o -es skeepslading, vrag

ca'ricature (n) karikatuur, spotprent

car'rillon kariljon, klokkespel; ~ play'er beiaar= dier

car'nage (n) slagting, bloedbad also mas'= sacre

carn'al (a) vleeslik, wellustig

carna'tion angelier (blom)

carn'ival karnaval

carniv'orous (a) vleisetend

ca'rol (n) lofsang, lied; voëlsang; Christ'mas ~s Kersliedere

carousel' (n) mallemeule also mer'ry-go-= round

carp[1] (n) karp (vis)

carp[2] (v) vit, brom

car'penter timmerman

car'pet (n) tapyt; mat; wall-to-wall ~ vol= vloertapyt

car'port motorskuiling, motorafdak

ca'rriage wa, rytuig; ~ paid vragvry

ca'rrier transportryer; (vrag)karweier; draer; bagasierak; ~ pi'geon posduif

ca'rrot (n) (geel)wortel

ca'rry dra, vervoer; bring; verdien (rente); ~ through voltooi; ~ weight gesag hê; ~cot drawieg(ie)

cart (n) kar; voertuig; (v) vervoer, ry; ~age vraggeld; ~age con'tractor vervoerkontrak= teur, karweier

cart'ilage kraakbeen

cartog'rapher kartograaf (mens)

cartoon' (n) spotprent; tekenprent

cart'ridge patroon; ~ belt bandelier

carve (v) uitsny, houtsny, graveer; voorsny; ~ry voorsnybuffet/voorsnygereg

case[1] (n) kis, kas; boks; handkoffer; sloop; boeksak

case[2] (n) geval, saak; naamval; in any ~ in alle geval; in every ~ in elke geval; in ~ in geval

case his'tory gevallestudie; siekteverslag

cash (n) kontant(geld); ~ on delivery kontant by aflewering; hard ~ kontant; (v) (in)wis= sel, kleinmaak; trek; ~book kasboek; ~box geldtrommel; ~ dis'count kontantkorting; ~ float wisselfonds, kontantvlot; ~-and- car'ry koop-en-loop, haal-en-betaal; ~ flow kontantvloei

cashier' (n) kassier (mens)

cash: ~ reg'ister kasregister also till; ~ slip kontantstrokie; ~ till kasregister

cas'ing oortreksel; voering (boorgat)

casi'no -s casino/kasino, dobbelhuis

cask vat, vaatjie, kuip

cask'et kissie (juwele), boksie; urn

cassette' kasset; ~ play'er kassetspeler

cast (n) gooi; vorm; soort; rolbesetting (dra= ma); gietvorm; (v) gooi, werp; uitwerp; neergooi; optel (syfers); uitbring (stem); giet (metaal); ~ lots loot; ~ a spell on be= tower

cast'away (n) skipbreukeling; verworpeling; (a) onbruikbaar, oud

caste (n) klas, kaste

cast'ing vote beslissende stem

cast i'ron gietyster, potyster

ca'stle kasteel; ~ in the air lugkasteel

cas'tor oil kasterolie

castrate' (v) sny, ontman, regmaak, kastreer

ca'sual toevallig, terloops, los, kasueel; smart ~ deftig informeel (gekleed); ~ la'bour los arbeid; ~ wear slenterdrag

ca'sualty ..ties ongeval; (pl) ongevalle (hospi= taal); ongeluk; gesneuwelde; (pl) verliese, ge= sneuweldes; ~ list ongevallelys; krukkelys

cat kat; kats (strafsweep); *let the ∼ out of the bag* die aap uit die mou laat; *rain ∼s and dogs* ou vroue met knopkieries reën; *fat ∼* dikvreter *see* gra′vy train

cat′alogue (n) katalogus, pryslys

catamaran′ katamaran, tweeromper (seilboot)

cat′apult slingervel, katapult; voëlrek, kettie

cat′aract waterval; oogpêrel, katarak

catarrh′ katar

catas′trophe ramp, onheil; katastrofe

cataw′ba catawba/katôba (druif)

cat: ∼ bur′glar klouterdief, sluipdief; ∼call kattegetjank; fluitroep

catch (n) -es vangs, buit; vanghou; voordeel; (v) vang, gryp; vat; haal (trein); betrap (dief); ∼ *a chill* koue vat; ∼ *a cold* verkoue kry; ∼ *up (with)* inhaal; ∼ *a train* 'n trein haal

catch′ment area opvanggebied (van water)

catch′y aantreklik; aansteeklik; ∼ que′stion strikvraag

cat′egory ..ries kategorie, klas, soort

cat′er (v) verskaf, voorsien, spyseneer/spyse= nier; ∼er (n) spysenier; leweransier; ∼ing spysenering/spyseniering, spysverskaffing; ∼ing depart′ment verversingsdepartement

cat′erpillar ruspe(r); ∼ trac′tor kruiptrekker

cat′erwauling katmusiek, kattegeskree(u)

cathe′dral domkerk, katedraal

cath′olic algemeen *also* univer′sal; katoliek; ∼ taste veelsydige/omvattende smaak

cat′napping indommel, 'n uiltjie knip/knap

cat-o′-nine′-tails kats (strafsweep)

cat′tery (n) kattery, kietsiesorg

catt′ish katterig; ∼ wo′man snip

catt′le vee, grootvee, beeste

cat′walk (n) stapvlak (vir modelle)

cauc′us (n) -es koukus, partyvergadering; (v) koukus

caul net; helm; agterstuk; *born with a ∼* met die helm gebore

caul′dron groot ketel, kookpot

caul′iflower blomkool

cause (n) oorsaak; beweegrede; rede; (v) ver= oorsaak, teweegbring; ∼ *damage* skade aan= rig

cause′way spoelbrug

caus′tic bytend, brandend; ∼ so′da seepsoda

caut′erise (v) uitbrand, toeskroei

cau′tion (n) omsigtigheid/versigtigheid; seker= heid; waarskuwing; (v) waarsku; berispe

cau′tious (a) versigtig, behoedsaam, omsigtig

cavalcade′ ruiterstoet, kavalkade

cav′alry ruitery, kavallerie

cave (n) grot; spelonk; ∼ *in* instort; ∼dwel′ler grotbewoner, troglodiet; ∼man oermens

cavia′re kaviaar

cav′ity ..ties holtes; ∼ wall holmuur

cay′man/cai′man kaaiman, alligator (dier)

CD-ROM drive CD-ROM-aandrywer (rek.)

cease (v) ophou, laat staan, staak; ∼fire (n) skietstaking, skietstilstand

ced′ar seder (boom)

cede (v) afstaan, opgee; sedeer, afstand doen

ceil′ing solder(ing), plafon; hoogtegrens

cel′ebrate (v) vier, besing; herdenk

celebra′tion (n) (fees)viering, herdenking; makietie

cel′ery seldery (groente)

celes′tial (n) hemelbewoner; (a) hemels; ∼ bod′ies hemelliggame

cel′ibacy ongetroude staat, selibaat

cell sel; kamertjie; hokkie

cell′ar (n) kelder

cell′o -s tjello, violonsel

cell′phone (n) selfoon *also* cell′ular tel′ephone

cement′ (n) sement; band (fig.); (v) saamvoeg

cem′etery kerkhof, begraafplaas

cen′otaph praalgraf, gedenksuil, senotaaf

cen′sor (n) sensor; sedemeester; (v) sensureer; ∼ship board sensuurraad

cen′sure (n) sensuur, berisping, bestraffing; (v) onder sensuur sit; bestraf; afkeur

cen′sus -es volkstelling, sensus

cent sent; *per ∼* persent, per honderd

cente′nary ..ries eeufees, honderdste bestaans= jaar

cen′tigrade honderdgradig; *4 degrees ∼ 4* grade Celcius

cen′timetre sentimeter

cen′tipede duisendpoot

cen′tral sentraal, middelste; vernaamste; ∼ bus′iness dis′trict (CBD) sentrale sake= gebied, sakekern

cen′tralise (v) sentraliseer

cen′tre (n) middel(punt); sentrum; senter (voetbal); ∼ *of gravity* swaartepunt; (v) ver= enig; ∼ punch kornael, senterpons

centrif′ugal middelpuntvliedend, sentrifugaal

centrip′etal middelpuntsoekend, sentripetaal

cen′tury ..ries eeu, honderd jaar; honderdtal (krieket); *turn of the ∼* eeuwisseling

ceram′ics keramiek, erdeware

cer′eal (n) graan; (a) graan=

ce′rebral harsing=, serebraal=; ∼-pal′sied

chil'dren serebraalgestremde kinders
ce'remony seremonie, plegtigheid; **mas'ter of ce'remonies** seremoniemeester, tafelheer
cer'tain seker, gewis; ~ly sekerlik, beslis; ~ty sekerheid
certif'icate sertifikaat, verklaring; diploma
cert'ify (v) sertifiseer, verklaar
chafe (n) skaafplek; wrywing; (v) vryf/vrywe, skuur, skaaf; irriteer
chaff (n) kaf; skerts; (v) liggies terg/pla
chain (n) ketting; reeks; (pl) boeie; (v) bind, boei, in kettings slaan; ~ **reac'tion** ketting= reaksie
chair (n) stoel; setel; leerstoel; *take the* ~ die voorsitterstoel inneem; (v) voorsit; ~**man** voorsitter *also* chair'person/chair; Mr ~**man** (Meneer die) Voorsitter; **Ma'dam** ~ Agbare Voorsitter; *she is* ~ *of the new com= mit'tee* sy is die nuwe komitee se voorsitter
cha'let (n) berghut; chalet
chal'ice kelk, Nagmaalsbeker
chalk (n) kryt; ~ *up* opskryf
chall'enge (n) uitdaging; aansporing; (v) uit= daag; ~ **cup** uitdaagbeker; ~**r** uitdager
cham'ber kamer; vertrek; grot; ~ **of com'= merce** kamer van koophandel, sakekamer; ~ **of hor'rors** gruwelgrot; ~ **of mines** kamer van mynwese
chame'leon trapsoetjies/trapsuutjies, verkleur= mannetjie, kameleon
cham'ois gems(bok); ~ **lea'ther** seemsleer
champagne' sjampanje, bruiswyn, vonkelwyn; ~ **break'fast** vonkelontbyt
cham'pion (n) kampioen; kampvegter (vir 'n saak); (v) verdedig; bepleit; ~ **play'er** baasspeler; ~**ship** kampioenskap
chance (n) kans; toeval; waarskynlikheid; vooruitsig; *stand a good* ~ 'n goeie kans hê; *take a* ~ 'n kans waag; (v) waag
chan'cellor kanselier (mens)
chan'cer (n) waaghans; kansvatter; opportunis
chandelier' (n) kandelaber, kroonlugter
change (n) verandering; kentering; klein= geld; (v) verander; ruil; (ver)wissel; klein= maak (geld); ~ *one's mind* van plan verander; ~**room** kleedkamer *also* **cloak'= room**
chann'el (n) kanaal, seestraat; (v) kanaliseer
cha'os (n) chaos, warboel, baaierd
chao'tic chaoties, deurmekaar(spul)
chap[1] (n) bars, skeur; (v) bars, skeur
chap[2] (n) kêrel; ou *also* **guy**; *a decent* ~ 'n

gawe vent/kêrel/ou; ~**pie** tjokkertjie; laitie, tjommie
cha'pel (v) kapel, kerkie; bidhuisie
chap'eron (n) begeleidster, chaperone; (v) begelei, beskerm, chaperonneer
chap'lain kapelaan, veldprediker
chap'ter hoofstuk, kapittel; ~ **and verse** vers en kapittel
char (v) verkool, brand, skroei; (n) skropvrou (huishulp)
cha'racter karakter; aard; kenmerk; letter; naam, reputasie; rol (toneel)
characteris'tic (n) karaktertrek; kenmerk; (a) karakteristiek; kenmerkend
char'coal houtskool
charge (n) opdrag *also* **brief**; bewaring; be= skuldiging; aanklag; stormloop; ~ **sheet** klagstaat; (v) opdra; aanval; beskuldig; hef (gelde)
charge' of'fice aanklagkantoor (polisie)
chargé d'affaires' saakgelastigde
cha'riot strydwa, triomfwa
cha'rity ..ties liefdadigheid; barmhartigheid *also* **compas'sion**; ~ *begins at home* die hemp is nader as die rok
charm (n) betowering; sjarme; gelukbringer; (v) betower, bekoor; verruk; toor; ~**er** sjarmiet (mens); ~**ing** betowerend, bekoor= lik; sjarmant; ~ **school** sjarmeskool
chart (see)kaart, tabel
chart'er (n) oktrooi, handves; oorkonde; (v) oktrooieer; huur; ~**ed flight** huurvlug; ~**ed plane** huurvliegtuig; ~**ed sec'retary** geok= trooieerde sekretaris, oktrooisekretaris
chase (n) jag; agtervolging; (v) jag, agtervolg; jaag; ~ *away* wegjaag
chasm (n) afgrond, kloof
chass'is (sing and pl) onderstel; raamwerk
chaste (a) kuis, rein, vlekloos
chastise' (v) kasty, tugtig
chat (n) praatjie/geselsie; gesels, babbel; ~**line** inbelprogram (radio); kletslyn (Internet); ~**show** geselsprogram (radio, TV)
chatt'er (v) babbel, klets, snater; ~**box** bab= belkous (vrou)
chauffeur' motorbestuurder, chauffeur
chauv'inism (v) nasionale eiewaan, chauvi= nisme
cheap goedkoop *also* **inexpen'sive**
cheat (n) bedrieër; (v) bedrieg, kul
check[1] (n) geruite materiaal, ruitgoed
check[2] (n) kontrole, verifikasie; beperking;

keep in ~ in toom hou; (v) nagaan, tjek, verifieer; ~ *out* uitklaar; ~ *up* optel, vergelyk; (medies) ondersoek/optjek; ~**er** laaimeester; ~**list** tjeklys; ~**mate** skaakmat; ~**up** (n) roetine-ondersoek, opvolgonder= soek, optjek

cheek[1] parmantigheid, vermetelheid

cheek[2] wang; ~**bone** wangbeen, kakebeen

cheek'y (a) parmantig, astrant, vermetel

cheer (n) toejuiging; vrolikheid; (v) opvrolik, toejuig; ~**ful** vrolik, opgeruimd; ~**lea'der** rasieleier; dirigent; ~**s!** gesondheid!

cheese kaas; ~ *and wine reception* kaas-en-wyn-onthaal; ~**bur'ger** kaasburger; ~ **spread** smeerkaas

cheet'ah jagluiperd, cheetah

chef -s hoofkok, sjef

chem'ical skeikundig, chemies; ~ **war'fare** chemiese oorlogvoering; ~ **weed control'** chemiese onkruidbeheer; ~**s** chemikalieë

chem'ist apteker *also* **phar'macist**; skeikun= dige, chemikus

chem'istry skeikunde, chemie

cheque tjek, wissel; **blank** ~ blanko tjek; ~**book** tjekboek

che'rish (v) koester, liefkoos, liefhê

che'rry (n) **cherries** kersie; kersieboom

chess skaakspel; *play at* ~ skaakspeel

chest bors; kis; ~ **of dra'wers** laaikas

chest'nut (n) kastaiing; sweetvos(perd)

chev'ron sign chevronteken/sjevronteken

chew (n) koutjie; pruimpie; (v) kou; pruim; nadink, oordink; ~ *the cud* herkou; bepeins; ~**ing gum** kougom

chic (a) sjiek, elegant *also* **smart**

chick. -ens, -s kuiken(tjie); kind

chick'en -s hoender, hoendervleis; snuiter; *a mere* ~ 'n piepjong ventjie; ~**feed** hoen= derkos; kleinigheidjie; ~**-hearted** lafhartig; ~ **mash** kuikenmeel; ~ **pox** waterpokkies

chic'ory sigorei

chief (n) -s hoof, kaptein; (a) vernaamste, hoogste, senior, opperste; ~ **exe'cutive** hoofbestuursleier; senior bestuurshoof; ~ **gen'eral man'ager** senior hoofbestuurder; ~ **jus'tice** hoofregter; ~**ly** hoofsaaklik, vernaamlik

chil'blain winterhande, wintervoete

child -ren kind; *backward* ~ geremde kind; *handicapped* ~ gestremde kind; *retarded* ~ vertraagde kind; ~ **abu'se** kindermishande= ling/kindermolestering *also* ~ **molesta'tion**;

~**birth** bevalling; ~**hood** kinderjare; ~**ish** kinderagtig *also* **friv'olous**; ~ **moles'ter** kindermolesteerder *also* **pae'dophile**; ~**ren's books** kinderboeke; ~**ren's home** kinderhuis/kinderhawe *see* **or'phanage**; ~ **wel'fare** kindersorg

chill (n) koue, koudheid; kilheid; *catch a* ~ kou(e) vat; (v) verkoel

chil'li (n) (brand)rissie; ~ **bite** brandhappie

chil'ly (a) koel, natterig, kil, kouerig

chime (n) klokkespel; welluidendheid

chim'ney -s skoorsteen; lampglas; ~**piece** skoorsteenmantel; ~ **sweep** skoorsteenveër

chimpanzee' sjimpansee

chin (n) ken; *double* ~ onderken

chin'a porselein, breekgoed *also* **por'celain**

Chi'na China (land)

Chine'se (n, a) Chinees/Sjinees

chip (n) spaander, splinter; skyfie/tjip; tjip (rek.); ~ *of the old block* aardjie na sy vaartjie; *he has had his* ~**s** sy doppie het geklap; *fish and* ~**s** vis en skyfies/slaptjips; (v) afsplinter; ~ *in* in die rede val

chirop'odist voetheelkundige *also* **po'diatrist**

chi'ropractor chiropraktisyn (mens)

chis'el (n) beitel; **cold** ~ koubeitel

chiv'alrous (a) ridderlik *also* **gal'lant**

chlor'oform (n) chloroform

chlor'ophyll bladgroen, chlorofil

choc'olate sjokolade, sjokkie, **slab of** ~ blok sjokolade

choice (n) keus(e), keur, ~ **gra'de** keurgraad

choir koor

choke (n) smoor(klep); demper; (v) stik, wurg, verstik; ~ **chain** glyketting/wurgketting

chol'era cholera/kolera

choles'terol cholesterol, galsteenvet

choose (v) kies, verkies; *for choosing* te kus en te keur

chop (n) hou, kap, slag; tjop (vleis); (v) kap, slaan; ~**shop** kapwerf (gesteelde motors)

chop'per (n) helikopter *also* **he'licopter**

chor'al (a) koraal; koor=; ~ **i'tem** koorsang

chord snaar; lyn, tou, koord; akkoord (mus.); **spi'nal** ~ rugmurg; **vo'cal** ~ stemband

chore werkie; ~**s** huispligte, sleurwerk

choreog'rapher choreograaf, dansontwerper

chor'us -es koor, refrein, rei; ~ **girl** koormei= sie; kabaretsangeres

cho'se(n) (a) uitverkore *see* **choo'se**

Christ Christus

chri'sten (v) doop, naam gee

Chris'tian (n) Christen; (a) Christelik; ~ **e'ra** Christelike jaartelling; ~ **name** voornaam *also* **first name**
Chris'tmas Kersfees; ~ *greetings and good wishes for the New Year* Kers- en Nuwe= jaarsgroete; ~ **box** Kersgeskenk; ~ **card** Kerskaart(jie); ~ **Day** Kersdag; ~ **Eve** Ou= kersaand; ~ **ho'liday** Kersvakansie; ~ **night** Kersaand; ~ **par'ty** Kersparty(tjie); ~ **sea'**= son Kerstyd/Kersgety; ~ **tree** Kersboom
chron'ic (a) chronies/kronies (siekte)
chronolog'ical chronologies, in tydsorde
chrysan'themum -s krisant (blom)
chuck (n) gooi; (v) gooi; opgee, laat staan; ~ *up* in wanhoop opgee; **chuck'er-out** uit= smyter *also* **boun'cer** (person)
chuc'kle (n) onderdrukte lag; gekloek; (v) lag; kloek
chum (n) maat, vriend, tjom *also* **pal**
church -es kerk; ~ **square** kerkplein; ~**war'**= **den** koster; ~**yard** kerkhof
chute glybaan, glygeut; waterval
chut'ney blatjang
cid'er appelwyn
cigar' sigaar; ~**band collec'tor** vitolfilis
cigarette' sigaret
Cinderell'a Aspoestertjie
cin'der track asbaan
cin'ema -s bioskoop, fliek; ~ **fan** fliekvlooi; ~**go'er** bioskoopganger/fliekvlooi
cinn'amon kaneel
cir'cle (n) sirkel; ring; kring; kroon; galery (teater); geselskap; (v) ronddraai; omsluit; **vi'cious** ~ bose kringloop
cir'cuit rondgang; kringloop; reeks (sport); stroombaan (elektr.); **short** ~ kortsluiting
cir'cular (n) omsendbrief, sirkulêre; (a) sirkel= vormig
cir'culate (v) sirkuleer, in omloop bring
circula'tion (n) sirkulasie; oplaag (koerant)
circumci'sion besnyding, besnydenis
circum'ference omtrek
circ'umflex -es kappie, sirkumfleks (^)
cir'cumstance omstandigheid; *in the* ~*s* on= der/in die omstandighede
circ'us -es sirkus
ciss'y (n) **cissies** verwyfde mens, papbroek
cis'tern (n) vergaarbak, spoelbak; dam; kuip
cita'tion aanhaling, sitaat; dagvaarding
cit'izen burger; stadsbewoner; **John C**~ Jan Burger; ~ **band ra'dio** burgerbandradio, kletsradio; ~**ship** burgerskap

cit'ron (n) sitroen
cit'rus sitrus, lemoenvrug
cit'y cities stad; ~ **coun'cil** stadsraad; ~ **hall** stadhuis (gebou); stadsaal (saal); ~ **slick'er** stadskalant, stadskoejawel (mens)
civ'et (cat) muskeljaatkat/musseljaatkat
civ'ic burgerlik, burger=; ~ **cen'tre** burger= sentrum; ~ **recep'tion** burgerlike onthaal; ~ **thea'tre** stadskouburg
ci'vil burgerlik; siviel; beleef; ~ **avia'tion** burgerlugvaart; ~ **defen'ce** burgerlike be= skerming; ~ **ser'vant** staatsamptenaar; ~ **war** burgeroorlog
civil'ian (n) burger; burgerlike (mens); (a) burgerlik, burger=; ~ **blind** burgerblindes
civilisa'tion beskawing
claim (n) eis, vordering; (v) eis, opvorder
clairvoy'ant heldersiende; fortuinverteller
clamm'y (a) klam, vogtig *also* **moist**
clam'our (n) geskree(u), geroep; (v) skree(u); ~ *for* roep om, aandring op
clamp (n) kram, klem; (v) klamp, vasklem
clan stam; familiegroep, clan; kliek
clap (n) klap, slag; donderslag; knal; (v) klap, toeslaan; ~**trap** mooipraatjies
cla'rify (v) verklaar/uiteensit; uitklaar
cla'rinet/clarionet' klarinet
clash (n) -es stamp; botsing *also* **con'flict**; (v) stamp, bons, bots; stry
clasp (n) haak, gespe, kram; omhelsing; (v) vashaak, toegespe; omhels; omarm
class (n) -es klas; orde; stand; (v) rangskik, orden; klassifiseer; klasseer (wol)
class'ic (n) klassieke werk/skrywer; (a) klas= siek; ~**al** klassiek (musiek); ~**s** klassieke
classifica'tion klassifikasie, indeling
class'ify klàssifiseer, indeel
clause sinsdeel; klousule; artikel; bysin
claustropho'bia engtevrees, noutevrees
claw (n) klou, poot; haak; (v) vasklou
clay (n) klei; (a) klei=; ~ **pig'eon shoot'ing** pieringskiet, kleiduifskiet
clean (v) skoonmaak, reinig; *make a* ~ *sweep* skoonskip maak; ~ *up* opruim; (a) skoon, sindelik; (adv) heeltemal, totaal; ~**er** skoonmaker (mens)
clear (v) reinig; ophelder; ooptrek (weer); (a) helder, duidelik; (adv) skoon; duidelik; ~**ance** vryhoogte; ~**ance sale** opruimver= koping; ~**ing bank** verrekeningsbank; ~**ly** duidelik, onomwonde; ~ **majo'rity** vol= strekte meerderheid

cleave (v) kloof/klowe; splits; **cleft pal'ate** gesplete verhemelte/gehemelte

clem'ency (n) begenadiging; goedertierenheid; sagtheid (die weer)

clench (vuiste) bal; omklink; vasbyt

cler'gy (pl) predikante, leraars; ~**man** predikant, geestelike

cler'ical geestelik, klerikaal; klerklik; ~ **er'= ror** skryffout; ~ **work** klerklike werk

clerk klerk; winkelbediende; opsigter

clev'er slim; handig; knap, oulik *also* **bright**

clich'é afgesaagde uitdrukking, cliché

click (n) tik, klink; klapklank; (v) tik, klink; klik (rekenaarmuis)

cli'ent kliënt (van geleerde beroep); klant (van winkel); ~**ele** klandisie; ~ **rela'tions** kliën= tebetrekkinge/klantesorg

cliff krans, rotswand

clim'ate klimaat

clim'ax hoogtepunt, klimaks *also* **zen'ith**

climb (n) klim; (v) klim, klouter; ~**ing lane** klimbaan (pad)

clinch (v) vasklem; omklink; beklink; beseël; ~ *a deal* 'n transaksie beklink

cling vashou, vaskleef; ~ *together* aanmekaar= klou; ~'**stone** taaipit (perske); ~**wrap** kleefplastiek *also* **glad'wrap**

clin'ic (n) kliniek; (a) klinies

clin'ical klinies; ~ **examina'tion** kliniese ondersoek; ~ **psychol'ogist** kliniese siel= kundige; ~ **thermom'eter** koorspennetjie

clip (n) knipsel, skeersel; (v) knip, snoei, skeer; kortwiek

clip: ~**board** knypbord; ~**per** knipper; skeer= masjien; skêr; ~**ping** (n) (uit)knipsel

clique (n) kliek, aanhang

cloak (n) mantel; dekmantel; ~**room** kleed= kamer; bewaarkamer

clock klok, horlosie; ~**wise** kloksgewys; ~**work** uurwerk

clod kluit, klont; domkop *also* **fat'head**; ~**hop'per** gomtor, lummel, gaip (mens)

clog (n) blok, hindernis; klomp (houtskoen); (v) verstop; belemmer

clois'ter klooster *also* **con'vent**; suilegang

clo'ne (n) kloon (genetiese duplikaat); (v) kloneer; **clo'ning** kloning

close (n) end, sluiting; slot; *at the* ~ *of play* met/ teen uitskeityd (krieket); (v) sluit, toemaak, toesluit; afsluit; (a) dig, diep (geheim); *a* ~ *friend* 'n intieme vriend; ~**d-cir'cuit TV** kringtelevisie, kabel-TV; ~ **corpora'tion**

(CC) beslote korporasie (BK); ~**-fis'ted** inhalig; vrekkerig

clos'et (n) kabinet; kleinhuisie; (v) opsluit

close'-up (n) digby-opname, nabybeeld

clos'ing sluiting; ~ **date** sluitdatum; ~ **hour** sluitingsuur; ~ **stage** eindstadium; ~ **time** sluittyd

clot (n) klont, kluit; **blood** ~ bloedklont

cloth kledingstof, laken

clothe (v) klee, beklee, bedek; inklee

clothes klere; ~ **peg** was(goed)pennetjie

cloth'ing kleding, klere; inkleding; ~ **in'dus= try** die klerebedryf

cloud (n) wolk; *be in the* ~s in vervoering wees; ~**burst** wolkbreuk; ~**y** bewolk

clout (n) lap, vadoek; hou; (v) iem. klap

clove (n) naeltjie

clov'er klawer; *live in* ~ lekker lewe; ~**leaf** klawerblad

clown (n) grapmaker, hanswors, harlekyn, nar

club (n) knuppel, knopkierie; klub; klawer (kaartspel); (v) doodslaan; saamwerk; ~**foot** klompvoet; horrelvoet; ~**house** klubhuis; ~**s** klawers (kaarte)

clue leidraad, spoor, aanduiding; ~**d up** ge= konfyt in; goed op hoogte wees van

clum'sy (a) onhandig, lomp; onhanteerbaar

clus'ter tros, trop, hoop, swerm; ~ **hou'sing** korfbehuising/trosbehuising

clutch[1] (n) greep, klou; koppelaar (motor), (v) gryp, vashou

clutch[2] (n) broeisel (eiers)

coach (n) rytuig, koets; passasierswa; afrigter, breier (sport); (v) afrig, brei

coal (n) steenkool

coali'tion verbond, samesmelting, koalisie

coarse kru, ru; grof; lomp *also* **rude**

coast (n) kus, strand; (v) luier, vry loop (motor); ~**er** kusboot; biermatjie/drupmat= jie; ~**guard** kuswag

coat (n) baadjie; jas; skil; laag (verf); ~ *of arms* wapenskild; familiewapen; ~**ing** laag (verf), aanpaksel

coax (v) vlei, pamperlang, mooipraat, paai

cob mieliekop; ponie; mannetjieswaan

cob'ble (n) straatsteen; stuk steenkool; (v) lap; saamflans; ~**r** skoenmaker

cob'ra koperkapel, geelslang, kobra; **brown** ~ bruinkapel; **Cape** ~ geelslang; **ringed** ~ bakkopslang

cob'web spinnerak

cocaine' kokaïen/kokaïne

cochineal' cochenille/kosjeniel (karmynkleur=stof; Mexikaanse luis)
cock[1] (n) haan; haan (geweer); mannetjie
cock[2] (v) oorhaal (geweer); spits (ore)
cockateel' kaketiel/kokketiel (voël)
cock: ~-**eyed** skeel; dwaas; ~**fight** hanege=veg; ~**pit** stuurkajuit (vliegtuig); ~**roach** kakkerlak, kokkerot
cock'tail skemerkelkie/mengeldrankie; kewer; ~ **bar** kelkiekroeg; ~ **par'ty** skemerparty/skemeronthaal
cock'y (a) verwaand, eiewys, hanerig
coc'oa kakao (warm sjokoladedrank)
co'co(a)nut (n) kokosneut; klapper
cocoon' papie, kokon
cod kabeljou (vis)
code wetboek, kode; ~ **of eth'ics** gedragsko=de; (v) (en)kodeer
cod'ling moth appelmot
cod'liver oil lewertraan, visolie
coeduca'tion koëdukasie; ~**al school** koëd=skool
coff'ee koffie; boeretroos (idiom.)
coff'er kis, kas, koffer; skatkis; ~ **dam** kof=ferdam, afsluitdam
coff'in (n) dood(s)kis; (v) kis
cog (kam)rat, tand (van 'n wiel)
cog'nisance kennisname; *take* ~ *of* kennis neem van; erkenning; kenmerk
cohab'it saamwoon, saamhuis; ~**a'tion** saam=bly(ery)
coil (n) kronkeling; draai; klos; (v) inmekaar=kronkel, opdraai
coin (n) muntstuk; *pay one in his own* ~ iem. in sy eie munt betaal; (v) (aan)munt; versin; ~ *new words* nuwe woorde skep
coin'cidence (n) sameloop; toeval(ligheid)
coir klapperhaar
coke kooks
cold (n) koue; verkoue; *bitterly* ~ snerpend koud; *catch* ~ koue vat; (a) koud, koel; on=verskillig; *in* ~ *blood* koelbloedig; ~-**blood'ed** koudbloedig; koelbloedig; ~ **sweat** angssweet
cole kool; ~**rape** koolraap
collab'orate saamwerk *also* **conspi're**
collab'orator medewerker; medepligtige (in misdaad); meeloper (met vyand)
collapse' (n) instorting, mislukking; (v) instort, inval; verslap; misluk
coll'ar (n) boordjie; kraag; halsband; (v) vang; ~**bone** sleutelbeen

collat'eral sydelings; bykomend; ~ **secu'rity** kollaterale sekuriteit (vir lening);
coll'eague kollega, ampsgenoot (mens)
collect' (v) versamel, kollekteer; ~ *money* geld insamel/in; ~ **call** kollekteeroproep; ~**ion** versameling; kollekte; ~**ive bar'gaining** kol=lektiewe bedinging; ~**or** versamelaar
coll'ege kollege; raad; ~ **of educa'tion** onder=wyskollege; **elec'toral** ~ kieskollege
collide' bots, teen mekaar stamp
coll'iery steenkoolmyn
colli'sion botsing; **head-on** ~ trompop botsing
collo'quial alledaags, gemeensaam; ~ **lan'=guage** gebruikstaal, gewone omgangstaal
collude (v) heul; saamspan, kop in een mus wees
collu'sion (n) samespanning, geheul
co'lon[1] dubbelpunt (:)
co'lon[2] dikderm
colonel (*pron.* **ker'nl**) kolonel
colo'nial (n) kolonis; kolonialer; (a) koloniaal
col'onist nedersetter, kolonis
col'ony kolonie; nedersetting; wingewes
coloss'al (a) kolossaal, reusagtig, tamaai
col'our (n) kleur, tint; (v) verf; kleur; ~-**blind** kleurblind; ~**ed** gekleur; ~**ed peo'ple** kleur=linge, bruin mense; ~**ful** kleurryk; ~**slide** kleurskyfie
colt jong hings; jong perd; groentjie
col'umn kolom; suil; rubriek (koerant)
co'ma (n) diep slaap; bedwelming, koma
comb (n) kam, haarkam; heuningkoek; (v) kam; kaard (wol)
com'bat (n) geveg; ~ **troops** vegtroepe
combina'tion (n) verbinding, kombinasie
combine' (n) vereniging; trust, sindikaat; stro=per (graan); (v) verbind, kombineer
combus'tion verbranding; **slow** ~ **stove** smeul=stoof
come kom, aankom; ~ *of age* mondig word; ~ *in handy* te pas kom
comed'ian komediant, grapmaker *also* **jes'ter**
com'edy komedie, blyspel
come'ly (a) aanvallig/bevallig; knap, gepas
co'met komeet, stertster
com'fort (n) troos; gemak, gerief; (v) troos, opvrolik/opbeur; ~**able** gemaklik, gerieflik; ~**er** trooster, fopspeen
com'fy (a) gesellig, snoesig *also* **cudd'ly**
com'ic grapperig, komies, snaaks; ~**s**, ~ **strips** prentverhaal, strokiesprent, strokies
comm'a -s komma (,)

command' (n) bevel, gebod; opdrag; be in ~ die bevel voer; (v) beveel, gebied
commandant' kommandant, bevelvoerder
commandeer' (v) kommandeer, oproep
comman'der bevelhebber; ~-in-chief com= manders-in-chief opperbevelhebber
command': ~ing of'ficer bevelvoerende of= fisier; ~ment gebod, bevel; the Ten Com= mand'ments die Tien Gebooie
comman'do kommando
commem'orate (v) herdenk, gedenk; vier
commence' (v) begin, aanvang; ~ment begin
commend' aanbeveel, prys, opdra; ~able hof= lik, prysenswaardig; ~a'tion aanprysing, eervolle vermelding
comm'ent (n) aanmerking, kommentaar; uitleg= (ging); (v) kritiseer; verklaar; ~ on kom= menteer/kommentaar lewer oor/op; ~ary uitleg, kommentaar; ~ator kommentator (radio); verklaarder
comm'erce handel, verkeer; cham'ber of ~ kamer van koophandel, sakekamer
commer'cial handels-, kommersieel; ~ ar'tist handelskunstenaar; ~ bank handelsbank; ~ law kommersiële reg; handelsreg; ~ trav'= eller handelsreisiger
commi'ssion (n) kommissie; opdrag; (v) op= dra, magtig; aanstel; ~aire' deurwagter, portier; opsigter; ~er kommissaris, kom= missielid; opsiener; ~er of oaths kommis= saris van ede; high ~er hoë kommissaris
commit' bedryf, uitvoer; ~ted to change verbind tot verandering; ~ murder moord pleeg
commit'ment verpligting; verbintenis; ~ fee bindgeld
committ'ee komitee; he serves on the ~ hy dien in/op die komitee
commod'ity ..ties gebruiksartikel, kommodi= teit; (pl) koopware, kommoditeite
comm'on (n) dorpsgrond; have much in ~ baie (met mekaar) gemeen hê; ~ law (die) ge= menereg; (a) gemeenskaplik; ~age dorps= grond, meent; ~ room geselskap(s)kamer; personeelkamer; ~place (n) gemeenplaas; (a) alledaags, gewoon; ~ sen'se gesonde verstand; ~wealth gemenebes
commo'tion beroering, drukte, opskudding
comm'une (n) gemeenskap; kommune
commu'nicate (v) meedeel, kommunikeer
communica'tion mededeling; kommunikasie= kunde/kommunikasieleer (as vak)

commun'ion gemeenskap, kommunie; Ho'ly C~ Nagmaal
com'munist kommunis (mens)
commu'nity ..ties gemeenskap, maatskappy; ~ cen'tre gemeenskapsentrum; ~ devel'opment gemeenskapsbou; ~ health gemeenskap(s)= gesondheid; ~ ser'vice gemeenskap(s)diens
commute' pendel; verwissel, verruil; versag (vonnis); ~r pendelaar; ~r train pendel= trein; voorstedelike trein
compact' (v) kompakteer, aaneensluit; ver= kort; (a) dig; beknop; kompak; ~ disc (CD) laserskyf/laserplaat, kompakskyf, CD
compan'ion maat, metgesel; ~ship geselskap
com'pany ..nies geselskap; maatskappy, fir= ma; organisasie; keep ~ with omgaan met; ~ car firmamotor; hol'ding ~ houermaat= skappy; subsi'diary ~ filiaal(maatskappy)
compar'ative vergelykend; betreklik; ~ de= gree' vergrotende trap
compare' (v) vergelyk; gelyk wees
compar'ison vergelyking; in ~ with vergeleke met, in vergelyking met, teenoor
compart'ment kompartement; afdeling
com'pass (n) omtrek; omvang; -es kompas; pair of ~es passer
compa'ssion deernis, medelye, erbarming also sym'pathy/em'pathy
compat'ible (a) verenigbaar (rekenaars)
compel' (v) dwing, verplig, noodsaak, noop
com'pensate (v) vergoed, kompenseer
compensa'tion (skade)vergoeding, kompensa= sie
compete' (v) wedywer, meeding; kompeteer
com'petence (n) bevoegdheid, bekwaamheid
com'petent (a) bevoeg, bekwaam; geskik
competi'tion (n) mededinging, wedywer(ing); wedstryd, kragmeting; kompetisie
compet'itor mededinger; deelnemer (aan wed= stryd/wedloop)
compile' saamstel, bymekaarmaak, versamel, kompileer; ~r samesteller, kompilator
complain' kla; ~ant klaer, eiser; ~er klaer
complaint' klag; kwaal, ongesteldheid; be= skuldiging; lay a ~ 'n klag indien
com'plement (n) aanvulling, komplement; volle getal; (v) aanvul; ~ary (a) aanvullend
complete' (v) voltooi; invul ('n vorm); (a) volkome; volledig, kompleet
com'plex (n) kompleks (winkels, woonstelle); samestel; (a) ingewikkeld; ~ sen'tence saamgestelde sin

comple'xion (n) gelaatskleur; voorkoms; aard
com'plicate (v) kompliseer, ingewikkeld maak
complica'tion (n) verwikkeling; komplikasie
compli'city medepligtigheid (in misdaad)
com'pliment (n) kompliment; pluimpie; (pl)
	groete; *the ~s of the season* geseënde Kers=
	fees en 'n voorspoedige Nuwe Jaar: *with ~s
	of* met (die) komplimente van; (v) geluk=
	wens, komplimenteer
complimen'tary komplimenteus; vry=; ~ **tick'**=
	et komplimentêre kaartjie
comply' nakom, inwillig, toestem; ~ *with*
	voldoen aan
compon'ent (n) bestanddeel, komponent
compose' (v) saamstel; opstel; komponeer;
	toonset (mus.); ~**d'** kalm, bedaard; ~**r**
	komponis, toonsetter; samesteller
composi'tion samestelling; opstel; toonsetting
	(mus.); komposisie; aard; skikking
com'post (n) kompos; mengsel
compo'sure (n) kalmte, bedaardheid
com'pound (n) samestelling; (v) verbind; skik;
	(a) saamgestel(d); ~ **in'terest** saamgestelde
	rente; ~ **sen'tence** veelvoudige sin
comprehen'sion begrip; bevatlikheid; omvang
comprehen'sive (veel)omvattend; ~ **insur'**=
	ance/pol'icy omvattende versekering/polis
compress' (v) saamdruk, saampers; ~**ed air**
	druklug
comprise' bevat, omvat, insluit
com'promise (n) skikking, kompromis; kom=
	promie; (v) skik
compul'sory (a) gedwonge, verpligtend; ~
	educa'tion verpligte onderwys
compute' bereken, skat, uitreken
compu'ter (n) rekenaar, komper; blikbrein
	(idiom.); ~ **disc/disk** rekenaardisket; ~
	hard'ware apparatuur/hardeware; ~**ise** reke=
	nariseer, komp; ~ **lit'erate** rekenaarbedrewe/
	rekenaarvaardig; **per'sonal** ~ (**PC**) per=
	soonlike rekenaar (PR); ~ **print-out** reke=
	naardrukstuk/komperdruk; ~ **science** reke=
	naarwetenskap, komperkunde; ~ **soft'ware**
	(rekenaar)programmatuur/sagteware
com'rade kameraad; maat
con (n): **pros and** ~**s** voor- en nadele; (v) kul,
	bedrieg, swendel *see* **con'man**
conceal' (v) wegsteek, verberg
concede' toestem, toegee, inwillig
conceit' eiewaan, inbeelding, verwaandheid,
	trots; ~**ed** (a) verwaand, eiewys
con'centrate (n) kragvoer; pitkos; (v) konsen=

treer; saamtrek; ~ *on* konsentreer/toespits op
concentra'tion sametrekking, konsentrasie
concen'tric konsentries
con'cept (n) denkbeeld, begrip, konsep
concern' (n) besigheid; onderneming, organi=
	sasie; besorgdheid; (v) betref, raak; ~**ed**
	besorg; betrokke; ~**ing** aangaande, betref=
	fende, met betrekking tot
con'cert[1] (n) ooreenstemming; konsert
concert'[2] (v) beraadslaag; skik; ~**ed** beraam;
	geskik; ~**ed ac'tion** gesamentlike optrede
concerti'na (n) konsertina; donkielong, kris=
	miswurm (idiom.)
conce'ssion (n) toegewing, konsessie
concilia'tion versoening, konsiliasie
concise' (a) kort, bondig, beknop, saaklik
conclude' (v) besluit, beslis; aflei; sluit; ~**d**
	geëindig, beslis; *to be* ~**d** slot volg
conclu'sion (n) besluit; gevolgtrekking, kon=
	klusie; afloop, end; *in* ~ ten slotte
conclus'ive (a) oortuigend, beslissend; ~
	ev'idence/proof afdoende getuienis/bewys
concoct' smee; brou; versin; ~**ion** fabrikasie,
	verdigsel; konkoksie
conc'rete (n) beton; **re'inforced** ~ gewapende
	beton
con'cubine bywyf, houvrou; handperd (idiom.)
concu'ssion (n) skok, botsing, skudding; ~ *of
	the brain* harsingskudding
condemn' (v) veroordeel; afkeur; ~**ed'** (n)
	veroordeelde (mens); (a) veroordeel
condensa'tion (n) kondensasie, verdigting
condense' kondenseer, verdik; ~**d milk** blik=
	kiesmelk, kondensmelk
condescend' verwaardig/verwerdig; ~**ing** neer=
	buigend
con'diment kruiery/kruidery
condi'tion (n) voorwaarde; kondisie; ~**al**
	voorwaardelik, kondisioneel; ~**s of ser'**=
	vice diensvoorwaardes
condole' (v) betreur, kondoleer; ~**nce** roube=
	klag, deelneming; **letter of** ~**nce** brief van
	deelneming/meegevoel/simpatie
con'dom (n) kondoom *see* **fem'idom** (for
	women)
condone' vergewe, kwytskeld, kondoneer
con'dor kondor (voël)
con'duct (n) gedrag; houding; handelwyse
conduct' (v) lei, aanvoer; bestuur; gelei; ~ *an
	interview* 'n onderhoud lei/voer; ~**ed tour**
	(be)geleide toer; rondleiding; ~**or** geleier
	kondukteur (trein); dirigent

con'duit leipyp; waterleiding, buis
cone keël; dennebol; konus
confec'tion banket, suikergoed; ~**er** banket=
bakker; ~**ery** soetgebak, banket
confedera'tion konfederasie, verbond
confer' (v) verleen, toeken ('n graad); beraad=
slaag, samespreking(s) voer
con'ference konferensie; byeenkoms
confess' bely, erken; bieg; ~**ion** belydenis;
bieg; ~**ional po'etry** biegpoësie
confet'ti (n) confetti/konfetti
con'fidence vertroue, geloof, sekerheid; oor=
moedigheid; ~ **trick'ster** vertrouewende=
laar, kulman/kulkalant *also* **con'man**
con'fident (a) vol vertroue, hoopvol; oortuig
confiden'tial (a) vertroulik, konfidensieel; ge=
heim; *stric'tly* ~ streng vertroulik
confine' (v) begrens, beperk; opsluit; ~
oneself to jou bepaal/beperk tot
confined' eng, nou; gevang; *be* ~ 'n bevalling
hê; ~ *to one's house* huisarres
confine'ment beperking; bevalling (kinderge=
boorte)
confirm' bevestig, bekragtig; versterk; ~**a'tion**
bevestiging; aanneming (in kerk)
con'fiscate konfiskeer, beslag lê op
con'flict[1] (n) botsing, stryd, konflik, geskil
conflict'[2] (v) bots, stry, worstel; ~**ing** teen=
strydig; ~**ing in'terests** strydige/botsende
belange
con'fluence sameloop, samevloeiing (riviere)
conform' (v) vorm/skik na; instem met; kon=
formeer; ~**ist** konformis
confound' verwar; ~ *it!* verbrands!; ~**ed** ver=
vloek, verdeksels
confront' (v) konfronteer; ~**a'tion** konfronta=
sie
confuse' (v) verwar, verbyster; ~**d** (a) verwar;
deurmekaar
confus'ion verwarring
congest' ophoop; *traf'fic* ~**ion** verkeersop=
hoping, verkeersdrukte
congrat'ulate (v) gelukwens, felisiteer
congratula'tion gelukwensing; ~**s!** veels ge=
luk!
con'gregate vergader, bymekaarkom
congrega'tion gemeente; vergadering
con'gress -es kongres, vergadering
con'ifer naaldboom (denneboom)
con'jugate (v) vervoeg; saamvloei; (a) ver=
want; toegevoeg; ooreenkomstig
conjuga'tion (n) vervoeging; verbinding

conjunc'tion verbinding, vereniging; voeg=
woord; sameloop; *in* ~ *with* saam met
con'jure (v) besweer; toor, goël
con'jurer kulkunstenaar, goëlaar *also* **magi=
c'ian**
con'man swendelaar *also* **swind'ler**
connect' verbind, konnekteer; aansluit
connec'tion verbinding; aansluiting; konnek=
sie; familie; *in* ~ *with* in verband met
connoisseur' kenner, fynproewer (mens)
con'queror oorwinnaar, veroweraar
con'quest oorwinning; verowering
con'science gewete, konsensie; *guilty* ~ skul=
dige gewete
conscien'tious (a) nougeset, konsensieus, pligs=
getrou; ~ **objec'tor** diensweieraar
con'scious bewus; ~ *of* bewus van
concrip'tion konskripsie, diensplig
con'secrate (v) wy, inseën, heilig
consec'utive opeenvolgend, gereeld, volgend;
~ **num'ber** volgnommer; ~**ly** agtereenvol=
gens, opeenvolgend
consen'sus (n) ooreenstemming; akkoord, kon=
sensus *also* **agree'ment**
consent' (n) toestemming; (v) inwillig
con'sequence gevolg, uitwerking; *in* ~ *of* as
gevolg van, ten gevolge van; weens
conser'vancy (n) bewarea/bewaararea; natuur=
reservaat
conserva'tion behoud, bewaring; *na'ture* ~
natuurbewaring
conserv'atism konserwatisme; behoudendheid
conserv'ative (n) preserveermiddel; (a) kon=
serwatief, behoudend
conserve' (n, pl) ingelegde vrugte; (v) bewaar,
behou
consid'er oorweeg, beredeneer; beskou
consid'erable aanmerklik, aansienlik, bedui=
dend; *a* ~ *time* 'n geruime tyd
consid'erate (a) sorgvuldig; omsigtig; bedag=
saam *also* **mind'ful**; hoflik; weloorwoë
considera'tion oorweging; konsiderasie; ver=
goeding; teenprestasie; *take into* ~ in aan=
merking neem
consign' versend; ~**ee'** geadresseerde; agent;
~**ment** besending/lading
consist' bestaan; ~ *of* bestaan uit
consist'ent bestendig, konsekwent; *she plays a*
~ *game* sy speel bestendig
consola'tion troos, vertroosting; ~ **prize**
troosprys
console' (v) troos, bemoedig; (n) konsool

consol'idate (v) konsolideer *also* **amal'gamate**
con'sonant (n) medeklinker, konsonant
con'sort (n) maat; metgesel; gade
consor'tium konsortium; sindikaat
conspic'uous opsigtig; beroemd; ~ *by one's absence* skitter deur afwesigheid
conspir'acy ..cies sameswering, komplot
conspir'ator samesweerder (mens)
conspire' saamsweer, 'n komplot smee
con'stable konstabel, polisieman, geregsdie=naar
con'stant (a) standvastig, konstant; getrou
con'stantly voortdurend, onafgebroke
constella'tion (n) sterrebeeld; konstellasie; ~ *of sta'tes* konstellasie van state
consterna'tion (n) ontsteltenis, konsternasie
constipa'tion hardlywigheid, konstipasie
constit'uency ..cies kiesafdeling; kiesers
con'stitute (v) saamstel; vorm, konstitueer
constitu'tion grondwet (van 'n land), konsti=tusie; grondreëls (van 'n klub/vereniging); gestel, konstitusie (iem. se liggaam)
constitu'tional grondwetlik, konstitusioneel; ~ **assem'bly** grondwetgewende vergade=ring; ~ **court** konstitusionele/grondwetlike hof; ~ **devel'opment** grondwetlike ontwik=keling
construct' bou, oprig, saamstel; ~**ion** kon=struksie; uitleg; ~**ive** opbouend
con'sul konsul; ~**ate** konsulaat
consult' (v) raadpleeg; beraadslaag, oorleg pleeg; ~**a'tion** raadpleging, konsultasie; ~**ing** (n) raadpleging; (a) raadplegend; raadgewend; ~**ing engineer'** raadgewende ingenieur; ~**ing hours** spreekure; ~**ing room(s)** spreekkamer
consume' (v) verteer, verbruik, opgebruik
consum'er verbruiker; ~ *friendly* verbruiker=vriendelik/verbruikergunstig; ~ **goods** ver=bruiksgoedere; ~ **price in'dex** verbrui=kersprysindeks; ~ **spen'ding** verbruiker(s)=besteding
consump'tion (n) verbruik, tering, uittering
con'tact (n) aanraking, voeling, kontak; ~ **len'ses** kontaklense; (v) (iem.) kontak
conta'gious besmetlik (deur aanraking), aan=steeklik *also* **infec'tious**
contain' bevat, insluit, behels; ~**er** houer; blik; ~**er ves'sel** houerskip; ~**erisa'tion** behouering
contam'inate besoedel, bevlek, besmet
contem'porary (n) tydgenoot (mens); (a) tydgenootlik, eietyds, kontemporêr
contempt' veragting, minagting; ~ *of court* minagting v.d. hof; ~**ible** veragtelik
contend' betwis, bestry; beweer; ~**er** aan=spraakmaker (op 'n titel)
content' (n) tevredenheid; *to one's heart's ~* na hartelus; (a) voldaan, vergenoeg
conten'tious kontensieus, omstrede (boek)
con'tents inhoud; omvang
con'test[1] (n) twis; (wed)stryd; kragmeting *also* **match** (n), **tri'al**
contest'[2] (v) betwis; wedywer; ~ *a seat* 'n setel betwis; ~**ant** deelnemer, mededinger; ~**ed** bestrede
con'tinent (n) vasteland, kontinent
continen'tal kontinentaal, vasteland=
contin'gency ..cies gebeurlikheid, toevallig=heid; ~ **fund** gebeurlikheidsfonds
contin'gent (a) gebeurlik; ~ **liabil'ity** voor=waardelike aanspreeklikheid
contin'ual (a) aanhoudend, onafgebroke
continua'tion voortsetting; verlenging
contin'ue voortsit; aanhou; vervolg; verleng. *to be ~d* word vervolg; ~**d support'** vol=gehoue steun; **contin'uing/on'going educa'=tion** voortgesette onderwys
contin'uous voortdurend, deurlopend
con'tour omtrek, hoogtelyn; kontoer
contracep'tive voorbehoedmiddel
con'tract (n) verdrag, ooreenkoms; kontrak; ~ **stu'dent** verbintenisstudent
contract' (v) inkrimp, saamtrek; ~ *out* uit=kontrakteer; ~**ion** sametrekking, verkorting; ~**or** kontrakteur/kontraktant; aannemer; le=weransier
contradict' (v) weerspreek, weerlê; ~**ion** teen=spraak, weerspreking
contrapt'ion uitvindsel *also* **gad'get**; kontrep=sie
con'trary: *on the ~* inteendeel; ~ *to* in stryd met; strydig met; (a) teenoorgestel(d), stry=dig; eiesinnig, dwars (mens)
con'trast (n) teenstelling, kontras
contrast' (v) teenstel, kontrasteer
contraven'tion oortreding; teenstand
contrib'ute (v) bydra, bevorder; meewerk
contribu'tion (n) bydrae, kontribusie; inset
contri'vance (n) uitvindsel, kontrepsie *see* **contrap'tion**
contrive' (v) uitvind; beraam, versin, prakseer; ~**d** bedag; gesog
control' (n) bestuur; beheer, kontrole; (v

kontroleer; beheer; monitor/moniteer; ~ler kontroleur; ~ling beheerend; ~ling com'=pany beheermaatskappy
controver'sial omstrede, tendensieus, kontro=versieel; ~ book omstrede boek
con'troversy (n) dispuut; strydpunt; polemiek
convales'cent (a) genesend; ~ home herstel=oord; ~ leave aansterkverlof
convene' (v) saamroep, belê; notice convening the meeting byeenroepende kennisgewing; ~r sameroeper (mens)
conven'ience gemak, gerieflikheid; for the sake of ~ geriefshalwe
conven'ient gemaklik; geskik; gerieflik
con'vent (nonne)klooster also nun'nery
conven'tion (n) byeenkoms, konvensie; ge=bruik; ~al gebruiklik, konvensioneel
conversa'tion gesprek, konversasie
converse'¹ (v) gesels, omgaan met, verkeer
con'verse² (a) teenoorgestelde, omgekeerde; ~ly omgekeerd
conver'sion omkering; omsetting; bekering; omrekening; doelskop (rugby)
con'vert (n) bekeerling, bekeerde (mens)
convert' (v) verdoel (rugby); bekeer
con'vex bolrond, konveks
convey' (v) vervoer, oordra; ~ancer akte-uit=maker; ~er belt (ver)voerband
con'vict (n) bandiet, prisonier (mens)
convict' (v) vonnis, veroordeel; ~ed gevonnis
convic'tion skuldigbevinding
convin'cing oortuigend
convoca'tion konvokasie; sameroeping
con'voy (n) -s konvooi, geleide
coo (v) koer, kir (duif)
cook (n) kok; (v) kook; ~ the books die boeke/syfers kook/vervals; ~ery kookkuns; ~ery book resepteboek; ~ing uten'sils kookgerei
cool (v) afkoel; bedaar; (a) koel; kalm; fanta,sties (studentetaal); ~ it, John! koel af, Jan!; ~bag koelsak, yssak; ~ing to'wer koeltoring
coop (n) fuik; hoenderhok; (v) opsluit; ~er vatmaker, kuiper (mens)
co-op'erate saamwerk, koöpereer
co-opera'tion samewerking; koöperasie/ko-=operasie
co-op'erative (n): ~ soci'ety koöperasie/ko-=operasie
co-opt' byvoeg, koöpteer/ko-opteer
cope (v) hanteer, cope also man'age/han'dle; ~ with regkom (met); opgewasse teen/vir

copp'er (n) koper; kopergeld; (a) koper=
cop'ulate kopuleer, paar; koppel, verbind
cop'y (n) copies kopie, afskrif; eksemplaar (boek); (v) afskryf, kopieer; ~right kopie=reg, outeursreg; ~wri'ter kopieskrywer (ad=vert.)
co'ral koraal; ~ is'land koraaleiland; ~ reef koraalrif; ~ tree koraalboom
cord (n) band, tou, lyn, koord; ~less tel'e=phone koordlose telefoon; spi'nal ~ rug=murg; umbi'lical ~ naelstring
cor'dial (a) hartlik; hartsterkend; ~ rela'tions hartlike betrekkinge/samewerking
cor'don kordon; snoer; ~ off afsper (straat)
cord'uroy ferweel; (pl) ferweelbroek
core kern, hart, pit; ~ syl'labus kernsillabus; ~ time kerntyd see flex'time
corian'der koljander
cork (n) kurk; prop; (v) toekurk; (a) kurk=; ~screw (n) kurktrekker
corn¹ (n) graan; koring; korrel; ~fla'kes graanvlokkies
corn² (n) liddoring; tread on one's ~s iem. op die tone trap
corn'ea -s horingvlies, kornea (oog)
cor'ner (n) hoek, hoekpunt; (v) vaskeer; vas=vra; ~stone hoeksteen
cor'onary koronêr, hart=; ~ thrombo'sis koro=nêre trombose, kroonaarverstopping
corona'tion kroning
corp'oral¹ (n) korporaal (soldaat)
corp'oral² (a) liggaamlik/lyflik; persoonlik; ~ pun'ishment lyfstraf
cor'porate korporaat/korporatief; bod'y ~ regspersoon; beheer/bestuursraad; ~ strat'=egy korporaatstrategie
corpora'tion stadsbestuur, korporasie; close ~ beslote korporasie; Small Bu'siness Devel'=opment C~ (SBDC) Kleinsake-Ontwikke=lingskorporasie (KSOK)
corpse lyk (dooie liggaam)
correct' (v) verbeter; nasien; (a) presies, juis, noukeurig, korrek
correc'tion verbetering; korreksie; regstelling; ~al ser'vices korrektiewe dienste
correla'tion korrelasie, verband
correspond' (v) korrespondeer; ooreenstem/saamval; ~ence briefwisseling, korrespon=densie; ~ence col'lege korrespondensiekol=lege; ~ent (n) korrespondent; beriggewer
corro'sion korrosie, wegvreting
cor'rugate rimpel, golf; ~d i'ron gegolfde

sinkplaat; ~**d road** sinkplaatpad

corrupt' (v) bederf; omkoop; (a) bedorwe; korrup; ~**ion** korrupsie

cors'et korset, borsrok; ~**ry** postuurdrag/ vormdrag

cosmet'ic(s) kosmetiek, skoonheidsmiddel; (pl) mooimaakgoed; ~ **change** kosmetiese/ oppervlakkige verandering; ~ **sur'gery** plastiese snykunde

cos'monaut (n) ruimtevaarder, ruimteman

cosmopol'itan (n) wêreldburger; kosmopoliet; (a) kosmopolities

cos'mos¹ wêreldorde, kosmos, heelal

cos'mos² nooientjie-in-die-groen, kosmos (blom)

cost (n) prys; (on)koste; (pl) onkoste; *at all* ~*s* tot elke prys; ~ *of li'ving allo'wance* duurtetoeslag; ~**-effec'tive** kostedoeltreffend/ kostelonend; (v) kos

cos'ting koste(be)rekening

cost: ~**ly** duur; kosbaar; ~ **price** (in)koopprys

cost'ume kleredrag, kostuum; pak

cos'y (n) **cosies** teemus; (a) gesellig, knus; snoesig

cot kinderkateltjie, bababed; hut; ~ **death** wiegiedood/wiegiesterfte

cott'age cottage, kothuis; ~ **cheese** maaskaas; ~ **in'dustry** tuisnywerheid; ~ **loaf** toringbrood; ~ **pie** herderspastei

cott'on katoen; garing; ~ **waste** poetskatoen; ~ **wool** watte

couch (n) **-es** rusbank, sofa; (v) inklee; uitdruk; ~ **pota'to** leunstoelpatat (voor TV)

cough (n, v) hoes, kug; ~ **loz'enge** hoesklontjie; ~ **rem'edy** hoesmiddel

coun'cil raad; raad(s)vergadering; ~ **cham'ber** raadsaal; ~**lor** raadslid

coun'sel (n) beraadslaging; raadgewer; (v) raad gee; aanraai; ~**lee** beradene (mens); ~**ling** berading; ~**lor** berader

count¹ (n) graaf (titel)

count² (n) telling; rekening; (v) tel; aftel; ~ *on* reken op; ~ *out* uittel; ~**down** aftelling (ruimtelansering)

coun'ter (n) toonbank; teller

coun'ter: ~**attack'** teenaanval; ~**-clock'wise** teen die wysers in; links om

coun'terfeit (n) namaaksel, vervalsing; (v) namaak; vervals; (a) nagemaak, oneg; ~**er** vervalser

coun'terfoil teenblad, kantstrokie

coun'ter: ~**mea'sures** teenmaatreëls; ~**offen'sive** teenoffensief; ~**part** ewleknie; ampsgenoot; ~**produc'tive** teenproduktief; ~**sig'nat-**

ure medeondertekening

coun'tess -es gravin

count'less talloos, ontelbaar

coun'try ..ries land; platteland; buitedistrik; country (sangstyl); ~ **club** buiteklub; ~**man** landgenoot; ~**wide** land(s)wyd

coun'ty ..ties graafskap (Engeland)

coup (d'état') staatsgreep, bewindoorname

coup de grâce' genadeslag

coupé' koepee

cou'ple (n) tweetal, paar; egpaar; (v) saamvoeg; koppel; paar

coup'let koeplet, tweereëlige vers

coup'on koepon

cou'rage (n) moed, dapperheid *also* .**val'our**

courag'eous (a) moedig, dapper, heldhaftig

cou'rier koerier, renbode; ~ **ser'vice** koerierdiens

course (n) loop; loopbaan; baan; kursus (studie); gang (ete); ~ **of ac'tion** gedragslyn, handelwyse

court¹ (n) (geregs)hof; landdroshof; baan; ~ *of justice* geregshof; *settle out of* ~ buite die hof skik; ~ **case** hofsaak, regsgeding; **high** ~ hoërhof; **supre'me** ~ hooggeregshof

court² (v) vry, kuier; ~ *a girl* 'n meisie/nooi die hof maak, by haar vleiksleep

court'eous (a) hoflik, beleef(d) *also* **poli'te**

court'esy ..sies hoflikheid, beleefdheid; *by* ~ *of* met goedkeuring van; goedgunstig geleen/geplaas/verskaf deur; ~ **bus/car** klantebus/motor; ~ **stand** selfdienstal(letjie); ~ **vi'sit/call** welwillendheidsbesoek, hoflikheidsbesoek

court: ~ **mar'tial** krygsverhoor; militêre hof; ~ **mes'senger** geregsbode

court'yard binneplaas *also* **enclo'sure**

cous'in neef, niggie; *first* ~ volle neef/niggie; *second* ~ kleinneef, kleinniggie

co'venant (n) verdrag, verbond; handves; *Day of the C*~ Geloftedag *now* **Day of Reconcilia'tion**

co'ver (n) deksel; bedekking; dekking (assuransie); omslag (van boek); buiteblad (boek); *seek* ~ skuiling soek; (v) bedek, oordek; dek; oortrek (kussing); aflê (afstand); bestryk (kanon); ~ *up* bedek; verswyg, geheim hou; ~**age** dekking (nuus); ~ **charge** tafelgeld; ~ **girl** voorbladnooi (tydskrif); ~**ing** bedekking, omhulsel; ~**ing bond** dekverband; ~**ing let'ter** begeleidende brief/dekbrief

cow (n) koei; ~**dung** beesmis; ~**'s milk** bees-

melk; ~**pea** akkerboon(tjie)
cow'ard lafaard, bangbroek; ~**ly** lafhartig
coy (a) sedig; verleë, beðees *also* **tim'id**
crab krap; kreef
crack (n) kraak, knak, bars; knal; (v) kraak; knak, bars; skeur; ~ *jokes* grappe verkoop; (a) beste, uithaler=, knap; ~**er** klapper
crac'kle (v) knetter, rinkel, kraak
crack'ling swoerd (gebraaide varkvel); ~**s** kaiings
cra'dle (n) wieg; bakermat; (v) wieg
craft (n) lis, sluheid; vaartuig; ~**s** (n) ambags= kunste; ~**s'man** ambagsman; ~**y** behendig; slu, geslepe *also* **sly, cun'ning**
cram (v) volprop, vasdruk; blok, inpomp (stu= die); ~ **col'lege** drilkollege
cramp (n) kramp; (v) beperk; ~**ed** nou; vas= gedruk
crane (n) kraanvoël; kraan, hysmasjien
crank[1] (n) slinger; (v) draai, slinger
crank[2] (n) gek; (a) gek *also* **cran'ky, cra'zy**; lendelam; los
crape *see* **crêpe**
crash (n) botsing; instorting; ramp; (v) kraak; instort; ~ **course** stapelkursus; ~ **hel'met** valhelm; ~ **lan'ding** buiklanding; ~ **tack'le** plettervat (rugby)
crate hok; krat; mandjie
crat'er krater
crave (v) smeek, eis; hunker
crav'ing (n) hunkering, begeerte
crawl (n) gekruip; kruipslag (in swem); (v) kruip, aansukkel; ~**er** kruiper
cray'fish varswaterkreef/rivierkreef; (see)krap
cray'on (n) tekenkryt
craze (n) manie, hartstog; mode
craz'y (a) gek, mal, kranksinnig; ~ **pa'ving** klipplaveisel, lapbestrating
creak (n) gekraak, geknars; (v) kraak
cream (n) room; ~ **of tar'tar** kremetart; (v) afroom; (a) liggeel; ~**ery** botterfabriek; sui= welfabriek; ~ **puff** roomsoes(ie); ~ **se'pa= rator** roomafskeier/romer
crease (n) vou, plooi, kreukel; kolfkampie (krieket); (v) kreukel, vou; ~**-resis'tant** kreukeltraag
create' (v) skep; vorm; voortbring, wek; ~ *the impression* die indruk wek
crea'tion skepping *also* **gen'esis**; heelal
creat'or skepper, maker
crea'ture skepsel, kreatuur; bees
crèche kinderhawe, bewaarskool, crèche

creden'tials (n) geloofsbrief
credibil'ity geloofwaardigheid, geloofbaar= heid; ~ **gap** vertrouensgaping
cre'dit (n) krediet; vertroue; *get* ~ *for* erken= ning kry vir; (v) krediteer; ~ **bal'ance** kredietsaldo/kredietbalans; ~ **card** krediet= kaart; ~**or** krediteur, skuldeiser (mens)
cre'do -s geloofsbelydenis, credo *also* **belief'**
creed geloof, godsdiens *also* **faith/belief'**
creek inham *also* **cove**; draai; spruit
creep kruip, sluip; seil; ~**er** klimop, slinger= plant, ranker; ~**y** grieselig, grillerig
cremat'e (v) veras/kremeer; *I want to be* ~*d* ek wil veras word
crema'tion verassing/kremasie; lykverbranding
cremator'ium -s krematorium
crêpe crêpe/kreip, lanfer; ~ **pa'per** krinkelpa= pier
cres'cent (n) (Turkse) halfmaan; singel (straat)
cress bronskors
crest kuif; kam; maanhaar; wapen
crev'ice skeur, bars, spleet
crew skeepsbemanning; trop; *a* ~ *of fifteen on the island* vyftien man op die eiland; **cab'in** ~ kajuitpersoneel (vliegtuig)
crib (n) krip; kinderbedjie; stal; (v) afkyk (in eksamen); bedrieg
crick'et[1] kriek (insek); **ground** ~ koringkriek
crick'et[2] krieket; ~ **enthu'siast** krieketgees= driftige (mens); ~ **bat** kolf; ~ **match** krie= ketwedstryd
crime misdaad; gruweldaad; ~ **preven'tion** misdaadvoorkoming; ~ **rate** misdaadsyfer
crim'inal (n) misdadiger; ~ **law** strafreg; **habit'ual** ~ gewoontemisdadiger; (a) mis= dadig, krimineel; ~ **proce'dure** strafproses= reg
crim'son karmosyn, dieprooi
cringe (v) ineenkrimp, kruip; ~**r** witvoetjie= soeker, kruiper
crip'ple (n) kreupele (mens); (a) kruppel/kreu= pel, mank
cris'is crises keerpunt, toppunt, krisis
crisp (n) kroes, krul; (v) krul; (a) kroes; bros; krakerig; ~**s** (n) tjips (in pakkie); ~**y** krul= lerig; bros
criter'ion ..teria maatstaf, norm, kriterium *also* **norm**; kenmerk
crit'ic beoordelaar, kritikus; ~**al** kritiek, hag= lik; krities; vitterig; ~**ism** kritiek, beoorde= ling; ~**ise** kritiseer, beoordeel
croak (v) kwaak, kras

cro'chet (n) hekelwerk; (v) hekel

crock (n) krukker; sukkelaar; knol; *old* ~*s* ou knolle; (v) seermaak

crock'ery (n) breekgoed, erdewerk, porselein= ware

croc'odile krokodil; ~ **tears** krokodiltrane, bob= bejaanhartseer

cron'y ..nies trawant; tjom(mie); kornuit

crook (n) boef, skelm, kroek, skurk; haak, staf

croon (v) neurie; ~**er** neuriesanger, sniksanger

crop (n) oes; gewas, gesaaide; krop (voël); ~ **far'mer** saaiboer; ~ **rota'tion** wisselbou; ~**per** knipper; kropduif; mislukking

cro'quet kroukie (spel)

cross (n) **-es** kruis; moeite; kruising; baster (van diere); (v) kruis; *a ~ed cheque* 'n gekruiste tjek; ~ *out* skrap *also* **dele'te**; (a) dwars; kwaad; ~**bow** kruisboog; ~**coun'try race** landloop; ~**examina'tion** kruisverhoor; ~**-exam'ine** kruisvra, onder/in kruisverhoor neem; ~**-eyed** skeel; ~**ing** kruising; oorweg; ~**-ref'erence** kruisverwys(ing); ~**road** kruis= pad, tweesprong; *at the ~roads* op die keerpunt; ~ **sec'tion** deursnee; ~**-street** dwars= straat; ~**word puzzle** blok(kies)raaisel

crouch (v) hurk, laag buk; kruip

crou'pier croupier/kroepier *also* **roulette' mas'ter**

crow (n) kraai; *as the ~ flies* reguit; (v) kraai; pronk; spog; ~**bar** koevoet, breekyster

crowd (n) skare; menigte, klomp; gepeupel

crown (n) kroon; kruin; (v) kroon

crow's-foot oogrimpel, lagplooitjie

cru'cial kritiek, beslissend *also* **criti'cal**

cru'cifix (n) **-es** kruis, kruisbeeld

crucifi'xion kruisiging, kruisdood

cru'cify (v) kruisig

crude ru, kru; onafgewerk; ongesuiwer; rou; ~ **oil** ruolie

cru'el wreed, wreedaardig, hardvogtig; ~**ty** wreedheid, onmenslikheid

cru'et stand sout-en-peperstel, kruiestel(letjie)

cruise (n) (rond)vaart; tog; (v) kruis, rondvaar; ~**r** kruiser; ~**rweight** ligswaargewig

cruis'ing speed togsnelheid

crul'ler (n) koe(k)sister *also* **koe(k)'sister**

crumb krummel, brokkie

crum'pet plaatkoekie, flappertjie

crunch (v) kraak, hard kou; knars

crusa'de kruistog; ~**r** kruisvaarder

crush drukgang; (v) verpletter, saampers; ~**ing** (a) verpletterend, vernietigend

crust (n) kors, korsie; roof (van seer)

crutch -es kruk, stut

crux (n) crux/kruks; kern; knoop

cry (n) **cries** skree(u), gil; (v) skree(u); uit= roep; huil; ~ *for joy* van vreugde huil; ~**ba'by** tjankbalie

crypt grafkelder; ~**ogram'** geheimskrif

cry'stal kristal; ~**lise** kristalliseer, versuiker; ~**lised fruit** suikervrugte

cub (n) welp; klein padvinder(tjie)

cubb'yhole paneelkassie, mossienes (idiom.)

cube (n) kubus; derde mag; ~ **root** derde= magswortel

cu'bic kubiek, van die 3e mag

cu'bicle afskorting; kleedhokkie

cuck'oo -s koekoek; idioot (mens)

cu'cumber komkommer

cud herkoutjie; *chew the ~* herkou

cud'dle omhels; liefkoos; lepel lê

cudd'ly (a) gesellig, snoesig

cud'gel (n) (knop)kierie; knots

cue[1] biljartstok

cue[2] wenk, aanwysing; wagwoord (toneel)

cuff (n) vuisslag; omslag; mouboordjie; (v) klap; ~ **link** mouskakel, mansjetknoop

cul-de-sac' culs-de-sac keerweer, doodloop= straat, keerom

cul'inary kombuis=, kook=; ~ **art** kookkuns

cull (v) uitdun; ~**ing** uitdun (van wild)

cul'minate (v) 'n toppunt bereik, kulmineer

culp'able strafbaar, toerekenbaar; ~ **hom'i= cide** strafbare manslag

cul'prit skuldige; oortreder, kwaaddoener

cul'tivar (n) kultivar; kweekvariëteit

cul'tivate (v) verbou, kweek (gewasse); teel (diere); kultiveer; beoefen; aanplant

cul'tural kultureel, beskawings=

cul'ture (n) kultuur; beskawing; **phys'ical** ~ lig= gaamsopvoeding/beweegkunde; ~**d pearls** kweekpêrels

cul'vert riool; stormsloot: duiker (onder 'n pad)

cum'ber (n) las, hindernis; ~**some** lastig, hinderlik; log, lomp

cum'quat/kum'quat koemkwat (vrug)

cu'mulate (v) ophoop, opstapel, kumuleer

cu'mulative ophopend, toenemend; kumula= tief, oplopend; ~ **prefe'rence shar'es** ku= mulatiewe voorkeuraandele

cunn'ing (n) lis, sluheid; (a) geslepe; uitge= slape, slinks, slu; behendig

cup (n) koppie; beker (sport); kelk (blom)

cup'board koskas; **built-in** ~ muurkas

cura'tor voog, kurator; opsigter (mens)

curb (n) kenketting (aan toom); bedwang; randsteen; (v) beteuel; bedwing

cure (n) geneesmiddel, kuur; genesing; (v) genees, gesond maak; ~ *skins* velle brei

cur'few (n) klokreël; aandklokreël(ing)

curios'ity nuuskierigheid, weetgierigheid; ~ *killed the cat* van uitvra is die tronk vol

cur'ious (a) nuuskierig; sonderling, snaaks

curl (n) krul, haarlok; kronkeling; (v) krul; oprol; kronkel; ~**ing iron,** ~**ing tongs** krul= yster, krultang; ~**y'head** krulkop

cu'rrant korent/korint

cu'rrency betaalmiddel, valuta, geld; looptyd (van 'n verband); koers (geld)

cu'rrent (n) stroom, stroming; (a) lopend; ~ **as'sets** bedryfsbates; ~ **liabil'ities** bedryfs= laste; ~ **price** heersende/huidige prys

curric'ulum -s kurrikulum, leerplan (van vak= ke); ~ **vi'tae** (CV) curriculum vitae, lewens= profiel, biodata

cu'rry[1] (n) **curries** kerrie

cu'rry[2] (v) roskam, brei; afransel; ~ *favour* witvoetjie soek; ~**comb** (n) roskam (perd)

curse (n) vloek; (v) vervloek, verwens; ~**d** vervloek; ~**d** *with* opgeskeep/gestraf met

curt (a) kortaf, bits(ig), kortweg

curtail' besnoei, verkort, verminder

curt'ain (n) gordyn; skerm; ~ **call** buiging; ~ **lec'ture** bedsermoen, bedpredikasie; ~**rais'er** voorstuk; voorwedstryd

curt'sy (n) . .**sies** kniebuiging, knieknik

curve (n) boog; ronding; kromme/kurwe (stat.)

cu'shion kussing (vir op/teen sit); biljartband

cus'tard vla

cus'tody aanhouding; voogdy; *in* ~ in aanhou= ding; *safe* ~ veilige bewaring

cus'tom gewoonte, gebruik; (pl) doeane; in= voerregte; ~**ary** gebruiklik; ~**er** klant, koper; klandisie; ~**-made**/~**ised** doelgebou; ~**-made gun** pasgeweer; ~**s du'ty** doeaneregte

cut (n) sny; hou, raps; keep; *short* ~ kort= paadjie; (v) sny; afsny; kap; kerf; raps; knip (hare); besnoei (salaris); verlaag (pryse); ~ *back* besnoei, inkort; ~ *and dried* kant en klaar; ~ *short a visit* 'n besoek kortknip

cute oulik (kindjie); skerpsinnig, skerp, fyn

cut'lery eetgerei, messeware; **canteen' of** ~ messestel

cut'let (n) kotelet (vleis)

cut: ~**throat** (n) moordenaar; barbier= (skeer)= mes; (a) genadeloos; ~**-throat competi'tion** genadelose mededinging

cut'ting uitgrawing; (uit)knipsel; stiggie/steg= gie; ~ **edge** voorpunt *also* **fo'refront;** ~ **ser'vice** knipseldiens; ~ **torch** blaasvlam

cy'ber kuber; rekenaarskepping; ~ **art** kuber= kuns; ~**punk** kubersltiper *also* **cy'berstalk'= er;** ~**space** kuberruimte

cy'cad sikadee, broodboom

cica'da (n) sonbesie, boomsingertjie, sikade

cy'cle (n) kringloop; siklus; sirkel; rywiel; reeks; (v) fiets; ~ **ra'cing** naelry, naelren

cy'clist fietsryer, fietser (mens) *also* **bi'ker**

cy'clone werwelstorm, tornado, sikloon

cyl'inder (n) silinder

cym'bal simbaal

cyn'ic (n) sinikus; ~**al** (a) sinies, smalend

cy'press sipres (boom)

D

dachs'hund dachshund, worshond(jie)

dab (n) tikkie; vlekkie; (v) aanraak; smeer

dab'ble sprinkel; plas; bolangs besig hou (met)

dad/dadd'y daddies pa, pappie, paps

daff'odil môresterretjie, affodil (blom)

daft (a) dwaas, mal *also* **mad, cran'ky**

dagg'er dolk, kris; kruisie

dahl'ia -s dahlia (blom)

dail'y (n) dagblad; (a) daagliks

daint'y (a) kieskeurig; fyn, sierlik; fraai

dair'y dairies melkery; ~ **pro'duce** suiwel= produkte

dais (n) podium; verhoog

dais'y daisies madeliefie; ma(r)griet (blom)

dale (n) dal, laagte, kom

dam[1] (n) moer (diere); moeder

dam[2] (n) dam; (v) opdam

dam'age (n) skade; (pl) skadevergoeding; *cause* ~ skade aanrig; (v) beskadig

dame (adellike) dame; huisvrou, mevrou

damn (n) vloek; *not worth a* ~ geen flenter werd nie; (v) veroordeel, vloek, verdoem; ~**ed** verdoem; vervloek; ~**ed nui'sance** vervlakste ergernis/oorlas

damp (n) damp, vogtigheid; (a) klam
dam'sel (n) meisie, maagd; jonkvrou
dance (n) dans(party), bal; ~ **mu'sic** dansmu= siek; ~**r** danser(es)
dan'druff (n) skilfers
dan'dy (n) modegek, laventelhaan, fat; (a) windmakerig, spoggerig
dan'ger gevaar, onraad; ~**ous** gevaarlik
dapp'er (a) agtermekaar; lewendig, fiks, viets
dare durf, waag; uitdaag; ~**de'vil** waaghals
dar'ing (n) durf; vermetelheid, astrantheid; (a) onverskrokke, waaghalsig; vermetel
dark (n) duisternis; (a) donker; somber; **D~ A'ges** Middeleeue; ~ **hor'se** onbekende me= dedinger; ~**ness** duisternis, donkerte
darl'ing (n) liefling, hartlam; skat, skattebol; (a) geliefde, liewe
darn (v) stop; ~**ing needle** stopnaald
dart (n) pyl(tjie); spies; veerpyltjie; sprong; (v) gooi; wegspring, pyl; *play* ~*s* (veer)= pyltjie speel; ~**board** pyltjiebord
dash (n) slag; aandagstreep; swier; (v) stoot; slaan; ~ *it!* vervlaks!; ~ *off* weghol; ~**board** paneelbord; ~**ing** (a) swierig, vurig
dat'a data, gegewens; ~ **bank** databank; ~= **ba'se** databasis; ~**base ser'ver** databasisbe= diener; ~ **pro'cessing** dataverwerking
date[1] (n) dadel
date[2] (n) datum; *a blind* ~ 'n molafspraak; *out of* ~ ouderwets; *up to* ~ modern; byderwets; *what is the* ~*?* die hoeveelste is dit?; (v) dateer; dagteken; *it dates from the 12th century* dit dagteken van die 12e eeu; ~ **rape** afspraakverkragting
daught'er dogter; ~**-in-law** skoondogter
daw'dle (v) teuter, lanterfanter; talm, sloer
dawn (n) dagbreek; (v) lig word, daag; *it* ~*ed upon me* dit het my bygeval
day (n) dag; daglig; *all* ~ *long* die hele dag; ~*s of grace* uitsteldae, respytdae; ~ *of the Mutt* Brakdag; *that will be the* ~*!* dank jou die duiwel!; *the* ~ *after tomorrow* oormôre; *the* ~ *before yesterday* eergister; ~**break** dagbreek, rooidag; ~ **la'bourer** dagloner; ~ **schol'ar** dagskolier
Day of Reconcilia'tion Versoeningsdag
daze (n) verbystering, bedwelming; (v) ver= byster; verblind, in verwarring bring
daz'zle (v) blikker; verblind *also* **glare**; verbyster
deac'on diaken, armeversorger; deken
dead (n) gesneuwelde; dooie; (a) dood; dooie= rig; ~ *as a doornail* so dood soos 'n mossie;

a ~ *heat* gelykop; (adv) in ergste graad; ~ *sure* so seker as wat; ~ **beat** doodmoeg, boeglam; ~ **drunk** smoordronk; ~**-end street** doodloopstraat; keerweer; ~**line** sper= tyd/perktyd; ~**lock** dooiepunt; ~**ly** dodelik
deaf (a) doof; ~ *and blind person* doofblinde; ~**-mute** doofstom
deal (n) deel; transaksie, akkoord; *make a* ~ akkoord sluit; *new* ~ nuwe bedeling; (v) deel; sake doen; onderhandel; ~ *in* handel dryf in; ~**er** winkelier, handelaar
dean deken (in sekere kerke); dekaan (univer= siteit)
dear (n) hartjie; (a) lief, dierbaar; geagte; duur, skaars; **D~ Sir/Mad'am** Geagte Heer/ Dame
death (n) dood, uiteinde; sterfgeval; afsterwe; *condemn to* ~ ter dood veroordeel; ~ **du'ties** boedelbelasting; ~**rate** sterftesyfer; ~ **sen'tence** doodsvonnis; ~ **toll** dodetol
debate' (n) debat; (v) debatteer; bespreek
debat'ing society debatsvereniging
deben'ture (n) skuldbrief, obligasie *also* **bond**
deb'it (n) debiet; (v) debiteer; belas; ~ **or'der** debietorder
deb'ris puin; opdrifsels; oorskot; **nu'clear** ~ kernafval, kernoorskot
debt skuld; ~ *of honour* ereskuld; ~ **collec'tor** skuldinvorderaar; ~**or** skuldenaar, debiteur
de'but (n) debuut, buiging, eerste optrede
dé'butante debutante (jong dame)
dec'ade tiental, dekade
dec'adent (a) in verval, dekadent
decant' (v) oorskink; ~**er** karaf/kraffie
decap'itate (v) onthoof *also* **behead'**
decath'lon tienkamp, dekatlon
decay' (n) verval; verrotting; (v) verval; ver= swak; verrot, vrot
decease' (n) sterf, doodgaan; ~**d'** (n) oorle= dene; afgestorwene; (a) oorlede; ~**d esta'te** bestorwe boedel
deceit' bedrog, lis, misleiding
deceive' bedrieg, mislei *also* **defraud**; verlei
Decem'ber Desember
de'cency (n) ordentlikheid, fatsoenlikheid
de'cent (a) fatsoenlik, ordentlik, betaamlik
decen'tralise desentraliseer
decep'tive misleidend
dec'ibel desibel (geluid-eenheid)
decide' (v) beslis; bepaal, vasstel; besluit; ~**d'** beslis, nadruklik; ~**dly** beslis
decid'uous bladwisselend (boom)

de'cimal (a) tientallig; desimaal; ~ **com'ma** desimaalkomma

deci'sion (n) beslissing, besluit; ~ **ma'ker** besluitnemer

deci'sive beslissend; deurslaggewend

deck (n) dek; (v) oortrek; bedek; versier; ~ **quoits** skyfgooi

declara'tion verklaring, deklarasie; ~ **of in-tent'** verklaring van voorneme

declare' verklaar; aankondig; ~ *war* oorlog verklaar

decline' (n) verval; afname; afdraand; daling (pryse); (v) verval; verwerp; verbuig (gram.)

deco'der (n) dekodeerder

decompress'ion (n) dekompressie, drukverlig-ting

dé'cor (n) dekor, toneelinkleding

dec'orate versier, dekoreer, optooi *also* **adorn'**

decora'tion versiering; ereteken, dekorasie

decoy' (n) lokaas, lokmiddel; lokvink (poli-sie); (v) aanlok; mislei; bedrieg

de'crease (n) vermindering, afname

decrease' (v) verminder, afneem

decree' (n) dekreet; (v) verorden, bepaal

decrep'it (a) afgeleef, oud, gebreklik *also* **in-firm', disa'bled**

ded'icate toewy; opdra; ~**d stu'dent** toege-wyde/konsensieuse student

deduct' aftrek, verminder; ~**ion** aftrekking; gevolgtrekking *also* **conclu'sion**

deed daad; akte; ~**s' office** aktekantoor

deem (v) beskou, oordeel, goeddink

deep (n) diepte; see; (a, adv) diep, diepsinnig; grondig; ~**free'ze** vrieskas

deer (n) takbok, hert

defama'tion (n) belastering, laster; ~ **of char'-acter** karakterskending

default' (n) versuim; gebrek; nalatigheid; wanbetaling; ~ **of payment** wanbetaling; *win by* ~ wen by verstek (sport)

defeat' (n) neerlaag; vernietiging; (v) verslaan, verydel; klop (sport)

de'fect (n) gebrek; fout; defek; tekort; ~**ive** (a) gebrekkig, onklaar, defek

defect' (v) oorloop (na vyand); afvallig word; ~**or** (n) oorloper, afvallige

defence' verdediging; verweer; ~ **for'ce** weer-mag; ~**less** weerloos, onbeskerm

defend' (v) verdedig, beskerm; ~**ant** verdedi-ger; verweerder/aangeklaagde (in hof)

defer' (v) uitstel; onderwerp aan

defi'ant (a) uitdagend, tartend

defi'cient gebrekkig; ontoereikend; *mentally* ~ geestelik gestrem; swaksinnig

def'icit (n) tekort, nadelige saldo (boekhou)

defile' (v) besmet, besoedel

define' bepaal, omskryf, definieer; omlyn

def'inite bepaald. definitief; ~**ly** beslis, op-sluit; ~*ly not!* volstrek nie!

defini'tion definisie, omskrywing

defla'tion deflasie; prysdaling

deform' (v) mismaak, skend, vervorm; ~**ed'** mismaak, wanskape; ~**ity** mismaaktheid, wanstaltigheid

defraud' bedrieg, kul *also* **cheat, con** (v)

defrost' ontvries (van koelkas); ontdooi (van voedsel)

defu'se (v) ontlont (krisis)

defy' (v) uitdaag, tart, trotseer *also* **confront'**

degen'erate (v) ontaard, versleg; verbaster

degrade' verneder, verlaag; degradeer

degra'ding (a) vernederend *also* **humil'iating**

degree' graad; rang; *to a certain* ~ in sekere mate; **hon'orary** ~ eregraad; ~ **course** graadkursus

dehyd'rate (v) ontwater, dehidreer

deject' ontmoedig; ~**ed** neerslagtig, bedruk

delay' (n) uitstel, oponthoud; *without* ~; onmiddellik/oombliklik; (v) uitstel; ver-traag; versuim; talm; weifel

del'egate (n) afgevaardigde, gevolmagtigde; kursusganger, kongresganger; (v) afvaardig; delegeer (pligte)

delega'tion afvaardiging, deputasie; ~ **of po'wers** delegering van magte/bevoegdhede

delete' skrap; uitkrap, uitwis; ~ *which is not applicable* skrap waar nodig

delib'erate (v) beraadslaag; (a) opsetlik; ~**ly** opsetlik, aspres/ekspres *also* **inten'tional**

delibera'tion oorlegpleging, beraadslaging

del'icacy keurigheid; ~**cies** lekkerny; ver-snapering

del'icate fyn; broos; tinger *also* **frail**; delikaat

delicates'sen delikatesse, fynkos

deli'cious (a) heerlik, verruklik; smaaklik

delight' (n) genoeë, genot, behae; (v) verheug, behaag; verruk; ~**ed** verruk, bly, opgetoë; ~*ed with* ingenome met; ~**ful** genotvol, genoeglik

delin'quency misdaad, vergryp; **ju'venile** ~ jeugwangedrag, jeugmisdadigheid

delin'quent (n) kwaaddoener, oortreder, skul-dige; **ju'venile** ~ jeugoortreder

delir'ious ylhoofdig, deliries

deliv'er aflewer; bevry; oorlewer

deliv'ery ..ries aflewering; lewering; verlos= sing; *cash on* ~ kontant by aflewering; ~ **van** bestelwa, bakkie

demand' (n) vraag; aanvraag; ~ *for* vraag na; *supply and* ~ vraag en aanbod; (v) vra; eis

dem'i half; ~**john** karba, mandjiefles

demise' (n) (af)sterwe, oorlyde; bemaking

demist'er (n) ontwasemer

demobilisa'tion demobilisasie

democ'racy ..cies volksregering, demokrasie

democrat'ic demokraties

demol'ish (v) afbreek, sloop; ~**er** sloper

dem'on bose gees, duiwel, demon/demoon

dem'onstrate bewys, uitlê; betoog (politiek); demonstreer (nuwe masjien)

demonstra'tion betoging, protesoptog (poli= tiek) *also* **dem'o**; demonstrasie

dem'onstrator/dem'o betoger (mens)

demure' (a) stemmig, sedig, preuts *also* **coy**

demur'rage lêgeld, staangeld

den (n) lêplek; hool, hol

de'nim denim; ~**s** denims, slenterdrag

denomina'tion benaming; kerkverband; klas; soort; ~**al** kerklik

denom'inator noemer

denounce' (v) veroordeel, afkeur; betig

dense (a) dig, dik; suf, dom, toe; ~**ly pop'ulat= ed** digbevolk

dent (n) duik; kerf, kepie; (v) duik, inkeep

den'tal tand=; ~ **floss** tandegare, tandevlos; ~ **sur'geon** tandarts

dentist tandarts

den'ture(s) (kuns)gebit, vals tande; winkel= tande (idiom.)

deny' (v) ontken; weerspreek *also* **contradict'**; misgun; ontsê

deo'dorant reukweerder, deodorant

depart' vertrek, verlaat; afwyk van; sterf; ~**ment** departement, afdeling; ~**ment of educa'tion** onderwysdepartement

depar'ture vertrek, trek; afsterwe

depend' (v) afhang; vertrou; ~ *upon* reken op (iemand); ~**able** vertroubaar/betroubaar; ~**ant** (n) afhanklike (mens); ~**ent** (a) afhank= lik; ~*ing on* afhangende van; na gelang van

deploy' (v) ontplooi, versprei; ~ *troops* troepe ontplooi

deport' (v) deporteer; (jou) gedra; ~**a'tion** verbanning, deportasie; ~**ment** houding, gedrag; houdingsleer (vak)

depos'it (n) storting, deposito; afsetting

(geol.); (v) stort, deponeer

depos'it book bankboek(ie); depositoboek

depos'itor belegger (mens); deposant (bank)

depos'it slip inlegstrokie

dep'ot bêreplek, opslagplek; depot

depre'ciate (v) depresieer; in waarde vermin= der; minag

deprecia'tion depresiasie (boekhou); waarde= vermindering

depress' (v) (ter)neerdruk; verneder; ~**ed** (a) neerslagtig, bedruk; ~**ion** neerslagtigheid; depressie, slapte (sake); insinking

deprive' ontneem; ontroof; ~**ed child** ver= waarloosde kind; ~**d/disadvan'taged com= mu'nity** agtergeblewe gemeenskap

depth diepte; diepsinnigheid, *a study in* ~ dieptestudie; ~ **charge** dieptebom

deputa'tion afvaardiging, deputasie

dep'uty ..ties plaasvervanger; adjunk=; ~ **may'or** onderburgemeester; ~ **pres'ident** adjunkpresident

derail' ontspoor; ~**ment** ontsporing

deregula'tion (n) deregulering

de'relict (n) verlate skip; (a) verlate, opgegee, prysgegee

deriva'tion afleiding, afkoms/herkoms

derive' (v) aflei, afstam; ontleen aan

dermatol'ogist huidarts, dermatoloog

derog'atory kleinerend, neerhalend; ~ **re= marks'** kwetsende aanmerkings

der'rick boortoring; hyskraan, hysbalk

descend' (v) (af)daal; afstam; (n) ~**ant** af= stammeling, nasaat (mens)

descent' (n) (neer)daling; afkoms; afdraand

describe' beskryf, omskryf, aandui

descrip'tion beskrywing; aard, klas

des'ecrate (v) ontheilig; ontwy (grafte)

des'ert[1] (n) woestyn; woesteny

desert'[2] (n) verdienste; (pl) verdiende loon; *get one's* ~**s** jou verdiende loon kry

desert'[3] (v) verlaat, wegloop, (weg)dros; ~**er** droster

deserve' verdien; ~**d'ly** na verdienste

deserv'ing (a) verdienstelik

design' (n) ontwerp, plan; voorneme; (v) ontwerp, skets; beoog

des'ignate aanwys; bestem; noem; **des'igna= tory title/ini'tials** kenletters

designa'tion (n) betiteling; ampsbenaming

design'er ontwerper; sketstekenaar

desir'able (a) wenslik; begeerlik

desire' (n) begeerte, verlange, wens; (v)

begeer, verlang, wens; *leave much to be* ∼d veel te wense oorlaat

desk lessenaar, skryftafel; skoolbank; ∼**top pub'lishing (DTP)** tafeltopdrukwerk, DTP

des'olate (a) verlate, eensaam, troosteloos

despair' (n) wanhoop; vertwyfeling; (v) wan= hoop, moed opgee/verloor

despatch *see* **dispatch**

des'perate (a) wanhopig; radeloos, desperaat

despera'tion wanhoop, vertwyfeling, rade= loosheid; *in* ∼ uit wanhoop

despic'able (a) veragtelik, laag, gemeen

despise' verag, verfoei

despite' (prep) nieteenstaande, ondanks/ongeag

despond' (v) wanhoop; ∼**ent** (a) moedeloos

des'pot despoot, dwingeland, tiran (mens)

des'potism despotisme, dwingelandy

dessert' (n) nagereg, dessert

destina'tion (n) bestemming

des'tiny (nood)lot; bestemming, voorland

des'titute (a) behoeftig, arm *also* **poor**

destroy' verniel, vernietig; verdelg

destruc'tion vernietiging, verwoesting

destruc'tive vernielend, afbrekend; ∼ **crit'i= cism** afbrekende/neerhalende kritiek

detach' losmaak, afsonder

de'tail (n) besonderheid, detail; *further* ∼*s* meer besonderhede; omstandigheid; uiteen= setting; *in* ∼ breedvoerig

detail' (v) omstandig vertel, opsom, aanwys/ aansê

de'tailed breedvoerig, uitvoerig; ∼ **report'** uitvoerige verslag

detain' aanhou, gevange hou; terughou; ∼**ee** aangehoudene (mens)

detect' (v) uitvind, betrap, ontdek; ∼**ive** speur= der; ∼**or** ontdekker; opspoorder; verklikker

deten'tion aanhouding, gevangehouding; de= tensie; skoolbly; ∼ *without trial* aanhouding sonder verhoor

deter'gent (n) suiweringsmiddel, detergent

deter'iorate ontaard; agteruitgaan; versleg

determina'tion (n) bepaling, beslissing; vas= beradenheid, beslistheid, wilskrag

deter'mine bepaal, besluit; beslis; eindig

deter'mined (a) vasberade (van aard); vas= beslote (om iets te doen)

dete'rrent (n) afskrikmiddel

detest' (v) verfoei, verafsku; ∼**able** verfoeilik

de'tour ompad, (pad)verlegging; omweg

detrimen'tal (a) nadelig, skadelik

deuce[1] twee; gelykop (tennis)

deuce[2] joos, duiwel; drommel; *what the* ∼ ? wat die/de drommel?

deval'uate (v) devalueer, in waarde verminder

devasta'tion verwoesting

devel'op (v) ontwikkel, ontvou, ontplooi; ∼**ed coun'tries** ontwikkelde lande; ∼**ing coun'= tries** ontwikkelende lande; ∼**er** ontwikke= laar (mens/toestel); ∼**ment** ontwikkeling

dev'iate afwyk, afdwaal; verlê

devia'tion verlegging (pad); afwyking; syspoor

device' (n) oogmerk; leus(e); ontwerp, uitvind= sel, apparaat; lis

dev'il duiwel; *between the* ∼ *and the deep sea* tussen twee vure; ∼**ish** duiwels; ∼**ry** dui= welskunste; slegtigheid; terglus; ∼**'s bones** dobbelstene; ∼ **wor'ship** duiwelaanbidding

devote' (toe)wy; oorlewer; ∼ *attention to* aandag skenk/gee aan; ∼**d** toegewy, toege= neë, geheg; verslaaf: *a* ∼*d husband* 'n toegewyde eggenoot/man

devo'tion toewyding; vroomheid *also* **pie'ty**; (pl) godsdiensoefening, gebede

devour' verslind, verteer

devout' (a) vroom, godsdienstig *also* **pi'ous**

dew (n) dou; (v) dou; ∼**drop** doudruppel

diabet'ic (n) suikersiektelyer (mens)

diabol'ic duiwelagtig, duiwels

diae'resis deelteken (¨)

di'agnose (v) diagnoseer, vasstel

diag'onal (a) diagonaal, oorhoeks

di'agram (n) figuur, skets, tekening, diagram

di'al (n) sonwyser *also* **sun'dial**; wyserplaat; (v) skakel (foon); ∼**ling tone** skakeltoon

di'alect (n) dialek, tongval, streekspraak

di'alogue tweegesprek; dialoog

diam'eter middellyn, deursnee

di'amond diamant; ∼**s** ruitens (kaartspel)

diarrhoe'a maagwerking, appelkoossiekte, diar= ree; **ver'bal** ∼ woordskittery (kru)

di'ary dagboek *diaries*

dice (n) dobbelstene; (v) dobbel; uitdaag

dictate' (v) dikteer; gebied; voorskryf

dictat'or diktator; ∼**ship** diktatuur

dic'tion (n) voordrag; styl, diksie

dic'tionary . .ries woordeboek/leksikon

didac'tic (a) didakties, lerend

die[1] (n) matrys; muntstempel; *the* ∼ *is cast* die besluit is (onherroeplik) geneem

die[2] (v) sterf, doodgaan; sneuwel; vrek (diere)

diet (n) dieet; leefreël; **slim'ming** ∼ verslan= kingsdieet

dietic'ian dieetkundige, voedselkundige (mens)

diff'er verskil; *I beg to* ~ ek is dit nie daarmee eens nie; moenie glo nie

diff'erence (n) verskil, onderskeid

diff'erent verskillend, onderskeie

diff'icult moeilik, swaar; ~**y** moeilikheid, moeite, haakplek; beswaar

diff'ident (a) verleë, skaam *also* **shy**; nederig

dig (n) stoot; (v) graaf/grawe, grou, delf, spit

di'gest¹ (n) opsomming, oorsig; keurblad

digest'² (v) verteer; oordink; verwerk; ~**ion** spysvertering *see* **in'digestion**

digg'er delwer (mens)

digg'ings delwery

di'git vinger; toon; syfer; **five** ~**s** vyfsyfer

di'gital (a) vinger-; toon-; syfer-; ~ **sound system** digitale klankstelsel; ~ **watch** syfer-horlosie, digitale horlosie

dig'nified (a) waardig, deftig; verhewe

dig'nitary ..ries hooggeplaaste, (hoog)waar-digheidbekleër, dignitaris (mens)

dig'nity waardigheid, deftigheid; *beneath one's* ~ benede jou waardigheid

digs blyplek, losies *also* **board, dig'gings** (sl)

dike damwal, dyk; gang (geol.)

dilap'idated (a) bouvallig, vervalle

dilemm'a verknorsing, penarie, dilemma

dilettan'te ..ti dilettant, leek, amateur

dil'igent (a) ywerig, fluks, vlytig

dill dille, vinkel

dilute' (v) verdun, verslap, verwater

dim (v) demp; benewel; verdonker; ~ *head-lights* hoofligte domp; (a) dof, skemerig; suf; wasig

dimen'sion afmeting, grootte, dimensie

dimin'ish verminder, verklein

dimin'utive (n) verkleinwoord; (a) klein; ver-kleining-; ~ **form** verkleinvorm

dim'ple (wang)kuiltjie

din (n) geraas, lawaai; (v) raas, baljaar

dingh'y rubberbootjie, opblaasbootjie

din'ing: ~ **car** eetsalon, eetwa; ~ **room** eet-kamer

dinn'er (n) aandete (meestal) *also* **sup'per**; middagete (soms) *also* **lunch**; dinee (for-meel); ~ **jack'et** aandbaadjie; ~ **ser'vice/**~ **set** eetservies

dip (n) dip; indompeling; duik; (v) dip (vee); indompel; *take a* ~ in die water spring

diphther'ia witseerkeel, difterie

diph'thong tweeklank, diftong

diplo'ma -s diploma, sertifikaat; getuigskrif

diplom'acy diplomasie; behendigheid, takt

dip'lomat diplomaat

diplomat'ic diplomaties *also* **tact'ful**; oulik

direct'¹ (v) rig; bestuur; adresseer; vestig op (aandag); beveel; aanstuur

di'rect'² (a) regstreeks, direk; dadelik; ~ **hit** voltreffer; ~ **speech** direkte rede

direc'tion (n) rigting; leiding; bevel; direksie

direct'or direkteur; ~**-general directors-gen-eral** direkteur-generaal/hoofdirekteur; ~**y** adresboek

dir'igible (n) bestuurbare lugballon, lugskip *also* **air'ship**; (a) bestuurbaar

dirt (n) vuilgoed, vuilis; (v) vuil maak, be-smeer; ~**box** vullisbak *also* **trash can**; ~**-cheap** spotgoedkoop; ~**track** asbaan

dirt'y (v) bevuil, bemors, besmeer; (a) vieslik; morsig, smerig; gemeen

disabil'ity gebrek; ongeskiktheid (vir werk)

disa'ble onbekwaam maak; buite geveg stel; vermink; ~**d** gestrem; gebreklik; ~**d per'-son** (liggaamlik) gestremde; ~**d sol'dier** in-valide/gewonde soldaat

disadvan'tage nadeel; skade; verlies; ~**d commu'nity** agtergeblewe/onderbevoorreg-te gemeenskap *also* **depri'ved commu'nity**

disagree' nie ooreenstem nie, verskil; vassit (oor iets); *it* ~*s with me* dit akkordeer nie met my nie; ~**able** onaangenaam *also* **un-plea'sant**; ~**ment** verskil, onenigheid

disappear' verdwyn, wegraak; ~**ance** ver-dwyning

disappoint' teleurstel; verydel; ~**ed** teleurge-stel(d); ~**ment** teleurstelling

disapprove' (v) afkeur, verwerp *also* **reject'**

disarm' ontwapen; ~**ament** ontwapening

disas'ter (n) ramp, ongeluk, onheil; ~ **a'rea** rampgebied; ~ **fund** rampfonds

disas'trous (a) noodlottig, rampspoedig

disburse' voorskiet; uitbetaal; ~**ment** voor-skot, uitbetaling; uitgawe, onkoste

disc skyf; rekenaarskyf; werpskyf; ~ **drive** skyfaandrywer; ~ **jock'ey** platejoggie

discard' (v) afdank; verwerp; weggooi

discharge' (n) ontslag; kwytskelding; betaling; (v) ontslaan; afdank; vervul (plig); betaal, delg (skuld)

disci'ple leerling, volgeling, dissipel (mens)

disciplinar'ian tugmeester, ordehouer

dis'ciplinary tug-, dissiplinêr-; ~ **commit'tee** tugkomitee

dis'cipline (n) tug, dissipline; (v) tugtig

disclose' (v) onthul, openbaar (maak), blootlê

disconnect' diskonnekteer; loskoppel
discontin'ue eindig/beëindig, ophou, staak
dis'cord (n) wanklank; tweedrag, onvrede; **ap'ple of** ~ twisappel
discotheque diskoteek; **dis'co dan'cing** dis= kodans
dis'count (n) korting; afslag, diskonto; *at a* ~ teen afslag; ~ **store** afslagwinkel
discou'rage (v) ontmoedig, afraai; afskrik
discourt'eous (a) onmanierlik; onbeleef
disco'ver ontdek, uitvind; onthul; ~y ontdek= king
discreet' oordeelkundig; beskeie; tak(t)vol
discrep'ancy ..cies verskil, teenstrydigheid; wanverhouding
discre'tion diskresie, oorleg, goeddunke; *use one's* ~ na goeddunke handel
discrim'inate (v) onderskei, diskrimineer
discrim'inating (a) skerpsinnig, onderskeidend *also* **discer'ning**
discrimina'tion diskriminasie; benadeling
dis'cus -es, disci werpskyf, diskus
discuss' bespreek; beraadslaag; ~**ion** samespre= king(s), bespreking, diskussie; ~**ion group** besprekingsgroep, diskussiegroep, gonsgroep
disease' siekte, kwaal *also* **ill'ness, ail'ment**
disgrace' (n) skande, ongenade; (v) te skande maak; ~**ful** skandelik/skandalig
disguise' (n) vermomming, masker; voor= wendsel; *a blessing in* ~ 'n bedekte seën; *in* ~ vermom; (v) vermom; verbloem
disgust' (n) afkeer, walging, teensin; *be* ~*ed with* walg van; ~**ing** walglik, stuitlik
dish (n) skottel; gereg; (pl) skottelgoed; (v) opskep; ~**cloth** vadoek
dishon'est oneerlik, bedrieglik *also* **croo'ked**; ~**y** oneerlikheid, bedrog
dishon'our (n) oneer, skande; (v) onteer; ~ *a cheque* 'n tjek dishonoreer
dish'washer opwasser, skottelgoedwasser
disinfect' ontsmet; ~**ant** ontsmetmiddel; ~**ion** ontsmetting
disinforma'tion (n) waninligting/fopinligting; disinformasie
disin'tegrate ontbind; verval; disintegreer, verbrokkel
disin'terested belangeloos; onpartydig
disket'te (n) disket, slapskyf *also* **flop'py disc**
dislike' (n) afkeer, teensin; (v) 'n afkeer hê van
dis'locate (v) ontwrig; verskuif, verstuit
disloy'al ontrou, dislojaal
dis'mal (a) somber, treurig, droewig, aaklig

disman'tle afbreek (stellasie); sloop
dismay' (n) skrik, ontsteltenis; (v) bang maak; ontmoedig; onthuts; ~**ed** verslae
dismiss' (v) ontslaan, afdank; verdaag (mil.); ~**al** ontslag, afdanking
dismount' afklim, afstyg (van perd)
disobe'dience (n) ongehoorsaamheid
disobe'dient (a) ongehoorsaam
disord'er (n) wanorde, verwarring; oproer; ongesteldheid; ~**ly** wanordelik
dispa'rity ongelykheid, verskil, wanbalans
dispa'ssionate (a) bedaard, kalm, nugter
dispatch'/despatch' (n) afsending, versending; (v) versend; afstuur; doodmaak; ~ **ri'der** rapportryer
dispen'sary ..ries mengapteek/resepteering
dispensa'tion bedeling; vrystelling; stelsel; **new** ~ nuwe bedeling
dispense' uitdeel; ~ *with* daarsonder klaarkom; ~**r** uitdeler (apparaat); toediener/resepteur (mens); **dispen'sable** weggooibaar; **dispen'= sing doc'tor** resepterende dokter
disperse' (v) verstrooi/versprei; uiteenjaag
displace' verplaas; vervang; ~**d per'son** ont= wortelde/ontheemde persoon
display' (n) uitstalling; vertoning; (v) tentoon= stel, vertoon; ~ **ca'binet/case** (ver)toonkas; ~ **di'ving** sierduik; ~ **room** toonlokaal *also* **show'room**; ~ **win'dow** toonvenster
dispos'al beskikking, skikking, reëling, *at your* ~ tot u beskikking
dispose' beskik, reël, orden; ~ *of* vervreem, verkoop; **dispo'sable** weggooibaar (inspuit= naald); ~**d'** geneig, gestem
disposi'tion aard, gesindheid; gesteldheid
dispute' (n) twis; geskil, dispuut; *the matter in* ~ die geskilpunt; *settle the* ~ die geskil besleg/bylê; (v) betwis; redetwis; ~**d** (a) betwis
disqualifica'tion ongeskiktheid, diskwalifika= sie; uitsluiting
disqual'ify diskwalifiseer; ongeskik verklaar; uit= sluit
disregard' (n) veron(t)agsaming; (v) veron(t)= agsaam *also* **igno're**; geringskat
disrep'utable berug; ~ **char'acter** ongure vent (mens)
disrepute' (n) skande, berugtheid; diskrediet, oneer; *fall into* ~ 'n slegte naam kry
disrespect' (n) oneerbiedigheid, disrespek
disrupt' ontwrig; verbrokkel; ~ *the class* die klas ontwrig

dissatisfac'tion ontevredenheid
dissect' dissekteer; ontleed
dissent' verskil van opinie; ~er afgeskeidene, andersgesinde; ~ing vote teenstem
disserta'tion verhandeling, dissertasie, proef= skrif, tesis *also* **the'sis, trea'tise**
dissolve' (v) oplos; ontbind; ~ *a partnership* 'n vennootskap ontbind
dissuade' (v) afraai, afskrik *see* **persuade'**
dis'tance (n) afstand, distansie; (v) distansieer; ~ **educa'tion/tea'ching** afstandonderrig
dis'tant ver/vêr weg; afgeleë; uit die hoogte
distaste' teensin, walging; ~**ful** (a) onsmaak= lik, afstootlik
distil' (v) distilleer, stook
distinct' onderskeie; bepaald; eie
distinc'tion (n) onderskeiding/lof; aansien; eer= betoon; *with* ~ met onderskeiding/lof
distin'guish (v) onderskei; ~**ed** beroemd, ver= naam; *our* ~*ed guests* ons geëerde/vername/ uitgelese gaste
distort' verdraai; verwring; ~**ion** verdraaiing; ~**ionist** lyfwringer, slangmens
distract' aftrek; aflei; ~**ed** afgetrokke
distress' (n) ellende; nood; *a damsel in* ~ 'n nooientjie in nood; ~**ed** behoeftig; ~ **call** noodroep; ~ **sig'nal** noodsein; ~ **syn'drome** noodsindroom
distrib'ute (v) uitdeel, verdeel, versprei
distribu'tion verspreiding, distribusie
distrib'utor (n) verspreider (van ware); vonk= verdeler (motor)
dis'trict distrik; streek, gebied; ~ **sur'geon** distriksgeneesheer
distrust' (n) wantroue; argwaan; (v) wantrou; verdink
disturb' (v) steur/stoor (iem.); versteur; ~**ance** versteuring; opskudding; (pl) onluste
ditch (n) -es sloot, voor; (v) oorboord gooi
dith'er (v) weifel, talm *also* **daw'dle**; bibber, beef/bewe
ditt'y ditties liedjie, deuntjie
divan' sofa, divan, rusbank
dive (n) duik; (v) duik; ~ **bom'ber** duikbom= werper; ~**r** duiker (mens)
diver'sify (v) afwisselend maak; verander, wysig, diversifeer
divers'ity verskeidenheid, verskil; diversiteit; ~ *of opinion* mening(s)verskil
divert' (v) aflei; wegkeer; verlê (pad)
divide (v) deel, verdeel; skei
divid'ed (ver)deel, afgeskei; onenig

div'idend dividend; deeltal; *pay a* ~ 'n divi= dend uitbetaal; **in'terim** ~ tussendividend
divine' (v) voorspel; (a) goddelik; verruklik; ~**r** waarsêer; waterwyser; ~ **ser'vice** ere= diens (in kerk), huisgodsdiens
divin'ing rod (n) wiggelroede, waterstok
divin'ity (n) godheid; godgeleerdheid
divi'sion deling; verdeling; afdeling; verdeeld= heid; divisie (leër); ~ **sum** deelsom
divorce' (n) egskeiding; ~**e'** geskeide vrou/ persoon
divulge' (v) onthul, openbaar *also* **disclo'se**
dizz'y duiselig, lighoofdig *also* **gid'dy**
do (v) **did, done** doen, maak, verrig; ~ *for* deug vir; *how* ~ *you* ~? hoe gaan dit?; ~ *mischief* kattekwaad aanrig
dock (n) skeepsdok; getuiebank (in hof)
dock'et dossier; faktuur; strook/strokie
dock'yard skeepswerf
doc'tor (n) dokter, geneesheer; arts; doktor (in die regte, lettere, ens.); (v) medies behandel, dokter; opknap
doc'torate (n) doktoraat; (v) doktoreer
doc'trine leer, leerstelling, doktrine
doc'ument (n) dokument, geskrif, bewysstuk; (v) dokumenteer
documen'tary dokumentêr; ~ **film** dokumen= têre film, feitefilm
dodge (v) ontwyk; ontglip, uitoorlê; ~**r** ont= duiker; draaijakkels
dog (n) hond; *let sleeping* ~*s lie* moenie sla= pende honde wakker maak nie; *top* ~ uit= blinker, bobaas; ~**fight** hondegeveg; ~**ged** (a) stuurs, koppig; vasberade *also* **deter'mined**
dog'gybag (n) brakkiesakkie (idiom.)
dog'kennel hondehok; (pl) hondehotel, woe= fietuiste (idiom.)
dog'ma leerstuk, dogma *also* **doc'trine**
doil'y doilies melklappie, kraaldoekie, doilie
do'ing doen, werk, doenigheid; ~**s** besigheid, bedryf; gedrag; doenigheid
dol'drums (streke van) windstilte
doll (n) (speel)pop
dol'phin dolfyn
domain' gebied; domein; heerskappy
dome koepel, dom
domes'tic (n) huishulp; (a) huislik, huishoude= lik; binnelands; ~ **an'imal** huisdier; ~ **scien'ce** huishoudkunde; ~ **ser'vant** huis= hulp/huisbediende; ~ **tra'de** binnelandse handel
dom'icile (n) woonplek, verblyf; (v) woon

dom'inant (a) (oor)heersend; dominant
dom'inate (v) heers; oorheers; domineer
don (n) don, hoof; **D**~ **Ju'an** pierewaaier; rokjagter, opperste vryer *also* **wo'maniser**
dona'te (v) skenk, gee; bydra
dona'tion skenking, donasie *also* **gift**
done (a) gedaan; gekook, gaar; klaar
don'ga **-s** spoelsloot, donga
don'key **-s** donkie, esel; domkop; *for* ~'s *years* jare lank, van toeka se dae af
don'or gewer; skenker, donateur (mens)
don't = do not moenie
doom (n) noodlot; ondergang; (v) verdoem; *prophet of* ~ doemprofeet
door deur, ingang; ~**bell** deurklok(kie); ~**kee'per/man** portier, deurwagter
dope (n) dwelmmiddel; toorgoed, doepa; (v) bedwelm; opkikker
dorm'itory **..ries** slaapsaal, slaapvertrek
dose (n) dosis; (v) doseer, medisyne ingee, dokter; **hoos'ter** ~ skraagdosis
doss'ier (n) dossier, lêer; strafregister
dot (n) punt, stippel; stip; (v) stippel; ~**ted line** stippellyn; stippelstreep (pad)
dott'y gestippel; versprei; suf, onnosel
dou'ble (n) duplikaat; dubbelganger; (pl) dubbelspel; (v) verdubbel; (a) dubbel; twee= voudig; ~ **stan'dards** dubbele standaarde/ maatstawwe; ~**-barrel** dubbelloop (ge= weer); ~**-fa'ced** huigelagtig, vals; ~**sto'rey** dubbelverdieping(huis)
doub'let doeblet; onderkleed
doubt (n) twyfel; argwaan; *give the benefit of the* ~ die voordeel van die twyfel gee; *be= yond a* ~/*no* ~/*without* ~ ongewyfeld; (v) twyfel, weifel; ~**ful** twyfelagtig, onseker; ~**less** ongetwyfeld
dough (n) deeg; ~**nut** oliebol; stormjaer
dour (a) streng, stug, stroef; hardnekkig
dove duif; ~**tail** (n) swaelstert(voeg)
down[1] (n) dons; melkbaard
down[2] (n) teenslag; *ups and* ~s wederwaardig= hede; (v) neergooi; neerslaan; ~ *tools* staak; (a) afdraand; neerslagtig; (adv) ondertoe; *knock* ~ platslaan; omry; *run* ~ inhaal; sleg maak; omry; ~**cast** neerslagtig, mismoedig; ~**fall** instorting, ondergang; ~**hear'ted** neer= slagtig, bedruk; ~**hill** afdraand; bergaf; ~**load** (v) aflaai (rek.); ~**pipe** afvoerpyp; ~**pour** stortbui, stortreën; ~**right** puur; gewoonweg; *a* ~*right lie* 'n onbeskaamde leuen; ~**town** sakekern *also* **CBD**

dowr'y **..ries** bruidskat; talent
do'yen doyen, oudste lid, nestor (mens)
doze (n) dutjie; (v) sluimer, dut, dommel
do'zen dosyn; **ba'ker's** ~ dertien
drab (a) vaal, ligbruin; saai, eentonig
draft (n) skets, plan; ontwerp; (v) ontwerp; opstel; ~ **bill** konsepwetsontwerp; ~ **consti= tu'tion** konsepgrondwet; ~ **legisla'tion** kon= sepwetgewing
drag (n) rem; sleepnet; (v) sleep; sleur; talm; ~ **queen** fopdosser (manlike transvestiet) *also* **cross-dresser**; ~ **ra'cing** versnelrenne; ~**ster** renstel
drag'on (n) draak
drain (n) riool; (v) dreineer; ~**age** dreinering, riolering *also* **se'werage**
drake (n) mannetjieseend
dra'ma **-s** toneelstuk, drama
dramat'ic (a) dramaties
dra'ma: ~**tist** dramaskrywer; toneeldigter; dramaturg; ~**tise** (v) dramatiseer
dras'tic drasties, kragtig *also* **rad'ical**
draught (n) trek; teug, sluk; drankie; ~ **beer** vatbier; ~ **horse** trekperd; ~**s** dambord/ damspel; ~**y** trekkerig/togtig
draw (n) trek; gelykopspel; loot/loting (sport); skyfie; skuifie (rook); (v) trek, sleep; teken, gelykop speel; onbeslis eindig (krieket); trek (wissel); ~ *comparisons* vergelykings tref; ~ *level* kop aan kop; ~**back** nadeel; ~**brid'ge** ophaalbrug; ~**er** trekker (van tjek); tekenaar; laaitjie; ~**ers** onderbroek; **chest of** ~**ers** spieëlkas, laaikas
draw'ing tekening, skets; ~ **board** tekenbord; ~ **pin** duimspyker(tjie); ~ **room** sitkamer
drawn getrek; onbeslis (geëindig); gelykop
dread (n) skrik, vrees, ontsetting; (v) vrees; ~**ful** verskriklik, ontsettend *also* **aw'ful**
dream (n) droom; hersenskim; (v) droom; ~**er** dromer (mens); ~**y** dromerig, vaak
drear'y (a) aaklig, somber *also* **dis'mal, gloo'my**
dredge (n) sleepnet; baggermasjien; (v) (uit)= bagger; ~**r** baggerboot
drench (v) drenk; deurweek; (a) ~**ed** sopnat
dress (n) **-es** rok; tabberd; (v) aantrek; afrig; dresseer (dier); verbind (wond); kap (klip); ~**ed chick'en** bevrore hoender; ~ **cir'cle** voorbalkon; ~**coat** manel *also* **tail'coat**
dress'er kombuiskas, spenskas
dress'ing (n) toebereiding, verband; loesing; ~ **gown** kamerjas; ~ **room** kleedkamer; ~ **table** spieëltafel

dress: ~**maker** kleremaakster; modiste; ~ **rehear'sal** kleedrepetisie; ~ **suit** aandpak; ~**y** keurig gekleed; smaakvol, swierig

drib'ble (n) druppel; motreën; (v) dribbel (voetbal); druppel; kwyl

drift (n) neiging, tendens *also* **trend**; drif (spruit); (v) wegdryf; aanspoel; rondswalk

drill (n) boor; (v) dril, oefen; boor

drink (n) drank, sopie; *stand a* ~ (op) 'n glasie trakteer; (v) drink; ~ *to* drink op; ~**er** drinker, dronklap; ~**ing par'ty** drinkparty

drip (n) gedrup; drup (med.); jandooi (mens); (v) drup, lek; ~**ping** (n) braaivet; druipvet; lek: ~**ping wet** papnat, sopnat

drive (n) ritjie; oprypad; rylaan; dryfhou (gholf); dryfkrag, stukrag; klopjag; (v) dryf, dwing; bestuur (motor), dryf (lorrie); ~ *to despair* tot wanhoop bring

drive'-in inrit; ~ **bank** inrybank; ~ **bi'oscope/** ~ **the'atre** inrybioskoop, veldfliek

dri'ver drywer; masjinis; bestuurder (motor); ~'**s licence** rybewys

dri'veway (op)rylaan, oprit/inrit (by huis)

dri'ving range dryfbaan/dryfbof (gholf)

driz'zle (n) motreën(tjie), stuifreën

drone (n) hommel, waterdraerby; luiaard; (v) gons, brom, zoem; ~**fly** brommer

droop (v) neerhang, kwyn; sink; ~**ing shoul'**= **ders** hangskouers

drop (n) druppel; skepskop; val; (v) drup; neerval, ophou; neerlaat; daal; ~ *a hint* 'n wenk gee; ~ *a line* 'n brief skryf; ~**kick** skepskop; ~**out** skoolstaker, uitsakker; mis= lukkeling; ~**per** stutpaaltjie, spar (vir draad= heining); ~**shot** valhou (tennis)

drop'sy watersug, water (siekte)

drought (n) droogte; (a) ~**-strick'en** droogte= geteister

drown (v) verdrink (mens); versuip (dier)

drow'sy (a) slaperig; vaak, soeserig, lomerig

drudge (n) slaaf, werkesel; (v) swoeg, afsloof, ploeter; ~**ry** sleurwerk

drug (n) geneesmiddel, medikasie (medies); dwelmmiddel, verslaafmiddel, dwelms; (v) verdoof; bedwelm; ~ **abu'se** dwelmmisbruik; ~ **ad'dict** dwelmslaaf; ~ **addic'tion** dwelm= verslawing; ~ **depen'dence** dwelmafhanklik= heid; ~**gist** drogis, apteker; ~**lord** dwelm= baas; ~ **ped'lar/pus'her** dwelmsmous; ~ **traff'icker** dwelmhandelaar (mens)

drum (n) tamboer, trom; konka, drom; ~ **majorette'** trompoppie, tamboernooi; ~**mer**

tamboerslaner

drunk (a) dronk, besope, beskonke, gekoring, getier, hoenderkop *also* **tip'sy**; ~**ard** dronk= aard, dronklap; ~**(en) dri'ving** dronkbestuur

dry (v) verdroog; opdroog; (a) droog, dor; ~**clea'ner** droogskoonmaker; ~**dock** droog= dok; ~ **rot** molm; houtswam

du'al (n) tweevoud, tweetal; (a) tweeledig; ~**-me'dium** dubbelmedium

dub (v) tot ridder slaan; verhef tot; noem; smeer; oorklank (TV); ~**bin** leervet; ~**bing** oorklanking (TV)

du'bious (a) twyfelagtig; onseker *also* **doubt'ful**

duch'ess -es hertogin

duck (n) (eend)voël; nul (krieket); liefling; (v) duik; koe(t)s *also* **dod'ge**; ~**ling** eendjie; ~**tail** eendstert

duct pyp, geleibuis; kanaal; ~**ile** rekbaar

dud (n) toiing, flenter; domkop (mens); (a) dom; nikswerd, onbruikbaar

due (a) skuldig, betaalbaar; *in* ~ *course* met= tertyd; ~ *date* vervaldatum; *money* ~ *to him* geld aan hom verskuldig

du'el (n) tweegeveg, duel; (v) duelleer

duet' duet; paar

dug (v) *see* **dig;** ~**-out** uitgrawing; boomkano; skuilplek

duke hertog

dull (v) dof maak; (a) dom; toe (mens); saai, eentonig; onnosel; ~**-wit'ted** dom

du'ly behoorlik, noukeurig; op tyd; ~ **com= ple'ted** behoorlik ingevul/voltooi

dumb stom; stemloos; stilswygend; *don't be so* ~ moenie so toe wees nie; ~**found** (v) dronkslaan, verstom, oorbluf; ~ **show** ge= barespel

dumm'y (n) **dummies** fopspeen; figurant; (a) nagemaak; (v) pypkan (rugby)

dump (n) mynhoop; opslagplek; (v) stort; dump (mark); *no* ~*ing* stort(ing) verbode; ~**ing site** stortterrein

dump'ling kluitjie *also* **dough'boy**

dumps (pl) bedruktheid; *down in the* ~ mis= moedig, op moedverloor se vlakte

dum'py le'vel (n) nivelleerder, bukswaterpas

dune duin

dung (n) mis; ~ **beetle** miskruier

dun'geon (n) kerker, ondergrondse sel

dunk (v) doop (beskuit in koffie)

du'plex (n) dupleks, tweevloerwoning

du'plicate (n) duplikaat, afskrif; *in* ~ in twee= voud; (v) dupliseer

du′rable (a) duursaam
du′ring gedurende, tydens
dusk (n) skemering; (a) skemer, duister
dust (n) stof; gruis; saagsel; (v) afstof; opvee; uitlooi; ~**bin** vullisblik; ~**cov′er** omslag (boek); ~**er** stoffer, stoflap; ~**man** Klaas Vakie; ~ **storm** stofstorm; ~**y** stowwerig
Dutch (n, a) Nederlands, Hollands; *we are going* ~ elkeen betaal vir homself; *Cape* ~ Kaaps-Hollands; ~**man** Hollander, Nederlander
dut′y duties plig; diens; belasting; *be off* ~

van diens af wees; *be on* ~ diens hê; op/aan diens wees
dwarf (n) -s dwerg; (v) verdwerg
dwell (v) woon, bly; ~**ing** woning, woonhuis
dwin′dle (v) inkrimp, verminder, wegkwyn
dye (n) kleursel, kleurstof; (v) kleur, tint
dy′ing (n) dood, (af)sterwe; (a) sterwende
dynam′ics bewegingsleer, dinamika
dy′namite (n) dinamiet, plofstof; (v) opblaas
dys′entery disenterie (siekte by mense); bloedpersie (diere)
dyslex′ia (n) disleksie, leergestremdheid

E

each elk(een), iedereen; ~ *other* mekaar
eag′er (a) gretig, begerig; ywerig, vurig
eag′le arend, adelaar; ~**t** jong arend
ear[1] (n) aar (koring); kop (mielie)
ear[2] (n) oor; *prick up one's* ~*s* die ore spits; ~*a′che* oorpyn; ~**drum** trommelvlies; ~ **guard** oorskut, oorskerm
earl graaf; ~**dom** graafskap
earl′y (a) vroeg, tydig; *at your earliest convenience* spoedig, so gou moontlik; ~ **bird** doutrapper (mens)
ear′mark (n) merk; (v) merk (dier); afsonder; bestem, oormerk, bewillig (fondse)
earn (v) verdien, verwerf
earn′est (n) erns; (a) ernstig, ywerig
earn′ings verdienste, loon, besoldiging
ear′ring oorbel, oorkrabbetjie
earth (n) aarde, grond; (v) aard (elektr.); ~**enwa′re** breekgoed, erdewerk; ~**quake** aardbewing; ~ **trem′or** aardskok/aardtrilling
ease (n) gemak; (v) gerusstel; versag; lenig
eas′el (n) (bord)esel
eas′ily maklik; fluit-fluit, tjop-tjop
east oos; ooste; *the E*~ die Ooste; ~ **coast** ooskus; ~**coast fe′ver** ooskuskoors
Eas′ter Pase, Paasfees; ~ **egg** Paaseier
East′ern Cape (province) Oos-Kaap
eas′y maklik; lig; *take it* ~ dit kalm opneem; ~ **chair** leunstoel
eat ate, eaten eet, opeet; ~**ery** (n) eetplek, restourant
eaves dakrand; ~**drop′per** luistervink (mens)
ebb (n) eb; ~ *and flow* eb en vloed; (v) afloop, eb; verval; ~ *away* wegvloei
eccen′tric (n) sonderling (mens); (a) snaaks,

eksentriek, sonderling *also* **queer/odd**
ec′ho (n) -es weerklank, eggo
eclipse′ (n) verduistering; **lu′nar** ~ maan(s)verduistering; **so′lar** ~ son(s)verduistering
ecol′ogy (n) ekologie, omgewingsleer
econom′ical (a) spaarsaam, ekonomies
econ′omist ekonoom (mens)
econ′omise (v) spaar, bespaar, besuinig
econ′omy (n) ekonomie, staatshuishoudkunde; **..mies** spaarsaamheid; besuiniging
e′co: ~**sys′tem** ekosisteem/ekostelsel; ~**tour′ism** ekotoerisme
ec′stasy verrukking, opgetoënheid, geesdrif, ekstase *also* **rap′ture**
ec′zema uitslag, ekseem; roos
edd′y (n) maalstroom; dwarrelwind
edge (n) kant, rand; skerp kant (mes); *be on* ~ gespanne wees; (v) ~ *on* aanhits
ed′ible eetbaar
ed′ict gebod, edik
ed′ifice imposante gebou/struktuur
ed′it redigeer, persklaar maak
edi′tion uitgawe, edisie *also* **is′sue**; oplaag
ed′itor redakteur (koerant); ~**-in-chief** hoofredakteur; redigeerder (film)
editor′ial (n) hoofartikel; (a) redaksioneel
ed′ucate (v) opvoed; onderwys; grootmaak
educa′tion opvoeding; opleiding, onderwys, onderrig; opvoedkunde; ~**al** opvoedkundig; ~**ist** opvoeder, opvoedkundige (mens)
eel (n) paling, aal (vis)
effect′ (n) uitwerking, gevolg; (pl) bates, besittings; *take* ~ in werking tree; *with* ~ *from 3 March* met ingang 3 Maart; (v) bewerk, teweegbring; ~**ive** doeltreffend, effektief;

~**ual** doeltreffend
effi'ciency (n) doeltreffendheid; bekwaamheid
effi'cient doeltreffend; bekwaam *also* **ca'pable**
eff'igy ..gies afbeeldsel, beeld, beeltenis
eff'luent (n) syrivier; afstroming; uitloop; afwater (fabriek)
eff'ort (n) poging, inspanning, probeerslag; ~**less** speel-speel, sonder inspanning
egg (n) eier; **bad** ~ vrot eier; ·niksnut (mens); **new'laid** ~**s** pasgelegde/vars eiers; **scram'-bled** ~**s** roereiers; ~ **flip** advokaat (drankie); ~**ti'mer** sandloper(tjie)
eg'o ek, ego; eie ek ~**ism** selfsug/egoïsme; ~**ist** egoïs; ~**tis'tical** selfsugtig, egoïsties
eid'er eidereend; ~**down (quilt)** donskombers, verekombers
eight ag(t); ~**een** ag(t)tien; ~**eenth** ag(t)-tiende; ~**h** ag(t)ste; **the E**~**ies** die jare (dekade van) Tagtig, die tagtigerjare; ~**ieth** tagtigste; ~**y** tagtig
eistedd'fod (n) **-au** sangfees, eisteddfod *also* **song/sin'ging fes'tival**
ei'ther (a, pron) albei; (adv, conj) of; ~ **or** óf . . . óf
eject' uitgooi; ~**ion seat** (uit)skietstoel
elab'orate (v) noukeurig uitwerk, verwerk; ~ *on* uitbrei op; (a) uitvoerig
el'and eland (bok)
elas'tic (n) rek, gomlastiek; (a) rekbaar, elasties; veerkragtig
el'bow (n) elmboog; (v) stoot, stamp (met die elmboog); ~ **chair** armstoel; ~ **grease** spierkrag; ~ **room** speling, staanplek
el'der (n) ouer persoon; ouderling; (a) ouer; **the** ~**ly** oumense, bejaardes; ~**ly** bejaard
el'dest oudste
elect' (v) uitverkies; (ver)kies; (a) uitgekies; verkose; ~*ed to council* tot die raad verkies/benoem; ~**ion** verkiesing, eleksie; ~**ion day** stemdag
elec'toral district kiesdistrik, kiesafdeling
elec'tric elektries; ~ **bulb** gloeilamp; ~ **cur'rent** elektriese stroom; ~ **plug** kragprop
electri'cian ekektrisiën (mens)
electri'city elektrisiteit
elec'trocardiogram (ECG) elektrokardiogram (EKG) *see* **car'diograph**
elec'trocute (v) doodskok; elektries teregstel
electro'nic (a) elektronies; ~ **control** elektroniese beheer; ~ **mail (e-mail/email)** elektroniese pos (e-pos)
el'egant sierlik, bevallig, smaakvol, elegant

el'egy elegies elegie, treursang/treurdig
el'ement element; (pl) elemente, beginsels
elemen'tary elementêr, eenvoudig
el'ephant olifant; ~ **tusk** olifanttand
el'evate (v) ophef, verhef; veredel; (a) verhewe, hoog; ~**d** verhewe
el'evator hyser/hysbak; graansuier, silo
elev'en elf; elftal (krieket); ~**th** elfde
elf' elves kaboutermannetjie, dwerg
el'igible (a) verkiesbaar, geskik; *being* ~, *he offers himself for re-election* hy is en stel hom herkiesbaar; ~ **bach'elor** hubare/gesogte (oujong)kêrel/vrygesel
elim'inate weglaat, elimineer; uitdun
eli'te (a) deftig *also* **smart**; (n) elite (mens); ~ **troops** keurtroepe
ell el *see* **el'bow**
ellipse' (n) ellips, ovaal
elocu'tion voordrag(kuns), elokusie
elope' (v) wegloop, dros; skaak
el'oquent welsprekend; veelseggend
else anders; *anyone* ~? iem. anders?, nog iem.?; ~**where** êrens anders, elders
e-mail/email e-pos
emancipa'tion vrymaking, vrywording, emansipasie
emas'culate (v) ontman, kastreer, sny
embank' indyk, opdam; ~**ment** dyk; afdamming; skuinste; wal
embar'go (n) verbod, embargo *also* **ban**
embark' inskeep; aanvaar; aanpak
embar'rass verleë maak; embarrasseer; *you* ~ *me* jy bring my in die verleentheid; ~**ment** verleentheid
em'bassy embassies ambassade
embez'zle (v) verduister, steel (geld, fondse)
embitt'er verbitter, versuur
em'blem (n) sinnebeeld, simbool, embleem
embrace' (v) omhels; omvat
embroid'er borduur
em'bryo -s vrug, embrio
em'erald (n) smarag; (a) smaraggroen
emerge' (v) opkom, te voorskyn kom, oprys
emer'gency ..cies nood(geval) *also* **cri'sis**; ~ **brake** noodrem; ~ **ex'it** nooduitgang; ~ **fund** (nood)hulpfonds; ~ **lan'ding** noodlanding (vliegtuig)
em'ery: ~ **pa'per** skuurpapier *also* **sand'paper**; ~ **wheel** slypwiel
em'igrant (n) emigrant, landverhuiser (mens)
em'inent (a) verhewe; voortreflik
em'issary ..ries gesant, afgesant (mens)

emit' uitstraal; uitvaardig

emol'ument besoldiging; salaris, loon

emo'tion aandoening, emosie, ontroering; ~**al** aandoenlik, emosioneel, roerend; ~**al sce'nes** roerende tonele

em'peror keiser

em'phasis (n) nadruk; klem *also* **stress**

em'phasise (v) benadruk, beklemtoon, uitlig *also* **high'light** (v)

em'pire keiserryk

employ' (n) diens; (v) gebruik; werk gee; be= sig hou; ~**ee'** werknemer; ~**er** werkgewer; ~**ment** werk, werkverband; werkverskaf= fing; indiensplasing, indiensneming; ~**ment a'gency** personeelagentskap, werkverskaf= fingsburo; **condi'tions of** ~**ment** diensvoor= waardes

empo'wer (v) mag gee/bemagtig; ~**ment** (n) bemagtiging

emp'ty (v) leegmaak; (a) leeg; ydel; ~**-headed** dom, onnosel

em'ulate (v) oortref *also* **surpass'**, **out'per= form**

ena'ble in staat stel, bekwaam maak, help

enam'el (n) glasuur; emalje/enemmel; erd; ~ **paint** glansverf *also* **gloss paint**

enchant' (v) bekoor, betower; ~**ed** betowerd, verruk; ~**ing** betowerend, bekoorlik

enclose' insluit; omhein, inkamp

enclo'sure omheining, kamp; bylae

encode' (v) (en)kodeer; kodifiseer

encore' (n) toegif (by opvoering); herhaling

encoun'ter (n) skermutseling/botsing; krag= meting; ontmoeting; (v) tref, slaags raak

encou'rage (v) aanmoedig, aanspoor; ~**ment** aanmoediging, aansporing

encyclopaed'ia ensiklopedie

end (n) end, einde; afloop; *be at one's wits'* ~ raadop wees; (v) end, eindig; ophou

endan'gered: ~ **spe'cies** bedreigde spesies

endeav'our (n) poging; strewe; (v) probeer

endem'ic inheems, endemies (siekte)

end'ing end, uiteinde, slot, einde

endorse' (v) endosseer; bevestig; ~**ment** en= dossement; goedkeuring

endow'ment skenking, bemaking; gawe, ta= lent; ~ **pol'icy** uitkeerpolis

endur'ance uithouvermoë

endure' (v) verduur; uitstaan, verdra; volhou

en'ema (n) lawement, enema

en'emy (n) **..mies** vyand; teenstander

energet'ic (a) kragtig, energiek; deurtastend

en'ergy **..gies** energie; arbeidsvermoë; krag

enforce' (af)dwing; deurdryf; ~ *the law* die wet toepas/uitvoer; ~**ment** toepassing

engage' (v) verloof; aanpak; aanneem; ~*d to* verloof aan; ~**ment** verlowing; ~**ment ring** verloofring

en'gine (n) enjin; motor (elektr.); ~ **dri'ver** enjindrywer, masjinis

engineer' (n) ingenieur; **civ'il** ~ siviele inge= nieur; **elec'trical** ~ elektrotegniese inge= nieur; **mechanical** ~ meganiese/werktuig= kundige ingenieur; (v) bewerk; bou; geni= eer; ~**ing** ingenieurswese (vak); geniëring (proses)

Eng'land Engeland

Eng'lish Engels; ~**man** **..men** Engelsman

engrave' graveer; inprent; ~**r** graveur (mens)

engrav'ing gravure, kunsplaat

enhance' (v) verhoog, verhef; verbeter

enjamb'ment enjambement, deurloop (vers= reël), oorvloeiing

enjoy' (v) geniet, vermaak; ~ *yourself (at the party)* geniet (die partytjie); ~**able** aange= naam, genotvol; ~**ment** genot, vermaak, plesier, pret *also* **fun**

enlarge' vergroot; ~**ment** vergroting

enlight'en verlig; voorlig; ~**ed** verlig

enorm'ous (a) ontsaglik, enorm, tamaai

enough' genoeg, voldoende

enquire' (v) navraag doen, verneem, infor= meer; ~ *after* verneem/vra na

enquir'y **..ries** navraag; (pl) navrae; *make enquiries* navraag doen *see* **in'quiry**

enrich' (v) verryk; vrugbaar maak

enrol' inskryf/registreer; aansluit; in diens neem; ~**ment** inskrywing

ensure' waarborg; verseker, seker maak

entail' (v) meebring; behels; veroorsaak

en'ter ingaan, intree; inskryf, registreer; aan= gaan; sluit (kontrak); ~ *for a race* inskryf vir 'n wedren

enter'ic fever/enteri'tis ingewandskoors

en'terprise onderneming; *free* ~ vrye onder= nemerskap, vrye markstelsel

entertain' (v) onthaal; vermaak; ~ *guests* gaste onthaal; ~**er** vermaaklikheidskunste= naar; ~**ing** onderhoudend, vermaaklik; ~**ment** onthaal; vermaaklikheid

enthu'siast entoesias; **sport/spor'ting** ~ sport= liefhebber (mens)

enthusias'tic (a) geesdriftig, entoesiasties

entice' verlok, verlei, in versoeking bring

232

entire′ volledig, volkome; ~**ly** heeltemal, geheel en al *also* **comple′tely**
enti′tle betitel, noem; reg gee op; ~**d** geregtig op; *be* ~**d** *to* geregtig wees op
en′tity entities wese, entiteit
entomol′ogist entomoloog, insektekundige
en′trance (n) ingang, toegang; intrede
en′trance: ~ **examina′tion** toelaateksamen; ~ **fee** intreegeld, inskryfgeld; ~ **require′ments** toelaatvereistes
en′trant kandidaat, nuweling, deelnemer
entreat′ (v) smeek, bid, soebat *also* **beseech′**
entrench′ verskans; ~**ed clau′ses** verskanste klousules
entrepreneur′ (sake)ondernemer, entrepreneur
en′try entries ingang, intrede; inskrywings; pos; ~ **form** inskryfvorm
enum′erate (v) opnoem; tel; lys (w)
en′velope koevert; omslag, omhulsel
en′vious (a) afgunstig, naywerig, jaloers
envir′on omring, omsingel; ~**ment** omgewing, milieu; ~**men′tal conserva′tion** omgewingsbewaring; ~**men′tally friend′ly** omgewingsvriendelik/omgewingsgunstig; ~**men′tal stud′ies** ekologie; omgewingsleer; ~**men′talist** omgewing(s)bewaarder
envi′sage beskou; beoog; voor die gees roep
en′voy -s gesant, afgesant *also* **go-between′**
en′vy (n) afguns, nyd; (v) beny, misgun
ep′ic (n) heldedig, epos; (a) epies, verhalend
epidem′ic (n) epidemie; (a) epidemies
ep′igram (n) puntdig, epigram
ep′ilepsy vallende siekte, epilepsie
epilep′tic (a) epilepties
ep′ilogue (n) narede, slottoespraak; oordenking *also* **medita′tion**
ep′isode voorval, episode; tussenverhaal
ep′itaph (n) grafskrif
ep′os -es heldedig, (mondelinge) epos
eq′ual (n) gelyke; weerga; (v) ewenaar; (a) dieselfde, gelyk; ~ *to* gelyk aan; opgewasse teen/vir; *on* ~ *footing* op gelyke voet
eq′ualise gelyk maak; gelykstel; ewenaar; ~**r** gelykmaker (van punte); effenaar (radio)
equal′ity (n) gelykheid; ~ *of votes* staking van stemme
eq′ually gelyk, eenders/eners, net so
equa′tion vergelyking; ewewig
equat′or ewenaar/ekwator; sonlyn, linie
eques′trian (n) perderuiter, ruiter; ~ **stat′ue** ruiterstandbeeld
equilib′rium (n) ewewig

eq′uinox -es dag- en nagewening
equip′ (v) toerus, uitrus; voorsien
equip′ment uitrusting, toerusting *also* **out′fit**
eq′uitable (a) billik, redelik, regverdig
eq′uity ..ties billikheid, onpartydigheid; (pl) ekwiteite, gewone aandele
equiv′alent ekwivalent; ~ *to* gelyk aan
er′a -s tydvak, era; jaartelling
erad′icate uitroei, verdelg; ontwortel
eras′e (v) skrap *also* **dele′te**; uitwis, uitvee; ~**r** uitveër, wisser
erect′ (v) oprig, stig, bou; (a) (pen)regop, penorent; ~**ion** oprigting, stigting; ereksie
erf erven erf; standplaas
erm′ine hermelyn
ero′sion (n) wegvreting, erosie, verwering, (grond)verspoeling
erot′ic eroties; ~ **film** hygfliek
err′ (v) fout maak, fouteer; dwaal, sondig
e′rrand boodskap; opdrag
errat′ic wisselvallig; onbestendig (sport)
errat′um errata drukfout, skryffout
erron′eous (a) verkeerd, onjuis, foutief
e′rror fout, dwaling, vergissing; *commit an* ~ ′n fout/flater begaan/maak; **un′forced** ~ ongedwonge fout (sport)
e′rudite (a) geleerd, belese *also* **lear′ned**
erupt′ uitbars (vulkaan); uitbreek; ~**ion** uitbarsting; uitslag
es′calate (v) eskaleer, progressief toeneem
es′calator (n) roltrap
escape′ (n) ontsnapping; **nar′row** ~ noue ontkoming; (v) ontsnap; ontkom
escarp′ment platorand/eskarp; skuinste
es′cort (n) begeleier; vrygeleide
escort′ (v) begelei, vergesel; ~ **a′gency** gesellin(ne)klub, huurmeisieklub
espe′cial besonder; ~**ly** veral, vernaamlik
espiona′ge spioenasie, bespieding; **indus′trial** ~ nywerheidspioenasie
esplanade′ (gras)plein, esplanade, wandelbaan
ess′ay (n) opstel, verhandeling, essay; ~**ist** essayis (mens)
ess′ence wese, essensie; grondbestanddeel
essen′tial (a) essensieel, noodsaaklik
essen′tially hoofsaaklik, in hoofsaak/wese
estab′lish (v) vasstel; oprig, stig, vestig; ~**ed** gevestig, opgerig; ~**ment** oprigting; vestiging; saak, onderneming
estate′ (n) besitting(s), eiendom; landgoed; boedel; ~ **du′ty** boedelbelasting; **real** ~

vaste eiendom

esteem' (n) agting; waardering; (v) ag, hoog=
ag; ~**ed** geag, gesien

es'timate (n) (be)raming, skatting, waardering;
(v) raam, skat, waardeer, begroot; *an* ~*d
R5 million* 'n geraamde R5 miljoen; ~ *the
cost at* raam die koste op

es'tuary ..**ries** riviermond, monding

et cet'era (etc.) ensovoort (ens.)

etch -es ets; ~**er** etser (mens); ~**ing** ets

etern'al (a) ewig, ewigdurend

etern'ity (n) ewigheid

eth'ics sedeleer, sedekunde, etiek; **code of** ~
gedragskode

eth'nic volkekundig; etnies

e'tiquette (n) etiket, wellewendheidsvorme

etymol'ogy woordafleiding, etimologie

eucalyp'tus ..**ti** bloekom(boom)

eu'logy (n) lofrede/lofspraak; lykrede

euph'emism (n) eufemisme, versagting

eupho'ria geluksgevoel, euforie

Eur'omart (n) Euromark

Eu'rope Europa

Europe'an (n) Europeaan, Europeër (mens);
(a) Europees

euthanas'ia (n) genadedood, eutanasie *also*
mer'cy kil'ling

evac'uate ontruim, verlaat; ~ *the building* die
gebou ontruim; ~ *the inhabitants* die in=
woners na veiligheid bring

evade' ontwyk; ontduik; ontgaan

evaluat'ion evaluering, waardebepaling

evan'gel: ~**isa'tion** evangelisasie; ~**ist** evan=
gelis

evap'orate (v) verdamp, vervlieg; uitwasem

eva'sive ontwykend, ontduikend; vaag

eve aand: vooraand; **Christ'mas E**~ Oukers=
aand; **New Year's E**~ Oujaarsaand; *on the*
~ *of* op/aan die vooraand van

e'ven[1] (v) gelykmaak; gelykstel; (a, adv) glad,
effe, egalig, reëlmatig; *odd and* ~ gelyk en
ongelyk; *we are* ~/*quits* ons is kiets;
~-**tem'pered** gelykmoedig *also* **plac'id**

e'ven[2] (adv) selfs, ook, eweneens; *not* ~ nie
eers/eens nie; ~ *now* selfs nou

eve'ning aand; ~ **dress** aanddrag; aandrok

event' gebeurtenis, voorval; (pl) gebeure; by=
eenkoms *also* **hap'pening**; *in the* ~ *of* in
geval van

even'tual moontlik, gebeurlik; toevallig

even'tually ten slotte, uiteindelik

ev'er ooit; steeds, altyd; *for* ~ ewig; *thank you*
~ *so much* hartlike dank; baie, baie dankie;
~**green** immergroen; ~**last'ing** ewigdu=
rend; ~**last'ings** sewejaartjies (blomme);
~**more** vir altyd, ewig

ev'ery elke, ieder, alle; ~ *other day* al om die
ander dag; ~ *person who* elkeen/iedereen
wat; ~ *time* telkens; ~**bo'dy** elkeen, ieder=
een; ~**day** daagliks; alledaags; ~**one** elk=
een, iedereen, almal; ~**thing** alles; ~**where**
oral(s)

ev'idence (n) bewys; getuie; getuienis; *give* ~
getuienis aflê

ev'ident (a) duidelik, klaarblyklik; ~**ly** blyk=
baar

ev'il (n) kwaad, euwel; (a) kwaad, sleg, son=
dig; ~**do'er** boosdoener

evolu'tion (n) ontwikkeling, evolusie/ewolusie

ewe ooi; ~ **lamb** ooilam

ex- gewese, oud=; ~**pu'pil** oudleerling

exact'[1] (v) afdwing, afpers *also* **force** (v)

exact'[2] (a) noukeurig, juis, presies, eksak

exa'ggerate oordryf, vergroot; ~**d** oordrewe

examina'tion/exam' eksamen, ondersoek;
pass an ~ (in) 'n eksamen slaag; *sit for an*
~ eksamen doen; ~ **pa'per** eksamenvraestel

exam'ine (v) ondersoek, eksamineer, onder=
vra; uitvra; verhoor; ~**r** eksaminator

exam'ple voorbeeld; monster, proef; eksem=
plaar; *for* ~ byvoorbeeld

exaspera'tion gramskap *also* **an'ger**; terging;
verbittering; *in* ~ tot frustrasie gedryf

excava'tion uitgrawing; opgrawing

exceed' (v) oortref; oorskry, *losses* ~ *revenue*
verliese oorskry inkomste; ~**ing(ly)** buiten=
gewoon, uitermate

excel' (v) oortref, uitmunt; ~ *in tennis* in ten=
nis uitmunt

ex'cellence voortreflikheid, uitmuntendheid

ex'cellency ..**cies** eksellensie (mens)

ex'cellent (a) uitstekend, voortreflik, uitmun=
tend, puik *also* **outstan'ding, superb'**

except' (v) uitsonder, uitsluit; (prep) uitge=
sonder(d), behalwe

excep'tion (n) uitsondering; *take* ~ *to* aanstoot
neem aan; ~**al** buitengewoon, besonder,
uitsonderlik

excess' -**es** oordaad, oormaat; ~**ive** oormatig,
buitensporig

exchange' (n) ruiling; wisselkoers, valuta;
telefoonsentrale; **bill of** ~ (geld)wissel; ~
control' valutabeheer; (v) wissel; ruil; ~
rate wisselkoers; ~ **stu'dent** (uit)ruilstudent

excite' (v) aanspoor; opwen; ~d opgewonde; ~ment opwinding; opgewòndenheid

excit'ing (a) opwindend, spannend

exclama'tion uitroep, skree(u); ~ mark uit= roepteken

exclude' (v) uitsluit, uitsonder

exclus'ive (a) uitsluitend, eksklusief; deftig, kieskeurig; ~ of met uitsluiting van; ~ residential area spog(woon)buurt; ~ sub= urb deftige voorstad also up'market a'rea

excru'ciating martelend, folterend (pyn)

excur'sion uitstappie, ekskursie; uitweiding; ~ tick'et ekskursiekaartjie

excuse' (n) verskoning, ekskuus; (v) verskoon, ekskuseer; ~ me! ekskuus (tog)!; pardon!

ex'ecute (v) uitvoer, voltrek; verrig, vervul; teregstel, ophang, onthoof, fusilleer

execu'tion uitvoering; voltrekking (doodstraf); teregstelling; onthoofding; beslaglegging; ~er laksman, beul

exec'utive (n) bestuurshoof, bestuursleier; be= dryfsleier; (uitvoerende) bestuur; chief ~ hoofbestuursleier; op'erating ~ bedryfs= hoof; (a) uitvoerend; ~ commit'tee uit= voerende komitee; dagbestuur; ~ direc'tor uitvoerende direkteur; ~ suite bestuurstel

exec'utor eksekuteur (van boedel)

exem'plar voorbeeld; toonbeeld; ~y (a) voor= beeldig, navolgenswaardig

exempt' (v) vrystel, ontslaan; ~ from a subject van 'n vak vrystel; (a) vrygestel, uitgeson= der(d); ~ion vrystelling

ex'ercise (n) oefening; (v) oefen, dril; ~ book skryfboek, oefenskrif, skrif

exert' (v) aanwend; inspan; beywer; ~ oneself jou inspan; ~ion inspanning

exhale' uitasem; uitdamp/uitwasem

exhaust'[1] (n) uitlaatpyp; knaldemper (motor)

exhaust'[2] (v) uitput, afmat; leegmaak; ~ed gedaan, kapot, uitgeput; ~ion uitputting, afmatting; heat ~ion hitte-uitputting; ~ive (a) volledig, grondig

exhib'it (n) insending; uitstalling; bewysstuk; (v) vertoon, ten toon stel, uitstal; ~ one's cattle jou beeste skou

exhibi'tion tentoonstelling, skou; vertoning

exhil'arating verfrissend, opwekkend

ex'ile (n) ballingskap; banneling/balling (mens); (v) verban

exist' bestaan, lewe

exist'ence bestaan, lewe; preca'rious ~ suk= kelbestaan

exist'ing bestaande; aanwesig

ex'it (n) deur, uitgang; (v) (gaan) af (toneel); ~ in'terview vertrekgesprek (met personeel)

ex'odus (n) uittog, eksodus

exorb'itant buitensporig, erg, verregaande

exot'ic (a) uitheems, vreemd, eksoties

expand' uitsprei (plant); uitbrei; uitsit; swel

expan'sion (n) uitsetting; uitbreiding; swel= ling, ontwikkeling; toename; ~ joint uit= sitvoeg

expat'riate (n) banneling; uitgewekene (mens)

expect' (v) verwag; veronderstel, vermoed; life ~ancy lewensverwagting; ~ant verwagtend; swanger (vrou) also preg'nant

expecta'tion verwagting; vooruitsig

exped'ient (n) hulpmiddel, noodhulp; (a) ge= skik, dienstig also appro'priate

ex'pedite (v) bespoedig; afstuur; verhaas

expedi'tion veldtog, ekspedisie

expel' verdryf; uitsit (uit skool); verban

expend' bestee, verkwis; ~able afskryfbaar

expen'diture (n) uitgawe, onkoste, besteding; in'come and ~ inkomste en uitgawes

expense' koste, onkoste

expen'sive duur also cost'ly; kosbaar

exper'ience (n) ondervinding, ervaring; (v) ondervind, ervaar; ~d (a) ervare (mens)

expe'riment (n) proefneming, eksperiment; (v) beproef, eksperimenteer

experimen'tal proefondervindelik, eksperimen= teel; ~ farm proefplaas

ex'pert[1] (n) deskundige, vakkundige, kundige/ kenner, ekspert; ~ise (sake)vernuf, kundig= heid also know'-how

ex'pert[2] (a) bedrewe; deskundig, vakkundig

expir'e uitasem, sterf; verval, verstryk; expi'ry date vervaldatum/verstrykdatum

explain' (v) uitlê, verklaar, verduidelik

explana'tion uitleg(ging), verklaring, verdui= deliking also clarifica'tion

expli'cit uitdruklik, stellig also express'

explode' ontplof, bars, spring; laat ontplof

exploit' (v) uitbuit; ontgin, bewerk

explora'tion (n) navorsing, eksplorasie; ont= dekking/ontginning

explore' ondersoek, navors, naspoor; ~r ont= dekkingsreisiger; navorser

explo'sion ontploffing, uitbarsting, slag, knal also blast; ~ shot plofhou (gholf)

explos'ive (n) plofstof; (pl) plofstof, springstof; (a) (ont)plofbaar; opvlieënd; ~s ex'pert plofstof(des)kundige

ex'po (n) uitstalling, skou, ekspo
ex'port[1] (n) uitvoer; uitvoerartikels
export'[2] (v) uitvoer, eksporteer
ex'port: ~ **du'ty** uitvoerreg; ~**er** uitvoerder (mens); ~ **trade** uitvoerhandel
expose' ontbloot, blootstel; openbaar; ~**d** onbeskut; ~**r** ontbloter *also* **flash'er** (man)
expo'sure blootstelling; gevaar
express' (v) uitdruk; uit; betuig; (a) spoed=; opsetlik, uitdruklik; ~**ion** uitdrukking, ge= segde; *beyond* ~**ion** onbeskryflik; ~**ive** uit= druklik, betekenisvol; veelseggend; ~ **mail/ post** spoedpos; ~ **way** snelweg
expro'priate (v) onteien, ontvreem (eiendom)
expul'sion uitsetting (uit skool); verdrywing
ex'quisite (a) keurig, voortreflik
extend' (v) uitstrek; uitbrei; verleng; ~ *our best wishes* die allerbeste toewens
exten'sion (n) uitbreiding; verlenging; bylyn (telefoon), verlengstuk; **Eloff Street E~** Eloffstraatverlenging; **Parkwood E~** Park= wood-uitbreiding; ~ **cord** verlengkoord; ~ **lad'der** skuifleer; ~ **of'ficer** voorlig(tings)= beampte, veldbeampte
extent' uitgestrektheid, omvang; *to the* ~ *of* tot die bedrag/omvang van; *to some* ~ in sekere mate
exten'uating versagtend; ~/**mit'igating cir'= cumstances** versagtende omstandighede
exter'ior (n) uiterlike, voorkome; buitekant; (a) uitwendig; uiterlik; buite=
exterm'inate (v) uitroei, verdelg *also* **destroy'**
extern'al (n) uiterlike; (pl) uiterlikhede; by= komstighede; (a) uitwendig, ekstern, buite=; ~

stu'dies eksterne studie
extinct' dood; uitgeblus; uitgesterf; uitgedoof, uitgewerk (vulkaan)
exting'uish (v) doodblaas, uitdoof, blus (vuur); ~**er** blusser; domper
extort' afpers, afdreig; ~**ion** afpersing
ex'tra (n) toegif, ekstratjie; *no* ~**s** alles in= begrepe; (a) buitengewoon, ekstra; ~**cur= ric'ular** buitekurrikulêr
ex'tract (n) uittreksel; ekstrak; aftreksel
extract' (v) uittrek; 'n uittreksel maak; ~**ion** afkoms, afstamming (familie)
extradi'tion (n) uitlewering
extramur'al buitemuurs (studie)
extraor'dinary (a) buitengewoon, sonderling
extrasens'ory: ~ **percep'tion (ESP)** buitesin= tuiglike waarneming
extrav'agance (n) buitensporigheid; verkwis= ting, oordaad
extrav'agant (a) buitensporig, uitspattig; on= matig; verkwistend, spandabel
extravagan'za musikale kykspel, extravaganza
extre'me (n) uiterste; ~**ly** uiters, uitermate
ex'trovert (n) ekstrovert (mens); (a) ekstrovert
eye (n) oog; lus (in tou); *turn the blind* ~ oogluikend toelaat; *see* ~ *to* ~ *with* dit vol= kome eens wees met; (v) dophou, bekyk, beskou, gadeslaan; ~**brow** wenkbrou; ~**hole** kykgaatjie/loerkyker(tjie) (in deur); ~**lash** ooghaar, wimper; ~**lid** ooglid; ~**o'pener** openbaring; verrassing; ~**sight** gesig; ~**sore** onooglik(heid); ~**wash** oogwater; oëverblin= dery (fig.), kaf; ~**wit'ness** ooggetuie *also* **wit'ness**

F

fa'ble (n) fabel, sprokie; verdigsel
fab'ric weefstof; bou; maaksel, fabrikaat; ~**a'tion** verdigsel, versinsel
fab'ulous (a) fabelagtig *also* **fantas'tic**
face (n) gesig, gelaat; voorkoms; ~ *the music* die gevolge dra; ~ *to* ~ onder die vier oë; ~**brick** siersteen; ~ **cream** gesigroom; ~**lift** ontrimpeling, gesig(s)kuur; verjongingskuur
fa'cet (n) vlak, faset
face'tious (a) grappig, geestig *also* **wit'ty**
face val'ue nominale waarde, sigwaarde
fa'cial gesig(s)=; ~ **tis'sue** gesigsnesie
facil'itate vergemaklik, (aan)help, fasiliteer;

verlig; ~ *matters* sake vergemaklik
facil'ity (pl) ~**ties** geriewe, fasiliteite
facsim'ile reproduksie, faksimilee *see* **fax**
fact (n) feit; daad; werklikheid; *in* ~ inder= daad; ~**find'ing mis'sion** feitesending
fac'tion party, partyskap; faksie, kliek; (poli= tieke) groep; ~ **fight** stamgeveg/faksiegeveg
fac'tor faktor, agent; oorsaak
fac'tory ..ries fabriek; ~ **waste** fabrieksafval; ~ **overheads'** fabrieksbokoste
facto'tum (n) handlanger, knaphand, faktotum
fac'ulty ..ties vermoë, bekwaamheid; talent; fakulteit (van 'n universiteit)

fad (n) gier, idee *also* **cra′ze/fan′cy**; stokperd=
jie
fade (v) verwelk; verlep; kwyn, verflou
fail (n) fout; *without* ~ seker; (v) misluk/faal;
sak/dop/druip (eksamen)
fail′ing (n) fout, gemis; tekortkoming; ~
subject ′n druipvak
fail′ure (n) mislukking; gebrek; druipeling (in
eksamen); ~ **rate** druipsyfer
faint (n) floute; (v) flou val, verwelk; (a) swak,
onduidelik; dof; ~**-heart′ed** halfhartig
fair[1] (n) kermis, jaarmark *also* **fê′te**
fair[2] (a) fraai, skoon; blond, lig; *the* ~*(er) sex*
die skone geslag; ~ **play** (n) eerlike spel; (a)
regverdig, reg, eerlik; ~**way** skoonveld
(gholf)
fair′y fairies fee; ~ **tale** sprokie, feëverhaal
faith (n) geloof; vertroue; (interj) regtig, so=
waar; ~**ful** getrou; ~ **heal′er** geloofsge=
neser
fake (n) vervalsing; bedrog *also* **for′gery**; (a)
vervals, namaak
fakir′ (n) fakir, bedelmonnik (Indies)
fal′con valk; ~**er** valkenier (mens)
fall (n) val; daling; ondergang; (v) val, daal,
sink; ~ *due* verval; ~ *in love* verlief raak
fall′ible (a) feilbaar *also* **imper′fect**
fall′-out uitval; kern-as (atoombom)
false (a) vals, skynheilig; ~**hood** valsheid;
leuen, bedrog
fal′sify vervals *also* **forge**; namaak
fal′ter hakkel, stamel; strompel, struikel
fame roem, beroemdheid; **house of ill-**~ bor=
deel, hoerhuis
famil′iar (a) vertroulik, eie; vrypostig; ~
surroundings bekende/vertroude omgewing;
~ *with the facts* vertroud met die feite
fam′ily . .**lies** familie, gesin; geslag; stam; *be
in the* ~ *way* in geseënde omstandighede
wees; ~ **cir′cle** familiekring; ~ **kil′ling** ge=
sinsmoord; ~ **plan′ning** gesinsbeplanning;
~ **practi′tioner** huisarts; ~ **tree** stamboom
Fam′ily Day Gesinsdag (vakansie)
fam′ine hongersnood; gebrek
fam′ous (a) beroemd, vermaard
fan[1] (n) bewonderaar, aanhanger; entoesias;
~**mail** bewonderaarsbriewe, dweeppos
fan[2] (n) waaier; wan; (v) koel waai; aanwak=
ker; ~**belt** waaierband
fanat′ic (n) dweper, fanatikus (mens); ~**al**
dweepsiek, fanatiek
fan′cy (n) . .**cies** verbeelding, inbeelding, gril,

nuk, gier; fantasie; *take a* ~ *to* aangetrokke
voel tot, hou van; (v) verbeel, baie hou van;
(interj) dink net!; ~ **dress** fantasiekostuum;
~**dress ball** kostuumbal, maskerbal; ~
goods snuisterye/sierware
fang slagtand; giftand (van slang)
fan′tail (n) waaierstert, pronkduif (pigeon)
fantas′tic grillig, fantasties *also* **fab′ulous**
fan′tasy inbeelding; fantasie; gril, inval
far (n): *by* ~ verreweg; (a) ver/vêr, afgeleë;
(adv) baie, veel; ver, ver(re)weg
farce (n) grap, klug *also* **com′edy**
fare (n) reisgeld, passasiersgeld; kos
farewell′ vaarwel, afskeid; ~ **din′ner** af=
skeid(s)dinee; ~ **gift/pres′ent** afskeid(s)ge=
skenk
farm (n) plaas, boerdery; (v) boer; ~**er** boer,
landbouer; ~**stall** plaaskiosk, padstal(le=
tjie); ~**stead** (plaas)opstal
far-reach′ing verreikend/vêrreikend; groot
far′-sighted versiende/vêrsiende
farth′er (a) verder; (adv) verder/vêrder
fas′cinating (a) boeiend; bekoorlik
fa′shion (n) mode; drag; fatsoen; maaksel; *out
of* ~ uit die mode; (v) fatsoeneer, vorm;
~**able** modies, modieus; deftig; fatsoenlik; ~
design′er mode-ontwerper; ~ **para′de** mo=
deparade; ~ **show** modeskou
fast[1] (n) vas; (v) vas, sonder kos bly
fast[2] (a, adv) vinnig; vas, standvastig, sterk;
the clock is too ~ die klok loop voor; ~
bowler snelbouler; ~ **col′our** vaste kleur;
vaskleur=; ~ **foods** kitskos, prulkos *also*
junk food
fas′ten (v) vasmaak; bevestig
fat (n, a) vet; ~ **cat** geiljan, dikvreter (mens)
fa′tal noodlottig, dodelik; fataal; ~ **ac′cident**
noodlottige ongeluk
fate (n) noodlot; lot, bestemming
fat′head domkop, skaap, pampoen *also* **clod**
Fa′ther Christ′mas Kersvader, Vader Krismis
also **San′ta Claus**
fa′ther (n) vader; (v) verwek; ~**-in-law** skoon=
vader; ~**land** vaderland; ~**ly** vaderlik
fath′om (n) vaam/vadem; (v) omvat, deur=
grond; *I can't* ~ *it* ek kan dit nie kleinkry
nie
fatigue′ (n) moegheid, vermoeienis, afmatting;
met′al ~ metaalverswakking
fat: ~**ten** vet maak; ~**ty** (n) vetsak; potjierol
(kind); (a) vetterig
fault fout, gebrek; skuld; *find* ~ *with* vit;

~**find′er** foutvinder, vitter; ~**less** onberis≈
pelik; foutloos; ~**y** gebrekkig, foutief, defek

faun (n) sater, bosgod, faun

faun′a -e dierewêreld, fauna

fav′our (n) guns; *by* ~ *of* deur (vriendelike)
bemiddeling van; *curry* ~ witvoetjie soek;
do one a ~ iem. 'n guns bewys; *in* ~ *of* ten
gunste van; (v) begunstig; ~**able** gunstig;
welwillend; ~**ite** (n) gunsteling; liefling;
kansperd; (a) lieflings≈; geliefkoosde: *my*
~*ite poet* my gunstelingdigter; *my* ~*ite dog*
my lieflingshond; ~**itism** voortrekkery

fax (n, v) faks (telef. faksimilee)

fear (n) vrees, angs; *for* ~ *of* uit vrees vir; (v)
bang wees, vrees; ~**less** onbevrees, onver≈
skrokke *also* **undaun′ted**

fea′sible (a) uitvoerbaar, haalbaar; prakties

feasibil′ity uitvoerbaarheid; ~ **study** uitvoer≈
baarheidstudie, haalbaarheidstudie

feast (n) fees, feesmaal; (v) feesvier; fuif

feat (n) kordaatstuk, prestasie; heldedaad

feath′er (n) veer; *a* ~ *in one's cap* 'n pluim≈
pie; ~**-brain′ed** dom; ~**weight** veergewig

fea′ture (n) gelaatstrek; hooftrek; kenmerk;
(pl) gelaatstrekke; (v) uitbeeld; ~ **pro′≈
gramme** glansprogram; hoorbeeld (radio)

Feb′ruary Februarie

fed gevoed; ~ *up* vies, keelvol; gatvol (*kru*)

fed′eral federaal

federa′tion federasie; verbond

fee (n) fooi *also* **tip**; professionele fooi/ver≈
goeding; honorarium; **medi′cal** ~**s** dokters≈
gelde, mediese koste

fee′ble (a) swak, kleinmoedig, halfhartig;
~**-min′ded** swaksinnig; ~**ness** swakheid

feed (n) voer, kos; (v) voer, voed; insleutel
(rek.); ~**back** terugvoer(ing); ~**er ser′vice**
toevoerdiens; ~**ing bottle** bababottel; ~**lot**
voerkraal

feel (n) gevoel; aanvoeling; (v) voel; bevoel;
~**er** voelhoring, voelspriet, ~**ing** (n) ge≈
voel, gedagte; opinie; (a) gevoelig; gevoel≈
vol

feint (n) voorwendsel; (v) liemaak; skrikmaak

felicita′tion gelukwensing *also* **congratula′t≈
ions**

fell (v) laat val; neerval; platslaan *see* **fall** (v)

fell′ow maat, kêrel, ou; lid(maat); genoot (van
'n vereniging); **good/jolly** ~ gawe kêrel;
~**-crea′ture** medemens; ~**ship** kameraad≈
skap; innige samesyn (kerk); genootskap
(van 'n vereniging)

fel′ony ..**nies** misdaad, misdryf

felt (n) vilt; (a) vilt≈; ~ **hat** vilthoed

fem′ale (n) vrou, vroumens; wyfie; (a) vroue≈;
vroulik; wyfie≈; ~ **doc′tor** dokteres; ~
suff′rage vrouestemreg

fem′idom (n) femidoom *see* **con′dom**

fem′inine (a) vroulik; verwyf

fem′inist feminis (mens)

fempower vrouekrag *see* **man′power**

fence (n) heining, draad; muur; *sit on the* ~
die kat uit die boom kyk; (v) omhein

fen′cing omheining; skermkuns

fend afweer, wegkeer; ~**er** modderskerm

fenn′el vinkel (kruie)

ferment′ (v) gis, fermenteer; ~**a′tion** gisting,
fermentasie

fern varing

fero′cious wild, wreed, woes *also* **sav′age**

fer′ret (n) fret (knaagdier); snuffelaar

fer′ry (n) veerboot, pont; (v) oorvaar

fert′ile vrugbaar

fert′ilise (v) bemes; ~**r** (n) kunsmis, misstof

ferv′ent (a) vurig, warm; ywerig

fes′ter (n) sweer, verswering; (v) etter

fes′tival (n) fees, feesdag; (a) feestelik

fes′tive feestelik, vrolik; ~ **sea′son** feestyd/
feesgety (Kersfees en Nuwejaar)

festiv′ity (n) feesviering, makietie

fetch (v) (gaan) haal, bring, te voorskyn bring

fête fees, kermis, basaar *also* **bazaar′**

feud (n) (bloed)vete *also* **vendet′ta**; twis, rusie

feud′al leen≈; feodaal; ~ **sys′tem** leenstelsel

fev′er koors; onrus; **scar′let** ~ skarlakenkoors;
~**ish** koorsig; koorsagtig

few party; 'n paar; min; weinig; ~ *and far
between* dun/yl gesaai; seldsaam

fian′cé verloofde, aanstaande (manlik); ~**e**
verloofde, aanstaande (vroulik)

fias′co -s mislukking, fiasko *also* **flop**

fib (n) leuen(tjie), kluitjie; *tell* ~**s** jok

fi′bre vesel; ~**glass** veselglas/glasvesel

fic′kle (a) wispelturig, veranderlik

fiction verdigsel; romankuns, fiksie; **science** ~
wetenskapfiksie

fid′dle (n) viool; *as fit as a* ~ so reg soos 'n
roer; (v) vermors (tyd); ~ *with* peuter aan;
~**stick** strykstok; ~**sticks!** gekheid!

fidel′ity (n) getrouheid, eerlikheid; ~ **guaran≈
tee′** getrouheidswaarborg; **high** ~ hoëtrou,
louterklank *also* **hi-fi**

fidg′et (v) woel, vroetel; ~**y** woelig

field (n) veld, vlakte; speelveld; gebied; (v)

veldwerk doen (krieket); ∼ **event'** veldnom=
mer; ∼ **mar'shal** veldmaarskalk
fiend (n) bose gees, demon *also* **de'vil,**
de'mon; ∼**ish** gemeen, demonies, hels
fierce wild, woes; fel, verbete; verwoed
fier'y vurig; gloeiend; driftig, opvlieënd
fifteen' vyftien; ∼**th'** vyftiende
fifth vyfde; ∼ **col'umn** vyfde kolonne
fif'tieth vyftigste
fif'ty fifties vyftig; ∼-∼ gelykop; half-om-
half
fig vy; vyeboom; *I don't care a* ∼ ek gee geen
flenter om nie
fight (n) geveg, twis, rusie; (v) veg, twis,
baklei; ∼**er** bakleier, vegter; ∼**er plane**
vegvliegtuig, straaljagter; ∼**ing spir'it** veg=
gees
fig'ment (n) verdigsel; versinsel
fig'urative figuurlik, sinnebeeldig
fig'ure (n) gedaante; gestalte, vorm; figuur;
syfer; *at a low* ∼ teen 'n lae prys; ∼ *of*
speech stylfiguur; (v) vorm; figure maak; ∼
out bereken; prakseer; uitreken; ∼**head**
(boeg)beeld (skip); strooipop, skynhoof
(mens)
file¹ (n) vyl; (v) vyl
file² (n) dossier; lêer; gelid; ry; *stand in* ∼
toustaan; (v) inryg; liasseer
fil'ibuster (n) vrybuiter, boekanier *also* **pi'rate;**
kaper *also* **hi'jacker**
fil'ing liassering; ∼ **cab'inet** liasseerkabinet
fill (v) vul; versadig; beklee (pos); stop (tand);
∼ *in* invul; ∼ *up* aanvul; invul; volgooi;
voltap (petrol); ∼**er** vuller(tjie)
fill'et (n) moot (vis); filet (beeshaas)
fill'ing aanvulling; vulsel, stopsel (tand); ∼
sta'tion vulstasie, petrolstasie
fill'y (n) merrievul; lewendige/wilde meisie
film (n) vlies; film, rolprent; (v) verfilm; ∼ **fan**
fliekvlooi; ∼ **li'brary** filmoteek
fil'ter (n) filter, suiweraar; (v) filtreer
filth vuilgoed, vullis; vuilheid; (a) ∼**y** vuil,
vieslik, morsig
fin vin; ∼ **di'ving** vinduik, swemduik
fin'al (n) eindeksamen; eindwedstryd; eind=
rondte, finaal; (a) finaal; beslissend; ∼
score eindtelling
fin'ally uiteindelik, ten slotte
finance'/fin'ance (n) inkoms(te); finansies,
geldmiddele; geldwese; (v) finansier; ∼
commit'tee finanskomitee
finan'cial geldelik, finansieel; ∼ **year** boek=

jaar, geldjaar; **an'nual** ∼ **sta'tements** finan=
siële jaarstate
finch -es vink (voël)
find (n) vonds (mv **vondste**); ontdekking; (v)
vind, kry, aantref; ∼ *fault with* afkeur; ∼
one's feet regkom; ∼ *guilty* skuldig bevind
fine¹ (n) (geld)boete; (v) beboet
fine² (a) mooi, fyn, fraai, suiwer; helder; ∼
arts skone/beeldende kunste
fing'er (n) vinger; *little* ∼ pinkie; *have a* ∼ *in*
the pie in die saak betrokke wees; (v)
bevoel, betas; ∼**print** vingerafdruk
fin'ical/fin'icky/fin'iking (a) puntene(u)rig
fin'ish (n) end, voltooiing; afwerking; (v)
klaarmaak, eindig; ∼**ed** klaar, gereed; ∼**ing**
(n) afwerking; ∼**ing line** wenstreep; ∼**ing**
school afrondingskool; slypskool
fiord' fjord
fire (n) brand; vuur, vlam; *the fat is in the* ∼
die poppe is aan die dans; (v) aansteek,
skiet; (summier) afdank; besiel; ∼ **alarm'**
brandalarm; ∼**arm** vuurwapen; ∼ **bomb**
brandbom; ∼ **briga'de** brandweer; ∼
esca'pe brandtrap; ∼ **exting'uisher** brand=
blusser; ∼ **fight'er** brandweerman; brand-
slaner; ∼**fly** vuurvlieg, glimwurm; ∼**hose**
brandslang; ∼ **insu'rance** brandversekering;
∼**man** stoker; brandweerman; ∼ **sta'tion**
brandweerstasie; ∼**wood** brandhout; ∼**works**
vuurwerk
fi'ring skietery, ontsteking; ∼ **squad** vuurpe=
loton
firm¹ (n) firma; (sake)onderneming, organisa=
sie *also* **concern** (n)
firm² (a, adv) standvastig, stewig, sterk; ∼
offer vaste aanbod; ∼**ly** vas, stewig
firm'ament (n) uitspansel, firmament
first (n) die eerste; begin; (a) eerste, ver=
naamste; *in the* ∼ *place* in die eerste plek, in
eerste instansie; (adv) eerste, eerstens, eers;
∼ *come* ∼ *served* eerste gesien eerste be=
dien; ∼ **aid** noodhulp; ∼-**class** eersteklas,
uitstekend; bakgat (*kru*); ∼ **floor** eerste
vloer/vlak; ∼ **name** voornaam; ∼-**rate** eer=
steklas
fir'tree den(neboom)
fish (n) **-es, fish** vis; ∼ *and chips* vis en
skyfies/(slap)tjips; *neither* ∼ *nor flesh* vis
nóg vlees; (v) visvang; uitvis; ∼ **bait** aas;
∼**bone** graat; ∼**erman** visser; visterman; ∼
paste vismeer; ∼**y** (a) visagtig; verdag/
suspisieus

fis'hing (a) vissers=, vis=; ~ **hook** (vis)hoek; ~ **rod** visstok; ~ **tack'le** hengelgerei

fist (n) vuis; handskrif

fit [1] (n) vlaag, aanval; nuk, gril

fit [2] (v) pas; aanpas; *the cap ~s* die skoen pas; ~*ter and turner* passer en draaier; (a) fiks, fris; *deem* ~ goedkeur/goedvind; ~**ter** monteur; passer; ~**ness** geskiktheid, fiks=heid; ~**ting** (pl) benodig(d)hede; toebehore, onderdele, bybehore; (a) passend, gepas

five vyf; ~**-course meal** vyfgang-ete; ~**-speed gearbox** vyfgangratkas

fix (n) verleentheid, moeilikheid; (v) vasmaak; verrig; *in a* ~ in 'n penarie; ~ **up** regmaak

fix'ture vaste toebehore; bepaling (sport); (pl) wedstrydreeks, program

flabb'ergasted (a) verbluf/oorbluf, dronkge=slaan

flabb'y (a) slap, pap(perig), week

flag (n) vlag; *hoist the* ~ die vlag hys; *lower/strike the* ~ die vlag stryk

flag'hoisting vlaghysing; ~ **cer'emony** vlag=hysseremonie

fla'grant (a) verregaand, skandalig, flagrant; berug *also* **outra'geous**

flair aanleg, instink *also* **knack**

flake (n) vlok; vonk; skilfer; snysel; (v) af=skilfer; afdop

flamboy'ant (a) flambojant, swierig *also* **orna'te**

flame (n) vlam, vuur, hartstog, *burst into* ~ aan (die) brand slaan; *fan the* ~s die vuur aanwakker/aanblaas; ~**thro'wer** vlamwerper

flaming'o -es flamink (voël)

flank (n) sy, flank; lies

flann'el flanel; (pl) flanelbroek; flennieonder=klere; ~**graph** flenniebord

flap (n) flap; deksel; valdeur(tjie); luik

flapp'er bakvissie (meisie); stert, vin

flare (n) seinfakkel (mil.); flikkerlig; (v) flikker, skitter; ~ **up** opvlam/opvlieg

flash (n) -es blits, flits; ~ *in the pan* 'n op=flikkering; 'n mislukking; (v) skitter; blits, uitstraal; ~ *back* weerkaats; ~**back** (n) te=rugflits; ~**er** ontbloter (man); ~ **in'dicator** rigtingflitser; ~**light** flits(lig); flikkerlig; ~**point** brandpunt; ~**y** (a) spoggerig

flask fles, bottel; **hip** ~ heupfles

flat [1] (n) woonstel

flat [2] (n) vlakte; laagte; mol (mus.); (v) plat maak; (a) plat; vlak; pap (band); ~ **beer** verslaande/verskaalde bier; ~ **rate** vaste tarief; ~ **footed** platvoet=; ~ **iron** stryk=

yster; ~**ly** ronduit; plat; ~**ten** plat slaan, plet; ~ **tyre** pap band

flatt'er (v) vlei, flikflooi; ~**er** vleier, witvoe=tjiesoeker; ~**y** vleiery, vleitaal

flav'our (n) smaak; geur; (v) kruie, geur

flaw (n) fout, gebrek; defek; gles (in diamant)

flax vlas

flea vlooi; ~**mar'ket** vlooimark, snuffelmark

fleck (n) vlek; sproet; stippie; (v) spikkel, vlek; ~**ed** bont, gespikkel(d)

fledg'ling klein voëltjie; snuiter (mens)

flee (v) vlug (uit die land); ontwyk; padgee

fleece (n) vlies; vag; skeersel; **gol'den** ~ gulde vlies; (v) (af)skeer; uitbuit

fleet [1] (n) vloot; seearm; ~ **ow'ner** vlooteienaar (motorkarre)

fleet [2] (v) vervlieg; (a) vinnig; ~ *of foot* vlugvoetig; ~**ing** verganklik; vlugtig

flesh (n) vlees (menslik); vleis (dierlik); lig=gaam; *make one's ~ creep* hoendervleis laat kry; ~**ly** vleeslik, sinlik

flex (n) elektriese koord; (v) buig; ~**time/flexi-time** skiktyd *see* **core time**

flex'ible buigsaam, soepel, fleksiel, plooibaar; meegaande (mens)

flick tik, raps, vee(g); ~ **knife** springmes

flick'er (n) geflikker; getril; (v) flikker, tril; klap (vlerke); ~ **light** flikkerlig

flight [1] (n) vlug; ontsnapping *also* **esca'pe**

flight [2] vlug (groep vliegtuie); swerm; *put to* ~ op loop jaag; ~ *of stairs* trap; ~ **plan/sched'ule** vlugplan/vlugrooster; ~ **recor'der** vlugopnemer, stemopnemer *also* **black box**

flim'sy dun; flenterig; flou (ekskuus)

flinch (v) aarsel, terugdeins, weifel

fling (n) gooi; dans; (v) gooi, slinger, smyt

flint vuurklip/vuursteen; vuurslag

flirt (n) flerrie, vryerige meisie, flirt; (v) koketteer, flankeer; ~ *with the girls* flankeer met die nooiens

flit (v) vlieg, fladder

float (n) vlot; dobber; sierwa (optog); (v) dryf, dobber; floteer (lening); vlot maak (skip); oprig (maatskappy); dobber; **cash** ~ kon=tantvlot/wisselfonds (boekhou)

floa'ting drywend, dryf=, vlottend; ~ **dock** dryfdok; ~ **tro'phy** wisseltrofee

flock (n) trop, kudde; ~ *together* saamstroom, saambondel

flog klop, pak gee, slaan; ~ *oneself* jouself moor; (n) ~**ging** pak slae, loesing *also* span'king, hi'ding

flood (n) vloed/oorstroming; sondvloed; (v) oorstroom; versuip (vergasser); ~**gate** sluis; ~ **disas'ter** vloedramp; ~**lights** spreiligte

floor (n) vloer; verdieping; vlak; **se'cond** ~ tweede vloer/vlak; ~ **shift** (car) vloerkierie, plesierkierie (idiom.)

flop (n) plof; mislukking/misoes; fladder; neer= plof

flop'py disc/disk (n) disket; slapskyf; ~ **drive** slapskyfaandrywer (rek.)

flor'a plantegroei, flora

flor'ist bloemis, blomkweker (mens)

floss dons; vloksy/vlos(sy); **den'tal** ~ tande= vlos

flot'sam wrakgoed, opdrifsel

floun'der (v) spartel, sukkel, kleitrap

flour meelblom; ~**bag** meelsak

flou'rish (n) bloei; glans; prag; (v) bloei, floreer; pronk; ~**ing** bloeiend, welvarend, voorspoedig

flow (n) vloei; stroming; *ebb and* ~ eb en vloed; (v) vloei, stroom; ~**chart** vloeikaart

flo'wer (n) blom; bloeisel; (v) blom, bloei; ~ **arrange'ment** blommerangskikking; ~ **girl** strooimeisie; blommeverkoopster; ~**ing peach** sierperske; ~ **show** blommeskou; ~**y** blomryk; breedsprakig, hoogdrawend

flu griep, influensa *see* **influen'za**

fluc'tuate (v) sweef, skommel; wissel; **fluc'= tuating prices** skommelende pryse

flue skoorsteenpyp; windpyp

flu'ent (a) vloeiend; glad, vlot, pront (praat)

fluff (n) dons, pluisie; ~**y** donserig, donsagtig

flu'id (n) vloeistof; (a) vloeiend, vloeibaar

fluke (n) gelukskoot, gelukslag; meevaller; *the perfect* ~ die volmaakte gelukhou, putjie-in-een/fortuinhou (gholf)

fluores'cent light buislig

flush (v) deurspoel; aanvuur; blos (op wange) (a) blosend; volop (geld); ~*ed with wine* deur wyn verhit; **hot** ~**es** warm gloede

flute fluit; fluitblaser; groef ~**d** gegroef

flut'ist fluitspeler

flutt'er (n) gefladder, gejaagdheid; (v) fladder; opja(ag); in die war bring

flux (n) stroming, saamvloeiing; *state of* ~ vloeibare toestand; (v) stroom

fly[1] (n) **flies** vlieg; *there are no flies on her* sy is wawyd wakker

fly[2] (n) **flies** vliegwiel; onrus (horlosie); gulp (broek); (v) vlieg, laat waai; ~ *into a pas=*

sion woedend word

fly[3] (a) geslepe; oulik, slim, gevat, oorlams

fly'half (n) losskakel (rugby)

fly'ing (a) vlieënd; ~ **ant** rysmier; ~ **sau'cer** vlieënde piering; ~ **squad** blitspatrollie

fly: ~**-over** oorbrug; ~ **swat(ter)** vlieëklap; ~**trap** vlieëvanger; ~**wheel** vliegwiel

foal (n, v) vul (perd)

foam (n, v) skuim; ~ **rub'ber** skuimrubber

foc'al (a) fokaal; ~ **point** brandpunt, fokus

foc'us (n) ..**ci**, -**es** brandpunt; fokus; (v) saamtrek, konsentreer; instel, fokus

fodd'er voer

foe -**s** vyand *also* en'emy

foet'us (n) ongebore vrug, fetus

fog (n) mis *also* **mist**; newel; ~**gy** mistig, newelig; dof, onduidelik; ~ **horn** misho= ring; ~ **patch** miskol

foil[1] (n) foelie; bladmetaal, bladgoud

foil[2] (v) verydel, fnuik, uitoorlê

fold[1] (n) trop; kudde; kraal; (v) omsluit

fold[2] (n) vou; plooi; (v) vou; ~**er** voublad; omslag; ~**ing chair** voustoel

fol'iage (n) loof, blare, lommer; **fa'cial** ~ welige baard

fol'io -**s** bladsy; folio; foliant (boek)

folk mense; *little* ~**s** die kleinspan; *old* ~**s** ou mense; ~ **dan'cing** volksdanse; ~**lore** volksoorlewering, volkskunde, folklore; ~ **medi'cine** boereraat *also* **ho'me rem'edy**; ~**song** volksliedjie; ~ **tale** sprokie

foll'ow volg, navolg; ~ **up** voortsit; opvolg; ~**er** navolger, volgeling; ~**ing** (n) aanhang; gevolg; (a) volgende, onderstaande; ~**-on** opvolgbeurt (krieket); ~**-up** opvolg(brief)

foll'y follies dwaasheid, gekheid

fond (a) versot, verlief; ~ *of* lief vir/gek na

fon'dle liefkoos, streel; betas, bevoel

font doopbak(kie), doopvont

food kos, voedsel; ~ *for thought* stof tot nadenke; pitkos; ~ **poi'soning** voedselver= gift(ig)ing; ~**stuffs** eetgoed, eetware

fool (n) dwaas, gek; domkop, swaap; *make a* ~ *of* vir die gek hou; ~*s' paradise* gekkepa= radys; (v) fop, flous; vir die gek hou; ~**har'dy** domastrant, onbesonne; ~**ishness** dwaasheid; ~**proof** flatervry/peutervry

foot (n) **feet** voet; *put one's* ~ *into it* 'n flater begaan; (v) ~ *the bill* opdok/betaal; ~**ball** voetbal; ~**hold** vastrapplek; ~**note** voet= noot; ~**path** sypaadjie; ~**print** spoor; ~**slog** voetslaan; ~**wear** skoene, skoeisel

fop (n) modegek, fat, ydeltuit (mens)

for (prep) vir, na, om, tot, teen; ~ *all I care* sover dit my aangaan; *go* ~ *a walk* 'n ent gaan loop; ~ *goodness' sake* in hemels= naam; *long* ~ verlang na; ~ *my part* wat my betref; ~ *my sake*, vir/om my ontwil; ~ *sale* te koop; (conj) want

forbid' verbied, belet, verhinder; *Heaven* ~ mag die Here dit verhoed; ~**den** ongeoor= loof, verbode, belet

force (n) krag, mag, geweld; (pl) troepe; ~ *of gravity* swaartekrag; *in* ~ van krag; *put in* ~ in werking stel; (v) dwing, forseer; ~**d** ge= maak, onnatuurlik; ~**d lan'ding** nood= landing *also* **crash lan'ding**

for'ceps (n) tang, tandetrekker, knyper

fore'arm (n) onderarm; voorarm

for(e)'bear (n) voorvader, voorsaat *also* **an'= cestor**

forebo'ding voorgevoel, voorspooksel

fore'cast (n) vooruitskatting, projeksie; bera= ming; **wea'ther** ~ weervoorspelling

fore'cast (v) vooruitskat, projekteer

fore'father voorvader *also* **for(e)'bear**

fore'finger voorvinger

fore'gone verby; afgedaan; ~ **conclu'sion** uit= gemaakte saak

fore: ~**ground** voorgrond; ~**hand** voorarm (tennis); ~**head** voorhoof/voorkop

for'eign buitelands, vreemd; uitheems; **F**~ **Affairs'** Buitelandse Sake; ~ **exchan'ge** buitelandse valuta; ~ **tra'de** buitelandse handel; ~**er** buitelander; vreemdeling

fore'man , **.men** voorman, opsigter

fore'most eerste, voorste, vernaamste

fore'name (n) voornaam; ~**d** voornoem(d)

forerunn'er (n) voorbode; voorloper

foresee' (v) verwag; voorsien, vooruitsien *also* **antic'ipate**; *in the* ~*able future* binne af= sienbare tyd

fore'shore voorstrand, strandgebied

fore'skin voorhuid

fo'rest (n) bos, woud; (v) bebos

fo'rester (n) bosbouer; boswagter, houtvester

fo'restry bosbou, boswese

fore'taste (n) voorsmaak

foretell' (v) voorspel, vooruitsê

fore'thought voorbedagtheid; voorsorg

forewarn' vooruit waarsku

fore'word voorwoord *also* **pref'ace**

forf'eit (v) verbeur *also* **surren'der** (v); ~ **mon'ey** roukoop

forge (v) smee (smid); vervals *also* **fake**; ~**d sig'nature** vervalste naamtekening/handte= kening

forg'ery ~**ries** vervalsing; namaking

forget' (v) vergeet, in gebreke bly; afleer; ~**ful** vergeetagtig

forget'-me-not vergeet-my-nietjie (blom)

forgive' (v) vergeef/vergewe; verskoon; ~**ness** vergifnis

fork (n) vurk; gaffel; mik (boom); (v) vertak; ~**lift** vurkhyser

forlorn' verlore, verlate; ellendig, wanhopig

form (n) vorm; gedaante; formulier; *be in good* ~ op sy stukke wees; (v) vorm; maak, vervaardig

form'al vormlik, stelselmatig, styf; formeel

formal'ity **..ties** plegtigheid; formaliteit

form'at formaat

forma'tion vorming, stigting, formasie

form'er (a) vroeër; vorig; voormalig, gewese; (pron) eersgenoemde; ~ **pre'sident** voor= malige president; ~**ly** (adv) voorheen, eer= tyds, vanmelewe, vroeër

form'idable (a) gedug, formidabel; impone= rend

form'ula **-e**, **-s** voorskrif, formule

fornica'tion (n) hoerery, owerspel, ontug

fort (n) vesting, skans, fort *also* **strong'hold**

forth voorwaarts, verder, vervolgens; *and so* ~ ensovoorts; ~**com'ing** eerskomende, vol= gende; ~**with** dadelik, oombliklik

fort'ieth veertigste

fortifica'tion (n) versterking; verskansing

fort'itude moed, sterkte *also* **cour'age**

fort'night veertien dae; *this day* ~ vandag oor veertien dae

fort'ress **-es** vesting, fort *also* **cas'tle**

fort'unate (a) gelukkig, voorspoedig; gunstig

fort'une geluk; lot; fortuin; *tell one's* ~ sy toekoms voorspel; iem. inklim; *try one's* ~ jou geluk beproef; ~ **hun'ter** fortuinsoeker; geluksoeker; ~ **tel'ler** waarsêer

fort'y veertig; ~ *winks* 'n dutjie, effens skuins= lê

for'ward (n) voorspeler; (v) (af)stuur, versend; (a) voorwaarts, voorbarig; parmantig; (adv) voorwaarts; *brought* ~ oorgebring, oorge= dra; ~ *child* vroegryp/oulike kind; *look* ~ *to* uitsien na

for'ward(s) vooruit, verder

foss'il (n) verstening, fossiel; (a) fossiel

fos'ter grootmaak; kweek; ~ **child** pleegkind;

∼ **pa′rents** pleegouers; ∼ **care** pleegsorg

foul (v) bemors; besmeer; (a) walglik, vuil; ongunstig (weer); ∼ **deed** gemene/veragte= like daad; ∼ **lang′uage** vuil taal; ∼**-mouth= ed** vuilbekkig; ∼ **play** gemene spel, vuil spel; ∼ **wea′ther** slegte/gure weer

founda′tion (n) stigting, grondslag; fonda= ment/fondasie; ∼ **gar′ment** vormdrag, pos= tuurdrag; ∼ **stone** hoeksteen

foun′ded opgerig, gestig (firma); gegrond

foun′der (n) oprigter, stigter; ∼ **mem′ber** stigterslid

found′ling (n) vondeling; optelkind

found′ry (n) (metaal)gietery; smeltery

foun′tain fontein; bron; ∼ **pen** vulpen; **wa′ter** ∼ spuitfontein *also* **lea′ping** ∼

four vier; *on all* ∼s hande-viervoet; ∼**footed** viervoetig; ∼**pos′ter** ledekant/hemelbed; ∼**some** vierspel

four′teen veertien; ∼**th** veertiende

fourth vierde; ∼**ly** vierdens

fourway stop (street) vierrigtingstop (straat)

four-wheel drive (n) vierwieldryf (voertuig)

fowl (n) hoender *see* **chick′en**; (pl) pluimvee; ∼**run** hoenderkamp

fox (n) jakkals, vos; (v) flous; ∼ **hunt** jak= kalsjag; ∼**terrier** foksterriër; ∼**trot** jakkals= draf (soort dans); ∼**y** slu, skelm *also* **cun′= ning, wi′ly**

fo′yer (n) voorportaal, foyer

frac′tion breuk; fraksie; deel; **de′cimal** ∼ desimale breuk; **vul′gar** ∼ gewone breuk

frac′ture (n) breuk, beenbreuk; (v) breek; ∼ *of the skull* skedelbreuk

frag′ile breekbaar; bros, swak

frag′ment (n) brokstuk, fragment

fra′grance geurigheid *also* **per′fume**

frail (a) broos; tingerig, swak; ∼ **a′ged** verswakte bejaardes; ∼**care** verswaktesorg; ∼**care u′nit** sorgeenheid

frame (n) raam, lys; kosyn (deur); (v) lys, omlys, raam; ∼**work** raamwerk

franc frank (geldeenheid)

France Frankryk

fran′chise stemreg, kiesreg; konsessie; ge= bruiksreg, franchise

frank (a) vrymoedig, openhartig *also* **can′did**; *quite* ∼*ly* om die waarheid te sê

fran′tic (a) woedend, waansinnig, rasend

fratern′ity ..ties broederskap, gilde

fraud (n) bedrog, bedrieëry; ∼**ulent** oneerlik; bedrieglik, vals

fray (n) twis, rusie, geveg; *enter the* ∼ tot die stryd toetree

freak nuk, gril, gier; frats; ∼ **ac′cident** frats= ongeluk; ∼ **of na′ture** natuurgril, natuur= frats; ∼ **wea′ther** fratsweer

frec′kle sproet, vlek

free (v) vrymaak, bevry, verlos; (a, adv) vry, gratis; ∼**boo′ter** vrybuiter; ∼**dom** vryheid; **F**∼**dom Day** Vryheidsdag (vakansie); ∼**dom figh′ter** vryheidsvegter; ∼**dom of the ci′ty** ereburgerskap; ∼ **en′terprise** vryemarkstel= sel, private inisiatief; ∼**hold prop′erty** vrypageiendom; ∼**kick** strafskop; ∼**lance** vryskut; ∼**-lance jour′nalist** vryskutjoerna= lis; **F**∼**man** ereburger; ∼**post** vrypos

Free′mason Vrymesselaar

free-range: ∼ **chick′en** skrophoender, werf= hoender

frees′ia -s freesia, kammetjie (blom)

Free State (province) Vrystaat

free: ∼**way** deurpad (tussenstedelik), snel= weg; ∼**wheel** vrywiel; ∼**will** (n) vrywillig= heid; (a) vrywillig, uit eie beweging

freeze (n) ryp; **deep**∼ vrieskas; (v) vries, bevries; stol (TV-beeld); ∼**r** vrieskas

freez′ing (a) ysig; ∼ **point** vriespunt

freight (n) vrag, lading; vraggeld; ∼**er** vrag= skip

French (n, a) Frans; *take* ∼ *leave* wegloop, dros; ∼ **drain** syferput; ∼ **pol′isher** lakver= nisser (mens)

fren′zy waansin, kranksinnigheid, dolheid

freq′uency (n) frekwensie; ∼ **modula′tion (FM)** frekwensiemodulasie (FM)

frequent′[1] (v) dikwels besoek; boer by

fre′quent[2] (a) herhaaldelik, gedurig, dikwels

fre′quently dikwels, herhaaldelik

fresh (a) vars, fris, koel; *as* ∼ *as a daisy* springlewendig; ∼**er**/∼**ette**/∼**man** nuwe= ling, groentjie (aan univ.)

fri′ar monnik (mens)

fric′tion (n) wrywing

Fri′day Vrydag

frid′ge (n) *see* **refrig′erator**

friend vriend/vriendin, maat; ∼**liness** vriende= likheid; ∼**ly** vriendelik, vriendskaplik; ∼**ly coun′try** bevriende land; ∼**ly match** vriend= skaplike wedstryd; ∼**ship** vriendskap

frig′ate fregat(skip)

fright (n) skrik; *take a terrible* ∼ oorhoeks skrik; ∼**en bang maak,** vrees aanja; ∼**ened** verskrik; ∼**ful** verskriklik, vreeslik

frig'id (a) yskoud; koel, kil *also* **aloof'**; styf
fringe' (n) fraiing; soom; ~ **ben'efits** byvoor=
dele *also* **perks**
frisk (v): ~ *a suspect* 'n verdagte visenteer;
~**y** (a) lewendig, dartel
friv'olous ligsinnig, kinderagtig; beuselagtig
frizz'ly kroes (hare)
frock (n) rok, jurk; manel; toga
frog padda *also* **toad**
frog'march (v) dra-sleep (onwillige persoon)
frol'ic (n) plesier, vermaak; skerts; (v) vrolik
wees, grappe maak, skerts; (a) vrolik
from van, vandaan; uit, vanuit; *apart* ~
afgesien van; behalwe, buiten; ~ *childhood*
van jongs af
front (n) voorkant, front; ~**age** voorgewel;
voorkant, front; ~**line sta'tes** frontliniestate;
~**loa'der** laaigraaf; hysvurk; ~**wheel drive**
voorwielaandrywing/voorwieldryf
front'ier grens *also* **bor'der**; ~ **war** grens=
oorlog
frost (n) ryp; (v) ryp; versier (koek); ~**bite** (n)
vriesbrand; ~**bit'ten** (a) gevriesbrand; ~**ed**
glass matglas
froth skuim; ~**y** skuimagtig, skuimend
frown (n) frons; (v) frons
froz'en (v) *see* **freeze**; (a) bevries, yskoud;
styf; ~ **meat** bevrore vleis
frug'al (a) spaarsaam *also* **thrif'ty**; suinig
fruit vrugte; resultaat, ~**fly** vrugtevlieg; ~**ful**
vrugbaar; ~ **juice** vrugtesap; ~ **sal'ad** vrug=
teslaai
frustra'tion verydeling, frustrasie
fry (v) braai; **small** ~ (n) onbeduidende
mense
fudge (n) fudge (lekkers); onsin
fu'el (n) brandstof; ~ **consump'tion** brand=
stofverbruik; ~ **injec'tion** brandstofinspui=
ting
fu'gitive (n) vlugteling; voortvlugtige (mens)
fulfil' (v) vervul; verwesenlik; uitvoer, vol=
bring, nakom
full (a) vol; gevul; voltallig; ~*time employ=
ment* voltydse/heeltydse werk; *in* ~ *swing* in
volle gang; (adv) ten volle, ruim; ~**back**
heelagter; ~ **speed** in volle vaart; ~**stop**
punt; ~**time** voltyds/heeltyds; ~**y** volkome,
heeltemal, ten volle
fum'ble (v) friemel, frommel; swak hanteer

fume (n) rook, damp; woede; (v) damp, rook;
briesend wees
fum'igate (v) berook, uitrook, fumigeer
fun pret; skerts; *poke* ~ *at* die gek skeer met;
~**fair** kermis, pretpark; ~**run** pretloop
func'tion (n) verrigting; byeenkoms, funksie;
(v) werk, fungeer, funksioneer; ~**al** funk=
sioneel
fund (n) fonds, kapitaal; (v) befonds; bekostig;
~**rai'sing** geldinsameling
fundamen'tal (a) fundamenteel; ~ **rights** men=
seregte *also* **hu'man rights**
fun'di (n) kenner, gesaghebbende, foendi
fun'eral (n) begrafnis; (a) begrafnis=, graf=,
lyk=, doods=; ~ **march** treurmars; ~ **pro=
ces'sion** lykstoet; ~ **ser'vice** roudiens; ~ **un=
derta'ker** begrafnisondernemer
fun'gus -es, ..gi fungus, swam; paddastoel
funic'ular kabel=, tou=, draad=; ~ **rail'way**
kabelspoor; tandratspoor *also* **ca'bleway**
funk (n) vrees; bangbroek; *get the* ~*s* bang
word; ~**y** bang, lafhartig
funn'el tregter; skoorsteen
funn'y (a) grappig, snaaks, koddig
fur (n) pels, bont; ~ **cloak** pelsmantel, ~ **coat**
pelsjas
fur'ious (a) woes, woedend, rasend *also*
ra'ging
fur'nace (smelt)oond; stookoond; smeltkroes
furn'ish verskaf, lewer; voorsien; meubileer/
meubeleer; uitrus; ~**er** meubileerder/meu=
beleerder
fur'niture (n) meubels, huisraad, meubelment/
meublement; **piece of** ~ meubelstuk
fu'rrow (n) voor, sloot *also* **ditch** (n)
furth'er (v) bevorder; aanhelp; (a, adv) verder,
bowendien; ~ *information* meer/nader(e) in=
ligting; ~**more** verder, bowendien; ~**most**
verste/vêrste, uiterste
furth'est verste/vêrste, uiterste
fur'y woede, raserny; *in a* ~ rasend
fuse (n) lont; smeltdraadjie, sekering
fu'sion (n) (ver)smelting; fusie (atoom)
fuss (n) ophef, gedoente, herrie, opskudding
fut'ile (a) vergeefs, vrugteloos, ydel
fu'ture (n) toekoms; *bright* ~ rooskleurige
toekoms; *the near* ~ die nabye/afsienbare
toekoms; (a) toekomstig, aanstaande; ~ **tense**
toekomende tyd

G

ga'ble (n) gewel (van huis)

gad (v) ronddrentel; ~ *about* rondslenter

gad'get (n) toestel(letjie); katoeter, kontrepsie

gaff (n) ysterhaak, vishaak, gaffel

gag (v) muilband; die mond snoer

gag'gle (n) trop ganse; (v) snater, kekkel

gai'ety (n) vrolikheid; joligheid/jolyt, pret *also* **mirth, mer'riment**; vertoon

gain (n) wins, profyt; aanwins; (v) wen, verkry; verwerf; ~ *the upper hand* die oormag kry; *not for* ~ sonder winsoogmerk; ~ings winste

gal'a -s fees, gala; **swim'ming** ~ swemgala, swembyeenkoms

gal'axy (n) sterrestelsel; melkweg, hemelstraat

gale (n) stormwind, windvlaag

gall (n) gal; bitterheid; (v) terg; vergal

gall'ant (n) galant; (a) galant; swierig, statig

gall'ery galery; *play to the* ~ effek soek

gall'ey -s galei (plat slaweskip); ~ **proof** galeiproef/strookproef; ~ **slave** galeislaaf

gal'livant (v) rondjakker, jollifikasie hou; flankeer, rinkink

gall'op (n) galop; *at a* ~ op 'n galop

gall'ows galg

galore' in oorvloed, volop, soos bossies

gal'vanise (v) galvaniseer; ~d (a) versink; ~d **iron** (sink)plaat, (ge)galvaniseerde yster

gam'ble (n) dobbelary, dobbelspel; (v) dobbel, verkwis; ~ *away* verwed, verdobbel; ~r dobbelaar

gam'bling dobbelary; ~ **house** dobbelhuis/kasino; ~ **table** dobbeltafel

gam'bol (n) bokkesprong; (v) huppel, bok-spring, baljaar, ravot

game[1] (n) spel, spel(l)etjie, pot(jie), wedstryd; wild; *big* ~ grootwild; *play the* ~ eerlik handel; *the* ~ *is up* die saak is verlore

game[2] (a) bereid; *I am* ~ ek is reg/bereid; moedig; lam, mank

game: ~ **farm** wildplaas; ~fish sportvis; ~keep'er wildopsigter, boswagter; ~ poa'-cher wilddief, stroper; ~ran'ger wildwag-ter; ~ reser've wildtuin, wildreservaat

gan'der gansmannetjie

gang bende; ~ lea'der bendeleier; ~ rape groepverkragting/bendeverkragting

gang'rene verrotting; kouevuur, gangreen

gang'ster rampokker, straatboef *also* **thug**

gaol (n) gevangenis, tronk *also* **jail;** ~bird tronkvoël; ~er tronkbewaarder, sipier

gap gaping, opening; bres; leemte; *narrow the* ~ die gaping vernou

gape (v) gaap; hunker; ~ *at* aangaap

ga'rage garage, vulstasie, motorhawe (pu-bliek); motorhuis (privaat)

garb'age afval, oorskiet; vullis; ~ **bin** vullis-blik *also* **trash bin**

gar'ble: ~d mes'sage deurmekaar boodskap

gard'en tuin; hof; ~er tuinier (as eienaar); tuinhulp/tuinman; ~ **hose** tuinslang

garden'ia -s katjiepiering (blom)

gar'den: ~ing tuinmaak/tuinbou; ~ **par'ty** tuinparty

gar'gle (n) gorreldrank; (v) gorrel

garl'ic knoffel

garm'ent kleding, kledingstuk; ~ **wor'kers** klerewerkers

ga'rrison (n) garnisoen; (v) beset

gart'er (n) kousband

gas (n) -es gas; ~bag gassak; windlawaai *also* **brag'gart, boas'ter;** ~ **cyl'inder** gassilin-der; ~ **en'gine** gasenjin

gash (n) -es sny, hou; (v) sny, kloof

gas'ket pakstuk; pakking, voering, vulsel

gasp (n) snik; *the last* ~ doodsnik; (v) snik, snak, hyg; ~ *for breath* snak na asem

gas'tric maag-, gastries; ~ **fe'ver** maagkoors; ~ **ul'cer** maagseer

gas'tronome (n) koskenner; smulpaap/lekker-bek

gate (n) hek, hekgeld; toegang; (v) insluit; hok; ~-crasher hekstormer; indringer (par-tytjie); ~kee'per hekwagter, portier; ~ mon'ey toegangsgeld, hekgeld

gath'er (v) vergader, byeenkom; versamel; *the clouds* ~ die wolke pak saam; ~ing (n) vergadering, byeenkoms, saamtrek

gaud'y (a) opsigtig, bont *also* **flash'y**

gauge (n) spoorwydte; maat; **nar'row** ~ smal-spoor; (v) (af)meet; **rain** ~ reënmeter

gauze (n) gaas; wasigheid/dynsigheid

gav'el (n) voorsittershamer; klophamer

gay[1] (a) lewendig, vrolik

gay[2] (a) homoseksueel; (n) gay; homosek-sueel

gaze (n) starende/verbaasde blik; (v) (aan)= staar, aangaap; tuur

gazelle' gasel (bok)

gazette' (n) koerant, gaset; **gov'ernment** ~ staatskoerant; (v) aankondig

gear (n) rat, tandrat; gereedskap; tuig; uitrus= ting; *change* ~ oorskakel; *in* ~ in rat; *low (high)* ~ laagste (hoogste) versnelling; ~**box** ratkas

geck'o (n) boomgeitjie, gekko

gei'ger coun'ter geigerteller

gel'atine gelatien

geld (v) sny, kastreer; ~**ed pig** burg

geld'ing reun (perd)

gem (n) edelsteen; juweel; briljant

gem' squash skorsie; lemoenpampoentjie

gen'der (n) geslag; ~**-ben'ding** uniseksing; ~ **eq'uity** geslagsgelykheid

ge'ne (n) -s geen (erflikheidsbepaler) *see* **gen= et'ic engineer'ing**

genealog'ical genealogies, geslags=; ~ **tree** stamboom, geslagregister

gen'eral (n) generaal (mens); *in* ~ oor/in die algemeen; (bw) deurgaans; (a) algemeen; gewoon; **G**~ **Assem'bly** Algemene Verga= dering (VN); ~ **practi'tioner** algemene praktisyn *also* **fam'ily practi'tioner**; ~ **man'ager** hoofbestuurder; ~ **meet'ing** al= gemene vergadering; ~ **pub'lic** die gewone/ algemene publiek; ~**ise** (v) veralgemeen

gen'erate opwek (elektrisiteit); ontwikkel (stoom); teel, voortplant

genera'tion (n) geslag, generasie; ~ **gap** ouder= domsgaping, generasiegaping

gen'erator kragopwekker; ontwikkelaar

gener'ic ~ **med'icines** generiese medisyne

generos'ity vrygewigheid; grootmoedigheid

gen'erous (a) grootmoedig, vrygewig; ruim

gen'et muskeljaatkat, musseljaatkat

genet'ic geneties; ~ **enginee'ring** genetiese manipulering; ~**s** erflikheidsleer, genetika

gen'itals (n, pl) geslagsorgane, skaamdele

gen'itive genitief

gen'ius (n) genie (mens); beskermgees

gen'ocide volksmoord; menseslagting

gen'tile (n) nie-Jood; Christen; heiden (vir Jode)

gen'tle (a) sagsinnig, meegaande, vriendelik; *the* ~ *sex* die skone geslag; ~**man** fatsoen= like man; heer/gentleman: ~**man's agree= ment** ereooreenkoms; ere-akkoord

gent'ly saggies, soetjies; vriendelik

gen'uine eg, opreg, onvervals; *the* ~ *article* die ware Jakob, die regte ding

geog'raphy aardrykskunde, geografie

geol'ogy aardkunde, geologie

geom'etry meetkunde, geometrie

geran'ium -s geranium, malva (blom)

geriat'ric ~ **prob'lems** ouderdomsprobleme; ~**s** (n) geriatrie, ouderdomskunde

germ (n) (siekte)kiem; oorsprong

Ger'man (n) Duitser; Duits; (a) Duits; ~ **mea'sles** Duitse masels, rooihond; ~ **sau= 'sage** metwors

Ger'many Duitsland

germ'inate (v) ontkiem, uitloop, opkom

ges'ture (n) gebaar, beweging; (v) gebare maak; deur gebare beduie

get (v) kry, verkry, bekom, verwerf; bereik; ~ *along with* met iem. klaarkom; ~ *going* val weg; kry koers, sny 'n lyn; ~ *the better of* die oorhand kry; ~ *the boot* in die pad gesteek word; ~ *a cold* koue vat; ~ *out of hand* handuit ruk; ~ *on* vooruitgaan; ~ *ready* klaarmaak; ~**-at'-able** bekombaar; bereikbaar; ~**-away'** car wegkommotor

gey'ser warm bron/spuitbron; geiser

ghast'ly afgryslik; vreeslik; aaklig

ghost spook, gees, skim; *give up the* ~ die gees gee; **Holy G**~ Heilige Gees *also* **Ho'ly Spir'it**; ~**ly** spookagtig, aaklig; ~ **squad** skimpatrollie; ~ **sto'ry** spookstorie; ~**wri'ter/au'thor** skimskrywer

ghoul (n) lykverslinder, grafskender; monster

gi'ant (n) reus; (a) reuse=, reusagtig; ~ **bull'd= ing** reusegebou

gidd'y (a) duiselig, lighoofdig, ligsinnig

gift geskenk, present; gawe; ~**ed** talentvol; ~**ed child** begaafde kind; ~ **vouch'er** geskenkbewys; ~ **wrap** geskenkpapier

gigan'tic reusagtig; ontsaglik *also* **hu'ge**

gig'gle (v) giggel *also* **snig'ger**

gig'olo (n) gigolo; kooivlooi, katelknapie *also* **toy'boy**

gild (v) verguld, verfraai; ~**ed** verguld; ryk

gill (n) kieu/kief (van 'n vis); ~ **net** kieunet

gilt (n) verguldsel; klatergoud; (a) verguld; ~**-ed'ged** goudgerand (boek); doodveilig, prima (belegging); ~**s** prima effekte

gim'mick (n) truuk, foefie *also* **trick**

gin (n) jenewer

gin'ger gemmer; rooikop; ~ **ale** gemmer= lim(onade); ~**bread** (n) gemmerbrood; ~**ly** versigtig, behoedsaam *also* **cau'tious**

gip'sy gipsies sigeuner; swartoog; vabond
giraffe' kameelperd, giraf *also* **camel'opard**
gird (v) omgord, ombind
gir'dle (n) gordel, lyfband, buikgord; (v) om=
gord; omsluit
girl meisie; meisiekind; nooi; ~ **Fri'day** nuts=
meisie; ~**friend** vriendin; nooi/bokkie;
~**hood** meisie(s)jare; ~**ish** skaam, meisie=
agtig; ~**s' high school** hoër meisieskool
gist (n) kern, hoofsaak, *also* **core, es'sence**; *the*
~ *of the report* die kern van die verslag
give (v) gee, oorgee; toegee; skenk, lewer; ~
chase agternasit; ~ *in* tou opgooi; ~ *notice*
kennis gee; ~ *offence* aanstoot gee; ~**n**
gegewe; ~**r** gewer
gla'cier (n) gletser
glad bly, verheug; ~**den** bly maak, verbly; ~
eye knipogie
gladiol'us -es ..li gladiolus, swaardlelie (blom)
glad: ~**ly** graag; blymoedig; ~**ness** blydskap,
vrolikheid; ~**wrap** (n) kleefplastiek
glam'orous (a) betowerend, verleidelik *also*
cap'tivating
glam'our (n) oëverblinding; betowering, aan=
treklikheid *also* **charm**; ~ **girl** prikkelpop
also **pin-up** (n)
glance (n) oogopslag; skramshou; flikkering;
(v) sydelings kyk, aanblik; flikker; ~ *off*
afskram; ~ *over* vlugtig deurkyk, glylees
gland klier
glare (n) glans, skittering; blikkering (affek=
teer sig in motor); (v) skitter, flikker; blikker
glar'ing (a) verblindend; skandelik; ~ **injus'=
tice** skreiende onreg; ~ **omis'sion** skande=
like versuim
glass (n) **-es** glas; ruit; (a) glas=, glaas=; ~=
blo'wer glasblaser; ~**es** bril *also* **spec'tacles**
glaze (n) glasuur; (v) verglaas (ruite insit)
glaz'ier glasmaker; glasenier (mens)
gleam (n) ligstraal, flikkering; glimp; glans;
(v) straal, flikker
glee vrolikheid, blydskap; ~**ful** bly, dartel
glen (n) dal, laagte, vlei
glib beweeglik; *a* ~ *tongue* 'n gladde tong
glide (v) gly, glip; sweef; ~**r** sweeftuig
glimm'er (n) flikkering, glinstering; (v) flik=
ker, glinster
glimpse (n) vlugtige blik; kykie; glimp; *catch*
a ~ *of* skrams raaksien
glint (n) skynsel, glinstering; (v) blink,
glinster; *a* ~ *in his eyes* 'n (ondeunde) kyk/
flikkering in sy oë

glitt'er (n) glans, glinstering; luister; (v
glinster; ~**ing** skitterend; ~**ing occa'sio**
glansgeleentheid
globe (n) (aard)bol; gla(a)skap (lamp)
gloom (n) somberheid; ~**y** somber, droefgees
tig, neerslagtig *also* **dis'mal/som'bre**
glor'ify (v) verheerlik, verhef; ophemel
glor'ious roemryk; heerlik
glor'y (n) roem, glorie; saligheid; (v) roen
trots wees, koning kraai; ~ *over* triomfee
oor
gloss[1] (n) **-es** kommentaar, kanttekening
gloss[2] (n) **-es** glans; opheldering; vals skyn; ~
paint glansverf; ~**y** **magazi'ne** glanstyd
skrif
gloss'ary ..ries glossarium, woordelys
glove handskoen; *be hand in* ~ kop in een mu
wees
glow (n) gloed, vuur; (v) gloei, blaak; ~**worn**
glimwurm
glu'cose glukose, druiwesuiker
glue (n) lym, gom; (v) vaslym, vasplak; ~
snif'fing gomsnuif
glum (a) somber, bedruk, droefgeestig
glut (n) oorvoorsiening; (v) oorlaai; oorvoor
sien (die mark); volprop
glutt'on vraat, smulpaap, gulsigaard (mens)
gly'cerine gliserien
gnash kners; ~ *the teeth* op die tande kners
gnat muggie
gnaw (v) knaag, kou, knabbel
gnu -s wildebees; **brin'dled** ~ blouwildebee=
go (n) gang; energie; (v) gaan; loop; ~ *halve*
gelykop deel; ~ *mad* gek word
goal (n) grenspaal; doelpunt; doel (sport,
oogmerk, doelwit; ~**keeper** doelwagter
~**kick** doelskop; ~**post** doelpaal: *move th*
~*posts* die doelpale verskuif
goat bok
gob'ble (v) gulsig eet, inlaai; ~**r** vraat
go-between tussenganger, bemiddelaar *als*
me'diator
gob'lin (n) spook, spooksel; bose gees
go'-cart kaskar *see* **go-kart**
God God; *for* ~*'s sake* in vadersnaam
god god; ~**child** peetkind; ~**dess** godir
~**fa'ther** peetoom; ~**fea'ring** godvresend
~**ly** godvresend; vroom; ~**send** uitreddins
go'-getter pasaangeër; voorslag; inpalmer (men=
go'ing (n) vertrek; gaan; *the* ~ *is good* dit gaa
voor die wind; ~ **concern'** gevestigde
lopende saak

goi'tre kropgeswel

go-kart (n) knortjor; ~ **ra'cing/kar'ting** knor=
tjorrenne

gold (n) goud; (a) goue, goud=

gol'den goue; gulde; ~ **age** goue eeu; ~
hand'shake afdankpasella, tatatjek; ~ **ol'=
dies** goue oues; ~ **rule** gulde reël; ~
wed'ding goue bruilof

gold: ~leaf bladgoud; ~**mine** goudmyn

golf (n) gholf; ~ **ball** gholfbal; ~ **club**
gholfklub; gholfstok; ~ **course** gholfbaan;
~er gholfspeler/gholfer

goll'iwog (n) paaiboelie, spookpop

gond'ola -s gondel

gone (a) gegaan; verlore

gong ghong

gonorrhoea' druiper, gonorree (geslagsiekte)

good (n) welsyn; nut; *for his own* ~ in sy eie
belang; (a, adv) goed, gaaf; ~ **gracious!**
grote genugtig!; ~ *heavens!* my goeie tyd!;
make ~ vergoed; regkom; (tekort) aanvul;
(belofte) nakom; *in* ~ *spirits* in opgewekte
stemming/luim; *do a* ~ *turn* 'n diens bewys;
~ **afternoon'** (goeie)middag; ~**bye'** tot
siens/totsiens/goedgaan!; ~ **day** goeiedag/
dagsê!; ~ **e'vening** (goeie)naand/naandsê!;
~ **fel'lowship** kameraadskap; ~-**for-
nothing** niksnuts (mens)

Good Friday Goeie Vrydag

good: ~-**look'ing** aantreklik; ~ **luck** geluk; ~
luck! sterkte!; ~ **mor'ning** (goeie)môre;
môresê!; ~-**na'tured** goedgeaard

good'ness goedheid, vriendelikheid; ~ *knows*
nugter weet; *for* ~' *sake* in hemelsnaam

good night (goeie)naand, naandsê! (w)

goods (pl) goedere, goed; ~ **train** goedere=
trein

good'timer (n) swierbol, pierewaaier, dartel=
dawie *also* **play'boy**

good'will goedgesindheid; klandisie(waarde)
(besigheid)

Good'will Day Welwillendheidsdag (vakansie)

good'y-goody skynheil, mamma se soet kind=
jie

goose geese gans; uilskuiken; ~**berry** appel=
liefie; ~**flesh/**~**pim'ples** hoendervleis (idi=
om.); ~**step** paradepas

Gord'ian Gordiaans, ingewikkeld; *cut the* ~
knot die Gordiaanse knoop deurhak

gorge (n) kloof, ravyn; (v) verslind, inwurg

gor'geous skitterend, pragtig *also* **magni'fi=
cent/exqui'site**

gorill'a -s gorilla

go-slow' strike sloerstaking

gos'pel evangelie; ~ **truth** heilige waarheid

goss'ip (n) skinderpraatjie; (v) skinder; ~er
babbelkous, skinderbek (mens)

gourm'et (n) fynproewer, gastronoom (mens)

gout (n) jig; pootjie, podagra

go'vern regeer, bestuur; ~ess goewernante;
~**ing bod'y** bestuursraad

go'vernment (n) regering, goewerment; (a)
regerings=, staats=; ~ **gazet'te** staatskoerant

go'vernor goewerneur; reëlaar (masjien)

gown (n) toga; tabberd; mantel; kamerjas

grab (v) gryp, beetpak

grace (n) genade, guns; tafelgebed; swier *also*
charm; grasie; respyt; *by the* ~ *of God* by
die grasie Gods; *days of* ~ respytdae; *say* ~
tafelgebed doen; ~**ful** (a) bekoorlik, be=
vallig

gra'cious (a) deugsaam, hoflik *also* **po'lite**;
good ~! goeie genade!/genugtig!

grade (n) graad; rang; (v) gradeer, sorteer; ~ **8**
graad 8 (st. 6); ~**r** (pad)skraper

grad'ient helling; helling(s)hoek; gradiënt

gra'ding: ~ **list** ranglys, keurlys (sport)

grad'ual geleidelik; trapsgewyse; ~**ly** lang=
samerhand, geleidelik, trapsgewyse

grad'uate (n) gegradueerde (mens); (v) pro=
moveer, gradueer; gradeer

gradua'tion: ~ **ce'remony** gradeplegtigheid

graft (n) ent; bedrog; (v) ent; oorplant

grain (n) graan, graankorrel; grein, bietjie;
draad; ~ **el'evator** graansuier/graansilo; ~
sorg'hum graansorghum

gram gram; *50* ~*s of sugar* 50 gram suiker

gramm'ar (n) spraakleer, spraakkuns, gram=
matika

gram'ophone (n) grammofoon; ~ **rec'ord**
grammofoonplaat

granadill'a grenadella (vrug)

grand (a) groot; groots; vernaam, verhewe;
~**child** kleinkind; ~**dad** oupa

gran'deur grootheid, grootsheid, aansienlik=
heid; *illusions of* ~ grootheidswaan

grand'father oupa/grootvader; ~ **clock** staan-
horlosie/staanoorlosie

grand: ~**mo'ther** ouma/grootmoeder; ~
occa'sion glansgeleentheid; ~ **pia'no** vleuel=
klavier; ~**stand** hoofpawiljoen.

gran'ite graniet

grann'y grannies ouma/grootjie; ~ **flat** tuin=
woonstel, herfshuisie

grant (n) toekenning; skenking; (v) toeken; skenk; verleen

grape druif; ~**fruit** pomelo; ~ **juice** druiwesap; ~**vine** wingerdstok; riemtelegram/bostamboer (idiom.)

graph (n) grafiek; (a) ~**ic** skilderend; lewendig, grafies

graph'ite grafiet, potlood

grasp (n) greep; bereik; houvas; *get a good* ~ ʼn goeie begrip/houvas kry; (v) gryp; begryp; vashou

grass (n) gras; weiveld; *keep off the* ~ bly weg van die gras; ~**hop'per** sprinkaan; ~**roots lev'el** grondvlak, voetsoolvlak; ~ **wid'ow** grasweduwee

grate (n) rooster; traliewerk; vuurherd; (v) knars; ~**ful** dankbaar, erkentlik

grat'er (n) rasper

gratifica'tion bevrediging, voldoening

grat'is (a) gratis, vry, kosteloos

grat'itude dankbaarheid

gratu'ity ..**ties** geskenk; fooi(tjie); beloning, toelae, gratifikasie; bonus

grave[1] (n) graf

grave[2] (a) ernstig; plegtig; swaar *see* **grav'ity**

grav'el (n) growwe sand, gruis; (v) gruis

grave: ~**stone** grafsteen; ~**yard** kerkhof

grav'ing dock (n) droogdok

grav'ity swaarte, gewig; *centre of* ~ swaartepunt; **speci'fic** ~ soortlike gewig

grav'y gravies (vleis)sous; ~ **train** soustrein, strooptrein, weeldetrein, mannawa

graze[1] (n) skaafplek; skramskoot; (v) skram

graze[2] (v) wei, laat wei, graas

graz'ing (n) weiding, weiveld *also* **pas'ture**

grease (n) vet; ghries; (v) smeer, ghries; ~ *the palm* omkoop; ~ **gun** ghriesspuit

greas'y (a) olierig, vetterig; smerig; salwend

great groot; lang; beroemd, aansienlik

Great Brit'ain Groot-Brittanje

great: ~**-grandfat'her** oorgrootvader, oupagrootjie; ~**-great-grand'mother** bet-oorgrootmoeder; ~**ly** grootliks; ~**ness** grootte *also* **size**; grootheid

greed'y (a) gulsig; inhalig, hebsugtig; snoep

green (n) grasbaan; setperk (gholf); (a) groen; fris; onryp; ~ **fee** baangeld; ~**fly** plantluis, bladluis; ~**gage** groenpruim; ~**gro'cer** groentehandelaar; ~**horn** nuweling, groentjie (mens); ~**house** kweekhuis; broeikas; ~**house effect'** kweekhuiseffek; ~ **pep'per** soetrissie; ~**stick frac'ture** knakbreuk

greet (v) groet, begroet; ~**ing** groet, groetnis; groeteboodskap, groetewens(e); ~**ings!** dagsê!, mooi loop; goedgaan!

grem'lin (n) tokkelos(sie), duiweltjie; setfout/setsatan/drukfout

grena'de' granaat; **stun** ~ skokgranaat

grenadel'la *see* **granadilla**

grenadier' grenadier (soldaat)

grey (a) grys, grou; wit, gespikkel, blou (perd); ~ **horse** (blou)skimmelperd; ~**hound** windhond; ~**ish** valerig

grid (n) rooster, tralie; motorhek; bagasierak; ~**i'ron** traliewerk; Amerikaanse voetbal

grief (n) droefheid, hartseer, verdriet; kommer

griev'ance grief; beswaar, ergernis

grill (n) rooster; braaigereg, braaivleis; **mix'ed** ~ allegaartjie; (v) braai; rooster; ~**room** (rooster)restourant, braaihuis/braais

grim grimmig; nors; meedoënloos; wreed; fel, hard; ~ **hu'mour** galgehumor

grime (n) vuiligheid; roet, koolstof

grim'y (a) vuil, morsig *also* **grub'by**

grin (n) gryns, grynslag; (v) gryns; grinnik

grind maal, vergruis; ~ *the teeth* die tande kners; ~**ing stone** maalklip; ~**stone** slypsteen

grip (n) greep; begrip; beheer; houvas; *come to* ~*s* handgemeen raak; (v) (vas)gryp

gripe (n) maagkramp; klagte; (pl) koliek; kramp, knaag; kla *also* **moan**

gris'ly (a) aaklig, grillerig; afskuwelik

grit (n) gruis; sand; durf, (waag)moed; (v) knars, skuur; ~**ty** sanderig, korrelrig

griz'zly (n) ..**lies** grysbeer (Noord-Amerika); (a) grys; gryserig, valerig

groan (n) gekreun/gesteun; (v) kreun, steun

gro'cer kruidenier; ~**y** kruidenierswinkel; (pl) kruideniersware

grog'gy (a) aangeklam, dronkerig *also* **tip'sy**; bewerig

groin lies

groom staljong; bruidegom; (v) roskam; skoonmaak; ~*ed for a senior post* opgelei/voorberei vir ʼn senior pos; *well* ~*ed* netjies uitgevat

groove (n) keep, groef; roetine; (v) ingroef

gross[1] (n) gros (12 dosyn)

gross[2] (a) lomp; grof; bruto; ~ **amount'** (groot)totaal; ~ **nat'ional prod'uct** bruto nasionale produk; ~ **neg'ligence** growwe nalatigheid; ~ **prof'it** bruto wins

ground[1] (n) grond; rede; *gain* ~ veld win

ground[2] (v) grond; grondves, bou; belet om te vlieg (vliegtuig); (a) gemaal, geslyp

ground: ~ **floor** grondvloer; onderste vloer/vlak; ~ **hos'tess** grondwaardin; ~**ing** grondslag; ~**nut** grondboon(tjie); ~**s'man** terreinopsigter

group (n) groep; (v) groepeer, rangskik; ~ **dyn'am'ics** groepdinamika; ~ **lea'der** groepleier

grouse (n) grief, klag; (v) mor, murmureer; ~**r** brompot, knorpot (mens) *also* **moa'ner**

grow groei, toeneem, aanwas; verbou/kweek (gewasse); ~ *up* groot word; ~ **veg'etables** groente kweek; ~**ing pains** groeipyne

growl (n) geknor; (v) knor, brom; ~**er** brompot, knorpot *also* **grum'bler**

grown begroei; gekweek; grootgeword; ~**-up** (n) volwassene; (a) volwasse

growth (n) groei; ~ **fund** groeifonds; ~ **point** groeipunt; ~ **rate** groeikoers

groyne (n) pier *also* **jet'ty, pier**

grudge (n) wrok *also* **mal'ice**; *bear a person a* ~ 'n wrok teen iem. koester; (v) beny, misgun

gru'elling (a) uitputtend, veeleisend; ~ **match** strawwe wedstryd

grue'some grusaam, afsigtelik; ~ **mur'der** grumoord

gruff (a) nors, stuurs, suur

grum'ble (v) mor, knor, brom; ~**r** brompot

grump'y ontevrede, knorrig

grunt (n) geknor, gebrom; (v) knor, brom

G'-string deurtrekker, genadelappie

gua'no ghwano/guano; voëlmis

guarantee' (n) waarborg, garansie; borg; (v) waarborg; borg staan *also* **war'rant** (v)

guard (n) wag; sekuriteitswag; beskerming, bewaking; brandwag; *rear* ~ agterhoede; (v) waghou; bewaak; ~ *against* waak teen

guard'ian voog, beskermer *also* **custo'dian**; ~ **an'gel** beskermengel, skutpatroon

gua'va -s koejawel (vrug)

guess (n) **-es** gissing, vermoede; (v) gis, raai; skat

guest gas, kuiergas; ~**house** gastehuis *also* **lod'ge**; ~ **speak'er** geleentheidspreker, gasspreker

guid'ance (n) leiding, bestuur; (beroeps)voorligting *also* **coun'sel** (n, v)

guide (n) gids, leidsman; wegwyser; raadgewer; handleiding; (v) lei; bestuur; raadgee; ~ **dog** gidshond; ~**d mis'sile** gerigte missiel; ~**d tour** begeleide toer/rondleiding; ~**line** riglyn

guild (n) gilde; vakvereniging

guillotine' (n) guillotine/gilotien, valbyl

guilt (n) skuld; misdaad; ~**y** skuldig, strafbaar: *found* ~*y of* skuldig bevind aan

guin'ea ghienie; ~**fowl** tarentaal, poelpetater; ~ **pig** marmotjie; proefkonyn (mens in proefrol)

guitar' (n) ghitaar/kitaar

gulf -s golf, baai; draaikolk

gull (n) seemeeu *also* **sea'gull**

gull'ible (a) liggelowig, goedgelowig

gull'y (n) geut, riool(put); (v) uitspoel

gulp (n) sluk; (v) insluk; wegsluk

gum[1] (n) gom; (v) gom, vasplak; ~**boot** waterstewel; ~**pole** teerpaal

gum[2] (n) tandvleis

gun geweer; roer; kanon; vuurwapen *also* **fire'arm**; ~ **bar'rel** geweerloop; ~**man** rampokker, gewapende boef/rower; ~**ner** kanonnier; ~**pow'der** kruit, buskruit; ~**run'ner** wapensmokkelaar; ~**shot** geweerskoot; ~**to'ting per'son** rolliepronker

gur'gle (n) borreling; gegorrel; (v) gorrel

gu'ru (n) (geestelike) leier, leermeester, ghoeroe *also* **lea'der, men'tor**

gush (v) uitstroom, oorborrel; ~**er** spuitbron; dweper (mens)

gust (n) windvlaag; stroom, vloed

gut (n) derm; dermsnaar; (pl) ingewande; fut, durf; ~ **fee'ling** intuïtiewe gevoel, kropgevoel; ~**string** dermsnaar

gutt'er (n) geut (aan dakrand)

guy (n) **-s** vent; kêrel(tjie), ou *also* **chap, fel'low**; voëlverskrikker

gym (n) springjurk; gimnasium/gimnastieksaal

gymkha'na (-s) ruitersport, gimkana

gymna'sium -s gimnasium *also* **gym**

gym'nast gimnas (mens)

gymnas'tics gimnastiek; ~ **display'** gimnastiekvertoning

gynaecol'ogist ginekoloog, vrouespesialis

gyp'sum gips; ~ **board** gipsbord

H

hab′erdasher (n) kramer; ~y kramery (naald=
werkafdeling)
hab′it (n) gewoonte; neiging; geaardheid;
(ry)kleed; kostuum; *force of* ~ mag van
die gewoonte
hab′itat woonplek, tuiste, habitat
habit′ual (n) gewoonlik, gebruiklik; ~ **crim′i=**
nal gewoontemisdadiger
hack′ney -s (n) drawwer (perd); huurrytuig;
~ed afgesaag, holruggery, verslete
hack′saw ystersaag
hadd′ock skelvis
haem′orrhage bloeding, bloedstorting
haem′orrhoids aambeie *also* **piles**
hag ou vrou/wyf, heks
hagg′ard verwilder(d), sku *also* **drawn** (a)
hag′gle (v) kibbel, kwansel, afding (prys)
hail¹ (n) hael; (v) hael; ~ **sho′wer** haelbui; ~=
stone haelkorrel; ~**storm** haelstorm
hail² (n) heilgroet; begroeting; (v) begroet;
roep; aanroep; ~ *from* afkomstig wees van;
~-**fellow-well-met** allemansvriend
hair haar; *split* ~s hare kloof; ~**dres′ser**
haarsnyer/haarkapper; ~**pin** haarnaald; ~**pin**
bend dubbele draai, s-draai; ~**splitting**
haarklowery, vittery; ~**spray** haarsproei;
~**style** **para′de** kapselparade; ~ **sty′list**
haarstileerder; ~y harig
hake stokvis
hale gesond, sterk; ~ *and hearty* gesond
half (n) **halves** helfte; halwe; (skrum)skakel;
better ~ wederhelf; ~ *an hour* 'n halfuur; ~
past three halfvier; (a, adv) half; ~**brother**
halfbroer; ~**mast** halfstok; ~**time** rustyd,
pouse; ~**vol′ley** skephou (tennis); ~-**wit′ted**
onnosel, simpel; ~-**year′ly** halfjaarliks *also*
bian′nual (a)
hall (n) saal; voorportaal, hal; ~**stand** hoede=
stander
hallucina′tion hersenskim, hallusinasie
hal′o stralekrans, ligkrans
halt (n) halt; halte (spoor); stilstand
hal′ter (n) halter; strop
halve (v) in die helfte deel, halveer
ham ham; dy; **ra′dio** ~ radio-amateur
ham′burger hamburger, frikkadelbroodjie
ham′let dorpie, gehug(gie)
hamm′er (n) hamer; ~ *and sickle* hamer en

sekel; (v) hamer
hamm′ock (n) hangmat
ham′per¹ (n) smulmandjie, keurpakket
ham′per² (v) belemmer, bemoeilik; hinder
ham′ster (n) hamster (troeteldier)
ham′string (n) dyspier; (v) verlam; kniehalter
(fig.)
hand (n) hand; wyser/wyster (horlosie); *at* ~
byderhand; *by* ~ per bode; *be* ~ *in glove*
kop in een mus wees; *second-*~ tweedehands; *under his* ~ deur hom onderteken;
~s *up!* han(d)sop!; *win* ~s *down* fluit-fluit
wen; (v) oorhandig; hand gee; ~ *in* inlewer,
indien; voorlê; ~ *in the assignment* die taak/
werkstuk inlewer; ~**bag** handsak; ~**bill**
strooibiljet; ~**book** handleiding; ~**cuff** (n)
handboei *also* **shack′les**; (v) boei; ~**feed**
hans grootmaak; ~ **grena′de** handgranaat;
~**gun** handwapen
hand′icap (n) voorgee; hendikep; (v) voorgee;
strem; *the* ~*ped* die gestremdes, gestremde
persone *also* **disa′bled**
han′dicraft handwerk, kunsvlyt
hand′kerchief -s sakdoek *also* **han′ky** (n)
handle (n) handvatsel; hingsel; (v) hanteer;
behandel; behartig; ~**bar** stuur(stang)
hand: ~-**out** strooibiljet, vlugskrif; ~**pick′ed**
staff handgekeurde personeel
hand′some mooi, fraai; aansienlik/aantreklik
hands-on (a): ~ **trai′ning** praktiese onderrig
hand′writing handskrif
han′dy handig, behendig; *come in* ~ goed te
pas kom; ~**man** handlanger, nutsman,
faktotum
hang¹ hang; helling; *get the* ~ *of a matter* die
slag kry
hang² (v) hang; behang; ophang
hang′ar vliegtuigloods, hangar
hang: ~**gli′der** vlerkswewer (mens); ~**gli′ding**
vlerksweef; ~**man** beul, laksman; ~**out** blyplek, lêplek; ~**over** bab(b)elaas, wingerd=
griep, wynpyn; ~-**up** inhibisie, fobie; obsessie
haphaz′ard (a) lukraak; ongeorden
happ′en gebeur, plaasvind, voorkom; *I* ~ *to*
know toevallig weet ek
happ′ening gebeurtenis; saamtrek, kunste=
naarsfees/happening; makietie
happ′iness (n) geluk, vreugde *also* **joy**

happy (a) gelukkig, voorspoedig; *many ~ returns* veels geluk met u/jou verjaardag; onbekommerd, onbesorg, sorg(e)loos; **~-go-luck′y**

harb′our (n) hawe; skuilplek; (v) herberg

hard (a) hard, swaar; streng; hardvogtig; *a ~ and fast rule* 'n vaste reël; (adv) hard, stewig; *~ of hearing* hardhorend; dowerig; *try ~* hard probeer; *be ~ up* platsak wees; **~-boiled** hardgekook (eier); hardkoppig; **~ cash** koue kontant/klinkende munt; **~-disc/ disk drive** hardeskyfaandrywer; **~en** hard maak, verhard; **~-hear′ted** hardvogtig; **~ la′bour** dwangarbeid/hardepad; **~ lines!**; **~ luck!** simpatie!/hoe jammer!; **~ly** nouliks, skaars; **~-pres′sed** verleë, in die knyp; **~ship** ontbering; **~ware** hardeware, yster= ware; apparatuur (rek.); **~-work′ing** arbeid= saam, fluks; **~y** sterk, gehard, taai

hare (n) haas; **~lip** haaslip, gesplete lip *also* **cleft lip**

harl′equin harlekyn, hanswors, nar *also* **jo′ker**

harm (n) skade, nadeel; (v) benadeel; **~ful** skadelik, nadelig; **~less** onskadelik

harmon′ica -s mondfluitjie, harmonika

harmon′ium harmonium, huisorrel/traporrel

harm′ony (n) harmonie; eendrag

harn′ess (n) **-es** tuig; (v) optuig; inspan

harp (n) harp; *~ on the same string* op dieselfde aambeeld hamer; **Jew′s ~** trompie

harpoon′ (n) harpoen

ha′rrow (n) eg; (v) eg/êe; kwel/teister

harsh (a) ru; hard; nors; skerp; *~ mea′sures* streng/strawwe maatreëls

hart′ebees hartbees (bok)

harv′est (n) oes; (v) oes; insamel

has′-been (n) uitgediende persoon; ou knol (mens)

hash (n) fynvleis; mengelmoes; *make a ~ of* verknoei, verbrou

hasp (n) grendel; werwel; *~ and staple* kram en oorslag

hassle (n) gesukkel; moeite *also* **nui′sance**

haste (n) haas, spoed; *more ~ less speed* hoe meer haas hoe minder spoed

hat hoed; *talk through one's ~* grootpraat; kaf verkoop

hatch[1] (n) **-es** luik; onderdeur; **~back** luikrug (kar)

hatch[2] (n) broeisel; (v) pik; uitbroei; uitdink, beraam; **~ery** broeiery

hatch′et handbyl; strydbyl; *bury the ~* vrede maak

hate (n) haat, afkeer; (v) haat, verafsku

ha′tred (n) haat, wrok, nyd

hat: *~ stand* kapstok; *~ trick* driekuns (krieket)

haught′y (a) hoogmoedig; trots *also* **proud**

haul (n) vangs; (v) trek, sleep, hys; **~ier** (vrag)karweier/vragryer *also* **car′rier**

haunch -es heup; dy; boud; (pl) hurke

haunt (n) druk besoekte plek; boerplek (diere); (v) boer; ronddwaal/spook

have (v) hê; besit; kry; *~ a heart!* moenie laf wees nie; *~ no doubt* nie daaraan twyfel nie; *he had no objection* hy had geen beswaar nie (het geen beswaar gehad nie)

ha′ven (n) (veilige) hawe, toevlug(soord)

hav′oc (n) verwoesting

hawk[1] (n) valk; **~er** valkenier (mens); be= drieër; (v) met valke jag

hawk[2] (v) rondvent, smous; **~er** straatsmous *also* **street ven′dor/in′formal tra′der**

hay hooi; *make ~ while the sun shines* die yster smee terwyl dit warm is; **~box** hooikis, prutkis(sie); **~fe′ver** hooikoors; **~stack** hooimied

haz′ard (n) gevaar; risiko; hindernis (gholf); (v) waag, riskeer; **~ous** gevaarlik

haze (n) dyns(er)igheid, mis

haz′y dyns(er)ig, mistig; vaag

he (n) mansmens; mannetjie; (pron) hy

head (n) hoof, kop; koppenent; verstand; *~ of cattle* stuk(s) vee; *~ of state* staatshoof; *~ over heels* bolmakiesie; *lose one's ~* die kluts kwytraak; *~s or tails* kruis of munt; (v) aanvoer, lei; **~a′che** hoofpyn/kopseer; **~hun′ter** koppesneller; **~lights** hoofligte (kar); **~line** opskrif; hooftrek; **~mas′ter** skoolhoof, prinsipaal; **~-on colli′sion** tromp= op botsing, kop teen kop botsing; **~quar′ters** hoofkwartier; **~rest** kopstut; slagkussing (motorkar); **~strong** koppig, eiewys *also* **stub′born**

heal (v) genees, heel, gesond maak/word; **~er** heler, heelmeester

health gesondheid; welstand; **~care** gesond= heidsorg; **~y** gesond

heap (n) hoop, klomp, stapel, menigte

hear (v) hoor; verneem; **~er** toehoorder, hoorder; **~ing** gehoor; verhoor; **~ing aid** (ge)hoorapparaat

hear′say hoorsê, gerug *also* **ru′mour**

hearse (n) roukoets/lykwa

heart hart; *to one's* ∼*'s content* na hartelus; *learn by* ∼ van buite leer; ∼ *to* ∼ openhartig; ∼**ache** hartseer, sielsmart; ∼ **attack′** hartaanval; ∼**-bro′ken** ontroosbaar; ∼**burn** sooibrand; ∼ **by′pass** hartomleiding; ∼ **do′nor** hartskenker; ∼ **fail′ure** hartversaking

hearth (n) vuurherd, haard *also* **fi′replace**

heart: ∼**ily** hartlik; ∼**ren′ding** hartverskeurend; ∼**s** hartens (kaarte); ∼ **pace′maker** hartpasaangeër; ∼ **trans′plant** hartoorplanting; ∼**y** hartlik; vrolik; gesond

heat (n) hitte, warmte; gloed; loopsheid (by diere); uitdun (wedstryd); *dead* ∼ gelykop; (v) verhit; ∼**er** verwarmer; ∼ **exhaus′tion** hitte-uitputting

heath′en (n) heiden (mens); (a) heidens

hea′ther heide; vlakte, heideveld

hea′ven hemel; lug; *move* ∼ *and earth* hemel en aarde beweeg; *for* ∼*'s sake* in vredesnaam; ∼**ly** hemels

hea′vy (a) swaar; gewigtig; moeilik; ∼**weight** swaargewig

He′brew (n) Hebreër (mens); (a) Hebreeus

hec′kle hekel; roskam; ∼**r** hekelaar (mens)

hec′tare hektaar

hec′tic (a) koorsagtig; woelig, wild

hedge (n) heining; (v) omhein; ∼**hog** krimpystervark

heed (n) aandag, sorg; hoede; (v) oppas, ag gee, oplet

heel (n) hakskeen; *take to one's* ∼*s* op loop sit, weghol; (v) haak (voetbal)

hef′ty (a) fris, sterk ('n man)

hei′fer vers (kalf)

height hoogte; lengte

heir (n) erfgenaam; ∼**loom** erfstuk

heist (n) (bank)roof, rooftog *also* **hold-up**

hel′icopter (n) helikopter, tjopper, wentelwiek

hel′ipad heliblad (op gebou)

hell hel; speelhol; ∼ *of a noise* helse lawaai; ∼**cat** tierwyfie (vrou); ∼**driver** jaagduiwel

Hellen′ic Helleens, Grieks

helm roer, helmstok; *at the* ∼ aan die roer (van sake)

hel′met helm; **crash** ∼ valhelm

help (n) hulp, steun, bystand; *I could not* ∼ *laughing* ek kon my lag nie hou nie; *by the* ∼ *of* met behulp van; (v) help, steun; ∼**ing push/shove** hupstootjie; ∼**er** helper, hulp; ∼**ful** behulpsaam, nuttig; ∼**ing** (n) porsie (kos, nagereg); ∼**less** hulpeloos

hem′isphere (n) halfrond, halfbol

hemp hennep; tou; **wild** ∼ dagga

hen hen, hoenderhen; =wyfie, wyfie=

hence van nou af, vandaar; ∼ *this problem* vandaar hierdie probleem

hench′man handlanger; trawant *also* **cro′ny**

hen: ∼**house** hoenderhok; ∼**peck′ed** onder die plak/pantoffelregering

hep′tagon sewehoek

her haar

her′ald (n) herout, voorloper, bode; heraldikus; (v) aankondig, uitroep

her′aldry (n) wapenkunde, heraldiek

herb kruid, bossie; (a) kruie=; ∼**alist′** kruiekundige; bossiedokter; ∼ **gar′den** kruietuin, fyntuin; ∼**ici′de** onkruiddoder

herd (n) trop, kudde (beeste) *also* **flock**

here hier; hierso; hiernatoe; *that's neither* ∼ *nor there* dit het niks met die saak te doen nie; ∼**af′ter** (n) hiernamaals; (adv) hierna, later; ∼**by′** hierby, hiermee

hered′itary (a) erflik, oorerflik

here: ∼**in′** hierin; ∼**on** hierop

her′esy kettery, dwaalleer

her′etic (n) ketter *also* **un′believer**, **in′fidel**

here: ∼**upon′** hierop, toe; ∼**with** hiermee

her′itage erf(e)nis, erfdeel; **H**∼ **Day** Erfenisdag

hermaph′rodite (n) trassie, hermafrodiet; (a) tweeslagtig, hermafrodities

herm′it kluisenaar, hermiet (mens)

hern′ia -e, -s breuk

he′ro -es held; ∼**es′ a′cre** heldeakker

hero′ic (a) heldhaftig, heroïes

her′on reier (watervoël)

he′ro worship heldeverering

her′ring haring

hers hare

herself′ haarself

hes′itate (v) aarsel, weifel; skroom, huiwer

hes′sian goiingsak, goiingstof

hex′agon seshoek

hey′day glorietyd/glansperiode; vrolikheid

hi′bernate (v) oorwinter; hiberneer

hibis′cus vuurblom, hibiskus

hic′cup (n) hik; (v) hik

hidd′en verborge; ∼**agen′da** verskuilde agenda

hide[1] (n) vel, huid; *dress a* ∼ 'n vel looi

hide[2] (v) wegkruip; wegsteek, verberg; ∼ *one's head* jou kop laat sak

hid′eous (a) afskuwelik, afsigtelik *also* **hor′rid**

hide′-out skuilplek; wegkruipplek

hid′ing pak (slae), afranseling, loesing; *be in*

~ wegkruip; ~ **place** skuilplek, skuiling

hi'erarchy kerkregering, hiërargie/gesagslyn

hi-fi set (n) hoëtroustel, klanktroustel

high (n) maksimum; toppunt; ~**-den'sity housing** hoëdigtheid(s)behuising; (a) hoog; verhewe; *in* ~ *spirits* uitgelate; (adv) hoog; ~ **al'titude** hoog bo seespieël/seevlak; ~**-al'titude ten'nis balls** hoëvlaktennisbal= le; ~ **blood pres'sure** hoë bloeddruk, hipertensie; ~ **court** hoërhof; ~ **fidel'ity** hoëtrou/klanktrou; ~**-lev'el talks** hoëvlak samesprekings; ~**light** hoogtepunt/glans= punt; (v) uitlig/kleur; beklemtoon; ~**light= er** uitligter/kleurder

high'ly hoog, baie, besonder; ~ *commended* sterk aanbeveel

high: ~**ness** hoogheid; hoogte; ~ **school** hoërskool *also* **sec'ondary school;** ~ **socie'= ty** glanskring(e); ~**-technol'ogy** (a) hoog= tegnies *also* **hi'tech;** ~ **tide** hoogwater; ~ **trea'son** hoogverraad; ~**way** (Am.), snel= weg, deurpad (tussenstedelik); ~**wayman** struikrower, rampokker *also* **ban'dit**

hi'jack (v) kaap; skaak; ~**er** kaper (vliegtuig), motor; ~**ing** motorkaping *also* **car'jacking**

hike (n) staptoer; (v) voetslaan

hik'er voetslaner, pakstapper

hi'king trail voetslaanpad, staproete

hilar'ious (a) lagwekkend; vrolik, opgeruimd, uitgelate

hill heuwel, bult, koppie

hilt (n) handvatsel, greep

him hom; ~**self** homself

hind (a) agter=, agterste; ~**sight** agternawysheid

hin'der (v) hinder, verhinder

hin'drance hindernis, belemmering

hinge (n) skarnier; hingsel; spil

hint (n) wenk, skimp

hip heup; ~ **flask** heupfles

hippopot'amus ..**mi** seekoei

hire (v) huur; verhuur; *for* ~ te huur; ~**pur'chase** huurkoop

his sy, syne, s'n

hiss (n) gesis; geblaas; gefluit; (v) sis, blaas; uitfluit; ~ *at* uitjou

histor'ical (a) geskiedkundig, histories

his'tory ..**ries** geskiedenis

hit (n) slag; treffer; (v) slaan; moker; ~ *and run case* tref-en-trapvoorval

hitch (n) lissie, haak; beletsel; (v) haak; vasmaak; ~ *on to* vashaak aan; ~**hike** ry= loop, duimry, duimgooi; ~**hi'ker** ryloper,

duimryer, duimgooier

hi'tech (a) hoogteg(nies) *see* **high-technol'ogy**

hit: ~**list** moordlys; ~**man** huurmoordenaar *also* **assas'sin;** ~ **para'de** trefferparade; ~**squad'** moordbende

hive (n) byekorf, heuningnes

hoard (v) opstapel; opgaar; oppot (goud)

hoar'frost (n) ruigryp, ysel

hoarse hees, skor; ~**ness** heesheid

hoar'y (a) grou, grys

hoax (n) **-es** grap, foppery; vals alarm; ~ **tel'ephone call** fop-oproep

hob'ble (n) strompelgang; (v) mank loop; strompel; ~ **skirt** hobbelrok

hobb'y hobbies stokperdjie, liefhebbery, tyd= verdryf; ~**horse** stokperdjie

hob'goblin kaboutermannetjie; paaiboelie

hob'nob (v) meng (met ryker/vernamer mense)

ho'bo (n) boemelaar *also* **tramp;** landloper

hock'ey hokkie

hoe (n) skoffelpik; (v) skoffel; losmaak

hog vark, swyn, burg; smeerlap; *the whole* ~ tot by oom Daantjie in die kalwerhok; ~**s'back** middelmannetjie (in plaaspad)

hog'sty ..**sties** varkhok *also* **pig'sty**

hoist (n) ligter; hystoestel; (v) hys, optrek

hold[1] (n) skeepsruim, (vrag)ruim

hold[2] (n) vat, handvatsel; (v) hou; besit; be= hou; bevat; beklee (pos); ~ *the line* bly aan asseblief; (ek skakel u) deur; ~ *an office* 'n pos beklee; ~ *one's tongue* jou mond hou; ~**er** houer; besitter, bekleer (pos); ~**-up** aanhouding, ophoping (verkeer); roof; (v) beroof

hole (n) gat; putjie (gholf); ~**-in-one** kolhou/ fortuinhou (gholf)

hol'iday -s vakansie, feesdag; **Christ'mas** ~ Kersvakansie; *on* ~ met/op vakansie; ~ **resort'** vakansieoord; plesieroord

Holl'and Holland, Nederland; ~**er** Hollander, Nederlander (mens)

holl'ow (n) holte; (v) uithol; (a) hol

ho'locaust (n) groot menseslagting *also* **car'= nage**

hol'ster (n) holster *also* **pis'tol case**

hol'y heilig; ~ **wa'ter** wywater

hom'age eerbetoon; hulde; *pay* ~ *to* hulde betoon aan

home (n) tuiste; tehuis; *at* ~ tuis; ~*, sweet* ~ oos, wes, tuis bes; (a) huislik, huis=; (adv) huis toe; ~ **affairs'** binnelandse sake; ~**craft** huisvlyt; ~ **econom'ics** huishoud=

kunde; ~ **in'dustry** tuisnywerheid; ~**ly** eenvoudig; huislik; ~**made** tuisberei/tuis=
gebak; ~ **man'agement** huisbestuur
hom'eopath homeopaat, homopaat
home'perm tuiskarteling
hom'er posduif
home: ~ **page** tuisblad (Internet); ~**sick:** *be* ~*sick* heimwee hê; ~**stead** woonhuis, opstal; ~ **stretch** pylvak (atletiek); ~**work** tuiswerk/huiswerk
hom'icide manslag *also* **man'slaughter**
ho'ming: ~ **devi'ce** aanpeiler; ~ **pig'eon** pos=
duif
homosex'ual (n, a) homoseksueel
hon'est (a) eerlik, opreg; ~**ly** regtig/rêrig
hon'esty eerlikheid, opregtheid; ~ *is the best policy* eerlikheid duur die langste
hon'ey (n) heuning; skat, hartlam; ~**comb** heuningkoek; ~**moon** wittebrood(sdae), hu=
weliksreis; ~**suckle** kanferfoelie
hon'ky-tonk (piano) tokkelklavier
honorar'ium ..ria, -s honorarium
hon'orary ere=; honorêr, eervol; ~ **life mem'bership** lewenslange erelidskap; ~ **mem'ber** erelid; ~ **profes'sor** ereprofessor, professor-honorêr; ~ **sec'retary** eresekretaris
hon'our (n) eer; waardigheid; *debt of* ~ ereskuld; *funeral* ~*s* laaste eer/eerbewys; *in* ~ *of* ter ere van; *word of* ~ erewoord; *Your H*~ Edelagbare; (v) eer, vereer, eer bewys; ~**able** edel; agbaar; eervol: *The H*~*able the President* Sy Edele die President
hon'ours degree honneursgraad
hood (n) hoofdeksel; kap; kleurserp
hood'lum (straat)boef, skobbejak *also* **thug**
hoo'doo (n) teenspoed, ongeluk; beswering, vloek; (v) toor, beheks
hood'wink (v) blinddoek; fop, kul, flous
hoof (n) hoef; klou
hook (n) hoek; haak; vishoek; *by* ~ *or by crook* eerlik of oneerlik; (v) haak, aanhaak; ~*ed on* verslaaf aan/versot op *also: addicted to*; ~**er** haker (rugby); dief, rampokker; straathoer, prostituut, sekswerker; ~**worm** haakwurm
hool'igan straatboef; ~**ism** straatboewery
hoop (n) hoepel; band
hoot (n) gejou; getoet (motor); *not care a* ~ geen flenter omgee nie; (v) uitjou; toeter; ~**er** toeter (van motor)
hop[1] (n) hop; ~**(s) beer** hopbier
hop[2] (n) sprong; (v) spring, huppel; wip; ~, *skip and jump* driesprong; ~**scotch** een=

beentjie/klippiehink (speletjie)
hope (n) hoop, verwagting; (pl) verwagtings; (v) hoop; ~**ful** veelbelowend; hoopvol; ~**ful'ly** hopelik; ~**less** hopeloos
horde (n) horde, bende; swerm, trop
hori'zon gesigseinder, horison
horizon'tal (n) horisontale lyn; (a) waterpas; horisontaal; ~ **bar** rekstok (gimn.)
hormo'ne (n) hormoon
horn horing; voelspriet
horn'et perdeby, wesp
ho'roscope horoskoop
ho'rrible afskuwelik, vreeslik, gruwelik
horrif'ic ysingwekkend, afgryslik
ho'rror (n) afsku, gruwel; afkeer/afgryse
hors d'oeuvre' -s voorspys, voorgereg
horse (n) perd; bok (gimn.) ~ *and trailer* voorhaker en treiler; ~**fly** perdevlieg; ~**man** (perde)ruiter; ~**manship** ruiterkuns/ rykuns; ~**play** ruwe spel; ~**po'wer** perde=
krag; ~ **ra'cing** perde(wed)renne; perde=
sport; ~**ri'ding competi'tion** ruiterkuns, perdesport; ~**shoe** hoefyster; ~**whip** peits, karwats *also* **quirt**
hort'iculture tuinbou
hosann'a -s hosanna, lofsang
hose kous; tuinslang; brandspuit; **pan'ty** ~ kousbroek *also* **pan'tihose**
hos'pice (n) hersteloord, hospies/hospitium
hos'pital hospitaal, siekehuis; **gen'eral** ~ al=
gemene hospitaal; ~**isa'tion** hospitalisasie; ~**ise** (v) in hospitaal opneem
hospital'ity (n) gasvryheid, herbergsaamheid
host[1] gasheer; *we are* ~*ing the event* ons is gasheer vir die byeenkoms
host[2] menigte *also* **crowd, mul'titude**; skare
hos'tage (n) gyselaar; *release of* ~ vrylating van gyselaar
hos'tel losieshuis; koshuis; hostel (myne)
hos'tess gasvrou; waardin; geselskap(s)dame; gesellin
hos'tile (a) vyandig; vyandelik (mil.); ~ **at'titude** vyandige houding
hot warm, heet; vurig; ~**bed** broeines; broeikas; ~**-air balloon'** (warm)lugballon; ~**blood'ed** warmbloedig; ~**cross bun** paasbolletjie, kruisbolletjie; ~**dog** worsbroodjie
hotch'potch mengelmoes, sameraapsel; alle=
gaartjie *also* **hash**
hotel' hotel; ~**kee'per/hotel'ier** hotelhouer, hotelier
hot: ~**head** vuurvreter, heethoof; ~**hou'se**

kweekhuis; broeikas; ~**li′ne** rooilyn, blits-lyn; ~ **pursuit′** hakkejag; ~**-tem′pered** opvlieënd; ~**wa′ter bottle** warmwatersak

hound (n) jaghond; (v) agtervolg, vervolg

hour uur; ~**glass** sandloper(tjie), uurglas; ~ **hand** uurwyser/uurwyster

house (n) huis, woonhuis; ~ *of ill fame* bordeel; (v) huisves; herberg; woon; ~ **arrest′** huisarres; ~**brea′king** huisbraak, inbraak

house′hold (n) huis(houding); huisgesin; (a) huishoudelik; ~ **appli′ances** huisgerei; ~ **effects′** huisraad; ~ **rem′edy** boereraat

house: ~ **jour′nal** firmablad, lyfblad; ~**keep′er** huishoudster; ~**maid′s knee** kniewater/skropknieë; ~ **rent** huishuur; ~**-trai′ned** (a) sindelik (huisdier); ~**war′ming** huisinwyding; ~**wife** huisvrou; ~**wives′ lea′gue** huisvroueliga

housing (n) huisvesting; behuising; omhulsel

hov′el pondok, strooihuis/stroois; krot *also* **shan′ty, shack**

ho′ver fladder; sweef; ~ *about* rondswerf; ~**craft** skeertuig/kussingtuig

how hoe; waarom/hoekom; ~ *are you?* hoe gaan dit?; ~ *do you do* aangenaam, aangename kennis, bly u te kenne; ~**-ever** egter, nogtans; nietemin

howl (v) huil, tjank; ~**er** huiler, tjanker; (eksamen)flater, blaps; ~**ing** (n) getjank

hubb′y **hubbies** manlief

hub′cap wieldop/naafdop (motor)

hud′dle (n) hoop; bondel; *go into a* ~ beraad/koukus hou

hue[1] kleur, tint

hue[2] geskree(u); *raise a* ~ *and cry* moord en brand skree(u)

huff (n) opvlieëndheid; *be in a* ~ beledig voel; kwaad/opgeruk wees

hug (n) omhelsing; (v) omhels, vasdruk

huge (a) reusagtig, kolossaal, tamaai *also* **colos′sal, vast**; ~ **buil′ding** reusegebou

hullabaloo′ (n) ophef, herrie, kommosie

hum (n) gegons; gemompel; (v) gons; neurie; mompel; zoem

hu′man (n) mens; (a) menslik; ~ **im′munodeficiency vi′rus (HIV)** menslike immuniteitsmorende virus (MIV/HIV); ~ **rela′tions** menseverhoudinge; ~ **resour′ces** mensebronne/menslike hulpbronne; ~ **rights** menseregte/fundamentele regte; ~ **scien′ces** geesteswetenskappe; **H**~ **Scien′ces Research′ Coun′cil** Raad vir Geesteswetenskaplike Navorsing

Hu′man Rights′ Day Menseregtedag (vakansie)

humane′ (a) mensliewend, humaan

human′ity mensheid, mensdom

hum′ble (a) nederig, beskeie; (v) verneder

hum′bug (n) bluf; grootpratery; swendelaar/bedrieër (mens)

humid′ity (n) vogtigheid, humiditeit

humil′iate (v) verneder, verlaag, (ver)kleineer

hu′miture (n) ongemak(likheid)syfer (klimaat) *also* **dis′comfort in′dex**

humm′ing (n) gegons; ~**bird** kolibrie

hu′morous (a) luimig, grappig, geestig

hum′our (n) bui, luim; humeur; (v) inwillig, sy sin gee

hump (n) boggel; skof (dier); hobbel (spoedbreker); ~**-backed** geboggel *see* **hunch′back**

hunch knop; boggel; voorgevoel; ~**back** boggelrug (mens)

hun′dred honderd, honderdtal; ~**fold** honderdvoud(ig); ~**th** honderdste

hung′er (n) honger; ~ **strike** eetstaking

hun′gry honger; hongerig; lus

hunt (n) jag; (v) jag; najaag; vervolg; ~**er** jagter; ~**ing expedi′tion** jagtog; ~**ing sea′son** jagseisoen

hur′dle (n) hekkie; (v) oorspring; ~ **race** hekkiewedloop

hurl (v) gooi, smyt, slinger

hu′rricane orkaan *also* **cy′clone**

hu′rry (n) gewoel, haastigheid; (v) jaag; gou maak; ~ *up* gou maak, opskud

hurt (v) seer maak, beseer; benadeel; *feel* ~ gekrenk voel; *I* ~ *my leg* ek het my been beseer

hus′band (n) man, eggenoot

hush (n) stilte, kalmte; (v) stil maak, bedaar; (interj) sjuut!; ~ **mon′ey** swyggeld

husk (n) dop, skil; bas; (v) uitdop; afskil

hu′stle (n) gedrang; harwar; (v) druk, stoot; ~ *and bustle* drukte

hut strooihuis, stroois, pondok, hut

hy′acinth naeltjie(blom), hiasint

hy′brid (n) baster, hibried; basterwoord; (a) baster-; ~**ise** baster, kruis; ~ **maize/mea′lies** bastermielies

hydran′gea (n) hortensia, krismisroos

hy′drant brandkraan, hidrant

hydraul′ic hidroulies, water-

hydro-elec′tric (a) hidroëlektries

hy′drogen (n) waterstof

hy′droplane skeerboot *also* **hy′drofoil**

hyen'a -s hiëna, (strand)wolf
hygien'ic (a) higiënies, gesondheids=
hymn (a) gesang, kerklied, himne
hyperb'ole oordrywing, hiperbool
hy'pertext hiperteks (rek.)
hy'phen (n) koppelteken; (v) ~**ate** koppel
hy'permarket hipermark, alleswinkel
hyperten'sion (n) hoë bloeddruk, hipertensie
hyp'notism hipnotisme
hyp'notise (v) hipnotiseer

hypochon'dria verbeelsiekte, hipokondrie; hipo=
konders, ipekonders
hypochon'driac (n) hipokonder/ipekonder
(mens); (a) hipokondries
hyp'ocrite (n) huigelaar, skynheilige, twee=
gatjakkals (mens)
hysterec'tomy (n) histerektomie, baarmoeder=
verwydering
hyster'ical (a) histeries *also* **uncontroll'ed
laugh'ing/cry'ing**

I

I ek; ~ *say* hoor ('n) bietjie
ib'is -es ibis (voël); **brown** ~ hadida
ice (n) ys; ~**berg** ysberg; ~**cream** roomys;
~**cream cone** roomyshorinkie
i'cing yskors; ~ **su'gar** (ver)siersuiker
i'cy (a) ysagtig; yskoud *also* **free'zing**
ide'a (n) -s idee, denkbeeld; begrip
ide'al (n) ideaal; (a) ideaal, volmaak; ~**ist**
idealis (mens); ~**ise** idealiseer
iden'tical identies, identiek, dieselfde
identifica'tion vereenselwiging; identifikasie;
~ **para'de** uitkenparade
iden'tify (v) vereenselwig; uitken, aantoon;
identifiseer; ~ *with* vereenselwig met
iden'tikit (n) gesigsamestelling, identikit
iden'tity identiteit; ~ **doc'ument** identiteits=
dokument
ideol'ogy (n) ideologie, begripsleer; dwepery
id'iom idioom, tongval; ~**a'tic** idiomaties
id'iot onnosele mens, idioot *also* **fool, dunce**
i'dle (v) leeglê, lanterfanter; luier (motor); (a)
ledig, werkloos; uitgeskakel (rat); ~ *talk*
kafpraatjies; ~**r** luiaard, leeglêer
id'ol (n) afgod; dwaalbegrip, skynbeeld
idyll'ic (a) idillies, landelik; rustig/bekoorlik
if (n) as; (conj) indien, as, so, ingeval; *funds
available,* ~ *any* beskikbare fondse, as daar
is; ~ *need be* desnoods; ~ *not* so nie
igni'tion ontbranding; ontsteking (motor)
ig'norance (n) onkunde, onwetendheid; *dis=
play his* ~ sy onkunde openbaar
ignore' (v) verbysien, ignoreer, verontagsaam
igua'na likkewaan
ilk klas, soort
ill (a) siek, ongesteld; (adv) sleg, kwalik;
skaars; ~ *at ease* nie op sy gemak nie; *be
taken* ~ siek word; ~**-advi'sed** onverstan=

dig, onbesonne, onwys
illeg'al onwettig, wederregtelik; ~ **im'migrant** onwettige immigrant
illeg'ible onleesbaar
illegit'imate onwettig; buite-egtelik (kind)
ill: ~**-feel'ing** kwaaivriendskap; ~**-for'tune**
teenspoed; ongeluk; ~ **health** swak gesond=
heid
illi'cit ongeoorloof, onwettig; ~ **dia'mond buy'=
ing** onwettige diamanthandel
illit'erate (a) ongeletterd, analfabeties
ill: ~**-mannered** ongemanierd; ~**ness** siekte,
ongesteldheid; ~**-tem'pered** humeurig, knor=
rig; ~**treat** (v) mishandel
illum'inate verlig *also* **light up**; versier;
opluister; ~**d address'** oorkonde, sieradres
illu'sion (n) sinsbedrog; waan, illusie
ill'ustrate ophelder, verduidelik/toelig; illu=
streer; ~**d** verduidelik; geïllustreer
illustra'tion (n) illustrasie, toeligting
illus'trious (a) beroemd, vermaard
im'age (n) beeld; afbeelding; ~ **buil'der** beeld=
bouer; **pub'lic** ~ beeld na buite
im'agery (n) beeldspraak; beeldrykheid
ima'ginary (a) denkbeeldig; onbestaanbaar
imagina'tion verbeelding, voorstelling
ima'gine (v) jou verbeel/voorstel; fantaseer
im'becile (n) swaksinnige, imbesiel (mens);
(a) geestelik gestrem, imbesiel
im'itate (v) navolg, namaak; naboots
imita'tion (n) navolging, namaaksel, naboot=
sing; ~ **lea'ther** kunsleer
immac'ulate (a) rein, onbevlek; onberispelik;
~ **concep'tion** onbevlekte ontvangenis
immate'rial geestelik; onbelangrik; *that's* ~
dis om 't ewe; dit maak nie saak nie
immature' (a) groen, onvolwasse; onryp

imme'diate onmiddellik, oombliklik; ~**ly** dadelik

immense' (a) onmeetlik, kolossaal

immer'sion onderdompeling, indompeling; ~ **hea'ter** dompelaar, dompelverwarmer

im'migrant (n) immigrant, inkomeling (mens)

immigra'tion verhuising *also* **reloca'tion**; immigrasie

imm'inent dreigend; naby

immo'bilise immobiliseer, lam lê, buite geveg stel; ~**r** immobiliseerder

immoral'ity onsedelikheid; ontug

immort'al (a) onsterflik; onverganklik

immortal'ity onsterflikheid

immo'vable onbeweeglik; onroerend; vas; ~ **prop'erty** vaste eiendom, vasgoed

immune' vry van, immuun

im'pact (n) skok, stamp, botsing, impak

impal'a rooibok

impar'tial (a) onpartydig, afsydig

impass'able ontoeganklik, onbegaanbaar (pad)

impa'tient (a) ongeduldig; driftig, moeilik

imped'iment hindernis, beletsel; belemmering; **speech** ~ spraakgebrek

impe'rative gebiedend

imperf'ect (n) onvoltooid verlede tyd; (a) onvolmaak/onvolkome; onvoltooid

imper'ial keiserlik, imperiaal; ~**ism** imperialisme, ~**ist** imperialis (mens)

impers'onal onpersoonlik

imper'sonate (v) verpersoonlik; vertolk; voorstel; ~ *a character* 'n karakter speel/vertolk

impert'inence astrantheid; vermetelheid

impert'inent parmantig, astrant, vermetel

impet'uous voortvarend, onstuimig, heftig

im'petus -es beweegkrag, aandrang; *give a fresh* ~ *to* nuwe stukrag gee aan

im'pi -s impie, Zoeloeregiment

im'pish (a) ondeund/onnutsig, speels

implant' (v) inprent; inplant(eer) (med.)

im'plement (n) gereedskap, werktuig; (pl) benodig(d)hede; implemente (plaasgereedskap); (v) uitvoer, toepas, implementeer

implica'tion (n) implikasie; gevolgtrekking; *by* ~ by implikasie; stilswyend

implied' stilswyend inbegrepe

implode' (v) inplof ('n ou gebou)

implo'sion (n) inploffing

implore' (v) bid, smeek *also* **beg, beseech'**

imply' bevat; behels; te kenne gee; sinspeel op

im'port (n) invoer; inhoud; belang; gewig; betekenis; (pl) invoerartikels

import' (v) invoer, importeer; te kenne gee

import'ance (a) belangrikheid; betekenis

import'ant belangrik, betekenisvol *also* **signi'ficant, vi'tal**

impose' (v) oplê; te laste lê; skenk

imposs'ible onmoontlik, onbegonne

impos'ter/impostor (n) bedrieër, kuller, swendelaar *also* **preten'der**

im'potent magteloos, impotent

impound' (v) skut (los diere); opsluit

imprac'ticable (a) onuitvoerbaar, onprakties

impreg'nate bevrug, beswanger; deurtrek, vervul; ~**d with** deurtrek van

im'press (n) **-es** stempel; merk, afdruk

impress' (v) indruk, beïndruk *also* **em'phasise**

impress'ion indruk; *create the* ~ die indruk wek; druk; uitgawe (van boek); ~**ism** impressionisme (in skilderkuns); ~**ist** impressionis (mens)

impress'ive (a) indrukwekkend, treffend

im'prest voorskot (boekhouding)

im'print (n) stempel; naam; indruk

impris'on (v) in die gevangenis sit

improb'able onwaarskynlik

impromp'tu (n) improvisasie; impromptu; (a, adv) uit die vuis (toespraak); onvoorberei(d)

improp'er (a) onbehoorlik, onbetaamlik

improve' (v) verbeter, veredel, verhoog; vooruitgaan (pasiënt); ~**ment** verbetering

im'provise (v) improviseer, uit die vuis lewer (toespraak); haastig prakseer

im'pudent parmantig, (dom)astrant

impul'sive (a) impulsief, voortvarend

impu'rity **..ties** onsuiwerheid; onreinheid

in (adv) in, binne; (prep) in, by, op, na, tot, met; ~ *Afrikaans* in/op Afrikaans; ~ *any case* in elk/alle geval, ~ *camera* agter geslote deure, in camera; ~ *fact* inderdaad; ~ *honour of* ter ere van; ~ *ink* met ink; ~ *a jiffy* in 'n kits; ~ *terms of* ingevolge, kragtens; ~ *this way* op hierdie manier; ~ *a week* oor 'n week; ~ *writing* op skrif

inabil'ity (n) onvermoë, onbekwaamheid

inacc'urate onnoukeurig, onakkuraat

inad'equate (a) onvoldoende, ontoereikend

inadvert'ent onoplettend, agteloos, onopsetlik; ~**ly** per abuis/ongeluk

inartic'ulate (a) onverstaanbaar; *he is quite* ~ hy kan hom nie behoorlik uitdruk nie

inasmuch': ~ *as* aangesien

inaug'ural intree-; wydings-; ~ **address'** intreerede; openingsrede; ~ **meet'ing** stigtingsvergadering

inaugura'tion (n) inwyding, ingebruikneming; inhuldiging; bevestiging

in'born (a) aangebore, ingeskape

incal'culable onberekenbaar (skade)

inca'pable (a) onbekwaam, onbevoeg

incen'diary (n) brandstigter *also* **ar'sonist**; (a) brandstigtend; opruiend; ~ **bomb** brandbom

in'cense[1] (n) wierook; (v) bewierook

incense'[2] (v) kwaad maak, terg, vertoorn

incen'tive (n) aansporing; prikkel; ~ **bo'nus** aanspoorbonus; ~ **sche'me** aanspoorskema

incep'tion begin, aanvang

incess'ant (a) onophoudelik, aanhoudend

in'cest (n) bloedskande

inch -es duim; *every* ~ *a gentleman* 'n regte heer/gentleman

in'cident (n) gebeurtenis, voorval, insident; (pl) gebeure; (a) bykomstig, toevallig

inciden'tal toevallig, onvoorsiens; ~**ly** toevallig, terloops; ~**s** bykomende/onvoorsiene uitgawes

incin'erator (n) verbrandingsoond; verasser

incite' (v) opstook/opsweep, aanhits *also* **in'stigate/stir up**; ~**ment** aanhitsing

inclem'ent onbarmhartig; stormagtig; wreed; ~ **wea'ther** gure weer

inclina'tion (n) neiging; helling; skuinste

incline' (n) helling, afdraand, opdraand; skuinste; (v) neig; oorhang; hel

incli'ned: *be* ~ *to* geneig wees om

include' insluit, behels, bevat; meereken; *not* ~**d** nie inbegrepe nie

inclus'ive insluitend; ingeslote, inklusief; *VAT*~ BTW inbegrepe/ingesluit

incoher'ent (a) onsamehangend (spraak)

in'come inkomste, inkome; ~ **sta'tement** inkomstestaat; ~ **tax** inkomstebelasting

in'-com'pany trai'ning indiensopleiding

incompat'ible onverenigbaar; ~ *with* strydig met

incom'petence (n) onbekwaamheid, onbevoegdheid

incom'petent (a) onbevoeg, onbekwaam

incomplete' onvoltooi; onvolledig

incomprehen'sible (e) onbegryplik, onverstaanbaar

inconceiv'able (a) ondenkbaar, onbegryplik

inconsid'erate (a) onbedagsaam, agte(r)losig

inconsis'tent (a) teenstrydig; onverenigbaar; ongerymd; ~ *with* strydig met

inconve'nience (n) ongerief, ongemak; *put to* ~ ongerief veroorsaak; (v) ontrief

inconve'nient (a) ongerieflik, ongeleë

incor'porate (v) inlyf, inkorporeer; (a) ingelyf; ~*d association not for gain* ingelyfde vereniging sonder winsoogmerk

incorrect' foutief, onjuis; inkorrek

inco'rrigible (a) onverbeterbaar (leerling)

in'crease (n) vermeerdering; aanwas (in bevolking); verhoging; *on the* ~ aan die toeneem

increase' (v) vermeerder, vergroot, verhoog

incred'ible ongelooflik *also* **unbeliev'able**

in'crement (n) verhoging; inkrement; aanwas

in'cubator broeimasjien; kweekmasjien

incum'bent (n) amp(s)bekleër; predikant

incur' (v) op die hals haal, blootstel aan; ~ *debt* skuld maak

incu'rable ongeneeslik

inda'ba indaba, (bos)beraad *also* **lekgot'la**; beraadslaging

indebt'ed verskuldig, verplig; *be* ~ *to* verskuldig wees aan

inde'cent onbetaamlik; onfatsoenlik; onwelvoeglik; ~ **assault'** onsedelike aanranding

indeed' inderdaad, regtig/rêrig

indef'inite onbepaald; onbeslis; ~ **pro'noun** onbepaalde voornaamwoord

indel'ible onuitwisbaar; ~ **pen'cil** inkpotlood

indem'nify (v) vrywaar; skadeloos stel

indem'nity vrywaring; skadeloosstelling

indent' (v) inkerf; inspring (drukwerk); inboek; bestel

indepen'dence (n) onafhanklikheid; **declara'tion of** ~ onafhanklikverklaring

indepen'dent (n) onafhanklike (mens); (a) onafhanklik, selfstandig

in'-depth study dieptestudie

indestruc'tible (a) onvernietigbaar

in'dex (n) **indices, -es** bladwyser, indeks; register; ~ **fin'ger** voorvinger/wysvinger

In'dian (n) Indiër; Indiaan (Amerika); (a) Indies; Indiaans; ~ **sum'mer** ontydige somer; ~ **wrest'ling** armdruk(wedstryd) *also* **arm wrest'ling**

in'dicate (v) aandui, aanwys; toon

indica'tion aanduiding, aanwysing; teken

indic'ative (a) aanwysend; ~ **mood** aantonende wys

in'dicator (n) wyser; nommerbord; aantoner; **flash** ~ flikkerlig

indict' (v) beskuldig, aankla; ~**ment** aanklag

In'dies Indië; **East** ~ Oos-Indië; **West** ~ Wes-Indië

indiff'erent (a) onverskillig, agte(r)losig; *his*

health is ~ sy gesondheid is swak

indig'enous inheems; aangebore; ~ **tree** in=heemse boom

indiges'tion slegte spysvertering, indigestie

indigna'tion verontwaardiging

indirect' indirek, onregstreeks; ~ **speech** indirekte rede

indiscreet' (a) onverstandig/onbesonne; takt=loos

indispen'sable onontbeerlik, onmisbaar

indispose' (v) ongesteld maak; ~**d'** ongesteld, olik, siek; ongeneë

indistinct' (a) onduidelik, dof, vaag

individ'ual (n) individu, persoon, enkeling; (a) individueel, afsonderlik

individ'ually een vir een; individueel, apart

indoctrina'tion (n) indoktrinasie/indoktrine=ring

in'dolent (a) lui, traag *also* **i'dle, laz'y**

Indone'sian (n) Indonesiër (mens); Indonesies (taal); (a) Indonesies

in'door huis=, binne=; ~ **game** kamerspeletjie; ~ **plants** binnehuise plante

in'doors (a) binnenshuis/binnehuis

induce (v) beweeg; oorhaal, oorreed; ~**ment** aansporing, lokmiddel *also* **incen'tive**

induct' installeer; inwy; bevestig (dominee); ~**ion** induksie; inwyding; bevestiging; in=burgering (groentjies)

indus'trial (a) industrieel, nywerheids=; ~ **ac'= tion** protesoptrede; arbeidsonrus; ~**ist** fabri=kant, nyweraar; ~ **psychol'ogist** bedryfsiel=kundige; ~ **rela'tions** arbeidsverhoudinge; ~ **school** nywerheidskool/ambagskool

indus'trious (a) werksaam, fluks, vlytig

in'dustry vlyt, ywer, werksaamheid; nywer=heid, industrie, bedryf

ine'briate (n) dronkaard; (a) dronk

ined'ible (a) oneetbaar

ineffic'iency (n) onbekwaamheid, onbevoegd=heid; ondoeltreffendheid

ineffic'ient (a) onbekwaam; ongeskik *also* **in=com'petent, inca'pable**; onbruikbaar

inequal'ity ongelykheid; verskil

iner'tia traagheid, bewegingloosheid, inersie; ~ **reel seat'belt** rukstopgordel

ines'timable onskatbaar, onberekenbaar; ~ **dam'age** onberekenbare skade

inev'itable onvermydelik *also* **unavoi'dable**

inexhaus'tible onuitputlik; onvermoeid *also* **ti'reless**

inexpen'sive goedkoop, billik

inexper'ience onervarenheid; ~**d** onervare

infall'ible onfeilbaar *also* **unfai'ling**

in'famous (a) skandalig; verfoeilik; berug

in'fant (n) babatjie, kleuter, suigeling; (a) klein, jong/jonk; minderjarig; ~ **mortal'ity rate** kindersterftesyfer

in'fantile kinderagtig, infantiel; kinderlik; ~ **paral'ysis** kinderverlamming

in'fantry (n) infanterie, voetsoldate

in'fant school kleuterskool *also* **nur'sery school**

infect' (v) besmet, aansteek; ~**ed** besmet, aan=gesteek; ~**ion** besmetting, infeksie; ~**ious' disea'se** aansteeklike siekte/infeksiesiekte

infe'rior (n) ondergeskikte, mindere (mens); (a) minderwaardig; ondergeskik

inferior'ity minderwaardigheid; ~ **com'plex** minderwaardigheidskompleks

infer'nal (a) hels, verfoeilik

infest' vervuil, verpes; wemel (van); teister; ~**ed with rats** vervuil van die rotte

in'fighting binnegevegte; broedertwis

in'filtrate insypel, infiltreer

infiltra'tor (n) insypelaar *also* **insur'gent**

in'finite (n) oneindigheid; (a) oneindig, grens=loos

infinites'imal oneindig klein

infin'itive (n) onbepaalde wys; (a) oneindig, eindeloos; ~ **mood** onbepaalde wys

infirm' (a) swak; gebreklik; ~**ary** siekehuis

inflamm'able (ont)vlambaar, brandbaar *also* **flam'mable**

inflamma'tion ontsteking, inflammasie (siekte)

infla'table (n) rubber/opblaasbootjie *see* **din'ghy**

infla'tion (n) inflasie (ekon.); opblasing

inflex'ion verbuiging, infleksie

inflict' (v) oplê; toebring; ~ *punishment* straf toedien

in'fluence (n) invloed; (v) beïnvloed

influen'tial (a) invloedryk (mense)

influen'za influensa, griep *also* **flu**

in'flux (n) instroming, toestroming

inform' (v) meedeel, verwittig; berig, aankondig

inform'al informeel; ~ **dress** informele drag; ~ **sec'tor** informele sektor; ~ **settle'ment** plakkerskamp

informa'tion (n) informasie, berig, inligting; *full* ~ volle/volledige inligting; *further* ~ meer inligting

inform'ed goed ingelig; saakkundig; *keep someone* ~ iem. op die hoogte hou

inform'er nuusdraer, informant (mens)

in'frastructure infrastruktuur

infre′quent seldsaam *also* sel′dom; ∼ly selde

infringe′ (v) oortree, inbreuk maak op

infu′riate (v) woedend/briesend maak, vertoorn

ingen′ious (a) vernuftig, vindingryk, knap

ingrat′itude (n) ondankbaarheid

ingred′ient (n) bestanddeel, ingrediënt

inhab′it bewoon; woon; ∼able bewoonbaar; ∼ant bewoner, inwoner

inhale′ (v) inasem, intrek

inher′ent aangebore/ingebore, inherent

inhe′rit (v) erf; ∼ance erfenis, erflating, erf=porsie; ∼ed geërf, oorgeërf

inhu′man (a) onmenslik, gevoelloos, barbaars

inim′itable onnavolgbaar, onkopieerbaar

ini′tial (n) voorletter; (pl) paraaf; (v) parafeer; (a) eerste, begin=; aanvangs=; ∼ investiga′= tion/explora′tion aanvang(s)ondersoek; ∼ly (adv) aanvanklik

ini′tiate (v) inlei; inwy, insout, inisieer; ont=groen, inburger (student)

initia′tion inwyding, inburgering; ontgroe=ning; ∼ school inisiasieskool, bergskool

ini′tiative (n) inisiatief, voortou; *take the* ∼ die leiding/inisiatief neem

inject′ (v) inspuit

injec′tion (n) inspuiting, injeksie

in′jure beseer; benadeel, beledig/krenk

in′jury ..ries besering; benadeling; letsel

injus′tice (n) onregverdigheid, onreg; *do an* ∼ iem. ′n onreg aandoen

ink (n) ink; *write in* ∼ skryf met ink

ink′ling vermoede, idee; wenk, snuf

in′land (a) binnelands; (adv) landwaarts

in-law′ aangetroude familielid; *my* ∼s my skoonfamilie

in′line ska′tes (n) inlynskaatse, rollemskaatse *also* rol′lerblades

in′mate bewoner, huisgenoot; inwoner (van ′n gestig)

in′most binneste; diepste, innigste

inn herberg *also* tav′ern; hotel

inn′er innerlik, inwendig; geheim; ∼most bin=neste, innigste

inn′ings beurt; kolfbeurt (krieket)

inn′keeper herbergier, waard

inn′ocence (n) onskuld; eenvoudigheid

inn′ocent (a) onskuldig; onnosel (mens)

innova′tion nuwigheid *also* nov′elty

inoc′ulate (v) inent, ent, okuleer

inoffen′sive (a) onskadelik; argeloos

inopportu′ne (a) ongeleë, ontydig

in′put (n) inset (produksiemiddele); *make an*

∼ ′n inset/bydrae lewer *see* out′put

in′quest geregtelike ondersoek; lykskouing

inquire′ ondersoek instel; ∼ *into the affairs of the company* ondersoek instel na die maat=skappy se sake

inquir′y (geregtelike) ondersoek *also* inves=tiga′tion, probe (n)

inquisi′tion inkwisisie

inquis′itive (a) nuuskierig; weetgierig

insane′ (a) kranksinnig, mal *also* mad

inscrip′tion inskrywing; inskripsie (op iets)

in′sect insek, gogga

insec′ticide insekdoder, insektegif

insecure′ (a) onveilig, onseker *also* unsa′fe

insemina′tion bevrugting, inseminasie; arti′=ficial ∼ (AI) kunsmatige bevrugting, kuns=matige inseminasie (KI)

insep′arable (a) onskei(d)baar; onafskeidelik (vriende)

insert′ invoeg, inlas; inskakel; ∼ion invoe=ging; opname, plasing (in koerant)

in′-service: ∼ trai′ning indiensopleiding; ∼ tui′tion (in)diensonderrig

in′set (n) bylae/byvoegsel; byblad; inlas

in′side (n) binnekant; binneste; inwendige; binnegoed; *know* ∼ *out* deur en deur ken; (a) binneste=; binne=; (adv) binnekant, binne(n)shuis; (prep) binne

in′sight insig; begrip; blik

insignif′icant onbeduidend

insincere′ (a) onopreg, huigelagtig

insin′uate (v) sinspeel, insinueer; te kenne gee

insip′id smaakloos, laf, flou

insist′ (v) aanhou, aandring; volhou; volhard by; ∼ *on* aandring op

insofar′: ∼ *as* in dié mate dat, vir sover

in′solence (n) onbeskoftheid, parmantigheid

insol′vency bankrotskap, insolvensie

insol′vent (n) insolvent (mens); (a) bankrot, insolvent

insom′nia slaaploosheid/slapeloosheid

inspan′ inspan

inspect′ (v) inspekteer; ∼ion inspeksie, onder=soek; ∼or inspekteur; opsiener

inspira′tion (n) besieling, inspirasie, ingewing

inspire′ inboesem; besiel; inspireer; aanvuur; inasem; ∼ *confidence* vertroue inboesem; ∼d besiel, geïnspireer, begeester(d)

inspir′ing (a) besielend, inspirerend

install′ (v) installeer, aanlê, aanbring, vestig

installa′tion installasie; aanleg (fabriek)

instal′ment paaiement; aflewering; *pay in* ∼s

in paaiemente afbetaal

in'stance (n) voorbeeld, geval; versoek; *in the first* ~ in die eerste plek, in eerste instansie; *for* ~ byvoorbeeld

in'stant (n) oomblik, tydstip; (a, adv) onmid= dellik, dadelik; dringend; kits=; *the 16th* ~ 16 deser; ~**a'neous** oombliklik; ~ **cof'fee** kitskoffie

instead' of in plaas van, pleks van

in'step (n) voetboog, wreef

in'stigate (v) aanhits, opstook, aanpor

in'stigator opstoker, aanhitser *also* **ag'itator**

instil' inboesem *see* **inspi're**; inprent

in'stinct (n) instink, natuurdrif

in'stitute (n) instelling; wet; instituut; (pl) in= stitute; (v) instel, stig, vestig; ~ *proceedings* regstappe doen/instel

institu'tion (n) instelling; inrigting; gestig

instruct' onderrig, leer; ~**ion** onderrig; bevel, instruksie; ~**ive** leersaam; ~**or** leermeester, instrukteur

in'strument (n) instrument, werktuig; middel

instrumen'tal (a) bevorderlik, behulpsaam

insubordina'tion (n) ongehoorsaamheid, ver= set, insubordinasie

insuffi'cient (a) ontoereikend, onvoldoende

in'sulate (v) afsonder, isoleer

insula'tion afsondering, isolering; ~ **tape** iso= leerband

in'sult (n) belediging, affront; **cal'culated** ~ berekende affront

insult' (v) beledig; ~**ing** krenkend, beledi= gend, kwetsend *also* **abu'sive**

insu'rance versekering, assuransie; **third par= ty** ~ derdepartyversekering; ~ **a'gent** assu= ransieagent; ~ **com'pany** versekering(s)= maatskappy; ~ **pol'icy** versekering(s)po= lis/assuransiepolis

insure' verseker, verassureer; seker maak; ~**d'** (n) die versekerde; (a) verseker, verassureer; ~**r** versekeraar; onderskrywer

insur'gent (n) opstandeling; insypelaar (mens)

insurrec'tion (n) opstand, muitery

intact' ongeskonde, onaangeroer, intak(t)

in'take inname; toevoer; opvanggebied

in'tegral (a) heel, volledig, integraal/integre= rend; ~ *part of* integrerende deel van

integra'tion (n) integrasie; inskakeling

integ'rity (a) opregtheid, egtheid; integriteit

in'tellect verstand, vernuf, gees, intellek

intellec'tual (n) intellektueel (mens); (a) ver= standelik, intellektueel; verstands=

intell'igence verstand; intelligensie; inlig= ting (mil.); ~ **quo'tient (I.Q.)** intelligensie= kwosiënt (I.K.)

intell'igent skrander, intelligent, slim, knap

intend' voornemens wees, wil; ~ *no harm* geen kwaad bedoel nie; ~**ed** (n) aanstaande (mens); (a) bestem(d), voorgenome

intense' hewig, kragtig, fel *also* **fierce**

inten'sify (v) versterk, verskerp

inten'sity hewigheid, intensiteit

inten'sive intensief; intens; ~ **care u'nit** (intensiewe) sorgeenheid, waakeenheid

intent' (n) oogmerk, voorneme; *to all* ~*s and purposes* vir alle praktiese doeleindes

inten'tion voorneme; bedoeling; ~**al** opsetlik, moedswillig

inter'[1] (v) begrawe, ter aarde bestel

in'ter[2] (adv) tussen; ~ **a'lia** onder andere

interact' (v) op mekaar inwerk; ~**ion** wis= selwerking; interaksie

intercept' onderskep; afsny; teenhou

in'terchange (n) wisseling; ruiling; **traf'fic** ~ (verkeers)wisselaar, wisselkruising

interchange' (v) wissel, ruil; verwissel

in'tercourse (n) omgang, verkeer; **sex'ual** ~ (geslags)gemeenskap

interdenomina'tional (a) interkerklik; inter= sektaries

in'terdict (n) verbod, interdik

interdict' (v) verbied, skors

in'terest (n) belang; belangstelling; rente; ~**ed** *parties* belangstellende/belanghebbende par= tye; *I am* ~*ed* in ek stel belang in; *in the* ~ *of* in (die) belang van; *take an* ~ *in* belang stel in; (v) belang stel, interesseer; **compound** ~ saamgestelde rente; **rate of** ~ rentekoers; **simple** ~ enkelvoudige rente; ~**ing** interes= sant, belangwekkend

in'terface (n) raakvlak/intervlak; (v) intervlak, koppel

interfere' (v) bemoei (met), inmeng (in)

in'terim (n) tussentyd; ~ **div'idend** tussen= tydse dividend/tussendividend

inte'rior (n) binneland; binneste; (a) binneste, binnelands; ~ **dec'orating** binneversiering

interjec'tion (n) tussenwerpsel; uitroep

in'terlude (n) tussenspel

intermar'ry ondertrou

intermed'iary (n) tussenganger *also* **go-be= tween'**; (be)middelaar (mens); (a) tussen=

intermed'iate tussenkomend, intermediêr; ~ **examina'tion** intermediêre eksamen

inter'ment (n) begrafnis, teraardebestelling *also* **fu'neral, bu'rial**
intermi'ssion onderbreking; tussenpouse
intermitt'ent (a) afwisselend; periodiek
in'tern[1] (n) intern, (proef)arts/huisarts (mens)
intern'[2] (v) interneer
inter'nal (a) inwendig, binne; binnelands; in= nerlik; ~ **check** interne kontrole; ~ **combus'tion en'gine** binnebrandmotor; ~ **control'** interne beheer; ~ **mat'ter** huishoude= like/interne saak/aangeleentheid
interna'tional (n) internasionale speler; (a) in= ternasionaal; ~ **air'port** internasionale lug= hawe; ~ **media'tion** internasionale bemid= deling
Internet Internet
inter'pret (v) verklaar, uitlê, vertolk; ~**a'tion** verklaring, vertolking, uitleg, interpretasie; ~**er** tolk; uitlêer; vertolker (musiek)
interprovin'cial interprovinsiaal
inter'rogate (v) ondervra, uitvra, kruisvra
interrupt' onderbreek; ~**ion** onderbreking
intersect' deursny, deurkruis, sny; ~**ion** sny= punt, kruispunt; kruising (strate)
in'terval (n) rustyd, pouse; tussenruimte; tus= sentyd; interval; *at* ~*s* met tussenposes
intervar'sity (n) ..**ties** intervarsity; (a) inter= universitêr
interven'tion (n) tussenkoms, intervensie
in'terview (n) onderhoud; vraaggesprek; (v) ondervra; 'n onderhoud voer; **ex'it** ~ ver= trekgesprek; ~**er** ondervraer, onderhoud= voerder; ~**ing** onderhoudvoering
intes'tine (n) derm; (pl) ingewande, derms
in-thing: *the* ~ die inding (om te doen)
in'timate[1] (v) te kenne gee, aandui
in'timate[2] (a) vertroulik, intiem; innig
intimida'tion (n) vreesaanjaging, intimidasie
in'to in, tot; ~ *the bargain* op die koop toe
intona'tion intonasie, stembuiging; aanhef
intoxica'tion dronkenskap; bedwelming
intraven'ous binneaars; ~ **fee'ding** aarvoeding
in'tricate (a) ingewikkeld; verwar(d)
intrigue' (n) intrige, komplot; gekonkel
introduce' voorstel (mense); invoer; inlei; ~ *a bill* 'n wetsontwerp indien
introduc'tion inleiding (tot boek); voorstel= ling; introduksie; voorspel (mus.)
in'trovert (n) introvert (mens); (a) in homself gekeer(d)
intrude' (v) indring; lastig val; opdring; inbreuk maak; steur; ~**r** indringer

intui'tion intuïsie, aanvoeling
invade' inval/aanval; ~**r** invaller
in'valid[1] (n) sieke, invalide (mens); (a) swak, siek; gestrem, invalide
inval'id[2] (a) ongeldig *also* **null and void**
inval'uable onskatbaar *also* **pri'celess**
inva'riably gereeld, deurgaans
inva'sion inval (van leër)
invent' (v) uitvind; uitdink; ~**ion** uitvinding; uitvindsel; ~**or** uitvinder
in'ventory (n) inventaris; voorraadopname; (v) voorraad opneem *also* **take stock**
in'verse (n) omgekeerde; (a) omgekeer; ~ **propor'tion/ra'tio** omgekeerde verhouding
invert' omkeer, omsit; ~**ed com'mas** aan= haaltekens *also* **quota'tion marks**
invest' (v) belê, investeer (geld); beklee
inves'tigate (v) ondersoek *also* **pro'be**; na= vors; ~ *into* ondersoek instel na *see* **inquire; inves'tigating of'ficer** ondersoek= beampte
investiga'tion ondersoek, navorsing
invest'ment (n) belegging (geld); investering
inves'tor belegger
invi'gilate (v) toesig hou oor, oppas
invi'gilator toesighouer (eksamen); opsiener
invin'cible onoorwinlik
invis'ible onsigbaar; ~ **men'ding** fynstop, kunsstop
invita'tion (n) uitnodiging
invite' (n) uitnodiging; (v) (uit)nooi; ~ *your friends* jou vriende nooi; ~ *tenders* tenders aanvra; ~ *trouble* moeilikheid soek
in'voice (n) faktuur; (v) faktureer
invol've (v) omvat; betrek; inwikkel; ~*d in* betrokke in/by ~**ment** betrokkenheid
in'ward (a) inwendig; innerlik; (adv) binne= waarts; die land in
i'odine (n) jodium, jood
irate' (a) kwaad, woedend, briesend
ir'is -es iris, reënboogvlies (oog); flap (blom)
i'ron (n) yster; strykyster; *have too many* ~*s in the fire* te veel hooi op die vurk hê; **cast** ~ gietyster; **wrought** ~ smeeyster; (a) yster=; ~ **foun'dry** ystergietery; ~**ware** ysterware
iron'ic(al) ironies
irrecov'erable (a) onverhaalbaar (skuld); ~ **debts** oninbare skuld, dooieskuld
irreg'ular (a) ongereeld; onreëlmatig
irregula'rity ..**ties** ongereeldheid; onreëlma= tigheid; afwyking, fout
irresis'tible (a) onweerstaanbaar, verleidelik

irrespec'tive: ~ *of* ongeag, afgesien van
irrespon'sible (a) onverantwoordelik
irrev'erent (a) oneerbiedig
ir'rigate besproei, natlei
irriga'tion besproeiing, irrigasie
ir'ritable (a) prikkelbaar, liggeraak *also* **touch'y**
ir'ritate (v) vererg, prikkel, irriteer
irrita'tion irritasie, ergernis; wrewel
Is'lam (n) Islam (geloof)
i'sland eiland; vlugheuwel (verkeer); ~**er** eilandbewoner
i'slet (n) eilandjie
i'solate afsonder, isoleer
isola'tion afsondering, isolasie; ~ **hos'pital** afsonderingshospitaal
Is'rael Israel; ~**i** (n) Israeli (mens); (a) Israe= lies; ~**ite** Israeliet (mens, histories)
iss'ue (n) uitgawe (boek); kwessie, knelpunt; uitgifte (aandele, banknote); afstamming;

~ *from* (voort)spruit uit; *without male* ~ sonder manlike afstammeling; *point at* ~ geskilpunt; kwessie; (v) uitreik
it dit; hy; sy; *face* ~ die gevolge dra; *with* ~ daarmee; **with-it** byderwets; bydertyds *also* **tren'dy**
ital'ic (n) kursiefletter; *in* ~*s* kursief; (a) kur= sief, skuins; ~**ise** (v) kursiveer
itch (n) (ge)jeuk (ge)juk; uitslag; hunkering; (v) j(e)uk, kriewel/kriebel
it'em item, nommer (op program); artikel
itin'erary (n) ..ries reisplan; reisgids
its sy, syne; haar, hare
i'vory (n) ivoor, olifantstand; **i'vories** dobbel= steen; biljartbal; *black* ~ ebbehout; (a) ivoor=, van ivoor; ~ **poach'er** ivoorstroper; ~ **to'wer** ivoortoring
iv'y ivies klimop *also* **(wall) cree'per**
ix'ia kalossie, ixia (blom)

J

jab (n) steek *also* **poke, prod,** (v) steek, stoot
jacaran'da -s jakaranda (boom)
Jack[1] Jan; ~ *of all trades* hansie-my-kneg; ~ *of all trades, master of none* twaalf am= bagte, dertien ongelukke
jack[2] (n) boer (kaartspel); domkrag; (v) opdomkrag
jack'al (n) jakkals (dier)
jack'ass eselhings, donkiehings; domkop
jack'boot (n) kapstewel
jack'et (n) baadjie; omhulsel; mantel
jack: J~ Frost die ryp; ~**-in-the-box** kaart= man(netjie); ~**knife** groot knipmes; jagmes; (v) knakvou (koppellorrie); ~**pot** boerpot
jag'uar Amerikaanse luiperd, jaguar
jail (n) gevangenis, tronk *also* **gaol, pris'on**; (v) in die tronk sit; ~**bird** tronkvoël; ~**break** tronkbraak; ~**er** tronkbewaarder; sipier
jam[1] (n) (fyn)konfyt
jam[2] (n) gedrang; verkeersknoop; haak; (v) (vas)klem; vasknel
jamboree' saamtrek; makietie; jamboree
jan'itor deurwagter, portier *also* **door'keeper**
Jan'uary Januarie
japon'ica -s japonika, kamelia (blom)
jar[1] (n) kruik; vrugtebottel (vir inmaak)
jar[2] (n) wanklank; rusie; (v) twis; skok

jarg'on (n) kliektaal, jargon; koeterwaals
jas'mine jasmyn; geelsuring (blom)
jas'per jaspis *also* **touch'stone**
jaun'dice (n) geelsug; nyd, jaloesie
jaunt (n) uitstappie; (v) rondflenter
jav'elin (n) werpspies (sport)
jaw (n) kaak, kakebeen; ~**bone** kakebeen; ~**brea'ker** tongknoper (swaar woord), snel= sêer *also* **tonguetwis'ter**
jay'walker bontloper, gansloper (in strate)
jazz jazz
jeal'ous (a) jaloers, afgunstig, naywerig; ~**y** jaloesie, naywer
jeans (n) jeans; slenterdrag
jeer (n) spot, beskimping; (v) spot, uitlag
jell'y jellies jellie; ~**beans** jellieboontjies; ~**fish** seekwal
jeo'pardise (v) in gevaar bring/stel; waag *also* **endan'ger**; ~ *your promotion* jou bevorde= ring verongeluk
jerk (n) ruk; stamp; *by* ~*s* met rukke en stote; (v) ruk, pluk; ~**y** (a) hortend
je'rrybuilder (n) knutselbouer, knoeibouer
jers'ey -s trui
jest (n) skerts, grap, korswel; (v) skerts, kors= wel; ~*ing apart* alle gekheid op 'n stok= kie; ~**er** (hof)nar, grapmaker, grapjas *also*

jo′ker, come′dian

Je′sus Jesus

jet[1] (n) git; (a) git=; ~**black** gitswart

jet[2] (n) straal; pit; straler (vliegtuig); tuit; spuit; (v) uitspuit; straal; ~**fighter** straaljagter, straalvegter; ~ **lag** straaldraal: *I am suffering from* ~ ek het straaldraal, ek is vliegvoos

jet′sam strandgoed; wrakstukke, opdrifsel

jet′liner (n) passasierstraler

jet′set stralerkliek; ~**ter** stralerjakker

jet′ski waterponie *also* **ski′-jet**

jett′y jetties hawehoof, pier *also* **pier**

Jew Jood

jew′el (n) juweel, kleinood; skat; ~**ler** juwe= lier; ~**lery** juwele, juweliersware

jiff′(y) ommesientjie, kits; *in a* ~ in ′n kits, in ′n japtrap, tjop-tjop

jigg′le bar (n) riffelstrook (spoeddemper)

jig′saw figuursaag; ~ **puz′zle** legkaart

jin′gle (n) reklamedeuntjie; klingel(rympie) *also* **chi′me, dit′ty**; (v) klingel, rinkel; ~ **bell** klingelklokkie

jit′terbug (n) ritteldans

jit′ters ritteltit; *get the* ~ op die senuwees kry

jive (n, v) jive (dans)

job (n) werk, betrekking, pos; taak; ~ **crea′= tion** werkskepping; ~ **descrip′tion** pos= beskrywing; ~ **evalua′tion** posevaluering; ~ **opportu′nity** werkgeleentheid; ~ **pla′ce= ment** indiensplasing; ~ **see′ker** werksoeker; ~ **satisfac′tion** werk(s)bevrediging

job: ~**ber** makelaar; knoeier; ~ **lot** rommelspul

jock′ey (n) -s jokkie (perde); snuiter, vent; **disc** ~ platejoggie

jog (v) draf, pretdraf; stamp, stoot, sukkel; ~ *along* voortsukkel; ~**ger** (pret)drawwer; ~**ging** (pret)draf, drafsport

jog′trot (n) sukkelgang; sukkeldraffie

johnn′y johnnies kêrel, vent *also* **guy**

join (n) voeg, naat, las; (v) verbind; saamvoeg; ~ *up* aansluit

join′er skrynwerker; meubelmaker

joint[1] (n) gewrig; lit; verbinding; las; *out of* ~ uit lit

joint[2] (a) mede-; gesamentlik; ~ **esta′te** ge= samentlike/gemeenskaplike boedel; ~**ly** ge= samentlik

joke (n) grap, frats; gekheid; *it is no* ~ dis geen/g′n kleinigheid nie; *play a practical* ~ *on someone* iem. ′n poets bak; (v) grappe maak; gekskeer; ~**r** grapmaker/grapjas; joker/asjas (kaartspel)

jollifica′tion vrolikheid, pret, joligheid

joll′y (a) vrolik, plesierig; aangeklam; ~ **jum′per** huppeltuig

jolt (n) stamp, stoot

jot[1] (n) jota, kleinigheid

jot[2] (v) aanteken, aanstip; ~ *down* aanstip

journ′al dagboek; joernaal, tydskrif; **house** ~ firmablad; ~ **en′try** joernaalinskrywing

journ′alism joernalistiek; die pers

journ′alist koerantskrywer, joernalis; verslag= gewer (mens)

journ′ey (n) -s reis; *a day′s* ~ ′n dagreis

jo′vial (a) vrolik, plesierig, opgeruimd, joviaal

jowl kakebeen; wang; krop; onderken; keel= vel; *cheek by* ~ kop in een mus

joy (n) blydskap, vreugde; *it gives me* ~ dit doen my genoeë; ~**ful** vrolik; bly/verheug; ~**ous** vreugdevol; ~**ride** plesierrit; ~**stick** stuur= stang

jub′ilee (n) jubileum; bestaansjaar *also* **fes= tiv′ity, ga′la**

judge (n) regter; beoordelaar; (v) oordeel; vonnis; beoordeel; ~ *by* oordeel volgens

judg′ment (n) oordeel; vonnis; opinie

judi′cious (a) oordeelkundig, verstandig

ju′do judo

jug kan, beker; wasbeker

jug′gle (v) goël, wiggel; ~**r** goëlaar/wiggelaar, jongleur *see* **magi′cian**

juice sop, sap

jui′cy (a) sapperig/sappig; smaaklik

jukebox blêrkas

juk′skei: ~ **club** jukskeilaer; ~ **lea′gue** jukskei= liga

July′ Julie; ~ **Han′dicap** Juliewedren

jum′ble (n) verwarring; mengelmoes; alle= gaartjie; ~ **sale** rommelverkoping

jum′bo lomperd, diksak; ~ **jet** makrostraler

jump (n) sprong; (v) spring

jum′per (n) springer; ~ **lead** aansitkabel *also* **boos′ter cable; jolly** ~ huppeltuig

junc′tion aansluiting (pad, spoorweg)

June Junie

jung′le (n) oerwoud; ruigte, wildernis; ~**-gym** klimraam, wouterklouter (speeltuig)

jun′ior jonger, junior

junk (n) rommel, uitskot; jonk (seilboot); ~ **food** prulkos, kafkos; ~ **mail** smouspos/ strooipos; ~ **shop** help-my-krapwinkel

jurisdic′tion regsgebied, jurisdiksie

jur′ist juris, regsgeleerde (mens)

jur′y (n) **juries** jurie (in hofsitting)

just (a) regverdig, onpartydig; juis, presies
just² (adv) net, presies; ~ *as* net soos, nes; ~ *now* netnou; ~ *as well* ook maar goed
jus'tice (n) reg, geregtigheid; regverdigheid; justisie; *court of* ~ geregshof; *do* ~ *to* reg laat geskied; ~ *of the peace* vrederegter
jus'tify regverdig, staaf, bewys *also* **val'idate**
jut (n) uitsteeksel; (v) uitsteek

jute goiing, jute/juut (tou, sakke)
ju'venile (n) jeugdige; (a) jong, jeugdig; ~ **court** kinderhof; ~ **delin'quency** jeugwan= gedrag; jeugmisdadigheid; ~ **delin'quent** jeugoortreder, jeugmisdadiger; ~ **lit'era= ture** jeuglektuur
juxtaposi'tion naasmekaarstelling, jukstaposisie

K

kaleid'oscope (n) kaleidoskoop
kangaroo' kangaroe; ~ **court** boendoehof, straathof
kart (n) renstel *see* **go'-cart**; ~**ing** knortjorrenne
keel (n) kiel; skip, vaartuig; (v) kiel; omslaan; omval; ~**haul** (v) kielhaal
keen (a) gretig, ywerig, skerp(sinnig) *also* **ea'ger**; *as* ~ *as mustard* uiters gretig; ~ *on* versot op *also* **hooked on**
keep (n) bewaring; onderhoud; toesig; *for* ~*s* om te hou; (v) hou; bêre; bewaar; in voorraad hou; ~ *an appointment* 'n af= spraak hou; ~ *a promise* 'n belofte nakom; ~ *time* maat hou; ~ *in touch with* in voeling/aanraking bly met; ~ *well* goed/ gesond bly; ~**er** bewaarder, opsigter; ~**sake** (n) aandenking, soewenier
keg (n) vaatjie
kenn'el dierehberg; hondehok, woefie= tuiste; kietsiesorg
kept *see* **keep**; ~ **wo'man** houvrou, handperd
kerb (n) randsteen
kern'el pit *also* **core, es'sence**; korrel
ketch'up (n) ketjap; kruiesous, tamatiesous
ket'tle ketel; *a pretty* ~ *of fish* 'n mooi spul/ gedoente; ~**drum** keteltrom, pouk
key (n) -**s** sleutel (van deur), klawer; toets; ~**board** klawers, toetsbord; ~**hole** sleutel= gat; ~ **in'dustry** sleutelnywerheid, sleutel= bedryf; ~**note** grondtoon; ~**note address'** tematoespraak; ~**stone** sluitsteen
kha'ki kakie; ~**bos** kakiebos
kibb'utz (n) kibboets (Israel); gemeenskaps= plaas
kick (n) skop; skok; (v) skop; ~ *the bucket* sterf, bokveld toe gaan; ~**back** gunsloon (oneerlike vergoeding); ~**box'ing** skopboks; ~**er** skop= per; ~-**off** afskop
kid¹ (n) boklam; bokvel; kidleer; kind, kan=

netjie, snuiter; (v) lam
kid² (v) kul, fop, die gek skeer
kid'dy kiddies kleintjie, kleinding
kid'nap (v) ontvoer, skaak, steel ('n kind); ~**per** kinderdief; ontvoerder *also* **abduc'= tor**; ~**ping** ontvoering
kid'ney -**s** nier; ~ **bean** nierboon(tjie)
kill (v) doodmaak; slag; vermoor; ~*ed in= stantly* op slag dood (padongeluk); ~ *time* tyd verdryf; ~**ing** (n) doodmaak; slagting; (a) dodelik; onweerstaanbaar; ~**joy** suur= pruim, pretbederwer/spelbreker
kiln (n) (droog)oond
kil'ogram kilogram
kil'ometre kilometer
kil'owatt kilowatt
kin (n) familie, bloedverwant; afkoms
kind¹ (n) soort, geslag; aard; natuur; *nothing of the* ~ niks daarvan nie
kind² (a) vriendelik, minsaam; lief; ~ *regards* vriendelike groete
kin'dergarten kleuterskool, bewaarskool
kind'hearted (a) goedhartig, goedgeaard
kin'dle (v) aansteek; ontvlam; opflikker
kind'ly (a) vriendelik, goedhartig
kind'ness vriendelikheid, goedheid, welwil= lendheid
kin'dred (a) verwant; passend; gelyksoortig
king (n) koning, vors; heer; ~**'s Eng'lish** standaard-Engels; ~**dom** koninkryk; ~**fisher** visvanger; ~**size** bieliegrootte, reusegrootte
kink (n) kinkel; nuk, gril; ~**y** eksentriek; (seksueel) afwykend *also* **queer; sex'ually de'viant**
kiosk' kiosk; tuinhuisie; stal(letjie) *also* **booth, stall**
kipp'er/kipp'ered her'ring gerookte haring, kipper
kiss (n) -**es** soen, kus; (v) soen; ~ *goodbye*

soengroet, 'n afskeidsoen gee; ~ **curl** oor=
krulletjie, koketkrulletjie
kit uitrusting; (op)boustel; ~**bag** knapsak
kitch'en kombuis; ~ **dres'ser** kombuiskas; ~
tea: *have a* ~ *tea* bruidskombuis/kombuis=
tee hou; ~ **uten'sils** kombuisgerei
kite vlieër; kuikendief (voël); inhaler, haai
(mens); *fly a* ~ 'n proefballon oplaat
kitt'en (n) katjie
kitt'y[1] **kitties** katjie, kietsie
kitty[2] (n) poel/pot (met geldbydraes)
knack slag, handigheid *also* **flair**; gewoonte
knap'sack bladsak, knapsak *also* **kitbag**
knead (v) knie (deeg); masseer
knee (n) knie; ~**cap** knieskyf; knieskut (by
voetbal); ~**joint** kniegewrig
kneel (v) kniel; ~ *down* neerkniel
knick'erbockers kniebroek, kuitbroek
knick'-knack snuistery, tierlantyntjie
knife (n) **knives** mes; ~ **blade** lem
knight (n) ridder; perd (skaak)
knit (v) brei; saamvleg; ~ *the brows* die
wenkbroue frons; ~**ting** breiwerk; ~**ting
machi'ne** breimasjien
knob (n) knop; ~**by** knoesterig; ~**ker'rie**
knopkierie
knock (n) klop, klap, raps; stamp; (v) klop, stoot;
stamp; ~ *spots off someone* iem. opdons;

~**er** klopper; ~**-kneed** met X-bene; lamlen=
dig; ~**knees** aankapknieë; ~**-on** aanslaan
knock'out: ~ **blow** uitklophou; ~ **competi'=
tion** uitklopkompetisie
knot (n) knoop; kwas; *cut the Gordian* ~ die
Gordiaanse knoop deurhak; (v) knoop; strik;
verbind; ~**ty** geknoop; knoesterig; netelig
('n probleem)
know (n) wete; *be in the* ~ ingelig wees; (v)
weet, ken; verstaan; ~ *for a fact* seker weet;
~ *by heart* van buite ken; ~ *the ropes*
gekonfyt wees in iets; ~**-all** beterweter
(mens); ~**-how** kundigheid; sakevernuf
also **experti'se**; ~**ingly** wetend; opsetlik
knowl'edge kennis; wete; *to the best of my* ~
na my beste wete; *it is common* ~ dis
algemeen bekend; *without my* ~ sonder my
medewete; *a working* ~ gangbare kennis
(van iets)
known (a) bekend
knuc'kle (n) kneukel; ~**-dus'ter** vuisyster
koek'sister koe(k)sister *also* **crul'ler**
kop'pie koppie (heuwel) *also* **hil'lock, knoll**
kosh'er (a) kosjer/kousjer; fatsoenlik
krans krans, rotswand *also* **cliff, prec'ipice**
ku'du koedoe (bok)
kum'quat/cum'quat koemkwat
kwashior'kor (n) kwasjiorkor, ondervoedingsiekte

L

laag'er (n) laer *also* **wag'on encamp'ment**; (v)
laer trek
la'bel (n) etiket; (v) merk, klassifiseer; be=
stempel, etiketteer
labor'atory ..ries laboratorium, werkvertrek
la'bour (n) arbeid, werk; **hard** ~ hardepad; ~
intensive arbeidintensief; (v) werk, arbei;
~**er** arbeider/werker; ~ **relations** arbeids=
verhouding
lab'yrinth doolhof, labirint *also* **ma'ze**
lace (n) kant, band; skoenveter/skoenriem; (v)
(toe)ryg; met kant versier; bymeng
lack (n) gebrek, gemis, behoefte; *for* ~ *of* by
gebrek aan; (v) ontbreek
lack'ey (n) lyfkneg; lakei/handlanger
lacq'uer (n) lak, vernis; (v) verlak, vernis
lad (n) seun, jongeling *also* **young'ster**; maat,
makker *also* **guy, pal**
ladd'er (n) leer; *go into* ~s lostrek

ladd'ie knapie, kêreltjie *also* **chap'pie**
la'ding lading, vrag; **bill of** ~ vragbrief
la'dle (n) (op)skeplepel, potlepel; (v) met 'n
lepel skep, opskep; ~ *out* uitskep
lad'y ladies dame; ~ *of the house* gasvrou,
huisvrou; ~**bird** liewe(n)heersbesie (insek);
~ **friend** vriendin; ~**like** damesagtig; fyn,
beskaaf, vroulik; ~**'s man** rokjagter; laven=
telhaan, ruikerridder
lag (v) draal *also* **daw'dle**; agterbly, deporteer;
~ *behind* agterbly
lagoon' (n) strandmeer, lagune
lake (n) meer; pan; ~ **dwel'ler** paal(be)woner
lamb (n, v) lam
lame (a) lam, mank, kruppel, gebreklik
lament' (n) weeklaag; (v) beween, betreur
lam'inate (v) lamelleer; uitklop, plat slaan;
lamineer; (a) skilferig; ~**d door** lameldeur
lamm'ergeyer (n) lammervanger (berghaan)

lammergier (Eur.)

lamp lamp; lig; ~ **chim'ney** lampglas; ~**post** lamppaal

lance (n) lans; harpoen; lansier; (v) deursteek; oopsny; ~**r** lansier (soldaat)

lan'cet (n) vlym, lanset

land (n) land, grond; landerye; (v) land, aan wal stap

land: ~**ing strip** landingstrook; ~**la'dy** losieshoudster, hospita; ~**lord** huisbaas; woonstelverhuurder; ~**mark** landmerk; ~**mine** landmyn; ~**scape gar'dening** tuinargitektuur; ~ **survey'or** landmeter

lane laning/laan; deurgang; baan (verkeer)

lang'uage taal, spraak; ~ **labor'atory** taallaboratorium; ~ **me'dium** voertaal

lank/lanky (a) skraal, dun; rank

lan'tern (n) lantern; **Chi'nese** ~ lampion; **mag'ic** ~ towerlantern

lap[1] (n) skoot; klap (van saal); holte; (v) inwikkel; toevou

lap[2] (n) voeg; las; rondte (sport); ~ **rec'ord** baanrekord (motorrenne)

la'pa (n) lapa, saamkomplek

lap'dog skoothondjie

lapel' (n) kraagomslag, lapel; ~ **bad'ge** lapelwapen, lapelknopie

lapse (n) verloop; glips; ~ **of time** tyd(s)verloop; (v) verval; verstryk

lap'top compu'ter skootrekenaar

lar'ceny ..nies diefstal also **theft'**

lard (n) varkvet, reusel; (v) deurspek, lardeer; ~**er** (voorraad)spens

large (a) groot; breed, wyd; ruim; as ~ as life lewensgroot; *the public at* ~ die groot/breë publiek; *to a* ~ *extent* in/tot 'n groot mate

lark[1] (n) lewerkie, leeurik (veldvoël)

lark[2] (n) gekskeerdery also **an'tics**; (v) gekskeer, grappe verkoop; ~**er** pretmaker

lark'spur ridderspoor

larv'a -e larwe, papie, maaier

laryngit'is keelontsteking, laringitis

lar'ynx -es, larynges strottehoof

lasciv'ious weelderig; wulps, wellustig also **sen'sual, lust'ful**

la'ser laser; ~ **beam** laserstraal; ~ **print'er** laserdrukker; ~ **scan'ner** lasertaster/laserskandeerder

lash (n) -es raps, sweepslag; voorslag; ooghaar; (v) raps, slaan, gésel

lass -es (n) meisie, nooientjie also **dam'sel, mai'den**

lasso' (n) -s vangriem, gooitou, lasso

last[1] lees (vir 'n skoen)

last[2] (n) laaste; *the* ~ *but one* op een na die laaste; ~ *but not least* les bes; *to the very* ~ tot die bitter end; (a, adv) laaste, vergange; eind=; ~ *night* gisteraand; *last Saturday* verlede/laas Saterdag

last[3] (n) uithouvermoë; (v) duur, uithou/volhou, aanhou; voldoende wees

last'comer heksluiter, laatlammetjie (kind)

last'ing duursaam; ~ **peace** blywende vrede

last'ly uiteindelik, ten laaste, ten slotte

latch (n) -es knip; ~**key** nagsleutel

late (a) laat; wyle, oorlede (mens); (adv) laat; onlangs; *sooner or* ~**r** vroeër of later

late'ly onlangs, pas, kort gelede

la'tent verborge; latent

lathe (n) draaibank

lath'er (n) seepsop, skuim; (v) inseep

lat'itude breedte; ruimte; beweegruimte

latt'er laasgenoemde; laaste; ~**ly** onlangs, in die jongste tyd

latt'ice traliewerk, rasterwerk

laud (v) prys, ophemel; ~**able** lofwaardig, prysenswaardig also **commen'dable**

laugh (n) lag, gelag; (v) lag, ~ *at* uitlag, ~**able** belaglik, snaaks also **lu'dicrous**

laugh'ing lag; gelag; *I could not help* ~ ek kon nie my lag hou nie; ~**ly** lag-lag; ~ **stock** die spot van iedereen

laugh'ter (n) gelag

launch[1] (n) -es plesierbootjie; barkas, sloep; lansering (ruimtetuig)

launch[2] (v) loods (skema), bekendstel; van stapel laat loop (skip); van stapel stuur; lanseer (ruimtetuig); gooi; slinger; aanpak; ~ *a project* 'n projek loods; ~**(ing) pad** lanseerblad

launderette'/laun'dromat wasseret/muntwasser

laun'dry ..dries wassery; waskamer

lau'rel (n) lourier; *rest on one's* ~**s** op jou louere rus; ~ **wreath** louerkrans

la'va lawa

lav'atory ..ries latrine, kleinhuisie, privaat, toilet(kamer); waskamer

lav'ender (n) reukwater, laventel

lav'ish (a) kwistig; volop, oorvloedig

law wet; regsgeleerdheid, die reg; *study/read* ~ in die regte studeer; **common** ~ gemenereg; ~ **of employment** arbeidsreg, diensreg; **international** ~ volkereg; **Roman Dutch** ~ Romeins-Hollandse reg; **statute** ~ wette=

reg, statutereg; ∼**-abi′ding** wetsgehoor=
saam; ordeliewend; ∼**court** geregshof; ∼
enforce′ment wetstoepassing; ∼**ful** wettig,
wetlik; ∼**less** wetteloos

lawn grasperk; grasveld; ∼ **mo′wer** grassnyer;
∼ **ten′nis** tennis

law′yer prokureur *also* **attor′ney**; regspraktisyn

lax (a) slap, los; laks; nalatig; ∼**ative** (n) lak=
seermiddel, purgeermiddel

lay¹ (v) lê (eier); indien ('n klag); voorlê; dek
(tafel) *see* **lie²**; ∼ *a bet* 'n weddenskap aan=
gaan/sluit

lay² (a) wêreldlik; leke=; ∼ **bro′ther** leke=
broeder; ∼ **prea′cher** lekeprediker

lay′-by bêrekoop; *on* ∼ op bêrekoop

lay′er laag; loot (plant); lêhoender

lay′man leek, oningewyde (mens)

lay-out (n) uiteensetting, inkleding, uitleg

la′ziness luiheid, traagheid

la′zy lui, traag; ∼**bo′nes** luilak; ∼ **Su′san**
draaistander (op eettafel)

lead¹ (n) lood; dieplood; koeël

lead² (n) leiding; leidraad; hoofrol; (honde)=
leiband/hondeketting; voortou (sport); *play
the* ∼ die hoofrol vertolk; *take the* ∼ die
leiding/voortou neem; (v) lei, voorgaan;
aanvoer; ∼ *a dog's life* 'n hondelewe hê/
voer; ∼ *the way* die pad wys

lead′er leier, voorman; hoofartikel (koerant);
∼**ship** leierskap

lead′ing (a) leidend, vernaamste; ∼ **ques′tion**
uitlokvraag

leaf (n) **leaves** blad; blaar; *turn over a new* ∼ 'n
nuwe blaadjie begin; ∼**let** blaartjie (boom);
vlugskrif, strooibiljet *also* **hand-out**

lea′gue (n) verbond; myl; liga; **L**∼ **of Na′tions**
Volke(re)bond (nou VN)

leak (n) lek(plek); lekkasie; (v) lek; uitlek
(inligting); ∼ *out* uitlek; ∼**age** lekkasie, lek

lean¹ (a) maer, skraal; ∼ **per′son** skarminkel

lean² (v) leun; oorhel; geneig wees; ∼ *on*
steun op

leap (n) sprong; (v) spring; huppel; oorspring;
∼**frog** hasieoor; ∼ **year** skrikkeljaar; ∼**ing
foun′tain** spuitfontein *also* **wa′ter fountain**

learn leer; verneem, hoor; ∼ *by heart* uit die
hoof leer; ∼**ed** geleerd; ∼**er** leerling;
beginner; leerder; ∼**er dri′ver's li′cence**
leer(ling)rybewys; ∼**ing** geleerdheid

lease (n) huurkontrak; bruikhuur; (v) verhuur;
uithuur; ∼**hold** huurbesit, huurpag

leash (n) **-es** leiriem, ketting (hond); *on* ∼ aan

'n tou/ketting

least (n) die minste; *at* ∼ minstens (tien vrae);
ten minste; *not in the* ∼ glad nie; *to say the*
∼ *of it* op sy sagste uitgedruk; (a) kleinste;
minste, geringste

leath′er leer, oorleer

leave¹ (n) verlof; vergunning; ∼ *of absence*
verlof; *on* ∼ met/op verlof

leave² (n) afskeid; *take* ∼ afskeid neem; (v)
laat staan; verlaat; ∼ *alone* met rus laat;
uitlos; ∼ *behind* agterlaat

lect′ern (a) lesingstander, koorlessenaar

lec′ture (n) lesing, voorlesing; (v) les gee; 'n
voorlesing hou; vermaan *also* **admon′ish** (v)

lec′turer lektor; dosent

lec′turing post doseerpos

ledge (n) rand; lys; bergrand

ledg′er grootboek (boekhou); dwarsbalk

leech -es bloedsuier; arts, heelmeester

left (n) linkerhand; *second from* ∼ naaslinks
(foto); *to the* ∼ links, aan die linkerkant; (a)
linker=; hot; (adv) links

left: ∼**hand dri′ve** linkerstuur; ∼**han′ded**
links, hotklou; onhandig; ∼**o′vers** oorskiet=
kos; ∼**-wing** (a) linksgesind(e) (studente,
werkers)

leg (n) been; poot; boud (vleis); *on one's last*
∼*s* op sy uiterste; ∼ *of mutton* skaapboud;
pull someone's ∼ met iem. die gek skeer;
skerts, korswel; ∼ *before wicket* been voor
paaltjie; ∼**-i′ron** voetboei

leg′acy (n) **..cies** erfenis; nalatenskap

leg′al (a) wetlik, wettig; regs=; ∼ **lang′uage**
regstaal; ∼ **procee′dings** geregtelike stappe;
∼ **represen′tative** regsverteenwoordiger; ∼
steps/ac′tion regstappe; ∼ **ten′der** wettige
betaalmiddel

leg′end (n) legende, sprokie; verklaring (op
padkaart); ∼**ary** legendaries

legg′ing(s) kamas(te) (soldate); beenkouse
also **leg′warmers, gai′ters**

leg′ible (a) leesbaar

le′gion keurbende, legioen; ∼**naire** legioen=
soldaat

legisla′tion (n) wetgewing

leg′islative (a) wetgewend; ∼ **assem′bly** wet=
gewende vergadering

legit′imate (a) wettig, eg *also* **law′ful**; ∼
sha′re regmatige (aan)deel

leguan′ likkewaan *also* **igua′na**

lei′sure ledige tyd, vrye tyd; ∼**ly** op sy/haar
gemak, kuier-kuier; ∼ **wear** slenterdrag

lem'on suurlemoen; ~ **squash** kwas
lemonade' limonade
lem'ur (n) lemur, vosaap, halfaap
lend (v) leen, uitleen; ~ *itself to* leen hom tot; ~**er** uitlener; ~**ing rate** uitleenkoers
length (n) lengte; duur, afstand; *go to any* ~ niks ontsien nie; ~**en** langer maak, verleng; ~**y** lang, langdurig, uitgerek
le'nient (a) versagtend, toegewend, toeskietlik
lens -es lens; brilglas
len'til lensie; ~ **soup** lensiesop
leo'pard luiperd (dier)
le'per melaatse (mens), lepralyer
lep'rosy (n) melaatsheid, lepra
les'bian (n) lesbiër (vrou); (a) lesbies, gay
less (n) minder; (a) minder, kleiner, geringer; *in* ~ *than no time* in 'n kits; (adv) minder; *none the* ~ nietemin; (prep) min; *for* ~ goedkoper; *five* ~ *four* vyf min vier
lessee' huurder (mens)
less'on (n) les, oefening; skriflesing
less'or verhuurder, huisbaas
let (v) laat; toelaat; verhuur; ~ *down* in die steek laat; ~ *go* loslaat/vrylaat; *to* ~ te huur
leth'al (a) dodelik, dodend *also* **dead'ly**
lett'er (n) letter; brief; (pl) lettere; ~ *of attorney* volmag; *by* ~ per brief; *capital* ~ hoofletter; *man of* ~s geleerde; ~**box** briewebus; ~**head** briefhoof
lett'uce (blaar)slaai, kropslaai *see* **sal'ad**
leukem'ia (n) leukemie, bloedkanker
lev'el (n) waterpas; vlak; *on the same* ~ op gelyke voet; *upper* ~ boonste vlak; (v) gelyk maak, aanlê; (a, adv) gelyk, waterpas; *do one's* ~ *best* jou uiterste bes doen; ~ **cros'sing** (spoorweg)oorgang; ~**-hea'ded** verstandig, ewewigtig, oorwoë
le'ver (n) hefboom; ligter; klawer (van slot)
lev'y (n) **levies** heffing, bybelasting; (v) hef; lig; oplê; invorder (geld); ~ *a fine* 'n boete oplê
lexicog'rapher leksikograaf, woordeboekmaker
lex'icon -s woordeboek, leksikon
liabil'ity (n) **..ties** aanspreeklikheid; verantwoordelikheid, verpligting; (pl) laste
li'able aanspreeklik; verantwoordelik; ~ *for* aanspreeklik vir
liais'on (n) skakeling/liaison; ~ **commit'tee** skakelkomitee; ~ **of'ficer** skakelbeampte/mediabeampte
li'ar leuenaar, spekskieter (mens)

lib'el (n) laster; (v) belaster, beklad; ~ **ac'tion** lasteraksie; ~**lous** lasterlik
lib'eral (n) vrysinnige, liberaal (mens); (a) liberaal, vrysinnig; onbekrompe; ~ **educa'tion** vrysinnige opvoeding; ~**ism** liberalisme
lib'erate (v) bevry, vrymaak, vrylaat
lib'ertine vrydenker; libertyn; losbol (mens)
lib'erty ..ties vryheid
librar'ian (n) bibliotekaris
li'brary ..ries biblioteek *also* **me'dia centre**; boekery (privaat)
li'cence (n) lisensie, permit; rybewys
li'cense (v) toelaat, vergun; lisensieer
licen'tiate lisensiaat (mens)
licen'tious (a) losbandig, ongebonde
lick (n) lek; (v) lek; uitstof, wen, klop; ~**ing** gelek/lekkery; loesing
lid deksel; ooglid
lie[1] (n) leuen; kluitjie; *tell a* ~ lieg, jok; **white** ~ noodleuen(tjie); (v) lieg, jok; ~ **detec'tor** leuenverklikker
lie[2] (n) ligging; (v) lê, rus; ~ *in state* in staatsie lê (gestorwene)
lien (n) retensiereg, retensiegeld
lieuten'ant luitenant; ~**-gen'eral lieutenants-general** luitenant-generaal
life lives lewe; lewensduur; leefwyse; *full of* ~ springlewendig; *not for the* ~ *of him* vir geen geld ter wêreld nie; *take one's* ~ *in one's hands* jou lewe waag; ~ **assur'ance** lewensversekering; ~**belt** redgordel; reddingsboei; ~**boat** reddingsboot; ~**buoy** reddingsboei; ~**guard** strandwag *see* **bo'dyguard**; ~**jack'et** reddingsbaadjie; ~**less** leweloos, dooierig; ~**long** lewenslank; ~**sa'ver** menseredder, strandwag; ~ **sen'tence** lewenslange gevangenisstraf; ~**size** lewensgrootte; ~**style** leefwyse/lewenswyse
lift (n) hyser, hysbak; *give a* ~ iem. oplaai; (v) optel, oplig; iem. oplaai; ~ **club** saamryklub; ~**-off** lansering (ruimtetuig) *see* **launch** (v)
lig'ament band, ligament
light[1] (n) lig; *bring to* ~ aan die lig bring; lig; verlig; aansteek; (a) lig, helder; blond; **flash**~ flitslig; **flood**~ spreilig; **lime**~ kalklig; **search**~ soeklig; **spot**~ kollig
light[2] (a, adv) los; lig; gou, vinnig; ~ **delive'ry van** (ligte) bestelwa, bakkie; ~ **rea'ding** ligte leesstof
light'er aansteker, vuurslag
light'-hearted (a) lughartig, vrolik, onbesorg

light'house vuurtoring
light'ning weerlig, blits; ~ **conduc'tor** weer= ligafleier
light: ~**-o-love** flerrie, snol (vrou); ~**weight** liggewig
like (n) gelyke; ewebeeld; *his* ~*s and dislikes* sy voorkeure en afkeure; (v) hou van, lief wees vir; (a, adv) gelyk; eenders/eners, soortgelyk; soos; ~**ly** waarskynlik, vermoe= delik *also* **prob'ably**
like'ness (n) gelykenis, ewebeeld
like'wise eweneens; ingelyks, net so
lik'ing behae, smaak, welgevalle; *not to my* ~ nie na my smaak nie
li'lac (n) sering; (a) pers, lila
lil'y (n) **lilies** lelie; (a) lelie=; ~**-white** leliewit, spierwit
limb (n) ledemaat; lit, tak; **artifi'cial** ~ kuns= ledemaat
lime[1] (n) kalk; voëlent; (v) vaslym
lime[2] lemmetjie; ~ **juice** lemmetjiesap
lime: ~ **kiln** kalkoond; ~**light** kalklig
lim'erick (n) bogrympie, limeriek
lim'it (n) grens, perk, limiet; *that's the* ~*!* dis darem te erg!; ~**a'tion** beperking; ~**ed** beperk, begrens; ~**ed liabil'ity com'pany** maatskappy met beperkte aanspreeklikheid
limp (v) mank loop, hink; (a) kruppel, mank; lenig, slap, buigsaam
lim'pet klipmossel; ~ **mine** kleefmyn *see* **stun grena'de**
line (n) reël; lyn; streep; verseël; ~ *of com= munication* verbindingslyn; *drop a* ~ 'n paar reëls skryf; *hard* ~*s!* simpatie!; hoe jammer!; *in* ~ *with* in lyn met; *read between the* ~*s* tussen die reëls lees; (v) lyne trek; onder= streep; ~ *the route* die roete belyn (soldate)
lin'en (n) linne; linnegoed; beddegoed
lines'man vlagman; lynregter
ling'er (v) talm, draal, vertoef; kwyn, sukkel
ling'erie linnegoed; onderklere (vir vrou)
ling'uist taalgeleerde, linguis (mens)
li'ning (n) voering; bekleding
link (n) skakel; fakkel; (v) (aaneen)skakel; ~**s** gholfbaan (aan die see); mansjetknoop/ mouskakel
lin'seed lynsaad; ~ **oil** lynolie
lin'tel latei (onderkant venster)
li'on leeu; ~**'s den** leeukuil; ~**'s share** leeue= aandeel; ~**ess** leeuwyfie; ~**-hear'ted** moe= dig, dapper; ~**ise** (v) 'n besoeker ophemel/ verafgo(o)d

lip lip; kant, rand; *keep a stiff upper* ~ moed hou; ~ **ser'vice** lippediens; ~**stick** lipstif(fie)
liqueur' likeur, soetsopie
liq'uid (n) vloeistof; (pl) vloeibare kos; (a) vloeibaar; ~ **as'sets** likiede bates; ~**ate** ver= effen, likwideer; uitdelg; ~**a'tion** likwida= sie; ~**iser** versapper
liq'uor (sterk) drank; *the worse for* ~ hoen= derkop, lekkerlyf, getier
liq'uorice drop, soethout
lisp (n) gelispel; (v) lispel, sleeptong praat
list (n) lys; naamlys; **stock exchan'ge** ~**ing** notering op effektebeurs; (v) lys (die items); noteer (effektebeurs); kwoteer (aandele)
lis'ten luister; ~ *in* (in)luister; ~**er** luisteraar; toehoorder; ~**ing post** luisterpos
list'less (a) lusteloos, dooierig *also* **dull**
lit'chi lietsjie (vrug)
lit'eral (a) letterlik, woordelik; (n) drukkers= duiwel, setsatan *also* **grem'lin**
lit'erary letterkundig; ~ **tal'ent** skryftalent
lit'erature letterkunde, literatuur
lit're liter; *two* ~*s of milk* twee liter melk
litt'er (n) drag, werpsel; ~ *of pups* werpsel hondjies; ~**bug** morsjors, rommelstrooier (mens); (v) omkrap, mors; ~**ing** rommel= strooi
lit'tle (n) bietjie, min; (a) klein; min, bietjie; ~ **fin'ger** pinkie; (adv) min, weinig
Little Red Ri'ding Hood Rooikappie
live[1] (v) leef, woon, bly; ~ *up to one's promise* jou belofte gestand doen/nakom
li've[2] (a) lewend; lewendig; vars; stroom= draend (elektr.); ~ **ammuni'tion** skerppunt= koeëls; ~ **broad'cast** lewende uitsending; ~ **wire** wakker persoon; 'n voorslag; ~**lihood** bestaan; ~**ly** lewendig, opgeruimd; woelig
live-in lo'ver blyervryer (man)
liv'er lewer
li'vestock (n) lewende hawe, vee; beeste
liv'ing (n) bestaan, broodwinning; *make a* ~ 'n bestaan vind/voer/maak; (a) lewend; lewendig; *within* ~ *memory* binne mense= heugenis; ~ **room** woonkamer; ~ **wage** be= staanbare/menswaardige loon
liz'ard akkedis
load (n) vrag, lading; (v) laai; belas; ~**ed dice** vals dobbelstene
loaf[1] (n) **loaves**: *a* ~ *of bread* 'n brood
loaf[2] (v) leeglê, slenter, lanterfanter; ~**er** leeglêer, lieplapper, niksdoener
loan (n) lening; geldlening; (v) leen, uitleen

loathe verfoei, verafsku *also* **disli'ke** (v)

lob'by (n) voorportaal; wandelgang (parlement)

lobe (oor)lel; lob

lob'ster (see)kreef

lo'cal (a) lokaal, plaaslik; ~ **anaesthet'ic** plaaslike verdowing; ~ **author'ity** plaaslike bestuur/owerheid; ~ **con'tent** plaaslike inhoud

local'ity omgewing; lokaliteit, plek, buurt

oca'tion ligging; aanduiding; plek

ock[1] (n) slot (van deur); *under* ~ *and key* agter slot en grendel; ~, *stock and barrel* romp en stomp; die hele boel; (v) sluit; opsluit; afsluit

ock[2] (n) krul (hare); klos (aan skape)

ock: ~**er** sluitkas; ~**et** hangertjie, medaljon; ~**jaw** klem in die kake *also* **tet'anus**; ~**smith** slotmaker

ocomo'tive (n) lokomotief; (a) bewegend

oc'ust sprinkaan

odge (n) hut; jaghuis *also* **cab'in**; losie (Vrymesselaars); (v) huisves; loseer; indien (klag); inwoon; ~ *a complaint* 'n klag indien/lê; ~ *an objection* beswaar opper; ~**r** loseerder, kosganger

odg'ing huisvesting, inwoning, losies

oft solder; solderkamer; duiwehok; (a) ~**y** verhewe, hoog; trots

og (n) blok; lys; puntelys; logboek; (v) aanteken (in logboek)

og'arithm logaritme

og: ~**book** logboek; skeepsjoernaal; ~ **cab'in** blokhuis

ogg'erhead: *at* ~*s* haaks, aan die twis

og'ic logika, redeneerkuns; (a) ~**al** logies

oin lende; (pl) lendene; *gird up the* ~*s* die lendene omgord; ~**cloth** lendedoek

oit'er (v) drentel, leeglê; draal, talm; sloer

oll'ipop stokkielekker/suigstokkie; suikerpop

one eensaam; verlate; ~**r** alleenloper/eenloper (mens); ~**ly** eensaam, allenig

ong[1] (n) lang tyd; (a) lang/lank; langdurig; *in the* ~ *run* op die duur; (adv) lang, lankal; ~ *ago* lankal, vanmelewe; *don't be* ~ moenie lank wegbly nie; *so* ~*!* tot siens/goedgaan!

ong[2] (v) verlang; ~ *for* hunker na

ong'ing (n) verlange, hunkering, heimwee; (a) verlangend

ong: ~**jump** vêrspring; ~ **play'ing rec'ord** langspeler

oo (n) kleinhuisie, toilet, privaat *also* **toi'let**

ook (n) voorkoms; uitdrukking; (pl) voorkoms; (v) kyk, sien, aanskou; ~ *after* oppas; ~ *ahead* vooruitsien; ~ *forward to* uitsien na; ~ *for trouble* moeilikheid soek; ~ *up* naslaan; besoek; ~**er-on** toeskouer; ~**out** uitkykpos

loom[1] (n) weefmasjien; handvatsel; steel

loom[2] (v) oprys, opdoem; skemer

loop (n) lissie, strop; ~ *the* ~ bol(le)makiesie slaan; ~**hole** skuiwergat; uitvlug, skietgat

loose (n) losspel (rugby); (v) losmaak; bevry; (a, adv) los, vry; ~**-leaf book** losbladboek; ~**ly** lossies; ~**n** losmaak

loot (n) buit, roof *also* **loo'ting**; (v) plunder, buit(maak); ~**er** plunderaar, buiter (mens)

Lord Here, Heer; *the* ~*'s prayer* die Onse Vader

lord (n) heer, baas; lord; *my* ~ edelagbare; ~ *and master* heer en meester; (v) kommandeer, baasspeel

lor'ry lorries vragmotor, lorrie; ~ **dri'ver** lorriedrywer, vragmotorbestuurder

lose (v) verloor; ~ *marks* punte verbeur; ~ *one's temper* kwaad word; ~ *one's way* verdwaal; ~**r** verloorder

loss (n) -es verlies, skade; ~ *of memory* geheueverlies

lost verlore; *get* ~ verdwaal; ~ *in thought* in gedagtes verdiep

lot (n) lot; aandeel; klomp; *draw* ~*s* lootjies trek

lott'ery ..ries lotery *also* **raf'fle, sweep'stake**

loud (a) luid; hard; luidrugtig; opsigtig; ~**hailer** luidroeper *also* **meg'aphone**; ~**spea'ker** luidspreker

lounge (n) sitkamer, voorhuis; (v) luier; ronddrentel, slenter; ~ *suit* dagpak

louse lice luis

lou'sy (a) luisbesmet; beroerd (toestand)

lout lummel, gomtor, bullebak (mens)

louv'er/louv're luggat, rookgat; ~ **blind** hortjieblinding, hortjieruit

love (n) liefde; skat, liefling; stroop (tennis); *fall in* ~ *with* verlief raak op; *send one's* ~ groete laat weet; (v) liefhê; *I* ~ *him* ek lief/bemin hom; ~ *affair'* (liefdes)verhouding; ~ **let'ter** minnebrief; ~**liness** lieflikheid; beminlikheid; ~**ly** lieflik; beminlik; ~ **poem** liefdesgedig, minnedig; ~**r** minnaar; ~ **sto'ry** liefdesverhaal

lo'ving liefhebbend, teer; *your* ~ *daughter* u liefhebbende dogter

low[1] (n) gebulk; (v) bulk (bees) *also* **moo**

low[2] (n) laagtepunt; (a) laag, sag; nederig; *in*

~ *spirits* neerslagtig; ~ *profile* lae profiel; (adv) *run* ~ opraak; ~-**class** (a) agterklas; ~**er** (v) verlaag, laat sak; (a) laer; swakker; minder; ~ **tide** laagwater; ~**veld** laeveld
loy'al (a) getrou, lojaal; ~**ist** lojalis
loz'enge (n) suiglekker/hoeslekker; tablet(jie)
lub'ricant smeerolie; masjienolie
lucerne' lusern
lu'cid (a) helder *also* **clear**; deurskynend
luck geluk, toeval; *bad* ~! simpatie!; *good* ~! die beste!/beste wense!; ~**ily** gelukkig
luck'y (a) gelukkig; *a* ~ *hit (shot)* 'n geluk= skoot; ~ **bean** sierboontjie, toorboontjie; ~ **dip/pack'et** gelukspakkie, grabbelsak
lu'crative (a) winsgewend, betalend, lonend
lu'dicrous belaglik, bespotlik *also* **ridic'ulous**
lugg'age bagasie *also* **bag'gage**; ~ **car'rier** bagasierak; dakrak
lull (n) stilte, kalmte; (v) kalmeer, sus
lull'aby ..**bies** slaapliedjie, wiegeliedjie
lum'bar punc'ture lumbaalpunksie, lendesteek
lum'ber (n) spul, rommel; timmerhout; ~**jack** boswerker, houtkapper; ~**jack'et** ritsbaad= jie, bosbaadjie; ~ **room** rommelkamer

lu'minous liggewend; stralend; ~ **di'al** glim= wyserplaat; ~ **paint** glimverf
lump (n)-stuk, klont; hoop; ~ *sum* ronde som; ~ *together* saamgooi; ~**y** klonterig
lu'nar maan=; ~ *eclip'se* maan(s)verduistering
lu'natic (n) kranksinnige (mens); (a) maan= siek, gek; ~ *asy'lum* kranksinnigegestig, sielsiekegestig; malhuis
lunch (n) -es middagete; (v) middagete geniet
lunch'eon formele middagete, noenmaal
lung long
lurch (n) -es ruk, swaai; *leave in the* ~ in die steek laat; (v) swaai, slinger
lu'rid (a) somber; donker; ~ *past* duister(e) verlede
lust (n) wellus; begeerte; (v) dors na
lus'tre (n) glans; roem, luister
lute luit
lux'ury (n) ..**ries** luukse, weelde; ~ *ar'ticle* weeldeartikel; ~ **bus** luuksebus; ~ **car** weeldemotor
lyre lier
ly'ric (n) liriese poësie; liriek(e), luisterliedjie; (a) liries (poësie)

M

ma ma *also* **mo'ther, mum'my**
mace ampstaf (parlement); ~**bearer** stafdraer
machine' masjien, werktuig; (v) masjineer; ~ **gun** (n) masjiengeweer
machi'nery masjinerie; **plant and** ~ aanleg en masjinerie
machi'nist masjinis, bediener (mens)
mack'erel makriel (vis)
mack'intosh -es reënjas *also* **rain'coat**
mad mal, gek, dol, kranksinnig; bossies (idiom.); *as* ~ *as a hatter/March hare* stapelgek; ~ *on* versot op
mad'am mevrou; juffrou; **Mad'am Chair** Ag= bare Voorsitter *see* **chair'person**
mad cow disea'se malbeessiekte
made gemaak; kunsmatig; ~-**up sto'ry** ver= sinsel
mad: ~**house** malhuis; ~**ness** malheid
magazine' tydskrif *also* **jour'nal**; magasyn
ma'gic (n) towerkuns; **black** ~ duiwelskuns; (a) ~ **lan'tern** towerlantern; ~ **wand** tower= staf
magi'cian (n) kulkunstenaar; goëlaar

ma'gistrate (n) magistraat, landdros; ~'s **court** magistraatshof, landdroshof
mag'nate (n) magnaat; kapitalis *also* **tycoon'**
mag'net magneet
magnet'ic magneties
mag'netism magnetisme, aantrekkingskrag
magnif'icent (a) pragtig, heerlik; manjifiek
mag'nify (v) vergroot, verheerlik; ophemel; ~**ing glass** vergrootglas
mag'nitude grootte, omvang, trefwydte
magno'lia magnolia, tulpboom
mag'pie ekster (voël); babbelkous
mahog'any mahoniehout
maid meisie, maagd; diensmeisie; huishulp *also* **domes'tic** (n); *old* ~ oujongnooi
maid'en (n) meisie; nooi; maagd; leë boul= beurt; (a) maagdelik; eerste; ongetroud; ~ *aunt* ongetroude tante; ~ *flight* eerste vlug; ~ *name* nooiensvan; ~ *speech* intreerede; nuwelingstoespraak (parlement)
mail (n) pos; posbesending; (v) pos; ~**bag** possak; ~**coach** poskar
maim (v) vermink *also* **disa'ble**; skend

main (n) hoofdeel; (a) hoof=; vernaamste, grootste; ~ **body** hoofmag; ~ **en′trance** hoofingang; ~**frame** hoofraam (rek.); ~**land** vasteland; ~**ly** hoofsaaklik, vernaamlik; ~ **road** hoofweg, grootpad; ~ **street** hoofstraat; **water** ~**s** hoofwaterleiding

maintain′ (v) handhaaf; onderhou; volhou; in stand hou; bewaar; ~**er** handhawer

main′tenance (n) instandhouding, onderhoud; handhawing; *pay* ~/*alimony to divorced wife* betaal onderhoud aan geskeide vrou; ~ **costs** instandhoukoste

maize mielies; ~ **far′mer** mielieboer; ~ **meal** mieliemeel

majes′tic (a) majestueus, verhewe

maj′esty ..ties majesteit; *Your M*~ U Majesteit

maj′or[1] (n) majoor (offisier)

maj′or[2] (n) meerderjarige, mondige; majeur (mus.); (a) mondig; hoof=; groot=; grootste, vernaamste

major′ity meerderheid; **ab′solute/clear** ~ volstrekte meerderheid; ~ **gov′ernment** meerderheidsregering

make (n) vorm, gedaante; soort; fabrikaat; (v) maak, doen; verrig; vervaardig; voer (oorlog); hou (toespraak); begaan/maak (fout); sluit (vrede); ~ *an example of* tot voorbeeld stel; ~ *a fool of* belaglik maak; ~ *good* vergoed (vir), opmaak, vooruitgaan; ~ *love* die hof maak; liefde maak; ~ *up one's mind* besluit; ~ *peace* vrede sluit; ~ *a speech* 'n toespraak afsteek/hou; ~ *sure of* verseker, sorg dat; ~ *up* inhaal (skade); goedmaak; versoen raak (ná rusie); versin (verhaal); ~**-believe** (n) voorwendsel; skyn; (a) oneg; ~**shift** redmiddel, noodhulp; ~**-up** grimering; vermomming; versinsel

mal′adjusted (a) wanaangepas *also* **unsta′ble**

Malay′ (n) Maleier (mens); (a) Maleis; ~**sia** Maleisië (land)

male (n) mansmens, manspersoon; mannetjie (by diere); (a) manlik; mans=; ~ **nurse** verpleër

mal′ice (n) boosaardigheid; (bose) opset; haat

malic′ious kwaadwillig, boosaardig

malig′nant (a) skadelik, kwaadaardig; ~ **growth/tu′mour** kwaadaardige groeisel/gewas/tumor

mall wandellaan; winkelplein, mall

malnutri′tion (n) wanvoeding, ondervoeding

malprac′tice (n) wanpraktyk; wangedrag

malt (n, v) mout

Mal′tese poodle Malteserpoedel, Maltees (hond)

maltreat′ (v) mishandel *also* **harm**

mam′ba mamba (slang)

mam(m)a′ mamma *also* **moth′er**

mamm′al soogdier

mam′moth (a) reusagtig, kolossaal

man (n) **men** man; mansmens; eggenoot; mens; ~ *of straw* strooipop; *the* ~ *in the street* die gewone man; Jan Alleman/Publiek; ~ *about town* pierewaaier, stadskoejawel; (v) beman; ~ *oneself* moed vat

man′age (v) bestuur; ~**ment** bestuur, leiding, beheer; ~**r** bestuurder; ~**ment by objec′tives** doelwitbestuur; ~**ment commit′tee** bestuurskomitee; dagbestuur

man′aging besturend; ~ **direc′tor** besturende direkteur

mand′arin[1] mandaryn (Chinese amptenaar)

mand′arin[2] (n) (geel) nartjie (vrug)

man′date (n) volmag; mandaat/magtiging

manda′tory (a) voorskriftelik, verpligtend

man′dolin mandolien (musiekinstrument)

mane maanhaar

mang′anese mangaan

man′ger krip, trog, voerbak

man′gle (n) strykmasjien; mangel (vir wasgoed); (v) vermink, verskeur; radbraak

man′go -es mango (vrug)

mang′rove wortelboom, munglict

man: ~**han′dle** toetakel, afransel; ~**ha′ter** mensehater; ~**hole** skouput/inspeksieput; ~**hood** manlikheid; ~**hunt** polisiesoektog

ma′niac (n) waansinnige, maniak (mens)

man′icure (v) manikuur; ~ **set** naelstel, manikuurstel

man′ifest (v) bekend maak, manifesteer; ~**a′tion** openbaring, manifestasie

manifes′to -es manifes, openbare bekendmaking *also* **pub′lic sta′tement**

man′ifold (n) spruitstuk; (a) baie, menigvuldig *also* **mul′tiple**

man′ikin (n) dwergie, mannetjie; model

manip′ulate (v) hanteer, bewerk, manipuleer

man: ~**kind** (die) mensdom, mensheid; ~**liness** manlikheid; ~**ly** manlik *also* **mas′culine**; (man)moedig

ma′nna manna

mann′equin mannekyn; modemodel; ~ **para′de** modeskou

mann′er (n) manier, gewoonte, wyse; ~**ism** gemaaktheid; aanwensel; ~**ly** beleef(d)

mann′ing (n) bemanning, personeelvoorsie= ning *also* **staf′fing**

manoeu′vre (n) maneuver, krygsoefening; (v) maneuvreer; bewerkstellig, manipuleer

man′-of-war oorlogskip, slagskip

man′or landgoed; herehuis (van adel) *also* **man′sion**

man′power (n) arbeidskrag, mannekrag *see* **fem′power**; ~ **research′** mannekragnavor= sing

man′rope valreep

man′sion herehuis *see* **man′or**

man′slaughter manslag *also* **hom′icide**

man′telpiece skoorsteenmantel, kaggelrak

man′tis (n) mantis

man′tle mantel; omhulsel; gloeikousie

man′ual (n) handleiding; handboek; ~ **la′bour** handearbeid; ~ **trai′ning** ambagsopleiding

manufac′ture (n) fabrikaat; (pl) fabrikate; (v) vervaardig; ~**r** fabrikant, vervaardiger

manure′ (n) mis; misstof *also* **fer′tiliser**; (v) bemes

man′uscript manuskrip; handskrif

ma′ny (a) baie, veel; ~ *happy returns* (veels) geluk met u/jou verjaardag

map (n) kaart, landkaart; plattegrond; (v) karteer; afbeeld

ma′ple esdoring, ahornboom

ma′rabou maraboe, Indiese ooievaar

mar′athon (n) marat(h)on (wedloop)

maraud′ (v) plunder, roof, buit; ~**er** buiter, plunderaar; ~**ing raid** plundertog

mar′ble (n) marmer; albaster; (a) marmer

March[1] Maart; *as mad as a* ~ *hare* stapelgek

march[2] **-es** (n) mars; (v) marsjeer; opruk; ~ *past* verbymarsjeer; (n) ~**-past** defileer= mars, parademars/verbymars

mare merrie

margarine′ kunsbotter, margarien

mar′gin rand; kantlyn, kantruimte; marge, speling; ~**al** marginaal, grens=, kant=; ~**al note** kant(aan)tekening

marg′uerite margriet(jie), gansblom

mar′igold afrikaner; gousblom

mari′na (n) marina, waterdorp

marine′ (n) vloot; seesoldaat/vlootsoldaat; **mer′cantile** ~ handelsvloot; ~ **cadet′** adel= bors; ~ **insu′rance** marine-assuransie

marionette′ marionet, draadpop

ma′rital huweliks=; egtelik; ~ **state** huwelik= staat

ma′ritime maritiem; ~ **law** seereg

mark[1] (n) mark (geldeenheid)

mark[2] (n) merk; teken; doel; punt (eksamen); skoonvang (rugby); *below the* ~ benede peil; *make one's* ~ naam maak; (v) merk; nasien; ~ *time* die pas markeer; ~**er** merker, teller; nasiener (eksamenskrifte)

mark′et (n) mark; afsetgebied; (v) bemark; **bull** ~ bulmark/stygmark; **bear** ~ beer= mark/daalmark (aandele); ~ **in′dicator** markaanwyser; ~**ing** bemarking; ~**ing direc′tor** direkteur bemarking; ~ **mas′ter** markmeester; ~ **price** markprys; ~ **rela′ted** markverwant; ~ **research′** marknavorsing

mark: ~**ing** merk; tekening; ~**ing ink** merk= ink, letterink; ~**s′man** skerpskutter

mar′lin marlyn (swaardvis)

marm′alade lemoenkonfyt, marmelade

maroon′ (a) maroen, bruinrooi

marquee′ markee(tent)/markiestent

mar′riage (n) huwelik; bruilof, troue; ~ **cer′= tif′icate** trousertifikaat; ~ **coun′sellor** hu= weliksberader

mar′ried getroud; ~ **to** getroud met; ~ **life** huwelikslewe; ~ **quar′ters** kwartiere vir ge= troudes

ma′rrow murg; ~ **bone** murgbeen

mar′ry (v) trou, in die huwelik/eg tree

marsh -es vlei, moeras *also* **swamp**

marsh′al (n) maarskalk; ordehouer (by beto= gings); (v) rangskik, orden; ~**ling yard** rangeerwerf, opstelterrein (spoorweë)

marsh: ~ **fe′ver** moeraskoors; malaria; ~**mal= low** malvalekker; ~**y** moerassig

mar′tial: ~**arts** verweerkuns; ~ **law** krygswet

mart mark; verkoopsaal; vandisielokaal

mart′yr (n) martelaar (mens)

mar′vel (v) verwonder, verbaas; ~**lous** won= derlik, verbasend *also* **ama′zing**

mas′cot talisman, gelukbringer *also* **charm**

mas′culine manlik; sterk, fors; kragtig

mash (n) meelkos, mengsel; (v) fynstamp; meng; ~**ed pota′toes** kapokaartappels

mask (n) masker; mombakkies; (v) vermom; ~**ed ball** maskerbal

mas′king tape maskeerband

ma′son (n) messelaar; klipkapper

Ma′sonry[1] Vrymesselary

ma′sonry[2] messelwerk

mass[1] (n) **-es** massa, menigte; massa/gewig; ~ **ac′tion** protesoptrede/massa-optrede *also* **in= dus′trial ac′tion**; ~ **attack′** massa-aanval; ~ **me′dia** massamedia; ~ **mee′ting** monsterver=

gadering; ~ **produc'tion** massaproduksie

mass² (n) mis (kerk)

mass'acre (n) bloedbad, menseslagting *also* **car'nage**; (v) verdelg, uitmoor

mass'age (v) masseer; ~ **par'lour** masseersa= lon; streelperseel (idiom.)

masseur' masseur/masseerder (man/vrou)

mass'ive (a) massief, swaar *also* **bul'ky**

mast (n) mas

ma'ster (n) meester; baas; weesheer; onder= wyser; jongeheer; bobaas; ~ *of ceremonies* seremoniemeester/tafelheer; ~ *and servant* werkgewer en dienaar; (v) oormeester, baasraak; (a) hoof=; ~ **buil'der** meester= bouer; ~ **key** loper, diewesleutel; ~**ly** mees= terlik; ~**mind** meesterbrein; ~**piece** mees= terstuk; ~**'s degree'** magister(graad)/mees= tersgraad

mas'tiff (n) boel(hond), boerboel

masturba'tion masturbasie

mat (n) mat; (v) vleg

mat'ador matador, stiervegter (mens)

match¹ (n) vuurhoutjie; ~**box** vuurhoutjiedo= sie/vuurhoutjieboksie

match² (n) -es paar; ewekneë; gelyke/portuur; wedstryd/kragmeting *also* **con'test**; *he a* ~ *for* opgewasse wees teen; (v) paar; pas; ~**less** weergaloos; ~**maker** huweliksmake= laar/paartjiemaker; ~ **point** wedstrydpunt

mate (n) maat/kameraad; metgesel, vriend; (v) maats maak; paar; trou

mater'ial (n) materiaal, stof, goed; (pl) hou= stof; (a) stoflik, materieel; ~**ism** materialis= me; ~**ist** materialis (mens); ~**ise** verwe= senlik, verwerklik

matern'al moederlik; ~ **love** moederliefde

matern'ity moederskap; ~ **home** kraaminrig= ting; ~ **leaf** kraamverlof; ~ **wear** kraam= drag/ooievaarsdrag

mathemat'ic(al) wiskundig, matematies

mathemat'ics (n) wiskunde, matesis; **applied'** ~ toegepaste wiskunde

mat'inee (n) middagvertoning

matric' matriek, matrikulasie

matrimon'ial huweliks=; egtelik; ~ **a'gency** huweliksburo

ma'tron (n) huismoeder; matrone

matt'er (n) stof, materie; saak; aangeleent= heid; kwessie; *what is the* ~? wat makeer?; ~ *of course* vanselfsprekend

matt'ress -es matras; **in'ner-spring** ~ binne= veermatras

mature' (v) ryp word/maak; verval (wissel); (a) ryp, beleë (wyn); volwasse; ~**d'** ryp; volgroei, volwasse

matur'ity rypheid; vervaldag; *at* ~ op (die) vervaldag

mauve ligpers, malvapers, mauve (kleur)

max'imise (v) maksimeer

max'imum (n) ..**ma** maksimum; (a) maksi= mum, grootste, maksimale

May¹ Mei; ~**pole** meipaal/meiboom

may² (v) mag, kan; *come what* ~ wat ook al (mag) gebeur

may'be dalk; altemit(s) *also* **perhaps'**

may'day noodsein *also* **alarm' call**

may'flower meiblom

may'or burgemeester; *lady* ~ burgemeesteres; ~**ess'** burgemeestersvrou; ~**'s par'lour** bur= gemeesterskamer

maze (n) doolhof; verleentheid; warboel

me my; ek; *poor* ~ arme ek

mea'gre (a) maer, skraal; armsalig

meal¹ meel

meal² maaltyd; *at* ~s aan tafel; ~s **on wheels** reisende spyse (idiom.)

mea'lie mielie *also* **maize**; ~ **gro'wer** mielie= boer *also* **maize far'mer**; ~ **meal** mie= liemeel *also* **maize**

meal'time etenstyd

mean¹ (n) middel, middelmaat; gemiddelde; (pl) middele; geld, vermoë, *by all* ~s alte seker; *beyond his* ~s bokant sy vermoë; *not by any* ~s glad nie; *the golden* ~ die gulde middel(l)weg; (a) gemiddeld; middelmatig, middel=

mean² (v) meen, bedoel, beteken; *what do you* ~? wat bedoel jy?

mean³ (a, adv) gemeen, laag *also* **nas'ty**

mean'ing betekenis *also* **connota'tion**; be= doeling; ~**ful** betekenisvol, sinvol; ~**less** betekenisloos, niksseggend

mean'time/mean'while intussen, ondertussen, onderwyl

mea'sels (n) masels

mea'sure (n) maat; maatstaf; maatreël; (v) meet, maat neem; takseer; ~**ment** maat, inhoud; meting

meat vleis; **min'ced** ~ maalvleis; ~ **pat'ty** frikkadel; ~ **pie** vleispastei

mechan'ic (n) werktuigkundige; ambagsman

mechan'ical meganies; ~ **engineer'** werktuig= kundige ingenieur; ~ **horse** voorhaker

mech'anism (n) meganisme, tegniek

mech'anise (v) meganiseer
med'al medalje; gedenkpenning; ~ of hon'our erepenning
medal'lion gedenkpenning, medaljon
med'dle (jou) bemoei, (jou) inlaat; ~r be= moeial, lolpot; ~some bemoeisiek
med'ia (pl) media; ~ cen'tre mediasentrum; mass ~ massamedia; ~ of'ficer mediaska= kel (mens); ~ wor'kers mediawerkers
med'ian (n) mediaan; middellyn
med'iate (v) bemiddel, tussenbei kom/tree
med'iator (be)middelaar; tussenganger
med'ic (n) mediese ordonnans
med'ical (a) medies, geneeskundig; ~ aid fund siekefonds, mediese fonds/skema; ~ examina'tion mediese/geneeskundige on= dersoek; ~ practi'tioner geneesheer, dok= ter, huisarts also fam'ily/gen'eral practi= tioner; ~ stu'dent mediese student
medica'tion (n) medikasie, (genees)middels
med'icine (n) medisyne, geneesmiddel; ~ chest medisynekassie, huisapteek
mediev'al (a) middeleeus
medita'tion oordenking; (be)peinsing, medi= tasie also ep'ilogue
med'ium (n) ..dia, -s middel; medium; (a) gemiddeld; lan'guage ~ voertaal
med'lar mispel(boom)
meek (a) sagmoedig, sagsinnig; nederig
meer'cat/meer'kat meerkat
meet (v) ontmoet, raakloop, teenkom; ~ with approval die goedkeuring wegdra; ~ half= way tegemoetkom; ~ one's liabilities jou verpligtinge nakom
meet'ing (n) vergadering, byeenkoms; saam= trek; adjourn a ~ 'n vergadering verdaag; convene a ~ 'n vergadering belê/byeenroep; ~ place vergaderplek also ven'ue
meg'abyte megagreep (rek.)
mel'ancholy (n) swaarmoedigheid, droefgees= tigheid
mell'ow (v) ryp word; saf/sag maak; laat oud word; ~ with age skafliker word met ouder= dom; (a) ryp; saf/sag; mals
melod'ious welluidend, melodies
melodramat'ic melodramaties
mel'ody ..dies melodie, wysie, deuntjie
mel'on (n) meloen; (waat)lemoen; ho'ney-sweet ~ spanspek
melt (v) smelt; ~ing (n) smelting; vertedering
mem'ber (n) lid; lidmaat (van kerk); ~ship lidskap (van klub); ledetal (aantal lede);

~ship card lidkaart; ~ship fee lidgeld
mem'orable (a) heuglik, gedenkwaardig
memoran'dum memorandum, voorlegging
memor'ial (n) gedenkteken; (a) gedenk=; ~ ser'vice roudiens/gedenkdiens
mem'orise (v) memoriseer, uit die hoof leer
mem'ory ..ries geheue; herinnering; nagedag= tenis; from ~ uit die hoof; a good ~ 'n goeie geheue; in ~ of ter gedagtenis aan
men mense; mans; manne (van daad)
men'ace (n) bedreiging; oorlas; (v) bedreig
mend (v) heelmaak, lap; stop (kouse)
mend'ing herstelwerk; invis'ible ~ fynstop= (werk)
meningit'is harsingvliesontsteking
men'opause menopouse, oorgangsleeftyd
menstrua'tion (n) maandstonde, menstruasie
men'tal geestelik, verstandelik; ~ arith'metic hoofrekene; ~ defic'iency swaksinnigheid; ~ fac'ulties geestesvermoë; ~ hos'pital sielsiekegestig
mental'ity geeskrag; denkwyse, mentaliteit
men'tally geestelik, verstandelik; ~ han'di= capped verstandelik gestrem; ~ retar'ded chil'dren verstandvertraagde kinders
men'tion (n) melding; don't ~ it nie te danke nie; hon'ourable ~ eervolle vermelding; (v) meld, noem
men'tor (n) leermeester, leidsman, mentor
men'u -s spyskaart, menu; kieslys (rek.)
merc'antile handels=, koopmans=, kommersi= eel; ~ law handelsreg see commer'cial law; ~ mar'ine handelsvloot
mer'cenary ..ries (n) huursoldaat
merch'andise (n) negosieware, koopware
merch'ant winkelier, handelaar, koopman also tra'der; ~ bank aksepbank
mer'ciful (a) genadig, barmhartig
mer'ciless onbarmhartig, meedoënloos
merc'ury kwik(silwer)
mer'cy (n) genade, barmhartigheid; have ~ upon us wees ons genadig; ~ kil'ling gena= dedood also euthana'sia
mere (a, adv) eenvoudig, bloot, maar net; ~ly net, slegs, bloot
merge indompel; sink; saamsmelt; ~r same= smelting/amalgamasie; oplossing
merid'ian (n) middaglyn, meridiaan
meringue' skuimpie, skuimkoekie
me'rit (n) verdienste, meriete; waarde; cer= tif'icate of ~ sertifikaat van verdienste
mer'maid meermin

me'rry vrolik, plesierig; ~ **Christ'mas** ge=
seënde Kersfees; ~**-go-round** mallemeule/
rondomtalie *also* **carousel'**; ~**ma'king** pret=
makery, jolyt, makietie (hou)

mesh (n) **-es** netwerk, maas; strik

mess (n) gemeenskaplike tafel; deurmekaar=
spul; menasie (militêr); *make a ~ of* ver=
knoei; (v) saameet; knoei; mors; ~ *up* be=
derf; verongeluk; **of'ficers'** ~ offisiersme=
nasie

ness'age (n) boodskap, berig

mess'enger boodskapper, bode; ~ **of the Court**
balju, geregsbode

messieurs' menere, here; ~ **Jo'nes & Co.** die
firma Jones & Kie

mess'y (a) vuil, smerig, morsig

met'al (n) metaal; (a) metaal=, metaalagtig; ~
detec'tor metaalverklikker; ~ **fati'gue** me=
taalverswakking

metamorpho'sis (n) gedaantewisseling, meta=
morfose

met'aphor (n) beeldspraak, metafoor

metapho'ric figuurlik, oordragtelik

met'eor (n) vallende ster, meteoor

net'eorite meteoriet, meteoorsteen

meteorol'ogist (n) weerkundige, meteoroloog

net'er meter; ~ **maid** boetebessie (idiom.)

neth'od metode, manier; werkwyse

neth'ylated spi'rits brandspiritus

metic'ulous (a) nougeset, noulettend

me'tre¹ meter

me'tre² versmaat, metrum

net'ric metriek; ~ **sys'tem** metrieke/tiende=
lige stelsel; ~**al** metries, tiendelig

netrop'olis (n) wêreldstad, metropolis/metro=
pool, moederstad *also* **meg'acity**

metropol'itan (a) metropolitaans; ~ **a'rea**
stedelike/metropolitaanse gebied; ~ **sub'=**
structure metropolitaanse substruktuur

net'tle ywer, moed; fut, vuur, gees *also* **guts,
spi'rit**; *show one's* ~ toon jou staal

news stalkompleks; winkelhof; mews

nezzanin'e (n) tussenvloer

nic'a mika

nic'robe mikrobe

nic'rochip (n) mikrovlokkie/mikroskyfie

nic'rocomputer mikrorekenaar/mikrokomper

nic'rofilm mikrofilm

ni'crolight: ~ **air'craft/plane** mikroligte vlieg=
tuig/mikrotuig

nic'rophone mikrofoon, klankversterker

nic'roscope mikroskoop

---

mic'rosurgery mikrochirurgie

mic'rowave mikrogolf; ~ **o'ven** mikrogolf=
oond

mid'air: *in* ~ tussen hemel en aarde

mid'day (n) middag; (a) middag=

mid'dle (n) middel; midde(l)weg; (v) verdeel;
(a) middel, middelste; **M~ Ages** Middeleeue; **M~ East** Midde-Ooste; ~**-aged** mid=
deljarig; ~**man** middelman, tussenganger
also **go-between'**

midge muggie; warmassie; dwergie

midg'et (n) dwerg; (a) klein; ~ **car** muggie=
motor; ~ **golf** miniatuurgholf

mid: ~**land** (n) middelland; (a) binnelands;
~**night** (n) middernag; (a) middernagtelik:
burn the ~*night oil* laat studeer; ~**night sun**
middernagson; ~**shipman** adelbors, see=
kadet

midst (n) middel; *in our* ~ in ons midde

mid'term break termynreses

mid'way halfpad

mid'wife (n) vroedvrou; kraamverpleegster;
~**ry** verloskunde, obstetrie

might mag, geweld; vermoë

might'y (a) magtig, groot, sterk; *high and* ~
hoog verhewe

mi'graine (n) skeelhoofpyn, migraine

mig'rant (n) trekvoël; (a) trek=, rondtrekkend;
~ **la'bourer** trekarbeider

migrate' (v) verhuis/trek *also* **re'locate**

mild mild, sag; koel; sagsinnig, meegaande
(mens); lig=(siekte)

mil'dew (n) skimmel, muf; (v) beskimmel

mile myl; **nau'tical** ~ seemyl; ~**age** mylaf-
stand; ~**stone** mylpaal

mil'itant (a) veglustig, strydend, militant

mil'itary (n) militêr, soldaat; (a) militêr, krygs=;
~ **court** krygshof *also* **court mar'tial**; ~
force krygsmag; ~ **intel'ligence** militêre in-
ligting/intelligensie; (**compulsory**) ~ **ser'vice**
diensplig

milk (n) melk; **conden'sed** ~ blikkiesmelk;
skim'med ~ afgeroomde melk; (v) melk; ~
bar melksalon; ~ **jug** melkbeker; ~ **sa'chet**
melksakkie; ~**shake** bruismelk; ~**tart**
melktert; ~**tooth** melktand; ~**y** melkagtig/
melkerig; soetsappig; ~**y way** melkweg

mill (n) meul(e); (v) maal; ronddraai

mill'er meulenaar (mens)

mill'iard miljard (1 000 miljoen) *also* **bil'lion**

mill'igram milligram

mill'ilitre milliliter

mill'imetre millimeter
mill'iner hoedemaakster, modiste
mill'ion miljoen; ~**aire'** miljoenêr (mens)
milt (n) milt; hom (van vis); (v) bevrug
mime (n) gebarespel, mimiek; (v) mimeer, naboots
mim'ic (n) na-aper, koggelaar; (v) (uit)= koggel, namaak *also* **im'itate**
mimos'a mimosa (doringboom)
mince (n) maalvleis; (v) maal; goedpraat; *do not* ~ *matters* moenie doekies omdraai nie; ~**meat** maalvleis: *make* ~**meat** *of* kafloop; ~ **pie** vleispastei; Kerspastei; ~**r** vleismeul(e)
mind (n) siel; gees, gemoed; verstand; me= ning; *change one's* ~ van plan verander; *presence of* ~ teenwoordigheid van gees; *speak one's* ~ reguit/padlangs praat; *be in two* ~*s* twyfel; (v) oppas; oplet; ~ *your own business* bemoei jou met jou eie sake; *I don't* ~ graag; *never* ~*!* toe maar!; *would you* ~*?* gee jy om?; wil jy asb.?
mine¹ (n) myn; (v) delf, grawe; ontgin; **lim'pet** ~ kleefmyn
mine² (pron) myne
mine: ~ **cap'tain** mynkaptein; ~**field** myn= veld; ~**r** mynwerker/myner
min'eral (n) mineraal, delfstof; koeldrank; ~ **baths** kruitbad(dens), borrelbad
mi'ners' phthis'is (n) myntering
mine: ~ **survey'or** mynopmeter; ~**swee'per** mynveër; ~ **wor'kers' u'nion** mynwerkers= unie
ming'le (v) meng; deurmekaar maak
min'i (n) mini; (a) mini; ~**bus tax'i** mini= bustaxi; ~**dic'tionary** miniwoordeboek; ~**skirt** miniromp
min'im (n) klein bietjie; halwe noot; ~**al** minimaal; ~**ise** verklein; minimeer/mini= miseer; ~**um** (n) minste; minimum; (a) kleinste, minimum
mi'ning (n) mynbou; mynwese; (a) myn=
min'ister (n) minister (parlement); predikant/ dominee/leraar; gesant; (v) versorg, hulp verleen
mink (n) nerts, mink
mi'nor (n) minderjarige (mens); mineur; (a) ondergeskik; mineur (mus.); minder, klei= ner; minderjarig
minor'ity ..ties minderheid; minderjarigheid; ~ **report'** minderheidsverslag
mint¹ (n) kruisement, peperment
mint² (n) munt; (v) munt; (a) eersteklas

minuet' menuet (mus.)
min'us min, minus
min'ute¹ (n) minuut; brief; memorandum; (pl notule; *in the* ~*s* in die notule; *just a* ~ ne 'n oomblikkie; (v) notuleer
minute'² (a) baie klein, gering, nietig
min'ute: ~ **book** notuleboek; ~ **hand** minuut wyster (horlosie)
mir'acle (n) wonderwerk, mirakel; *work* ~ wondere verrig; ~ **play** mirakelspel
mirage' lugspieëling, opgeefsel (fata morgana *also* **illu'sion**
mi'rror (n) spieël; toonbeeld; (v) weerkaats weerspieël
mirth (n) vrolikheid, opgeruimdheid; joligheid
misappropria'tion wanbesteding, verduiste ring (geld, fondse)
miscal'culate (v) misreken, verreken
miscar'riage mislukking; miskraam *als* **abor'tion**
miscellan'eous gemeng; diverse, allerlei
mis'chief (n) onheil, kwaad; kattekwaad; on nutsigheid; *be up to* ~ iets in die skild voei ~ **ma'king** kwaadstokery
mis'chievous (a) ondeund, onnutsig
mis'er gierigaard, vrek (mens)
mis'erable (a) ellendig, miserabel, naar
mis'ery ..ries ellende, nood, narigheid
mis'fit (n) slegpassende kledingstuk; misbak sel/misgewas, mislukkeling (mens)
misfort'une (n) ongeluk, teenspoed
mis'hap ongeluk, ongeval *also* **ac'cident**
mislaid' verlê, weg (artikel)
mislead' (v) mislei; kul; (a) ~**ing** misleidenc
misman'age (v) wanbestuur; (n) ~**ment** wan bestuur, wanbeheer
miss¹ (n) -es (me)juffrou
miss² (n) -es misskoot; gemis; (v) mis; ~ *th bus* die bus mis
miss'ile missiel; projektiel, werptuig
miss'ing verlore, ontbrekend; *reported* ~ a vermis aangegee
mis'sion sending; opdrag; missie; ~**ary** (n sendeling; (a) sending=; **fact-fin'ding** ~ fei tesending; ~ **work** sendingwerk
mist (n) mis, newel *also* **fog**; (v) misreën
mistake' (n) fout, vergissing; *by* ~ per abui *make a* ~ 'n fout maak/begaan; ~**n** ver keerd
mis'ter meneer; (die) heer; **Mr Chair'ma Chairper'son** Meneer die voorsitter/Agbar voorsitter

mis'tletoe (n) mistel; voëlent

mis'tress -es mevrou; meesteres, nooi, ounooi; onderwyseres; houvrou/bywyf/minnares; *the* ~ *of the house* die huisvrou/gasvrou

mistrust' (v) wantrou, verdink

mist'y mistig, bewolk, dynserig *also* **ha'zy**

misunderstand' misverstaan; (n) ~**ing** misverstand

misuse' (n) misbruik; mishandeling; (v) misbruik; mishandel

mit'igate (v) versag, verlig; **mit'igating cir'cumstances** versagtende omstandighede *also* **exten'uating cir'cumstances**

mix (v) meng, vermeng

mixed gemeng, deurmekaar; *be* ~ *up with* betrokke wees in; ~ **grill** allegaartjie, gemengde braaigereg; ~ **pickles** suurtjies, atjar

mix'ture mengsel, mikstuur

mix'-up warboel, deurmekaarspul

moan (n) gekerm; (v) kerm, steun; ~**er** sanikpot (mens); ~**ing** gekerm, gekla

mob (n) gepeupel, oproerige skare

mob'ilise (v) mobiliseer; oproep (troepe)

mock (n) bespotting; namaaksel; (v) spot, (uit)koggel; bespot; ~ **fight** skyngeveg; ~**ingbird** piet-my-vrou; ~ **lob'ster** kammakreef; ~ **shut'ters** kammahortjies; ~ **tri'al** skynverhoor

mode (n) metode, manier, gewoonte

mod'el (n) model, voorbeeld; (v) vorm, modelleer; ~**ling** (n) boetseerkuns; model(leer)werk

mod'erate (v) matig; modereer (eksamen); kalmeer; (a) matig, redelik

mod'erating commit'tee modereerkomitee

mod'erator moderator; bemiddelaar

mod'ern (a) modern, nuwerwets, bydertyds *also* **with-it, tren'dy**

mod'est (a) beskeie, ingetoë *also* **shy, demu're**; matig; ~**y** beskeidenheid

mod'ify (v) wysig, verander; matig

mod'ule eenheidsmaat, maatstaf; module

mo'hair bokhaar, angorahaar

Mohamm'ed Mohammed

moist (a) kalm, vogtig; ~**en** natmaak, bevogtig; ~**ure** vog, klammigheid; ~**uriser** (n) bevogter

mol'ar (n) kiestand, maaltand

molass'es swartstroop, triakel, melasse

mole[1] (n) mol (dier); (v) ondergrawe; uithol

mole[2] (n) moesie, moedervlek

mole[3] (n) seehoof/hawehoof, pier; golfbreker

mol'ecule stofdeeltjie, molekule

mole'hill molshoop; *make a mountain out of a* ~ van 'n muggie 'n olifant maak

molest' (v) pla, lastig val; molesteer; lol (met kinders)

mo'ment oomblik, rukkie, kits, moment; *half a* ~ wag 'n bietjie; *in a* ~ in 'n kits/oogwenk

mon'arch (n) monarg, alleenheerser; potentaat; ~**ist** monargis (mens); ~**y** monargie

mon'astery (n) ..**ries** klooster (vir monnike)

Mon'day Maandag; *blue* ~ blou Maandag

mo'netary geldelik, monetêr; **Internat'ional M**~ **Fund (IMF)** Internasionale Monetêre Fonds (IMF)

mo'ney -s geld, munt; betaalmiddel; ~ *galore* geld soos bossies; *be out of* ~ platsak wees; ~**box** spaarpot, spaarbus; geldtrommel; ~ **len'der** geldskieter (mens); ~ **or'der** poswissel; ~ **spin'ner** geldmaker

mon'goose muishond; **yel'low** ~ rooimeerkat

mo'ngrel (n) baster; basterbrak; (a) basteragtig

mon'itor monitor; klasleier (skool); (v) moniteer/monitor; kontroleer, verifieer

monk (n) monnik, kloosterling

mon'key (n) aap; (v) na-aap; ~**nut** grondboon(tjie); ~ **trick** bobbejaanstreek; ~ **wrench** moersleutel

mon'ochrome (a) eenkleurig, monochroom

mon'ocle oogglas, monokel

mon'ologue (n) alleenspraak, monoloog

monop'oly , .lies monopolie, alleenhandel

monosyllab'ic (a) eenlettergrepig

monot'onous (a) eentonig, monotoon

monsoon' passaatwind, moeson

mon'ster (n) monster, gedrog; dierasie

mon'strous (a) monsteragtig, wanskape, afskuwelik, vreeslik *also* **hid'eous**

month maand

month'ly (n) maandblad; (pl) maandstonde/menstruasie; (a) maandeliks, maand=; ~ **mee'ting** maandvergadering

mon'ument (n) monument, gedenkteken

mood (n) stemming, bui, luim; *in a good* ~ in 'n goeie bui; ~**iness** humeurigheid; ~**y** buierig, knorrig *also* **grum'py**

moon maan; maand (poëties); *once in a blue* ~ 'n enkele keer; ~**bag** maansak, pensportefeulje; ~**light** maanlig; ~**light'ing** sluikwerk/privaat werk *also* **double-job'bing**; ~**shine** maanskyn; onsin; ~**shi'ner** dranksmokkelaar; ~**struck** maansiek, mal

moor¹ (n) heide; vlei, moeras *also* **marsh**
moor² (v) vasmeer, anker
moot (v) bespreek, debatteer; (a) betwisbaar; *a* ∼ *point* 'n ope vraag
mop (n) stofdoek, dweil, opvryflap; (v) afvee, opvrywe; ∼ *the floor with somebody* iem. kafloop; ∼*ping up* opruim, bymekaarmaak
mop'ed kragfiets
mor'al (n) moraal; sedeles; boodskap; (a) sedelik; moreel; *one's* ∼ *duty* jou morele plig; ∼ **decay'** sedelike verval
morale' moed, volharding; moreel (van 'n leër); *improve the* ∼ *of his soldiers* sy soldate se moreel verstewig; ∼ **boos'ter** moreelkikker
moral'ity sedelikheid, sedeleer, moraliteit; **..ties** sinnespel, moraliteit (drama)
mor'als sedes
mor'bid (a) sieklik, ongesond, morbied
more meer, groter; *the* ∼ *the better* hoe meer, hoe beter; ∼ *or less* min of meer; *the* ∼ *the merrier* hoe meer siele, hoe meer vreug(de); ∼*over* bowendien, buitendien
morg'en (n) morg (oppervlakte)
mor'gue lykhuis; dodehuis *also* **mor'tuary**
morn'ing (n) môre, môreoggend, voormiddag; (a) môre=, môreoggend=; *good* ∼ goeiemôre; *tomorrow* ∼ môreoggend; ∼ **glo'ry** purper= winde, trompettertjie; ∼ **gown** kamerjas; ∼ **pa'per** oggendblad/oggendkoerant
mor'on moron/moroon, volwasse swaksinnige
morph'ia/morph'ine morfien, morfine
mors'el (n) stukkie, happie, krummel
mor'tal (n) sterfling; (a) sterflik; dodelik; menslik; ∼ **en'emy** doodsvyand; ∼ **remains'** stoflike oorskot
mortal'ity sterflikheid, sterfte; **in'fant** ∼ **rate** kindersterftesyfer
mortg'age (n) verband; (v) onder verband plaas, verband; verpand; ∼ **bond** verband=; (akte); ∼**e'** verbandhouer; ∼**r/mort'gagor** verbandgewer
mort'uary (n) lykhuis *also* **mor'gue**
mosa'ic (n) mosaïek; (a) mosaïek=
Mos'lem (n) Moslem/Moesliem *also* **Mus'lim**
mosque (n) moskee
mosquit'o muskiet; ∼ **net** muskietnet
most (a) meeste, uiterste, grootste; *at the* ∼ hoogstens; *for the* ∼ *part* grotendeels; ∼ *probably* heel waarskynlik; ∼ *of us* die meeste van ons; (adv) hoogs, baie, uiters, besonders; ∼**ly** mees(t)al, merendeels,

hoofsaaklik
mote stofdeeltjie, stof; stipseltjie; splinter (in 'n ander se oog)
motel' motel *see* **hotel'**
moth mot; ∼**-eaten** motgevreet
mo'ther (n) moeder, mamma; (v) vertroetel; (a) moeder=; ∼ **coun'try** vaderland; ∼**-in-law'** skoonmoeder; ∼**ly** moederlik; ∼**-of-pearl'** perlemoen *also* **ab'alone/perlemoen'**; ∼ **super'=ior** moederowerste; ∼ **ton'gue** moedertaal
mo'tion (n) beweging; mosie; ∼ *of no con= fidence* mosie van wantroue; *in slow* ∼ in stadige aksie, in traagtempo; (v) wink; 'n teken gee; ∼**less** botstil, bewegingloos; ∼ **pic'tures** rolprent; bioskoop *also* **mo'vies**
mot'ivate (v) aanspoor, motiveer
motiva'tion (n) motivering
mot'ive (n) beweegrede, motief (vir 'n moord)
mot'ley (a) (kakel)bont; vreemdsoortig; ∼ **crowd** bont menigte
mot'ocross motocross, motorfietsveldrenne
mot'or (n) motor; (a) dryf=; ∼ **boat** motorboot; ∼**cade** motorstoet, motorkade; ∼**car** motor, motorkar; kar; vuurwa (idiom.); ∼**coach** toerbus; ∼**cy'cle** motorfiets; ∼**ist** motoris/ motorryer; ∼ **ral'ly** motortydren; ∼ **truck** vragmotor; ∼ **van** bestelwa; ∼ **ve'hicle** motorvoertuig; ∼**way** deurpad (stedelik), motorweg
mot'tle (v) vlek; (a) bont, gevlek; gemarmer; ∼**d** bont, gestreep; ∼**d soap** blouseep
mott'o -es (n) leuse, slagspreuk, motto
mould¹ (n) (giet)vorm; matrys; (v) vorm, giet; modelleer
mould² (n) skimmel; (v) skimmel, kim
moult (v) verveer (hoender); verhaar (dier); vervel (slang)
mound (n) hoop, heuweltjie; wal, skans
mount (n) rydier; berg; (v) monteer, opplak; opklim; ∼*ing costs* stygende koste; ∼*ed in gold* in goud geset
moun'tain berg; *make* ∼*s of molehills* van 'n muggie 'n olifant maak; ∼ **bike** bergfiets; ∼**eer'** bergklimmer/bergenier; ∼**eer'ing** berg= klim; ∼**ous** bergagtig; ∼ **pass** bergpas, poort, nek; ∼ **range** bergreeks; ∼ **slide** bergstorting
moun'ted berede, te perd; ∼ **poli'ce** berede polisie
mourn (v) rou, treur *also* **lament'**; ∼**er** rouklaer
mouse (n) **mice** muis; ∼**trap** muisval
moustache' (n) snor(baard)

mouth (n) mond; bek; monding (rivier); ~**ful** mond vol; ~ **harp** trompie; ~ **or'gan** mondfluitjie; ~**piece** woordvoerder, segs= man; mondstuk; ~ **wash** (n) mondspoeling

mo'vable beweegbaar, verplaasbaar; ~ **prop'er= ty** losgoed, roerende eiendom

move (n) beweging; (v) beweeg, roer; verhuis; ~ *heaven and earth* hemel en aarde beweeg; ~ *in* intrek; (a) ~**d** bewoë, aangedaan; ~**ment** beweging; ~**r** voorsteller (van mosie)

mo'vie (n) rolprent, fliek; film; ~ **fan** fliek= vlooi

mo'ving bewegend, beweeg=; roerend, aan= doenlik; ~ **viola'tion** ry-oortreding

much more, most baie, veel; *nothing* ~ niks besonders nie; ~ *worse* veel erger

muck (n) mis *also* **dung**; bog; smerigheid; ~ **heap** mishoop; ~ **worm** miswurm

mud modder; **stick-in-the-**~ agterblyer, rem= skoen (mens)

mud'dle (n) verwarring, warboel; (v) verwar; verbrou; ~**d** deurmekaar *also* **confu'sed**; ~**r** knoeier (mens)

mud: ~**dy** (a) modderig; troebel; ~**guard** modderskerm

muezz'in (n) muezzin/muedzin, gebedsroeper (Islam)

muf'fin roosterkoekie, plaatkoekie

muf'ti burgerdrag, siviele drag

mug (n) kommetjie; beker; bakkies, gevreet; domkop; (v) volprop; grimeer; straatroof; ~**ger** straatrower

mul'berry mulberries moerbei

mule muil, esel; hardekop; ~ **kick** volstruis= skop (by stoei)

mull'et harder (vis)

mul'ti veel=, meer=; multi=; ~**col'oured** veel= kleurig; ~**cul'tural** multikultureel; ~**grade** meergraad; ~ **me'dia** multimedia (rek.); ~**millionai're** multimiljoenêr; ~**na'tional** veelvolkig

mul'tiped duisendpoot

mul'tiple (n) veelvoud; (a) veelvoudig/veel= vuldig; ~**-choi'ce ques'tions** veelkeusevrae; ~ **in'juries** veelvuldige beserings

mul'tiply (v) vermenigvuldig; toeneem

mul'tiracial (a) veelrassig

mul'titude (n) menigte, skare *also* **crowd**

mum[1] (n) mams, mamma

mum[2] (v) stilbly; vermom; (a) stil, soet; (interj) stil!; st! ~*'s the word!* stilbly!, geen kik nie; ~ *on the issue* swyg oor die kwessie

mum'ble (v) mompel; prewel

mumm'y[1] **mummies** mummie (gebalsem)

mumm'y[2] **mummies** mammie, mamsie

mumps pampoentjies (siekte), parotitis

munici'pal munisipaal, stedelik; ~ **coun'cil** stadsraad; ~ **rates** erfbelasting

municipal'ity (n) ..**ties** munisipaliteit, stads= raad, plaaslike owerheid/bestuur

mur'der (n) moord; *commit* ~ moord pleeg/ begaan; *horrible* ~ grumoord; (v) vermoor; ~**er** moordenaar; ~**ous** moorddadig

murm'ur (v) murmel; mompel

mu'scle (n) spier; spierkrag; ~ **relax'ant** spierverslapper

muse'um (n) **-s, ..sea** museum

mush'room paddastoel, sampioen

mu'sic (n) musiek, toonkuns; *classical* ~ klas= sieke musiek; *face the* ~ die gevolge dra; *set to* ~ toonset; ~**al** musikaal, welluidend; (n) musiekblyspel; ~ **box** musiekdoos; ~ **cen'tre** musieksentrum

musi'cian musikus, toonkunstenaar; musikant (speler)

musk'et roer, geweer; ~**eer'** musketier

Mus'lim Moslem/Moeslicm *also* **Mos'lem**

muss'el mossel

must (v) **must** moet, verplig wees

mus'tard mosterd; ~ **gas** mosterdgas

mus'ter (v) monster, oproep, versamel; ~ *up courage* moed skep

must'roll mosholletjie *also* **mustbun**

mus'ty (a) muf, beskimmel, suf

mu'ti (n) toormedisyne, doepa/moetie

mut'ilate (v) vermink, skend *also* **maim**

mutineer' (n) muiter, oproerling (mens)

mut'iny (n) muitery, oproer; (v) muit

mutt'er (v) mompel; brom, prewel

mutt'on skaapvleis; skaap; *as dead as* ~ so dood soos 'n mossie; **leg of** ~ skaapboud

mut'ual wedersyds; wederkerig *also* **reci'= procal**; (a) gemeenskaplik; ~ **friend** ge= meenskaplike vriend

muz'zle (n) snoet, bek; loop (van geweer); muilband; (v) muilband; besnuffel; ~ **loa'= der** voorlaaier (geweer)

my my; *oh* ~! goeie genade!

my'nah (n) Indiese spreeu *also* (**In'dian**) **star'ling**

myop'ic (a) bysiende, stiksienig, miopies

myself' ekself, myself; *by* ~ alleen; *I am not* ~ ek voel nie lekker nie

myster'ious (a) geheimsinnig, misterieus; ver=
borge, duister *also* **dark, cryp'tic**
mys'tery ..ries geheim, misterie; raaisel

mys'tic (n) mistikus; (a) misties, geheimsin=
nig, duister; ~**ism** mistiek
myth (n) mite, fabel *also* **leg'end**; ~**ol'ogy**
mitologie *also* **folk'lore**; godeleer

N

naar'tjie = **nartjie**
nab (v) betrap, gryp, arresteer
nag (v) pla; lol, sanik, seur, neul
nag: ~**ger** plaer, sanikpot, terger; ~**ging** ge=
sanik, gelol, vittery, geneul
nail (n) spyker; nael; *a* ~ *in his coffin* 'n spy=
ker in sy doodkis; (v) vasspyker; inslaan;
~**brush** naelborsel; ~**pol'ish** naellak
naïve (a) naïef, eenvoudig, kinderlik
nak'ed nakend/naak, kaal; *stark* ~ poedelna=
kend; *the* ~ *truth* die blote/naakte waarheid;
~**ness** naaktheid
Nama'qualand: ~ **dai'sy** Namakwalandse
gousblom
name (n) naam, benaming; *first (Christian)* ~
voornaam; *make a* ~ spore afdruk; (v)
noem, naam gee; opnoem; ~**board** naam=
bord *also* **sign'post**; ~**ly** naamlik; ~**sake**
genant, naamgenoot; ~**tag** kenstrokie/
naamplaatjie
Namib'ia Namibië; ~**n econ'omy** Namibiese
ekonomie; ~**n** Namibiër (mens)
nan'ny (n) kinderoppasser; ~ **goat** bokooi
nap¹ (n) nop (klere, setperkgras); dons (vrug=
te); (v) pluis
nap² (n) dutjie, sluimering; *catch one* ~*ping*
iem. onverwags betrap; *take a* ~ 'n uiltjie
knyp/knip; (v) dut, sluimer
nap'kin (n) servet; doek; luier (vir baba)
narcism' (n) narsisme, selfliefde
narciss'us -es, ..cissi narsing (plant)
narcot'ic (n) verdowingsmiddel/doofmiddel;
(a) narkoties, verdowend; ~**s bur'eau** nar=
kotikaburo
narra'tion vertelling, verhaal; relaas; **min'=
utes of** ~ notule van relaas
narra'tor verteller, verhaler (mens)
nar'row (v) vernou; beperk; (a) nou, smal; *a* ~
escape 'n noue ontkoming; ~ *views* be=
krompe idees; ~ *the wage gap* die loonga=
ping vernou; ~**-min'ded** kleingeestig; be=
krompe
nar'tjie -s nartjie *see* **man'darin, tan'gerine**
na'sal (a) nasaal, neus=; ~ **cav'ity** neusholte;

~**ise** (v) nasaleer
nastur'tium kappertjie (blom); bronkors
nas'ty (a) naar, aaklig; gemeen, haatlik; vuil;
~ **feel'ing** nare gevoel; ~ **fel'low** onaange=
name/skurwe vent
na'tion (n) volk, nasie; moondheid; **Unit'ed
N~s** Verenigde Nasies; ~**wide** land(s)=
wyd
nat'ional (n) burger, landgenoot; (a) nasio=
naal; vaderlands; volks=, staats=; ~ **an'them**
volkslied; ~ **flag** landsvlag; ~**ism** na=
sionalisme; ~**ist** nasionalis (mens); ~**ity**
nasionaliteit
National Council of Provinces Nasionale
Raad van Provinsies
Nat'ional Wo'men's Day Nasionale Vrouedag
(vakansie)
na'tive¹ (n) inboorling/boorling (van land/
streek)
na'tive² (a) aangebore; oorspronklik; eie; in=
heems; vry; natuurlik
nat'ural (a) natuurlik; natuur=; ongekunstel(d);
~ **death** natuurlike dood; ~ **gas** aardgas; ~
resour'ces natuurbronne; ~**ly** natuurlik;
~**ise** naturaliseer; ~ **science** natuur=
wetenskap/natuurkunde
na'ture (n) natuur; karakter; aard, geaardheid,
inbors; *freak of* ~ natuurfrats; *in* ~*'s garb* in
Adamspak; ~ **conserva'tion** natuurbewa=
ring; ~ **resort'** natuuroord
nat'uropath natuurgeneser (mens)
naught (n) niks, nul *also* **nought**; (a) niks=
werd, waardeloos
naught'y (a) ondeund, stout; ~ **boy** karnallie,
rakker *also* **little ras'cal**
naus'eous mislik; walglik
naut'ical see=, skeeps=, seevaart=; ~ **batt'le**
seeslag; ~ **mile** seemyl (1 852 m)
na'val see=, skeeps=, vloot=; ~ **battle** seeslag; ~
cadet' adelbors; ~ **po'wer** seemoondheid (land)
na'vel nawel (lemoen); nael (op maag); ~
cord/string naelstring
nav'igate vaar; bevaar *also* **cruise** (v)
naviga'tion skeepvaart; lugvaart

nav′igator seevaarder (mens); koerspeiler (lugv.); navigator (tydrenne)

na′vy navies seemag, vloot; ~ **blue** marine= blou

neap′tide laagwater/laaggety, dooie gety

near (v) nader (kom); (a) naby, digby, by; ~ **fu′ture** afsienbare toekoms; ~**est rel′ative** naaste bloedverwant/aanverwant; (adv) naby, digby, byna; ~**ly** amper, byna *also* **near′= ly, al′most**; ~**-sighted** bysiende

neat (a) netjies, sindelik; keurig

neat: ~**ly** netjies; ~**ly done** mooi/knap gedoen; ~**ness** netheid; ~ **whis′key** skoon whiskey

ne′cessary (a) nodig, noodsaaklik

necess′ity ..ties noodsaaklikheid/noodsaak; behoefte; ~ *knows no law* nood breek wet

neck (n) nek (van mense, diere); pas, engte (tussen berge); ~**lace** halsketting, halssnoer; ~**lace mur′der** halssnoermoord; ~**tie** das

nec′tar nektar, godedrank; heuning (van plante)

nec′tarine kaalperske, nektarien

need (n) nood, behoefte; *in time of* ~ as die nood druk; (v) nodig hê, makeer; *you* ~ *not come* jy hoef nie te kom nie; *you* ~ *not have come* jy hoef nie te gekom het nie; (a) nodig, noodsaaklik

need′le naald; wyser; *on pins and* ~*s* op hete kole; ~ **case** naaldekoker

need′less (a) onnodig, nodeloos

need′lework naaldwerk/naaiwerk

needs (n) behoeftes, benodig(d)hede

need′y arm/armoedig, behoeftig

ne′er-do-well niksnuts *also* **rot′ter** (person)

neg′ative (n) negatief; ontkenning; ~ **growth** negatiewe groei; ~ **sign** minusteken

neglect′ (n) verwaarlosing, versuim; (v) verwaarloos

neg′ligence nalatigheid, versuim

neg′ligent (a) nalatig, agte(r)losig

neg′ligible nietig, onbeduidend

nego′tiable verhandelbaar; reëlbaar; *salary* ~ salaris reëlbaar

nego′tiate (v) onderhandel; behartig

negotia′tion (n) onderhandeling, beraad(slaging)

nego′tiator onderhandelaar (mens)

Neg′ro -es Neger

neigh′bour (n) buurman; ~**ing coun′tries** buur= lande; (v) grens aan; (a) naburig; ~**hood** buurt; buurskap; ~**hood watch** buurtwag; ~**ing** naburig, aangrensend

neith′er (adv) ewemin, ook nie; (conj) nie een

nie; *that's* ~ *here nor there* dit maak geen saak nie; ~ . . . *nor* nóg . . . nóg

neol′ogism (n) nuutskepping, neologisme

neph′ew neef/nefie, broerskind, susterskind

nerd nerd (asosiale slimkop), vaaljan/noffie

nerve (n) senuwee; spierkrag; moed, durf; (pl) senuwees; *get on a person's* ~*s* op iem. se senuwees werk; ~**-rack′ing** senutergend

ner′vous senuweeagtig; ~ **attack′** senuaanval; ~ **strain** stres *also* **stress**

nest (n) nes; *feather one's* ~ jou verryk; (v) nes maak, nestel; ~ **egg** neseier

net[1] (n) net; spinnerak; netwerk; (v) vang; inbring, oplewer; ~**work** netwerk

net[2] (a) netto; suiwer; ~ **prof′it** netto wins

Neth′erlander Nederlander/Hollander

nett′ing netwerk, gaas; ~ **wire** ogiesdraad, sif= draad

nett′le (n) brandnetel; (v) vererg, prikkel; ~ **rash** netelroos

neural′gia (n) senu(wee)pyn, sinkings

neurot′ic (n) senulyer; senuweemiddel; (a) neuroties

neut′er (n) onsydige geslag; (a) geslagloos; (v) kastreer, regmaak; spei (wyfiedier)

neut′ral (a) neutraal, onpartydig, onsydig

nev′er nooit, nimmer; ~ *mind* toe maar; dit maak g'n saak nie; ~**more** nooit meer/weer nie; ~**theless** nieteenstaande, nietemin, tog *also* **notwithstan′ding, despi′te**

new nuut, vars; ~**co′mer** nuweling, aankome= ling; ~**-fang′led** nuwerwets, bydertyds *also* **tren′dy**; ~**ly appoin′ted** pas aangestel(de)

news nuus, tyding; *the latest* ~ die jongste nuus; ~ **a′gent** nuusagent; ~**cast** nuus (radio, TV); ~**flash** flitsberig (radio); ~**group** diskussie= groep (Internet); ~**pa′per** koerant, nuusblad; ~**let′ter** nuusbrief

New Year′ Nuwejaar; ~**'s day** Nuwejaarsdag; ~**'s eve** Oujaarsaand; ~**'s resolu′tion** Nu= wejaarsvoorneme

next (n) (die) volgende; (a) volgende, aan= staande; ~ **best** naasbeste; ~ **door** langsaan; ~ **of kin** naasbestaande(s); (prep) langsaan

nib (n) pen(punt)

nib′ble (v) knaag, peusel

nice (a) lekker; gaaf, lief; oulik; ~ **mess** mooi gemors

nick (n) kerf; stippie; kabouter; *in the very* ~ *of time* op die nippertjie; (v) inkerf; kul

nick′el nikkel; ~**-pla′ted** vernikkel

nick: ~**name** bynaam; ~**stick** kerfstok

nic′otine nikotien; pypolie
niece nig(gie); susterskind, broerskind
nigg′le (v) neul, sanik, seur *also* nag, fuss; (n) ~r neuler, neulpot, sanikpot (mens)
night nag, aand; *all* ~ die hele nag; *last* ~ gisteraand; ~ ad′der nagadder; ~cap slaapmus; aandsnapsie, slaapdop; ~class aandklas; ~club nagklub
night′ingale nagtegaal (voël)
night: ~ly nagtelik, snags; ~mare nagmerrie; ~shift nagskof
nil niks, nul; zero
nim′ble (a) lenig, vinnig, rats *also* ag′ile
nine nege; ~ o'clock nege-uur; ~teen negen= tien; ~teenth negentiende; ~teenth hole gholfklubkroeg; ~tieth negentigste; ~ty negentig
ninth negende
nip¹ (v) byt, knyp; ~ *in the bud* in die kiem smoor
nip² (n) halfbottel; snapsie
nip′ple (n) tepel (mens); speen (dier)
Nko′si Sikelel′ iAfrika God seën Afrika
no (n) -es nee, weiering; (a) geen, g'n; ~ *parking* geen parkering (nie); *in* ~ *time* in 'n kits/japtrap, tjop-tjop; (adv) nee; ~ *sooner said than done* so gesê, so gedaan
nob (n) knop; hoë meneer *also* big shot
nobil′ity adel, adeldom
no′ble (a) edel; adellik; ~man edelman
no′body niemand
noc′turne naglied, nokturne; nagtafereel
nod (n) knik, wenk; (v) knik; *getting the* ~ die jawoord/goedkeuring kry
noise (n) geraas, lawaai, rumoer; big ~ groot kokkedoor; (v) raas; ~less stil, geruisloos
nois′y (a) luidrugtig, rumoerig, lawaaierig
nom′ad swerwer, nomade (mens)
no-man's-land niemandsland
nom de plume′ skuilnaam, skryfnaam
nom′inal: ~ val′ue nominale waarde
nomina′tion benoeming, nominasie
nominee′ benoemde, genomineerde
nonaggress′ion pact nie-aanvalsverdrag
non′chalant (a) onverskillig, ongeërg
nonconform′ist nonkonformis (mens)
none (a) niks, geen; (pron) geeneen, niemand; (adv) niks; ~ *the worse for* glad nie slegter nie; ~theless nietemin, nogtans
nonfic′tion niefiksie
nonpay′ment wanbetaling/niebetaling
non′profit underta′king onderneming sonder

winsoogmerk
nonra′cial (a) nierassig
non′sense onsin, bog, kaf, twak *also* trash
non′stop deurlopend, ononderbroke
noon (n) middag, twaalfuur
noose (n) strop; galgtou; lus, strik
nor ook nie, nóg; *neither ...* ~ nóg ... nóg
norm (n) standaard, maatstaf, norm
nor′mal normaal; ~ col′lege onderwyskollege
north (n) die noorde; (a) noord; noordelik; (adv) noordwaarts; N~ Pole Noordpool; ~ward noordwaarts
Nor′thern Cape (province) Noord-Kaap
Northern Province Noordelike Provinsie
North West (province) Noordwes
nose (n) neus; *blow your* ~ snuit jou neus; *under his* ~ vlak voor hom; (v) ruik; snuffel; ~dive (v) neusduik
nos′tril neusgat
no′sy par′ker nuuskierige agie (mens)
not nie; ~ *at all* glad nie; ~ *yet* nog nie
no′tary ..ries notaris (regsman)
notch (n) -es kerf, keep; (v) kerf; aanteken; uitkeep; ~ stick kerfstok
note (n) aantekening; toon, nota; noot (geld, musiek); ~ *of exclamation* uitroepteken; ~ *of interrogation* vraagteken; *make* ~s aan= tekeninge maak; (v) oplet, let wel (L.W.), opmerk; ~book aantekeningboek; ~d (a) beroemd/vermaard; ~paper skryfpapier, briefpapier; ~wor′thy merkwaardig *also* remark′able
noth′ing niks, glad nie; ~ *at all* glad niks nie; *next to* ~ so goed as niks; ~ *to speak of* onbenullig; ~ *like trying* aanhouer wen
no′tice (n) kennis; kennisgewing, berig; ~ *calling the meeting* byeenroepende kennis= gewing; *until further* ~ tot nader kennisge= wing; ~ *is hereby given* geliewe kennis te neem van . . .; (v) opmerk, bemerk, oplet; ~able merkbaar; ~ board aanspeldbord
not′ify (v) meedeel, aankondig, verwittig; notifi′able disea′se aanmeldbare siekte
no′tion (n) denkbeeld, opvatting, idee, begrip
notor′ious (a) berug, wêreldkundig
notwithstand′ing nieteenstaande, desnieteen= staande, nietemin, ondanks, tog
nought niks, nul, zero *also* ze′ro; ~s-and-cros′ses tik-tak-tol
noun selfstandige naamwoord
nou′rish voed *also* nur′ture; koester; ~ing voedsaam; ~ment voedsel/voeding

nov'el[1] (n) roman (boek)

nov'el[2] (a) nuut, modern *also* **new**; eienaardig

nov'el: ~ette' novelle; ~ist romanskrywer, romansier (mens)

nov'elty (n) nuwigheid; (pl) fantasieware

Novem'ber November

nov'ice (n) nuweling, groentjie *also* **fresh'er**; beginner *also* **lay'man**

now (n) hede, teenswoordige; (adv) nou, tans, teenswoordig; *every ~ and then* telkens; *~ and then* af en toe; partykeer; (conj) nou; ~adays teenswoordig, deesdae

no'where nêrens, niewers

noz'zle nossel, sproeipyp; spuitkop; tuit

nu'clear kern=; ~ **fall-out** kern-as; ~ **deb'ris** kernoorskot; ~ **reac'tion** kernreaksie; ~ **war** kernoorlog; ~ **waste** kernafval

nu'cleus nuclei kern, pit *also* **core**

nude (a) kaal, naak, bloot; ~ **ba'ther** kaal= (bas)swemmer/kaalbaaier

nu'dist (n) naakloper, nudis; kaalbas

nuis'ance (n) oorlas, plaag; laspos; ~ **val'ue** irritasiewaarde, steurfaktor

null nietig; ongeldig; ~ *and void* van nul en gener waarde; nietig (kontrak)

numb gevoelloos; verkluim (van koue)

number (n) nommer; aflewering (blad); getal, aantal; klomp; *his ~ goes up* dis klaar(praat) met hom; (v) nommer; tel, reken; ~ **plate** nommerplaat

nu'meral telwoord; syfer

numer'ical numeriek, getal=; ~ly *stronger* getalsterker; ~ **or'der** getal(s)orde

nu'merous (a) talryk, baie

numismat'ics muntkunde, numismatiek

num'skull dwaas, domkop *also* **fool, dunce**

nun (n) non; ~nery nonneklooster *see* **mon'= astery** (for monks)

nup'tial huweliks=, bruilofs=; ~s bruilof

nurse (n) verpleegster; verpleegsuster; kinder= oppasser; (v) verpleeg, soog; kweek (plan= te); ~ *a grievance* 'n grief koester; ~maid kindermeisie; **male ~** verpleër

nurs'ery kinderkamer; kwekery; ~ **rhyme** kleuterversie; ~ **school** kleuterskool

nurs'ing verpleging, verpleegkunde; ~ **home** verpleeginrigting; ~ **sister** verpleegsuster; ~ **staff** verpleegpersoneel

nut neut; moertjie; ~crack'er neutkraker; ~= **grass** uintjie; ~meg neutmuskaat

nutri'tion voeding, kos; voedingsleer (vak)

nut'sedge uintjie *also* **nutgrass**

nut'shell neut(e)dop; *in a ~* baie beknop, kort en saaklik

nymph (n) nimf; ~oma'niac nimfomaan, seks= beheepte vrou; (a) mansiek

O

oak eike(hout); (a) eike=; ~ **table** eikehouttafel; ~ **tree** eikeboom; *oak trees bear acorns* eikebome dra akkers

oar (n) roeispaan; roeiriem; ~sman roeier

oa'sis (n) oases oase

oath eed; vloek; ~ **of alle'giance** eed van ge= trouheid

oat: ~meal hawermeel; ~s hawer

obe'dient gehoorsaam, dienswillig

obey' gehoorsaam, luister na; ~ *traffic rules* verkeersreëls eerbiedig/gehoorsaam

obit'uary (n) ..ries doodsberig

ob'ject (n) voorwerp; doel, oogmerk; bedoe= ling; *money is no ~* geld is bysaak

object' (v) beswaar maak, teenwerp, objekteer; ~ion beswaar, objeksie; *raise ~ions* be= sware opper; ~ionable aanstootlik, afkeu= renswaardig; ~ive (n) doelwit, doel; (a) objektief; **aims and** ~ives doelstellings; **man'agement by** ~ives doelwitbestuur

object'or beswaarmaker; **conscien'tious ~** gewetensbeswaarde (mens)

obliga'tion (n) verpligting

oblige' verplig; diens bewys; *feel ~d* gedwonge/ verplig voel; *much ~d* baie dankie

ob'long (n) reghoek; (a) langwerpig

ob'oe -s hobo (musiekinstrument)

ob'oist hobospeler (mens)

obsce'ne (a) onwelvoeglik, vuil, liederlik, ob= seen

obscu're (v) verduister; (a) duister, onbekend; ~ *poetry* duister(e) poësie

observ'ant (a) oplettend; gedienstig

observa'tion opmerking; waarneming; vie= ring; nakoming; ~ **post** observasiepos

observ'atory (n) ..ries sterrewag

observe' (v) bemerk/opmerk, waarneem; ~ *the law* die wet eerbiedig; ~**r** waarnemer (mens)

obsess'ion obsessie, manie *also* **hang-up**

obsoles'cense veroudering; *planned* ~ beplande veroudering

obsole'te (a) verouder(d); uitgedien

ob'stacle hinderpaal, beletsel, belemmering; ~ **race** hindernis(wed)ren

obstetri'cian verloskundige (geneesheer)

obstet'rics verloskunde, obstetrie

ob'stinate (a) (hard)koppig, steeks *also* **stub'-born**

obstrep'erous weerspannig, opstandig *also* **unru'ly**

obstruct' (v) verhinder, belemmer, versper; teenhou; ~**ion** versperring

obtain' verkry, verskaf; ~**able** verkry(g)baar

ob'vious (a) klaarblyklik; vanselfsprekend

occa'sion (n) geleentheid; geselligheid; plegtigheid; (v) veroorsaak, teweegbring; ~**ally** af en toe

occ'upant (n) besitter; bewoner; insittende (in 'n kar)

occupa'tion beroep, ambag, besigheid, bedryf; ~**al disea'se** beroepsiekte; ~ **haz'ard** beroepsrisiko; ~**al ther'apy** arbeidsterapie

occ'upy (v) besit; besig hou; bewoon, gebruik, okkupeer; beklee ('n pos)

occur' (v) voorkom, voorval, gebeur; byval; *it* ~*red to me* dit het my bygeval

o'cean (n) oseaan, wêreldsee

o'clock' op die klok; *it is ten* ~ dis tienuur

octag'onal agthoekig

octane' oktaan

o'ctave oktaaf

Octob'er Oktober

oc'topus -es, ..pi seekat, oktopus

oc'ulist oogdokter, oogarts; oogkundige

odd onewe, ongelyk; snaaks, koddig; ~ *and even* gelyk en ongelyk; ~**ly** snaaks, koddig; ~**ments** oorskietsels, afvalstukke

odds onenigheid; ongelykheid; waarskynlikheid; *the* ~ *are* die kans bestaan; *fight against* ~ teen die oormag stry

ode (n) ode, lofsang/lofdig

o'dious haatlik, verfoeilik, walglik

o'dour geur, reuk *also* **aro'ma**

of van, uit, aan; *she* ~ *all people* dat dit juis sy moet wees; *the city* ~ *Pretoria* die stad Pretoria

off (a) ander; regter=; *the* ~ *season* die slap tyd; (adv) af, weg, ver/vêr vandaan, van;

hands ~*!* hande tuis!; *be well* ~ welgesteld wees; (prep) van, van . . . af; ~ *Church Street* uit Kerkstraat; ~ *duty* van diens af

o'ffal afval (vleis); oorskiet

off'-chance moontlikheid; geluk; vir geval

off-col'our van stryk; kroes, olik

off'-course (a) buitebaan (totalisator)

off'-cut afvalstuk

offence' (n) oortreding, misdryf; *give* ~ aanstoot gee

offend' (v) beledig; ~**ed** beledig, kwaad; ~**er** oortreder, misdadiger

offen'sive (n) aanval, offensief; (a) beledigend aanstootlik; stuitig

off'er (n) aanbod, aanbieding; bod; (v) aanbied, bied; offer; ~ *an apology* verskoning maak; ~**ing** offerande

off'-hand (a) kortaf, hooghartig; ongeërg

off'ice kantoor; amp, diens; ~ **bear'er** beampte, ampsdraer; amp(s)bekleër; ~ **hours** kantoorure

off'icer offisier; amptenaar, beampte

offi'cial (n) amptenaar, beampte; (a) amptelik offisieel; ~ **car** ampsmotor; ~ **coun'terpart** ampsgenoot; ~ **jour'nal** lyfblad

offi'ciate optree; ~ *as* optree/fungeer as

off'ish uit die hoogte, eenkant (houding)

off'-peak afspits; ~ **traf'fic** slapverkeer

off'-ramp afrit, uitrit (verkeer)

off'-road ra'cing veldrenne (motorkarre)

off'-sales buiteverkope/buiteverbruik (drank)

off'-season buiteseisoen(s)

off'set (n) teenrekening; (v) verreken (teen) goedmaak; neutraliseer

off'shoot loot, uitspruitsel, tak

off'-shore aflandig, seewaarts (wind)

off'side onkant (sport)

off'spring (n) kroos, spruite, nakomelingskap

off'-street par'king buitenstraatse parkering

off'-white naaswit

o'ften dikwels, baiemaal/baiekeer, baie maal baie keer

oil (n) olie; (v) olie (gee); ~ **consump'tion** olieverbruik; ~ **pipe'line** oliepypleiding; ~ **pain'ting** olieverfskildery; ~ **rig** olieboor ~ **slick** olieslik/oliekol; ~**stone** oliesteen slypsteen

oint'ment (n) salf, smeergoed

O.K. reg, okei *also* **okay'**

oka'pi -s boskameelperd, okapi (dier)

old oud, ou; ouderwets; *as* ~ *as the hills* so oud soos die Kaapse wapad; *of* ~ vanouds

vanmelewe; ~-**fash'ioned** ouderwets, ou=
tyds; ~-**a'ge home** ouetehuis, tehuis vir be=
jaardes; ~ **pupil/ex-pu'pil** oudleerling; **O**~
Tes'tament Ou Testament; ~-**ti'mer** ringkop
olean'der selonsroos, oleander (blom)
o'live (n) olyf; ~ **oil** olyfolie
olym'piad (n) olimpiade (wisk., wetenskap)
Olym'pic Olimpies; ~ **games** Olimpiese spele
om'budsman ombudsman, burgerregtewaker
see **pub'lic protec'tor**
om'elet (n) (eier)struif, omelet
om'en (n) voorteken; (v) voorspel
om'inous (a) onheilspellend, dreigend
omi'ssion weglating, uitlating, versuim
omit' (v) weglaat, uitlaat; versuim
on (a) aangeskakel; (adv) aan, deur, op; ver=
der; (prep) op, in, aan, te, na, bo, met, teen;
~ *account of* as gevolg van/weens; ~
business met/vir sake; ~ *duty* op/aan diens;
~ *call* op roep (dokter); ~ *form* op stryk; ~
holiday met/op vakansie; ~ *purpose* op=
setlik; ~ *time* betyds, op tyd
once (n) eenmaal; (a) vroeër; (adv) eendag,
eens, eenmaal; ~ *again* nog 'n keer, nog
eenmaal; *at* ~ dadelik; ~ *in a blue moon*
baie selde; ~ *upon a time* eendag
on'coming (a) naderende; ~ **traf'fic** aanko=
mende verkeer, teenverkeer
one (n) een; *little* ~*s* die kleintjies; (a) een,
enigste, ~ *for the road* loopdop (drinkie);
(pron) een; iemand, 'n mens; ~ *and all*
almal; *every* ~ elkeen; ~-**act play** eenbe=
dryf; ~-**horse town** dooiedonkiedorp
on'ion ui
on'line compu'ter (n) inbaanrekenaar
on'looker toeskouer, aanskouer (mens)
on'ly (a) enigste; *the* ~ *of its kind* enig in sy
soort; (adv) alleen, slegs, maar net; ~ *too*
glad maar alte bly
onomatopoe'ia (n) klanknabootsing, onoma=
topee
on'ramp oprit, inrit (verkeer)
on'slaught aanval, bestorming
on'us (no pl) (bewys)las; verpligting; onus; *the*
~ *rests on/upon him* die onus rus op hom
on'ward voorwaarts, verder
on'yx -es oniks; ~ **mar'ble** oniksmarmer
ooze (n) slyk, slik; sug (wond); (v) sypel/syfer
op'al opaal
op'en (n) ruimte; oopte; (v) oopmaak; open
(konferensie); oopstel; begin; (a, adv) oop/
deursigtig; openhartig; blootgestel; ~-**air**

muse'um opelugmuseum; ~ **cast** oopgroef
(myn); ~ **day** ope dag; ~-**en'ded** oopkeuse
(vraag); ~**er** inleier (debat); oopmaker,
oopsnyer; ~**ing** opening, kans; ~**ly** openlik
op'era opera; ~ **com'pany** operageselskap; ~
glas'ses toneelkyker
op'erate (v) werk; opereer; bedien (masjien)
op'erating: ~ **costs** bedryfskoste; ~ **the'atre**
operasiesaal/teater
opera'tion operasie; bewerking; werking;
verrigting; bediening; *in* ~ in werking
op'erative (a) werksaam; operatief; doeltref=
fend; *become* ~ in werking tree
op'erator (n) werker, bediener; operateur
ophthal'mic (a) oog=; ~ **sur'geon** oogarts,
oftalmoloog
opin'ion (n) opinie; mening; sienswyse; oor=
deel; *be of* ~ van mening wees; *have a high*
~ *of* 'n hoë dunk hê van; *in my* ~ na/vol=
gens my mening; *public* ~ openbare me=
ning; ~ **for'mer** meningvormer; ~ **poll** me=
ningspeiling/meningsopname
op'ium (n) opium, heulsap
oppo'nent teenstander, opponent
opportu'nity . .ties geleentheid, kans
oppose' (v) opponeer, teenwerk
opp'osite (n) die teenoorgestelde; (a) teen=
oorgestel; teengestel; ~ *number* teëhanger;
the ~ *sex* die ander geslag; (adv) oorkant,
anderkant; (prep) teenoor, regoor
opposi'tion (n) teenstand, opposisie; teenparty
oppress' (v) onderdruk, verdruk; ~**ion** onder=
drukking, verdrukking; neerslagtigheid; ~**or**
onderdrukker, tiran
op'tical gesigs=, opties; ~ **illu'sion** gesigs=
bedrog
opti'cian (n) brilmaker, optisiën, optikus
optimis'tic optimisties, hoopvol
op'timum optimaal (produksie), gunstigste
op'tion (n) opsie, keuse; *the* ~ *of a fine* boe=
tekeuse; ~**al** opsioneel; ~**al sub'ject** keu=
sevak
op'ulent (a) ryk, vermoënd *also* **af'fluent**
op'us (no pl) werk, opus
or of; *either* . . . ~, óf . . . óf
or'acle (n) godspraak, orakel
or'al mondeling; mond=; ~ **examina'tion**
mondelinge eksamen
or'ange lemoen, soetlemoen; oranje(kleur); ~
squash lemoenkwas
orang'utang' orangoetang
or'ator spreker, redenaar (mens)

orb'it (v) wentel; (n) wentelbaan; oogholte
orch'ard boord, vrugteboord
or'chestra orkes
or'chid orgidee (blom)
ord'er (n) orde, volgorde; order, bevel; op=
    drag; bestelling (van goedere); *cash with* ∼
    kontant met bestelling; *in* ∼ *that* sodat; *out*
    of ∼ buite werking, stukkend; *place an* ∼
    bestel; (v) bestel; reël; beveel; ∼ *about*
    rondkommandeer; ∼ **form** bestelvorm; ∼**ly**
    (n) lyfdienaar, ordonnans; (a) ordelik
ord'inal (n) rangtelwoord
ord'inance reglement; ordinansie (kerklik);
    ordonnansie (provinsie); voorskrif
ord'inary (a) gewoon, gebruiklik; *something*
    out of the ∼ iets ongewoons/buitengewoons
ore erts; ∼ **crusher** ertsbreker, vergruiser
or'gan (n) orgaan; orrel (mus.); werktuig; ∼**s**
    of speech spraakorgane; ∼ **do'nor** orgaan=
    skenker; ∼ **reci'tal** orreluitvoering
org'anist orrelis (mens)
organisa'tion inrigting/instelling, organisasie
org'anise (v) organiseer; inrig; ∼**d** georgani=
    seer; ∼**r** organiseerder, organisator
org'anising commit'tee reëlingskomitee
or'gy orgies swelgparty, drinkparty, orgie
or'ibi (n) oorbietjie, oribie (bokkie)
orienta'tion oriëntering; ontgroening, inbur=
    gering, induksie *also* **induc'tion**
o'rigin (n) oorsprong, bron; herkoms
ori'ginal (n) oertipe; (a) oorspronklik
orn'ament (n) sieraad, ornament; (pl) tierlan=
    tyntjies; (v) versier, tooi, verfraai
ornamen'tal (a) sierlik, versierend; fraai, de=
    koratief; ∼ **shrub** sierstruik
ornithol'ogist voëlkenner, ornitoloog (mens)
orph'an (n) weeskind; (a) wees=, ouerloos;
    ∼**age** weeshuis
orthodon'tist (n) ortodontis (tandheelkundige)
orth'odox (a) regsinnig, ortodoks
orthog'raphy ortografie, spellingleer
orthopae'dic ortopedies; ∼**s** ortopedie; ∼
    sur'geon ortopedis/ortopeed
os'trich -es volstruis; ∼ **farm** volstruisplaas;
    ∼ **fea'ther** volstruisveer
o'ther (n, pron, a) ander; anders; *the* ∼ *day*
    nou die dag; *on the* ∼ *hand* aan die ander
    kant; ∼ *than* behalwe
o'therwise anders(ins); origens
ott'er otter (waterdier)
ought (v) behoort, moet; *you* ∼ *to do it* jy
    behoort dit te doen; *he* ∼ *to have said it* hy

behoort dit te gesê het
ounce ons
our ons
ours ons s'n; *he likes* ∼ *better* hy hou meer
    van ons s'n
our'selve/our'selves ons, onsself
out (a) nie tuis nie; (adv, prep) uit, weg, buite;
    ∼ *of breath* uitasem; ∼ *of print* uit druk; ∼
    of the question buite die kwessie; ∼ *of town*
    uitstedig; ∼ *of work* werkloos
out'board buiteboords; ∼ **mo'tor** buiteboord=
    motor
out: ∼**come** uitbreking; uitbraak (van epide=
    mie); ∼**buil'ding** buitegebou; ∼**burst** uitbars=
    ting; ∼**cast** (n) balling; verstoteling (mens)
outclass' vêr oortref/oorskadu; *we were* ∼*ed*
    hulle was veels te sterk vir ons
out: ∼**come** resultaat, uitslag; ∼**cry** lawaai,
    geskree(u); ∼**do** oortref; ∼*do someone* iem.
    ore aansit; ∼**door** buite=, buitelug=
out'er buite; uiterste; ∼ **dark'ness** buitenste
    duisternis
out'fit uitrusting, uitset; ∼**ter** uitruster
out: ∼**flow** uitvloei(ing); uitloop; ∼**going** af=
    tredende; uittredende (voorsitter); ∼**house**
    buitegebou; ∼**ing** uitstappie, kuier
outland'ish vreemd, uitlands, uitheems
outlast' (v) oorleef, langer duur
out'law (n) balling, voëlvryverklaarde; (v)
    ban, voëlvry verklaar
out'lay (n) uitgawe, koste; besteding
out'let verkooppunt, afsetpunt
out'line (v) skets; *in* ∼ in hooftrekke
out'look (n) vooruitsig; beskouing
out'lying·ver/vêr, afgeleë (distrik)
outnum'ber oortref; *they were* ∼*ed* hulle was
    in die minderheid
out-of-date verouder *also* **outmo'ded/obso=**
    le'te onvanpas
out'-of-doors' buite(ns)huis, buite
out-of-pock'et: ∼ **expen'ses** klein/los uitga=
    wes; sakgeld
out: ∼**patient** buitepasiënt; ∼**post** voorpos,
    buitepos; ∼**put** opbrengs, produksie, uitset
outra'geous skandelik/skandalig, verregaande
out'reach: ∼ **pro'gramme** uitreikprogram
out'right volkome, volstrek; openlik, onom=
    wonde; ∼ **major'ity** volstrekte meerderheid
out'room buitekamer
out'set begin, aanvang; *at (from) the* ∼ uit die
    staanspoor
out'side (n) uiterlik; buitekant; (a) buite=,

uiterste; (prep) buite, buitekant; ∼r oninge=
wyde; buitestander; outsider (lett.); buite=
perd; ∼ **chance** buitekans

out′size buitemaat, ekstra groot

out′skirts grens, buitewyk (van stad)

out′span (n) uitspanning, uitspanplek; (v) uit=
span

outspo′ken openhartig, reguit

out′standing onbetaal/uitstaande (skulde); uit=
stekend; uitmuntend

out′ward (n) uiterlik; (a) uiterlik, uitwendig;
(adv) uitwaarts; ∼ **jour′ney** heenreis, uit=
reis; ∼ **pol′icy** uitwaartse beleid

out′wit uitoorlê, flous, fnuik *also* **out′smart**

ov′al (n) krieketveld; (a) ovaal

ov′ary ..ries eierstok, vrugbeginsel (bot.)

ova′tion (n) hulde, ovasie, toejuiging

o′ven oond

ov′er (n) boulbeurt (krieket); (adv) oor; om,
onderstebo; *hand* ∼ oorhandig; *run* ∼ iem.
raakry; (prep) oor, uit, bo, op; ∼ *and above*
bo en behalwe, boonop, bowendien

ov′erall (n) oorpak; (pl) oorklere; (a) totaal;
algeheel; ∼ **win′ner** algehele wenner

o′verboard oorboord

overburd′en (v) oorlaai (met take, opdragte)

overcast′ (a) bewolk, betrokke

over′charge (n) oorvordering *also* **rip-off**; (v)
he ∼*d me* hy het my oorvra

ov′ercoat (oor)|as

overcome′ (v) oormeester; oorkom, baasraak;
(a) aangedaan, verslae; ∼ *with grief* deur
droefheid oormeester

over′con′fident oormoedig; oorgerus

ov′erdraft (n) oortrokke bankrekening

ov′erdrive (n) snelrat, spoedrat

overdue′ agterstallig (skuld, paaiemente)

overgrow′ oorgroei, toegroei

ov′ergrowth (n) uitwas, oorgroeisel

overhaul′ (v) herstel; opknap/opdoen

ov′erhead (a) lug=, oorhoofs, oorkoepelend;
bogronds; ∼ **cam′shaft** bo-nokas; ∼ **ex=
pen′ses** bokoste; ∼ **projec′tor** truprojektor;
∼ **rail′way** lugspoor

overjoy′ed (a) verruk, opgetoë *also* **delight′ed**

overlap′ (v) oorvleuel

overleaf′ keersy; *see* ∼ blaai om *also* **PTO**

overlock′er (sewing machine) omkap(naai)=
masjien

overlook′ oor die hoof sien, verskoon

ov′ernight die vorige nag, oornag

ov′erpopulated (a) oorbevolk

overpow′er (v) oorweldig, oorstelp

overrate′ oorskat; ∼**d** (a) oorskat

overreact′ (v) oorreageer

overrule′ verwerp (voorstel) *also* **overri′de,
coun′termand**; van die hand wys (be=
swaar)

ov′erseas oorsee; ∼ **mail** oorsese pos

ov′erseer (n) opsigter, opsiener, toesighouer

overshad′ow oorskadu, oortref *also* **out′class**

ov′ersight (n) vergissing, fout, versuim

oversleep′ (v) jou verslaap

ov′erstatement oorbeklemtoning

overstrung′ (a) oorspanne *also* **tense**

over′supply (n) oorvoorsiening (mark); oor=
aanbod

overtake′: ∼ *a car* 'n motor/kar verbysteek

overthrow′ (v) omverwerp, oorwin; tot 'n val
bring (regering)

ov′ertime (n) oortyd (diens); ∼ **pay** oortyd=
betaling

ov′erture (n) voorspel, ouverture; uitnodiging;
voorstel; *make* ∼*s* toenadering soek

overturn′ onderstebo keer, omkeer

overwhelm′ (v) oorweldig, oorrompel; ∼**ing**
oorweldigend, verpletterend; ∼**ing support′**
oorweldigende steun/belangstelling

overwork′ oorwerk, te veel werk

ov′um ova eier; eiersel (bot.)

owe (v) skuld, verskuldig wees, te danke

ow′ing (a) onbetaal, verskuldig; *the amount* ∼
die verskuldigde bedrag; (prep) weens,
vanweë; danksy; ∼ *to an error* weens 'n
fout

owl uil (voël); uilskuiken, domkop, swaap

own¹ (v) besit; erken, erken

own² (a) eie; *of one's* ∼ *accord* uit eie
beweging; ∼**er** eienaar; besitter; ∼**ership**
eiendomsreg; eienaarskap (van 'n huis)

ox -en os; *young* ∼ tollie; ∼**bow** rivierdraai;
∼**bow lake** kronkelmeer; ∼**braai** osbraai

oxida′tion oksidasie

ox′wagon ossewa

ox′ygen suurstof; ∼ **thief (OT)** nuttelose mens

oys′ter oester; ∼ **cul′ture** oesterteelt

oz′one (n) osoon; ∼ **friend′ly** osoonvrien=
delik

P

pace (n) tree, pas; gang; tempo; vaart; *keep ~ with* tred hou met; (v) stap; aftree; die pas aangee; ~**ma'ker** pasaangeër (hart); ~**set'ter** pasmaker (mens)

paci'fic vreedsaam, stil; **P~ O'cean** Stille Oseaan

pa'cifist (n) pasifis, vrede(s)voorstander (mens)

pack (n) pak; vrag; ~**ed hall** stampvol saal; ~ **of ro'gues** bende skurke; (v) pak, inpak; ~**age** pakket (salaris; uittrede); ~**age deal** pakketakkoord; ~**age tour** groeptoer; ~**et** pakkie/pakket; ~**ing** verpakking

pact (n) verdrag, verbond, ooreenkoms, pakt

pad (n) kussinkie; skryfblok; beenskut; (v) opvul; volstop; ~**ding** vulsel

padd'le¹ (v) plas; speel; waggel

padd'le² (n) roeispaan; skepper; (v) pagaai; roei; ~ **skiing** skiroei; ~ **skier** skiroeier; ~ **wheel** skeprat

padd'ling pool plaspoel, plasdammetjie

pad'dock kamp; renbaanperk

pad'lock (n) hangslot; (v) toesluit

pad're (n) priester; kapelaan, veldprediker

paediatri'cian kinderarts, pediater (mens)

paedophi'lia pedofiel *also* **child moles'ter**

pa'gan (n) heiden; (a) heidens

page¹ (n) (hotel)bode, hoteljoggie; livreikneg; (v) spoor, roepsoek; ~**er** roepradio, spoorder

page² (n) bladsy, pagina; (v) pagineer

pag'eant optog, skouspel, vertoning; **pomp and** ~**try** prag en praal

page' boy -s hoteljoggie; slipdraertjie

paid betaal; voldaan; *reply* ~ antwoord betaal(d) *see* **pay**

pail (n) emmer, dopemmer *also* **buck'et**

pain (n) pyn, smart, leed; (pl) moeite, inspanning; (v) seer maak, pyn; kwel; bedroef; ~**ful** pynlik, seer, smartlik; ~**kil'ler** pyndoder, pynstiller; ~**less** pynloos

painsta'king (a) fluks, vlytig; presies

paint (n) verf; (v) verf; skilder; ~ *the town red* fuif, jollifikasie hou; ~**brush** verfkwas; ~**er** verwer (ambag); (kuns)skilder; ~**ing** skildery; skilderkuns; ~ **remo'ver** verfstroper

pair (n) paar; ~ *of scissors* skêr; ~ *of spectacles* bril; ~ *of trousers* broek; (v) paar; saampas; ~ *off* afpaar

pal (n) maat, makker; tjom(mie); *jobs for* ~*s*

baantjies vir boeties; (v) omgaan met; ~ *up* maats maak

pal'ace (n) paleis

pal'ate verhemelte/gehemelte; **cleft** ~ gesplete verhemelte

pale (v) verbleek; (a) bleek, vaal, flets; dof

pall'bearer (slip)draer (by begrafnis)

pall'et pottebakkerskyf, palet; hegstrook; laaikis, laaiplank (vir vrag)

palm¹ (n) palm(boom); segepalm

palm² (n) palm (hand); (v) inpalm; hanteer; streel; omkoop; ~ *off upon* afsmeer aan; ~ **grea'sing** omkopery; omkoopgeld; ~**ist** handkyker/handleser; ~ **oil** palmolie

pal'pitate klop (hart)

pal'sied verlam; gestrem; geraak; **cer'ebral** ~ serebraal verlam/gestrem

pam'per (v) vertroetel, bederf, piep *also* **spoil**

pamph'let pamflet; bladskrif, vlugskrif, voublad, strooibiljet, blaadjie

pan (n) pan; pan (watervlak); (v) was

pan'cake (n) pannekoek

pandemon'ium (n) uitbarsting, hel, pandemonium *also* **bed'lam, ut'ter confu'sion**

pane ruit; paneel; vak

pan'el (n) paneel; naamlys; strook; ~**bea'ter** duikklopper/paneelklopper; ~**ling** paneelwerk; ~ **van** paneelwa

pan'ga kapmes, panga

pan'golin ietermagô, miervreter

pan'handle pypsteel (straat)

pan'ic (n) skrik, paniek; (a) paniekerig; ~**ky** paniekerig; ~ **but'ton** angsknop(pie); ~ **sta'tions** skarreltyd; ~**-strick'en** paniekbevange

panora'ma (n) panorama, vergesig *also* **vis'ta**

pan'sy pansies gesiggie, viooltjie; verwyfde mansmens (neerh.)

pant (n) gehyg; (v) hyg, snak, kortasem wees

pan'ther panter; ~ **lil'y** tierlelie

pan'tie knapbroekie, damesbroekie

pan'tihose kousbroekie

pan'try pantries spens *also* **lar'der**

pants' broek (in VSA); onderbroek (Eng.)

papa' (n) pa, pappie

pa'paw papaja (vrug)

pa'per (n) papier; vraestel; koerant; verhandeling; *read a* ~ 'n (voor)lesing hou; (v) plak, behang; (a) papier=; ~**back** slapband(boek);

~ **bag** kardoes, papiersakkie; ~ **chase** snipperjag; ~ **clip** skuifspeld; papierknyper; ~ **fas'tener** papierspy; ~ **han'ger** plakker, behanger; ~ **knife** papiermes; ~ **mill** papierfabriek; ~ **mon'ey/cur'rency** papiergeld
par pari, gelykheid; (baan)syfer (gholf)
par'able (n) gelykenis, parabel
pa'rachute (n) valskerm; (v) valspring
pa'rachutist val(skerm)springer (mens)
para'de (n) parade, vertoon, optog; wapenskou(ing); (a) paradeer
pa'radise (n) paradys, lushof; hemel
pa'radox -es paradoks; teenstrydigheid
pa'raffin paraffien, lampolie; ~ **stove** paraffienstoof, pompstofie
pa'ragraph (n) paragraaf; (v) paragrafeer
pa'rakeet parkiet; **grass** ~ budjie
pa'rallel (n) parallel, ewewydige lyne; *without* ~ sonder weerga; (a) parallel, ewewydig; ~ **bars** brug; ~**ism** parallelisme, vergelyking; ~**-me'dium school** parallel(medium)skool
pa'ralyse (v) verlam; magteloos maak
para'lysis (n) verlamming, beroerte; magteloosheid; **in'fantile** ~ kinderverlamming
paramed'ic paramedikus/mediese ordonnans *also* **med'ic** (person)
pa'ramount hoogste, vernaamste; *of* ~ *importance* van die allergrootste belang; ~ **chief** opperhoof
parapherna'lia bybehore; rommel *also* **odd'ments**
pa'raphrase (n) parafrase; (v) parafraseer
puraple'gic (n) parapleeg (mens); (a) paraplegies
pa'rasite (n) parasiet; woekerplant; klaploper
par'asol (son)sambreel, sonskerm
pa'ratroops valskermtroepe
par'cel (n) pakkie, pakket; (v) inpak; verdeel; ~ **post** pakketpos
parch opdroog, verseng, versmag; ~**ed** verdroog, verskroei; (n) ~**ment** perkament
pard'on (n) vergifnis, pardon, ekskuus; *I beg your* ~ ekskuus, verskoon my; (v) vergewe, kwytskeld; begenadig; verskoon
par'ent (n) ouer; vader, moeder; (a) oorspronklik, moeder=; ~**age** afkoms
paren'tal ouerlik; ~ **care** ouersorg
paren'thesis ..ses parentese, hakies ( ); *in* ~ tussen hakies *also* **in brack'ets**
Pa'ris Parys; **plas'ter of** ~ gips
pa'rish (n) gemeente *also* **congrega'tion**; parogie

pa'rity gelykheid, pariteit, pari
park (n) park, wildtuin; (v) parkeer; *no* ~*ing* geen parkering; ~**ade** parkade; ~**ing a'rea/bay** staanplek/parkeerplek; ~**ing atten'dant** parkeerbeampte
Park'town prawn (n) koringkriek *also* **corn/har'vester cricket**
parl'iament (n) parlement
parl'our sitkamer, voorkamer; ontvang(s)kamer; ontvanglokaal (burgemeester); **beauty** ~ skoonheidsalon
pa'rody (n) parodie; spotskrif; (v) parodieer
parole' parool; erewoord, wagwoord
parq'uet: ~ **floor(ing)** blokkiesvloer
par'rot (n) papegaai; na-aper; (v) napraat
pars'ley pietersielie (groente)
pars'on predikant, dominee; ~**age** pastorie
part (n) deel; onderdeel, aandeel; *pirate* ~ roofonderdeel; ~*s of speech* rededele; *take* ~ *in* deelneem aan; *take somebody's* ~ iem. se kant kies; (v) deel, verdeel; ~ *with* afstand doen van
partake' (v) deelneem, deel in
par'tial gedeeltelik; partydig; *be* ~ *to* voortrek, partydig wees vir
parti'cipant (n) deelnemer; deelhebber
parti'cipate (v) deelneem, meedoen (aan spel/sport)
participa'tion deelneming, deelname; inspraak; ~ **bond** deelneemverband
par'ticiple deelwoord
part'icle (n) deeltjie, greintjie, sprankie
partic'ular (n) besonderheid; *in* ~*s* in besonderhede; (a) kieskeurig, puntene(u)rig; noukeurig; *a* ~ *friend* 'n intieme vriend
partic'ularly veral, vernaamlik; by uitstek
part'ing (n) deling, skeiding; paadjie (in die hare); ~ **meal** galgemaal
partisan' (n) partyganger; volgeling; partisaan
parti'tion (n) afdeling; partisie; afskorting; (v) afskort
part'ly gedeeltelik
part'ner (n) maat; deelhebber; vennoot; *sleeping* ~ stil/rustende vennoot; ~**ship** vennootskap: *dissolve a* ~*ship* 'n vennootskap ontbind; **spar'ring** ~ skermmaat (boks)
part'ridge patrys (voël)
part-time deeltyds; ~ **cour'ses** deeltydse/na-uurse kursusse; ~ **min'ister** tentmaker (predikant, geestelike)
part'y ..ties party, instansie; party(tjie), makietie; ~ **whip** partysweep

pass[1] (n) **-es** nek, bergpas; deurgang (by berge)
pass[2] (n) **-es** pas; aangee (voetbal); slaag
(eksamen); (v) verbygaan; passeer; aangee;
slaag (eksamen); vel (vonnis); ~ *away* ver=
dwyn; sterf; ~ *a bill* 'n wetsontwerp aan=
neem; ~ *an examination* (in) 'n eksamen
slaag; ~ *a sentence* vonnis; ~**able** gangbaar
also **ad'equate**; begaanbaar, rybaar (pad);
~**mark** slaagpunt
pass'age (n) gang, deurgang; oortog; reisgeld;
birds of ~ trekvoëls
pass'book bankboek, depositoboek; bewysboek
pass'enger passasier; ~ **li'ner** passasierskip;
~ **plane** passasierstraler
pa'ssing (a) verbygaande; ~**-out para'de** voor=
stel(lings)parade
pas'sion (n) hartstog, drif, passie/liefde; woede
pas'sionate (a) hartstogtelik, vurig
pas'sion: ~ **flo'wer** passieblom; ~ **play** pas=
siespel; **P~ Week** Lydensweek
pass'ive (n) lydende vorm; ~ **resis'tance**
lydelike verset; ~ **voice** lydende vorm
Passov'er Joodse Paasfees
pass'port paspoort
pass'word (n) wagwoord
past (n) verlede; (a) verlede, oud=; (adv, prep)
verby, langs, oor; **ten** ~ **nine** tien na/oor
nege; ~ **stu'dent** oudstudent
paste (n) gom; deeg; pasta (vir tande)
pas'tel (n) pastel, papierkryt
pas'time (n) tydverdryf, stokperdjie
pas'tor predikant, herder; pastor (Prot.); pas=
toor (R.K./Prot.) *also* **cler'gyman**
pas'toral: ~ **play** herderspel; ~ **vis'it** huisbe=
soek
pas'try ..ries deeg; tert, soetgebak
pas'ture (n) weiveld, gras; weiding; (v) wei
pat (n) tikkie, klappie; (v) tik, streel; (adv)
vanpas, toepaslik; *know off* ~ op jou duim=
pie ken; ~**-a-cake** handjie-klap
patch (n) **-es** lap, stuk; (v) lap, heelmaak; ~ *up*
lap, saamflans; ~**work** lapwerk; laplas=
(werk)
pâté' patee (gereg)
pa'tent (n) patent, oktrooi; (a) vanselfspre=
kend; ~ **leat'her** glansleer; ~ **med'icine**
huismiddel
patern'al vaderlik; ~**ism** paternalisme
path pad, weg, baan
pathet'ic (a) aandoenlik, pateties, roerend
pathol'ogist patoloog (spesialis)
pa'tience (a) geduld, lydsaamheid

pa'tient (n) pasiënt, sieke; (a) geduldig
pa'tio (n) patio, (buite)stoep
pat'riarch aartsvader, patriarg
pat'riotism vaderlandsliefde, patriotisme
patrol' (n) patrollie; (v) patrolleer
pa'tron (n) beskermheer; gereelde besoeker;
(pl) klandisie; ~ **saint** beskermheilige
patt'ern (n) patroon, voorbeeld; model
pat'typan (n) krulpampoentjie
paunch -es pens; ~**-bel'lied** boepens=
paup'er armlastige, behoeftige, pouper
pause (n) pouse, verposing, rustyd; (v) rus,
wag, pouseer
pave plavei, bevloer; uitlê; ~ *the way for* die
weg baan vir; ~**ment** plaveisel; sypaadjie
also **si'dewalk**
pavil'ion pawiljoen/paviljoen; tent
paw (n) poot, klou; (v) krap, skop; betas
pawn (n) pand; pion; (v) verpand; ~**bro'ker**
pandjieshouer; ~**shop** pandjieswinkel
pay (n) betaling, loon, soldy; (v) betaal;
beloon; vereffen; ~ *one a compliment* iem.
'n kompliment maak; ~ *a dividend* 'n divi=
dend uitbetaal/uitkeer; ~ *off* afbetaal; af=
dank; ~ *out* uitbetaal; ~ *up* opdok, betaal;
~ *a visit* besoek; ~**able** betaalbaar; ~**-as-
you-earn (PAYE)** lopende belastingstelsel
(LBS); ~ **chan'nel** betaalkanaal (TV);
~**day** betaaldag; ~**ee'** ontvanger; ~**er** be=
taler; ~**mas'ter** betaalmeester; ~**ment** beta=
ling; ~**roll**/~**sheet** betaalstaat
pea ertjie; **green** ~ dop-ertjie; **sweet** ~*s*
pronk-ertjies, blom-ertjies
peace (n) vrede, rus; kalmte; *justice of the* ~
vrederegter; ~**-loving** vredeliewend; ~ **of'-
fering** soenoffer
peach (n) **-es** perske; *a* ~ *of a girl* 'n beeld van
'n nooi; ~ **bran'dy** perskebrandewyn, pers=
kesnaps; mampoer
pea: ~**cock** pou; ~**hen** pouwyfie
peak (n) punt, spits; top; (v) piek
peak: ~ **pe'riod** spitstyd, spitsuur; ~ **traf'fic**
spitsverkeer
pea'nut grondboon(tjie); ~ **but'ter** grond=
boontjiebotter
pear peer (vrug)
pearl (n) pêrel; (a) pêrel=; *cast* ~*s before (the)
swine* pêrels voor die swyne werp/gooi; ~
di'ver pêrelvisser
pea'sant (klein)boer, landman; ~**ry** boerestand
pea' soup ertjiesop
peat (n) veen, (moeras)turf

peb'ble spoelklippie
pe'cannut pekanneut
peck (n) hap; pik; (v) pik; ~ at pik na; vit op;
~ing order (n) pikprioriteit; gesagsorde
pecu'liar (a) eienaardig; buitengewoon, snaaks
pecu'niary geldelik, geld=; ~ troubles geld=
nood
pedagog'ic opvoedkundig, pedagogies; ~s
opvoedkunde, pedagogie
ped'al (n) pedaal; trapper; (v) trap; fiets; ~ car
trapkar
pedant'ic (a) pedanties, verwaand
ped'estal voetstuk, onderstuk
pedes'trian (n) voetganger; (a) voet=, voetgan=
ger=; alledaags; ~ mall wandellaan; ~
traf'fic light voetganger(verkeers)lig
ped'igree (n) stamboom; geslagsregister; stam=
boek; (a) volbloed= also pu'rebred; ~ cattle/
stock stamboekvee
ped'lar (n) smous, venter also haw'ker
peel (n) skil; dop; (v) afskil; afdop
peep (n) kykie; (v) gluur, loer; P~ing Tom
(af)loerder, loervink; ~hole loergaatjie;
~show kykspel; ~sight gaatjievisier
peer (n) edelman; gelyke, eweknie/portuur; ~
group portuurgroep
peer (v) loer, gluur
peg (n) (tent)pen; kapstok; wasgoedknyper;
(v) vasslaan; afpen; ~ prices pryse vaspen
pel'ican pelikaan (voel)
pell'et (n) balletjie; pilletjie; koeëltjie; korrel;
~ gun windbuks
pel'met (n) gordynkap
pel'vic (a) bekken=; ~ massa'ge bekkenmasse=
ring
pel'vis (n) pelves bekken
pen¹ (n) hok, kraal; kampie
pen² (n) pen; (v) neerpen, skryf/skrywe
pen'al straf=; strafbaar; ~ise straf, beboet, pe=
naliseer
pen'alty (n) ..ties straf, (straf)boete; strafskop,
strafpunt
pen'cil potlood; write in ~ skryf met potlood;
~ box/~ case potloodkoker
pend (v) (laat) oorstaan
pen'dant (n) hangkroon; hanger(tjie), pendant
pen'dent (a) hangend; hang=; ~ watch hang=
horlosie; halshorlosie
pend'ing (a) hangende ('n gebeurtenis); onbeslis
pen'dulum -s slinger; pendule/pendulum
pen'etrate deurdring, penetreer
pen'etrating deurdringend, skerp; ~ oil pene=

treerolie
peng'uin pikkewyn
penicil'lin penisillien/penisilline
penin'sula skiereiland
pe'nis (n) penis also fal'lus
pen'itent (n) boeteling; (a) berouvol
peniten'tiary (n) strafgevangenis
pen: ~ name skuilnaam; skryfnaam; also
pseu'donym; ~pal penvriend; ~ por'trait
penskets; ~push'er pennelekker (mens),
klerk
penn'ant wimpel also strea'mer; driehoek=
vlaggie
penn'y pence, pennies pennie, dubbeltjie, oulap;
~ hor'rible sensasieverhaal; ~whis'tle kwe=
lafluit; ~wise agterstevoor suinig
pen'sion (n) pensioen; old-age ~ ouderdoms=
pensioen; retire on ~ met pensioen aftree;
(v) pensioeneer; (a) pensioens=; ~ed gepen=
sioeneer; ~er pensioentrekker, pensioe=
naris; ~ fund pensioenfonds; ~ mon'ey
kieriegeld (idiom.)
pen'sive (a) peinsend; swaarmoedig
pen'tagon vyfhoek
pentam'eter pentameter; iam'bic ~ vyfvoe=
tige jambe (versmaat)
pentath'lon vyfkamp (sport)
Pen'tecost Pinkster
pent'house (n) dakwoonstel; skermdak; ~
suite dakstel
peo'ple (n) mense; volk; nasie; he of all ~ juis
hy; (v) bevolk
pep (n) fut, lewe, pit; ~ pill opkikker(pil); ~
talk opkikpraatjie/motiveerpraatjie
pepp'er (n) peper; (v) peper; ~corn peper=
korrel; ~mint peperment/pipperment
per per, deur, deur middel van; ~ annum
jaarliks; ~ cent persent
peram'bulator (n) kinderwaentjie/stootwaen=
tjie also pram; meetwiel
per cent' persent; per honderd
percent'age (n) persentasie
percep'tion (n) insig, begrip, persepsie
perch (n) -es stokkie (in 'n voëlkou); slaap=
stok (hoenders)
percus'sion (n) skok, slag; ~ band slagorkes
perenn'ial (a) meerjarig (plant); standhoudend
(water)
perf'ect (n) voltooid teenwoordige tyd; (a)
volmaak; ideaal, volkome, perfek; ~ fluke
kolhou (gholf); ~ non'sense klinkklare onsin
perfect' (v) (ver)volmaak; voleindig, perfek=

sioneer; ~ *the art* die kuns verfyn

perfect′: ~**ion** volmaaktheid, perfeksie, voor=treflikheid; ~**ionist** perfeksionis (mens)

perf′orate (v) deurboor, perforeer

perform′ uitvoer; opvoer, voordra; verrig; ~ **a play** 'n toneelstuk opvoer

perform′ance (n) opvoering (toneel); uitvoe=ring (mus.); vervulling; werkverrigting, prestasie; ~ **apprai′sal** prestasiemeting

perform′ing: ~ **arts** uitvoérende kunste; ~ **group/com′pany** toneelgeselskap

perf′ume (n) reukwater, parfuum, laventel

perg′ola (n) prieel, pergola

perhaps′ miskien, dalk, altemit *also* **may′be**

pe′ril (n) gevaar; ~**ous** gevaarlik

perim′eter (n) omtrek, buitelyn, buitekant

per′iod tydperk, tydvak, tyd, periode; punt; volsin; termyn; ~**ic** periodiek

period′ical (n) tydskrif *also* **jour′nal, maga=zi′ne**; (a) gereeld, periodiek

per′iods maandstonde *also* **menstrua′tion**

periph′erals (n) randapparatuur (rek.)

pe′riscope periskoop

pe′rish vergaan, omkom; bederf; ~**able** be=derfbaar (vrugte)

pe′ri-urban buitestedelik, omstedelik

pe′riwig (n) pruik *also* **wig**

pe′riwinkle alikreukel/alikruik; katoog (plant)

perj′ury (n) meineed, woordbreuk

perk orent sit; ~**s** (n) byvoordele *also* **per′=quisites**; ~**y** astrant, parmantig

perlemoen′ (n) perlemoen *also* **ab′elone**; **moth′er-of-pearl**

perm′anent blywend, permanent; ~ **force** staande mag; ~ **wave** vasgolf (hare)

permiss′ible toelaatbaar, geoorloof

permiss′ion (n) verlof, vergunning, permissie; *give* ~ toestemming gee, die jawoord gee

permiss′ive toelaatbaar, permissief; ~**ness** permissiwiteit, toegeeflikheid

perm′it (n) permit, vrybrief, pas

permit′ (v) toelaat, veroorloof, vergun

perpendic′ular (n) loodlyn; (a) penregop; ver=tikaal, loodreg

perpet′ual onophoudelik, ewigdurend; ~ **mo′=tion** ewigdurende beweging

perplex′ (v) verwar, oorbluf, verbouereer

perq′uisite (n) byvoordeel *also* **fringe ben′efit, perk**

persecu′tion vervolging; ~ **ma′nia** vervol=gingswaan

persever′ance (n) volharding; uithouvermoë

persevere′ (v) volhard, aanhou, deurdruk

persimm′on tamatiepruim, persimmon

persist′ aanhou, volhard; volhou; ~**ent cough** aanhoudende hoes

pers′on persoon, mens; persoonlikheid; *every* ~ *who* elkeen/iedereen wat; *in* ~ persoon=lik; ~**age** persoon; ~**al** persoonlik, self; ~**al liabil′ity** persoonlike aanspreeklikheid, ~**al compu′ter (PC)** persoonlike rekenaar (PR)

personal′ity ..ties persoonlikheid

pers′onally persoonlik

personifica′tion (n) verpersoonliking, perso=nifiëring, personifikasie

personnel′ personeel *also* **staff**; ~ **man′age=ment** personeelbestuur

perspec′tive (n) perspektief; uitsig, vergesig

perspire′ (v) sweet, perspireer

persuade′ (v) oorhaal, ompraat; oorreed

persua′sion oorreding; oortuiging, geloof

pert′inent geskik, gepas, saaklik, ter sake

peru′sal deurlesing; *for* ~ ter insae

perverse′ pervers; eiewys; befoeterd

pes′simist pessimis (mens)

pessimis′tic (a) pessimisties, swaarmoedig

pest pes, plaag; ~ **control′** plaagbeheer; ~**ici′de** plaagdoder, insekdoder

pe′stle (n) (vysel)stamper

pet (n) troeteldier, hansdier; (v) vertroetel, streel; (a) geliefde; hans=; *one's* ~ *aversion/hate* jou doodsteek, jou grootste hekel; ~ **dog** skoothondjie; ~ **lamb** hanslam

pet′al (n) blomblaar

pet′er: ~ *out* doodloop, opraak

petit′ion (n) versoekskrif, beswaarskrif, petisie

pet name lieflingsnaam, troetelnaam

pet′rify (v) versteen *also* **har′den**; verstar

pe′trol petrol; ~ **atten′dant** pompjoggie; ~ **consump′tion** petrolverbruik

petrol′eum petroleum; aardolie

pet′rol: ~ **pump** petrolpomp; ~ **sta′tion** vul=stasie; ~ **tank** petroltenk

pet′shop (n) arkmark, troeteldierwinkel

pett′icoat onderrok; vrou; ~ **govern′ment** vroueregering

pett′y (a) onbeduidend *also* **insignif′icant**; nietig; ~ **cash** kleinkas

pew kerkbank

pew′ter (n) piouter, edeltin; tinkan

phan′tom spook, verskyning; (hersen)skim

pha′raoh farao

pha′risee fariseër, huigelaar, skynheilige

pharmaceut′ical (a) farmaseuties

pharm'acy apteek; artsenykunde

phase toestand, voorkome, verskynsel, stadi=
um, fase; ~ **out** uitfaseer

phea'sant fisant (voël)

phenom'enal (a) buitengewoon, merkwaardig

phenom'enon ..**mena** (natuur)verskynsel

philan'thropist filantroop, mensevriend

philat'elist posseëlversamelaar, filatelis

philharmon'ic filharmonies, musiekliewend

philos'opher wysgeer, filosoof (mens)

philos'ophy wysbegeerte, filosofie

pho'bia (n) fobie, sieklike vrees

phone (n) telefoon; (v) (op)bel, skakel; **cell**~
selfoon; ~**-in chat show** (radio) inbelpro=
gram

phonet'ics klankleer, fonetiek

pho'ney vals, nageboots *also* **hoax** (n)

phos'phate fosfaat

phos'phorus fosfor

pho'to -s (*abbrev. of* **pho'tograph**) foto, por=
tret; ~**copy** (n) fotokopie; (v) fotokopieer;
~**-finish** fotobeslissing (wedrenne); ~**gen'ic**
fotogenies

pho'tograph (n) portret, foto; (v) afneem,
fotografeer; ~ **al'bum** foto-album

photog'rapher afnemer, fotograaf (mens)

photog'raphy fotografie

phot'ostat fotostaat; fotostatiese afdruk

phrase (n) frase, sinsnede; (v) fraseer

phthis'is (n) longtering, myntering

phys'ical natuurkundig, fisies; liggaamlik, fi=
siek; ~ **educa'tion** liggaamsopvoeding/
menslike beweegkunde; ~ **science** natuur-
en skeikunde

physi'cian internis (spesialis); geneesheer, arts

phys'ics natuurkunde, fisika

physiol'ogy fisiologie, natuurleer

physiothe'rapist (n) fisioterapeut (mens)

physiothe'rapy fisioterapie

physique' liggaamsbou

pi'anist pianis, klavierspeler

pian'o -s piano, klavier; ~ **accom'paniment**
klavierbegeleiding

pick[1] (n) keuse; (die) beste; *the* ~ *of the bunch*
die allerbeste; (v) uitsoek

pick[2] (n) pik; tandestokkie; (v) pik; pluk; ~ *a*
bone with appeltjie skil met; ~ *and choose*
te kus en te keur; ~ *a quarrel with* rusie/
skoor soek met; ~ *up* optel, oplaai; oplig

pick'ax(e) kiel(houer)pik

pick'et brandwag; stakerswag/staakwag

pi'ckle (n) moeilikheid; pekel; (v) insout, inlê,
inmaak; ~**s** piekels; atjar, suurtjies

pick'-me-up (n) opknapper(tjie), sopie

pick'pocket sakkeroller, goudief

pick'-up toonopnemer (grammofoon); bakkie
(motor); ~ **van** bestelwa(entjie)

pic'nic (n) piekniek, veldparty; (v) piekniek
(hou) *also* **pic'nicking**

pic'ture (n) prent, skildery; afbeelding; (v)
beskryf; afbeeld; ~ **book** prenteboek; ~
puzzle soekprentjie

picturesque' (a) skilderagtig *also* **viv'id**

pie (n) pastei, tert; *have a finger in the* ~ in
iets betrokke wees

piece (n) stuk, deel; *give a* ~ *of one's mind*
goed die waarheid vertel; ~**work** stukwerk

pied bont, geskakeer; **P**~ **Pi'per** rottevanger
(van Hameln)

pier hawehoof, pier; pyler

pierce (v) deursteek, deurboor, 'n gat steek in

pi'ety vroomheid, piëteit

pif'fle bog, kaf, twak *also* **trash, tri'pe**

pig (n) vark, otjie; **gelded** ~ burg; **suck'ling** ~
speenvark

pi'geon (n) duif; ~**hole** (n) (pos)vakkie, loket

pig: ~**gery** varkboerdery, ottery; ~**gy-back**
heart abbahart; ~**gy bank** spaarvarkie/otpot;
~**-head'ed** eiesinnig, dom; ~**-iron** ruyster

pig'ment (n) kleurstof, pigment

pig: ~**sty** varkhok; ~**tail** varkstert; (pruik)=
stert; ~**weed** misbredie

pike[1] spies; lans; varswatersnoek

pike[2] tol, tolhek/tolboom *see* **toll'gate**

pil'chard sardyn, pelser (vis)

pile[1] (n) paal; pyler (brug); heipaal

pile[2] (n) hoop, massa, stapel; fortuin

piles aambeie

pil'fer (v) gaps, vaslê; ~**ing** stelery/vaslê

pil'grim pelgrim, ~**age** (n) pelgrimstog

pi'ling (n) heiwerk

pill (n) pil; **contracep'tive** ~ voorbehoedpil

pill'ar (n) pilaar; steunpilaar; *from* ~ *to post*
van Pontius na Pilatus

pill'ion (n) saal, kussing, agtersaaltjie

pill'ow (kop)kussing; peul; ~**case**/~**slip** kus=
singsloop

pil'ot (n) gids; stuurman (van boot); loods,
vlieënier; **automa'tic** ~ stuuroutomaat; (v)
lei, loods (vliegtuig)

pimp (n) koppelaar, pooier *also* **procu'rer**

pim'ple puisie

pin (n) speld; skroef; kegel; *be on* ~**s** *and*
needles op hete kole sit; (v) vasspeld; ~

al′ley kegelbaan

pin′cers (n) tangetjie; knyper, pinset

pinch (n) **-es** knyp; nood, verleentheid

pine[1] (n) pyn, den; pynappel

pine[2] (v) kwyn; ~ *away* wegkwyn; ~ *for* smag/hunker na

pine: ~**ap′ple** pynappel; ~ **cone** dennebol; ~ **tree** denneboom; ~**wood** dennehout, greinhout

pink[1] (n) toonbeeld; die beste; (a) pienk; ligrooi

pink[2] (v) pingel, klop (motor)

pinn′acle toppunt *also* **peak**; toringspits

pint pint; ~**-si′zed** klein (van gestalte)

pin′table spykertafel

pin′-up girl prikkelpop, kalendermeisie

pioneer′ (n) pionier, baanbreker

pi′ous (a) vroom, godvrugtig *also* **devout′**

pip[1] (n) vrugtepit

pip[2] (v) kafloop; raak skiet; troef/uitknikker

pipe (n) pyp; fluit; (pl) doedelsakke; ~**line** pypleiding (olie); ~**r** fluitspeler; ~**wrench** pypsleutel

pir′ate (n) seerower; letterdief; (v) plunder; ~ **part** roofonderdeel (motorhandel); ~ **vie′wer** roofkyker (TV)

piss (n, v) water, piepie; pis (*kru*)

pis′tol (n) pistool; **automat′ic** ~ outomatiese pistool

pis′ton (n) suier; klep; ~ **ring** suierring

pit (n) put, kuil; graf; afgrond; kuip (motorwedren); ~ *one's strength against* kragte meet met; ~ **bullter′rier** (Amerikaanse) veghond

pitch[1] (n) pik; ~**-dark** (a) pikdonker

pitch[2] (n) **-es** hoogte, toppunt; toonhoogte (mus.); kolfblad (krieket); (v) opslaan (tent); gooi (bal); ~ *camp* kamp opslaan; ~**ed roof** staandak

pitch′er kruik; kan

pit′fall (n) vangkuil/valkuil; valstrik

pit′iful (a) armsalig, ellendig; treurig

pit′y (n) medelye, jammer(te); *take* ~ *on* medelye hê met; *what a* ~ hoe jammer tog; (v) jammer kry

piv′ot (n) spil, draaipunt

plac′ard (n) plakkaat, aanplakbiljet

place (n) plek, plaas; verblyf; (v) plaas, neersit; ~ *an order* bestel; bestelling plaas; ~**kick** stelskop; ~**name** pleknaam

placen′ta (n) nageboorte, plasenta

pla′cid (a) kalm, vreedsaam *also* **peace′ful**

pla′giarism plagiaat, letterdiefstal

pla′gue (n) plaag, pes; (v) kwel, pla

plain (n) vlakte; (a) eenvoudig; *the* ~ *truth* die naakte waarheid; (adv) duidelik; ~**ly** duidelik, klaarblyklik

plain′tiff klaer, eiser (mens)

plain′tive (a) klaend

plan (n) plan; voorneme; ontwerp, skets; (v) beplan, ontwerp

plane[1] (n) plataanboom

plane[2] (n) skaaf; (v) skaaf/skawe

plane[3] (n) vlak; hoogte, gelykte; vliegtuig; (v) vlieg; skeer oor (die water); (a) plat

plan′et (n) planeet

planetar′ium ..ria, -s planetarium

plank (n) plank; beginsel; doelstelling

plann′er beplanner, ontwerper

plant (n) plant; aanleg, installasie; (v) plant, beplant; ~ **and machin′ery** aanleg en masjinerie; ~**a′tion** plantasie; ~**er** planter

pla′que (n) gedenkplaat, plakket; plaak (tande)

plas′ter (n) pleister; gips; ~ **of Pa′ris** gips

plas′tic beeldend, plasties, plastiek=; ~ **arts** beeldende kuns(te); ~ **cup** plastiekkoppie, plastiekbeker; ~ **sur′gery** plastiese snykunde

plate (n) bord; plaat; prys; ~ **event′** plaatkompetisie (sport)

plateau′ plato, hoogvlakte, hoogland

plate glass (n) spieëlglas, winkelglas

plat′form verhoog, platform, perron

plat′inum platinum, witgoud (element); platina (erts)

platoon′ peloton (soldate)

play (n) vermaak; speelruimte; spel; toneelstuk; (v) speel; bespeel; ~ *the fool* die gek skeer; ~ *tricks* poetse bak; ~ *truant* stokkies draai; ~**boy** pierewaaier, darteldawie, swierbol *also* **good′timer**; ~**er** speler, toneelspeler; ~**ful** spelerig, dartel, speels; ~**ground** speelterrein; ~**ing card** speelkaart; ~**ing field:** *level the* ~*ing field* die speelveld gelyk maak; ~**mate** speelmaat; ~**-off** uitspeelwedstryd; ~**school** peuterskool; ~**time** speeltyd, pouse; ~**wright** toneelskrywer; dramaturg; ~**wri′ter** draaiboekskrywer

plead (v) soebat, smeek, pleit; ~ *guilty* skuld beken

plea′sant aangenaam, prettig *also* **enjoy′able**

please (v) beval, behaag, genoeë doen; ~ *God* as dit God behaag; *if you* ~ asseblief; (interj) asseblief; ~**d** ingenome, tevrede, bly: ~*d with his marks* bly oor/ingenome met sy punte

plea'sure (n) genot, vermaak, genoeë, plesier; *I have* ~ *in* dis my 'n genoeë om; ~ **resort'** plesieroord

pledge (n) pand; waarborg; (v) verpand, plegtig belowe; ~**e'** pandhouer; ~**r/pledgor'** pand= geër

plen'ary volledig; voltallig (vergadering); ~ **po'wers** volmag; ~ **ses'sion** volsessie

plenipoten'tiary gevolmagtigde (mens)

plen'tiful (a) oorvloedig, volop

plen'ty (n) oorvloed; (a) oorvloedig, volop *also* **abun'dant**

ple'onasm oortolligheid (van woorde), pleo= nasme

pleur'isy borsvliesontsteking

pli'able buigsaam, lenig, soepel; plooibaar

pli'ers draadtang, knyptang

plod (v) swoeg, ploeter; ~ *along* aansukkel; ~**der** ploeteraar

plot (n) (klein)hoewe, perseel, plot *also* **small'= holding**; sameswering, komplot; intrige, knoop (roman); (v) saamsweer, saamspan

plough (n) ploeg; (v) ploeg, braak; ~**share** ploegskaar

plo'ver klewiet; strandloper(tjie) (voël)

ploy (n) voorwendsel, set, streek, slenter, bluf

pluck (n) moed, durf; (v) ruk, pluk; kul; ~ *up courage/heart/spirits* moed skep; ~**y** moe= dig, dapper *also* **bold, brave**

plug (n) prop, stop; vonkprop; muurprop; (v) toestop, beskiet; dop/druip (eksamen)

plum pruim; die beste

plumb'er loodgieter

plume (n) pluim; veerbos; (v) pronk

plump (a) dik, vet; mollig (meisie)

plum'pudding (n) doekpoeding, Kerspoeding

plun'der (n) buit, roof; (v) buit, roof, plunder

plunge (n) indompeling; *take the* ~ die sprong waag; (v) plons; indompel; stort

plur'al meervoud

plus (n) plusteken; (a) ekstra; (adv) meer, plus; ~**fours** pofbroek, kardoesbroek

plush wolfluweel; (a) weelderig, luuks

ply (v) **plies** draad (wol); laag (hout); (v) beoefen (beroep); behartig; gebruik; hanteer

ply'wood laaghout, plakhout

pneumat'ic lug=; pneumaties

pneumon'ia (n) longontsteking

poach[1] posjeer (eier)

poach[2] vertrap; wild steel

poached' egg posjeereier, kalfsoog

poach'er (n) wildstroper/wilddief

pock'et (n) sak; beursie; (v) wegbêre; toe-eien; ~ **knife** knipmes/sakmes; ~ **mon'ey** sak= geld; ~**-size** (a) sakformaat; sakpas *also* **afford'able**

pod (n) dop, skil, peul; (v) uitdop

pod'ium podia verhoog, podium

po'em (n) gedig, vers

po'et digter, poëet (albei geslagte)

poet'ic (a) digterlik, poëties; ~ **li'cence** dig= terlike vryheid

po'etry (n) digkuns, poësie

poign'ant skerp, skrynend; pynlik

poinset'tia (n) karlienblom, poinsettia

point (n) punt; onderwerp, kwessie; piek; (pl) wissel (treinspoor); *up to a* ~ tot op sekere hoogte; ~ *of view* gesig(s)punt; (v) skerp maak; wys; ~**blank'** trompop, reguit; ~**du'ty** puntdiens/verkeersdiens; ~**ed** skerp; geestig, gevat; ~**er** wyser, pylflits (vir skerm); pointer (patryshond); ~**less** sinloos; ~**s'man** wisselwagter, verkeerreëlaar

pois'on (n) gif, gifstof; (v) vergiftig; **food** ~**ing** voedselvergift(ig)ing; ~**ous** giftig

poke[1] (v) pook, oppor; steek; ~ *fun at* gek= skeer met

poke[2] sak; *buy a pig in a* ~ 'n kat in die sak koop

pok'er vuuryster/vuurpook; poker (kaartspel)

pol'ar pool=, polêr; ~ **bear** ysbeer

polarisat'ion polarisasie/polarisering

pole paal; disselboom (kar); roede

pole'cat muishond (SA)

pole'vault paalspring (atletiek)

pol'ice (n) polisie; ~ **investiga'tion** polisie-on= dersoek; ~**man** konstabel; polisiebeampte; ge= regsdienaar; ~ **ser'vices** polisiedienste; **polic'= ing** polisiëring; ~ **sta'tion** polisiekantoor

pol'icy[1] (n) ..**cies** polis (assuransie)

pol'icy[2] beleid (mv beleide, beleidrigtings); ~ **ma'ker** beleidvormer

pol'io(myelitis) kinderverlamming

pol'ish -es politoer, waks; verfyning; (v) poleer, poets; ~ *off* kafloop; ~**ed** beskaaf(d); gepo= leer

polite' beleef(d), beskaaf, hoflik, verfynd

polit'ical (a) staatkundig, staats=; politiek, polities; ~ **science** staatsleer

politi'cian politikus (mens)

pol'ka polka (Tsjeggiese dans)

poll[1] (n) stembus; verkiesing; stemlys; *go to the* ~**s** gaan stem; (v) stem

poll² (n) poenskop(dier); (v) top, snoei
poll'en stuifmeel
poll'ing (n) stemmery, stem; ~ **booth** stembus/stemhokkie; ~ **of'ficer** stemopnemer, stembeampte; ~ **sta'tion** stemlokaal
pollute' (v) besoedel, verontreinig, bevuil
pollu'tion besoedeling, bevuiling
pol'o polo; ~ **neck** rolhals (trui)
polon'y ..nies polonie, dikwors
polyg'amist poligamis, veelwywer (mens)
pol'yglot (n) veeltalige (persoon), poliglot
pol'yp poliep (groeisel)
pomegran'ate granaat (vrug)
pomp (n) prag, praal; staatsie
pom'pous (a) verwaand; hoogdrawend
pond vywer, poel; pan
pon'der (v) peins, dink, oorweeg
pontoon' ponton, brug, pont
pon'y ponies ponie; ~**tail** poniestert
pooch: ~ **par'lour** woefieboetiek
poo'dle poedel
pool¹ (n) poel, kuil; (private) swembad
pool² (n) inset; ring; sindikaat; poel; **ty'ping** ~ tikpoel; (v) poel; winste deel
poor: (n) *the* ~ arm mense, die armes; (a) arm, behoeftig; *a* ~ *show* 'n swak vertoning
pop¹ (n) knal, slag; (v) skiet; ~ *up* opduik
pop² (a) populêr, pop=; ~ **mu'sic** popmusiek
pop'corn (n) springmielies, kiepiemielies
pope pous; ~**dom** pousdom
pop'gun speelgeweertjie; propgeweertjie
pop'lar populier (boom)
popp'y poppies papawer, klaproos
pop'ular (a) populêr; bemind, gewild
popula'rity gewildheid, populariteit
popula'tion (n) bevolking, populasie; ~ **explo'sion** bevolkingsontploffing
pop'-up: ~ **menu** opwipkieslys (rek.); ~ **toas'ter** wiprooster
porce'lain porselein
porch -es portaal; stoep, veranda
porc'upine ystervark (dier)
pore (n) sweetgaatjie, porie
pork varkvleis; ~**er** vleisvark
porn: ~ **book/film** pornoboek/pornofilm
pornograph'ic (a) pornografies, obseen
pornog'raphy pornografie, prikkellektuur
porp'oise (n) to(r)nyn (seevark)
po'rridge pap
port¹ (n) hawe; ingang
port² (n) bakboord (linkerkant van skip)
port'able (a) draagbaar; vervoerbaar; ~ **ra'dio** draradio; ~ **televi'sion set** draagbare televisiestel
por'ter kruier; portier; pakdraer
portfo'lio -s portefeulje; ministerspos
port'hole patryspoort/kajuitvenster (skip)
por'tion (n) deel; porsie *also* **hel'ping**; gedeelte; aandeel; (v) verdeel, uitdeel
port'ly (a) swaarlywig, dik
por'trait (v) portret; beeld/beeltenis
portray' afbeeld, uitbeeld; beskryf; ~**al** beskrywing; uitbeelding
pose¹ (n) houding, pose; aanstellery; (v) poseer; 'n houding aanneem; voordoen
pose² vasvra; ~**r** strikvraag
posh (a) deftig, vernaam *also* **grand**; eksklusief (woonbuurt); ~ **occa'sion** glansparty
posi'tion stand; toestand, posisie; ligging; (v) plaas, staanmaak, posisioneer
pos'itive (a) bevestigend, positief, seker
possess' besit, hê; bemagtig; beheers
possessed' besete *also* **demen'ted**; ~ *by the devil* deur die duiwel besete
posse'ssion besitting, besit, eiendom
possess'ive (n) tweede naamval; (a) besitlik
possibil'ity ..ties moontlikheid
poss'ible (a) moontlik, doenlik; haalbaar
poss'ibly miskien, straks, dalk, moontlik
post¹ (n) pos; poskantoor; poswese; betrekking; *by return of* ~ per kerende pos; (v) pos; oorboek
post² (n) paal, stut; styl (van deur)
post³ (voorvoegsel) na=; later
pos'tage posgeld; ~ **stamp** posseël
post: ~**bag** possak, briewesak; ~**card** poskaart
postdate' (v) vooruitdateer; ~**d che'que** vooruitgedateerde tjek
pos'ter aanplakbiljet, plakkaat *also* **bill'board**
poster'ity nageslag, nakomelingskap
postgrad'uate (n) gegradueerde (student); (a) nagraads; ~ **stu'dies** nagraadse studie
post'humous (a) postuum, nagelate
post: *keep* ~*ed* op die hoogte hou; ~**ing box** briewebus; ~**man** posbesteller, briewebesteller, posbode; ~**mas'ter** posmeester
postmort'em examina'tion (n) lykskouing; nadoodse ondersoek *also* **autop'sy**
post: ~ **of'fice** poskantoor; ~ **box** (pos)bus
postpone' (v) uitstel, verdaag; ~**ment** verdaging, uitstel, verskuiwing
post: ~**script** naskrif; ~**war** naoorlogs

pos'ture (n) houding, postuur

pot (n) pot, kan; blompot; ~s of money geld soos bossies

potat'o -es aartappel/ertappel; sweet ~ patat-(ta); ~ **chips** aartappelskyfies

pot'ent magtig, kragtig, potent

poten'tial (n) potensiaal; moontlikheid

pot'hole slaggat; rotsholte; maalgat

po'tion drank; gifdrank; doepa

pot'jiekos (n) potjiekos, ysterpotbredie also iron-pot stew

pot'luck wat die pot verskaf

pott'er (n) pottebakker; (v) peuter, knutsel; ~'s **wheel** pottebakkerskyf; ~**ing** (v) knutsel; ~**y** pottebakkery; erdewerk

pouch (n) -es sak, tabaksak; beurs; buidel

poul'try (n) pluimvee; hoenders; ~ **far'ming** hoenderboerdery

pounce (v) aanval, gryp; afspring op

pound[1] (n) pond (geld); pond (massa, gewig)

pound[2] (n) skut; (v) skut (losloopdiere)

pour (v) giet, uitstort; inskink; stortreën; ~**ing** rain gietende reën

pov'erty (n) armoede, gebrek

powd'er (n) poeier; kruit; (v) (be)poeier; fyn-stamp; ~ **box** poeierdoos; ~**ed** fyn; ge-poeier; ~ **puff** poeierkwas

pow'er (n) mag, krag; gesag; moondheid; bevoegdheid; ~ of attorney volmag, proku-rasie; ~ of resistance weerstandsvermoe; ~ **boat** kragboot; ~ **brakes** kragremme; ~ **sharing** mag(s)deling; ~**ful** magtig, kragtig; ~**ful bomb** kragtige bom; ~**house** krag-bron; ~**less** magteloos, kragteloos; ~ **lift'-ing** kragoptel; ~ **plug** kragprop; ~ **source** kragbron; ~ **sta'tion** kragsentrale; krag-stasie; ~ **stee'ring** kragstuur

pox pokke; **chick'en** ~ waterpokkies

prac'tical prakties; play a ~ joke 'n poets bak; ~ **expe'rience** praktiese ondervinding; ~ **teach'ing** praktiese onderwys, proefonder-wys (vir studente)

prac'tically feitlik; prakties; ~ everyone was there feitlik almal was daar

prac'tice (n) praktyk; oefening; gebruik; ge-woonte; ~ makes perfect oefening baar kuns; in ~ in die praktyk; out of ~ van stryk; ~ **run** oefenlopie; ~ **ses'sion** oefensessie

prac'tise (v) oefen; instudeer, praktiseer; ~ a profession 'n beroep beoefen

practi'tioner praktisyn; **gen'eral** ~ algemene praktisyn, huisarts; **le'gal** ~ regspraktisyn

praise (n) lof, roem, eer; (v) loof, prys, verheerlik, ophemel; ~ **sin'ger** lofsanger (imbongi); ~**wor'thy** loflik, prysenswaardig

pram kinderwaentjie, stootwaentjie

prank (n) (kwajong)streek, poets; (v) pronk

prawn steurgarnaal, (swem)krewel

pray (v) bid, smeek, versoek

prayer (n) gebed; smeking; the Lord's P~ die Onse Vader; say one's ~s, bid; ~ **mee'ting** biduur

pray'ing man'tis bidsprinkaan, mantis

preach (v) preek, verkondig; ~**er** predikant, prediker

precau'tionary voorsorg-; ~ **mea'sures** voor-sorgmaatreëls/voorsorg

precede' voorafgaan, voorgaan

prec'edent (n) voorbeeld, presedent; create a ~ 'n presedent skep

pre'cious kosbaar, kostelik; ~ little bloedwei-nig; ~ **stone** edelsteen also **gem'stone**

pre'cipice afgrond, krans; steilte

préc'is opsomming, samevatting, précis

precise' (a) noukeurig, presies; nougeset

preci'sion noukeurigheid, presiesheid, juist-heid, presisie

pred'atory roofsugtig, roof-; ~ **an'imal** roof-dier, predator

predeces'sor (n) voorganger (mens)

predestina'tion voorbeskikking; uitverkie-sing, predestinasie

predic'ament (n) penarie, verknorsing also **dilem'ma**

predict' voorspel; ~**ion** voorspelling

pre-empt' voorspring; vooruitloop ('n besluit)

prefab'ricated: ~ **house** opslaanhuis, mon-teerhuis/montasiehuis

pref'ace (n) voorwoord also **fo'reword**; (v) in-lei

pref'ect (n) prefek, klasleier/klasvoog

prefer' (v) verkies, die voorkeur gee aan; ~ tea to coffee verkies tee bo koffie

pref'erence voorkeur; voorrang; voorliefde

pref'ix (n) -es voorvoegsel

preg'nant (a) verwagtend, swanger (vrou); dragtig (dier); vrugbaar; veelseggend

prehistor'ic (a) voorhistories, prehistories

pre'judice (n) vooroordeel; (v) benadeel

prelim'inary (a) inleidend, voorlopig, preli-minêr; ~ **match** voorwedstryd

prel'ude (n) voorspel, prelude, inleiding

prem'ature (a) ontydig, voortydig; voorbarig

premed'itate: ~**d** voorbedag; ~**d mur'der**

moord met voorbedagte rade

pre′mier (n) premier; eerste minister; (a) eers=te, vernaamste

prem′ise (n) veronderstelling; (pl) werf, per=seel; gebou; *on the* ∼*s* op die perseel

prem′ium premie; prys, beloning

premoni′tion (n) voorgevoel, voorbode

prepaid′ posvry, vooruitbetaal

prepara′tion voorbereiding, gereedmaking; in=studering

prepa′ratory voorbereidend; inleidend; ∼ **school** voorbereidingskool

prepare′ voorberei (taak); berei (ete); gereed maak

preposi′tion voorsetsel

prepos′terous (a) ongerymd, dwaas, onsinnig

prereq′uisite (n) voorvereiste

prero′gative voorreg, prerogatief

preschool′ (a) voorskools

prescribe′ (v) voorskryf; behandel; ∼**d** voor=geskrewe; verjaar (skuld); ∼**d book** voor=geskrewe boek

prescrip′tion (n) voorskrif/preskripsie

pres′ence (n) voorwoordigheid; ∼ *of mind* teen=woordigheid van gees

pres′ent[1] (n) present, geskenk *also* **gift**

pres′ent[2] (n) die teenwoordige, hede; *at* ∼ tans; (a) teenwoordig, aanwesig; ∼ **tense** teenwoordige tyd

present′[3] (v) aanbied, skenk; oorhandig; ∼ *oneself* jou aanmeld; ∼ *prizes* pryse oor=handig; ∼**able** (ver)toonbaar; presentabel; ∼**a′tion** aanbieding; oorhandiging; ∼**er** aan=bieder (radio/TV)

pres′ently netnou, nou-nou, aanstons, straks

preserve′ (n) ingelegde vrugte; konfyt; (v) bewaar, preserveer; inmaak

preside′ (v) voorsit, presideer; lei, bestuur

pres′idency presidentskap; presidentswoning/presidensie; voorsitterskap

pres′ident president, staatshoof; voorsitter

presiden′tial: ∼ **address′** voorsittersrede

press (n) pers, koerantwese; drukpers; druk=kery; (v) pers, druk; aanpor

press: ∼**butt′on tel′ephone** drukknoptelefoon; ∼ **cut′ting** koerant(uit)knipsel; ∼**ing** drin=gend; dreigend; ∼ **photog′rapher** persfoto=graaf; ∼ **relea′se** persverklaring

pre′ssure (n) druk, drukking; **atmospher′ic** ∼ lugdruk; ∼ **burst** drukbars; ∼ **cooker** druk=kastrol/drukkoker; ∼ **group** drukgroep

prestige′ invloed; prestige, aansien

pretence′ (n) voorwendsel *also* **pre′text**

pretend′ (v) voorgee; ∼**er** aanspraakmaker; ∼*er to the throne* aanspraakmaker op die kroon/koningskap

pre′text (n) voorwendsel; *on/under the* ∼ *of* onder voorwendsel/die skyn van

pre′tty (a) mooi, bevallig *also* **attrac′tive**; *cost a* ∼ *sum* 'n mooi sommetjie kos; ∼ *sure* taamlik seker

prevail′ (v) heers; in swang wees

prevent′ (v) belet, verhinder; voorkom

preven′tion voorkoming, verhindering

preven′tive (n) voorbehoedmiddel; (a) voor=komend, voorbehoed=; ∼ **mea′sures** voor=komende maatreëls

prev′iew (n) voorskou; voorbesigtiging

prev′ious voorafgaande, vroeër, vorige; ∼**ly** voorheen, vantevore

prey (n) prooi; buit; slagoffer; *bird of* ∼ roofvoël; (v) roof, aas

price (n) prys; waarde; *at any* ∼ tot elke prys; ∼ **control′** prysbeheer; ∼ **fix′ing** prysbin=ding; ∼ **in′crease** prysstyging; **recommen′**=**ded** ∼ rigprys; ∼**less** onskatbaar *also* **in**=**val′uable**; ∼**list** pryslys

prick (n) steek; prikkel; (v) steek, prik; ∼ *up the ears* die ore spits; ∼**ly pear** turksvy

pride (n) trots, hoogmoed; (v) trots wees

priest priester; geestelike (mens)

prim styf, sedig, preuts; ∼ **and prop′er** net=jies; agtermekaar

pri′mary (a) .eerste; aanvanklik; laer, primêr; ∼ **health care** primêre gesondheidsorg; ∼ **school** primêre skool/laerskool

prime: ∼ **mini′ster** eerste minister; ∼ **lend′**=**ing rate** prima uitleenkoers

pri′mer eerste leesboek, abc-boek; grondverf

primev′al (a) oer=, oeroud; ∼ **for′est** oerwoud

prim′itive oorspronklik, primitief, vroegste

prim′rose sleutelblom, paasblom, primula

prim′ula primula (blom) *also* **prim′rose**

prince prins; ∼*ly reward* vorstelike beloning; **crown** ∼ kroonprins

prin′cess -es prinses, koningsdogter; ∼ **roy′al** koninklike prinses

prin′cipal (n) hoof, skoolhoof *also* **head′**=**master**; prinsipaal; opdraggewer; (a) ver=naamste; ∼ **sen′tence** hoofsin

prin′ciple beginsel, grondbeginsel, prinsiep

print (n) merk, spoor; druk; *out of* ∼ uit=verkoop; (v) druk; merk, stempel; uitgee

print′er drukker; ∼**'s devil** drukkersduiwel,

setsatan *also* **grem'lin**

print'ing drukkuns, drukwerk; ~ **press** druk=
pers

print-out (n) drukstuk; komperstaat

pri'or (a) vroeër, eerder, voorafgaande; ~
approval voorafgaande goedkeuring

prio'rity voorrang, prioriteit; *get your ..ties
right* stel jou prioriteite reg; ~ **mail** voor=
keurpos

prism prisma

pris'on gevangenis *also* **jail, gaol**; tronk

pris'oner gevangene, prisonier

pris'on warder bewaarder, sipier

pri'vacy afsondering, privaatheid

priv'ate (n) manskap, weerman; (a) privaat;
vertroulik

priv'ate: ~ **bag** privaatsak; ~**ly** privaat; ~
parts geslagdele; ~ **sec'retary** privaat se=
kretaresse (dame); privaat sekretaris (man);
~ **sec'tor** private sektor

privatisa'tion privatisering (proses); privati=
sasie (produk)

priv'ilege (n) voorreg; privilege

priv'y (n) privies kleinhuisie *also* **loo, toi'let**

prize (n) prys *also* **award'**; voordeel; (v) op
prys stel/waardeer

prize: ~**-fight'er** beroepsbokser; ~**-giving**
prysuitdeling; ~ **ring** bokskryt; ~**win'ner**
pryswenner

pro voor; *pros and cons* voor= en nadele

prob'able waarskynlik

proba'tion proeftyd; *on* ~ op proef; ~ **of'ficer**
proefbeampte; ~**ary per'iod** proeftyd

probe (n) (geregtelike) ondersoek; (v) onder-
soek/ondervra *also* **inves'tigate, in'quire** (in=
to)

prob'lem probleem, vraagstuk; raaisel; ~ **sol'v=
ing** probleemoplossing

proced'ure (n) handel(s)wyse, werkwyse, pro=
sedure

proceed' (v) aangaan, voortgaan, verder gaan

proceed'ing (n) handel(s)wyse, handeling,
gedragslyn; (pl) handelinge, verslae; ver=
rigtinge/werksaamhede (op 'n vergadering)

pro'ceeds opbrengs/opbrings, wins

pro'cess (n) verloop; regsgeding; proses; (v)
verwerk/prosesseer

proces'sion (n) optog, prosessie; stoet; reeks

pro'cessor verwerker; **word** ~ teksverwerker/
woordverwerker

proclama'tion afkondiging, proklamasie

procrastina'tion (n) uitstel, getalm; ~ *is the
thief of time* van uitstel kom afstel

procure' (v) verkry, verskaf, besorg; ~**r** ver=
skaffer; koppelaar (vir prostitute) *also* **pimp**

prod (v) steek; priem; aanpor

prod'igal (a) verkwistend, spandabel *also*
extra'vagant; ~ **son** verlore seun

prod'igy ..gies seldsaamheid; wonderkind

prod'uce (n) produk; oes, opbrengs/opbrings

produce' (v) voortbring; oplewer, produseer;
~ *a play* 'n toneelstuk opvoer; ~**r** produ=
sent; produksieleier, regisseur

prod'uct opbrengs; produk

produc'tion vervaardiging, produksie; opvoe=
ring (toneel)

productiv'ity produktiwiteit; vrugbaarheid

profane' (a) profaan; godslasterlik; ~ **lan=
guage** skeldtaal, vloektaal

profess' (v) bely, erken; beoefen ('n beroep)

profes'sion beroep, professie; *by* ~ van be=
roep; *follow a* ~ 'n beroep beoefen

profes'sional (n) beroepsman; beroepspeler;
(pl) beroepslui; (a) beroeps=, professioneel;
~ *code of conduct/ethics* professionele
gedragskode; ~ **know'ledge** vakkennis *also*
experti'se, know-how; ~ **play'er** beroep=
speler, ~ **rug'by** geldrugby, ~ **soc'cer**
beroepsokker

profess'or (n) professor, hoogleraar; ~**ship**
professoraat

profi'ciency (n) bedrewenheid, bekwaamheid;
vaardigheid, kundigheid

profi'cient (a) bedrewe, vaardig, bekwaam

pro'file (n) profiel; buitelyn; *keep a low* ~ jou
eenkant hou

prof'it (n) wins, profyt; ~ *after tax* (na)belaste
wins; ~ *before tax* voorbelaste wins; ~
mar'gin winsgrens; (v) wins maak; voor=
deel trek uit; ~**able** winsgewend

profound' (a) diep, diepsinnig, grondig

prog'eny nageslag, nakomelingskap

prog'ramme/pro'gram (n) program; ~**r** pro=
grammeerder (mens)

prog'ress (n) vordering, vooruitgang

progress' (v) vorder, vooruitgaan

progress'ive vooruitstrewend; progressief

prohib'it (v) belet, verbied

proj'ect (n) plan, ontwerp, projek

project' (v) ontwerp, beraam; uitsteek; ~**ile**
projektiel; ~**ing** uitstekend (rots); ~**ion** ont=
werp, projeksie; vooruitskatting *also* **fo're=
cast**

proletar'iat proletariaat; Jan Rap en sy maat

pro'logue (n) voorrede, voorwoord; proloog
prolong' (v) verleng, uitrek; ~**ed ill'ness** langdurige siekte
prom'inent uitstekend; prominent; ~ **per'son** vername/vooraanstaande persoon
prom'ise (n) belofte; *keep one's* ~ jou belofte nakom; (v) beloof/belowe
prom'ising (veel)belowend
prom'issory: ~ **note** promesse, (skuld)bewys
promote' (v) bevorder; aanmoedig; loods; promoveer; ~ *(launch) a new product* 'n nuwe produk loods/bevorder
promo'ter (n) oprigter; promotor; vegknoper/vegventer (boks, stoei)
promo'tion bevordering, promosie; produkbe= vordering
prompt (v) aanspoor; voorsê; (a) stip, vaardig; ~ *payment* stipte betaling; ~**er** voorsêer, souffleur (toneel)
prong hooivurk, gaffel, tand (van eg, tuin= vurk)
pron'oun (n) voornaamwoord
pronounce' (v) uitspreek, uiter; ~ *sentence of death* die doodvonnis uitspreek
pronuncia'tion uitspraak; spraak, tongval
proof (n) -**s** bewys; proef; (a) beproef; ~**reader** proefleser
prop (n) stut; steun; stutpaal; ~ *up* onder= skraag
propagan'da propaganda
prop'agate (v) voortplant, verbrei, versprei
propel' voortdryf, beweeg; ~**ler** skroef (vlieg= tuig)
prop'er (a) betaamlik, behoorlik; ~**ly** behoor= lik; eintlik; ~ **name** eienaam
prop'erty ..ties eiendom, besitting; eienskap; ~ **devel'oper** eiendomontwikkelaar; **fixed** ~ vasgoed, vaste eiendom; **mo'vable** ~ losgoed, roerende goed
proph'ecy (n) ..**cies** profesie, voorspelling
proph'et profeet; ~ *of doom* doemprofeet
propor'tion (n) eweredigheid, proporsie; *in* ~ *to* in verhouding tot
propor'tional (a) eweredig/proporsioneel
propo'sal voorstel, aanbod; huweliksaansoek
propose' voorstel, aanbied, vra; ~ *a vote of thanks* die dankwoord rig; ~**r** voorsteller
proposi'tion aanbod, proposisie; **bus'iness** ~ saketransaksie *also* **bus'iness deal**
propri'etary (a) eienaars=, eiendoms=; **P**~ **Limited** Eiendoms Beperk; ~ **med'icines** patente medisyne

propri'etor eienaar (van winkel)
prosa'ic (a) prosaïes, alledaags
prose (n) prosa; (a) prosa=; prosaïes
pros'ecute (v) vervolg; uitoefen; *trespassers will be* ~*d* oortreders word vervolg
pros'ecutor aanklaer; **pub'lic** ~ staatsaanklaer
prose'writer prosaskrywer, prosaïs
pros'pect (n) vooruitsig, verwagting
prospect' (v) prospekteer, ondersoek; ~**or** prospekteerder
prospec'tus -es prospektus (brosjure)
prospe'rity (n) voorspoed, welvaart
pros'perous voorspoedig; welvarend, bloeiend
pros'titute (n) prostituut, straathoer, seks= werker *also* **hoo'ker**
prostitu'tion hoerery, prostitusie
pros'trate (v) neerwerp, neerkniel; (a) neer= gebuig; ootmoedig; verslaan
pro'tea suikerbos, protea
protect' beskerm, beveilig; ~**ion** beskerming
protec'tive beskermend; ~ **clo'thing** skerm= drag
protec'tor beskermer; ~**ate** protektoraat; **pub'lic** ~ openbare beskermer
prot'est (n) protes, verset
protest' (v) beswaar maak, protesteer
pro'tocol (n) protokol, voorrangkode
protrude' (v) vooruitsteek, uitpeul (oë)
proud trots, hoogmoedig *also* **haugh'ty**
prove (v) bewys; beproef; bewys lewer
prov'erb spreekwoord, spreuk, segswyse
provide' (v) verskaf, voorsien, lewer; ~ *with* voorsien van; ~**d** mits, met dien verstande
prov'idence (n) voorsiening, spaarsaamheid
prov'ident sorgvuldig, spaarsaam; ~ **fund** voorsorgfonds
provid'er (n) verskaffer, leweransier, lewe= raar; **ser'vice** ~ diensverskaffer, dienslewe= raar
prov'ince provinsie; afdeling; vak
provin'cial (a) provinsiaal; bekrompe
provi'sion (n) voorsiening, voorsorg; bepa= ling; (pl) lewensmiddele, proviand; padkos (vir 'n reis); ~**al** voorlopig
provoc'ative (a) tartend, uitdagend, provoka= tief
provoke' (v) uitlok, (uit)tart, provokeer
prowl (v) rondsluip; uit op roof; ~**er** rond= sluiper (mens)
prox'imo aanstaande (maand)
prox'y (n) volmag; gevolmagtigde; *marry by* ~ met die handskoen trou

pru'dence (n) versigtigheid, verstandigheid
also **discre'tion**; ~ *is the best part of valour*
versigtigheid is die moeder v.d. wysheid
pru'dent (a) wys, verstandig, taktvol
pru'dish (a) preuts, skynsedig; *I am no prude*
ek is nie preuts nie
prune[1] (n) pruimedant, gedroogde pruim
prune[2] (v) snoei; knot; ~**r** snoeiskêr
psalm psalm; ~**ist**/~**odist** psalmdigter
pseud'o- vals, oneg; half=, pseudo=
pseud'onym (n) pseudoniem, skuilnaam
psychi'atrist psigiater (mens)
psycholog'ical (a) sielkundig, psigologies
psychol'ogy (n) sielkunde, psigologie
pub (n) kantien, kroeg; tappery/taphuis; ~
craw'ler kroegvlieg *also* **bar'fly**
pub'erty (n) puberteit, geslagsrypheid
pub'ic skaam=; ~ **hair** skaamhare
pub'lic (n) publiek; *in* ~ in die openbaar; (a)
openbaar, publiek; ~ **address' sys'tem** luid=
sprekerstelsel; ~**a'tion** uitgawe, publikasie;
~ **im'age** openbare beeld, beeld na buite;
~**'ity** openbaarmaking, publisiteit; ~
opin'ion openbare mening; ~ **protec'tor**
openbare beskermer *see* **om'budsman**; ~
rela'tions openbare betrekkinge; ~ **rela'=
tions offi'cial/of'ficer** (openbare) skakel=
amptenaar; mediaskakel; ~ **sec'tor** ower=
heidsektor; ~ **ser'vice** staatsdiens; ~ **school**
regeringskool; privaatskool (in Engeland);
~ **spea'king** openbare redevoering, (die)
redenaarskuns
pub'lish (v) uitgee, publiseer; aankondig; ~**er**
uitgewer; uitgewery
puck kaboutermannetjie, elf; stouterd
pu'dding poeding; nagereg; (soort) wors
pud'dle (n) poel; gemors; warboel
puff (n) geblaas, rukwind; poeierkwas; (v)
blaas, hyg, pof; ~ **ad'der** pofadder
pug (n) mopshondjie (mopar); kabouter
pull (n) trek, ruk, pluk; (v) trek, ruk; roei; ~
faces skewebek trek; ~ *one's leg* iem. vir
die gek hou; ~ *oneself together* jou reg=
ruk
pu'llet jong hennetjie
pu'lley -s katrol
pull'over langmoutrui/oortrektrui *also* **jer'sey**
pulp (n) murg; pap; pulp (papier); moes (van
vrugte); (v) fynmaak; verpulp
pu'lpit (n) preekstoel, kansel
pulse (n) pols; *feel one's* ~ die pols voel
pum'a (n) poema, bergleeu

pum'ice puimsteen
pump (n) pomp; (v) pomp; ~ **atten'dant** pomp=
joggie, petroljoggie
pump'kin (boer)pampoen
pun (n) woordspeling
punch (n) vuisslag; deurslag; (v) knip; perfo=
reer; ~ **sys'tem** ponsstelsel
Punch: ~ **and Ju'dy** poppekas/poppespel *also*
pup'pet show
punc'tual stip, presies
punctua'tion (n) interpunksie, leestekens
punc'ture (n) lek(plek); (v) prik
pun'ish (v) straf, kasty; toetakel; ~**able** straf=
baar; ~**ment** straf; boete
punk (n) punk (mens, anti-establishment); ~
mu'sic punkmusiek
punt (v) hoog skop; vlugskop; vir geld speel;
~**er** waagspeler (perde); vlugskopper
pup (n) jong hondjie; **lit'ter of** ~**s** werpsel
hondjies
pup'il leerling; oogappel; kyker, pupil (oog);
~ **tea'cher** kwekelingonderwyser
pupp'et (n) handpop, marionet; strooipop *also*
stoo'ge (mens); ~ **show** poppekas
pupp'y puppies jong hondjie; ~ **fat** jeugvet;
~ **love** kalwerliefde
purch'ase (n) koop, aankoop; (pl) inkope; (v)
koop; ~ **price** koopprys; ~**r** (aan)koper;
klant; **pur'chasing po'wer** koopkrag
pure (a) suiwer, rein, kuis, louter; ~ **non'=
sense** pure onsin/kaf
purge (n) (uit)suiwering, reiniging; (v) (uit)=
suiwer *also* **exter'minate**; reinig
pur'ist taalsuiweraar, puris (mens)
pur'ity suiwerheid; reinheid
pur'ple (n) purper (kleur); (a) purper, pers
purp'ose (n) voorneme, doel, oogmerk; *for* ~*s*
of vir die doel van; *on* ~ opsetlik; (v) be=
doel, beoog; ~**ly** opsetlik
purr (v) spin (kat), snor (w)
purse (n) beurs(ie); ~**r** betaalmeester (op skip)
pursue' (v) vervolg; agtervolg; nastreef/na=
strewe; beoefen (beroep); volg (beleid)
pursuit' vervolging; (pl) werksaamhede; ~ **of**
know'ledge die strewe na kennis
pus (n) etter, sug, pus (van wond)
push (n) -es stamp, stoot; deursettingsvermoë;
when it comes to the ~ in geval van nood;
(v) stamp; stoot; bespoedig; ~**bike** trapfiets;
~**-up** (n) opstoot
pu'ssy pussies katjie
put (v) neersit, stel, plaas; ~ *down an animal*

'n dier uitsit; ~ *out of action* buite geveg stel; ~ *in order* regmaak; ~ *up for sale* te koop aanbied; ~ *on weight* swaarder word; ~ *in writing* dit op skrif stel

put'-off uitstel; uitvlug
putt (n) sethou; (v) set, put (gholf)
putt'er setyster; setter, putter (gholf)
putt'-putt set-set
putt'y stopverf; ~ **plas'ter** fynpleister

puz'zle (n) raaisel; verleentheid; (v) verleë maak; verbyster; ~**d** verwar(d), deurme= kaar; ~ **pic'ture** soekprentjie
pyg'my pygmies dwerg, pigmee
pyja'mas (n) slaapklere, pajamas; slaappak
py'lon spanmas; kragmas
pyr'amid piramide/piramied
py'roman'iac (n) piromaan (brandstigter)
pyth'on (n) luislang, piton; orakel

Q

quack[1] (n) gekwaak; (v) kwaak
quack[2] (n) kwaksalwer (mens); ~ **doc'tor** kwaksalwer; ~ **med'icine** kwaksalwermiddels
qua'drangle (n) vierkant; vierhoek; binneplein
qua'druple (n) viervoud; (a) viervoudig
quadrupleg'ic (n) kwadrupleeg (mens); (a) kwadruplegies
qua'druplet vierling; viertal; ~**s** vierling
quagg'a kwagga
quag'mire modderpoel; drilgrond, welsand
quail (n) kwartel (patrysvoël)
quaint (a) snaaks, koddig; ouderwets
quake (n) bewing, siddering; (v) beef, tril
qualifica'tion (n) kwalifikasie; vereiste; be= voegdheid, bekwaamheid
qua'lified (a) bevoeg, gekwalifiseer
qua'lify (v) kwalifiseer; jou bekwaam; ~ *for* in aanmerking kom vir, kwalifiseer vir
qua'lity **..ties** hoedanigheid, eienskap, kwali= teit; aanleg; gehalte; ~ **of life** lewens= gehalte; ~ **control'** gehaltebeheer
qualm mislikheid; gewetenswroeging; ~**s** *of conscience* gewetenswroeging
quan'dary (n) **..ries** verleentheid, penarie, verknorsing; *be in a* ~ in die knyp sit
quan'tity (n) **..ties** hoeveelheid, kwantiteit, menigte; ~ **survey'or** bourekenaar (mens)
qua'rantine (n) kwarantyn; (v) onder kwa= rantyn stel, afsonder, isoleer
qua'rrel (n) twis, rusie; *pick a* ~ rusie/skoor soek; (v) rusie maak; twis; ~**ling** getwis; ~**some** twissiek
qua'rry[1] (n) **quarries** prooi; buit; wild
qua'rry[2] (n) **quarries** steengroef, gruisgat
quar'ter (n) kwartier; vierde deel; kwartaal; kwart; (pl) kwartiere; *give no* ~ geen ge= nade betoon nie; ~ *of an hour* 'n kwartier; *married* ~**s** kwartiere vir getroudes; *single*

~**s** enkelkwartiere; ~**ly** (n) kwartaalblad; (a) driemaandeliks, kwartaal=; ~**ly test** kwartaaltoets; ~**mas'ter** kwartiermeester, betaalmeester
quartet' kwartet
quartz kwarts; ~ **watch** kwartshorlosie
quash (v) nietig verklaar; verwerp *also* **crush**
quas'i kamtig, kastig, kwansuis, kwasi=
quat'rain vierreëlige vers, kwatryn
quav'er (n) agtste noot, triller; (v) tril
quay -s hawehoof, kaai *also* **wharf**
queen (n) koningin; ~**ly** vorstelik, statig
queer (n) (*derog.*) homo(seksueel); (v) ver= brou; (a) snaaks, sonderling; *be in Q*~ *street* in die verknorsing wees
quell (v) demp, onderdruk ('n opstand)
quench blus; les, bekoel; laat stilbly; ~ *thirst* dors les; ~**er** blusser; drankie
quer'y (n) navraag, twyfelvraag; vraagteken; (v) betwyfel, bevraagteken
quest (n) ondersoek; soektog *also* **pursuit'**; *the* ~ *for* die soeke/strewe na
ques'tion (n) vraag; kwessie; *beyond* ~ sonder twyfel; *out of the* ~ geen sprake van nie; (v) vra, ondervra; betwyfel; ~ *the accused* die beskuldigde ondervra; ~**able** twyfelagtig; ~ **bank** vraagbank; ~**ing** ondervraging; ~ **mark** vraagteken; ~**naire'** vraelys
queue (n) ry, tou; haarvlegsel; ~ *up/form a* ~ toustaan; (v) toustaan
quick (n) lewe; (a, adv) lewendig; vinnig, rats; *be* ~ *about it!* roer jou!; *a* ~ *eye* 'n skerp oog; ~**grass** kweek; ~**sand** welsand/wil= sand, dryfsand; ~**silver** kwiksilwer; ~**-tem'= pered** opvlieënd, kortgebonde; ~**-wit'ted** gevat
quid tabakpruimpie, tabakkoutjie
quid pro quo' teenprestasie, quidproquo

qui'et (n) stilte, rus; bedaardheid; *on the* ∼ stilletjies; (v) stilmaak; kalmeer; (a) rustig, stil, bedaard; *keep* ∼ stilbly; iets stil hou

quilt (n) donskombers/verekombers

quince kweper; ∼ **jam** kweperkonfyt

quinine' kina, kinien/kinine

quint kwint; vyfkaart

quintess'ence kern, kwintessens

quintet' kwintet; vyftal

quin'tuple (n) vyfvoud; (a) vyfvoudig; ∼t vyftal; ∼ts vyfling (kinders)

quip (n) kwinkslag, geestigheid *also* **plea'= santry**; spitsvondigheid; skimpskoot

quit (v) verlaat *also* **aban'don**; tou opgooi; ∼ **a job** 'n werk/pos los

quite heeltemal, glad, volkome; *I* ∼ *like him* ek hou nogal van hom; ∼ *warm* taamlik warm

quits gelyk, kiets; *we are* ∼ *now* nou is ons kiets

quiv'er (n) pylkoker;. trilling; *in a* ∼ sidde= rend; (v) tril, beef/bewe, ritsel

quixot'ic (a) buitensporig, avontuurlik

quiz (n) vasvrawedstryd; spotterny; (v) on= dervra, uitvra *also* **inter'rogate**; belaglik maak

quoit (n) gooiskyf, gooiring

quor'um kworum

quot'a -s aandeel, kwota *also* **share**

quota'tion (n) aanhaling; kwotasie; notering; prysopgawe; ∼ **marks** aanhaaltekens

quote (v) aanhaal, kwoteer, siteer; ∼ . . . *un= quote* aanhaal . . . afhaal

quo'tient resultaat (van deling), kwosiënt

R

rabb'i -s rabbi, rabbyn

rab'bit konyn *see* **hare**; nuweling

rabb'le (n) gespuis, hoipolloi, gepeupel

rab'id woes, onstuimig *also* **berserk'**

rab'ies hondsdolheid

race[1] (n) ras, geslag; ∼ **rela'tions** rassever= houdinge

race[2] (n) wedloop (atletiek), wedren/ren (per= de, motors); wedvaart (kano's, (seil)jagte); wedvlug (vlieg- en sweeftuie); (v) reisies/ resies ja; hardloop; ren; ∼**course** renbaan, re(i)siesbaan

race: ∼**horse** renperd; ∼ **mee'ting** wedren(ne)

ra'cial ras=; ∼ **discrimina'tion** rassediskrimi= nasie; ∼**ism** rassehaat

ra'cing renne, wedrenne, resies (ja); ∼ **dri'ver** renjaer (mens); ∼ **car** renmotor

rac'ism rassisme; rasseleer

rac'ist rassis (mens); (a) rassisties

rack (n) pynbank; rak; (v) rek, strek; ∼ *one's brains about*... jou hoof breek oor...

rack'et[1] (n) raket, spaan (tennis)

rack'et[2] (n) geraas/rumoer; moeilikheid; be= drogspul; (v) baljaar; lawaai (maak)

racketeer' rampokker, afperser, boef, swende= laar *also* **spiv, con'man**

ra'dar radar; ∼ **op'erator** radaroperateur

ra'dial ply straallaag(band)

ra'diant (a) glansryk, glinsterend; ∼ *with joy* stralend van geluk

radia'tion (uit)straling; bestraling

ra'diator (n) verwarmer; radiator, verkoeler

rad'ical (a) radikaal, ingrypend *also* **fanat'i= cal**; ∼ *change* radikale verandering

ra'dio (n) radio, draadloos; (v) uitsaai

ra'dioactive radioaktief

ra'dio: ∼ **announ'cer** (radio)omroeper; ∼ **drama** hoorspel, radiodrama

ra'dio ham radio-amateur (mens)

ra'diologist radioloog (spesialis)

ra'dio: ∼ **pa'ger** roepradio; ∼ **play** hoorspel

rad'ish -es radys; **black** ∼ ramenas

ra'dius radii straal, radius

raff'ia (n) raffia (palmdrade vir vleg)

raf'fle (n) kantoorloting; lotery; (v) uitloot

raft (n) vlot, dryfhout

raf'ter (n) dakbalk; kap, dakspar

rag[1] (n) vod, flard, toiing, flenter; ∼*s to riches* lompe tot luukse; vodde na vere

rag[2] (n) (studente)jool; (v) skerts

rag'amuffin skobbejak, smeerlap, lieplapper

rag' doll (n) lappop

rage (n) raserny; hartstog; *all the* ∼ hoog in die mode; (v) woed; tier

rag: ∼ **magazi'ne** joolblad; ∼ **proces'sion** jool= optog; ∼**time** gesinkopeerde musiek

raid (n) rooftog, inval, strooptog; klopjag

rail (n) leuning; reling; treinspoor; spoorstaaf; *by* ∼ per spoor; (v) spoorversend

rail'age spoorvrag, vraggeld; vervoerkoste

rail'ing reling, tralie; leuning

rail'road/rail'way -s spoorweg, treinspoor

rail'way: ~ **car'riage** spoorwa; ~ **compart'** **ment** (spoorweg)kompartement; ~ **cros'** **sing** spooroorgang; ~ **line** spoorlyn; ~ **tick'et** treinkaartjie; ~ **track** spoorbaan, trajek

rain (n) reën; (v) reën; *it's* ~*ing cats and dogs* dit reën outannies met hekelpenne; ~**bow** reënboog; ~**bow people** reënboogmense; ~**fall** reënval; ~ **gauge** reënmeter; ~**storm** stortbui; ~**water** reënwater; ~**y** reënerig

raise (n) verhoging (salaris); opslag; (v) optel, ophef, oplig; verhoog; verhef (stem); ~ *an objection* beswaar maak; ~ *objections* be= sware opper

rais'in (n) rosyn(tjie)

rake (n) hark; *as lean as a* ~ so maer soos 'n kraai; (v) hark; oprakel; versamel

rall'y (n) byeenkoms, saamtrek; tydren (mo= tors); (v) vergader (mense); houe wissel (tennis); ~ *to the support* te hulp snel

ram (n) (storm)ram; stamper; (v) vasstamp

ram'ble (v) rondloop; afdwaal; ~**r** swerwer (mens); klimplant; rankroos

ramp (n) helling, opdraand; laaibrug; oprit

ram'rod (n) laaistok

ram'shackle (a) bouvallig, lendelam

ranch (n) (groot) beesplaas/veeplaas

ran'cid (a) suur, rens; goor, galsterig

rand[1] rand (geldeenheid); ~ *for* ~ *system* rand-vir-randstelsel

rand[2] rant; **the R**~ die Witwatersrand *also* **the Reef**

ran'dom (n) toeval; geluk; *at* ~ blindweg, luk= raak; (a) ewekansig; ~ **sam'ple** steekproef *also* **spot check**

ran'dy (a) jags, wulps *also* **lech'erous**; **on heat**

range (n) ry, reeks; speelruimte; ~ **fin'der** af= standmeter

ran'ger veldwagter/boswagter; swerwer

rank[1] rang; ry; gelid; staanplek; (pl) geledere; (v) rangskik; ~*ed/seeded third* derde op die ranglys; ~ *with* gelyk staan met; ~**ing** gra= dering, ranglys *also* **see'ding**

rank[2] (a) welig, geil; onbeskof; ~ **non'sense** pure kaf, klinkklare onsin

ran'sack (v) plunder; deursnuffel, fynkam

ran'som (n) losgeld, losprys; *hold/put to* ~ losgeld vra; (v) vrykoop, verlos

rant (v) grootpraat, spog; uitvaar (teen)

ranunc'ulus ranonkel, botterblom

rap (n) tik; klop; *take the* ~ die blaam/straf kry (vir iem. anders); (v) klop, tik; uitblaker; ~ **(mu'sic)** rap(musiek), kletsrym

rape (n) verkragting; roof; (v) verkrag; onteer; ~ **case** verkragtingsaak

rap'id (n) stroomversnelling; (a) gou, snel, rats; ~ **fire** snelvuur

ra'pier rapier (kort swaard); ~ **fish** swaardvis

ra'pist (n) verkragter (man)

rapt opgetoë, verruk; gespanne; ~ **atten'tion** die ene aandag

rap'ture (n) verrukking; *in* ~*s* verruk

rare seldsaam, skaars; buitengewoon; yl, dun; ~ **collec'tion** seldsame versameling

rare'bit roosterbrood met kaassous; **Welsh** ~ Walliese kaasroosterbrood

rare'ly selde

ra'scal (n) skurk, skelm, vabond, karnallie

rash[1] (n) uitslag (op vel); roos *see* **shin'gles**

rash[2] (a) onbesonne, voortvarend

rasp (n) rasper; gekrap; (v) raspe(r)

ra'spberry ..berries framboos (vrug)

rat (n) rot; oorloper

rat'catcher rot(te)vanger (mens)

ratch'et (n) (sper)rat, tandskyf

rate[1] (n) prys; graad; syfer; koers; ~ **of** **exchan'ge** wisselkoers; ~ **of in'terest** ren= tekoers; **mortal'ity** ~ sterftesyfer; (v) tak= seer, valueer; ~**payer** belastingbetaler (mu= nisipaal); ~**s** erfbelasting

rate[2] (v) uitskel, inklim, uitvaar

ra'ther liewer(s), taamlik; nogal; ~ *not* liewer nie; ~ *pretty* nogal mooierig

ra'tio -s verhouding, ratio

rat'ion (n) rantsoen; porsie; (pl) kosvoorraad, proviand; (v) rantsoeneer

rationale' (n) grondrede/beweegrede, rasionaal

rat'race (n) rotren/rotresies, suksesjag

rattan' bamboes, rottang, spaansriet

ratt'le (n) geratel, gerammel; rammel(aar); (v) ratel, rammel; klets; ~**snake** ratelslang

rat'trap (n) muisval

rauc'ous hees, skor; ~ **voice** rasperstem

rav'age (v) verwoes, plunder; onteer

rave (v) raas, uitvaar; ~ *about* dweep met

rav'en (n) raaf (voël); (v) verslind; roof; (a) ~**ous** roofgierig, vraatsugtig

ravine' kloof, ravyn, skeur *also* **gorge**

ra'ving (a) rasend *also* **fren'zied**; ylend; ~ *mad* stapelgek

rav'ish (v) ontroof; verkrag; bekoor

aw (a) ru; rou; ~ **mate'rial** grondstof, ru=
materiaal; ~ **recruit'** baar rekruut

ay (n) -s straal; (v) uitstraal

'aze (v) uitkrap; sloop, afbreek; ~d *to the*
ground met die grond gelykgemaak

'a'zor skeermes; ~ **blade** skeerlem(metjie); ~
strop slypriem; ~ **wire** lemmetjiesdraad

'e = regar'ding insake

each (n) -es bereik; grens; *above my* ~
bokant my vuurmaakplek; *within* ~ binne
bereik; (v) aanreik, aangee; uitstrek

'eact', reageer, terugwerk; ~ion reaksie,
terugwerking; ~ion com'pany reaksiemaat=
skappy (beveiliging); ~ionary (n) opstan=
deling; (a) opstandig, reaksionêr

'ead lees; ~ *aloud* hardop lees, luidlees; ~ *for*
an examination vir 'n eksamen studeer;
~able leesbaar; ~er leser; leesboek

'ea'dily geredelik, graag

'ea'diness (n) bereidwilligheid; paraatheid

'ead'ing (n) lees; (voor)lesing, belesenheid;
vertolking; *light* ~ ligte lektuur; (a) lesend,
lees=; ~ **book** leesboek; ~ **desk** lessenaar;
~ **lamp** leeslamp; ~ **room** leeskamer

'ea'dy klaar, gereed; ~ **cash** kontant; ~-**made**
klaargemaak(te); ~ **reck'oner** kitsrekenaar

'eaffirm' (v) herbevestig, herbeklemtoon

'e'al (a) wesenlik; werklik, reëel; eg; ~ **esta'te**
vaste eiendom; ~ **esta'te a'gent** eiendoms=
agent; ~ **Mackay** die ware Jakob

'e'alism (n) realisme

'ealisa'tion verwesenliking; besef; realisering
(van bates)

'e'alise (v) besef, realiseer (geld oplewer)

'ealis'tic (a) realisties

'e'ally regtig/rêrig, inderdaad, werklik

'ealm (n) ryk, koninkryk

'eap (v) oes; insamel; win; ~ *advantage* voor=
deel trek; ~er/~ing machine snymasjien

'ear¹ (n) agterhoede, agtergrond

'ear² (v) kweek, teel; grootmaak; oplei; ~
children kinders grootmaak

'ear: ~-ad'miral skout-by-nag; skoutadmi=
raal; ~guard agterhoede

'ear'view mir'ror truspieël(tjie)

'eas'on (n) rede, verstand; *by* ~ *of* weens; *it*
stands to ~ dit spreek vanself; (v) redeneer;
bespreek; ~able redelik, billik; verstandig;
~ing redenering

'eassure' (v) herverseker; gerusstel

'e'bate (n) korting, afslag *also* **dis'count**

'eb'el (n) oproerling, rebel; (a) opstandig

rebel' (v) rebelleer; ~lion opstand, rebellie;
~lious oproerig, opstandig

re'born: ~ **Chris'tian** wedergebore/weerge=
bore Christen

rebound' (n) terugstuiting, terugslag; reaksie;
(v) terugstuit, terugkaats

recall' (v) herroep; terugtrek; *you will* ~ *that*
. . ., jy sal onthou dat . . .

recap' (v) versool (bande) *also* **retread'**

recapit'ulate kortliks herhaal, saamvat/opsom

receipt' (n) ontvangs; bewys, kwitansie; *on* ~
of by ontvangs van; ~ **book** kwitansieboek

receive' (v) ontvang; onthaal; opvang; kry

receiv'er ontvanger; hoorstuk/handstuk (te=
lef.); ~ **of rev'enue** ontvanger van belas=
tings/inkomste, (belasting)gaarder; Jan Taks

re'cent (a) nuut, vars, onlangs, pas gelede; ~ly
onlangs, kort gelede

recep'tion (n) ontvangs; onthaal; verwelko=
ming; ~ist ontvangsdame; ~ **room** ontvang=
kamer

recess' (n) skuilplek; pouse; vakansie, reses;
~ion slapte, resessie (handel)

recharge' (v) herlaai; ~able herlaaibaar

re'cipe (n) resep, voorskrif

recip'ient (n) ontvanger (mens)

recip'rocate (v) terugdoen (gunstig); vergeld

reciproc'ity (n) wederkerigheid, resiprositeit

recit'al verhaal, vertelling; voorlesing; uitvoe=
ring (mus.)

recita'tion voordrag, resitasie; opsomming

recite' (v) opsê, voordra, resiteer

reck'less roekeloos, onverskillig; ~ dri'ving
roekelose bestuur

reck'on reken, tel, skat, glo; ~ *on* staatmaak
op; *day of* ~ing vergeldingsdag

reclama'tion terugwinning; drooglegging

recline' (v) leun, agteroor lê, rus, neervly

recluse' (n) kluisenaar *also* **her'mit**

recogni'tion herkenning; erkenning, waarde=
ring; *in* ~ *of* ter erkenning van

rec'ognise (v) herken; erken, insien

recollec'tion herinnering, geheue

recommend' (v) aanbeveel, aanprys, aanraai;
~ed price aanbevole prys; rigprys

recommenda'tion aanbeveling; *letter of* ~
aanbevelingsbrief

rec'oncile (v) versoen; herenig; bylê

reconcilia'tion (n) versoening, rekonsiliasie;
toenadering

Reconcilia'tion Day Versoeningsdag (vakan=
sie)

recondi'tion (v) opknap, vernu, opdoen
reconn'aissance verkenning, spioentog, spioe=
nasie; ~ **flight** verken(nings)vlug
reconsid'er heroorweeg
reconstruc'tion heropbou, rekonstruksie; ~
and devel'opment heropbou en ontwikke=
ling
rec'ord (n) verslag; register; dokument; re=
kord; (grammofoon)plaat; *beat/break a* ~ 'n
rekord slaan/oortref/breek; *keep a* ~ *of*
rekord hou van (rekordhouding); *on* ~ aan=
geteken, op rekord; ~ **turn'over** rekord=
omset
record' (v) opteken; inskryf; boekstaaf; ver=
meld; opneem (klank); ~**ed mu'sic** musiek=
opname (CD/plaat/band); ~**ing** opname
(klank, beeld)
record'er notulehouer; blokfluit
rec'ord: ~ **li'brary** diskoteek; ~ **play'er** pla=
tespeler
recov'er (v) terugkry *also* **regain'**; terug=
vorder; herstel, gesond word; verhaal (geld);
~ *consciousness* weer bykom;. ~ *damages*
skadevergoeding verhaal/kry; ~**y** herstel=
(ling); terugvordering; (her)winning (myn)
recrea'tion (n) tydverdryf, vermaak, vryetyd=
besteding, ontspanning; rekreasie (vak); ~**al**
facil'ities ontspangeriewe
recruit' (n) rekruut; (v) werf, rekruteer; ~**ment**
(n) werwing; rekrutering
rectang'ular (a) reghoekig
rec'tify (v) aansuiwer; regstel, reghelp
rec'tor rektor; universiteitshoof/prinsipaal;
predikant; ~**ship** rektorskap; leraarskap;
~**y** pastorie (van kerk)
rec'tum recta endelderm, vetderm, rektum
recup'erate (v) herstel, aansterk (pasiënt)
recur' terugkom, herhaal; repeteer (desimaal);
~**rence** terugkeer, herhaling; ~**ring dec'i=
mal** repeterende breuk
recy'cle (v) herwin, hergebruik; hersikleer;
herraffineer (olie)
red: *in the* ~ in die skuld; (a, adv) rooi; **R**~
Cross Soci'ety Rooikruisvereniging; **R**~
Ri'ding Hood Rooikappie; ~**breast** rooi=
borsie; ~**-car'pet recep'tion** vorstelike ver=
welkoming/onthaal
redeem' (v) loskoop, vrykoop; delg (skuld);
~**ing death** soendood
Redeem'er Verlosser, Heiland
redemp'tion (n) verlossing; bevryding; del=
ging, aflossing; ~ **period** delgtermyn

red: ~**-handed** op heter daad/heterdaad
~**-hot** gloeiend warm, vuurwarm
redirect' heradresseer, aanstuur
red'-letter gedenkwaardig, besonder; ~ **day**
gedenkwaardige dag
red' tape burokrasie; rompslomp
reduce' (v) herlei; verminder; ~*d to despair* to
wanhoop gedryf; ~*d rate* verlaagde tarief
reduc'tion vermindering, afslag; inkorting
redun'dant oortollig (personeel); oorbodig
red'water rooiwater (dier); bilharziase (mens)
reed riet; matjiesgoed, biesie; (pl) riete
fluitjiesriet; ~ **war'bler** rietvink
reef (n) -s rif; klipbank, rotslaag
reel¹ (n) rolletjie; garetolletjie; (v) oprol, op=
draai; ~ *off* afrol (tou)
reel² (v) 'n riel dans; wankel; waggel; *my head*
~*s* my kop draai
re-elect' herkies; ~**ion** herkiesing
re-examina'tion hereksamen
re-exam'ine (v) hereksamineer; herondersoek
refer' verwys; ~ *to* verwys na
referee' (n) skeidsregter; referent (om te getuig
ref'erence (n) verwysing; referensie; getuig=
skrif; *with* ~ *to* met betrekking tot; met ver=
wysing na; ~ **guide** naslaangids; ~ **li'brary**
naslaanbiblioteek; ~ **num'ber** verwysnom=
mer
referen'dum referendum, volkstemming
re'fill (n) hervulling; vuller; (v) byvul
refine' (v) verfyn; raffineer (suiker, olie); ~**d**
verfyn; gesuiwer; ~**d man'ners** beskaafde
maniere; ~**ment** verfyning, beskawing; ~**ry**
raffinadery/raffineerdery; suiweringsaanleg
reflec'tion weerkaatsing; weerspieëling; ver=
wyt; *cast a* ~ *upon* blaam werp op
reflec'tor weerkaatser; trukaatser/kaatser; ~
strip/~ **tape** glimstrook
ref'lex (n) -es refleks
reflex'ive wederkerend, refleksief; ~ **verb** we=
derkerende werkwoord
reform' (v) hervorm, verbeter; ~**a'tion** her=
vorming, reformasie; ~**atory** (n) verbete=
ringsgestig; ~**ed** hervormd, gereformeerd
~**er** hervormer; ~ **school** verbeteringskool
refrain'¹ (n) refrein
refrain'² (v) beteuel, bedwing, terughou, weer=
hou; ~ *from* jou weerhou van
refresh' (v) verfris, verkwik, verkoel; ~**er
course** opknapkursus; lenteskool *see* **crash
course**; (a) ~**ing** verfrissend, verkwikkend
refresh'ments verversings

refrig'erator (n) yskas/koelkas; koelkamer (fabriek)

ref'uge (n) toevlug, skuilplek, toevlugsoord

refugee' vlugteling, uitgewekene (mens)

refund' (n) terugbetaling; (v) terugbetaal

refur'bish opknap, herstel also ren'ovate

refuse'¹ weiering, verwerping

ref'use¹ (n) afval, vullis; oorskiet, rommel; ~ bin vullisblik; ~ dump vullishoop

refuse'² (v) weier, verwerp, afwys

regain' herwin, terugkry; ~ consciousness by= kom

eg'al (a) koninklik, vorstelik

regal'ia koninklike waardigheidstekens; kroon= sierade; ampsierade; in full ~ in volle ornaat/ regalia

regard' (n) agting; opsig, betrekking; (pl) groete; in ~ to met betrekking tot; kind ~s to (hartlike) groete aan; in this ~ in hierdie opsig; with ~ to met betrekking tot; (v) beskou, ag; as ~s myself wat my betref; ~ing aangaande, betreffende, rakende also concer'ning

regard'less: ~ of expense ongeag die koste

regatt'a -s wedvaart/roeiwedstryd, regatta

re'gent (n) regent, vors

egime' (n) regering; bewind, regime; under the old ~ onder die ou bedeling/bewind

eg'iment regiment

e'gion (n) streek, landstreek, gebied

e'gional (a) streek(s)=; regionaal, gewestelik; ~ commi'ttee streekkomitee

eg'ister (n) register; rol; (v) registreer; aan= teken; inskryf; ~ a letter 'n brief laat aan= teken/registreer; ~ed ow'ner geregistreer= de/regmatige eienaar; ~ed stu'dent inge= skrewe/geregistreerde student

eg'istrar (n) registrateur (universiteit); kli= niese assistent (med.); griffier (hof)

egistra'tion registrasie; inskrywing

egret' (n) spyt, berou, verdriet, hartseer; hear with ~ met leedwese verneem; (v) spyt hê, betreur; I ~ to say dit spyt my om te sê; ~table (a) betreurenswaardig

eg'ular (a) gereeld, reëlmatig; ~ ar'my staan= de mag; ~ hours vaste ure; ~ mee'tings gereelde vergaderings

eg'ulate (v) reël, rangskik, reguleer

egula'tion regulasie; voorskrif, reglement

eg'ulator balans; slinger (aan uurwerk); reëlaar (aan enjin)

ehears'al (n) repetisie, instudering

rehearse' (v) repeteer, instudeer/inoefen

reign (n) regering; bestuur; (v) regeer; ~ of terror skrikbewind

reimburse' (v) terugbetaal, vergoed; goedmaak

rein (n) teuel, leisel; (v) beteuel, in toom hou

rein'deer rendier (bok)

reinforce' (v) versterk, verstewig; inskerp; ~ment/reinforcing versterking; wapening

reit'erate herhaal

re'ject (n) afgekeurde goed; (pl) uitskot

reject' (v) verwerp, afwys; weier; verstoot

rejoice' (v) verheug/bly wees; juig

rejuv'enate verjong, verlewendig

relate' (v) vertel, verhaal; ~d verwant

rela'tion (n) betrekking; verwantskap; in ~ to met betrekking tot; ~ship verwantskap; verhouding; verband (tussen)

rel'ative (n) bloedverwant/familielid; (pl) familie; (a) betreklik, relatief; ~ pro'noun betreklike voornaamwoord

relativ'ity relatiwiteit

relax' (v) verslap; ontspan; verlig; ~a'tion verslapping; ontspanning; versagting

relay' (n) -s aflosspan; heruitsending (radio); (v) heruitsaai; ~ race afloswedloop

release' (n) loslating, ontslag; (v) loslaat; ont= slaan; vrylaat; ~ of hostages vrylating van gyselaars; press ~ persverklaring

rel'evant toepaslik, ter sake, relevant

reli'able (a) betroubaar, vertroubaar; deeglik

relief' (n) verligting, oplugting; ondersteuning, noodleniging; what a ~! wat 'n verligting!; ~ fund noodlenigingsfonds

relieve' (v) verlig, ondersteun; aflos; ~ the guard die wag aflos

reli'gion (n) godsdiens; geloof also faith

reli'gious godsdienstig, vroom; stip; ~ deno= mina'tion kerkverband; kerkgroep; ~ in= struc'tion godsdiensonderrig

relinq'uish (v) afsien van, laat vaar, opgee

rel'ish (n) smaak, geur; voorsmaak; neiging; eat with ~ smaaklik eet

reloca'te (v) (weg)trek, verhuis also mo've

reluc'tant (a) weerstrewig, teensinnig; ~ly teensinnig, onwillig, langtand

rely' (v) vertrou/reken op, staatmaak op

remain' bly; oorbly; ~der oorblyfsel, oorskot; res; ~s oorblyfsels; stoflike oorskot

remark' (n) aanmerking (ongunstig); opmer= king; (v) aanmerk (ongunstig); opmerk; ~able merkwaardig, opmerklik

remed'ial (a) heilsaam; helend/genesend; re=

mediërend; ~ **educa'tion** remediërende on=
derwys/onderrig
rem'edy (n) geneesmiddel/boereraat; kuur;
regsmiddel; (v) regstel, herstel; genees; re=
medieer
remem'ber onthou; byval; ~ *me to your
friends* sê groete aan jou vriende
remem'brance aandenking; gedagtenis; **day
of** ~ gedenkdag
remind' herinner, help onthou; ~**er** aanma=
ning; wenk
remit' (v) terugstuur; terugkeer; terugbetaal;
~**tance** geldsending
rem'nant (n) oorblyfsel, oorskot; restant, oor=
skietlap; ~ **sale** restantverkoping
remorse' (n) (gewetens)wroeging, berou
remote' ver/vêr, afgeleë, verwyderd; ~ **con=
trol'** afstand(s)beheer; *not the* ~*st idea* nie
die vaagste benul nie
remov'al verwydering; verhuising; verplasing;
~**s van** verhuiswa, meubelwa
remove' (v) verwyder; verplaas; verhuis *also*
re'locate; ontslaan/afdank
remunera'tion (n) vergoeding, besoldiging
ren'der (v) lewer; oorgee; ~ *assistance* hulp
verleen; ~ *a service* 'n diens bewys;
account' ~**ed** gelewerde rekening
ren'dering lewering; vertolking (musiekstuk)
ren'dezvous (n) vergaderplek, versamelplek,
saamtrek, rendezvous
ren'egade (n) renegaat; droster
renew' (v) vernuwe; hernu(we); hervat; *please*
~ *your subscription* geliewe u intekening/
subskripsie te hernu; ~**al** hernuwing; ~**al
no'tice** hernuwingkennisgewing
renova'tion vernuwing, opknapping
rent (n) huur; huurgeld; (v) huur, verhuur; ~**al**
huur(geld)
reo'pen heropen (skool)
reorganisa'tion (n) herindeling, reorganisasie
repair' (n) herstel(ling), reparasie; (pl) herstel=
werk; *out of* ~ onklaar; stukkend; (v) reg=
maak, herstel; vergoed
repay' terugbetaal; ~**able** terugbetaalbaar;
~**ment** terugbetaling
repeat' (n) herhaling; (v) herhaal, repeteer;
~**edly** herhaaldelik
repel' (v) verdryf, terugdryf; **odour** ~**lent**
reukweerder, deodorant
repent' spyt hê, berou hê; ~**ance** berou
repercus'sion terugslag; nasleep, reperkussie;
cause ~**s** opslae maak

repeti'tion herhaling, repetisie
replace' verplaas, vervang; terugsit
re'play (n) trubeeld, kyk weer (TV)
replen'ish aanvul, vol maak *also* **restock'**
rep'lica ewebeeld; replika (kopie)
reply' (n) **replies** antwoord; *in* ~ *to* in ant=
woord op; (v) antwoord (gee)
report' (n) berig, verslag, rapport; (v) aan=
meld; berig, verslag doen/lewer; rapporteer:
~ *back* terugrapporteer; *he must* ~ *to the
trainer* hy moet hom by die afrigter
aanmeld; ~**er** verslaggewer *also* **jour'nalist**
represent' (v) verteenwoordig; voorstel
represent'ative (n) verteenwoordiger; (a) ver=
teenwoordigend; ~ **commit'tee** skakelko=
mitee *also* **liai'son commit'tee**
reprieve' (n) uitstel, opskorting; *grant a* ~
begenadig; (v) uitstel, opskort
rep'rimand (n) berisping, teregwysing; (v)
berispe, teregwys, bestraf *also* **admon'ish**
re'print herdruk; oordruk
repri'sal (n) vergelding, weerwraak; ~ **attack**
wraakaanval
reproach' (n) verwyt, berisping; blaam; (v)
verwyt, berispe
reproduce' (v) kopieer, reproduseer; namaak
reproduc'tion reproduksie, weergawe
rep'tile (n) reptiel; kruipende gedierte
repub'lic republiek; ~**an** (n) republikein
repud'iate (v) repudieer; loën, ontken
repul'sive weersinwekkend, afstootlik
rep'utable (a) fatsoenlik, agtenswaardig, res=
pektabel; betroubaar (firma)
reputa'tion aansien, eer, agting, reputasie
request' (n) versoek, vraag; *by* ~ op versoek
(v) versoek; vra; ~ *the company of* hartlik
vriendelik (uit)nooi; ~ **item** versoeknom=
mer (radio)
require' (ver)eis; ~**d** gevra, verlang; ~**men'
vereiste, benodig(d)heid, behoefte
requisi'tion (n) rekwisisie; (v) opkommandee:
res'cue (n) redding; (v) red, bevry; ~ **attempt**
redpoging; ~ **par'ty** reddingspan; ~**r** redde:
research' (n) navorsing; ondersoek; (v) na
vors, naspoor; ~ **work** navorsing, bronne
studie
resem'blance (n) ooreenkoms, gelykenis
resent' kwalik neem, beledig voel; ~**ful** lig
geraak, gevoelig; ~**ment** wrok, wrewel
reserva'tion (n) voorbehoud; bedenking; be
waring; bespreking (plek)
reserve' (n) reserwe, noodvoorraad; terug

houdendheid; reservaat; *without* ~ sonder
voorbehoud; (v) voorbehou; agterhou, re=
serveer; bespreek (sitplek); ~ *the right* die
reg (voor)behou
reserv'ist reservis (polisie)
res'ervoir (n) reservoir, opgaardam
reset'tle hervestig; ~**ment** hervestiging
reside' (v) woon, bly *also* **live, stay**; setel
res'idence woonplek; verblyf, inwoning;
board and ~ kos en inwoning; *be in* ~
inwoon; tuis/terug wees
res'ident (n) bewoner; inwoner; (a) woon=
agtig; inwonend; ~ **doc'tor** inwonende ge=
neesheer; ~ **engineer'** resident-ingenieur;
~**'s per'mit** verblyfpermit
residen'tial woon=; verblyf=; inwonend; ~
area/quar'ter woonbuurt
resign' (v) bedank, ontslag neem; ~ *from a*
committee uit 'n komitee bedank; ~**a'tion**
bedanking, ontslag; gelatenheid
resil'ience veerkrag, elastisiteit, fleksiteit
res'in (n) harpuis
resist' (v) weerstaan; teenstribbel; ~ *the*
temptation die versoeking weerstaan
resis'tance weerstand, teenstand; *the line of*
least ~ die weg van die geringste weer=
stand; *passive* ~ lydelike verset; ~ **move'=**
ment weerstand(s)beweging
resolu'tion (n) besluit, beslissing; resolusie
(vergaderings); *good* ~*s* goeie voornemens
resolve' (v) voorneem; besluit, beslis; oplos
('n probleem)
resort' (n) toevlugsoord; redmiddel; (v) sy
toevlug neem tot; ~ *to force* geweld ge=
bruik; **hol'iday** ~ vakansieoord; **pleas'ure**
~ plesieroord
resound' (v) weergalm, weerklink, skal
resource' hulpbron, redmiddel; (pl) geldmid=
dele, talente; **hu'man** ~**s** menslike hulp=
bronne, mensebronne; **nat'ural** ~**s** natuur=
bronne; ~**ful** slim, vindingryk, skerpsinnig
also **in'novative**
respect' (n) eerbied; agting; (pl) groete; *in all*
~*s* in alle opsigte; *in* ~ *of* met betrekking
tot; betreffende, rakende; uit hoofde van;
pay last ~*s* die laaste eer bewys; *with* ~ *to*
met betrekking tot; ~**able** fatsoenlik; res=
pektabel; ~**ed** geëer, geag; ~**ful** eerbiedig,
beleef(d); ~**ive** betreklik, respektief; ~**ive**
cap'tains onderskeie kapteins
respira'tion asemhaling *also* **brea'thing**
respond' antwoord, reageer; ~**ent** verweerder,

respondent (hofsaak)
response' (n) antwoord; respons(ie); weer=
klank; *make no* ~ nie reageer nie
responsibil'ity ..**ties** verantwoordelikheid;
aanspreeklikheid
respon'sible verantwoordelik; betroubaar
rest¹ (n) oorskiet, res
rest² (n) rus, pouse; blaaskans; *for the* ~
origens; *lay to* ~ ter ruste lê (begrawe); (v)
rus; slaap; *the decision* ~*s with you* jy moet
besluit
res'taurant restourant/restaurant; eetplek
rest: ~ **camp** ruskamp; ~ **cure** ruskuur; ~**ful**
rustig, stil; ~ **house** herberg
rest'less rusteloos, woelig
restore' teruggee; herstel; restoureer
restrain' bedwing, beteuel, beperk, inhou.
restrict' (v) beperk, begrens, bepaal; inperk
restric'tion beperking, restriksie, inperking
result' (n) gevolg, uitslag, resultaat; (v) volg,
ontstaan, voortspruit; **examina'tion** ~**(s)**
eksamenuitslag
resume' (v) hervat; saamvat; vervolg
resurrec'tion wederopstanding, verrysenis
retail' (v) rondvertel; ~ *at* verkoop teen
ret'ail (n) kleinhandel; ~ **dea'ler** kleinhande=
laar; ~**er** kleinhandelaar; ~ **price** klein=
handelprys, verbruikersprys
retain' behou; ~**ing fee/**~**er** bindgeld; reten=
siegeld; ~**ing wall** stutmuur
retal'iate (v) vergeld, terugbetaal, terugveg
retard' vertraag, uitstel, belemmer; ~**ed child**
(verstandelik) gestremde/vertraagde kind
ret'ina (n) netvlies (oog), retina
retire' (v) (jou) terugtrek; ontslag neem;
aftree; uittree; ~ *on a pension* met pensioen
aftree; ~**d** oud=, gewese; stil; teruggetrok=
ke; gepensioeneer; ~**d chair'person** uitge=
trede voorsitter; ~**ment** aftrede; uittrede;
~**ment annu'ity** aftreeannuïteit; ~**ment**
vil'lage aftreeoord
retir'ing stil, beskeie; ingetoë; ~ **chair'man/**
chair'person uittredende voorsitter
retract' terugtrek (jou woorde); herroep
retread' (v) versool; ~**s** versoolde bande
retreat' (n) aftog, terugtog; skuilplek; *sound*
the ~ die aftog blaas; (v) (jou) terugtrek
retrench' besnoei (personeel); afdank; ~**ment**
besnoeiing, inkorting; afdanking
retribu'tion vergelding, weerwraak *also*
repri'sal; *war of* ~ vergeldingsoorlog
retrieve' (v) terugkry; red; opspoor; ~ *in=*

formation inligting ontsluit; ~**r** jaghond
ret′rospect/retrospec′tion terugblik; *in* ~ agterna beskou, terugskouend
retrospec′tive terugwerkend
return′ (n) terugkeer, terugkoms; opbrengs, rendement (op belegging); opgawe; *many happy* ~*s* nog baie jare; (v) terugkom; terugstuur, teruggee; ~ **date/**~ **day** keerdatum, keerdag; ~ **jour′ney** terugreis; ~ **match** teenwedstryd; ~ **tic′ket** retoerkaartjie
reun′ion (n) hereniging, reünie/re-unie
revamp′ (v) opknap; restoureer
reveal′ openbaar, blootlê; onthul
rev′el (v) jolyt/rumoer/pret maak; fuif; swelg, bras; ~ *in* jou verlustig in
revela′tion openbaring, onthulling
rev′eller jolytmaker, pretmaker *also* **mer′rymaker**
revenge′ (n) wraak; (v) wreek; ~**ful** wraakgierig, wraaksugtig
rev′enue (n) inkomste; ~ **ser′vices** inkomstedienste; ~ **stamp** inkomseseël
rev′erence (n) eerbied, hoogagting, ontsag; *hold in* ~ eer; *pay* ~ eer betoon
rev′erend (n) eerwaarde; dominee; (a) eerwaarde
rev′erie (n) mymering, dromery, gepeins
reverse′ (n) keersy, agterkant; teenspoed; neerlaag; trurat; (v) omkeer; omdraai; tru; nietig verklaar (uitspraak); ~ *a judgment* ’n uitspraak omverwerp/ter syde stel; ~ **gear** trurat; ~ **side** keersy
revert′ (v) omkeer; terugkeer; terugval
review′ (n) oorsig; resensie/boekbespreking; (v) beoordeel, bespreek, resenseer; ~**er** beoordelaar, resensent (mens)
revise′ (v) hersien, bywerk; verbeter; wysig; ~**d edi′tion** hersiene uitgawe
revi′sion hersiening, revisie
revi′val (n) herlewing; oplewing; opwekking
revive′ (v) herleef; opwek; bykom; ~ *a patient* ’n pasiënt bybring
revoke′ (v) herroep (’n wet); vernietig; intrek
revolt′ (n) opstand, oproer; (v) in opstand kom; ~**ing** weersinwekkend
revolu′tion revolusie/rewolusie; omwenteling; kringloop, wenteling, toer; ~**ary** (n) opstandeling, revolusionêr; (a) revolusionêr, opstandig; ~**s coun′ter** toereteller (masjien) *also* **rev coun′ter**; ~**ise** omkeer
revol′ver rewolwer
revol′ving draai=; wentel=; ~ **cred′it** wentel=

krediet; ~ **restaurant** wentelrestourant
revue′ (n) musiekkomedie, revue
reward′ (n) beloning, vergoeding; *due* ~ verdiende loon; (v) beloon; vergeld
rhap′sody **..dies** rapsodie (mus.)
rhet′oric retoriek, welsprekendheid; ~**al** retories, hoogdrawend; welsprekend
rheumat′ic (n) rumatieklyer; ~ **fe′ver** rumatiekkoors, sinkingkoors
rheum′atism rumatiek
rhinoc′eros -es renoster *also* **rhi′no** (sing + pl)
Rhode′sia Rhodesië (tans Zimbabwe); ~**n ridge′back** rifrug(hond), pronkrughond
rhu′barb rabarber (groente)
rhyme (n) rym; rympie; poësie; (v) rym, dig
rhy′thm (n) ritme, maat; ~**ic(al)** ritmies
rib (n) rib, ribbetjie, ribbebeen
ribb′on lint, band; *tear to* ~*s* in flenters/flarde skeur; ~ **worm** snoerwurm *see* **tape′worm**
rice rys; ~ **pa′per** ryspapier
rich (a) ryk; kosbaar, vrugbaar (grond); voedsaam (kos); ~ **food** ryk kos; ~**es** rykdom; weelde; ~**ness** rykheid, oorvloed
rick′ets ragitis, Engelse siekte
rick′ety (a) slap, lendelam *also* **tot′tering**
rick′shaw riksja
ric′ochet (n) opslagkoeël; (v) opslaan
rid vry maak, ontslaan; verlos; verwyder; *be* ~ *of* kwyt wees; *get* ~ *of* ontslae raak van; ~**dance** bevryding, verlossing; *good* ~*dance* ’n ware oplugting, dankie bly
rid′dle (n) raaisel; (v) raai
ride (n) rit, toer; (v) ry, bery; ~**r** ruiter
ridge (n) rug; nok (dak); kant; krans; bult, bergrug; middelmannetjie; (v) rimpel, riffel; ~**back** rifrug(hond)
ridic′ulous (a) belaglik, verspot *also* **lu′dicrous**
ri′ding: ~ **bree′ches** rybroek; ~ **hab′it** rykostuum; ~ **whip/crop** rysweep, karwats, peits
riem riem; ~**pie** riempie
riff′-raff uitvaagsel, gespuis, skorriemorrie, hoipolloi *also* **rab′ble**
ri′fle (n) geweer; roer; ~ **club** skietvereniging; ~ **comman′do** skietkommando; ~**man** skutter; skerpskutter, skut; ~ **range** skietbaan
rift (n) skeur, bars; ~ **val′ley** slenkdal
rig (n) uitrusting; touwerk (skip); boortoring; (v) aantrek, optooi; manipuleer (verkiesing); ~**ger** takelaar (ambagsman)
right (n) reg, aanspraak; (pl) regte; *keep to the* ~ hou regs; *might is* ~ mag is reg; (v) reg=

stel; verbeter; (a) billik; regverdig; *at ~ angles* reghoekig; *in his ~ mind* by sy volle verstand; (adv) presies, reg; ~**-about** regs om; ~ **angle** regte hoek; ~**eous** regverdig, regskape; ~**ful** regmatig, wettig; ~**-handed** regs; ~**ly** tereg, presies, juis; ~**wing** regtervleuel; regsgesind (politiek)

rig′id (a) styf; streng; vas; rigied

rig′marole kaf; kletsery; gedoente

rim (n) rand; lys; velling (wiel)

ring[1] (n) ring; kring; kryt; (v) omring/omkring

ring[2] (n) klank; gelui; geluid; *have a familiar ~* bekend klink; (v) lui; telefoneer; bel

ring: ~**fin′ger** ringvinger, naaspinkie; ~**lea′der** belhamel, voorbok; ~**let** ringetjie; ~ **road** ringpad/sirkelpad; ~**worm** omloop

rink (n) baan, skaatsbaan/ysbaan; (v) skaats

rinse (v) uitspoel, afspoel

ri′ot (n) oproer, muitery; (v) muit, oproer maak; ~**er** oproermaker; ~**ous** oproerig; ~ **poli′ce** onluspolisie

rip (n) skeur; (v) oopskeur; ~**cord** trekkoord (valskerm)

ripe ryp; oud; beleë (wyn); ~ **age** hoë ouderdom; ~**n** ryp word; ryp maak

rip′ple (n) rimpeling, kabbeling; (v) kabbel, rimpel; ~ **effect′** rimpeleffek

rise (n) styging, opgang; opkoms (son); verhoging (salaris); toename; opdraand; *give ~ to* aanleiding gee tot; (v) styg; opkom; ontstaan

risk (n) gevaar, risiko; (v) waag, riskeer; ~**y** gewaag, riskant

rite (n) plegtigheid, ritus/rite, seremonie

rit′ual (n) kerkgebruik; ritueel; (a) ritueel; ~ **mur′der** rituele moord

riv′al (n) mededinger; teenstander *also* **oppo′nent**; (v) meeding, wedywer; (a) mededingend; ~**ry** mededinging, wedywer(ing)

riv′er rivier, stroom; ~ **ba′sin** stroomgebied; ~**bed** rivierbedding; ~**side** rivieroewer; ~ **tor′toise** waterskilpad

riv′et (n) klinknael; kram; (v) (vas)klink

road (n) pad, weg; *rules of the ~* verkeersregulasies; ~**block** padblokkade, padversperring; ~**hog** padvark; jaagduiwel; ~**house** padkafee; ~**race** padwedloop, padren; ~ **sa′fety** padveiligheid; ~**sign** padteken; ~**wor′thy** padwaardig; ~**wor′thy certif′icate** padwaardig(heid)sertifikaat

roam rondswerf/rondswerwe; ronddool; ~**ing** swerming (selfoon)

roan skimmel (perd)

roan′ an′telope bastergemsbok

roar (n) gebrul; gebulder; (v) brul; raas; ~ *with laughter* skater van die lag

roar′ing (a) brullend; dreunend; eersteklas, uitstekend; *a ~ time* groot pret/plesier; ~ *trade* lewendige handel, goeie besigheid

roast (n) braaivleis; (v) braai, bak

rob (v) (be)roof, steel; besteel; plunder; ~**ber** rower, dief; ~**bery** roof, rooftog *see* **heist**

robe (n) japon; toga; mantel; ~**s of of′fice** ampsgewaad

rob′in rooiborsie (voël)

ro′bot robot; outomaat

robust′ (a) sterk, gespierd, kragtig *also* **vir′ile**

rock[1] (n) rots, kliprots; ~**drill** klipboor, diamantboor; ~**ery′** rotstuin

rock[2] (v) skud, skommel; wieg; wankel; *~ to sleep* aan die slaap wieg

rock[3] rock (musiekstyl) *see* **soul, coun′try**

rock′-'n'-roll ruk-en-rol, ruk-en-pluk

rock′et vuurpyl; ~ **laun′cher** vuurpylrigter

rock′ing: ~ **chair** skommelstoel; ~ **horse** hobbelperd

rock: ~**fall** rotsstorting; drukbars (myn); ~ **pi′geon** bosduif, kransduif; ~**rab′bit** das (sie); ~**y** rotsagtig, klipperig

rod stang, staaf; (tug)roede

ro′dent (n) knaagdier; (a) knaag-; ~ **exter′minator** rot(te)vanger

roe takbokooi; ~**buck** gemsbok (Bybel)

rogue skurk, boef, booswig; skelm, vabond; ~ **el′ephant** dwaalolifant

role rol, funksie; ~ **play′er** rolspeler

roll (n) rol, register; broodjie; ~ *of honour* ererol; (v) rol, oprol; ~ *one's R's* bry; ~ *up* oprol; opdaag; ~**call** appèl, naamlesing

roll′er roller; rolstok; ~**bla′des** rollemskaatse, inlynskaatse *also* **in′line ska′tes**; ~ **blind** rolgordyn; ~ **coas′ter** wipwaentjie, tuimeltrein(tjie); ~ **skate** rolskaats

roll′ick (v) baljaar, vrolik wees

roll′ing golwend, rollend; ~ **pin** deegroller; ~ **stock** rollende materiaal (spoorweg)

ro′ly-po′ly (n) rolpoeding; klein vetsak, potjierol (kind)

Ro′man (n) Romein; romein (letter); (a) Romeins; Rooms; ~ **Cath′olic** Rooms-Katoliek

roman′tic (a) romanties; ~**ism** romantiek

Rome Rome; *do in ~ as the Romans do* skik jou na die omstandighede

romp (v) stoei, baljaar, jakker, ravot; ~ *home*

maklik eerste kom; fluit-fluit wen
ronda'vel rondawel
roof (n) -s dak; verhemelte (van mond); gewelf; *thatched* ~ grasdak; ~ **car'rier** dakrak, bagasierak (motor); ~**clut'cher** dakvink (motoris); ~ **gar'den** daktuin; ~**wet'ting** dakviering, huisinwyding *also* **house-war'ming**
room (n) kamer, vertrek; ~s spreekkamer (dokter); ~y ruim, groot *also* **spa'cious**
roost (n) slaapplek; slaapstok; *go to* ~ gaan slaap; *rule the* ~ baasspeel
roos'ter (hoender)haan
root (n) wortel; stam; oorsprong; *the* ~ *of all evil* die wortel van alle kwaad; (v) wortelskiet; ~ *up* uitroei
rope (n) tou, lyn; *know the* ~s goed ingelig/touwys wees; ~**lad'der** touleer; ~**wal'ker** koordloper
ro'sary rosekrans, paternoster; roostuin
rose (n) roos; roset; sproeier (gieter); *under the* ~ in die geheim; (a) rooskleurig; ~ **apple** jamboes; ~**bud** roosknop
rose'mary ..ries roosmaryn
rosette' roset, kokarde
ros'in (n) hars; vioolhars *also* **res'in**
ros'ter (n) rooster, tydtafel; skedule
ros'trum rostrum, podium; snawel, bek
ro'sy (a) rooskleurig, blosend
rot (n) verrotting; onsin; *dry* ~ vermolming; *tommy*~ kaf, onsin; (v) verrot, vergaan, verkwyn; terg, pla
Rota'rian Rondariër (mens)
ro'tary ronddraaiend, roterend
rotate' (v) draai, wentel *also* **revol've**; roteer; afwissel (gesaaides)
rota'tion rotasie, wenteling; *by* ~ om die beurt, rotasiegewys; ~ *of crops* wisselbou
rott'en (a) verrot, bederf; vrotsig, beroerd
rough (n) ruveld/sukkelveld (gholf); (v) ru/grof maak; touwys maak; ~ *it* jou ongerief/ongemak getroos; (a) ru, grof; ruig; *make a* ~ *guess* naastenby skat; ~**-and-tum'ble** (n) geveg, worsteling; ~**book** kladboek; ~ **draft** konsep; ~**ly** naastenby, ruweg; ~**man'ners** onbeskaafde maniere; ~**ness** ruheid; oneffenheid; ~ **play** ruwe spel; ~**ri'der** perdetemmer, baasruiter
roulette' roulette/roelet, dobbelwiel
round (n) rondte (om baan); rondgang, kring; ronde (boks, stoei); (a) rond; gerond; ~ *figures* rondesyfers/rondesom (geld); (adv, prep) rondom, in die rondte; *bring* ~

bybring (na 'n floute); *show* ~ rondneem; ~**ed** gerond, afgerond; ~**ly** ronduit, botweg; ~**ness** rondheid, volheid; ~ **rob'in** rondomtalie (speelpatroon); ~ **up** bymekaarmaak (vee); klopjag
Round Table (n) Tafelronde; ~**r** Tafelaar
rouse (v) wakker maak; wek, opja
route (n) pad, koers, roete; *en* ~ onderweg
routine' (n) sleur, gewoonte, roetine
row[1] (n) ry; reeks; *in* ~s in rye
row[2] (v) roei
row[3] (n) geraas, lawaai; rusie; *kick up a* ~ lawaai maak; ~**dy** rumoerig *also* **noi'sy**
roy'al koninklik *also* **impe'rial**; rojaal, uitstekend, eersteklas; *a* ~ *time* 'n heerlike tyd; ~ **game** kroonwild; ~**ist** rojalis, koning(s)gesinde; ~**ty** koningskap; die koningshuis; outeursaandeel (aan skrywer); vrugreg (myn)
rub (n) wrywing; moeilikheid, *there's the* ~ daar lê die knoop; (v) blink maak; vryf, skuur; ~ *shoulders with* in aanraking kom met
rubb'er (n) gomlastiek, rubber; uitveër; ~ **stamp** stempel, tjap
rubb'ish vullis, vuilis *also* **trash**; rommel; onsin, kaf; ~ **remo'val** vullisverwydering
rub'ble puin; bourommel
ru'by rubies robyn; robynkleur
ruck'sack rugsak, knapsak *also* **knap'sack**
ruc'tion (n) rusie, twis; onenigheid
rudd'er roer, stuur (van boot)
rude (a) onbeskof; onbeskaaf *also* **cru'de**; ~**ness** onbeskoftheid
ru'diment grondslag, beginsel; (pl) grond)eginsels, eerste beginsels
ruff'ian (n) booswig, skurk, molesmaker
ruf'fle (v) frommel, kreukel; iem. vererg/ontstel; ~**d hair** deurmekaar hare
rug (reis)deken; vloerkleed
rug'by rugby(voetbal)
ru'in (n) bouval, puinhoop; ruïne/murasie
rule (n) reël; reglement; bewind; liniaal; *the golden* ~ die gulde reël; *hard and fast* ~s vaste reëls; ~ *of law* regsoewereiniteit; ~ *of the road* verkeersreël; (v) reël, vasstel; regeer; linieer; ~ *out* uitskakel; ~ *the roost* baasspeel; ~**r** heerser/regeerder; bewindhebber; liniaal
rul'ing (n) beslissing; uitspraak; reëling; (a) regerend, bewindhebbend; heersend; ~ **par'ty** bewindhebbende/regerende party; ~

price heersende prys
rum (n) rum
rum'ble (n) gerommel, geratel; (v) rommel, ratel, dreun; ~ **strip** dreunstrook (teerpad)
rum'our (n) gerug; *mere* ~ riemtelegram
rump'steak kruisstuk/kruisskyf, rumpsteak
rum'pus (n) herrie, moles, opstootjie; ~ **room** jolkamer, gesinskamer
run' (n) lopie (krieket); verloop; wedloop; *have a ~ for one's money* waarde vir jou geld hê; (v) hardloop/hol; draf; stroom; dryf (saak); ~ *up bills,* ~ *into debt* skuld maak; ~ *down* omry/omloop; opspoor; slegmaak; ~ *the risk* die risiko loop; ~ *a shop* 'n winkel bestuur/bedryf; ~ *the show* baas wees
run'away (n) wegloper; (a) gevlug; op hol; ~ **vic'tory** wegholoorwinning
rung (n) sport (van 'n leer)
runn'er loper; boodskapper; hardloper; ~ **bean** rankboon; ~-**up** naaswenner
runn'ing (a) stromend, lopend; *three days* ~ drie dae aanmekaar; ~ **com'mentary** (deur)lopende kommentaar; ~ **costs** loop-

koste (motor); ~ **expen'ses** daaglikse uitgawes; ~ **no'se** snotneus (kind); ~ **shorts** drafbroekie; ~ **stom'ach/tum'my** loopmaag
run'way (n) aanloopbaan/stygbaan (vliegtuig); stroombed (rivier)
rup'ture (n) breuk *also* **frac'ture**; skeuring
rur'al (a) landelik; plattelands
rush (v) stormloop; voortsnel; haastig maak; ~ *at* bestorm; ~ *matters* oorhaastig te werk gaan; ~ **hour** spitsuur *also* **peak hour**
rusk (boer)beskuit (droog)
Ru'ssia Rusland; ~**n** (n) Rus; (a) Russies
rust (n) roes; (v) roes; verroes
rus'tic (a) landelik; vreedsaam; onbedorwe
ru'stle (n) geritsel; (v) ritsel, suisel; veediefstal pleeg; ~**r** veedief/veestroper
rust: ~**proof'ing** roeswering; ~ **resis'tant** (a) roeswerend
rut (n) groef; gewoonte, roetine; sleur
ruth'less (a) onbarmhartig, meedoënloos, wreed *also* **mer'ciless**
rutt'ish bronstig, loops, op hitte (diere)
rye rog; ~ **bread** rogbrood

S

Sabb'ath (n) Sabbat, rusdag
sabbat'ic sabbat-; ~**al leave** sabbatsverlof (vir studie/navorsing)
sa'ble an'telope swartwitpens(bok)
sab'otage (n) sabotasie; (v) saboteer, ondermyn, rysmier, ondergrawe
sab'oteur saboteur, ondermyner (mens)
sa'bre (n) sabel; ~ **rattling** wapengekletter
sach'et (n): **milk** ~ melksakkie
sack[1] (n) sak *also* **bag**
sack[2] (n) ontslag; plundering; *give the* ~ ontslaan, in die pad steek; *get the* ~ die trekpas kry; (v) afdank/ontslaan *also* **dismiss', fire**; plunder; afsê ('n kêrel)
sac'rament (n) sakrament
sa'cred (a) heilig, gewyd
sac'rifice (n) offer, offerande; opoffering; *make the supreme* ~ die hoogste offer bring; (v) offer; opoffer
sac'rilege (n) heiligskennis, ontheiliging
sad treurig, droewig, somber *also* **dis'mal**
sad'dle (n) saal; stut; (v) opsaal; belas; *be* ~*d*

with opgeskeep sit met; ~ **girth** buikgord; ~ **horse** ryperd; ~**r** saalmaker; ~**ry** saalmakery; ~**tree** saalboom
sadis'tic (a) sadisties
sad'ness droefheid, treurigheid, verdriet
safa'ri safari, jagtog; ~ **suit** safaripak
safe[1] (n) brandkas, kluis *also* **strong'room**
safe[2] (a) veilig, seker; ~ *and sound* fris en gesond; ~ **con'duct** vrygeleide; ~ **cus'tody** versekerde/veilige bewaring; ~**guard** (n) beskerming, beveiliging; (v) beskerm; vrywaar (van)
safe'ty veiligheid; sekerheid; ~ **belt** veiligheidsgordel, redgordel; ~ **clo'thing** glimdrag; ~ **match** (Sweedse) vuurhoutjie; ~ **pin** haakspeld
sag (v) afsak, hang, verslap
sa'ga -s sage, volksverhaal, legende; familieroman; saga (Noors), heldegeskiedenis
sage (n) salie (plant)
sag'o sago; ~ **tree** meelboom
said het gesê; genoemde

sail (n) seil; (v) vaar, uitseil; ~ **boar'ding** bordseil (sport); ~**cloth** seildoek

sail'ing afvaart; ~ **ves'sel** seilskip

sail'or matroos

saint (n) heilige; (a) heilig; ~**ly** heilig

sake: *for the* ~ *of* ter wille van; *for your* ~ om jou ontwil; *for goodness'* ~ in hemelsnaam

sal'ad slaai *see* **let'tuce;** ~ **dres'sing** slaaisous

sal'amander koggelmander; sal(a)mander

sal'ary (n) **..ries** salaris, loon, besoldiging; ~ *negotiable* salaris reëlbaar; (v) besoldig; ~ **pack'age** salarispakket

sale verkoop, (uit)verkoping, prysfees; veiling; vandisie/vendusie; *for* ~ te koop; ~ **price** uitverkoopprys

sales (n) verkope, afset

sales: ~**man** verkoper, verkoop(s)man; ~**manship'** verkoopkuns; ~ **man'ager** verkoopbestuurder; ~ **talk** smouspraatjies

sal'ient uitstaande; treffend, opvallend

sal'ine (n) soutbron; soutoplossing; (a) soutagtig

sali'va (n) spoeg/spuug, speeksel

salm'on (n) salm; (a) salmkleurig

saloon' (n) saal, salon; eetsaal, kantien

salt (n) sout; (v) insout, pekel; ~**less** soutloos, laf; ~**pan** soutpan

saltpet're (n) salpeter

saluta'tion groet, begroeting; aanhef (brief)

salute' (n) saluut; (v) salueer

sal'vage (n) berging; bergloon; wrakgoedere; (v) berg, red; ~ **ship/ves'sel** bergingskip

salva'tion (n) saligheid, redding, verlossing

Salva'tion Ar'my Heilsleër

Sama'ritan (n) Samaritaan; *good* ~ barmhartige Samaritaan

same (die)selfde; eenders/eners; gelyksoortig; *one and the* ~ presies dieselfde

samp (n) stampmielies

sa'mple (n) monster/proefmonster; steekproef; **ran'dom** ~ steekproef; (v) monsters neem; proe; toets; ~ **room** uitstallokaal

sa'mpling monsterneming

sanator'ium ..ria sanatorium, hersteloord

sanctimon'ious (a) skynheilig, skynvroom

sanc'tion (n) goedkeuring; toestemming; (ekonomiese) strafmaatreël, sanksie; (v) bekragtig, goedkeur *also* **appro've**

sanc'tuary ..ries toevlugsoord, heiligdom *also* **retreat'; bird** ~ voëlreservaat

sand (n) sand; (pl) strand, sandoewer

san'dal (n) sandaal

sand: ~ **glass** sandloper; ~**man** Klaas Vakie; ~**pa'per** skuurpapier

sand'wich (n) **-es** toebroodjie; (v) inskuif; ~ **course** stapelkursus *also* **crash course**

sane (a) verstandig, gesond (van gees)

san'itary sanitêr, gesondheids=

San'ta Claus sinterklaas; Kersvader

sap (n) sap, sop, vog; lewenskrag

sap'ling jong boompie

sapp'er sappeur, geniesoldaat

sapph'ire saffier

sarcas'tic (a) sarkasties, spottend, bytend

sardine' sardien(tjie)

sash[1] **-es** lyfband, serp

sash[2] **-es** raam; ~ **win'dow** skuifraam

Sat'an Satan; duiwel

satch'el boeksak, skooltas; handsakkie

sat'ellite satelliet; volgeling, naloper

sat'in (n) satyn; (a) satyn=

sat'ire (n) satire; spotskrif, hekelskrif

sati'rical satiries, spottend

satisfac'tion (n) voldoening, bevrediging

satisfac'tory (a) bevredigend; voldoende, toereikend, genoegsaam

sat'isfied tevrede; versadig; ~ *with* tevrede met, daarvan oortuig

sat'isfy (v) bevredig; voldoen aan; versadig; gerusstel; ~ *the examiners* slaag

Sat'urday Saterdag

sat'yr (n) sater, faun, bosgod; wellusteling

sauce (n) sous; ~**boat** souskom(metjie); ~**pan** kastrol, pot

sau'cer piering

saun'ter (n) slentergang; (v) slenter, drentel

sau'sage wors, sosys; ~ **roll** worsbroodjie

sav'age (n) barbaar; (v) toetakel, mishandel; (a) woes, barbaars *also* **barba'ric**

savann'ah savanne, grasvlakte *also* **prai'rie**

save[1] (v) red, verlos, salig maak; spaar, bêre; bewaar, behoed; ~ *one's skin* jou bas red

save[2] (prep) behalwe; uitgesonder; (conj) tensy; *the last* ~*/but one* die voorlaaste

sa'ving (n) besparing; (pl) spaargeld; (a) spaarsaam; ~**s bank** spaarbank

Sa'viour Heiland, Saligmaker

sa'vour (v) proe; ruik; ~**y** (n) soutigheid, southappie; (a) smaaklik, geurig

saw (n) saag; (v) saag; ~**dust** saagsel; ~**pit** saagkuil; ~**yer** saer (mens)

sax'ophone saxofoon/saksofoon

say (n) mening, bewering; *have a* ~ *in the matter* seggenskap in die saak hê; (v) sê, vertel, beweer; *never ~ die* moenie moed opgee nie; *so to ~ as* 't ware

say'ing (n) gesegde, spreekwoord *also* **expres'sion**; *it goes without ~* dit spreek vanself

scab roof; skurfte; brandsiek(te)

scaff'old steier; skavot (vir teregstelling); ~**ing** steierwerk, stellasie

scald (v) skroei, brand; opkook; uitkook

scale[1] (n) skaal; toonleer; *on a large ~* grootskaals; grootskeeps; (v) opklim; ~ *down* afskaal

scale[2] (n) skub (vis); skilfer; dopluis

scale[3] (n) weegskaal; *pair of ~s* (weeg)skaal; (v) weeg; trek

scall'op (n) kammossel; skulp; skulpwerk; (v) uitskulp; ~**ed ed'ge** skulprand

scalp (n) skedel; kopvel; (v) skalpeer; kwaai kritiseer; ~ **hun'ter** trofeejagter

scal'pel (n) ontleedmes, skalpeermes

sca'ly skubberig, skilferig

scam (n) swendelary, bedrogspul *also* (**finan'cial) fraud**

scan (v) skandeer/aftas; vluglees/glylees; (af)tas; (n) tasting, skandering; **brain ~** breinskandering/breintasting; **la'ser** ~**ner** lasertaster

scan'dal (n) skandaal, skande; ~**mon'ger** skinderbek, kwaadspreker; ~**ous** skandelik, skandalig *also* **disgra'ceful**

scan'sion skandering (poësie)

scant (a) skraal; *with ~ success* met weinig sukses

scant'y karig, skraps; ~**-pan'ty** amperbroekie, einabroekie, sjoebroekie

scape'goat sondebok, skuldlose (mens)

scar (n) litteken; (v) skram; littekens vorm

scarce (a) skaars, skraps; seldsaam, ~**ly** nouliks, kwalik, ternouernood

scare (n) paniek; (v) skrik maak; afskrik; ~ *away* wegjaag; ~*d stiff* lamgeskrik; ~**crow** voëlverskrikker

scarf (n) **scarves** serp, halsdoek *also* **shawl**

scar'let (n) skarlaken, skarlakenrooi; (a) skarlakenrooi; ~ **fe'ver** skarlakenkoors

scathe (n) letsel; *without ~* ongedeer(d)

scatt'er (v) verstrooi, versprei; ~**-brai'ned** deurmekaar, verward

scav'enge opruim; skoonmaak; ~**r** aasvoël; ~**r beetle** miskruier *also* **dung beetle**

scenar'io (n) draaiboek, filmteks; toekomsbeeld, scenario

scene toneel, tafereel; skouspel; *it is not my ~*

dis nie vir my nie; ~**ry** natuurskoon, landskap; toneeldekorasie, dekor

scen'ic toneel=; skilderagtig; ~ **rail'way** bergspoor; ~ **road/drive** uitsigpad

scent (n) geur, reuk; reukwerk, laventel

scep'tic (a) skepties, ongelowig

scep'tre septer, staf; *wield the ~* die septer swaai

sched'ule (n) lys, skedule, opgawe, tabel; (v) skeduleer; lys; ~**d flight** roostervlug

scheme (n) skema, plan, ontwerp; skets; (v) ontwerp; planne maak; konkel

schol'ar (n) leerling; geleerde; beurshouer; ~**ly** geleerd, (vak)kundig; ~ **patrol'** skolierpatrollie; ~**ship** studiebeurs

school[1] (n) skool; skoolgebou; leerskool; *at ~* op skool; *keep after ~* laat skoolsit; (v) onderwys, leer, onderrig; skool

school[2] (n) skool (visse)

school: ~**board** skoolraad; ~**boy** skoolseun; ~ **hol'iday(s)** skoolvakansie; ~**ing** opvoeding; onderrig; skoling; ~ **inspec'tor** skoolinspekteur; ~**lea'ver** skoolverlater; ~**mas'ter** skoolmeester, onderwyser; ~**mis'tress** onderwyseres; ~ **prin'cipal** skoolhoof, hoofonderwyser, ~**room** skoolkamer, klaskamer; ~**tea'cher** onderwyser

schoon'er skoener (skip)

sci'ence natuurwetenskap; wetenskap; kennis, kunde; ~ **fic'tion** wetenskapfiksie

sci'entist (n) wetenskaplike, natuurkundige

scis'sors skêr; *a pair of ~* 'n skêr

scoff (v) spot, skimp; ~**ing** smalend

scold (v) uitskel, berispe, bestraf; ~**ing** (n) uitbrander; berisping

scone (n) skon, botterbroodjie

scoop (n) potlepel, skeplepel; nuustreffer, scoop (joernalistiek); (v) uitskep; uithol; wins maak; ~ **wheel** skeprat

scoot'er (n) bromponie; ryplank; skopfiets

scope omvang; speling; *beyond the ~ of* buite die bestek van

scorch (v) brand, skroei; ~*ed earth* verskroeide aarde; ~**er** doodhou/kishou, pragstuk

score (n) kerf; rekening; twintigtal; (punte)telling; partituur (mus.); *keep the ~* telling hou; ~*s of times* baiemaal; (v) inkerf; aanteken; tel; onderstreep; ~**board** telbord; punteleer; ~**r** teller; puntemaker (mens)

scorn (n) veragting, hoon; (v) verag, versmaai

scorp'ion skerpioen

scotch (n) **-es** kerf, keep; wig; (v) kerf;

onskadelik maak; verydel; ~**cart** skotskar;
~**light** glimstrokies, glimplate
scot-free ongedeerd; ongestraf, skotvry
scoun'drel skelm, skurk, boef, skobbejak
scour (v) skuur, vryf; rondsoek; ~ *the area* die
omgewing fynkam
scourge gésel; plaag; (v) kasty, teister
scout (n) spioen, verkenner; padvinder; (v)
spioeneer, verken
scowl (n) suur gesig; (v) suur kyk, frons
scrabb'le gekrabbel, gekrap; (v) krap
scrag (a) brandmaer; ~**gy** dun, rietskraal,
(brand)maer; verpot
scram (sl.) (v) trap; (interj) trap!; siejy!
scram'ble (n) gewoel; (v) klouter; woel; grab-
bel; huts (syfers); ~**d eggs** roereiers; ~**r**
veldfiets
scram'bling veldrenne *see* **kar'ting**
scrap[1] (n) stuk; oorskot, afval, skroot; (pl) uitskot; *not care a* ~ geen flenter omgee nie; ~
val'ue oorskotwaarde; (v) skrap; weggooi;
afkeur; sloop
scrap[2] (n) vegparty; (v) baklei
scrap'book plakboek/knipselboek; kladboek
scrape (n) moeilikheid; (v) skraap, kras; ~
through net deurglip; ~ *together* bymekaar-
skraap; ~**r** krapper, krapyster; skraper (pad)
scrap'heap ashoop/asgate; afvalhoop
scrap: ~ **iron** afvalyster, skroot; ~ **val'ue**
sloopwaarde; ~**yard** skrootwerf/wrakwerf
scratch (n) -es krap; (v) krap, skraap; ~ *a horse*
'n perd onttrek (aan 'n wedren); ~ *through*
skrap, deurhaal, doodtrek
scrawl (n) slordige skrif, gekrap; (v) krap
scream (n) skree(u), gil; *a perfect* ~ iets om
jou oor slap te lag; (v) skreeu, gil; ~ *with
laughter* skater van die lag
screech (n) -es gekras, gekrys; (v) kras, krys,
gil; ~ **owl** steenuil, kerkuil
screen (n) skerm; (silwer)doek; (v) beskerm,
beskut; ~ *off* afskort; ~ **wi'per** ruitveër
screw (n) skroef; (v) vasskroef; ~**dri'ver**
skroewedraaier; ~**jack** domkrag; ~**nut** moer
scrib'ble (n) gekrap; (v) krap, krabbel; ~**r**
kladboek, kladskrif
scribb'ling gekrabbel; ~ **pad** kladblok
scribe skrywer; skriba (kerk); skrifgeleerde
script geskrif; manuskrip; draaiboek (film);
antwoordskrif (eksamen); ~**ure** die Heilige
Skrif, die Bybel
scroll (n) rol; lys; krul; (v) oprol, opkrul
scrounge (v) (rond)bedel, aas, skaai; ~**r**

gapser, klaploper (mens)
scrub (n) bossies; ruigte, struikgewas; (v)
skrop, skuur; ~**bing board** wasplank;
~**bing brush** skropborsel; ~**by** dwergagtig,
klein; ruig
scruff nekvel; *take by the* ~ *of the neck* agter
die nek beetkry
scrum (n) skrum; (v) skrum; ~**half** skrum-
skakel
scru'ple (n) gewetensbeswaar; *a man without*
~ 'n gewetenlose persoon
scru'pulous (a) nougeset, sorgvuldig; noukeurig; ~*ly clean* silwerskoon
scrutineer' stemopnemer (by verkiesing)
scru'tinise (v) noukeurig bestudeer/bekyk
scuf'fle (n) skermutseling, stoeiery; geharwar
scull'ery ..**ries** opwasplek; waskamer
sculp beeldhou; ~**tor** beeldhouer; ~**ture** (n)
beeldhouwerk; beeldhoukuns; (v) beeldhou
scum (n) skuim, afval; uitvaagsel (mens)
scurv'y skeurbuik
scut'tle[1] (n) luik; (v) kelder (skip), laat sink
scut'tle[2] (v) vlug, weghardloop
scythe (n) sens, seis
sea see; ~ **breeze** seebries; ~ **cap'tain** skeepskaptein; ~**front** strandgedeelte; ~**grass** seegras; wier; ~ **gull** seemeeu; ~ **lev'el** see-
spieël/seevlak
seal[1] (n) rob, seehond
seal[2] (n) seël, stempel; (v) verseël, toelak; ~**ed
or'ders** verseëlde instruksies
seal'ing wax (seël)lak
seal ring seëlring
seal'skin robbevel
seam (n) soom, naat; ~ **bow'ler** naatbouler
(krieket)
sea'man seeman, matroos; **able** ~ bevare seeman; ~**ship** seemanskap
sé'ance (n) sitting, séance (spiritisme)
search (n) soek(tog); (v) soek, ondersoek;
~**ing** (a) deurdringend; skerp; ~**light** soeklig; ~ **par'ty** soekgeselskap; ~ **war'rant**
lasbrief (vir visentering)
sea: ~**shell** seeskulp; ~**sick** seesiek; ~**side
resort** strandoord
seas'on (n) seisoen, jaargety; speelvak (teater)
out of ~ buiteseisoen; *the* ~**s** die jaargetye
(v) toeberei; ~**al** seisoenaal; ~**ed** gekrui
beleë; ~**ing** kruie; ~ **tick'et** seisoenkaartjie
seat (n) sitplek; setel; sitting; sitvlak, boom
(broek); ~**belt** (sitplek)gordel
sea: ~**weed** seewier; ~**worthy** seewaardig

seclude' uitsluit, afsonder; ~**d** afgesonder(d), afgeleë *also* **remo'te, i'solated**

sec'ond (n) sekonde (horlosie); tweede; ~ *from left* naaslinks (op foto); (v) sekondeer; ~ *a motion* 'n voorstel/mosie sekondeer; (a) tweede; ~ **cou'sin** kleinneef; ~ **floor** tweede vloer/verdieping/vlak

second' (v) sekondeer (na ander plek/pos)

sec'ondary (a) sekondêr; ondergeskik; ~ **school** sekondêre skool, hoërskool

sec'ond class tweede klas

sec'ond: ~ **best** naasbeste; ~ **hand** (n) sekondewyser; ~**hand** (a) tweedehands; ~**ly** tweedens; ~-**rate** tweederangs; minderwaardig

sec'ret (n) geheim; *let out a* ~ 'n geheim verklap; (a) geheim, heimlik

secretar'ial sekretaris=, sekretarieel; ~ **post** sekretariële betrekking

sec'retary ..ries sekretaris; **pri'vate** ~ privaat sekretaris (meestal man); privaat sekretaresse; ~ **bird** sekretarisvoël; ~-**gen'eral** sekretaris-generaal

sec'ret: ~**ly** stilletjies; ~ **ser'vice** geheime diens

sect (n) sekte

sec'tion afdeling, seksie; deursnee; ~**al ti'tle** deeltitel

sec'tor sektor; **pri'vate** ~ privaat sektor; **pub'lic** ~ owerheidsektor

sec'ular (a) wêreldlik, sekulêr; ~ **po'wer** wêreldlike mag; ~ **school** staatskool (teenoor kerkskool)

secure' (v) verseker, waarborg, beveilig; vasmaak; verkry, ~**d** *by a bond* gedek deur 'n verband

secur'ity (n) veiligheid, sekuriteit; beveiliging, sekerheid; waarborg; (pl) aandele, effekte, obligasies; **collat'eral** ~ kollaterale sekuriteit; **so'cial** ~ bestaansbeveiliging; **clear'ance** sekerheidsklaring; **S~ Coun'cil** Veiligheidsraad (VN); ~ **guard** sekerheidswag, sekuriteitswag; lyfwag; ~ **staff** sekerheidspersoneel

sed'ative (n) pynstiller; (a) pynstillend

sed'iment besinksel, afsaksel, sediment

seduce' (v) verlei, verlok; ~**r** verleier (mens)

seduc'tive verleidelik, aanloklik

see (v) sien, kyk; ~ *a doctor* 'n dokter raadpleeg/sien; ~ *the manager* die bestuurder spreek/sien; ~ *off* wegsien, afsien; ~ *to it* sorg daarvoor

seed (n) saad; (v) saai; keur (sport) *also* **rank/**

grade (v); *the first* ~ die eerste gekeurde (speler); eerste op die ranglys; ~**ling** saailing; ~ **pota'to** aartappelmoer; ~**y** (a) olik, oes, siekerig

see'ing (n) gesigsvermoë; sien; (conj) aangesien; omdat; ~ **eye** loerkyker(tjie)

seek (v) soek; beoog; ~ *advice* raad vra

seem lyk, skyn; *it* ~*s to me* dit lyk vir my; ~**ing** skynbaar, oënskynlik; ~**ly** betaamlik, geskik *also* **prop'er**

seep (v) lek, deursyfer

se'er siener; profeet (mens)

see-saw (n) wip(plank); (v) wipplank ry

seethe (v) kook, borrel, sied

segrega'tion afskeiding, segregasie

seis'mograph seismograaf (apparaat)

seize (v) gryp; konfiskeer; vasbrand (enjin)

sel'dom selde, min

select' (v) uitkies, keur, uitsoek; (a) uitgekies, keurig; vernaam; ~ **commit'tee** gekose komitee; ~**ion** keuse, keur; keuring/sifting/seleksie; versameling; ~**ive** selektief: ~*ive re- porting* selektiewe beriggewing; ~**or** selektor (tegn.); keurder (sport)

self selves self; ~-**ca'tering** selfsorg (op vakansie); ~-**con'fidence** selfvertroue; ~-**con'- scious** selfbewus; ~-**defen'ce** selfverdediging, noodweer; ~-**determina'tion** selfbeskikking; ~-**esteem'** selfbeeld; selfrespek; ~-**ev'ident** klaarblyklik, vanselfsprekend, ~-**in'terest** eiebelang; ~**ish** selfsugtig; ~-**respect'** selfrespek; ~ **ser'vice** selfbediening; ~**star'ter** aansitter (motor); ~-**suffi'cient** selfgenoegsaam; ~-**suppor'ting** selfonderhoudend

sell (v) verkoop, van die hand sit; bedrieg, kul; ~ *by auction* laat opveil; ~**er** verkoper

se'men (n) semen (mens); sperma (dier)

semes'ter semester, halfjaar

sem'i half=; ~-**cir'cle** halfsirkel; ~-**co'lon** kommapunt (;); ~**detach'ed house** skakelhuis; ~-**fi'nal** voorlaaste (wedstryd), halfeindronde, semifinaal

sem'inar (n) seminaar, kursus; slypskool

sem'inary ..ries kweekskool, seminarie

sem'i-precious: ~ **sto'nes** halfedelstene

sen'ate senaat; ~ **house** senaatsaal

sen'ator senator (mens)

send (v) stuur, wegstuur, versend; ~**er** versender, afsender; ~-**off** vaarwel; afskeidsfees

sen'ile (a) kinds; ouderdoms=; afgeleef, seniel

sen'ior (n) superior; senior; (a) ouer, senior; oudste; hoogste; ~ **cit'izen** senior burger; ~

part'ner oudste/senior vennoot

senior'ity voorrang, senioriteit

sensa'tion (n) opskudding, sensasie; *cause a* ~ opskudding veroorsaak; ~**al** sensasioneel/ sensasiewekkend, opspraakwekkend

sense (n) sintuig; betekenis; *common* ~ gesonde verstand; *in every* ~ in elke opsig; *five* ~*s* vyf sintuie; ~ *of humour* humorsin; (v) voel, besef, begryp; ~**less** bewusteloos; dwaas

sen'sible verstandig *also* **wise, pru'dent**

sen'sitive fyngevoelig, liggeraak; sensitief

sen'sual sinlik, wellustig, vleeslik

sen'tence (n) sin; vonnis; (v) vonnis, (ter dood) veroordeel

sentimen'tal oorgevoelig, sentimenteel

sen'try ..tries skildwag

sep'arate (v) skei; afsonder; verdeel; (a) afsonderlik, apart; *send in a* ~ *envelope* stuur afsonderlik

separa'tion skeiding; afsondering

sep'arator afskeier; roomafskeier/romer

Septem'ber September

sep'tic verrottend; septies; ~ **tank** septiese tenk, rottingsput

seq'uel vervolg, gevolg, uitvloeisel/resultaat; vervolgprogram/verhaal

seq'uence volgorde, opeenvolging

serenade' (n) serenade; (v) serenadeer

serene' kalm, bedaard *also* **tran'quil**

serge'ant sersant; ~**-at-arms** stafdraer *also* **ma'cebearer**; ~**-major** sersant-majoor

ser'ial (n) vervolgverhaal; ~ **kil'ler** reeks= moordenaar; ~ **num'ber** volgnommer; ~ **port** seriepoort (rek.); ~ **ra'pist** reeksver= kragter

ser'ies (same pl), serie, reeks

ser'ious (a) ernstig, plegtig; bedenklik (siekte= toestand)

serm'on preek, predikasie; vermaning; *the S*~ *on the Mount* die Bergrede

ser'pent slang; serpent

ser'um (n) sera, **-s** serum, entstof

serv'ant bediende, huisbediende, diensmeisie; dienaar; kneg; **domes'tic** ~ huishulp; **pub'lic** ~ staatsamptenaar

serve (v) dien, bedien; afslaan (tennis); uitdien (tronkstraf); ~ *its purpose* aan sy doel beantwoord; ~*s you right* jou verdiende loon; ~**r** afslaner (tennis); bediener (rek.)

serv'ice (n) diens; kerkdiens; afslaan (tennis); versiening/diens (motor); servies; *at your* ~ tot u diens; (v) versorg, onderhou; versien/

diens (motor); ~**able** diensbaar; ~ **charge** diensheffing; tafelgeld (restourant); ~**d flat** dienswoonstel; ~**d stands** dienserwe; ~ **provi'der** diensverskaffer; ~ **sta'tion** mo= torhawe/vulstasie

serviette' servet; **damp** ~ jammerlappie

ser'ving hatch dienluik

serv'itude serwituut, beperking

se'ssion sitting, sessie *also* **assem'bly**; **ple'nary** ~ volle/voltallige sitting, volsessie

sestet' sekstet (laaste 6 reëls van sonnet)

set (n) servies; stel; (v) sit; bring; plaas; skik; spalk (arm); rig; dek (tafel); vasstel; onder= gaan (son); ~ *an example* 'n voorbeeld stel; ~ *fire to* aan (die) brand steek; ~ *off* ver= reken; ~ *the pace* die pas aangee; ~ *the table* die tafel dek; (a) *a* ~ *book* 'n voor= geskrewe boek *also* **prescri'bed**; ~**back** teenslag/teenspoed, terugslag; ~**-off** skuld= verrekening; ~ **point** stelpunt (tennis)

settee' rusbank, sofa

sett'er jaghond, setter

sett'ing toonsetting; (toneel)dekor; agtergrond

sett'le vestig; vasstel; regmaak; vereffen; be= paal; bylê (twis); ~ *an account* 'n rekening vereffen; ~**d** vas; vasgesteld; betaal; ~**ment** nedersetting; vereffening; ~**ment plan** skikplan; ~**r** kolonis, nedersetter, setlaar

sev'en sewe; ~**-single** solus-sewe; ~**teen** se= wentien; ~**teenth** sewentiende; ~**th** sewen= de; ~**tieth** sewentigste; ~**ty** sewentig; ~**ty four** streepvis

se'ver (v) skei, afsonder; skeur, afsny; ~ *rela= tions with* betrekkinge verbreek met

sev'eral (a) verskeie, verskillende; (pron) ver= skeie, 'n hele paar; ~ *others* baie/heelparty ander; ~**ly** afsonderlik

sev'erance pack'age skeidingspakket, uittree= pakket

severe' streng; ernstig; kwaai; *a* ~ *blow* 'n swaar slag; *a* ~ *winter* 'n strawwe winter

sew werk (met naald en gare), naai; ~ *on* aanwerk

sew'age rioolvuil, rioolwater

sew'er (n) riool *also* **drain**; ~**age** riolering

sew'ing naaldwerk; ~ **machi'ne** naaimasjien

sex -es geslag; seks; *they had* ~ hulle het seks/ gemeenskap gehad

sex' appeal seksprikkeling, seksstraling *see* **sex'y**

sex: ~ **drive/urge** geslagsdrang; ~ **educa'tion** geslagsvoorligting; ~**ism** seksisme; ~

kit'ten sekska(a)tjie

sex'ton koster *also* bea'dle

sex'ual geslags=, seksueel; ~ har'assment seksuele teistering

sex'y (a) sexy; seksprikkelend; wulps

shabb'y kaal; toiingrig/verslete; gemeen

shack (n) pondok, hut *also* shan'ty

shac'kle (n) skakel; boei, ketting; (pl) boeie

shadd'ock (n) pampelmoes/pompelmoes

shade (n) skadu(wee); koelte; sweempie; *a* ~ *better* 'n ietsie/rapsie beter

shad'ow (n) skaduwee; *without a* ~ *of doubt* sonder die minste twyfel; (v) ongemerk volg

sha'dy skaduryk, lommerryk; verdag (vent)

shaft pyl; skag (myn); steel (gholf); straal (lig); ~ sin'king skagdelwing

shag'gy ruig, harig; ~ *dog* wolhaarhond

shake (n) skud; skok; (v) skud, skok; uitskud; *badly* ~*n* baie onthuts; ~ *with fear* van angs bewe; ~ *hands with* die hand gee; blad skud; ~ *off* afskud; ontslae raak van; ~**down** ker= misbed; ~**-up** drastiese hervorming

sha'ky (a) bouvallig; bewerig; onvas

shale skalie, leiaarde (geol.)

shall should sal; moet

shallot' salot *also* spring on'ion

shall'ow (a) vlak; ondiep; oppervlakkig

sham (n) bedrog, voorwendsel; skyn; (v) be= drieg, fop, kul, veins *also* feign

sham'bles deurmekaarspul, warboel; slagplek; bloedbad

shame (n) skande; skaamte, (v) skaam, be= skaam; (interj) foei tog!; sies tog!; ~ful skandelik; ~less skaamteloos

sham: ~ fight spieëlgeveg, skyngeveg; ~mer aansteller; bedrieër *also* con'man

shamm'y seemsleer *also* cham'ois lea'ther

shampoo' (n) harewas(middel), sjampoe

sham'rock klawer(blaar)

shan'dy shandy, lim(onade)bier, limbier

shan'ty ..ties pondok, krot *also* shack; ~town blikkiesdorp; krotbuurt; slum

shape (n) vorm; gedaante; gestalte; *take* ~ vaste vorm aanneem; (v) vorm; fatsoeneer; *see how things* ~ kyk/sien hoe sake ont= wikkel; ~ly welgevorm (meisie) *also* cur= va'ceous

share[1] (n) deel, porsie; aandeel; (v) deel, ver= deel; ~ *alike* gelykop deel

share[2] (n) ploegskaar

share: ~ bro'ker aandelemakelaar/effektema= kelaar; ~ cap'ital aandelekapitaal; ~hold'=

er aandeelhouer; ~ware deelware (rek.)

shark haai; swendelaar (mens) *also* con'man

sharp (n) kruis (mus.); (a) skerp; skerpsinnig; bitsig; listig; ~ *contrast* skrille kontras; ~ *practices* kullery, knoeiery; (adv) presies; gou; *at five* ~ klokslag vyfuur; ~en skerp maak, slyp; ~shoo'ter skerpskutter; sluip= skutter *also* sni'per; ~-sighted skerpsiende; skerpsinnig; ~-witted geestig, gevat

shatt'er (v) verbrysel, verpletter; verstrooi; ~proof splintervry

shave (n) skeer; noue ontkoming; *a close* ~ naelskraap; (v) skeer; skaaf; ~ *off* afskeer; ~r skeerder (mens, masjien)

sha'ving skeerdery; (pl) krulle, skaafsels; ~ brush skeerkwas; ~ strop skeerriem

shawl tjalie, sjaal *also* scarf

she sy

sheaf (n) sheaves gerf; (v) in gerwe bind

shear (v) skeer; knip; pluk; ~s skaapskêr; tuinskêr

shebeen' (n) sjebien, smokkelkroeg

she'-cat katwyfie

shed[1] (n) loods, skuur, afdak

shed[2] (v) stort, laat val; ~ *blood* bloed vergiet; ~ *light upon* lig werp op; ~ *a skin* vervel; ~ *tears* trane stort

sheen (n) glans, skittering, skynsel

sheep (sing and pl) skaap; ~ish onnosel, dom; ~ pen skaapkraal; ~skin skaapvel; bokjol (dans); ~'s trot'ters skaappootjies

sheer (a) louter, volstrek; ~ *coin'cidence* blote toeval; ~ *non'sense* pure onsin

sheet (n) laken; vel/blad (papier); plaat (sink)

she'-goat bokooi

sheik sjeik (man)

shelf shelves plank; rak; plaat; rotslaag; *on the* ~ afgedank, gebêre; op die bakoond (mei= sie); ~ *life* rak(leef)tyd, raklewe

shell (n) skil; skulp; peul; dop; (v) uitdop (van erte); skil; bombardeer; ~fish skulpdier; ~shock bomskok

shel'ter (n) skuilplek; beskerming *also* sanc'= tuary; ~ed occupa'tion beskutte/beskerm= de werk/beroep; (v) beskut, beskerm

shelve (v) bêre, weglê, wegsit; van rakke voor= sien; op die lange baan skuif *also* postpone'

shel'ving (n) rakke; rakplanke

shep'herd (n) skaapwagter, herder

sher'iff -s balju, geregsbode

sher'ry sjerrie (wyn)

shield (n) skild; beskerming; (v) beskerm

shift (n) verskuiwing/verwisseling; skof; (v) verwissel; vervang; verhuis; ~**ing** (n) ver= skuiwing; (a) veranderlik; ~**ing span'ner** skroefsleutel; ~**y** (a) skelm *also* **craf'ty**

shin (n) skeen, maermerrie

shine (n) skyn, glans; (v) skyn, glinster, blink; straal; uitblink/presteer

shin'gle (n) dakspaan; (v) stomp knip (hare); ~**d roof** spaandak

shin'gles (n) gordelroos ('n veluitslag)

shin'guard skeenskut/beenskut

shi'ny blink, glansend

ship (n) skip; (v) verskeep; ~**load** skeepslading, skeepsvrag; ~**ment** lading; ~**ping** skeep= vaart; verskeping; ~**ping a'gent** skeepsagent; ~**ping firm/line** skeepsredery; ~**'s cap'tain** skeepskaptein; ~**shape** in orde, agtermekaar; ~**hold** skeepsruim; ~**wreck** (n) skipbreuk; (v) skipbreuk ly; strand, vergaan; ~**yard** skeepswerf

shirk (v) vermy, ontduik; wegskram; ~**er** pligversaker, ontduiker *also* **dod'ger**

shirt hemp; *keep your* ~ *on* moenie kwaad word nie; ~ **col'lar** hempsboordjie; ~ **slee've** hempsmou

shit (*vulgar*) (n) kak, stront; vrotsige vent

shiv'er (n) rilling, siddering; (v) bewe, bibber; sidder, ril *also* **shud'der**

shiv'ering bewend, rittelend

shoal[1] (n) skool (visse); trop

shoal[2] (n) sandbank; vlak plek; (a) vlak

shock (n) skok, botsing; (v) skok; aanstoot gee; vererg; **delay'ed** ~ vertraagde skok

shock' absorb'er skokbreker, skokdemper

shock'ing (a) verskriklik, yslik; skokkend

shodd'y (a) verslons, armoedig; ~ **work** knoei= werk

shoe (n) skoen; hoefyster; (v) beslaan; ~**brush** skoenborsel; ~**horn** skoenlepel; ~**lace** skoenriem/skoenveter; ~**last** skoenlees; ~**maker** skoenmaker; ~**shine** skoenpoetser (mens); ~**string**: *on a* ~*string* op die goedkoopste manier

shoot[1] (n) skoot; (v) skiet; verskiet (ster); ~ *down* neerskiet; *prices shot up* pryse het die hoogte ingeskiet

shoot[2] (n) spruit, loot; (v) uitbot, uitloop

shoot'ing (n) skiet; jag; (a) skietend, skiet=; ~ **li'cence** jaglisensie; ~ **ran'ge** skietbaan *also* **ri'fle range**; ~ **sea'son** jagtyd; ~ **star** vallende ster

shoot'out (n) skietery, skietgeveg

shop (n) winkel; *closed* ~ geslote geledere; *talk* ~ vakpraatjies praat/gesels; (v) inkope doen; (gaan) winkel; ~ **assis'tant** winkelbediende; ~**brea'king** winkelinbraak; ~**keep'er** winke= lier *also* **dea'ler**; ~**lif'ter** winkeldief; ~**lift'= ing** winkeldiefstal/winkeldiewery; ~**per** win= kelaar (mens); ~**ping** (in)kopery: *go* ~*ping* inkopies doen; (gaan) winkel (w); ~**ping bag** winkelsak; ~**ping cen'tre** winkelsentrum; ~**soi'led** winkelslyt; ~**ste'ward** werkerska= kel/vloerleier (fabriek); ~**win'dow** winkel= venster, toonvenster

shore (n) kus, strand

short (n) tekort; kortsluiting; (a) kort, klein; beperk; *a* ~ *cut* kortpad; ~ *story* kort= verhaal; *fall* ~ *of* te kort skiet; ~ *but sweet* kort maar kragtig; ~**age** tekort; ~**bread** brosbeskuit; ~ **cir'cuit** kortsluiting; ~**en** verkort

short'hand (n) snelskrif, stenografie; ~ **ty'pist** snelskriftikster; ~ **wri'ter** stenograaf

short: ~**list** groslys; ~**ly** netnou, binnekort; ~**s** kortbroek; ~**-sigh'ted** kortsigtig; by= siende, miopies; ~**staf'fed** onderbeman; ~**-tem'pered** opvlieënd; ~**wave** kortgolf; ~**-winded** kortasem(ig)

shot (n) skut (persoon); hael; skoot (geweer); *like a* ~ bliksemsnel; *putting the* ~ gewig= stoot; ~**gun** haelgeweer; ~**put** gewig= stoot

shoul'der (n) skouer; skof; blad (dier); *give the cold* ~ die rug toekeer; *straight from the* ~ op die man af

shout (n) skree(u); (v) uitroep; skree(u); juig; ~ *for joy* jubel van vreugde; ~ *with laughter* skaterlag; ~**ing dis'tance** roepaf= stand

shove (n) stoot, stamp; (v) skuif, stoot

shov'el (n) skopgraaf *also* **spa'de**; skep

show (n) tentoonstelling, skou, vertoning; *put= ting his chickens on* ~ sy hoenders skou; *Easter S*~ Paasskou; (v) wys, toon; tentoon= stel, skou; ~ *mercy* genade betoon; ~ *off* spog, pronk; ~**bus'iness/show'biz** teaterbe= dryf; verhookguns; ~**case** toonkas/toonkabi= net; ~**down** beslissende konfrontasie

show'er (n) reënbui; stortbad; (v) besproei; reën, stort; ~ *upon* oorlaai met

show: ~**girl** pronkpoppie; verhoogmeisie; ~**ground** skougrond; ~**house** skouhuis; ~**-in** aandeel, seggenskap; ~ **jum'ping** ruitersport, perdespringkompetisie; ~**room**

toonlokaal; ~ **win'dow** toonvenster
shrap'nel (n) granaatkartets, skrapnel
shred (n) reep; snipper; *torn to* ~s in flenters;
(v) snipper, kerf; ~**der** snipperaar (masjien)
shrew feeks, wyf, heks, geitjie (vrou)
shrewd (a) slu *also* **sly**; listig; oorlams
shriek (n) skree(u), gil; (v) gil; ~ *with laugh=
ter* brul/gier van die lag, skaterlag
shrike janfiskaal, laksman (voël)
shrill (a) skril, skel, skerp
shrimp garnaal *see* **prawn**; dwerg
shrine (n) altaar; graftombe, heilige plek
shrink krimp; ~ *from* terugdeins vir
shroud (n) lykkleed
shrub (n) struik, bossie; ruigte; **ornamen'tal**
~ sierstruik; ~**bery** struiktuin
shrug (n) skouerophaling; (v) die skouers
optrek/ophaal
shudd'er (n) siddering; *it gives one the* ~s dit
laat 'n mens gril; (v) huiwer, sidder
shuf'fle (v) skuifel; skommel (kaarte); ~ *along*
aansukkel
shun (v) vermy, ontwyk *also* **eva'de**
shunt (n) regstoot, rangeer; ~**er** rangeerder; ~**ing**
yard rangeerwerf, opstelterrein
shu-shu (n) sjoesjoe (rankplant)
shut (v) sluit, toemaak; ~ *one's mouth* jou
mond hou; ~**ter** luik, blinder, hortjie; sluiter
(kamera); **mock** ~**ter** kammahortjie
shut'tle spoel(tjie), **space** ~ pendeltuig; ~
ser'vice pendeldiens *see* **commu'te**
shy (a) skaam, bedees, skugter *also* **tim'id**
sick (n) sieke (mens); (a) siek, krank; mislik;
naar; *feel* ~ naar voel; ~**bay** siekeboeg;
~**en** siek word/maak; naar word; walg;
~**fund** siekefonds
sic'kle sekel; ~**moon** sekelmaan
sick: ~ **leave** siekteverlof, ~**ness** siekte,
krankheid; mislikheid; ~ **vis'itor** sieke=
trooster
side (n) sy, kant; rand; *take* ~s kant kies; (v) ~
with iem. se kant kies; (a) sy=; ~**board**
buffet; ~**car** syspan(wa); ~**-effect'** ne=
we-effek; ~**line** byverdienste, liefhebbery;
·sylyn; ~**step** (n) systap; swenk; (v) verby=
spring, swenk; liemaak; ~**track** (n) syspoor;
wisselspoor; (v) ontwyk; ~**walk** sypaadjie;
~ **whis'kers** wangbaard, bakkebaard
si'ding (spoorweg)halte; wisselspoor
siege (n) beleg, beleëring
sieve (n) sif
sift sif; uitvra, uitpluis

sigh (n) sug, versugting; (v) sug
sight (n) gesig; skouspel; vertoning; korrel
(geweer); besienswaardigheid; *a* ~ *for sore
eyes* 'n verruklike gesig; *make a* ~ *of one=
self* jou belaglik maak; (v) sien; korrelvat;
~**ly** mooi, fraai; ~**see'ing tour** besigtigings=
toer; kykrit
sign (n) teken, merk; uithangbord; (v) (onder)=
teken; ~ *on* aansluit
sig'nal (n) sein, teken, sinjaal; ~ **of distress'**
noodsein; (v) sein; (a) merkwaardig; buiten=
gewoon; ~ **hon'our** besondere/buitengewo=
ne eer
sig'nature handtekening, naamtekening; ~ **tune**
kenwysie
sig'net seël; ~ **ring** seëlring
signif'icant (a) betekenisvol, beduidend
sign: ~ **lan'guage** gebaretaal; ~**post** pad=
teken, predikant; ~**wri'ter** letterskilder
si'lence (n) stilte; stilswye; (v) laat swyg, laat
bedaar; ~**r** klankdemper (motor); knaldem=
per (pistool)
si'lent (a) swygend; stil; *remain* ~ stilbly
silhouette' (n) silhoeët, skadubeeld
silk (n) sy; (a) sy=; ~**en** sy=; syagtig; ~ **hat**
keil; ~**worm** sywurm; ~**y** syerig; stroperig
sill (n) drumpel; vensterbank
sill'y (a) onnosel, verspot, kinderagtig, laf *also*
fool'ish, child'ish
si'lo (n) silo, graansuier; voerkuil
silt (n) afsaksel, slik; ~ *up* toeslik
sil'ver (n) silwer; (v) versilwer; (a) silwer=; ~
coin silwermunt; ~ **foil** bladsilwer; ~ **leaf**
silwerblaar, silwerblad; ~**-pla'ted** versil=
wer; ~**smith** silwersmid; ~**ware** silwer=
goed, silwerware; ~ **wed'ding** silwerbrui=
lof
sim'ilar (a) soortgelyk; gelyksoortig; eenders/
eners
similar'ity ..ties gelyksoortigheid; gelykheid;
ooreenkoms
sim'ilarly net so, op dieselfde manier
sim'mer prut, sag kook, stoof; sing (ketel)
sim'ple (a) eenvoudig; onnosel; ~ **in'terest**
enkelvoudige rente; ~**-min'ded** eenvoudig
(van gees)
sim'pleton swaap, dwaas, uilskuiken
simplic'ity eenvoud; natuurlikheid
sim'ply eenvoudig, gewoonweg
sim'ulate (v) naboots, simuleer; veins
sim'ulator nabootser (apparaat)
sim'ulcast (n, v) koppeluitsend(ing) (TV)

simultan'eous gelyktydig *also* **concur'rent**; ∼**ly** tegelyk(ertyd)

sin (n) sonde; *as ugly as* ∼ so lelik soos die nag; (v) sondig, oortree

since (adv) gelede; daarna; (prep) sinds, se= dert; (conj) nadat, sinds; omdat, aangesien; vandat; *ever* ∼ van toe af

sincere' (a) oopreg, suiwer, eg, eerlik; **Yours** ∼**ly** Opreg die uwe, Geheel die uwe

sincer'ity (n) opregtheid, openhartigheid

sin'ew sening, spier; ∼**y** gespierd, taai

sing (v) sing; besing; ∼ *one's praises* iem. se lof verkondig

singe (v) seng, skroei *also* **scorch**

sin'ger sanger (albei geslagte)

sing'ing sang, gesing; sangkuns; ∼ **bird** sang= voël; ∼ **les'son** sangles

sing'le (n) enkelspel; (v) ∼ *out* uitsoek; (a) enkelvoudig; enkel; *he lost in the* ∼*s* hy het in die enkelspel verloor; ∼ **file** agter me= kaar; ∼**-hand'ed** sonder hulp; ∼**s** enkelspel

sing'ly alleen, afsonderlik; een vir een

sing'song jolsang; deuntjie; sangoefening

sing'ular (n) enkelvoud; (a) enkelvoudig; seldsaam; vreemd; sonderling *also* **stran'ge**

sin'ister (a) onheilspellend, skrikwekkend, sinister; ∼ **phiz** boewetronie (van 'n mens)

sink (n) wasbak, aanreg; (v) sink; sak; delf (skag); delg (skuld); ∼ *differences* geskille laat rus; ∼ *a shaft* 'n skag grawe; ∼ *a ship* 'n skip kelder (laat sink); ∼**er** dieplood; ∼**hole** sinkgat

sink'ing (n) sink; keldering (skip); ∼ **fund** delgingsfonds

si'nus -es kromming; (sinus)holte; baai

sip (n) mondjie vol, slukkie; (v) bietjie-bietjie drink

si'phon (n) hewel, sifon; spuitwaterfles; (v) opsuig; oortap; ∼ *petrol out of the tank* petrol uit die tenk hewel/uitsuig

sir heer, meneer; sir

sire (n) sire; vader; vaar (dier); (v) verwek

si'ren sirene, mishoring; loeier; verleidster

si'sal sisalplant; garingboom

sis'ter suster; verpleegsuster; non; ∼**-in-law** skoonsuster; ∼**ly** susterlik, teer

sit (v) sit, gaan sit; ∼ *for an examination* eksa= men skryf/aflê; ∼ *for one's portrait* poseer; ∼**com(edy)** sitkom(edie); ∼**down strike** sitstaking; ∼**-in** sitbetoging

site ligging; bouterrein; perseel

sitt'ing (n) sitting; sessie; broeisel (eiers); (a)

sitting; ∼ **hen** broeishen; ∼ **room** sitkamer, voorhuis

sit'uated geleë

situa'tion (n) ligging; plek; toestand, situasie, betrekking, pos; *the* ∼ *causes concern* die toestand wek kommer

six -es ses; ∼ *of one and half a dozen of the other* dis vinkel en koljander; ∼**fold** sesvou= dig; ∼**shoo'ter** rewolwer; ∼**teen** sestien; ∼**teenth** sestiende; ∼**th** sesde; ∼**tieth** ses= tigste; ∼**ty** sestig

size (n) grootte, omvang; maat; afmeting

siz'zle (v) sis, knetter, spat

sjam'bok sambok; aapstert

skate (n) skaats; (v) skaats; ∼**board** skaats= plank

ska'ting rink skaatsbaan/ysbaan

skeet shoo'ting (n) pieringskiet, kleiduif skiet

skel'eton (n) geraamte, skelet; *a* ∼ *in the cupboard* 'n pynlike geheim; ∼ **key** diewe= sleutel, loper; ∼ **staff** kaderpersoneel, ska= dupersoneel; kernstaf (mil.)

sketch (n) skets, ontwerp, uitbeelding; (v) skets

ski/skiing (n, v) ski, sneeuskaats; ∼**boat** skiboot; ∼**jet** waterponie *also* **jet'ski**

skid (v) gly, rondskuif; sleep, rem

skier skiër (mens)

skil'ful (a) bekwaam, bedrewe, handig, knap

skill bedrewenheid; vaardigheid; kundigheid *also* **experti'se**; ∼**ed la'bour** geskoolde arbeid

skim (v) afskuim, afskep; vluglees/glylees; ∼**med milk** afgeroomde melk

skimp'y skraal, skraps, karig, afgeskeep

skin (n) vel; vlies; bas; *save one's* ∼ heelhuids daarvan afkom; *by the* ∼ *of one's teeth* hittete, naelskraap; (v) afslag; ∼**deep** oppervlakkig; ∼**di'ving** vinduik/swemduik; ∼**head** kalbas= kop/beenkop (mens); ∼ **magazi'ne** sekstyd= skrif; ∼**ny** maer *also* **scrag'gy**; ∼**ny-dip'per** kaalbaaier

skip[1] (n) hysbak; skip (mynbou)

skip[2] (n) sprong; (v) touspring; oorslaan

skip[3] (n) kaptein

ski'pants (n) knersbroek, kameelkouse

skip'per kaptein; skipper (rolbal)

skip'ping rope springtou

skirm'ish (n) -es skermutseling

skirt (n) romp; rok; slip, pant; kant, rand; (v) omsoom, omboor; langs die kus vaar; ∼**ing board** vloerlys

skit (n) parodie, spotskrif, skimpskrif

skit'tle kegel; ~ **al'ley** kegelbaan; ~ **pin** kegel *see* **ten'pin bow'ling**

skol'ly skollie, leeglêer, kwaaddoener

skull skedel; doodskop; ~**cap** kalotjie

skunk (n) muishond *also* **pole'cat**; smeerlap, vuilis (mens)

sky skies lug, hemel(ruim); ~**di'ving** lugduik; ~**lark** lewerkie; ~**scra'per** wolkekrabber; ~**wri'ting** rookskrif

slab (n) plaat, steen; reep, skyf; ~ *of chocolate* blok sjokolade; sjokkie

slack (n) slapte; (pl) slenterbroek; (v) vertraag, verslap, verflou; (a, adv) slap; traag, lui; laks; ~**en** laat skiet, verslap; ~**er** luiaard/lamsak; ~**ness** laksheid; ~**suit** broekpak

slake (v) les; blus; ~**d lime** gebluste kalk

slam (n) harde slag; kap, slag (kaartspel); (v) toeslaan (deur); kritiseer, verdoem

slan'der (n) skinderpraatjies, laster; (v) belaster; ~**er** lasteraar, kwaadspreker; ~**ous** lasterlik

slang (n) sleng; groeptaal, jargon

slant (n) skuinste, helling; ~**ed news** skewe beriggewing

slap (n) klap, slag; (v) 'n klap gee; (adv) reg; plotseling; ~**dash** (a) voortvarend; ongeërg; halsoorkop; (adv) onverskillig

slash (n) sny; balkteken (/); (v) sny, raps; ~ **prices** pryse kerf

slate (n) lei; leiklip; (a) lei=, leikleurig

slate: ~ **pen'cil** griffel; ~ **quar'ry** leigroef

slaught'er (n) slagting; bloedbad; (v) slag; ~ **cattle** slagbeeste, slagvee

slave (n) slaaf; werkesel; (v) swoeg, slaaf

sla'very (n) slawerny

slay (v) doodmaak, vermoor

sled/sledge/sleigh (n) slee; (v) slee

sledge'hammer voorhamer, smidshamer

sleek (v) blink maak; (a) glad, glansend, blink; geslepe, slu, salwend

sleep (n) slaap, vaak; (v) slaap, rus; ~**er** slaper; dwarslêer (spoor)

sleep'ing slapend; ~ **accommoda'tion** slaapplek; ~ **bag** slaapsak; ~ **part'ner** rustende vennoot; ~ **pill** slaappil; ~ **sick'ness** slaapsiekte

sleep: ~ **wal'ker** slaapwandelaar *also* **somnam'bulist**; ~**y** vaak, slaperig, dooierig

sleet (n) dryfsneeu, ysreën

sleeve mou; mof; *have something up one's* ~ iets in die skild voer; ~ **link** mouskakel, mansjetknoop *also* **cuff'link**

sleigh slee

slen'der (a) skraal, maer, slank, dun; gering

sleuth speurder; ~**hound** speurhond *also* **track'er dog**

slice (n) sny, skyf; ~ **of bread** sny brood

slick (a) handig, rats; glad, blink (diere); (adv) presies; glad, skoon; **city** ~**er** stadskoejawel (mens)

slide (n) gly; skuif; skyfie (fot.); haarknip; (v) gly, glip; skuif; ~ **rule** rekenliniaal

sli'ding glyend, dalend; skuif=; ~ **door** skuif= deur; ~ **scale** glyskaal

slight (a) gering, min, effentjies; ~ **injury** ligte besering; ~**ly** effentjies, 'n rapsie

slim (v) verslank; (a) slank, skraal *also* **lean**

slime slyk, modder, slym

slim'ming verslanking, vermaering

sli'my slymerig, glibberig; inkruiperig

sling (n) slingervel; draagband (vir arm); (v) slinger; swaai; ~**shot** slingervel

slink (v) wegsluip

slip (n) vergissing, fout; stiggie/steggie; kussingsloop; onderrok; *give one the* ~ iem. ontglip; *a* ~ *of the pen* 'n skryffout; (v) gly, glip; 'n fout maak; ~**ped disc** skyfletsel; ~**per** pantoffel, sloffie; ~**pery** glibberig, glyerig; ~**shod** slordig, onpresies; ~**way** skeepshelling; glipweg (verkeer); sleephelling (vir bote)

slit (n) slip, spleet; bars, skeur; (v) kloof, splits; bars (hout)

slobb'er (v) kwyl, teem; slobber; mors; knoei

slog (v) moker, hard slaan; swoeg

slo'gan (n) leuse, slagspreuk, motto; wagwoord; wekroep *also* **mot'to, catch'word**

sloop sleep (boot)

slop (n) (pl) vuil water; slap drank; (v) mors, vuil maak; ~ **pail** slopemmer; ~**py** morsig; huilerig, oordrewe sentimenteel; ~ **sink** opwasbak

slope (n) skuinste, hang, helling; afdraand

slot gleuf, opening; program-item; ~ **machine'** (munt)outomaat, slotmasjien

sloth (n) luidier; ai (indien 3 tone)

slouch (v) lomp loop; slof, sleep

slo'ven: ~**liness** slordigheid; ~**ly** slordig, morsig, vieslik *also* **mes'sy, slop'py**

slow (v) stadiger gaan; ~ *down* vertraag, verlangsaam; (a) stadig, langsaam; traag; agter (horlosie); ~**coach** draaikous, drel, drentelaar; ~**combus'tion stove** smeulstoof; ~ **mo'tion** stadige aksie *also* **slo'mo**

sludge modder, slik/slyk; boorslik; rioolslyk

slug slak; ~**gard**, leegloper, luilak; ~**gish** lui, traag

sluice (n) sluis; watervoor; ~ **gate** sluisdeur

slum (n) agterbuurt, krotbuurt, slum, gopse

slum'ber (n) sluimering; (v) sluimer

slump (n) in(een)storting; slapte (in ekono= mie); (v) inmekaar sak, in(een)stort

slur (n) vlek, smet; slordige uitspraak; (v) sleg uitspreek; bemors, besmet; trek (noot)

slush slyk, slik, modder; smeltende sneeu; sentimentaliteit; kletspraatjies

slut (n) sloerie; slet (vrou) *also* **tart, bitch**

sly (n): *on the* ~ tersluiks; (a) slu, uitgeslape, listig; slim; skelm *also* **cun'ning, craf'ty**; ~ **lod'ger** sluipslaper

smack[1] (n) klap, slag; klapsoen; (v) 'n klap gee; (adv) smak pardoems; ~ *up against* reg teenaan

smack[2] (n) geur, smakie; sweem; (v) smaak

small (a, adv) klein; gering, weinig, min; *in the* ~ *hours* ná middernag; ~**hol'ding** (land= bou)hoewe, kleinhoewe; ~**pox** (kinder)pok= kies; ~ **talk** kafpraatjies, geklets

smart[1] (v) skryn, seermaak, pynig

smart[2] (a) knap; oulik, wakker, slim; modieus; netjies, viets; keurig, elegant; ~*ly dressed* fyn uitgevat; ~ *cas'ual* deftig informeel; ~**card** knapkaart

smash (n) botsing; breekspul; mokerhou (ten= nis); (v) moker; ~**-up** botsing; in(een)stor= ting

smear (n) vlek, kol; (v) besmeer, besoedel; ~ **campaign'** smeerveldtog

smell (n) reuk, geur; ruik (van die see); snuf; (v) ruik; snuffel; ~ *a rat* lont ruik; ~**ing salts** vlugsout

smelt smelt; ~**ing fur'nace** smeltoond/smel= tery *also* **smel'ter**

smile (n) glimlag; (v) glimlag; *fortune* ~*s on us* die geluk lag ons toe

smi'ling vrolik, glimlaggend; *keep* ~*!* hou die blink kant bo!

smirch (n) **-es** klad, vlek, smet

smith smid *see* **black'smith**

smithereens' flenters, stukkies

smog (n) rookmis

smoke (n) rook, damp; (v) rook; uitrook; ~**d** rook=, gerook(te); ~ **detec'tor** rook(ver)klik= ker; ~**less** rookloos; ~**r** roker; ~**r's empo'r= ium** tabakboetiek; ~**screen** rookskerm

smooth (v) gelyk maak, laat bedaar; versag; (a) gelyk, glad, sag; vriendelik; vloeiend (styl); *a*

~ *tongue* 'n gladde tong; ~**-ton'gued** vleiend

smoth'er (v) smoor, verstik; onderdruk

smoul'der (n) smeulvuur; (v) smeul

smudge (n) vlek, vuil kol; smet; (v) besmeer

smug (n) selfgenoegsame mens; jansalie; (a) selfvoldaan, selfingenome; huigelagtig

smug'gle (v) smokkel; ~**r** smokkelaar (mens)

smugg'ling (n) smokkelary

smut (n) roet (van vuur); smerigheid; ~**ty** besmet, vuil; ~**ty joke** skurwe grap

snack porsie, happie, peuselhappie; snoepe= ry(e); ligte maaltyd; ~**bar** peuselkroeg; ~**s** versnaperings

snag kwas/knoes; haakplek; *I struck a* ~ ek het moeilikheid opgetel/teenspoed gekry

snail slak; ~**'s pace** slakkegang

snake slang; *cherish a* ~ *in one's bosom* 'n adder aan jou bors koester; ~ **char'mer** slangbesweerder; ~ **ex'pert** slangkenner; ~ **pit** slangkuil

snap (n) kiekie; slag; hap, byt; pit, energie; *a cold* ~ 'n skielike (vlaag) koue; (v) kraak; klap; breek; kiek; ~ *at* toesnou; ~ **deba'te** blitsdebat (parlement); ~**drag'on** leeubek= kie (blom); ~**pish** snipperig; ~**py** vurig, opgewerk; ~**shot** (n) kiekie; (v) kiek, afneem/fotografeer

snare (n) strik (vir kleinwild); wip (vir voëls); val

snarl (n) knor, snou; (v) knor, grom; **traf'fic** ~ verkeersknoop

snatch (n) ruk; (v) gryp, wegruk; ~**-and-grab thief** grypdief *also* **smash-and-grab thief**

sneak (v) sluip, verklap; ~ **thief** sluipdief; ~**y** gluiperig, agterbaks

sneer (n) spotlag, bytende skerts, hoonlag

sneeze (n) nies; (v) nies; *not to be* ~*d at* nie te versmaai nie; ~**wood** nieshout

snide (a) snedig, kwetsend; ~ **remark'** sne= dige aanmerking

sniff (n) gesnuffel; ruik; (v) snuffel, snuif; ~**er dog** snuffelhond, speurhond

snigg'er (n) skelm gegiggel; (v) grinnik

snipe (n) snip (voël); domkop; (v) sluipskiet; ~**r** sluipskutter (mens)

sniv'el (n) getjank, huigelary; (v) snotter, huil

snob (n) snob; flikflooier, inkruiper; ~**bery** snobisme; ~**bish** snobisties

snook'er snoeker, potspel

snooze (n) dutjie, slapie; (v) dut; 'n uiltjie knip/knap

snore (n) gesnork; (v) snork

snort (n) snork; snorkel, snort (van duikboot); (v) snuif (perd); proes

snot (n) snot *also* **mu'cus**; ~**ty nose** snotneus

snout snuit, snoet; ~ **bee'tle** snuitkewer

snow (n) kapok, sneeu; ~**ball** sneeubal; ~**drop** sneeuklokkie; ~**flake** sneeuvlok= (kie); ~**-white** sneeuwit, spierwit; **S~-White** Sneeuwitjie; ~**y** spierwit

snub[1] (n) afjak, teregwysing; (v) afsnou; ver= werp; vermy *also* **shun**

snub[2] (a) stomp; ~**nose** stompneus, mopsneus

snuff (n) snuif; snuitsel; (v) snuif; besnuffel; snuit (kers); ~**box** snuifdoos; ~**ers** (kers)= snuiter

snuf'fle (n) gesnuif; (v) deur die neus praat

snug (a) gesellig, behaaglik, knus *also* **co'sy**

snug'gle warm toemaak, toedraai; knuffel; ~ *up to* nader skuif; aanvly teen

so so, dus, sodanig; *and* ~ *forth* ensovoorts; *quite* ~! presies; ~ *to say* as 't ware

soak (v) week, deurweek, drink; ~*ed in* deur= trek van; ~**ing** deurweek

soap (n) seep; (v) inseep; ~**box** (cart) kaskar; ~ **bub'ble** seepblaas, seepbel; ~**y** (n) sepie, strooisage (TV) *also* **soap op'era**; (a) sepe= rig, vleierig

soar (v) hoog vlieg, opstyg; sweef/swewe

sob (n) snik; (v) snik

so'ber (a) matig; sober, nugter; beskeie

so'-called sogenaamd/sogenoemd; kastig

soc'cer sokker; ~ **hoo'ligans** sokkerboewe

so'ciable gesellig, aangenaam

so'cial (n) geselligheid, partytjie; (a) sosiaal, maatskaplik; ~ **secu'rity** bestaansbeveili= ging, sosiale sekerheid, ~ **wor'ker** maat= skaplike werker; ~**ism** sosialisme; ~**ite** so= sialiet; sosiale vlinder

soci'ety (n) samelewing, gemeenskap; ge= nootskap, vereniging; **buil'ding** ~ bouver= eniging

sociol'ogy sosiologie

sock (n) -s sokkie; *pull up your* ~*s* roer jou riete, doen jou bes

sock'et (n) holte; kas (van oog); potjie (heup); sok, huls; ~ **span'ner** soksleutel

sod (n) sooi, kluit

so'da soda; ~ **water** sodawater, spuitwater

sod'omy (n) sodomie, homoseksuele omgang

so'fa sofa, rusbank

soft (a) sag/saf, week; soetsappig; gevoelig; ver= wyf; ~**ball** sagtebal; ~**drink** koeldrank; ~**en**

versag; ~ **goods** weefstowwe/wolstowwe, tekstielware; ~**-hear'ted** teerhartig; ~ **job** maklike baantjie; ~ **porn(og'raphy)** prikkel= lektuur; ~ **serve** (n) stroomys/roomdroom; ~**soap** (n) groenseep; vleiery; (v) vlei; ~ **spot** teer plek; ~ **tar'get** sagte teiken; ~**wa're** sagteware/programmatuur (rek.); ~**y** goeierd; slapjas, papperd (mens)

sogg'y papnat, deurweek

soil[1] (n) grond, aarde; ~ **conserva'tion** grond= bewaring

soil[2] (n) smet; (v) besmeer, besoedel

so'lar son=; ~ **eclip'se** sonsverduistering; ~ **en'ergy** sonenergie; ~ **hea'ting** sonverhit= ting; ~ **po'wer** sonkrag; ~ **sys'tem** son(ne)= stelsel

sol'der (n) soldeersel; (v) soldeer; ~**ing i'ron** soldeerbout

sol'dier soldaat, krygsman; ~**'s pay** soldy

sole[1] (n) sool; (v) versool

sole[2] (n) tong(vis)

sole[3] (a) enkel, alleen, enigste; ~ **a'gent** al= leenagent; ~ **rights** alleenreg

sole'ly enkel, alleenlik

sol'emn (a) plegtig, statig, indrukwekkend

soli'cit lok, uitlok, lastig val; onsedelike voor= stelle maak; ~ *support* steun werf, ~**a'tion** aansoek; ~**ing** uitlokking

soli'citor prokureur (regsman)

sol'id (n) soliod, massief; stewig, bestendig; ~**ar'ity** eensgesindheid, solidariteit; ~ **con'=tents** kubieke inhoud

solil'oquy (n) alleenspraak *also* **mon'ologue**

sol'itary (a) eensaam, verlate, allenig; ~ **con= fi'nement** alleenopsluiting

sol'itude (n) eensaamheid, verlatenheid

solo soli, -s solo; ~**ist** solis, solosanger

solu'tion oplossing; ontbinding; rubberlym

solve (v) oplos; ~ *a problem* 'n probleem op= los/uitstryk

som'bre (a) somber, duister *also* **gloo'my**

some (pron) party, sommige; (a) party, som= mige, enige; *to* ~ *extent* tot op sekere hoogte; (adv) erg, danig, baie; ~**body** iemand; ~**how** op een of ander manier; ~**one** iemand

som'ersault (n) bolmakiesie, salto, buiteling

some'thing iets; ~ *nice* iets lekkers

some: ~**times** soms, somtyds, partymaal; ~**where** êrens/iewers

somnam'bulist (n) slaapwandelaar, slaaploper

son (n) seun; ~ *of a gun* swernoot, skobbejak

sona′ta sonate

song (n) lied, sangstuk; poësie; *make a* ~ *about it* 'n ophef maak van; *for a mere* ~ vir 'n kleinigheid/bakatel; ~ **fes′tival** sangfees

son′-in-law sons-in-law skoonseun

sonn′et sonnet, klinkdig

son′ny (n) seuntjie, boetie, mannetjie

soon gou, gou-gou, spoedig, binnekort; *as* ~ *as* sodra; *the* ~*er the better* hoe eerder, hoe beter

soot roet; ~**flake** roetkorreltjie

sooth′ing versagtend; troostend; ~ **mu′sic** strelende musiek

sooth′sayer waarsêer, voorspeller, siener

sophis′ticate verfyn; ~**d** verfynd, kundig; gesofistikeer(d)

sop′ping: ~ *wet* deurweek, sopnat/kletsnat

sopp′y papnat; sentimenteel, soetsappig

sopra′no . .ni, -s sopraan

sor′bet bruissuiker, vrugtedrank, sorbet

sor′cerer towenaar, goëlaar *also* **wiz′ard**

sor′did (a) laag, gemeen, vuil; inhalig

sore (n) seer, sweer, wond; (a) seer, pynlik; *a* ~ *point* 'n teer plek; *a sight for* ~ *eyes* 'n verruklike gesig

sorg′hum graansorghum

sor′row (n) droefheid, smart, verdriet; ~**ful** verdrietig, droewig, treurig; (v) treur

sor′ry (a) jammer, spyt; *be* ~ spyt wees; (interj) ekskuus (tog), jammer

sort[1] (n) soort, aard, klas; *nothing of the* ~ niks van die aard nie

sort[2] (v) sorteer; ~ *out* uitsoek; uitsorteer (sake); ~**er** sorteerder

sosa′tie (n) sosatie *also* **ke′bab**

soul siel, gees, wese; soul (musiekstyl); *not a* ~ nie 'n lewende wese nie; ~**-search′ing** selfondersoekend; ~**-stir′ring** aangrypend

sound[1] (n) geluid, klank; (v) klink, lui; ~ *the retreat* die aftog blaas; ~ **bar′rier** klankgrens; ~**board** klankbord; ~ **card** klankkaart (rek.); ~ **effects′** byklanke

sound[2] (a) gesond, gaaf, sterk; *a* ~ *beating/thrashing* 'n gedugte pak slae; ~ *reasons* gegronde redes; (adv) vas; ~ *asleep* vas aan die slaap

sound: ~**film** klankfilm; ~**proof** klankdig, geluidvry; ~**track** klankbaan

soup sop; *be in the* ~ in die verknorsing wees; ~ **kit′chen** sopkombuis; ~ **plate** sopbord

sour (v) versuur; (a) suur; nors; ~ *grapes* suur druiwe; ~**puss** suurknol (mens)

source (n) bron, oorsprong; ~ **stu′dy** bronnenavorsing

south (n) suide; (a) suidelik, suid; (adv) suidwaarts

South Afr′ica Suid-Afrika; ~**n** (n) Suid-Afrikaner, Suid-Afrikaan (mens); (a) Suid-Afrikaans; ~**n War** Anglo-Boereoorlog, Tweede Vryheidsoorlog

south: ~**east′** suidoos; ~**eas′ter** suidooster, Kaapse dokter; ~**ern** suidelik; ~**paw** hotklou (links); **S**~ **Pole** Suidpool; ~**ward** suidwaarts; ~**wes′ter** suidwestewind; reënjas/oliejas

South′ern Afr′ica Suider-Afrika

souv′enir (n) soewenier, aandenking; herinnering, gedagtenis

sov′ereign (n) vors, heerser; (a) oppermagtig, soewerein; vernaamste

Sov′iet Sowjet; ~ **Repub′lics** Sowjet-Unie (voormalige USSR)

sow[1] (n) (vark)sog

sow[2] (v) saai; strooi; versprei; ~ *discord* tweedrag saai; ~**er** saaier

soy′bean sojaboon(tjie)

spa (n) badplaas, kruitbad, spa

space (n) ruimte; plek; spasie; (v) spasieer; ~ **de′bris** ruimterommel; ~**man** ruimtevaarder; ~**ship** ruimteskip; ~ **shut′tle** pendeltuig; ~ **tra′vel** ruimtevaart

spa′cing spasiëring

spa′cious (a) ruim, wyd, uitgestrek

spade[1] skoppens (kaarte); *ace of* ~*s* skoppenaas

spade[2] (spit)graaf; *call a* ~ *a* ~ geen doekies omdraai nie; ~**work** aanvoorwerk

span (n) span; spanning (brug); (v) oorspan/oorbrug; ~ *of life* lewensduur

span′iel patryshond, spanjoel

spank (n) klap, slag; ~**ing** (n) loesing; (a) groot, sterk; gaaf, uitstekend

spann′er (n) skroefsleutel, skroefhamer

spanspek′ (n) spanspek *also* **musk′melon**

spare[1] (n) ekstra; (pl) onderdele

spare[2] (v) spaar, bespaar; ~ *no expense* geen koste ontsien nie; ~ *oneself the trouble* jou die moeite bespaar

spare[3] (a) maer; skraal; ~ *diet* skraal kos

spare: ~ *part* onderdeel; ~ *room* vrykamer; ~ *time* vrye tyd; ~ *tyre* noodband; ~ *wheel* noodwiel

spark[1] (n) windmakerige kêrel, swierbol

spark² (n) vonk; sprank, greintjie; (v) vonk; ~**plug** vonkprop

spark'le (n) glans, vonkeling; (v) vonkel, flik= ker; bruis; ~**r** diamant

spark'ling vonkelend, skitterend; ~ **wine** von= kelwyn, bruiswyn

spar'ring skerm, boks; ~ **part'ner** oefenmaat, skermmaat

spa'rrow (n) mossie; ~ **hawk** sperwer, wit valk

spasm kramp, trekking; ~**od'ic** krampagtig; spasmodies

spas'tic (a) krampagtig, spasties

spawn (n) viseiertjies, saad, kuit; (v) eiers lê

spay (v) regmaak, spei (wyfiedier)

speak praat, spreek; sê; ~ *one's mind* padlangs praat; ~**er** spreker; *Mr S~er* mnr. die Speaker (parlement); ~**ing** (n) praat; (a) pratend; *not on ~ing terms* kwaai= vriende; **pub'lic** ~**ing** (die) redenaarskuns

spear (n) spies, speer; wig; (v) deurboor; ~**head** speerpunt; ~ **fish'ing** spieshengel

spe'cial (n) spesiale uitgawe (koerant); dis van die dag (restourant); (a) spesiaal, besonder; ~**ist** spesialis (mens)

special'ity besonderheid, spesialiteit (bv. koek bak)

spe'cialise (v) spesialiseer; wysig, beperk

spe'cies (sing and pl) soort, spesie(s)

specif'ic soortlik, spesifiek; ~**a'tion** spesifika= sie; ~ **gra'vity** soortlike gewig

spe'cify (v) spesifiseer

spe'cimen (n) (proef)monster *see* **sam'ple**; eksemplaar; ~ **sig'nature** proefhandteke= ning

spec'tacle (n) skouspel, vertoning; spektakel; toneel, gesig; (pl) bril; ~**d** gebril

spectac'ular (a) skouspelagtig, opsienbarend

specta'tor toeskouer, aanskouer

spec'tre (n) spook, skim, gestalte

spec'ulate bespiegel; spekuleer (geld, beeste); ~ *about the future* bespiegel oor die toe= koms

specula'tion spekulasie; bespiegeling

spec'ulator spekulant (mens)

speech -es redevoering, toespraak; *make a* ~ 'n toespraak hou/lewer/afsteek; *parts of* ~ rededele; **after-din'ner** ~ tafelrede; ~ **im= ped'iment** spraakgebrek; ~**less** spraakloos, stom; ~ **ther'apist** spraakterapeut

speed (n) snelheid, spoed, vaart; *at full* ~ in volle vaart; (v) spoed, haastig/gou maak; jaag; ~**boat** snelboot, kragboot; ~**cop** spietkop/

padvalk; ~ **hump** (spoed)hobbel; ~ **lim'it** snelperk/spoedperk; ~**om'eter** snelheidsme= ter; ~**ster** jaagduiwel *also* **hell'dri'ver**; ~ **trap** snelstrik/jaagstrik; ~**way** jaagbaan; snel= weg, motorweg, deurpad; ~**way** **ra'cing** (motor)fietsrenne; ~ **wob'ble** spoedwaggel; ~**y** (a): ~ *recovery* spoedige herstel

spell¹ (n) towerkrag; betowering; *fall under the* ~ *of* onder die bekoring kom van

spell² (n) beurt; tyd, rukkie; *a cold* ~ 'n skielike koue

spell³ (v) spel; voorspel; ~ *out policy* beleid uitstippel

spell'bound betower(d), gefassineer

spell: ~ **check'er** spelgids; ~**ing** spelling; ~**ing er'ror/mistake'** spelfout

spend (n): *consumer* ~**ing** verbruiker(s)be= steding; (v) uitgee, spandeer; bestee; ~ *time on* tyd bestee aan; ~**thrift** deurbringer, ver= kwister (mens)

sperm saad, sperma

sphere (n) kring; sfeer, bol; omvang

sphinx (n) sfinks

spice (n) spesery, kruie; (v) krui

spick'-and-span' (a) piekfyn, agtermekaar

spi'der spinnekop; spaider (rytuig); ~**'s web** spinnerak

spike (n) lang spyker; spykerskoen (atletiek); briefpriem; (v) vaspen; vasspyker

spill (n) val; *have a nasty* ~ lelik val; (v) mors, uitstort, verspil

spill'way uitloop, oorloop (uit dam/rivier)

spin (n) draai; tolvlug (vliegtuig); toertjie, ritjie; *go for a* ~, gaan ry; (v) spin, weef; draai; wentel; ~ *a yarn* 'n storie vertel; kluitjies bak; ~ **bow'ler** draaibalbouler

spin'ach spinasie

spi'nal ruggraats=; ~ **col'umn** ruggraat; ~ **cord** rugmurg

spin'dle spil, as; ~**leg'ged** met speekbene

spin'drier toldroër (vir wasgoed)

spine (n) ruggraat, rugstring; ~**less** ruggraat= loos, slapgat; papbroekig

spinn'ing spin; ~ **mill** spinfabriek, spinnery; ~ **wheel** spinwiel

spin'ster (n) oujongnooi (dame)

spi'ral (n) spiraal; (v) kronkel, draai; ~ **stair'= case** wenteltrap

spir'it (n) gees; geeskrag, lewe, vuur; (pl) be= wussyn; brandspiritus; *in high* ~*s* opge= ruimd; (v) aanwakker, besiel, aanvuur; ~ *away* wegtoor; ~**ed** lewendig, opgeruimd;

~ **lamp** spirituslamp; ~ **le′vel** waterpas; ~ **stove** pompstofie

spir′itual (n) geestelike lied (Afro-Am.); (a) geestelik, onstoflik; ~**ism** spiritisme; ~**ist** spiritis (mens)

spit (n) spoeg/spuug; (braai)spit; (v) spoeg/spuug; ~ *out* uitspoeg

spite (n) spyt, wrok; *in* ~ *of* ten spyte van; in weerwil van; (v) krenk, vermaak; vererg; ~**ful** vermakerig; haatlik, geniepsig

spittoon′ (n) spoegbakkie, kwispedoor

spiv (n) vertroueswendelaar *also* **con′man**

splash (n) plas, plons; spatsel; (v) bespat, plas; ~**board** modderskerm; ~ **lan′ding** plons= landing (ruimtetuig); ~**y** (a) windmakerig

spleen (n) milt; ergernis

splen′did (a) pragtig, kostelik, luisterryk; uit= stekend, puik *also* **superb′**

splen′dour prag, glans, grootsheid

splice (n) splitsing; las (tou); (v) splits; las

splint (n) splinter; splytpen; (v) spalk

splin′ter (n) splinter; spaander; (v) (ver)splin= ter

split (n) skeuring, tweespalt; skeur, bars; (v) splits; ~ *personality* gesplete persoonlik= heid; *in a* ~ *second* oombliklik, blitsvinnig; (a) gesplits, verdeel; ~**peas** spliterte; ~**pin** splitpen; ~**pole fence** paaltjiesheining

spoil (n) buit, roof; ~*s of war* buit; (v) bederf; verwoes; verfomfaai (klere); ~**ed**, ~**t** be= dorwe; ~**sport** pretbederwer, spelbreker *al= so* **kill′joy**

spoke (n) speek; *put a* ~ *in a person's wheel* iem. dwarsboom

spokes′man woordvoerder, segsman *also* **spokesper′son**; mondstuk, spreekbuis

sponge (n) spons; klaploper/parasiet; *throw up the* ~ tou opgooi; (v) afspons; ~ *on one* op iem. teer; iem. uitsuig; ~ **cake** suikerbrood; ~**r** klaploper, opskeploerder, inhaler; nek= lêer (mens)

spon′sor (n) borg; stigter; (v) borg staan vir; borg *also* **promote′, fund**; ~ *a tournament* 'n toernooi borg; ~**ship** borgskap

spontan′eous (a) spontaan, ongedwonge

spook spook; ~**ish**, ~**y** spookagtig

spool (n) spoel(etjie), tolletjie, klos

spoon (n) lepel; (v) skep, (op/uit)lepel

spoon: ~**-feed** met die lepel voer; ~**ful** lepel vol

sporad′ic verspreid(e), sporadies

sport (n) sport; grap, korswel; grapmaker; (v)

jou vermaak; ~ *a gold watch* pronk met 'n goue horlosie; ~**ing** spelend; sport=, sportief

sports: sport; ~**man** sportman; ~**manlike** edelmoedig, sportief; ~**manship′** sport= manskap

spot (n) kol, merk, vlek; (v) merk; bespat; reg raai (vrae); ~ **cash** kontant; ~ **check** kol= toets, steekproef; ~ **col′our** pletterkleur; ~**fine** afkoopboete; ~**less** vlekloos; ~**light** soeklig, kollig; ~**ted** bont, gespikkel(d)

spouse (n) eggenoot; eggenote, gade

spout (n) tuit, geut; spuit; (v) spuit (walvis)

sprain (v) verrek, verstuit, verswik (enkel)

spray (n) skuim; sproeireën; (v) sproei; ~**er** spuit, sproeier; ~**can** spuitkan(netjie); ~ **paint** spuitverf

spread (n) omvang, uitgestrektheid; maaltyd; *prepare a* ~ 'n feestelike onthaal (voor)be= rei; (v) versprei; ontplooi; voortplant; ~**sheet** (elektroniese) werkblad (rek.)

spree (n) drinkparty, fuif, makietie; (v) fuif, jol, rinkink *also* **rev′el**

spright′ly lewendig, vrolik, dartel

spring¹ (n) lente, voorsomer; *in* ~ in die lente

spring² (n) bron, fontein *also* **well**

spring³ (n) veer; spring, sprong; (v) spring; ontspring; ~ *a surprise* verras; ~ **bal′ance** veerbalans, trekskaaltjie; ~**board** spring= plank; duikplank; afspringplek (vir aanval= le); ~**bok** springbok; ~ **chick′en** piep= kuiken; bakvissie (opgeskote meisie); ~ **tide** springvloed, springty; ~**time** lente; jeug

sprin′kle (v) sprinkel, besproei; (be)strooi; ~ **irriga′tion** sprinkelbesproeiing; ~**r** sprinke= laar, sproeier

sprint (n) naelwedloop, naelren; (v) nael; sny (hardloop); ~**er** naelloper (atleet)

sprite (n) spook(gedaante); kabouter, fee

sprout (n) spruit, loot; (v) uitspruit, groei; opskiet; ~**s** spruitkool

spruce (v) opskik, mooi maak; (a) netjies, keurig; viets, piekfyn

spunk (n) moed, fut; durf; koerasie

spur (n) spoor; spoorslag; aansporing, prikkel; (v) aanspoor

spurn (v) veragting; (v) verag; wegskop, ver= stoot, versmaai

spurt (v) uitspuit; spat; weglê; laat nael

spur′-toed frog/toad platanna, plandoeka

spur′ wheel tandrat, kamwiel

spy (n) **spies** spioen, verspieder; (v) spioeneer,

bespied; ~**glass** verkyker; ~**hole** loergat; ~**ing** spioenasie

squab'ble (n) rusie, twis; (v) twis, dwarstrek, kibbel; ~**r** dwarstrekker, korrelkop (mens)

squad seksie; afdeling (soldate); ~ **car** blits= motor; **fly'ing** ~ blitspatrollie

squad'ron eskadron (ruiters); eskader (vloot, lugmag)

squa'lid vuil, morsig, smerig

squa'lor (n) morsigheid, smerigheid

squan'der (v) verkwis, verspil, deurbring

square (n) vierkant; kwadrant; plein; winkel= haak; ouderwetse persoon; (v) vierkantig maak; vereffen; ~ *accounts with* afreken met; ~ *up* betaal, in orde bring; (a) vier= kantig; kwadraat; reghoekig; regskape; (adv) vierkant; eerlik; *they are* ~ *now* hulle is nou kiets; ~ **dealing** eerlikheid; ~**d** kwa= draat (x²); geruit; ~ **root** vierkantswortel

squash¹ (n) kwas, suurlemoendrank; muurbal; (v) kneus; verbrysel; die mond snoer

squash² (n) -es skorsie; **gem** ~ lemoenpam= poen(tjie)

squat (v) neerhurk; plak; (a) gehurk; ~**ter** plakker; ~**ter camp** plakkerskamp *also* **infor'mal settle'ment**; ~**ting** plakkery

squeak (n) gepiep; gil; (v) piep, gil

squeal (n) gil, skree(u); (v) tjank; verklik/verkla

squeeze (n) drukking; gedrang; (v) druk, vas= druk; uitpers; ~ *money out of* geld afpers; ~ *to death* dooddruk

squid pylinkvis; **com'mon** ~ tjokka

squint (v) skeel kyk; (a) skeel; *slightly* ~**ing** soetskeel; ~**eyed** skeeloog

squi'rrel (n) eekhorinkie (boomdiertjie)

squirt (n) spuit, straal, grootprater/windma= ker; (v) (uit)spuit

stab (n) (dolk)steek; belediging; (v) deursteek; ~ *to death* doodsteek

stabil'ity (n) vastheid, standvastigheid, be= stendigheid, stabiliteit

stab'ilise (v) stabiliseer ('n pasiënt); bestendig

sta'ble¹ (n) stal; renperde; (v) stal

sta'ble² (a) stabiel, standvastig, bestendig

stack (n) mied (hooi); hoop, stapel; (v) mied pak; opstapel

sta'dium -s stadion (sportpawiljoen)

staff (n) staf (militêr); personeel (skool, kan= toor); **edito'rial** ~ redaksie

stag takbok, hert; kortspekulant (beurs) *see* **bull, bear**; ~ **par'ty** ramparty

stage (n) toneel; stadium; trek (bus); *at that* ~

in daardie stadium; (v) opvoer; ~ **fe'ver** plankekoors; ~ **fright** plankevrees; ~ **man'agement** toneelleiding, regie; ~ **writ'= er** toneelskrywer

stagg'er (v) waggel, wankel; steier; ~**ed hours** verspreide werkure; skiktyd; ~**ing** (a) wan= kelend; verbluffend, verbysterend (koste) *also* **baff'ling, stun'ning**

stain (n) vlek, klad, smet; kleur; (v) vlek, be= smet, beklad; ~**ed** besoedel, besmet; ~**ed glass** kleurglas; brandskilderglas; ~**less** rein, skoon; vlekvry, roesvry (staal); ~ **re= mo'ver** vlekverwyderaar

stair (n) trap; *a flight of* ~*s* 'n trap; **up**~**s** bo; ~ **carpet** traploper; ~**case** trap

stake (n) paal; inset; (pl) wedgeld; *have a* ~ belange hê in; (v) waag; wed; ~**hol'der** deelgenoot, aandeelhouer; belanghebber

stal'actite (hangende) druipsteen, stalaktiet

stal'agmite (staande) druipsteen, stalagmiet

stale (a) oud; verslete, afgesaag; ~ **beer** ver= slaande bier; ~**mate** dooiepunt

stalk¹ (n) steel, stingel; skag (van veer)

stalk² (v) deftig stap; wild bekruip

stall (n) stal; loket; padstal, (plaas)kiosk; (v) staak (motor)

stall'ion (n) (dek)hings

stal'wart (n) staatmaker (mens)

stam'ina uithouvermoë, stamina

stamm'er (v) stotter, hakkel; ~**er** hakkelaar *also* **stut'terer**; ~**ing** (n) gehakkel

stamp (n) stempel; seël, merk; posseël; (v) stempel; ~ **collec'tor** (pos)seëlversamelaar; ~ **du'ty** seëlreg

stampede' (n) dolle vlug; stormloop; (v) in 'n paniek vlug (diere)

stand (n) stand, posisie; standplaas; pawiljoen; stalletjie; (v) staan; uithou; trakteer; *can't* ~ *the fellow* ek kan die vent nie verdra nie; *it* ~*s to reason* dit spreek vanself

stan'dard (n) standerd (skool, nou graad); standaard, peil, gehalte; banier; maatstaf, norm; (a) standaard; ~ **bea'rer** vaandel= draer; ~**isa'tion** standaardisering; (v) ~**ise** standaardiseer

stand'by bystand *also* **back-up**; steun; gereed= heidsdiens; nooddiens; *on* ~ op bystand/ roep

stand'ing (n) rang, stand; posisie, status, naam; *a man of high* ~ iem. van aansien; (a) staan= de; duursame; ~ **joke** ou grap; ~ **room** staanplek; ~ **rule** vaste reël

stand-off fish eenkant, terughoudend

stand'point (n) standpunt/gesigpunt

stan'za stansa, vers, strofe; koeplet

sta'ple[1] (n) kram; (v) kram

sta'ple[2] (n) stapel; (a) stapel=, vernaamste; ~ **food** stapelkos/stapelvoedsel

sta'pler kramdrukker; krambinder

star (n) ster; ~**board** stuurboord (regterkant)

starch (n) stysel; (v) styf/stywe

stare (v) aanstaar, aangaap; tuur

stark (a) sterk; styf; (adv) heeltemal, gans; ~ **mad** stapelgek; ~ **na'ked** poedelnakend

starl'ing spreeu; **watt'led** ~ sprinkaanvoël

start (n) begin, aanvang; voorsprong; (v) be= gin, vertrek; aansit (motor); ~**er** aansitter; afsitter (sport); voorgereg

start'ing begin, wegspring; ~ **block** weg= springblok (naellope); ~ **point** wegspring= plek, uitgangspunt

star'tle (v) ontstel, skrikmaak, laat skrik

starva'tion (n) uithongering, hongersnood

starve uithonger; van honger omkom

state[1] (n) staat; toestand; *lie in* ~ in staatsie lê; ~ **of affairs'** toedrag van sake; ~ **of emer'gency** noodtoestand

state[2] (v) meld, vermeld, berig, konstateer, vas= stel

state: ~ **aid** staatsteun; ~ **fu'neral** staatsbe= grafnis; ~**ly** statig, deftig, groots

state'ment (n) opgawe, staat; verklaring, bewering, stelling; formulering

state: ~ **pres'ident** staatspresident; ~**s'man** staatsman; ~**s'manship** staatsmanskap; ~ **witness** staatsgetuie

stat'ic (a) staties; vas

sta'tion (n) stasie; standplaas; ~ **wag'on** sta= siewa

sta'tionary (a) stilstaande, vas, onbeweeglik

sta'tioner handelaar in skryfware; boekhande= laar; ~**y** skryfgoed, skryfbehoeftes

statis'tics statistiek

stat'ue standbeeld

stat'ure (n) gestalte, grootte, statuur

stat'us stand, rang, status; posisie, aansien; ~ **sym'bol** statussimbool

stat'ute (n) wet, instelling, statuut; ~ **law** wettereg, statutereg, (die) landswette

staunch sterk, stewig, trou *also* **stur'dy**

stave (n) duig (van vat); staf; notebalk (mus.); (v) verbrysel; duie insit (vat); ~ *off* afwend/ afweer

stay (n) verblyf; stut; (pl) korset; (v) bly,

vertoef, loseer; ~ *with* loseer/woon by; ~**-away' ac'tion** wegbly-aksie

stead stede, plaas; *stand one in good* ~ goed te pas kom; *in* ~ *of* in plaas van; ~**fast** stand= vastig

stead'y (v) tot bedaring bring; (a) vas, gereeld; bestendig

steak steak/biefstuk; moot (vis); ~**house** braai= huis/braais, braairestourant; steakhuis

steal (v) steel; sluip; ~**ing** stelery, diefstal

steam (n) stoom; (v) stoom, damp; ~ **boi'ler** stoomketel; ~**ed pud'ding** doekpoeding; ~**er** stoomskip, stoomboot

steel (n) staal; (v) staal; (a) staal=, ~ **plate** staalplaat; ~ **trunk** trommel

steen'bok steenbok, vlakbok(kie)

steen'bras steenbras (vis)

steep[1] (a) steil; kras; *a* ~ *price* 'n hoë prys, baie duur; *a* ~ *turn* 'n skerp draai

steep[2] (v) inloop, indompel; ~*ed in alcohol* deurtrek van die drank; ~*ed in French* gekonfyt in Frans

stee'ple kloktoring; ~**chase** hinderniswedren, hinderniswedloop *also* **ob'stacle race**

steer[1] (n) bul; stier; jong os

steer[2] (v) stuur, rig; lei; ~ *clear of* vermy, omseil; ~**ing commit'tee** reëlingskomitee; ~**ing wheel** stuurwiel; stuurrat

stem[1] (n) stam, stingel, steel

stem[2] (v) stuit, teenhou

stench (n) stank

sten'cil (n) patroonplaat; wasvel; sjabloon

stenog'rapher snelskrywer, stenograaf (mens)

step (n) stap, tree; sport; trappie; voetstap; maatreël; (pl) trapleer; *take* ~*s* stappe doen; (v) stap, tree, betree, loop; ~**bro'ther** stief= broer; ~**lad'der** trapleer; ~**pa'rents** stief= ouers

ste'reo stereo=; ~**phon'ic** stereofonies

ste'reotype (n) stereotiep(druk); (v) stereoti= peer; (a) stereotiep, onveranderlik

ste'rile (a) onvrugbaar, steriel, dor

ste'rilise (v) steriliseer; spei (wyfiedier), kas= treer

sterl'ing sterling; eg, suiwer, onvervals; ~ **fel'low** eersteklas kêrel

stern[1] (n) agterstewe (skip); stert, agterste

stern[2] (a) ernstig, streng *also* **rig'id**; stroef

steth'oscope stetoskoop, gehoorpyp

steve'dore stuwadoor, dokwerker

stew (n) bredie *also* **bre'die/ragout'**; *be in a* ~ in die knyp sit; (v) stoof; smoor

stew'ard kelner; bottelier *see* **but'ler**; beampte (sport); ordehouer (by betoging)

stick (n) stok, lat; kierie; ~ *in the mud* (mens) sukkelaar; (v) steek; kleef, vassit; ~**er** plak= ker(tjie); kleefstrook; aanhouer; ~**iness** taai= heid, klewerigheid; ~**ing plas'ter** kleef= pleister/hegpleister; ~**y** klewerig/taai

stiff (n) stywe vent; niksnuts; (a) styf, stram; koppig; *a* ~ *examination* 'n moeilike eksa= men; *that's pretty* ~ dis nogal kras; *scared* ~ doodgeskrik

stiffy (n) stiffie; disket *also* **(computer) disk= ette'**

sti'fling (a) drukkend, bedompig (klimaat)

stig'ma brandmerk, skandvlek, stigma

still¹ (n) distilleerketel; stookketel

still² (v) stilmaak, bedaar; (a) stil, kalm; ~ *waters run deep* stille waters, diepe grond; (adv) nog, steeds

still: ~**born** doodgebore; ~ **life** stillewe (skildery)

stilt (n) stelt; *on* ~**s** op stelte; ~**ed** hoog= drawend; ~**wal'ker** steltloper

stim'ulate (v) aanspoor, stimuleer

stim'ulating prikkelend, stimulerend

sting (n) angel; prikkel; steek; (v) steek, prik, brand; ~**ing net'tle** brandnetel/brandnekel

stin'gy inhalig, gierig, vrekkerig (mens)

stink (n) stank; (v) stink; ~**bomb** stinkbom; ~**wood** stinkhout

stip'ulate (v) bepaal, voorskryf, neerlê, stipuleer

stir (n) beweging, opskudding; (v) roer, be= weeg; *not* ~ *a finger* nie 'n vinger verroer nie

sti'rrup stiebeuel; ~ *strap* stiegriem

stitch (n) -**es** steek; hegsteek (wond); (v) stik

stock (n) voorraad; veestapel; aandele/effekte; vilet (blom); *of good* ~ van goeie familie/ afkoms; *in* ~ in voorraad; (v) voorsien van

stock: ~**bree'der** veeboer; ~**bro'ker** effekte= makelaar; ~ **car** stampmotor; ~ **exchange'** aandelebeurs; ~ **far'mer** beesboer; ~ **let'ter** vormbrief; ~ **ra'cing** stampmotor(wed)renne

stock'ing kous; windhoos (lughawe)

stockpile (v) opberg; oppot

stock'taking voorraadopname; ~ **sale** opruim= verkoping

stoep stoep; patio/buitestoep *also* **pat'io/porch**

stoke stook; volstop; ~**r** stoker (mens)

stok'vel stokvel, spaarklub/begrafnisklub *also* **bu'rial socie'ty**

sto'mach (n) -**s** maag; pens (dier); *on an empty* ~ op jou nugter maag; (v) sluk, verdra; ~ **ache** maagpyn

stone (n) klip, steen; *leave no* ~ *unturned* hemel en aarde beweeg; (v) stenig; (a) klip=, steen=, (adv) totaal, heeltemal; ~ **age** steen= tydperk; ~ **blind** stokblind; ~ **dead** mors= dood; ~ **deaf** stokdoof; ~**fruit** pitvrugte; ~ **quar'ry** steengroef, klipgat; ~**thro'wing** klipgooiery; ~**ware** erdewerk

stooge (n) strooipop, pion *also* **pup'pet**

stool stoel (sonder leuning); stoelgang

stoop (v) buk, buig; jou verlaag/verneder; ~**ing** krom, inmekaar

stop (n) halte (spoorweg); stilstand; end; (v) ophou; teenhou, keer; stelp (bloed); staak; stop; ~ *at nothing* vir niks stuit nie; ~ *pay= ment* betaling staak; ~**cock** afsluitkraan; ~ **or'der** aftrekorder *also* **deb'it order;** ~**per** prop, kurk; ~**street** stopstraat; ~**watch** stophorlosie

stor'age ophoping; (op)berging; bergloon; bêreplek; pakhuisruimte; ~ **dam** opgaardam

store (n) voorraad; pakhuis; winkel; stoor= (kamer); (v) bêre, opberg; opstapel; stoor; ~ *away* bêre, stoor; ~**house** pakhuis; stoor; ~**keep'er** winkelier; magasynmeester; ~**room** pakkamer, stoor

stor'ey -**s** verdieping; *double* ~ *(house)* dubbelverdieping(huis); *the first* ~ die eers= te verdieping/vloer

stork ooievaar; ~ **par'ty** ooievaarstee *also* **ba'by show'er;** *black* ~ swart sprinkaanvoël

storm (n) storm; uitbarsting; (v) storm; ~**wa'ter** vloedwater; ~**y** stormagtig

stor'y ..**ries** storie, verhaal, vertelling; *tell stories* spekskiet; ~**book** storieboek; ~**tel'ler** verteller; leuenaar

stout (a) fris, fors, sterk; dapper; swaarlywig; ~**-hear'ted** moedig, dapper

stove (n) stoof

stow (v) bêre; wegsit; ~ *away* wegpak; ~**away** verstekeling (op skip, ens.)

strag'gle dwaal, swerf; streep-streep loop; ~**r** agterblyer, afdwaler; sukkelaar (mens)

straight (n) pylvak (in sport); (a) reguit, direk; eerlik, opreg; ~ *talk* openhartige gesprek; (adv) onmiddellik; reguit; ~ *away* op staande voet; ~**en** reguit maak; ~**forward** reguit, padlangs; openhartig; ~ **sets** skoon stelle (tennis)

strain (n) inspanning; spanning; verstuiting (van enkel); *in the same* ~ in dieselfde trant; (v) inspan; verstuit; ~**ed** gespanne; ~**er** melkdoek; siffie (tee); filtreerder

strait (n) seestraat; bergpas; ~**jack'et** dwang=
baadjie; (a) ~-**laced** gedwonge; preuts
strand¹ (n) string; draad; vesel; ~**ed cot'ton**
stringgare, breikatoen
strand² (n) kus, strand; (v) strand; ~**ed**
gestrand; verleë *also* **help'less**
strange (a) vreemd, snaaks, eienaardig; ~ *but*
true raar maar waar
stran'ger vreemdeling, onbekende (mens)
stran'gle (v) verwurg; ~**hold** wurggreep
strap (n) platriem, riem, band; (v) vasgord;
vasmaak; ~**ping** sterk
strate'gic strategies
strat'egy krygskunde, strategie
strat'osphere stratosfeer
straw (n) strooi; nietigheid
straw'berry (n) **..ries** aarbei
stray (n) verdwaalde dier; (v) verdwaal; (a)
afgedwaal; dakloos; ~ **bul'let** dwaalkoeël;
~ **dog** losloperhond/losloophond
streak (n) streep; strook; kaalhollery; (v) kaal
hol/hardloop; poedel; ~**er** kaalholler/kaal=
naeler, stryker
stream (n) stroom; spruit; (v) stroom, vloei;
~**er** wimpel, spandoek, papierlint; ~**let**
stroompie; spruitjie; ~**li'ned** vaartbelyn
street straat; *the man in the* ~ die groot
publiek, Jan Publiek; ~ **ar'ab** straatkind,
skollie; ~ **light'ing** straatverligting; ~
ven'dor straatsmous, sypaadjiesmous;
~**wal'ker** straatmeisie, straatvlinder (pros=
tituut) *also* **hoo'ker**
strength sterkte, krag; *on the* ~ *of* op grond
van; ~**en** versterk
stren'uous (a) veeleisend; kragtig, energiek
stress (n) nadruk, klem(toon); stres; spanning;
lay ~ *on* klem lê op; (v) beklemtoon, be=
nadruk; ~ **man'agement** streshantering
stretch (n) **-es** uitgestrektheid; streek; *a long*
~ *of road* 'n lang ent pad; (v) rek, uitrek;
span; inspan; ~**er** voukatel(tjie), kampbed=
(jie); draagbaar; ~**er bea'rer** draagbaar=
draer
strict (a) streng, stip; nougeset; presies; ~**ly**
confiden'tial streng vertroulik
stride (n) tree; *get in one's* ~ op dreef kom
strife (n) twis, tweedrag, onenigheid, onmin
strike (n) (werk)staking; *go-slow* ~ sloersta=
king; (v) stryk (vlag); trek (vuurhoutjie);
staak (werkers); ~**r** staker (wegblywerker);
slaner (van bal)
strik'ing (a) treffend, opvallend

string (n) lyn, tou; seilgare; snaar (viool)
vlegsel (hare); koord; snoer, string (pêrels)
(v) besnaar; ~ **band** strykorkes; ~ **bean**
snyboon, rankboon; ~**ed in'strument** snaar=
instrument; ~ **quar'tet** strykkwartet
strip (n) strook; (v) ontklee, afstroop; beroof
~ *bare* poedelnakend uittrek
stripe streep, striem; ~**d** gestreep
strip'per ontkleedanser(es), poedeltart
strip'tease ontkleedans, lokdans
strive streef/strewe; wedywer; ~ *for* streef na
beywer vir
stroke (n) hou, raps; slag; beroerte-aanval; ◄
~ *of apoplexy* 'n beroerte-aanval; *a* ~ *o,*
luck 'n gelukslag; *on the* ~ *of one* op die
kop (klokslag) eenuur; (v) streel, liefkoos
stroll (n) wandeling; (v) wandel, slenter
strong (a) sterk, kragtig; ~**hea'ded** koppig
~**hold** vesting/burg *also* **cas'tle**; ~**room**
(brand)kluis
strop (n) skeerriem/slypriem; (v) slyp
struc'ture bou, struktuur, bouwerk
strug'gle (n) worsteling; struggle/stryd; (v
baklei; sukkel, spook (w); ~**r** sukkelaar
stub stomp(ie), entjie
stubb'orn (a) hardnekkig/hardekwas, koppig
~**ness** koppigheid
stuck'-up trots; verwaand *also* **ar'rogant**
stud¹ (n) stoetery (diere); (a) stoet= ~ **horse**
volbloedperd
stud² (n) boordjieknoop; klinknael; stut
stu'dent student; leerling; ~ **coun'cil** leerling=
raad; studenteraad; ~ **tea'cher** aspirant=
onderwyser
stu'dio -s ateljee; studio; ~ **or'chestra** atel=
jeeorkes
stu'dious (a) fluks, ywerig, vlytig, leergierig
stud'y (n) **..dies** studeerkamer; studie; *tak*
your studies seriously jou studie ernstig op=
neem; (v) studeer, bestudeer; instudee=
(toneel); ~ *law/medicine* in die regte/medi=
syne studeer
stuff (n) goed; goeters; (v) opstop, stoffeer
~**ed an'imals** opgestopte diere; ~**y** bedom
pig, benoud
stum'ble (v) struikel, strompel
stum'bling block struikelblok
stump (n) stomp; pen; paaltjie (krieket); (v
stonk (krieket); vasvra
stun (v) verbyster, verbaas; bedwelm; ~
bat'on porstok; ~ **grenade'** skokgranaat
~**ner** pragstuk (meisie)

stun'ning bedwelmend; pragtig *also* **gor'geous**

stunt[1] (n) toer, kordaatstuk, streek; (v) toere/kunsies uithaal; ~ **flier/fly'er** lugakrobaat; ~**man** waagarties

stunt[2] (n) dwerg; (v) die groei belemmer; teenhou; ~**ed** dwergagtig, verpot

stu'pid (n) domkop; (a) dom, onnosel; toe

stupid'ity/stup'idness dwaasheid, domheid

stur'dy (a) kragtig, stoer, fors, robuus

stutt'er (n) (ge)stotter; (v) stotter; hakkel *see* stam'mer; ~er stotteraar

sty[1] (n) sties varkhok

sty[2] (n) karkatjie (op die oog)

style (n) styl, mode, manier; benaming; *live in* ~ op groot voet lewe; (v) noem, betitel

styl'ish deftig, modieus, stylvol *also* **chic**

sua've (a) vriendelik, goedig; glad, vleiend

sub'committee onderkomitee, subkomitee

subcon'scious (a) onderbewus, halfbewus; ~**ness** (n) onderbewussyn

subdivi'sion onderverdeling; gedeelte

subdue' (v) onderwerp, oorwin; demp (lig)

sub'ject (n) (studie)vak; onderdaan; onderwerp (gram.); individu; ~ *of study* leervak; (a) onderworpe, onderhorig; ~ *to approval* onderworpe aan goedkeuring

subject' (v) onderwerp, ondergeskik maak; blootstel aan; ~**ive** subjektief

sublime' (a) verhewe, voortreflik, subliem

sub'marine (n) duikboot, (a) ondersees

submerge' (v) onderdompel, onderduik

submis'sion (n) onderwerping, voorlegging

submit' (v) voorlê, indien; (jou) onderwerp

subord'inate (n) ondergeskikte (mens); (a) ondergeskik, onderhorig; ~ **sen'tence** ondergeskikte sin

subpoen'a (n) dagvaarding; (v) dagvaar

subscribe' inteken; bydra; ondertekend; ~ *to a newspaper* op 'n koerant/nuusblad inteken; ~**r** intekenaar

subscrip'tion (n) subskripsie, intekengeld; bydrae; lidgeld (vir klub)

sub'sequent volgend, daaropvolgende, naderhand; ~**ly** daarna, vervolgens

subside' (v) sak, bedaar; wegsak/insak

subsid'iary (n) ..ries plaasvervanger, noodhulp; filiaal; (a) hulp=, aanvullend; ~ **com'pany** filiaalmaatskappy

sub'sidise (v) geldelik steun, subsidieer

sub'sidy ..dies toelae/bydrae, subsidie

subsist'ence bestaan, broodwinning; ~ **econ'omy** bestaansekonomie

sub'stance selfstandigheid; kern, inhoud; wesenlikheid; *man of* ~ vermoënde/welgestelde man

substan'tial (a) wesenlik; aansienlik/groot

sub'stitute (n) plaasvervanger; (v) vervang; ~ *nylon for cotton* katoen vervang deur nylon

sub'structure (n) substruktuur (metropolitaans); onderbou, fondament

sub'tle (a) listig, slu, subtiel, geslepe; fyn, skerpsinnig; ~ **distinc'tion** fyn onderskeid

subtract' (v) aftrek, verminder

subtrop'ical subtropies

sub'urb voorstad; stadswyk; woonbuurt

suburb'an voorstedelik (trein)

subver'sion ondermyning, ondergrawing

subver'sive (a) ondermynend, opruiend

sub'way duikweg; tonnel; ~ **train** moltrein

succeed' (v) opvolg; slaag

success' -es sukses, welslae; ~**ful** suksesvol, geslaag (kandidaat)

succes'sion opvolging; opeenvolging; *in rapid* ~ vinnig na mekaar

success'or opvolger; erfgenaam (mens)

succ'ulent (n) vetplant; (a) sappig

succumb' (v) beswyk, swig; ~ *to* swig voor/vir

such (a) sulke, sodanig; so; (pron) sulke mense, sulkes; *as* ~ (as) sodanig; *all* ~ *persons who* almal wat

suck (v) suig; ~**er** pypkan; suier; loot; domkop/dwaas; stokkielekker; ~**ing pig** speenvark

su'ction suiging; ~ **pump** suigpomp

sudd'en(ly) plotseling, onverwags, skielik

sue (v) vervolg (geregtelik), dagvaar, aanskryf; ~ *for damages* dagvaar vir skadevergoeding

suede (n) sweedsleer, suède

su'et niervet, harde vet; ~ **dump'ling** vetkoek

suff'er (v) ly, verduur; ~ *defeat* die neerlaag ly; ~ *from* ly aan; ~**er** lyer, pasiënt; ~**ing** (n) lyding; (a) lydend

suffice' genoeg/voldoende wees; volstaan met; ~ *to say* voldoende om te sê

suffi'cient (a) voldoende, toereikend

suff'ix (n) -es agtervoegsel, suffiks

suff'ocate (v) verstik, versmoor *also* **choke**

suffragette' stemregvrou, suffrajet

sug'ar (n) suiker; mooipraatjies; (v) versuiker; ~**bird** suikerbekkie, jangroentjie; ~ **bowl** suikerpot; ~ **can'dy** kandysuiker, teesuiker; ~**cane** suikerriet; ~**dad'dy** paaipappie, vroe=

telvader (mens); ~ **mill** suikerfabriek; ~ **re= fi′nery** suikerraffinadery; ~ **stick** borssuiker
suggest′ (v) opper, aan die hand doen, sug= gereer, voorstel; *I* ~ *that* ek doen aan die hand dat; ~**ion** voorstel; ingewing
su′icide selfmoord; *commit* ~ selfmoord pleeg
suit (n) (hof)saak; pak klere; kleur (kaartspel); (v) pas; voldoen; bevredig, deug; ~**abil′ity** geskiktheid; ~**able** paslik, geskik; ~**case** (hand)koffer, reistas
suite *(pron. sweet)* stel, suite; **bed′room** ~ (slaap)kamerstel; **exe′cutive** ~ bestuurstel; **pent′house** ~ dakstel; ~ **of rooms** stel ka= mers
suit′or vryer, vryerklong; minnaar *also* **lov′er**
sulk (v) pruil; ~**y** pruilerig; suur, nors, nuk= ′kerig *also* **sul′len**
sul′ky sulkies drafkarretjie
sul′phur (n) swa(w)el, sulfer; (v) swa(w)el
sul′tan sultan
sulta′na sultana(rosyntjie); sultane (vrou van sultan)
sul′try (a) drukkend, bedompig, broeierig
sum (n) som; totaal; ~ *up* saamvat; optel; ~ *total* totaalbedrag
summ′arise opsom; saamvat
summ′ary (n) opsomming, (kort) samevatting; ~ **dismis′sal** summiere ontslag/afdanking
summ′er (n) somer; ~**house** tuinhuis
sum′mit toppunt, piek; ~ **meet′ing/**~ **talks** spitsberaad, leiersberaad
summ′on (v) dagvaar; oproep; opeis
summ′ons (n) dagvaarding; (v) dagvaar; *serve a* ~ *on someone* 'n dagvaarding aan iem. bestel/beteken
sump oliebak; sinkput; mynput
sump′tuous (a) weelderig, luuks *also* **lav′ish, luxu′rious, plush**
sun (n) son; *rise with the* ~ douvoordag op= staan; ~**ba′ther** sonbaaier; ~**beam** son= straal; ~**blind** rolgordyn; ~**bon′net** kap= pie; ~**burnt** (son)gebruin, songebrand
sun′dae (n) vrugte-ys; vrugteroomys
Sun′day Sondag; *his* ~ *best* sy kisklere *also* **Sun′day-go-to-mee′ting**
sun: ~**dial** sonwyser; ~**down** sononder, son(s)= ondergang; ~**downer** skemerkelkie/drankie
sun′dry allerlei, verskeie, diverse *also* **mis= cella′neous**; ~ **expen′ses** diverse uitgawes
sun: ~**flo′wer** sonneblom; ~**light** sonlig; ~**ny** (a) sonnig; opgewek, vrolik; ~**po′wer** son= krag *also* **so′lar po′wer**; ~**rise** sonop; ~**set**

sononder; ~**shade** sambreel, sonskerm; ~**shine** sonskyn; ~**stroke** sonsteek; ~ **wor′shipper** sonaanbidder
superb′ (a) voortreflik, pragtig, puik
su′perbitch (n) superfeeks (vrou)
superfi′cial oppervlakkig; oppervlak=
super′fluous (a) oortollig, oorbodig
superhum′an bo(we)menslik
superimpose′ (v) superponeer, bo-op sit
superintend′ (v) toesig hou; ~**ent** superinten= dent; toesighouer
supe′rior (n) meerdere (mens); (a) hooghartig; hoër, beter; *with a* ~ *air* uit die hoogte; ~ *numbers* oormag
super′lative (n) oortreffende trap; (a) oortref= fend; hoogste
su′perman (n) oppermens, supermens
su′permarket supermark, selfdienwinkel
superna′tural bonatuurlik *also* **occult′**
superson′ic supersonies; ~ **flight** supersoniese vlug
supersti′tion bygeloof
supersti′tious (a) bygelowig
sup′ertax bybelasting, bobelasting
su′pervise (v) toesig hou, kontroleer
su′pervisor toesighouer (fabriek); opsigter (woonstelle); opsiener
supp′er aandete *also* **din′ner**
sup′ple (a) lenig, buigsaam, soepel, slap
supp′lement (n) bylae/bylaag, byvoegsel
supplement′ (v) aanvul, byvoeg; ~**ary** aan= vullend, supplementêr; ~**ary examina′tion** aanvulling(s)eksamen
suppli′er verskaffer, leweransier; leweraar
supply′ (n) **..lies** voorraad; toevoer; (pl) benodig(d)hede; ~ *and demand* vraag en aanbod; (v) verskaf, voorsien, lewer; ~ **dump** opslagplek; ~ **ship** voorraadskip
support′ (n) steun, bystand, hulp; onderhoud; (v) steun, ondersteun, onderskraag, help; onderhou; staaf; ~ *a family* 'n gesin onder= hou; ~**er** ondersteuner; helper (mens); ~ **price** stutprys
suppose′ (v) veronderstel, gestel; vermoed
suppress′ (v) onderdruk; bedwing; demp; ~**ion** onderdrukking; geheimhouding
sup′purate (v) etter, sweer *also* **fes′ter** (v)
suprem′acy oppergesag; heerskappy
supreme′ (a) oppermagtig; opperste, hoogste; **S**~ **Being** Allerhoogste/Opperwese; ~ **command′** oppergesag; **S**~ **Court** Hoog= geregshof

sur'charge (n) bybetaling; byslag, toeslag

sure (a) gewis, seker, veilig; (adv) seker(lik); ~**ly** seker(lik), stellig, ongetwyfeld

sure'ty ..**ties** borg; *stand* ~ *for* borg staan vir; ~**ship** borgskap *see* **spon'sorship**

surf (n) branders, branding; (v) branderplank ry, branders ry

sur'face (n) oppervlak; vlak; blad (van pad); *on the* ~ op die eerste gesig; aan die oppervlak; (v) opduik, opkom

surf: ~**board** branderplank; ~**boat** reddings= boot; ~ **skiing** branderski

surge (n) golf, deining; (v) dein, golf

sur'geon snydokter, chirurg/sjirurg

sur'gery (n) snykunde, chirurgie; **plastic** ~ plastiese chirurgie/snykunde

sur'icate stokstertmeerkat, graatjiemeerkat

sur'ly (a) nors, stuurs, suur *also* **grum'py**

surmount' (v) oorwin, oorkom (probleme)

sur'name van, familienaam

surpass' (v) oortref, verbystreef; uitblink

surp'lus (n) oorskot, surplus; (a) oortollig; ~ **popula'tion** oorbevolking

surprise' (n) verrassing; *take by* ~ verras, oor= rompel; (v) verras; betrap; ~ *in the act* op heter daad/heterdaad betrap; ~ **attack'** verrassingsaanval; ~ **pack'et** verrassings= pakket; ~ **par'ty** invalparty; ~ **vis'it** onver= wagte besoek

surren'der (n) oorgawe; (v) oorgee; hen(d)s= op; uitlewer; ~ *an insurance policy* 'n assu= ransiepolis afkoop; ~ **val'ue** afkoopwaarde

sur'rogate: ~ **mo'ther** surrogaatmoeder, leen= moeder, dra-ma

surround' (v) omring, omsingel, insluit; (n) ~**ings** omgewing, buurt

surveill'ance (n) toesig; waarneming; *under* ~ onder bewaking/toesig

sur'vey (n) -s opmeting; opname; **mar'ket** ~ markopname

survey' (v) opmeet; ~**or** landmeter

surviv'al oorlewing; voortbestaan; ~ *of the fittest* oorlewing van die sterkste; ~ **course** oorlewingskursus

survive' (v) oorleef, lewend bly, voortleef

surviv'or oorlewende; langslewende; agter= blywende; opvarende (van gestrande skip)

suscep'tible (a) gevoelig, vatbaar

sus'pect (n) verdagte (mens/misdadiger)

suspect' (v) verdink; vermoed; ~*ed of arson* verdink van brandstigting

suspend' (v) ophang; opskort; skors; intrek; ~

payment betalings staak; ~**ed sen'tence** op= geskorte vonnis; ~**er** kousophouer, sokkie= ophouer; ~**er belt** kousgordel .

suspense' (n) spanning, angs; opskorting

suspen'sion staking, opskorting; vering (kar); ~ **bridge** swaaibrug/hangbrug

suspi'cion (n) agterdog, suspisie, argwaan; *be under* ~ onder verdenking

suspi'cious (a) verdag, suspisieus, agterdogtig

swab (n) dweillap; skropbesem; depper

swagg'er (v) spog, uithang, grootpraat *also* **brag;** bluf; (a) windmakerig, spoggerig; ~ **cane** spogkierietjie

swa'llow[1] (n) sluk; (v) sluk, verswelg

swa'llow[2] (n) swael, swa(w)eltjie; ~ **tail** swael= stert

swamp (n) moeras, vlei; (v) oorstroom; ~**y** moerassig, drassig

swan (n) swaan; seejuffer (vloot)

swank (v) spog, pronk; ~**y** windmaker(ig), spoggerig; bakgat *(kru)*

swan: ~**nery** swaanboerdery; ~ **song** swane= sang

swarm (n) swerm; menigte; (v) swerm; we= mel, krioel

swat (v) doodslaan ('n vlieg)

swatt'er vlieëplak/vlieëklap

sway (v) swaai, slinger; beheers; bestuur; ~ *the sceptre* die septer swaai

sweat (v) vloek, swets; beëdig, sweer; ~ *in* beëdig, inhuldig (burgemeester); ~ *an oath* 'n eed aflê

sweat (n) sweet; (v) sweet; swoeg; ~**er** oortrui/oortrektrui; uitbuiter; ~**ing** sweet; ~**y** natgesweet

sweep (n) veeg, slag; swaai; lotery; *make a clean* ~ skoonskip maak; (v) vee, wegvee; ~ *the board* alles wen

sweep'ing allesomvattend; ingrypend, deurtas= tend; *a* ~ *majority* 'n verpletterende meer= derheid; ~ **sta'tement** wilde stelling; verre= gaande/oordrewe bewering

sweep'stake (n) (pos)lotery; wedren (prys)

sweet (n) soetigheid; skat, liefling; (pl) lekkers, lekkergoed; (a, adv) soet, lieflik; bevallig; aangenaam; dierbaar; ~**en** versoet; veraan= genaam; ~**ener** versoeter; ~**heart** soetlief, skat, hartjie, liefste; ~**mel'on** spanspek *also* **spanspek;** ~ **pea** pronk-ertjie; ~ **pota'to** (soet) patat(ta); ~ **tooth** lekkerbek (mens); ~**y** hartjie, liefste, liefling; lekkertjie

swell (n) swelsel, geswel; deining (see); (v)

swel, opswel; (a) puik, (piek)fyn; ~ *clothes* spoggerige/windmakerige klere; ~**ing** ge= swel/swelsel

swel'ter (v) verdroog, verskroei; versmag; ~**ing** snikwarm, skroeiend (hitte)

swerve (v) swenk; wegswaai; afwyk

swift (a, adv) vinnig, rats, gou; ~**-footed** rats

swim (v) swem; *my head* ~*s* ek word duiselig; ~**mer** swemmer; ~**ming bath** swembad; ~**ming pool** (private) swembad; ~**ming trunks** swembroek(ie)

swind'le (n) bedrog, swendelary; (v) swendel, bedrieg; ~**r** bedrieër, swendelaar, verneuker *also* **con'man**

swine vark, swyn

swing (n) skoppelmaai; swaai; (v) swaai; slinger; ~**bar** rekstok; ~ **bridge** draaibrug

swipe (n) mokerhou; (v) slaan, moker

swirl (n) warreling, wirwar; draaikolk; (v) draai, warrel

swish (n) geruis, ritseling; (v) swiep, suis

Swiss (n) Switser; (a) Switsers; ~ **roll** rolkoek/konfytrol

switch (n) -es skakelaar; wisselspoor; (v) (in)= skakel; aanskakel (lig); verwissel; ~ *off* af= draai, afskakel; ~ *on* aanskakel; ~**board** skakelbord; ~**board op'erator** skakelbord= operateur/operatrise

swiv'el (n) draaiskyf, spil; ~ **chair** draaistoel

swoon (n) beswyming, floute; (v) swymel; flou word

swoop (n) verrassingsaanval; *with one* ~ met een slag; (v) neerskiet; neerstryk

swop ruil; uitruil, omruil; ~**shop** ruilwinkel, ruilhoekie

sword swaard, sabel; *put to the* ~ om die lewe bring; ~**s'man** swaardvegter; ~**s'man= ship** skermkuns *also* **fen'cing**

sworn beëdig, geswore; ~ **en'emies** geswore vyande; ~ **sta'tement** beëdigde verklaring

also **affada'vit**

swot (v) blok (vir eksamen); instudeer (toneel= rol)

syll'able lettergreep, sillabe

syll'abus -es leergang, sillabus

sym'bol (n) sinnebeeld, simbool

symbol'ic simbolies, sinnebeeldig

symmet'rical simmetries, eweredig

sympathet'ic (a) medelydend, deelnemend simpatiek *also* **compas'sionate/conge'nial**

sym'pathy (n) medely(d)e, meegevoel, sim= patie

sym'phony simfonie

sympo'sium (n) simposium; seminaar; same= spreking

symp'tom verskynsel, (ken)teken, simptoom

syn'agogue (n) sinagoge

syn'chronise saamval, reguleer, sinchroniseer; sinkroniseer

syn'copate (v) saamtrek, verkort, sinkopeer

syn'dicate sindikaat, kartel, sakegroep

syn'drome (n) siektebeeld, sindroom

synec'doche sinekdogee

syn'od sinode; ~**al** sinodaal

syn'onym (n) sinoniem

synop'tic sinopties, oorsigtelik; ~ **chart** sinop= tiese kaart

syn'tax sintaksis, sinsbou; woordvoeging

syn'thesis syntheses samevoeging, samestel= ling, sintese

synthet'ic samestellend, sinteties; ~ **rub'ber** kunsrubber

syph'ilis (n) geslagsiekte, sifilis

syph'on spuitwaterfles; sifon, hewel

syringe' (n) spuit; **hypoder'mic** ~ onder= huidse spuit; (v) spuit, inspuit

sy'rup stroop; **gol'den** ~ geelstroop

sys'tem (n) stelsel, sisteem; metode; **so'lar** ~ sonnestelsel; ~**at'ic** stelselmatig, sistema= ties

T

tabb'y (n) **tabbies** gestreepte kat; oujongnooi; (a) gestreep; gevlam

tab'ernacle (n) tabernakel; tent; *Feast of the T*~*s* Loofhuttefees

ta'ble (n) tafel, dis; tabel, lys; *the* ~*s are turned* die bordjies is verhang; (v) ter tafel (lê)

ta'ble: ~ **boar'der** kosganger, dagloseerder;

~**cloth** tafeldoek; ~**-knife** tafelmes; ~**land** plato, hoogvlakte

Ta'ble Mountain Tafelberg

ta'ble: ~**spoon** eetlepel; ~ **ten'nis** tafeltennis

tab'loid: ~ **(news)pa'per** poniekoerant

taboo' (n) verbod, taboe; (v) verbied, in die ban doen; (a) taboe, verbode

ab′ulate (v) tabelleer, tabuleer

ack (n) hegspyker, platkopspyker(tjie); ryg‑ steek; (v) keer, laveer; ∼ *together* aanme‑ kaarryg; ∼**ies** (n) tekkies

ac′kle (n) takel; duikwerk (voetbal); (v) duik; inspan, optuig; **block and** ∼ katrolstel; **fish′ing** ∼ hengelgerei

ack′y tackies seilskoen, tekkie; (a) klewerig

act (n) takt; ∼**ful** tak(t)vol; ∼**ical** takties, mees‑ terlik; ∼**ics** taktiek, krygskunde; ∼**less** dom, taktloos

ad′pole paddavis(sie)

ag (n) stif; lissie; etiket; naamplaatjie; ken‑ strokie; (v) aanheg

ail (n) stert; stuitjie; keersy (munt); ∼**coat** swaelstert(manel); ∼**less** stompstert; ∼**light** agterlig/stertlig

ail′or (n) kleremaker, snyer; ∼**made** aange‑ meet; pasklaar; ∼**made suit** snyerspak

aint (n) kleur, tint; vlek; smet, besoedeling; (v) besmet, bevlek, besoedel *also* **tar′nish**; ∼**ed** onrein, besoedel; ∼**worm** miet

ake (n) vangs; ontvangste; (v) neem, vat; gryp; ontvang; ∼ *account of* rekening hou met; ∼ *after* aard na; ∼ *aim* korrel vat; ∼ *care* oppas, pas op!; ∼ *a chance* 'n kans waag; ∼ *into consideration* in aanmerking neem; ∼ *a fancy to* lief word vir; ∼ *to heart* ter harte neem; ∼ *a holiday* met/op vakansie gaan; ∼ *ill* siek word; ∼ *minutes* notule hou; ∼ *notes* aantekeninge maak, ∼ *offence* aanstoot neem; ∼ *the opportunity* die ge‑ leentheid gebruik; ∼ *part* deelneem; ∼ *steps*, maatreëls tref; stappe doen; ∼*n up* ingenome, bly, verheug; ∼ *a walk* wandel, gaan stap; ∼**-aways′** wegneemetes, koop‑ en-loophappies, vat-'n-waai; ∼**-in** bedrog, kullery; ∼**-off** wegspring; opstyging (vlieg‑ tuig, vuurpyl); ∼**over** oorname

a′king (a) innemend, bekoorlik; ∼**s** ontvang‑ ste

alc talk

ale (n) storie, vertelling, verhaal, sprokie; *tell* ∼**s** klik; ∼**bea′rer** nuusdraer

al′ent talent, gawe, aanleg; ∼**ed** begaaf, talentvol; ∼**ed/gif′ted child** begaafde kind; ∼ **scout** talentjagter

al′isman talisman, gelukbringer *also* **mas′cot**

alk (n) gesprek; gerug; praatjie; onderhoud; samespreking; *have* ∼**s** *with* samesprekings voer met; (v) praat, gesels, spreek; ∼ *non‑ sense* kaf/twak praat; ∼ *shop* vakpraatjies

maak; ∼**ative** spraaksaam; ∼**er** prater, spre‑ ker; ∼**ie** klank(rol)prent, klankfilm *also* **mo′vie**; ∼**ing** (n) gepraat, pratery; ∼**ing-to** skrobbering *also* **reprimand′** (n)

tall groot; lang/lank; hoog; *a* ∼ *story* 'n on‑ gelooflike verhaal; ∼**boy** (hoë) laaikas

tall′ow kersvet, harde vet; talk; ∼ **candle** vetkers; ∼**-fa′ced** bleek

tall′y (n) kerfstok; keep; *take* ∼ *of* tel; (v) inkerf; ooreenstem; klop (syfers); ∼ *with* klop/strook/rym met

tame (v) mak maak, tem; (a) mak; gedwee

tam′per: ∼ *with* knoei met, peuter aan; ∼**proof** peutervry

tan (n) looibas; (v) looi; sonbruin; (a) geel‑ bruin; taan (kleur); *going to* ∼ *on the beach* op die strand gaan sonbraai/sonsoen

tan′dem (n) tweelingfiets; tandem

tangerine′ (n) (rooi) nartjie

tan′gible voelbaar, tasbaar; ∼ *proof of* tasbare bewys van

tan′gle (n) verwikkeling, warboel

tank (n) tenk, waterbak; tenk (vir oorlogvoe‑ ring); ∼**ard** drinkkan; ∼**er** tenkskip; tenk‑ wa; *fill up your* ∼ jou tenk voltap

tan: ∼**ner** looier; ∼**nery** looiery; ∼**nin** looi‑ suur, tannien

tan′talise (v) watertand; tempteer, tantaliseer; ∼**r** kweller, tempteerder (mens)

tan′trum (onbeheerste) woedebui; stresprotes; *throw a* ∼ vloerstuipe gooi/vang

tap[1] (n) tikkie; (v) tik; klop; ∼**dan′cer** klop‑ danser

tap[2] (n) kraan; kantien; tap; *beer on* ∼ bier uit die vat; (v) aftap (vloeistof); uittap; ∼ *a telephone* meeluister; 'n luistervlooi los

tape (n) band, lint; maatband; *red* ∼ romp‑ slomp; (v) vasbind, vasmaak; opneem; ∼ **aid** bandhulp (vir blindes); ∼**deck** banddek; ∼ **li′brary** bandoteek; ∼**line/**∼ **meas′ure** maatband/meetlint

ta′per (v) taps maak; afspits; (a) taps

tape: ∼ **recor′der** bandopnemer, bandma‑ sjien; ∼ **recor′ding** bandopname; ∼ **slide se′quence** klankskyfiereeks

tap′estry ..tries muurtapyt, tapisserie

tape′worm lintwurm

tap′root (n) penwortel

tar (n) teer; matroos, janmaat; **Jack T**∼ pik‑ broek, matroos; (v) teer; ∼ *and feather* teer en veer

taran′tula bobbejaanspinnekop, tarantula

tard'y traag, onwillig *also* slug'gish
tare eiegewig, eiemassa, tarra (massa)
targ'et skyf; mikpunt, teiken; *your* ~ *readers* jou teikenlesers; ~ date teikendatum/streef= datum; ~ prac'tice skyfskiet
ta'riff (n) tarief; ~ u'nion tolunie
tarn'ish (v) besoedel, bevlek; dof maak
tarpaul'in bokseil/kapseil; matrooshoed
tart (n) tert (koek); flerrie, snol (vrou)
tar'tan tartan, Skotse ruitwol; ~ track tartan= baan (atletiek)
tar'tar (n) wynsteen; cream of ~ kremetart
task (n) taak, werk; ~ force taakmag; ~ group taakgroep; ~mas'ter tugmeester
tass'el (n) tossel, kwas, klossie
taste (n) smaak; voorsmaak; bysmaak; voor= liefde; styl; (v) proe; smaak; *he* ~*s the pudding and it* ~*s nice* hy proe die poeding en dit smaak lekker; ~ful smaakvol (meu= bilering); ~less laf, smaakloos
tas'ty smaaklik, lekker *also* sa'voury
tatt'er flenter, toiing, flard; ~ed toiingrig
tat'tle (n) geklets, gebabbel; (v) babbel, kek= kel; ~r babbelaar; kekkelbek (mens)
tattoo'[1] (n) -s tatoeëring; (v) tatoeëer
tattoo'[2] (n) taptoe (militêr)
tav'ern (n) taverne, herberg; ~ keeper her= bergier *also* inn'keeper
tax (n) -es belasting; (v) takseer; belas; ~able belasbaar; ~a'tion belasting; ~ collec'tor belastinggaarder, ontvanger van belasting, Jan Taks; ~-free belastingvry
tax'i -s taxi (uitspraak: taksie); ~ driver taxi= drywer
tax'idermist (n) diere-opstopper, taksidermis
tax'ing (a) moeilik, veeleisend *also* demand'= ing
tax'payer belastingpligtige, belastingbetaler
tea tee; ligte ete; high ~ teemaaltyd
teach onderwys (gee), onderrig, skoolhou, leer; ~er onderwyser, leerkrag, (skool)= meester; ~er stu'dent student-onderwyser; ~ing (n) onderwys, leer; (a) onderwys=; ~ing aids leermiddele; ~ing expe'rience proefonderwys; praktiese onderwys (vir stu= dente)
tea: ~ co'sy teemus(sie); ~cup teekoppie
teak kiaat(hout), teak
team (n) span; ~ spi'rit spangees
tear[1] (n) skeur; *fair wear and* ~ billike sly= tasie; (v) skeur, losruk; ~ *up* stukkend skeur; ~-off slip skeurstrokie

tear[2] (n) traan; *shed* ~*s* trane stort; ~-jer'ker tranetrekker (film, boek)
tea'room teekamer, koffiehuis, kafee
tear'smoke (n) traanrook
tease (n) terggees; (v) pla, terg; treiter; pluis kam (hare); ~r plaaggees, plaer
tea: ~ service/~ set teestel, teeservies
tea'spoon teelepel; ~ful . .fuls teelepel vol
teat tepel (mens) *also* nip'ple; speen (dier)
tech'nical vak=, tegnies; ~ knock'out (k.o. tegniese uitklophou
techni'cian tegnikus (mens)
tech'nikon -s technikon
technique' tegniek
technol'ogy (n) tegnologie
ted'dy bear teddiebeer, speelbeertjie
ted'ious vervelig/vervelend, saai *also* bo'ring
tee bof (gholf); pennetjie (ringspel)
teem (v) wemel, krioel; ~ *with* krioel/weme van
teen'age tien(d)erjarig, tiener=; ~ dress tie nerdrag; ~ par'ty tienerpartytjie; ~r tien derjarige, tiener *also* (pl) teens
teens (n) tien(d)erjare, tiener; *in one's* ~ nog nie twintig jaar nie; in jou tienerjare
teeto'taller geheelonthouer, afskaffer (mens)
teff tef (gras)
telecommunica'tion telekommunikasie
tel'egram telegram
tel'egraph (n) telegraaf; (v) telegrafeer
telep'athy telepatie, gedagteoordrag
tel'ephone (n) telefoon; (v) bel, lui, skakel telefoneer; ~ call telefoonoproep; ~ ex chan'ge telefoonsentrale; ~ op'erator tele fonis(te); ~ recei'ver gehoorbuis, hoorstuk
teleph'onist telefonis(te)
tel'escope (n) verkyker/vêrkyker; teleskoop (v) teleskopeer
tel'etuition afstand(s)onderrig *also* dis'tance lear'ning/teach'ing
tel'evise (v) beeldsaai, beeldsend
televi'sion televisie; beeldradio; kykkas(sie)
tell sê, vertel, meedeel, berig; ~ *that to the marines* maak dit aan die swape wys; ~ *tales* jok; (ver)klik; ~er verteller; kassie (bank)
tell'ing vertel; verhaal; *you're* ~ *me!* weet el dit nie!; ~-off uitbrander/skrobbering
tell'tale verklikker, klikbek, nuusdraer
tem'per (n) aard, temperament; humeur; ~ tan'trum *see* tan'trum; (v) temper, matig
tem'perament (n) temperament, geaardheid

temperamen'tal (a) temperamenteel, buierig
em'perance matigheid, onthouding; ~ **socie'-ty** matigheidsbond, afskaffersbond
em'perature (n) temperatuur, warmtegraad; *have a* ~ koorsig wees, koors hê
em'pest storm, orkaan
em'ple¹ tempel
em'ple² slaap (aan kop)
em'po -s tempo, maat
em'porary (a) tydelik, voorlopig; ~ **ap-point'ment** tydelike pos/betrekking
empt (v) in versoeking bring; ~**a'tion** versoeking; *yield to the* ~*ation* swig voor die versoeking
en tien
ena'cious (a) taai, hardnekkig *also* **tough**
en'ant (n) huurder; bewoner (van huis)
end (v) geneig wees; versorg, bedien
en'dency ..**cies** strekking, neiging; aanleg; tendens *also* **trend**
enden'tious (a) tendensieus, omstrede (boek)
en'der¹ (n) tender, aanbod; inskrywing; *legal* ~ wettige betaalmiddel; (v) tender; ~ *one's resignation* jou bedanking/ontslag indien
en'der² (a) sag, mals (vleis); teer, delikaat; ~**-hearted** teerhartig, gevoelig; ~**ness** sagt-heid, teerheid
en'don (n) sening, pees
en: ~**fold** tienvoudig; ~**ner** tienrandnoot
enn'is tennis; ~ **court** tennisbaan; ~ **tour'na-ment** tennistoernooi
enniset'te tenniset/dwergtennis
en'or tenoor (stem); gees, strekking
en'pin: ~ **bow'ling** kegelspel/kegelbal
ense¹ (n) tyd; tempus (gram.)
ense² (a) strak, styf, gespan(ne)
en'sion trek; spanning *also* **stress; spankrag; high** ~ hoogspanning
ent (n) tent; kap; (v) kampeer/uitkamp
en'tacle voelorgaan, voelhoring; tentakel
en'tative (a) voorlopig, tentatief
en'terhook spanhaak; *on* ~*s* op hete kole
enth tiende; ~**ly** in die tiende plek
en'ure eiendomsreg, besit; ~ **of of'fice** diens-tyd, ampstermyn
er'cet terset (in sonnet); tersine; drieling
erm (n) termyn, dienstyd; kwartaal; term; (pl) voorwaardes; *on* ~*s and conditions* onder/op bepalings en voorwaardes; *on equal* ~*s* op gelyke voet; *in* ~*s of* ingevolge, krag-tens; ooreenkomstig; *not on speaking* ~*s* kwaaivriende; (v) noem, benoem

term'inal (n) eindpunt; terminaal; ~ **pa'tient** terminale/ongeneeslike pasiënt
term'inate (v) beëindig *also* **disconti'nue;** eindig, verstryk
terminol'ogy (n) terminologie
term'inus -es eindpunt/eindhalte, terminus
term'ite rysmier, termiet
te'rrace (n) terras; (v) terrasseer
te'rrapin (n) varswaterskilpad
te'rrible (a) verskriklik, yslik, vreeslik
terrif'ic verskriklik; wonderbaarlik
te'rrified (a) skrikbevange, doodbang
te'rritory (n) (grond)gebied, landstreek; terrein
te'rror skrik, ontsteltenis, angs; *reign of* ~ skrik-bewind; ~**ism** terrorisme, terreur; **ur'ban** ~**ism** stedelike terreur; ~**ist** terroris; ~**ise** skrik aanja, terroriseer; ~**-strick'en** angsbe-vange/doodverskrik
terse beknop, bondig *also* **brief, succinct'**
ter'tiary: ~ **educa'tion** tersiêre onderwys
test (n) toets, proef; *the acid* ~ die vuurproef; *stand the* ~ die toets deurstaan; (v) toets
tes'tament (n) testament *also* **last will** (n)
test: ~ **case** toetssaak; ~**ed** beproef
tes'ticle (n) teelbal, saadbal, testikel
tes'tify (v) getuig, plegtig verklaar
testimon'ial getuigskrif *also* **ref'erence**
test: ~ **match** toetswedstryd; ~ **pi'lot** toets-vlieënier; ~ **tube** proefbuis; ~**-tube baby** proefbuisbaba
tet'anus (n) klem in die kaak/kake, tetanus
text teks; onderwerp; ~**book** handboek/hand-leiding
tex'tile (a) geweef(de), tekstiel-, weef-; ~ **fac'tory** tekstielfabriek
tex'ture (n) weefsel, tekstuur
than as; *bigger* ~ groter as
thank (v) dank, bedank, dankie sê; ~ *you* dankie; ~**ful** dankbaar; ~**less** ondankbaar; ~ **of'fering** dankoffer
thanks! dankie!; *many* ~ baie dankie; ~ *to Tom, we won;* danksy Tom het ons gewen
thank-you card/let'ter dankkaart(jie), dank-brief, dankiebrief
that¹ (a) soveel, sodanig; *in* ~ *way* op daardie manier; (pron) dié, daardie; wat
that² (conj) dat, sodat
thatch (n) dekgras; strooidak; (v) dek; ~**ed roof** grasdak; strooidak, rietdak
thaw (v) smelt (sneeu); ontdooi
the die; ~ *sooner* ~ *better* hoe eerder hoe beter
the'atre teater, skouburg; toneel; operasiesaal;

~**go′er** toneelganger
theat′rical (a) toneelmatig; teatraal
thee u (verouderd, intieme aanspreekvorm)
theft (n) diefstal, stelery
their hulle, hul; ~**s** van hulle, hulle s'n
them hulle, hul
theme (n) onderwerp, tema; opstel; ~ **tune** kenwysie *also* **sig′nature tune**
themselves′ hulleself
then (a) destyds, toenmalig; (adv) dan, toe; *by* ~ teen daardie tyd; *every now and* ~ kort-kort; *now and* ~ af en toe; nou en dan; (conj) dan, dus
theod′olite hoogtemeter, teodoliet
theol′ogy godgeleerdheid, teologie
theoret′ic (a) teoreties
the′ory theories teorie; *in* ~ *and practice* in die teorie en praktyk
ther′apist terapeut (mens)
ther′apy geneeskuns, terapie; **phy′sio**~ fisio= terapie
there daar, daarso; daarnatoe, soontoe; daar= heen; ~**after** daarna; ~**by** daardeur; ~**fore** daarom, dus, derhalwe; ~**from** daaruit; ~**upon′** daarop, daarna
thermom′eter termometer; koorspennetjie
ther′mos flask (n) termosfles/koffiefles
therm′ostat termostaat
these hierdie, dié
thes′is (n) **theses** stelling; tesis, proefskrif, verhandeling, dissertasie
they hulle, hul; ~ *say* daar word gesê
thick (n): *in the* ~ *of* in die middel van
thick: ~**-hea′ded** dom, onnosel; ~**ness** dikte; ~**set** dig begroei; dik, geset (mens); ~**-skin′ned** dikvellig; ~**-skul′led** hardkop= pig, dom; ~**-wit′ted** dom, bot
thief thieves dief
thieve (v) steel *also* **steal**
thigh dy; ~ **bone** dybeen
thill disselboom *also* **beam** (wagon)
thim′ble vingerhoed
thin (v) verdun; (a) dun, maer; deursigtig; yl; *a* ~ *excuse* 'n flou ekskuus/verskoning; ~**ner** verdunner
thing (n) ding, goed; iets; (pl) goed, goeters; dinge; *he knows a* ~ *or two* hy is nie vandag se kind nie; *poor* ~ arme drommel; *the very* ~ net die regte ding
think dink, nadink; ~ *alike* eenders/eners dink; *if you* ~ *it fit* as jy dit goed vind; ~ *it over* daaroor nadink; ~**er** denker; filosoof;

~**ing** (n) dink; gedagte; denke; ~**-tank** dinkskrum, harsinggalop
third (n) derde deel; terts (mus.); (a) derde; ~ **degree′** afdreiging van bekentenis; ~ **floor** derde vloer/vlak; ~**ly** derdens, in die derde plek; ~ **par′ty** derde party; ~**-par′ty in**= **su′rance** derdepartyversekering; ~**-rate** der= derangs, minderwaardig; ~**-world coun′try** derdewêreldland
thirst (n) dors; begeerte; *quench* ~ dors les; (v) verlang; ~**y** dors, dorstig
thirteen′ dertien; ~**th** dertiende
thirt′ieth dertigste
thir′ty ..ties dertig
this dit, hierdie, dié; ~ *day week* vandag oor 'n week; ~ *month* vandeesmaand; ~ *morning* vanmôre; ~ *way* hiernatoe; ~ *week* van= deesweek, hierdie week; ~ *year* vanjaar
thi′stle distel/dissel (steekstruik)
thong (n) riem *also* **riem**; agterslag; (v) looi; **beach** ~**s** plakkies *also* **slip-slops**
thorn (n) doring; ~**y** doringrig; netelig, lastig
tho′rough (a) grondig, deeglik; ~**bred** (n) volbloedperd, renperd/resiesperd; (a) vol= bloed=; ~**fare** deurgang; ~**ly** deeglik
those daardie, diegene, dié
though hoewel, ofskoon, tog; *even* ~ selfs as
thought (n) gedagte; mening; *in deep* ~ diep ingedagte; *on second* ~**s** na verdere oorwe= ging; ~**ful** bedagsaam, sorgsaam *also* **con**= **sid′erate**
thou′sand duisend
thrash (v) uitlooi, afransel; oortref, verslaan; ~**ing** pak slae, loesing
thread (n) draad; rafel; skroefdraad; ~ **beads** krale inryg; ~**bare** kaal, verslyt/verslete *al*= *so* **shab′by, tat′ty**; afgesaag
threat (n) bedreiging, dreigement
threat′en dreig, bedreig; ~**ing** (a) dreigend
three drie; *the* ~ *R′s* lees-, skryf- en reken= kuns; ~**fold** drievoudig; ~**leg′ged** driebeen=; ~**ply** drielaag (hout); ~**quar′ter** (n) drie= kwart; (a) driekwart=
thresh (v) dors (koring); ~**er/**~**ing machi′ne** dorsmasjien
thresh′old drumpel; ingang, begin
thrift spaarsaamheid; ~**y** spaarsaam *also* **fru′gal** (a)
thrill (n) tinteling, ontroering, sensasie; (v) ontroer, aangryp; ~**er** riller; sensasieverhaa (boek, film); ~**ing** opwindend
thriv′ing (a) voorspoedig, florerend (besig

heid), bloeiend

throat keel; gorrel; *jump down one's* ~ iem. invlieg

throb (v) klop, hyg; bons; ~**bing** (n) klop, geklop; (a) kloppend

throe -s hewige pyn, doodsangs, barensweë; ~**s of death** doodsworsteling

thrombos'is aarverstopping, trombose

throne troon

throng (n) gedrang, gewoel; (v) toestroom

throt'tle (n) keelgorrel; strot, lugpyp; ver= snelklep (motor); (v) verwurg

through (a) deurgaande; (adv) deur; *fall* ~ deur die mat val; (prep) deur; ~**out'** dwars= deur; deurgaans; ~**put** (n) deurset (produk= sie); ~**way** deurpad, deurweg

throw (n) gooi; *a stone's* ~ 'n hanetreetjie; (v) gooi, werp; ~ *into prison* in die tronk smyt; ~ *up the sponge* tou opgooi; ~**er** gooier

thrush[1] spru/sproei (siekte)

thrush[2] lyster (voël)

thrust (n) stoot, steek; dryfkrag; (v) stoot, steek *also* **drive**

thud' (n) plof, bons; (v) plof

thug boef, skurk *also* **scoun'drel, ro'gue**

thumb (n) duim; *hold* ~*s for a person* vir iem. duim vashou; *Tom T-* Klein Duimpie, ~*s up* hou moed; (v) beduimel; deurblaai; ~**latch** deurknip; ~**screw** duimskroef; ~ **tack** duimspyker

thump (n, v) stoot, stamp, ~**ing** kolossaal

thun'der (n) donder; (v) donder, bulder; ~**bolt/** ~**clap** donderslag; ~**cloud** donderwolk; ~**ing** (a) donderend, oorverdowend; (adv) verba= send; ~**storm** donderstorm, swaarweer; ~**struck** verbaas, verstom

Thurs'day Donderdag

thus dus, so, aldus; ~ *far* tot sover/sovêr

thyme tiemie (plant)

thyr'oid skildvormig; ~ **gland** (n) skildklier

tick[1] (n) bosluis; luis

tick[2] (n) tik; merk; strepie; kruisie; *in two* ~*s* in 'n kits/japtrap; tjop-tjop; (v) tik; afmerk/ regmerk

tick[3] (n) krediet; *buy on* ~ op krediet koop

ticker-tape: ~ **para'de** lintreën (in motor= stoet)

tick'et (n) kaartjie; (v) beboet; ~ **exam'iner** kaartjie(s)ondersoeker; ~ **of'fice** kaartjies= kantoor; loket *also* **box of'fice**

tick'ey -s trippens; ~ **box** munthuisie (met telefoon); ~ **so'cial** tiekieaand

tick'-fever bosluiskoors (mense); ooskuskoors (beeste)

tic'kle (v) kielie; kriebel/kriewel

tick'lish (a) kielierig; liggeraak; netelig, deli= kaat *also* **trick'y, sen'sitive**

ti'dal: ~ **pool** getypoel; ~ **wave** vloedgolf

tiddlywinks' (n) vlooiespel

tide (n) gety, eb en vloed; tyd; stroming; *high* ~ hoogwater; *low* ~ laagwater; *neap* ~ dooiety; *spring* ~ springty, springvloed; ~ **gate** sluisdeur

ti'diness (n) netheid

ti'dings berig, tyding, nuus

ti'dy (v) opknap; (a) netjies/ordelik

tie (n) band, knoop; das; (v) gelykop speel; bind, vasknoop; ~ *up* vasbind; verbind; ~ *with* gelyk staan met; ~**brea'ker** valbylpot (tennis); ~**s of friend'ship** vriendskapsbande

tiff (n) slegte bui; rusie(tjie)

ti'ger tier; ~**'s eye** tieroog (halfedelsteen); ~ **li'ly** tierlelie

tight nou, eng; gierig; dronk/geswael; *be in a* ~ *corner* in die knyp wees; (adv) styf; *hold* ~ hou vas; ~**en** vaster maak; ~**fis'ted** vrek= kerig, inhalig; ~**-fit'ting** nousluitend; ~**rope dan'cer** koorddanser; ~**s** spanbroek/spanpak

tile (n) dakpan, teël; (v) teel; geteël

till[1] (n) kasregister *also* **cash reg'ister**; geld= laai(tjie)

till[2] (prep) tot; ~ *now* tot nog toe; ~ *then* tot dan, (conj) tot, totdat

tilt (n) skuinste; (v) steek, laat oorhel; ~ *over* skeef staan; oorhel; ~ *at windmills* teen windmeulens veg

tim'ber (n) timmerhout; ~ **yard** houtwerf

tim'bre timbre, toonkleur/klankkleur

time (n) tyd; maat; keer; maal; tempo; ~ *and again* herhaaldelik; *ask the* ~ vra hoe laat dit is; *for the* ~ *being* tot tyd en wyl; *in the nick of* ~ net betyds; *in no* ~ in 'n kits; *on* ~ betyds/op tyd; *at the same* ~ terselfdertyd; *ten* ~*s five* tien maal/keer vyf; ~ *is up* die tyd is om; *what is the* ~? hoe laat is dit?; (v) maat hou; ~ *his speech* sy toespraak klok; ~ **bomb** tydbom; ~**keep'er** tydopnemer; ~ **lim'it** tydgrens; ~**ly** tydig, betyds; ~**piece** uurwerk, klok; ~**s** maal/keer; ~ **sig'nal** tydsein; ~ **slot** tydgleuf; ~ **switch** tyd= skakelaar; ~**table** (les)rooster, werkplan

tim'id (a) skaam/skamerig, skugter, bedees

tim'ing tydreëling, tydinstelling (motor), tyd= opname, tyd(s)berekening

tin   344   tongue

tin (n) blik; tin; (v) vertin; inmaak, blik; ~**ned meat** blikkiesvleis; ~ o'**pener** bliksnyer

tin'der tontel; ~**box** tonteldoos

tin' foil (n) bladtin; foelie *also* **foil**

tin'sel (n) verguldsel; klatergoud; opskik; (v) verguld; (a) oppervlakkig

tint (n, v) tint, kleur

ti'ny (a) klein, nietig, gering *also* **small, minute'**

tip[1] (n) tip, top; punt

tip[2] (n) fooi, bedien(ings)geld *also* **gratu'ity**; wenk; (v) gooi; omkantel; 'n fooi gee; ~**-off** nuttige wenk/waarskuwing

tip'sy (a) hoenderkop, lekkerlyf, aangeklam, getier; ~ **cake** wynkoek

tip'toe (v) op die tone loop; (adv) suutjies, kat= voet, doekvoet

tip'top eersteklas, hoogste, beste, puik

tip truck wiplorrie

tip-up door wipdeur, opklapdeur

tirade' (n) tirade, woordevloed

tire (v) vermoei, verveel; ~**d** moeg, tam, mat; ~**less** onvermoeid; ~**some** vermoeiend; ver= velend

tiss'ue (n) weefsel; sneesdoekie/snesie; *get a* ~ *and blow your nose* kry 'n snesie en snuit jou neus; ~ **pa'per** snesie/traantrosie

tit (n) tepel, tiet; ~ *for tat* botter vir vet

titan'ic (a) reusagtig, tamaai, groot, titanies

tit'bit lekker, happie, lekkerny *also* **treat**

tithe (n) tiende, tiende gedeelte

tit'illate kielie; prikkel *also* **stim'ulate**

tit'ivate (v) opsmuk, mooi maak

ti'tle (n) titel; naam; aanspraak; (v) betitel, noem; ~**d** getitel; ~ **deed** transportakte; titelbewys; ~ **page** titelblad; ~ **role** titelrol

T-junction T-aansluiting

to (adv) toe; (prep) tot, na, na . . . toe, om te; ~ *the best of my ability* na my beste vermoë; ~ *the best of my knowledge* na my beste wete; *compared* ~ in vergelyking met, ver= geleke met; *face* ~ *face* van aangesig tot aangesig; *five* ~ *six* vyf minute voor ses; ~ *my mind* na/volgens my mening; ~ *the point* ter sake

toad padda; ~**stool** paddastoel; ~**y** (n) inkrui= per (mens); (a) inkruiperig, vleierig

toast (n) roosterbrood; heildronk; (v) braai; 'n heildronk instel; ~**er** (brood)rooster; ~**ed sand'wich** rooster(toe)broodjie; ~**mas'ter** seremoniemeester

tobacc'o tabak; twak; ~**nist** tabakwinkel(ier), tabakboetiek; ~ **pouch** tabaksak

to-be' toekomstig, aanstaande (bruid)

to'by (n) blaasoppie (vis)

today' vandag; teenswoordig, deesdae

tod'dle (v) waggel; ~**r** peuter *see* **kleu'ter**

to-do' drukte, gedoente, ophef

toe (n) toon; *big* ~ groottoon; *little* ~ klein= toontjie; ~ *the line* gehoorsaam wees; ~**nail** toonnael

toff'ee (n) toffie; tameletjie; ~**ap'ple** toffie-ap= pel

tog (n) kleding(stuk); (pl) sportklere, voetbal= klere; (v) aantrek

tog'a toga *also* **academ'ic gown**

togeth'er saam, bymekaar, gesamentlik; *all of us* ~ almal saam

toil (v) swoeg; ~ *and moil* swoeg en sweet

toil'et toilet; latrine, kleinhuisie *also* **loo**; ~ **pa'per** toiletpapier; ~ **soap** badseep/toilet= seep; ~ **set** wasstel, toiletstel; ~ **ta'ble** kleedtafel

to'ken teken; kenteken; aandenking; ~ *of appreciation* blyk van waardering

tol'erance (n) verdraagsaamheid; speling; tole= ransie, toelaatbare afwyking (tegnies)

tol'erant (a) verdraagsaam, meegaande

tol'erate (v) verdra, duld *also* **allow'/permit'**

toll[1] (n) tol, tolgeld; *take* ~ *of* eis, verg

toll[2] (n) klokgelui; (v) lui; tamp (van klokto= ring)

toll: ~**bar** slagboom; ~**free** tolvry; ~*free number* vrybelnommer; ~**gate** tolhek; ~ **plaza** tolplaza; ~ **road** tolpad

Tom: ~, **Dick and Har'ry** Jan Rap en sy maat; ~ **Thumb** Klein Duimpie

tom'ahawk strydbyl

toma'to -es tamatie; ~ **sauce** tamatiesous

tomb (n) graftombe, graf

tom'boy -s rabbedoe (wilde meisie)

tomb'stone grafsteen *also* **grave'stone**

tom'cat mannetjie(s)kat/katmannetjie, kater

tomm'y tommie; ~**rot** bog, kaf, twak

tomor'row more/môre; *the day after* ~ oor= môre; ~ *morning* môreoggend

ton ton; ~*s of people* hope mense

tone (n) klank; ~ *down* bedaar

tongs (n) (gryp)tang (vir kole)

tongue tong; taal, spraak; klepel (klok); *with one's* ~ *in one's cheek* skertsend; *confusion of* ~*s* spraakverwarring; *a slip of the* ~ 'n onbedagsame woord; ~**-tied** spraakloos; ge= muilband; ~ **twi'ster** snelsêer, tongknoper

ton'ic (n) versterkmiddel, opknapper, tonikum; ~ **sol'fa** letternota, solfanotering

tonight' vanaand; vannag

ton'nage tonnemaat; skeepsruimte/lading

ton'sil mangel; ~**lit'is** mangelontsteking, tonsilitis

too te, alte, ook, eweneens; ~ *much of a good thing* darem te erg; *only* ~ *true* maar alte waar

tool (n) werktuig; gereedskap; (v) bewerk; ~**box** gereedskapkis

toot (n) getoeter; (v) toeter/toet

tooth (n) **teeth** tand; kam; *artificial* ~ vals tand, winkeltand; *long in the* ~ oud; *fight* ~ *and nail* met hand en tand beveg; *by the skin of the teeth* naelskraap; ~**a'che** tandpyn; ~**brush** tandeborsel; ~**paste** (tande)pasta; ~**pick** tandekrapper; ~**pow'der** tandepoeier; ~**some** smaaklik *also* **tas'ty**

top[1] (n) tol (speelding)

top[2] (n) top; toppunt, kruin; ~ *of one's class* eerste in die klas; *on* ~ bo-op; (v) aftop, snoei; uitmunt bo; ~ *the poll* die meeste stemme kry; (a) boonste; beste; (interj) goed!; eersteklas!

top'az topaas (vuurgeel edelsteen)

top: ~**boot** kapstewel; ~**dog** bobaas; ~**dressing** bolaag, bobemesting; ~ **gear** hoogste versnelling; bokerf; ~ **hat** keil; ~**heavy** topswaar

top'ic onderwerp, tema *also* **the'me, sub'ject**

top'ical aktueel *also* **cur'rent**; geleentheids-

top: ~**less** (a) kaalbuus (meisie); ~ **man'agement** topbestuur; ~**not'cher** bobaas, doring, uithaler

top'ple (v) omval, omkantel, omtuimel

top: ~ **qua'lity** topgehalte; ~ **se'cret** uiters geheim; ~**soil** bogrond; ~**spin** botol (van bal)

topsy-tur'vy (a) onderstebo, bolmakiesie

torch -**es** toorts, fakkel; flitslig; ~**bea'rer** fakkeldraer; ~**light proces'sion** fakkelloop

to'reador toreador, berede stiervegter

torment' (v) folter, pynig, kwel

tornad'o -**es** werwelstorm, tornado

torped'o (n) -**es** torpedo; (v) torpedeer

tor'rent stortvloed; *in* ~**s** in strome

tor'rid dor, verskroeiend; ~ **zone** trope

tor'so -**s** romp (liggaam), bolyf; torso

tor'toise skilpad; ~ **shell** skilpaddop

tor'ture (v) folter, martel; ~ **cham'ber** folterkamer, martelkamer; ~**r** folteraar

toss (n) -**es** loot; *win the* ~ die loot wen; (v) loot; skud; ~ *aside* opsy gooi; ~-**up** (n) onuitgemaakte saak, gelyke kans

tot[1] (n): **ti'ny** ~ kleuter/peuter; snuiter

tot[2] (n) snaps/sopie/dop (drank); ~ **mea'sure** dopmaat/sopiemeter

tot'al (n) volle som, totaal *also* **ag'gregate**; (v) optel; (a) volkome, totaal; ~ **ab'stinence** geheelonthouding; ~ **eclip'se** algehele verduistering

tot'alisator totalisator; ~ **jack'pot** boerpot

tot'ally heeltemal, glad, volslae

tott'er (v) waggel, wankel; ~**ing** waggelend

touch (n) aanraking; tik; aanslag (mus.); ~ *and go* naelskraap; *keep in* ~ *with* in voeling bly met; (v) voel, tas, aanraak; *no one can* ~ *him* sy maters is dood; ~ *down* neerstryk (vliegtuig); ~ *up* opknap; bywerk; ~-**and-go** so hittete, amper(tjies); ~**ing** (a) roerend, aandoenlik; ~ **kick** buiteskop; ~ **line** kantlyn; ~**ty'ping** blindtik; ~**y** liggeraak

tough taai; hard; styf; moeilik, lastig; *have a* ~ *time* les opsê, dit hotagter kry; ~ **cus'tomer** moeilike/lastige kalant/klant

tour (n) reis, toer; rondreis; (v) toer, rondreis; ~**ism** toerisme; ~**ist** reisiger, toeris; ~**ist attrac'tion** besienswaardigheid, toeriste-aantreklikheid

tour'nament toernooi, wedstrydreeks

tour'niquet knelverband, toernikct

tout (n) klientelokker; (v) klante/kliënte lok

tow (n) sleep; sleeptou; *take in* ~ op sleeptou neem; (v) sleep, treil; ~-**away ser'vice** insleepdiens; ~**bar** trekstang/sleephaak; ~**truck'er** insleper/wegsleper

toward' (a) gewillig, volgsaam, leergierig

towards' na, tot, teen, jeens; *his attitude* ~ *me* sy houding teenoor my

tow'el (n) handdoek; *throw in the* ~ tou opgooi

tow'er (n) toring; ~ *of strength* steunpilaar

town (n) dorp, stad; *man about* ~ windmakerige niksdoener; stadskoejawel; *paint the* ~ *red* die dorp op horings neem; ~**clerk** stadsklerk; ~ **coun'cil** stadsraad; ~ **coun'cillor** stadsraadslid; ~ **hall** stadhuis/stadsaal; ~**house** meenthuis; ~**ship** township, woonbuurt; ~**s'man** stedeling, dorpenaar

tox'ic giftig; gif; ~ **waste** gevaarlike/giftige afval

toy (n) -**s** speelding; (pl) speelgoed; (v) speel; ~**boy** gigolo; kooivlooi, katelknapie (idiom.);

~ **dog** skoothondjie; ~**pom** dwergkees (hond)

toy'i-toyi(ng) (v) toi-toi

trace[1] (n) string (van tuig); *kick over the* ~*s* oor die tou trap

trace[2] (n) spoor; voetspoor; (v) opspoor; na= trek; ~**r-bu'llet** ligspoorkoeël

tra'cing paper natrekpapier, aftrekpapier

track (n) spoor; pad; spoorlyn; (ren)baan; *be on one's* ~ op iem. se hakke wees; (v) na= speur; ~ *down* opspoor; ~**er** spoorsnyer; speurhond; ~**ing devi'ce** opspooraparaat; ~ **rec'ord** diensrekord; reputasie; ~ **ste'**= **ward** baanbeampte; ~**suit** sweetpak

trac'tor (n) trekker

trade (n) handel, sake; bedryf, ambag; *a chemist by* ~ apteker van beroep; (v) handel dryf, sake doen; ~ *in* inruil; ~**-in val'ue** inruilwaarde (van 'n motor); ~ **dis'count** handelskorting; ~ **jour'nal** vakblad; ~**mark** handelsmerk; ~**r** winkelier, handelaar; ~**s'man** koopman, winkelier; ~ **u'nion** vak(ver)bond, vakunie; ~ **wind** passaat(wind)

trad'ing (n) handeldryf; handel; ~ **com'pany** handelsmaatskappy; ~ **prof'it** bedryfswins

tradi'tion (n) oorlewering, tradisie; ~**al** tradi= sioneel; ~**al lea'der/ru'ler** tradisionele leier; hoofman, kaptein

traff'ic (n) verkeer; (v) handel dryf; ~ **calm'ing** verkeerdemping; ~ **control'** verkeerbeheer; ~ **in'terchange** verkeerswisselaar; wisselkrui= sing; ~ **is'land** vlugheuwel; ~ **jam** verkeers= knoop; ~ **light** verkeerslig; ~ **of'ficer** ver= keersbeampte; spietkop *also* **speed'cop**

tra'gedy ..dies treurspel, tragedie

tra'gic (a) tragies; treurig, droewig

trail (n) sleep; spoor; voetpad; stert (komeet); *hiking* ~ voetslaanpad; wandelpad; (v) sleep, agtervolg; ~**er** rankplant; sleepwa/ treiler; lokfilm; ~**er truck** laslorrie *also* **artic'ulated truck**; ~**net** treknet

train (n) trein; *by* ~ per spoor; (v) oefen, dril; oplei; afrig; ~**ed** opgelei; geoefen; ervare, geskool; gedresseer (dier); ~ **bearer** slip= draer; ~ **dri'ver** treindrywer, masjinis

trainee' (n) kwekeling, kadet, opleideling

train'er instrukteur, afrigter, breier; opleier

train' fare (n) reisgeld, treingeld

train'ing opleiding; *be in* ~ opgelei word; ge= oefen wees; ~ **col'lege** oplei(dings)kollege, onderwyskollege; ~ **ses'sion** oefensessie

train-oil fac'tory traankokery, walvisfabriek

trait (n) (karakter)trek; eienskap; streep/streek

trait'or verraaier

traject'ory (n) baan; koeëlbaan; trajek

tram trem; koolwa; ~**line** tremspoor

tramp (n) landloper/rondloper *also* **va'grant**; boemelaar

tram'ple (v) trap; vertrap; ~ *to death* doodtrap

tramp'oline (n) wipmat, trampolien

trance (n) verrukking; beswyming, skyndood; droomtoestand

tranquill'ity rus, stilte, kalmte

tranq'uillise gerusstel, sus; ~**r** kalmeermid= del/susmiddel; bedaarmiddel, sedatief

transact' (v) onderhandel; verhandel; verrig; ~**ion** onderhandeling, transaksie *also* **deal**

transcribe' oorskryf; transkribeer; kopieer

trans'fer (n) transport; oordrag; oorplasing; afdruk; **deed of** ~ transportakte

transfer' (v) verplaas; oordra; oorplaas; ~*red to Cape Town* na Kaapstad verplaas

transform' (v) vervorm, transformeer; her= skep; ~**a'tion** transformasie; omvorming; ~**er** transformator (elektr.)

transfu'sion (n) oortapping (bloed)

transis'tor (n) transistor

transi'tion (n) oorgang (fig.); ~**al pe'riod** oorgangstydperk

translate' (v) vertaal, oorsit; ~*d from Afri= kaans* uit Afrikaans vertaal

transla'tion vertaling, oorsetting

transla'tor vertaler (mens)

transmi'ssion oorsending; transmissie (mo= tor); uitsending (radio)

transmit' (v) oorsend, oorsein (berig); oor= lewer; uitsend (radio); ~**ter** sender (radio)

transpar'ency (n) deursigtigheid/oopheid/open= heid; transparant (film)

transpar'ent deurskynend, deursigtig; opreg

transpire' uitlek; uitwasem; sweet; gebeur

transplant' verplant, oorplant; verplaas; **heart** ~ hartoorplanting

trans'port (n) transport, vervoer; ~ **allow'**= **ance** vervoertoelae; ~ **and subsis'tence** reis en verblyf; ~ **ser'vices** vervoerdienste

transport' (v) vervoer, transporteer

trap (n) val, strik; slagyster; lokvink; *set a* ~ 'n val stel; (v) vasstrik; ~**door** valdeur

trapeze' (n) sweefstok

trap: ~**ped** vasgepen (in motorongeluk); in 'n strik gevang; ~**per** wildvanger, pelsjagter; ~**pings** tooi(sel), versiering(s)

trash afval; vullis; bog, kletspraatjies, kaf;

~can vullisblik *also* **ref'use bin**
trau'ma (n) trauma/trouma; ~ **coun'selling** traumaberading
trav'el (v) reis, bereis; ~ **a'gent** reisagent; ~**a'tor** rolloper (lughawe)
trav'eller reisiger; ~'s **cheque** reis(iger)tjek
trav'elling reis; ~ **compan'ion** reisgenoot; ~ **expen'ses** reiskoste; ~ **li'brary** reisbiblio= teek
trawl (v) treil; ~**er** vistreiler; ~ **net** sleepnet
tray -s skinkbord; bakkie, (plat)kissie
trea'cherous (a) verraderlik, vals
trea'chery (n) verraad; valsheid
trea'cle (n) (swart) suikerstroop; melasse
tread (n) tree, tred, voetstap, skrede; loopvlak (band); (v) tree, stap, betree, bewandel; ~ *on thin ice* op gevaarlike terrein wees
tread'mill (n) trapmeul; sleurwerk
treas'on verraad; *high* ~ hoogverraad
treas'ure (n) skat; ~ **house** skatkamer; ~ **hunt** skattejag; ~**r** tesourier, penningmees= ter/sentmeester
trea'sury (n) skatkis, tesourie (regering)
treat (n) onthaal; (v) onthaal, trakteer; ~ *as a joke* as 'n grap beskou; ~ *a patient* 'n pasiënt behandel; ~**ment** behandeling
trea'tise (n) verhandeling *also* **disserta'tion**
treat'y (n) verdrag, traktaat; ooreenkoms
tree (n) boom; lees (vir skoene); ~ **fern** boomvaring; ~**fel'ler** boomkapper/boom= veller (mens); ~ **snake** boomslang
trek (n) trek; (v) trek; ~ **ox** trekos
trell'is (n) tralie(werk); prieel; ~ **work** tralie= werk, latwerk
trem'ble (n) bewing, bewerasie; (v) beef, sid= der; ~ *with fear* beef van angs/vrees
trem'bling (n) bewing, siddering, trilling; (a) bewend
tremen'dous (a) verskriklik, yslik, ontsaglik
trem'or aardskudding; bewing, siddering
trench (n) -es loopgraaf; voor; riool
trend (n) tendens; neiging, strekking; ~**s** *in literature* tendense in die literatuur; ~**y** by= derwets/bydertyds *also* **with-it**; ~**set'ter** by= derwetser/pasaangeër (mens)
tres'pass (n) -es oortreding, vergryp; sonde; *forgive us our* ~**es** vergeef ons ons oortre= dings; (v) oortree, vergryp; sondig; ~**er** oortreder; ~**ing** betreding
tress -es haarlok, haarstring, vlegsel
tre'stle stellasie, bok; skraag
tri'al (n) beproewing; proefneming; verhoor/

hofsaak; ~ **run** oefenlopie; proeflopie; *stand* ~ *for murder* weens moord teregstaan; ~**s and tribula'tions** beproewinge
tri'angle driehoek; triangel (mus.)
tri'bal stam=; ~ **war** stamoorlog
tribe (n) stam, volkstam; ras; geslag
tribun'al regbank, geregshof, tribunaal
trib'utary (n) syrivier, takrivier
trib'ute (n) hulde, huldeblyk; *floral* ~*s* kranse; ruikers; *pay* ~ *to* hulde betoon/betuig aan/ teenoor
trick (n) kultoertjie, kunsie, behendigheid; skelmstreek, truuk, foefie; *play* ~*s* poetse bak; *the* ~*s of the trade* fabrieksgeheime; (v) bedrieg; fop; kul; ~**ster** bedrieër, kuller *also* **con'man**; ~**ery** kullery, bedrieëry, verneukery
tric'kle (v) druppel, aftap; *tears* ~*d down her cheeks* trane het oor haar wange gerol/ gebiggel
trick'y (a) bedrieglik, listig *also* **craft'y**; oulik gewaag; ~ **ques'tion** strikvraag; ~ **situa'= tion** netelige situasie
tri'cycle driewiel(er)
tri'dent (n) drietand
tri'fle (n) kleinigheid/bakatel; koekstruif; (v) korswel, skerts; *he is not to be* ~*d with* hy laat nie met hom speel nie; (adv) bietjie
tri'fling (a) niksbeduidend, nietig, onbenullig
trigg'er sneller, ~**-hap'py** skietlustig
trigonom'etry driehoeksmeting, trigonometrie
tril'ogy (n) ..gies trilogie; drieluik; triptiek
trim (n) opskik, tooisel; (v) tooi, versier; snoei, knip; afwerk; (a) netjies; mooi, in orde; ~**mer** afwerker; ~**ming** opsmuk; ~**park** trimpark
trin'ity drie-eenheid; drietal
trink'et (n) sieraad *also* **or'nament**; kleinood, snuistery; ~ **box** juwelekissie
tri'o (n) drietal; trio (mus.)
trip (n) uitstappie, rit; dwelmtoer; (v) struikel, val; pootjie
tripe beespens; bog, kaf
trip'let drieling; tersine (poësie); drietal
tri'pod (n) driepoot, drievoet
trip'switch (n) uitskopskakelaar
trite (a) alledaags; uitgedien; banaal
tri'umph (n) triomf; (v) triomfeer, seëvier; ~ *over all difficulties* alle moeilikhede oorwin
trium'phant (a) triomfant(e)lik, seëvierend
triv'ial (a) vervelig, plat, triviaal; ~ *matters* kleinighede, beuselagtighede
trocha'ic (n) trogee; (a) trogeïes

trog'lodyte grotbewoner, troglodiet *also* **ca've dwel'ler**

trol'ley (n) trollie; ~**bus** trembus

trom'bone tromboon, skuiftrompet

troop (n) trop, hoop, menigte; afdeling; (pl) troepe, soldate; *deploy* ~**s** troepe ontplooi; ~ **car'rier** transportskip; troepevliegtuig; troepedraer; ~**ie** troepie (rekruut)

troph'y ..**phies** trofee, beker; **floa'ting** ~ wisseltrofee

trop'ic (n) keerkring; (pl) trope; **T**~ **of Can'cer** Kreefskeerkring; **T**~ **of Cap'ricorn** Steenbokskeerkring

trop'ical tropies; ~ **disea'ses** tropiese siektes

trot (n) draf; *go for a* ~ 'n entjie gaan draf; (v) draf; laat draf; ~**ter** drawwer; pootjie, afval (van vark, skaap)

troub'adour (n) minnesanger, troebadoer

trou'ble (n) moeite, sorg, moeilikheid; *be in* ~ in die knyp sit; (v) moeite doen, lastig val; pla; neul; ~**ma'ker** skoorsoeker; ~**shoo'ter** foutspeurder; ~**some** lastig, neulerig

trough (n) trog, bak

troupe geselskap (toneelspelers); troep

trouss'eau -s (bruids)uitset, trousseau

trout forel (vis)

trow'el (n) troffel

tru'ant (n) stokkiesdraaier; *play* ~ stokkies draai; (a) lui, pligversakend

truce wapenstilstand, verposing

truck (n) goederewa, trok; vragmotor; ~ **dri'ver** lorriedrywer; (v) trok; ~**er** karweier *also* **car'tage contrac'tor/truck'er**

trudge (v) aansukkel, strompel, swoeg

true (a, adv) waar; eg; opreg; suiwer; *his words have come* ~ sy woorde is bewaarheid; ~**bred** raseg, opreg; ~ **cop'y** ware afskrif; ~**love** soetlief, hartjie, skattebol

tru'ly regtig/rêrig, inderdaad; **yours** ~ hoogagtend *also* **yours since'rely**

trump (n) troefkaart; (v) troef; oortroef; ~ *up* uit die duim suig; ~ **card** troefkaart

trump'et (n) trompet; *blow one's own* ~ jou eie basuin blaas; (v) uitbasuin; ~ **call** trompetgeskal; ~**er** trompetblaser

trunk stomp; romp; stronk; koffer, kis; slurp (olifant); ~ **call** hooflynoproep; ~ **road** hoofweg, deurpad; ~**s** (n) draf/swembroek(ie)

trust (n) vertroue; trust; geloof; (v) vertrou; toevertrou; *I* ~ *that* ek hoop dat; ~ **deed** trustakte; ~**ee'** trustee, gevolmagtigde; ~ **mon'ey** trustgeld; ~**wor'thy** betroubaar; ~**y**

eerlik; beproef; ~**y fel'low** staatmaker

truth waarheid; ~**ful** waarheidliewend, betroubaar; ~**less** ontrou, vals

try (n) **tries** poging; proef; 'n drie (rugby); *convert a* ~ 'n drie verdoel; (v) verhoor; op die proef stel, probeer, beproef; ~**ing** lastig, moeilik, veeleisend; ~ **line** doellyn; ~ **square** winkelhaak

tset'se fly tsetsevlieg, gifvlieg

tsot'si -s tsotsi, boef *also* **ruf'fian**

T-shirt (n) T-hemp, frokkiehemp

T'-square tekenhaak, winkelhaak

tub (n) balie, kuip, bad; ~**by** vatvormig

tube pyp, buis; binneband; ~**less tyre** lugband; ~ **rail'way** moltrein

tuberculos'is tuberkulose, tering (siekte)

tuck (n) opnaaisel; (pl) eetgoed, snoepgoed; (v) plooi, intrek; ~ *in* lekker toe maak; instop, wegslaan (kos); ~**shop** snoepwinkel(tjie)/snoepie

Tues'day Dinsdag

tuft (n) bos, kuif, kwas, pluim; pol (gras)

tug (n) sleepboot; ~ **of war** toutrek; (v) trek, ruk; sleep

tui'tion onderwys, onderrig; **tel'e**~ afstand(s)onderrig

tul'ip tulp; ~ **bulb** tulpbol

tum'ble (n) val, tuimeling; warboel; (v) bolmakiesie slaan; rol; val-val loop; ~ *down* instort; afrol; ~**bug** miskruier *also* **dung bee'tle**; ~ **dry'er** tuimeldroër; ~**r** drinkglas; tuimelaar (duif); akrobaat; ~ **switch** tuimelskakelaar

tumm'y tummies magie, pensie

tu'mour (n) gewas/groeisel; tumor

tu'mult opskudding, rumoer, lawaai

tun'dra toendra, mossteppe; moeraswêreld

tune (n) toon, klank, wysie; (v) stem, instem (radio); ~ *in to* instem/instel op (radio); ~**ful** melodieus, welluidend; ~**r** stemmer (mens); stemvurk; instemmer (radio)

tun'ic (n) uniform, skooldrag, springjurk

tun'ing (n) stem, gestem; ~ **fork** stemvurk

tunn'el (n) tonnel; gang, skag; (v) tonnel

tunn'y tunnies tornyn, tuna (vis)

tur'ban tulband (hoofbedekking)

tur'bine turbine

tur'bulence onstuimigheid; oproerigheid; turbulensie (wolke)

tureen' sopkom

turf turf, sooi; grasveld, baan; renbaan/reisiesbaan; ~ **club** renbaanklub

turk'ey (n) **-s** kalkoen; ~ **cock** kalkoenman=
netjie; ~ **hen** kalkoenwyfie

turm'oil (n) onrus, gewoel *also* **confu'sion**

turn (n) draai, wending; beurt (by spele); *do
somebody a good* ~ iem. 'n guns bewys; ~
of the century eeuwending; (v) draai; om=
keer; wend; ~ *one's back on* die rug toe=
keer; ~ *hundred* honderd jaar oud word; ~
out for practice vir oefening opdaag; ~ *the
tables* die bordjies verhang; ~ *up* opdaag; ~
upside down onderstebo keer; ~**coat** man=
teldraaier, oorloper; ~**er** draaier (ambag)

turn'ing (a) draaiend; ~ **point** keerpunt

turn'ip raap

turn: ~**key** (tronk)bewaarder, sipier; ~**-out**
opkoms (van mense); ~**over** omset; ~**pike**
tolsnelweg (Am.); slagboom, draaihek/tol=
hek; ~**stile** draaihek; ~**table** draaitafel

turp'entine terpentyn

turq'uoise (n) turkoois (steen)

tu'rret torinkie; skiettoring

tur'tle[1] torelduif

tur'tle[2] waterskilpad; *turn* ~ omslaan

tusk (n) olifant(s)tand; slagtand; (v) oopskeur

tus'sle (n) worsteling, gestoei; (v) stoei

tu'tor (n) private onderwyser/leermeester; stu=
dieleier, afrigter; **private** ~ goewernant(e),
(v) onderrig; privaat les gee

tutor'ial (n) studieklas/groepklas; (a) groep=

twad'dle (n) bogpraatjies; gebabbel; ~**-r** klet=
ser, babbelaar

twang (n) snaarklank; neusklank; (v) tokkel

tweedledum': ~ **and tweedledee'** vinkel en
koljander (die een is soos die ander)

tweet (n) getjilp; (v) tjilp

tweez'ers (haar)tangetjie; pinset

twelfth twaalfde

twelve twaalf

twen'tieth twintigste; ~ **cen'tury** twintigste eeu

twen'ty ..ties twintig; ~**-four hours' ser'vice**
etmaaldiens

twice twee maal/keer

twid'dle (n) draaitjie, krul; (v) draai; lol

twig takkie, twyg; waterwysstokkie

twi'light (aand)skemering, skemerlig, skemer=
aand; ~ **sleep** pynlose bevalling

twin (n) tweeling; dubbelganger; ~ **broth'er**
tweelingbroer

twi'nkle (n) flikkering, vonkeling; oogknip

twi'nkling flikkering; kits; *in the* ~ *of an eye*
in 'n oogwink

twirl (n) draai; krul; (v) dwarrel, draai

twist (n) draai; kronkel; krul; rinkhalsdans; (v)
(ver)draai; vleg; ~ *evidence* getuienis ver=
draai; ~ *someone's arm* iem. se arm draai

twitch (n) **-es** senuweetrekking; (v) (ver)trek

twitt'er (n) gekwetter, getjilp; (v) kwetter;
kweel; giggel

two -s twee; *cut in* ~ middeldeur sny; *put* ~
and ~ *together* jou gesonde verstand ge=
bruik; ~**ply** tweelaag=; ~**sea'ter** tweesitplekmotor; ~**some** twee=
spel, dubbelspel; ~**-tongued** vals

tycoon' (n) geldmagnaat *also* **plu'tocrat**

type (n) tipe, soort; setsel (drukkery); (v) tik;
~**wri'ting** tikmasjien; ~**wri'ting** tikskrif

typh'oid: ~ **fe'ver** ingewandskoors/maagkoors

typhoon' tifoon (sikloon)

typh'us tifuskoors, vlektifus, luiskoors

typ'ical tipies *also* **characteris'tic**

ty'ping tik, tikwerk; ~ **pool** tikpoel

ty'pist tikster/tikker

tyr'anny (n) tirannie, dwingelandy

ty'rant tiran, dwingeland *also* **dicta'tor**

tyre buiteband; **tube'less** ~ lugband; ~ **le'ver**
bandwipper; ~ **pres'sure** banddruk

U

ud'der (n) uier

ug'ly (a) lelik; gemeen; skandelik; *an* ~ *cus=
tomer* 'n nare/gevaarlike vent; ~ *weather*
onaangename/gure weer

ul'cer (n) sweer, geswel; maagseer

ulter'ior (a) aan die ander kant; verborge; ge=
heim; ~ **mo'tive** bybedoeling

ul'timate laaste, uiterste; beslissend

ultimat'um -s, ..ta ultimatum; laaste eis

ul'timo laaslede, van die vorige maand

ul'tra: ~**son'ic** ultrasonies; ~**vi'olet** ultravio=
let (bestraling)

umbil'ical nael=; ~ **cord** naelstring

umbrell'a sambreel; ~ **bod'y** oorkoepelende
liggaam; ~ **stand** sambreelstander; ~ **tree**
kiepersolboom, nooiensboom *also* **cab'bage
tree**

um'pire (n) skeidsregter; beoordelaar

una'ble (a) onbekwaam, nie in staat nie
unaffect'ed (a) natuurlik, ongekunstel(d)
unan'imous eenparig; eenstemmig
unarmed' ongewapen(d)
unashamed' onbeskaamd, onbeskof
unassum'ing (a) beskeie *also* **mod'est**; pre= tensieloos
unauth'orised ongemagtig, onwettig
unavoid'able onvermydelik *also* **inev'itable**
unaware' onbewus, onwetend
un'ban (v) ontban, ontperk
unbear'able ondraaglik, onuithoubaar
unbeat'en (a) onoorwonne
unbecom'ing onbetaamlik, onwelvoeglik *also* **unseem'ly**
unbeliev'able ongelooflik
unbi'ased onbevooroordeel(d), onpartydig
unbun'dle (v) ontknoop ('n maatskappy)
uncall'ed: ∼ *for* onvanpas, ongevra
uncer'tain onseker, wisselvallig
unchart'ed ongekaart (oseane)
unchecked' los, vry, ongedwonge
unciv'il onbeleef(d), ongemanierd; ∼**ised** on= beskaaf, barbaars
unclaimed' onopgeëis
un'cle oom; U∼ **Sam** die VSA
uncom'fortable ongemaklik, ongerieflik
uncomm'on ongewoon, seldsaam
uncondi'tional onvoorwaardelik; ∼ **surren'**= **der** onvoorwaardelike oorgawe
uncon'scious (a) bewusteloos; onwetend, on= bewus
unconstitu'tional (a) ongrondwetlik
uncontest'ed onbetwis, onbestrede; ∼ **seat** on= betwiste setel (verkiesing)
uncouth' (a) ru, grof, onbeskaaf *also* **rude**
uncov'er ontdek, afdek; blootlê
uncrossed' ongekruis; onbelemmer; ∼ **cheq'ue** ongekruiste tjek
uncut' ongekerf; ongesny; ongeslyp (diamante)
undam'aged onbeskadig, heel
undaunt'ed (a) onversaag, onverskrokke
undelivered' onafgelewer; nie verlos nie
undeni'able onweerlegbaar, onbetwisbaar
undepend'able onbetroubaar
un'der (a) onderste; (adv) onder, onderkant; (prep) onder; benede; ∼ *one's hand* ge= teken; ∼ *way* op pad; onderweg
under'achie'ver onderpresteerder (student)
undercharge' (v) te min vra/bereken
un'derclothes/un'derclothing onderklere
un'dercurrent onderstroom; neiging

un'dercut[1] (n) opstopper (boks)
undercut[2] (v) ondergrawe; pryse verlaag; on= derbie; onderkruip
un'derdeveloped onderontwikkel *see* **un'de vel'oped**
un'derdog verdrukte/ondergeskikte (mens) lydende party
underdone' halfgaar (biefstuk); halfrou
underes'timate (v) onderskat
underexpose' onderbelig, te kort belig (foto)
undergo' (v) ondergaan, ly, verduur
undergrad'uate (n) ongegradueerde (student (a) voorgraads *see* **post'graduate**
un'derground (n) moltrein; (a) ondergronds onderaards; (adv) heimlik, stilletjies
un'dergrowth (n) ruigte, struikgewas
underhand' (a) agterbaks, onderduims
underline' (v) onderstreep
underly'ing grond=; fundamenteel; ∼ **prin'ci ples** grondbeginsels
undermen'tioned ondergenoemde, onder staande
undermine' ondermyn, benadeel; uitgrawe
underneath' benede, onder
underpaid' onderbetaal, te min betaal
underpriv'ileged (a) onderbevoorreg *also* **dis advan'taged/impov'erished** (community)
underrate' onderskat; minag
undersell' goedkoper verkoop as, onderbie
undersigned' ondergetekende
un'derstaffed onderbeman (kantoor)
understand' verstaan, begryp; *I was given t* ∼ hulle het my te kenne gegee
understand'ing (n) begrip, verstandhouding *come to an* ∼ tot 'n skikking kom; *on the* ∼ *that* met dien verstande dat
understate' versag, verklein; ∼**ment** onder beklemtoning, onderskatting
understood' verstaan; vanselfsprekend
un'derstudy (n) poswaarnemer, plaasvervange
undertake' onderneem, aanpak; ∼**r** onderne mer, entrepreneur (sakeman)
un'dertaker (n) lykbesorger, begrafnisonder nemer
undertak'ing onderneming; verpligting
un'derwear onderklere
un'derwood (n) ruigte, struikgewas
un'derworld onderwêreld; boewewêreld; dc deryk
un'derwriter onderskrywer (assuransie); ve sekeraar
undeserved' onverdien(d)

undesir'able (a) onwenslik, ongewens; ~ **publica'tion** ongewenste publikasie
undetect'ed onopgemerk; onontdek
undevel'oped onontwikkel(d)
undig'nified onwaardig
undis'ciplined ongedissiplineer *also* **unru'ly**
undisput'ed onbetwis; onbestrede
undisturbed' kalm, bedaard *also* **calm, plac'id**
undivid'ed onverdeel(d)
undo' losmaak; ongedaan maak; ~**ing** verderf, ondergang
undone' ongedaan, los; *what is done can not be* ~ gedane sake het geen keer nie
undoubt'ed ongetwyfeld, stellig, seker; ~**ly** ongetwyfeld, beslis
undress' (v) uittrek, ontklee; ~**ed'** uitgetrek, ongeklee; ongekap (klip)
un'dulating golwend, wegdeinend (vlakte)
undy'ing (a) ewig, onverganklik
unearth' opgrawe, openbaar; opdiep
uneas'y ongemaklik, onrustig; besorg
uned'ucated onopgevoed, ongeletterd
unemployed' (n, pl) werkloses; (a) werkloos; ongebruik, onaangewend
unemploy'ment werkloosheid; ~ **insur'ance** werkloosheid(s)versekering
unend'ing oneindig, eindeloos
unenlight'ened dom, oningelig, onkundig
uneq'ual ongelykmatig; nie opgewasse nie; ~ *to the task,* nie teen/vir die taak opgewasse nie; ~**led** ongeëwenaard, weergaloos *also* **unpar'alleled**
une'ven ongelyk, onewe; ~ **num'ber** ongelyke getal
unexpect'ed onverwags, onvoorsien
unfail'ing onfeilbaar; seker
unfair' (a) onbillik; oneerlik, onopreg
unfaith'ful ontrou, trouleoos; ongelowig
unfamil'iar vreemd, onbekend; onvertroud
unfa'sten losmaak; losgespe
unfav'ourable ongunstig
unfin'ished onvoltooi, onafgewerk; ~ **sym'phony** onvoltooide simfonie
unfit' (a) onbekwaam, ongeskik; ~ *for a person* nie vir predikant deug nie
unflinch'ing onverskrokke; onwrikbaar
unfold' ontvou, uitlê; ontplooi, uitsprei
unforeseen' onvoorsien (uitgawes)
unforget'table onvergeetlik; gedenkwaardig
unfort'unate (a) ongelukkig; rampspoedig; ~**ly** ongelukkig
unfound'ed ongegrond, vals *also* **fab'ricated**;

~ **ru'mour** riemtelegram
unfriend'ly onvriendelik; onbevriend (land)
unfulfilled' onvervul
unfurn'ished ongemeubileer(d) (huis)
ungain'ly (a) lomp *also* **clum'sy**; onhandig
ungen'tlemanly onwellewend, onhoflik
unglazed' onverglaas; sonder ruite
ungov'ernable onregeerbaar; wild, woes
ungrate'ful (a) ondankbaar; onerkentlik
unguard'ed onbewaak; onbedagsaam
unham'pered onbelemmer(d), ongehinder
unhapp'y ongelukkig, hartseer
unharmed' onbeskadig/ongedeerd; veilig
unhealth'y ongesond; onveilig
unhurt' ongedeerd, onbeseer *also* **unharmed'**
unhygien'ic onhigiënies
u'nicorn (n) eenhoring (dier)
unifica'tion eenwording, unifikasie
u'niform (n) uniform, mondering; (a) eenvormig/gelykvormig; gelyk
uniform'ity eenvormigheid, uniformiteit
unilat'eral eensydig
unili'ngual eentalig
unima'ginative (a) verbeeldingloos
unimport'ant onbelangrik
uninhab'ited onbewoon
unin'jured onbeseer, ongedeerd
uninten'tional onopsetlik
unin'terested onbelangstellend
unin'teresting oninteressant, vervelend
uninterrup'ted onafgebroke, ononderbroke, deurlopend
u'nion unie, vereniging; vakbond/vakunie; samesmelting; ~ *is strength* eendrag maak mag
uniq'ue enig, ongeëwenaard, uniek; ~ *of its kind* enig in sy soort
u'nisex enkelgeslag, uniseks; ~ **school** enkelgeslagskool (*teenoor* **koëdskool**)
u'nison harmonie, ooreenstemming; *in* ~ eenstemmig, eensgesind
u'nit (n) eenheid; ~ **trust** effektetrust/eenheidtrust
unite' (v) verenig; byeenvoeg; verbind, saamsmelt; ~**d** verenig; U~**d** Na'tions Verenigde Nasies; U~**d States of America (USA)** Verenigde State van Amerika (VSA)
u'nity eenheid; eensgesindheid
univer'sal algemeen, universeel; ~ **peace** wêreldvrede
u'niverse (n) heelal
univer'sity (n) universiteit, hoëskool; (a) universiteits-; universitêr

unjust' onregverdig, onbillik *also* **unfair'**

umkempt' ongekam; onversorg (voorkoms)

unkind' onvriendelik

unknown' (n) onbekende; (a) onbekend

unlad'ylike onvroulik, onfyn, onverfyn

unlaw'ful onwettig; ongeoorloof

unlead'ed (a): ~ **pet'rol** ongelode/loodvry(e) petrol

unless' tensy, so nie, behalwe

unlike' ongelyk; verskillend, anders; ~**ly** on= waarskynlik

unlim'ited onbegrens, onbeperk

unload' (v) aflaai, afpak *also* **off'load**

unlock' oopsluit, ontsluit; onthul

unluck'y ongelukkig; rampspoedig; ~ **num= ber** ongeluksgetal

unman'ageable onbeheerbaar; onregeerbaar *also* **intrac'table**

unmann'erly ongemanierd, onhebbelik

unmarked' ongemerk; onopgemerk; onnage= sien (opstelle)

unmarr'ied: ~ **moth'er** ongetroude/ongehude moeder

unmistak'able onmiskenbaar, seker

unmoved' onbewoë, koel; roerloos

unnamed' ongenoem; naamloos

unna'tural onnatuurlik

unne'cessary onnodig, oorbodig, oortollig

unnot'iced ongemerk, onopgemerk

unobli'ging ontegemoetkomend, ontoeskietlik; onsimpatiek

unobstruct'ed onbelemmer; ongehinder(d); ~ **view** onbelemmerde uitsig

unobtain'able onverkry(g)baar

unocc'upied onbewoon, leeg; onbeset

unoffi'cial nie-amptelik, onoffisieel

unopposed' onbestrede; ongehinder; ~ **seat** onbestrede setel (in verkiesing)

unorth'odox ketters, onortodoks

unpaid' onbetaal(d)

unpar'alleled ongeëwenaard, weergaloos

unpard'onable onvergeeflik, onverskoonbaar

unperturbed' onversteur(d), houtgerus

unpleas'ant onaangenaam; onplesierig

unpop'ular onpopulêr, ongewild

unprac'tical onprakties; onuitvoerbaar

unprepared' onvoorberei; onklaar

unprin'cipled beginselloos

unprotect'ed onbeskerm, onbeskut

unpun'ished ongestraf; *go* ~ ongestraf bly

unqual'ified ongekwalifiseer, onbevoeg

unques'tionable onbetwisbaar *also* **undeni'able**

unreas'onable onredelik, onbillik

unreli'able onbetroubaar

un'rest (n) onrus, angs; beroering

unrestrict'ed onbelemmer, onbeperk

unriv'alled weergaloos, ongeëwenaar(d)

unrul'y wild, losbandig, onhanteerbaar; on= stuimig, weerspannig

unsafe' onveilig, gevaarlik

unsatisfac'tory onbevredigend

unsav'oury onsmaaklik; walglik; ~ **char'ac= ter** ongure vent

unscathed' ongedeerd, ongeskaad

unscrup'ulous gewete(n)loos; beginselloos

un'seeded ongekeur; ~ **play'er** ongekeurde speler (sport)

unseem'ly onwelvoeglik, onbetaamlik

unseen' (n) (die) ongesiene; onvoorbereide vertaling; (a) ongesien, onsigbaar

unsett'le (v) verwar, van stryk bring; ~**d** rus= teloos; onbestendig (weer)

unsex': ~**ed** ongeseks (kuikens)

unsight'ly onooglik, lelik *also* **repul'sive, ug'ly**

unskilled' ongeskool; onbedrewe, onervare; ~ **la'bour** ongeskoolde arbeid

unso'ciable ongesellig, onsosiaal

unsold' onverkoop

unsoli'cited ongevra; onuitgelok; ~ **support'** spontane steun

unsolved' (a) onopgelos

unsophis'ticated (a) onvervals, eg; onskuldig, onbedorwe, ongesofistikeer(d)

unsound' ongesond; bederf; swak; sieklik; on= betroubaar; *of* ~ *mind* swaksinnig

unspoilt' (a) onbedorwe (kind); ~ **na'ture** on= gerepte natuur

unsports'manlike onsportief

unstab'le onvas, veranderlik, onstabiel

unsuccess'ful onsuksesvol, vergeefs

unsuit'able ongeskik, onvanpas

unsurpassed' onoortroffe

unsuspect'ing argeloos, niksvermoedend, dood= gerus

unsympathet'ic onsimpatiek

unsystemat'ic onstelselmatig, onsistematies

unthank'ful ondankbaar

unthink'ing onbedagsaam, onnadenkend

untid'y (a) slordig, onnet *also* **shod'dy**

until' tot, totdat; *not* ~ *then* toe eers

untime'ly ontydig; ongeleë

untir'ing onvermoeid *also* **perseve'ring**

un'to tot, aan

untold' talloos; onvermeld; onberekenbaar

untouched' onaangeroer; ongedeerd
untrained' onopgelei, ongeoefen; onafgerig
untrue' onwaar, vals; ontrou
untrust'worthy onbetroubaar
unu'sual ongewoon, buitengewoon
unveil' onthul (standbeeld); inwy
unwant'ed onbegeer; ongewens, ongevra; *an* ~ *child* 'n ongewenste kind
unwell' onwel, siek, ongesteld, olik
unwiel'dy (a) onhanteerbaar, swaar, log
unwill'ing onwillig; ongeneë, onbereid
unwind' afrol, losdraai; ontspan; loswikkel
unwise' onverstandig, dom *also* **indiscreet'**
unwitt'ing(ly) onwetend
unworth'y onwaardig
unwritt'en ongeskrewe; ~ **law** ongeskrewe wet
unyield'ing onversetlik, koppig, eiesinnig *also* **stub'born/ob'stinate**
up (n): ~*s and downs* voor- en teenspoed; (v) oplig; styg; (adv) op, bo, boontoe; (prep) op; *cheer* ~ opvrolik; *hurry* ~ maak gou; wikkel; *time is* ~ die tyd is om/verstreke
up'bringing (n) opvoeding; grootmaak
up-country binneland(s)
up'date bywerk; hersien; *an* ~*d edition* 'n bygewerkte/hersiene uitgawe
up'grade (v) opgradeer, kwaliteit verhoog
upheav'al (n) opstand, oproer; omwenteling
up'hill opdraand; swaar (werk)
uphold' handhaaf; staande hou; hooghou
uphol'ster stoffeer; ~**er** stoffeerder (mens)
up'keep onderhoud; instandhouding
uplift' (v) oplig, ophef
up'market (a): ~ **sub'urb** hoëklasbuurt
upon' op, bo-op, by; aan; *once* ~ *a time* eendag; op 'n goeie dag
upp'er (a) bo, hoër, boonste; *gain the* ~ *hand* die oorhand kry; ~ **hand** oorhand; ~ **lip** bolip; ~**most** hoogste, boonste; ~ **sto'rey** boonste vloer/verdieping/vlak
up'right regop; opreg, eerlik, regskape
upri'sing opstand, oproer
up'roar oproer, lawaai, herrie
uproot' (v) uitroei, ontwortel
upset' (n) omval; verwarring; (v) omverwerp, omgooi; omkrap; verydel; ~ *someone* iem. omkrap/ontstel
up'shot (n) gevolg, uiteinde, uitslag; nadraai
up'side down' onderstebo, deurmekaar

up'stairs (a) bo=, boonste; hoogmoedig; (adv) op die boonste vloer/verdieping, boontoe
up'start (n) (o) astrant; astrante/vrypostige mens; (a) verwaand
up'swing (n) oplewing, opswaai (ekonomie)
up'take begrip; *slow in the* ~ traag van begrip
up-to-date' byderwets/bydertyds, nuwerwets; op die hoogte, tot datum
up'turn oplewing (ekonomie) *also* **up'swing**
up'ward opwaarts
up'wards opwaarts, boontoe; *pupils of seven and* ~ leerlinge van sewe jaar en daarbo
uran'ium uraan; ~ **enrich'ment** uraanverryking
ur'ban (a) stedelik, stads=; ~ **ter'rorism** stedelike terreur; ~ **trans'port** stedelike vervoer
ur'banise (v) verstedelik
urge (n) aandrang; **sex'ual** ~ geslagsdrang; (v) aandring, aanspoor; aanpor
ur'gent (a) dringend, spoedeisend; *an* ~ *matter* 'n dringende saak
ur'ine urine/urien; pis, piepie
us ons
u'sage gebruik, gewoonte; behandeling
use (n) gebruik; nut; gewoonte; *it is no* ~ *talking* praat help tog nie; *put to good* ~ goed benut; (v) gebruik; aanwend; *get* ~*d to* gewoond raak aan; ~**d car** gebruikte motor; ~**ful** nuttig, handig; ~**less** nutteloos; ~**r friend'ly** (a) gebruikervriendelik
ush'er (n) plekaanwyser; deurwagter; (v) binnelei; ~ *in a new era* 'n nuwe tydvak inlui
u'sual gewoon(lik); gebruiklik; *as* ~ soos gewoonlik; ~**ly** gewoonlik
u'sufruct (n) vruggebruik
uten'sil (n) gereedskap; (kombuis)gerei
u'terus baarmoeder *also* **womb**
util'ity nut, nuttigheid; ~ **com'pany** nutsmaatskappy
u'tilise (v) benut, gebruik, aanwend
ut'most uiterste, beste; *do one's* ~ jou uiterste (bes) doen
utt'er[1] (v) uiter; uit; in omloop bring; **for'ging and** ~**ing** vervalsing en uitgifte
utt'er[2] (a) volkome, volslae, algeheel; ~ **mis'ery** die diepste ellende
utt'erly heeltemal, volkome *also* **whol'ly**
utt'ermost verste, uiterste
u'vula (n) kleintongetjie, uvula

V

va'cancy (n) **..ies** vakature
va'cant (a) vakant, leeg; oop, onbeset; ~ **post** vakante pos; ~ **stare** wesenlose blik
vacate' (v) leeg maak; afstand doen van; ont= ruim
vaca'tion vakansie *also* **hol'iday**; vrye tyd; ~ **course** vakansiekursus
vac'cinate (v) inent, vaksineer
vac'uum ..cua, -s vakuum, lugleegte; ~ **cleaner** stofsuier; ~ **flask** koffiefles/termosfles
vag'abond (n) vagebond, swerwer *also* **ro'ver**
vagi'na (n) vagina, skede
vag'rant (n) rondloper, landloper; leeglêer
vag'ue vaag, onduidelik; *not the ~st notion* nie die flouste/vaagste benul nie
vain (a) ydel, verwaand; (te)vergeefs; *in* ~ te= vergeefs
valedic'tory afskeids=; ~ **address'** afskeidsrede
Val'entine's Day Valentynsdag
val'iant dapper, moedig *also* **bold/brave**.
val'id geldig, van krag; gegrond; ~ **rea'son** gegronde rede
vall'ey (n) laagte, vallei, dal; kloof
val'uable kosbaar, waardevol; **-s** (pl) kosbaar= hede
valua'tion waardering/waardasie; evaluering
val'ue (n) waarde, prys; *to the ~ of* ter waarde van; ten bedrae van; (v) waardeer, skat; op prys stel; ~ **added tax (VAT)** belasting op toegevoegde waarde (BTW)
valve klep; radiolamp; ventiel (band)
vam'pire bloedsuier, vampier
van (n) bagasiewa; kon019kteurswa (trein); be= stelwa; bakkie; **light deliv'ery** ~ **(LDV)** ligte bestelwa; **poli'ce** ~ patrolliewa
van'dal vandaal (mens); **~ism** vandalisme
van'guard voorhoede, voorpunt
vanill'a vanielje/vanilla
van'ish (v) verdwyn, wegraak; wegsterf
van'ity ydelheid; skyn; ~ **case** smuktassie/ tooitassie; ~ **mir'ror** smukspieëltjie
va'pour (n) damp, wasem; (v) (ver)damp
var'iable (n) veranderlike(s); (a) veranderlik; onbestendig
varia'tion variasie; verskeidenheid
va'ricose (op)geswel; ~ **veins** spatare
var'ied verskeie, verskillend
vari'ety ..ties verskeidenheid, variëteit; ~

con'cert verskeidenheid(s)konsert
var'ious verskillend; verskeie
varn'ish (n) vernis; glans; (v) vernis
vars'ity (n) universiteit; (a) universiteits=
va'ry (v) verander, afwissel; *tastes* ~ smaak verskil; **~ing** afwisselend
vase vaas, blompot
vast (a) groot, uitgestrek *also* **huge/spa'cious**
vat (n) vat, kuip
vault (n) (brand)kluis; (graf)kelder; (v) oor= spring; **~ing horse** bok, perd (gimn.)
veal kalfsvleis
veg'etable (n) groente; (pl) groente; (a) plant= aardig; ~ **king'dom** planteryk
vegetar'ian (n) vegetariër, groente-eter
vegeta'tion plantegroei; plantwêreld
ve'hement (a) vurig, hewig, heftig, driftig
ve'hicle (n) voertuig; vervoermiddel; medium
veil (n) sluier; masker; dekmantel; *take the ~* non word; *under the ~ of* onder die dek= mantel van; (v) omsluier; bewimpel
vein (n) aar; luim, gees; aanleg; trant; *in the same ~* in dieselfde gees/trant
veld veld; ~ **school** veldskool
velo'city snelheid, vinnigheid
vel'skoen (n) veldskoen
vel'vet (n) fluweel
vendett'a bloedwraak; (bloed)vete, vendetta
ven'ding machi'ne (n) muntoutomaat
ven'dor verkoper; smous *also* **haw'ker**
veneer' (n) fineer; (v) fineer; **~ed brick** glasuur= steen; **~ed door** fineerdeur
ven'erable (a) eerwaardig, eerbiedwaardig
vener'eal veneries; ~ **disea'se** geslagsiekte
Vene'tian (a) Venesiaans; ~ **blind** hortjie(s)= blinding, hortjie(s)blinder
ven'geance (n) (weer)wraak; *with a ~* kwaai
ven'ison wildvleis, wildbraad
ven'om gif; venyn; **~ous** giftig; venynig
vent (n) opening, luggat; *give ~ to* uiting gee aan; (v) lug, uiting gee, uit
ven'til klep, ventiel; **~ate** lug gee, ventileer; **~a'tion** ventilasie, lugverversing
ventril'oquist buikspreker (mens)
ven'ture (n) onderneming, waagstuk; (v) waag; ~ *an opinion* 'n mening waag
ven'ue plek, vergaderplek; sentrum
veran'da veranda, (oordekte) stoep *also* **pat'io**

verb werkwoord
ver'bal (werk)woordelik; mondeling, verbaal; ~ **transla'tion** letterlike vertaling
verben'a -s verbena, ysterkruid (blom)
ver'dict (n) uitspraak, vonnis; bevinding
verge (n) rand, grens; staf
ve'rify (v) ondersoek, toets, tjek, verifieer; moniteer/monitor; bekragtig
verm'in (n) ongedierte, goggas; gespuis
vernac'ular (n) landstaal, volkstaal, spreek= taal; (a) inheems *also* **indi'genous**
vers'atile veelsydig; alsydig
verse (n) vers, versreël, poësie, gedig; koeplet; **blank** ~ rymlose verse
ver'sion (n) weergawe, bewerking; vertolking
vers'us teen/teenoor, versus
vert'ebral werwel=; ~ **col'umn** ruggraat
ver'tical (a) regop, vertikaal, loodreg
ver'vet mon'key blouaap/blouapie
ve'ry (a) eg, waar, opreg, werklik; *the* ~ *thing* net die regte ding; (adv) baie, regtig, erg, uiters; *the* ~ *best* die allerbeste
ves'per aand; aandster; aandgebed
vess'el vat; vaartuig/skip; kom, kruik
vest[1] (n) onderhemp; frokkie; onderbaadjie
vest[2] (v) beklee; toevertrou; ~ *with power* met mag/bevoegdheid beklee
vest'ed bestaande; ~ **in'terests** gevestigde be= lange
ves'tibule (voor)portaal, vestibule *also* **foy'er**
ves'try ..tries konsistoriekamer, sakristie
vet'eran (n) veteraan, oudgediende, oudstry= der *also* **old-tl'mer**; ringkop; (a) oud, be= proef; ~ **car** noagmotor, veteraanmotor
veterinar'ian (n) veearts, dierearts *also* **vet**
vet'erinary veeartsenykundig, veeartseny=; ~ **clin'ic** diereklinick; ~ **sur'geon** veearts
ve'to (n) -es verbod, veto; (v) veto
vi'a oor, via
viabil'ity lewensvatbaarheid; ~ **stu'dy** lewens= vatbaarhcidstudic/haalbaarhcidstudic *also* **feasibi'lity stu'dy**
vi'able lewensvatbaar, ekonomies uitvoerbaar; haalbaar *also* **fea'sible**
vi'be (n) aanvoeling, atmosfeer (tussen mense)
vibra'tion trilling; slingering; vibrasie
vic'ar vikaris; predikant; ~**age** pastorie
vice[1] (n) ondeug; fout, gebrek; onsedelikheid
vice[2] (n) skroef; (v) vasdraai; vasknel; ~ **grip** klemtang/kloutang
vice[3] (prep) in die plek van, vise=; onder=; ~**-chair'man** ondervoorsitter, visevoorsit=

ter; ~**-chan'cellor** visekanselier; ~**-prin= cipal** viseprinsipaal, onderhoof; ~**roy** on= derkoning
vice vers'a vice versa, andersom, omgekeerd
vicin'ity (n) buurt; omgewing, omstreke
vi'cious (a) boosaardig, venynig; kwaai; ~ **an'imal** dierasie; ~ **cir'cle/spi'ral** bose kringloop, duiwelspiraal
vic'tim (n) slagoffer, prooi; ~**ise** viktimiseer
vic'tor oorwinnaar (mens) *also* **con'querer**
vic'tory ..ries oorwinning, sege
vi'deo ~ **casset'te** videokasset; ~ **li'brary** videoteek; ~ **recor'der** video-opnemer; ~ **ta'pe** videoband
view (n) vergesig/vêrgesig; uitsig; mening/ beskouing; (v) kyk (TV); besigtig, beskou; ~**er** kyker (TV); ~**point** gesig(s)punt
vi'gil wag; **-s** nagwaak; *keep* ~*s* waak; ~**an'te** (n) hulpkonstabel; vigilante/burgerwaker
vig'orous (a) kragtig, sterk; gespierd
vill'age dorp; ~**r** dorpeling/dorpenaar
vil'lain skurk, booswig (mens)
vim (n) fut, pit, oemf, vitaliteit, woema
vindic'tive wraakgierig, wraaksugtig
vine wingerdstok, wynstok; ~ **cul'ture** wyn= bou *see* **vi'ticulture**
vin'egar (n) asyn; (a) asyn=, asynsuur=
vine'yard wingerd (druiwe)
vin'tage (n) wynjaar; (a) uitstekend; oud; ~ **car** veteraanmotor, toekamotor, noagmotor; ~ **year** oesjaar
vio'la[1] -s altviool, viola
vio'la[2] somerviooltjie; (klein) gesiggie (blom)
vi'olate (v) skend, oortree; verkrag; onthei= lig
vi'olence (n) geweld, geweldpleging; *die by* ~ 'n gewelddadige dood sterf; **contin'uing** ~ voortslepende geweld
vi'olent geweldig, verskriklik; gewelddadig
vi'olet (n) viooltjie; (a) perskleurig
violin' viool; ~**ist** violis, vioolspeler
vi'per (n) adder (slang)
virag'o -s mannetjiesvrou; tierwyfie *also* **bitch'= y woman**
vir'gin (n) maagd *also* **mai'den**; (a) maagde= lik; ongerep, suiwer; ~ **fo'rest** ongerepte (oer)woud
vir'ile manlik, manhaftig; gespierd, viriel
virt'ual wesenlik, werklik, feitlik, eintlik; *he is* ~*ly broke* hy is feitlik bankrot; ~ **real'ity** virtuele werklikheid; skynwerklikheid (rek.)
vir'tue (n) deug; krag; kuisheid; *by* ~ *of* krag=

tens; *of easy* ~ los van sedes
vi'rus gif, smetstof; virus; bitsigheid
vi'sa (n) visum; ondertekening
viscos'ity viskositeit, taaivloeibaarheid (van olie)
vis'count (*pron.* **vi'count**) burggraaf
visibil'ity sigbaarheid, sig
vis'ible sigbaar, duidelik, aanskoulik
vis'ion (n) gesig, visioen; visie, gesigskerpte
vis'it (n) besoek, kuier; *pay a* ~ besoek; (v) besoek, (gaan) kuier; ~**a'tion** beproewing, besoeking; ~**ing card** naamkaartjie, visitekaartjie; ~**or** besoeker; kuiergas
vis'ta (n) uitsig, verskiet, vergesig/vêrgesig
vis'ual gesigs=, visueel; ~ **educa'tion** aanskouingsonderwys; ~**ise** visualiseer
vi'tal lewensnoodsaaklik; beslissend/essensieel; *of* ~ *importance* van die (aller)hoogste belang
vital'ity lewenskrag, vitaliteit
vit'amin vitamine/vitamien
vit'iculture wynbou, wingerdbou
viva'cious (a) lewendig, lewenslustig, vrolik
viv'id duidelik, helder; ~ **imagina'tion** lewendige/sterk verbeelding(skrag)
vix'en wyfiejakkals; feeks, helleveeg (vrou)
vocab'ulary ..ries woordeskat, taalskat
voc'al (n) klinker, vokaal; (a) stem=; ~ **cord** stemband; ~**ist** sanger
voca'tion (n) beroep/professie; ambag; roeping
voca'tional beroeps=, vak=; ~ **guidance/counselling** beroepsleiding; ~ **trai'ning** beroepsopleiding, beroepsgerigte opleiding
voet'sak! (interj) voetsek! *also* **be off!**
vogue swang, mode *also* **cus'tom, fash'ion**
voice (n) stem, spraak; *active* ~ bedrywende vorm; *have no* ~ *in* geen seggenskap/inspraak hê nie in; *passive* ~ lydende vorm;

(v) uitspreek; ~ *my opinion* my mening lug
void (n) leegte, gaping; (a) leeg; *declare* ~ nietig verklaar; *null and* ~ van nul en gener waarde
vol'atile vlugtig; ongedurig; opvlieënd; ~ **oil** vlugtige olie; ~ **salts** vlugsout
volcan'ic (a) vulkanies; ~ **erup'tion** vulkaniese uitbarsting
volcan'o (n) -es vulkaan, vuurspuwende berg
voll'ey (n) -s sarsie, salvo; vlughou (tennis); ~**ball** vlugbal
volt volt; ~**age** stroomspanning
vol'uble woordryk *also* **talk'ative**; glad
vol'ume (n) boekdeel, bundel; grootte, omvang, volume; *speak* ~s boekdele spreek
vol'untary (a) vrywillig; spontaan
volunteer' (n) vrywilliger; (v) vrywillig onderneem; *he* ~*ed* hy het gevrywil
vom'it (v) braak, opgooi
vote (n) stem; stemreg; begrotingspos; *casting* ~ beslissende stem; ~ *of no-confidence* mosie van wantroue; *put to the* ~ tot stemming bring; (v) stem, stem uitbring; ~ *by ballot* per stembrief(ie) stem; ~**r** kieser, stemgeregtigde; ~**rs' roll** kieserslys
vot'ing stemming, stem(mery); ~ **pa'per** stembrief(ie)
vouch bevestig; instaan vir; ~ *for the truth of* instaan vir die waarheid van; ~**er** kwitansie; bewys, bewysstuk
vow (n) eed, gelofte; (v) 'n gelofte doen; sweer, plegtig beloof
vow'el (n) klinker, vokaal
voy'age (n) seereis, vaart; ~**r** seereisiger
vul'gar (a) plat, ordinêr, vulgêr; ~ **expres'sion** plat uitdrukking; ~ **frac'tion** gewone breuk; ~**ism** platheid; plat uitdrukking
vul'nerable (a) kwesbaar; wondbaar
vul'ture (n) aasvoël; uitsuier (mens)

W

wad (n) pluisie, prop, watte; ~**ding** watte, kapok
wa'ddle (v) waggel, strompel
wa'fer wafel (koek); hostie; ouel
wa'ffle wafel; (v) gorrel (in eksamen)
wag (v) kwispel, swaai; *the dog* ~*s his tail* die hond kwispel
wage[1] (n) verdienste, loon, besoldiging; ~ **de-**

mand' looneis; ~ **ear'ner** loontrekker, broodwinner; ~ **dispu'te** loongeskil
wage[2] (v) voer, maak; ~ *war* oorlog voer
wa'ger (n) weddenskap; *lay a* ~ 'n weddenskap aangaan; (v) wed *also* **bet**
wag'on wa, bokwa; ~ **dri'ver** wadrywer; ~ **house** waenhuis; ~ **load** wavrag
wag'tail kwikstertjie/kwikkie (voël) *also* **Wil'=**

lie **Wag'tail**
wail (v) weeklaag, kerm; ~**ing wall** klaag=
muur
waist middel; lyfie; ~**band** gordel, lyfband;
~**coat** onderbaadjie; ~ **cloth** lendedoek
wait (n) wagtyd; (v) vertoef; wag; ~ *a minute*
wag 'n bietjie; ~ *one's turn* jou beurt
afwag; ~**er** tafelbediende/kelner; ~**ing** (n)
wag; opwagting; bediening; (a). wagtend;
~**ing list** waglys; ~**ing room** wagkamer
waive (v) laat vaar, afstand doen van, kwyt=
skeld
wake[1] (n) kielwater; volgstroom
wake[2] (v) wakker word; wakker maak/wek
walk (n) wandeling; pas, gang; voetpad; *go for*
a ~ gaan stap; (v) loop, wandel, stap; ~**er**
stapper, wandelaar; ~**ie-tal'kie** loopgesel=
ser, tweerigtingradio; ~**ing ring** loopring;
~**ing stick** wandelstok, kierie; ~**ing tour**
wandeltog, staptoer; ~**o'ver** wegholoorwin=
ning
wall (n) muur; wal; (v) ommuur
wall clock hangklok
wal'let (sak)portefeulje; knapsak; notetas
wa'llop (v) afransel, looi; ~**ing** (n) loesing
wall: ~**paper** plakpapier; ~**-to-**~ **car'pet**
volvloermat, volvloertapyt
wal'nut okkerneut
wal'rus walrus (dier)
waltz (n) -es wals; (v) wals
wand (n) staf; **mag'ic** ~ towerstaf
wan'der dwaal, swerf; ronddool; yl; *his mind*
~*s* hy yl; ~**er** swerwer/swerfling; ~**lust**
swerfsug/wanderlust
wan'dering (a) ronddwalend, swerwend; **W**~
Jew Wandelende Jood
want (n) gebrek, behoefte, armoede, skaarste;
for ~ *of* by gebrek aan; (v) wil, wens, ver=
lang
war (n) oorlog, stryd *also* **war'fare**; *declare* ~
oorlog verklaar; *make* ~ oorlog voer; **civ'il**
~ burgeroorlog; **cold** ~ senuoorlog, koue
oorlog
war'ble (v) kweel, sing; ~**r** sangvoël
ward (n) wyk; saal, afdeling (hospitaal); (v)
bewaak; beskerm, beskut; ~ *off* afweer
war: ~ **cry** oorlogskreet/strydkreet; ~ **dance**
krygsdans; ~ **debt** oorlogskuld
war'den hoof, opsigter; voog; bewaarder
war'der bewaarder (gevangenis), korrektiewe
beampte; sipier
ward'robe klerekas; klere *also* **out'fit**

ware (n) ware, goed; (pl) koopware
ware'house (n) pakhuis; loods; (v) (op)berg
war'lord (n) krygsheer, strydleier
warm (v) warm maak, verwarm; (a) warm;
innig, hartlik; *a* ~ *reception* 'n hartlike ont=
vangs; ~**-bloo'ded** warmbloedig; ~**-hear'ted**
hartlik; ~**th** warmte; geesdrif
warn (v) waarsku, vermaan; ~**ing** waar=
skuwing; aanmaning; ~**ing light** kliklig(gie)
warp (n) skering (draad); ~ **and woof** skering
en inslag; (v) kromtrek, skeeftrek
wa'rrant (n) volmag; lasbrief, magtiging; (v)
vrywaar; waarborg; magtig; wettig; ~**ee'**
gevolmagtigde; ~**er/**~**or** borg, waarborger;
volmaggewer; ~ **of'ficer** adjudant-offisier;
~**y** volmag; waarborg/garansie
wa'rrior krygsman/kryger; vegsman
wart vratjie; knoes, kwas
wart'hog vlakvark (dier)
wa'ry (a) behoedsaam, versigtig *also* **cau'tious**
wash (n) wasgoed; (v) (uit)was; spoel; afspoel;
~ *one's dirty linen in public* onenigheid in
die openbaar uitmaak; ~*ed out* pootuit;
~**ba'sin** waskom; ~**er** wasser/waster (ring);
~**ing machi'ne** wasmasjien; ~**ing pow'der**
waspoeier; ~**stand** wastafel; ~**tub** wasbalie
wasp wesp, perdeby
wast'age verkwisting, vermorsing, verspilling;
afval; slytasie
waste[1] (n) verkwisting; afval; oorskiet; **atom'ic**
~ kernafval; (v) weggooi, verkwis, mors; ~
time tyd verspil; ~ *not, want not* wie spaar,
vergaar
waste[2] (a) verlate; ongebruik, woes, onbebou
waste: ~**ful** verkwistend; ~**pa'per** skeurpapier;
~**paper bas'ket** snippermandjie; ~**pipe** af=
voerpyp
watch (n) -es horlosie/oorlosie; wag; waak=
saamheid; (v) waghou; oplet; bewaak; ~**dog**
waghond; ~**ful** waaksaam; ~ **hand** horlo=
siewyser; ~**ma'ker** horlosiemaker; ~**tow'er**
wagtoring; ~**word** wagwoord
wa'ter (n) water; (v) water gee, natmaak/
natlei; water (oë); laat suip (dier); ~ *down*
verdun, verwater; ~**buck** waterbok; ~
chute glygeut; ~**col'our** waterverf; **divi'ner** waterwyser *also* **dow'ser** (person);
~**fall** waterval; ~**foun'tain** spuitfontein
also **leap'ing fountain**; ~**ing can** gieter;
~ **lev'el** waterpas *also* **spir'it** level;
~**mel'on** waatlemoen; ~**proof** (n) reënjas;
(a) waterdig; ~ **resis'tant** waterwerend;

~**spout** waterhoos; ~**shed** waterskeiding; ~**tight** waterdig; ~**y** pap, waterig; laf

wat'tle looibasboom, wattelboom; ~**-and-daub hut** hartbeeshuisie

wave (n) golf, brander; wuif; *permanent* ~ vasgolf, permanente karteling; (v) golf; waai, wuif; ~**length** golflengte

wa'ver (v) weifel, aarsel *also* **hes'itate**

wax[1] (n) was; byewas; lak; (v) opvryf, waks

wax[2] (v) was, groei (maan); ~**ing moon** wassende maan

wax: ~**bill** rooibekkie (voël); ~ **can'dle** waskers; ~ **doll** waspop; ~**en** wasagtig

way (n) -s weg, pad, rigting; manier; wyse; *by* ~ *of* by wyse van; *by the* ~ terloops; *in the family* ~ swanger; verwagtend; *get one's* ~ jou sin kry; ~**side** (n) die kant van die pad; (a) langs die pad; ~**ward** eiewys, eiesinnig *also* **head'strong**

we ons

weak (a) swak; flou, pap; ~**-hear'ted** weekhartig; ~**ling** swakkeling (mens); ~**ness** swakheid

wealth (n) rykdom *also* **af'fluence**; welvarendheid; ~**y** welgesteld, ryk, vermoënd

wean (v) speen; afleer, afwen

wea'pon (n) wapen; ~**ry** wapentuig

wear (n) drag; slytasie; *fair* ~ *and tear* billike slytasie; (v) dra; ~**er** draer; ~**ied** vermoeid; ~**iness** moegheid, vermoeidheid; ~**isome** vervelig; vermoeiend *also* **exhaus'ting**; ~**y** (a) vermoeid/tam; afmattend

weas'el wesel (diertjie)

wea'ther[1] (n) weer; ~ *permitting* as die weer goed is

wea'ther[2] (v) deurstaan; verweer, verkrummel; ~ *the storm* die storm deurstaan

wea'ther: ~ **bureau'** weerburo; ~**cock** weerhaan; ~ **fore'cast** weervoorspelling; ~ **glass** weerglas, barometer

weave (v) weef; vleg; ~**r** wewer; ~**r bird** wewervoël, vink

wea'ving weef/wewery

web web, spinnerak; ~**foot** swempoot

web'site (n) webtuiste/webblad (rek.)

wed (v) trou *also* **mar'ry**; verenig

wedd'ed getroud; ~ **life** getroude lewe

wedd'ing (n) bruilof, troue; huwelik *also* **mar'riage**; ~ **cake** bruidskoek; ~ **card** troukaart(jie); ~ **day** troudag; ~ **recep'tion** huweliksonthaal; ~ **ring** trouring

wedge (n) wig, keil; punt; *the thin end of the* ~

die skerp kant van die wig

wed'lock huwelik, eg; *born out of* ~ buite-egtelik gebore *see* **illegit'imate child**

Wed'nesday Woensdag

wee baie klein; *a* ~ *bit* 'n baie klein bietjie

weed (n) onkruid, vuilgoed; *ill* ~*s grow apace* onkruid vergaan nie; (v) skoffel, skoonmaak; ~ *out* uitroei, suiwer; ~**-eat'er** randsnyer/randsnoeier; ~**kil'ler** onkruiddoder *also* **herb'icide**

week week; *this day* ~ vandag oor 'n week; ~**day** werkdag, weekdag; ~**end** naweek; ~**ly** (n) weekblad; (a) weekliks

weep (v) huil, ween *also* **cry**; treur; ~ *for joy* van vreugde huil; ~**ing** (a) huilend; ~**ing wil'low** treurwilg(er)

weev'il kalander

weigh (v) weeg; oorweeg; bedink

weight (n) gewig/massa; swaarte; *pick up* ~ vet word; (v) beswaar; ~**lif'ter** kragopteller/gewigopteller; ~**y** swaar; gewigtig; gesaghebbend

weir (n) stuwal; studam, keerwal

weird (a) eienaardig; spookagtig; bonatuurlik

wel'come (n) welkom, verwelkoming; *bid one* ~ iem. welkom heet; ~ *home* welkom tuis; (v) verwelkom, welkom heet; (a) welkom

weld (v) sweis; ~**ing rod** sweisstaaf

wel'fare welsyn; welvaart, voorspoed; ~ **work** maatskaplike werk; welsynswerk

well[1] (n) put, bron; fontein

well[2] (n) die goeie; *wish someone* ~ iem. die beste toewens; (a) wel; gesond; *get* ~ beter word; (adv) goed; terdeë; *be* ~ *aware* ten volle bewus wees; ~ *done!* goed so!; *be* ~ *off* welgesteld wees; *very* ~ goed

well[3] (interj) wel

well: ~**-beha'ved** fatsoenlik; ~**be'ing** welstand; welsyn; ~**bred** goed opgevoed; volbloed; ~**do'er** weldoener *also* **benefac'tor**; ~**-infor'med** goed ingelig; ~**-man'nered** welgemanierd; ~ **off** welgesteld; ~**-read** belese; ~**-spo'ken** wel ter tale; ~**-to-do** welgesteld/welaf, gegoed

Welsh (n) Wallies (taal); ~**man** Wallieser; ~ **ra'rebit** kaasroosterbrood

wel'ter (n) beroering; harwar; (v) slinger, rol, wentel; ~**weight** weltergewig (boks)

wench (n) meisie(mens), vroumens; slet

wend (v) gaan, jou begeef

were'wolf ..wolves weerwolf

west (n) in die weste; (a) weste-, westelik;

(adv) na die weste, wes; *go* ~ bokveld toe gaan; ~**erly** westelik; **W**~**ern Cape** (province) Wes-Kaap; **W**~**ernise** (v) verwester(s); ~**ward** weswaarts

wet (n) nattigheid; (v) natmaak; bevogtig; ~ *the roof* huisinwyding vier; (a) nat, vogtig; klam; ~ **blan'ket** remskoen, pretbederwer; **drip'ping** ~ papnat/sopnat; ~**bike** waterponie

weth'er hamel (skaap)

whack (n) slag; deel; (v) slaan, moker

whale (n) walvis; ~**bone** balein; ~ **oil** walvistraan; ~**r** walvisvaarder (skip)

wharf (n) kaai *also* **quay**, **jet'ty**; (v) vasmeer

what (a) wat, watter; (pron) wat; hoe; *come* ~ *may* wat ook al gebeur; *so* ~ ? en wat daarvan?; (adv) hè?; nè?

whatev'er wat ook al; *nothing* ~ niks hoegenaamd nie

wheat koring; ~ **flour** meelblom

wheel (n) wiel, rat; (v) draai, rol; ~ *round* swenk; ~ **align'ment** wielsporing; ~**bar'row** kruiwa; ~ **cap** wieldop; ~**chair** rolstoel; ~**wright** wamaker

when (adv, conj) wanneer; toe

whence waarvandaan; vanwaar

whene'er/whenev'er/whensoev'er wanneer ook al

where (n) wanneer; (pron) waarheen, waarvandaan; (adv) waar; waarheen/waarnatoe, waarso, ~**about(s)** (n) verblyfplek; adres; (a) waaromtrent; waar; ~**as'** aangesien, daar; ~**by'** waardeur, waarby; ~**fore** waarom; ~**of'** waarvan; ~**on'** waarop; ~**to'** waarby, waarnatoe; ~**upon'** waarop

wher'ever waar ook al

whet (v) slyp; (op)wek (eetlus); prikkel

wheth'er (pron) watter van twee; (conj) hetsy; of; ~ *we go or not* of ons nou gaan al dan nie

whey (n) wei, dikmelkwater

which watter, wie, wat; ~**e'ver**, ~**soev'er** wat/ watter ook (al)

while[1] (n) rukkie; *after a* ~ kort daarna/daarop; *once in a* ~ af en toe

while[2] (conj) terwyl, onderwyl, solank as

whim (n) gril, nuk, gier, frats

whim'per (v) kerm, kreun; sanik, grens

whim'sical (a) wispelturig, vol nukke/fiemies

whine (v) kerm, tjank, grens

whip (n) sweep, peits; karwats; sweep (parlement); (v) slaan, piets, raps; ~**-handle** sweepstok; ~**lash** voorslag

whipped' cream slagroom

whipp'et windhond/renhond

whipp'ing pak slae, loesing *also* **beat'ing**; ~ **bag** slaansak; ~ **boy** sondebok *also* **scape'goat**

whirl (v) dwarrel, draai; maal (water); ~**pool** draaikolk, maalstroom; ~**wind** (n) (d)warrelwind; windhoos

whisk (n) stoffer; eierklitser; (v) rondfladder; klits, klop; ~ *away* vinnig wegvoer

whis'ker wangbaard; bak(ke)baard

whis'per (n) gefluister; geritsel; (v) fluister

whis'tle (n) gefluit; *wet one's* ~ 'n dop steek; (v) fluit

white (n) wit; blank; blanke/wit man; (a) wit; bleek; blank; ~ **lie** noodleuen; ~ **ant** rysmier; ~**col'lar crime** handelsmisdaad; ~**wash** (n) witsel, witkalk; (v) wit, afwit

whit'low fyt; omloop

whiz (v) sis, gons, fluit; ~**kid** jong ster/uitblinker/genie

who wie, wat; ~**dunn'it** speurverhaal; ~**ev'er/** ~**soev'er** wie ook (al)

whole (n) geheel; alles; totaal; *on the* ~ oor/in die algemeen; (a) heel; volkome; ~**-heart'ed** hartlik, opreg: *I agree with you* ~**-heart'edly** ek stem volmondig/volkome met jou saam

whole'sale (n) groothandel; (a) groothandel-; (adv) op groot skaal; ~ **dea'ler** groothandelaar; ~ **pri'ces** groothandelpryse

whole'some (a) gesond, voedsaam

whole'wheat volgraan, volkoring

wholl'y heeltemal, volkome

whom wat, vir wie; ~**ev'er/**~**soev'er** wie ook (al)

whoop optrek (by kinkhoes); ~**ing cough** kinkhoes

whop (v) oorwin; verslaan; ~**per** deeglike loesing; 'n groot leuen

whore hoer, prostituut *also* **pros'titute, hook'er**

whose wie s'n, wie se, van wie

why: *go into the* ~*s and wherefores* alle besonderhede wil weet; (adv) hoekom, waarom

wick pit (van lamp of kers)

wick'ed (a) goddeloos, sondig, sleg, boos; onnutsig, ondeund

wick'er riet; rottang; ~ **chair** rottangstoel; ~ **cra'dle** biesiewieg; ~ **work** rottangwerk

wick'et deurtjie; paaltjie (krieket); baan;

~**kee′per** paaltjiewagter

wide (a, adv) wyd, breed, ruim; *a* ~ *difference* 'n hemelsbreë verskil; ~**-awa′ke** wawyd wakker; uitgeslape; ~ **know′ledge** breë kennis; ~**spread** uitgebrei; wyd versprei

wid′ow (n) weduwee, weduvrou; ~**er** wewenaar; ~**'s weeds** rouklere

width (n) wydte; breedte; uitgestrektheid

wield (v) hanteer; swaai; ~ *the sceptre* die septer swaai

wife wives vrou, eggenote; ~ **bea′ter/bat′terer** vrou(e)slaner

wig pruik, vals hare *also* **hair′piece**

wig′wam Indiaanse tent/hut, wigwam

wild (n) wildernis, woesteny; (a, adv) wild, woes; onstuimig; *make a* ~ *guess* blindweg raai; *a* ~-*looking fellow* 'n wildewragtig; ~**cat** (n) wildekat; (a) onbesonne; ~**cat stri′ke** wilde/onwettige staking

wil′debees (n) wildebees *also* **gnu**

wil′derness wildernis, woesteny

wild-goo′se cha′se (n) dwase/onbesonne onderneming

wild′life natuurlewe; ~ **socie′ty** natuurlewevereniging

wil′ful (a) opsetlik; moedswillig; eiewys

will[1] (n) wil; wilskrag; wens; testament; (v) wil, begeer; bemaak (in testament)

will[2] (v) **would** sal; ~**ing** gewillig; bereid; ~**ingness** gewilligheid

Will′ie Wink′ie Klaas Vakie, Sandmannetjie

will′ow (n) wilg, wilgerboom

will′power wilskrag *also* **determina′tion**

will′y-nill′y noodgedwonge, teen wil en dank

wilt (v) kwyn, verwelk, verlep *also* **droop**

wi′ly (a) listig, geslepe, uitgeslape; oorlams

wimp (n) bleeksiel, papperd (mens)

win (n) oorwinning; (v) wen; verdien

wince (v) terugdeins; huiwer; ineenkrimp

winch -es windas; slinger; hystoestel

wind[1] (v) hys; slinger; draai, opwen; ~ *up* opwen (horlosie); likwideer

wind[2] (n) wind; lug; *find out how the* ~ *blows* die kat uit die boom kyk; (v) blaas; asem skep; ~**break** windskerm; ~**break′er** windjekker; ~**-chill fac′tor** aanvoeltemperatuur; ~**fall** buitekans; meevaller(tjie) *also* **bonan′za/jack′pot**; ~ **gauge** windmeter

wind′ing (a) kronkelend, draai; ~ **stair′case** wenteltrap; ~**-up** likwidasie

wind′mill windmeul; windpomp

win′dow venster, raam; ~ **en′velope** ruitkoevert/vensterkoevert; ~ **pa′ne** vensterruit; ~ **shop′ping** kuierkoop, loerkoop; ~ **shut′ter** hortjie(s); ~ **sill** vensterbank

wind: ~ **resis′tance** windweerstand; ~**screen** vooruit (kar); ~**screen wi′per** ruitveër; ~ **surf′ing** seilplankry; ~**y** winderig; windmakerig; ydel (mens)

wine wyn, kromhoutsap; ~ **bib′ber** wynvlieg, drinkebroer (mens); ~**glass** wynkelkie, wynglas; ~**ry** wynkelder; ~ **tas′ting** wynproe(wery)

wing (n) vlerk (voël); vleuel; *clip one's* ~*s* iem. kortwiek; ~**span** vlerkwydte

wink (n) (oog)wink; knipogie; *for′ty* ~*s* dutjie; (v) wink; ~ *at* knik vir

winn′er (n) wenner, oorwinnaar

winn′ing (a) wen; innemend (geaardheid); *the* ~ *side* die wenkant; ~ **post** wenpaal; ~ **shot** kishou (sport)

win′some (a) bevallig, bekoorlik *also* **hand′some, attrac′tive**

win′ter (n) winter; (v) oorwinter; ~ **sports** wintersport

win′try (a) winteragtig; koud, ysig (weer)

wipe (v) afvee, afdroog; ~ *one's eyes* jou oë afvee/uitvee; ~ *out* uitwis *also* **exter′minate**

wire (n) draad; **bar′bed** ~ doringdraad; **live** ~ wakker/lewendige mens; (v) bedraad; ~**cut′ter** draadtang; ~**dan′cer** koorddanser; ~**less** draadloos *also* **ra′dio**; ~ **net′ting** sifdraad, ogiesdraad; ~**pul′ler** draadtrekker; konkelaar (mens)

wis′dom (n) wysheid, verstand; ~ **tooth** verstand(s)kies/verstand(s)tand

wise[1] (n) manier, wyse *also* **man′ner**; *in this* ~ op hierdie manier

wise[2] (a) verstandig, wys; raadsaam; *nobody would have been the* ~*r* daar sou geen haan na gekraai het nie; ~**acre** wysneus, beterweter *also* **know-all** (person)

wish (n) wens, begeerte; *good* ~*es* beste wense; (v) wens, begeer; ~ *one well* iem. die beste toewens; ~**bone/**~**ing bone** geluksbeentjie

wish′ful: ~ **think′ing** wensdenkery

wish′ing well (n) wensput

wistar′ia eeloureent, wistaria (blom)

wit (n) geestigheid; vernuf; verstand; **rea′dy** ~ gevatheid *see* **wit′ty**

witch -es (n) (tower)heks, towenares; (v) toor, beheks; ~**craft** toordery; ~**doc′tor** toordokter

with met, saam (met); *put up* ~ verdra;

tremble ~ *fear* bewe van angs

withdraw' (v) terugtrek; herroep; ~ *from the match* hom onttrek aan die wedstryd; ~**al** opvraging, terugtrekking; ~**al slip** opvrastrokie; ~**al symp'tom** onttrek(king)simptoom; ~**n** (a) teruggetrokke

with'er (v) verwelk, verlep; kwyn; uitdor

withhold' (v) terughou, weerhou

with-it byderwets/bydertyds *also* **tren'dy**

without' (adv) buitekant; *do* ~ sonder klaarkom; (prep) sonder, buite; ~ *doubt* ongetwyfeld

withstand' weerstaan *also* **endu're**

wit'ness (n) -es getuie (mens); getuienis; (v) sien; getuig; ~ **box** getuiebank

wit: ~**ticism'** kwinkslag; ~**tingly** opsetlik; ~**ty** (a) geestig, gevat; snedig

wiz'ard towenaar; kulkunstenaar

woe (n) wee, ellende, ramp

wolf wolves wolf; ~**call/whis'tle** roepfluit

wo'man (n) vrou; vroumens; (a) vroue=; ~ **doc'tor** dokteres; ~ **ha'ter** vrouehater; ~**iser** rokjagter *also* **la'dykiller**; ~**ly** vroulik; ~ **pow'er** vrouekrag *also* **fem'power**

womb (n) baarmoeder, moederskoot, uterus

wom'en's: ~ **lib(erty)** vrouevryheid; ~ **res'idence** dameskoshuis

won'der (n) wonder, wonderwerk; *work* ~**s** wondere verrig; (v) wonder; ~**ful** wonderlik; verbasend; ~**land** towerland

woo (v) die hof maak *also* **court**; (v) flikflooi

wood (n) bos, woud; (pl) bosse; ~**bine** kanferfoelie; ~**car'ving** houtsnykuns; ~**cock** houtsnip; ~**cut** houtsnee; ~**cut'ter** houtkapper; ~**ed** bosryk; ~**en** van hout; houterig; ~ **nymph** bosnimf; ~**peck'er** houtkapper/speg (voël); ~**pig'eon** bosduif; ~**work** houtwerk; ~**y** bosryk

wool (n) wol; wolgoed; ~**gro'wer** skaapboer/wolboer; ~**len** van wol, wol=; ~**len blan'ket** wolkombers; ~**ly** wollerig, ~**pack** wolbaal; ~**shears** skaapskêr; ~**trade** wolhandel; wolbedryf

word (n) woord; berig/tyding; *too funny for* ~**s** baie snaaks; ~ *of honour* erewoord; *in other* ~**s** met ander woorde; ~**ing** bewoording; ~**-per'fect** rolvas; ~**play** woordspeling; ~ **pro'cessor** woordverwerker/teksverwerker; ~ **split'ting** haarklowery

work (n) werk, arbeid; (pl) fabriek, werkplek; (v) werk, arbei; ~ *together* saamwerk; ~**ahol'ic** werkolis, werkslaaf; ~**box** werk=

kissie; ~**day** werkdag; ~**er** werker, arbeider

Wor'kers' Day Werkersdag (vakansie)

work'ing (n) bewerking; beheer; (a) werkend; ~ **cap'ital** bedryfskapitaal; ~ **hours** werkure; ~ **know'ledge** gangbare kennis

work: ~**man** werk(s)man; ~**manship** vakmanskap; ~ **ses'sion** werksitting, werksessie; ~**shop** werksessie, werkwinkel, slypskool/slypsessie; werklokaal; ~ **shy** werksku, lui

world wêreld; *all the* ~ *is a stage* die wêreld is 'n speeltoneel; ~**ling** wêreldling; ~**ly** wêrelds; ~**wide** wêreldwyd *also* **glo'bal**; ~**wide web** wêreldwye web (rek.)

worm (n) wurm; ruspe(r); (v) kruip; wurm

worn afgeleef, verslyt *see* **wear**

wo'rry (n) **worries** kwelling, bekommernis, sorg; (v) kwel, pla, lol; ~ *oneself to death* jou doodkwel; ~ **beads** kommerkrale

worse (n) ergste, slegste; (a, adv) *from bad to* ~ van kwaad tot erger; *for better and for* ~ in lief en leed

wor'ship (n) aanbidding, verering; godsdiens; **His W~ the May'or** Sy Edelagbare die Burgemeester; (v) aanbid, vereer, dien; verafgo(o)d; ~ *the Lord* die Here aanbid; ~**per** aanbidder, kerkganger

worst (n) ergste; (a) ergste, slegste

worth (n) waarde, prys; (a) werd; nie die moeite werd nie ~**less** waardeloos; ~**while** (a) waardevol, lonend, verdienstelik; *not* ~**while**

wor'thy eerbaar, (agtens)waardig

would won *see* **will**; *he* ~ *like to know* hy wil graag weet; ~**-be** kastig, sogenaamd

wound (n) wond, besering, seerplek; (v) wond, verwond, kwes; grief; ~**ed** gekwes; gewond; ~**ed sol'dier** gewonde soldaat

wra'ngle (n) twis, rusie; (v) twis, ~**r** rusiemaker, skoorsoeker *also* **trou'blemaker**

wrap (n) (om)hulsel; omslag; tjalie, serp, halsdoek; (v) inwikkel, inrol; ~**ped in paper** in papier toegedraai; ~**per** omslag; ~**ping** omhulsel, omslag; ~**ping pa'per** toedraaipapier; *gift* ~ geskenkpapier

wrath (n) gramskap, toorn *also* **an'ger, rage**

wreath (n) krans (begrafnis); vlegwerk

wreck (n) wrak; gestrande skip; *go to* ~ *and ruin* te gronde gaan; (v) strand; verongeluk; ~**ed sai'lors** skipbreukelinge; ~**age** wrakstukke

wren winterkoninkie (voël)

wrench skroefsleutel *also* **shif'ting span'ner**

wres'tle (v) worstel, stoei; ~**r** stoeier

wres'tling (n) stoei, worsteling; **all-in** ~ rofstoei; **arm** ~ armdruk *also* **In'dian** ~; **profes'sional** ~ beroepstoei; ~ **ring** stoei= kryt

wretch (n) ellendeling; skurk; ~**ed** (a) ellen= dig/vervlakste/vervloekste/armsalig *also* **for= lorn', pathet'ic**

wrig'gle (v) woel, kronkel, kriewel

wring (v): ~ *the neck of* die nek omdraai

wri'nkle (n) rimpel, plooi; ~**d** gerimpel

wrist (n) handgewrig, pols; ~**band** armband; ~ **guard** polsskerm; ~**watch** polshorlosie

write skryf, neerskryf, opskryf; ~ *a cheque* 'n tjek uitskryf; ~**r** skrywer, outeur; ~**r's cramp** skryfkramp; ~**-up** (n) volledige ver=

slag/berig; opvyseling (deur 'n verslag/be= rig)

writhe (ineen)krimp, (ver)wring; ~ *with pain* krimp van die pyn

wri'ting skrif, geskrif; *in* ~ op skrif; ~ **desk/ table** lessenaar, skryftafel; ~ **pad** skryfblok; ~ **pa'per** skryfpapier

writt'en geskrewe; skriftelik (eksamen)

wrong (n) onreg, oortreding; (a) verkeerd; *what is* ~ *?* wat makeer?; (adv) mis, ver= keerd; ~**do'er** kwaaddoener *also* **e'vildoer**; ~**do'ing** oortreding; ~**ful** onwettig

wrought gevorm, bewerk; ~ **i'ron** smeeyster

wry (a) skeef, verdraai; *with a* ~ *smile* met 'n skewe glimlag

X

Xho'sa -s Xhosa (mens, volksgroep); isiXhosa, Xhosa (taal)

X'mas Kersfees

X'-ray (n) **-s** X-straal, röntgenstraal

xyl'ograph (n) houtsnede, houtgravure

xyl'ophone (n) xilofoon, houtharmonika

xyl'ose (n) houtsuiker

Y

yacht (n) (seil)jag; ~ **club** jagklub; ~**ing** seiljagvaart; ~ **ra'cing** seiljagwedvaart

yam broodwortel

yap blaf, kef; klets

yard[1] agterplaas, werf; ~**snea'ker** sluipslaper

yard[2] jaart, tree; ~ **mea'sure** duimstok

yarn (n) storie, grap; draad, garing

yawn (n) gaap; (v) gaap; ~**ing** gegaap

year jaar; *the* ~ *before last* voorverlede jaar; ~**book** jaarboek; ~**-end** jaareinde; ~**ling** jaaroud (dier); ~**ly** jaarliks

yearn (v) smag, hunker *also* **crave, long (for)**; ~**ing** (n) verlange; (a) verlangend

yeast suurdeeg; gis

yell (n) gil, angskreet; (v) gil, skree(u)

yell'ow geel; jaloers; agterdogtig; lafhartig; ~ **peach** geelperske; ~ **press** sensasiepers; ~**wood** geelhout

yelp (v) tjank, kef (hond)

yes ja; ~**-man** jabroer (mens)

yes'terday gister; *the day before* ~ eergister

yet (adv) nog; egter; nogtans, tog; ~ *he comes to school* tog kom hy skool toe

yield (n) opbrengs/opbrings; produksie; (v) (op)lewer; toegee (by pad); ~ *profit* wins oplewer/afwerp; ~ *to temptation* vir die versoeking/verleiding swig; ~**sign** toegee= teken/voorrangteken

yod'el (v) jodel (falset sing)

yo'ga joga, yoga (Indiese mistiek)

yo'gi jogi (volgeling van joga)

yog'hurt jogurt (soort suurmelk)

yoke (n) juk; band; skouerstuk; ~**pin/skey** jukskei *also* **juk'skei**

yok'el (n) takhaar, agtervelder, javel/jafel

yolk eiergeel, dooier

you jou; jy; julle; u (beleef); ~ *never can tell* 'n mens weet nooit nie

young (n) kleintjie; (a) jong, jeugdig; *her* ~ *man* haar kêrel/vryer; ~**ster** seun, jongeling

your u; jou; julle/jul

yours joue; julle s'n; van u; ~ *faithfully*

hoogagtend/hoogagtend die uwe; ~ *sincere=ly* opreg die uwe
yourself' jouself, uself
Youth Day Jeugdag (vakansie)
youth jeug; **-s** jeugdige (mens); jongkêrel; ~**ful**

jeugdig; jong/jonk; ~ **hostel** jeugherberg
yo'-yo (n) klimtol, jojo
Yule Kersfees *also* **Christ'mas**; ~**tide** Kerstyd
yup'pie jappie; ~ **flu** jappiegriep *also* **chron'ic fati'gue syn'drome**

Z

zeal (n) ywer, geesdrif
zeal'ous (a) ywerig, vurig, geesdriftig, vlytig
zeb'ra sebra, kwagga; ~ **cros'sing** sebraoor=gang; ~ **reflec'tor** sebrakaatser
zen'ith toppunt, hoogtepunt, senit
zeph'yr sefier, luggie, windjie
zep'pelin (n) lugskip, zeppelin
zer'o -es zero, nul; vriespunt
zest (n) smaak, gretigheid, genot; geesdrif; ~ *for life* lewensvreugde
zig'zag (n) sigsag(pad); kronkel(pad); (a) sig=sag=, slingerend, kwing-kwang
Zimbab'we Zimbabwe; ~**an econ'omy** Zimbab=wiese ekonomie; ~**an** Zimbabwiër (mens)
zinc sink; ~ **oint'ment** sinksalf
zinn'ia jakobregop (blom)
zip gerits; gogona, pit/fut, rits; ~ **tas'tener/**

~**per** rits(sluiter), treksluiter; rit(s)sluiting
zith'er siter (musiekinstrument)
zo'diac diereriem (volgens sterre), sodiak
zol (n) (sl) daggasigaret; handgerolde sigaret; (v) steel, gaps
zom'bi (n) zombi, wandelende lyk
zone songordel; sone; landstreek
zon'ing streekindeling; sonering; **re**~ hersonering
zoo (n) dieretuin
zoolog'ical dierkundig; diere=; ~ **gar'den** diere=tuin *also* **zoo**
zool'ogy dierkunde, soölogie
zoom zoem; ~ *away* zoem weg; ~ *in* zoem in; ~ **appara'tus** zoemer *see* **buz'zer**; ~ **lens** zoemlens/skuiflens
Zu'lu -s Zoeloe/Zulu (mens, volksgroep); isiZulu, Zoeloe/Zulu (taal)

Abbreviations/Acronyms

A

a./adj. adjective ☐ byvoeglike naamwoord **b.nw.**

@ at ☐ teen @

AA¹ Automobile Association ☐ Automobiel-Assosiasie **AA**

AA² Alcoholics Anonymous ☐ Alkoholiste-Anoniem **AA**

AA³ affirmative/corrective action ☐ regstel-lende/herstellende optrede —

AC/a.c. alternating current ☐ wisselstroom **WS/ws.**

a/c account ☐ rekening **rek.**

actg. acting ☐ waarnemend(e) **wnd.**

AD *Anno Domini* (in the Year of our Lord) ☐ *Anno Domini* (in die jaar van ons Here); ná Christus **n.C./nC**

ad. advertisement ☐ advertensie **advt.**

ad inf. *ad infinitum* (to the infinite) ☐ *ad infinitum* (tot die oneindige) **ad inf.**

adj. adjective ☐ byvoeglike naamwoord **b.nw.**

ad lib. *ad libitum* (at pleasure) ☐ *ad libitum* (na goedvinde) **ad lib.**

Adm. Admiral ☐ admiraal **adm.**

Admin. Administration/Administrator ☐ ad-ministrasie/administrateur **admin.**

Adv. Advocate ☐ advokaat **adv.**

adv. adverb ☐ bywoord **bw.**

Afr. Afrikaans; Afrikaner; African ☐ Afri-kaans; Afrikaner; Afrikaan **Afr.**

AGM/agm Annual General Meeting ☐ alge-mene jaarvergadering —

AHI — ☐ Afrikaanse Handelsinstituut **AHI**

AI artificial insemination ☐ kunsmatige inseminasie **KI**

Aids acquired immunodeficiency syndrome ☐ verworwe immuniteitgebreksindroom **vigs**

ald(.) alderman ☐ raadsheer **rdh(.)**

alt. altitude ☐ hoogte bo seespieël **h.b.s./hbs**

a.m. *ante meridiem* (before noon) ☐ *ante meridiem* (voormiddag) **vm.**

ANC African National Congress ☐ — **ANC**

app. appendix ☐ aanhangsel/bylae **aanh./byl.**

appro. approval ☐ op sig —

Apr. April ☐ April **Apr.**

art. article ☐ artikel **art.**

ASA Advertising Standards Authority ☐ Ge-sagvereniging vir Reklamestandaarde **GRS**

asst. assistant ☐ assistent **asst.**

ATKV — ☐ Afrikaanse Taal- en Kultuurver-eniging **ATKV**

ATM automatic tellermachine ☐ outomatiese tellermasjien/kitsbank **OTM**

Aug. August ☐ Augustus **Aug.**

AWB — ☐ Afrikaner-Weerstandsbeweging **AWB**

awol absent without official leave ☐ afwesig sonder amptelike verlof **asav/awol**

AWS — ☐ Afrikaanse Woordelys en Spel-reëls **AWS**

AZAPO Azanian People's Organisation ☐ — **AZAPO**

B

b. born/née; bowled ☐ gebore; geboul **geb.**

B.A. *Baccalaureus Artium* (Bachelor of Arts) ☐ *Baccalaureus Artium* **B.A.**

BBC British Broadcasting Corporation ☐ — **BBC**

BC before Christ ☐ voor Christus **v.C./vC**

B.Comm. *Baccalaureus Commercii* (Bachelor of Commerce) ☐ *Baccalaureus Commercii* **B.Com.**

Bd. Boulevard ☐ boulevard **bd.**

B.D. *Baccalaureus Divinitatis* (Bachelor of Divinity) ☐ *Baccalaureus Divinitatis* **B.D.**

B.Ed. *Baccalaureus Educationis* (Bachelor of Education) ☐ *Baccalaureus Educationis* **B.Ed.**

B.Mus. *Baccalaureus Musicae* (Bachelor of Music) ☐ *Baccalaureus Musicae* **B.Mus.**

bn billion (1 000 million) ☐ miljard —

B/P bill payable ☐ betaalwissel **BW/bw**

B/R bill receivable ☐ ontvangwissel **OW/ow**

Bros Brothers ☐ gebroeders (firma) **gebrs.**

B.Sc. *Baccalaureus Scientiae* (Bachelor of Science) ☐ *Baccalaureus Scientiae* **B.Sc.**

B.V.Sc. *Baccalaureus Veterinariae Scientiae* (Bachelor of Veterinary Science) ☐ *Bacca-laureus Veterinariae Scientiae* **B.V.Sc.**

365

C

C Celsius/Centigrade □ Celsius **C**
c cent(s) □ sent **c**
c/ca *circa* (about) □ *circa* (ongeveer) **ca/ong.**
CA Chartered Accountant □ Geoktrooieerde Rekenmeester **GR**
CA Constitutional Assembly □ Grondwetge= wende Vergadering **GV**
CAI computer aided instruction □ rekenaar= gesteunde onderrig/opleiding **RGO/RO**
caps. capital letters □ hoofletters **hfl.**
car./ct. carat □ karaat **kar.**
CBD central business district □ sakekern; sentrale sakegebied **SSG**
CC close corporation □ beslote korporasie **BK**
cc cubic centimetre(s) □ kubieke sentimeter **cc**
cc carbon copy □ afskrif aan **aa**
CD compact disc □ laserplaat/laserskyf **CD**
CE chief executive □ (senior) bestuurshoof, hoofbedryfsleier —
CEO Chief Executive Officer □ hoofbedryfs= leier **HBL**
cert. certificate □ sertifikaat **sert.**
cf./cp. *confer* (compare) □ vergelyk **vgl./cf.**
cg centigram(s) □ sentigram **cg**
CID Criminal Investigation Department □ Speurdiens —
CIS Institute of Chartered Secretaries and Administrators □ Instituut van Geok= trooieerde Sekretarisse en Administrateurs **GIS**
CIS Commonwealth of Independent States (Russia) □ Gemenebes van Onafhanklike State (Rusland) **GOS**
cl centilitre(s) □ sentiliter **cl**
clr councillor □ raadslid **rdl**
cm centimetre(s) □ sentimeter **cm**
Co Company □ Kompanjie/Maatskappy **Kie./My.**
c/o care of □ per adres **p.a.**
CO Commanding Officer □ bevelvoerende offisier **BO**
COD cash on delivery □ kontant by aflewe= ring **k.b.a.**
comp. computer (science) □ rekenaar(weten= skap) **rek.**
conj. conjunction □ voegwoord **voegw.**
contd. continued □ vervolg **verv.**
Contralesa Congress of traditional leaders of SA □ — **Contralesa**
co-op co-operative (society) □ koöperasie/

ko-operasie **koöp./ko-op.**
cor./cnr. corner □ hoek van **h.v.**
Cosas Congress of SA Students □ — **Cosas**
Cosatu Congress of SA Trade Unions □ — **Cosatu**
CP Conservative Party □ Konserwatiewe Party **KP**
Cr. credit/creditor □ krediet/krediteur **kt./kr.**
CSA Christian Students' Association □ Christelike Studentevereniging **CSV**
CSIR Council for Scientific and Industrial Research □ Wetenskaplike en Nywerheid= navorsingsraad **WNNR**
cu(b). cubic □ kubiek(e) **kub.**
CV *Curriculum Vitae* □ *Curriculum Vitae* (lewensprofiel), biodata **CV**
CWO/cwo cash with order □ kontant met bestelling **k.m.b.**
cwt centiweight □ centiweight **cwt**

D

D Roman 500 □ Romeinse 500 **D**
d. *denarius* (penny) □ *denarius* (pennie/ dubbeltjie) **d.**
Dalro Dramatic, Artistic and Literary Rights Organisation □ Dramatiese, Artistieke en Letterkundige Regte Organisasie **Dalro**
DBSA Development Bank of Southern Africa □ Ontwikkelingsbank van Suider-Afrika **OBSA**
Dec. December □ Desember **Des.**
def. definition □ definisie/bepaling **def./bep.**
dept. department □ departement **dept.**
Dg decagram(s) □ dekagram **Dg**
dg decigram(s) □ desigram **dg**
DG Director-General □ direkteur-generaal **DG**
dict./lex. dictionary □ woordeboek **wdb.**
DIN *Deutsche Industrie-Norm* (German Indus= trial Standard) □ Duitse Industrienorm **DIN**
dip. diploma □ diploma **dipl.**
dist. district □ distrik **distr.**
div. division □ afdeling **afd.**
div. dividend(s) □ dividend(e) **div.**
DIY do it yourself □ doen dit self **DDS**
Dl decalitre(s) □ dekaliter **Dl**
dl decilitre(s) □ desiliter **dl**
Dm decametre(s) □ dekameter **Dm**
dm decimetre(s) □ desimeter **dm**
DMS decoration for meritorious service □ dekorasie vir voortreflike diens **DVD**

do. *ditto* (the same) ☐ *ditto* (dieselfde) **do.**

doz. dozen ☐ dosyn **dos.**

DP Democratic Party ☐ Demokratiese Party **DP**

Dr. Drive ☐ rylaan/ryweg **rln(.)**

Dr Doctor ☐ doktor; dokter **dr(.)**

Dr. debtor ☐ debiteur **dr.**

DRC Dutch Reformed Church ☐ Nederduitse Gereformeerde Kerk **NGK**

DTP desktop publishing ☐ tafeltopdrukwerk **TTD/DTP**

d.t./DT delirium tremens ☐ delirium tremens (horries) **d.t./DT**

DV *Deo volente* (God willing) ☐ *Deo volente* (so die Here wil) **DV**

dwt. pennyweight ☐ pennyweight **dwt.**

E

EC European Community *see* **EEC** ☐ Euro= pese Gemeenskap **EG**

ECG electrocardiogram ☐ elektrokardiogram **EKG**

ECU European currency unit ☐ Europese geldeenheid **EGE**

Ed. Editor ☐ redakteur/redaksie **red.**

ed. edition ☐ druk/edisie/uitgawe **dr./ed.**

EEC European Economic Community ☐ Europese Ekonomiese Gemeenskap **EEG**

E & OE errors and omissions excepted ☐ foute en weglatings uitgesonder **F en WU**

e.g. *exempli gratia* (for example) ☐ byvoor= beeld **bv.**

encl. enclosure ☐ bylae **byl.**

e-mail/email electronic mail ☐ elektroniese pos **e-pos**

Eskom Electricity Supply Commission ☐ Elektrisiteitvoorsieningskommissie **Eskom**

ESP extrasensory perception ☐ buitesintuig= like waarneming **BSW**

Esq. Esquire ☐ Weledele Heer **Weled. Hr.**

est. established ☐ gestig/opgerig **gest.**

et al. *et alii* (and others) ☐ *et alii* (en ander(e)/ en so meer) **e.a./e.s.m.**

etc. *et cetera* (and so forth) ☐ ensovoorts/en dergelike (dies) meer/en so meer **ens./ e.d.m./e.s.m.**

EU European Union *see* **EC** ☐ Europese Unie **EU**

exam. examination ☐ eksamen **eks.**

Exc. Excellency ☐ Eksellensie **Eks.**

ex off. *ex officio* (by virtue of his office) ☐ *ex officio* (ampshalwe) **ex off.**

F

F Fahrenheit ☐ — **F**

FAK — ☐ Federasie van Afrikaanse Kultuur- verenigings **FAK**

fax facsimile ☐ faksimilee **faks**

FBI Federal Bureau of Investigation ☐ — **FBI**

FCIS Fellow of the Chartered Institute of Secretaries and Administrators ☐ Genoo van die Instituut van Geoktrooieerde Sekre tarisse en Administrateurs **FCIS**

FCS Fellowship of the College of Surgeons ☐ Genootskap van die Kollege van Chirurge **GKC**

Feb. February ☐ Februarie **Feb.**

FF Freedom Front ☐ Vryheidsfront **VF**

FM frequency modulation ☐ frekwensiemo dulasie **FM**

Finrand financial Rand ☐ finansiële Rand **Finrand**

forex foreign exchange ☐ buitelandse valuta —

Frelimo *Frente de Libertação de Moçambique* (Front for the Liberation of Mozambique ☐ — **Frelimo**

Fri. Friday ☐ Vrydag **Vr.**

FS Free State ☐ Vrystaat **VS**

ft. foot, feet ☐ voet **vt.**

G

g gram(s) ☐ gram **g**

gal. gallon(s) ☐ gelling/gallon **gell./gall.**

Gasa Gay Association of South Africa ☐ — **Gasa**

Gen. General ☐ generaal **genl.**

geog. geography ☐ aardrykskunde/geografie **Aard./Geogr.**

geol. geology ☐ aardkunde/geologie **Aardk. Geol.**

geom. geometry ☐ meetkunde **Meetk.**

Glow Gay and Lesbian Organisation ☐ — **Glow**

GMT Greenwich Mean Time ☐ Greenwich tyd **GT**

GNU Government of National Unity ☐ Re gering van Nasionale Eenheid **RNE**

GP general/family practitioner ☐ huisarts mediese praktisyn —

gym. gymnastics/gymnasium ☐ gimnastiek gimnasium **gimn.**

H

ha hectare(s) □ hektaar **ha**
HDE Higher Diploma in Education □ Hoër Onderwysdiploma **HOD**
hg hectogram(s) □ hektogram **hg**
HH Her Highness □ Haar Hoogheid **HH**
His Hon. His Honour □ Sy Edele/Edelagbare **S.Ed./S.Ed. Agb.**
HIV human immunosuppressive virus □ menslike immuniteitsmorende virus **MIV/HIV**
hℓ hectolitre(s) □ hektoliter **hℓ**
HM His/Her Majesty □ Sy/Haar Majesteit **SM/HM**
hm hectometre(s) □ hektometer **hm**
HNP — □ Herstigte Nasionale Party **HNP**
Hon. Honourable □ Edelagbare/Edele **Agb./Ed.**
Hon. Sec. Honorary Secretary □ Eresekretaris **eresekr.**
h.p. horsepower □ perdekrag **pk**
HSRC Human Sciences Research Council □ Raad vir Geesteswetenskaplike Navorsing **RGN**

I

IBA Independent Broadcasting Authority □ Onafhanklike Uitsaai-owerheid **OUO**
ICU intensive care unit □ waakeenheid/waaksaal, intensiewe sorgeenheid —
ID identity document □ identiteitsdokument **ID**
IDC Industrial Development Corporation □ Nywerheidontwikkelingskorporasie **NOK**
i.e. *id est* (that is) □ dit is; dit wil sê **d.i./d.w.s./dws**
IEB Independent Examinations Board □ Onafhanklike Eksamenraad **OER**
IFP Inkatha Freedom Party □ Inkatha Vryheidsparty **IVP**
illus. illustrated □ geïllustreer **geïll.**
IMF International Monetary Fund □ Internasionale Monetêre Fonds **IMF**
in. inch(es) □ duim **dm.**
incl. inclusive/including □ insluitende/inklusief **insl./inkl.**
infra dig. *infra dignitatem* (beneath one's dignity) □ *infra dignitatem* (benede sy waardigheid) **infra dig.**
INMDC Interim National Medical and Dental Council □ — **INMDC**
inst. instant (this month) □ deser **des.**
interj. interjection □ tussenwerpsel **tw.**
inv. invoice □ faktuur **fakt.**
IOC International Olympic Committee □ Internasionale Olimpiese Komitee **IOK**
IOU I owe you □ skuldbewys —
IQ intelligence quotient □ intelligensiekwosiënt **IK**
IRA Irish Republican Army □ Ierse Republikeinse Leër **IRL**
i.r.o in respect of □ ten aansien van **t.a.v.**
ISBN International Standard Book Number □ Internasionale Standaardboeknommer **ISBN**
Iscor (South African) Iron and Steel Corporation □ — **Iscor**
ital. italics □ kursief **kurs.**

J

Jan. January □ Januarie **Jan.**
JP Justice of the Peace □ Vroderegter **VR**
JSE Johannesburg Stock Exchange □ Johannesburgse Aandelebeurs **JA**
Jul. July □ Julie **Jul.**
Jun. June □ Junie **Jun.**
jun. *junior* (the younger) □ junior **jr.**

K

kg kilogram(s) □ kilogram **kg**
KGB *Komitet Gosudarstvennoi Bezopasnosti* (Russian Secret Police) □ — (Russiese geheimpolisie) **KGB**
kℓ kilolitre(s) □ kiloliter **kℓ**
km kilometre(s) □ kilometer **km**
km/h kilometre per hour □ kilometer per uur **km/h**
kW kilowatt(s) □ kilowatt **kW**
KWV — □ Koöperatiewe Wynbouersvereniging **KWV**
KZN KwaZulu-Natal □ KwaZulu-Natal **KZN**

L

ℓ litre(s) □ liter **ℓ**
ℓ/100 km litres per 100 km □ liter per 100 km **ℓ/100 km**
L Roman 50 □ Romeinse 50 **L**

£ *librae* (pounds, money) ☐ *librae* (pond, geld) **£**

lb *libra(e)* (pound, weight) ☐ *libra(e)* (pond, gewig) **lb/pd.**

l.b.w./lbw leg before wicket ☐ been voor paaltjie(s) **b.v.p./bvp**

LDV light delivery van ☐ ligte afleweringswa **LAW/l.a.w.**

LL.B. *Legum Baccalareus* (Bachelor of Laws) ☐ *Legum Baccalareus* **LL.B.**

LS *Lectori Salutem* (the reader, hail) ☐ *Lectori Salutem* (heil die leser) **LS/H.d.L.**

Ltd Limited ☐ Beperk **Bpk**

M

m metre(s) ☐ meter **m**

m. mile(s) ☐ myl **m.**

M Roman 1 000 ☐ Romeinse 1 000 **M**

M.A. *Magister Artium* (Master of Arts) ☐ *Magister Artium* **M.A.**

Mar. March ☐ Maart **Mrt.**

Masa Medical Association of SA ☐ Mediese Vereniging van SA **MVSA**

MBA Master's degree in Business Administration ☐ Magister in Bedryfsleiding/ Besigheidsadministrasie **MBL/MBA**

MC¹ master of ceremonies ☐ seremoniemeester/tafelheer —

MC² Metropolitan Council ☐ Metropolitaanse Raad **MR**

MCC Marylebone Cricket Club ☐ — **MCC**

MCQ Multiple Choice Question ☐ Veelkeusevraag **VKV**

MD managing director ☐ besturende direkteur **BD**

ME *myalgic encephalomyelitis* (yuppie flu) ☐ — **ME**

Medunsa Medical University of Southern Africa ☐ Mediese Universiteit van Suider-Afrika **Medunsa**

Messrs *Messieurs* (gentlemen) ☐ menere/ (die) firma **mnre./firma**

mg milligram(s) ☐ milligram **mg**

Mintek Council for Mineral Technology ☐ Raad vir Mineraaltegnologie **Mintek**

MK Umkhonto we Sizwe ☐ — **MK**

mℓ millilitre(s) ☐ milliliter **mℓ**

mm millimetre(s) ☐ millimeter **mm**

M-Net Electronic Media Network ☐ Elektroniese Medianetwerk **M.Net.**

MOH Medical Officer of Health ☐ stadsgeneesheer —

M(on). Monday ☐ Maandag **Ma.**

MOTH/Moths Memorable Order of Tin Hat(s) ☐ — **Moths**

Moz. Mozambique ☐ Mosambiek —

MP Member of Parliament ☐ Lid van die Parlement **LP**

mpg miles per gallon ☐ myl per gelling **m.p.g./mpg**

mph miles per hour ☐ myl per uur **m.p.u./mpu**

MPLA *Movimento Popular de Libertação de Angola* (Angolan Peoples' Liberation Movement) ☐ — **MPLA**

Mr Mister ☐ meneer **mnr(.)**

MRC Medical Research Council ☐ Mediese Navorsingsraad **MNR**

MRI Medical Rescue International ☐ — **MRI**

Mrs Mistress ☐ mevrou **mev(.)**

Ms manuscript ☐ manuskrip/handskrif **ms., hs.**

Ms Mizz ☐ mejuffrou-mevrou **me(.)**

MSS Metropolitan substructure ☐ Metropolitaanse substruktuur **MSS**

MTN Mobile Telephone Network ☐ — **MTN**

MWU Mineworkers' Union ☐ Mynwerkersunie **MWU**

N

n. noun ☐ selfstandige naamwoord **s.n.w.**

n. *natus* (born); née ☐ *natus* (gebore) **geb.**

n.a./NA not applicable ☐ nie van toepassing **n.v.t./NVT**

Nasrec National sport, recreation and exhibition centre ☐ Nasionale sport-, ontspan- en uitstalsentrum **Nasrec**

NATO/Nato North Atlantic Treaty Organisation ☐ Noord-Atlantiese Verdrag(s)organisasie **NAVO/Navo**

NB *Nota Bene* (mark well) ☐ *Nota Bene* (let wel) **NB/LW**

NCOP National Council of Provinces ☐ Nasionale Raad van Provinsies **NRP**

No. *numero* (number) ☐ *numero* (nommer) **no./nr.**

NOCSA National Olympic Committee of SA ☐ Nasionale Olimpiese Komitee van SA **NOKSA**

Nov. November ☐ November **Nov.**

NP National Party ☐ Nasionale Party **NP**

NT New Testament ☐ Nuwe Testament **NT**

NUM National Union of Mineworkers ☐ Nasionale Unie van Mynwerkers **NUM**

O

OAU Organisation for African Unity ☐ Organisasie vir Afrika-Eenheid **OAE**
ob *obiit* (died) ☐ *obiit* (oorlede) **ob./oorl.**
OBE Outcomes Based Education ☐ Resul= taatgegronde Onderwys **RGO**
Oct. October ☐ Oktober **Okt.**
OK all correct ☐ goed/reg/okei **OK**
OPEC/Opec Organisation of Petroleum Ex= porting Countries ☐ Organisasie van Pe= troleumuitvoerlande **OPUL/OPEC**
OSEO Office for serious economic offences ☐ Kantoor vir ernstige ekonomiese mis= drywe **KEEM**
OT[1] Old Testament ☐ Ou Testament **OT**
OT[2] oxygen thief (useless person) ☐ suur= stofsteler **ss**
oz. ounce ☐ onza **oz.**

P

p. page ☐ pagina/bladsy **p./bl.**
p.a. *per annum* (per year) ☐ *per annum* (per jaar) **p.a./p.j.**
PAC Pan Africanist Congress ☐ — **PAC**
part. participle ☐ deelwoord **dw.**
PAYE pay as you earn ☐ lopende betaalstel= sel **LBS**
P/B private bag ☐ privaatsak/private possak **ps/ps.**
PC/pc personal computer ☐ persoonlike rekenaar **PR**
PC politically correct ☐ politiek/polities kor= rek **PK**
p.c. per cent ☐ persent **p.s.**
pd. paid ☐ betaal(d) **bet.**
per pro./p.p. *per procurationem* (by proxy) ☐ *per procurationem* (by volmag) **per pro./p.p.**
PI private investigator/eye ☐ privaat speurder **PS**
pl. plural ☐ meervoud/pluralis **mv./pl.**
PLO Palestinian Liberation Organisation ☐ Palestynse Bevrydingsorganisasie **PBO**
p.m. *post meridiem* (after noon) ☐ namiddag **nm.**

p.m. *per mensem* (per month) ☐ *per mensem* (per maand) **p.m.**
PO Post Office ☐ Poskantoor **Pk**
POPCRU Police and Prisons Civil Rights Union ☐ — **POPCRU**
POW prisoner(s) of war ☐ krygsgevangene(s) —
PP Public Protector ☐ Openbare Beskermer **OB**
pp. pages ☐ paginas/bladsye **bl.**
p.p./per pro. *per procurationem* (by proxy) ☐ — (by volmag) **p.p./per pro.**
p.p. past participle ☐ verlede deelwoord **verl. dw.**
PRC People's Republic of China *also see* **RoC** ☐ — Volksrepubliek China (vaste= land) —
pred. predicate ☐ predikaat **pred.**
pref. preface; prefix ☐ voorwoord; voorvoeg= sel **voorw.; voorv.**
prep. preposition ☐ voorsetsel **v(oor)s.**
Pres./pres. president ☐ president **Pres./pres.**
PRO public relations officer ☐ skakelampte= naar/mediaskakel —
Prof(.) Professor ☐ professor/hoogleraar **prof./hoogl.**
pron. pronoun ☐ voornaamwoord **vnw.**
prox. *proximo* (next) ☐ *proximo* (aanstaande maand) **as.; eerskomende ek.**
PS *post scriptum* (postscript) ☐ *post scriptum* (naskrif) **PS/Ns.**
pt. pint(s); point ☐ pint; punt **pt**
PTO please turn over ☐ blaai om/sien ommesy **b.o./SOS**
Pty Ltd Proprietary Limited ☐ Eiendoms Beperk **Edms Bpk**
PU Potchefstroom University ☐ Potchef= stroomse Universiteit vir Christelike Hoër Onderwys **PUCHO**

Q

QED *quod erat demonstrandum* (that which had to be demonstrated) ☐ *quod erat de= monstrandum* (wat te bewys was) **QED**
qt. quart(er) ☐ kwart(aal) **kw.**

R

R Rand(s) ☐ Rand/rand **R**
R radius ☐ radius/straal **r.**
RAU Rand Afrikaans University ☐ Randse Afrikaanse Universiteit **RAU**
RC Roman Catholic ☐ Rooms-Katoliek(e) **RK**
R/D refer to drawer ☐ verwys na trekker **VT**
RDP Reconstruction and Development Pro= gramme ☐ Heropbou- en Ontwikkelings= program **HOP**
re regarding ☐ betreffende/insake **is.**
Ref. Reformed ☐ Gereformeerd(e)/Hervorm= d(e) **Herv.**
ref. reference ☐ referensie/verwysing **ref./verw.**
rel. pron. relative pronoun ☐ betreklike voornaamwoord **betr.vnw.**
Renamo Resistência Nacional Moçambicana ☐ — **Renamo**
rev. Reverend ☐ Eerwaarde **eerw.**
RIP *requiescat in pace* (may he (she) rest in peace) ☐ — (rus in vrede) **RIP**
r/min revolutions per minute ☐ omwentelin= ge per minuut **r/min (opm)**
RoC Republic of China ☐ (Taiwan) —
ROEP rescue our endangered platteland ☐ red ons eensame platteland **ROEP**
RSA Republic of South Africa ☐ Republiek (van) Suid-Afrika **RSA**
RSC (former) regional services council ☐ (voormalige) streekdiensteraad **SDR**
RSVP *répondez s'il vous plaît* (please reply) ☐ — (antwoord asseblief) **RSVP/ a.asb.**
Rt. Hon. Right Honourable ☐ Hoogedele **H.Ed.**
Rt. Rev. Right Reverend ☐ Hoogeerwaarde/ Weleerwaarde **H. Eerw./Weleerw.**
RU Rhodes University ☐ Universiteit Rhodes **UR**

S

SA South Africa ☐ Suid-Afrika **SA**
SAA South African Airways ☐ Suid-Afri= kaanse Lugdiens **SAA**
SAAF South African Air Force ☐ Suid-Afri= kaanse Lugmag **SALM**
SABC South African Broadcasting Corpora= tion ☐ — **SABC**

SABS South African Bureau of Standards ☐ SA Buro vir Standaarde **SABS**
SACC South African Council of Churches ☐ SA Raad van Kerke **SARK**
SACOB SA Chamber of Business ☐ SA Besigheidskamer **SABEK**
SACP SA Communist Party ☐ SA Kommu= nisteparty **SAKP**
SAFA South African Football Assosiation ☐ — **SAFA**
SAMDC (former) SA Medical and Dental Council *see* **INMDS**
Samro SA Music Rights Organisation ☐ SA Musiekregte-Organisasie **Samro**
SANDF South African National Defence Force ☐ SA Nasionale Weermag **SANW**
SAPS South African Police Services ☐ SA Polisiedienste **SAPD**
Sapa South African Press Association ☐ Suid-Afrikaanse Pers-Assosiasie **Sapa**
SARS SA Revenue Services ☐ SA Inkoms= tedienste —
Sasol SA Coal, Oil and Gas Corporation ☐ Suid-Afrikaanse Steenkool-, Olie- en Gas= korporasie **Sasol**
Sat. Saturday ☐ Saterdag **Sa.**
SBDC Small Business Development Corpora= tion ☐ Kleinsake-Ontwikkelingskorporasie **KSOK**
Sci fi Science fiction ☐ wetenskapfiksie —
scuba self-contained underwater breathing apparatus ☐ — **scuba**
Sen. Senate/Senator ☐ senaat/senator **sen.**
sen. *senior* (the elder) ☐ *senior* (die oudste) **sr.**
Sept. September ☐ September **Sept.**
Sergt. Sergeant ☐ sersant **sers.**
SG specific gravity ☐ soortlike gewig **s.g.**
sgd. signed ☐ (was) geteken **w.g./get.**
SIDS Sudden Infant Death Syndrome ☐ Skielike Babasterftesindroom **SBSS**
Sim subscriber identity module ☐ — **sim**
sitcom situation comedy ☐ situasiekomedie **sitkom**
slomo slow motion ☐ stadige aksie/traagtem= po **staksie**
sing. singular ☐ enkelvoud **enkv.**
Soekor Southern Oil Exploration Corporation ☐ Suidelike Olie-Eksplorasiekorporasie **Soekor**
SOS last signal for help ☐ internasionale nood= sein **SOS**
SPCA Society for the Prevention of Cruelty to

Animals □ Dierebeskermingvereniging/Diere= sorg **DBV**

sq. square □ vierkant(e) **vk.**

SRC Students' Representative Council □ (Ver= teenwoordigende) Studenteraad **VSR/SR**

St. Street □ straat **str.**

St. Saint □ Sint/Heilige **St.**

Sun. Sunday □ Sondag **So.**

superl. superlative □ oortreffend(e)/superla= tief **oortr./sup.**

s.v.p. *s'il vous plaît* (if you please) □ — (asseblief) **asb./s.v.p.**

Swapo South West African People's Organi= sation □ — **Swapo**

T

t ton(s) (metric) □ ton **t**

t. *tare* (own weight) □ tara (eiegewig) **t.**

TB tuberculosis □ tuberkulose **TB**

Telkom Telecommunication Services □ Tele= kommunikasiedienste **Telkom**

temp. temperature □ temperatuur **temp.**

theol. theology □ teologie(s)(e) **teol.**

Thur. Thursday □ Donderdag **Do.**

TKO/tko technical knockout □ tegniese uit= klophou —

TRC Truth and Reconciliation Commission □ Waarheid- en Versoeningskommissie **WVK**

t.t. *totus tuus* (wholly yours) □ *totus tuus* (geheel die uwe) **t.t.**

Tues. Tuesday □ Dinsdag **Di.**

TV television □ televisie **TV**

twinkie twin income couple no kiddies (*see* yuppie) □ —

U

UAE United Arab Emirates □ Verenigde Arabiese Emirate **VAE**

UCT University of Cape Town □ Universiteit Kaapstad **UK**

UFO unidentified flying object □ vreemde vlieënde voorwerp **VVV**

UFS University of the Free State □ Univer= siteit van die Vrystaat **UVS**

UK United Kingdom □ Verenigde Koninkryk **VK**

ULP unleaded petrol □ ongelode petrol **OLP**

ult. *ultimo* (last) □ *ultimo* (laaslede/jongslede) **ult./ll./jl.**

UN United Nations □ Verenigde Nasies **VN**

UN University of Natal □ Universiteit Natal **UN**

Unesco United Nations Educational, Scientific and Cultural Organisation □ — **Unesco**

Unibo University of Bophuthatswana □ Universiteit Bophuthatswana **Unibo**

Unisa University of South Africa □ Univer= siteit van Suid-Afrika **Unisa**

Unita *União Nacional para a Independencia Total de Angola* □ — **Unita**

Unitra University of the Transkei □ — **Unitra**

UP University of Pretoria □ Universiteit (van) Pretoria **UP**

UPE University of Port Elizabeth □ Univer= siteit (van) Port Elizabeth **UPE**

US University of Stellenbosch □ Universiteit (van) Stellenbosch **US**

USA United States of America □ Verenigde State van Amerika **VSA**

UW University of the Witwatersrand (Wits) □ Universiteit Witwatersrand **UW**

UWC University of the Western Cape □ Universiteit Wes-Kaap **UWK**

UZ University of Zululand □ — **UZ**

V

V Roman 5 □ Romeinse 5 **V**

v./vs *versus* (against) □ *versus* (teen) **vs./v.**

VAT value added tax □ belasting op toege= voegde waarde **BTW**

v./vb verb □ *verbum* (werkwoord) **verb./ww.**

VD venereal disease □ geslagsiekte —

vet. veterinary surgeon □ veearts/dierearts —

VIP very important person □ baie belangrike persoon **BBP**

viz. *videlicet* (namely) □ *videlicet* (naamlik/te wete) **viz./nl./t.w.**

Vodacom Voice and Data Communication □ — **Vodacom**

vol. volume □ volume/deel/jaargang **vol./dl./jg.**

W

w. week □ week **w.**

w.c. water closet □ privaat/toilet —

WCC World Council of Churches □ Wêreld=

raad van Kerke **WRK**
Wed. Wednesday □ Woensdag **Wo.**
WHO World Health Organisation □ Wêreld‎
gesondheidsorganisasie **WGO**
wpm words per minute □ woorde per minuut
w.p.m./wpm

X

X Roman 10 □ Romeinse 10 **X**
Xmas Christmas □ Kersfees —

Y

yd. yard(s) □ jaart **jt.**

YMCA Young Men's Christian Association □
Christelike Jongmannevereniging **CJMV‎**
YMCA
Your Hon. Your Honour □ U Edele/Edel‎
agbare (in die hof) **U Ed./Ed.Agb.**
Yuppie young (urban) upwardly mobile pro‎
fessional person □ jong opkomende pro‎
fessionele persoon **Jappie**
YWCA Young Women's Christian Associa‎
tion □ Christelike Jongvrouevereniging‎
CJVV/YWCA

Z

Zim. Zimbabwe □ Zimbabwe **Zim.**

Provinces of South Africa

Eastern Cape ☐ Oos-Kaap
Free State ☐ Vrystaat
Gauteng ☐ Gauteng
KwaZulu-Natal ☐ KwaZulu-Natal
Mpumalanga ☐ Mpumalanga
Northern Cape ☐ Noord-Kaap
Northern Province ☐ Noordelike Provinsie
North West ☐ Noordwes
Western Cape ☐ Wes-Kaap

Official languages of South Africa

The versions **printed in bold** are according to the Constitution of the Republic of South Africa (1994). The bracketed versions are commonly used.

Afrikaans ☐ **Afrikaans**
English ☐ **Engels**
isiNdebele (Ndebele) ☐ **isiNdebele** (Ndebele)
Sepedi/Sesotho sa Leboa (Northern Sotho) ☐ **Sepedi/Sesotho sa Leboa** (Noord-Sotho)
Sesotho (Southern Sotho) ☐ **Sesotho** (Suid-Sotho)
Setswana (Tswana) ☐ **Setswana** (Tswana)
siSwati (Swazi) ☐ **siSwati** (Swazi)
Tshivenda (Venda) ☐ **Tshivenda** (Venda)
isiXhosa (Xhosa) ☐ **isiXhosa** (Xhosa)
Xitsonga (Tsonga) ☐ **Xitsonga** (Tsonga)
isiZulu (Zulu) ☐ **isiZulu** (Zulu, Zoeloe)

African Language Titles from Hippocrene ...

Afrikaans-English/English-Afrikaans Practical Dictionary
14,000 entries • 430 pages • 4½ x 6½ • ISBN 0-7818-0052-8 • $11.95pb

Amharic-English/English-Amharic Dictionary
27,000 entries • 472 pages • 5½ x 8½ • ISBN 0-7818-0115-X • $27.50hc

Bemba-English/English-Bemba Concise Dictionary
10,000 entries • 233 pages • 4 x 6 • ISBN 0-7818-0630-5 • $13.95pb

Hausa-English/English-Hausa Practical Dictionary
18,000 entries • 431 pages • 5 x 7 • ISBN 0-7818-0426-4 • $16.95pb

Igbo-English/English-Igbo Dictionary & Phrasebook
3,000 entries • 186 pages • 3¾ x 7 • ISBN 0-7818-0661-5 • $11.95pb

Malagasy-English/English-Malagasy Dictionary & Phrasebook
2,500 entries • 170 pages • 3¾ x 7½ • ISBN 0-7818-0843-X • $11.95pb

Pulaar-English/English-Pulaar Standard Dictionary
30,000 entries • 276 pages • 5½ x 8½ • ISBN 0-7818-0479-5 • $19.95pb

Beginner's Shona (ChiShona)
215 pages • 5½ x 8½ • ISBN 0-7818-0864-2 • $14.95pb

Shona-English/English-Shona Dictionary & Phrasebook
1,500 entries • 174 pages • 3¾ x 7 • ISBN 0-7818-0813-8 • $11.95pb

Somali-English/English-Somali Dictionary & Phrasebook
1,400 entries • 176 pages • 3¾ x 7 • ISBN 0-7818-0621 • $13.95pb

Swahili-English/English-Swahili Practical Dictionary
35,000 entries • 596 pages • 4 x 7 • ISBN 0-7818-0480-9 • $19.95pb

Swahili-English/English-Swahili Dictionary & Phrasebook
5,000 entries • 200 pages • 3¾ x 7 • ISBN 0-7818-0905-3 • $11.95pb

Twi-English/English-Twi Concise Dictionary
8,000 entries • 332 pages • 4 x 6 • ISBN 0-7818-0264-4 • $12.95pb

Venda-English Dictionary
20,000 entries • 490 pages • 6 x 8½ • ISBN 0-6270-1625-1 • $39.95hc

Yoruba-English/English-Yoruba Practical Dictionary
26,000 entries • 674 pages • 5½ x 8½ • ISBN 0-7818-0263-6 • $22.50pb

Beginner's Yoruba
268 pages • 5 ½ x 8 ½ • ISBN 0-7818-1069-8 • $14.95pb

Scholar's Zulu-English/English-Zulu Dictionary
25,000 entries • 519 pages • ISBN 0-7818-0255-5 • 4¾ x 7¼ • $22.50pb

All prices are subject to change without prior notice. To order Hippocrene Books, contact your local bookstore, call (718) 454-2366, visit www.hippocrenebooks.com, or write to: Hippocrene Books, 171 Madison Avenue, New York, NY 10016. Please enclose check or money order adding $5.00 shipping (UPS) for the first book and $.50 for each additional title.